2014

W9-CPO-498

NOVEL & SHORT STORY WRITER'S MARKET

includes a 1-year online subscription to **Novel & Short Story Writer's Market** on

Where & How to Sell What You Write

THE ULTIMATE MARKET RESEARCH TOOL FOR WRITERS

To register your *2014 Novel & Short Story Writer's Market* book and **start your 1-year online genre-only subscription**, scratch off the block below to reveal your activation code, then go to www.WritersMarket.com. Find the box that says "Have an Activation Code?" then click on "Sign Up Now" and enter your contact information and activation code. It's that easy!

UPDATED MARKET LISTINGS FOR YOUR INTEREST AREA
EASY-TO-USE SEARCHABLE DATABASE • RECORD-KEEPING TOOLS
PROFESSIONAL TIPS & ADVICE • INDUSTRY NEWS

Your purchase of *Novel & Short Story Writer's Market* gives you access to updated listings related to this genre of writing (valid through 12/31/14). For just $9.99, you can upgrade your subscription and get access to listings from all of our best-selling Market Books. Visit **www.WritersMarket.com** for more information.

WritersMarket.com

Where & How to Sell What You Write

Activate your WritersMarket.com subscription to get instant access to:

- **UPDATED LISTINGS IN YOUR WRITING GENRE:** Find additional listings that didn't make it into the book, updated contact information, and more. WritersMarket.com provides the most comprehensive database of verified markets available anywhere.

- **EASY-TO-USE SEARCHABLE DATABASE:** Looking for a specific magazine or book publisher? Just type in its name. Or widen your prospects with the Advanced Search. You can also search for listings that have been recently updated!

- **PERSONALIZED TOOLS:** Store your best-bet markets, and use our popular recording-keeping tools to track your submissions. Plus, get new and updated market listings, query reminders, and more—every time you log in!

- **PROFESSIONAL TIPS & ADVICE:** From pay rate charts to sample query letters, and from how-to articles to Q&A's with literary agents, we have the resources writers need.

YOU'LL GET ALL OF THIS WITH YOUR INCLUDED SUBSCRIPTION TO

WritersMarket.com

Where & How to Sell What You Write

33RD ANNUAL EDITION

2014

NOVEL & SHORT STORY WRITER'S MARKET

Rachel Randall, Editor

WD
WRITER'S DIGEST
BOOKS
WritersDigest.com
Cincinnati, Ohio

2014 Novel & Short Story Writer's Market. Copyright © 2013 F+W Media, Inc. Published by Writer's Digest Books, an imprint of F+W Media, Inc., 10151 Carver Road, Suite 200, Blue Ash, OH 45242.

Publisher: Phil Sexton

Writer's Market website: www.writersmarket.com

Writer's Digest website: www.writersdigest.com

Distributed in Canada by Fraser Direct
100 Armstrong Avenue
Georgetown, Ontario, Canada L7G 5S4
Tel: (905) 877-4411

Distributed in the U.K. and Europe by F&W Media International
Brunel House, Newton Abbot, Devon, TQ12 4PU, England
Tel: (+44) 1626-323200, Fax: (+44) 1626-323319
E-mail: postmaster@davidandcharles.co.uk

Distributed in Australia by Capricorn Link
P.O. Box 704, Windsor, NSW 2756 Australia
Tel: (02) 4577-3555

ISSN: 0897-9812
ISBN 13: 978-1-59963-729-7
ISBN 10: 1-59963-729-4

Attention Booksellers: This is an annual directory of F+W Media, Inc.
Return deadline for this edition is December 31, 2014.

Edited by: Rachel Randall
Cover Designed by: Claudean Wheeler
Designed by: Geoff Raker
Production coordinated by: Greg Nock

CONTENTS

MARKETING & PROMOTION

MARKETS

RESOURCES

INDEX

FROM THE EDITOR

Many writers start writing because for them, the novel or the short story holds a certain power—the ability to transport, to captivate, to frighten or delight—and they want to harness that power. As they move forward, they begin to explore their craft. They learn the techniques of crafting memorable characters and creating tension and conflict. They write and revise. They hone their skills. They practice. A writer could spend the rest of her career at this stage, but eventually she turns her eye to getting published and to the business of writing. She still writes because she loves to write, but now she has aspirations: of publication, of recognition, of success.

Wherever you are in your writing journey, you hold in your hands an invaluable tool, one that combines your love for the craft with the business of fiction writing. *Novel & Short Story Writer's Market* has something for every writer. In addition to providing the trusted resources for which *NSSWM* is renowned—listings for book publishers, agents, online markets, contests and awards, and more—I've focused on curating a variety of content focused on the topics that matter the most to *you*, the writer.

Inside *NSSWM* you'll learn how to raise your characters above the status quo from master storyteller Steven James (page 12) and how to turn any idea into story gold from prize-winning author Elizabeth Sims (page 6). You'll master the long synopsis with the help of writing instructor James Scott Bell (page 58), and you'll delve into the mind of the publicist to learn how to effectively promote your work (page 88).

Writing fiction in the twenty-first century presents its own set of exciting challenges. Writers must now concern themselves not only with producing excellent novels and short stories, but also with promoting themselves and their work across several platforms, improving their query-writing skills, and being mindful of the many ways in which their work can be published. *Novel & Short Story Writers Market* will aid you with all of these considerations and will serve as both map and compass wherever your writing journey may take you.

Rachel Randall
Content Editor, Writer's Digest Books

HOW TO USE
NSSWM

To make the most of *Novel & Short Story Writer's Market*, you need to know how to use it. And with more than five hundred pages of fiction publishing markets and resources, a writer could easily get lost amid the information. This quick-start guide will help you navigate through the pages of *Novel & Short Story Writer's Market*, as well as the fiction publishing process, and emerge with your dream to see your work in print accomplished.

1. READ, READ, READ. Read numerous magazines, fiction collections, and novels to determine if your fiction compares favorably with work currently being published. If your fiction is at least the same caliber as what you're reading, then move on to step two. If not, postpone submitting your work and spend your time polishing your fiction. Writing and reading the work of others are the best ways to improve craft.

For help with craft and critique of your work: You'll find advice and inspiration from best-selling authors and seasoned writers in the articles found in the first few sections of this book (**Craft & Technique, Getting Published,** and **Marketing & Promotion**). You'll find contest listings in the **Contests & Awards** section and even more listings to help you locate various events where you can hone your craft in the **Conferences & Workshops** section.

2. ANALYZE YOUR FICTION. Determine the type of fiction you write to best target markets most suitable for your work. Do you write literary, genre, mainstream, or one of many other categories of fiction? For definitions and explanations of genres and subgenres, check out the **Glossary** and the **Genre Glossary** in the **Resources** section of the book. There are magazines and presses seeking specialized work in each of these areas as well as numerous others.

For editors and publishers with specialized interests, see the **Category Index** in the back of the book.

3. LEARN ABOUT THE MARKET. Read *Writer's Digest* magazine (F+W Media, Inc.); *Publishers Weekly*, the trade magazine of the publishing industry; and *Independent Publisher*, which contains information about small- to medium-sized independent presses. And don't forget the Internet. The number of sites for writers seems to grow daily, and among them you'll find www.writersmarket.com and www.writersdigest.com.

4. FIND MARKETS FOR YOUR WORK. There are a variety of ways to locate markets for fiction. The periodical section in bookstores and libraries is a great place to discover new journals and magazines that might be open to your type of short stories. Read writing-related magazines and newsletters for information about new markets and publications seeking fiction submissions. Also, frequently browse bookstore shelves to see what novels and short story collections are being published and by whom. Check acknowledgment pages for names of editors and agents, too. Online journals often have links to the websites of other journals that may publish fiction. And last but certainly not least, read the listings found here in *Novel & Short Story Writer's Market*.

Also, don't forget to utilize the various category **Indexes** at the back of this book to help you target the market for your fiction.

5. SEND FOR GUIDELINES. In the listings in this book, we try to include as much submission information as we can get from editors and publishers. Over the course of the year, however, editors' expectations and needs may change. Therefore, it is best to request submission guidelines by sending a self-addressed stamped envelope (SASE). You can also check each magazine's and press's website—they usually contain a page with guideline information. For an even more comprehensive and continually updated online markets list, you can obtain a subscription to www.writersmarket.com.

6. BEGIN YOUR PUBLISHING EFFORTS WITH JOURNALS AND CONTESTS OPEN TO BEGINNERS. If this is your first attempt at publishing your work, your best bet is to begin with local publications or those you know are open to beginning writers. After you have built a publication history, you can try the more prestigious and nationally distributed magazines. For markets most open to beginners, look for the ○ symbol preceding listing titles. Also, look for the ◑ symbol that identifies markets open to exceptional work from beginners as well as work from experienced, previously published writers.

7. SUBMIT YOUR FICTION IN A PROFESSIONAL MANNER. Take the time to show editors that you care about your work and are serious about publishing. By following a publication's or book publisher's submission guidelines and practicing standard submission etiquette, you can increase your chances that an editor will want to take the time to read your work and consider

⊕ market new to this edition

Ⓐ market accepts agented submissions only

⊘ market does not accept unsolicited submissions

🏆 award-winning market

🍁 Canadian market

🌐 market located outside of the U.S. and Canada

⑀ market pays (in magazine sections)

💬 comment from the editor of *Novel & Short Story Writer's Market*

○ actively seeking new writers

◐ seeks both new and established writers

● prefers working with established writers, mostly referrals

◎ market has a specialized focus

◍ imprint, subsidiary or division of larger book publishing house (in book publishers section)

😀 publisher of graphic novels or comics

it for publication. Remember, first impressions last; a carelessly assembled submission packet can jeopardize your chances before your story or novel manuscript has had a chance to speak for itself.

8. KEEP TRACK OF YOUR SUBMISSIONS. Know when and where you have sent fiction and how long you need to wait before expecting a reply. If an editor does not respond in the time indicated in his or her market listing or guidelines, wait a few more months, and then follow up with a letter (and SASE) asking when the editor anticipates making a decision. If you still do not receive a reply from the editor within a month or two, send a letter withdrawing your work from consideration and move on to the next market on your list.

9. LEARN FROM REJECTION. Rejection is the hardest part of the publication process. Unfortunately rejection happens to every writer, and every writer needs to learn to deal with the negativity involved. On the other hand, rejection can be valuable when used as a teaching tool rather than a reason to doubt yourself and your work. If an editor offers suggestions with his or her rejection slip, take those comments into consideration. You don't have to agree with an editor's opinion of your work. It may be that the editor has a different perspective on the piece than you do. Or you may find that the editor's suggestions give you new insight into your work and help you improve your craft.

10. DON'T GIVE UP. The best advice for you as you try to get published is to be persistent and to always believe in yourself and your work. By continually reading other writers' work, constantly working on the craft of fiction writing, and relentlessly submitting your work, you will eventually find that magazine or book publisher that's the perfect match for your fiction. *Novel & Short Story Writer's Market* will be here to help you every step of the way.

GUIDE TO LISTING FEATURES

Below is an example of the market listings contained in *Novel & Short Story Writer's Market* with callouts identifying the various format features of the listings. (For an explanation of the icons used, see the sidebar on the opposite page).

EASY-TO-USE REFERENCE ICONS

E-MAIL AND WEBSITE INFORMATION

SPECIFIC CONTACT NAMES

DETAILED SUBMISSION GUIDELINES

EDITOR'S COMMENTS

① ⑤ ❻ ❼ THE SOUTHERN REVIEW

Old President's House, Louisiana State University, Baton Rouge, LA 70803-5001. (225)578-5108. Fax: (225)578-5098. E-mail: southernreview@lsu.edu (**Website:** www.lsu.edu/thesouthern review/.

Contact Cara Blue Adams, editor. Magazine: 6 ¼ × 10; 240 pages; 50 lb. Glatfelter paper; 65 lb. #1 grade cover stock. Quarterly. Circ. 3,000.

- Several stories published in The Southern Review were Pushcart Prize selections.

NEEDS Literary. "We select fiction that conveys a unique and compelling voice and vision." Receives approximately 300 unsolicited mss/month. Accepts 4-6 mss/issue. Reading period: September-June. Publishes ms 6 months after acceptance. Agented fiction 1%. Publishes 10-12 new writers/year. Recently published work by Jack Driscoll, Don Lee, Peter Levine, and Debbie Urbanski. Also publishes literary essays, literary criticism, poetry and book reviews.

HOW TO CONTACT Mail hard copy of ms with cover letter and SASE. No queries. "Prefer brief letters giving author's professional information, including recent or notable publications. Biographical info not necessary." Responds within 10 weeks to mss. Sample copy for $8. Writer's guidelines online. Reviews fiction, poetry.

PAYMENT/TERMS Pays $30/page. Pays on publication for first North American serial rights. Sends page proof to author via e-mail. Sponsors awards/contests.

TIPS "Careful attention to craftsmanship and technique combined with a developed sense of the creation of story will always make us pay attention."

HOW TO DEVELOP ANY IDEA INTO A GREAT STORY

....

Elizabeth Sims

A while ago I attended an inventors' club meeting. Some of the members had already launched successful products and were working on more, while others were merely beginners with great ideas. The beginners were commiserating about how hard it is to deal with financing, raw materials, manufacturing, promotion and all the rest, when one of the experienced inventors suddenly stood up. "Look," he said impatiently, "ideas are a dime a dozen. It's the *development* that puts you over the top. Do what you have to do to make it real and get it to market."

I was surprised, because I'd always thought that a brilliant idea could make you a fortune. But I quickly realized my new friend was right: Idea is just the beginning.

Fiction writers share a lot with those inventors. It's not hard to get inspired by a great concept, to take it to your table or toolshed or cellar and do some brainstorming, and even to start putting the story on paper—but eventually, many of us lose steam. Why? Because development doesn't happen on its own. In fact, I've come to think that idea development is the No. 1 skill an author should have.

How do great authors develop stunning narratives, break from tradition and advance the form of their fiction? They take whatever basic ideas they've got, then move them away from the typical. No matter your starting point—a love story, buddy tale, mystery, quest—you can do like the great innovators do: Bend it. Amp it. Drive it. Strip it.

Bend. Amp. Drive. Strip.

It's BADS, baby, it's BADS.

BEND IT.

Chuck Palahniuk is on record as saying he drew heavily from *The Great Gatsby* to create his novel *Fight Club*. I've read both books (multiple times) but would not have perceived that parallel. He said, "Really, what I was writing was just *The Great Gatsby* updated a little. It was 'apostolic' fiction—where a surviving apostle tells the story of his hero. There are two men and a woman. And one man, the hero, is shot to death." Palahniuk took a traditional love story set in the high society of America's Roaring Twenties and transformed it into a violent and bloody tale of sexual obsession, cultism and social disruption, set in a rotten world.

He bent the ideas behind *Gatsby* into something all his own.

The next time you get a great idea for a story, don't stop there. Bend your initial concept, making it more unique—and more powerful—with every turn:

- **GET OUT OF YOUR HEAD AND INTO YOUR PELVIS.** Give your characters inner yearnings (sexual or otherwise) that they don't understand and can't deal with cognitively. Palahniuk took his idea for an apostolic main character and gave him an unnamable urge, a gland-level longing that drives him to pretend to be a cancer patient and participate in support groups where hugging and crying are not only okay, but expected. Breaking the taboo against exploiting nonexistent pain does more than give the character relief: It moves the story forward in huge leaps.

  Brainstorm who your own characters might be by starting with their motivations. Let's say you've come up with the idea that your main character is an insomniac who needs chocolate to fall asleep. Take that urge and bend it into something else that would be totally disquieting to anybody *but* your protagonist. Wouldn't it be more compelling if she has to, say, shoplift an expensive item precisely one hour before bedtime?

- **BREAK AWAY FROM FAMILIAR PARAMETERS.** Most authors write characters who have backgrounds similar to their own, at least with respect to class, education, and money. Throw that out. Write billionaires, bums, addicts, the hopeless, the heroic. Give them crappy, selfish habits, resentments, grudges. Mix traits. Make feral creatures out of urban sophisticates and urban sophisticates out of feral creatures.

- **ADD INSANITY.** The key to making a character believably and compellingly crazy is to give him a way to rationalize his behavior, from the slightly weird to the outrageous. Is your character actually nuts, or is there something else going on? How can anybody tell? Crazy characters wind up needing a lot of resources to keep them out of trouble—and they usually have a major impact on everybody else. Have fun with that.

- **QUESTION CONVENTION.** Use existential questions to bend the life lessons your readers think they've already learned: What is suffering? What is pleasure? What is a waste? What is worthwhile? Can something be both, or neither? Invite your characters to reject common wisdom and look for answers themselves.

AMP IT.

Brief Encounter is a British film adapted from Nöel Coward's play *Still Life*. It's the story of two quiet people who meet and fall in love in spite of being married to others, but then, conscience-stricken, break off the relationship before it really gets going. The small, exquisite tragedy resonated with the genteel, romantic codes of conduct valued in prewar England.

But then along comes Tennessee Williams with his play *Cat on a Hot Tin Roof*, a love story that has similar themes at its core but rips us away from any semblance of civilization. Williams sure could amp drama! For one thing, he knew that a story about noble ideals wouldn't cut it anymore. Setting his play in the emotionally brutal mélange of the postwar American South, he slashed into the secret marrow of his protagonists and antagonists alike, exposing the weaknesses and delusions that bind people together on the surface while tearing them apart below decks.

Take the essence of your story, and amp it:

- **ADD CHARACTERS AND PILE ON THE EMOTION.** Playwrights used to limit the number of characters in their stories, not wanting to overcrowd the stage. But when Williams crams six or eight people into the scene at once and sets them all at one another's throats, we get a chance to *feel* their emotional claustrophobia and unwanted interdependence. Amp up your action by adding cunning, vindictiveness, jealousy, fear of exposure, stupidity, even death.
- **MAKE EVEN MINOR CHARACTERS FIERCE AND ELEMENTAL.** Consider Mae and Gooper's five children in *Cat on a Hot Tin Roof*, who lesser authors would describe (boringly) as "brats" and leave offstage. Before you even see them, you witness their havoc (ruining Maggie's dress) and listen to Maggie call them "no-neck monsters." You don't even have to meet them to fear them. Then Williams gives them stage time, every second of which makes you squirm with discomfort.
- **EXPOSE INTERNAL BLEEDING.** The deepest, most painful wounds are the invisible ones humans inflict on one another and ourselves in a hundred ways: betrayal, selfishness, abandonment. Strive to write characters who feel vulnerable to pain, whose secrets are so close to the surface that they can't afford to be polite. Put in a truth teller and watch the inner flesh rip and sizzle.
- **CREATE BLOOD TIES.** Kinship is story gold. Take your pick of, and take your time with, its darker aspects: scapegoating, favoritism, jealousy. A blood link can instantly heighten *any* conflict. Why? Because kinship is the one thing in life you can't change or walk away from. Make your characters learn this the hard way.

DRIVE IT.

Many great modern stories spring from the same seeds as old folk tales. The subjugation of young women, for instance, is not only one of the oldest oppressions, it's one of the most pernicious—hence, it still resonates with audiences of all sorts. We first meet Cinderella in the scullery, a slave to the rough demands of her stepmother and older stepsisters. When Cinderella tries to take some initiative to improve her situation, she's squelched and punished. (I might add that the step-relationship is especially lush ground for storytellers, given the schizophrenic strength of the half-kin, half-stranger link.)

Margaret Atwood, in her landmark dystopian novel *The Handmaid's Tale*, steers the Cinderella archetype away from any home whatsoever and from any relationships, besides. She multiplies Cinderella a thousand times, and all the Cinderellas are kept alive for the sole asset they possess that can't be synthesized (at least, not yet!): their fertile wombs. Their purpose is to procreate a society that would be better off dead. And there are no handsome princes to come along and change anything.

Atwood drove Cinderella to a point almost—but not quite—beyond recognition. And that's the power.

You, too, can make gut-wrenching magic out of your fiction by driving your tale to a conclusion further than you ever thought it could go:

- **START AT THE CRUX OF YOUR PREMISE AND HIT THE GAS.** Agents and editors often tell new writers, "Don't start at the beginning, start in the middle," which usually means, "Don't waste pages setting up the core of your story." Wise advice. Try *starting* at your knottiest point, and then drive it forward using the same techniques that got your concept there. Everybody's bloody and panting, everybody's heart is broken, everybody's hanging on by their fingernails. Now what? Let the story begin!

- **MAKE IT BIGGER THAN THE INDIVIDUAL.** How would an organization intimidate and subjugate? Make it legal; go step by small step. Lawlessness isn't as frightening as a breakdown of the social order with the wrong people in charge. An organization can be as small as a truck stop, a fraternity house, or a bridal party. Let everything seem normal at first, and then gradually let things devolve, deteriorate, go wrong. Make your characters passengers trapped on a train that's barreling toward disaster.

- **ADD THE COMPLICITY OF A VICTIM.** Polite, politically correct society isn't at all comfortable with a victim being complicit in his or her own oppression. Good! The discomfort comes from the fact that everybody knows but doesn't *want* to know that such perversion of the human spirit exists; it's real because self-deceit is real. Break the taboo and use it to *make* your tale breathtaking, like a ship breaking apart on a reef.

- **PUT IN AN IMPOSSIBLE CHOICE.** The women in Atwood's novel live an impossible choice every day: Do they go along, or rebel? To go along is to destroy yourself from within; to rebel is to invite certain destruction from without. An impossible choice can confront someone who's being blackmailed, or someone who absolutely must have two conflicting things, or any number of other possibilities. And it can steer your story in new directions like nothing else.

STRIP IT.

War has been the seed of innumerable creative works. In developing *War and Peace*, Leo Tolstoy put in everything he could think of because war is so big. To represent the French invasion of Russia and the accompanying Napoleonic era, he wrote an epic that followed dozens of characters. The sheer pounding weight of detail in *War and Peace* helps us understand the impact of war on individuals and the institutions they thought to be unshakable.

But Ernest Hemingway, a young man reeling from his own experiences in World War I, stripped away everything he could think of because war is as small as one man. Confronted with the realities of war, he wrote what came to him, then stripped it and sanded it until nothing but hard, bright pieces were left. The result, *In Our Time*, is a collection of vignettes and short stories that evokes the immediate horror and lingering pain of that most awful of human activities.

When it starts to seem as if no number of words can truly represent the reality of anything, explore what might happen if you strip your idea down to allow the miniature to suggest the infinite:

- **ADOPT A MINIMALIST ATTITUDE.** If you've taken to heart my BAD advice (!), you might have a notebook or file with ideas, hunks of story, character notes, lists of heart-clutching moments you want to include. Great material! Now, instead of trying to develop all that further by squeezing out more, look closely at what you have. Sort through it for gems, or what could become gems with some tough love. Look for quality over quantity. Continue to apply this mentality throughout your writing and revision.
- **CONVEY EMOTION THROUGH ACTION, NOT DESCRIPTION.** Inexperienced storytellers often try—alas, unsuccessfully—to do what Tolstoy did well: to not only show what happens, but to tell in deep, ruminative detail how everybody feels about it. To Siberia with that! Do like Papa Hemingway: When Joe's dad in "My Old Man" gets crushed to death on the horse track, Hemingway simply lets Joe tell us that the cops held him back, and what his father's dead face looked like, and that it was pretty hard to stop

crying right then. You, too, can present life-and-death emotion without saying a word about it. Adopting this approach from the outset of your idea development can save you a lot of writing and rewriting later.

- **USE SMALL PARTICULARS TO BRING BIG THINGS TO LIFE.** A mushroom cloud, or a burned, crying baby? A wedding with a cast of thousands, or the intimate taste of a lover? A travelogue, or the feel of acceleration down a mountain road? It's not too early to start thinking about your details. Be choosy. What makes *your* heart quicken? Those glancing moments may offer up all the description you need.

When you implement these techniques, don't bear down hard on any one; take a light, relaxed approach and allow idea to build on idea. If you do that, your innate creativity will take over. It knows what it's doing! At times when you're really rolling, your ideas will seem to develop themselves; they'll pop brighter and bite deeper.

And like the best inventors who combine brilliant ideas with the guts and drive to make them reality, you won't be stuck drumming your fingers on the drafting table. You'll be producing well-developed stories with the optimum chance of success.

Elizabeth Sims (elizabethsims.com) is a prize-winning novelist as well as a contributing editor for Writer's Digest. She holds degrees in English from Michigan State University and Wayne State University, and is currently working on new fiction. Her book, *You've Got a Book In You: A Stress-Free Guide to Writing the Book of Your Dreams*, was released in April 2013 by Writer's Digest Books.

RAISE YOUR CHARACTERS ABOVE THE STATUS QUO

....

Steven James

You've sweated over your manuscript, crafted your characters, honed your story line, and rooted your novel in a location organic to and inseparable from your plot. Now, as you begin tweaking and revising your story, it's the perfect time to take a closer look at the depth and dimensionality of your characters.

One of the most effective ways of doing this is something most writers have never even heard of: managing status.

I first learned about status years ago while studying physical comedy, mime, and improvisation. I remember listening to acting instructor Keith Johnstone (author of *IMPRO* and *Impro for Storytellers*) explain how dominance and submission affect actors on stage and how stillness raises status. As he spoke, I kept thinking of how essential it is for writers to capture the same characterizations on the page.

Since then, I've been on the lookout for ways to fine-tune the status of my characters. Here are four essential principles I've discovered.

1. VARIABLE STATUS IS THE KEY TO DIMENSIONALITY

So what exactly is status?

Simply put, in every social interaction, one person has (or attempts to have) more of a dominant role. Those in authority or those who want to exert authority use a collection of verbal and nonverbal cues to gain and maintain higher status. But it's not just authority figures who do this. In daily life all of us are constantly adjusting and negotiating the amount of status we portray as we face different situations and interact with different people.

Novelists have the daunting task of showing this dynamic of shifting submission and dominance through dialogue, posture, pauses, communication patterns, body language, action, and inner dialogue. To do so, you'll need to recognize some basic status cues:

- Dominant individuals exude confidence through a relaxed demeanor and loose gestures and gait; submissive people constrict their stride, voice, posture, gestures. Looking down, crossing your legs, biting your lip and holding your hands in front of your face are all ways of hiding. Concealment lowers status.
- Eye contact is a powerful way of maintaining dominance. Cultures differ, but North Americans prolong eye contact to intimidate, control, threaten, or seduce.
- Stillness is power. Dominant people delay before replying to questions not because they can't think of anything to say, but in order to control the conversation. They blink less frequently than submissive people and keep their heads still as they speak. The more fidgety, bedraggled, or frazzled a person is, the less status he has.
- Submissive people apologize and agree more than dominant ones. They try to please and are easily intimidated. To act as if you need something lowers your status; telling someone they can be helpful to you raises it.
- Effective negotiators mirror the status of the people with whom they're doing business. This way they neither appear too aggressive (intimidatingly high status) or too willing to compromise (unimpressively low status).

Status varies with respect to three things: relationship (a father has higher relational status than his eight-year-old), position (a boss has higher positional status than her employees), and situation (if you're attacked by a team of ninjas and you've never studied martial arts, you'd have significantly lower situational status than your assailants).

Although the level of relational, positional and situational status might be out of our hands, our response to it is not. The daughter might manipulate her father, the employee might quit, and you might summon up enough moxie to frighten off those ninjas. So, in determining status, choices matter more than circumstances.

When readers complain that a character is one-dimensional, flat or "cardboard," they may not realize it, but they're actually noting that the character—regardless of the social context in which she appears—always has the same degree of status. She might always be angry or ruthless or heroic, but the more uniformly she responds to everyone and everything, the less interesting she'll be.

People in real life are complex.

Fictional characters need to be, as well.

So what's the key to a well-rounded character? Simple: She doesn't have the same status in every situation.

Each supporting cast member is in the story to bring out different traits of the main characters. Dimensionality, depth, and complexity are all brought out by showing subtle shifts in your character's status as he interacts with the other players.

In my novels featuring FBI Special Agent Patrick Bowers, I'm careful not to let him appear weak or cowardly: I want readers to respect and admire him. Whenever he's at a crime scene or standing up to a bad guy, he has the highest status. He'll never back down, never give in, never give up.

But to have dimensionality he also needs relationships in which he has *low* status. So, as a single dad he struggles with knowing how to handle his sharp-witted and surly teenage daughter, and, lacking some social graces, he fumbles for the right things to say to women he's attracted to. Without his daughter or a love interest to reveal those low status aspects of his characterization, he'd be one-dimensional, and certainly not engaging enough to build a series around.

If you want readers to invest in your protagonist, you'll need to find areas where he has a weakness, low status or something to overcome. Remember, even Indiana Jones is afraid of snakes, and Superman is vulnerable to Kryptonite.

Status at a Glance

LOW STATUS	HIGH STATUS
Arrogance	Confidence
Loss of control	Self-control
Cries or weeps often	Reserved, might cry when grieving
Slouches	Good posture
Tense	At ease, relaxed
Avoids eye contact	Steady gaze
Postures, shows off	Exhibits poise, doesn't try to impress
Brags, narcissistic	Doesn't draw attention to self, humble
Shrinks from danger	Rises to the occasion
Cowardly	Courageous
Shy	Outgoing
Self-congratulatory	Self-effacing
Needy	Self-reliant
Argumentative, interrupts others	Listens attentively
Tries to be cool	Can't help but be cool
Worries about reputation	Cares more about ideals
Dependent	Independent but also relational

LOW STATUS	HIGH STATUS
Vies for control	Naturally has control
Gives in, conforms	Sets trends
Makes threats	Takes action

2. WORD CHOICE DETERMINES CHARACTERIZATION

In theater the phrase "stealing the scene" refers to instances in which another person upstages the star. Actually, it's just another way of saying that the star (or protagonist) no longer has the highest status.

When this happens on stage, it will annoy the star.

When it happens in your novel, it'll turn off your readers.

And you can shatter hundreds of pages of careful characterization with one poorly chosen word.

A person with high status might *shout, holler, call,* or *yell*, but if she *screams, screeches, bawls,* or *squeals*, her status is lowered. Similarly, a character who *quivers, trembles, whines,* or *pleads* has lower status than one who tries to control the pain. For example:

1. Adrian drew the blade across Sylvia's arm. She shrieked and begged him to stop.
2. Adrian drew the blade across Sylvia's arm. She clenched her teeth, refused to give him the satisfaction of seeing her cry.

In the first example, Sylvia's uncontrolled reaction lowers her status beneath that of her assailant. In the second, however, her resolve raises her status above that of Adrian, who has evidently failed to intimidate her. Rather than appearing victimized, she has become heroic.

Your protagonist must never act in a way that lowers her status below that of the antagonist.

Take a moment to let that sink in.

You might find it helpful to imagine high-status movie stars playing your protagonist. I'm not sure about you, but I have a hard time imagining Liam Neeson, Jason Statham, or Bruce Willis pleading for mercy or screaming for help.

Remember, choices determine status. So, while revising, continually ask yourself what you want readers to feel about each character. Do you want them to be on this character's side? To cheer for him? Fear, despise, or discount him? Every action, every word of dialogue, every gesture—even every speaker attribution—communicates a certain status, so be sure the words you choose support the impression you're trying to make. If Betty *stomps* across the floor (showing lack of self-control) or *struts* across it (implying the need for attention), she'll have lower status than someone who *strides* across it (showing composure and confidence).

Even punctuation affects status:

1. "I know you heard me! Move away from Anna! If you lay a hand on her, I guarantee you will regret it!"
2. "I know you heard me. Move away from Anna. If you lay a hand on her, I guarantee you will regret it."

In the first example, the exclamation points cause the speaker to come across as frantic or desperate. In the second, the periods show him to be controlled, measured, authoritative. That's how a hero responds.

A wimpy protagonist isn't interesting.

A wimpy antagonist isn't frightening.

In marketable fiction, both heroes and villains need high status. When villains aren't frightening or heroes aren't inspiring, it's usually because the author let them act in a way that undermines their status. Don't make that mistake.

3. PROTAGONISTS NEED OPPORTUNITIES TO BE HEROIC

When I was writing my novel *The Rook*, one section gave me a particularly difficult time. Agent Bowers is at the scene of a suicide when Detective Dunn, a street-smart local homicide cop, shows up. Dunn is tough. He's used to calling the shots, to having the highest status. In this scene, he makes an aggressive, high-status move by getting in Bowers' face and then taunting him. I struggled with showing that as bold and brash as Dunn is, my hero still has higher status. After hashing through numerous drafts, here's how the encounter finally played out (from Bowers' point of view):

> *[Dunn] stepped close enough for me to smell his garlicky breath.*
>
> *"This is my city. The next time you and your pencil-pushing lawyer buddies from Quantico decide to stick your nose into an ongoing investigation, at least have the courtesy to go through the proper channels."*
>
> *"I'd suggest you back away," I said. "Now."*
>
> *He backed up slowly.*

Bowers refuses to be baited and isn't intimidated by Dunn's aggressive posturing. If he were, readers would lose faith in him and side with Dunn. Instead, Bowers remains calm and, by exhibiting poise and self-control, induces Dunn's submission. (Also, by adding the speaker attribution "I said," I inserted a slight pause in Bowers' response, subtly adding to his status even more. To see the difference, read the sentence aloud with and without the pause.)

At the end of the scene, when Dunn steps back, there's no doubt in the mind of the reader who is in charge.

Readers will not empathize with a weak protagonist. They expect protagonists who have strength of conviction, moral courage, and noble aspirations. It's true, of course, that during the story the protagonist might be struggling to grow in these areas, but readers need to see her as someone worth cheering for along the way.

If you can spot weaknesses in your protagonist and are grappling with how to strengthen her, try one of these ways:

- Have your protagonist sacrifice for the good of others. The sacrifice might be physical (stepping in front of a bullet), financial (anonymously paying another's debt), material (volunteering for the Peace Corps), or emotional (forgiving someone for a deep offense).
- Have her stand up for the oppressed. I've seen all too many authors try to show how "tough" their protagonist is by portraying her as cold or unfeeling—especially at a crime scene. Bad idea. Readers want the hero (or heroine) to be compassionate and life affirming. Let's say your female medical examiner is at a crime scene and one of the other cops gestures toward the corpse and quips, "They stab 'em; you slab 'em." Your protagonist needs to uphold the dignity and value of human life. She might reproach the cop, or remind him of the victim's grieving family. If you let her make light of something as precious as life itself, you'll end up devastating her status.
- Have her turn the other cheek. If someone slaps your protagonist and she looks the guy in the eye and refuses to fight back, her self-control raises her status above that of the attacker. Strength isn't shown only by what a person can do, but by what she *could do* but *refrains from doing*. Self-restraint always raises status.

4. STATUS CRYSTALLIZES AS THE STORY ESCALATES

As your story builds toward its climax, the status of both your hero and your villain will also rise. The bad guy will become more and more coldhearted or unstoppable, and the good guy will need to summon unprecedented strength or courage to save the day.

Status has more to do with actions than motives, so even though the hero and villain have completely different agendas, you can raise the status of either one by giving him more 1) self-control, 2) courage, and/or 3) resolve.

Remember, stillness is power, so if you decide you need to make a villain more imposing, try slowing him down. Show readers that he's in no hurry to commit his evil deed—he has such high status that he can walk slowly and still catch the person fleeing frantically through the woods.

Villains become less frightening when they're self-congratulatory or cocky. You actually *lower* a villain's status by giving him the need to prove himself. Sadistic, chortling, hand-wringing villains aren't nearly as unnerving as calm, relentless ones who are simply indifferent to the suffering of others.

If your story calls for multiple villains, try staggering their status levels so that the top-tier bad guy has the highest status and is therefore the most threatening and dangerous person for your protagonist to encounter at the story's climax.

Let your protagonist enter the final showdown at a disadvantage—weaponless, injured, poisoned, or exhausted from fighting his way past all the antagonist's henchmen. An underdog who overcomes impossible odds is a hero we can believe in.

And one we will want to read about again.

....

Steven James is the national best-selling author of four critically acclaimed thrillers: *The Pawn, The Rook, The Knight,* and *The Bishop.* He has a master's degree in storytelling and has taught writing and creative storytelling on three continents.

....

3 SECRETS TO GREAT STORYTELLING

....

Steven James

As a novelist and writing instructor, I've noticed that three of the most vital aspects of story craft are left out of many writing books and workshops. Even best-selling novelists stumble over them.

But they're not difficult to grasp. In fact, they're easy.

And if you master these simple principles for shaping great stories, your writing will be transformed forever. Honest. Here's how to do it.

SECRET #1: CAUSE AND EFFECT ARE KING.

Everything in a story must be caused by the action or event that precedes it.

Now, this sounds like an almost embarrassingly obvious observation, and when I mention it in my writing seminars I don't often see people furiously taking notes, muttering, "Man, are you getting this stuff? This is amazing!" But humor me for a few minutes. Because you might be surprised by how more careful attention to causation will improve your writing.

As a fiction writer, you want your reader to always be emotionally present in the story. But when readers are forced to guess why something happened (or didn't happen), even for a split second, it causes them to intellectually disengage and distances them from the story. Rather than remaining present alongside the characters, they'll begin to analyze or question the progression of the plot. And you definitely don't want that.

When a reader tells you that he couldn't put a book down, often it's because everything in the story followed logically. Stories that move forward naturally, cause to effect, keep the reader engrossed and flipping pages. If you fail to do this, it can confuse readers, kill the pace and telegraph your weaknesses as a writer.

Let's say you're writing a thriller and the protagonist is at home alone. You might write:

With trembling fingers she locked the door. She knew the killer was on the other side.

But, no. You wouldn't write it like that.

Because if you did, you would fracture, just for a moment, the reader's emotional engagement with the story as he wonders, *Why did she reach out and lock the door?* Then he reads on. *Oh, I get it, the killer is on the other side.*

If you find that one sentence is serving to explain what happened in the sentence that preceded it, you can usually improve the writing by reversing the order so that you render rather than explain the action.

It's stronger to write the scene like this:

The killer was on the other side of the door. She reached out with a trembling hand to lock it.

Cause: The killer is on the other side of the door.

Effect: She locks it.

Think about it this way: If you've written a scene in which you could theoretically connect the events with the word *because*, then you can typically improve the scene by structuring it so that you could instead connect the events with the word *so*.

Take the example about the woman being chased by the killer:

She locked the door *because* she knew the killer was on the other side.

If written in this order, the sentence moves from effect to cause. However:

She knew the killer was on the other side of the door, so she locked it.

Here, the stimulus leads naturally to her response.

Of course, most of the time we leave out the words *because* and *so*, and these are very simplified examples—but you get the idea.

Remember in rendering more complex scenes that realizations and discoveries happen after actions, not before them. Rather than telling us what a character realizes and then telling us why she realizes it—as in, "She finally understood who the killer was when she read the letter"—write it this way: "When she read the letter, she finally understood who the killer was." Always build on what has been said or done, rather than laying the foundation after the idea is built. Continually move the story forward, rather than forcing yourself to flip backward to give the reason something occurred.

One last example:

Greg sat bored in the writer's workshop. He began to doodle. He'd heard all this stuff before. Suddenly he gulped and stared around the room, embarrassed, when the teacher called on him to explain cause and effect structure.

This paragraph is a mess. As it stands, at least seven events occur, and none are in their logical order. Here is the order in which they actually happened:

1. Greg sits in the workshop.
2. He realizes he's heard all this before.
3. Boredom ensues.
4. Doodling ensues.
5. Greg gets called on.
6. Embarrassment ensues.
7. He gulps and stares around the room

Each event causes the one that follows it.

Your writing will be more effective if you show us what's happening *as it happens* rather than explain to us *what just happened*.

With all of that said, there are three exceptions, three times when you can move from effect to cause without shattering the spell of your story.

First, in chapter or section breaks. For example, you might begin a section by writing:

> *"How could you do this to me?" she screamed.*

Immediately, the reader will be curious who is screaming, at whom she is screaming, and why. This would make a good hook, so it's fine (good, even!) to start that way. If this same sentence appeared in the middle of a scene in progress, though, it would be wiser to move from cause to effect:

> *He told her he was in love with another woman.*
> *"How could you do this to me?" she screamed.*

The second exception is when one action causes two or more simultaneous reactions. In the paragraph about Greg, he gulps and looks around the room. Because his embarrassment causes him to respond by both gulping and looking around, the order in which you tell the reader he did them could go either way.

And the final exception is when you write a scene in which your character shows his prowess by deducing something the reader hasn't yet concluded. Think of Sherlock Holmes staring at the back of an envelope, cleaning out the drainpipe, and then brushing off a nearby stick of wood and announcing that he's solved the case. The reader is saying, "Huh? How did he do that?" Our curiosity is sparked, and later when he explains his deductive process, we see that everything followed logically from the preceding events.

SECRET #2: IF IT'S NOT BELIEVABLE, IT DOESN'T BELONG.

The narrative world is also shattered when an action, even if it's impossible, becomes unbelievable.

In writing circles it's common to speak about the suspension of disbelief, but that phrase bothers me because it seems to imply that the reader approaches the story *wanting* to disbelieve and that she needs to somehow set that attitude aside in order to engage with the story. But precisely the opposite is true. Readers approach stories wanting *to believe them*. Readers have both the intention and desire to enter a story in which everything that happens, within the narrative world that governs that story, is believable. As writers, then, our goal isn't to convince the reader to suspend her disbelief, but rather to give her what she wants by continually *sustaining* her belief in the story.

The distinction isn't just a matter of semantics; it's a matter of understanding the mindset and expectations of your readers. Readers want to immerse themselves in deep belief. We need to respect them enough to keep that belief alive throughout the story.

Let's say you create a world in which gravity doesn't exist. Okay, if you bring the world to life on the page and through your characters, the reader will accept that—but now she'll want you to be consistent. As soon as someone's hair doesn't float above or around her head, or someone is able to drink a cup of coffee without the liquid floating away, the consistency of that world is shattered. The reader will begin to either lose interest and eventually stop reading or will disengage from the story and begin to look for more inconsistencies—neither of which you want her to do.

All else being equal, as soon as readers stop believing your story, they'll stop caring about your story. And readers stop believing stories when characters act inexplicably.

When I'm shaping a story, I continually ask myself, "What would this character naturally do in this situation?"

And then I let him do it.

Always.

Why?

Because the reader, whether he's conscious of it or not, is asking the same question: "What would this character naturally do?"

As soon as characters act in ways that aren't believable, either in reference to their characterizations or to the story's progression, the reader loses faith in the writer's ability to tell that story.

In a scene in my first novel, *The Pawn*, my protagonist is interviewing the governor of North Carolina, and the governor is responding oddly. Now, if my hero, who's supposed to be one of the best investigators in the world, doesn't notice *and respond to* the governor's inexplicable behavior, the reader will be thinking, *What's wrong with this Bowers guy? There's obviously something strange going on here. Why doesn't he notice? He's a moron.*

So, I had Bowers think, *Something wasn't clicking. Something wasn't right.*

Then the reader will agree, *Ah, good! I thought so. Okay, now let's find out what's going on here.* Rather than drive the reader away from identifying with the protagonist, this was a way of drawing the reader deeper into the story.

So when something that's unbelievable or odd happens, don't be afraid to let your character notice and respond: "I never expected her to say that," "What? That just doesn't make sense," or "Obviously there's more going on here than I thought when I first found the necklace."

If a character acts in an unbelievable way, you'll need to give the reader a reason why—and it'd better be a good one. Remember: Always give the reader what he wants, or something better. If you don't give the reader what he wants (believability), you must satisfy him with a twist or a moment of story escalation that satisfies him more than he ever expected.

SECRET #3: IT'S ALL ABOUT ESCALATION.

At the heart of story is tension, and at the heart of tension is unmet desire. At its core, a story is about a character who wants something but cannot get it. As soon as he gets it, the story is over. So, when you resolve a problem, it must always be within the context of an even greater plot escalation.

As part of the novel-writing intensives that I teach, I review and critique participants' manuscripts. Often I find that aspiring authors have listened to the advice of so many writing books and included an engaging "hook" at the beginning of their story. This is usually a good idea; however, all too often the writer is then forced to spend the following pages dumping in background to explain the context of the hook.

Not a good idea.

Because you've killed escalation.

This is also why dream sequences typically don't work—the protagonist thinks she's in a terrible mess, then wakes up and realizes none of it was real.

So things weren't really that bad after all.

That's the opposite of escalation—and the death of the forward movement of the story.

Tension drives a story forward. When tension is resolved, the momentum of the story is lost. I've heard writing instructors differentiate between "character-driven" and "plot-driven" stories, but the truth is that neither character nor plot really drives a story forward—only unmet desire does.

You might include page after page of interesting information about your character, but that won't move the story along; it'll cause it to stall out. Until we know what the character wants, we don't know what the story is about, and we won't be able to worry or care about whether or not the character's desires are eventually met.

Somewhat similarly, plot is simply the casually related series of events that the character experiences as he moves through a crisis or calling into a changed or transformed life. So you might include chase scene after chase scene, but eventually the reader could care less that one car is following another down the street. Until we know what the stakes are, we don't care. A story isn't driven forward by events happening, but by tension escalating.

All stories are "tension-driven" stories.

Now, to create depth in your characters, typically you'll have two struggles that play off each other to deepen the tension of the story. The character's external struggle is a problem that needs to be solved; her internal struggle is a question that needs to be answered. The interplay of these two struggles is complementary until, at the climax, the resolution of one gives the protagonist the skills, insights, or wherewithal to resolve the other.

To some extent the genre in which you write will have expectations and conventions that'll dictate the precedence of the internal or external struggle in your story. However, readers today are very astute and narratively aware. If you intend to write commercially marketable fiction, you'll need to include both an internal struggle that helps us empathize with the protagonist, and an external struggle that helps drive the movement of the story toward its exciting climax.

So, as you shape your novel, ask yourself, "How can I make things worse?" Always look for ways to drive the protagonist deeper and deeper into an impossible situation (emotionally, physically, or relationally) that you then eventually resolve in a way that is both surprising and satisfying to the reader.

The story needs to progress toward more and more conflict, with more intimate struggles and deeper tension.

The plot must always thicken; it must never thin. Because of that, repetition is the enemy of escalation. Every murder you include decreases the impact that each subsequent murder will have on the reader. Every explosion, prayer, conversion, sex scene means less and less to the reader, simply because repetition, by its very nature, serves to work against that escalation your story so desperately needs.

Strive, instead, to continually make things worse for the protagonist. In doing so, you'll make them better and better for the reader.

All three of these storytelling secrets are interwoven. When every event is naturally caused by the one that precedes it, the story makes sense. As characters act in ways that are credible and convincing in the quest for their goals, the story remains believable, and the deepening tension and struggles keep the reader caring about what's happening as well as interested in what's going to happen next.

By consistently driving your story forward through action that follows naturally, characters who act believably, and tension that mounts exponentially, you'll keep readers flipping pages and panting for more of your work.

THE BUSINESS OF FICTION WRITING

//

It's true there are no substitutes for talent and hard work. A writer's first concern must always be attention to craft. No matter how well presented, a poorly written story or novel has little chance of being published. On the other hand, a well-written piece may be equally hard to sell in today's competitive publishing market. Talent alone is just not enough.

To be successful, writers need to study the field and pay careful attention to finding the right market. While the hours spent perfecting your writing are usually hours spent alone, you're not alone when it comes to developing your marketing plan. *Novel & Short Story Writer's Market* provides you with detailed listings containing the essential information you'll need to locate and contact the markets most suitable for your work.

Once you've determined where to send your work, you must turn your attention to presentation. We can help here, too. We've included the basics of manuscript preparation, along with information on submission procedures and how to approach markets. We also include tips on promoting your work. No matter where you're from or what level of experience you have, you'll find useful information here on everything from presentation to mailing to selling rights to promoting your work—the "business" of fiction.

APPROACHING MAGAZINE MARKETS

A query letter by itself is usually not required by most magazine fiction editors. If you are approaching a magazine to find out if fiction is accepted, a query is fine, but editors looking for short fiction want to see the actual piece. A cover letter can be useful as a letter of introduction, but the key here is brevity. A successful cover letter is no more than one page (20-lb. bond paper). It should be single spaced with a double space between paragraphs, proofread carefully, and neatly typed in a standard typeface (not script or italic). The writer's name, address, phone number, and e-mail address must appear at the top, and the letter should be addressed, ideally, to a specific editor. (If the editor's name is unavailable, use "Fiction Editor.")

The body of a successful cover letter contains the name and word count of the story, a brief list of previous publications, if you have any, and the reason you are submitting to this particular publication. Mention that you have enclosed a self-addressed, stamped envelope or postcard for reply. Also, let the editor know if you are sending a disposable manuscript (not to be returned; more and more editors prefer disposable manuscripts that save them time and save you postage). Finally, don't forget to thank the editor for considering your story.

Note that more and more publications prefer to receive electronic submissions, both as e-mail attachments and through online submission forms. See individual listings for specific information on electronic submission requirements and always visit magazines' websites for up-to-date guidelines.

APPROACHING BOOK PUBLISHERS

Some book publishers do ask for queries first, but most want a query plus sample chapters or an outline or, occasionally, the complete manuscript. Again, make your letter brief. Include the essentials about yourself: name, address, phone number, e-mail address, and publishing experience. Include a three or four sentence "pitch" and only the personal information related to your story. Show that you have researched the market with a few sentences about why you chose this publisher.

BOOK PROPOSALS

A book proposal is a package sent to a publisher that includes a cover letter and one or more of the following: sample chapters, outline, synopsis, author bio, publications list. When asked to send sample chapters, send up to three consecutive chapters. An outline covers the highlights of your book chapter by chapter. Be sure to include details on main characters, the plot, and subplots. Outlines can run up to thirty pages, depending on the length of your novel. The object is to tell what happens in a concise, but clear, manner. A synopsis is a shorter summary of your novel, written in a way that expresses the emotion of the story in addition to just explaining the essential points. Evan Marshall, literary agent and author of *The Marshall Plan for Getting Your Novel Published* (Writer's Digest Books), suggests you aim for a page of synopsis for every twenty-five pages of manuscript. Marshall also advises you write the synopsis as one unified narrative, without section, subheads, or chapters to break up the text. The terms synopsis and outline are sometimes used interchangeably, so be sure to find out exactly what each publisher wants.

A FEW WORDS ABOUT AGENTS

Agents are not usually needed for short fiction and most do not handle it unless they already have a working relationship with you. For novels, you may want to consider working with an agent, especially if you intend to market your book to publishers who do not look at unsolicited submissions. For more on approaching agents and to read listings of agents willing to work with beginning and established writers, see our Literary Agents section. You can also refer to this year's edition of *Guide to Literary Agents*, edited by Chuck Sambuchino.

MANUSCRIPT MECHANICS

A professionally presented manuscript will not guarantee publication. But a sloppy, hard-to-read manuscript will not be read—publishers simply do not have the time. Here's a list of suggested submission techniques for polished manuscript presentation:

- For a short story manuscript, your first page should include your name, address, phone number, and e-mail address (single spaced) in the upper left corner. In the upper right, indicate an approximate word count. Center the name of your story about one-third of the way down the page, skip a line, and center your byline (byline is optional). Skip four lines and begin your story. On subsequent pages, put your last name and page number in the upper right-hand corner.

- For book manuscripts, use a separate title page. Put your name, address, phone number, and e-mail address in the lower right corner and word count in the upper right. If you have representation, list your agent's name and address in the lower right. (This bumps your name and contact information to the upper left corner.) Center your title and byline about halfway down the page. Start your first chapter on the next page. Center the chapter number and title (if there is one) one-third of the way down the page. Include your last name and the novel's title in all caps in the upper left header and put the page number in the upper right header of this page and each page to follow. Start each chapter with a new page.

- Proofread carefully. Keep a dictionary, thesaurus, and stylebook handy and use the spell-check function on your computer.

- Include a word count. If you work on a computer, chances are your word processing program can give you a word count.

- Suggest art where applicable. Most publishers do not expect you to provide artwork and some insist on selecting their own illustrators, but if you have suggestions, let them know. Magazine publishers work in a very visual field and are usually open to ideas.

- Keep accurate records. This can be done in a number of ways, but be sure to keep track of where your stories are and when you sent them out. Write down submission dates. If you do not hear about your submission for a long time—about one to two months longer than the reporting time stated in the listing—you may want to contact the publisher. When you do, you will need an accurate record for reference.

Electronic Submissions:

- If sending electronic submissions via e-mail or online submission form, check the publisher's website first for specific information and follow the directions carefully.

Hard Copy Submissions:

- Use white 8½" × 11" bond paper, preferably 16- or 20-lb. weight. The paper must be heavy enough not to show pages underneath and strong enough to take handling by several people.

- Type your manuscript on a computer and print it out using a laser or ink-jet printer (or, if you must, use a typewriter with a new ribbon).

- An occasional spot of white-out is okay, but don't send a marked-up manuscript with many typos.

- Always double space and leave a 1" margin on all sides of the page.

- Don't forget word count. If you are using a typewriter, there are several ways to count the number of words in your piece. One way is to count the words in five lines and divide that number by five to find an average. Then count the number of lines and multiply to find the total words. For long pieces, you may want to count the words in the first three pages, divide by three and multiply by the number of pages you have.

- Always keep a copy. Manuscripts do get lost. To avoid expensive mailing costs, send only what is required. If you are including artwork or photos but you are not positive they will be used, send photocopies. Artwork is hard to replace.

- Enclose a self-addressed, stamped envelope (SASE) if you want a reply or if you want your manuscript returned. For most letters, a business-size (#10) envelope will do. Avoid using any envelope too small for an 8½" × 11" sheet of paper. For manuscripts, be sure to include enough postage and an envelope large enough to contain it. If you are requesting a sample copy of a magazine or a book publisher's catalog, send an appropriate-size envelope.

- Consider sending a disposable manuscript that saves editors time (this will also save you money).

ABOUT OUR POLICIES

We occasionally receive letters asking why a certain magazine, publisher, or contest is not in the book. Sometimes when we contact listings, the editors do not want to be listed because they:

- do not use very much fiction.
- are overwhelmed with submissions.
- are having financial difficulty or have been recently sold.
- use only solicited material.
- accept work from a select group of writers only.
- do not have the staff or time for the many unsolicited submissions a listing may bring.

Some of the listings do not appear because we have chosen not to list them. We investigate complaints of unprofessional conduct in editors' dealings with writers and misrepresentation of information provided to us by editors and publishers. If we find these reports to be true, after a thorough investigation, we will delete the listing from future editions.

There is no charge to the companies that list in this book. Listings appearing in *Novel & Short Story Writer's Market* are compiled from detailed questionnaires, phone interviews, and information provided by editors, publishers, and awards and conference directors. The publishing industry is volatile and changes of address, editor, policies, and needs happen frequently. To keep up with the changes between editions of the book, we suggest you check the market information on the Writer's Market website at www.writersmarket.com or on the Writer's Digest website at www.writersdigest.com. Many magazine and book publishers offer updated information for writers on their websites. Check individual listings for those website addresses.

Organization newsletters and small magazines devoted to helping writers also list market information. Several offer online writers' bulletin boards, message centers, and chat lines with up-to-the-minute changes and happenings in the writing community.

We rely on our readers, as well, for new markets and information about market conditions. E-mail us if you have any new information or if you have suggestions on how to improve our listings to better suit your writing needs.

RIGHTS

The Copyright Law states that writers are selling one-time rights (in almost all cases) unless they and the publisher have agreed otherwise. A list of various rights follows. Be sure you know exactly what rights you are selling before you agree to the sale.

Copyright is the legal right to exclusive publication, sale, or distribution of a literary work. As the writer or creator of a written work, you need simply to include your name, date, and the copyright symbol © on your piece in order to copyright it. Be aware, however, that most editors today consider placing the copyright symbol on your work the sign of an amateur and many are even offended by it.

....

Some people are under the mistaken impression that copyright is something they have to send away for.

....

To get specific answers to questions about copyright (but not legal advice), you can call the Copyright Public Information Office at (202)707-3000 weekdays between 8:30 A.M. and 5 P.M. EST. Publications listed in *Novel & Short Story Writer's Market* are copyrighted unless otherwise stated. In the case of magazines that are not copyrighted, be sure to keep a copy of your manuscript with your notice printed on it. For more information on copyrighting your work, see *The Copyright Handbook: How to Protect & Use Written Works, 11th edition*, by Stephen Fishman (Nolo Press, 2011).

Some people are under the mistaken impression that copyright is something they have to send away for and that their writing is not properly protected until they have "received" their copyright from the government. The fact is, you don't have to register your work with the Copyright Office in order for your work to be copyrighted; All writing is copyrighted the moment it is put to paper.

Although it is generally unnecessary, registration is a matter of filling out an application form (for writers, that's Form TX) and sending the completed form, a nonreturnable copy of the work in question and a check for $45 to the Library of Congress, Copyright Office, Register of Copyrights, 101 Independence Ave. SE, Washington, DC 20559-6000. If the thought of paying $45 each to register every piece you write does not appeal to you, you can cut costs by registering a group of your works with one form, under one title for one $45 fee.

Most magazines are registered with the Copyright Office as single collective entities themselves; that is, the individual works that make up the magazine are not copyrighted individually in the names of the authors. You'll need to register your article yourself if you wish to have the additional protection of copyright registration.

For more information, visit the United States Copyright Office online at www .copyright.gov.

First Serial Rights

This means the writer offers a newspaper or magazine the right to publish the article, story, or poem for the first time in a particular periodical. All other rights to the material remain with the writer. The qualifier "North American" is often added to this phrase to specify a geographical limit to the license.

When material is excerpted from a book scheduled to be published and it appears in a magazine or newspaper prior to book publication, this is also called first serial rights.

One-Time Rights

A periodical that licenses one-time rights to a work (also known as simultaneous rights) buys the nonexclusive right to publish the work once. That is, there is nothing to stop the author from selling the work to other publications at the same time. Simultaneous sales would typically be to periodicals with different audiences.

Second Serial (Reprint) Rights

This gives a newspaper or magazine the opportunity to print an article, poem, or story after it has already appeared in another newspaper or magazine. Second serial rights are nonexclusive; that is, they can be licensed to more than one market.

All Rights

This is just what it sounds like. All rights means a publisher may use the manuscript anywhere and in any form, including movie and book club sales, without further payment to the writer (although such a transfer, or assignment, of rights will terminate after thirty-five years). If you think you'll want to use the material more than once, you must avoid submitting to such markets or refuse payment and withdraw your material. Ask the editor whether he is willing to buy first rights instead of all rights before you agree to an assignment or sale. Some editors will reassign rights to a writer after a given period, such as one year. It's worth an inquiry in writing.

Subsidiary Rights

These are the rights, other than book publication rights, that should be covered in a book contract. These may include various serial rights; movie, television, audiotape, and other electronic rights; translation rights, etc. The book contract should specify who controls these rights (author or publisher) and what percentage of sales from the licensing of these subrights goes to the author.

Dramatic, Television, and Motion Picture Rights

This means the writer is selling his material for use on the stage, in television, or in the movies. Often a one-year option to buy such rights is offered (generally for 10 percent of the total price). The interested party then tries to sell the idea to actors, directors, studios, or television networks. Some properties are optioned over and over again, but most fail to become dramatic productions. In such cases, the writer can sell his rights again and again—as long as there is interest in the material. Though dramatic, TV, and motion picture rights are more important to the fiction writer than the nonfiction writer, producers today are increasingly interested in nonfiction material; many biographies, topical books and true stories are being dramatized.

Electronic Rights

These rights cover usage in a broad range of electronic media, from online magazines and databases to CD-ROM magazine anthologies and interactive games. The editor should specify in writing if—and which—electronic rights he's requesting. The presumption is that the writer keeps unspecified rights.

Compensation for electronic rights is a major source of conflict between writers and publishers, as many book publishers seek control of them and many magazines routinely include electronic rights in the purchase of print rights, often with no additional payment. Writers can suggest an alternative way of handling this issue by asking for an additional 15 percent to purchase first rights and a royalty system based on the number of times an article is accessed from an electronic database.

MARKETING AND PROMOTION

Everyone agrees writing is hard work whether you are published or not. Yet once you achieve publication the work changes. Now not only do you continue writing and revising your next project, you must also concern yourself with getting your book into the hands of readers. It's time to switch hats from artist to salesperson.

While even best-selling authors whose publishers have committed big bucks to marketing are asked to help promote their books, new authors may have to take it upon themselves to plan and initiate some of their own promotion, usually dipping into their own pockets. While this does not mean that every author is expected to go on tour, sometimes at their own expense, it does mean authors should be prepared to offer suggestions for promoting their books.

Depending on the time, money, and personal preferences of the author and publisher, a promotional campaign could mean anything from mailing out press releases to setting up book signings to hitting the talk-show circuit. Most writers can contribute to their own promotion by providing contact names—reviewers, hometown newspapers, civic groups, organizations—that might have a special interest in the book or the writer.

Above all, when it comes to promotion, be creative. What is your book about? Try to capitalize on it. Focus on your potential audiences and how you can help them connect with your book.

IMPORTANT LISTING INFORMATION

- Listings are not advertisements. Although the information here is as accurate as possible, the listings are not endorsed or guaranteed by the editors of *Novel & Short Story Writer's Market.*
- *Novel & Short Story Writer's Market* reserves the right to exclude any listing that does not meet its requirements.

THE NEW ERA OF PUBLISHING:

Making It Work for You

....

April Eberhardt

Newsflash: Book publishing in the United States is undergoing tumultuous change. (If you're surprised by that, you've got some serious catching up to do!)

One of the biggest changes, and definitely among the most exciting, is your heightened ability as an author to choose how to publish your work. Whereas just a few years ago the "Big Six" publishers (Random House, HarperCollins, Penguin Group, Macmillan, Simon & Schuster and Hachette Book Group) were the gatekeepers to a book's success, and self-publishing was considered by many to be the option of last resort, perceptions—and the realities driving them—have shifted dramatically in recent months. With the rise of electronic publishing, and the ease with which authors can now use the Internet and print-on-demand technology to produce their own books and reach readers directly, many have opted to bypass the "middlemen" in traditional publishing and take matters into their own hands. And for a growing number of those authors, their efforts have proven to be both successful and satisfying—financially as well as personally.

In my role as both literary agent and author advocate, I view these changes not as the end of traditional publishing as we know it, but as the beginning of an exciting era in which more power has shifted into the hands of authors. But that doesn't necessarily mean that these new routes around the gatekeepers make it easier to navigate the publishing landscape. In fact, you may find that your path suddenly seems unclear *because* there are now so many viable options from which to choose.

How have the writers who've succeeded on these more independent paths made the leap? How have they attracted readers? And are their approaches right for you?

UNDERSTANDING HOW PUBLISHING IS CHANGING

The truth is that constant change has become the new normal. Choosing the routes of self-publication and/or electronic publication requires a mind shift for many. Writers are still in the process of embracing these methods as feasible ways to take control of their careers, while gradually letting go of the belief that the only "real" book is a traditionally published print book. On the other side of the desk, agents and publishers are still grappling with the implications of these new shifts, which can complicate their own business models significantly.

Regardless of which avenue to publication you ultimately pursue—and we'll talk more in a moment about ways to approach that decision—there are three principles to keep in mind:

1. **THERE IS NO ONE RIGHT WAY TO PUBLISH.** Success comes in all shapes and sizes. What appeals to one author may be wrong for you. The only rule that applies across the board is that, for your book to be embraced by readers, it must be edited and packaged with professional quality, whether you achieve that yourself or contract with others to do it for you.

2. **AUTHORS AND READERS NO LONGER NEED THE "BIG SIX" TO FIND AND ENGAGE ONE ANOTHER.** While traditional publishers continue to bring a great deal to the table, emerging models also provide all sorts of effective ways for writers and readers to connect. If you're willing to consider different ways to reach your audience directly, you'll likely be pleasantly surprised.

3. **NEW MODELS ARE POPPING UP DAILY.** Some mainstream publishers have expanded their business models to include assisted self-publishing services for authors (Thomas Nelson, Harlequin and even WD's own Abbott Press are a few examples). A few literary agencies now offer consulting services for authors who've chosen the self-publishing route and/or provide hybrid publishing opportunities (Waxman Literary Agency's launch of e-publisher Diversion Books is one example), in which they may share in the author's publication costs as well as profits. The lines between publishing models are blurring rapidly—and not without controversy, as they can create potential conflicts of interest among the agents and publishers that offer these services in addition to their traditional roles.

Regardless of how you feel about these trends, it behooves you as an author to stay attuned to changes, and periodically reassess the success of your chosen model based on new developments and opportunities in the industry. The route you choose today doesn't have to be the route you choose tomorrow.

THE FIRST 3 STEPS TO SUCCESS

Before you make a single move down any path to publication, take these three steps:

1. **MAKE SURE YOUR STORY IS GOOD.** The same rule applies to self-published e-books as it does to print books. You have to start with an enticing, top-notch story in order to persuade readers to keep turning the pages.

2. **EDIT, EDIT, EDIT.** If you can, hire a good freelance editor. Agents and publishers will reject a manuscript pretty quickly if it's not well edited. And if you go the self-publishing route, this step is even more important. To reverse the perception of self-published books as amateur, assume they'll need to be even better than traditionally published books, at least for a while.

3. **BUILD YOUR MARKETING SKILLS.** Given that publishers offer increasingly limited promotional support, and self-publishing authors are entirely on their own, much of book marketing in today's environment is in creating "discoverability." You can't sell a book if no one knows it exists, so you'll need to create awareness however you can, whether it's through social media or blogging or passing out fliers on a street corner. Apply "the rule of setting one hundred small fires": The best way to start a roaring bonfire is to strike many matches, because you can never know which one is going to catch on and create a conflagration.

RE-ESTABLISHING YOUR PUBLICATION GOALS

Let's begin by taking a close look at your personal objectives. What's appealing to you about being published?

Is it the validation of a well-known publisher choosing, printing, distributing, and promoting your book? If so, there's nothing wrong with that—but there are two unfavorable trends you should be prepared to face: 1) given the number of writers vying for fewer slots on publishers' lists, the statistical chances of your manuscript being selected are, unfortunately, getting slimmer, and 2) of those authors who are offered traditional deals, many are finding their advances are smaller and/or paid out over longer periods than were previously standard—or sometimes even that the contract is offered "advance-free."

What if you mainly want the satisfaction of sharing your story with others interested in the same subject you are? Whether you're writing about baseball or butterflies, rockets or rock 'n' roll, there *are* readers out there who are hungry for good writing about your shared passion—and there are now many effective means by which you can reach out to them, with or without the assistance of a publisher.

What if it's your own personal story you want to tell, one that will appeal primarily to family and friends? If that's the case, your audience is certainly well within reach—and through easier and less expensive methods than ever before.

As you're contemplating the best route for you, it's worthwhile to consider the successes of "track-switching" authors who've made headlines. Barry Eisler, a well-known thriller writer, turned down a six-figure advance from a major publisher in order to self-publish, and then he subsequently decided to sign with Amazon when the retailer formed its own imprint. Amanda Hocking, a self-published author who made her name (not to mention a nice income) with e-books, accepted an offer from a major publisher *after* her titles went viral. Will these and other authors return to self-publishing their work down the line? It's too soon to tell—but it's encouraging that not only has self-publishing launched the careers of wildly successful unknowns, it also has surfaced as an appealing alternative to more established writers.

EVALUATING POTENTIAL ROUTES

Even if you know where you want to head, the best way to get there may be unclear. If you're still not sure, ask yourself these questions:

1. **WHAT'S YOUR PATIENCE LEVEL?** Be honest with yourself about your expectations, and be realistic about what you'll be getting into, no matter which path you choose. Are you willing to take the chance that you'll find an agent who believes in your work as you do, and that that agent will be able to place your manuscript? If so, how long are you prepared to give it? Pursuing traditional publication takes time and effort—and is by no means guaranteed. Finding an agent can take a year or more of diligently sending queries, attending pitch sessions at conferences, and/or refining your materials based on feedback. Then, if and when you do secure representation, you'll likely work with your agent for several more months to further edit your manuscript and refine your pitch before the process of submitting your book to publishing houses begins. Finding a willing acquisitions editor can *again* take a year or more—and there's no guarantee that your agent will be able to place your book.

    At the opposite end of the spectrum, you could theoretically format and upload your e-book for sale before you go to bed tonight (not that I'd recommend rushing any release, but you get the point).

    As you weigh your options, I'd recommend you give some thought to what your Plan B would be, if Plan A falls short of your expectations. That way, you can prevent small obstacles from becoming big setbacks.

2. **WHAT'S YOUR WILLINGNESS TO EXPERIMENT?** The Internet can be a wonderful way to find your audience, and if you're game to try different techniques—creating a compelling website, participating in blogs and online forums, communicating via social media, finding creative ways to reach out to everyone you know to let them

know you've published a book—your chances of becoming a successful author are much greater. While this is true whether you are traditionally or independently published, a willingness to try new approaches is particularly important if you choose to do it yourself.

3. **WHAT'S YOUR FINANCIAL SITUATION?** Publishing well on your own will require some investment, whether you e-publish or create a print book (or both). Costs vary tremendously, from a few hundred dollars to many thousands, depending on how you decide to proceed. Doing it all yourself will require more time, and likely (but not necessarily) less money, than outsourcing elements to experienced pros such as website designers, freelance editors and publicists. Then again, quality is key. And if you purchase top-notch assistance, you'll have more time to focus on your writing. As with so many decisions, it's a trade-off—but remember that as self-published books proliferate, the good will rise above the not so good, and you'll want your book to be a clear contender in the first group, regardless of how you get it there.

MOVING AHEAD

So what should you do? And why, you may be wondering, would I, a literary agent, suggest you consider publishing models outside the traditional paradigm? After all, agents traditionally make a living selling authors' manuscripts to big publishers. I'll answer the second question first, which may provide guidance and insight into the first.

As an author advocate foremost, I want to see good stories make their way to interested readers in whatever ways they can. I'm particularly passionate about helping new authors launch their work. Despite my continued optimism that the publishing world will welcome new work, over the past year I've seen a distinct diminishment in publishers' willingness to take a chance on new authors, particularly authors of fiction. While I continue to welcome submissions from writers seeking traditional publication and do all I can to make that dream a reality for the few I'm able to represent each year, I'm a realist at heart. After one, two, three, even four dozen queries or more to suitable editors on behalf of an author, I often see a pattern among responses: "This is a terrific manuscript—but we can't take a chance on a new author." For authors with the determination and willingness to try a different path—and, very importantly, the ability to set aside any lingering prejudice against publishing independently, and commit to publishing with a quality that will help raise the bar—I see great opportunity and the possibility for astounding success.

If mainstream publication is your dream, and you're willing to wager that your manuscript will make it through the gates, then by all means pursue that path with hope and confidence. Go forth with the blessings of all the agents who would love to see you achieve that. As you enter the fray, develop the ability to occupy yourself as you wait to hear back from agents and editors. While you wait, ramp up your website, expand your social media network, begin your next novel—and be sure to stay on top of what's happening in publishing, because today's experiments with new publishing models could easily become tomorrow's most appealing alternatives.

No matter what path you choose, try to let go of the idea that only traditionally published books are "real." Forward-thinking writers are best equipped to face the challenges that lie ahead on *every* publishing route.

Predictions as to the uncertain future of publishing abound these days, and they vary widely. Only time will tell who (if anyone) is right, but in the meantime, here's mine: Within the year, a new order will emerge, one in which a select and growing group of authors, ones who have carefully crafted their books—not only in writing them well but investing in good editing and overall design—will establish a direct pipeline to their readers, bypassing traditional publishers and finding their markets independently of the legacy model. Readers, in turn, will begin to shift perceptions, developing trust and confidence in certain self-published authors as they see quality emerging in a distinct subset. Respected reviewers of self-published books will emerge.

While traditional publishers will continue to mediate between many authors and their readers for some time to come, I see much excitement and success in authors' ability to find their own readers more quickly, engaging them in dialogue and discussion, playing off of their dreams and desires in order to create new kinds of work they'll find appealing, and doing so in a rapid, free-flowing, satisfying, and—dare I say it?—profitable way. Are you ready for the adventure?

Literary change agent and author advocate **April Eberhardt** founded April Eberhardt Literary in early 2011 in order to assist and advise authors as they navigate the increasingly complex world of publishing. In addition to representing authors in the traditional publishing world, she works with clients who wish to pursue nontraditional means of publication.

REVISING YOUR PATH TO PUBLICATION

....

Jane Friedman

Don't you wish someone could tell you how close you are to getting published? Don't you wish someone could say, "If you just keep at it for three more years, you're certain to make it!"?

Or, even if it would be heartbreaking, wouldn't it be nice to be told that you're wasting your time, so that you could move on, try another tack, or simply write what brings you personal pleasure, with no other aim in mind?

I've counseled thousands of writers over the years, and even if it's not possible for me to read their work, I can usually say something definitive about what their next steps should be. I often see when they're wasting their time.

No matter where you are on your own publishing path, it's smart to periodically take stock of where you're headed, and revise as necessary. Here are some steps you can take to do just that.

RECOGNIZING STEPS THAT AREN'T MOVING YOU FORWARD

Let's start with five common time-wasting behaviors. You may be guilty of one or more. Most writers have been guilty of the first.

Time-Waster #1: Submitting manuscripts that aren't your best work

Let's be honest. We all secretly hope that some editor or agent will read our work, drop everything, and call us to say: *This is a work of genius! YOU are a genius!*

Few writers give up on this dream entirely, but in order to increase the chances of this ever happening, you have to give each manuscript *everything* you've got, with nothing held back. Too many writers save their best effort for some future work, as if they were going to run out of good material.

You can't operate like that.

Every single piece of greatness must go into your current project. Be confident that your creative well will refill. Make your book better than you ever thought possible—that's what it needs to compete. It can't be good. *Good* gets rejected. Your work has to be the *best*.

How do you know when it's ready, when it's your best? I like how *Guide to Literary Agents* Editor Chuck Sambuchino typically answers this question at writing conferences: "If you think the story has a problem, it does—and any story with a problem is not ready."

It's common for a new writer who doesn't know any better to send off his manuscript without realizing how much work is left to do. But experienced writers are just as guilty of sending out work that is not ready. Stop wasting your time.

Time-Waster #2: Self-publishing when no one is listening

There are many reasons writers choose to self-publish, but the most common is the inability to land an agent or a traditional publisher.

Fortunately, it's more viable than ever for a writer to be successful without a traditional publisher or agent, primarily due to the rise of e-books and e-readers. However, when writers chase self-publishing as an alternative to traditional publishing, they often have a nasty surprise in store: No one is listening. They don't have an audience.

Bowker estimated that in 2009, more than 760,000 new titles were "nontraditionally" published, meaning print-on-demand and self-published work. How many new titles were traditionally published? About 288,000. And none of these numbers take into account the growing number of writers releasing their work in electronic-only editions.

If your goal is to bring your work successfully to the marketplace, it's a waste of time to self-publish that work—in any format—if you haven't yet cultivated an audience for it or can't market and promote it effectively through your network. Doing so will not likely harm your career in the long run, but it won't move it forward, either.

Time-Waster #3: Publishing your work digitally when your audience wants print

E-books have become the darlings of the self-publishing world, and for good reason. They're easy to create, require little investment, and can reach an international market overnight. They also allow you to experiment, to have a direct line to a readership, and to see what effectively grows that readership.

But it won't do you a bit of good if your audience is still devoted to print. If you don't know what format your readers prefer, then find out before you waste your time developing a product no one will read or buy.

Rework this maxim as needed for your particular audience (e.g., don't focus on producing print if your readers favor digital).

Time-Waster #4: Looking for major publication of regional or niche work

The cookbook-memoir that your local church ladies produced this year is probably not appropriate for one of the major New York publishers.

That may seem obvious, but every year agents receive thousands of submissions for work that does not have national appeal and does not deserve shelf space at every chain bookstore in the country. (And that's typically why you get an agent: to sell your work to the big publishers, which specialize in national distribution and marketing.)

Now, if those church ladies were famous for producing the award-winning Betty Crocker recipe twenty years in a row, we'd be onto something with a national market. But few regional works have that broader angle.

As a writer, one of the most difficult tasks you face is having sufficient distance from your work to understand how a publishing professional would view the market for it or to determine if there's a commercial *angle* to be exploited. You have to view your work not as something precious to you, but as a product to be positioned and sold. That means pitching your work only to the most appropriate publishing houses, even if they're in your own backyard rather than New York City.

Time-Waster #5: Focusing on publishing when you should be writing

Some writers are far too concerned with queries, agents, marketing, or conference-going, when they should be busy producing the best work possible.

Don't get me wrong—for some types of nonfiction, it's essential to have a platform in place before you write the book. The fact that nonfiction authors don't typically write the full manuscript until after acceptance of their proposal (with the exception of memoir and creative nonfiction) is indicative of how much platform means to their publication.

But for everyone else (those of us who are *not* selling a book based solely on the proposal): Don't get consumed with finding an agent until you're a writer ready for publication.

And now we come to that tricky matter again. How do you know it's *that* time? Let's dig a little deeper.

EVALUATING YOUR PLACE ON THE PUBLICATION PATH

Whenever I sit down for a critique session with a writer, I ask three questions early on: How long have you been working on this manuscript, and who has seen it? Is this the first manuscript you've ever completed? And finally: How long have you been actively writing?

These questions help me evaluate where the writer might be on the publication path. Here are a few generalizations I can often make:

- Most first manuscript attempts are not publishable, even after revision, yet they are necessary and vital for a writer's growth. A writer who's just finished her first manuscript probably doesn't realize this and will likely take the rejection process very hard. Some writers can't move past this rejection. You've probably heard experts advise that you should always start working on the next manuscript, rather than waiting to publish the first. That's because you need to move on and not get stuck on your first attempt.

- A writer who has been working on the same manuscript for years and years—and has written *nothing else*—might have a motivation problem. There isn't usually much valuable learning going on when someone tinkers with the same pages over a decade.

- Writers who have been actively writing for many years, have produced multiple full-length manuscripts, and have one or two trusted critique partners (or mentors) are often well-positioned for publication. They probably know their strengths and weaknesses, and have a structured revision process. Many such people require only luck to meet preparedness.

- Writers who have extensive experience in one medium, then attempt to tackle another (e.g., journalists tackling the novel) may overestimate their abilities to produce a publishable manuscript on the first try. That doesn't mean their effort won't be good, but it might not be *good enough*. Fortunately, any writer with professional experience will probably approach the process with more of a business mind-set, a good network of contacts to help him understand next steps, and a range of tools to overcome the challenges.

Notice I have not mentioned talent. I have not mentioned creative writing classes or degrees. I have not mentioned online presence. These factors are usually less relevant in determining how close you are to publishing a book-length work.

The two things that *are* relevant:

1. **HOW MUCH TIME YOU'VE PUT INTO WRITING.** I agree with Malcolm Gladwell's 10,000-hour rule in *Outliers*: The key to success in any field is, to a large extent, a matter of practicing a specific task for a total of around 10,000 hours.

2. WHETHER YOU'RE READING ENOUGH TO UNDERSTAND WHERE YOU ARE ON THE SPECTRUM OF QUALITY. In his series on storytelling (available on YouTube), Ira Glass says:

> *The first couple years that you're making stuff, what you're making isn't so good. It's not that great. It's trying to be good, it has ambitions, but it's not that good. But your taste, the thing that got you into the game, your taste is still killer. Your taste is good enough that you can tell that what you're making is kind of a disappointment to you. You can tell that it's still sort of crappy. A lot of people never get past that phase. A lot of people at that point quit. … Most everybody I know who does interesting creative work, they went through a phase of years where they had really good taste [and] they could tell that what they were making wasn't as good as they wanted it to be.*

If you can't perceive the gap—or if you haven't gone through the "phase"—you probably aren't reading enough. How do you develop good taste? You read. How do you understand what quality work is? You read. What's the best way to improve your skills aside from writing more? You read. You write, and you read, and you begin to close the gap between the quality you *want* to achieve, and the quality you can achieve.

In short: You've got to produce a lot of crap before you can produce something publishable.

SIGNS YOU'RE GETTING CLOSE TO PUBLICATION

- You start receiving personalized, "encouraging" rejections.
- Agents or editors reject the manuscript you submitted, but ask you to send your next work. (They can see that you're on the verge of producing something great.)
- Your mentor (or published author friend) tells you to contact his agent, without you asking for a referral.
- An agent or editor proactively contacts you because she spotted your quality writing somewhere online or in print.
- You've outgrown the people in your critique group and need to find more sophisticated critique partners.
- Looking back, you understand why your work was rejected, and see that it deserved rejection. You probably even feel embarrassed by earlier work.

KNOWING WHEN IT'S TIME TO CHANGE COURSE

I used to believe that great work would eventually get noticed—you know, that old theory that quality bubbles to the top?

I don't believe that anymore.

Great work is overlooked every day, for a million reasons. Business concerns outweigh artistic concerns. Some people are just perpetually unlucky.

To avoid beating your head against the wall, here are some questions that can help you understand when and how to change course.

1. **IS YOUR WORK COMMERCIALLY VIABLE?** Indicators will eventually surface if your work isn't suited for commercial publication. You'll hear things like: "Your work is too quirky or eccentric." "It has narrow appeal." "It's experimental." "It doesn't fit the model." Possibly: "It's too intellectual, too demanding." These are signs that you may need to consider self-publishing—which will also require you to find the niche audience you appeal to.

2. **ARE READERS RESPONDING TO SOMETHING YOU DIDN'T EXPECT?** I see this happen all the time: A writer is working on a manuscript that no one seems interested in but has fabulous success on some side project. Perhaps you really want to push your memoir, but it's a humorous tip series on your blog that everyone loves. Sometimes it's better to pursue what's working, and what people express interest in, especially if you take enjoyment in it. Use it as a stepping-stone to other things if necessary.

3. **ARE YOU GETTING BITTER?** You can't play the poor, victimized writer and expect to get published. As it is in romantic relationships, pursuing an agent or editor with an air of desperation, or with an Eeyore complex, will not endear you to them. Embittered writers carry a huge sign with them that screams, "I'm unhappy, and I'm going to make you unhappy, too."

   If you find yourself demonizing people in the publishing industry, taking rejections very personally, feeling as if you're owed something, and/or complaining whenever you get together with other writers, it's time to find the refresh button. Return to what made you feel joy and excitement about writing in the first place. Perhaps you've been focusing too much on getting published, and you've forgotten to cherish the other aspects. Which brings me to the overall theory of how you should, at various stages of your career, revisit and revise your publication strategy.

REVISING YOUR PUBLISHING PLAN

No matter how the publishing world changes, consider these three timeless factors as you make decisions about your next steps forward:

1. **WHAT MAKES YOU HAPPY:** This is the reason you got into writing in the first place. Even if you put this on the back burner in order to advance other aspects of your writing and publishing career, don't leave it out of the equation for very long. Otherwise your efforts can come off as mechanistic or uninspired, and you'll eventually burn out.

2. **WHAT EARNS YOU MONEY:** Not everyone cares about earning money from writing—and I believe that anyone in it for the coin should find some other field—but as you

gain experience, the choices you make in this regard become more important. The more professional you become, the more you have to pay attention to what brings the most return on your investment of time and energy.

3. **WHAT REACHES READERS OR GROWS YOUR AUDIENCE:** Growing readership is just as valuable as earning money. It's like putting a bit of money in the bank and making an investment that pays off as time passes. Sometimes you'll want to make trade-offs that involve earning less money in order to grow readership, because it invests in your future. (E.g., for a time you might focus on building a blog or a site, rather than writing for print publication, to grow a more direct line to your fans.)

It is rare that every piece of writing you do, or every opportunity presented, can involve all three elements at once. Commonly you can get two of the three. Sometimes you'll pursue certain projects with only one of these factors in play. You get to decide based on your priorities at any given point in time.

At the very beginning of this article, I suggested that it might be nice if someone could tell us if we're wasting our time trying to get published.

Here's a little piece of hope: If your immediate thought was, *I couldn't stop writing even if someone told me to give up,* then you're much closer to publication than someone who is easily discouraged. The battle is far more psychological than you might think. Those who can't be dissuaded are more likely to reach their goals, regardless of the path they ultimately choose.

....

Jane Friedman, a former publisher and editorial director of Writer's Digest, is an industry author-ity on commercial, literary, and emerging forms of publishing. She blogs at janefriedman.com.

....

FREE MONEY:

How to Find Grants, Fellowships, and Residencies to Support Your Writing Career

....

Gigi Rosenberg

Cheryl Strayed has won seventeen grants totaling more than $33,000 over the course of her career to support her work as a writer. The grants have bought her time to write but have also funded a research trip, child care, travel expenses to attend a writing retreat, and even the development of her website. Along with many essays, she's published a novel, *Torch* (released by Houghton Mifflin in 2006), and a memoir, *Wild* (released by Knopf in 2012), both with partial support from grants and residencies.

Without grants, she would still be a writer—and most writers can't live solely on grant money—but grants have helped her write more, market more, earn prestige and hone her craft. In short, grants can propel a writing career. And even just the act of applying for a grant, regardless of the outcome, can help you better define both your work and your goals—an exercise that benefits every writer.

So what's the catch? Where is all this "free money," and how do you get some?

First of all, grants are not exactly free. Applying for one takes work, including researching where to apply and then writing a detailed proposal. Grants are also not for every writer. To be a competitive applicant for most of these opportunities, you'll need to be at a stage in your career where you have some body of work—even a small one—to show your talent. So though you will find grants for "emerging" writers, you'll need to demonstrate that you've been working at your craft for at least a few years and have some publishing credits to your name—even modest ones. (The idea is to demonstrate that you're seriously pursuing your writing. The good news is that the actual work sample you submit is more important than past accolades.)

The grant-writing process is similar to the query/submission process: You study each organization offering a grant to ensure your project is the right match, and then you follow the directions for applying. If you've had success submitting your work, you already have the skills you need to win grants to support your writing.

EXPLORING THE OPPORTUNITIES

You can find grants to pay for taking a class, attending a conference, traveling to do research, producing a project, hiring a consultant, or to support you while you write. The types of grants available fall into these main categories:

- **FELLOWSHIPS AND AWARDS:** Many writers find these to be the most attractive kinds of grants because they're usually "no strings attached," which means you can use the funds to support your writing in any way you want—it's up to you what you work on.
- **PROFESSIONAL DEVELOPMENT GRANTS:** These funds pay for you to advance your career. Frequently, they'll pay your tuition to attend a workshop or writing conference. For example, I used a professional development grant to take a voice workshop at the Banff Centre for the Arts when I was performing dramatic monologues and needed help translating the written word to the spoken voice. These grants might also pay for marketing materials, the cost of hiring a consultant, or anything else that develops you professionally.
- **PROJECT GRANTS:** These grants pay for a specific project that usually culminates in a public event. In your applications for these grants, you'll need to consider and define your audience. Examples of projects would be a performance of a stage play, a reading series, or any literary event that engages an audience.
- **RESIDENCIES:** Technically, residencies are not grants because they offer time and space, not money (though some residencies do offer stipends). However, time and space can be as useful as money, and the application process is similar to that of grants. You can find residencies across the country and around the globe. Most offer a place to live and write in community with writers and/or artists from other disciplines. Some residencies require you to teach a workshop or give a reading during your time there.

WHERE TO FIND GRANTS ///////////////////////////////////////

Start your search small and local by investigating grant opportunities in your own town, region, and state. Peruse the websites of your town's art council and your state's arts commission. To help guide your efforts, visit the website of the National Assembly of State Arts Agencies (**nasaa-arts.org**), which provides links to arts agencies in all fifty states and a range of helpful publications.

- **THE NEW YORK FOUNDATION FOR THE ARTS' SOURCE** (**nyfasource.org**) is an online national directory of awards for all types of artists. The Source lists about one thousand opportunities for literary artists nationwide, including residencies, fellowships, professional development grants, and so on. This list is updated daily, and access is free.
- **MIRA BARTÓK'S BLOG FOR ARTISTS, WRITERS, AND COMPOSERS** (**miraslist.blogspot. com**) includes information, resources, and deadlines for grants, fellowships, and international residencies (along with encouraging posts).
- C. Hope Clark offers a comprehensive monthly **FUNDS FOR WRITERS E-NEWSLETTER** (**funds forwriters.com**) for $15 per year that lists contests, awards, grants, and fellowships.
- **PEN AMERICAN CENTER** (**pen.org**) offers a comprehensive directory for writers with its Grants and Awards Database, which comprises more than one thousand grants, fellowships, scholarships, and residencies for writers. Subscriptions are available for $12 per year.
- Nonprofit literary organization **POETS & WRITERS** (**pw.org**) lists grants, awards, and competitions.
- **THE FOUNDATION CENTER WEBSITE** (**foundationcenter.org/getstarted/individuals**) offers a comprehensive database for individual grant seekers. For a fee, you can subscribe for a month or more. See if your local library has a subscription you can use for free.

FOCUSING YOUR EFFORTS

Grant money comes from either public sources (like the federal, state, or local government) or private sources (namely individuals or foundations). But before you surf the Web or wander the library, begin your research with your own career plans and dreams.

What project are you most excited about right now? Make a list of what it would take to get that project completed. For example, when Debra Gwartney was writing her memoir, *Live Through This*, she needed time more than money. So she put her efforts into applying for residencies. She ultimately won two—a month at Hedgebrook in Washington State and three months at the Helene Wurlitzer Foundation in New Mexico—and the resulting book was published by Houghton Mifflin in 2009.

Residencies also made an enormous difference to Ellen Sussman, who wrote the bulk of her novel *French Lessons*, published by Ballantine, at Ragdale, Ucross Foundation and the Ledig House International Writers' Residency. "I can write at home," Sussman says, "but I can find a focus, sustained and intense, over two or three weeks at a residency that allows me to lose myself in the kind of first-draft-writing dream state that I love."

Deciding what you want can sometimes be the biggest hurdle. If you're like me, your project list is long. How do you decide which is the right project to pursue next?

An exercise I recently discovered in Priscilla Long's *The Writer's Portable Mentor* is one way to start. Long advises writers to make a chronological "List of Works," starting with the very first poem, essay, novel, or other piece you ever wrote. You need only to have completed a first draft of the work for it to qualify for the list.

To compile my list, I sorted through boxes stashed at the back of my closet, where I discovered abandoned screenplays, poems, dramatic monologues, personal essays, and book-length manuscripts. The first item on my list—from 1972—is a letter of complaint I wrote and mailed to the director of a summer camp I attended when I was fourteen. I have almost 150 entries, many published, most not.

My "List of Works" helped me see that the fourteen-year-old writer, the twenty-one-year-old writer, and the thirty-five-year-old writer have been exploring the same themes and concerns at different stages of experience and writing skill. This powerful exercise showed me in concrete terms where I was coming from.

When the list was complete, I saw the trajectory of my passions as a writer and I knew exactly what I wanted to work on next.

Begin your grant research with your own desire and passion for your work. This will ground you and focus your efforts throughout the process.

PREPARING THE APPLICATION

What makes grant writing daunting is that no two applications are exactly alike. However, the more applications you write, the more you realize that they all require similar elements. At a minimum, you'll need to submit at least three items:

- **ARTIST STATEMENT:** Think of the artist statement as your manifesto. It speaks for your work and answers the question of why you write what you write. It tells the story of where you've been, where you are, and where you're taking your writing next. It might divulge your process, your research techniques, your themes, obsessions, and influences.

- **WORK SAMPLE:** This is the most crucial piece of any application. Because even if you write the most stunning artist statement and compelling project description, if your work sample doesn't live up to the promise, you won't get funded, no matter what.

  "Make sure the work sample is your best work," advises Jim Tomlinson, author of *Things Kept, Things Left Behind*. Tomlinson has won grants from the Kentucky Arts Council and the National Endowment for the Arts. The NEA grant paid his living expenses for a year while he finished his second book of stories, *Nothing Like an Ocean*, which was later published by the University Press of Kentucky.

  "[Work] that you are just finishing and polishing might seem absolutely magnificent at that moment," Tomlinson says, "but a few weeks down the road, you might wish you'd gone with something tried and true."

  Ensure the sample is a good match for the grant you're applying for. For example, if I were applying for a grant for Jewish writers, I'd make sure my writing sample was a strong piece with a Jewish theme.
- **PROJECT DESCRIPTION:** You'll need to describe in concrete terms what the project is, why it's needed, what the goals are, who the intended audience is, and how the project will serve that audience. If you're applying for a project grant, the application will require a detailed budget and a plan for how you will evaluate the success of your venture.

BEING A MODEL APPLICANT

To stand out from the hordes, ensure you and your project are a good match for the funder and follow the directions to the letter.

Ask yourself: Is your project exactly the kind of undertaking this funder likes supporting? If not, can you tweak your idea so it lines up? If you can't, find a better match.

Even if the directions sound like a person with obsessive-compulsive disorder wrote them, they are ridiculously specific for several reasons: to ease the strain of an already overworked staff, to make the applications easy to review, and to make the process fair. If all the applications follow the same format, the system is more equitable and it's easier to compare applicants. By following directions, you're showing respect for the organization.

You may need to review the directions several times to discern nuances. For instance, the instructions may say, "Submit up to five poems." If so, then submitting four poems would be fine. If they say, "Submit six poems," you can submit only six, not five or seven.

Those reviewing the applications are looking for ways to reduce the pile. If two applications are equally strong, but one applicant didn't follow directions and one did, the applicant who did is going to make the cut.

DISCOVERING HIDDEN ADVANTAGES

Grants and fellowships are very competitive. There are more worthy and eligible applicants than funds and opportunities to go around. You do your best and it still feels like a crap-shoot—because it is.

But applying for a grant helps you articulate and organize your next project—a benefit even when you don't win.

"Every time I write one of those damn artist statements, I learn something new," Sussman says. "In my most recent statement, I talk about how I seem to reinvent the novel every time I write one … [and] while writing that, I realized that I needed to think way outside the box for my next novel. … In a matter of moments, I came up with a new framework for this complicated new work."

David Shields recalls his application for a Guggenheim fellowship to support his writing of *The Thing About Life Is That One Day You'll Be Dead* (which was later published by Knopf): "I had to encounter that the book as such wasn't hanging together well yet. Writing the proposal, I actually discovered what the core of *The Thing About Life* was."

Writing a grant will bring you clarity, focus, and momentum. As you hone the description for your next project, you make discoveries. You'll notice that you talk about your project in a more concise way. Back at the writing desk, you'll find that now you know what to emphasize, what to cut, what to push to the background. The grant-writing process helps you edit, expand, and bring the project into its fullness.

"Everyone else complains about writing grant proposals," Shields says. "I must admit I sort of love the process because it forces one to confront what the work is trying to do." And when he actually wins the grants, he notices another benefit besides the money: "The thing I like most about grants is the guilt: One feels duty-bound to deliver on the grant's implicit promise."

The truth is, it's humbling to ask for something—especially money. But the process of asking will toughen you up in good ways—the more you clarify, the stronger your conviction becomes. You'll also realize that "no" won't kill you.

In fact, a rejection can help you discern how much you want to complete your project. If one "no" is enough to make you quit, then perhaps you didn't have the passion the idea required. If you're still determined, this is your chance to persevere and pursue the next funding opportunity. Being a writer requires the sensitivity of a poet and the toughness of a rhino—and grant writing helps you practice both. This process is not for the weak willed. It takes courage to be a writer. Now use that courage to push your writing further into the world.

....

Gigi Rosenberg is a writer, speaker, and the author of *The Artist's Guide to Grant Writing*.

....

WRITING AN IRRESISTIBLE QUERY

Jennifer D. Foster

Crafting a query with the perfect mix of clarity, impact, and intrigue—so desired by agents, editors, and publishers—to showcase your novel or short story may seem like an intimidating, insurmountable task. Sigh not. Eight expert insider tips and success techniques from these agents, authors, editors, educators, and publishers will have you writing your best query yet.

DO YOUR HOMEWORK. Visit a bricks-and-mortar book shop to see what's selling. "Your idea shouldn't copy what's already out there, but going to a bookstore will help you determine what is working and whether or not your manuscript is marketable," says Jennifer MacKinnon, an editor at Scholastic Canada Ltd. in Toronto. Read up on how to write queries, take a workshop, and research—ad nauseum—to qualify the right agents, editors, or publishers for you.

"You should know the deal history of the agents you approach, and why you want to work with a particular person," imparts Sam Hiyate, a Toronto literary agent and founder of The Rights Factory. "Finding an agent is like dating; you want someone with the right chemistry." Check out books' acknowledgment pages, then target specific editors or agents who've worked on books similar to yours, to make an educated submission and "greatly reduce your rejection rate," emphasizes Helen Zimmermann, president of Zimmermann Literary in New York. According to Crissy Boylan, managing editor at Toronto's ECW Press, "The author-publisher relationship is so much about making a perfect match, and the query letter is your chance to make a great first impression." And, adds Zimmermann, "always pay particular attention to each agent's submission guidelines and follow them to a T."

OWN YOUR QUERY, BUT ... Your query is *the* opportunity to impress and cover all the bases. "It's the very first introduction to your writing style, so it's pretty important to put your best words and style out there from the beginning," emphasizes Tonya Martin, publisher and editor-in-chief of McKellar & Martin Publishing Group, Ltd. in Vancouver. Inherent in a great query is "a well-crafted prose style and a sense of the writer's ambition, discipline, and personality," says Hiyate. Gráinne Fox, a literary agent with Fletcher & Company in New York, agrees: "Who you are should come across in how you write about your book." But, she warns, "please don't tell me it's brilliant and will be a surefire bestseller. Part of the real trick of a writing life is not only to have confidence in what you are doing creatively, but also to practice humility." Boylan concurs: "While it's great to be confident in describing your work, saying a book is the 'best ever' or unlike anything ever before written in the history of mankind makes the reader wary you're making grand claims you won't be able to live up to."

Kevin Smoker, San Francisco-based blogger and author of *Practical Classics: 50 Reasons to Reread 50 Books You Haven't Touched Since High School*, adds: "Don't praise yourself. It's juvenile and sends the message you don't trust the judgment of the person you're querying." Taking ownership also means that "you need to convince the reader why you're *the* person, why no one else in the world could possibly write this book," says Lynn Wiese Sneyd, owner of LWS Literary Services in Tuscon, Arizona, and author of *Holistic Parenting and Healthy Solutions*.

COME OUT SWINGING. "Always begin with your biggest strength. If it's your characters, tell me about them. If it's the plot, start there. If your bio stands out, start by talking about yourself," says Zimmermann. Best-selling New Jersey-based author Lisa Collier Cool calls this the "powerhouse lead paragraph." Collier Cool, who's authored *How to Write Irresistible Query Letters* and co-authored *Beat the Heart Attack Gene*, stresses effective queries have a "tantalizing summary of the book and a compelling reason why readers will want to read about the topic, such as telling the query reader something she doesn't already know." And that's what Wiese Sneyd refers to as the "great hook: the first sentence and paragraph that stand out and convince the agent or editor to continue reading."

"The most important part of the letter is describing your book effectively," ensures Cynthia Good, director of the Creative Book Publishing program at Toronto's Humber College and former president of Penguin Canada. Katharine Sands, a literary agent with the New York-based Sarah Jane Freymann Literary Agency and author of *Making the Perfect Pitch: How to Catch a Literary Agent's Eye*, expands on this: "If the writing is capable yet safe, intelligent yet stilted, I simply say, '*I'm outta here.*' I have to be." Sands is "hoping to have an *aha* moment of discovery. The hook can be the writing itself and it can be one sentence or one moment. I love to see a 'rope-trick.' A writer shows me writing chops with a sentence that jumps out at me. It could be that the use of language is lovely or bold, unexpected in some way.

Or there might be a well-constructed moment of observation, humor, or conflict. But one moment, one well-wrought sentence speaks volumes. And it makes me want to see more."

And, says Wiese Sneyd, "a good title also helps." While it may not be the final one, a title that connects to the book's content shows you're serious. Wiese Sneyd also says, "Delineating the market for the book is important." Why? Because, while reading your query, "some of the first questions a publisher, agent, or editor will ask are, 'Who is going to read this book? And how is it going to be positioned in the marketplace?'". Adds MacKinnon: "Tell me why you think your book is right for us, and why it will sell. However, be succinct. We look at these very quickly, so I want to see the highlights, not an in-depth analysis of the market."

INCLUDE COMPARABLES. Comparing your novel or short story to another author's work helps the query reader gain an immediate understanding of its genre. "It helps me think we share the same sensibility," clarifies Fox. Hiyate agrees: "I recently used the example of '*Twilight* meets Murakami' to pitch something myself. If someone else had used such comps, I would have asked to see the manuscript." Zimmermann also applauds the use of comps. "Be familiar with other books in your genre and compare your project to others, as appropriate. That's a great way to really nail your audience."

But, cautions Fox, "don't get wrapped up in ludicrous comparisons, such as *Sophie's Choice* meets *Twilight* meets *Gone Girl*. There's a fine line between the author using comparable titles that can be illuminating and just going off on a tangent, trying to be all things to all people." Adds Martin: "Inadvertently compare yourself to a literary genius when *genius* may not *yet* describe your work, and the outcome probably won't be great."

ENSURE ERROR-FREE COPY. Sloppy, error-laden text spells probable disaster. The query must be unhindered by grammatical and spelling errors for it to stand a chance. Be sure to "have people whose opinions you trust read and critique it" before submitting, recommends Boylan. And having a professional (copy) editor eyeball the final version is wise, but only after "you've polished it and tested it out through several revisions," recommends Hiyate. Translation? "You should feel like you're Don Draper trying out a pitch, and present it to qualified agents only when it's perfect," he urges.

MacKinnon agrees, advising to "be professional and think of this as a cover letter for a job. You wouldn't send a letter off to a prospective employer without having it carefully proofread, and you wouldn't give out personal details, either." Stresses MacKinnon: "The editor/agent wants to know you take this seriously." Personalizing your query is an additional way to ensure blunder-free text. It's no secret agents and editors abhor "feeling that the query might be spam sent to a zillion people," states Hiyate. "Don't start with 'Dear Agent,'" warns Zimmermann. This form of misaddressing is what Sands refers to as a "querial killer." However, stresses Good, don't confuse personalizing with "attempting to be overly familiar with the query reader." Finding a balance between a professional and personal tone is key.

SECURE A PLATFORM. Clarifying who are you and how you can help market your work is crucial. "Make sure you don't ignore your qualifications," stresses Good, "whether it's writing credits or your connection to the material. And it's important to have some kind of marketing hook, some reason your book would sell or some audience you know you could target." But "ditch the hard sell," warns Martin. Demanding, "'You have to publish this book! It will make you money and be a super-bestseller!'" is an absolute no-no, she stresses, as is "predicting your sales volume."

So, what's a platform, exactly? People with whom the author already has a connection. "Maybe it's through Facebook or blog followers, or maybe the author is already giving talks or doing radio shows or has a newspaper column," states Wiese Sneyd. "Having a good platform is like having a ready-made audience when your book comes out." Boylan explains further: "It's important to see an author is committed to working past the publication date by being involved in promotional efforts. Are you involved in the community [that is] connected to your book's topic or genre? Do you have an online presence? As much as a publisher can and will work with the author to find the audience for his or her book, the author, as expert, is almost always the best point of contact for a community of readers, and when we see in a pitch letter that the writer understands his/her role in this process, it's very encouraging." Yet, while publishers often prefer to work with authors with established platforms or a publishing history," if you haven't had much experience, that's okay, too. Just be honest. It gives a true sense of the writer if I know you've been working a night-time security job, but writing a crime novel in the daylight hours," says Fox.

EMBRACE BREVITY. Tell the reader what the book's about. As Sands says, "Ask yourself: 'Have you taken me in, introduced a character, and shown me why I want to spend time in this world?'"). But keep the query brief. How brief? "It's not easy to reduce the entire contents of your book into two sentences, but it's necessary," says Boylan. "Try out your short pitch on friends or relatives; if they get it instantly, the editor/agent receiving your query probably will, too."

Martin agrees: "The first sentence of a query letter is usually the time you have to make your case. Not unlike the first sentence of your manuscript." Fox believes, "If you have to explain it too much or fill in your note with caveats, then you'll need to redraft it." The rest of your query must include why you're *the* person to write it, who the audience is, and how you're going to market it (think platform). And Zimmerman advises to do it all in just three paragraphs. Why? "Since we're reading so very many, seeing a L-O-N-G query is just daunting." Good says a single-spaced page is best, as does Martin. Her reason? "We're often reading information on our phones these days, and this fact should become a careful consideration when submitting." And never send one query for multiple projects.

PERSEVERE. If the first—or fifteenth—agent or editor rejects your novel or short story, don't give up. "If an agent just simply doesn't *get* your book, that's okay. She or he isn't the right person for you, so move on," says Fox. "If your query is rejected, dust yourself off and send it out again the same day. Keep trying until you've either made a sale, exhausted every possible market, or your topic has become outdated," encourages Collier Cool. Martin advises to "love what you do. *Know,* intrinsically, that you love what you do. This love and knowledge of the craft will be apparent in your letter and your manuscript." Strengthen your perseverance by joining a writers' group or professional writer's organization. "The insight and connections from your peers can be very helpful," says MacKinnon. She also proposes "following a few authors, agents, and reviewers you admire; they often give great tips on writing and getting published." And don't discount the many good book publishing blogs and digital magazines that allow you to stay current for free.

Still struggling with your query? Perhaps the most succinct advice for avoiding the dreaded slush pile belongs to Sands: "Show, don't tell. You want to use the pitch to deliver enough of the flavor of the book to whet the reader's appetite for more." As she says in *Making the Perfect Pitch*, "Publishing begins with a pitch. … [Pitching with aplomb is] about finding the right words and the right people to read them."

Jennifer D. Foster is a freelance writer, editor, and aspiring novelist, and her company is Planet Word. She lives in Toronto, Ontario, Canada, with her husband and their tween son. She's been freelancing since 2003 and has been "in the biz" for seventeen years. Her clients are from the book publishing, magazine, newspaper, corporate communication, and arts and culture fields and include the Art Gallery of Ontario, The Globe and Mail, James Lorimer & Company, Ltd., Quill & Quire, and Canadian House & Home. Jennifer has two university degrees, including a bachelor of applied arts in journalism from Ryerson University. She is an adult English literacy tutor and an avid traveler and gardener who loves dogs, Japan, pumpkin pie, Scrabble, and boules. She is a longtime member of the Professional Writers Association of Canada and the Editors' Association of Canada and can be reached via her website, lifeonplanetword.wordpress.com or her LinkedIn profile.

MASTERING THE LONG SYNOPSIS:

An Interview With James Scott Bell

Janice Gable Bashman

The dreaded long synopsis. The format is easy, but the execution is difficult, often more difficult than writing your book. When writing a long synopsis you must reveal voice and show plot development, relationships, tension, resolution, and more, but in a concise way. You must show the critical moments of your story. So how do you cover the novel from beginning to end in so few words and convey this information in a way that makes editors and agents want to read your manuscript?

Best-selling writing coach James Scott Bell knows how. He frequently contributes to *Writer's Digest* magazine and has written four craft books for Writer's Digest Books: *Plot & Structure; Revision & Self-Editing; The Art of War for Writers;* and *Conflict & Suspense.* He is also a thriller author. His books include: *Deceived; Try Dying; Watch Your Back;* and *One More Lie* (International Thriller Writers Award finalist).

What makes a good long synopsis?

The synopsis has one primary aim, and that is to help sell the project. A good synopsis motivates a reader (*reader* here meaning anyone reading for possible purchase or representation of the author) to move on to the actual pages of a proposal. It can also result in a request for a full manuscript. A good synopsis provides the plot information that tells the reader this project has sales potential and then gets out of the way.

A weak synopsis has things in it that do not add to, or may even detract from, the above.

For example, a synopsis that has anything in it about the author, or the author's motivations for writing the novel, is not good. That kind of information belongs in the cover letter.

Keep sales copy out. Nothing like this: *For those who love James Patterson and Harlan Coben comes the next big author of thrills and chills!* should appear in the synopsis.

A good synopsis is not like the egotistic boor at a party. It is polite. It thinks about the other person (the reader). What does this reader want? A project to get excited about. That doesn't come from vainglorious sales patter. It comes from a solid plot summary.

As a technical matter, the sharp long synopsis renders character names in ALL CAPS the first time they are mentioned. Thus:

TICK ANDERSON is a local news anchor in Los Angeles. His director, LEENA MAR-GOLIS, has been trying to get him fired. When Tick comes in to work one Friday after-noon, Leena confronts him with a statement from a page that says Tick molested her.

Is it important to begin and end the synopsis with action? Why?

The synopsis is *all* action. It's a present tense summary of the main plot and important subplots. So yes, begin with action, but you can drop in key infor-mation along the way. For example:

BUCK SAVAGE, a recently divorced fireman, arrives at the station just as a call comes in. He's about to jump in his suit when the captain, DAVE IRONSIDE, calls him in and tells him he's not going to be going on the call. "You're a danger to your-self and everyone else," he says.

Now you can add the pivotal backstory, but keep it as short and relevant as possible:

Buck's drinking has led to a divorce and estrangement from his teenage son. The only thing that keeps him going is his job.

What action should you start with? Utilize what I call the opening *disturbance*. This is the moment (and I advocate that it happen in the first few pages, if not the first paragraph) where the character's "ordinary world" is disturbed by something. It's an event or bit of news or impending change—anything that doesn't happen every day. It doesn't have to be all that big, but it does have to get the character's attention:

DOROTHY GALE, a Kansas farm girl, runs home with her dog, TOTO, because the town busybody, MISS GULCH, is after them. Toto has been digging in Miss Gulch's garden, and she has vowed to have the dog destroyed.

SCARLETT O'HARA, a spoiled Southern belle, is flirting with a couple of young men when one of them says the man she loves, ASHLEY WILKES, is going to marry his cousin, MELANIE HAMILTON. The news rocks Scarlett, threatening her dreams of a marriage and a life of privilege in the Old South.

LUKE SKYWALKER, a farm boy on the planet Tatooine, is tinkering with a secondhand droid when a hologram suddenly appears. A beautiful girl says, "Help me, Obi-Wan Kenobi. You're my only hope!" and then disappears.

For novels with many characters, how do you decide which characters to discuss?
Step back from the story and ask yourself how you would explain this as a movie plot to a friend. What would you stress so it doesn't become too confusing, or boring? In fact, you may want to record yourself doing this out loud and make adjustments after listening to it.

Remember, once again, this is a selling document, intended to get the reader to go to actual pages. The old advertising adage is, "Sell the sizzle, not the steak." You should not be exhaustive in the telling. Synopses are limited vis-à-vis fiction technique. So you have to depend on tweaking the imagination where you can.

You can sometimes use a summary paragraph to indicate the largeness of the cast. For example, in a historical epic about Custer's last stand at Little Bighorn, where Custer and a rival are the main characters, you might do something like this:

Riding along are PATRICK HUSK, a reporter from the East, determined to expose the general as a fraud; MOLLY SAVANNAH, a former prostitute who is now a spy for the War Department; DYLAN McKENZIE, twelve-year-old drummer boy whose father is the notorious deserter, RANDALL "BLACK EYE" McKENZIE; and OLD JOE, a veteran of the Mexican War who, unbeknownst to Custer, is half-Lakota. Each character will complicate the mission of the 7th Calvary on its way to disaster.

How do you balance covering plot points vs. characters' emotional arcs?
You handle them simply and directly.

PLOT POINT:

One night Buck is awakened by a screaming neighbor. Her house is on fire and her dog is stuck inside. Stumbling out of bed in his underwear, still fighting off last night's drinking bout, he charges into the house to save the dog. He does, but is severely burned in the process.

CHARACTER ARC:

In the hospital, immobile and without booze, Buck is forced to look at the wreckage he's made of his life. When his ex-wife comes to visit, he begs her to forgive him.

The key to every line in a synopsis is brevity. Say what you need to say and move on.

Is voice the key when writing the long synopsis? How do you transfer the voice of your book into the voice of your synopsis?
The synopsis is a tool to get the reader to the real voice, which is in the pages. If you can convey a sense of the voice and tone, that's great. You just don't want to get too cute

with it. You don't want to seem like you're leaving the main purpose of the synopsis to show how clever you are as a writer of synopses. You can certainly provide a hint of voice and even drop in one or two lines of dialogue. Just make sure they sparkle. What you don't want is to turn the synopsis into a creative writing project. A little bit can go a long way. Compare the following examples:

A beautiful blonde enters, unannounced, the office of Los Angeles private detective PHILIP MARLOWE.

That's fine. That works. Here's something with a little more of the voice:

The office door of LA private dick PHILIP MARLOWE swings open, and in walks a blonde that could make a bishop kick a hole in a stained-glass window.

A sprinkling of that type is fine. But only a sprinkling. Get on with the story.

It's important to build tension in the synopsis just like in a novel. How do you build that tension and write the synopsis so the work comes alive?

The tension should be evident from the plot summary. It's a delicate balance. You don't want to engage in novelistic techniques that stretch it out as you would in a scene. That takes you away from synopsizing into narrative. So choose the right words and right scene moments to emphasize.

For example, Chapter 13 of *The Hunger Games* begins with Katniss Everdeen dodging the fireballs that have begun to rain upon her. This goes on for five pages. You certainly would want this in the synopsis, but not beat-for-beat. It would be enough to say,

Now Katniss must dodge deadly fireballs being shot at her by the Gamemakers. Her jacket catches on fire and she is vomiting, but she survives.

Of course, if a sequence goes on for several chapters, you can put in a few more beats. But a synopsis cannot compete with the actual scene in a book. It's not supposed to. So don't put that burden on it.

What are the most common mistakes writers make in writing a long synopsis?

Losing the focus of the structure. Sometimes I'll read a synopsis that starts off well but then meanders, losing the thread of the essential story.

And as with a novel, the middle can sometimes sag. We need to know why readers are going to be caught up in that long Act 2. This is a crucial point. A reader will be asking questions like: Why should I care what happens? Are the stakes high enough? Is there enough happening to pack all those pages in the middle?

A good long synopsis will have the feel of three acts: A crisp opening, a substantial middle, and a wrap-up at the end.

What shouldn't you include in the synopsis?

As stated above, anything relating to the author's background, the motivations for writing the book, hopes for marketing, who should play the lead role in the movie, what the cover should look like, and so on. Anything, in other words, that is not in some way a rendition of story.

How can writing a long synopsis help the writer think about a manuscript's true structures and aid in revision?

The discipline of writing a long synopsis (which writers generally hate doing, by the way) is a great way to solidify what your novel is all about. There is, in fact, a method of writing a novel that was championed by British writer John Braine. He advocated doing a full draft quickly, and then writing a 2,000-word synopsis. That synopsis becomes a working document in and of itself. You revise as needed in order to make the story better before going on to do a full second draft.

Another method is this: Write a synopsis in four sections, going on as long as you like in each one. The first section is Act 1. The next is the first part of Act 2. Then the second part of Act 2 and, finally, Act 3, the resolution.

Dividing it up this way helps you focus on the strengths and weaknesses of each part. When you finally get those parts in fighting shape, you can put the whole thing together, editing it as needed to make it flow.

A writer can do this before writing the book, or afterward. For those who are commonly known as "pantsers" (writers who write "by the seat of their pants", for whom writing a synopsis beforehand is like injecting bamboo under the fingernails), here's an alternative: Keep a record of what you write after you write it. Summarize each scene in a line or two. When you're finished with your draft, you can put all the summaries together and you'll have the rough material from which to forge a long synopsis.

Why is the ability to write a good long synopsis an important tool for every writer to have in his/her toolbox?

Because a writer will be asked to write one at some point, if the writer is seeking a publishing contract or an agent. Also, it can become a tool for creating marketing copy when the time comes. While publishing houses have people who do that, the author might want to be involved so he or she has a say in what's important and what to leave out. Some of my author friends have had cover copy done that gives away key plot secrets. You definitely don't want that! And, if a writer eventually self-publishes, the synopsis can become the basis of an effective book description for the online stores.

....

Janice Gable Bashman is co-author of *Wanted Undead or Alive*, nominated for a Bram Stoker award. She is the managing editor of The Big Thrill, the International Thriller Writers' e-zine. Visit Janice at janicegablebashman.com.

....

HOOKING AN AGENT:

Seeking Representation for Your Novel

....

Jack Smith

You've finished your novel, and now you're ready to market it. If you're planning to send it to an independent or university press, you won't need an agent, but if you're hoping to find a commercial publisher, you will. Several issues come up in the submission process, and you'll need to handle each one professionally and to your advantage.

APPROACHING AN AGENT

What about querying an agent? Must you have an agent referral? What if you have to go in cold—on your own? What do authors with novels at commercial presses say?

Ellen Sussman, author of *French Lessons*, states, "You're lucky if you have an agent referral—if so, use it! And be sure to mention it in the letter!" But another avenue might be open to you beyond a referral: "If you've met an agent at a writers conference, contact them and remind them of your meeting." If you have to go in cold, Sussman says, "Find the agents who represent work like yours and write a fabulous cover letter."

How necessary is a referral—assuming the agent doesn't require it?

According to Josh Weil, author of *The New Valley* and forthcoming debut novel, *The Great Glass Sea*, "It probably helps to have a referral, but it's not necessary. I got my first agent with a cold query but my second—whom I stayed with—via referral. That said, doing your homework about an agent is important: Know some books they represent, some authors, and have a reason for writing them in particular."

Kristen-Paige Madonia, author of *Fingerprints of You*, agrees that either way—by referral or going in cold—will work. But again, the important thing is to do your homework, targeting the agents "that specifically publish the kind of work you are writing." A referral, says Madonia, will most likely get an agent's attention and, if you've sent a sample of your manuscript, increase the chances of getting a faster read, "but if the project is strong enough and the letter is well written and shows them you have done the work, an agent will respond."

Vaddey Ratner preferred going it alone when she queried agents on her debut novel, *In the Shadow of the Banyan*: "I didn't want to depend on knowing another author or someone in publishing to get me in the door. I wanted the writing to speak for itself. While I didn't have any referrals, I did research the agencies thoroughly, seeking ones that I felt would fit the project. But ultimately, whether you go in cold or not, the writing has to stand on its own."

Timing can be an important factor. Harriet Chessman, author of the acclaimed *Lydia Cassatt Reading the Morning Paper,* states: "It certainly helps to have an agent referral—this is ideal—yet if you get lucky and hit the right agent at the right time with the right project, you don't need a referral."

There is, of course, the sheer numbers issue. How can you help beat the odds in an increasingly competitive market? "It's always best," says Susan Henderson, author of *Up from the Blue*, "to have a referral from an agent's client. Agents get hundreds of manuscripts a week and anything that separates you from the slush pile helps."

Ed Falco, whose latest novel is *The Family Corleone,* switches the argument: "The best way to find an agent is to have one find you." This usually happens, says Falco, when an agent sees a story in a magazine or journal and takes an interest in either the story or the writer. Agents aren't usually interested in short story collections because they don't sell well, says Falco, but if the story looks like it could be expanded into a novel, this could certainly interest the agent. Or, the agent may simply be impressed with the writing itself and want to represent this writer. An agent referral, to Falco, is, in fact, the "second-best route to finding representation." This assumes you know some published writers. "If you don't," says Falco, "if you're a lone wolf writing in solitude, then you're best advised to do some research: Get online, go to your library, check out Literary Market Place (a reference book that lists agents), and try to find several agents who appear to represent work similar to your own."

HOW MANY AGENTS TO APPROACH

Whether you have a referral or not, make sure that your work is solid and it's the kind of work the agent is currently representing. Once you've done that, how many agents should you approach at a given time? Answers vary.

For Ed Falco, it all depends on the circumstances. You need to go with multiple submissions if you're sending a query letter with your opening chapter "because, unfortunately, at least a few of your queries will go unanswered." But if the agent has contacted you, send only to that agent, and the same goes for an agent referral.

Josh Weil advises approaching no more than five agents with referrals, and if you're sending an entire manuscript, he limits the number to three or four at a time. "If they want an exclusive read, give it to just the one. But they should get back to you in two to three weeks, tops."

Kristen-Paige Madonia has a strategy and process: "My golden number is six, and I always recommend starting with your dream-team list. Aim high and go from there. I suggest creating a list of twenty-five agents, so that when you begin to hear back you already know who you will send your letter to next."

Susan Henderson recommends about the same number "so you don't waste your own time but also not so many that you can't take tepid feedback as a reason to change your query letter or your approach." Ellen Sussman suggests up to ten, and she makes the same point about the opportunity for revision—but in this case, the novel submission itself: "You don't want to burn all your bridges, because you might get comments from those agents, suggesting changes you should make to your novel. If you choose to do a rewrite, then you want another round of agents to approach with the new draft."

Still, here's another point of view—as to the number of query letters you should send out at any given time: "As many as possible," says Kim McLarin, whose most recent novel is *Jump at the Sun*. "Maybe back in the good old days of gentlemanly agreements a writer could approach one agent, wait for her reply and then move on to the second. But doing so today puts you at a distinct disadvantage. Some agents will sit on your work and not respond for six months or more. That's valuable time lost for you. As long as you do not represent yourself as having submitted solely to any particular agent, I think you're under no obligation to go steady with someone who has yet to indicate she wants to go steady with you."

QUERY LETTER

What should your query letter look like? How should it come off? Ellen Sussman states: "There are tons of reference guides out there for writing query letters. Just read a few and write many drafts until you get it right." For help on professional format, Harriet Chessman suggests Agentquery.com as a great resource.

In a nutshell, published writers suggest making sure your letter has the following good qualities:

Professional, Polite, Appreciative

One aspect of professionalism making sure you target agents who represent the kind of work you're submitting. This demonstrates that you have a clear sense of audience and purpose. A second is the mechanics of the submission itself. This means "no cute tricks like colored paper or unusual font," says Kristen-Paige Madonia. "It should follow traditional business letter guidelines and include your contact info, the date, and the agent's contact info before the body of the letter begins. The goal is to get their attention but simultaneously prove you are serious about writing as a profession." Related to professionalism is the attitude that comes through in your letter. According to Josh Weil, you need to show that you are "conscious of the time someone is giving you—even if just by reading your letter. Thank the agent for his or her time. Make it genuine." Madonia has this to say: "Agents are unbelievably overworked, and it's good to acknowledge that you appreciate them taking the time to read your letter and consider your work."

Concise, Relevant, Well-Stated

"Keep it short," says Josh Weil. "One paragraph. And this is not a plot summary. It's a synopsis of the project; you want to get across the plot, but also the *feel* of it." According to Susan Henderson, the letter needs to be "as short as you can get it." Get the novel's plot and themes down in two to three sentences. Your bio needs to demonstrate that you have "credibility" with your targeted audience or readership. "For example, if your book is about a veterinarian and you are a former veterinarian who regularly participates in animal rescue conferences, that's exactly what will grab an agent's attention." Says Ed Falco: "Brevity is the key. A brief letter in which you say whatever you think will most likely interest the agent in your project. Don't alienate the agent by being smug or pompous; don't annoy him by sending a long letter in which you tell him all about your fascinating life. Be brief. Try to interest the agent in reading your first chapter." And, says Ellen Sussman, "It should tell the story of your novel in dazzling language."

Unique

"It should stand out by articulating the uniqueness of your work," says Vaddey Ratner. "It should convey the passion or excitement, the seriousness or lightness of your project. In other words, your query letter should reflect not only who you are as a writer, but the spirit of your work." It must demonstrate how your project is "different from all the other projects" the agent considers, says Kristen-Paige Madonia. And Ellen Sussman states: "Try to capture your own particular voice in the writing style."

Impressive in Bio

"Put in anything that distinguishes you as a writer," says Josh Weil. Don't leave anything out that might play well in your favor: "Certainly," says Ed Falco," if you've already published work, let the agent know what you've published and where. If you don't have publications, maybe you've studied somewhere impressive. If you're a recent MFA, you can tell them that.

If you graduated first in your class from MIT, let them know. The agent will think, *huh, this one sounds smart,* and read your first chapter."

MANUSCRIPT SUBMISSION

The Novel Manuscript

What about the manuscript itself? If a portion is called for, what must you do to meet professional standards?

Are you really ready to submit?

Of the various parts of one possible submission package—brief cover letter, synopsis or outline, and first chapter—Ed Falco says, "What counts the most here is that first chapter. If you've written a brief but interesting cover letter, one that suggests you might be a writer worth exploring, the agent will take the time to read that opening chapter. If she likes it (by which I mean if she thinks she can sell it), she will ask to see the rest of the work. If, after reading the whole book she thinks she can sell it, you'll have yourself an agent."

But how do you get that first chapter—or however many chapters you're asked to submit—in shape for an agent to make this decision? How do you get your whole novel in this shape?

"It's a very hard process," states Ellen Sussman. "And sometimes a manuscript gets rejected forty times and finally finds an agent who falls in love with it. So you have to keep believing in it. You also have to listen hard if you keep hearing the same comments. Your manuscript might need another draft before it goes out again."

Before you submit it the first time, Kristen-Paige Madonia urges: "Rewrite, rewrite, rewrite, and then begin editing on the sentence level. Find readers and ask for feedback." These readers, says Josh Weil, "should be people you can trust to tell the hard truth." Once you've considered this feedback and made changes that make sense to you, are you finally ready? "When you think it's ready to send out, reread it at least one more time," says Madonia. Susan Henderson agrees: "Let it simmer. When you think it's done, put it away in a drawer for a month or so and read the very best books of the same genre. Then go back and read it again to see if it needs more edits. It does."

To get an absolutely clean, edited copy, "proofread, proofread, proofread!" says Kristen-Paige Madonia. "I worked as an intern in a literary agency a number of years ago, and I can attest to the fact that finding basic grammar mistakes on the first few pages will make a reader want to stop reading." But more is at hand than grammar—there are other professional submission mechanics to consider: "Don't be sloppy, and follow traditional formatting rules in terms of font and margins. Always use page numbers and include your last name and the title in the header on every page." And Josh Weil adds: "No fancy fonts or frilliness. It looks unprofessional."

Book Doctor

Should you hire a book doctor? For Harriet Chessman, it depends on the project. "This can certainly help sometimes! Certainly, agents and editors rarely edit anymore, so the more polished and market-ready your manuscript is, the better. The question is, what is viable on the market?"

Susan Henderson discourages it. "Most book doctors are horrible. The good ones cost a fortune. Better to find a writer's workshop via Zoetrope or Backspace, or ask about freelance editors on their forums."

For Kristen-Paige Madonia it comes down to several considerations, cost among them. "You absolutely need readers, I'd say at least three," says Madonia, but she values other options besides paying a professional to read your work: exchanging work with fellow writers from a writing group or with acquaintances made from taking classes or attending conferences—or enlisting family members. In making your decision, there are two principal considerations, notes Madonia: budget and time. A book doctor can be quite expensive, but will at least meet a definite time line. Writing associates, friends, and family won't affect your budget, but they may take longer to read your manuscript. If you plan to hire a professional, says Madonia, "do your homework and request references and a resume or a list of previous clients. Contact other authors that have worked with the editor to learn more about their style and their level of expertise and commitment."

Synopsis and Outline

As submission blurbs in *Novel & Short Story Writer's Market* reveal, some agents require a synopsis, and some don't. Some call for an outline. "You absolutely need a synopsis," says Kim McLarin, "because at some point both the agent and potential editor will ask for one. Learn to write one and to do it well." Susan Henderson finds value in both synopsis and outline: "It's helpful to have these so you can talk about your book more succinctly."

Sending the Manuscript

What about actual submission of the manuscript—the packing it off? "Each agency is different," Vaddey Ratner notes. "Some will want the manuscript as a PDF file, some as a Word document, some will request three chapters or fifty pages. Read the directions carefully. The agency is doing you the courtesy of reviewing your work; the least you can do is provide it in the format they require."

"Almost everyone is reading digital manuscripts these days," says Ed Falco, "which means that, once the agent agrees to read the whole book, you can send it via a PDF or Word file, unless the agent requests something different. As for the initial submission of a letter and first chapter, I'd probably send a hard copy through the postal service, if only because it's a lot easier to ignore an e-mail than a nice crisp envelope delivered in the daily mail."

FOLLOWING UP QUERIES

You've submitted your work to agents, and now you're waiting for a response. Should you follow up on queries at some point? If so, how long should you wait? How should you communicate—by e-mail or phone call? Authors' recommendations vary.

Josh Weil has no problem with a phone call. "Though I might follow up with an e-mail first. And I'd wait a month, unless something comes up that will affect the agent's take on the work (i.e., you win a significant award, etc.), in which case send a brief update e-mail."

Kristen-Paige Madonia doesn't recommend phone calls. It can seem "intrusive," she says, and, given the fact that agents are "one-hundred percent overworked," they probably won't respond by phone to a nonclient. "But e-mailing is perfectly appropriate, and I suggest waiting three or four weeks." What you want to avoid, she says, is appearing "demanding or high maintenance." Just send a polite note mentioning that you sent your query letter and are looking forward to their response when they have time to consider your proposal. "Again," emphasizes Madonia, "be polite and gracious."

"I'd wait six weeks and then send a follow-up e-mail," says Ellen Sussman. "Just ask what the status of the manuscript is at this point in time."

Ed Falco agrees on the six-week time frame for query letter and first chapter—and a couple of months in the case of a whole novel manuscript. "I don't recommend following up with a phone call. It usually gets you nowhere. You can follow up with an e-mail, and if you still don't hear anything back, then just move on."

Harriet Chessman suggests two months. "I'd follow up first with an e-mail, and only after that hasn't worked, a phone call. Agents are just totally overwhelmed. Always be diplomatic and polite. Never act as if you think you're the only writer in the world!"

Susan Henderson recommends not following up at all. "Any follow-up will probably tip the answer toward a no. You have to remember that you're seeking a long-term relationship with an agent, so any behavior that comes off as impatient, annoying, or aggressive will give the agent an easy reason to turn you down."

Vaddey Ratner points out: "Most agencies will say in what time frame you should expect a response. After that period, if you haven't heard from them, you should take it as a rejection. So move on—your energy is better spent in researching and approaching new agencies."

Kim McLarin takes the same basic position: "I don't think most agents will appreciate being bugged via phone. Finding an agent really is like dating, from the woman's perspective: If you haven't heard from him, he's not interested. Bugging him will not help. I believe six or eight weeks is more than reasonable. If you haven't received, in that time, at least an e-mail saying, 'Please send me more!' or 'I'm reading, please give me a bit of time!' then I'd move on."

SUMMING UP

Once you've completed your manuscript, fine-tuned it, put it aside, and finished the final round of editing, you're ready to begin the query process. First, read the blurbs. Which agents represent your kind of fiction? Then, decide: Should you try to get a referral to improve your chances of getting more attention or a faster read? Decide on how many agents you'll approach at a time and work up a query letter, making sure it's tightly written, professional, and stylistically strong. Be prepared to send only what the agent asks for—and in the manner called for. Once you've made your submission, be prepared to wait. Agents are flooded, but if your letter or submission package gets their attention, you've got a shot at representation.

Jack Smith has published twenty articles in *Novel & Short Story Writer's Market*. His creative writing book, *Write and Revise for Publication: A 6-Month Plan for Crafting an Exceptional Novel and Other Works of Fiction*, was published in 2013 by Writer's Digest Books. His novel *Hog to Hog* won the 2007 George Garrett Fiction Prize and was published by Texas Review Press in 2008. He has published stories in a number of literary magazines, including *Southern Review, North American Review, Texas Review, X-Connect, In Posse Review*, and *Night Train*. His reviews have appeared widely in such publications as *Ploughshares, Georgia Review, American Book Review, Prairie Schooner, Mid-American Review, Pleiades*, the *Missouri Review*, and *Environment* magazine. His co-authored nonfiction environmental book entitled *Killing Me Softly* was published by Monthly Review Press in 2002. Besides writing, Smith co-edits the *Green Hills Literary Lantern*, an online literary magazine published by Truman State University.

HABITS OF HIGHLY SUCCESSFUL SHORT STORY WRITERS

Erika Dreifus

Once we send our short stories out for an editor's consideration, there's little we can do to enhance our chances for acceptance and publication. That gives us all the more reason to do whatever we can to strengthen those chances *before* the stories go out. The stakes are even higher for anyone who hopes to publish an entire book of short stories; in nearly all cases, agents and publishers look more favorably on collections in which at least some of the component stories have been previously published by magazine and journal editors.

After more than a decade of submitting my stories, including those in my collection, *Quiet Americans*—and discussing the process with fellow writers, editors, and teachers—I've noticed a number of practices that seem helpful. Let's call them "habits of highly successful short story writers."

First, let's emphasize one habit that every writer must cultivate. It's so seemingly self-evident that I didn't even include it in the original list that I shared with my three expert interviewees. But my wisdom in choosing these sources was confirmed when one of them, Roxane Gay (whose multiple professional hats include short story writer—her collection *Ayiti* was published in 2011—and co-editor of the journal *PANK*), stated the obvious: "Writing regularly is my best habit," she told me. "I like to keep that fiction muscle warm by remembering that a writer needs to actually write."

With that said, let's continue with some other useful practices:

- **READ MAGAZINES AND JOURNALS.** This, too, may seem like common sense. But as the saying goes, common sense can be sadly uncommon. If you want to be published in magazines and literary journals, you simply must read them. "It's impossible to read every literary magazine out there," concedes Midge Raymond, author of the award-winning story collection *Forgetting English* and co-founder of Ashland Creek Press. "[But] I have to say I've read the vast majority of the ones I submit to, at least once. And over the years I've subscribed to many of them. It's great to support them, for one, but also to get a feel for what they publish." Raymond adds that in one case, she purchased and perused a copy of a literary magazine shortly *after* having submitted a story to its editors. She quickly realized that her story was unlikely to fit. "So, it really does help [to read before] submitting!"

- **UNDERSTAND EACH MAGAZINE'S MISSION AND FOLLOW ITS GUIDELINES.** Again, seems pretty simple, right? And again, you'd be surprised how often this advice needs repeating. As Gay phrases it: "If you're serious about being published, you will do your homework. With most magazines having substantial online presences, there's no excuse for having no clear understanding of a market. You cannot subscribe to every magazine, but you can know that *Cat Fancy* isn't interested in stories about turtles."

- **SUBSCRIBE.** Beyond simply supporting publications and having full access to their content, purchasing a subscription can confer privileges. Some magazines extend submission-related benefits to their subscribers. For instance, both *New Ohio Review* and *Agni* have time-limited submission periods, but they will receive submissions from subscribers year-round. Others, including *Grist* and *Carve*, waive their online submission fees for writers who subscribe to their print journals.

  But these days, there are many types of subscriptions, and some of them won't cost you anything. For example, by subscribing to a journal's free electronic newsletter or blog, you may receive news and information—including calls for submissions—before announcements make their way to an official website. Employ social media, too. Following a journal on Twitter or "liking" its Facebook page is another way to get to know the editors and the work that they are most interested in publishing.

- **REVISE AND PROOFREAD.** "As an editor," says Gay, "I cannot tell you how often there are typos in the title, first line, or first paragraph, and it's frustrating. There will always be some small mechanical issue that gets through, but the more of these issues you have, and the earlier in the work an editor finds them, the less likely your work will receive serious consideration."

  Reading your story aloud is one helpful revision practice. When Gay reads her finished drafts aloud, she "always find[s] new things to revise or reconsider." And it's not all about finding problems to fix. Sometimes,

Gay says, reading aloud helps spotlight "what is working well," which is an equally useful discovery.

And slow down! Raymond shares: "If you put your story aside for a while before sending it out (which I've learned the hard way is essential!), you're more likely to ensure that it's truly a great piece [and] find errors if you've had a little time away from it."

- **SUBMIT YOUR WORK.** You can be the most talented writer in the world, but if you don't put your work out there, it won't be published. There's obviously no guarantee that a particular submission will be accepted. But there is a guarantee that if it's not submitted, it won't be published. (It takes some time, and a track record, before one reaches the level of having work solicited.)

  Raymond concurs: "A writer friend of mine likes to quote Wayne Gretzky: 'You miss one hundred percent of the shots you never take.' So true." For her part, Gay compares getting work accepted to the lottery: "You have to play to win."

- **PERSEVERE IN THE FACE OF REJECTION.** "Rejection is inevitable," says Michael Griffith, whose current roles include editing fiction for *Cincinnati Review*. "Think of the arithmetic: At *Cincinnati Review* we get around three thousand stories per year. We can accept roughly twelve. That's .4 percent, or 1 in 250."

  Griffith emphasizes that just because a story isn't accepted by *Cincinnati Review* doesn't mean that it lacks merit. "I'd say that at least 10 percent of the stories we get strike us as potentially publishable somewhere, and I'd say there are a hundred every year that we would be glad to publish," he says. "Which means that we reject seven-eighths of the stories that one or more of us would love to print. What I'm getting at is that even an excellent story doesn't have the odds in its favor if you think of it as a solo submission. So you shouldn't. If you get to the point where you have a 1 in 8 shot rather than 1 in 100, the math is in your favor, as long as you keep submitting. The scale needs recalibration: The fiction writer who hits .125 percent is highly successful. Ignore the rejections; it only takes one editor to say yes, and I know terrific stories that have been rejected thirty or more times before finally finding a great home."

  You read that correctly. *Thirty or more times*. This rings true with several of my own published stories, too.

  Arithmetic aside, it helps to keep some other points in mind. Says Raymond: "[T]here are so many reasons for being rejected that have nothing to do with our stories—it could be that an issue is full, that it didn't connect with a certain reader (these things are so subjective), that it is too similar in theme to something they've already accepted, etc. It's not always about your piece specifically. And even if it is, it's not about you at all—I always try to remember this and not take rejections personally. Which is fortunate because I've gotten so many!" Raymond's experience is instructive: "I have several stories that received dozens and dozens of rejections before being published—and not only being published but winning prizes and Pushcart nominations. It's so subjective—and so competitive—that you just have to keep sending it out until the right editor reads it."

- **BELIEVE IN—AND ACT ON—THE "ENCOURAGING" REJECTIONS.** At times, a rejection will be accompanied by a personal message from an editor that expresses apparently sincere regret for turning down the story and invites you to submit another story soon. But something within you may doubt this advice. The editor probably encourages everyone, right?

  Wrong. "The encouraging responses absolutely should be taken seriously," says Raymond. "No one can afford the time to write these unless they really mean it, so this means you've got something that really resonated with someone and you should take that to heart." Griffith echoes that sentiment. "If an editor sends an encouraging rejection, *believe* him or her. No one wants to add to his or her own workload in vain. In such instances, strike while the iron is hot; if an editor expresses a willingness to see more, send something new as soon as you can."

- **AIM HIGH—BUT REMAIN REASONABLE.** If I defined "successful" only as being published in *The New Yorker*, I'd be setting an extremely high—and likely unattainable—bar. To date, I wouldn't have published a single story, let alone a full collection.

  Raymond agrees. "Always send pieces out to your dream journals, but don't neglect all the other great ones that may pay more attention to emerging writers or unagented submissions. Also, the more you publish and succeed, the easier it'll be to get the attention of the 'unattainable' journals."

  You might try Gay's approach: "I submit in a three-tiered manner by sending a given piece out to a magazine I feel is well within my reach, a magazine that is moderately within my reach, and a magazine that is a long shot. Writers need to be realistic about the likelihood of being published in certain magazines. The odds are not in our favor. It can and does happen, but know that your submission is often one of thousands or tens of thousands."

- **BE PROFESSIONAL—AND POLITE.** "Editors and writers have long memories and everybody talks," says Gay. So it's wise to conduct yourself courteously and professionally.

  This advice applies to the oft-dreaded cover letter. Raymond notes that cover letters should never receive as much attention as stories themselves. Her advice is to keep cover letters or messages that accompany electronic submissions "short, sweet, and professional. I know that editors can get turned off by weird or offensive cover letters—and why do that if it might influence the way they read your story?"

Griffith agrees. "Short, simple cover letters, please. Nothing bespeaks amateurishness like an overlong, overcomplicated cover letter."

Once a story has been accepted, there's more etiquette to follow. Assuming that you've followed the advice to send a single story out to several magazines, you may still be waiting for responses from other editors when the acceptance arrives. As soon as you are certain that your story is, in fact, "taken," be sure to withdraw the piece from further consideration elsewhere. It's the polite and professional thing to do, an extension of courtesy not only to the editors who might otherwise be spending time and resources on a story that's no longer available to them, but also to your fellow writers.

If you're worrying that all of these suggestions will cramp your style and cause you to remain too cautiously within certain limits, perhaps you'll take heart in Griffith's closing counsel: "Take risks, take risks, take risks. To me the most depressing stories I read are the careful, stolid, well-wrought ones that never attempt anything daring or fresh. We use a five-point scoring system [when considering submissions at *Cincinnati Review*] in which three denominates a story that may be solid but unremarkable, and the saddest cases are those that aim directly at three and hit their bull's-eye. These stories are, as Padgett Powell says, "executed to conception"—a withering bit of faint praise that indicates competence that never aimed at anything higher. No matter how much of this process seems to be within an editor's control, your writing is something that remains absolutely, resolutely within yours.

Erika Dreifus is the author of *Quiet Americans: Stories* (Last Light Studio), which was an American Library Association Sophie Brody Medal Honor Title (for outstanding Jewish literature). Erika's short fiction has been published in numerous literary magazines and featured on National Public Radio. Erika blogs about writing and publishing at Practicing Writing and publishes a free monthly newsletter for fictionists, poets, and writers of creative nonfiction. Please visit www. erikadreifus.com to learn more about Erika and her work.

EMERGING VOICES

Debut Authors Discuss
Their Paths to Publication

Chuck Sambuchino

ALISON ATLEE

The Typewriter Girl
(historical fiction, Gallery Books)
Scandalous, 'ruined' Betsey Dobson fights to make an independent living among the upper class at an 1890s seaside resort.

What did you do prior to writing *The Typewriter Girl*?
I'd been trying to break into the romance genre but was told several times that my voice wasn't "right" for romance. I didn't quite understand or believe that until the person who became my agent said, "There's more to this story and place you've created; let's bring it out." [It became historical fiction.]

What was the time frame for the book?
This book was really about the revisions, which took about two years with my agent, and then even more with my editor. I'd always thought of myself as a writer who worked meticulously on a first draft and thus avoided heavy revisions. Learning I don't have to work that way was both tough and valuable.

How did you meet your agent?
I made an initial query list by looking at agent rosters for smaller regional writing conferences, thinking those agents were seeking new clients more actively. A valid rationale? I don't know, but Emmanuelle Morgen [of Stonestong, who became my agent] was in that first list. What I learned: How long the [book] contract takes. I knew of

things going horribly wrong even after the deal, so I was eager to have the actual contract in my hand.

What did you do right?

One, studied craft. Two, never quit.

Would you do anything differently?

I do wonder if taking time off from my day job would have led to selling earlier.

What's next for you?

I'm working on another historical novel.

Alison Atlee writes from Kentucky. Visit her website at alisonatlee.com.

F.T. BRADLEY

Double Vision
(middle-grade thriller, HarperCollins Children's)
When 12-year-old Linc Baker replaces a junior secret agent for a mission, he has only his quick wits to crack secret codes and find a dangerous painting—before the bad guys do.

What did you do prior to writing *Double Vision*?

I wrote short crime fiction for years, getting published in small press magazines and e-zines. I still write shorts when I can—it's the best way to stay sharp craft-wise. I also wrote freelance articles to pay the bills.

What was the time frame for the book?

I'm one of those freak success stories: the Double Vision series (three books) sold on proposal. I had only written seventy-five pages, and about half [of those] didn't even make it into the first draft. From first draft to copyedited manuscript, it took about eight months.

How did you meet your agent?

I had pitched Stephen Barbara at Foundry Literary + Media two different YA manuscripts, but no luck. We spoke on the phone, and he suggested, based on my writing, that I try middle-grade. We worked on the sample pages and proposal for about six months before he sold *Double Vision*.

What did you learn along the way?

I'm still amazed by how great editors are at what they do. If I'm ever stuck creatively, they always have the key to unlock the story and make it better.

What did you do right?

I kept writing something new. I'm not afraid to throw stuff out—I'll cut chapters, passages or plotlines that don't work. I even have six manuscripts in the drawer that'll never see print.

Tell us a little about your platform.

I have a blog and am active on Facebook and Twitter. I'm on Goodreads and Skype now and attending conventions to connect with librarians and booksellers.

F.T. Bradley writes from Biloxi, Mississippi. Visit her website at ftbradley.com.

TARA CONKLIN

The House Girl

(literary/historical fiction, William Morrow)
The lives of two indomitable young women—a slave in antebellum Virginia and a lawyer in modern-day New York—intersect in a story about truth, love and justice.

What did you do prior to writing *The House Girl*?

I had written stories since childhood, but I never tried seriously to have anything published. When I began *The House Girl*, I didn't think I was writing a novel, but I couldn't get the characters out of my head.

How did you meet your agent?

My agent is the fabulous Michelle Brower of Folio Literary Management. I found her the old-fashioned way: with a cold query. On the Folio website, her description of the fiction she was looking to represent summarized exactly the book that I had written.

What did you do right?

I wrote and rewrote and rewrote again before sending the manuscript off to agents. I also carefully researched agents and only contacted those whom I felt certain would love the book.

What was the biggest surprise?

After hearing so many horror stories about big publishing houses, I've been wonderfully surprised by the warmth and enthusiasm of everyone I've been lucky enough to work with.

Tell us a little about your platform.

I'm a regular contributor to Popcorn The Blog, a site about all things writing. I have a website, Facebook author page and Twitter feed.

What's next for you?

I'm working on my second novel, tentatively titled *This Is the Sea.*

EMILY HAINSWORTH

Through to You

(young adult, Balzer + Bray)
Seventeen-year-old Camden Pike, a boy grieving for his girlfriend who was killed in a car accident, discovers a parallel world where she's still alive—but she isn't quite the same girl he remembers.

What did you do prior to writing *Through to You*?

This is my first published book, but I had been rewriting and submitting one other YA manuscript to literary agents for four years before realizing I needed to try something different.

What was the time frame for the book?

From idea to query letter, *Through to You* took a little less than a year to write in my spare time.

How did you meet your agent?

I initially found my agent, Mary Kole [of Movable Type Management], through her children's literature blog, kidlit.com. Mary actually passed on my first project, but offered such great advice when she turned me down that she was one of the first agents I queried with my new book.

What did you do right?

I learned a lot while writing and rewriting my first manuscript, but I couldn't really apply the knowledge and skills until I gave myself permission to move beyond that project. Writing something new was the best move I ever made.

What was the biggest surprise?

I was totally taken by surprise when *Through to You* sold so quickly. I was fully prepared for a long wait, but the book sold at auction in less than two weeks.

Tell us a little about your platform.

I have a blog, Facebook page and Twitter feed.

What's next for you?

I'm currently working on a second stand-alone YA novel.

JAY CASPIAN KANG

The Dead Do Not Improve
(literary suspense, Hogarth)
A literary crime/surf novel featuring a writer on the run.

What did you do prior to writing *The Dead Do Not Improve*?
I was in San Francisco, mostly surfing badly and drinking coffee. For five years, I had been working on a long, overworked novel about a television show. When that fell through, I had built up so much nervous energy that this story just sort of flew out of me. … I [had also done] some reporting on a shooting in Oakland for *The New York Times Magazine* and found myself really enjoying the writing process.

What was the time frame for the book?
I wrote most of it in a barn on Whidbey Island, Washington. My parents run a small lavender farm there. They were out of the country for a few months, so I went up there, bought a ton of Red Man and really churned out the pages.

How did you meet your agent?
My agent is Jim Rutman [of Sterling Lord Literistic]. He came highly recommended by a friend.

What was the biggest surprise?
That anyone wanted to buy a literary crime/surf novel about a writer on the run! What I did right: I'm very hardheaded and shortsighted. I think that really helps writers. I probably should have given up when I turned thirty and still hadn't made a penny as a writer. But I couldn't really think of any other career options, and I wasn't good enough at anything else to consider a different job.

Would you do anything differently?
I think I would have been a bit more serious about the amount of work it takes to be a writer. For a while, I got caught up in the whole "my malaise is beautiful" trap.

What's next for you?
I want to keep building [my website] and do more crime reporting for *The New York Times Magazine.*

Jay Caspian King writes from Los Angeles. Visit his website at grantland.com.

JULIE KIBLER

Calling Me Home
(women's fiction, St. Martin's Press)
Eighty-nine-year-old Isabelle asks Dorrie, her young African-American hairstylist and friend, to drive her halfway across the country to a funeral.

What did you do prior to writing *Calling Me Home*?
I was making a decent living as a freelance editor, writer and researcher for a nonprofit think tank. I had one short [essay] published by an online literary journal.

What was the time frame for the book?
I wrote the first draft between April and November of 2010. I enjoy participating in [the annual book-in-a-month challenge of] National Novel Writing Month, though I like to make up my own rules (i.e., word count goal). ... I've called it NaNoFiMo, or National Novel Finishing Month, twice.

How did you meet your agent?
Elisabeth Weed [of Weed Literary] was my dream agent. I knew one of her clients fairly well online. The client sent Elisabeth a recommendation. The deal: I sold my book at auction, and I asked to speak with each editor by phone before the auction took place. I still think it was a great idea, and I recommend it.

What did you do right?
I believe the first and most important thing you can do is write the very best manuscript you can, and the second is to be patient before you begin to submit it.

Tell us a little about your platform.
I have worked hard to build a strong base of relationships with regular, everyday readers, mostly on Facebook. I hope to make a lot of book clubs excited about reading [the book] when the time comes.

What's next for you?
Another story that ... explores the marginalization of certain groups, with some unexpected relationships thrown in for good measure!

Julie Kibler writes from Arlington, Texas. Visit her websites at juliekibler.com and book pregnant.blogspot.com.

ROBERT K. LEWIS

Untold Damage
(crime fiction, Midnight Ink)
Mark Mallen, a former narcotics officer who is also a recovering junkie, tries to find the answer to the mystery of his best friend's death.

What did you do prior to writing *Untold Damage*?
I'd written the original first Mark Mallen novel, but it didn't sell. During the time it was [on submission], I wrote a draft of what I thought would be the second Mallen book. When the first one didn't sell, I put the second book aside and figured I'd try something different—with a different protagonist, etc. That didn't work out. So, there I was, feeling desperate, when I came across this second book in my desk drawer. I had really forgotten all about it. I read it, and it worked for me.

How did you meet your agent?
I found my agent through the website AgentQuery Connect [when querying the first Mallen novel]. My agent is Barbara Poelle of the Irene Goodman Literary Agency, and I'm very lucky to have her in my corner. … She's been a great mentor, sounding board and advocate.

What did you learn along the way?
The biggest learning experience was adapting to the fact that my book was no longer really an artistic endeavor but was now a product that needed to sell units. It becomes a business, and you need to conduct yourself accordingly.

What did you do right?
I believe that having patience, never giving up and working on my craft all went together to help me break in. I mean, I had been trying to get published for over seven years!

Tell us a little about your platform.
Barbara hooked me up with a blogging job at the place for fans of crime fiction: CriminalElement.com. And I'm on Twitter.

What's next for you?
The [next] Mallen book.

Robert K. Lewis writes from Berkeley, California. Visit his website at robertklewis.com.

DENNIS MAHONEY

Fellow Mortals

(literary fiction, Farrar, Straus and Giroux)
Relationships are strained and forged after a mailman accidentally starts
a tragic neighborhood fire.

What did you do prior to writing *Fellow Mortals*?

I'd written a few failed novels. … I just kept trying to write better books until one of
them was good enough to publish. [This book] started with a good protagonist. I wanted
to stick him in a catastrophe of his own making and watch him try to fix it.

How did you meet your agent?

My early novels didn't garner book deals but drew the attention of a few agents. I was
a client of two different agents, only to part ways amicably with each. I finished *Fellow
Mortals* and queried again. Dozens of rejections later, an agent signed me. In the middle of submitting, that agent retired. An editor who was interested in the book at FSG
referred me to my current agent, Jim Rutman at Sterling Lord Literistic.

What did you learn along the way?

During my many years of submissions, I must have contacted almost every agent in New
York. [All of them] struck me as hardworking, passionate book lovers. They truly want
to find great material in the slush pile and, while they often miss terrific books because
they're simply overwhelmed, a talented author who doesn't quit will eventually succeed.

What did you do right?

It's all about tenacity. Finish one book, start the next, and keep submitting. The ones
who make it are the ones who keep trying.

Would you do anything differently?

I would've established my writing discipline sooner. I wasted most of my twenties writing halfhearted blog posts and wishing I were a published novelist instead of working
on a novel five days a week.

Tell us a little about your platform.

I blog at Giganticide.com and write for other sites, including The Morning News.

What's next for you?

A mystery/adventure about a young woman in an alternate Colonial America.

Dennis Mahoney writes from Upstate New York. Visit his website at authordennis
mahoney.com.

BEN MASTERS

Noughties
(mainstream fiction, Hogarth)
A comedy about a group of friends on their last night at university as they try to come to terms with the past and their untold futures.

What did you do prior to writing *Noughties*?

I had just finished doing a master's at Oxford and stayed in the city to do a summer job as a waiter [at] my college. That's when I started writing the novel. Besides two regrettable short stories, *Noughties* was the first piece of fiction I had written.

What was the time frame for the book?

I wrote the first draft in about six months. I then had to find an agent, after which I did a couple [more drafts].

How did you meet your agent?

I didn't have any useful contacts, so I … bought *The Writer's Handbook* [a now defunct guide to U.K. publishing], circled the agents who sounded best for me and submitted the opening couple of chapters. Fortunately, my first-choice agent, Georgia Garrett [of Rogers, Coleridge & White], got in touch and foolishly took me on. I owe her a lot for taking that chance.

What did you do right?

I have no idea. You can only write what you want to write or what suggests itself to you, do the best job you can at the time, and then hope for the best. Too much calculation will hamper you.

Tell us a little about your platform.

I don't do anything wacky or attention grabbing to that end. Thinking about that kind of stuff can be too much of a distraction from writing. I do the typical things, though—readings, festivals … etc.

What's next for you?

I'm currently completing the first draft of my second novel.

Ben Masters writes from Cambridge, U.K.

JENNY MILCHMAN

Cover of Snow
(literary thriller, Ballantine)
When her police detective husband commits suicide in the middle of a frozen Adirondack winter, Nora Hamilton must lay bare the secrets a town has always kept—as well as her own.

What did you do prior to writing *Cover of Snow*?

Cover of Snow is my debut novel, but it's the eighth one I wrote. At a certain point, when the rejections were flying so fast and furious that I didn't even see them any more (that's a lie), I realized that published writers wrote roughly a book a year, so I might as well do the same. I wrote eight books in eleven years, slowing down some when I had two babies.

What was the time frame for the first book?

Cover of Snow took me five months.

How did you meet your agent?

My agent is Julia Kenny of the Markson Thoma Literary Agency. She is my third agent and—with great gratitude to the others who believed in me early on—I hope my forever agent. She knows when to bolster me and when to tell me to get outside in the sun. I came across Julia's listing on Publishers Marketplace.

What did you learn along the way?

That an agent doesn't sell all of the projects she takes on and that having an editor at a house that wants to acquire your book doesn't guarantee a deal.

What did you do right?

I did some pretty outside-the-box things, but the two most important were: First, I made friends with booksellers and authors by attending readings and signings and events. Second, I did not give up. There were a thousand points along the way when I wanted to.

Would you do anything differently?

[I wouldn't change] one single thing.

What's next for you?

Getting out and meeting the writers, booksellers, and readers I've been dreaming of all these years.

....

Jenny Milchman writes from New Jersey. Visit her website at jennymilchman.com.

....

TIM O'MARA

Sacrifice Fly
(mystery, Minotaur)
Schoolteacher and ex-cop Raymond Donne gets dragged back to the mean streets of Williamsburg when a student and his sister go missing.

What did you do prior to writing *Sacrifice Fly*?
I was actually working on a second Raymond Donne [novel when] I took *Sacrifice Fly* out of the closet to give it one more go, and the story finally fell into place.

What was the time frame for the book?
Between first word on the first page and the final version I was willing to show people, it took almost twenty years.

How did you meet your agents?
A friend of mine, TV producer Matt Bennett, was kind enough to read the book. He passed it on to his agent, Maura Teitelbaum at Abrams Artists, who asked Erin Niumata at Folio Literary to take a read. They both liked it, and I ended up with two agents.

Would you do anything differently?
I would have eliminated all the excuses for not writing and found the time to get it done. The time is there. We just have to see it.

Tell us a little about your platform.
I've served as a New York City public schoolteacher for nearly twenty-five years; my publishers and I plan to advertise in the major teachers' magazines and periodicals this fall. I'm a member of the three major teachers' unions, the International Thriller Writers and the Mystery Writers of America.

What's next for you?
I'm working on the second Raymond Donne book, *Chin Music*.

Tim O'Mara writes from New York City. Visit his website at timomara.net.

VADDEY RATNER

In the Shadow of the Banyan
(literary fiction, Simon & Schuster)
"The story of a seven-year-old girl who comes to maturity amidst the atrocity of the Khmer Rouge revolution."

What did you do prior to writing *In the Shadow of the Banyan*?

Having survived the Khmer Rouge, I knew that I would one day write this story. I began the book after I returned to live in Cambodia with my husband and daughter.

What was the time frame for the book?

Over the years, I had tried writing the book in various versions, among which was memoir. Yet it was only in Cambodia, in such proximity to the past, that I began the book as a work of fiction. It isn't my own life I wanted to draw attention to; instead, I wanted my work to honor the lives of those who perished.

How did you meet your agent?

When I finished the manuscript, I sent out queries to agents. Several weeks later, I heard back from Emma Sweeney [of the Emma Sweeney Agency].

What was your biggest surprise?

I'd read so many scary stories about the publishing process. It has been nothing but a lovely experience for me.

What did you do right?

Absolutely nothing. I don't tweet or blog. I've never been to a writers' workshop. I just closeted myself and wrote. Despite people constantly bemoaning the decline of quality publishing, I still have faith there are those in the industry looking for good writing. I wrote always with the belief that my job as a writer is to produce the best work I can and the rest will take care of itself.

Would you do anything differently?

If I had known with absolute certainty I would be published, I may have despaired less. There were moments when I stopped to ask myself, "Who will care?" In such moments, I thought maybe I should pursue something like dentistry. I would have been a terrible dentist!

What's next for you?

I've started on my second novel, *Music of the Ghosts*.

....

Vaddey Ratner writes from Potomac, Maryland. Visit her website at vaddeyratner.com.

....

INSIDE THE MIND OF THE PUBLICIST

Janice Hussein

Whether authors are e-publishing or combining e-publishing with the more traditional publishing track, marketing is now a key activity in a successful writing career. Discoverability, a term that has been coined in this past year, is the name of the game. However, many traditionally published authors feel that house publicists don't do enough and don't give their books the time and attention that would make a real difference in the book's success. With all the books and authors assigned to them, publicists often just don't have enough time. And many e-published authors either won't or don't hire a publicist, partly due to the expense; even if they did, authors would still be doing some of the legwork. So what can you do to get word-of-mouth buzz started and moving among your readership or potential readers?

Your own marketing and promotion efforts will benefit greatly from using the same marketing plan that publicists use for developing their own marketing campaigns. The process involves asking and answering a number of questions, starting with the Author Question and Answer Worksheet. With that in hand, you will then develop an Author Marketing Plan. When these tools are applied, they will give you a clear, personalized, and effective marketing plan for your book that will increase your discoverability and help maximize your book's potential.

Before creating your marketing plan, though, you should first familiarize yourself with the common tools and tropes of book promotion.

BRANDING

Carefully consider your options when developing an authorial brand. Branding is about making your name memorable, about differentiating yourself from the crowd so that readers remember you and your books. It's about promising something—a type of book and a reading experience (i.e., romances promise a happy ending; mysteries promise a killer brought to justice)—and then consistently meeting that expectation.

MARKETING TOOLKIT

You should consider all the traditional tools of marketing (while keeping your budget in mind): selling, advertising, publicity, promotion, and public relations.

- Selling is the personal component of marketing. It happens anytime authors and readers connect, like book signings and conferences or national and regional book festivals, such as BEA, the Romantic Times Booklovers Convention, International Thriller Writers Conference, or Wordstock.
- Advertising differs from the other tools in that it is paid for—a commercial or paid ad. Consider placing ads in magazines or on websites (www.freshfiction.com for example).
- Publicity is free. It's comprised of news releases, reviews, or product announcements.
- Promotions, like publicity, can be free: in-store displays, giveaways, contests, coupons, two for one's, samples, sweepstakes, and rebates.
- Public relations creates an image for the public that is attached to the book and author; for example, a PR representative may organize an event that benefits someone else, like an organization or nonprofit.

PRESS KITS

Maintain an up-to-date press or media kit, both in hard-copy format and as a web page that acts as an online press or media kit (in PDF or .zip file form). Make sure that the online kit is easy to find. Traditionally, the press kit contains the following:
- Cover letter
- Press release, usually for the book launch
- Sell sheet: Important information on the book—title, cover image, publication date, page count, retail price, ISBN, summary of the book, key selling points, contact and/or ordering information
- Professional photo of author and book cover
- Blurb(s)
- Biography
- Interviews
- Reviews
- Advertisements

- A list of past and present events (public relations events, workshops, conferences, book signings)
- For hard-copy kits: excerpts of novels, like booklets or sample chapters

I suggest creating hard-copy new release press kits to send to booksellers, book reviewers, newspapers, television and radio stations, historical societies, libraries, and so on. Most of these people are very busy and don't always have time to stop and check your website or blog for a media kit, but if they have the materials in hand, you have a much better chance of receiving a response.

A FICTIONAL EXAMPLE

To illustrate how the Author Marketing Plan works, I'll use a fictional example. Let's say an author writes a romantic suspense novel, *Countdown in Greece*, about a woman whose mother, on her deathbed, reveals that her real father is Greek. While researching her genealogy and trying to find her roots in Cyprus, the woman becomes enmeshed in the Greek/Turkey conflict, but encounters a handsome Greek Cypriot who must save her while attempting to unite his country.

This author would fill out the Author Question and Answer Worksheet as follows:

AUTHOR QUESTION AND ANSWER WORKSHEET

AUTHOR: Ava Brooks

HIGH SCHOOL: Graduated in Boston, MA

COLLEGE: Seattle, WA. Graduate of University of Washington

CURRENT RESIDENCE: Portland, OR

OCCUPATION: College Professor, Political Science, Portland State University

1. WHO ARE YOUR TARGET READERS?
WHO READS THE KIND OF BOOKS YOU WRITE?

Romance readers: 91 percent are women. Thriller readers.

WHAT ARE THEIR DEMOGRAPHICS, AGES, INTERESTS? PLAN ACCORDINGLY.

COMMUNITY:

Suburban residents tend to be middle-aged and have higher incomes than either rural or urban residents.

Suburban or urban residents are more likely to have an e-reader or tablet computer.

Urban readers tend to prefer e-books; rural readers tend to prefer print. (Pew Research, December 2012)

TRENDS:

Fifty-four percent of romance is still purchased in printed format, and 55 percent of Romance book buyers do not read e-books [yet] (2012 Romance Book Consumer Survey on the RWA website).

Fifty-nine percent of readers had "no interest" in buying an e-book (2012 Bowker Market Research survey). From "Don't Burn Your Book--Print is Here to Stay" by Nicholas Carr, Wall Street Journal, January 5, 2013.

SPECIAL INTERESTS: Genealogy; Greek/Cyprus politics and history; political science; higher education; travel; romance; international intrigue.

2. MAKE A LIST OF WHO WOULD BE MOST INTERESTED IN YOUR BOOK, BASED ON WHO YOU ARE: E-BOOK AND PRINT MARKETS.

WHERE YOU LIVE, SINCE MANY PEOPLE BUY FROM LOCAL AUTHORS: Portland, OR.
OTHER AUTHORS OF THE SAME GENRE OR TYPE OF BOOK.

PEOPLE AND PLACES ASSOCIATED WITH YOU WHO MIGHT BE INTERESTED:

LOCAL BOOKSTORES

University where you attended and/or graduated. Seattle, WA; University of Washington.

LOCAL AND REGIONAL LIBRARIES

Where you went to high school: Boston, MA.

People who have interests that are highlighted in the book: multicultural families.

ORGANIZATIONS AND/OR PUBLICATIONS THAT REFLECT INTERESTS HIGHLIGHTED IN THE BOOK: Genealogy organizations and clubs, historical organizations and clubs, family-oriented organizations and publications

Colleagues

Family and friends

Writers' organizations or groups that author belongs to or not.

Friends on social networking sites: Facebook (facebook.com), Twitter (twitter.com), LinkedIn (linkedin.com).

3. LIST AT LEAST TEN BOOKSTORES OR RETAIL OUTLETS IN YOUR AREA WHERE YOU WOULD MOST LIKE TO DO AN EVENT.

Portland State Bookstore, Portland, OR

Powells Books, Beaverton, OR

Barnes & Noble, Clackamas Town Center

Oregon Historical Society, Portland

Alexis Restaurant, Portland

The Agora Shop, Seattle

4. LIST COLLEAGUES, ALUMNI, COMMUNITY, FAMILY AND FRIENDS. THESE ARE THE CONTACTS WHO CAN HELP SPREAD THE WORD ABOUT YOUR NEW BOOK.

Academic groups, peace groups, Portland State professors and staff, other college professors, Greek community in Portland and Seattle, genealogical societies, historical societies, and book clubs.

5. HOW COMFORTABLE ARE YOU WITH BEING INTERVIEWED? IN FRONT OF A LIVE AUDIENCE?

Very comfortable. College professor.

TALKING ON THE RADIO? Comfortable. Done this before.

APPEARING ON TELEVISION? No experience with this.

6. ARE YOU COMFORTABLE SPEAKING IN PERSON TO AN AUDIENCE? DESCRIBE YOUR STRENGTHS AND WEAKNESSES.

Very comfortable. With a large group, a microphone is needed.

7. LIST TELEVISION AND RADIO STATIONS IN YOUR AREA THAT WOULD BE APPROPRIATE FOR YOU AND YOUR BOOK. INCLUDE SHOWS, HOST CONTACT NAMES, ADDRESSES, PHONE NUMBERS, AND E-MAIL ADDRESSES.

Oregon Public Broadcasting—Radio & TV. KATU Channel 2

Northwest News Channel 8. KOIN 6 TV

KPTV Cable

8. WHO OR WHAT DO YOU THINK ARE THE BEST MARKETS FOR THIS BOOK?

Romance and thriller readers; those interested in recent history and international conflicts.

9. ARE YOU A MEMBER OF A PROFESSIONAL ORGANIZATION? DO YOU HAVE ANY GROUP AFFILIATIONS THAT WOULD BE INTERESTED?

Peace organizations, Organization of University Women

10. WHAT ARE THE NEWSPAPERS AND PRINT MEDIA IN YOUR AREA? INCLUDE NAMES, ADDRESSES, E-MAIL, PHONE NUMBERS, AND CONTACT NAMES WHERE POSSIBLE.

The Oregonian, Seattle Times, The Columbian newspaper, The Boston Globe .

11. IN YOUR WORDS, WHAT WAS THE IMPETUS FOR WRITING THIS BOOK?

Interest in genealogy; how the search for our roots can affect us .

Interest in international conflicts and how they affect us personally.

12. WHAT IS MY BRAND?
    Romantic suspense/thrillers, with international settings.

The author would then use these answers to fill out the Marketing Plan and Marketing Strategy worksheets.

MARKETING PLAN

What are the book's unique features?
THE BOOK COMBINES A HISTORICAL PERSPECTIVE WITH GENEALOGY RESEARCH.
Genealogy chart and tips, with a list of genealogy websites.

What are the book's competitive advantages?
THE BOOK STANDS OUT FROM OTHER ROMANTIC SUSPENSE AND FICTION BECAUSE OF ITS
connections with genealogy and the Cyprus conflict.

Audience/Markets:
Fiction market, print and e-book readers
Family-oriented organizations and publications, multicultural families
Boston, MA, community
Seattle, WA, community; University of Washington
Portland, OR, community; Portland State University
Trade/Bookstores: chains and independents
Libraries
Genealogy organizations and clubs
Historical organizations and clubs
Online bookstores and book clubs
Brick-and-mortar bookstores and book clubs

Strongest selling features:
Suspense in Cyprus
Greek/Turkey conflict
Appeal to both romance and thriller readers
The successful search for one's roots and identity

MARKETING STRATEGY

General

PRESS KITS: Bookstores, book reviewers, newspapers, television and radio stations, historical societies, libraries, travel organizations, and magazines.

GALLEYS: Newspapers, magazines, bookstores, universities.

REVIEW COPIES: Academia, booksellers, reviewers (print and online), societies, organizations, Publishers Weekly, Kirkus, Romantic Times, Booklist.

MAILING LISTS TO RENT: Libraries, academics, book clubs (depends on budget). Most libraries carry reference books that list media across the country. (Of course, many organizations can be e-mailed.)

PROMOTION MATERIALS: NPR, booksellers, conferences, book launch.

BOOK SIGNINGS AND OTHER EVENTS:

BOOK EXCERPT: Clubs, societies, fiction clubs, websites.

COLLATERAL: Bookmarks, postcards, flyers, posters, booklets.

ARTICLES: Will hire freelancer to write.

PRESS RELEASES: Launch announcement and events.

SOCIETIES/ORGANIZATIONS, INTERESTED IN THE BOOK: Booksellers; historical; Romance Writers of America (RWA); International Thriller Writers, Inc. (ITW); libraries.

SPECIAL SALES:
Book catalogs. Copies for consignment to gift shops, retail outlets like Greek stores and restaurants, home improvement stores, travel outlets.

Strategy: Online

WEBSITE: www.avabrooks.com

BLOG: www.avabrooks.com/blog

REVIEW SITES: GoodReads, Story Cartel, Amazon.com, Bookpage

Social Networking sites: Twitter, Facebook, Google+, GoodReads

AUTHOR PAGES, WITH BOOK COVER AND EXCERPTS, AND LISTINGS FOR THE BOOK SET UP ON THESE WEBSITES: RWA, Amazon, Goodreads, Facebook, Bublish.com, ITW, Criminal Element, publisher's website.

PINTEREST, VISUAL.LY: Images of the book cover, Greece; links to news articles on Greek/Turkey conflict, genealogy

OTHER: Guest blogs, blog tours, blog hops, mass e-mails, podcasts, audio, teleclasses, telecasts, webinars, YouTube, SlideShare.

Strategy: Media—Print

PRESS KITS AND ADVANCED READER COPIES (ARCS) SENT TO: Publishers Weekly, Romantic Times, history and Greek and genealogical magazines, Library Journal, university newspapers, Oregonian, New York Times, Writer's Digest magazine, Barnes & Noble Booksellers, the Wall Street Journal, AAA magazine, New York Times Book Review, key media personalities.

Media—Radio

SET UP RADIO STATION INTERVIEWS:

Oregon: KLCC, Eugene; KOAB, Bend; KBOO, Portland

Washington: KUOW, Seattle

Massachusetts: WUMB, Boston

Send press kits to local and national radio shows focused on fiction

Contact BlogTalkRadio for an interview

Media—TV

SEND PRESS KITS TO LOCAL AND NATIONAL MORNING SHOWS IN CITIES WHERE THE AUTHOR WILL BE DOING BOOK SIGNINGS, SUCH AS: AM Northwest, CBS This Morning, and Good Morning America,in Portland, Seattle, Boston.

SEND PRESS KITS TO LOCAL AND NATIONAL TV SHOWS FOCUSED ON GENEALOGY OR FICTION: KPTV, OPB, ABC, The View, and Charlie Rose.

ADVERTISING:

ADS PREPARED FOR: Publishers Weekly, Romantic Times magazine, Romance Writers Report.

Flyers for reading

Posters for book launch

EVENTS:

INTERVIEWS/TOURS/SIGNINGS:

SET UP MEDIA INTERVIEWS AND BOOK SIGNINGS AT:

Powell's Books in Portland, OR

Local high schools and colleges

SPECIAL SALES/INTERESTS: Family History Fair (exhibits) in May

Tentative Schedule: Book Tour

BOOK LAUNCH: Date and place to be arranged

PRESENTATION AND BOOK SIGNING AT: Portland State University

PRESENTATION AND BOOK SIGNING AT: University of Washington

OTHER BOOKSTORES: Elliot Bay Book Company and Third Place Books in Seattle, WA; Barnes & Noble Booksellers; Jan's Paperbacks in Hillsboro, OR

Blog tour to be set up.

OTHER POSSIBLE BOOK TOUR SITES:

EXHIBITS/CONFERENCES: RT BookLovers Convention; RWA Conference; Write on the Sound conference; Wordstock Festival in Portland, OR; BEA; International Thriller Writers (ITW); Seattle Book Festival.

LAUNCH PARTY:

PRE-LAUNCH:

Host book giveaways on your website, blog, Goodreads, other authors' websites, reviewer websites.

Press releases sent to major news sites and search engines on the web. (Check out PRWeb and other sites that distribute press releases for a relatively small fee.)

List the launch in local newspapers, newsletters, advertisements.

Send out announcements to writing groups and organizations, and other groups.

Send out electronic invitations with time, date, and request an RSVP.

In the current publishing climate, marketing and promotion are no longer optional exercises—they are essential strategies for building a perennial readership for your book. After developing your marketing plan and strategy, you'll be armed with the same tools and techniques used by professional publicists, which will only increase your chances of success. Don't let your book come and go without notice. Send it out into the world with a bang.

....

Janice Hussein is a professioinal freelance editor with ten years of editing experience and a Master of Science in Writing. In her first three years as an editor she worked for a literary agent. Her published articles on writing craft, marketing, and other topics have been featured in Writer's Digest's *Novel & Short Story Writer's Market* and the *Romance Writer's Report*. She offers workshops at conferences and through her website: www.documentdriven.com. She blogs at documentdriven.com/SmartWriterBlog. Some of her short stories and an essay appear in online anthologies at http://www.columbiaarts.org/arts-more.html.

....

AUTHORIAL SELF-PROMOTION AND MARKETING

....

Jack Smith

Publishers today, both commercial and small press, expect authors to play a significant role in marketing their work. And so we hear a lot about branding, creating an author's platform, and effectively utilizing social media. Must you brand yourself? If you want to create an authorial brand, how do you go about it? What about cost and time? How do you make use of social media to promote yourself or your book? Are there different ways to look at the process? Is there a best process? And what's the payoff for all your effort?

DEVELOPING A BRAND

So how do you go about creating a "brand"? Authors view it differently—and approach it differently.

Authorial branding suggests "product recognition." In developing her own brand, Susan Wingate, author of ten novels, including *Drowning* and *Bobby's Diner*, seeks uniformity. "I've [made] all of my online and business marketing tools look the same. My website has the same logo, 'Writing from the Couch,' and the same photo as my Facebook and my Twitter pages, and any other online sites I might employ. You'll find the same logo and color scheme on my business cards and bookmarks."

How does one go about this? How much technical expertise do you need? According to Wingate, "The art of developing a brand can be an elusive one unless you do extensive research or hire an expert." But these marketing and publicity experts can be very expensive, with "price tags of anything from $2,000 for basic services to $20,000 and up." Wingate says doing your own research is certainly cost-effective, but time-consuming. She adds: "I still don't feel I've branded myself as well as a professional might, but I've opted for the road of least expense."

Elizabeth Spann Craig is author of three mystery series: the Memphis Barbeque mystery series (as Riley Adams), the Southern Quilting mysteries, and the Myrtle Clover series. She also sees the importance of authorial branding, but her approach is different from Wingate's: "If you're creating exposure for yourself as an author, the best way is to build a stable online presence, portray yourself as a professional, and offer yourself as a helpful resource for others."

Still, it should be noted that the very prospect of authorial branding doesn't sit too well with some writers. Cathy Day, author of *Comeback Season* and *The Circus in Winter*, states: "Honestly, I can't stand words like *branding, platform*, and *self-promotion*. Really, I loathe those words. And yet," says Day, "I also realize that it's no longer my publisher's job to find an audience for my work. I've come to terms with the fact that it's my job to self-promote and build relationships with other writers and readers." She works to make the process "as organic and genuine as possible. I am not branding myself. I am simply being exactly who I already am in a more public way."

Laura van den Berg is author of two story collections, *What the World Will Look Like When All the Water Leaves Us: Stories* and *The Isle of Youth*. In a similar vein as Day, she states: "I frankly can't imagine entering into any situation with brand awareness on the brain." Instead, thinking of the Internet "as one giant conversation," she seeks to find "the parts of the conversation I'd like to join."

If authorial branding has an objectionable ring to it for some authors, Thaisa Frank, author of several works of fiction, including *Heidegger's Glasses* and *Enchantment,* shifts the emphasis from author to work: "This may sound simplistic, but I think about what I do in fiction that no one else I know or read does, and then I try to characterize it. It's always a work in process. The hubris may be in believing that my sensibility is unique. The work is figuring out 'how,' and the humility is realizing that I want to reach people."

Elizabeth Searle, author of four works of fiction, including *Girl Held in Home*, also links brand to work, but since she writes in more than one medium—fiction as well as theater and film—this becomes a bit "tricky," she says. "However, my works in each genre do have common themes [which relate to] our crazed celebrity culture and its warping effects." Searle's advice to those who work in more than one genre is to "think about what common themes or elements or subject matter might link your works."

Lise Haines has authored three novels, including *In My Sister's Country* and *Girl in the Arena*. She maintains that "the real 'brand' has to come from the work itself." She realizes the importance of the business side, but there's a risk here, she says: "I'm not saying we don't have to pay attention to platforms. The business side has become a second career for most authors. But if we become living, breathing ads more than authors writing essential books, that's a loss."

USE OF WEBSITE AND SOCIAL MEDIA

Whatever your position on branding, creating a platform, or promoting and marketing your work, and whatever your degree of commitment, an important question certainly arises: How *do* you create exposure for yourself as an author, or for your work, through your website and various forms of social media? And what are some potential benefits of doing so?

A website is, of course, a very useful tool.

An author's website, says Elizabeth Spann Craig, can function as "an information hub." This is usually the first place readers go to find out about an author: "I use my website as a way to inform readers—I'm letting them know what I'm currently working on and what will be released next in my different series. The website also provides readers my contact information so they can reach me in a variety of ways."

Thaisa Frank likens a website to the old calling card. "It gives people quick information about yourself." She keeps her website current with information about her books, upcoming events, reviews, and links. Her bio lets readers know "where I've been, where I am, and where I'm going." She's easily reached by curious readers, as well as those who want to invite her to events or ask her to write something.

For many writers, a website is a good first step in creating a wide variety of platform avenues. Blogging is another important means of connecting with other writers. It's the primary tool for Elizabeth Spann Craig. "[By blogging], I network with others in the writing community and share ideas on the writing craft and resources that I've come across." Because of these valuable posts, her blog has received several awards that have provided her with recognition and exposure. Elizabeth Searle states, "I use my blog to sound off on pop culture issues. Luckily I have a whole network of writing friends and former students who regularly supply me with guest posts." On her blog, "The Big Thing," Cathy Day blogs about both novel writing and teaching novel writing. Her success has created a niche among students and teachers of creative writing.

Blogs can also connect writers with readers. Thaisa Frank finds blogging useful in terms of reaching readers with her particular sensibility. "I use blogs to talk about writing; I've been using a great site called Red Room and am planning to move my blog over to my website (it will still be linked on Red Room) and I am also planning to focus on a few issues in writing that will involve interviews. The advantage of Red Room is that what I write gets read by a lot of people, but the advantage of a blog on a website is that it helps broadcast the brand."

Facebook and Twitter have both become vital means of professional networking. For Elizabeth Spann Craig, Facebook serves two important functions: networking with other writers and supporting them by cross promoting their releases on her wall—practices which have helped build her brand and have allowed her to gain exposure "in a way that's professional and less self-serving." Through Twitter, Craig regularly shares helpful web resources for writers, a habit which has given her a large following. "This method has also helped me build my personal brand as someone who tries to offer help and support to others online." If you want to extend your reach to writers and readers in other time zones in the world, Craig suggests scheduling tweets on Twitter. "If you've found a great writing-related craft post or a publishing-related news story, you can use a free program like SocialOomph.com to schedule a tweet of the link and a short description of the post."

Facebook serves Lise Haines in several different ways: "I spend time on Facebook networking, picking up articles on publishing, and learning about new books." Haines prefers Facebook over Twitter because Facebook is more in keeping with her own visual orientation. Thaisa Frank credits the overwhelming response she's gotten to *Enchantment*, which appeared on the "Best Books of 2012" in the *San Francisco Chronicle*, to the provocative, entertaining articles she posted on both her personal Facebook page (with over 660 subscribers) and her author Facebook page (with over two thousand "likes"). Over time, she feels that she has grown to appreciate the usefulness of this platform in gaining exposure for both author and work. "I'm about to make my website more personal, drawing people from Facebook to read my columns."

Elizabeth Searle is actively involved in both Facebook and Twitter, with more than one thousand friends and followers. She uses these social media outlets to post links to her projects and other authors' projects she wants to promote. On Facebook, she also updates friends on local literary and theatrical events. "I like the feeling of being part of an online community where we can cheer each other on with thumbs-up in good times and writerly advice in not-so-good times. I have definitely found that connecting over Facebook can lead to in-person support at readings and other literary opportunities. It also provides comfort and camaraderie in the solitary writing life."

OTHER INTERNET TOOLS AND SITES

Jabari Asim has authored four books for adults, including *A Taste of Honey*, and six books for children. In addition to fan pages on Facebook and guest hosting #blacklitchat on Twitter, he has posted promotional videos on YouTube and excerpts from his fiction and poetry on Soundcloud. He also posts on Goodreads. Asim states, "I think you get as much out of these tools as you put into them."

Elizabeth Spann Craig also recommends actively using other Internet tools and sites: Google+, says Craig, is "a great way to get your name ranked higher in Google's search engine. Claim your name there and try to regularly update the page. Google tends to reward Google+ users with higher visibility on its [search] engine." Craig also recommends LinkedIn, Pinterest, and Goodreads. "LinkedIn," she says, "is perhaps the easiest way to connect online for writers. [Pinterest allows writers] an easy way to connect with readers online. Writers can create different bulletin boards for book-related topics and pin images that correspond." Readers go to Goodreads to find out about new books, and Craig values this site as "another contact point for readers to reach me."

THE BEST PROCESS

Is there a "right way" of thinking and going about this whole matter of promoting your work—or yourself as author? Is there a best process, and is one process better than another? Writers differ in their outlooks, but you should keep the following principles, practices, and issues in mind.

Supporting Your Fellow Writers

For Elizabeth Searle, "posting a link for a fellow writer's event takes only minutes and is a favor that's often kindly returned." It's even better if you can attend each other's events. For Searle, authors shouldn't bemoan the great numbers of writers who make for such stiff competition in publishing; instead, they should find ways to promote each other, making for "'safety' (and support) in numbers."

Doing Only What You Enjoy

Laura van den Berg states that she doesn't really enjoy blogging and confesses that she's not especially good at it, so she doesn't do it very much. "I enjoy Twitter, so I use that resource more consistently. [With so many social media options available, you might] think you need to do everything," says van den Berg, "[but] it's probably more effective to focus your energies on what you enjoy doing and have some aptitude for." Elizabeth Spann Craig states: "If you don't enjoy the site, you're likely not going to use it." The most important thing, Lise Haines believes, is to be passionate about what you're doing, whether it's starting a journal, publishing in magazines, taking time to build Klout scores, or making Skype visits. "I don't think you can take these things on unless you're really passionate about this kind of effort, and prepared to hustle and meet endless deadlines."

Studying Proven Techniques

Jabari Asim offers this advice: "I'd start out by studying the social media techniques of authors I admire or whom I envision reaching a similar audience—and model my approach after them. Most of the things I've done were fairly easy to figure out; other stuff, like posting videos, I leave to my kids."

Handling Graphic Design Issues

Susan Wingate acknowledges that she struggles with graphic design issues in terms of product recognition: "I don't like to see the same colors all of the time or the same logo or photo on every piece of marketing material. It bores me." She is tempted to change her website's background color, shuffle around pages, and even switch to a new website template. But, she says, to keep things consistent, she fights her urges because the website isn't for her own pleasure—"it's a business tool that people can land on and think, 'Ah, yes. This is Susan Wingate.'"

Finding a Way to Present Your Unique Vision to Your Readers

For Thaisa Frank, you must demonstrate that you have something unique to offer. "If you really don't have something unique to offer, you have to change your game plan." Don't worry about readers 'getting it', she says. "[They're] more intelligent and sensitive than writers think, and you're not so 'special' that a reader won't 'get' you. They will. Figuring out how to tell them they will is the challenge and the mystery."

Deciding How Much Time You Can Give to the Promotional Process

Lise Haines points out that for breakthrough books and big sellers, publishers do a lot of the promotional work—blog tours, advertising space, and dedicated websites. "And then there are all those independent publicists who make critical connections for large sums and commissioned services that set up readings." But, says Haines, if you're a new or midlist author, it's a catch-22: "How do you get enough attention to get enough attention? Most authors cut out huge chunks of their writing lives or their sleep in order to promote their work." Timers are one way to address the "time-suck" problem with social media, says Elizabeth Spann Craig. "Using a free program like Countdown Timer enables me to keep track of how long I've been answering e-mails or connecting with others on Facebook."

Dealing With the Marketing Perspective in Your Own Way

Cathy Day rejects the standard marketing viewpoint: "It's not selling. It's not networking. It's about being a good literary citizen." This includes several kinds of people-oriented activities: "Friending and following. Commenting on blogs. Talking about other people's books and readings. Sharing links and information that add value to a community. Just being interested in what other people are doing." Day wants to take the emphasis off the profit motive: "It's not about saying 'Hey! Here's my book! Go buy it!'" Even so, one should be aware of the marketing realities, and Day believes being a good literary citizen might well pay off in the end. "I have this Theory of the Five Pops: In order for someone to feel compelled to buy a book, it has to 'pop' up on their radar five times. If your book is reviewed in the *New York Times* or *People,* or you get a spot on *Fresh Air,* well, that's like fifty pops. If your publisher pays to have your book strategically placed on a table or on an end cap at a bookstore, that's a lot of pops, too. But what if your book doesn't get 'the big push?' What if you don't publish it traditionally? That's where social media comes in. By creating a digital presence, you give your book a chance to find its audience by creating the opportunity for more pops."

THE PAYOFF

What's the potential payoff for all your efforts at self-promotion, marketing, and branding? The answer to this question is manifold.

You can create a brand at little or no cost. For Elizabeth Spann Craig, "the largest payoff is the fact that I've got great name recognition in the industry and have paid really nothing to attain this." She has created her brand on her own, at home. "Not only have I created a brand for myself in the States, but I've extended my reach to other countries for the cost of an Internet connection."

If you work for uniformity and consistency, you can achieve brand recognition. Susan Wingate states, "People feel comfortable with your website simply because they recognize your branding and, therefore, they recognize you." Even though achieving consistency "can be a bit tricky" with book covers each being different, says Wingate, "much of it can be handled with fonts and back cover art."

Outside of the question of authorial branding, what about simply getting your work out there—and noticed?

For Thaisa Frank, the payoff includes two things: "Knowing that the arc of the story is going to be re-created by a stranger. And money!"

Cathy Day also sees the double payoff. First, there's the nonmaterial benefit. "Our lives are improved by expanding our circles in conscious, mindful ways. My life has been greatly enriched by the people I've met online." She's optimistic about her online efforts leading to book sales, but even if they don't, she states: "I still feel that the time I've spent doing this work has been worth it."

Laura van den Berg also values expanding her circles. She says: "If you're active on social media, it's a chance to meet people you wouldn't cross paths with in your regular life." She finds that an online presence provides company for a lonely writer, but also expands one's knowledge of the literary landscape. Like Cathy Day, she also sees potential sales: "When a book goes out into the world, the kindness of friends and acquaintances can go a long way."

And, finally, whatever happens, you know you've done your best to promote your work, says Elizabeth Searle. "To me, the payoff of promoting my works online or in person is simply that I have the satisfaction of knowing—in this most challenging of fields—that I have done my best to get my words 'out there.' I am not one to write 'for the drawer' or for a tiny group of family and real-life friends. The social media world provides a relatively easy way to link up to the larger world."

SUMMING UP

You may set out to create a brand, or you may set out only to sell books. You may see so-cial media as a great way to network with other writers and to gain exposure with read-ers. Or you may set out to get involved in social media because you really enjoy an online presence—and you see a double payoff, in being linked to other writers and in potential sales as you gain more and more exposure. It makes sense to find out as much as you can about all aspects and realities of marketing and then decide on the nature and the extent of your commitment. First determine your personal marketing goals, and then determine what you are willing to do to meet them.

TAKE YOUR WEBSITE TO THE NEXT LEVEL

....

Karen M. Rider

A professionally designed website is your business card to the world, one that should evolve with your writing career. Your website should make a dynamic presentation of the wares you have to offer—books, articles, or writing and editing services. Unlike a standard blog that aims to engage people in discussion, the purpose of a website is to *inform* people about who you are and to *market* your writing efforts to your target audience: potential readers or clients, publishers, editors, or agents.

As such, your website should pay you back for the time and money you invested in it. It's easy to tell when that's not happening: No one is contacting you, buying from you, or hiring you.

To take your website to the next level, where there's an engaged audience and a click-through rate that soars, you'll want to do four things: Make sure all the key essentials are in place, stock it with the best content, get a little tech savvy and maintain a strong buzz.

1. DOUBLE-CHECK THE BASICS.

Whether you're an unpublished writer building a platform, a seasoned freelancer, a self-published scribe or a midlist author, your website has to meet your visitors' basic expectations. "You'll want to hone the content so it has structure and provides visitors with compelling and current information," says Mark Hollis, president of Hollis Internet Marketing. Visitors get that structure from the way information is organized, so your first step is to check that your website contains all the right pages:

- A home page with a welcome message
- A portfolio page presenting published fiction/nonfiction (or links to it)

- A reviews or testimonials page
- An about page with short and long bios
- A contact page with your info or agent/publicist info
- An events page or calendar
- A services page informing visitors about what you do—copywriting, editing, etc.
- A press page or FAQ page, as necessary.

After you have all the right pages, ensure the essentials are in place throughout your site:

- Use high-resolution author photos and book cover images.
- Use familiar menu names ("portfolio," not "library").
- Keep drop-down menus simple.
- Check that active links connect to the appropriate pages within your site.
- Avoid Flash and music intros that slow down page-load time.
- Make sure your site loads properly on all popular Internet browsers (Firefox, Internet Explorer, Chrome).

2. SHARPEN THE CONTENT.

Once the basics are good to go, you can focus on buffing up your content to engage readers.

"Authors can woo visitors by going beyond jacket copy to give readers a feel for what makes the author tick," says Steve Bennett, founder of AuthorBytes. For instance, novelists can reveal secrets, illuminate character backstory or show images that inspired the setting for a book.

Freelancers can offer bonus material that didn't appear in a published article but deepens a visitor's experience of a subject. A "behind-the-interview" pop-up could give readers little-known details about an interviewee.

Karin Bilich, president of SmartAuthorSites.com, says unpublished authors seeking an agent should include video or audio clips of themselves to show that they know how to present themselves. Also, even if you're not published, provide fun details, such as what inspired you to write a particular story—and no matter what you write, address visitors in your unique voice (not your favorite author's), so that you stand out in your own way. Keep a link to your website on Facebook and Twitter, too—and record your social media fan and follower numbers, because they can come in handy when querying agents.

"Show you know how to market yourself, and you're successfully doing it," Bilich says.

Ultimately, the golden rule is that content is king—so make it good. Even the coolest features—videos, etc.—become hackneyed quickly on the Web. "You *don't* have a captive audience," Bennett says. "It takes but one click for visitors to go elsewhere."

Stale content derails website traffic, reducing the number of repeat visits and potential sales. "To keep traffic moving to your site," says Carol Fitzgerald, president of AuthorsOn-TheWeb.com, "assess whether or not readers are getting *current* information and the calls to action necessary to encourage a presale order or to hire you for an assignment."

This call to action, a "do this now" prompt that entices visitors to do X and to get Y from you in return, is key. On your website, you won't sell books, build a platform or get hired without it. Examples include "buy" links to purchase books; e-newsletter sign-ups; registration for exclusive content; and so on.

As for keeping content current, Fitzgerald advises writers to review material monthly and to time-release new additions. "Don't give everything away at once," she says. "Think about the timing of your message about a book release, an appearance or when a feature article will publish."

Then, update accordingly. On your home page, designate an area that alerts visitors to new content within the site. Clean up your events calendar. (No events scheduled? Fill that space with a call to action: "Book Now for Spring.") Visitors want to read fresh testimonials and reviews, check out recently published clips, and see recent photos.

3. KNOW SEO.

The technology that makes Internet search results more accurate evolves daily. Getting savvy to technical elements such as search engine optimization (SEO) and analytics can ensure your website has what it needs to get to the next level and pull in the visitors you want: readers, editors, publishers, and agents.

In a nutshell, search engines scan content on websites in response to queries typed into a search field. When keywords in the website code and text are a relevant match, that site appears in the search results.

What makes for relevant keywords for writers? That depends on what you do. For novelists, relevant keywords could be your name, book titles, even character names. For freelancers, subjects you've written about will most likely be the terms a person surfing the Web will use.

So make a list of your keywords. Then, if you don't know how to tweak your own website code to put the keywords in, don't freak out: You can find tutorials online and learn more about this topic in resources such as Google's Search Engine Optimization Starter Guide (available for free at http://bit.ly/d29DIe) and the *Yahoo! Style Guide* (free articles are available at styleguide.yahoo.com). Moreover, website/blogging software such as WordPress has simple SEO plug-ins you can use, which will have a similar, though not quite as precise, effect.

Overall, writers unfamiliar with basic Web design may be better off hiring an experienced webmaster to optimize their website. But if you're up to the task, Hollis says one of the best ways to make sure search engines can find you is to place keywords in heading-level tags <h1> through <h6>. "Just as writers use headlines to indicate to readers the kind of information presented in an article, heading-level tags act as 'headlines' for search engines crawling through your Web copy."

For example, a freelance writer specializing in do-it-yourself grooming for specific dogs wants those breed names located in <h1> and <h2>, the top of the hierarchy. When someone searches "grooming poodles," websites with those keywords properly placed in HTML "headlines" will come up in the search results.

Regardless of whether you tweak the tags yourself or have a pro do it, track your results by monitoring how many monthly page views you get, the number of people signing up for an offer, the sales of books or services—all part of what is called Web analytics. Analytics packages that track website performance range in both price (free to $80 a month) and the quality of information they provide (one excellent free resource is Google Analytics—google.com/analytics).

Track your stats, then adjust your keywords accordingly … and save the data.

Agents and publishers respond to statistics because numbers drive business. Showing your stats provides convincing evidence about the market for your work. An aspiring novelist who has detailed analytics in hand is able to say to an agent, "My website has averaged X unique visitors and Y repeat hits per month over the past four months. Visitors spend an average of Z minutes reading my content."

Book deals aside, no matter how many visitors you get, making your site a meaningful investment of your time and money is about more than simply pulling people in.

"Magic doesn't happen just because someone lands on your site," says Penny Sansevieri, president of Author Marketing Experts. "The trick is to convert 1 to 2 percent of your traffic into consumers by getting them to sign up for something: your blog, newsletter, coupon."

To keep traffic flowing so you can reach people with those crucial calls to action, you've got to maintain the *buzz* at your website.

4. STAY BUZZED.

Be proactive: Building buzz begins with actively promoting your website by talking it up and listing that link wherever your name appears, from press releases to e-mail messages. To stay buzzed, you'll need to do a little online marketing—and, well, resist the urge to get completely lost in it!

Online marketing drives traffic to your website through publicity and promotion. Unlike SEO, any writer can easily do a fair amount of it herself. For starters, place a link to your website on *everything* you do online. Comment on blogs that align with the audience you want to reach. Trade links with other writers' websites (your link on their site, their link on yours). Share reviews of your books or write articles for digital magazines that link back to you. Social networking sites like Facebook and Twitter can provide link areas to keep your site humming with visitors ready to take action.

Once you start buzzing about your first novel or writing services or latest article, keep it up. "Never go dark," states M.J. Rose, novelist and founder of AuthorBuzz.

It's imperative to be consistent and to keep your audience engaged with compelling content that makes them want to come back for more. Sure, there'll be quiet times (like when you are actually working on your novel), but with a little strategic effort on your part, your website will make it to the next level—and take your writing career along with it.

Karen M. Rider has published nearly two hundred articles for print and digital magazines on topics ranging from energy medicine to writer's block. She applied all she learned writing this article to her website, karenmrider.com, and is thrilled with the results.

PLATFORM FOR FICTION WRITERS

....

Chuck Sambuchino

If you write nonfiction, creating a platform is a mandatory step to getting published. But what if you write fiction? Do you still need a platform? The quick answer is that while you don't absolutely need one by any means, building a platform will without a doubt help your writing career. It will help you sell more books and control your destiny (as much as that is possible). It also allows you channels where you can reach out to fans and prospective readers. All of these are beneficial to have and will make you more valuable as an author.

Take it from Elana Johnson, author of the young adult novels *Possession* and *Surrender*. Johnson created a popular blog in the writing community and usually gets forty to one hundred comments on each post. (Consistently getting any number of comments on posts—even seven to ten—is a good thing.)

In a blog column where she discusses the upsides of platform, Johnson stated what she thought were the benefits of the hard work she put in before she even had a book deal: "I believe that MTV asked me to blog for them because of my blogging experience here … [and] I believe that blogging has brought me more than $25,000 more on my debut deal. I've done what I set a goal to do: make meaningful connections." And Johnson is not alone in her personal story. Novelists Billy Coffey and Gina Holmes attribute a portion of their payments directly to the blog platform they created before they had a book deal.

Plenty of times, novelists shy away from platform building, saying something along the lines of, "I believe my job is to write a great book and hope that it finds an audience." And just to be clear, yes, this answer is very valid. The number one thing you can do to sell more novels is write a damn good story; the quality of the prose is paramount, according to Beth Gissinger, former digital marketing director for F+W Media: "When I sit in title acquisition meetings, it's my job to help ensure we are signing projects from authors with decent platforms. That said, I'd take a chance on a [book] with great writing and no platform vs. a [book] with lousy writing and decent platform most days."

But you must understand that building a platform can only help your success and worth as an author. Think of it from the perspective of a publishing executive. Sales are a bit down, so she's acquiring fewer books and being careful about what gets published. Then an employee appears in her office holding two manuscripts to consider and notes that they can only say yes to one. The executive reads both books, and neither disappoints. Good plots, good characters, good series potential—both of them. The executive can't decide which one to choose. Then she asks the employee about both writers' platforms. It turns out Writer #1 is an enthusiastic guest blogger for some big sites and has 7,500 followers on Twitter, among other accomplishments. Writer #2 actually "hates social media sites" and is "not a fan of being interviewed."

If you were this executive, whom would you choose? I personally would choose Writer #1, and there is no logical reason why anyone else wouldn't do the same thing. The first things an editor looks for in a novel are exactly what you think: quality, salability, and across-media potential. But a certain small factor in their decision-making methods is indeed platform—because your personal reach is money for them.

WHAT CONSTITUTES A FICTION NICHE?

Nonfiction writers have a relatively clear route to platform. If a man in Michigan wants to make a name for himself as an expert on restaurants in the state, he can start a blog and Twitter account and newspaper column all about his specialty. Boom. Done. The train is off and running; let's all wish him good luck.

But what's a novelist's specialty? These are much more difficult to pin down because often no clear answer exists. However, that's not necessarily a bad thing. Not being forced into one "clear" niche allows a writer to decide what she wants to blog about. It gives writers openness and opportunity. In my opinion, fiction writers have three different platform routes they can take:

- The "loose subject connection" niche
- The "altogether different" niche
- The "writing focus" niche

1. The "Loose Subject Connection" Niche
This approach means choosing a major theme in your book and making that your focus. Perhaps your books always feature detectives of Native-American descent—

most of the time solving cases on reservations. You likely have a great interest in Native-American culture, so how can that translate into a blog? Perhaps you can write about news involving First Peoples communities or inspiring stories of what's going on in the West today. Or perhaps you can do some research and share interesting stories from the past that many people aren't familiar with. You're creating content that has a major relation to what you're writing, so those who come to your site and also read fiction would be target readers for you.

Here's a loose connection niche in practice: Delilah Marvelle is a successful romance writer who's had many books published. On her blog each month, she posts a true story about sex in the context of history. Her fiction genre is romance, so discussing true stories about sex in history is a fascinating and successful way to build a readership and platform. Not only has it gained her blog readers and friends, but it was this "sex and history" column that caught the attention of a big-time literary agent who later offered to represent her.

2. The "Altogether Different" Niche

This approach entails building a platform of some size while acknowledging that it has little or no connection to your novels. For example, maybe you're a literary fiction writer who is sitting around brainstorming what to blog about. You ask yourself, "What do I love to discuss in life?" Perhaps the answer you keep coming back to is, of all things, mountain biking. Okay. If this is your true passion in life and you won't easily get bored writing about it, then I say go for it. Create content with passion and gusto, and build a community around yourself. The goal is simply to create a huge readership and to hope that some of that visibility translates to book sales. No doubt it will, though exact numbers will be difficult to come by.

In a manner of speaking, I myself fall into the "altogether different" niche because I write two distinctly different types of nonfiction books: how-to titles on writing, and quirky humor books. When I started writing humor books, I debated on building a second platform by submitting articles to humor sites and such but ultimately decided against it. My opinion was that my publishing platform was already amply successful in one arena, and the sheer size of it was enough to ensure that a small percentage of people who visited my blog would also buy my humor books. I expected some crossover and am confident there has been plenty.

Having a platform outside your niche runs directly contrary to popular teaching, but it can work. In my case, my humor books fall into a more general category that can be marketed to any group. The goal is that in meeting people online and in person, readers will connect with me through my writing advice but also get to know me, Chuck Sambuchino, the person, the husband, the dog lover, the wannabe rock star, the chocolate chip cookie addict. When that happens, the brand they follow becomes me, not Guide to Literary Agents. That's the goal. And achieving that goal to some degree or another allows me to sell humor books.

3. The "Writing Focus" Niche

The primary focus of this blog is your own writing journey, along with your personal successes and challenges along the way. These blogs are extremely common with new writers, which means there is good news and bad news if you try this approach.

The good news is that there are plenty of up-and-coming writers who will immediately identify with your subject matter—that is to say, readership exists for your website. The bad news is that there are so many "new writer" blogs out there already. Here's what happens: An unpublished writer writes a book and then hears that he should be online, so he starts a simple blog. He doesn't know what to write about, so he defaults to chronicling his attempts to get published.

What a blogger will likely not realize is that there must be more than five thousand of these "new writer" blogs out there. And that means you are immediately facing stiff competition everywhere in every direction. Remember that you want to carve out a unique niche, not compete against as many people as possible.

These warnings are not to say that this plan can't work. It actually works plenty of times. Look at young adult writer Elana Johnson again. She blogs about writing, does it well, gets tons of reader interaction, and credits a huge chunk of change to her hard work. There are and will continue to be success stories with writing blogs—but beware of focusing only on your writing journey. Brainstorm what else you can bring to the table. I'll start you off with some ideas:

- Can you interview professionals or authors? Stick to a specific niche (e.g., science fiction writers), so your blog/site gains an identity.
- Can you review books?
- Can you round up industry news in a certain genre or subject area?
- Can you answer reader questions? Again, try to be specific. I've seen writers have some success answering questions about "writing about psychology" or "writing about hospitals." These approaches are specific—and specific is good.

Try to come up with different dimensions and elements you can give your brand other than "writer trying to make it who wants to update you about his writing journey." It's not very original or entertaining on its own, and so many people are doing it already. Plus, having this focus often makes the blog more for you than for others. It also lends itself to writing posts about the slog of trying to get published, and that might easily include complaints about editors and agents in the industry. Not a good thing to publicly vent!

6 TIPS ON BUILDING A BRAND *by Robert Brewer*

Carving out a niche as an editor who understands the publishing industry has afforded me several opportunities that other editors have not enjoyed. Likewise, branding myself as a poet with a popular blog has led to my being named Poet Laureate of the Blogosphere. I was also invited to be a National Feature Poet at the 2011 Austin International Poetry Festival. Building a brand is easy on paper, but it requires rolling up your sleeves in real life. Here are six simple tips:

1. Make a list of who you are as a person. Are you nice? Are you helpful? Are you outrageous? Are you funny? Are you authoritative? Try not to answer yes to every question you ask yourself.
2. Make a list of who you are as a writer. Answer the same questions above. Hopefully the answers align with step 1.
3. Define how you'd like others to view you. Again, it would be nice if this aligned with steps 1 and 2.
4. List your writing specialties and successes up to this point. It's okay if you don't have a long list.
5. List what you'd like to do with your writing in the short term. Then begin working toward these goals while keeping in mind how these goals align with steps 1 through 3 and/or build off step 4.
6. List what you'd like to do with your writing in the long term. In a perfect world, this will build off step 5.

The main thing you want to do is identify who you are and who you want to be. Then everything you do should be an extension of this identity. I would strongly advise against dramatically changing who you are in an attempt to find success. Instead, build upon who you are by emphasizing your strengths and working on your weaknesses.

....

Chuck Sambuchino (chucksambuchino.com) is an editor, best-selling humor book author, and authority on how to get published. He works for Writer's Digest Books and edits the *Guide to Literary Agents* as well as the *Children's Writer's and Illustrator's Market*. His Guide to Literary Agents Blog (guidetoliteraryagents.com/blog)—all about agents, submissions, and platform—is one of the largest blogs in publishing. Chuck is also a freelance book/query editor, husband, cover band guitarist, piano lover, chocolate chip cookie fiend, and owner of a flabby-yet-lovable dog named Graham. Find him on Twitter (@chucksambuchino).

....

MAN MARTIN

Self-Promotion Is Generosity

....

Jack Smith

 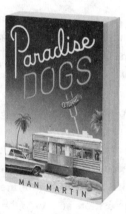

Man Martin has published two novels: *Days of the Endless Corvette* (Carroll & Graf, 2007) and *Paradise Dogs* (Thomas Dunne Books, 2011). His first novel won the 2008 George Author of the Year Award for First Novel. *Publishers Weekly* wrote of Man Martin's second book: "A full-bore slapstick marathon in the tradition of Carl Hiassen." Still, if Martin's work is pure farce at times, he doesn't see himself as a satirist like Hiassen. "I'm too mild. I'm much more in the camp of Dickens. At the end of the day, I can't help believing in the fundamental goodness of life, the world, and people," he says. And one certainly sees this in his two novels. Martin knows how to milk his material for any signs of human folly, irony, or ignorance, but at the same time one feels the presence of an understanding, sympathetic author behind it all.

As an artist, Martin is a real risk taker. In *Days of the Endless Corvette*, set in fictional Humble County, Georgia, he adopts an unusual point of view: omniscient first person.

Told from the vantage point of the local librarian, who makes only sporadic appearances in the novel, Martin somehow seamlessly weaves together a mythic tale of a bleak region with the sad but comic story of two lovers doomed to live apart, to settle for much less than their heart's desires. If he uses an unconventional technical device in his first novel, in his second, *Paradise Dogs*, he risks an unsympathetic protagonist in the person of Adam Newman: alcoholic, inveterate mess up, imposter. He *risks* this—and yet, as with his first novel, Martin skillfully pulls it all off, endearing the reader to his bungling but well-intentioned protagonist and creating a heartfelt genial comedy.

Novel writing is only part of the process for Man Martin. Self-promotion of one's work must follow: "Writers do a certain amount of bitching and moaning about how little publicity effort publishers put forth. For my part, I'm grateful for whatever my publisher does, but I don't expect them to carry the whole load. They've already paid me an advance, edited my manuscript, designed the cover, paid to have the book printed, and arranged for distribution; what else do I expect from them—that they write the book? If the author is not the person on the planet most interested in promoting his own book, there's a problem."

Can you comment on your comic vision?

Make things simultaneously as funny and sad as you possibly can. Flannery O'Connor said it best: Some things are terrible because they're funny and funny because they're terrible. My first book is about a high-school dropout who spends his life waiting for a woman who will never be his, and my second is about an alcoholic who is like a wrecking ball in his own life. Go figure. Coleridge wrote of the reconciliation of opposites, which seems to me the wrong term, or maybe the meaning of reconciliation has shifted in the past two hundred years, but in any case, I fully believe in the juxtaposition of opposites. Reconciliation sounds like you mix hot and cold and end up with tepid, but the real trick is to take two opposites, make them sit side by side, while sacrificing none of their opposition, and not only make them sit by each other, but join them at the hip so they can't be separated. Bear in mind they're opposites and can't possibly be together and yet they are—if you can pull that off, you're an artist. The particular opposites I work with happen to be humor and sadness.

What's your sense for the craft?

Nothing at all should be in a story—whether it's a single word or an entire chapter— without earning its keep. There's a real temptation for the novelist to think that since the novel is a form of indefinite length, there's room for extraneous matter. Not so. Northrop Frye once suggested [writers] ought to refer to every written work, whether it's a sonnet or an algebra textbook, as a poem. And everything within the work, whether it's a comma or a description of a suicide, is a symbol. It's a terrifying and exhilarating thought, but think of your next novel as a poem. Not that you'll strive for the density of a short poem, but [for] a strict, ruthless, economy.

What advice can you give on the writing process?

Write every day. Read more than you write. Writers need to fill their heads with words like painters fill their heads with light. Listen to what the story wants to say instead of what you want to write. My mother had a notion that in heaven there was a library of all the books—*all* the books—the ones that hadn't been written as well as the ones that had. And if you wanted to be a writer, all you had to do was gain access to the shelves of books that hadn't been written yet, and just take one down, and copy it. I really believe there's a lot of truth in this. I often feel like the process of writing is more akin to discovering than creating; it's about making what ends up on the page as close a match as possible to the story that already exists in an ideal form. When I see bad writing, my own or somebody else's, usually the problem is that the writer is getting in the way of the story, trying to show what a great writer he is rather than allowing the story to come through.

Where do you write? And when? Do you have a schedule?

My schedule is very busy. I get up around 5:00 in the morning and write on weekdays, and on weekends I write in the morning and again later in the day. It's hard for me to write after the day begins and my head is full of the clutter and minutiae of the daily round. But whenever you choose to write, sit down and do it. I think it's extremely important to have a schedule for anything you're serious about doing.

What is the act of self-promotion like for you?

For a long time I thought self-promotion was a matter of walking around like a one-piece band, beating on your drum, blowing into a harmonica, and clashing cymbals between your knees to attract attention. What I've slowly discovered is self-promotion is not, contrary to expectations, a matter of being selfish. [It's] just the opposite: It's an act of generosity, or more accurately, continuing acts of generosity. You have to be generous with readers, booksellers, the community, and other writers. I live in Atlanta and a very instructive place for a writer to visit is the Margaret Mitchell House. There's a gallery of photostatic blow ups of feature articles Mitchell wrote as a columnist for the *Atlanta Journal*. No matter how you feel about *Gone with the Wind*, the message is clear: Long before Mitchell published her novel, she'd already connected with readers in a big way; there were a lot of people out there—primarily women—who were her fans and ready to line up at the bookseller when the novel came out. In short, Mitchell had already given herself to her readers. The novelist who says, "Well, I've written a novel, now come and read it," without making or having made any effort to engage the public is not only being unrealistic, but profoundly selfish.

Can you comment on the current emphasis on branding and having a platform?

I don't have any issue with branding oneself; it's just not something I'm likely to do. It's not that I wouldn't want to; I just don't think I'd be able to. The nice thing about branding oneself is the reader knows what to expect from you, and that builds reader loyalty. And there's nothing especially "current" about it; writers have been branding themselves since forever. Mark Twain got to the point where he never wore anything in public but a white linen suit. He was branding himself. When Oscar Wilde toured America, he addressed audiences wearing a purple smoking jacket. He was living up to the Oscar Wilde Brand. I'm sure if you looked into it, you'd discovered when Gutenberg printed his first Bible, there was a little sticker on the back cover: "You can be sure it's *gut* if it's a Gutenberg."

What about blogging?

When it comes to social media, I'm something of a techno-troglodyte, but I'm slowly learning. I have a bare-bones website, but I blog every day on manmartin.blogspot.com. I almost never mention my writing on my blog; I just try to write humorous and sometimes thought-provoking pieces that I think would genuinely be of interest to my readers. Things I'd like to see myself. I label these to make them easier to find for the casual Internet browser, I use pictures as much as possible (I'm also a cartoonist), and I tweet my blogs as well. I don't yet tweet for the sake of tweeting because ... well, it's just hard for a novelist to say anything worth hearing in so few words. I'm not one of the big boys yet as far as number of [page] hits, but each month I've seen a gratifying increase in the size of my audience. I really think regular blogging is one of the most important things an author can do; not that there's necessarily any correlation between the number of hits you get and the number of books you sell, but it's an instantaneous way to reach your audience and offer them something of value—yourself. Again, it's all a matter of generosity.

Besides use of social media, do you do readings? What's that like for you?

When it comes to readings, I do everything I can to give my audience the best experience possible. Let's face it, hearing someone read an excerpt from his novel is not exactly a hot ticket. So I don't just read—whenever possible I memorize, so I'm not reading but performing. I'm not saying I dress up in costumes or use hand puppets, but instead of looking at the pages of a book, I'm looking at the audience. And I give the very best I can, whether I'm speaking to a group of a hundred or just the bookstore owner and the cashier. To the greatest extent possible, I take on the burden of promoting the reading myself. I like to do readings at bookstores I'm familiar with—Eagle Eye and Peerless Books here in Atlanta—and get the word out through every conduit I can. When out of town, I focus on stores where I have a close friend or family member living in the area who can help get me an audience. Above all else, I want the bookstore to be glad I came.

What other efforts do you make at promoting your work?

In my community, I do what I can to share my talents—the only two I have are as a writer and reader. For the last three years, I've taught a Lenten class at my church: the first two years [I focused] on Flannery O'Connor, and last year on Walker Percy. (I'm thinking of Isaac Bashevis Singer for next year.) I've also begun teaching adult writing classes at a local bookstore. Periodically I appear in something called Write Club, which is the damndest blend of a reading and performance art. Two writers create pieces on assigned topics and go head-to-head in competition for which piece the audience prefers. The winner's charity of choice then gets a donation. It's an offshoot of an event in Chicago.

What about your connection with other authors?

I post reviews on Goodreads. I've also written reviews for *Pleiades* and other journals. By the way, for new writers, book reviews are a fun and easy way to get your first publication. You get to read interesting work, and sometimes you get these really cool-looking ARCs [Advance Reader Copies]. I never trash a book in a review. If I come across a book I don't like—and I come across plenty—I just don't write about it one way or the other. What's the point in today's market of telling people not to read a book? And I've started writing fan letters to my favorite authors—not e-mails but actual letters. I try to restrain myself from asking anything in return—and it is so difficult—but just offer my heartfelt praise for their work. Other writers, it turns out, are also generous with their time and rarely fail to be touched by the written word.

What's your final word on self-promotion and marketing?

There are so many opportunities for promotion out there, it is a poor and unimaginative sort who couldn't easily spend his entire waking life doing nothing but promotion, but of course you also have to make time to write. That's the selfish part.

LITERARY AGENTS

///

Many publishers are willing to look at unsolicited submissions but most feel having an agent is in the writer's best interest. In this section, we include agents who specialize in or represent fiction.

The commercial fiction field is intensely competitive. Many publishers have small staffs and little time. For that reason, many book publishers rely on agents for new talent. Some publishers even rely on agents as ``first readers'' who must wade through the deluge of submissions from writers to find the very best. For writers, a good agent can be a foot in the door—someone willing to do the necessary work to put your manuscript in the right editor's hands.

It would seem today that finding a good agent is as hard as finding a good publisher. Yet those writers who have agents say they are invaluable. Not only can a good agent help you make your work more marketable, an agent also acts as your business manager and adviser, protecting your interests during and after contract negotiations.

Still, finding an agent can be very difficult for a new writer. If you are already published in magazines, you have a better chance than someone with no publishing credits. (Some agents read periodicals searching for new writers.) Although many agents do read queries and manuscripts from unpublished authors without introduction, referrals from their writer clients can be a big help. If you don't know any published authors with agents, attending a conference is a good way to meet agents. Some agents even set aside time at conferences to meet new writers.

Almost all the agents listed here have said they are open to working with new, previously unpublished writers as well as published writers. They do not charge a fee to cover the time and effort involved in reviewing a manuscript or a synopsis and chapters, but their time is still extremely valuable. Only send an agent your work when you feel it is as complete and polished as possible.

USING THE LISTINGS

It is especially important that you read individual listings carefully before contacting these busy agents. The first information after the company name includes the address and phone, fax, e-mail address (when available), and website. **Member Agents** gives the names of individual agents working at that company. (Specific types of fiction an agent handles are indicated in parentheses after that agent's name). The **Represents** section lists the types of fiction the agency works with. Reading the **Recent Sales** gives you the names of writers an agent is currently working with and, very important, publishers the agent has placed manuscripts with. **Writers Conferences** identifies conferences an agent attends (and where you might possibly meet that agent). **Tips** presents advice directly from the agent to authors.

Also, look closely at the openness to submissions icon that precedes most listings. It indicates how willing an agency is to take on new writers.

THE AHEARN AGENCY, INC.

2021 Pine St., New Orleans, LA 70118. **E-mail:** pahearn@aol.com. **Website:** www.ahearnagency.com. **Contact:** Pamela G. Ahearn. Other memberships include MWA, RWA, ITW. Represents 35 clients. 20% of clients are new/unpublished writers. Currently handles novels (100%).

○ Prior to opening her agency, Ms. Ahearn was an agent for 8 years and an editor with Bantam Books.

REPRESENTS **Considers these fiction areas:** action, adventure, contemporary issues, crime, detective, ethnic, family saga, feminist, glitz, historical, humor, literary, mainstream, mystery, police, psychic, regional, romance, supernatural, suspense, thriller.

⚷ Handles women's fiction and suspense fiction only. Does not want to receive category romance, science fiction or fantasy.

HOW TO CONTACT Query with SASE or via e-mail. Accepts simultaneous submissions. Responds in 8 weeks to queries. Responds in 10 weeks to mss. Obtains most new clients through recommendations from others, solicitations, conferences.

TERMS Agent receives 15% commission on domestic sales. Agent receives 20% commission on foreign sales. Offers written contract, binding for 1 year; renewable by mutual consent.

RECENT SALES *The Ronin's Mistress*, by Laura Joh Rowland; *How to Woo a Reluctant Lady*, by Sabrina Jeffries; *The Things That Keep Us Here*, by Carla Buckley.

WRITERS CONFERENCES Moonlight & Magnolias; RWA National Conference; Thriller Fest; Florida Romance Writers; Bouchercon; Malice Domestic.

TIPS "Be professional! Always send in exactly what an agent/editor asks for—no more, no less. Keep query letters brief and to the point, giving your writing credentials and a very brief summary of your book. If one agent rejects you, keep trying—there are a lot of us out there!"

AITKEN ALEXANDER ASSOCIATES

18-21 Cavaye Place, London, England SW10 9PT United Kingdom. (020)7373-8672. **Fax:** (020)7373-6002. **E-mail:** reception@aitkenalexander.co.uk. **Website:** www.aitkenalexander.co.uk. Estab. 1976. Represents 300+ clients. 10% of clients are new/unpublished writers.

MEMBER AGENTS Gillon Aitken, agent; Clare Alexander, agent; Andrew Kidd, agent.

REPRESENTS Nonfiction books, novels. **Considers these fiction areas:** historical, literary.

⚷ "We specialize in literary fiction and nonfiction." Does not represent illustrated children's books, poetry, or screenplays.

HOW TO CONTACT Query with SASE. Submit synopsis, first 30 pages, and SASE. Aitken Alexander Associates. Address submission to an individual agent or to the Submissions Department. Responds in 6-8 weeks to queries. Obtains most new clients through recommendations from others, solicitations.

TERMS Agent receives 15% commission on domestic sales. Agent receives 20% commission on foreign sales. Offers written contract; 28-day notice must be given to terminate contract. Charges for photocopying and postage.

RECENT SALES Sold 50 titles in the last year. *My Life with George*, by Judith Summers (Voice); *The Separate Heart*, by Simon Robinson (Bloomsbury); *The Fall of the House of Wittgenstein*, by Alexander Waugh (Bloomsbury); *Shakespeare's Life*, by Germane Greer (Picador); *Occupational Hazards*, by Rory Stewart.

TIPS "Before submitting to us, we advise you to look at our existing client list to establish whether your work will be of interest. Equally, you should consider whether the material you have written is ready to submit to a literary agency. If you feel your work qualifies, then send us a letter introducing yourself. Keep it relevant to your writing (e.g., tell us about any previously published work, be it a short story or journalism; you may be studying or have completed a postgraduate qualification in creative writing; when it comes to nonfiction, we would want to know what qualifies you to write about the subject)."

ALIVE COMMUNICATIONS, INC.

7680 Goddard St., Suite 200, Colorado Springs, CO 80920. (719)260-7080. **Fax:** (719)260-8223. **E-mail:** submissions@alivecom.com. **Website:** www.alivecom.com. **Contact:** Rick Christian. Member of AAR. Other memberships include Authors Guild. Represents 100+ clients. 5% of clients are new/unpublished writers. Currently handles nonfiction books (50%), novels (40%), juvenile books (10%).

MEMBER AGENTS Rick Christian, president (blockbusters, bestsellers); Lee Hough (popular/commercial nonfiction and fiction, thoughtful spirituality, children's); Andrea Heinecke (thoughtful/inspirational nonfiction, women's fiction/nonfiction, popular/commercial nonfiction and fiction); Joel Kneedler popular/commercial nonfiction and fiction, thoughtful spirituality, children's).

REPRESENTS Nonfiction books, novels, short story collections, novellas. **Considers these fiction areas:** adventure, contemporary issues, crime, family saga, historical, humor, inspirational, literary, mainstream, mystery, police, religious, satire, suspense, thriller.

☞ This agency specializes in fiction, Christian living, how-to, and commercial nonfiction. Actively seeking inspirational, literary, and mainstream fiction, and work from authors with established track records and platforms. Does not want to receive poetry, scripts or dark themes.

HOW TO CONTACT Query via e-mail. "Be advised that this agency works primarily with well-established, best-selling, and career authors. Always looking for a breakout, blockbuster author with genuine talent." New clients come through recommendations from others.

TERMS Agent receives 15% commission on domestic sales. Offers written contract; 2-month notice must be given to terminate contract.

RECENT SALES Sold 300+ titles in the last year. Alive's best-selling titles include: *Heaven Is for Real*, by Todd Burpo with Lynn Vincent (Nelson); *Loving*, by Karen Kingsbury (Zondervan); *A Hole in Our Gospel*, by Rich Stearns (Nelson); *The Chance*, by Karen Kingsbury (Howard); *Unfinished*, by Rich Stearns (Nelson); *The Pastor: A Memoir*, by Eugene Peterson (Harper One); *The Bridge*, by Karen Kingsbury (Howard); *Adapt or Die*, by Lt. Gen. (ret) Rick Lynch with Mark Dagostino (Baker); *C.S. Lewis: A Life*, by Alister McGrath (Tyndale); *7*, by Jen Hatmaker (B&H); *Successful Women Think Differently*, by Valorie Burton (Harvest House); *Same Kind of Different as Me*, by Ron Hall and Denver Moore (Nelson); *Lifelong Love Affair*, by Jimmy Evans with Frank Martin (Baker); *Days of War*, by Cliff Graham (Zondervan); *Realm Walkers*, by Donita K. Paul (Zondervan).

TIPS "Rewrite and polish until the words on the page shine. Endorsements and great connections may help, provided you can write with power and passion. Network with publishing professionals by making contacts, joining critique groups, and attending writers conferences in order to make personal connections and to get feedback. Alive Communications, Inc., has established itself as a premiere literary agency. We serve an elite group of authors who are critically acclaimed and commercially successful in both Christian and general markets."

AMBASSADOR LITERARY AGENCY

P.O. Box 50358, Nashville, TN 37205. (615)370-4700. **E-mail:** wes@ambassadoragency.com; info@ambassadoragency.com. **Website:** www.ambassadoragency.com. **Contact:** Wes Yoder. Represents 25-30 clients. 10% of clients are new/unpublished writers. Currently handles nonfiction books (95%), novels (5%).

○ Prior to becoming an agent, Mr. Yoder founded a music artist agency in 1973; he established a speakers bureau division of the company in 1984.

REPRESENTS Nonfiction books, novels.

☞ "This agency specializes in religious market publishing dealing primarily with A-level publishers." Actively seeking popular nonfiction themes, including the following: practical living; Christian spirituality; literary fiction. Does not want to receive short stories, children's books, screenplays, or poetry.

HOW TO CONTACT Ambassador Literary's department represents a growing list of best-selling authors. We represent select authors and writers who are published by the leading religious and general market publishers in the United States and Europe, and television and major motion picture rights for our clients. Authors should e-mail a short description of their manuscript with a request to submit their work for review. Guidelines for submission will be sent if we agree to review a manuscript. Accepts simultaneous submissions. Responds in 2-4 weeks to queries. Obtains most new clients through recommendations from others.

TERMS Agent receives 15% commission on domestic sales. Agent receives 20% commission on foreign sales. Offers written contract.

RECENT SALES Sold 20 titles in the last year. *The Death and Life of Gabriel Phillips*, by Stephen Baldwin (Hachette); *Amazing Grace: William Wilberforce and the Heroic Campaign to End Slavery*, by Eric Mataxas (Harper San Francisco); *Life@The Next Level*, by Courtney McBath (Simon and Schuster); *Women, Take Charge of Your Money*, by Carolyn Castleberry (Random House/Multnomah).

BETSY AMSTER LITERARY ENTERPRISES

6312 SW Capitol Hwy #503, Portland, OR 97239. **Website:** www.amsterlit.com. **Contact:** Betsy Amster (adult); Mary Cummings (children's and YA). Estab. 1992. Member of AAR. Represents more than 65 clients. 35% of clients are new/unpublished writers. Currently handles nonfiction books (65%), novels (35%).

○ Prior to opening her agency, Ms. Amster was an editor at Pantheon and Vintage for 10 years and served as editorial director for the Globe Pequot Press for 2 years.

REPRESENTS Nonfiction books, novels. **Considers these fiction areas:** ethnic, literary, women's, high quality.

⊶ "Actively seeking strong narrative nonfiction, particularly by journalists; outstanding literary fiction (the next Jennifer Haigh or Jess Walter); witty, intelligent commerical women's fiction (the next Elinor Lipman); mysteries that open new worlds to us; and high-profile self-help and psychology, preferably research based." Does not want to receive poetry, children's books, romances, Western, science fiction, action/adventure, screenplays, fantasy, techno-thrillers, spy capers, apocalyptic scenarios, or political or religious arguments.

HOW TO CONTACT For adult titles: b.amster.assistant@gmail.com. "For fiction or memoirs, please embed the first three pages in the body of your e-mail. For nonfiction, please embed your proposal." For children's and YA: b.amster.kidsbooks@gmail.com. See submission requirements online at website. "For picture books, please embed the entire text in the body of your e-mail. For novels, please embed the first three pages." Accepts simultaneous submissions. Responds in 1 month to queries. Responds in 2 months to mss. Obtains most new clients through recommendations from others, solicitations, conferences.

TERMS Agent receives 15% commission on domestic sales. Agent receives 20% commission on foreign sales. Offers written contract, binding for 1 year; 3-month notice must be given to terminate contract. Charges for photocopying, postage, messengers, galleys/books used in submissions to foreign and film agents and to magazines for first serial rights.

WRITERS CONFERENCES Los Angeles Times Festival of Books; USC Masters in Professional Writing; San Diego State University Writers Conference; UCLA Extension Writers Program; The Loft Literary Center; Willamette Writers Conference.

MARCIA AMSTERDAM AGENCY

41 W. 82nd St., Suite 9A, New York, NY 10024-5613. (212)873-4945. **Contact:** Marcia Amsterdam. Signatory of WGA. Currently handles nonfiction books (15%), novels (70%), movie scripts (5%), TV scripts (10%).

○ Prior to opening her agency, Ms. Amsterdam was an editor.

REPRESENTS Novels, movie scripts, feature film, sitcom. **Considers these fiction areas:** adventure, detective, horror, mainstream, mystery, romance (contemporary, historical), science, thriller, young adult.

HOW TO CONTACT Query with SASE. Responds in 1 month to queries.

TERMS Agent receives 15% commission on domestic sales. Agent receives 20% commission on foreign sales. Agent receives 10% commission on film sales. Offers written contract, binding for 1 year. Charges clients for extra office expenses, foreign postage, copying, legal fees (when agreed upon).

RECENT SALES *Hidden Child*, by Isaac Millman (FSG); *Lucky Leonardo*, by Jonathan Canter (Sourcebooks).

TIPS "We are always looking for interesting literary voices."

THE AXELROD AGENCY

55 Main St., P.O. Box 357, Chatham, NY 12037. (518)392-2100. **E-mail:** steve@axelrodagency.com. **Website:** www.axelrodagency.com. **Contact:** Steven Axelrod. Member of AAR. Represents 15-20 clients. 1% of clients are new/unpublished writers. Currently handles novels (95%).

○ Prior to becoming an agent, Mr. Axelrod was a book club editor.

REPRESENTS Novels. **Considers these fiction areas:** mystery, romance, women's.

HOW TO CONTACT Query with SASE. Accepts simultaneous submissions. Responds in 3 weeks to queries. Responds in 6 weeks to mss. Obtains most new clients through recommendations from others.

TERMS Agent receives 15% commission on domestic sales. Agent receives 20% commission on foreign sales. No written contract.

WRITERS CONFERENCES RWA National Conference.

BARER LITERARY, LLC

20 W. 20th St., Suite 601, New York, NY 10011. (212)691-3513. **E-mail:** submissions@barerliterary .com. **Website:** www.barerliterary.com. **Contact:** Julie Barer. Estab. 2004. Member of AAR.

○ Before becoming an agent, Julie worked at Shakespeare & Co. Booksellers in New York City. She is a graduate of Vassar College.

MEMBER AGENTS Julie Barer.

REPRESENTS Nonfiction books, novels, short story collections. Julie Barer is especially interested in working with emerging writers and developing long-term relationships with new clients. **Considers these fiction areas:** contemporary issues, ethnic, historical, literary, mainstream.

8—π This agency no longer accepts young adult submissions. No health/fitness, business/investing/finance, sports, mind/body/spirit, reference, thrillers/suspense, military, romance, children's books/picture books, screenplays.

HOW TO CONTACT Query with SASE; no attachments if query by e-mail. "We do not respond to queries via phone or fax."

TERMS Agent receives 15% commission on domestic sales. Agent receives 20% commission on foreign sales. Offers written contract. Charges for photocopying and books ordered.

RECENT SALES *The Unnamed*, by Joshua Ferris (Reagan Arthur Books); *Tunneling to the Center of the Earth*, by Kevin Wilson (Ecco Press); *A Disobedient Girl*, by Ru Freeman (Atria Books); *A Friend of the Family*, by Lauren Grodstein (Algonquin); *City of Veils*, by Zoe Ferraris (Little, Brown).

BARONE LITERARY AGENCY

385 North St., Batavia, OH 45103. (513)732-6740. **Fax:** (513)297-7208. **E-mail:** baroneliteraryagency@ roadrunner.com. **Website:** www.baroneliteraryagen cy.com. **Contact:** Denise Barone. Estab. 2010. RWA Represents 7 clients. 100% of clients are new/unpublished writers.

○ Denise Barone still maintains an active law degree but is "hoping, increasingly, to focus [my] efforts more on agenting."

REPRESENTS Fiction. **Considers these fiction areas:** action, adventure, cartoon, comic books, commercial, confession, contemporary issues, crime, detective, erotica, ethnic, experimental, family saga, fantasy, feminist, frontier, gay, glitz, hi-lo, historical, horror, humor, inspirational, juvenile, lesbian, literary, mainstream, metaphysical, military, multicultural, multimedia, mystery, New Age, occult, plays, psychic, regional, religious, romance, science fiction, sports, thriller, women's, young adult.

8—π Actively seeking adult contemporary romance. Does not want textbooks, plays, or screenplays.

HOW TO CONTACT Submit query letter, SASE, and synopsis. Accepts simultaneous submissions. Obtains new clients by queries/submissions, Facebook, recommendations from others.

TERMS 15% commission on domestic sales, 20% on foreign sales. Offers written contract.

RECENT SALES *The Cinderella Files*, by Rebekah Purdy (Astrea Press); *The Trouble with Charlie*, by Cathy Bennett (Astrea Press).

TIPS "In the immortal words of Sir Winston Churchill, if you want to get published, you must never give up!"

LORETTA BARRETT BOOKS, INC.

220 E. 23rd St., 11th Floor, New York, NY 10010. (212)242-3420. **E-mail:** query@lorettabarrettbooks .com. **Website:** www.lorettabarrettbooks.com. **Contact:** Loretta A. Barrett; Nick Mullendore; Gabriel Davis. Estab. 1990. Member of AAR. Currently handles nonfiction books (50%), novels (50%).

○ Prior to opening her agency, Ms. Barrett was vice president and executive editor at Doubleday and editor-in-chief of Anchor Books.

MEMBER AGENTS Loretta A. Barrett; Nick Mullendore.

REPRESENTS Nonfiction books, novels. **Considers these fiction areas:** contemporary, psychic, adventure, detective, ethnic, family, historical, literary, mainstream, mystery, thriller, young adult.

8—π "The clients we represent include both fiction and nonfiction authors for the general adult trade market. The works they produce encompass a wide range of contemporary topics and themes including commercial thrillers, mysteries, romantic suspense, popular science, memoirs, narrative fiction and current affairs." No children's, juvenile, cookbooks, gardening, science fiction, fantasy novels, historical romance.

HOW TO CONTACT See guidelines online. Use e-mail (no attachments) or if by post, query with SASE. For hardcopy queries, please send a 1-2 page query letter and a synopsis or chapter outline for your project. In your letter, please include your contact information, any relevant background information on yourself or your project, and a paragraph of description of your project. If you are submitting electronically, then all of this material may be included in the body of your e-mail. Accepts simultaneous submissions. Responds in 3-6 weeks to queries.

TERMS Agent receives 15% commission on domestic sales. Agent receives 20% commission on foreign sales. Offers written contract. Charges clients for shipping and photocopying.

● **BARRON'S LITERARY MANAGEMENT**

4615 Rockland Dr., Arlington, TX 76016. **E-mail:** barronsliterary@sbcglobal.net. **Contact:** Adele Brooks, president.

REPRESENTS Nonfiction books, novels. **Considers these fiction areas:** historical, horror, all mysteries, detective/pi/police, romance (suspense, paranormal, historical, chick lit and lady lit), science fiction, thriller, crime thriller, medical thriller.

☛ Barron's Literary Management is a small Dallas/Fort Worth-based agency with good publishing contacts. Seeks tightly written, fast-moving fiction, as well as authors with a significant platform or subject area expertise for nonfiction book concepts.

HOW TO CONTACT Contact by e-mail initially. Send bio and a brief synopsis of story or a nonfiction proposal. Obtains most new clients through e-mail submissions.

TIPS "Have your book tightly edited, polished, and ready to be seen before contacting agents. I respond quickly and, if interested, may request an electronic or hard copy mailing."

●◗ **LORELLA BELLI LITERARY AGENCY (LBLA)**

54 Hartford House, 35 Tavistock Crescent, Notting Hill, London, England W11 1AY United Kingdom. (44)(207)727-8547. **Fax:** (44)(870)787-4194. **E-mail:** info@lorellabelliagency.com. **Website:** www.lorella belliagency.com. **Contact:** Lorella Belli. Membership includes AAA.

REPRESENTS Nonfiction books, novels. **Considers these fiction areas:** historical, literary genre fiction, women's,, crime.

☛ "We are interested in first-time novelists, journalists, multicultural and international writ-

ing, and books about Italy." Does not want children's books, fantasy, science fiction, screenplays, short stories, or poetry.

HOW TO CONTACT For fiction, send query letter, first 3 chapters, synopsis, brief CV, SASE. For nonfiction, send query letter, full proposal, chapter outline, 2 sample chapters, SASE.

TERMS Agent receives 15% commission on domestic sales. Agent receives 20% commission on foreign sales.

TIPS "Please send an initial query letter or e-mail before submitting your work to us."

THE BENT AGENCY

Bent Agency, The, 204 Park Place, Number 2, Brooklyn, NY 11238. **E-mail:** info@thebentagency.com. **Website:** www.thebentagency.com. **Contact:** Jenny Bent; Susan Hawk; Molly Ker Hawn; Nicole Steen; Gemma Cooper. Estab. 2009.

◓ Prior to forming her own agency, Ms. Bent was an agent and vice president at Trident Media.

MEMBER AGENTS Jenny Bent (all adult fiction, except for science fiction); Susan Hawk (young adult and middle grade books; within the realm of kids stories, she likes fantasy, science fiction, historical fiction, and mystery); Molly Ker Hawn (young adult and middle grade books, including contemporary, historical science fiction, fantasy, thrillers, mystery; Nicole Steen (literary and commercial fiction, narrative nonfiction, and memoir); Gemma Cooper (all ages of children's and young adult books, including picture books, likes historical, contemporary, thrillers, mystery, humor, and science fiction).

REPRESENTS **Considers these fiction areas:** commercial, crime, historical, horror, mystery, picture books, romance, suspense, thriller, women's, young adult literary.

HOW TO CONTACT For Jenny Bent, e-mail: queries@thebentagency.com; for Susan Hawk, e-mail: kidsqueries@thebentagency.com; for Molly Ker Hawn, e-mail: hawnqueries@thebentagency.com; for Nicole Steen, e-mail: steenqueries@thebent agency.com; for Gemma Cooper, e-mail: cooperqu eries@thebentagency.com. "Tell us briefly who you are, what your book is, and why you're the one to write it. Then include the first 10 pages of your material in the body of your e-mail. We respond to all queries; please resend your query if you haven't had a response within 4 weeks." Accepts simultaneous submissions.

RECENT SALES *The Ghost Bride*, by Yangsze Choo (Morrow); *The Life List*, by Lori Nelson Spielman (Bantam); *17 First Kisses*, by Rachael Allen (Harper); *Starter House*, by Sonja Condit (Morrow); *Disalmanac*, by Scott Bateman (Perigee); *Moms Who Drink and Swear*, by Nicole Knepper (NAL); *Movies R Fun*, by Josh Cooley (Chronicle); *Lark Rising*, by Sandra Waugh (Random House); *Chickens in the Road*, by Suzanne McMinn (HarperOne); *The Secret Diamond Sisters*, by Michelle Maddow (HarlequinTeen).

BLEECKER STREET ASSOCIATES, INC.

217 Thompson St., #519, New York, NY 10012. (212)677-4492. **Fax:** (212)388-0001. **E-mail:** bleeckerst@hotmail.com. **Contact:** Agnes Birnbaum. Member of AAR. Other memberships include RWA, MWA. Represents 60 clients. 20% of clients are new/unpublished writers. Currently handles nonfiction books (75%), novels (25%).

○ Prior to becoming an agent, Ms. Birnbaum was a senior editor at Simon & Schuster, Dutton/Signet, and other publishing houses.

REPRESENTS Nonfiction books, novels. **Considers these fiction areas:** ethnic, historical, literary, mystery, romance, thriller, women's.

⚬━ "We're very hands-on and accessible. We try to be truly creative in our submission approaches. We've had especially good luck with first-time authors." Does not want to receive science fiction, Westerns, poetry, children's books, academic/scholarly/professional books, plays, scripts, or short stories.

HOW TO CONTACT Query with SASE. No e-mail, phone, or fax queries. Accepts simultaneous submissions. Responds in 2 weeks to queries. Responds in 1 month to mss. "Obtains most new clients through recommendations from others, solicitations, conferences, plus, I will approach someone with a letter if his/her work impresses me."

TERMS Agent receives 15% commission on domestic sales. Agent receives 25% commission on foreign sales. Offers written contract; 1-month notice must be given to terminate contract. Charges for postage, long distance, fax, messengers, photocopies (not to exceed $200).

RECENT SALES Sold 14 titles in the last year. *Following Sarah*, by Daniel Brown (Morrow); *Biology of the Brain*, by Paul Swingle (Rutgers University Press); *Santa Miracles*, by Brad and Sherry Steiger (Adams); *Surviving the College Search*, by Jennifer Delahunt (St. Martin's).

TIPS "Keep query letters short and to the point; include only information pertaining to the book or background as a writer. Try to avoid superlatives in description. Work needs to stand on its own, so how much editing it may have received has no place in a query letter."

◑ BOOKENDS, LLC

136 Long Hill Rd., Gillette, NJ 07933. **Website:** www.bookends-inc.com. **Contact:** Kim Lionetti, Jessica Alvarez. Member of AAR. RWA, MWA. Represents 50+ clients. 10% of clients are new/unpublished writers. Currently handles nonfiction books (50%), novels (50%).

MEMBER AGENTS Jessica Faust (**no longer accepting unsolicited material**) (fiction: romance, erotica, women's fiction, mysteries and suspense; nonfiction: business, finance, career, parenting, psychology, women's issues, self-help, health, sex); Kim Lionetti (only currently considering romance, women's fiction, and young adult queries. "If your book is in any of these 3 categories, please be sure to specify 'Romance,' 'Women's Fiction,' or 'Young Adult' in your e-mail subject line. Any queries that do not follow these guidelines will not be considered."); Jessica Alvarez (romance, women's fiction, erotica, romantic suspense).

REPRESENTS Nonfiction books, novels. **Considers these fiction areas:** detective, cozies, mainstream, mystery, romance, thrillers, women's.

⚬━ "BookEnds is currently accepting queries from published and unpublished writers in the areas of romance (and all its subgenres), erotica, mystery, suspense, women's fiction, and literary fiction. We also do a great deal of nonfiction in the areas of self-help, business, finance, health, pop science, psychology, relationships, parenting, pop culture, true crime, and general nonfiction." BookEnds does not want to receive children's books, screenplays, science fiction, poetry, or technical/military thrillers.

HOW TO CONTACT Review website for guidelines, as they change. BookEnds is no longer accepting unsolicited proposal packages or snail mail queries. Send query in the body of e-mail to only 1 agent.

BOOKS & SUCH LITERARY AGENCY

52 Mission Circle, Suite 122, PMB 170, Santa Rosa, CA 95409. **E-mail:** representation@booksandsuch.com. **Website:** www.booksandsuch.biz. **Contact:** Janet Kobobel Grant, Wendy Lawton, Rachel Kent, Mary Keeley, Rachelle Gardner. Member of AAR. Member of CBA (associate), American Christian Fiction Writers. Represents 150 clients. 5% of clients are new/unpublished writers. Currently handles nonfiction books (50%), novels (50%).

○ Prior to becoming an agent, Ms. Grant was an editor for Zondervan and managing editor for *Focus on the Family*; Ms. Lawton was an author, sculptor, and designer of porcelein dolls. Ms. Keeley accepts both nonfiction and adult fiction. She previously was an acquisition editor for Tyndale publishers.

REPRESENTS Nonfiction books, novels. **Considers these fiction areas:** contemporary, family, historical, mainstream, religious, romance.

⚷ This agency specializes in general and inspirational fiction, romance, and in the Christian booksellers market. Actively seeking well-crafted material that presents Judeo-Christian values, if only subtly.

HOW TO CONTACT Query via e-mail only; no attachments. Accepts simultaneous submissions. Responds in 1 month to queries. "If you don't hear from us asking to see more of your writing within 30 days after you have sent your e-mail, please know that we have read and considered your submission but determined that it would not be a good fit for us." Obtains most new clients through recommendations from others, conferences.

TERMS Agent receives 15% commission on domestic sales. Agent receives 20% commission on foreign sales. Offers written contract; 2-month notice must be given to terminate contract. No additional charges.

RECENT SALES Sold 125 titles in the last year. *One Perfect Gift*, by Debbie Macomber (Howard Books); *Greetings from the Flipside*, by Rene Gutteridge and Cheryl Mckay (B&H Publishing); *Key on the Quilt*, by Stephanie Grace Whitson (Barbour Publishing); *Annotated Screwtape Letters, Annotations*, by Paul Mccusker, (Harper One). Other clients include: Lauraine Snelling, Lori Copeland, Rene Gutteridge, Dale Cramer, BJ Hoff, Diann Mills.

WRITERS CONFERENCES Mount Hermon Christian Writers Conference; Writing for the Soul; American Christian Fiction Writers Conference; San Francisco Writers Conference.

TIPS "The heart of our agency's motivation is to develop relationships with the authors we serve, to do what we can to shine the light of success on them, and to help be a caretaker of their gifts and time."

THE BARBARA BOVA LITERARY AGENCY

3951 Gulf Shore Blvd. N., Unit PH 1-B, Naples, FL 34103. (239)649-7263. **Fax:** (239)649-7263. **E-mail:** michaelburke@barbarabovaliteraryagency.com. **Website:** www.barbarabovaliteraryagency.com. **Contact:** Ken Bova, Michael Burke. Represents 30 clients. Currently handles nonfiction books (20%), fiction (80%).

REPRESENTS Nonfiction books, novels. **Considers these fiction areas:** adventure, crime, detective, mystery, police, science fiction, suspense, thriller, women's, young adult teen lit.

⚷ This agency specializes in fiction and nonfiction, hard and soft science. "We also handle foreign, movie, television, and audio rights." No scripts, poetry, or children's books.

HOW TO CONTACT Query through website. No attachments. "We accept short (3-5 pages) e-mail queries. All queries should have the word *Query* in the subject line. Include all information as you would in a standard, snail mail query letter, such as pertinent credentials, publishing history, and an overview of the book. Include a word count of your project. You may include a short synopsis. We're looking for quality fiction and nonfiction." Obtains most new clients through recommendations from others.

TERMS Agent receives 15% commission on domestic sales. Agent receives 20% commission on foreign sales. Charges clients for overseas postage, overseas calls, photocopying, shipping.

RECENT SALES Sold 24 titles in the last year. *The Green Trap* and *The Aftermath*, by Ben Bova; *Empire and a War of Gifts*, by Orson Scott Card; *Radioman*, by Carol E. Hipperson.

BRADFORD LITERARY AGENCY

5694 Mission Center Rd., #347, San Diego, CA 92108. (619)521-1201. **E-mail:** queries@bradfordlit.com. **Website:** www.bradfordlit.com. **Contact:** Laura Bradford, Natalie Lakosil. Member of AAR. RWA, SCBWI, ALA Represents 50 clients. 20% of clients are new/

unpublished writers. Currently handles nonfiction books (5%), novels (95%).

REPRESENTS Nonfiction books, novels, novellas, stories within a single author's collection anthology. **Considers these fiction areas:** adventure, detective, erotica, ethnic, historical, humor, mainstream, mystery, romance, thriller psychic/supernatural.

⚷ Actively seeking romance (historical, romantic suspense, paranormal, category, contemporary, erotic), urban fantasy, women's fiction, mystery, thrillers, children's (Natalie Lakosil only), and young adult. Does not want to receive poetry, screenplays, short stories, Westerns, horror, new age, religion, crafts, cookbooks, gift books.

HOW TO CONTACT Accepts e-mail queries only; send to queries@bradfordlit.com. The entire submission must appear in the body of the e-mail and not as an attachment. The subject line should begin as follows: QUERY: (the title of the ms or any short message that is important should follow). For fiction: e-mail a query letter along with the first chapter of ms and a synopsis. Include the genre and word count in cover letter. Nonfiction: e-mail full nonfiction proposal including a query letter and a sample chapter. Accepts simultaneous submissions. Responds in 2-4 weeks to queries. Responds in 10 weeks to mss. Obtains most new clients through solicitations.

TERMS Agent receives 15% commission on domestic sales. Agent receives 20% commission on foreign sales. Offers written contract, nonbinding for 2 years; 45-day notice must be given to terminate contract. Charges for extra copies of books for foreign submissions.

RECENT SALES Sold 68 titles in the last year. *All Fall Down,* by Megan Hart (Mira Books); *Body and Soul,* by Stacey Kade (Hyperion Children's); *All Things Wicked,* by Karina Cooper (Avon); *Circle Eight: Matthew,* by Emma Lang (Kensington Brava); *Midnight Enchantment,* by Anya Bast (Berkley Sensation); *Outpost,* by Ann Aguirre (Feiwel and Friends); *The One That I Want,* by Jennifer Echols (Simon Pulse); *Catch Me a Cowboy,* by Katie Lane (Grand Central); *Back in a Soldier's Arms,* by Soraya Lane (Harlequin); *Enraptured,* by Elisabeth Naughton (Sourcebooks); *Wicked Road to Hell,* by Juliana Stone (Avon); *Master of Sin,* by Maggie Robinson (Kensington Brava); *Chaos Burning,* by Lauren Dane (Berkley Sensation); *If I Lie,* by Corrine Jackson (Simon Pulse); *Renegade,* by J.A. Souders (Tor).

WRITERS CONFERENCES RWA National Conference; Romantic Times Booklovers Convention.

◐ ANDREA BROWN LITERARY AGENCY, INC.

1076 Eagle Dr., Salinas, CA 93905. (831)422-5925. **Fax:** (831)422-5915. **E-mail:** andrea@andreabrownlit.com; caryn@andreabrownlit.com; lauraqueries@gmail.com; jennifer@andreabrownlit.com; kelly@andreabrownlit.com; jennL@andreabrownlit.com; jamie@andreabrownlit.com; jmatt@andreabrownlit.com; lara@andreabrownlit.com. **Website:** www.andreabrownlit.com. **Contact:** Andrea Brown, president. Member of AAR. 10% of clients are new/unpublished writers.

◓ Prior to opening her agency, Ms. Brown served as an editorial assistant at Random House and Dell Publishing and as an editor with Knopf.

MEMBER AGENTS Andrea Brown (President); Laura Rennert (Senior Agent); Caryn Wiseman (Senior Agent); Kelly Sonnack (Agent); Jennifer Rofé (Agent); Jennifer Laughran (Agent); Jamie Weiss Chilton (Agent); Jennifer Mattson (Associate Agent); Lara Perkins (Associate Agent, Digital Manager).

REPRESENTS Nonfiction, fiction, juvenile books. **Considers these fiction areas:** juvenile, literary, picture books, women's, young adult middle-grade, all juvenile genres.

⚷ Specializes in "all kinds of children's books—illustrators and authors." 98% juvenile books. Considers: nonfiction, fiction, picture books, young adult.

HOW TO CONTACT For picture books, submit complete ms. For fiction, submit query letter, first 10 pages. For nonfiction, submit proposal, first 10 pages. Illustrators: submit a query letter and 2-3 illustration samples (in .jpeg format), link to online portfolio, and text of picture book, if applicable. "We only accept queries via e-mail. No attachments, with the exception of .jpeg illustrations from illustrators." Visit the agents' bios on our website and choose only one agent to whom you will submit your e-query. Send a short e-mail query letter to that agent with *QUERY* in the subject field. Accepts simultaneous submissions. If we are interested in your work, we will certainly follow up by e-mail or by phone. However, if you haven't heard from us within 6-8 weeks, please assume that we are passing on your project. Obtains most new clients through referrals from editors, clients, and agents. Check website for guidelines and information.

TERMS Agent receives 15% commission on domestic sales. Agent receives 25% commission on foreign sales. Offers written contract.

RECENT SALES *The Scorpio Races*, by Maggie Stiefvater (Scholastic); *The Raven Boys*, by Maggie Stiefvater (Scholastic); *Wolves of Mercy Falls* series, by Maggie Stiefvater (Scholastic); *The Future of Us*, by Jay Asher; *Triangles*, by Ellen Hopkins (Atria); *Crank*, by Ellen Hopkins (McElderry/S&S); *Burned*, by Ellen Hopkins (McElderry/S&S); *Impulse*, by Ellen Hopkins (McElderry/S&S); *Glass*, by Ellen Hopkins (McElderry/S&S); *Tricks*, by Ellen Hopkins (McElderry/S&S); *Fallout*, by Ellen Hopkins (McElderry/S&S); *Perfect*, by Ellen Hopkins (McElderry/S&S); *The Strange Case of Origami Yoda*, by Tom Angleberger (Amulet/Abrams); *Darth Paper Strikes Back*, by Tom Angleberger (Amulet/Abrams); *Becoming Chloe*, by Catherine Ryan Hyde (Knopf); Sasha Cohen autobiography (HarperCollins); *The Five Ancestors*, by Jeff Stone (Random House); *Thirteen Reasons Why*, by Jay Asher (Penguin); *Identical*, by Ellen Hopkins (S&S).

WRITERS CONFERENCES SCBWI; Asilomar; Aloha Writers Conference; SouthWest Writers Conference; San Diego State University Writers Conference; Big Sur Children's Writing Workshop; William Saroyan Writers Conference; Columbus Writers Conference; Willamette Writers Conference; La Jolla Writers Conference; San Francisco Writers Conference; Hilton Head Writers Conference; Pacific Northwest Conference; Pikes Peak Conference.

TIPS "ABLA is consistently ranked #1 in juvenile sales in Publishers Marketplace. Several clients have placed in the top 10 of the NY Times Bestseller List in the last year, including Tom Angleberger, Jay Asher, Ellen Hopkins, and Maggie Stiefvater. Awards recently won by ABLA clients include the Michael L. Printz Honor, the APALA Asian/Pacific Award and Honor, Charlotte Zolotow Honor, Cybils Award, EB White Read Aloud Award and Honor, Edgar Award Nominee, Indies Choice Honor Award, Jack Ezra Keats New Writer Award, Odyssey Honor Audiobook, Orbis PIctus Honor, Pura Belpré Illustrator Honor Book; SCBWI Golden Kite Award; Stonewall Honor; Texas Bluebonnet Award; Theodore Seuss Geisel Honor; William C. Morris YA Debut Award."

CURTIS BROWN, LTD.

10 Astor Place, New York, NY 10003-6935. (212)473-5400. **E-mail:** gknowlton@cbltd.com. **Website:** www.curtisbrown.com. **Contact:** Ginger Knowlton. Alternate address: Peter Ginsberg, president at CBSF, 1750 Montgomery St., San Francisco, CA 94111; (415)954-8566. Member of AAR. Signatory of WGA.

MEMBER AGENTS Ginger Clark; Katherine Fausset; Holly Frederick; Emilie Jacobson; Elizabeth Hardin; Ginger Knowlton, executive vice president; Timothy Knowlton, CEO; Laura Blake Peterson; Mitchell Waters. San Francisco office: Peter Ginsberg (president).

REPRESENTS Nonfiction books, novels, short story collections, juvenile. **Considers these fiction areas:** contemporary, glitz, New Age, psychic, adventure, comic, confession, detective, erotica, ethnic, experimental, family, fantasy, feminist, gay, gothic, hi lo, historical, horror, humor, juvenile, literary, mainstream, military, multicultural, multimedia, mystery, occult, picture books, plays, poetry, regional, religious, romance, science, short, spiritual, sports, thriller, translation, Western, young adult, women's.

HOW TO CONTACT Prefers to read materials exclusively. *No unsolicited mss.* Query with SASE. If a picture book, send only 1 picture book ms. Considers simultaneous queries, "but please tell us." Returns material only with SASE. Responds in 3 weeks to queries; 5 weeks to mss. Obtains most new clients through recommendations from others, solicitations, conferences.

TERMS Agent receives 15% commission on domestic sales; 20% on foreign sales. Offers written contract. 75-day notice must be given to terminate contract. Offers written contract. Charges for some postage (overseas, etc.).

RECENT SALES This agency prefers not to share information on specific sales.

● KIMBERLEY CAMERON & ASSOCIATES

1550 Tiburon Blvd., #704, Tiburon, CA 94920. **Fax:** (415)789-9191. **E-mail:** info@kimberleycameron.com. **Website:** www.kimberleycameron.com. **Contact:** Kimberley Cameron. Member of AAR. 30% of clients are new/unpublished writers.

Kimberley Cameron & Associates (formerly The Reece Halsey Agency) has had an illustrious client list of established writers, including the estate of Aldous Huxley, and has represented Upton Sinclair, William Faulkner, and Henry Miller.

MEMBER AGENTS Kimberley Cameron, Elizabeth Kracht, Pooja Menon, Amy Cloughley, and Ethan Vaughan.

REPRESENTS Nonfiction, fiction. **Considers these fiction areas:** adventure, contemporary issues, ethnic, family saga, historical, horror, mainstream, mystery, interlinked short story collections, thriller, women's, and sophisticated/crossover young adult.

8—☞ "We are looking for a unique and heartfelt voice that conveys a universal truth."

HOW TO CONTACT Query via e-mail. "See our website for submission guidelines." Obtains new clients through recommendations from others, solicitations.

TERMS Agent receives 15% on domestic sales; 10% on film sales. Offers written contract, binding for 1 year.

WRITERS CONFERENCES Pacific Northwest Writers Association Conference; Women's Fiction Festival in Matera, Italy; Willamette Writers Conference; San Francisco Writers Conference; Book Passage Mystery and Travel Writers Conferences; Chuckanut Writers Conference; many others.

TIPS "Please consult our submission guidelines and send a polite, well-written query to our e-mail address."

Ⓞ MARIA CARVAINIS AGENCY, INC.

Rockefeller Center, 1270 Avenue of the Americas, Suite 2320, New York, NY 10020. (212)245-6365. **Fax:** (212)245-7196. **E-mail:** mca@mariacarvainisagency .com. **Website:** http://mariacarvainisagency.com. **Contact:** Maria Carvainis, Chelsea Gilmore. Member of AAR. Signatory of WGA. Other memberships include Authors Guild, Women's Media Group, ABA, MWA, RWA. Represents 75 clients. 10% of clients are new/unpublished writers. Currently handles nonfiction books (35%), novels (65%).

Ⓞ Prior to opening her agency, Ms. Carvainis spent more than 10 years in the publishing industry as a senior editor with Macmillan Publishing, Basic Books, Avon Books, and Crown Publishers. Ms. Carvainis has served as a member of the AAR Board of Directors and AAR Treasurer, as well as serving as chair of the AAR Contracts Committee. She presently serves on the AAR Royalty Committee. Ms. Gilmore started her publishing career at Oxford University Press, in the Higher Education Group. She then worked at Avalon Books as associate editor. She is most interested in women's fiction, literary fiction, young adult, pop culture, and mystery/suspense.

MEMBER AGENTS Maria Carvainis, president/literary agent; Chelsea Gilmore, literary agent.

REPRESENTS Nonfiction books, novels. **Considers these fiction areas:** contemporary issues, historical, literary, mainstream, mystery, suspense, thriller, women's, young adult, middle-grade.

8—☞ Does not want to receive science fiction or children's picture books.

HOW TO CONTACT Query with SASE. No e-mail accepted. Responds in up to 3 months to mss and to queries 1 month. Obtains most new clients through recommendations from others, conferences, query letters.

TERMS Agent receives 15% commission on domestic sales. Agent receives 20% commission on foreign sales. Offers written contract. Charges clients for foreign postage and bulk copying.

RECENT SALES *A Secret Affair*, by Mary Balogh (Delacorte); *Tough Customer*, by Sandra Brown (Simon & Schuster); *A Lady Never Tells*, by Candace Camp (Pocket Books); *The King James Conspiracy*, by Phillip Depoy (St. Martin's Press).

WRITERS CONFERENCES BookExpo America; Frankfurt Book Fair; London Book Fair; Mystery Writers of America; Thrillerfest; Romance Writers of America.

Ⓞ CASTIGLIA LITERARY AGENCY

1155 Camino Del Mar, Suite 510, Del Mar, CA 92014. **E-mail:** castigliaagency-query@yahoo.com. **Website:** www.castigliaagency.com. Member of AAR. Other memberships include PEN. Represents 65 clients. Currently handles nonfiction books (55%), novels (45%).

MEMBER AGENTS Julie Castiglia (not accepting queries at this time); Win Golden (fiction: thrillers, mystery, crime, science fiction, YA, commercial/literary fiction; nonfiction: narrative nonfiction, current events, science, journalism).

REPRESENTS Nonfiction books, novels. **Considers these fiction areas:** contemporary issues, ethnic, literary, mainstream, mystery, suspense, women's.

8—☞ Does not want to receive horror, screenplays, poetry, or academic nonfiction.

HOW TO CONTACT Query via e-mail. No unsolicited submissions. No snail mail submissions accepted.

Obtains most new clients through recommendations from others, solicitations, conferences.

TERMS Agent receives 15% commission on domestic sales. Agent receives 25% commission on foreign sales. Offers written contract; 6-week notice must be given to terminate contract.

RECENT SALES *Germs Gone Wild*, by Kenneth King (Pegasus); *The Insider* by Reece Hirsch (Berkley/Penguin); *The Leisure Seeker*, by Michael Zadoorian (Morrow/HarperCollins); *Beautiful: The Life of Hedy Lamarr*, by Stephen Shearer (St. Martin's Press); *American Libre*, by Raul Ramos y Sanchez (Grand Central); *The Two Krishnas*, by Ghalib Shiraz Dhalla (Alyson Books).

WRITERS CONFERENCES Santa Barbara Writers Conference; Southern California Writers Conference; Surrey International Writers Conference; San Diego State University Writers Conference; Willamette Writers Conference.

TIPS "Be professional with submissions. Attend workshops and conferences before you approach an agent."

JANE CHELIUS LITERARY AGENCY

548 Second St., Brooklyn, NY 11215. (718)499-0236. **Fax:** (718)832-7335. **E-mail:** queries@janechelius.com. **Website:** www.janechelius.com. Member of AAR. **REPRESENTS** Nonfiction books, novels. **Considers these fiction areas:** literary, mystery, suspense.

➣ Does not want to receive fantasy, science fiction, children's books, stage plays, screenplays, or poetry.

HOW TO CONTACT Please see website for submission procedures. Does not consider e-mail queries with attachments. No unsolicited sample chapters or mss. Responds in 3-4 weeks usually.

ELYSE CHENEY LITERARY ASSOCIATES, LLC

78 Fifth Avenue, 3rd Floor, New York, NY 10011. **Website:** www.cheneyliterary.com. **Contact:** Elyse Cheney; Adam Eaglin; Alex Jacobs.

Prior to her current position, Ms. Cheney was an agent with Sanford J. Greenburger Associates.

REPRESENTS Nonfiction, novels. **Considers these fiction areas:** upmarket commercial fiction, historical fiction, literary, suspense, upmarket women's fiction. **HOW TO CONTACT** Query this agency with a referral. Include SASE or IRC. No fax queries. Snail mail or e-mail (submissions@cheneyliterary.com) only.

RECENT SALES *Moonwalking with Einstein: The Art and Science of Remembering Everything*, by Joshua Foer; *The Possessed: Adventures with Russian Books and the People Who Read Them*, by Elif Batuman (Farrar, Strauss & Giroux); *The Coldest Winter Ever*, by Sister Souljah (Atria); *A Heartbreaking Work of Staggering Genius*, by Dave Eggers (Simon and Schuster); *No Easy Day*, by Mark Owen; *Malcom X: A Life of Reinvention*, by Manning Marable.

DON CONGDON ASSOCIATES INC.

110 William St., Suite 2202, New York, NY 10038. (212)645-1229. **Fax:** (212)727-2688. **E-mail:** dca@doncongdon.com. **Website:** http://doncongdon.com. **Contact:** Michael Congdon, Susan Ramer, Cristina Concepcion, Maura Kye Casella, Katie Kotchman, Katie Grimm. Member of AAR. Represents 100 clients. Currently handles nonfiction books (60%), other (40% fiction).

REPRESENTS Nonfiction books fiction. **Considers these fiction areas:** action, adventure, contemporary issues, crime, detective, literary, mainstream, mystery, police, short story collections, suspense, thriller, women's.

➣ Especially interested in narrative nonfiction and literary fiction.

HOW TO CONTACT Query with SASE or via e-mail (no attachments). Responds in 3 weeks to queries. Responds in 1 month to mss. Obtains most new clients through recommendations from other authors. **TERMS** Agent receives 15% commission on domestic sales. Agent receives 19% commission on foreign sales. Charges client for extra shipping costs, photocopying, copyright fees, book purchases.

TIPS "Writing a query letter with an SASE is a must. We cannot guarantee replies to foreign queries via standard mail. No phone calls. We never download attachments to e-mail queries for security reasons, so please copy and paste material into your e-mail."

THE DOE COOVER AGENCY

P.O. Box 668, Winchester, MA 01890. (781)721-6000. **E-mail:** info@doecooveragency.com. **Website:** www.doecooveragency.com. Represents 150+ clients. Currently handles nonfiction books (80%), novels (20%).

MEMBER AGENTS Doe Coover (general nonfiction, including business, cooking/food writing, health and science); Colleen Mohyde (literary and commercial fiction, general nonfiction); Associate: Frances Kennedy.

REPRESENTS Considers these fiction areas: commercial, literary.

⚬—⚞ The agency specializes in narrative nonfiction, particularly biography, business, cooking and food writing, health, history, popular science, social issues, gardening, and humor; literary and commercial fiction. The agency does not represent poetry, screenplays, romance, fantasy, science fiction, or unsolicited children's books.

HOW TO CONTACT Accepts queries by e-mail only. Check website for submission guidelines. No unsolicited mss. Accepts simultaneous submissions. Responds within 4-6 weeks, only if additional material is required. Obtains most new clients through solicitation and recommendation.

TERMS Agent receives 15% commission on domestic sales, 10% of original advance commission on foreign-sales. No reading fees.

RECENT SALES *Vegetable Literacy*, by Deborah Madison (Ten Speed Press); *Frontera: Margaritas, Guacamoles, and Snacks*, by Rick Bayless and Deann Groen Bayless (W.W. Norton); *Silvana's Gluten-Free Kitchen*, by Silvana Nardone (Houghton Mifflin Harcourt); *The Essay*, by Robin Yocum (Arcade Publishing); *The Flower of Empire*, by Tatiana Holway (Oxford University Press); *Confederates Don't Wear Couture*, by Stephanie Strohm (Houghton Mifflin Harcourt); Dulcie Schwartz mystery series, by Clea Simon (Severn House UK), *Gourmet Weekday* and *Gourmet Italian*, by Conde Nast Publications (Houghton Mifflin Harcourt); Untitled Biography of Eunice Kennedy Shriver, by Eileen McNamara (Simon & Schuster); Movie/TV MOW scripts optioned: *Keeper of the House*, by Rebecca Godwin. Other clients include: WGBH, New England Aquarium, Duke University, Blue Balliett, David Allen, Jacques Pepin, Cindy Pawlcyn, Joann Weir, Suzanne Berne, Paula Poundstone, Anita Silvey, Marjorie Sandor, Tracy Daugherty, Carl Rollyson, and Joel Magnuson.

● **CRICHTON & ASSOCIATES**

6940 Carroll Ave., Takoma Park, MD 20912. (301)495-9663. **Fax:** (202)318-0050. **E-mail:** query@crichton-associates.com. **Website:** www.crichton-associates.com. **Contact:** Sha-Shana Crichton. 90% of clients are new/unpublished writers. Currently handles nonfiction books 50%, fiction 50%.

💬 Prior to becoming an agent, Ms. Crichton did commercial litigation for a major law firm.

REPRESENTS Nonfiction books, novels. **Considers these fiction areas:** ethnic, feminist, inspirational, literary, mainstream, mystery, religious, romance, suspense chick lit.

⚬—⚞ Actively seeking women's fiction, romance, and chick lit. Looking also for multicultural fiction and nonfiction. Does not want to receive poetry, children's, YA, science fiction, or screenplays.

HOW TO CONTACT "In the subject line of e-mail, please indicate whether your project is fiction or nonfiction. Please do not send attachments. Your query letter should include a description of the project and your biography. If you wish to send your query via snail mail, please include your telephone number and e-mail address. We will respond to you via e-mail. For fiction, include short synopsis and first 3 chapters with query. For nonfiction, send a book proposal." Responds in 3-5 weeks to queries.

TERMS Agent receives 15% commission on domestic sales. Agent receives 20% commission on foreign sales. Offers written contract, binding for 45 days. Only charges fees for postage and photocopying.

RECENT SALES *The African American Entrepreneur*, by W. Sherman Rogers (Praeger); *The Diversity Code*, by Michelle Johnson (Amacom); *Secret & Lies*, by Rhonda McKnight (Urban Books); *Love on the Rocks*, by Pamela Yaye (Harlequin). Other clients include Kimberley White, Beverley Long, Jessica Trap, Altonya Washington, Cheris Hodges.

WRITERS CONFERENCES Silicon Valley RWA; BookExpo America.

D4EO LITERARY AGENCY

7 Indian Valley Rd., Weston, CT 06883. (203)544-7180. **Fax:** (203)544-7160. **E-mail:** bob@d4eo.com; mandy.hubbard.queries@gmail.com; kristin.d4eo@gmail.com; bree@d4eo.com; samantha@d4eo.com. **Website:** www.d4eoliteraryagency.com. **Contact:** Bob Diforio. Represents 100+ clients. 50% of clients are new/unpublished writers. Currently handles nonfiction books (70%), novels (25%), juvenile books (5%).

💬 Prior to opening his agency, Mr. Diforio was a publisher.

MEMBER AGENTS Bob Diforio, Many Hubbard, Kristin Miller-Vincent, Bree Odgen, Samantha Dighton, Joyce Holland (currently closed to submissions).

REPRESENTS Nonfiction books, novels. **Considers these fiction areas:** adventure, detective, erotica, historical, horror, humor, juvenile, literary, mainstream, mystery, picture books, romance, science, sports, thriller, Western, young adult.

HOW TO CONTACT Query with SASE. Accepts and prefers e-mail queries. Prefers to read material exclusively. Responds in 1 week to queries. Obtains most new clients through recommendations from others.

TERMS Agent receives 15% commission on domestic sales. Agent receives 25% commission on foreign sales. Offers written contract, binding for 2 years; 60-day notice must be given to terminate contract. Charges for photocopying and submission postage.

◑ DANIEL LITERARY GROUP

1701 Kingsbury Dr., Suite 100, Nashville, TN 37215. (615)730-8207. **E-mail:** submissions@danielliter arygroup.com. **Website:** www.danielliterarygroup .com. **Contact:** Greg Daniel. Represents 45 clients. 30% of clients are new/unpublished writers. Currently handles nonfiction books (85%), novels (15%).

○ Prior to becoming an agent, Mr. Daniel spent 10 years in publishing—6 at the executive level at Thomas Nelson Publishers.

REPRESENTS Nonfiction books, novels. **Considers these fiction areas:** action, adventure, contemporary issues, crime, detective, family saga, historical, humor, inspirational, literary, mainstream, mystery, police, religious, satire, suspense, thriller.

⚬━ The agency currently accepts all fiction topics, except for children's, romance, and sci-fi. "We take pride in our ability to come alongside our authors and help strategize about where they want their writing to take them in both the near and long term. Forging close relationships with our authors, we help them with such critical factors as editorial refinement, branding, audience, and marketing." The agency is open to submissions in almost every popular category of nonfiction, especially if authors are recognized experts in their fields. No screenplays, poetry, science fiction/fantasy, romance, children's, or short stories.

HOW TO CONTACT Query via e-mail only. Submit publishing history, author bio, brief synopsis of work, key selling points; no attachments. For fiction, send first 5 pages pasted in e-mail. Check submissions guidelines before querying or submitting. "Please do not query via telephone." Responds in 2-3 weeks to queries.

● DARHANSOFF & VERRILL LITERARY AGENTS

236 W. 26th St., Suite 802, New York, NY 10001. (917)305-1300. **Fax:** (917)305-1400. **E-mail:** submis sions@dvagency.com. **Website:** www.dvagency.com. Member of AAR. Represents 120 clients. 10% of clients are new/unpublished writers. Currently handles nonfiction books (25%), novels (60%), story collections (15%).

MEMBER AGENTS Liz Darhansoff, Chuck Verrill, Michele Mortimer.

REPRESENTS Novels, juvenile books narrative nonfiction, literary fiction, mystery and suspense, young adult.

HOW TO CONTACT Send queries via e-mail or by snail mail with SASE. Obtains most new clients through recommendations from others.

◑ THE JENNIFER DECHIARA LITERARY AGENCY

31 East 32nd St., Suite 300, New York, NY 10016. (212)481-8484. **Fax:** (212)481-9582. **E-mail:** jenndec@ aol.com; stephenafraser@verizon.net. **Website:** www .jdlit.com. **Contact:** Jennifer DeChiara, Stephen Fraser. Represents 100 clients. 50% of clients are new/unpublished writers. Currently handles nonfiction books (25%), novels (25%), juvenile books (50%).

○ Prior to becoming an agent, Ms. DeChiara was a writing consultant, freelance editor at Simon & Schuster and Random House, and a ballerina and an actress.

MEMBER AGENTS Jennifer DeChiara, Stephen Fraser, Dorothy Spencer (adult fiction and nonfiction).

REPRESENTS Nonfiction books, novels, juvenile. **Considers these fiction areas:** confession, crime, detective, ethnic, family saga, fantasy, feminist, gay, historical, horror, humor, juvenile, lesbian, literary, mainstream, mystery, picture books, police, regional, satire, sports, suspense, thriller, young adult, chick lit, psychic/supernatural, glitz.

⚬━ "We represent both children's and adult books in a wide range of ages and genres. We are a full-service agency and fulfill the potential of every book in every possible medium—stage, film, television, etc. We help writers every step of the way, from creating book ideas to editing and promotion. We are passionate about helping writers further their careers but are just as eager to discover new talent, regardless of age or lack of prior publishing experience. This agency is committed to managing a writer's entire career. For us, it's not just about selling books, but about making dreams come true. We are especially attracted to the downtrodden, the discouraged, and the downright disgusted." Actively seeking literary fiction, chick lit, young adult fiction, self-help, pop culture, and celebrity biographies. Does not want Westerns, poetry, or short stories.

HOW TO CONTACT Query with SASE. Accepts simultaneous submissions. Responds in 3-6 months to queries. Responds in 3-6 months to mss. Obtains most new clients through recommendations from others, conferences, query letters.

TERMS Agent receives 15% commission on domestic sales. Agent receives 20% commission on foreign sales. Offers written contract.

RECENT SALES Sold more than 100 titles in the past year. PEN Award-winner YA novel: *Glimpse*, by Carol LynchWilliams (St. Martin's); PEN and Edgar Award-winning middle-grade: *Icefall*, by Matthew Kirby (Scholastic); Newbery Honor Medal-winner and *New York Times* Best-selling middle-grade: *Heart of a Samurai*, by Margi Preus (Abrams); Lambda Award-winner YA novel: *Split Screen*, by Brent Hartinger (HarperCollins); *A Moose That Says Moo*, by Jennifer Hamburg (Farrar, Straus & Giroux); *Naptime for Barney*, by Danny Sit (Sterling); *The 30-Day Heartbreak Cure*, by Catherine Hickland (Simon & Schuster); *The One-Way Bridge*, by *New York Times* Best-selling Author Cathie Pelletier (Sourcebooks); *New York Times* Best-selling: *Not Young, Still Restless*, by Jeanne Cooper (HarperCollins). Other clients include *New York Times* Best-selling author Sylvia Browne, Sonia Levitin, Susan Anderson.

DEFIORE & CO.

47 E. 19th St., 3rd Floor, New York, NY 10003. (212) 925-7744. **Fax:** (212)925-9803. **E-mail:** info@defioreandco.com; submissions@defioreandco.com. **Website:** www.defioreandco.com. **Contact:** Lauren Gilchrist. Member of AAR. Represents 75 clients. 50% of clients are new/unpublished writers. Currently handles nonfiction books (70%), novels (30%).

Prior to becoming an agent, Mr. DeFiore was publisher of Villard Books (1997-1998), edi-

tor-in-chief of Hyperion (1992-1997), and editorial director of Delacorte Press (1988-1992).

MEMBER AGENTS Brian DeFiore (popular nonfiction, business, pop culture, parenting, commercial fiction); Laurie Abkemeier (memoir, parenting, business, how-to/self-help, popular science); Kate Garrick (literary fiction, memoir, popular nonfiction); Matthew Elblonk (young adult, popular culture, narrative nonfiction); Caryn Karmatz-Rudy (popular fiction, self-help, narrative nonfiction); Adam Schear (commercial fiction, humor, YA, smart thrillers, historical fiction, and quirky debut literary novels. For nonfiction: popular science, politics, popular culture, and current events); Meredith Kaffel (smart upmarket women's fiction, literary fiction [especially debut] and literary thrillers, narrative nonfiction, nonfiction about science and tech, sophisticated pop culture/humor books); Rebecca Strauss (literary and commercial fiction, women's fiction, urban fantasy, romance, mystery, YA, memoir, pop culture, and select nonfiction).

REPRESENTS Nonfiction books, novels. **Considers these fiction areas:** ethnic, literary, mainstream, mystery, suspense, thriller.

☛ "Please be advised that we are not considering children's picture books, poetry, adult science fiction and fantasy, romance, or dramatic projects at this time."

HOW TO CONTACT Query with SASE or e-mail to submissions@defioreandco.com. "Please include the word *Query* in the subject line. All attachments will be deleted; please insert all text in the body of the e-mail. For more information about our agents, their individual interests, and their query guidelines, please visit our About Us page." Accepts simultaneous submissions. Responds in 3 weeks to queries. Responds in 2 months to mss. Obtains most new clients through recommendations from others.

TERMS Agent receives 15% commission on domestic sales. Agent receives 20% commission on foreign sales. Offers written contract; 10-day notice must be given to terminate contract. Charges clients for photocopying and overnight delivery (deducted only after a sale is made).

WRITERS CONFERENCES Aloha Writers Conference; Pacific Northwest Writers Conference; North Carolina Writers Network Fall Conference.

● JOELLE DELBOURGO ASSOCIATES, INC.

101 Park St., 3rd Floor, Montclair, NJ 07042. (973)773-0836. **Fax:** (973)783-6802. **E-mail:** info@delbourgo.com. **Website:** www.delbourgo.com. **Contact:** Joelle Delbourgo, Molly Lyons, Jacquie Flynn. Represents more than 100 clients. Currently handles nonfiction books (75%), novels (25%).

○ Prior to becoming an agent, Ms. Delbourgo was an editor and senior publishing executive at HarperCollins and Random House.

MEMBER AGENTS Joelle Delbourgo (narrative nonfiction, serious "expert-driven" nonfiction, self-help, psychology, business, history, science, medicine, quality fiction); Jacquie Flynn (thought-provoking and practical business, parenting, education, personal development, current events, science, and other select nonfiction and fiction titles); Carrie Cantor (current events, politics, history, popular science and psychology, memoir, and narrative nonfiction).

REPRESENTS Nonfiction books, novels. **Considers these fiction areas:** historical, literary, mainstream, mystery, suspense.

⊶ "We are former publishers and editors with deep knowledge and an insider perspective. We have a reputation for individualized attention to clients, strategic management of authors' careers, and creating strong partnerships with publishers for our clients." Actively seeking history, narrative nonfiction, science/medicine, memoir, literary fiction, psychology, parenting, biographies, current affairs, politics, young adult fiction and nonfiction. Does not want to receive genre fiction, science fiction, fantasy, or screenplays.

HOW TO CONTACT Query by mail with SASE. Accepts simultaneous submissions. Responds in 3 weeks to queries. Responds in 2 months to mss.

TERMS Agent receives 15% commission on domestic sales. Agent receives 20% commission on foreign sales. Offers written contract. Charges clients for postage and photocopying.

RECENT SALES *Alexander the Great*, by Philip Freeman; *The Big Book of Parenting Solutions*, by Dr. Michele Borba; *The Secret Life of Ms. Finkelman*, by Ben H. Wintners; *Not Quite Adults*, by Richard Settersten Jr. and Barbara Ray; *Tabloid Medicine*, by Robert Goldberg, PhD; *Table of Contents*, by Judy Gerlman and Vicky Levi Krupp.

TIPS "Do your homework. Do not cold call. Read and follow submission guidelines before contacting us. Do not call to find out if we received your material. No e-mail queries. Treat agents with respect, as you would any other professional, such as a doctor, lawyer or financial advisor."

●● JIM DONOVAN LITERARY

5635 SMU Blvd., Suite 201, Dallas, TX 75206. **E-mail:** jdliterary@sbcglobal.net. **Contact:** Melissa Shultz, agent. Represents 30 clients. 10% of clients are new/unpublished writers. Currently handles nonfiction books (75%), novels (25%).

MEMBER AGENTS Jim Donovan (history—particularly American, military and Western; biography; sports; popular reference; popular culture; fiction—literary, thrillers, and mystery); Melissa Shultz (parenting, women's issues, memoir).

REPRESENTS Nonfiction books, novels. **Considers these fiction areas:** action, adventure, crime, detective, literary, mainstream, mystery, police, suspense, thriller.

⊶ This agency specializes in commercial fiction and nonfiction. "Does not want to receive poetry, children's, short stories, inspirational, or anything else not listed above."

HOW TO CONTACT "For nonfiction, I need a well-thought query letter telling me about the book: What it does, how it does it, why it's needed now, why it's better or different than what's out there on the subject, and why the author is the perfect writer for it. For fiction, the novel has to be finished, of course; a short (2-5 page) synopsis—not a teaser, but a summary of all the action, from first page to last—and the first 30-50 pages is enough. This material should be polished to as close to perfection as possible." Accepts simultaneous submissions. Responds in 3 weeks to queries. Responds in 1 month to mss. Obtains most new clients through recommendations from others.

TERMS Agent receives 15% commission on domestic sales. Agent receives 20% commission on foreign sales. Offers written contract, binding for 1 year; 30-day notice must be given to terminate contract. This agency charges for things such as overnight delivery and manuscript copying. Charges are discussed beforehand.

RECENT SALES Sold 31 titles in the past year. *Manson: The Life and Times of Charles Manson*, by Jeff Guinn (Simon and Schuster); *Shot All to Hell*, by Mark

Lee Gardner (Morrow); *Grant and Lee*, by William C. Davis (Da Capo); *Below*, by Ryan Lockwood (Kensington); *The Dead Lands*, by Joe McKinney (Kensington); *Perfect: Don Larsen's Miraculous World Series Game and the Men Who Made It Happen*, by Lew Paper (NAL); *Undefeated: America's Heroic Fight for Bataan and Corregidor*, by Bill Sloan (Simon and Schuster).

TIPS "Get published in short form—magazine reviews, journals, etc.—first. This will increase your credibility considerably, and make it much easier to sell a full-length book."

DUNHAM LITERARY, INC.

110 William St., Suite 2202, New York, NY 10038. (212)929-0994. **E-mail:** dunhamlit@yahoo.com. **E-mail:** query@dunhamlit.com. **Website:** www.dunhamlit.com. **Contact:** Jennie Dunham. Member of AAR. SCBWI Represents 50 clients. 15% of clients are new/unpublished writers. Currently handles nonfiction books (25%), novels (25%), juvenile books (50%).

- Prior to opening her agency, Ms. Dunham worked as a literary agent for Russell & Volkening. The Rhoda Weyr Agency is now a division of Dunham Literary, Inc.

REPRESENTS Nonfiction books, novels, short story collections, juvenile. **Considers these fiction areas:** ethnic, juvenile, literary, mainstream, picture books, young adult.

HOW TO CONTACT Query with SASE. Responds in 1 week to queries; 2 months to mss. Obtains most new clients through recommendations from others, solicitations.

TERMS Agent receives 15% commission on domestic sales. Agent receives 20% commission on foreign sales.

RECENT SALES Sold 30 books for young readers in the last year. *Peter Pan*, by Robert Sabuda (Little Simon); *Flamingos on the Roof*, by Calef Brown (Houghton); *Adele and Simon in America*, by Barbara McClintock (Farrar, Straus & Giroux); *Caught Between the Pages*, by Marlene Carvell (Dutton); *Waiting For Normal*, by Leslie Connor (HarperCollins), *The Gollywhopper Games*, by Jody Feldman (Greenwillow); *America the Beautiful*, by Robert Sabuda; *Dahlia*, by Barbara McClintock; *Living Dead Girl*, by Tod Goldberg; *In My Mother's House*, by Margaret McMulla; *Black Hawk Down,* by Mark Bowden; *Look Back All the Green Valley*, by Fred Chappell; *Under a Wing*, by Reeve Lindbergh; *I Am Madame X*, by Gioia Diliberto.

DUPREE/MILLER AND ASSOCIATES INC. LITERARY

100 Highland Park Village, Suite 350, Dallas, TX 75205. (214)559-BOOK. **Fax:** (214)559-PAGE. **Website:** www.dupreemiller.com. Member of ABA. Represents 200 clients. 20% of clients are new/unpublished writers. Currently handles nonfiction books (90%), novels (10%).

MEMBER AGENTS Jan Miller, president/CEO; Shannon Miser-Marven, senior executive VP; Annabelle Baxter; Nena Madonia; Cheri Gillis.

REPRESENTS Nonfiction books, novels, scholarly, syndicated religious, inspirational/spirituality. **Considers these fiction areas:** action, adventure, crime, detective, ethnic, experimental, family saga, feminist, glitz, historical, humor, inspirational, literary, mainstream, mystery, picture books, police, psychic, religious, satire, sports, supernatural, suspense, thriller.

- This agency specializes in commercial fiction and nonfiction.

HOW TO CONTACT Submit 1-page query, summary, bio, how to market, SASE through U.S. postal service. Obtains most new clients through recommendations from others, conferences, lectures.

TERMS Agent receives 15% commission on domestic sales. Offers written contract.

WRITERS CONFERENCES Aspen Summer Words Literary Festival.

TIPS "If interested in agency representation, it is vital to have the material in the proper working format. As agents' policies differ, it is important to follow their guidelines. Work on establishing a strong proposal that provides sample chapters, an overall synopsis (fairly detailed), and some biographical information. Do not send your proposal in pieces; it should be complete upon submission. Your work should be in its best condition."

EAST/WEST LITERARY AGENCY, LLC

1158 26th St., Suite 462, Santa Monica, CA 90403. (310)573-9303. **Fax:** (310)453-9008. **E-mail:** dwarren@eastwestliteraryagency.com; rpfeffer@eastwestliteraryagency.com. Estab. 2000. Currently handles juvenile books (90%), adult books (10%).

MEMBER AGENTS Deborah Warren, founder; Rubin Pfeffer, partner content agent and digital media strategist.

HOW TO CONTACT By referral only. Submit proposal and first 3 sample chapters, table of contents (2 pages or fewer), synopsis (1 page). For picture books, submit entire ms. Requested submissions should be sent by mail as a Word document in Courier, 12-pt., double-spaced with 1.20-inch margin on left, ragged right text, 25 lines per page, continuously paginated, with all your contact info on the first page. Only responds if interested, no need for SASE. Responds in 60 days. Obtains new clients through recommendations from others.

TERMS Agent receives 15% commission on domestic sales. Agent receives 25% commission on foreign sales. Offers written contract; 30-day notice must be given to terminate contract. Charges for out-of-pocket expenses, such as postage and copying.

ANNE EDELSTEIN LITERARY AGENCY

404 Riverside Dr., #12D, New York NY 10025. (212)414-4923. **Fax:** (212)414-2930. **E-mail:** info@ aeliterary.com. **E-mail:** submissions@aeliterary.com. **Website:** www.aeliterary.com. Member of AAR.

MEMBER AGENTS Anne Edelstein; Krista Ingebretson.

REPRESENTS Nonfiction, fiction. **Considers these fiction areas:** literary.

This agency specializes in fiction and narrative nonfiction.

HOW TO CONTACT E-mail queries only; consult website for submission guidelines.

RECENT SALES *Amsterdam*, by Russell Shorto (Doubleday); *The Story of Beautiful Girl*, by Rachel Simon (Grand Central).

THE NICHOLAS ELLISON AGENCY

Affiliated with Sanford J. Greenburger Associates, 55 Fifth Ave., 15th Floor, New York, NY 10003. (212)206-5600. **Fax:** (212)463-8718. **E-mail:** nellison@sjga.com. **Website:** www.greenburger.com. **Contact:** Nicholas Ellison. Represents 70 clients. Currently handles nonfiction books (50%), novels (50%).

Prior to becoming an agent, Mr. Ellison was an editor at Minerva Editions and Harper & Row, and editor-in-chief at Delacorte.

MEMBER AGENTS Nicholas Ellison; Chelsea Lindman.

REPRESENTS Nonfiction books, literary novels, mainstream children's books. **Considers these fiction areas:** literary, mainstream.

HOW TO CONTACT Submit query in the body of an e-mail; no attachments. Responds in 6 weeks to queries.

TERMS Agent receives 15% commission on domestic sales. Agent receives 20% commission on foreign sales.

THE ELAINE P. ENGLISH LITERARY AGENCY

4710 41st St. NW, Suite D, Washington DC 20016. (202)362-5190. **Fax:** (202)362-5192. **E-mail:** queries@ elaineenglish.com. **E-mail:** elaine@elaineenglish .com. **Website:** www.elaineenglish.com/literary.php. **Contact:** Elaine English, Lindsey Skouras. Member of AAR. Represents 20 clients. 25% of clients are new/unpublished writers. Currently handles novels (100%).

Ms. English has been working in publishing for more than 20 years. She is also an attorney specializing in media and publishing law.

MEMBER AGENTS Elaine English (novels).

REPRESENTS Novels. **Considers these fiction areas:** historical, multicultural, mystery, suspense, thriller, women's romance (single title, historical, contemporary, romantic, suspense, chick lit, erotic), general women's fiction. The agency is slowly but steadily acquiring in all mentioned areas.

Actively seeking women's fiction, including single-title romances. Does not want to receive any science fiction, time travel, or picture books.

HOW TO CONTACT Generally prefers e-queries sent to queries@elaineenglish.com. If requested, submit synopsis, first 3 chapters, SASE. "Please check our website for further details." Responds in 4-8 weeks to queries; 3 months to requested submissions. Obtains most new clients through recommendations from others, conferences, submissions.

TERMS Agent receives 15% commission on domestic sales. Agent receives 20% commission on foreign sales. Offers written contract; 30-day notice must be given to terminate contract. Charges only for shipping expenses; generally taken from proceeds.

RECENT SALES Sourcebooks, Tor, Harlequin.

WRITERS CONFERENCES RWA National Conference; Novelists, Inc.; Malice Domestic; Washington Romance Writers Retreat, among others.

FAIRBANK LITERARY REPRESENTATION

P.O. Box 6, Hudson, NY 12534-0006. (617)576-0030. **Fax:** (617)576-0030. **E-mail:** queries@fairbankliter ary.com. **Website:** www.fairbankliterary.com. **Contact:** Sorche Fairbank. Member of AAR. Represents 45 clients. 20% of clients are new/unpublished writers. Currently handles nonfiction books (60%), novels (22%), story collections (3%), other (15% illustrated).

MEMBER AGENTS Sorche Fairbank (narrative nonfiction, commercial and literary fiction, memoir, food and wine); Matthew Frederick, matt@fairbankliterary.com (scout for sports nonfiction, architecture, design).

REPRESENTS Nonfiction books, novels, short story collections. **Considers these fiction areas:** action, adventure, feminist, gay, lesbian, literary, mainstream, mystery, sports, suspense, thriller, women's Southern voices.

❧ ⚷ "I have a small agency in Harvard Square, where I tend to gravitate toward literary fiction and narrative nonfiction, with a strong interest in women's issues and women's voices, international voices, class and race issues, and projects that simply teach me something new about the greater world and society around us. We have a good reputation for working closely and developmentally with our authors and for loving what we do." Actively seeking literary fiction, international and culturally diverse voices, narrative nonfiction, topical subjects (politics, current affairs), history, sports, architecture/design, and pop culture. Does not want to receive romance, poetry, science fiction, pirates, vampire, young adult, or children's works.

HOW TO CONTACT Query with SASE. Submit author bio. Accepts simultaneous submissions. Responds in 6 weeks to queries. Responds in 10 weeks to mss. Obtains most new clients through recommendations from others, solicitations, conferences, ideas generated in-house.

TERMS Agent receives 15% commission on domestic sales. Agent receives 20% commission on foreign sales. Offers written contract, binding for 12 months; 45-day notice must be given to terminate contract.

WRITERS CONFERENCES San Francisco Writers Conference, Muse and the Marketplace/Grub Street Conference, Washington Independent Writers Conference, Murder in the Grove, Surrey International Writers Conference.

TIPS "Be professional from the very first contact. There shouldn't be a single typo or grammatical flub in your query. Have a reason for contacting me about your project other than I was the next name listed on some website. Please do not use form query software! Believe me, we can get a dozen or so a day that look identical—we know when you are using a form. Show me that you know your audience—and your competition. Have the writing and/or proposal at the very, very best it can be before starting the querying process. Don't assume that if someone likes it enough they'll 'fix' it. The biggest mistake new writers make is starting the querying process before they—and the work—are ready. Take your time and do it right."

◑ FAYE BENDER LITERARY AGENCY

19 Cheever Place, Brooklyn, NY 11231. **E-mail:** info@fbliterary.com. **Website:** www.fbliterary.com. **Contact:** Faye Bender. Estab. 2004. Member of AAR.

MEMBER AGENTS Faye Bender.

REPRESENTS Nonfiction books, novels, juvenile. **Considers these fiction areas:** commercial, literary, women's, young adult (middle-grade).

❧ ⚷ "I choose books based on the narrative voice and strength of writing. I work with previously published and first-time authors." Faye does not represent picture books, genre fiction for adults (Western, romance, horror, science fiction, fantasy), business books, spirituality, or screenplays.

HOW TO CONTACT Query with SASE and 10 sample pages via mail or e-mail (no attachments). Guidelines online. "Please do not send queries or submissions via registered or certified mail, or by FedEx or UPS requiring signature. We will not return unsolicited submissions weighing more than 16 ounces, even if an SASE is attached. We do not respond to queries via phone or fax."

TIPS "Please keep your letters to the point, include all relevant information, and have a bit of patience."

◑ FELICIA ETH LITERARY REPRESENTATION

555 Bryant St., Suite 350, Palo Alto, CA 94301-1700. (650)375-1276. **Fax:** (650)401-8892. **E-mail:** feliciaeth.literary@gmail.com. **Website:** http://ethliterary.com. **Contact:** Felicia Eth. Member of AAR. Represents 25-35 clients. Currently handles nonfiction books (75%), novels (25% adult).

REPRESENTS Nonfiction books, novels. **Considers these fiction areas:** literary, mainstream.

❧ ⚷ This agency specializes in high-quality fiction (preferably mainstream/contemporary) and provocative, intelligent, and thoughtful nonfiction on a wide array of commercial subjects.

HOW TO CONTACT Query with SASE. Accepts simultaneous submissions. Responds in 3 weeks to queries. Responds in 4-6 weeks to mss.

TERMS Agent receives 15% commission on domestic sales. Agent receives 20% commission on foreign sales. Agent receives 20% commission on film sales. Charges clients for photocopying and express mail service.

RECENT SALES Sold 70-100 titles in the last year. *Bumper Sticker Philosophy*, by Jack Bowen (Random House); *Boys Adrift* by Leonard Sax (Basic Books); *A War Reporter*, by Barbara Quick (HarperCollins); *Pantry*, by Anna Badkhen (Free Press/S&S).

WRITERS CONFERENCES "Wide array—from Squaw Valley to Mills College."

TIPS "For nonfiction, established expertise is certainly a plus—as is magazine publication—though not a prerequisite. I am highly dedicated to those projects I represent but highly selective in what I choose."

DIANA FINCH LITERARY AGENCY

116 W. 23rd St., Suite 500, New York, NY 10011. E-mail: diana.finch@verizon.net. **Website:** http://diana finchliteraryagency.blogspot.com. **Contact:** Diana Finch. Member of AAR. Represents 40 clients. 20% of clients are new/unpublished writers. Currently handles nonfiction books (85%), novels (15%), juvenile books (5%), multimedia (5%).

Seeking to represent books that change lives. Prior to opening her agency in 2003, Ms. Finch worked at Ellen Levine Literary Agency for 18 years.

REPRESENTS Nonfiction books, novels, scholarly. **Considers these fiction areas:** action, adventure, crime, detective, ethnic, historical, literary, mainstream, police, thriller, young adult.

Actively seeking narrative nonfiction, popular science, memoir and health topics. "Does not want romance, mysteries, or children's picture books."

HOW TO CONTACT Query with SASE or via e-mail (no attachments). Accepts simultaneous submissions. Obtains most new clients through recommendations from others.

TERMS Agent receives 15% commission on domestic sales. Agent receives 20% commission on foreign sales. Offers written contract. "I charge for photocopying, overseas postage, galleys, and books purchased, and try to recoup these costs from earnings received for a client, rather than charging outright."

RECENT SALES *Heidegger's Glasses*, by Thaisa Frank; *Genetic Rounds*, by Robert Marion, MD (Kaplan); *Honeymoon in Tehran*, by Azadeh Moaveni (Random House); *Darwin Slept Here* by Eric Simons (Overlook); *Black Tide*, by Antonia Juhasz (HarperCollins); *Stalin's Children*, by Owen Matthews (Bloomsbury); *Radiant Days*, by Michael Fitzgerald (Shoemaker & Hoard); *The Queen's Soprano*, by Carol Dines (Harcourt Young Adult); *What to Say to a Porcupine*, by Richard Gallagher (Amacom); *The Language of Trust*, by Michael Maslansky et al.

TIPS "Do as much research as you can on agents before you query. Have someone critique your query letter before you send it. It should be only 1 page and describe your book clearly—and why you are writing it—but also demonstrate creativity and a sense of your writing style."

FINEPRINT LITERARY MANAGEMENT

115 W. 29th, 3rd Floor, New York, NY 10001. (212)279-1282. **E-mail:** stephany@fineprintlit.com. **Website:** www.fineprintlit.com. Member of AAR.

MEMBER AGENTS Peter Rubie, CEO (nonfiction interests include narrative nonfiction, popular science, spirituality, history, biography, pop culture, business, technology, parenting, health, self-help, music, and food; fiction interests include literate thrillers, crime fiction, science fiction and fantasy, military fiction and literary fiction, middle-grade and YA fiction and nonfiction for boys); Stephany Evans (Nonfiction: health and wellness, especially women's health; spirituality, environment/sustainability, food and wine, memoir, and narrative nonfiction; Fiction: stories with a strong and interesting female protagonist, both literary and upmarket commercial/book club fiction, romance—all subgenres; mysteries); Janet Reid (Nonfiction: narrative nonfiction, history and biography; Fiction: thrillers); Brooks Sherman, (Nonfiction: narrative nonfiction, history, pop culture, and food; Fiction: literary, upmarket, crime, science fiction grounded in realistic settings, high/contemporary/dark fantasy, magical realism, middle-grade, young adult, and picture books); Becky Vinter (Nonfiction: travel, food, health, wellness, business/management, environment, current events, memoir; Fiction: women's fiction, romance, mysteries, literary, book club, young adult); Laura Wood (Nonfiction: nonfiction books, business, dance, economics, history, humor, law, science, narrative nonfiction, popular science; Fiction: fantasy, science fiction, suspense).

HOW TO CONTACT Query with SASE. Submit synopsis and first 3-5 pages of ms embedded in an e-mail proposal for nonfiction. Do not send attachments or manuscripts without a request. See contact page onilne at website for e-mails. Obtains most new clients through recommendations from others, solicitations.

TERMS Agent receives 15% commission on domestic sales. Agent receives 20% commission on foreign sales.

FOUNDRY LITERARY + MEDIA

33 West 17th St., PH, New York, NY 10011. (212)929-5064. **Fax:** (212)929-5471. **Website:** www.foundry media.com.

MEMBER AGENTS Peter H. McGuigan (smart, offbeat nonfiction, particularly works of narrative nonfiction on pop culture, niche history, biography, music and science; fiction interests include commercial and literary, across all genres, especially first-time writers); Yfat Reiss Gendell (favors nonfiction books focusing on all manners of prescriptive: how-to, science, health and well-being, memoirs, adventure, travel stories and lighter titles appropriate for the gift trade genre. Yfat also looks for commercial fiction highlighting the full range of women's experiences—young and old—and also seeks science fiction, thrillers and historical fiction); Stéphanie Abou (in fiction and nonfiction alike, Stéphanie is always on the lookout for authors who are accomplished storytellers with their own distinctive voice, who develop memorable characters, and who are able to create psychological conflict with their narrative. She is an across-the-board fiction lover, attracted to both literary and smart upmarket commercial fiction. In nonfiction she leans towards projects that tackle big topics with an unusual approach. Pop culture, health, science, parenting, women's and multicultural issues are of special interest); Chris Park (memoirs, narrative nonfiction, Christian nonfiction and character-driven fiction); David Patterson (outstanding narratives and/or idea-driven works of nonfiction); Hannah Brown Gordon (fiction, YA, memoir, narrative nonfiction, history, current events, science, psychology and pop culture); Lisa Grubka; Mollie Glick (literary fiction, narrative nonfiction, YA, and a bit of practical nonfiction); Stephen Barbara (all categories of books for young readers in addition to servicing writers for the adult market); Brandi Bowles (idea and platform-driven nonfiction in all categories, including music and pop culture, humor, business, sociology, philosophy, health, and relationships. Quirky, funny, or contrarian proposals are always welcome in her in-box, as are big-idea books that change the way we think about the world. Brandi also represents fiction in the categories of literary fiction, women's fiction, urban fantasy, and YA).

REPRESENTS Considers these fiction areas: literary, religious.

HOW TO CONTACT Query with SASE. Should be addressed to one agent only. Submit synopsis, 3 sample chapters, author bio, For nonfiction, submit query, proposal, sample chapter, TOC, bio. Put submissions on your snail mail submission.

TIPS "Consult website for each agent's submission instructions."

FOX LITERARY

110 W. 40th St., Suite 410, New York, NY 10018. **E-mail:** submissions@foxliterary.com. **Website:** www .foxliterary.com.

REPRESENTS Considers these fiction areas: erotica, fantasy, literary, romance, science, young adult, science fiction, thrillers, historical fiction, literary fiction, graphic novels, commercial fiction, women's fiction, gay and lesbian, erotica historical romance.

✎ Does not want to receive screenplays, poetry, category Westerns, horror, Christian/inspirational, or children's picture books.

HOW TO CONTACT E-mail query and first 5 pages in body of e-mail. E-mail queries preferred. For snail mail queries, must include an e-mail address for response and no response means NO. Do not send SASE.

LYNN C. FRANKLIN ASSOCIATES, LTD.

1350 Broadway, Suite 2015, New York, NY 10018. (212)868-6311. **Fax:** (212)868-6312. **E-mail:** agency@ fsainc.com. **E-mail:** agency@franklinandsiegal.com. **Contact:** Lynn Franklin, president; Claudia Nys, foreign rights. Other memberships include PEN America. Represents 30-35 clients. 50% of clients are new/ unpublished writers. Currently handles nonfiction books (90%), novels (10%).

REPRESENTS Nonfiction books, novels. **Considers these fiction areas:** literary, mainstream, commercial; juvenile, middle-grade, and young adult.

8—• "This agency specializes in general nonfiction with a special interest in self-help, biography/memoir, alternative health, and spirituality."

HOW TO CONTACT Query via e-mail to agency@franklinandsiegal.com. No unsolicited mss. No attachments. For nonfiction, query letter with short outline and synopsis. For fiction, query letter with short synopsis and a maximum of 10 sample pages (in the body of the e-mail). Please indicate "query adult" or "query children's") in the subject line. Accepts simultaneous submissions. Responds in 2 weeks to queries. Responds in 6 weeks to mss. Obtains most new clients through recommendations from others, solicitations.

TERMS Agent receives 15% commission on domestic sales. Agent receives 20% commission on foreign sales. Offers written contract.

RECENT SALES Adult: *Made for Goodness*, by Archbishop Desmond Tutu and Reverend Mpho Tutu (HarperOne); *Children of God Storybook Bible*, by Archbishop Desmond Tutu (Zondervan for originating publisher Lux Verbi); *Playing Our Game: Why China's Economic Rise Doesn't Threaten the West*, by Edward Steinfeld (Oxford University Press); *The 100 Year Diet*, by Susan Yager (Rodale); Children's/YA: *I Like Mandarin*, by Kirsten Hubbard (Delacorte/Random House); *A Scary Scene in a Scary Movie*, by Matt Blackstone (Farrar, Straus & Giroux).

● **SARAH JANE FREYMANN LITERARY AGENCY**

59 W. 71st St., Suite 9B, New York, NY 10023. (212)362-9277. **E-mail:** sarah@sarahjanefreymann.com; Submissions@SarahJaneFreymann.com. **Website:** www.sarahjanefreymann.com. **Contact:** Sarah Jane Freymann, Steve Schwartz. Represents 100 clients. 20% of clients are new/unpublished writers. Currently handles nonfiction books (75%), novels (23%), juvenile books (2%).

MEMBER AGENTS Sarah Jane Freymann; (nonfiction books, novels, illustrated books); Jessica Sinsheimer, Jessica@sarahjanefreymann.com (young adult fiction); Steven Schwartz, steve@sarahjanefreymann.com; Katharine Sands.

REPRESENTS Considers these fiction areas: ethnic, literary, mainstream.

HOW TO CONTACT Query with SASE. Responds in 2 weeks to queries. Responds in 6 weeks to mss.

Obtains most new clients through recommendations from others.

TERMS Agent receives 15% commission on domestic sales. Agent receives 20% commission on foreign sales. Offers written contract. Charges clients for long distance, overseas postage, photocopying. 100% of business is derived from commissions on ms sales.

RECENT SALES *How to Make Love to a Plastic Cup: And Other Things I Learned While Trying to Knock Up My Wife*, by Greg Wolfe (Harper Collins); *I Want to Be Left Behind: Rapture Here on Earth*, by Brenda Peterson (a Merloyd Lawrence Book); *That Bird Has My Name: The Autobiography of an Innocent Man on Death Row*, by Jarvis Jay Masters with an Introduction by Pema Chodrun (HarperOne); *Perfect One-Dish Meals*, by Pam Anderson (Houghton Mifflin); *Birdology*, by Sy Montgomery (Simon & Schuster); *Emptying the Nest: Launching Your Reluctant Young Adult*, by Dr. Brad Sachs (Macmillan); *Tossed & Found*, by Linda and John Meyers (Steward, Tabori & Chang); *32 Candles*, by Ernessa Carter; *God and Dog*, by Wendy Francisco.

TIPS "I love fresh, new, passionate works by authors who love what they are doing and have both natural talent and carefully honed skill."

● **FREDRICA S. FRIEDMAN AND CO., INC.**
136 E. 57th St., 14th Floor, New York, NY 10022. (212)829-9600. **Fax:** (212)829-9669. **E-mail:** info@fredricafriedman.com; submissions@fredricafriedman.com. **Website:** www.fredricafriedman.com. **Contact:** Ms. Chandler Smith. Represents 75+ clients. 50% of clients are new/unpublished writers. Currently handles nonfiction books (95%), novels (5%).

REPRESENTS Nonfiction books, novels anthologies. **Considers these fiction areas:** literary.

8—• "We represent a select group of outstanding nonfiction and fiction writers. We are particularly interested in helping writers expand their readership and develop their careers." Does not want poetry, plays, screenplays, children's books, sci-fi/fantasy, or horror.

HOW TO CONTACT Submit e-query, synopsis; be concise, and include any pertinent author information, including relevant writing history. If you are a fiction writer, we also request a one-page sample from your manuscript to provide its voice. We ask that you keep all material in the body of the e-mail. Accepts simultaneous submissions. Responds in 4-6 weeks to queries. Responds in 4-6 weeks to mss. Obtains most new clients through recommendations from others.

TERMS Agent receives 15% commission on domestic sales. Agent receives 25% commission on foreign sales. Offers written contract. Charges for photocopying and messenger/shipping fees for proposals.

RECENT SALES *A World of Lies: The Crime and Consequences of Bernie Madoff*, by Diana B. Henriques (Times Books/Holt); *Polemic and Memoir: The Nixon Years* by Patrick J. Buchanan (St. Martin's Press); *Angry Fat Girls: Five Women, Five Hundred Pounds, and a Year of Losing It . . . Again*, by Frances Kuffel (Berkley/Penguin); *Life with My Sister Madonna*, by Christopher Ciccone with Wendy Leigh (Simon & Schuster Spotlight); *The World Is Curved: Hidden Dangers to the Global Economy*, by David Smick (Portfolio/Penguin); *Going to See the Elephant*, by Rodes Fishburne (Delacorte/Random House); *Seducing the Boys Club: Uncensored Tactics from a Woman at the Top*, by Nina DiSesa (Ballantine/Random House); *The Girl from Foreign: A Search for Shipwrecked Ancestors, Forgotten Histories, and a Sense of Home*, by Sadia Shepard (Penguin Press).

TIPS "Spell the agent's name correctly on your query letter."

◑ FULL CIRCLE LITERARY, LLC

7676 Hazard Center Dr., Suite 500, San Diego, CA 92108. **E-mail:** submissions@fullcircleliterary.com. **Website:** www.fullcircleliterary.com. **Contact:** Lilly Ghahremani, Stefanie Von Borstel. Represents 55 clients. 60% of clients are new/unpublished writers. Currently handles nonfiction books (70%), novels (10%), juvenile books (20%).

◯   Before forming Full Circle, Ms. Von Borstel worked in both marketing and editorial capacities at Penguin and Harcourt; Ms. Ghahremani received her law degree from UCLA and has experience in representing authors on legal affairs.

MEMBER AGENTS Lilly Ghahremani (Lilly is only taking referrals: young adult, pop culture, crafts, green living, narrative nonfiction, business, relationships, Middle Eastern interest, multicultural); Stefanie Von Borstel (Latino interest, crafts, parenting, wedding/relationships, how-to, self-help, middle grade/teen fiction/YA, green living, multicultural/bilingual picture books); Adriana Dominguez (fiction areas of interest: children's books—picture books, middle-grade novels, and (literary) young adult novels; on the adult side, she is looking for literary, women's, and historical fiction. Nonfiction areas of interest: multicultural, pop culture, how-to, and titles geared toward women of all ages).

REPRESENTS Nonfiction books, juvenile. **Considers these fiction areas:** ethnic, literary, young adult.

☞   "Our full-service boutique agency, representing a range of nonfiction and children's books (limited fiction), provides a one-stop resource for authors. Our extensive experience in the realms of law and marketing provide Full Circle clients with a unique edge. Actively seeking nonfiction by authors with a unique and strong platform, projects that offer new and diverse viewpoints, and literature with a global or multicultural perspective. We are particularly interested in books with a Latino or Middle Eastern angle and books related to pop culture." Does not want to receive screenplays, poetry, commercial fiction or genre fiction (horror, thriller, mystery, Western, sci-fi, fantasy, romance, historical fiction).

HOW TO CONTACT Agency accepts e-queries. See website for fiction guidelines, as they are in flux. For nonfiction, send full proposal. Accepts simultaneous submissions. Responds in 1-2 weeks to queries. Responds in 4-6 weeks to mss. Obtains most new clients through recommendations from others, solicitations, conferences.

TERMS Agent receives 15% commission on domestic sales. Agent receives 20% commission on foreign sales. Offers written contract; up to 30-day notice must be given to terminate contract. Charges for copying and postage.

TIPS "Put your best foot forward. Contact us when you simply can't make your project any better on your own, and please be sure your work fits with what the agent you're approaching represents. Little things count, so copyedit your work. Join a writing group and attend conferences to get objective and constructive feedback before submitting. Be active about building your platform as an author before, during, and after publication. Remember this is a business and your agent is a business partner."

DON GASTWIRTH & ASSOCIATES

265 College St., New Haven, CT 06510. (203)562-7600. **Fax:** (203)562-4300. **E-mail:** Donlit@snet.net. **Con-**

tact: Don Gastwirth. Signatory of WGA. Represents 26 clients. 10% of clients are new/unpublished writers. Currently handles nonfiction books (30%), scholarly books (60%), other (10% other).

Prior to becoming an agent, Mr. Gastwirth was an entertainment lawyer and law professor.

REPRESENTS Nonfiction books, scholarly. **Considers these fiction areas:** mystery, thriller.

This is a selective agency and is rarely open to new clients that do not come through a referral.

HOW TO CONTACT Query with SASE.

TERMS Agent receives 15% commission on domestic sales. Agent receives 10% commission on foreign sales.

GELFMAN SCHNEIDER LITERARY AGENTS, INC.

250 W. 57th St., Suite 2122, New York, NY 10107. (212)245-1993. **Fax:** (212)245-8678. **E-mail:** mail@gelfmanschneider.com. **Website:** www.gelfmanschneider.com. **Contact:** Jane Gelfman, Deborah Schneider. Member of AAR. Represents 300+ clients. 10% of clients are new/unpublished writers.

REPRESENTS Fiction and nonfiction books. **Considers these fiction areas:** literary, mainstream, mystery, women's.

Does not want to receive romance, science fiction, Westerns, or children's books.

HOW TO CONTACT Query with SASE. Send queries via snail mail only. No unsolicited mss. Please send a query letter, a synopsis, and a SAMPLE CHAPTER ONLY. Consult website for each agent's submission requirements. Responds in 1 month to queries. Responds in 2 months to mss.

TERMS Agent receives 15% commission on domestic sales. Agent receives 20% commission on foreign sales. Agent receives 15% commission on film sales. Offers written contract. Charges clients for photocopying and messengers/couriers.

THE SUSAN GOLOMB LITERARY AGENCY

540 President St., 3rd Floor, Brooklyn, NY 11215. **Fax:** (212)239-9503. **E-mail:** susan@sgolombagency.com; krista@sgolombagency.com. **Contact:** Susan Golomb; Krista Ingebretson. Currently handles nonfiction books (50%), novels (40%), story collections (10%).

MEMBER AGENTS Susan Golomb (accepts queries); Krista Ingebretson (accepts queries).

REPRESENTS Novels, short story collections. **Considers these fiction areas:** ethnic, historical, humor, literary, mainstream, satire, thriller, women's, young adult chick lit.

"We specialize in literary and upmarket fiction and nonfiction that is original, vibrant and of excellent quality and craft. Nonfiction should be edifying, paradigm shifting, fresh and entertaining." Actively seeking writers with strong voices. Does not want to receive genre fiction.

HOW TO CONTACT Query via mail with SASE or by e-mail. Will respond if interested. Submit outline/proposal, synopsis, a sample chapter, author bio. Obtains most new clients through recommendations from others, solicitations, and unsolicited queries.

TERMS Offers written contract.

RECENT SALES *The Kraus Project*, by Jonathan Franzen (FSG); *The Word Exchange*, by Alena Graedon (Doubleday); *The Flamethrowers*, by Rachel Kushner (Scribner); *The Book of Jonah*, by Joshua Feldman (Holt); *Last Stories* and *Other Stories* and *The Dying Grass*, by William T. Vollmann (Viking)

IRENE GOODMAN LITERARY AGENCY

27 W. 24th St., Suite 700B, New York, NY 10010. **E-mail:** irene.queries@irenegoodman.com. **Website:** www.irenegoodman.com. **Contact:** Irene Goodman, Miriam Kriss. Member of AAR.

MEMBER AGENTS Irene Goodman; Miriam Kriss; Barbara Poelle; Jon Sternfeld.

REPRESENTS Nonfiction, novels. **Considers these fiction areas:** historical, intelligent literary, modern urban fantasies, mystery, romance, thriller, women's.

"Specializes in the finest in commercial fiction and nonfiction. We have a strong background in women's voices, including mysteries, romance, women's fiction, thrillers, suspense. Historical fiction is one of Irene's particular passions and Miriam is fanatical about modern urban fantasies. In nonfiction, Irene is looking for topics on narrative history, social issues and trends, education, Judaica, Francophilia, Anglophilia, other cultures, animals, food, crafts, and memoir." Barbara is looking for commercial thrillers with strong female protagonists; Miriam is looking for urban fantasy and edgy sci-fi/young adult. No children's picture books, screenplays, poetry, or inspirational fiction.

HOW TO CONTACT Query. Submit synopsis, first 10 pages. E-mail queries only! See the website submission page. No e-mail attachments. Responds in 2 months to queries. Consult website for each agent's submission guidelines.

RECENT SALES *The Ark*, by Boyd Morrison; *Isolation*, by C.J. Lyons; *The Sleepwalkers*, by Paul Grossman; *Dead Man's Moon*, by Devon Monk; *Becoming Marie Antoinette*, by Juliet Grey; *What's Up Down There*, by Lissa Rankin; *Beg for Mercy*, by Toni Andrews; *The Devil Inside*, by Jenna Black.

TIPS "We are receiving an unprecedented amount of e-mail queries. If you find that the mailbox is full, please try again in two weeks. E-mail queries to our personal addresses will not be answered. E-mails to our personal inboxes will be deleted."

GOUMEN & SMIRNOVA LITERARY AGENCY

Nauki pr., 19/2 fl. 293, St. Petersburg 195220 Russia. **E-mail:** info@gs-agency.com. **Website:** www.gs-agency.com. **Contact:** Julia Goumen, Natalia Smirnova. Represents 20 clients. 10% of clients are new/unpublished writers. Currently handles nonfiction books (10%), novels (80%), story collections (5%), juvenile books (5%).

○ Prior to becoming agents, both Ms. Goumen and Ms. Smirnova worked as foreign rights managers with an established Russian publisher selling translation rights for literary fiction.

MEMBER AGENTS Julia Goumen (translation rights, Russian language rights, film rights); Natalia Smirnova (translation rights, Russian language rights, film rights).

REPRESENTS Nonfiction books, novels, short story collections, novellas, movie, TV, TV movie, sitcom. **Considers these fiction areas:** adventure, experimental, family, historical, horror, literary, mainstream, mystery, romance, thriller, young adult, women's.

⚷ "We are the first full-service agency in Russia, representing our authors in book publishing, film, television, and other areas. We are also the first agency representing Russian authors worldwide, based in Russia. The agency also represents international authors, agents and publishers in Russia. Our philosophy is to provide an individual approach to each author, finding the right publisher both at home

and across international cultural and linguistic borders, developing original marketing and promotional strategies for each title." Actively seeking manuscripts written in Russian, both literary and commercial; and foreign publishers and agents with the high-profile fiction and general nonfiction lists to represent in Russia. Does not want to receive unpublished manuscripts in languages other than Russian or any information irrelevant to our activity.

HOW TO CONTACT Submit synopsis, author bio. Accepts simultaneous submissions. Responds in 14 days to mss. Obtains most new clients through recommendations from others, solicitations.

TERMS Agent receives 20% commission on domestic sales. Agent receives 20% commission on foreign sales. Offers written contract, binding for 1 year; 2-month notice must be given to terminate contract.

SANFORD J. GREENBURGER ASSOCIATES, INC.

55 Fifth Ave., New York, NY 10003. (212)206-5600. **Fax:** (212)463-8718. **E-mail:** queryHL@sjga.com. **Website:** www.greenburger.com. Member of AAR. Represents 500 clients.

MEMBER AGENTS Heide Lange; Faith Hamlin; Dan Mandel; Matthew Bialer; Courtney Miller-Callihan, Brenda Bowen (authors and illustrators of children's books for all ages as well as graphic novelists); Lisa Gallagher.

REPRESENTS Nonfiction books and novels. **Considers these fiction areas:** action, adventure, crime, detective, ethnic, family saga, feminist, gay, glitz, historical, humor, lesbian, literary, mainstream, mystery, police, psychic, regional, satire, sports, supernatural, suspense, thriller.

⚷ No Westerns. No screenplays.

HOW TO CONTACT Submit query, first 3 chapters, synopsis, brief bio, SASE. Consult website for submission guidelines. Accepts simultaneous submissions. Responds in 2 months to queries and mss. Responds to mss. Obtains most new clients through recommendations from others.

TERMS Agent receives 15% commission on domestic sales. Agent receives 20% commission on foreign sales. Charges for photocopying and books for foreign and subsidiary rights submissions.

THE GREENHOUSE LITERARY AGENCY

11308 Lapham Dr., Oakton, VA 22124. **E-mail:** submissions@greenhouseliterary.com. **Website:** www.greenhouseliterary.com. **Contact:** Sarah Davies, vice president; John M. Cusick, agent (US); Julia Churchill, agent (UK). Member of AAR. Other memberships include SCBWI. Represents 20 clients. 100% of clients are new/unpublished writers. Currently handles juvenile books (100%).

Sarah Davies has had an editorial and management career in children's publishing spanning 25 years; for 5 years prior to launching the Greenhouse she was publishing director of Macmillan Children's Books in London, where she published leading authors from both sides of the Atlantic.

REPRESENTS Juvenile. **Considers these fiction areas:** juvenile, young adult.

"We exclusively represent authors writing fiction for children and teens. The agency has offices in both the USA and UK, and Sarah Davies (who is British) personally represents authors to both markets. The agency's commission structure reflects this—taking 15% for sales to both US and UK, thus treating both as 'domestic' market.'" All genres of children's and YA fiction—ages 5+. Does not want to receive nonfiction, poetry, picture books (text or illustration), or work aimed at adults; short stories, educational or religious/inspirational work, preschool/novelty material, or screenplays.

HOW TO CONTACT E-mail queries only; short letter containing a brief outline, biography, and any writing credentials. The first five pages of text should be pasted into the e-mail. All submissions are answered. Responds in 2-6 week to queries; 6-8 weeks to requested mss. Obtains most new clients through recommendations from others, solicitations, conferences.

TERMS Agent receives 15% commission on domestic sales. Agent receives 25% commission on foreign sales. Offers written contract. This agency occasionally charges for submission copies to film agents or foreign publishers.

RECENT SALES *Fracture*, by Megan Miranda (Walker); *Paper Valentine*, by Brenna Yovanff (Razorbill); *Uses for Boys*, by Erica L. Scheidt (St Mar-

tin's); *Dark Inside*, by Jeyn Roberts (Simon & Schuster); *Breathe*, by Sarah Crossan (HarperCollins); *After the Snow*, by SD Crockett (Feiwel/Macmillan); *Sean Griswold's Head*, by Lindsey Leavitt (Hyperion).

WRITERS CONFERENCES Bologna Children's Book Fair, ALA and SCBWI conferences, BookExpo America.

TIPS "Before submitting material, authors should read the Greenhouse's Top 10 Tips for Authors of Children's Fiction and carefully follow our submission guidelines, which can be found on the website."

KATHRYN GREEN LITERARY AGENCY, LLC

250 West 57th St., Suite 2302, New York, NY 10107. (212)245-4225. **Fax:** (212)245-4042. **E-mail:** query@kgreenagency.com. **Contact:** Kathy Green. Other memberships include Women's Media Group. Represents approximately 20 clients. 50% of clients are new/unpublished writers. Currently handles nonfiction books (50%), novels (25%), juvenile books (25%).

Prior to becoming an agent, Ms. Green was a book and magazine editor.

REPRESENTS Nonfiction books, novels, short story collections, juvenile, middle grade, and young adult only). **Considers these fiction areas:** crime, detective, family saga, historical, humor, juvenile, literary, mainstream, mystery, police, romance, satire, suspense, thriller, women's, young adult women's.

Keeping the client list small means that writers receive my full attention throughout the process of getting their project published. Does not want to receive science fiction or fantasy.

HOW TO CONTACT Query to query@kgreenagency.com. Send no samples unless requested. Accepts simultaneous submissions. Responds in 1-2 months to mss. Obtains most new clients through recommendations from others, solicitations, conferences.

TERMS Agent receives 15% commission on domestic sales. Agent receives 20% commission on foreign sales. No written contract.

RECENT SALES The Touch Series by Laurie Stolarz; *How Do You Light a Fart*, by Bobby Mercer; *Creepiosity*, by David Bickel; *Hidden Facets: Diamonds for the Dead* by Alan Orloff; *Don't Stalk the Admissions Officer*, by Risa Lewak; *Designed Fat Girl*, by Jennifer Joyner.

TIPS "This agency offers a written agreement."

🌑🌓 GREGORY & CO. AUTHORS' AGENTS

3 Barb Mews, Hammersmith, London W6 7PA England. (44)(207)610-4676. **Fax:** (44)(207)610-4686. **E-mail:** info@gregoryandcompany.co.uk. **E-mail:** maryjones@gregoryandcompany.co.uk. **Website:** www.gregoryandcompany.co.uk. **Contact:** Jane Gregory. Other memberships include AAA. Represents 60 clients. Currently handles nonfiction books (10%), novels (90%).

MEMBER AGENTS Stephanie Glencross.

REPRESENTS Nonfiction books, novels. **Considers these fiction areas:** crime, detective, historical, literary, mainstream, police, thriller, contemporary women's fiction.

⊶ As a British agency, we do not generally take on American authors. Actively seeking well-written, accessible modern novels. Does not want to receive horror, science fiction, fantasy, mind/body/spirit, children's books, screenplays, plays, short stories, or poetry.

HOW TO CONTACT Query with SASE. Submit outline, first 10 pages by e-mail or post, publishing history, author bio. Send submissions to Mary Jones, submissions editor: maryjones@gregoryandcompany .co.uk. Accepts simultaneous submissions. Returns materials only with SASE. Obtains most new clients through recommendations from others, conferences.

TERMS Agent receives 15% commission on domestic sales. Agent receives 20% commission on foreign sales. Offers written contract; 1-month notice must be given to terminate contract. Charges clients for photocopying of whole typescripts and copies of book for submissions.

RECENT SALES *Ritual*, by Mo Hader (Bantam UK/Grove Atlantic); *A Darker Domain*, by Val McDermid (HarperCollins UK); *The Chameleon's Shadow*, by Minette Walters (Macmillan UK/Knopf Inc); *Stratton's War*, by Laura Wilson (Orion UK/St. Martin's).

WRITERS CONFERENCES CWA Conference; Bouchercon.

🌓 JILL GROSJEAN LITERARY AGENCY

1390 Millstone Rd., Sag Harbor, NY 11963. (631)725-7419. **E-mail:** JillLit310@aol.com. **Contact:** Jill Grosjean.

○ Prior to becoming an agent, Ms. Grosjean managed an independent bookstore. She also worked in publishing and advertising.

⊶ Actively seeking literary novels and mysteries.

HOW TO CONTACT E-mail queries preferred, no attachments. No cold calls, please. Accepts simultaneous submissions, though when manuscript requested, requires exclusive reading time. Accepts simultaneous submissions. Responds in 1 week to queries; month to mss. Obtains most new clients through recommendations and solicitations.

TERMS Agent receives 15% commission on domestic sales; 20% commission on foreign and film sales.

RECENT SALES *A Spark of Death*, *Fatal Induction*, and *Capacity for Murder*, by Bernadette Pajer (Poison Pen Press); *Neutral Ground*, by Greg Garrett (Bond-fire Books); *Threading the Needle*, by Marie Bostwick (Kensington Publishing).

WRITERS CONFERENCES Thrillerfest; Texas Writer's League; Book Passage Mystery Writers Conference.

⬤ LAURA GROSS LITERARY AGENCY

P.O. Box 610326, Newton Highlands, MA 02461. (617)964-2977. **Fax:** (617)964-3023. **E-mail:** query@lg-la.com. **Website:** www.lg-la.com. **Contact:** Laura Gross. Estab. 1988. Represents 30 clients. Currently handles nonfiction books (40%), novels (50%), scholarly books (10%).

○ Prior to becoming an agent, Ms. Gross was an editor.

REPRESENTS Nonfiction books, novels. **Considers these fiction areas:** historical, literary, mainstream, mystery, suspense, thriller.

HOW TO CONTACT Submit online using submissions manager. Query with SASE or by e-mail. Submit author bio. Responds in several days to queries. Obtains most new clients through recommendations from others.

TERMS Agent receives 15% commission on domestic sales. Agent receives 20% commission on foreign sales. Offers written contract.

THE MITCHELL J. HAMILBURG AGENCY

149 S. Barrington Ave., #732, Los Angeles, CA 90049. (310)471-4024. **Fax:** (310)471-9588. **Contact:** Michael Hamilburg. Estab. 1937. Signatory of WGA. Represents 70 clients. Currently handles nonfiction books (70%), novels (30%).

REPRESENTS Nonfiction books, novels. **Considers these fiction areas:** glitz, New Age, adventure, experimental, feminist, humor, military, mystery, occult, regional, religious, romance, sports, thriller, crime, mainstream, psychic.

HOW TO CONTACT Query with outline, 2 sample chapters, SASE. Responds in 1 month to mss. Obtains most new clients through recommendations from others, conferences, personal search.

TERMS Agent receives 10-15% commission on domestic sales.

HARTLINE LITERARY AGENCY

123 Queenston Dr., Pittsburgh, PA 15235-5429. (412)829-2483. **Fax:** (412)829-2432. **E-mail:** joyce@ hartlineliterary.com. **Website:** www.hartlineliterary .com. **Contact:** Joyce A. Hart. Represents 40 clients. 20% of clients are new/unpublished writers. Currently handles nonfiction books (40%), novels (60%).

MEMBER AGENTS Joyce A. Hart, principal agent; Terry Burns: terry@hartlineliterary.com; Tamela Hancock Murray: tamela@hartlineliterary.com; Diana Flegal: diana@hartlineliterary.com.

REPRESENTS Nonfiction books, novels. **Considers these fiction areas:** action, adventure, contemporary issues, family saga, historical, inspirational, literary, mystery, regional, religious, suspense, thriller amateur sleuth, cozy, contemporary, gothic, historical, and regency romances.

8—**¬** "This agency specializes in the Christian bookseller market." Actively seeking adult fiction, self-help, nutritional books, devotional, and business. Does not want to receive erotica, gay/lesbian, fantasy, horror, etc.

HOW TO CONTACT Submit summary/outline, author bio, 3 sample chapters. Accepts simultaneous submissions. Responds in 2 months to queries. Responds in 3 months to mss. Obtains most new clients through recommendations from others.

TERMS Agent receives 15% commission on domestic sales. Offers written contract.

RECENT SALES *Aurora, An American Experience in Quilt, Community and Craft*, and *A Flickering Light*, by Jane Kirkpatrick (Waterbrook Multnomah); *Oprah Doesn't Know My Name* by Jane Kirkpatric (Zondervan); *Paper Roses, Scattered Petals, and Summer Rains*, by Amanda Cabot (Revell Books); *Blood Ransom*, by Lisa Harris (Zondervan); *I Don't Want a Divorce*, by David Clark (Revell Books); *Love Finds You in Hope, Kansas*, by Pamela Griffin (Summerside Press); Journey to the Well, by Diana Wallis Taylor (Revell Books); *Paper Bag Christmas, The Nine Lessons* by Kevin Milne (Center Street); *When Your Aging Parent Needs Care,* by Arrington & Atchley (Harvest House); *Katie at Sixteen* (Zondervan) and *A Promise of Spring*, by Kim Vogel Sawyer (Bethany House); *The Big 5-OH!*, by Sandra Bricker (Abingdon Press); *A Silent Terror & A Silent Stalker*, by Lynette Eason (Steeple Hill); Extreme Devotion series, by Kathi Macias (New Hope Publishers); *On the Wings of the Storm*, by Tamira Barley (Whitaker House); Tribute, by Graham Garrison (Kregel Publications); *The Birth to Five Book*, by Brenda Nixon (Revell Books); *Fat to Skinny Fast and Easy*, by Doug Varrieur (Sterling Publishers).

JOHN HAWKINS & ASSOCIATES, INC.

71 W. 23rd St., Suite 1600, New York, NY 10010. (212)807-7040. **Fax:** (212)807-9555. **E-mail:** jha@ jhalit.com; moses@jhalit.com; Frazier@jhalit. com; Ahawkins@jhalit.com. **Website:** www.jhalit. com. **Contact:** Moses Cardona (rights and translations); Liz Free (permissions); Warren Frazier, literary agent; Anne Hawkins, literary agent. Member of AAR. Represents over 100 clients. 5-10% of clients are new/unpublished writers. Currently handles nonfiction books (40%), novels (40%), juvenile books (20%).

MEMBER AGENTS Moses Cardona; Liz Free; Warren Frazier; Anne Hawkins.

REPRESENTS Nonfiction books, novels. **Considers these fiction areas:** action, adventure, crime, detective, ethnic, experimental, family saga, gay, glitz, hi-lo, historical, inspirational, literary, mainstream, multicultural, multimedia, mystery, police, short story collections, sports, supernatural, suspense, thriller, translation, war, Westerns, women's, young adult.

HOW TO CONTACT Submit query, proposal package, outline, SASE. Accepts simultaneous submissions. Responds in 1 month to queries. Obtains most new clients through recommendations from others.

TERMS Agent receives 15% commission on domestic sales. Agent receives 20% commission on foreign sales. Charges clients for photocopying.

RECENT SALES The Doll, by Taylor Stevens; *Flora*, by Gail Godwin; *The Affairs of Others*, by Amy Loyd.

RICHARD HENSHAW GROUP

145 W. 28th St., 12th Floor, New York, NY 10001. (212)414-1172. **E-mail:** submissions@henshaw.com.

Website: www.richardhenshawgroup.com. **Contact:** Rich Henshaw. Member of AAR. Other memberships include SinC, MWA, HWA, SFWA, RWA. 20% of clients are new/unpublished writers. Currently handles nonfiction books (35%), novels (65%).

○ Prior to opening his agency, Mr. Henshaw served as an agent with Richard Curtis Associates, Inc.

REPRESENTS Nonfiction books, novels. **Considers these fiction areas:** action, adventure, crime, detective, ethnic, family saga, historical, humor, literary, mainstream, mystery, police, psychic, romance, satire, science fiction, sports, supernatural, suspense, thriller.

⌐ This agency specializes in thrillers, mysteries, science fiction, fantasy, and horror.

HOW TO CONTACT Query with SASE. Accepts multiple submissions. Responds in 3 weeks to queries. Responds in 6 weeks to mss. Obtains most new clients through recommendations from others, solicitations, conferences.

TERMS Agent receives 15% commission on domestic sales. Agent receives 20% commission on foreign sales. No written contract. Charges clients for photocopying and book orders.

RECENT SALES *Though Not Dead*, by Dana Stabenow; *The Perfect Suspect*, by Margaret Coel; *City of Ruins*, by Kristine Kathryn Rusch; *A Dead Man's Tale*, by James D. Doss, *Wickedly Charming*, by Kristine Grayson, History of the World series, by Susan Wise Bauer; *Notorious Pleasures*, by Elizabeth Hoyt.

TIPS "While we do not have any reason to believe that our submission guidelines will change in the near future, writers can find up-to-date submission policy information on our website. Always include a SASE with correct return postage."

◑ HIDDEN VALUE GROUP

1240 E. Ontario Ave., Ste. 102-148, Corona, CA 92881. **E-mail:** bookquery@hiddenvaluegroup.com. **Website:** www.hiddenvaluegroup.com. **Contact:** Nancy Jernigan. Represents 55 clients. 10% of clients are new/unpublished writers.

MEMBER AGENTS Jeff Jernigan, jjernigan@hiddenvaluegroup.com (men's nonfiction, fiction, Bible studies/curriculum, marriage and family); Nancy Jernigan, njernigan@hiddenvaluegroup.com (nonfiction, women's issues, inspiration, marriage and family, fiction).

REPRESENTS Nonfiction books and adult fiction; no poetry. **Considers these fiction areas:** action, adventure, crime, detective, fantasy, frontier, inspirational, literary, police, religious, thriller, Westerns, women's.

⌐ "The Hidden Value Group specializes in helping authors throughout their publishing career. We believe that every author has a special message to be heard and we specialize in getting that message out." Actively seeking established fiction authors and authors who are focusing on women's issues. Does not want to receive poetry or short stories.

HOW TO CONTACT Query with SASE. Submit synopsis, 2 sample chapters, author bio, and marketing and speaking summary. Accepts queries to bookquery@hiddenvaluegroup.com. No fax queries. Responds in 1 month to queries. Responds in 1 month to mss. Obtains most new clients through recommendations from others, solicitations.

TERMS Agent receives 15% commission on domestic sales. Agent receives 15% commission on foreign sales. Offers written contract.

WRITERS CONFERENCES Glorieta Christian Writers Conference; CLASS Publishing Conference.

HOPKINS LITERARY ASSOCIATES

2117 Buffalo Rd., Suite 327, Rochester, NY 14624-1507. (585)352-6268. **Contact:** Pam Hopkins. Member of AAR. Other memberships include RWA. Represents 30 clients. 5% of clients are new/unpublished writers. Currently handles novels (100%).

REPRESENTS Novels. **Considers these fiction areas:** mostly women's genre romance, historical, contemporary, category, women's.

⌐ This agency specializes in women's fiction, particularly historical, contemporary, and category romance, as well as mainstream work.

HOW TO CONTACT Regular mail with synopsis, 3 sample chapters, SASE. Accepts simultaneous submissions. Responds in 2 weeks to queries. Responds in 1 month to mss. Obtains most new clients through recommendations from others, solicitations, conferences.

TERMS Agent receives 15% commission on domestic sales. Agent receives 20% commission on foreign sales. No written contract.

RECENT SALES Sold 50 titles in the last year. *The Wilting Bloom Series* by Madeline Hunter (Berkley);

The Dead Travel Fast, by Deanna Raybourn; *Baggage Claim*, by Tanya Michna (NAL).

WRITERS CONFERENCES RWA National Conference.

ANDREA HURST LITERARY MANAGEMENT

P.O. Box 1467, Coupeville, WA 98239. **E-mail:** andrea@andreahurst.com. **Website:** www.andreahurst.com. **Contact:** Andrea Hurst, Judy Mikalonis, Gordon Warnock, Vickie Motter. For Gordon Warnock: P.O. Box 19010, Sacramento, CA 95819. Represents 100+ clients. 50% of clients are new/unpublished writers. Currently handles nonfiction books (50%), novels (50%).

Prior to becoming an agent, Ms. Hurst was an acquisitions editor as well as a freelance editor and published writer; Ms. Mikalonis was in marketing and branding consulting; Gordon Warnock was a freelance editor and marketing consultant.

MEMBER AGENTS Andrea Hurst, andrea@andreahurst.com (adult fiction, women's fiction, nonfiction—including personal growth, health and wellness, science, business, parenting, relationships, women's issues, animals, spirituality, women's issues, metaphysical, psychological, cookbooks, and self-help); Judy Mikalonis, judy@andreahurst.com (YA fiction, Christian fiction, Christian nonfiction). Gordon Warnock, gordon@andreahurst.com, P.O. Box 19010, Sacramento, CA 95819. Gordon represents nonfiction: Memoir, political and current affairs, health, humor and cookbooks. Fiction: Commercial narrative with a literary edge. Vickie Motter, vickie@andreahurst.com, P.O.Box 1467, Coupeville, WA 98239. Vickie represents YA fiction and nonfiction and adult nonfiction.

REPRESENTS Nonfiction, novels, juvenile books. **Considers these fiction areas:** inspirational, juvenile, literary, mainstream, psychic, religious, romance, supernatural, thriller, women's, young adult.

"We work directly with our signed authors to help them polish their work and their platform for optimum marketability. Our staff is always available to answer phone calls and e-mails from our authors, and we stay with a project until we have exhausted all publishing avenues." Actively seeking "well-written nonfiction by authors with a strong platform; superbly crafted fiction with depth that touches the mind and heart and all of our listed subjects." Does not want to receive sci-fi, horror, Westerns, poetry, or screenplays.

HOW TO CONTACT E-mail query with SASE. Submit outline/proposal, synopsis, 2 sample chapters, author bio. Query a specific agent after reviewing website. Use (agentfirstname)@andreahurst.com. Accepts simultaneous submissions. Obtains most new clients through recommendations from others, solicitations, conferences.

TERMS Agent receives 15% commission on domestic sales. Agent receives 20% commission on foreign sales. Offers written contract, binding for 6-12 months; 30-day notice must be given to terminate contract. This agency charges for postage. No reading fees.

RECENT SALES *No Buddy Left Behind,* by Terri Crisp and Cindy Hurn (Lyons Press); *A Year of Miracles* Dr. Bernie Siegel (NWL); *Selling Your Crafts on Etsy* (St. Martin's); *The Underground Detective Agency* (Kensington); *Alaskan Seafood Cookbook* (Globe Pequot); *Faith, Hope and Healing,* by Dr. Bernie Siegel (Rodale); *Code Name: Polar Ice*, by Jean-Michel Cousteau and James Fraioli (Gibbs Smith); *How to Host a Killer Party*, by Penny Warner (Berkley/Penguin).

WRITERS CONFERENCES San Francisco Writers Conference; Willamette Writers Conference; PNWA; Whidbey Island Writers Conference.

TIPS "Do your homework and submit a professional package. Get to know the agent you are submitting to by researching their website or meeting them at a conference. Perfect your craft: Write well and edit ruthlessly over and over again before submitting to an agent. Be realistic: Understand that publishing is a business and be prepared to prove why your book is marketable and how you will market it on your own. Be persistent! Andrea Hurst is no longer accepting unsolicited query letters. Unless you have been referred by one of our authors, an agent or publisher, please check our website for another appropriate agent. www.andreahurst.com."

INTERNATIONAL TRANSACTIONS, INC.

P.O. Box 97, Gila, NM 88038-0097. (845)373-9696. **Fax:** (480)393-5162. **E-mail:** submissions@intltrans.com; submission-fiction@intltrans.com; submission-nonfiction@intltrans.com. **Website:** www.intltrans.com. **Contact:** Peter Riva. Represents 40+ clients. 10% of clients are new/unpublished writers. Currently handles nonfiction books (60%), novels (25%), story collections (5%), juvenile books (5%), scholarly books (5%).

MEMBER AGENTS Peter Riva (nonfiction, fiction, illustrated; television and movie rights placement); Sandra Riva (fiction, juvenile, biographies); JoAnn Collins (fiction, women's fiction, medical fiction).

REPRESENTS Nonfiction books, novels, short story collections, juvenile, scholarly illustrated books, anthologies. **Considers these fiction areas:** action, adventure, crime, detective, erotica, experimental, family saga, feminist, gay, historical, humor, lesbian, literary, mainstream, mystery, police, satire, spiritual, sports, suspense, thriller, women's, young adult, chick lit.

⚬┅ "We specialize in large and small projects, helping qualified authors perfect material for publication." Actively seeking intelligent, well-written innovative material that breaks new ground. Does not want to receive material influenced by TV (too much dialogue); a rehash of previous successful novels' themes, or poorly prepared material.

HOW TO CONTACT E-query with an outline or synopsis. E-queries only! Responds in 3 weeks to queries. Responds in 5 weeks to mss. Obtains most new clients through recommendations from others, solicitations.

TERMS Agent receives 15% (25% on illustrated books) commission on domestic sales. Agent receives 20% commission on foreign sales. Offers written contract; 120-day notice must be given to terminate contract.

TIPS "'Book'—a published work of literature. That last word is the key. Not a string of words, not a book of (TV or film) 'scenes,' and never a stream of consciousness unfathomable by anyone outside of the writer's coterie. A writer should only begin to get 'interested in getting an agent' if the work is polished, literate, and ready to be presented to a publishing house. Anything less is either asking for a quick rejection or is a thinly disguised plea for creative assistance—which is often given but never fiscally sound for the agents involved. Writers, even published authors, have difficulty being objective about their own work. Friends and family are of no assistance in that process either. Writers should attempt to get their work read by the most unlikely and stern critic as part of the editing process, months before any agent is approached. In another matter: The economics of our job have changed as well. As the publishing world goes through the transition

to e-books (much as the music industry went through the change to downloadable music)—a transition we expect to see at 95% within 10 years—everyone is nervous and wants 'assured bestsellers' from which to eke out a living until they know what the new e-world will bring. This makes the sales rate and, especially, the advance royalty rates, plummet. Hence, our ability to take risks and take on new clients' work is increasingly perilous financially for us and all agents."

JABBERWOCKY LITERARY AGENCY
24-16 Queens Plaza S, Suite 505, Long Island City, NY 11101. (718)392-5985. **Website:** www.awfulagent.com. **Contact:** Joshua Bilmes. Other memberships include SFWA. Represents 40 clients. 15% of clients are new/unpublished writers. Currently handles nonfiction books (15%), novels (75%), scholarly books (5%), other (5% other).

MEMBER AGENTS Joshua Bilmes; Eddie Schneider.

REPRESENTS Novels. **Considers these fiction areas:** action, adventure, contemporary issues, crime, detective, ethnic, family saga, fantasy, gay, glitz, historical, horror, humor, lesbian, literary, mainstream, police, psychic, regional, satire, science fiction, sports, supernatural, thriller.

⚬┅ This agency represents quite a lot of genre fiction and is actively seeking to increase the amount of nonfiction projects. It does not handle children's or picture books. Book-length material only—no poetry, articles, or short fiction.

HOW TO CONTACT "We are currently open to unsolicited queries. No e-mail, phone, or fax queries, please. Query with SASE. Please check our website, as there may be times during the year when we are not accepting queries. Query letter only; no manuscript material unless requested." Accepts simultaneous submissions. Responds in 3 weeks to queries. Obtains most new clients through solicitations and recommendations by current clients.

TERMS Agent receives 15% commission on domestic sales. Agent receives 20% commission on foreign sales. Offers written contract, binding for 1 year. Charges clients for book purchases, photocopying, international book/ms mailing.

RECENT SALES Sold 30 U.S. and 100 foreign titles in the last year. *Dead in the Family*, by Charlaine Harris; *The Way of Kings*, by Brandon Sanderson; *The Desert Spear*, by Peter V. Brett; *Oath of Fealty*, by

Elizabeth Moon. Other clients include Tanya Huff, Simon Green, Jack Campbell, Kat Richardson, and Jon Sprunk.

TIPS "In approaching with a query, the most important things to us are your credits and your biographical background to the extent it's relevant to your work. I (and most agents) will ignore the adjectives you may choose to describe your own work."

J DE S ASSOCIATES, INC.

9 Shagbark Road, Wilson Point, South Norwalk, CT 06854. (203)838-7571. **Website:** www.jdesassociates .com. **Contact:** Jacques de Spoelberch. Represents 50 clients. Currently handles nonfiction books (50%), novels (50%).

○ Prior to opening his agency, Mr. de Spoelberch was an editor with Houghton Mifflin.

REPRESENTS Nonfiction books, novels. **Considers these fiction areas:** crime, detective, frontier, historical, juvenile, literary, mainstream, mystery, New Age, police, suspense, Westerns, young adult.

HOW TO CONTACT Query with SASE. "Kindly do not include sample proposals or other materials unless specifically requested to do so." Responds in 2 months to queries. Obtains most new clients through recommendations from authors and other clients.

TERMS Agent receives 15% commission on domestic sales. Agent receives 20% commission on foreign sales. Charges clients for foreign postage and photocopying.

◑ JET LITERARY ASSOCIATES

941 Calle Mejia, #507, Santa Fe, NM 87501. (505)780-0721. **E-mail:** etp@jetliterary.com. **Website:** www .jetliterary.com. **Contact:** Liz Trupin-Pulli. Represents 75 clients. 35% of clients are new/unpublished writers.

MEMBER AGENTS Liz Trupin-Pulli (adult and YA fiction/nonfiction; romance, mysteries, parenting); Jim Trupin (adult fiction/nonfiction, military history, pop culture); Jessica Trupin, associate agent based in Seattle (adult fiction and nonfiction, children's and young adult, memoir, pop culture).

REPRESENTS Nonfiction books, novels, short story collections. **Considers these fiction areas:** action, adventure, crime, detective, erotica, ethnic, gay, glitz, historical, humor, lesbian, literary, mainstream, mystery, police, romance, suspense, thriller, women's, young adult.

⚬━ "JET was founded in New York in 1975, so we bring a wealth of knowledge and contacts, as well as quite a bit of expertise to our represen-

tation of writers." Actively seeking women's fiction, mysteries, and narrative nonfiction. JET represents the full range of adult and YA fiction and nonfiction, including humor and cookbooks. Does not want to receive sci-fi, fantasy, horror, poetry, children's, or religious.

HOW TO CONTACT An e-query only is accepted. Responds in 1 week to queries. Responds in 8 weeks to mss. Obtains most new clients through recommendations from others, solicitations, conferences.

TERMS Agent receives 15% commission on domestic sales. Agent receives 10% commission on foreign sales. Offers written contract, binding for 3 years. This agency charges for reimbursement of mailing and any photocopying.

RECENT SALES Sold 22 books in 2009, including several ghostwriting contracts. *Mom-in-Chief*, by Jamie Woolf (Wiley, 2009); *Dangerous Games* by Charlotte Mede (Kensington, 2009); *So You Think You Can Spell!* by David Grambs and Ellen Levine (Perigee, 2009); *Cut, Drop & Die*, by Joanna Campbell Slan (Midnight Ink, 2009).

WRITERS CONFERENCES Women Writing the West; Southwest Writers Conference; Florida Writers Association Conference.

TIPS "Do not write cute queries—stick to a straightforward message that includes the title and what your book is about, why you are suited to write this particular book, and what you have written in the past (if anything), along with a bit of a bio."

● VIRGINIA KIDD AGENCY, INC.

538 E. Harford St., P.O. Box 278, Milford, PA 18337. (570)296-6205. **Fax:** (570)296-7266. **Website:** www .vk-agency.com. Other memberships include SFWA, SFRA. Represents 80 clients.

MEMBER AGENTS Christine Cohen.

REPRESENTS Novels. **Considers these fiction areas:** fantasy, historical, mainstream, mystery, science fiction, suspense, women's speculative.

⚬━ This agency specializes in science fiction and fantasy.

HOW TO CONTACT *This agency is not accepting queries from unpublished authors at this time.* Submit synopsis (1-3 pages), cover letter, first chapter, SASE. Snail mail queries only. Responds in 6 weeks to queries.

TERMS Agent receives 15% commission on domestic sales. Agent receives 20-25% commission on foreign sales. Agent receives 20% commission on film sales.

Offers written contract; 2-month notice must be given to terminate contract. Charges clients occasionally for extraordinary expenses.

RECENT SALES *Sagramanda*, by Alan Dean Foster (Pyr); *Incredible Good Fortune*, by Ursula K. Le Guin (Shambhala); *The Wizard and Soldier of Sidon*, by Gene Wolfe (Tor); *Voices and Powers*, by Ursula K. Le Guin (Harcourt); *Galileo's Children*, by Gardner Dozois (Pyr); *The Light Years Beneath My Feet* and *Running From the Deity*, by Alan Dean Foster (Del Ray); *Chasing Fire*, by Michelle Welch. Other clients include Eleanor Arnason, Ted Chiang, Jack Skillingstead, Daryl Gregory, Patricia Briggs, and the estates for James Tiptree Jr., Murray Leinster, E.E. "Doc" Smith, R.A. Lafferty.

TIPS "If you have a completed novel that is of extraordinary quality, please send us a query."

HARVEY KLINGER, INC.

300 W. 55th St., Suite 11V, New York, NY 10019. (212)581-7068. **E-mail:** queries@harveyklinger.com. **Website:** www.harveyklinger.com. **Contact:** Harvey Klinger. Member of AAR. Represents 100 clients. 25% of clients are new/unpublished writers. Currently handles nonfiction books (50%), novels (50%).

MEMBER AGENTS David Dunton (popular culture, music-related books, literary fiction, young adult, fiction, and memoirs); Sara Crowe (children's and young adult, adult fiction and nonfiction, foreign rights sales); Andrea Somberg (literary fiction, commercial fiction, romance, sci-fi/fantasy, mysteries/thrillers, young adult, middle grade, quality narrative nonfiction, popular culture, how-to, self-help, humor, interior design, cookbooks, health/fitness).

REPRESENTS Nonfiction books, novels. **Considers these fiction areas:** action, adventure, crime, detective, family saga, glitz, literary, mainstream, mystery, police, suspense, thriller.

This agency specializes in big, mainstream, contemporary fiction and nonfiction.

HOW TO CONTACT Use online e-mail submission form or query with SASE. No phone or fax queries. Don't send unsolicited manuscripts or e-mail attachments. Responds in 2 months to queries and mss. Obtains most new clients through recommendations from others.

TERMS Agent receives 15% commission on domestic sales. Agent receives 25% commission on foreign sales. Offers written contract. Charges for photocopying mss and overseas postage for mss.

RECENT SALES *Woman of a Thousand Secrets*, by Barbara Wood; *I Am Not a Serial Killer*, by Dan Wells; untitled memoir, by Bob Mould; *Children of the Mist*; by Paula Quinn; *Tutored*, by Allison Whittenberg; *Will You Take Me As I Am*, by Michelle Mercer. Other clients include: George Taber, Terry Kay, Scott Mebus, Jacqueline Kolosov, Jonathan Maberry, Tara Altebrando, Alex McAuley, Eva Nagorski, Greg Kot, Justine Musk, Alex McAuley, Nick Tasler, Ashley Kahn, Barbara De Angelis.

KRAAS LITERARY AGENCY

E-mail: irenekraas@sbcglobal.net. **Website:** www.kraasliteraryagency.com. **Contact:** Irene Kraas. Represents 35 clients. 75% of clients are new/unpublished writers. Currently handles novels 100%.

MEMBER AGENTS Irene Kraas, principal.

REPRESENTS Novels. **Considers these fiction areas:** literary, thriller, young adult.

This agency is interested in working with published writers, but that does not mean self-published writers. "The agency is ONLY accepting new manuscripts in the genre of adult thrillers and mysteries. Submissions should be the first ten pages of a completed manuscript embedded in an e-mail. I do not open attachments or go to websites." Does not want to receive short stories, plays, or poetry. This agency no longer represents adult fantasy or science fiction.

HOW TO CONTACT Query and e-mail the first 10 pages of a completed ms. Requires exclusive read on mss. Attachments aren't accepted. Accepts simultaneous submissions.

TERMS Offers written contract.

TIPS "I am interested in material—in any genre—that is truly, truly unique."

EDITE KROLL LITERARY AGENCY, INC.

20 Cross St., Saco, ME 04072. (207)283-8797. **Fax:** (207)283-8799. **E-mail:** ekroll@maine.rr.com. **Contact:** Edite Kroll. Represents 45 clients. 20% of clients are new/unpublished writers. Currently handles nonfiction books (40%), novels (5%), juvenile books (40%), scholarly books (5%), other.

Prior to opening her agency, Ms. Kroll served as a book editor and translator.

REPRESENTS Nonfiction books, novels (very selective), juvenile, scholarly. **Considers these fiction**

areas: juvenile, literary, picture books, young adult, middle grade, adult.

🗝 "We represent writers and writer-artists of both adult and children's books. We have a special focus on international feminist writers, women writers and artists who write their own books (including children's and humor books)." Does not want to receive genre (mysteries, thrillers, diet, cookery, etc.), photography books, coffee table books, romance, or commercial fiction.

HOW TO CONTACT Query with SASE. Submit outline/proposal, synopsis, 1-2 sample chapters, author bio, entire ms if sending picture book. No phone queries. Responds in 2-4 weeks to queries. Responds in 4-8 weeks to mss. Obtains most new clients through recommendations from others.

TERMS Agent receives 15% commission on domestic sales. Agent receives 20% commission on foreign sales. Offers written contract; 30-day notice must be given to terminate contract. Charges clients for photocopying and legal fees with prior approval from writer.

RECENT SALES Sold 12 domestic/30 foreign titles in the last year. This agency prefers not to share information on specific sales. Clients include Shel Silverstein estate, Suzy Becker, Geoffrey Hayes, Henrik Drescher, Charlotte Kasl, Gloria Skurzynski, Fatema Mernissa.

TIPS "Please do your research so you won't send me books/proposals I specifically excluded."

○ KT LITERARY, LLC

9249 S. Broadway, #200-543, Highlands Ranch, CO 80129. (720)344-4728. **Fax:** (720)344-4728. **E-mail:** contact@ktliterary.com. **Website:** http://ktliterary.com. **Contact:** Kate Schafer Testerman. Member of AAR. Other memberships include SCBWI. Represents 20 clients. 60% of clients are new/unpublished writers. Currently handles nonfiction books (5%), novels (5%), juvenile books (90%).

◯ Prior to her current position, Ms. Schafer was an agent with Janklow & Nesbit.

REPRESENTS Nonfiction books, novels, juvenile books. **Considers these fiction areas:** action, adventure, fantasy, historical, juvenile, romance, science fiction, women's, young adult.

🗝 "I'm bringing my years of experience in the New York publishing scene, as well as my lifelong love of reading, to a vibrant area for writers, proving that great work can be found, and sold, from anywhere. Actively seeking brilliant, funny, original middle-grade and young adult fiction, both literary and commercial; witty women's fiction (chick lit); and pop culture, narrative nonfiction. Quirky is good." Does not want picture books, serious nonfiction, and adult literary fiction.

HOW TO CONTACT E-mail queries only. Keep an eye on the KT Literary blog for updates. Responds in 2 weeks to queries. Responds in 2 months to mss. Obtains most new clients through recommendations from others, solicitations, conferences.

TERMS Agent receives 15% commission on domestic sales. Agent receives 20% commission on foreign sales. Offers written contract; 30-day notice must be given to terminate contract.

WRITERS CONFERENCES Various SCBWI conferences, BookExpo.

TIPS "If we like your query, we'll ask for (more). Continuing advice is offered regularly on my blog 'Ask Daphne,' which can be accessed from my website."

● THE LA LITERARY AGENCY

P.O. Box 46370, Los Angeles, CA 90046. (323)654-5288. **E-mail:** ann@laliteraryagency.com; mail@laliteraryagency.com. **Website:** www.laliteraryagency.com. **Contact:** Ann Cashman.

◯ Prior to becoming an agent, Mr. Lasher worked in publishing in New York and Los Angeles.

MEMBER AGENTS Ann Cashman, Eric Lasher, Maureen Lasher.

REPRESENTS Nonfiction books, novels. **Considers these fiction areas:** action, adventure, crime, detective, family saga, feminist, historical, literary, mainstream, police, sports, thriller.

HOW TO CONTACT Prefers submissions by mail, but welcomes e-mail submissions as well. Nonfiction: query letter and book proposal; fiction: query letter and first 50 (double-spaced) pages. Query with outline, 1 sample chapter.

RECENT SALES *Full Bloom: The Art and Life of Georgia O'Keeffe*, by Hunter Druhojowska-Philp (Norton); *And the Walls Came Tumbling Down*, by H. Caldwell (Scribner); *Italian Slow & Savory*, by Joyce Goldstein (Chronicle); *A Field Guide to Chocolate Chip Cookies*, by Dede Wilson (Harvard Common Press); *Teen Knitting Club* (Artisan); *The Framingham Heart Study*, by Dr. Daniel Levy (Knopf).

PETER LAMPACK AGENCY, INC.

The Empire State Building, 350 Fifth Ave., Suite 5300, New York, NY 10118. (212)687-9106. **Fax:** (212)687-9109. **E-mail:** alampack@verizon.net. **E-mail:** submissions-andrew@peterlampackagency.com. **Website:** www.peterlampackagency.com. **Contact:** Andrew Lampack. Represents 50 clients. 10% of clients are new/unpublished writers. Currently handles nonfiction books (20%), novels (80%).

MEMBER AGENTS Peter Lampack (president); Rema Delanyan (foreign rights); Andrew Lampack (new writers).

REPRESENTS Nonfiction books, novels. **Considers these fiction areas:** adventure, crime, detective, family saga, literary, mainstream, mystery, police, suspense, thriller contemporary relationships.

8—¬ "This agency specializes in commercial fiction, and in nonfiction by recognized experts." Actively seeking literary and commercial fiction, thrillers, mysteries, suspense, and psychological thrillers. Does not want to receive horror, romance, science fiction, Westerns, historical literary fiction, or academic material.

HOW TO CONTACT Query via e-mail. *No unsolicited mss.* Responds within 2 months to queries. Obtains most new clients through referrals made by clients.

TERMS Agent receives 15% commission on domestic sales. Agent receives 20% commission on foreign sales.

RECENT SALES *Spartan Gold,* by Clive Cussler with Grant Blackwood; *The Wrecker,* by Clive Cussler with Justin Scott; *Medusa,* by Clive Cussler and Paul Kemprecos; *Silent Sea* by Clive Cussler with Jack Dubrul; *Summertime,* by J.M. Coetzee; *Dreaming in French,* by Megan McAndrew; *Time Pirate,* by Ted Bell.

WRITERS CONFERENCES BookExpo America; Mystery Writers of America.

TIPS "Submit only your best work for consideration. Have a very specific agenda of goals you wish your prospective agent to accomplish for you. Provide the agent with a comprehensive statement of your credentials—educational and professional accomplishments."

LAURA LANGLIE, LITERARY AGENT

63 Wyckoff St., Brooklyn, NY 11201. (718)855-8102. **Fax:** (718)855-4450. **E-mail:** laura@lauralanglie.com. **Contact:** Laura Langlie. Represents 25 clients. 50% of clients are new/unpublished writers. Currently handles nonfiction books (15%), novels (58%), story collections (2%), juvenile books (25%).

Prior to opening her agency, Ms. Langlie worked in publishing for 7 years and as an agent at Kidde, Hoyt & Picard for 6 years.

REPRESENTS Nonfiction books, novels, short story collections, novellas, juvenile. **Considers these fiction areas:** crime, detective, ethnic, feminist, historical, humor, juvenile, literary, mainstream, mystery, police, suspense, thriller, young adult mainstream.

8—¬ "I'm very involved with and committed to my clients. Most of my clients come to me via recommendations from other agents, clients, and editors. I've met very few at conferences. I've often sought out writers for projects, and I still find new clients via the traditional query letter." Does not want to receive how-to, children's picture books, hardcore science fiction, poetry, men's adventure, or erotica.

HOW TO CONTACT Query with SASE. Accepts queries via fax. Accepts simultaneous submissions. Responds in 1 week to queries. Responds in 1 month to mss. Obtains most new clients through recommendations, submissions.

TERMS Agent receives 15% commission on domestic sales. Agent receives 20% commission on foreign and dramatic sales. No written contract.

RECENT SALES Sold 15 titles in the last year. *As Close As Hands and Feet,* by Emily Arsenault (William Morrow); *The Aviator's Wife,* by Melanie Benjamin (Delacorte Press); *Free Verse* and *Ashes to Asheville,* by Sarah Dooley (G.P. Putnam's Son's/Penguin Young Reader's Group); *Miss Dimple Suspects,* by Mignon F. Ballard (St. Martin's Press); *Awaken,* by Meg Cabot (Scholastic, Inc.); *Size 12 and Ready to Rock,* by Meg Cabot (William Morrow); *Adaptation* and *Inheritance,* by Malinda Lo (Little, Brown & Co Books for Young Readers); *One Tough Chick,* by Leslie Margolis (Bloomsbury); *The Elite Gymnasts,* by Dominique Moceanu and Alicia Thompson (Disney/Hyperion); *The Lighthouse Road,* by Peter Geye (Unbridled Books); *The Nazi and the Psychiatrist,* by Jack El-Hai (Public Affairs Books); *The Last Animal,* by Abby Geni (Counterpoint Press); *Something Resembling Love,* by Mary Hogan (William Morrow); *Little Wolves,* by Thomas Maltman (Soho Press).

TIPS "Be complete, forthright, and clear in your communications. Do your research as to what a particular agent represents."

LANGTONS INTERNATIONAL AGENCY

124 West 60th St., #42M, New York, NY 10023. (646)344-1801. **E-mail:** langton@langtonsinterna tional@com; llangton@langtonsinternational.com. **Website:** www.langtonsinternational.com. **Contact:** Linda Langton, president.

○ Prior to becoming an agent, Ms. Langton was a co-founding director and publisher of the international publishing company, The Ink Group.

REPRESENTS Nonfiction books and literary fiction. **Considers these fiction areas:** literary, political thrillers, young adult, and middle-grade books.

⌐ "Langtons International Agency is a multimedia literary and licensing agency specializing in nonfiction, inspirational, thrillers, and children's middle-grade and young adult books, as well as the the visual world of photography."

HOW TO CONTACT Please submit all queries via hard copy to the address above or e-mail outline/proposal, synopsis, publishing history, author bio. Only published authors should query this agency. Accepts simultaneous submissions.

RECENT SALES *Talking with Jean-Paul Sartre: Conversations and Debates*, by Professor John Gerassi (Yale University Press); *The Obama Presidency and the Politics of Change*, by Professor Stanley Renshon (Routledge Press); *I Would See a Girl Walking*, by Diana Montane and Kathy Kelly (Berkley Books); *Begin 1913-1992*, by Avi Shilon (Yale University Press); *This Borrowed Earth*, by Robert Emmet Hernan (Palgrave McMillan); *The Perfect Square*, by Nancy Heinzen (Temple Uni Press); *The Honey Trail* by Grace Pundyk (St. Martin's Press); *Dogs of Central Park* by Fran Reisner (Rizzoli/Universe Publishing).

① MICHAEL LARSEN/ELIZABETH POMADA, LITERARY AGENTS

1029 Jones St., San Francisco, CA 94109. (415)673-0939. **E-mail:** larsenpoma@aol.com. **Website:** www .larsenpomada.com. **Contact:** Mike Larsen, Elizabeth Pomada. Member of AAR. Other memberships include Authors Guild, ASJA, PEN, WNBA, California Writers Club, National Speakers Association. Represents 100 clients. 40-45% of clients are new/unpublished writers. Currently handles nonfiction books (70%), novels (30%).

○ Prior to opening their agency, Mr. Larsen and Ms. Pomada were promotion executives for major publishing houses. Mr. Larsen worked for Morrow, Bantam, and Pyramid (now part of Berkley); Ms. Pomada worked at Holt, David McKay, and Dial Press. Mr. Larsen is the author of the 4th edition of *How to Write a Book Proposal* and *How to Get a Literary Agent* as well as the co-author of *Guerilla Marketing for Writers: 100 Weapons for Selling Your Work*, which was republished in September 2009.

MEMBER AGENTS Michael Larsen (nonfiction); Elizabeth Pomada (fiction and narrative nonfiction).

REPRESENTS Considers these fiction areas: action, adventure, contemporary issues, crime, detective, ethnic, experimental, family saga, feminist, gay, glitz, historical, humor, inspirational, lesbian, literary, mainstream, mystery, police, religious, romance, satire, suspense, chick lit.

⌐ We have diverse tastes. We look for fresh voices and new ideas. We handle literary, commercial and genre fiction, and the full range of nonfiction books. Actively seeking commercial, genre, and literary fiction. Does not want to receive children's books, plays, short stories, screenplays, pornography, poetry, or stories of abuse.

HOW TO CONTACT Query with SASE. Elizabeth Pomada handles literary and commercial fiction, romance, thrillers, mysteries, narrative nonfiction and mainstream women's fiction. If you have completed a novel, please e-mail the first 10 pages and 2-page synopsis to larsenpoma@aol.com. Use 14-point typeface, double-spaced, as an e-mail letter with no attachments. For nonfiction, please read Michael's *How to Write a Book Proposal* book—available through your library or bookstore and through our website—so you will know exactly what editors need. Then, before you start writing, send him the title, subtitle, and your promotion plan via conventional mail (with SASE) or e-mail. If sent as e-mail, please include the information in the body of your e-mail with NO attachments. Please allow up to 2 weeks for a response. See each agent's page on the website for contact and submission information. Responds in 8 weeks to pages or submissions.

TERMS Agent receives 15% commission on domestic sales. Agent receives 20% (30% for Asia) commission on foreign sales. May charge for printing, postage for multiple submissions, foreign mail, foreign phone calls, galleys, books, legal fees.

RECENT SALES Sold at least 15 titles in the last year. *Secrets of the Tudor Court*, by D. Bogden (Kensington); *Zen & the Art of Horse Training*, by Allan Hamilton, MD (Storey Pub.); *The Solemn Lantern Maker* by Merlinda Bobis (Delta); *Bite Marks*, the fifth book in an urban fantasy series by J.D. Rardin (Orbit/Grand Central); *The Iron King*, by Julie Karawa (Harlequin Teen).

WRITERS CONFERENCES This agency organizes the annual San Francisco Writers Conference (www.sfwriters.org).

TIPS "We love helping writers get the rewards and recognition they deserve. If you can write books that meet the needs of the marketplace and you can promote your books, now is the best time ever to be a writer. We must find new writers to make a living, so we are very eager to hear from new writers whose work will interest large houses, and nonfiction writers who can promote their books. For a list of recent sales, helpful info, and three ways to make yourself irresistible to any publisher, please visit our website."

⊙ THE STEVE LAUBE AGENCY

5025 N. Central Ave., #635, Phoenix, AZ 85012. (602)336-8910. **E-mail:** krichards@stevelaube.com. **Website:** www.stevelaube.com. **Contact:** Steve Laube. Other memberships include CBA. Represents 60+ clients. 5% of clients are new/unpublished writers. Currently handles nonfiction books (48%), novels (48%), novella (2%), scholarly books (2%).

🖉 Prior to becoming an agent, Mr. Laube worked 11 years as a Christian bookseller and 11 years as editorial director of nonfiction with Bethany House Publishers.

REPRESENTS Nonfiction books, novels. **Considers these fiction areas:** religious.

🖙 Primarily serves the Christian market (CBA). Actively seeking Christian fiction and religious nonfiction. Does not want to receive children's picture books, poetry, or cookbooks.

HOW TO CONTACT Submit proposal package, outline, 3 sample chapters, SASE. For e-mail submissions, attach as Word doc or PDF. Consult website for guidelines. Accepts simultaneous submissions. Responds in 6-8 weeks to queries. Obtains most new clients through recommendations from others, solicitations, conferences.

TERMS Agent receives 15% commission on domestic sales. Agent receives 20% commission on foreign sales.

Offers written contract; 30-day notice must be given to terminate contract.

RECENT SALES Sold 80 titles in the last year. Clients include Deborah Raney, Allison Bottke, H. Norman Wright, Ellie Kay, Jack Cavanaugh, Karen Ball, Tracey Bateman, Susan May Warren, Lisa Bergren, John Rosemond, Cindy Woodsmall, Karol Ladd, Judith Pella, Michael Phillips, Margaret Daley, William Lane Craig, Tosca Lee, Ginny Aiken.

WRITERS CONFERENCES Mount Hermon Christian Writers Conference; American Christian Fiction Writers Conference.

⏻ ROBERT LECKER AGENCY

4055 Melrose Ave., Montreal QC H4A 2S5 Canada. (514)830-4818. **Fax:** (514)483-1644. **E-mail:** leckerlink@aol.com. **Website:** www.leckeragency.com. **Contact:** Robert Lecker. Represents 20 clients. 20% of clients are new/unpublished writers. Currently handles nonfiction books (80%), novels (10%), scholarly books (10%).

🖉 Prior to becoming an agent, Mr. Lecker was the co-founder and publisher of ECW Press and professor of English literature at McGill University. He has 30 years of experience in book and magazine publishing.

MEMBER AGENTS Robert Lecker (popular culture, music); Mary Williams (travel, food, popular science).

REPRESENTS Nonfiction books, novels, scholarly syndicated material. **Considers these fiction areas:** action, adventure, crime, detective, erotica, literary, mainstream, mystery, police, suspense, thriller.

🖙 RLA specializes in books about popular culture, popular science, music, entertainment, food, and travel. The agency responds to articulate, innovative proposals within 2 weeks. Actively seeking original book mss only after receipt of outlines and proposals.

HOW TO CONTACT Query first. Only responds to queries of interest. Discards the rest. Accepts simultaneous submissions. Responds in 2 weeks to queries. Responds in 1 month to mss. Obtains most new clients through recommendations from others, conferences, interest in website.

TERMS Agent receives 15% commission on domestic sales. Agent receives 15-20% commission on foreign sales. Offers written contract, binding for 1 year; 6-month notice must be given to terminate contract.

LEVINE GREENBERG LITERARY AGENCY, INC.

307 Seventh Ave., Suite 2407, New York, NY 10001. (212)337-0934. **Fax:** (212)337-0948. **E-mail:** submit@levinegreenberg.com. **Website:** www.levinegreenberg.com. Member of AAR. Represents 250 clients. 33% of clients are new/unpublished writers. Currently handles nonfiction books (70%), novels (30%).

○ Prior to opening his agency, Mr. Levine served as vice president of the Bank Street College of Education.

MEMBER AGENTS James Levine, Daniel Greenberg, Stephanie Kip Rostan, Lindsay Edgecombe, Danielle Svetcov, Elizabeth Fisher, Victoria Skurnick.

REPRESENTS Nonfiction books, novels. **Considers these fiction areas:** literary, mainstream, mystery, thriller, psychological, women's.

⛏ This agency specializes in business, psychology, parenting, health/medicine, narrative nonfiction, spirituality, religion, women's issues, and commercial fiction.

HOW TO CONTACT See website for full submission procedure at "How to Submit." Or use our e-mail address, if you prefer, or online submission form. Do not submit directly to agents. Prefers electronic submissions. Cannot respond to submissions by mail. Obtains most new clients through recommendations from others.

TERMS Agent receives 15% commission on domestic sales. Agent receives 20% commission on foreign sales. Offers written contract. Charges clients for out-of-pocket expenses—telephone, fax, postage, photocopying—directly connected to the project.

WRITERS CONFERENCES ASJA Writers Conference.

TIPS "We focus on editorial development, business representation, and publicity and marketing strategy."

◑ PAUL S. LEVINE LITERARY AGENCY

1054 Superba Ave., Venice, CA 90291. (310)450-6711. **Fax:** (310)450-0181. **E-mail:** paul@paulslevinelit.com. **Website:** www.paulslevinelit.com. **Contact:** Paul S. Levine. Other memberships include the State Bar of California. Represents over 100 clients. 75% of clients are new/unpublished writers. Currently handles nonfiction books (60%), novels (10%), movie scripts (10%), TV scripts (5%), juvenile books (5%).

MEMBER AGENTS Paul S. Levine (children's and young adult fiction and nonfiction, adult fiction and

nonfiction except sci-fi, fantasy, and horror); Loren R. Grossman (archaeology, art/photography/architecture, gardening, education, health, medicine, science).

REPRESENTS Nonfiction books, novels, episodic drama, movie, TV, movie scripts, feature film, TV movie of the week, sitcom, animation, documentary, miniseries syndicated material, reality show. **Considers these fiction areas:** action, adventure, comic books, confession, crime, detective, erotica, ethnic, experimental, family saga, feminist, frontier, gay, glitz, historical, humor, inspirational, lesbian, literary, mainstream, mystery, police, regional, religious, romance, satire, sports, suspense, thriller, Westerns.

⛏ Does not want to receive science fiction, fantasy, or horror.

HOW TO CONTACT Query with SASE. Accepts simultaneous submissions. Responds in 1 day to queries. Responds in 6-8 weeks to mss. Obtains most new clients through conferences, referrals, listings on various websites, and in directories.

TERMS Agent receives 15% commission on domestic sales. Offers written contract. Charges for postage and actual out-of-pocket costs only.

RECENT SALES Sold 8 books in the last year.

WRITERS CONFERENCES Willamette Writers Conference; San Francisco Writers Conference; Santa Barbara Writers Conference and many others.

TIPS "Write good, sellable books."

◐ LIPPINCOTT MASSIE MCQUILKIN

27 West 20th Street, Suite 305, New York, NY 10011. **Fax:** (212)352-2059. **E-mail:** info@lmqlit.com. **Website:** www.lmqlit.com.

MEMBER AGENTS Maria Massie (fiction, memoir, cultural criticism); Will Lippincott (politics, current affairs, history); Rob McQuilkin (fiction, history, psychology, sociology, graphic material); Jason Anthony (young adult, pop culture, memoir, true crime, and general psychology).

REPRESENTS Nonfiction books, novels, short story collections, scholarly graphic novels. **Considers these fiction areas:** action, adventure, cartoon, comic books, confession, family saga, feminist, gay, historical, humor, lesbian, literary, mainstream, regional, satire.

⛏ "LMQ focuses on bringing new voices in literary and commercial fiction to the market, as well as popularizing the ideas and arguments of scholars in the fields of history, psychology, sociology, political science, and current affairs. Actively seeking fiction writers who already have credits in magazines and quarterlies, as well as nonfiction writers who already have a media platform or some kind of a university affiliation." Does not want to receive romance, genre fiction, or children's material.

HOW TO CONTACT "We accepts electronic queries only. Only send additional materials if requested." Accepts simultaneous submissions. Responds in 1 week to queries. Responds in 1 month to mss. Obtains most new clients through recommendations from others, solicitations, conferences.

TERMS Agent receives 15% commission on domestic sales. Agent receives 20% commission on foreign sales. Offers written contract; 30-day notice must be given to terminate contract. Only charges for reasonable business expenses upon successful sale.

RECENT SALES Clients include: Peter Ho Davies, Kim Addonizio, Natasha Trethewey, Anne Carson, David Sirota, Katie Crouch, Uwen Akpan, Lydia Millet, Tom Perrotta, Jonathan Lopez, Chris Hayes, Caroline Weber.

THE LITERARY GROUP INTERNATIONAL

330 W. 38th St., Suite 408, New York, NY 10018. (646)442-5896. **E-mail:** js@theliterarygroup.com. **Website:** www.theliterarygroup.com. **Contact:** Frank Weimann. 1900 Ave. of the Stars, 25 Fl., Los Angeles, CA 90067; Tel: (310)282-8961; **Fax:** (310) 282-8903 65% of clients are new/unpublished writers. Currently handles nonfiction books (50%), (50% fiction).

MEMBER AGENTS Frank Weimann.

REPRESENTS Nonfiction books, novels, graphic novels. **Considers these fiction areas:** adventure, contemporary issues, detective, ethnic, experimental, family saga, fantasy, feminist, historical, horror, humor, literary, multicultural, mystery, psychic, romance, sports, thriller, young adult regional, graphic novels.

This agency specializes in nonfiction (memoir, military, history, biography, sports, how-to).

HOW TO CONTACT Query with SASE. Prefers to read materials exclusively. Only responds if interested. Obtains most new clients through referrals, writers conferences, query letters.

TERMS Agent receives 15% commission on domestic sales. Agent receives 20% commission on foreign sales.

Offers written contract; 30-day notice must be given to terminate contract.

RECENT SALES *One From the Hart*, by Stefanie Powers with Richard Buskin (Pocket Books); *Sacred Trust, Deadly Betrayal*, by Keith Anderson (Berkley); *Gotti Confidential*, by Victoria Gotti (Pocket Books); Anna Sui's illustrated memoir (Chronicle Books); *Mania*, by Craig Larsen (Kensington); *Everything Explained through Flowcharts*, by Doogie Horner (HarperCollins); *Bitch*, by Lisa Taddeo (TOR); film rights for *Falling Out of Fashion*, by Karen Yampolsky to Hilary Swank and Molly Smith for 2S Films.

WRITERS CONFERENCES San Diego State University Writers Conference; Aloha Writers Conference; Agents and Editors Conference; NAHJ Convention in Puerto Rico, others.

LITERARY MANAGEMENT GROUP, INC.

P.O. Box 40965, Nashville, TN 37204. (615)812-4445. **E-mail:** brucebarbour@literarymanagementgroup.com; brb@brucebarbour.com. **Website:** http://literarymanagementgroup.com; www.brucebarbour.com. **Contact:** Bruce Barbour.

Prior to becoming an agent, Mr. Barbour held executive positions at several publishing houses, including Revell, Barbour Books, Thomas Nelson, and Random House.

REPRESENTS Nonfiction books, novels.

"Although we specialize in the area of Christian publishing from an Evangelical perspective, we have editorial contacts and experience in general interest books as well." Does not want to receive gift books, poetry, children's books, short stories, or juvenile/young adult fiction. No unsolicited mss or proposals from unpublished authors.

HOW TO CONTACT Query with SASE. E-mail proposal as an attachment. Consult website for each agent's submission guidelines.

TERMS Agent receives 15% commission on domestic sales.

LOWENSTEIN ASSOCIATES INC.

121 W. 27th St., Suite 501, New York, NY 10001. (212)206-1630. **Fax:** (212)727-0280. **E-mail:** assistant@bookhaven.com. **Website:** www.lowensteinassociates.com. **Contact:** Barbara Lowenstein. Member of AAR. Represents 150 clients. 20% of clients are

new/unpublished writers. Currently handles nonfiction books (60%), novels (40%).

MEMBER AGENTS Barbara Lowenstein, president (nonfiction interests include narrative nonfiction, health, money, finance, travel, multicultural, popular culture, and memoir; fiction interests include literary fiction and women's fiction); Kathleen Ortiz, associate agent and foreign rights manager at Lowenstein Associates. She is seeking children's books (chapter, middle grade, and young adult) and young adult nonfiction.

REPRESENTS Nonfiction books, novels. **Considers these fiction areas:** crime, detective, erotica, ethnic, fantasy, feminist, historical, literary, mainstream, mystery, police, romance, suspense, thriller, young adult.

⌐☞ "This agency specializes in health, business, creative nonfiction, literary fiction, and commercial fiction—especially suspense, crime and women's issues. We are a full-service agency, handling domestic and foreign rights, film rights and audio rights to all of our books." Barbara Lowenstein is currently looking for writers who have a platform and are leading experts in their field, including business, women's issues, psychology, health, science, and social issues, and is particularly interested in strong new voices in fiction and narrative nonfiction.

HOW TO CONTACT Please send us a one-page query letter, along with the first 10 pages pasted in the body of the message (if fiction; for nonfiction, please send only a query letter), by e-mail. Please put the word *QUERY* and the title of your project in the subject field of your e-mail and address it to the agent of your choice. Please do not send an attachment. We reply to all queries and generally send a response within 2-4 weeks. By mail: For Fiction: Mail a query letter, short synopsis, first chapter and a SASE. For Nonfiction: Mail a query letter, proposal, if available, or else a project overview and a SASE. Responds in 4 weeks to queries. Obtains most new clients through recommendations from others, solicitations, conferences.

TERMS Agent receives 15% commission on domestic sales. Agent receives 20% commission on foreign sales. Offers written contract. Charges for large photocopy batches, messenger service, international postage.

WRITERS CONFERENCES Malice Domestic

TIPS "Know the genre you are working in and read! Also, please see our website for details on which agent to query for your project."

◑ LYONS LITERARY, LLC

In Association with Curtis Brown, Ltd., 10 Astor Place, 3rd Floor, New York, NY 10003. (212)255-5472. **Fax:** (212)851-8405. **E-mail:** info@lyonsliterary.com. **Website:** www.lyonsliterary.com. **Contact:** Jonathan Lyons. Member of AAR. Other memberships include the Author's Guild, American Bar Association, New York State Bar Associaton, New York State Intellectual Property Law Section. Represents 37 clients. 15% of clients are new/unpublished writers. Currently handles nonfiction books (60%), novels (40%).

REPRESENTS Nonfiction books, novels. **Considers these fiction areas:** contemporary issues, crime, detective, fantasy, feminist, gay, historical, humor, lesbian, literary, mainstream, mystery, police, psychic, regional, satire, science fiction, sports, supernatural, suspense, thriller, women's, chick lit.

⌐☞ "With my legal expertise and experience selling domestic and foreign language book rights, paperback reprint rights, audio rights, film/TV rights and permissions, I am able to provide substantive and personal guidance to my clients in all areas relating to their projects. In addition, with the advent of new publishing technology, Lyons Literary, LLC, is situated to address the changing nature of the industry while concurrently handling authors' more traditional needs."

HOW TO CONTACT Only accepts queries through online submission form. Accepts simultaneous submissions. Responds in 8 weeks to queries. Responds in 12 weeks to mss. Obtains most new clients through recommendations from others.

TERMS Agent receives 15% commission on domestic sales. Agent receives 20% commission on foreign sales. Offers written contract.

WRITERS CONFERENCES Agents and Editors Conference.

TIPS "Please submit electronic queries through our website submission form."

● DONALD MAASS LITERARY AGENCY

121 W. 27th St., Suite 801, New York, NY 10001. (212)727-8383. **E-mail:** info@maassagency.com. **Website:** www.maassagency.com. Member of AAR. Oth-

er memberships include SFWA, MWA, RWA. Represents more than 100 clients. 5% of clients are new/unpublished writers. Currently handles novels (100%).

○ Prior to opening his agency, Mr. Maass served as an editor at Dell Publishing (New York) and as a reader at Gollancz (London). He also served as the president of AAR.

MEMBER AGENTS Donald Maass (mainstream, literary, mystery/suspense, science fiction, romance); Jennifer Jackson (commercial fiction, romance, science fiction, fantasy, mystery/suspense); Cameron McClure (literary, mystery/suspense, urban, fantasy, narrative nonfiction and projects with multicultural, international, and environmental themes, gay/lesbian); Stacia Decker (fiction, memoir, narrative nonfiction, pop-culture [cooking, fashion, style, music, art], smart humor, upscale erotica/erotic memoir and multicultural fiction/nonfiction); Amy Boggs (fantasy and science fiction, especially urban fantasy, paranormal romance, steampunk, YA/children's, and alternate history. historical fiction, multicultural fiction, Westerns).

REPRESENTS Novels. **Considers these fiction areas:** crime, detective, fantasy, historical, horror, literary, mainstream, mystery, police, psychic, science fiction, supernatural, suspense, thriller, women's romance (historical, paranormal, and time travel).

⚬━ This agency specializes in commercial fiction, especially science fiction, fantasy, mystery, and suspense. Actively seeking to expand in literary fiction and women's fiction. We are fiction specialists. All genres are welcome. Does not want to receive nonfiction, picture books, prescriptive nonfiction, or poetry.

HOW TO CONTACT Query with SASE. Returns material only with SASE. Accepts simultaneous submissions. Responds in 2 weeks to queries. Responds in 3 months to mss.

TERMS Agent receives 15% commission on domestic sales. Agent receives 20% commission on foreign sales.

RECENT SALES *Codex Alera 5: Princep's Fury*, by Jim Butcher (Ace); *Fonseca 6: Bright Futures*, by Stuart Kaimsky (Forge): *Fathom*, by Cherie Priest (Tor); *Gospel Grrls 3: Be Strong and Curvaceous*, by Shelly Adina (Faith Words); *Ariane 1: Peacekeeper,* by Laura Reeve (Roc); *Execution Dock*, by Anne Perry (Random House).

WRITERS CONFERENCES Donald Maass: World Science Fiction Convention; Frankfurt Book Fair;

Pacific Northwest Writers Conference; Bouchercon. Jennifer Jackson: World Science Fiction Convention; RWA National Conference.

TIPS "We are fiction specialists, also noted for our innovative approach to career planning. Few new clients are accepted, but interested authors should query with a SASE. Works with subagents in all principle foreign countries and Hollywood. No prescriptive nonfiction, picture books, or poetry will be considered."

● **MACGREGOR LITERARY INC.**
2373 N.W. 185th Ave., Suite 165, Hillsboro, OR 97124. (503)277-8308. **E-mail:** submissions@macgregorliterary.com. **Website:** www.macgregorliterary.com. **Contact:** Chip MacGregor. Signatory of WGA. Represents 40 clients. 10% of clients are new/unpublished writers. Currently handles nonfiction books (40%), novels (60%).

○ Prior to his current position, Mr. MacGregor was the senior agent with Alive Communications. Most recently, he was associate publisher for Time-Warner Book Group's Faith Division and helped put together their Center Street imprint.

MEMBER AGENTS Chip MacGregor, Sandra Bishop, Amanda Luedeke.

REPRESENTS Nonfiction books, novels. **Considers these fiction areas:** crime, detective, historical, inspirational, mainstream, mystery, police, religious, romance, suspense, thriller, women's chick lit.

⚬━ "My specialty has been in career planning with authors—finding commercial ideas, then helping authors bring them to market, and in the midst of that, assisting the authors as they get firmly established in their writing careers. I'm probably best known for my work with Christian books over the years, but I've done a fair amount of general market projects as well." Actively seeking authors with a Christian worldview and a growing platform. Does not want to receive fantasy, sci-fi, children's books, poetry, or screenplays.

HOW TO CONTACT Query with SASE. Accepts simultaneous submissions. Responds in 3 weeks to queries. Obtains most new clients through recommendations from others. Not looking to add unpublished authors except through referrals from current clients.

TERMS Agent receives 15% commission on domestic sales. Agent receives 15% commission on foreign sales. Offers written contract; 30-day notice must be given to terminate contract. Charges for exceptional fees after receiving author's permission.

WRITERS CONFERENCES Blue Ridge Christian Writers Conference; Write to Publish.

TIPS "Seriously consider attending a good writers conference. It will give you the chance to be face-to-face with people in the industry. Also, if you're a novelist, consider joining one of the national writers organizations. The American Christian Fiction Writers (ACFW) is a wonderful group for new as well as established writers. And if you're a Christian writer of any kind, check into The Writers View, an online writing group. All of these have proven helpful to writers."

⬤ CAROL MANN AGENCY

55 Fifth Ave., New York, NY 10003. (212)206-5635. **Fax:** (212)675-4809. **E-mail:** submissions@carolmannagency.com. **Website:** www.carolmannagency.com. **Contact:** Eliza Dreier. Member of AAR. Represents roughly 200 clients. 15% of clients are new/unpublished writers. Currently handles nonfiction books (90%), novels (10%).

MEMBER AGENTS Carol Mann (health/medical, religion, spirituality, self-help, parenting, narrative nonfiction, current affairs); Laura Yorke; Gareth Esersky; Myrsini Stephanides (nonfiction areas of interest: pop culture and music, humor, narrative nonfiction and memoir, cookbooks; fiction areas of interest: offbeat literary fiction, graphic works, and edgy YA fiction). Joanne Wyckoff (nonfiction areas of interest: memoir, narrative nonfiction, personal narrative, psychology, women's issues, education, health and wellness, parenting, serious self-help, natural history); fiction.

REPRESENTS Nonfiction books, novels. **Considers these fiction areas:** commercial, literary.

⌐**➤** This agency specializes in current affairs, self-help, popular culture, psychology, parenting, and history. Does not want to receive genre fiction (romance, mystery, etc.).

HOW TO CONTACT Please see website for submission guidelines. Responds in 4 weeks to queries.

TERMS Agent receives 15% commission on domestic sales. Agent receives 20% commission on foreign sales. Offers written contract.

⬤ MANUS & ASSOCIATES LITERARY AGENCY, INC.

425 Sherman Ave., Suite 200, Palo Alto, CA 94306. (650)470-5151. **Fax:** (650)470-5159. **E-mail:**

manuslit@manuslit.com. **Website:** www.manuslit.com. **Contact:** Jillian Manus, Jandy Nelson, Penny Nelson. Member of AAR. Represents 75 clients. 30% of clients are new/unpublished writers. Currently handles nonfiction books (70%), novels (30%).

◯ Prior to becoming an agent, Ms. Manus was associate publisher of two national magazines and director of development at Warner Bros. and Universal Studios; she has been a literary agent for 20 years.

MEMBER AGENTS Jandy Nelson, jandy@manuslit.com (self-help, health, memoirs, narrative nonfiction, women's fiction, literary fiction, multicultural fiction, thrillers). Nelson is currently on sabbatical and not taking on new clients. Jillian Manus, jillian@manuslit.com (political, memoirs, self-help, history, sports, women's issues, Latin fiction and nonfiction, thrillers); Penny Nelson, penny@manuslit.com (memoirs, self-help, sports, nonfiction); Dena Fischer (literary fiction, mainstream/commercial fiction, chick lit, women's fiction, historical fiction, ethnic/cultural fiction, narrative nonfiction, parenting, relationships, pop culture, health, sociology, psychology); Janet Wilkens Manus (narrative fact-based crime books, religion, pop psychology, inspiration, memoirs, cookbooks); Stephanie Lee (not currently taking on new clients).

REPRESENTS Nonfiction books, novels. **Considers these fiction areas:** literary, mainstream, multicultural, mystery, suspense, thriller, women's quirky/edgy fiction.

⌐**➤** "Our agency is unique in the way that we not only sell the material, but we edit, develop concepts, and participate in the marketing effort. We specialize in large conceptual fiction and nonfiction, and always value a project that can be sold in the TV/feature film market." Actively seeking high-concept thrillers, commercial literary fiction, women's fiction, celebrity biographies, memoirs, multicultural fiction, popular health, women's empowerment and mysteries. No horror, romance, science fiction, fantasy, Western, young adult, children's, poetry, cookbooks, or magazine articles.

HOW TO CONTACT Consult website for specific fiction and nonfiction guidelines. Accepts simultaneous submissions. Responds in 3 months to queries. Responds in 3 months to mss. Obtains most new clients through recommendations from others, solicitations, conferences.

TERMS Agent receives 15% commission on domestic sales. Agent receives 20-25% commission on foreign sales. Offers written contract, binding for 2 years; 60-day notice must be given to terminate contract. Charges for photocopying and postage/UPS.

RECENT SALES *Nothing Down for the 2000s* and *Multiple Streams of Income for the 2000s*, by Robert Allen; *Missed Fortune 101*, by Doug Andrew; *Cracking the Millionaire Code*, by Mark Victor Hansen and Robert Allen; *Stress Free for Good*, by Dr. Fred Luskin and Dr. Ken Pelletier; *The Mercy of Thin Air*, by Ronlyn Domangue; *The Fine Art of Small Talk*, by Debra Fine; *Bone Men of Bonares*, by Terry Tamoff.

WRITERS CONFERENCES Aloha Writers Conference; San Diego State University Writers Conference; Willamette Writers Conference; BookExpo America; MEGA Book Marketing University.

TIPS "Research agents using a variety of sources."

THE EVAN MARSHALL AGENCY

6 Tristam Place, Pine Brook, NJ 07058-9445. (973)882-1122. **Fax:** (973)882-3099. **E-mail:** evanmarshall@ thenovelist.com. **Contact:** Evan Marshall. Member of AAR. Other memberships include MWA, Sisters in Crime. Currently handles novels (100%).

REPRESENTS Novels. **Considers these fiction areas:** action, adventure, erotica, ethnic, frontier, historical, horror, humor, inspirational, literary, mainstream, mystery, religious, satire, science fiction, suspense, Western romance (contemporary, gothic, historical, regency).

HOW TO CONTACT "Do not query. Currently accepting clients only by referral from editors and our own clients." Responds in 1 week to queries. Responds in 3 months to mss. Obtains most new clients through recommendations from others.

TERMS Agent receives 15% commission on domestic sales. Agent receives 20% commission on foreign sales. Offers written contract.

RECENT SALES *Watch Me Die*, by Erica Spindler (St. Martin's Press); *The First Day of the Rest of My Life*, by Cathy Lamb (Kensington); *Highland Protector*, by Hannah Howell (Zebra); *Devoured by Darkness*, by Alexandra Ivy (Kensington).

THE MARTELL AGENCY

1350 Avenue of the Americas, Suite 1205, New York, NY 10019. **Fax:** (212)317-2676. **E-mail:** afmartell@aol

.com. **E-mail:** submissions@themartellagency.com. **Website:** www.themartellagency.com. **Contact:** Alice Martell.

REPRESENTS Nonfiction, novels. **Considers these fiction areas:** commercial, mystery, suspense, thriller.

HOW TO CONTACT Query with SASE. Submit sample chapters. "Please send a query first to Alice Martell, by e-mail or mail." Consult website for complete submission guidelines.

RECENT SALES *Peddling Peril: The Secret Nuclear Arms Trade* by David Albright and Joel Wit (Five Press); *America's Women: Four Hundred Years of Dolls, Drudges, Helpmates, and Heroines*, by Gail Collins (William Morrow). Other clients include Serena Bass, Janice Erlbaum, David Cay Johnston, Mark Derr, Barbara Rolls, PhD.

MARGRET MCBRIDE LITERARY AGENCY

P.O. Box 9128, La Jolla, CA 92038. (858)454-1550. **Fax:** (858)454-2156. **E-mail:** staff@mcbridelit.com. **Website:** www.mcbrideliterary.com. **Contact:** Michael Daley, submissions manager. Member of AAR. Other memberships include Authors Guild.

Prior to opening her agency, Ms. McBride worked at Random House, Ballantine Books, and Warner Books.

REPRESENTS Nonfiction books, novels. **Considers these fiction areas:** action, adventure, crime, detective, historical, humor, literary, mainstream, mystery, police, satire, suspense, thriller.

This agency specializes in mainstream fiction and nonfiction. PLEASE DO NOT SEND: screenplays, romance, poetry, or children's.

HOW TO CONTACT The agency is only accepting new clients by referral at this time. Query with synopsis, bio, SASE. Do not fax queries. Accepts simultaneous submissions. Responds in 4-6 weeks to queries. Responds in 6-8 weeks to mss.

TERMS Agent receives 15% commission on domestic sales. Agent receives 25% commission on foreign sales. Charges for overnight delivery and photocopying.

TIPS "Our office does not accept e-mail queries!"

THE MCCARTHY AGENCY, LLC

7 Allen St., Rumson, NJ 07660. **Phone:** (732)741-3065. **E-mail:** McCarthylit@aol.com; ntfrost@hotmail.com. **Contact:** Shawna McCarthy. Member of AAR. Currently handles nonfiction books (25%), novels (75%).

MEMBER AGENTS Shawna McCarthy, Nahvae Frost.

REPRESENTS Nonfiction books, novels. **Considers these fiction areas:** fantasy, juvenile, mystery, romance, science, women's.

HOW TO CONTACT Query via e-mail or regular mail to The McCarthy Agency, c/o Nahvae Frost, 101 Clinton Avenue, Apartment #2, Brooklyn, NY 11205. Accepts simultaneous submissions.

MCCARTHY CREATIVE SERVICES

625 Main St., Suite 834, New York, NY 10044-0035. (212)832-3428. **Fax:** (212)829-9610. **E-mail:** paulmccarthy@mccarthycreative.com. **Website:** www.mccarthycreative.com. **Contact:** Paul D. McCarthy. Memberships include the Authors Guild, American Society of Journalists & Authors, National Book Critics Circle, Authors League of America. Represents 5 clients. 0% of clients are new/unpublished writers. Currently handles nonfiction books (95%), novels (5%).

○ Prior to his current position, Mr. McCarthy was a professional writer, literary agent at the Scott Meredith Literary Agency, senior editor at publishing companies (Simon & Schuster, HarperCollins, and Doubleday), and a public speaker. Learn much more about Mr. McCarthy by visiting his website.

MEMBER AGENTS Paul D. McCarthy.

REPRESENTS Nonfiction books, novels. **Considers these fiction areas:** glitz, adventure, confession, detective, erotica, ethnic, family, fantasy, feminist, gay, historical, horror, humor, literary, mainstream, mystery, regional, romance, science, sports, thriller, Western, young adult, women's.

⊶ "I deliberately founded my company to be unlimited in its range. That's what I offer, and the world has responded. My agency was founded so that I could maximize and build on the value of my combined experience for my authors and other clients, in all of my capacities and more. I think it's *very* important for authors to know that because I'm so exclusive as an agent, I may not be able to offer representation on the basis of the manuscript they submit. However, if they decide to invest in their book and lifetime career as authors, by engaging my professional, near-unique editorial services, there is the possibility that at the end of the process, when they've achieved the very best, most salable, and competitive book they can write, I may see sufficient potential in the book and their next books, that I do offer to be their agent. Representation is never guaranteed." Established authors of serious and popular nonfiction, who want the value of being one of Mr. McCarthy's very exclusive authors who receive special attention, and of being represented by a literary agent who brings such a rich diversity and depth of publishing/creative/professorial experience, and distinguished reputation. No first novels. "Novels by established novelists will be considered very selectively."

HOW TO CONTACT Submit outline, one chapter (either first or best). Queries and submissions by e-mail only. Send as e-mail attachment. Responds in 3-4 weeks to queries. Obtains most new clients through recommendations from others.

TERMS Agent receives 15% commission on domestic sales. Agent receives 20% commission on foreign sales. Offers written contract; 30-day notice must be given to terminate contract. "All reading done in deciding whether or not to offer representation is free. Editorial services are available. Mailing and postage expenses incurred on the author's behalf are always approved by them in advance."

TIPS "Always keep in mind that your query letter/proposal is only one of hundreds and thousands that are competing for the agent's attention. Therefore, your presentation of your book and yourself as author has to be immediate, intense, compelling, and concise. Make the query letter 1 page, and after a short introductory paragraph, write a 150-word KEYNOTE description of your manuscript."

⦿ THE MCGILL AGENCY, INC.

10000 N. Central Expressway, Suite 400, Dallas, TX 75231. (214)390-5970. **E-mail:** info.mcgillagency@gmail.com. **Contact:** Jack Bollinger. Estab. 2009. Represents 10 clients. 50% of clients are new/unpublished writers.

MEMBER AGENTS Jack Bollinger (eclectic tastes in nonfiction and fiction); Amy Cohn (nonfiction interests include women's issues, gay/lesbian, ethnic/cultural, memoirs, true crime; fiction interests include mystery, suspense and thriller).

REPRESENTS Considers these fiction areas: historical, mainstream, mystery, romance, thriller.

HOW TO CONTACT Query via e-mail. Responds in 2 weeks to queries and 6 weeks to mss. Obtains new clients through conferences.

TERMS Agent receives 15% commission.

● MENDEL MEDIA GROUP, LLC

115 W. 30th St., Suite 800, New York, NY 10001. (646)239-9896. **Fax:** (212)685-4717. **E-mail:** scott@ mendelmedia.com. **Website:** www.mendelmedia. com. Member of AAR. Represents 40-60 clients.

○ Prior to becoming an agent, Mr. Mendel was an academic. "I taught American literature, Yiddish, Jewish studies, and literary theory at the University of Chicago and the University of Illinois at Chicago while working on my PhD in English. I also worked as a freelance technical writer and as the managing editor of a healthcare magazine. In 1998, I began working for the late Jane Jordan Browne, a long-time agent in the book publishing world."

REPRESENTS Nonfiction books, novels, scholarly, with potential for broad/popular appeal. **Considers these fiction areas:** action, adventure, contemporary issues, crime, detective, erotica, ethnic, feminist, gay, glitz, historical, humor, inspirational, juvenile, lesbian, literary, mainstream, mystery, picture books, police, religious, romance, satire, sports, thriller, young adult Jewish fiction.

○━ "I am interested in major works of history, current affairs, biography, business, politics, economics, science, major memoirs, narrative nonfiction, and other sorts of general nonfiction." Actively seeking new, major or definitive work on a subject of broad interest, or a controversial, but authoritative, new book on a subject that affects many people's lives. I also represent more lighthearted nonfiction projects, such as gift or novelty books, when they suit the market particularly well." Does not want "queries about projects written years ago that were unsuccessfully shopped to a long list of trade publishers by either the author or another agent. I am specifically not interested in reading short category romances (regency, time travel, paranormal, etc.), horror novels, supernatural stories, poetry, original plays, or film scripts."

HOW TO CONTACT Query with SASE. Do not e-mail or fax queries. For nonfiction, include a com-

plete, fully edited book proposal with sample chapters. For fiction, include a complete synopsis and no more than 20 pages of sample text. Responds in 2 weeks to queries. Responds in 4-6 weeks to mss. Obtains most new clients through recommendations from others.

TERMS Agent receives 15% commission on domestic sales. Agent receives 20% commission on foreign sales.

WRITERS CONFERENCES BookExpo America; Frankfurt Book Fair; London Book Fair; RWA National Conference; Modern Language Association Convention; Jerusalem Book Fair.

TIPS "While I am not interested in being flattered by a prospective client, it does matter to me that she knows why she is writing to me in the first place. Is one of my clients a colleague of hers? Has she read a book by one of my clients that led her to believe I might be interested in her work? Authors of descriptive nonfiction should have real credentials and expertise in their subject areas, either as academics, journalists, or policy experts, and authors of prescriptive nonfiction should have legitimate expertise and considerable experience communicating their ideas in seminars and workshops, in a successful business, through the media, etc."

◐ DEE MURA LITERARY

P.O. Box 131, Massapequa, NY 11762. (516)795-1616. **Fax:** (516)795-8797. **E-mail:** query@deemuraliterary .com. **Website:** www.deemuraliterary.com. **Contact:** Dee Mura. Signatory of WGA. 50% of clients are new/ unpublished writers.

○ Prior to opening her agency, Mura was a public relations executive with a roster of film and entertainment clients. She is the president and CEO of both Dee Mura Literary and Dee Mura Entertainment.

MEMBER AGENTS Dee Mura, Kimiko Nakamura, Kaylee Davis.

REPRESENTS Considers these fiction areas: action, adventure, erotica, ethnic, experimental, fantasy, gay, historical, lesbian, mystery, romance, satire, science fiction, women's, young adult chick lit, contemporary fiction, Jewish, middle grade, paranormal, paranormal romance, teens, thriller/espionage.

○━ Fiction with crossover film potential. "No children's books please."

HOW TO CONTACT Query with SASE or e-mail query@deemuraliterary.com (e-mail queries are preferred). Please include first 25 pages in the body of

165

the e-mail as well as a short author bio and synopsis of the work. Accepts multiple submissions. Accepts simultaneous submissions. Responds to queries in 3-4 weeks. Responds to mss in 8 weeks. Obtains new clients through recommendations, solicitation, and conferences.

TERMS Agent receives 15% commission on domestic sales. Agent receives 20% commission on foreign sales. Offers written contract. Charges clients for photocopying, mailing expenses, overseas/long-distance phone calls.

WRITERS CONFERENCES BEA Expo, San Francisco Writers Conference.

TIPS "Please include a short author bio, even if you have no literary background, and a brief synopsis of the project."

◑ MUSE LITERARY MANAGEMENT

189 Waverly Place., #4, New York, NY 10014. (212)925-3721. **E-mail:** museliterarymgmt@museliterary.com. **Website:** www.museliterary.com. **Contact:** Deborah Carter. Associations: NAWE, International Thriller Writers, Historical Novel Society, Association of Booksellers for Children, The Authors Guild, Children's Literature Network, and American Folklore Society. Represents 10 clients. 90% of clients are new/unpublished writers.

◔ Prior to starting her agency, Ms. Carter trained with an AAR literary agent and in the music business as a talent scout for record companies and in artist management. She has a BA in English and music from the College of Arts & Sciences at NYU.

REPRESENTS Considers these fiction areas: historical, literary, mystery, thriller, literary fiction, multicultural and international fiction that's relatable to American readers, children's, and teen.

⚷ Specializes in development of book manuscripts and associated journalism, the sale and administration of print, performance, and foreign rights. Actively seeking "writers with formal training who bring a unique outlook to their manuscripts. Those who submit should be receptive to editorial feedback and willing to revise during the submission process to remain competitive." Does not want romance, chick lit, sci-fi, fantasy, horror; stories about pets, vampires, or serial killers; fiction

or nonfiction with religious or spiritual subject matter."

HOW TO CONTACT Query with SASE. Query via e-mail (no attachments). Discards unwanted queries. Responds in 1-2 weeks to queries; 2-3 weeks to mss. Obtains most new clients through referrals and conferences.

TERMS Agent receives 15% commission on gross domestic sales, 20% on gross foreign sales. One-year contract offered when writer and agent agree that the manuscript is ready for submission. All expenses are preapproved by the client.

TIPS "Since we all look for books by familiar names, new writers need a plan for building an audience through their professional affiliations and in freelance journalism. All agreements are signed by the writers. Reimbursement for expenses is subject to client's approval, limited to photocopying and postage."

● JEAN V. NAGGAR LITERARY AGENCY, INC.

216 E. 75th St., Suite 1E, New York, NY 10021. (212)794-1082. **E-mail:** jweltz@jvnla.com; jvnla@jvnla.com. **E-mail:** jweltz@jvnla.com; jregel@jvnla.com; atasman@jvnla.com; atasman@jvnla.com. **Website:** www.jvnla.com. **Contact:** Jean Naggar. Member of AAR. Other memberships include PEN, Women's Media Group, Women's Forum, SCBWI. Represents 450 clients. 20% of clients are new/unpublished writers. Currently handles nonfiction books (35%), novels (45%), juvenile books (15%), scholarly books (5%).

◔ Ms. Naggar has served as president of AAR.

MEMBER AGENTS Jennifer Weltz (subrights, children's, adults); Jessica Regel (young adult, adult, subrights); Jean Naggar (taking no new clients); Alice Tasman (adult, children's); Elizabeth Evans (adult nonfiction, some fiction and YA).

REPRESENTS Nonfiction books, novels. **Considers these fiction areas:** action, adventure, crime, detective, ethnic, family saga, feminist, historical, literary, mainstream, mystery, police, psychic, supernatural, suspense, thriller.

⚷ This agency specializes in mainstream fiction and nonfiction and literary fiction with commercial potential.

HOW TO CONTACT Query via e-mail. Prefers to read materials exclusively. No fax queries. Consult website for specific guidelines for each agent. Responds in 1 day to queries. Responds in 2 months to mss. Obtains most new clients through recommendations from others.

TERMS Agent receives 15% commission on domestic sales. Agent receives 20% commission on foreign sales. Offers written contract. Charges for overseas mailing, messenger services, book purchases, long-distance telephone, photocopying—all deductible from royalties received.

RECENT SALES *Night Navigation*, by Ginnah Howard; *After Hours at the Almost Home*, by Tara Yelen; *An Entirely Synthetic Fish: A Biography of Rainbow Trout*, by Anders Halverson; *The Patron Saint of Butterflies*, by Cecilia Galante; *Wondrous Strange*, by Lesley Livingston; *6 Sick Hipsters*, by Rayo Casablanca; *The Last Bridge*, by Teri Coyne; *Gypsy Goodbye*, by Nancy Springer; *Commuters*, by Emily Tedrowe; *The Language of Secrets*, by Dianne Dixon; *Smiling to Freedom*, by Martin Benoit Stiles; *The Tale of Halcyon Crane*, by Wendy Webb; *Fugitive*, by Phillip Margolin; *BlackBerry Girl*, by Aidan Donnelley Rowley; *Wild Girls*, by Pat Murphy.

WRITERS CONFERENCES Willamette Writers Conference; Pacific Northwest Writers Conference; Bread Loaf Writers Conference; Marymount Manhattan Writers Conference; SEAK Medical & Legal Fiction Writing Conference.

TIPS "Use a professional presentation. Because of the avalanche of unsolicited queries that flood the agency every week, we have had to modify our policy. We will now only guarantee to read and respond to queries from writers who come recommended by someone we know. Our areas are general fiction and nonfiction— no children's books by unpublished writers, no multimedia, no screenplays, no formula fiction, and no mysteries by unpublished writers. We recommend patience and fortitude: the courage to be true to your own vision, the fortitude to finish a novel and polish it again and again before sending it out, and the patience to accept rejection gracefully and to wait for the stars to align themselves appropriately for success."

NELSON LITERARY AGENCY

1732 Wazee St., Suite 207, Denver, CO 80202. (303)292-2805. **E-mail:** query@nelsonagency.com. **Website:** www.nelsonagency.com. **Contact:** Kristin Nelson, president and senior literary agent; Sara Megibow, associate literary agent. Member of AAR. RWA, SCBWI, SFWA.

Prior to opening her own agency, Ms. Nelson worked as a literary scout and subrights agent for agent Jody Rein.

REPRESENTS Novels, select nonfiction. **Considers these fiction areas:** commercial, literary, mainstream romance (includes fantasy with romantic elements, science fiction, fantasy, young adult).

NLA specializes in representing commercial fiction and high-caliber literary fiction. Actively seeking stories with multicultural elements. Does not want short story collections, mysteries, thrillers, Christian, horror, children's picture books, or screenplays.

HOW TO CONTACT Query by e-mail only.

RECENT SALES *Prodigy*, by Marie Lu (young adult); *Wool*, by Hugh Howey (science fiction); *The Peculiar*, by Stefan Bachmann (middle grade); *Catching Jordan*, by Miranda Kenneally (young adult); *Broken Like This*, by Monica Trasandes (debut literary fiction); *The Darwin Elevator*, by Jason Hough (debut science fiction).

NORTHERN LIGHTS LITERARY SERVICES, LLC

2323 State Rd. 252, Martinsville, IN 46151. (888)558-4354. **Fax:** (208)265-1948. **E-mail:** queries@northernlightsls.com. **Website:** www.northernlightsls.com. **Contact:** Sammie Justesen. Represents 25 clients. 35% of clients are new/unpublished writers. Currently handles nonfiction books (90%), novels (10%).

MEMBER AGENTS Sammie Justesen (fiction and nonfiction); Vorris Dee Justesen (business and current affairs).

REPRESENTS Nonfiction books, novels. **Considers these fiction areas:** action, adventure, crime, detective, ethnic, family saga, feminist, glitz, historical, inspirational, mainstream, mystery, police, psychic, regional, religious, romance, supernatural, suspense, thriller, women's.

"Our goal is to provide personalized service to clients and create a bond that will endure throughout the writer's career. We seriously consider each query we receive and will accept hardworking new authors who are willing to develop their talents and skills. We enjoy working with health-care professionals and writers who clearly understand their market and have a platform." Actively seeking general nonfiction—especially if the writer has a platform. Does not want to receive fantasy, horror, erotica, children's books, screenplays, poetry, or short stories.

HOW TO CONTACT Query with SASE. Submit outline/proposal, synopsis, 3 sample chapters, author bio. E-queries preferred. No phone queries. All queries considered, but the agency only replies if interested. If you've completed and polished a novel, send a query letter, a 1- or 2-page synopsis of the plot, and the first chapter. Also include your biography as it relates to your writing experience. Do not send an entire mss unless requested. If you'd like to submit a nonfiction book, send a query letter along with the book proposal. Include a bio showing the background that will enable you to write the book. Consult website for complete submission guidelines. Accepts simultaneous submissions. Responds in 2 months to queries. Responds in 2 months to mss. Obtains most new clients through solicitations, conferences.

TERMS Agent receives 15% commission on domestic sales. Agent receives 20% commission on foreign sales. Offers written contract; 30-day notice must be given to terminate contract.

RECENT SALES *Intuitive Parenting*, by Debra Snyder, PhD (Beyond Words); *The Confidence Trap*, by Russ Harris (Penguin); *The Never Cold Call Again Toolkit*, by Frank Rumbauskas Jr. (Wiley); *Thank You for Firing Me*, by Candace Reed and Kitty Martini (Sterling); *The Wal-Mart Cure: Ten Lifesaving Supplements for Under $10* (Sourcebooks).

TIPS "If you're fortunate enough to find an agent who answers your query and asks for a printed manuscript, always include a letter and cover page containing your name, physical address, e-mail address, and phone number. Be professional!"

● KATHI J. PATON LITERARY AGENCY

P.O. Box 2236 Radio City Station, New York, NY 10101. (212)265-6586. **E-mail:** KJPLitBiz@optonline .net. **Website:** www.PatonLiterary.com. **Contact:** Kathi Paton. Currently handles nonfiction books (85%), novels (15%).

REPRESENTS Nonfiction books, novels, short story collections, book-based film rights. **Considers these fiction areas:** literary, mainstream, multicultural short stories.

⌐ This agency specializes in adult nonfiction.

HOW TO CONTACT Accepts e-mail queries only. Accepts simultaneous submissions. Accepts new clients through recommendations from current clients.

TERMS Agent receives 15% commission on domestic sales. Agent receives 20% commission on foreign sales. Offers written contract. Charges clients for photocopying.

WRITERS CONFERENCES Attends major regional panels, seminars, and conferences.

ALISON J. PICARD, LITERARY AGENT

P.O. Box 2000, Cotuit, MA 02635. **Phone/Fax:** (508)477-7192. **E-mail:** ajpicard@aol.com. **Contact:** Alison Picard. Represents 48 clients. 30% of clients are new/unpublished writers. Currently handles nonfiction books (40%), novels (40%), juvenile books (20%).

⭕ Prior to becoming an agent, Ms. Picard was an assistant at a literary agency in New York.

REPRESENTS Nonfiction books, novels, juvenile. **Considers these fiction areas:** action, adventure, contemporary issues, crime, detective, erotica, ethnic, family saga, feminist, gay, glitz, historical, horror, humor, juvenile, lesbian, literary, mainstream, multicultural, mystery, New Age, picture books, police, psychic, romance, sports, supernatural, thriller, young adult.

⌐ "Many of my clients have come to me from big agencies, where they felt overlooked or ignored. I communicate freely with my clients and offer a lot of career advice, suggestions for revising manuscripts, etc. If I believe in a project, I will submit it to a dozen or more publishers, unlike some agents who give up after four or five rejections." No science fiction/fantasy, Westerns, poetry, plays, or articles.

HOW TO CONTACT Query with SASE. Accepts simultaneous submissions. Responds in 2 weeks to queries; 4 months to mss. Obtains most new clients through recommendations from others, solicitations.

TERMS Agent receives 15% commission on domestic sales. Agent receives 20% commission on foreign sales. Offers written contract, binding for 1 year; 1-week notice must be given to terminate contract.

RECENT SALES *Zitface*, by Emily Ormand (Marshall Cavendish); *Totally Together*, by Stephanie O'Dea (Running Press); *The Ultimate Slow Cooker Cookbook*, by Stephanie O'Dea (Hyperion); Two Untitled Cookbooks, by Erin Chase (St. Martin's Press); *A Journal of the Flood Year*, by David Ely (Portobello Books, United Kingdom; L'Ancora, Italy); *A Mighty Wall*, by John Foley (Llewellyn/Flux); *Jelly's Gold*, by David Housewright (St. Martin's Press).

TIPS "Please don't send material without sending a query first via mail or e-mail. I don't accept phone or fax queries. Always enclose a SASE with a query."

LINN PRENTIS LITERARY

155 East 116th St., #2F, New York, NY 10029. **Fax:** (212)875-5565. **E-mail:** ahayden@linnprentis.com; linn@linnprentis.com. **Website:** www.linnprentis.com. **Contact:** Amy Hayden, acquisitions director; Linn Prentis, agent; Jordana Frankel assistant. Represents 18-20 clients. 25% of clients are new/unpublished writers. Currently handles nonfiction books (5%), novels (65%), story collections (7%), novella (10%), juvenile books (10%), scholarly books (3%).

○ Prior to becoming an agent, Ms. Prentis was a nonfiction writer and editor, primarily in magazines. She also worked in book promotion in New York. Ms. Prentis then worked for and later ran the Virginia Kidd Agency. She is known particularly for her assistance with manuscript development.

REPRESENTS Nonfiction books, novels, short story collections, novellas (from authors whose novels I already represent), juvenile (for older juveniles), scholarly anthology. **Considers these fiction areas:** adventure, ethnic, fantasy, feminist, gay, glitz, historical, horror, humor, juvenile, lesbian, literary, mainstream, mystery, thriller.

⚷ "Because of the Virginia Kidd connection and the clients I brought with me at the start, I have a special interest in sci-fi and fantasy, but, really, fiction is what interests me. As for my nonfiction projects, they are books I just couldn't resist." Actively seeking hard science fiction, family saga, mystery, memoir, mainstream, literary, women's. Does not want to "receive books for little kids."

HOW TO CONTACT Query with SASE. Submit synopsis. No phone or fax queries. No snail mail. E-mail queries to ahayden@linnprentis.com. Include first ten pages and synopsis as either attachment or as text in the e-mail. Accepts simultaneous submissions. Obtains most new clients through recommendations from others, solicitations.

TERMS Agent receives 15% commission on domestic sales. Agent receives 20% commission on foreign sales. Offers written contract; 60-day notice must be given to terminate contract.

RECENT SALES Sold 15 titles in the last year. *The Sons of Heaven, The Empress of Mars,* and *The House of the Stag,* by Kage Baker (Tor) (the last of those titles has also been sold to Dabel Brothers to be published as a comic book/graphic novel); *Indigo Springs* and a sequel, by A.M. Dellamonica (Tor); Wayne Arthurson's debut mystery plus a second series book; *Bone Crossed* and *Cry Wolf* for *New York Times* #1 best-selling author Patricia Briggs (Ace/Penguin). "The latter is the start of a new series."

TIPS "Consider query letters and synopses as writing assignments. Spell names correctly."

○ P.S LITERARY AGENCY

20033 - 520 Kerr St., Oakville, ON L6K 3C7 Canada. **E-mail:** query@psliterary.com. **Website:** www.psliterary.com. **Contact:** Curtis Russell, principal agent; Carly Watters, agent. Estab. 2005. Currently handles nonfiction books (50%), novels (50%).

REPRESENTS Nonfiction, novels, juvenile books. **Considers these fiction areas:** action, adventure, detective, erotica, ethnic, family saga, historical, horror, humor, juvenile, literary, mainstream, mystery, picture books, romance, sports, thriller, women's, young adult biography/autobiography, business, child guidance/parenting, cooking/food/nutrition, current affairs, government/politics/law, health/medicine, history, how-to, humor, memoirs, military/war, money/finance/economics, nature/environment, popular culture, science/technology, self-help/personal improvement, sports, true crime/investigative, women's issues/women's studies.

⚷ "What makes our agency distinct: We take on a small number of clients per year in order to provide focused, hands-on representation. We pride ourselves in providing industry-leading client service." Actively seeking both fiction and nonfiction. Seeking both new and established writers. Does not want to receive poetry or screenplays.

HOW TO CONTACT Queries by e-mail only. Submit query, synopsis, and bio. "Please limit your query to one page." Accepts simultaneous submissions. Responds in 4-6 weeks to queries/proposals; mss 4-8 weeks. Obtains most new clients through solicitations.

TERMS Agent receives 15% commission on domestic sales. Agent receives 25% commission on foreign sales. We offer a written contract, with 30-days notice terminate. "This agency charges for postage/messenger services only if a project is sold."

TIPS "Please review our website for the most up-to-date submission guidelines. We do not charge reading fees. We do not offer a critique service."

RAINES & RAINES

103 Kenyon Rd., Medusa, NY 12120. (518)239-8311. **Fax:** (518)239-6029. **Contact:** Theron Raines (member of AAR); Joan Raines; Keith Korman. Member of AAR. Represents 100 clients.

REPRESENTS Nonfiction books, novels. **Considers these fiction areas:** action, adventure, crime, detective, fantasy, frontier, historical, mystery, picture books, police, science fiction, suspense, thriller, Westerns, whimsical.

HOW TO CONTACT Query with SASE. Responds in 2 weeks to queries.

TERMS Agent receives 15% commission on domestic sales. Agent receives 20% commission on foreign sales. Charges for photocopying.

THE REDWOOD AGENCY

474 Wellesley Ave., Mill Valley, CA 94941. (415)381-2269, ext. 2. **E-mail:** info@redwoodagency.com. **E-mail:** query@redwoodagency.com. **Website:** www.redwoodagency.home.comcast.net. **Contact:** Catherine Fowler, founder. Adheres to AAR canon of ethics. Currently handles nonfiction books (100%).

Prior to becoming an agent, Ms. Fowler was an editor, subsidiary rights director, and associate publisher for Doubleday, Simon & Schuster, and Random House during her 20 years in New York publishing. Content exec for web startups Excite and WebMD.

REPRESENTS Nonfiction books, novels. **Considers these fiction areas:** literary, mainstream, suspense, women's quirky.

"Along with our love of books and publishing, we have the desire and commitment to work with fun, interesting, and creative people, to do so with respect and professionalism, but also with a sense of humor." Actively seeking high-quality, nonfiction works created for the general consumer market, as well as projects with the potential to become book series. Does not want to receive fiction. Do not send packages that require signature for delivery.

HOW TO CONTACT Query via e-mail only. While we redesign website, submit "quick query" to: query@

redwoodagency.com. See all guidelines online. Obtains most new clients through recommendations from others, solicitations.

TERMS Offers written contract. Charges for copying and delivery charges, if any, as specified in author/agency agreement.

HELEN REES LITERARY AGENCY

14 Beacon St., Suite 710, Boston, MA 02108. (617)227-9014. **Fax:** (617)227-8762. **E-mail:** reesagency@reesagency.com. **Website:** http://reesagency.com. **Contact:** Joan Mazmanian, Ann Collette, Helen Rees, Lorin Rees. Estab. 1983. Member of AAR. Other memberships include PEN. Represents more than 100 clients. 50% of clients are new/unpublished writers. Currently handles nonfiction books (60%), novels (40%).

MEMBER AGENTS Ann Collette (literary, mystery, thrillers, suspense, vampire, and women's fiction; in nonfiction, she prefers true crime, narrative nonfiction, military and war, work to do with race and class, and work set in or about Southeast Asia. Ann can be reached at: Agent10702@aol.com). Lorin Rees (literary fiction, memoirs, business books, self-help, science, history, psychology, and narrative nonfiction. lorin@reesagency.com).

REPRESENTS Nonfiction books, novels. **Considers these fiction areas:** historical, literary, mainstream, mystery, suspense, thriller.

HOW TO CONTACT Query with SASE, outline, 2 sample chapters. No unsolicited e-mail submissions. No multiple submissions. Consult website for each agent's submission guidelines. Responds in 3-4 weeks to queries. Obtains most new clients through recommendations from others, conferences, submissions.

TERMS Agent receives 15% commission on domestic sales. Agent receives 20% commission on foreign sales.

RECENT SALES Sold more than 35 titles in the last year. *Get Your Ship Together*, by Capt. D. Michael Abrashoff; *Overpromise and Overdeliver*, by Rick Berrara; *Opacity*, by Joel Kurtzman; *America the Broke*, by Gerald Swanson; *Murder at the B-School*, by Jeffrey Cruikshank; *Bone Factory*, by Steven Sidor; *Father Said*, by Hal Sirowitz; *Winning*, by Jack Welch; *The Case for Israel*, by Alan Dershowitz; *As the Future Catches You*, by Juan Enriquez; *Blood Makes the Grass Grow Green*, by Johnny Rico; *DVD Movie Guide*, by Mick Martin and Marsha Porter; *Words That Work*, by Frank Luntz; *Stirring It Up*, by Gary Hirshberg; *Hot Spots*, by Martin Fletcher; *Andy Grove: The Life* and *Times of an American*, by Richard Tedlow; *Girls Most Likely To*, by Poonam Sharma.

JODIE RHODES LITERARY AGENCY

8840 Villa La Jolla Dr., Suite 315, La Jolla, CA 92037-1957. **Website:** jodierhodesliterary.com. **Contact:** Jodie Rhodes, president. Member of AAR. Represents 74 clients. 60% of clients are new/unpublished writers. Currently handles nonfiction books (45%), novels (35%), juvenile books (20%).

○ Prior to opening her agency, Ms. Rhodes was a university-level creative writing teacher, workshop director, published novelist, and vice president/media director at the N.W. Ayer Advertising Agency.

MEMBER AGENTS Jodie Rhodes; Clark McCutcheon (fiction); Bob McCarter (nonfiction).

REPRESENTS Nonfiction books, novels. **Considers these fiction areas:** ethnic, family saga, historical, literary, mainstream, mystery, suspense, thriller, women's, young adult.

⚭ "Actively seeking witty, sophisticated women's books about career ambitions and relationships; edgy/trendy young adult and teen books; narrative nonfiction on groundbreaking scientific discoveries, politics, economics, military; and important current affairs by prominent scientists and academic professors." Does not want to receive erotica, horror, fantasy, romance, science fiction, religious/inspirational, or children's books (does accept young adult/teen).

HOW TO CONTACT Query with brief synopsis, first 30-50 pages, SASE. Do not call. Do not send complete ms unless requested. This agency does not return unrequested material weighing a pound or more that requires special postage. Include e-mail address with query. Accepts simultaneous submissions. Responds in 3 weeks to queries. Obtains most new clients through recommendations from others, agent sourcebooks.

TERMS Agent receives 15% commission on domestic sales. Agent receives 20% commission on foreign sales. Offers written contract; 1-month notice must be given to terminate contract. Charges clients for fax, photocopying, phone calls, postage. Charges are itemized and approved by writers upfront.

RECENT SALES Sold 42 titles in the last year. *The Ring*, by Kavita Daswani (HarperCollins); *Train to Trieste*, by Domnica Radulescu (Knopf); *A Year with Cats and Dogs*, by Margaret Hawkins (Permanent Press); *Silence and Silhouettes*, by Ryan Smithson (HarperCollins); *Internal Affairs*, by Constance Dial (Permanent Press); *How Math Rules the World*, by James Stein (HarperCollins); *Diagnosis of Love*, by Maggie Martin (Bantam); *Lies, Damn Lies, and Science*, by Sherry Seethaler (Prentice Hall); *Freaked*, by Jeanne Dutton (HarperCollins); *The Five Second Rule*, by Anne Maczulak (Perseus Books); *The Intelligence Wars*, by Stephen O'Hern (Prometheus); *Seducing the Spirits*, by Louise Young (the Permanent Press), and more.

TIPS "Think your book out before you write it. Do your research, know your subject matter intimately, and write vivid specifics, not bland generalities. Care deeply about your book. Don't imitate other writers. Find your own voice. We never take on a book we don't believe in, and we go the extra mile for our writers. We welcome talented new writers."

THE RIGHTS FACTORY

P.O. Box 499, Station C, Toronto, ON M6J 3P6 Canada. (416)966-5367. **Website:** www.therightsfactory.com.

MEMBER AGENTS Sam Hiyate, Ali McDonald.

⚭ "The Rights Factory is an agency that deals in intellectual property rights to entertainment products, including books, comics and graphic novels, film, television, and video games. We license rights in every territory by representing 3 types of clients."

HOW TO CONTACT There is a submission form on this agency's website.

RECENT SALES *Beauty, Pure & Simple*, by Kristen Ma; *Why Mr. Right Can't Find You*, by J.M. Kearns; *Tout Sweet: Hanging Up My High Heels for a New Life in France*, by Karen Wheeler; *The Orange Code*, by Arkadi Kuhlmann and Bruce Philp.

ANN RITTENBERG LITERARY AGENCY, INC.

15 Maiden Lane, Suite 206, New York, NY 10038. **Website:** www.rittlit.com. **Contact:** Ann Rittenberg, president; Penn Whaling, associate. Member of AAR. Currently handles fiction 75%, nonfiction (25%).

REPRESENTS Considers these fiction areas: literary, thriller upmarket fiction.

⚭ This agent specializes in literary fiction and literary nonfiction. Does not want to receive screenplays, straight genre fiction, poetry, self-help.

HOW TO CONTACT Query with SASE. Submit outline, 3 sample chapters, SASE. Query via postal mail *only*. Accepts simultaneous submissions. Responds in 6 weeks to queries. Responds in 2 months to mss. Obtains most new clients through referrals from established writers and editors.

TERMS Agent receives 15% commission on domestic sales. Agent receives 20% commission on foreign sales. Offers written contract. This agency charges clients for photocopying only.

RECENT SALES *The Given Day*, by Dennis Lehane; *My Cat Hates You*, by Jim Edgar; *Never Wave Goodbye*, by Doug Magee; *House and Home*, by Kathleen McCleary; *Nowhere to Run*, by C.J. Box; and *Daughter of Kura*, by Debra Austin.

◑ RLR ASSOCIATES, LTD.

Literary Department, 7 W. 51st St., New York, NY 10019. (212)541-8641. **Fax:** (212)262-7084. **E-mail:** sgould@rlrassociates.net. **Website:** www.rlrassociates.net. **Contact:** Scott Gould. Member of AAR. Represents 50 clients. 25% of clients are new/unpublished writers. Currently handles nonfiction books (70%), novels (25%), story collections (5%).

REPRESENTS Nonfiction books, novels, short story collections, scholarly. **Considers these fiction areas:** action, adventure, cartoon, comic books, crime, detective, ethnic, experimental, family saga, feminist, gay, historical, horror, humor, lesbian, literary, mainstream, multicultural, mystery, police, satire, sports, suspense.

⚸ "We provide a lot of editorial assistance to our clients and have connections." Actively seeking fiction, current affairs, history, art, popular culture, health and business. Does not want to receive screenplays.

HOW TO CONTACT Query by either e-mail or mail. Accepts simultaneous submissions. Responds in 4-8 weeks to queries. Obtains most new clients through recommendations from others.

TERMS Agent receives 15% commission on domestic sales. Agent receives 20% commission on foreign sales. Offers written contract.

RECENT SALES Clients include Shelby Foote, The Grief Recovery Institute, Don Wade, Don Zimmer, The Knot.com, David Plowden, PGA of America, Danny Peary, George Kalinsky, Peter Hyman, Daniel Parker, Lee Miller, Elise Miller, Nina Planck, Karyn Bosnak, Christopher Pike, Gerald Carbone, Jason Lethcoe, Andy Crouch.

TIPS "Please check out our website for more details on our agency."

◑ B.J. ROBBINS LITERARY AGENCY

5130 Bellaire Ave., North Hollywood, CA 91607-2908. **E-mail:** Robbinsliterary@gmail.com. **E-mail:** amy.bjrobbinsliterary@gmail.com. **Contact:** (Ms.) B.J. Robbins, or Amy Maldonado. Member of AAR. Represents 40 clients. 50% of clients are new/unpublished writers. Currently handles nonfiction books (50%), novels (50%).

REPRESENTS Nonfiction books, novels. **Considers these fiction areas:** crime, detective, ethnic, literary, mainstream, mystery, police, sports, suspense, thriller.

HOW TO CONTACT Query with SASE. Submit outline/proposal, 3 sample chapters, SASE. Accepts e-mail queries (no attachments). Accepts simultaneous submissions. Responds in 2-6 weeks to queries. Responds in 6-8 weeks to mss. Obtains most new clients through conferences, referrals.

TERMS Agent receives 15% commission on domestic sales. Agent receives 20% commission on foreign sales. Offers written contract; 3-month notice must be given to terminate contract. This agency charges clients for postage and photocopying (only after sale of ms).

RECENT SALES Sold 15 titles in the last year. *The Sweetness of Tears*, by Nafisa Haji (William Morrow); *Paper Dollhouse: A Memoir*, by Dr. Lisa M. Masterson; *The Sinatra Club*, by Sal Polisi and Steve Dougherty (Gallery Books); *Getting Stoned with Savages*, by J. Maarten Troost (Broadway); *Hot Water*, by Kathryn Jordan (Berkley); *Between the Bridge and the River*, by Craig Ferguson (Chronicle); *I'm Proud of You* by Tim Madigan (Gotham); *Man of the House*, by Chris Erskine (Rodale); *Bird of Another Heaven*, by James D. Houston (Knopf); *Tomorrow They Will Kiss*, by Eduardo Santiago (Little, Brown); *A Terrible Glory*, by James Donovan (Little, Brown); *The Writing on My Forehead*, by Nafisa Haji (Morrow); *Seen the Glory*, by John Hough Jr. (Simon & Schuster); *Lost on Planet China*, by J. Maarten Troost (Broadway).

WRITERS CONFERENCES Squaw Valley Writers Workshop; San Diego State University Writers Conference.

THE ROSENBERG GROUP

23 Lincoln Ave., Marblehead, MA 01945. (781)990-1341. **Fax:** (781)990-1344. **Website:** www.rosenberggroup.com. **Contact:** Barbara Collins Rosenberg. Estab. 1998. Member of AAR. Recognized agent of the RWA. Represents 25 clients. 15% of clients are new/unpublished writers. Currently handles nonfiction books (30%), novels (30%), scholarly books (10%), (30% college textbooks).

○ Prior to becoming an agent, Ms. Rosenberg was a senior editor for Harcourt.

REPRESENTS Nonfiction books, novels, textbooks, college textbooks only. **Considers these fiction areas:** romance, women's.

⚷ Ms. Rosenberg is well-versed in the romance market (both category and single title). She is a frequent speaker at romance conferences. Actively seeking romance category or single title in contemporary romantic suspense, and the historical subgenres. Does not want to receive inspirational, time travel, futuristic, or paranormal.

HOW TO CONTACT Query with SASE. See guidelines on website. Responds in 2 weeks to queries. Responds in 4-6 weeks to mss. Obtains most new clients through recommendations from others, solicitations, conferences.

TERMS Agent receives 15% commission on domestic sales. Agent receives 15% commission on foreign sales. Offers written contract; 1-month notice must be given to terminate contract. Charges maximum of $350/year for postage and photocopying.

RECENT SALES Sold 27 titles in the last year.

WRITERS CONFERENCES RWA National Conference; BookExpo America.

JANE ROTROSEN AGENCY LLC

318 E. 51st St., New York, NY 10022. (212)593-4330. **Fax:** (212)935-6985. **Website:** www.janerotrosen.com. Estab. 1974. Member of AAR. Other memberships include Authors Guild. Represents more than 100 clients. Currently handles nonfiction books (30%), novels (70%).

MEMBER AGENTS Jane R. Berkey; Andrea Cirillo; Annelise Robey; Meg Ruley; Christina Hogrebe; Peggy Gordijn, director of rights.

REPRESENTS Nonfiction books, novels. **Considers these fiction areas:** crime, family saga, historical, mystery, police, romance, suspense, thriller, women's.

HOW TO CONTACT Query with SASE to the attention of "Submissions." Find appropriate agent contact/e-mail on website. Responds in 2 weeks to writers who have been referred by a client or colleague. Responds in 2 months to mss. Obtains most new clients through recommendations from others.

TERMS Agent receives 15% commission on domestic sales. Agent receives 20% commission on foreign sales. Offers written contract, binding for 3 years; 2-month notice must be given to terminate contract. Charges clients for photocopying, express mail, overseas postage, book purchase.

VICTORIA SANDERS & ASSOCIATES

241 Avenue of the Americas, Suite 11 H, New York, NY 10014. (212)633-8811. **Fax:** (212)633-0525. **E-mail:** queriesvsa@gmail.com. **Website:** www.victoriasanders.com. **Contact:** Victoria Sanders, Diane Dickensheid. Estab. 1992. Member of AAR. Signatory of WGA. Represents 135 clients. 25% of clients are new/unpublished writers. Currently handles nonfiction books (30%), novels (70%).

MEMBER AGENTS Tanya McKinnon, Victoria Sanders, Chris Kepner (open to all types of books as long as the writing is exceptional. Include the first three chapters in the body of the e-mail. At the moment, he is on the lookout for quality nonfiction).

REPRESENTS Nonfiction books, novels. **Considers these fiction areas:** action, adventure, contemporary issues, ethnic, family saga, feminist, gay, lesbian, literary, thriller.

HOW TO CONTACT Query by e-mail only. "We will not respond to e-mails with attachments or attached files."

TERMS Agent receives 15% commission on domestic sales. Agent receives 20% commission on foreign sales. Offers written contract. Charges for photocopying, messenger, express mail. If in excess of $100, client approval is required.

RECENT SALES Sold 20+ titles in the last year.

TIPS "Limit query to letter (no calls) and give it your best shot. A good query is going to get a good response."

SCHIAVONE LITERARY AGENCY, INC.

236 Trails End, West Palm Beach, FL 33413-2135. (561)966-9294. **Fax:** (561)966-9294. **E-mail:** profschia@aol.com. **Website:** www.publishersmarketplace.com/members/profschia; blog site: www.schiavoneliteraryagencyinc.blogspot.com. **Contact:** Dr.

James Schiavone, CEO, corporate offices in Florida; Jennifer DuVall, president, New York office. New York office: 3671 Hudson Manor Terrace, No. 11H, Bronx, NY, 10463-1139, phone: (718)548-5332; fax: (718)548-5332; e-mail: jendu77@aol.com. Other memberships include National Education Association. Represents 60+ clients. 2% of clients are new/unpublished writers. Currently handles nonfiction books (50%), novels (49%), textbooks (1%).

○ Prior to opening his agency, Dr. Schiavone was a full professor of developmental skills at the City University of New York and author of 5 trade books and 3 textbooks. Jennifer DuVall has many years of combined experience in office management and agenting.

REPRESENTS Nonfiction books, novels, juvenile, scholarly, textbooks. **Considers these fiction areas:** ethnic, family saga, historical, horror, humor, juvenile, literary, mainstream, science fiction, young adult.

☞ This agency specializes in celebrity biography and autobiography and memoirs. Does not want to receive poetry.

HOW TO CONTACT Query with SASE. Do not send unsolicited materials or parcels requiring a signature. Send no e-attachments. Accepts simultaneous submissions. Responds in 2 weeks to queries. Responds in 6 weeks to mss. Obtains most new clients through recommendations from others, solicitations, conferences.

TERMS Agent receives 15% commission on domestic sales. Agent receives 20% commission on foreign sales. Offers written contract. Charges clients for postage only.

WRITERS CONFERENCES Key West Literary Seminar; South Florida Writers Conference; Tallahassee Writers Conference, Million Dollar Writers Conference; Alaska Writers Conference.

TIPS "We prefer to work with established authors published by major houses in New York. We will consider marketable proposals from new/previously unpublished writers."

◑◉ SUSAN SCHULMAN LITERARY AGENCY

454 W. 44th St., New York, NY 10036. (212)713-1633. **Fax:** (212)581-8830. **E-mail:** schulmanqueries@yahoo.com. **Contact:** Susan Schulman. Estab. 1980. Member of AAR. Signatory of WGA. Other memberships include Dramatists Guild. 10% of clients are new/unpublished writers. Currently handles nonfiction books (50%), novels (25%), juvenile books (15%), stage plays (10%).

MEMBER AGENTS Linda Kiss, director of foreign rights; Katherine Stones, theater; Emily Uhry, submissions editor.

REPRESENTS Considers these fiction areas: action, adventure, crime, detective, feminist, historical, humor, inspirational, juvenile, literary, mainstream, mystery, picture books, police, religious, suspense, women's, young adult.

☞ "We specialize in books for, by, and about women and women's issues including nonfiction self-help books, fiction, and theater projects. We also handle the film, television, and allied rights for several agencies as well as foreign rights for several publishing houses." Actively seeking new nonfiction. Considers plays. Does not want to receive poetry, television scripts, or concepts for television.

HOW TO CONTACT Query with SASE. Submit outline, synopsis, author bio, 3 sample chapters. Accepts simultaneous submissions. Responds in 6 weeks to queries/mss. Obtains most new clients through recommendations from others, solicitations, conferences.

TERMS Agent receives 15% commission on domestic sales. Agent receives 20% commission on foreign sales. Offers written contract; 30-day notice must be given to terminate contract.

RECENT SALES Sold 50 titles in the last year; hundreds of subsidiary rights deals.

WRITERS CONFERENCES Geneva Writers Conference (Switzerland); Columbus Writers Conference; Skidmore Conference of the Independent Women's Writers Group.

TIPS "Keep writing!" Schulman describes her agency as "professional boutique, long-standing, eclectic."

● SCRIBBLERS HOUSE, LLC LITERARY AGENCY

P.O. Box 1007, Cooper Station, New York, NY 10276-1007. (212)714-7744. **E-mail:** query@scribblershouse.net. **Website:** www.scribblershouse.net. **Contact:** Stedman Mays, Garrett Gambino. 25% of clients are new/unpublished writers.

MEMBER AGENTS Stedman Mays, Garrett Gambino.

REPRESENTS Nonfiction books, occasionally novels. **Considers these fiction areas:** crime, historical, literary, suspense, thriller, women's.

HOW TO CONTACT "Query via e-mail. Put 'nonfiction query' or 'fiction query' in the subject line followed by the title of your project (send to our submissions e-mail on our website). Do not send attachments or downloadable materials of any kind with query. We will request more materials if we are interested. Usually respond in 2 weeks to 2 months to e-mail queries if we are interested (if we are not interested, we will not respond due to the overwhelming amount of queries we receive). We are only accepting e-mail queries at the present time." Accepts simultaneous submissions.

TERMS Agent receives 15% commission on domestic sales. Charges clients for postage, shipping, and copying.

TIPS "If you must send by snail mail, we will return material or respond to a U.S. Postal Service-accepted SASE. (No international coupons or outdated mail strips, please.) Presentation means a lot. A well-written query letter with a brief author bio and your credentials is important. For query letter models, go to the bookstore or online and look at the cover copy and flap copy on other books in your general area of interest. Emulate what's best. Have an idea of other notable books that will be perceived as being in the same vein as yours. Know what's fresh about your project and articulate it in as few words as possible. Consult our website for the most up-to-date information on submitting."

O SCRIBE AGENCY, LLC

5508 Joylynne Dr., Madison, WI 53716. **E-mail:** whattheshizzle@scribeagency.com. **E-mail:** submissions@scribeagency.com. **Website:** www.scribeagency.com. **Contact:** Kristopher O'Higgins. Represents 11 clients. 18% of clients are new/unpublished writers. Currently handles novels (98%), story collections (2%).

O "With more than 15 years experience in publishing, with time spent on both the agency and editorial sides, with marketing experience to boot, Scribe Agency is a full-service literary agency, working hands-on with its authors on their projects. Check the website (www.scribeagency.com) to make sure your work matches the Scribe aesthetic."

MEMBER AGENTS Kristopher O'Higgins.

REPRESENTS Novels, short story collections, novellas, anthologies. **Considers these fiction areas:** experimental, fantasy, feminist, gay, horror, lesbian, literary, mainstream, science fiction, thriller.

Actively seeking excellent writers with ideas and stories to tell.

HOW TO CONTACT E-queries only: submissions@scribeagency.com. See the website for submission info, as it may change. Responds in 3-4 weeks to queries. Responds in 5 months to mss.

TERMS Agent receives 15% commission on domestic sales. Agent receives 20% commission on foreign sales. Offers written contract. Charges for postage and photocopying.

RECENT SALES Sold 3 titles in the last year.

WRITERS CONFERENCES BookExpo America; WisCon; Wisconsin Book Festival; World Fantasy Convention; WorldCon.

SECRET AGENT MAN

P.O. Box 1078, Lake Forest, CA 92609. (949)698-6987. **E-mail:** query@secretagentman.net. **Website:** www.secretagentman.net. **Contact:** Scott Mortenson.

Selective mystery, thriller, suspense, and detective fiction. Does not want to receive scripts or screenplays.

HOW TO CONTACT Query via e-mail only; include sample chapter(s), synopsis, and/or outline. Prefers to read the real thing rather than a description of it. Obtains most new clients through recommendations from others.

LYNN SELIGMAN, LITERARY AGENT

400 Highland Ave., Upper Montclair, NJ 07043. (973)783-3631. **Contact:** Lynn Seligman. Other memberships include Women's Media Group. Represents 32 clients. 15% of clients are new/unpublished writers. Currently handles nonfiction books (60%), novels (40%).

O Prior to opening her agency, Ms. Seligman worked in the subsidiary rights department of Doubleday and Simon & Schuster, and served as an agent with Julian Bach Literary Agency (which became IMG Literary Agency). Foreign rights are represented by Books Crossing Borders, Inc.

REPRESENTS Nonfiction books, novels. **Considers these fiction areas:** detective, ethnic, fantasy, feminist, historical, horror, humor, literary, mainstream, mystery, romance, contemporary, gothic, historical, regency, science fiction.

8—☛ "This agency specializes in general nonfiction and fiction. I also do illustrated and photography books and have represented several photographers for books."

HOW TO CONTACT Query with SASE. Prefers to read materials exclusively. Accepts simultaneous submissions. Responds in 2 weeks to queries. Responds in 2 months to mss. Obtains most new clients through referrals from other writers and editors.

TERMS Agent receives 15% commission on domestic sales. Agent receives 25% commission on foreign sales. Charges clients for photocopying, unusual postage, express mail, telephone expenses (checks with author first).

RECENT SALES Sold 15 titles in the last year. *Lords of Vice* series, by Barbara Pierce; *Untitled* series, by Deborah Leblanc.

◑ THE SEYMOUR AGENCY

475 Miner St., Canton, NY 13617. (315)386-1831. E-mail: marysue@twcny.rr.com; nicole@theseymour agency.com. **Website:** www.theseymouragency.com. **Contact:** Mary Sue Seymour, Nicole Resciniti. Member of AAR. Signatory of WGA. Other memberships include RWA, Authors Guild. Represents 50 clients. 5% of clients are new/unpublished writers. Currently handles nonfiction books (50%), other (50% fiction).

○ Ms. Seymour is a retired New York State certified teacher.

MEMBER AGENTS Mary Sue Seymour (accepts queries in Christian, inspirational, romance, and nonfiction); Nicole Resciniti (accepts queries in same categories as Ms. Seymour, plus action/suspense/thriller, mystery, sci-fi, fantasy, and YA/children's).

REPRESENTS Nonfiction books, novels. **Considers these fiction areas:** action, fantasy, mystery, religious, romance, science fiction, suspense, thriller, young adult.

HOW TO CONTACT Query with SASE, synopsis, first 50 pages for romance. Accepts e-mail queries. Accepts simultaneous submissions. Responds in 1 month to queries. Responds in 3 months to mss.

TERMS Agent receives 12-15% commission on domestic sales.

RECENT SALES Dinah Bucholz's *The Harry Potter Cookbook* (Adams Media); Vannetta Chapman's *A Simple Amish Christmas* (Abingdon Press); Shelley

Shepard Gray's current book deal (HarperCollins); Shelley Galloway's multibook deal (Zondervan); Beth Wiseman's Christmas two novellas and multibook deal (Thomas Nelson); Mary Ellis's multibook deal (Harvest House); Barbara Cameron's novellas (Thomas Nelson) and multibook deal (Abingdon Press).

● SHEREE BYKOFSKY ASSOCIATES, INC.

P.O. Box 706, Brigantine, NJ 08203. **E-mail:** sheree bee@aol.com. **E-mail:** submitbee@aol.com. **Website:** www.shereebee.com. **Contact:** Sheree Bykofsky. Member of AAR. Memberships include ASJA, WNBA. Currently handles nonfiction books (80%), novels (20%).

○ Prior to opening her agency, Ms. Bykofsky served as executive editor of the Stonesong Press and managing editor of Chiron Press. She is also the author or co-author of more than 20 books, including *The Complete Idiot's Guide to Getting Published*. Ms. Bykofsky teaches publishing at NYU and SEAK, Inc.

MEMBER AGENTS Janet Rosen, associate.

REPRESENTS Nonfiction, novels. **Considers these fiction areas:** contemporary issues, literary, mainstream, mystery, suspense.

8—☛ This agency specializes in popular reference nonfiction, commercial fiction with a literary quality, and mysteries. "I have wide-ranging interests, but it really depends on quality of writing, originality, and how a particular project appeals to me (or not). I take on fiction when I completely love it—it doesn't matter what area or genre." Does not want to receive poetry, material for children, screenplays, Westerns, horror, science fiction, or fantasy.

HOW TO CONTACT "We only accept e-queries now and will only respond to those in which we are interested. E-mail short queries to submitbee@aol .com. Please, no attachments, snail mail, or phone calls. Fiction: 1-page query, 1-page synopsis, and first page of ms in the body of the e-mail. Nonfiction: 1-page query in the body of the e-mail. We cannot open attached Word files or any other types of attached files. These will be deleted." Accepts simultaneous submissions. Responds in 1 month to requested mss. Obtains most new clients through recommendations from others.

TERMS Agent receives 15% commission on domestic sales. Agent receives 20% commission on foreign sales.

Offers written contract, binding for 1 year. Charges for postage, photocopying, fax.

RECENT SALES *Red Sheep: The Search for My Inner Latina*, by Michele Carlo (Citadel/Kensington); *Bang the Keys: Four Steps to a Lifelong Writing Practice*, by Jill Dearman (Alpha, Penguin); *Signed, Your Student: Celebrities on the Teachers Who Made Them Who They Are Today*, by Holly Holbert (Kaplan); *The Five Ways We Grieve*, by Susan Berger (Trumpeter/Shambhala).

WRITERS CONFERENCES ASJA Writers Conference; Asilomar; Florida Suncoast Writers Conference; Whidbey Island Writers Conference; Florida First Coast Writers Festival; Agents and Editors Conference; Columbus Writers Conference; Southwest Writers Conference; Willamette Writers Conference; Dorothy Canfield Fisher Conference; Aloha Writers Conference; Pacific Northwest Writers Conference; IWWG.

TIPS "Read the agent listing carefully and comply with guidelines."

● WENDY SHERMAN ASSOCIATES, INC.

27 W. 24th St., New York, NY 10010. (212)279-9027. **E-mail:** wendy@wsherman.com. **E-mail:** submissions@wsherman.com. **Website:** www.wsherman.com. **Contact:** Wendy Sherman; Kim Perel. Member of AAR. Represents 50 clients. 30% of clients are new/unpublished writers.

○ Prior to opening the agency, Ms. Sherman served as vice president, executive director, associate publisher, subsidiary rights director, and sales and marketing director for major publishers.

MEMBER AGENTS Wendy Sherman (board member of AAR), Kim Perel.

REPRESENTS Considers these fiction areas: Mainstream fiction that hits the sweet spot between literary and commercial.

○—¬ "We specialize in developing new writers, as well as working with more established writers. My experience as a publisher has proven to be a great asset to my clients."

HOW TO CONTACT Query via e-mail only. Accepts simultaneous submissions. Responds in 1 month to queries. Obtains most new clients through recommendations from other writers.

TERMS Agent receives standard 15% commission. Offers written contract.

RECENT SALES *Z, A Novel of Zelda Fitzgerald*, by Therese Anne Fowler; *The Silence of Bonaventure Arrow*, by Rita Leganski; *Together Tea*, by Marjan Kamali; *A Long Long Time Ago and Essentially True*, by Brigid Pasulka; *Illuminations*, by Mary Sharratt; *The Accounting*, by William Lashner; *Lunch in Paris*, by Elizabeth Bard; *The Rules of Inheritance*, by Claire Bidwell Smith; *Love in Ninety Days*, by Dr. Diana Kirschner; *The Wow Factor*, by Jacqui Stafford; *Humor Memoirs*, by Wade Rouse.

TIPS "The bottom line is: Do your homework. Be as well prepared as possible. Read the books that will help you present yourself and your work with polish. You want your submission to stand out."

●● JEFFREY SIMMONS LITERARY AGENCY

15 Penn House, Mallory St., London NW8 8SX England. (44)(207)224-8917. **E-mail:** jasimmons@unicombox.co.uk. **Contact:** Jeffrey Simmons. Represents 43 clients. 40% of clients are new/unpublished writers. Currently handles nonfiction books (65%), novels (35%).

○ Prior to becoming an agent, Mr. Simmons was a publisher. He is also an author.

REPRESENTS Nonfiction books, novels. **Considers these fiction areas:** action, adventure, confession, crime, detective, family saga, literary, mainstream, mystery, police, suspense, thriller.

○—¬ "This agency seeks to handle good books and promising young writers. My long experience in publishing and as an author and ghostwriter means I can offer an excellent service all around, especially in terms of editorial experience where appropriate." Actively seeking quality fiction, biography, autobiography, showbiz, personality books, law, crime, politics, and world affairs. Does not want to receive science fiction, horror, fantasy, juvenile, academic books, or specialist subjects (e.g., cooking, gardening, religious).

HOW TO CONTACT Submit sample chapter, outline/proposal, SASE (IRCs if necessary). Prefers to read materials exclusively. Responds in 1 week to queries. Responds in 1 month to mss. Obtains most new clients through recommendations from others, solicitations.

TERMS Agent receives 10-15% commission on domestic sales. Agent receives 15% commission on foreign sales. Offers written contract, binding for lifetime of book in question or until it becomes out of print.

TIPS "When contacting us with an outline/proposal, include a brief biographical note (listing any previous publications, with publishers and dates). Preferably tell us if the book has already been offered elsewhere."

◑● BEVERLEY SLOPEN LITERARY AGENCY

131 Bloor St. W., Suite 711, Toronto, ON M5S 1S3 Canada. (416)964-9598. **E-mail:** beverly@slopenagency.ca. **Website:** www.slopenagency.ca. **Contact:** Beverley Slopen. Represents 70 clients. 20% of clients are new/unpublished writers. Currently handles nonfiction books (60%), novels (40%).

○ Prior to opening her agency, Ms. Slopen worked in publishing and as a journalist.

REPRESENTS Nonfiction books, novels, scholarly. **Considers these fiction areas:** literary, mystery, suspense.

⚷ "This agency has a strong bent toward Canadian writers." Actively seeking serious nonfiction that is accessible and appealing to the general reader. Does not want to receive fantasy, science fiction, or children's books.

HOW TO CONTACT Query by e-mail. Returns materials only with SASE (Canadian postage only). Accepts simultaneous submissions. Responds in 2 months to queries.

TERMS Agent receives 15% commission on domestic sales. Agent receives 10% commission on foreign sales. Offers written contract, binding for 2 years; 3-month notice must be given to terminate contract.

RECENT SALES *Solar Dance*, by Modris Eksteins (Knopf Canada, Harvard University Press. U.S.); *The Novels*, by Terry Fallis; *God's Brain*, by Lionel Tiger and Michael McGuire (Prometheus Books); *What They Wanted*, by Donna Morrissey (Penguin Canada, Premium/DTV Germany); *The Age of Persuasion*, by Terry O'Reilly and Mike Tennant (Knopf Canada, Counterpoint US); *Prisoner of Tehran*, by Marina Nemat (Penguin Canada, Free Press US, John Murray UK); *Race to the Polar Sea*, by Ken McGoogan (HarperCollins Canada, Counterpoint US); *Transgression*, by James Nichol (HarperCollins US, McArthur Canada, Goldmann Germany); *Midwife of Venice* and *The Harem Midwife*, by Roberta Rich; *Vermeer's Hat*, by Timothy Brook (HarperCollins Canada, Blooms-

bury US); *Distantly Related to Freud*, by Ann Charney (Cormorant).

TIPS "Please, no unsolicited manuscripts."

VALERIE SMITH, LITERARY AGENT

1746 Route 44-55, Box 160, Modena, NY 12548. **Contact:** Valerie Smith. Represents 17 clients. Currently handles nonfiction books (2%), novels (75%), story collections (1%), juvenile books (20%), scholarly books (1%), textbooks (1%).

REPRESENTS Nonfiction books, novels, juvenile, textbooks. **Considers these fiction areas:** fantasy, historical, juvenile, literary, mainstream, mystery, science, young women's/chick lit.

⚷ "This is a small, personalized agency with a strong long-term commitment to clients interested in building careers. I have strong ties to science fiction, fantasy, and young adult projects. I look for serious, productive writers whose work I can be passionate about." Does not want to receive unsolicited mss.

HOW TO CONTACT Query with synopsis, bio, 3 sample chapters, SASE. Contact by snail mail only. Obtains most new clients through recommendations from others.

TERMS Agent receives 15% commission on domestic sales. Agent receives 20% commission on foreign sales. Offers written contract; 6-week notice must be given to terminate contract.

◐ SPECTRUM LITERARY AGENCY

320 Central Park W., Suite 1-D, New York, NY 10025. **Fax:** (212)362-4562. **Website:** www.spectrumliteraryagency.com. **Contact:** Eleanor Wood, president. Estab. 1976. SFWA. Represents 90 clients. Currently handles nonfiction books (10%), novels (90%).

MEMBER AGENTS Eleanor Wood, Justin Bell.

REPRESENTS Nonfiction books, novels. **Considers these fiction areas:** fantasy, historical, mainstream, mystery, romance, science fiction, suspense.

⚷ Mr. Bell is actively seeking mystery submissions and a select amount of nonfiction

HOW TO CONTACT Query with SASE. Submit author bio, publishing credits. No unsolicited mss will be read. Queries and submissions by snail mail only. Ms. Wood and other agents have different addresses—see the website for full info. Responds in 1-3 months to queries. Obtains most new clients through recommendations from authors.

TERMS Agent receives 15% commission on domestic sales. Deducts for photocopying and book orders. **TIPS** "Spectrum's policy is to read only book-length manuscripts that we have specifically asked to see. Unsolicited manuscripts are not accepted. The letter should describe your book briefly and include publishing credits and background information or qualifications relating to your work, if any."

SPENCERHILL ASSOCIATES

P.O. Box 374, Chatham, NY 12037. (518)392-9293. **Fax:** (518)392-9554. **E-mail:** submissions@spencer hillassociates.com. **Website:** www.spencerhillassoci ates.com. **Contact:** Karen Solem or Jennifer Schober (please refer to their website for the latest information). Member of AAR. Represents 96 clients. 10% of clients are new/unpublished writers.

Prior to becoming an agent, Ms. Solem was editor-in-chief at HarperCollins and an associate publisher.

MEMBER AGENTS Karen Solem; Jennifer Schober. **REPRESENTS** Novels. **Considers these fiction areas:** crime, detective, historical, inspirational, literary, mainstream, police, religious, romance, thriller, young adult.

"We handle mostly commercial women's fiction, historical novels, romance (historical, contemporary, paranormal, urban fantasy), thrillers, and mysteries. We also represent Christian fiction. No nonfiction." No poetry, science fiction, children's picture books, or scripts.

HOW TO CONTACT Query submissions@spencer hillassociates.com with synopsis and first three chapters attached as a .doc or .rtf file. "Please note: We no longer accept queries via the mail." Responds in 6-8 weeks to queries "if we are interested in pursuing." **TERMS** Agent receives 15% commission on domestic sales. Agent receives 20% commission on foreign sales. Offers written contract; 3-month notice must be given to terminate contract.

THE SPIELER AGENCY

27 W. 20 St., Suite 305, New York, NY 10011. **E-mail:** thespieleragency@gmail.com. **Contact:** Joe Spieler. Represents 160 clients. 2% of clients are new/unpublished writers.

Prior to opening his agency, Mr. Spieler was a magazine editor.

MEMBER AGENTS Joe Spieler, Eric Myers.

REPRESENTS Nonfiction books, novels children's books. **Considers these fiction areas:** feminist, gay, lesbian, literary, mystery children's books, middlegrade and young adult novels.

HOW TO CONTACT Accepts electronic submissions, or send query letter and sample chapters. Returns materials only with SASE; otherwise materials are discarded when rejected. Accepts simultaneous submissions. Cannot guarantee a personal response to all queries. Obtains most new clients through recommendations, listing in *Guide to Literary Agents*. **TERMS** Agent receives 15% commission on domestic sales. Charges clients for messenger bills, photocopying, postage.

WRITERS CONFERENCES London Book Fair. **TIPS** "Check http://www.publishersmarketplace. com/members/spielerlit/."

NANCY STAUFFER ASSOCIATES

P.O. Box 1203, Darien, CT 06820. (203)202-2500. **E-mail:** StaufferAssoc@optonline.net. **Website:** pub lishersmarketplace.com/members/nstauffer. **Contact:** Nancy Stauffer Cahoon. Other memberships include Authors Guild. 5% of clients are new/unpublished writers. Currently handles nonfiction books (10%), novels (90%).

"Over the course of my more than 20-year career, I've held positions in the editorial, marketing, business, and rights departments of *The New York Times*, McGraw-Hill, and Doubleday. Before founding Nancy Stauffer Associates, I was director of foreign and performing rights, then director of subsidiary rights for Doubleday, where I was honored to have worked with a diverse range of internationally known and best-selling authors of all genres."

REPRESENTS **Considers these fiction areas:** contemporary, literary, regional.

HOW TO CONTACT Accepts simultaneous submissions. Obtains most new clients through referrals from existing clients.

TERMS Agent receives 15% commission on domestic sales. Agent receives 20% commission on foreign sales. Agent receives 15% commission on film sales. **RECENT SALES** *Blasphemy*, by Sherman Alexi; *Benediction*, by Kent Haruf; *Bone Fire*, by Mark Spragg; *The Carry Home*, by Gary Ferguson.

◐ STEELE-PERKINS LITERARY AGENCY

26 Island Ln., Canandaigua, NY 14424. (585)396-9290. **Fax:** (585)396-3579. **E-mail:** pattiesp@aol.com. **Contact:** Pattie Steele-Perkins. Member of AAR. Other memberships include RWA. Currently handles novels (100%).

REPRESENTS Novels. **Considers these fiction areas:** romance, women's category romance, romantic suspense, historical, contemporary, multicultural, and inspirational.

HOW TO CONTACT Submit synopsis and one chapter via e-mail (no attachments) or snail mail. Snail mail submissions require SASE. Accepts simultaneous submissions. Responds in 6 weeks to queries. Obtains most new clients through recommendations from others, queries/solicitations.

TERMS Agent receives 15% commission on domestic sales. Offers written contract, binding for 1 year; 1-month notice must be given to terminate contract.

RECENT SALES Sold 130 titles last year. This agency prefers not to share specific sales information.

WRITERS CONFERENCES RWA National Conference; BookExpo America; CBA Convention; Romance Slam Jam, Romantic Times.

TIPS "Be patient. E-mail rather than call. Make sure what you are sending is the best it can be."

● STERNIG & BYRNE LITERARY AGENCY

2370 S. 107th St., Apt. #4, Milwaukee, WI 53227. (414)328-8034. **Fax:** (414)328-8034. **E-mail:** jackbyrne@hotmail.com. **Website:** www.sff.net/people/jackbyrne. **Contact:** Jack Byrne. Other memberships include SFWA, MWA. Represents 30 clients. 10% of clients are new/unpublished writers. Currently handles nonfiction books (5%), novels (90%), juvenile books (5%).

REPRESENTS Nonfiction books, novels, juvenile. **Considers these fiction areas:** fantasy, horror, mystery, science fiction, suspense.

8—⚷ "Our client list is comfortably full, and our current needs are therefore quite limited." Actively seeking science fiction/fantasy, and mystery by established writers. Does not want to receive romance, poetry, textbooks, or highly specialized nonfiction.

HOW TO CONTACT Query with SASE. Prefers e-mail queries (no attachments); hard copy queries also acceptable. Responds in 3 weeks to queries. Responds in 3 months to mss.

TERMS Agent receives 15% commission on domestic sales. Agent receives 20% commission on foreign sales. Offers written contract; 2-month notice must be given to terminate contract.

TIPS "Don't send first drafts, have a professional presentation (including cover letter), and know your field. Read what's been done—good and bad."

● THE STROTHMAN AGENCY, LLC

P.O. Box 231132, Boston, MA 02123. (617)742-2011. **Fax:** (617)742-2014. **E-mail:** info@strothmanagency.com. **Website:** www.strothmanagency.com. **Contact:** Wendy Strothman, Lauren MacLeod. Member of AAR. Other memberships include Authors' Guild. Represents 50 clients. Currently handles nonfiction books (70%), novels (10%), scholarly books (20%).

◐ Prior to becoming an agent, Ms. Strothman was head of Beacon Press (1983-1995) and executive vice president of Houghton Mifflin's trade and reference division (1996-2002).

MEMBER AGENTS Wendy Strothman; Lauren MacLeod.

REPRESENTS Nonfiction books, novels, scholarly young adult and middle grade. **Considers these fiction areas:** literary, young adult, middle grade.

8—⚷ "Because we are highly selective in the clients we represent, we increase the value publishers place on our properties. We specialize in narrative nonfiction, memoir, history, science and nature, arts and culture, literary travel, current affairs, and some business. We have a highly selective practice in literary fiction, young adult and middle-grade fiction, and nonfiction. We are now opening our doors to more commercial fiction from authors who have a platform. If you have a platform, please mention it in your query letter. The Strothman Agency seeks out scholars, journalists, and other acknowledged and emerging experts in their fields. We are now actively looking for authors of well-written young-adult fiction and nonfiction. Browse the 'Latest News' [on our website] to get an idea of the types of books we represent. For more about what we're looking for, read 'Pitching an Agent: The Strothman Agency' on the publishing website www.strothmanagency.com." Does not want to receive commercial fiction, romance, science fiction, or self-help.

HOW TO CONTACT Accepts queries only via e-mail at strothmanagency@gmail.com. See submission guidelines online. Accepts simultaneous submissions. Responds in 4 weeks to queries. Responds in 6 weeks to mss. Obtains most new clients through recommendations from others.

TERMS Agent receives 15% commission on domestic sales. Agent receives 20% commission on foreign sales. Offers written contract; 30-day notice must be given to terminate contract.

EMMA SWEENEY AGENCY, LLC

245 E 80th St., Suite 7E, New York, NY 10075. **E-mail:** queries@emmasweeneyagency.com. **Website:** www .emmasweeneyagency.com. Member of AAR. Other memberships include Women's Media Group. Represents 80 clients. 5% of clients are new/unpublished writers. Currently handles nonfiction books (50%), novels (50%).

- Prior to becoming an agent, Ms. Sweeney was director of subsidiary rights at Grove Press. Since 1990, she has been a literary agent.

MEMBER AGENTS Emma Sweeney, president; Noah Ballard, rights manager and agent (represents literary fiction, young adult novels, and narrative nonfiction). Considers these nonfiction areas: popular science, pop culture and music history, biography, memoirs, cooking, and anything relating to animals. Considers these fiction areas: literary (of the highest writing quality possible), young adult.

REPRESENTS Nonfiction books, novels.

- "We specialize in quality fiction and nonfiction. Our primary areas of interest include literary and women's fiction, mysteries and thrillers, science, history, biography, memoir, religious studies and the natural sciences." Does not want to receive romance, Westerns, or screenplays.

HOW TO CONTACT Send query letter and first 10 pages in body of e-mail (no attachments) to queries@ emmasweeneyagency.com. No snail mail queries.

TERMS Agent receives 15% commission on domestic sales. Agent receives 10% commission on foreign sales.

WRITERS CONFERENCES Nebraska Writers Conference; Words and Music Festival in New Orleans.

TALCOTT NOTCH LITERARY

2 Broad St., Second Floor, Suite 10, Milford, CT 06460. (203)876-4959. **Fax:** (203)876-9517. **E-mail:** editorial@talcottnotch.net. **Website:** www.talcottnotch.net.

Contact: Gina Panettieri, President. Represents 35 clients. 25% of clients are new/unpublished writers. Currently handles nonfiction books (50%), novels (20%), story collections (5%), juvenile books (20%), scholarly books (10%).

- Prior to becoming an agent, Ms. Panettieri was a freelance writer and editor.

MEMBER AGENTS Gina Panettieri (nonfiction, mystery); Rachel Dowen (children's fiction, mystery).

REPRESENTS Nonfiction books, novels, juvenile, scholarly, textbooks. **Considers these fiction areas:** action, adventure, crime, detective, fantasy, juvenile, mystery, police, romance, suspense, thriller, young adult.

HOW TO CONTACT Query via e-mail (preferred) with first 10 pages of the ms within the body of the e-mail, not as an attachment, or with SASE. Consult website for detailed submission guidelines. Accepts simultaneous submissions. Responds in 1 week to queries. Responds in 4-6 weeks to mss.

TERMS Agent receives 15% commission on domestic sales. Agent receives 20% commission on foreign sales. Offers written contract, binding for 1 year.

RECENT SALES Sold 36 titles in the last year. *Delivered From Evil*, by Ron Franscell (Fairwinds) and *Sourtoe* (Globe Pequot Press); *Hellforged*, by Nancy Holzner (Berkley Ace Science Fiction); *Welcoming Kitchen; 200 Allergen- and Gluten-Free Vegan Recipes*, by Kim Lutz and Megan Hart (Sterling); *Dr. Seth's Love Prescription*, by Dr. Seth Meyers (Adams Media); *The Book of Ancient Bastards,* by Brian Thornton (Adams Media); *Hope in Courage*, by Beth Fehlbaum (Westside Books).

TIPS "Know your market and how to reach them. A strong platform is essential in your book proposal. Can you effectively use social media? Are you a strong networker: Are you familiar with the book bloggers in your genre? Are you involved with the interest-specific groups that can help you? What can you do to break through the 'noise' and help present your book to your readers? Check our website for more tips and information on this topic."

PATRICIA TEAL LITERARY AGENCY

2036 Vista Del Rosa, Fullerton, CA 92831-1336. **Phone:** (714)738-8333. **Contact:** Patricia Teal. Member of AAR. Other memberships include RWA, Authors Guild. Represents 20 clients. Currently handles nonfiction books (10%), (90% fiction).

REPRESENTS Nonfiction books, novels. **Considers these fiction areas:** glitz, mainstream, mystery, romance, suspense.

⚮ This agency specializes in women's fiction, commercial how-to, and self-help nonfiction. Does not want to receive poetry, short stories, articles, science fiction, fantasy, or regency romance.

HOW TO CONTACT Published authors only may query with SASE. Accepts simultaneous submissions. Responds in 10 days to queries. Responds in 6 weeks to mss. Obtains most new clients through conferences, recommendations from authors and editors.

TERMS Agent receives 10-15% commission on domestic sales. Agent receives 20% commission on foreign sales. Offers written contract, binding for 1 year. Charges clients for ms copies.

RECENT SALES Sold 30 titles in the last year. *Texas Rose*, by Marie Ferrarella (Silhouette); *Watch Your Language*, by Sterling Johnson (St. Martin's Press); *The Black Sheep's Baby*, by Kathleen Creighton (Silhouette); *Man With a Message*, by Muriel Jensen (Harlequin).

WRITERS CONFERENCES RWA Conferences; Asilomar; BookExpo America; Bouchercon; Aloha Writers Conference.

TIPS "Include SASE with all correspondence. I am taking on published authors only."

◑ TRACY BROWN LITERARY AGENCY

P.O. Box 88, Scarsdale, NY 10583. (914)400-4147. **Fax:** (914)931-1746. **E-mail:** tracy@brownlit.com. **Contact:** Tracy Brown. Represents 35 clients. Currently handles nonfiction books (90%), novels (10%).

💬 Prior to becoming an agent, Mr. Brown was a book editor for 25 years.

REPRESENTS Nonfiction, novels anthologies. **Considers these fiction areas:** contemporary issues, feminist, literary, mainstream, women's.

⚮ Specializes in thorough involvement with clients' books at every stage of the process from writing to proposals to publication. Actively seeking serious nonfiction and fiction. Does not want to receive YA, sci-fi, or romance.

HOW TO CONTACT Submit outline/proposal, synopsis, author bio. Accepts simultaneous submissions. Responds in 2 weeks to queries. Obtains most new clients through referrals.

TERMS Agent receives 15% commission on domestic sales. Agent receives 20% commission on foreign sales. Offers written contract.

RECENT SALES *Why Have Kids?* by Jessica Valenti (HarperCollins); *Hotel Notell: A Novel*, by Daphne Uviller (Bantam); *Healing Sexual Pain*, by Deborah Coady, MD, and Nancy Fish, MSW, MPH (Seal Press).

◑● TRANSATLANTIC LITERARY AGENCY

2 Bloor St., Suite 3500, Toronto, ON M4W 1A8 Canada. **E-mail:** info@tla1.com. **Website:** www.tla1.com. Represents 250 clients. 10% of clients are new/unpublished writers. Currently handles nonfiction books (30%), novels (15%), juvenile books (50%), textbooks (5%).

MEMBER AGENTS Lynn Bennett, Lynn@tla1.com, (juvenile and young adult fiction); Shaun Bradley, Shaun@tla1.com (literary fiction and narrative nonfiction); Marie Campbell, Marie@tla1.com (literary juvenile and young adult fiction); Andrea Cascardi, Andrea@tla1.com (literary juvenile and young adult fiction); Samantha Haywood, Sam@tla1.com (literary fiction, narrative nonfiction and graphic novels); Don Sedgwick, Don@tla1.com (literary fiction and narrative nonfiction).

REPRESENTS Nonfiction books, novels, juvenile. **Considers these fiction areas:** juvenile, literary, mainstream, mystery, suspense, young adult.

⚮ "In both children's and adult literature, we market directly into the United States, the United Kingdom, and Canada." Actively seeking literary children's and adult fiction, nonfiction. Does not want to receive picture books, poetry, screenplays, or stage plays.

HOW TO CONTACT Submit e-query with synopsis, 2 sample chapters, bio. Always refer to the website, as guidelines will change. Also refer to website for appropriate agent contact info to send e-query. Responds in 2 weeks to queries. Obtains most new clients through recommendations from others.

TERMS Agent receives 15% commission on domestic sales. Agent receives 20% commission on foreign sales. Offers written contract; 45-day notice must be given to terminate contract. This agency charges for photocopying and postage when it exceeds $100.

RECENT SALES Sold 250 titles in the last year.

TRIADA U.S. LITERARY AGENCY, INC.

P.O. Box 561, Sewickley, PA 15143. (412)401-3376. **E-mail:** uwe@triadaus.com. **Website:** www.triadaus.com. **Contact:** Dr. Uwe Stender. Member of AAR. Represents 65 clients. 20% of clients are new/unpublished writers.

REPRESENTS Fiction, nonfiction. **Considers these fiction areas:** action, adventure, crime, detective, ethnic, historical, horror, juvenile, literary, mainstream, mystery, occult, police, romance, women's, especially young adult, women's fiction, and mysteries.

- "We are looking for great writing and story platforms. Our response time is fairly unique. We recognize that neither we nor the authors have time to waste, so we guarantee a 5-day response time. We usually respond within 24 hours. " Actively looking for both fiction and nonfiction in all areas.

HOW TO CONTACT E-mail queries preferred; otherwise query with SASE. "We do not respond to postal submission that aren't accompanied by a SASE." Accepts simultaneous submissions. Responds in 1-5 weeks to queries. Responds in 2-6 weeks to mss. Obtains most new clients through recommendations from others, conferences.

TERMS Agent receives 15% commission on domestic sales. Agent receives 20% commission on foreign sales. Offers written contract; 30-day notice must be given to terminate contract.

RECENT SALES *The Man Whisperer*, by Samantha Brett and Donna Sozio (Adams Media); *Whatever Happened to Pudding Pops*, by Gael Fashingbauer Cooper and Brian Bellmont (Penguin/Perigee); *86'd*, by Dan Fante (Harper Perennial); *Hating Olivia*, by Mark SaFranko (Harper Perennial); *Everything I'm Not Made Me Everything I Am*, by Jeff Johnson (Smiley Books).

TIPS "I comment on all requested manuscripts that I reject."

THE UNTER AGENCY

23 W. 73rd St., Suite 100, New York, NY 10023. (212)401-4068. **E-mail:** Jennifer@theunteragency.com. **Website:** www.theunteragency.com. **Contact:** Jennifer Unter. Estab. 2008.

- Ms. Unter began her book publishing career in the editorial department at Henry Holt & Co. She later worked at the Karpfinger Agency while she attended law school. She then be-came an associate at the entertainment firm of Cowan, DeBaets, Abrahams & Sheppard LLP where she practiced primarily in the areas of publishing and copyright law.

REPRESENTS **Considers these fiction areas:** commercial, mainstream, picture books, young adult.

- This agency specializes in children's and non-fiction, but does take quality fiction.

HOW TO CONTACT Send an e-query.

UPSTART CROW LITERARY

P.O. Box 25404, Brooklyn, NY 11202. **E-mail:** info@upstartcrowliterary.com. **E-mail:** danielle.submission@gmail.com; alexandra.submission@gmail.com. **Website:** www.upstartcrowliterary.com. **Contact:** Danielle Chiotti, Alexandra Penfold. Estab. 2009.

MEMBER AGENTS Michael Stearns; Chris Richman (special interest in books for boys, books with unforgettable characters, and fantasy that "doesn't take itself too seriously"); Danielle Chiotti (books ranging from contemporary women's fiction to narrative nonfiction, from romance to relationship stories, humorous tales, and YA fiction); Ted Malawer (accepting queries only through conference submissions and client referrals); Alexandra Penfold (children's—picture books, middle grade, YA; illustrators and author/illustrators).

REPRESENTS **Considers these fiction areas:** picture books, women's, young adult, middle grade.

HOW TO CONTACT Upstart Crow agents that are currently accepting submissions are Danielle Chiotti and Alexandra Penfold. See website for what they are seeking.

VENTURE LITERARY

2683 Via de la Valle, G-714, Del Mar, CA 92014. (619)807-1887. **Fax:** (772)365-8321. **E-mail:** submissions@ventureliterary.com. **Website:** www.ventureliterary.com. **Contact:** Frank R. Scatoni. Represents 50 clients. 40% of clients are new/unpublished writers. Currently handles nonfiction books (80%), novels (20%).

- Prior to becoming an agent, Mr. Scatoni worked as an editor at Simon & Schuster.

MEMBER AGENTS Frank R. Scatoni (general nonfiction, biography, memoir, narrative nonfiction, sports, serious nonfiction, graphic novels, narratives).

REPRESENTS Nonfiction books, novels graphic novels, narratives. **Considers these fiction areas:** action, adventure, crime, detective, literary, mainstream, mystery, police, sports, suspense, thriller, women's.

☛ Specializes in nonfiction, sports, biography, gambling, and nonfiction narratives. Actively seeking nonfiction, graphic novels, and narratives. Does not want fantasy, sci-fi, romance, children's picture books, or Westerns.

HOW TO CONTACT Considers e-mail queries only. *No unsolicited mss* and no snail mail whatsoever. See website for complete submission guidelines. Obtains most new clients through recommendations from others.

TERMS Agent receives 15% commission on domestic sales. Agent receives 20% commission on foreign sales. Offers written contract.

RECENT SALES *The 9/11 Report: A Graphic Adaptation*, by Sid Jacobson and Ernie Colon (FSG); *Having a Baby*, by Cindy Margolis (Perigee/Penguin); *Phil Gordon's Little Blue Book*, by Phil Gordon (Simon & Schuster); *Atomic America*, by Todd Tucker (Free Press); *War as They Knew It*, by Michael Rosenberg (Grand Central); *Game Day*, by Craig James (Wiley); *The Blueprint* by Christopher Price (Thomas Dunne Books).

◐ BETH VESEL LITERARY AGENCY

80 Fifth Ave., Suite 1101, New York, NY 10011. (212)924-4252. **E-mail:** kezia@bvlit.com. **Contact:** Kezia Toth, assistant. Represents 65 clients. 10% of clients are new/unpublished writers. Currently handles nonfiction books (75%), novels (10%), story collections (5%), scholarly books (10%).

○ Prior to becoming an agent, Ms. Vesel was a poet and a journalist.

REPRESENTS Nonfiction books, novels. **Considers these fiction areas:** crime, detective, literary, police Francophone novels.

☛ "My specialties include serious nonfiction, psychology, cultural criticism, memoir, and women's issues." Actively seeking cultural criticism, literary psychological thrillers, and sophisticated memoirs. No uninspired psychology or run-of-the-mill first novels.

HOW TO CONTACT Query with SASE. Accepts simultaneous submissions. Responds in 2 weeks to queries. Responds in 1 month to mss. Obtains most new clients through referrals, reading good magazines, contacting professionals with ideas.

TERMS Agent receives 15% commission on domestic sales. Agent receives 20% commission on foreign sales. Offers written contract.

RECENT SALES *Neurotribes*, by Steve Silberman (Penguin); *Blessing the Hands That Feed Us*, by Vicki Robin (Viking); *Phantom Street*, by Christina Baker Kline (William Morrow); *James Browns' Body*, by Greg Tate (FSG); *Remembering Ritalin*, by Lawrence Diller (Perigee Publishers); *The Use and Abuse of Literature*, by Marjorie Garber (Pantheon).

WRITERS CONFERENCES Squaw Valley Writers Workshop, Iowa Summer Writing Festival.

TIPS "Try to find out if you fit on a particular agent's list by looking at his/her books and comparing yours. You can almost always find out who represents a book by looking at the acknowledgments."

◐ JOHN A. WARE LITERARY AGENCY

392 Central Park W., New York, NY 10025. (212)866-4733. **Fax:** (212)866-4734. **Contact:** John Ware. Represents 60 clients. 40% of clients are new/unpublished writers. Currently handles nonfiction books (75%), novels (25%).

○ Prior to opening his agency, Mr. Ware served as a literary agent with James Brown Associates/Curtis Brown, Ltd., and as an editor for Doubleday.

REPRESENTS Nonfiction books, novels. **Considers these fiction areas:** detective, mystery, thriller, accessible literary, noncategory fiction.

☛ Does not want personal memoirs.

HOW TO CONTACT Query with SASE. Send a letter only. Accepts simultaneous submissions. Responds in 2 weeks to queries.

TERMS Agent receives 15% commission on domestic sales, 20% commission on foreign sales, film.

RECENT SALES *One Shot at Forever*, by Chris Ballard (Hyperion); *Knights of The Sea*, by David Hanna (New American Library); *Becoming Clementine*, by Jennifer Niven (Plume); *Kosher USA*, by Roger Horowitz (Columbia); *The River's Own*, by Travis Hugh Culley (Random House).

TIPS "Writers must have appropriate credentials for authorship of proposal (nonfiction); no publishing track record required. I am open to good writing and interesting ideas by new or veteran writers."

● CHERRY WEINER LITERARY AGENCY

28 Kipling Way, Manalapan, NJ 07726. (732)446-2096. **Fax:** (732)792-0506. **E-mail:** cherry8486@aol

.com. **Contact:** Cherry Weiner. Represents 40 clients. 10% of clients are new/unpublished writers. Currently handles nonfiction books (10-20%), novels (80-90%). **REPRESENTS** Nonfiction books, novels. **Considers these fiction areas:** action, adventure, contemporary issues, crime, detective, family saga, fantasy, frontier, historical, mainstream, mystery, police, psychic, romance, science fiction, supernatural, thriller, Westerns.

> *This agency is currently not accepting new clients except by referral or by personal contact at writers conferences.* Specializes in fantasy, science fiction, Westerns, mysteries (both contemporary and historical), historical novels, Native-American works, mainstream, and all genre romances.

HOW TO CONTACT Query with SASE. Prefers to read materials exclusively. Does not accept e-mail queries. Responds in 1 week to queries. Responds in 2 months to requested mss.

TERMS Agent receives 15% commission on domestic sales. Agent receives 15% commission on foreign sales. Offers written contract. Charges clients for extra copies of mss, first-class postage for author's copies of books, express mail for important documents/mss.

RECENT SALES Sold 70 titles in the last year. This agency prefers not to share information on specific sales.

TIPS "Meet agents and publishers at conferences. Establish a relationship, then get in touch with them and remind them of the meeting and conference."

THE WEINGEL-FIDEL AGENCY

310 E. 46th St., 21E, New York, NY 10017. (212)599-2959. **Contact:** Loretta Weingel-Fidel. Currently handles nonfiction books (75%), novels (25%).

> Prior to opening her agency, Ms. Weingel-Fidel was a psychoeducational diagnostician.

REPRESENTS Nonfiction books, novels. **Considers these fiction areas:** literary, mainstream.

> This agency specializes in commercial and literary fiction and nonfiction. Actively seeking investigative journalism. Does not want to receive genre fiction, self-help, science fiction, or fantasy.

HOW TO CONTACT Accepts writers by referral only. *No unsolicited mss.*

TERMS Agent receives 15% commission on domestic sales. Agent receives 20% commission on foreign

sales. Offers written contract, binding for 1 year with automatic renewal. Bills sent back to clients are all reasonable expenses, such as UPS, express mail, photocopying, etc.

TIPS "A very small, selective list enables me to work very closely with my clients to develop and nurture talent. I only take on projects and writers about which I am extremely enthusiastic."

LARRY WEISSMAN LITERARY, LLC

526 8th St., #2R, Brooklyn, NY 11215. **E-mail:** lwsubmissions@gmail.com. **Contact:** Larry Weissman. Represents 35 clients. Currently handles nonfiction books (80%), novels (10%), story collections (10%). **REPRESENTS** Nonfiction books, novels, short story collections. **Considers these fiction areas:** literary.

> "Very interested in established journalists with bold voices. Interested in anything to do with food. Fiction has to feel 'vital' and short stories are accepted, but only if you can sell us on an idea for a novel as well." Nonfiction, including food and lifestyle, politics, pop culture, narrative, cultural/social issues, journalism. No genre fiction, poetry, or children's.

HOW TO CONTACT "Send e-queries only. If you don't hear back, your project was not right for our list."

TERMS Agent receives 15% commission on domestic sales. Agent receives 20% commission on foreign sales.

WHIMSY LITERARY AGENCY, LLC

310 E. 12th St., Suite 2C, New York, NY 10003. (212)674-7161. **E-mail:** whimsynyc@aol.com. **Website:** http://whimsyliteraryagency.com/. **Contact:** Jackie Meyer. Other memberships include Center for Independent Publishing Advisory Board. Represents 30 clients. 20% of clients are new/unpublished writers. Currently handles nonfiction books (100%).

> Prior to becoming an agent, Ms. Meyer was with Warner Books for 19 years; Ms. Vezeris and Ms. Legette have 30 years experience at various book publishers.

MEMBER AGENTS Jackie Meyer; Olga Vezeris (fiction and nonfiction); Nansci LeGette, senior associate in LA.

REPRESENTS Nonfiction books. **Considers these fiction areas:** mainstream, religious, thriller, women's.

> "Whimsy looks for projects that are concept- and platform driven. We seek books that edu-

cate, inspire, and entertain." Actively seeking experts in their field with good platforms.

HOW TO CONTACT Send a query letter via e-mail. Send a synopsis, bio, platform, and proposal. No snail mail submissions. Responds "quickly, but only if interested" to queries. *Does not accept unsolicited mss.* Obtains most new clients through recommendations from others, solicitations.

TERMS Agent receives 15% commission on domestic sales. Agent receives 20% commission on foreign sales. Offers written contract. Charges for posting and photocopying.

● WM CLARK ASSOCIATES

186 Fifth Ave., Second Floor, New York, NY 10010. (212)675-2784. **Fax:** (347)-649-9262. **E-mail:** general@wmclark.com. **Website:** www.wmclark.com. Estab. 1997. Member of AAR. 50% of clients are new/unpublished writers. Currently handles nonfiction books (50%), novels (50%).

○ Prior to opening WCA, Mr. Clark was an agent at the William Morris Agency.

REPRESENTS Nonfiction books, novels. **Considers these fiction areas:** contemporary issues, ethnic, historical, literary, mainstream Southern fiction.

⚷ "William Clark represents a wide range of titles across all formats to the publishing, motion picture, television, and new media fields on behalf of authors of first fiction and award-winning, best-selling narrative nonfiction, international authors in translation, chefs, musicians, and artists. Offering individual focus and a global presence, the agency undertakes to discover, develop, and market today's most interesting content and the talents that create it, and forge sophisticated and innovative plans for self-promotion, reliable revenue streams, and an enduring creative career. Referral partners are available to provide services including editorial consultation, media training, lecture booking, marketing support, and public relations. Agency does not respond to screenplays or screenplay pitches. It is advised that before querying you become familiar with the kinds of books we handle by browsing our Book List, which is available on our website."

HOW TO CONTACT Accepts queries via online form only at www.wmclark.com/queryguidelines.html. We respond to all queries submitted via this form. Responds in 1-2 months to queries.

TERMS Agent receives 15% commission on domestic sales. Agent receives 20% commission on foreign sales. Offers written contract.

TIPS "WCA works on a reciprocal basis with Ed Victor Ltd. (UK) in representing select properties to the U.S. market and vice versa. Translation rights are sold directly in the German, Italian, Spanish, Portuguese, Latin American, French, Dutch, and Scandinavian territories in association with Andrew Nurnberg Associates Ltd. (UK); through offices in China, Bulgaria, Czech Republic, Latvia, Poland, Hungary, and Russia; and through corresponding agents in Japan, Greece, Israel, Turkey, Korea, Taiwan, and Thailand."

○ WOLFSON LITERARY AGENCY

P.O. Box 266, New York, NY 10276. **E-mail:** query@wolfsonliterary.com. **Website:** www.wolfsonliterary.com. **Contact:** Michelle Wolfson. Estab. 2007. Adheres to AAR canon of ethics. Currently handles nonfiction books (20%), novels (80%).

○ Prior to forming her own agency in December 2007, Ms. Wolfson spent two years with Artists & Artisans, Inc. and two years with Ralph Vicinanza, Ltd.

⚷ Actively seeking commercial fiction: young adult, mainstream, mysteries, thrillers, suspense, women's fiction, romance, practical, or narrative nonfiction (particularly of interest to women).

HOW TO CONTACT E-queries only! Accepts simultaneous submissions. Responds only if interested. Positive response is generally given within 2-4 weeks. Responds in 3 months to mss. Obtains most new clients through queries or recommendations from others.

TERMS Agent receives 15% commission on domestic sales. Agent receives 25% commission on foreign sales. Offers written contract; 30-day notice must be given to terminate contract.

WRITERS CONFERENCES SDSU Writers Conference; New Jersey Romance Writers of America Writers Conference; American Independent Writers Conference in Washington DC.

TIPS "Be persistent."

● WRITERS' REPRESENTATIVES, LLC

116 W. 14th St., 11th Floor, New York, NY 10011-7305. **Fax:** (212)620-0023. **E-mail:** transom@writersreps

.com. **Website:** www.writersreps.com. Represents 130 clients. 10% of clients are new/unpublished writers. Currently handles nonfiction books (90%), novels (10%).

○ Prior to becoming an agent, Ms. Chu was a lawyer; Mr. Hartley worked at Simon & Schuster, Harper & Row and Cornell University Press.

MEMBER AGENTS Lynn Chu, Glen Hartley, Christine Hsu.

REPRESENTS Nonfiction books, novels. **Considers these fiction areas:** literary.

○— Serious nonfiction and quality fiction. No motion picture or television screenplays.

HOW TO CONTACT Query with SASE. Prefers to read materials exclusively. Considers simultaneous queries, but must be informed at time of submission. Consult website section "FAQ" for detailed submission guidelines.

TERMS Agent receives 15% commission on domestic sales. Agent receives 20% commission on foreign sales.

TIPS "Always include a SASE; it will ensure a response from the agent and the return of your submitted material."

① HELEN ZIMMERMANN LITERARY AGENCY

3 Emmy Lane, New Paltz, NY 12561. **E-mail:** Helen@ZimmAgency.com. **Website:** www.zimmermannlit erary.com. **Contact:** Helen Zimmermann. Estab. 2003. Currently handles nonfiction books (80%), other (20% fiction).

○ Prior to opening her agency, Ms. Zimmermann was the director of advertising and promotion at Random House and the events coordinator at an independent bookstore.

REPRESENTS Nonfiction books, novels. **Considers these fiction areas:** family saga, historical, literary, mystery, suspense.

○— "As an agent who has experience at both a publishing house and a bookstore, I have a keen insight for viable projects. This experience also helps me ensure every client gets published well, through the whole process." Actively seeking memoirs, pop culture, women's issues, and accessible literary fiction. Does not want to receive horror, science fiction, poetry, or romance.

HOW TO CONTACT Accepts e-mail queries only. E-mail should include a short description of project and bio, whether it be fiction or nonfiction. Accepts simultaneous submissions. Responds in 2 weeks to queries. Responds in 1 month to mss. Obtains most new clients through recommendations from others, solicitations.

TERMS Agent receives 15% commission on domestic sales. Offers written contract; 30-day notice must be given to terminate contract. Charges for photocopying and postage (reimbursed if project is sold).

WRITERS CONFERENCES BEA/Writer's Digest Books Writers Conference; Portland, ME Writers Conference; Berkshire Writers and Readers Conference; La Jolla Writers Conference; The New School Writers Conference; Vermont Writers Conference.

MAGAZINES

This section contains magazine listings that fall into one of several categories: literary, consumer, small circulation, and online. Our decision to combine magazines under one section was two-fold: All of these magazines represent markets specifically for short fiction, and many magazines now publish both print and online versions, making them more difficult to subcategorize. Below, we outline specifics for literary, online, consumer, and small circulation magazines.

LITERARY MAGAZINES

Although definitions of what constitutes literary writing vary, editors of literary journals agree they want to publish the best fiction they can acquire. Qualities they look for in fiction include fully developed characters, strong and unique narrative voice, flawless mechanics, and careful attention to detail in content and manuscript preparation. Most of the authors writing such fiction are well read and well educated, and many are students and graduates of university creative writing programs.

Stepping Stones to Recognition

Some well-established literary journals pay several hundred or even several thousand dollars for a short story. Most, though, can only pay with contributor's copies or a subscription to their publication. However, being published in literary journals offers the important benefits of experience, exposure, and prestige. Agents and major book publishers regularly read literary magazines in search of new writers. Work from these journals is also selected for inclusion in annual prize anthologies.

You'll find most of the well-known prestigious literary journals listed here. Many, including *The Southern Review* and *Ploughshares*, are associated with universities, while others like *The Paris Review* are independently published.

Selecting the Right Literary Magazine

Once you have browsed through this section and have a list of journals you might like to submit to, read those listings again carefully. Remember, this is information editors provide to help you submit work that fits their needs. Note that you will find some magazines that do not read submissions all year long. Whether limited reading periods are tied to a university schedule or meant to accommodate the capabilities of a very small staff, those periods are noted within listings (when the editors notify us). The staffs of university journals are usually made up of student editors and a managing editor who is also a faculty member. These staffs often change every year. Whenever possible, we indicate this in listings and give the name of the current editor and the length of that editor's term. Also be aware that the schedule of a university journal usually coincides with that university's academic year, meaning that the editors of most university publications are difficult or impossible to reach during the summer.

Furthering Your Search

It cannot be stressed enough that reading the listings for literary journals is only the first part of developing your marketing plan. The second part, equally important, is to obtain fiction guidelines and to read with great care the actual journal you'd like to submit to. Reading copies of these journals helps you determine the fine points of each magazine's publishing style and sensibility. There is no substitute for this type of hands-on research.

Unlike commercial periodicals available at most newsstands and bookstores, it requires a little more effort to obtain some of the literary magazines listed. The super-chain bookstores are doing a better job these days of stocking literaries, and you can find some in independent and college bookstores, especially those published in your area. The Internet is an invaluable resource for submission guidelines, as more and more journals establish an online presence. You may, however, need to send for a sample copy. We include sample copy prices in the listings whenever possible. In addition to reading your sample copies, pay close attention to the Advice section of each listing. There you'll often find a very specific description of the style of fiction the editors at that publication prefer.

Another way to find out more about literary magazines is to check out the various prize anthologies and take note of journals whose fiction is being selected for publication in them. Studying prize anthologies not only lets you know which magazines are publishing award-winning work, but it also provides a valuable overview of what is considered to be the best fiction published today. Those anthologies include:

- *Best American Short Stories*, published by Houghton Mifflin.
- *New Stories from the South: The Year's Best*, published by Algonquin Books of Chapel Hill.
- *The O. Henry Prize Stories*, published by Doubleday/Anchor.
- *Pushcart Prize: Best of the Small Presses,* published by Pushcart Press.

CONSUMER MAGAZINES

Consumer magazines are publications that reach a broad readership. Many have circulations in the hundreds of thousands or millions. And among the oldest magazines listed in this section are ones not only familiar to us, but also to our parents, grandparents, and even great-grandparents: *The Atlantic Monthly* (1857), *Esquire* (1933), and *Ellery Queen's Mystery Magazine* (1941).

Consumer periodicals make excellent markets for fiction in terms of exposure, prestige, and payment. Because these magazines are well known, however, competition is great. Even the largest consumer publications buy only one or two stories an issue, yet thousands of writers submit to these popular magazines.

Despite the odds, it is possible for talented new writers to break into consumer magazines. Your keys to breaking into these markets include careful research, professional presentation, and, of course, top-quality fiction.

SMALL-CIRCULATION MAGAZINES

Small-circulation magazines include general interest, special interest, regional, and genre magazines with circulations under ten thousand. Although these magazines vary greatly in size, theme, format, and management, the editors are all looking for short stories. Their specific fiction needs present writers of all degrees of expertise and interests with an abundance of publishing opportunities. Among the diverse publications in this section are magazines devoted to almost every topic, every level of writing, and every type of writer. Some of these markets publish fiction about a particular geographic area or by authors who live in that locale.

Although not as high-paying as the large-circulation consumer magazines, you'll find some of the publications listed here do pay writers 1–5¢/word or more. Also, unlike the big consumer magazines, these markets are very open to new writers and relatively easy to break into. Their only criterion is that your story be well written, well presented, and suitable for their particular readership.

ONLINE MARKETS

As production and distribution costs go up and the number of subscribers falls, more and more magazines are giving up print publication and moving online. Relatively inexpensive to maintain and quicker to accept and post submissions, online fiction sites are growing fast in numbers and legitimacy. The benefit for writers is that your stories can get more attention in online journals than in small literary journals. Small journals have small print runs—five hundred to one thousand copies—so there's a limit on how many people will read your work. There is no limit when your work appears online.

There is also no limit to the types of online journals being published, offering outlets for a rich and diverse community of voices. These include genre sites, particular those for science fiction/fantasy and horror, and mainstream short fiction markets. Online literary journals range from the traditional to those with a decidedly quirkier bent. Writers will also find online outlets for more highly experimental and multimedia work.

While the medium of online publication is different, the traditional rules of publishing apply to submissions. Writers should research the site and archives carefully, looking for a match in sensibility for their work. Follow submission guidelines exactly and submit courteously. True, these sites aren't bound by traditional print schedules, so your work theoretically may be published more quickly. But that doesn't mean online journals have larger staffs, so exercise patience with editors considering your manuscript.

A final note about online publication: Like literary journals, the majority of these markets are either nonpaying or very low paying. In addition, writers will not receive print copies of the publications because of the medium. So in most cases, do not expect to be paid for your exposure.

SELECTING THE RIGHT MARKET

First, zero in on those markets most likely to be interested in your work. Begin by looking at the Category Index. If your work is more general—or conversely, very specialized—you may wish to browse through the listings, perhaps looking up those magazines published in your state or region.

In addition to browsing through the listings and using the Category Index, check the openness icons at the beginning of listings to find those most likely to be receptive to your work. This is especially true for beginning writers, who should look for magazines that say they are especially open to new writers **O** and for those giving equal weight to both new and established writers **◑**. For more explanation about these icons, see the inside back cover of this book.

Once you have a list of magazines you might like to try, read their listings carefully. Much of the material within each listing carries clues that tell you more about the magazine. "How to Use NSSWM" describes in detail the listing information common to all the markets in our book.

The physical description appearing near the beginning of the listings can give you clues about the size and financial commitment to the publication. This is not always an indication of quality, but chances are a publication with expensive paper and four-color artwork on the cover has more prestige than a photocopied publication featuring a clip-art cover. For more information on some of the paper, binding, and printing terms used in these descriptions, see "Printing and Production Terms Defined."

FURTHERING YOUR SEARCH

It cannot be stressed enough that reading the listing is only the first part of developing your marketing plan. The second part, equally important, is to obtain fiction guidelines and read the actual magazine. Reading copies of a magazine helps you determine the fine points of the magazine's publishing style and philosophy. There is no substitute for this type of hands-on research.

Most of the magazines listed here are published in the U.S. You will also find some English-speaking markets from around the world. These foreign publications are denoted with a ◑ symbol at the beginning of listings. To make it easier to find Canadian markets, we include a ◌ symbol at the start of those listings.

ACM (ANOTHER CHICAGO MAGAZINE)

P.O. Box 408439, Chicago, IL 60640. **E-mail:** edi tors@anotherchicagomagazine.net. **Website:** www.an otherchicagomagazine.net. **Contact:** Jacob S. Knabb, editor-in-chief; Caroline Eick Kasner, managing editor. Estab. 1977. "*Another Chicago Magazine* is a biannual literary magazine that publishes work by both new and established writers. We look for work that goes beyond the artistic and academic to include and address the larger world. The editors read submissions in fiction, poetry, creative nonfiction, etc., year round. We often publish special theme issues and sections. We will post upcoming themes on our website."

Work published in *ACM* has been included frequently in *The Best American Poetry* and the *Pushcart Prize* anthology.

NEEDS Fiction: Short stories and novel excerpts of 15-20 pages or less. Poetry: Usually no more than 4 pages. Creative Nonfiction: Usually no more than 20 pages. Et Al: Work that doesn't quite fit into the other genres such as word and image texts, satire, and interviews.

HOW TO CONTACT "Please include the following contact information in your cover letter and on your ms: Byline (name as you want it to appear if published), mailing address, phone number, and e-mail. Include a self-addressed stamped envelope (SASE). If a SASE is not enclosed, you will only hear from us if we are interested in your work. Include the genre (e.g., fiction) of your work in the address."

PAYMENT/TERMS Pays small honorarium when possible, contributor's copies and 1 year subscription.

TIPS "Support literary publishing by subscribing to at least one literary journal—if not ours, another. Get used to rejection slips, and don't get discouraged. Keep introductory letters short. Make sure your manuscript has name and address on every page, and that it is clean, neat, and proofread. We are looking for stories with freshness and originality in subject angle and style, and work that encounters the world."

THE ADIRONDACK REVIEW

Black Lawrence Press, 8405 Bay Parkway, Apt C8, Brooklyn, NY 11214. **E-mail:** editors@theadiron dackreview.com. **Website:** www.adirondackreview .homestead.com. **Contact:** Angela Leroux-Lindsey, editor; Kara Christenson, senior fiction editor; Nicholas Samaras, poetry editor. Estab. 2000. *The Adiron-dack Review*, published quarterly online, is a literary journal dedicated to quality free verse poetry and short fiction, as well as book and film reviews, art, photography, and interviews. "We are open to both new and established writers. Our only requirement is excellence. We would like to publish more French and German poetry translations, as well as original poems in these languages. We publish an eclectic mix of voices and styles, but all poems should show attention to craft. We are open to beginners who demonstrate talent, as well as established voices. The work should speak for itself."

Uses online submissions manager.

NEEDS Length: 700-8,000 words.

HOW TO CONTACT Send complete ms with cover letter. Include estimated word count, brief bio, list of publications, and "how they learned about the magazine." Submit via online submissions manager.

TIPS "*The Adirondack Review* accepts submissions all year long, so send us your poetry, fiction, nonfiction, translation, reviews, interviews, and art and photography. Please note that we've recently shifted our submission management to Submittable."

ADVOCATE, PKA'S PUBLICATION

1881 Little Westkill Rd., Prattsville, NY 12468. (518)299-3103. **Website:** Advocatepka.weebly.com; www.facebook.com/Advocate/PKAPublications; www.facebook.com/GaitedHorseAssociation. **Contact:** Patricia Keller, publisher. Estab. 1987. *Advocate, PKA's Publication*, published bimonthly, is an advertiser-supported tabloid using "original, previously unpublished works, such as feature stories, essays, 'think' pieces, letters to the editor, profiles, humor, fiction, poetry, puzzles, cartoons, or line drawings. Advocates for good writers and quality writings. We publish art, fiction, photos, and poetry. *Advocate*'s submitters are talented people of all ages who do not earn their livings as writers. We wish to promote the arts and to give those we publish the opportunity to be published."

"This publication has a strong horse orientation." Includes Gaited Horse Association newsletter. Horse-oriented stories, poetry, art, and photos are currently needed.

NEEDS "Nothing religious, pornographic, violent, erotic, pro-drug or anti-enviroment."

HOW TO CONTACT Send complete ms.

TIPS "Please, no simultaneous submissions, work that has appeared on the Internet, pornography, overt religiousity, anti-environmentalism, or gratuitous violence. Artists and photographers should keep in mind that we are a black-and-white paper. Please do not send postcards. Use envelope with SASE."

◑ ⑤ AFRICAN AMERICAN REVIEW

St. Louis University, 317 Adorjan Hall, 3800 Lindell Blvd., St. Louis, MO 63108. (314)977-3688. **Fax:** (314)977-1514. **E-mail:** ngrant2@slu.edu; keenanam@slu.edu. **Website:** http://aar.slu.edu. Estab. 1967. Essays on African-American literature, theater, film, art, and culture generally; interviews; poetry and fiction by African-American authors; book reviews.

◔ *African American Review* is the official publication of the Division of Black American Literature and Culture of the Modern Language Association. The magazine received American Literary Magazine Awards in 1994 and 1995.

NEEDS No children's, juvenile, young adult, teen. Length: No more than 1,500 words.

PAYMENT/TERMS Pays 1 contributor's copy and 5 offprints.

◑ AFRICAN VOICES

African Voices Communications, Inc., 270 W. 96th St., New York, NY 10025. (212)865-2982. **Fax:** (212)316-3335. **E-mail:** africanvoicesmag@gmail.com. **Website:** www.africanvoices.com. Estab. 1992. *African Voices*, published quarterly, is an "art and literary magazine that highlights the work of people of color. We publish ethnic literature and poetry on any subject. We also consider all themes and styles: avant-garde, free verse, haiku, light verse, and traditional. We do not wish to limit the reader or author."

◔ Considers poetry written by children. Has published poetry by Reg E. Gaines, Maya Angelou, Jessica Care Moore, Asha Bandele, Tony Medina, and Louis Reyes Rivera. *African Voices* is about 48 pages, magazine-sized, professionally printed, saddle-stapled, with paper cover. Receives about 100 submissions/year, accepts about 30%. Press run is 20,000. Single copy: $4; subscription: $12.

NEEDS Length: 500-2,500 words.

HOW TO CONTACT Send complete ms. Include short bio. Send SASE for return of ms. Responds in 3 months to queries. Accepts simultaneous and reprints submissions. Reviews fiction.

PAYMENT/TERMS Pays $25-50. Pays on publication for first North American serial rights.

TIPS "A ms stands out if it is neatly typed with a well-written and interesting story line or plot. Originality is encouraged. We are interested in more horror, erotic, and drama pieces. *AV* wants to highlight the diversity in our culture. Stories must touch the humanity in us all. We strongly encourage new writers/poets to send in their work. Accepted contributors are encouraged to subscribe."

◑ A GATHERING OF THE TRIBES

P.O. Box 20693, Tompkins Square Station, New York, NY 10009. (212)674-3778. **Fax:** (212)388-9813. **E-mail:** info@tribes.org. **Website:** www.tribes.org. **Contact:** Steve Cannon. Estab. 1992. *A Gathering of the Tribes* is a multicultural and multigenerational publication featuring poetry, fiction, interviews, essays, visual art, musical scores. Audience is anyone interested in the arts from a diverse perspective."

◔ Magazine: 8½" × 10"; 130 pages; glossy paper and cover; illustrations; photos. Receives 20 unsolicited mss/month. Publishes 40% new writers/year. Has published work by Carl Watson, Ishle Park, Wang Pang, and Hanif Kureishi. Sponsors awards/contests.

NEEDS "Would like to see more satire/humor. We are open to all; just no poor writing/grammar/syntax." Publishes short shorts. Length: 2,500-5,000 words.

HOW TO CONTACT Send complete ms. Send SASE for reply, return of ms or send a disposable copy of ms. Accepts simultaneous and reprints submissions.

PAYMENT/TERMS Pays 1 contributor's copy; additional copies $12-50.

TIPS "Make sure your work has substance."

◔ AGNI

Creative Writing Program, Boston University, 236 Bay State Rd., Boston, MA 02215. (617)353-7135. **Fax:** (617)353-7134. **E-mail:** agni@bu.edu. **Website:** www.agnimagazine.org. **Contact:** Sven Birkerts, editor. Estab. 1972. "Eclectic literary magazine publishing first-rate poems, essays, translations, and stories."

◔ Reading period is September 1-May 31 only. Online magazine carries original content not found in print edition. All submissions are considered for both. Founding editor Askold Melnyczuk won the 2001 Nora Magid Award for Magazine Editing. Work from *AGNI* has been included and cited regularly in the *Push-cart Prize* and *Best American* anthologies.

NEEDS Buys stories, prose poems. "No science fiction or romance."

HOW TO CONTACT Query by mail.

PAYMENT/TERMS Pays $10/page up to $150, a 1-year subscription, and for print publication: 2 contributor's copies and 4 gift copies.

TIPS "We're also looking for extraordinary translations from little-translated languages. It is important to read work published in *AGNI* before submitting, to see if your own might be compatible."

●❶❸ ALBEDO ONE

2 Post Rd., Lusk, Co Dublin, Ireland. (353)1 8730 177. **E-mail:** bobn@yellowbrickroad.ie. **Website:** www.albedo.com. **Contact:** Bob Nielson. Estab. 1993. "We hope to publish interesting and unusual fiction by new and established writers. We will consider anything, as long as it is well written and entertaining, though our definitions of both may not be exactly mainstream. We like stories with plot and characters that live on the page. Most of our audience are probably committed genre fans, but we try to appeal to a broad spectrum of readers."

NEEDS Length: 2,000-9,000 words.

PAYMENT/TERMS Pays €3 per 1,000 words, and 1 contributor's copy.

TIPS "We look for good writing, good plot, good characters. Read the magazine, and don't give up."

❶ ALIMENTUM, THE LITERATURE OF FOOD

P.O. Box 210028, Nashville, TN 37221. **E-mail:** editor@alimentumjournal.com. **Website:** www.alimentumjournal.com. **Contact:** Paulette Licitra, publisher/editor-in-chief; Peter Selgin, fiction and nonfiction editor; Cortney Davis, poetry editor. Estab. 2005. *Alimentum* is 128 pages, perfect-bound, with matte coated cover with 4-color art, interior black-and-white illustration includes ads. Contains illustrations. "All of our stories, poems and essays have food or drink as a theme." Semiannual. "We do not read year round. Check website for reading periods."

NEEDS Literary. Special interests: food related. Receives 100 mss/month. Accepts 20-24 mss/issue. Manuscript published 1 to 2 years after acceptance. **Publishes average of 2 new writers/year.** Published Mark Kurlansky, Oliver Sacks, Dick Allen, Ann Hood, Carly Sachs. Length: 3,000 words (max). Average length:

1,000-2,000 words. Publishes short shorts. Also publishes literary essays, poetry, spot illustrations. Rarely comments on/critiques rejected mss.

HOW TO CONTACT Send complete ms with cover letter. Snail mail only. No previously published work. 5-poem limit per submission. Simultaneous submissions okay. Responds to queries and mss in 1-3 months. Send either SASE (or IRC) for return of ms or disposable copy of ms and #10 SASE for reply only. Sample copy available for $10. Guidelines available on website. Check for submission reading periods, as they vary from year to year. Send complete ms.

PAYMENT/TERMS Writers receive 1 contributor's copy. Additional contributor's copies $8. Pays on publication. Acquires first North American serial rights. Publication is copyrighted.

TIPS "No e-mail submissions, only snail mail. Mark outside envelope to the attention of Poetry, Fiction, or Nonfiction Editor."

❶❸ ALIVE NOW

1908 Grand Ave., P.O. Box 340004, Nashville, TN 37203. (615)340-7254. **Fax:** (615)340-7267. **E-mail:** alivenow@upperroom.org. **Website:** www.alivenow.org; www.upperroom.org. **Contact:** Beth A. Richardson, editor. *Alive Now*, published bimonthly, is a devotional magazine that invites readers to enter an ever-deepening relationship with God. "*Alive Now* seeks to nourish people who are hungry for a sacred way of living. Submissions should invite readers to see God in the midst of daily life by exploring how contemporary issues impact their faith lives. Each word must be vivid and dynamic and contribute to the whole. We make selections based on a list of upcoming themes. Manuscripts which do not fit a theme will be returned."

◯ Considers avant-garde and free verse. *Alive Now* is 64 pages. Circulation is 70,000. Subscription: $17.95/year (6 issues); $26.95 for 2 years (12 issues). Additional subscription information, including foreign rates, available on website.

NEEDS Accepts 20 poems/year. Themes can be found on website.

HOW TO CONTACT Prefers electronic submissions, pasted into body of e-mail or attached as Word document. Postal submissions should include SASE. Include name, address, theme on each sheet. Payment will be made at the time of acceptance for publication. "We will notify contributors of manuscript status when we make final decisions for an issue, approximately 2 months before the issue date."

THE ALLEGHENY REVIEW

Allegheny College, P.O. Box 32, Meadville, PA 16335. **Website:** http://alleghenyreview.wordpress.com. **Contact:** Senior editor. Estab. 1983. "*The Allegheny Review* is one of America's only nationwide literary magazines exclusively for undergraduate works of poetry, fiction, and nonfiction. Our intended audience is persons interested in quality literature."

Annual. Magazine: 6" × 9"; 100 pages; illustrations; photos. Has published work by Dianne Page, Monica Stahl, and DJ Kinney.

NEEDS Receives 50 unsolicited mss/month. Accepts 3 mss/issue. Publishes ms 2 months after deadline. Publishes roughly 90% new writers/year. Also publishes short shorts (up to 20 pages), nonfiction, and poetry. "We accept nothing but fiction by currently enrolled undergraduate students. We consider anything catering to an intellectual audience."

HOW TO CONTACT Send complete mss with a cover letter. Accepts submissions on disk. Send disposable copy of ms and #10 SASE for reply only.

PAYMENT/TERMS Pays 1 contributor's copy; additional copies $3. Sponsors awards/contests; reading fee of $5.

TIPS "We look for quality work that has been thoroughly revised. Unique voice, interesting topic, and playfulness with the English language. Revise, revise, revise! And be careful how you send it—the cover letter says a lot. We definitely look for diversity in the pieces we publish."

ALLEGORY

P.O .Box 2714, Cherry Hill, NJ 08034. **E-mail:** submissions@allegoryezine.com. **Website:** www.allegoryezine.com. **Contact:** Ty Drago, editor. Estab. 1998. "We are an e-zine by writers for writers. Our articles focus on the art, craft, and business of writing. Our links and editorial policy all focus on the needs of fiction authors."

Peridot Books won the Page One Award for Literary Contribution.

NEEDS Receives 150 unsolicited mss/month. Accepts 8 mss/issue; 24 mss/year. Agented fiction 5%. Publishes 10 new writers/year. Also publishes literary essays, literary criticism. Often comments on rejected mss. "No media tie-ins (*Star Trek*, *Star Wars*, etc., or

space opera, vampires)." Length: 1,500-7,500 words; average length: 4,500 words.

HOW TO CONTACT "All submissions should be sent by e-mail (no letters or telephone calls) in either text or RTF format. Please place 'Submission [Title]-[first and last name]' in the subject line. Include the following in both the body of the e-mail and the attachment: your name, name to use on the story (byline) if different, your preferred e-mail address, your mailing address, the story's title, and the story's word count."

PAYMENT/TERMS $15/story or article.

TIPS "Give us something original, preferably with a twist. Avoid gratuitous sex or violence. Funny always scores points. Be clever, imaginative, but be able to tell a story with proper mood and characterization. Put your name and e-mail address in the body of the story. Read the site and get a feel for it before submitting."

ALL GENRES LITERARY MAGAZINE

4625 Mormon Coulee Rd., #100, La Crosse, WI 54601. **E-mail:** editor@allgenres24.com. **Website:** www .mikesharlowwritercom.fatcow.com/allgenres24. **Contact:** Michael Miller, managing editor; Elizabeth Miller. Estab. 2011. "'All Genres' means we accept any writing as long as we like it. We are very open to new and emerging writers. Your chances of publication in All Genres is presently about 50/50. So send us your work! *All Genres Literary Magazine* is an independent online periodical not affiliated with or sponsored by any educational system's creative writing program. It is funded by donations and small fees."

NEEDS Length: no more than 6,000 words.

HOW TO CONTACT Submit complete ms.

TIPS "We are seeking anything that trips our triggers. It can be literary, fantasy, science fiction, speculative fiction, erotic, western.... We believe that good writing is not genre specific. Accepted pieces will be published on the website and may be published in an annual hardcopy issue."

AMERICAN CINEMATOGRAPHER

American Society of Cinematographers, 1782 N. Orange Dr., Hollywood, CA 90028. (800)448-0145; outside U.S.: (323)969-4333. **Fax:** (323)876-4973. **E-mail:** stephen@ascmag.com. **Website:** www.theasc.com. **Contact:** Stephen Pizzello, executive editor. Estab. 1919. "*American Cinematographer* is a trade publication devoted to the art and craft of cinematography. Our readers are predominantly film-industry professionals."

TIPS "Familiarity with the technical side of film production and the ability to present that information in an articulate fashion to our audience are crucial."

⊙ AMERICAN LITERARY REVIEW

University of North Texas, P.O. Box 311307, Denton, TX 76203-1307. (940)565-2755. **Fax:** (940)565-4355. **E-mail:** americanliteraryreview@gmail.com; bond@unt.edu. **Website:** www.engl.unt.edu/alr. Estab. 1990. Publishes quality, contemporary poems and stories. "The *American Literary Review* welcomes submissions of previously unpublished poems, short stories, and creative nonfiction. We also accept submissions for cover art. Please include a SASE and cover letter with your submission. Also include enough postage to return your work. Please mark envelopes and cover letters Fiction, Poetry, or Nonfiction. Simultaneous submissions are acceptable if noted in your cover letter. For any questions not covered in this section, please refer to our 'Frequently Asked Questions' page. Our reading period extends from October 1 to May 1. Unsolicited manuscripts received outside this reading period will be returned unread. Online submissions are accepted via the website. Submissions should be directed to the appropriate editor (Fiction, Poetry, Nonfiction, or Art)." Receives 150-200 unsolicited mss/month. Accepts 5-6 mss/issue; 12-16 mss/year. Reading period: October 1-May 1. Publishes ms within 2 years after acceptance. Recently published work by Marylee MacDonald, Michael Isaac Shokrian, Arthur Brown, Roy Bentley, Julie Marie Wade, and Karin Forfota Poklen. Also publishes creative nonfiction, poetry. Critiques or comments on rejected mss.

◯ Magazine: 6" × 9"; 128 pages; 70 lb. Mohawk paper; 67 lb. Wausau Vellum cover. " Semiannual.

NEEDS Literary, mainstream. "No genre works. We would like to see more short shorts and stylistically innovative and risk-taking fiction. We like to see stories that illuminate the various layers of characters and their situations with great artistry. Give us distinctive character-driven stories that explore the complexities of human existence." Looks for "the small moments that contain more than at first possible, that surprise us with more truth than we thought we had a right to expect." Length: 8,000 words or less.

HOW TO CONTACT Send complete ms with cover letter. Responds in 2-4 months to mss. Accepts simultaneous submissions. Sample copy for $8. Writ-

er's guidelines for #10 SASE. "Submit only 1 story at a time. Please mark envelopes and cover letters Fiction. We have no set maximum for length, but stories under 8,000 words have the best chance of publication. We generally avoid novel excerpts unless they can stand alone as stories." Send complete ms with cover letter.

PAYMENT/TERMS Pays in contributor's copies. Acquires one time rights.

TIPS "We encourage writers and artists to examine our journal. The *American Literary Review* publishes semiannually. If you would like to subscribe to our journal, subscription rates run $14 for a 1-year subscription, $26 for a 2-year subscription, and $36 for a 3-year subscription. You may also obtain a sample copy of the *American Literary Review* for $7 plus $1 per issue for shipping and handling in the U.S. and Canada ($2 for postage elsewhere)."

⊙ AMOSKEAG, THE JOURNAL OF SOUTHERN NEW HAMPSHIRE UNIVERSITY

2500 N. River Rd., Manchester, NH 03106. **E-mail:** m.brien@snhu.edu. **Website:** www.amoskeagjournal.com. **Contact:** Michael J. Brien, editor. Estab. 1983; literary journal since 2005. "We select fiction, creative nonfiction, and poetry that appeals to general readers, writers, and academics alike. We accept work from writers nationwide, but also try to include New England writers. We tend not to accept much experimental work, but the language of poetry or prose must nevertheless be dense, careful, and surprising." Annual.

◯ Magazine has revolving editor and occasional themes (see website). Editorial term: 3 years. Literary magazine/journal: 6" × 9", 105-130 pages. Contains photographs. Receives 200 mss/month. Accepts 10 prose mss and 20-25 poems/issue. Does not read December-July. Reading period is August-December. Ms published in late April. Published Ann Hood, Donald Hall, Allan Gurganus, Leslie Jamison, Ayana Mathis, Craig Childs, Diane Les Becquets, Maxine Kumin, Jonathan Blake, Philip Dacey, Charles Harper Webb.

NEEDS Does not want genre fiction.

HOW TO CONTACT Send complete ms with cover letter. Include brief bio, list of publications. Send either SASE (or IRC) for return of ms or disposable copy of ms and #10 SASE or e-mail address for reply only.

Considers multiple submissions. Pays 2 contributor's copies; additional copies $7.

PAYMENT/TERMS Pays 2 contributor's copies.

TIPS "We're looking for quality and pizzazz. Stories need good pacing, believable characters and dialogue, as well as unusual subjects to stand out. Read the news, live an exciting life. Write about remarkable people."

ⓘⓒⓢ ANALOG SCIENCE FICTION & FACT

Dell Magazines, 267 Broadway, 4th Floor, New York, NY 10007-2352. (212)686-7188. **Fax:** (212)686-7414. **E-mail:** analog@dellmagazines.com. **Website:** www .analogsf.com. **Contact:** Dr. Stanley Schmidt, editor. Estab. 1930.

⚫ Fiction published in *Analog* has won numerous Nebula and Hugo Awards.

NEEDS "Basically, we publish science fiction stories. That is, stories in which some aspect of future science or technology is so integral to the plot that, if that aspect were removed, the story would collapse. The science can be physical, sociological, or psychological. The technology can be anything from electronic engineering to biogenetic engineering. But the stories must be strong and realistic, with believable people doing believable things—no matter how fantastic the background might be." No fantasy or stories in which the scientific background is implausible or plays no essential role. Prefers lengths: 2,000-7,000 words for shorts, 10,000-20,000 words for novelettes, and 40,000-80,000 for serials

HOW TO CONTACT Submit via online submissions manager.

PAYMENT/TERMS Analog pays 6-8 cents per word for short stories up to 7,500 words, $450-600 for stories between 7,500 and 10,000 words, and 5-6 cents per word for longer material.

TIPS "I'm looking for irresistibly entertaining stories that make me think about things in ways I've never thought before. Read several issues to get a broad feel for our tastes, but don't try to imitate what you read. In your query give clear indication of central ideas and themes and general nature of story line—and what is distinctive or unusual about it. We have no hard-and-fast editorial guidelines, because science fiction is such a broad field that I don't want to inhibit a new writer's thinking by imposing 'Thou Shalt Not's.' Besides, a really good story can make an editor swallow his preconceived taboos. I want the best

work I can get, regardless of who wrote it—and I need new writers. So I work closely with new writers who show definite promise, but of course it's impossible to do this with every new writer." No occult or fantasy.

ⓘⓒ ANDERBO.COM

Anderbo Publishing, 270 Lafayette St., Suite 705, New York, NY 10012-3364. **E-mail:** editors@anderbo.com. **Website:** www.anderbo.com. **Contact:** Rick Rofihe, editor-in-chief. Online literary magazine/journal. "Quality fiction, poetry, 'fact' and photography on a website with 'print-feel' design." Receives 200 mss/ month. Accepts 20 mss/year. Publishes 6 new writers/ year. Has published Lisa Margonelli, Margot Berwin, Jeffrey Lent, and Susan Breen. Member CLMP.

⚫ Received the Best New Online Magazine or Journal, *storySouth* Million Writers Award in 2005.

NEEDS "We're interested only in literary fiction, poetry, and literary 'fact.'" Also publishes literary essays. Rarely comments on/critiques rejected mss. Does not want any genre literature. Length: 3,500. Average length: 1,750 words. Also publishes short shorts. Average length of short shorts: 1,400 words.

HOW TO CONTACT Send complete ms with cover letter. Accepts submissions by e-mail. Include brief bio, list of publications.

PAYMENT/TERMS Does not pay.

TIPS "We are looking for fiction that is unique, urgent, accessible, and involving. Look at our site and read what we've already published."

ANDROIDS2 MAGAZINE

Man's Story 2 Publishing Co., 1321 Snapfinger Rd., Decatur, GA 30032. **E-mail:** mansstory2@aol.com. **Website:** www.androids2.com; www.mansstory2 .com. Estab. 2001. *"Androids 2 Magazine* strives to re-create the pulp fiction that was published in the magazines of the 1920s through the 1970s with strong emphasis on 3D graphic art."

⚫ Online e-zine. Story subjects tend to slant toward the "damsel in distress."

NEEDS Length: 1,500-3,500 words.

HOW TO CONTACT Send complete ms.

PAYMENT/TERMS Pays $25.

TIPS "We suggest interested writers visit our website. Then read the 1960s style pulp fiction stories posted in our online mini-magazine and/or read 1 of our magazines, or find an old pulp fiction magazine that was published in the 1960s. If all else fails, e-mail us."

THE ANTIGONISH REVIEW

St. Francis Xavier University, P.O. Box 5000, Antigonish, NS B2G 2W5 Canada. (902)867-3962. **Fax:** (902)867-5563. **E-mail:** tar@stfx.ca. **Website:** www.antigonishreview.com. **Contact:** Bonnie McIsaac, office manager. Estab. 1970.

NEEDS No erotica. Length: 500-5,000 words.

HOW TO CONTACT Send complete ms. Accepts submissions by fax. Accepts electronic (disk compatible with WordPerfect/IBM and Windows) submissions. Prefers hard copy.

PAYMENT/TERMS Pays $50 and 2 contributor's copies for stories.

TIPS "Send for guidelines and/or sample copy. Send ms with cover letter and SASE with submission."

ANTIOCH REVIEW

P.O. Box 148, Yellow Springs, OH 45387-0148. E-mail: mkeyes@antiochreview.org. **Website:** www.antiochreview.org. **Contact:** Robert S. Fogarty, editor; Judith Hall, poetry editor. Estab. 1941. Literary and cultural review of contemporary issues, and literature for general readership. *The Antioch Review* "is an independent quarterly of critical and creative thought. For well over 70 years, creative authors, poets, and thinkers have found a friendly reception—regardless of formal reputation. We get far more poetry than we can possibly accept, and the competition is keen. Here, where form and content are so inseparable and reaction is so personal, it is difficult to state requirements or limitations. Studying recent issues of *The Antioch Review* should be helpful." Has published poetry by Richard Howard, Jacqueline Osherow, Alice Fulton, Richard Kenney, and others. Receives about 3,000 submissions/year.

> Work published in the *Antioch Review* has been included frequently in *The Best American Stories, Best American Essays,* and *The Best American Poetry.* Finalist for National Magazine Award for essays in 2009 and 2011, and for fiction in 2010.

NEEDS Quality fiction only, distinctive in style with fresh insights into the human condition. No science fiction, fantasy, or confessions. Length: generally under 8,000 words.

HOW TO CONTACT Send complete ms with SASE, preferably mailed flat.

PAYMENT/TERMS Pays $20/printed page, plus 2 contributor's copies.

ANY DREAM WILL DO REVIEW

250 Jeanell Dr., Carson City, NV 89703. (775)786-0345. **E-mail:** cassjmb10@att.net. **Website:** www.willigocrazy.org/Ch08.htm. **Contact:** Dr. Jean M. Bradt, editor and publisher. Estab. 2001. The 52-page *Any Dream Will Do Review* showcases a new literary genre, Psych-Inspirational Fiction, which attempts to fight the prejudice against consumers of mental-health services by touching hearts by exposing consumers' deepest thoughts and emotions. In the *Review's* stories, accomplished authors honestly reveal their most intimate secrets. See website for detailed instructions on how to write psych-inspirational fiction. Does not accept queries. Annual magazine written by, for, and about persons living with mental illness.

NEEDS No pornography, true-life stories, black humor, political material, testimonials, experimental fiction, or depressing accounts of hopeless or perverted people. Length: 400-4,000 words.

HOW TO CONTACT *Currently not accepting stories.* Often comments on rejected mss.

PAYMENT/TERMS Pays in contributor's copies; additional copies $10

TIPS "Read several stories on the website before starting to write. Proof your story many times before submitting. Make the readers think. Above all, present people (preferably diagnosed with mental illness) realistically rather than with prejudice."

APALACHEE REVIEW

Apalachee Press, P.O. Box 10469, Tallahassee, FL 32302. (850)644-9114. **E-mail:** arsubmissions@gmail.com (for queries outside of the U.S.). **Website:** apalacheereview.org. **Contact:** Michael Trammell, editor; Mary Jane Ryals, fiction editor. Estab. 1976. "At *Apalachee Review*, we are interested in outstanding literary fiction, but we especially like poetry, fiction, and nonfiction that addresses intercultural issues in a domestic or international setting/context." Annual.

> *Apalachee Review* is 120 pages, digest size, professionally printed, perfect-bound, with card cover. Press run is 700. Subscription: $15 for 2 issues ($30 foreign). Includes photographs. Receives 60-100 mss/month. Accepts 5-10 mss/issue. Agented fiction: 0.5%. Publishes 1-2 new writers/year. Sample: $5. Has published Lu Vickers, Joe Clark, Joe Taylor, Jane Arrowsmith Edwards, Vivian Lawry, Linda

Frysh, Charles Harper Webb, Reno Raymond Gwaltney. Member CLMP.

NEEDS Also publishes short shorts. Does not want cliché-filled genre-oriented fiction. Length: 600-5,500 words; average length: 3,500 words. Average length of short shorts: 250 words.

HOW TO CONTACT Send complete ms with cover letter. Include brief bio, list of publications. Send either SASE (international authors should see website for "international" guidelines: no IRCs, please) for return of ms or disposable copy of ms and #10 SASE for reply only. Considers simultaneous submissions.

PAYMENT/TERMS Pays 2 contributor's copies.

APEX MAGAZINE

Apex Publications, LLC, P.O. Box 24323, Lexington, KY 40524. (859)312-3974. **E-mail:** jason@apexbookcompany.com. **Website:** www.apexbookcompany.com. Estab. 2004. "An elite repository for new and seasoned authors with an otherworldly interest in the unquestioned and slightly bizarre parts of the universe. We want science fiction, fantasy, horror, and mash-ups of all three of the dark, weird stuff down at the bottom of your little literary heart."

Monthly e-zine publishing dark speculative fiction. Circ. 10,000 unique visits per month. Buys 24 mss/year.

NEEDS "We publish dark speculative fiction with horror elements. Our readers are those that enjoy speculative fiction with dark themes." Does not want monster fiction. Length: 100-7,500 words.

HOW TO CONTACT Send complete ms with cover letter. Include estimated word count, brief bio.

PAYMENT/TERMS Pays $20-200.

TIPS See submissions guidelines at submissions@apex-digest.com.

APPALACHIAN HERITAGE

CPO 2166, Berea, KY 40404. (859)985-3699. **Fax:** (859)985-3903. **E-mail:** george_brosi@berea.edu; appalachianheritage@berea.edu. **Website:** http://community.berea.edu/appalachianheritage. **Contact:** George Brosi. Estab. 1973. "We are seeking poetry, short fiction, literary criticism, and biography, book reviews, and creative nonfiction, including memoirs, opinion pieces, and historical sketches. Unless you request not to be considered, all poems, stories, and articles published in *Appalachian Heritage* are eligible for our annual Plattner Award. All honorees are rewarded with a sliding book rack with an attached commemo-

rative plaque from Berea College Crafts and first place winners receive an additional stipend of $200."

NEEDS "We do not want to see fiction that has no ties to Southern Appalachia." Length: up to 3,500 words.

HOW TO CONTACT Submit complete ms. Send SASE for reply, return of ms.

PAYMENT/TERMS Pays 3 contributor's copies.

TIPS "Sure, we are *Appalachian Heritage* and we do appreciate the past, but we are a forward-looking contemporary literary quarterly, and, frankly, we receive too many nostalgic submissions. Please spare us the "Papaw Was Perfect" poetry and the "Mamaw Moved Mountains" manuscripts and give us some hard-hitting prose, some innovative poetry, some inventive photography, and some original art. Help us be the groundbreaking, stimulating kind of quarterly we aspire to be."

APPLE VALLEY REVIEW: A JOURNAL OF CONTEMPORARY LITERATURE

88 South 3rd St., Suite 336, San Jose, CA 95113. **E-mail:** editor@leahbrowning.net. **Website:** www.applevalleyreview.com. **Contact:** Leah Browning, editor. Estab. 2005. *Apple Valley Review: A Journal of Contemporary Literature*, published semiannually online, features "beautifully crafted poetry, short fiction, and essays." Receives 100+ mss/month. Accepts 1-4 mss/issue; 2-8 mss/year. Published Barry Jay Kaplan, Jenny Steele, Tai Dong Huai, Matthew Grice, Arrie Brown.

Considers poetry by children and teens: "Our audience includes teens and adults of all ages."

NEEDS Wants "work that has both mainstream and literary appeal. All work must be original, previously unpublished, and in English. Translations are welcome if permission has been granted." Does not want "erotica, work containing explicit language or violence, or work that is scholarly, critical, inspirational, or intended for children." Also publishes short shorts. Length: 100-3,000+ words. Average length: 2,000 words. Average length of short shorts: 800 words.

HOW TO CONTACT Send complete ms with cover letter.

THE APUTAMKON REVIEW: VOICES FROM DOWNEAST MAINE AND THE CANADIAN MARITIMES (OR THEREABOUTS)

The WordShed, LLC, P.O. Box 190, Jonesboro, ME 04648. **E-mail:** thewordshed@tds.net. **Website:** http://thewordshed.com. Estab. 2006. "*The Aputamkon Review will present a mismash of truths, half truths and outright lies, including but not limited to short fiction, tall tales, creative nonfiction, essays, (some) poetry, haiku, black-and-white visual arts, interviews, lyrics and music, quips, quirks, quotes that should be famous, witticisms, follies, comic strips, cartoons, jokes, riddles, recipes, puzzles, games. Stretch your imagination. Practically anything goes. "All age groups living in downeast Maine and the Canadian Maritimes, or thereabouts, are invited to participate."

Magazine, approx. 190 pages. Contains black-and-white illustrations. Includes photographs.

HOW TO CONTACT Send complete ms with cover letter. Accepts submissions in the body of an e-mail and on disk via USPS. Submission period is 12 months a year; responding time varies depending on scheduling on next publication. Include age if under 18, and a bio will be requested upon acceptance of work. Send SASE (or IRC) for return of ms or a disposable copy of ms and #10 SASE for reply only. Considers simultaneous submissions, multiple submissions.

PAYMENT/TERMS Submissions receive $10-35 depending on medium, plus 1 copy.

TIPS "Be colorful and heartfelt, not mainstream. Write what you want and then submit."

ARKANSAS REVIEW

A Journal of Delta Studies, Department of English and Philosophy, P.O. Box 1890, Office: Wilson Hall, State University, AR 72467-1890. (870) 972-3043; (870)972-2210. **Fax:** (870)972-3045. **E-mail:** arkansasreview@astate.edu. **E-mail:** jcollins@astate.edu; arkansasreview@astate.edu. **Website:** http://altweb.astate.edu/arkreview. **Contact:** Dr. Janelle Collins, general editor/associate professor of English. Estab. 1998. "All material, creative and scholarly, published in the *Arkansas Review*, must evoke or respond to the natural and/or cultural experience of the Mississippi River Delta region."

Arkansas Review is 92 pages, magazine size, photo offset printed, saddle stapled, with 4-color cover. Press run is 600; 50 distributed free to contributors. Receives 30-50 unsolicited mss/month. Accepts 2-3 mss/issue; 5-7 mss/year. Receives about 500 poems/year; accepts about 5%. Publishes ms 6-12 months after acceptance. Agented fiction 1%. Publishes 3-4 new writers/year. Subscription: $20. Make checks payable to ASU Foundation.

NEEDS "No genre fiction. Must have a Delta focus." 10,000 words maximum. Has published work by Susan Henderson, George Singleton, Scott Ely and Pia Erhart.

HOW TO CONTACT Send complete ms. "Submit via mail. E-mails are more likely to be overlooked or lost. Submit a cover letter, but don't try to impress us with credentials or explanations of the submission."

PAYMENT/TERMS Pays 3 contributor's copies.

TIPS "Immerse yourself in the literature of the Delta, but provide us with a fresh and original take on its land, its people, its culture. Surprise us. Amuse us. Recognize what makes this region particular as well as universal, and take risks. Help us shape a new Delta literature."

ARTFUL DODGE

Dept. of English, College of Wooster, Wooster, OH 44691. (330)263-2577. **E-mail:** artfuldodge@wooster.edu. **Website:** www.wooster.edu/artfuldodge. **Contact:** Daniel Bourne, editor-in-chief; Karin Lin-Greenberg, fiction editor; Marcy Campbell, associate fiction editor; Carolyne Wright, translation editor. Estab. 1979. There is no theme in this magazine, except literary power. "We also have an ongoing interest in translations from Central/Eastern Europe and elsewhere."

NEEDS "We judge by literary quality, not by genre. We are especially interested in fine English translations of significant prose writers. Translations should be submitted with original texts."

PAYMENT/TERMS Pays 2 contributor's copies and honorarium of $5/page, thanks to funding from the Ohio Arts Council.

TIPS "Poets may send books for review consideration; however, there is no guarantee we can review them."

ARTS & LETTERS JOURNAL OF CONTEMPORARY CULTURE

Campus Box 89, Georgia College & State University, Milledgeville, GA 31061. **E-mail:** al.journal@gcsu.edu. **Website:** http://al.gcsu.edu. Estab. 1999. *Arts & Letters Journal of Contemporary Culture*, published semiannually, is devoted to contemporary arts and literature, featuring ongoing series such as The World Poetry Translation Series and The Mentors Interview Series. Wants work that is of the highest literary and artistic quality.

Work published in *Arts & Letters Journal* has received the Pushcart Prize.

NEEDS No genre fiction.

PAYMENT/TERMS Pays $10 per printed age, 1 contributor's copy, and 1-year subscription.

ART TIMES

A Literary Journal and Resource for All the Arts, P.O. Box 730, Mount Marion NY 12456. (845)246-6944. **Fax:** (845)246-6944. **E-mail:** info@ArtTimesJournal .com. **Website:** www.arttimesjournal.com. **Contact:** Raymond J. Steiner, editor. Estab. 1984. *"Art Times* covers the art fields and is distributed in locations most frequented by those enjoying the arts. Our copies are distributed throughout the lower part of the northeast as well as metropolitan New York area; locations include theaters, galleries, museums, schools, art clubs, cultural centers, and the like. Our readers are mostly over 40, affluent, art conscious, and sophisticated. Subscribers are located across U.S. and abroad (Italy, France, Germany, Greece, Russia, etc.)."

NEEDS Looks for quality short fiction that aspires to be literary. Publishes 1 story each issue. "Nothing violent, sexist, erotic, juvenile, racist, romantic, political, offbeat, or related to sports or juvenile fiction." Length: up to 1,500 words.

HOW TO CONTACT Send complete ms.

PAYMENT/TERMS Pays $25 and a 1-year subscription.

TIPS "Competition is greater (more submissions received), but keep trying. We print new as well as published writers. Be advised that we are presently on an approximate 3-year lead for short stories, 2-year lead for poetry. We are now receiving 300-400 poems and 40-50 short stories per month. Be familiar with *Art Times* and its special audience."

ASCENT ASPIRATIONS

1560 Arbutus Dr., Nanoose Bay BC C9P 9C8 Canada. **E-mail:** ascentaspirations@shaw.ca. **Website:** www .ascentaspirations.ca. **Contact:** David Fraser, editor. Estab. 1997. *"Ascent Aspirations* magazine publishes monthly online and once a year in print. The print issues are operated as contests. Please refer to current guidelines before submitting. *Ascent Aspirations* is a quality electronic publication dedicated to the promotion and encouragement of aspiring writers of any genre. The focus, however, is toward interesting experimental writing in dark mainstream, literary, science fiction, fantasy, and horror. Poetry can be on any

theme. Essays need to be unique, current, and have social, philosophical commentary."

Magazine: 40 electronic pages; illustrations; photos. Receives 100-200 unsolicited mss/ month. Accepts 40 mss/issue; 240 mss/year. Publishes ms 3 months after acceptance. Publishes 10-50 new writers/year. Has published work by Taylor Graham, Janet Buck, Jim Manton, Steve Cartwright, Don Stockard, Penn Kemp, Sam Vargo, Vernon Waring, Margaret Karmazin, Bill Hughes; and recently spoken word artists Sheri-D Wilson, Missy Peters, Ian Ferrier, Cathy Petch, and Bob Holdman.

NEEDS Length: 1,000 words or less. Publishes short shorts.

HOW TO CONTACT Query by e-mail with Word attachment. Include estimated word count, brief bio, and list of publications. "If you have to submit by mail because it is your only avenue, provide a SASE with either International Coupons or Canadian stamps only."

PAYMENT/TERMS "No payment at this time."

TIPS "Short fiction should, first of all tell, a good story, take the reader to new and interesting imaginary or real places. Short fiction should use language lyrically and effectively, be experimental in either form or content and take the reader into realms where they can analyze and think about the human condition. Write with passion for your material, be concise and economical and let the reader work to unravel your story. In terms of editing, always proofread to the point where what you submit is the best it possibly can be. Never be discouraged if your work is not accepted; it may just not be the right fit for a current publication."

ASIMOV'S SCIENCE FICTION

Dell Magazine Fiction Group, 267 Broadway, 4th Floor, New York, NY 10007. (212)686-7188. **Fax:** (212)686-7414. **E-mail:** asimovssf@dellmagazines .com. **Website:** www.asimovs.com. **Contact:** Sheila Williams, editor; Victoria Green, senior art director; June Levine, associate art director. Estab. 1977. Magazine: $5^7/_8" \times 8^5/_8"$ (trim size); 112 pages; 30 lb. newspaper; 70 lb. to 8 pt. C1S cover stock; illustrations; rarely photos. Magazine consists of science fiction and fantasy stories for adults and young adults. Publishes "the best short science fiction available." Receives approximately 800 unsolicited mss/month. Accepts 10 mss/issue. Publishes ms 6-12 months after acceptance. Agented fiction 10%. **Publishes 10 new writers/**

year. Recently published work by Robert Silverberg and Larry Niven. Publishes short shorts. Sometimes comments on rejected mss. Reviews fiction.

○ Named for a science fiction "legend," *Asimov's* regularly receives Hugo and Nebula Awards. Editor Gardner Dozois has received several awards for editing including Hugos and those from *Locus* magazine.

NEEDS Fantasy, science fiction (hard science, soft sociological). No horror or psychic/supernatural. Would like to see more hard science fiction. "Science fiction primarily. Some fantasy and humor but no sword and sorcery. No explicit sex or violence that isn't integral to the story. It is best to read a great deal of material in the genre to avoid the use of some very old ideas. Would like to see more hard science fiction. Length: 750-15,000 words.

HOW TO CONTACT Send complete ms with SASE. Responds in 2 months to queries; 3 months to mss. No simultaneous or reprint submissions. Sample copy for $5. Writer's guidelines for #10 SASE or online.

PAYMENT/TERMS Pays 5-8¢/word. Pays on acceptance. Buys first North American serial, nonexclusive foreign serial rights; reprint rights occasionally. Sends galleys to author.

TIPS "In general, we're looking for 'character-oriented' stories, those in which the characters, rather than the science, provide the main focus for the reader's interest. Serious, thoughtful, yet accessible fiction will constitute the majority of our purchases, but there's always room for the humorous as well. Borderline fantasy is fine, but no sword and sorcery, please. A good overview would be to consider that all fiction is written to examine or illuminate some aspect of human existence, but that in science fiction the backdrop you work against is the size of the universe. Please do not send us submissions on disk or via e-mail. We've bought some of our best stories from people who have never sold a story before."

○○ THE ATLANTIC MONTHLY

The Watergate, 600 New Hampshire Ave., NW, Washington DC 20037. (202)266-6000. **Website:** www.the atlantic.com. **Contact:** James Bennet, editor; C. Michael Curtis, fiction editor; David Barber, poetry editor. Estab. 1857. General magazine for an educated readership with broad cultural and public-affairs interests. Receives 1,000 unsolicited mss/month. Accepts 7-8 mss/year. **Publishes 3-4 new writers/year.**

Recently published work by Mary Gordon, Tobias Wolff. Accepts multiple submissions. Writer's guidelines online. "A general familiarity with what we have published in the past is the best guide to our needs and preferences. Manuscripts must be typewritten and double-spaced." No longer publishes fiction in the regular magazine. Instead, it will appear in a special newsstand-only fiction issue.

○ TheAtlantic.com no longer accepts unsolicited submissions.

NEEDS Literary and contemporary fiction. "Seeks fiction that is clear, tightly written with strong sense of 'story' and well-defined characters." Preferred length: 2,000-6,000 words

HOW TO CONTACT Send complete ms. Responds in 2 months. Receipt of manuscripts will be acknowledged if accompanied by a self-addressed stamped envelope. Manuscripts will not be returned. **At this time, the print magazine does not read submissions sent via fax or e-mail.**

PAYMENT/TERMS Pays $3,000. Pays on acceptance for first North American serial rights.

TIPS "Writers should be aware that this is not a market for beginner's work (nonfiction and fiction), nor is it truly for intermediate work. Study this magazine before sending only your best, most professional work. When making first contact, cover letters are sometimes helpful, particularly if they cite prior publications or involvement in writing programs. Common mistakes: melodrama, inconclusiveness, lack of development, unpersuasive characters and/or dialogue."

AUTHORSHIP

National Writers Association, 10940 S. Parker Rd., #508, Parker, CO 80134. (303)841-0246. **E-mail:** natl writersassn@hotmail.com. **Website:** www.nation alwriters.com. Estab. 1950s. "Association magazine targeted to beginning and professional writers. Covers how-to, humor, marketing issues."

HOW TO CONTACT "Disk and e-mail submissions preferred."

TIPS "Members of National Writers Association are given preference."

THE AVALON LITERARY REVIEW

CCI Publishing, P.O. Box 780696, Orlando, FL 32878. (407)574-7355. **E-mail:** submissions@avalonliter aryreview.com. **Website:** www.avalonliteraryreview .com. **Contact:** Valerie Rubino, managing editor. Estab. 2011. Quarterly magazine. "*The Avalon Literary*

Review welcomes work from both published and un-published writers and poets. We accept submissions of poetry, short fiction, and personal essays. The author's voice and point of view should be unique and clear. We seek pieces which spring from the author's life and experiences. Submissions which explore both the sweet and bitter of life, with a touch of humor, are a good fit for our *Review*. While we appreciate the genres of fantasy, science fiction and horror, our magazine is not the forum for such work."

NEEDS No erotica, science fiction, or horror. Length: 250-2,500 words.

HOW TO CONTACT Submit complete ms. Only accepts electronic submissions.

PAYMENT/TERMS Pays 5 contributor's copies.

TIPS "We seek work that is carefully structured. We like vivid descriptions, striking characters, and realistic dialogue. A humorous but not ridiculous point of view is a plus."

BABEL: THE MULTILINGUAL, MULTICULTURAL ONLINE JOURNAL AND COMMUNITY OF ARTS AND IDEAS

E-mail: submissions@towerofbabel.com. **Website:** http://towerofbabel.com. **Contact:** Malcolm Lawrence, editor-in-chief. Estab. 1995. Publishes regional reports from international stringers all over the planet, as well as features, roundtable discussions, fiction, columns, poetry, erotica, travelogues, and reviews of all the arts and editorials. "Our bloggers include James Schwartz, the first out gay poet raised in the Old Order Amish community in Southwestern Michigan and author of the book *The Literary Party*; Susanna Zaraysky, author of the book *Language Is Music: Making People Multilingual*; James Rovira, assistant professor of English and program chair of humanities at Tiffin University and author of the book *Blake & Kierkegaard: Creation and Anxiety*; and Paul B. Miller, assistant professor, department of French and Italian at Vanderbilt University. We're interested in fiction, nonfiction, and poetry from all over the world, including multicultural or multilingual work."

Babel is recognized by the U.N. as one of the most important social and human sciences online periodicals.

NEEDS "We are currently looking for WordPress bloggers in the following languages: Arabic, Bulgarian, Bengali, Catalan, Czech, Welsh, Danish, German, English, Esperanto, Spanish, Persian, Finnish, Faroese, French, Hebrew, Croatian, Indonesian, Italian, Japanese, Korean, Latvian, Malay, Dutch, Polish, Portuguese, Russian, Albanian, Serbian, Swedish, Tamil, Thai, Ukrainian, Urdu, Uzbek, Vietnamese, and Chinese." Reviews novels, short story collections, books/chapbooks of poetry and other magazines, single- and multibook format. Open to unsolicited reviews. Send materials for review consideration.

HOW TO CONTACT Send queries/mss by e-mail. "Please send submissions with a resumé/cover letter or biography attached to the e-mail."

PAYMENT/TERMS Does not pay.

TIPS "We would like to see more fiction with first-person male characters written by female authors, as well as more fiction first-person female characters written by male authors. We would also like to see that dynamic in action when it comes to other languages, cultures, races, classes, sexual orientations, and ages. Know what you are writing about and write passionately about it."

THE BALTIMORE REVIEW

P.O. Box 36418, Towson, MD 21286. **E-mail:** editor@baltimorereview.org. **Website:** www.baltimorereview.org. **Contact:** Barbara Westwood Diehl, senior editor; Kathleen Hellen, senior editor. Estab. 1996. "*The Baltimore Review* publishes poetry, fiction, and creative nonfiction from Baltimore and beyond." Submission periods are August 1 through November 30 and February 1 through May 31.

In 2012, *The Baltimore Review* began its new life as a quarterly online literary.

NEEDS No genre fiction. "No science fiction, westerns, children's, romance, etc." Length: 100-6,000 words.

HOW TO CONTACT Send complete ms using online submission form.

PAYMENT/TERMS Pays in contributor's copies.

TIPS "Please read what is being published in other literary journals, including our own. As in any other profession, writers must know what the trends and the major issues are in the field. We look for compelling stories and a masterful use of the English language. We want to feel that we have never heard this story, or this voice, before. Read the kinds of publications you want your work to appear in. Make your reader believe and care."

BARBARIC YAWP

BoneWorld Publishing, 3700 County Rt. 24, Russell, NY 13684-3198. (315)347-2609. **Website:** www.bone worldpublishing.com.

NEEDS "We publish what we like. Fiction should include some bounce and surprise. Our publication is intended for the intelligent, open-minded reader." "We don't want any pornography, gratuitous violence, or whining."

HOW TO CONTACT Send SASE for reply, return of ms or send a disposable copy of ms. Accepts simultaneous, multiple submissions, and reprints.

PAYMENT/TERMS Pays 1 contributor's copy; additional copies $3.

TIPS "Don't give up. Read much, write much, submit much. Observe closely the world around you. Don't borrow ideas from TV or films. Revision is often necessary—grit your teeth and do it. Never fear rejection."

THE BARCELONA REVIEW

Correu Vell 12-2, Barcelona 08002 Spain. (00 34) 93 319 15 96. **E-mail:** editor@barcelonareview.com. **Website:** www.barcelonareview.com. **Contact:** Jill Adams, editor.

NEEDS Length: no more than 4,500 words.

HOW TO CONTACT Submit one story at a time. To submit via e-mail, send an attached document; do not send in the body of an e-mail. Include "Submission/ Author Name" in the subject box. Accepts hard copies, but they will not be returned.

PAYMENT/TERMS "We cannot offer money to contributors, but in lieu of pay we can sometimes offer an excellent Spanish translation (worth quite a bit of money in itself). Work is showcased along with two or more known authors in a high quality literary review with an international readership."

TIPS "Send top drawer material that has been drafted two, three, four times—whatever it takes. Then sit on it for a while and look at it afresh. Keep the text tight. Grab the reader in the first paragraph and don't let go. Keep in mind that a perfectly crafted story that lacks a punch of some sort won't cut it. Make it new, make it different. Surprise the reader in some way. Read the best of the short fiction available in your area of writing to see how yours measures up. Don't send anything off until you feel it's ready and familiarize yourself with the content of the review/magazine to which you are submitting."

BAYOU

English Dept. University of New Orleans, 2000 Lakeshore Dr., New Orleans, LA 70148. (504)280-5423. **E-mail:** bayou@uno.edu. **Website:** www.uno.edu/bayou. **Contact:** Joanna Leake, editor. Estab. 2002. "A nonprofit journal for the arts, each issue of *Bayou Magazine* contains beautiful fiction, nonfiction, and poetry. From quirky shorts to more traditional stories, we are committed to publishing solid work. Regardless of style, at *Bayou* we are always interested first in a well-told tale. Our poetry and prose are filled with memorable characters observing their world, acknowledging both the mundane and the sublime, often at once, and always with an eye toward beauty. *Bayou* is packed with a range of material from established, award-winning authors as well as new voices on the rise. Recent contributors include Eric Trethewey, Virgil Suarez, Marilyn Hacker, Sean Beaudoin, Tom Whalen, Mark Doty, Philip Cioffari, Lyn Lifshin, Timothy Liu, and Gaylord Brewer. And in one issue every year, *Bayou* features the winner of the annual Tennessee Williams/New Orleans Literary Festival One-Act Play Competition."

Does not accept e-mail submissions. Reads submissions from September 1 to June 1.

NEEDS "Flash fiction and short shorts are welcome. No novel excerpts, please, unless they can stand alone as short stories." No horror, gothic, or juvenile fiction. Length: no more than 7,500 words.

HOW TO CONTACT Send complete ms. Send disposable copy of the ms and #10 SASE for reply only.

PAYMENT/TERMS Pays 2 contributor's copies and one year subscription.

TIPS "Do not submit in more than one genre at a time. Don't send a second submission until you receive a response to the first."

THE BEAR DELUXE MAGAZINE

Orlo, 810 SE Belmont, Studio 5, Portland, OR 97214. (503)242-1047. **E-mail:** bear@orlo.org. **Website:** www .orlo.org. **Contact:** Tom Webb, editor-in-chief; Kristin Rogers Brown, art director. Estab. 1993. "*The Bear Deluxe Magazine* is a national independent environmental arts magazine publishing significant works of reporting, creative nonfiction, literature, visual art, and design. Based in the Pacific Northwest, it reaches across cultural and political divides to engage readers on vital issues effecting the environment. Published twice per year, *The Bear Deluxe* includes a wider array and a higher percentage of visual artwork and design than many other publications. Artwork is included both as editorial support and as stand-alone or independent art. It has included nationally recognized artists as well as emerging artists. As with any publication, artists are encouraged to review a sample copy for a clearer understanding of the magazine's approach. Unsolicited submissions and samples are accepted and encouraged."

NEEDS "Stories must have some environmental context, but we view that in a broad sense." No detective, children's, or horror. Length: 750-4,500 words.

HOW TO CONTACT Query or send complete ms.

PAYMENT/TERMS Pays free subscription to the magazine, contributor's copies and $25-400, depending on piece; additional copies for postage

TIPS "Offer to be a stringer for future ideas. Get a copy of the magazine and guidelines, and query us with specific nonfiction ideas and clips. We're looking for original magazine-style stories, not fluff or PR. Fiction, essay, and poetry writers should know we have an open and blind review policy and should keep sending their best work even if rejected once. Be as specific as possible in queries."

BELLEVUE LITERARY REVIEW

NYU Langone Medical Center, Department of Medicine, 550 First Ave., OBV-A612, New York, NY 10016. (212)263-3973. **E-mail:** info@BLReview.org. **E-mail:** stacy.bodziak@nyumc.org. **Website:** www.blreview .org. **Contact:** Stacy Bodziak, managing editor. Estab. 2001. *Bellevue Literary Review*, published semiannually, prints "works of fiction, nonfiction, and poetry that touch upon relationships to the human body, illness, health, and healing."

Receives 100 unsolicited mss/month. Accepts 10-12 mss/issue; 24 mss/year. *Bellevue Literary Review* is 160 pages, digest size, perfect-bound; includes ads. Press run is 5,000; distributed free to literary magazine conferences, promotions, and other contacts. Single copy: $9; subscription: $15/year, $35 for 3 years (plus $5/year postage to Canada, $8/year postage foreign). Make checks payable to *Bellevue Literary Review*. Work published in *Bellevue Literary Review* has appeared in the *Pushcart Prize* anthology. Recently published work by Rafael Campo, Paul Harding, Tom Sleigh.

NEEDS Agented fiction 1%. Publishes 3-6 new writers/year. Publishes short shorts; also publishes literary essays and poetry. Sometimes comments on rejected mss. No genre fiction. Length: 5,000 words. Average length: 2,500 words.

HOW TO CONTACT Submit online at www.blreview.org (preferred). Also accepts mss via regular mail. Send complete ms. Send SASE (or IRC) for return of ms or disposable copy of the ms and #10 SASE for reply only.

PAYMENT/TERMS Pays 2 contributor's copies, 1-year subscription, and 1-year gift subscription; additional copies $6.

BELLINGHAM REVIEW

Mail Stop 9053, Western Washington University, Bellingham, WA 98225. (360)650-4863. **E-mail:** bh review@wwu.edu. **Website:** www.bhreview.org. **Contact:** Tyler Koshakow, managing editor. Estab. 1977. Annual nonprofit magazine published once a year in the spring. Seeks "literature of palpable quality: poems stories and essays so beguiling they invite us to touch their essence. The *Bellingham Review* hungers for a kind of writing that nudges the limits of form or executes traditional forms exquisitely."

The editors are actively seeking submissions of creative nonfiction, as well as stories that push the boundaries of the form. The Tobias Wolff Award in Fiction Contest runs December 1-March 15; see website for guidelines or send SASE.

NEEDS Experimental, humor/satire, literary, regional (Northwest). Does not want anything nonliterary. 6,000 words maximum.

HOW TO CONTACT Send complete ms.

PAYMENT/TERMS Pays as funds allow.

TIPS "Open submission period is from September 15-December 1. Manuscripts arriving between December 2 and September 14 will be returned unread. The *Bellingham Review* holds 3 annual contests: the 49th Parallel Award for poetry, the Annie Dillard Award for Nonfiction, and the Tobias Wolff Award for Fiction. Submissions: December 1-March 15. See the individual listings for these contests under 'Contests & Awards' for full details."

BELOIT FICTION JOURNAL

Box 11, Beloit, 700 College St., Beloit, WI 53511. (608)363-2079. **E-mail:** bfj@beloit.edu. **Website:** www.beloit.edu/english/fictionjournal. **Contact:**

Chris Fink, editor-in-chief. Estab. 1985. "We are interested in publishing the best contemporary fiction and are open to all themes except those involving pornographic, religiously dogmatic, or politically propagandistic representations. Our magazine is for general readership, though most of our readers will probably have a specific interest in literary magazines."

◑ Receives 200 unsolicited mss/month. Accepts 20 mss/year. Publishes ms 9 months after acceptance. **Publishes 3 new writers/year.** Sometimes comments on rejected mss. Annual literary magazine: 6" × 9"; 250 pages; 60 lb. paper; 10 pt. C1S cover stock; illustrations; photos on cover; ad-free. Work first appearing in *Beloit Fiction Journal* has been reprinted in award-winning collections, including the Flannery O'Connor and the Milkweed Fiction Prize collections, and has won the Iowa Short Fiction award. Has published work by Dennis Lehane, Silas House, and David Harris Ebenbach.

NEEDS No pornography, religious dogma, science fiction, horror, political propaganda, or genre fiction. Length: 250-10,000 words; average length: 5,000 words.

HOW TO CONTACT "Our reading period is August 1-December 1 only. " No fax, e-mail, or disk submissions. Accepts simultaneous submissions if identified as such. Please send one story at a time. Always include SASE. Sample copy for $10 (new issue), $8 (back issue, double issue), $6 (back issue, single issue). Writer's guidelines for #10 SASE or on website.

PAYMENT/TERMS Payment in copies.

TIPS "Many of our contributors are writers whose work we had previously rejected. Don't let one rejection slip turn you away from our—or any—magazine."

◐ BERKELEY FICTION REVIEW

10B Eshleman Hall, University of California, Berkeley, CA 94720. (510)642-2892. **E-mail:** bfictionreview@ yahoo.com. **Website:** www.ocf.berkeley.edu/~bfr. Estab. 1981.

NEEDS Length: no more than 25 pages.

HOW TO CONTACT Submit via e-mail with "Submission: Name, Title" in subject line. Include cover letter in body of e-mail, with story as an attachment.

PAYMENT/TERMS Pays 1 contributor's copy.

TIPS "Our criteria is fiction that resonates. Voices that are strong and move a reader. Clear, powerful prose (either voice or rendering of subject) with a

point. Unique ways of telling stories—these capture the editors. Work hard, don't give up. Ask an honest person to point out your writing weaknesses, and then work on them. We look forward to reading fresh new voices."

◐ ◑ BIG MUDDY: A JOURNAL OF THE MISSISSIPPI RIVER VALLEY

Southeast Missouri State University Press, One University Plaza, MS 2650, Cape Girardeau, MO 63701. (573)651-2044. **Website:** www6.semo.edu/universi typress/bigmuddy. **Contact:** Susan Swartwout, publisher/editor. Estab. 2001. "*Big Muddy* explores multidisciplinary, multicultural issues, people, and events mainly concerning, but not limited to, the 10-state area that borders the Mississippi River. We publish fiction, poetry, historical essays, creative nonfiction, environmental essays, biography, regional events, photography, art, etc."

◑ Magazine: 8½" × 5½" perfect-bound; 150 pages; acid-free paper; color cover stock; lay flat lamination; illustrations; photos. Receives 50 unsolicited mss/month. Accepts 20-25 mss/issue. Accepts multiple submissions.

NEEDS No romance, fantasy, or children's.

PAYMENT/TERMS Pays 2 contributor's copies; additional copies $5.

TIPS "We look for clear language, avoidance of clichés except in necessary dialogue, a fresh vision of the theme or issue. Find some excellent and honest readers to comment on your work-in-progress and final draft. Consider their viewpoints carefully. Revise if needed."

THE BINNACLE

University of Maine at Machias, 116 O'Brien Ave., Machias, ME 04654. **E-mail:** ummbinnacle@maine .edu. **Website:** www.umm.maine.edu/binnacle. Estab. 1957. "Please see our website (www.umm.maine .edu/binnacle) for details on our Annual Ultra-Short Competition (Prize a minimum of $300)." Semiannual, Fall edition is the Ultra-Short Competition editon. Publishes ms 3-9 months after acceptance. Sample copy for $7. Writer's guidelines online at website only. Acquires one-time rights. "We are interested in fresh voices, not Raymond Carver's, and not the Iowa Workshop's. We want the peculiar and the idiosyncratic. We want playful and experimental, but understandable. Please see our website for details on our Annual Ultra-Short Competition. We accept submissions for the Fall Ultra-Short Edition from December 1 to March 15 and report to writers in early June. We accept submissions for the Spring Edition from September 1 to November 30 and report to writers between February 1 and March 1."

○ Does not accepted paper submissions. Electronic/e-mail submissions only.

NEEDS Ethnic/multicultural, experimental, humor/satire, mainstream, slice-of-life vignettes, but any genre attuned to a general audience can work. No extreme erotica, fantasy, horror, or religious, but any genre attuned to a general audience can work. 2,500 words maximum.

HOW TO CONTACT Submissions by e-mail only. Responds in 1 month to queries; 3 months to mss. Accepts simultaneous submissions. Send complete ms via e-mail only.

PAYMENT/TERMS $300 in prizes for Ultra-Short Competition. $50 per issue for one work of editor's choice.

TIPS "We want fiction, poetry, and images that speak to real people, people who have lives, people who have troubles, people who laugh, too."

THE BITTER OLEANDER

4983 Tall Oaks Dr., Fayetteville, NY 13066. **Fax:** (315)637-5056. **E-mail:** info@bitteroleander.com. **Website:** www.bitteroleander.com. **Contact:** Paul B. Roth, editor and publisher. Zine specializing in poetry and short fiction.

○ 6" × 9"; 128 pages; 55 lb. paper; 12 pt. CIS cover stock; photos. Bi-annual. Receives 200 unsolicited mss/month. Accepts 4-5 mss/issue; 8-10 mss/year. Always comments on rejected mss. Does not read in July. Recently published work by Mark Joseph Kiewlak, Judith Taylor Gold, Edwin García Lopez, Eros Alegra Clarke, Norberto Luis Romero (Spain), and Samanta Schweblin (Argentina).

NEEDS: "We're interested in the surreal; deep image particularization of natural experiences." Max length: 2,500 words. Publishes short shorts. Also publishes literary essays, poetry. Does not want family stories with moralistic plots, and no fantasy that involves hyper-reality of any sort. Length: 300-2,500 words.

HOW TO CONTACT Query. Send mss by mail with SASE for response. Whether you live in the U.S. or outside, we accept e-mail submissions or regular mail submissions if SASE is enclosed.

PAYMENT/TERMS Pays contributor's copies.

TIPS "If you are writing poems or short fiction in the tradition of 95% of all journals publishing in this country, your work will usually not be fit for us. If within the first 100 words my mind drifts, the rest rarely makes it. Be yourself and listen to no one but yourself."

❶ BLACKBIRD

Virginia Commonwealth University Department of English, P.O. Box 843082, Richmond, VA 23284. (804)827-4729. **E-mail:** blackbird@vcu.edu. **Website:** www.blackbird.vcu.edu. Estab. 2001. *Blackbird* is published twice a year.

NEEDS "We primarily look for short stories, but novel excerpts are acceptable if self-contained."

HOW TO CONTACT Submit using online submissions manager or by postal mail. Online submission is preferred.

TIPS "We like a story that invites us into its world, that engages our senses, soul, and mind. We are able to publish long works in all genres, but query *Blackbird* before you send a prose piece over 8,000 words or a poem exceeding 10 pages."

❶❸ BLACK LACE

P.O. Box 83912, Los Angeles, CA 90083. (310)410-0808. **Fax:** (310)410-9250. **E-mail:** newsroom@blk .com. **Website:** www.blacklace.org. Estab. 1991.

NEEDS Length: 2,000-4,000 words.

HOW TO CONTACT Submit complete ms via postal mail or e-mail.

TIPS "*Black Lace* seeks erotic material of the highest quality, but it need not be written by professional writers. The most important thing is that the work be erotic and that it feature black women in the life or ITL themes. We are not interested in stories that demean black women or place them in stereotypical situations."

❶❷❸ BLACK WARRIOR REVIEW

P.O. Box 862936, Tuscaloosa, AL 35486. (205)348-4518. **E-mail:** interns.bwr@gmail.com. **Website:** www.bwr.ua.edu. **Contact:** Jenny Gropp Hess, editor. Estab. 1974. "We publish contemporary fiction, poetry, reviews, essays, and art for a literary audience. We publish the freshest work we can find."

○ Work that appeared in the *Black Warrior Review* has been included in the *Pushcart Prize* anthology, *Harper's Magazine, Best American*

Short Stories, Best American Poetry, and *New Stories from the South.*

NEEDS Wants work that is conscious of form and well-crafted "We are open to good experimental writing and short-short fiction. No genre fiction please. Publishes novel excerpts if under contract to be published." Length: no more than 7,000 words.

HOW TO CONTACT One story/chapter per envelope.

PAYMENT/TERMS "BWR pays a one-year subscription and a nominal lump-sum fee for all works published."

TIPS "We look for attention to language, freshness, honesty, a convincing and sharp voice. Send us a clean, well-printed, proofread manuscript. Become familiar with the magazine prior to submission."

◑ BLOOD LOTUS

Wales. **E-mail:** bloodlotusjournal@gmail.com; bloodlotusfiction@gmail.com. **Website:** www.bloodlotusjournal.com. **Contact:** Stacia M. Fleegal, managing editor. *Blood Lotus*, published quarterly online, publishes "poetry, fiction, and anything in between!" Wants "fresh language, memorable characters, strong images, and vivid artwork." Will not open attachments. Reads submissions year round.

NEEDS Must be stand-alone, self-contained stories. No excerpts. Stories should be no longer than 4,500 words.

TIPS "Don't be boring."

◑ BLUELINE

120 Morey Hall, Department of English and Communication, Postdam, NY 13676. (315)267-2043. **E-mail:** blueline@potsdam.edu. **Website:** www2.potsdam.edu/blueline. **Contact:** Donald McNutt, editor; Caroline Downing, art editor. Estab. 1979. "*Blueline* seeks poems, stories, and essays relating to the Adirondacks and regions similar in geography and spirit, or focusing on the shaping influence of nature. Payment in copies. Submission period is July through November. *Blueline* welcomes electronic submissions, either in the body of an e-mail message or in Word or html formatted files. Please avoid using compression software."

◐ Magazine: 6" × 9"; 200 pages; 70 lb. white stock paper; 65 lb. smooth cover stock; illustrations; photos. Receives 8-10 unsolicited mss/month. Accepts 6-8 mss/issue. Does not read January-August. Publishes 2 new writers/year. Recently published work by Joan Connor, Laura Rodley, and Ann Mohin.

NEEDS No urban stories or erotica. Length: 500-3,000 words. Average length: 2,500 words.

PAYMENT/TERMS Pays 1 contributor's copy; charges $7 each for 3 or more copies.

TIPS "We look for concise, clear, concrete prose that tells a story and touches upon a universal theme or situation. We prefer realism to romanticism but will consider nostalgia if well done. Pay attention to grammar and syntax. Avoid murky language, sentimentality, cuteness, or folkiness. We would like to see more good fiction related to the Adirondacks and more literary fiction and prose poems. If manuscript has potential, we work with author to improve and reconsider for publication. Our readers prefer fiction to poetry (in general) or reviews. Write from your own experience, be specific and factual (within the bounds of your story), and if you write about universal features such as love, death, change, etc., write about them in a fresh way. Triteness and mediocrity are the hallmarks of the majority of stories seen today."

BLUE MESA REVIEW

E-mail: bmreditr@unm.edu. **Website:** www.unm.edu/~bluemesa/index.htm. **Contact:** Suzanne Richarson, editor; Bonnie Arning, managing editor. "Originally founded by Rudolfo Anaya, Gene Frumkin, David Johnson, Patricia Clark Smith, and Lee Bartlette in 1989, the *Blue Mesa Review* emerged as a source of innovative writing produced in the Southwest. Over the years the magazine's nuance has changed, sometimes shifting towards more craft-oriented work, other times realigning with its original roots."

◐ Open for submissions from September 1 to May 31. Only accepts submissions through online submissions manager.

HOW TO CONTACT Submit up to 30 pages.

BLUESTEM

English Deptartment, Eastern Illinois University, E-mail: info@bluestemmagazine.com. **Website:** www.bluestemmagazine.com. **Contact:** Olga Abella, editor. Estab. 1966. "*Bluestem*, formerly known as *Karamu*, produces a quarterly online issue (December, March, June, September) and an annual print issue. Submissions are accepted year-round. Print contributors receive a complimentary copy of the issue containing their work and may purchase extra copies at a discounted price. There is no compensation for online contributors but we will promote your work enthusiastically and widely. Past issues have included themes such as: The Humor Issue, The Music Issue, The Millennium."

○ Only accepts submissions through online submissions manager.

NEEDS Length: no more than 5,000 words.

HOW TO CONTACT Submit only one short story at a time. Include bio (less than 100 words) with submission. Query if longer than 5,000 words.

⊙⑤ BOMB MAGAZINE

New Arts Publications, 80 Hanson Place, Suite 703, Brooklyn, NY 11217. (718)636-9100. Fax: (718)636-9200. E-mail: firstproof@bombsite.com; generalin quiries@bombsite.com. Website: www.bombsite .com. Contact: Monica de la Torre, senior editor. Estab. 1981. "Written, edited, and produced by industry professionals and funded by those interested in the arts. Publishes work which is unconventional and contains an edge, whether it be in style or subject matter."

NEEDS No genre: romance, science fiction, horror, western. Length: less than 25 pages.

HOW TO CONTACT Submit complete ms. E-mailed submissions will not be considered.

PAYMENT/TERMS Pays $100, and contributor's copies.

TIPS "Manuscripts should be typed, double-spaced, proofread and should be final drafts. Purchase a sample issue before submitting work."

⊙⑦⑤ BOSTON REVIEW

PO Box 425786, Cambridge, MA 02142. (617)324-1360. Fax: (617)452-3356. E-mail: review@boston review.net. Website: www.bostonreview.net. Estab. 1975. "The editors are committed to a society and culture that foster human diversity and a democracy in which we seek common grounds of principle amidst our many differences. In the hope of advancing these ideals, the *Review* acts as a forum that seeks to enrich the language of public debate."

○ *Boston Review* is a recipient of the Pushcart Prize in Poetry.

NEEDS Looking for "stories that are emotionally and intellectually substantive and also interesting on the level of language. Things that are shocking, dark, lewd, comic, or even insane are fine so long as the fiction is *controlled* and purposeful in a masterly way. Subtlety, delicacy, and lyricism are attractive, too." No romance, erotica, genre fiction. Length: 1,200-5,000 words. Average length: 2,000 words.

HOW TO CONTACT Send complete ms. "Simultaneous submissions are fine as long as we are notified of the fact. We accept submissions through our **online submissions system**."

PAYMENT/TERMS Pays $25-300 and contributor's copies.

TIPS "The best way to get a sense of the kind of material *Boston Review* is looking for is to read the magazine. (Sample copies are available for $6.95 plus shipping.) We do not consider previously published material."

⊙⑦⑤ BOULEVARD

Opojaz, Inc., 6614 Clayton Rd., Box 325, Richmond Heights, MO 63117. (314)862-2643. Fax: (314)862-2982. E-mail: richardburgin@att.net; jessicarogen@ boulevardmagazine.org; kellyleavitt@boulevard magazine.com. Website: www.boulevardmagazine. org. Contact: Richard Burgin, editor; Jessica Rogen, managing editor; Kelly Leavitt, associate editor. Estab. 1985. "*Boulevard* is a diverse literary magazine presenting original creative work by well-known authors, as well as by writers of exciting promise. *Boulevard* has been called 'one of the half-dozen best literary journals' by Poet Laureate Daniel Hoffman in *The Philadelphia Inquirer*. We strive to publish the finest in poetry, fiction and nonfiction." Also sponsors the Short Fiction Contest for Emerging Writers. $1,500 and publication in *Boulevard* awarded to the winning story by a writer who has not yet published a book of fiction, poetry, or creative nonfiction with a nationally distributed press. Entry fee is $15 for each individual story, with no limit per author. Entry fee includes a 1-year subscription to *Boulevard* (one per author). Make check payable to *Boulevard*.

○ Triannual. Receives over 600 unsolicited mss/ month. Accepts about 10 mss/issue. Does not accept manuscripts between May 1 and October 1. Publishes ms 9 months after acceptance. **Publishes 10 new writers/year.** Recently published work by Joyce Carol Oates, Floyd Skloot, Alice Hoffman, Stephen Dixon, and Frederick Busch. Sometimes comments on rejected mss. Accepts multiple submissions. No simultaneous submissions. Sample copy for $9. Writer's guidelines online.

NEEDS Confessions, experimental, literary, mainstream, novel excerpts. "We do not want erotica, science fiction, romance, western, or children's stories."

Also publishes short shorts, literary essays, literary criticism, poetry. Length: 8,000 words maximum.

HOW TO CONTACT Send complete ms. "We strongly urge you to submit electronically rather than through the mail." Accepts online submissions: .pdf, .doc, .docx, .txt, .rtf, .jpg, .gif, .mp3, .mp4, .m4a, .zip, .tiff, .png. Responds in 2 weeks to queries; 3-4 months to mss.

PAYMENT/TERMS Pays $50-500 (sometimes higher) for accepted work.

TIPS "Read the magazine first. The work *Boulevard* publishes is generally recognized as among the finest in the country. We continue to seek good literary or cultural essays. Send only your best work."

◐◯ BRAIN, CHILD

Erielle Media, LLC, 341 Newtown Turnpike, Wilton, CT 06897. (203)563-9149. **E-mail:** submissions@brainchildmag.com. **Website:** www.brainchildmag.com. **Contact:** Marcelle Soviero, editor-in-chief. Estab. 2000. *"Brain, Child: The Magazine for Thinking Mothers,* reflects modern motherhood—the way it really is. It is the largest print literary magazine devoted to motherhood. *Brain, Child* as a community, for and by mothers who like to think about what raising kids does for (and to) the mind and soul. *Brain, Child* isn't your typical parenting magazine. We couldn't cupcake-decorate our way out of a paper bag. We are more 'literary' than 'how-to,' more *New Yorker* than *Parents.* We shy away from expert advice on child rearing in favor of firsthand reflections by great writers (Jane Smiley, Barbara Ehrenreich, Anne Tyler) on life as a mother. Each quarterly issue is full of essays, features, humor, reviews, fiction, art, cartoons, and our readers' own stories. Our philosophy is pretty simple: Motherhood is worthy of literature. And there are a lot of ways to mother, all of them interesting. We're proud to be publishing articles and essays that are smart, down to earth, sometimes funny, and sometimes poignant."

NEEDS "We publish fiction that has a strong motherhood theme." No genre fiction. Length: 800-5,000 words.

HOW TO CONTACT Send complete ms.

PAYMENT/TERMS Payment varies.

TIPS Prefers e-mail submissions. No attachments.

BREAD FOR GOD'S CHILDREN

P.O. Box 1017, Arcadia, FL 34265. (863)494-6214. **Fax:** (863)993-0154. **E-mail:** bread@breadministries.org. **Website:** www.breadministries.org. **Contact:** Judith M. Gibbs, editor. Estab. 1972. An interdenominational Christian teaching publication published 6-8 times/year written to aid children and youth in leading a Christian life.

NEEDS "We are looking for writers who have a solid knowledge of Biblical principles and are concerned for the youth of today living by those principles. Our stories must be well written, with the story itself getting the message across—no preaching, moralizing, or tag endings." Young readers, middle readers, young adult/teen: adventure, religious, problem solving, sports. Looks for "teaching stories that portray Christian lifestyles without preaching." Buys approximately 10-15 mss/year. Length: young children, 600-800 words; older children, 900-1,500 words.

HOW TO CONTACT Send complete ms.

PAYMENT/TERMS Pays $40-50.

TIPS "We want stories or articles that illustrate overcoming obstacles with faith and living solid, Christian lives. Know our publication and what we have used in the past. Know the readership and publisher's guidelines. Stories should teach the value of morality and honesty without preaching. Edit carefully for content and grammar."

◐◯ THE BRIAR CLIFF REVIEW

3303 Rebecca St., Sioux City, IA 51104. (712)279-5477. **E-mail:** tricia.currans-sheehan@briarcliff.edu (editor); jeanne.emmons@briarcliff.edu (poetry). **Website:** www.briarcliff.edu/bcreview. **Contact:** Tricia Currans-Sheehan, Jeanne Emmons, Phil Hey, Paul Weber, editors. Estab. 1989. *The Briar Cliff Review,* published annually in April, is "an attractive, eclectic literary/art magazine." The *Briar Cliff Review* focuses on (but is not limited to) "Siouxland writers and subjects. We are happy to proclaim ourselves a regional publication. It doesn't diminish us; it enhances us."

◯ Magazine: 8½" × 11"; 125 pages; 70 lb. 100# Altima Satin Text; illustrations; photos; perfectbound, with 4-color cover on dull stock. Accepts 5 mss/year. Reads mss only between August 1 and November 1. **Publishes 10-14 new writers/year.** Publishes ms 3-4 months after acceptance. Recently published work by Leslie Barnard, Daryl Murphy, Patrick Hicks, Siobhan Fallon, Shelley Scaletta, Jenna Blum, Brian Bedard, Rebecca Tuch, Scott H. Andrews, and Josip Novakovich. Member: CLMP; Humanities International Complete.

NEEDS "No romance, horror, or alien stories." Length: 2,500-5,000 words; average length: 3,000 words.

HOW TO CONTACT Send SASE for return of ms. Does not accept electronic submissions (unless from overseas). Responds in 4-5 months to mss. Seldom comments on rejected mss. Accepts simultaneous submissions.

PAYMENT/TERMS Pays 2 contributor's copies; additional copies available for $12.

TIPS "So many stories are just telling. We want some action. It has to move. We prefer stories in which there is no gimmick, no mechanical turn of events, no moral except the one we would draw privately."

◑ BRILLIANT CORNERS: A JOURNAL OF JAZZ & LITERATURE

Lycoming College, 700 College Place, Williamsport PA, 17701. **Website:** www.lycoming.edu/brilliant corners. **Contact:** Sascha Feinstein. Estab. 1996. "We publish jazz-related literature—fiction, poetry, and nonfiction. We are open as to length and form." Semiannual.

◒ Journal: 6" × 9"; 90 pages; 70 lb. Cougar opaque, vellum, natural paper; photographs. Does not read mss May 15-September 1. Receives 10-15 unsolicited mss/month. Accepts 1-2 mss/issue; 2-3 mss/year. Rarely comments on rejected mss.

HOW TO CONTACT Submit with SASE for return of ms or send disposable copy of ms. Accepts unpublished work only.

TIPS "We look for clear, moving prose that demostrates a love of both writing and jazz. We primarily publish established writers, but we read all submissions carefully and welcome work by outstanding young writers."

THE BROADKILL REVIEW

Broadkill Publishing Associates c/o John Milton & Company, 104 Federal St., Milton, DE 19968. **E-mail:** the_broadkill_review@earthlink.net. **Website:** www.thebroadkillreview.blogspot.com; https://sites.google.com/site/thebroadkillreview. **Contact:** Jamie Brown, editor; Scott Whitaker, Web editors. Estab. 2005. "*The Broadkill Review* accepts the best fiction, poetry, and nonfiction by new and established writers. We have published Pushcart nominated fiction and poetry."

NEEDS No erotica, fantasy, sci-fi "unless these serve some functional, literary purpose; most do not." Length: 6,000 words/maximum.

HOW TO CONTACT Send complete ms with cover letter online at https://thebroadkillreview.submittable.com/submit. Include estimated word count, brief bio, list of publications.

PAYMENT/TERMS Pays contributor's copy.

TIPS "Query the editor first. Visit our website to familiarize yourself with the type of material we publish. Request and read a copy of the magazine first!"

◯ BROKEN PENCIL

P.O. Box 203, Station P, Toronto, ON M5S 2S7 Canada. **E-mail:** editor@brokenpencil.com. **Website:** www.brokenpencil.com. Estab. 1995. "*Broken Pencil* is one of the few magazines in the world devoted exclusively to underground culture and the independent arts. We are a great resource and a lively read! *Broken Pencil* reviews the best zines, books, websites, videos, and artworks from the underground and reprints the best articles from the alternative press. From the hilarious to the perverse, *Broken Pencil* challenges conformity and demands attention."

◒ Reads fiction submissions only between February 1 and September 15.

NEEDS "We're particularly interested in work from emerging writers." Length: 50-3,000 words.

HOW TO CONTACT Submit using online submissions manager.

PAYMENT/TERMS Pays $30-300.

TIPS "Remember, we are a guide to alternative and independent culture. We don't want your thoughts on Hollywood movies or your touching tale about coming of age on the prairies! Make sure you have some sense of the kind of work we use before getting in touch. Do not send us something if you haven't at least read *Broken Pencil*. Always include your address, phone number, and e-mail, so we know where to find you, and a little something about yourself, so we know who you are."

◑ BRYANT LITERARY REVIEW

Faculty Suite F, Bryant University, 1150 Douglas Pike, Smithfield, RI 02917. **E-mail:** blr@bryant.edu. **Website:** http://bryantliteraryreview.org. **Contact:** Tom Chandler, editor; Stasia Walmsley, managing editor; Lucie Koretsky, associate editor. Estab. 2000. *Bryant Literary Review* is an international magazine of poetry and fiction published annually in May. Features poetry, fiction, photography, and art. "Our only standard is quality." Has published poetry by Michael S. Harper, Mary Crow, Denise Duhamel, and Baron Wormser.

◐ Bryant Literary Review is 125 pages, digest size, offset printed, perfect-bound, with 4-color cover with art or photo. Single copy: $8; subscription: $8. Reads submissions September 1-December 31.

HOW TO CONTACT "To submit work, please review the submission guidelines on our website."

TIPS "We expect readers of the *Bryant Literary Review* to be sophisticated, educated, and familiar with the conventions of contemporary literature. We see our purpose to be the cultivation of an active and growing connection between our community and the larger literary culture. Our production values are of the highest caliber, and our roster of published authors includes major award and fellowship winners. The *BLR* provides a respected venue for creative writing of every kind from around the world. Our only standard is quality. No abstract expressionist poems, please. We prefer accessible work of depth and quality."

◐⑤ BUGLE

5705 Grant Creek Rd., Missoula, MT 59808. (406)523-4500. **Fax:** (800)225-5355. **E-mail:** bugle@rmef.org. **Website:** www.elkfoundation.org. **Contact:** P.J. DelHomme, hunting/human interest editor. Estab. 1984. Magazine: 114-172 pages; 55 lb. Escanaba paper; 80 lb. Sterling cover, black-and-white, 4-color illustrations; photos. "Our readers are predominantly hunters, many of them conservationists who care deeply about protecting wildlife habitat."

◐ *Bugle* is the membership publication of the Rocky Mountain Elk Foundation, a nonprofit wildlife conservation group. Bimonthly. Receives 20-30 unsolicited mss/month. Accepts 3-4 mss/issue; 18-24 mss/year. Publishes ms 1-36 months after acceptance. **Publishes 12 new writers/year.**

NEEDS "We accept fiction and nonfiction stories pertaining in some way to elk, other wildlife, hunting, habitat conservation, and related issues. We would like to see more humor." Publishes short shorts. Also publishes literary essays and poetry about elk. Length: 1,500-4,500 words; average length: 2,500 words.

HOW TO CONTACT Query with or without published clips or send complete ms. Prefers submissions

by e-mail. Send SASE for reply or return of ms, or send a disposable copy of ms. Accepts reprints.

TIPS "Hunting stories and essays should celebrate the hunting experience, demonstrating respect for wildlife, the land, and the hunt. Articles on elk behavior or elk habitat should include personal observations and entertain as well as educate. No freelance product reviews or formulaic how-to articles accepted. Straight action-adventure hunting stories are in short supply, as are 'Situation Ethics' mss."

◐ BURNSIDE REVIEW

P.O. Box 1782, Portland, OR 97207. **Website:** www.burnsidereview.org. Estab. 2004. *Burnside Review*, published every 9 months, prints "the best poetry and short fiction we can get our hands on." Each issue includes one featured poet with an interview and new poems. "We tend to publish writing that finds beauty in truly unexpected places; that combines urban and natural imagery; that breaks the heart."

◐ *Burnside Review* is 80 pages, 6" × 6", professionally printed, perfect-bound.

NEEDS "*Burnside Review* accepts submissions of poetry and fiction. If you have something else that you think would be a perfect fit for our journal, please query the editor before submitting."

HOW TO CONTACT Submit 1 short story at a time. Accepts submissions through online submission manager only.

PAYMENT/TERMS Pays $50 plus 1 contributor's copy.

TIPS "We like work that breaks the heart, that leaves us in a place we didn't expect to be. We like the lyric. We like the narrative. We like when the two merge. We like whiskey. We like hourglass figures. We like crying over past mistakes. We like to be surprised. Surprise us. Read a past issue and try to to understand our tastes. At the least, please read the sample poems that we have linked from our prior issues."

●⑤ BUTTON

P.O. Box 77, Westminster, MA 01473. **E-mail:** sally@moonsigns.net. **Website:** www.moonsigns.net. Estab. 1993. "*Button* is New England's tiniest magazine of poetry, fiction, and gracious living, published once a year. As 'gracious living' is on the cover, we like wit, brevity, cleverly conceived essay/recipe, poetry that isn't sentimental, or song lyrics. I started *Button* so that a century from now, when people read it in landfills or, preferably, libraries, they'll say, 'Gee, what a great time to have lived. I wish I lived back then.'"

○ *Button* is 16-24 pages, saddle stapled, with cardstock offset cover with illustrations that incorporate 1 or more buttons. Press run is 500. Subscription: $5 for 3 issues. Receives 20-40 unsolicited mss/month. Accepts 3-6 mss/issue; 3-6mss/year. Has published poetry by Amanda Powell, Brendan Galvin, Jean Monahan, Mary Campbell, KevinMcGrath, and Ed Conti.

NEEDS Seeks quality fiction. No genre fiction, science fiction, techno-thriller. "Wants more of anything Herman Melville, Henry James, or Betty MacDonald would like to read." Length: 300-2,000 words.

HOW TO CONTACT "We don't take e-mail submissions, unless you're living overseas, in which case we respond electronically. But we strongly suggest you request writers' guidelines (send an SASE). Better still, look over our online issue or order a sample copy for $2.50, which includes postage." Send complete ms with bio, list of publications, and explain how you found the magazine. Include SASE.

PAYMENT/TERMS Pays honorarium and subscriptions.

TIPS "*Button* writers have been widely published elsewhere, in virtually all the major national magazines. They include Ralph Lombreglia, Lawrence Millman, They Might Be Giants, Combustible Edison, Sven Birkerts, Stephen McCauley, Amanda Powell, Wayne Wilson, David Barber, Romayne Dawnay, Brendan Galvin, and Diana DerHovanessian. Follow the guidelines, make sure you read your work aloud, and don't inflate or deflate your publications and experience. We've published plenty of new folks on the merits of the work."

○ ☻ ⑤ CADET QUEST MAGAZINE

P.O. Box 7259, Grand Rapids, MI 49510-7259. (616)241-5616. **Fax:** (616)241-5558. **E-mail:** submissions@calvinistcadets.org. **Website:** www.calvinistcadets.org. **Contact:** G. Richard Broene, editor. Estab. 1958. "*Cadet Quest Magazine* shows boys 9-14 how God is at work in their lives and in the world around them."

NEEDS Middle readers, boys/early teens: adventure, arts/craft, games/puzzles, hobbies, how-to, humor, interview/profile, multicultural, problem solving, religious, science, sports. Fast-moving stories that appeal to a boy's sense of adventure or sense of humor are welcome. Avoid preachiness. Avoid simplistic answers to complicated problems. Avoid long dialogue and little action. No fantasy, science fiction, fashion, horror, or erotica. Length: 900-1,500 words.

HOW TO CONTACT Send complete ms. Accepts submissions by mail or by e-mail (must include ms in text of e-mail; will not open attachments).

PAYMENT/TERMS Pays 4-6 cents/word, and 1 contributor's copy.

TIPS "Best time to submit stories/articles is early in the year (January-April). Also remember readers are boys ages 9-14. Stories must reflect or add to the theme of the issue and come from a Christian perspective."

○ ⑦ ⑤ THE CAFE IRREAL

E-mail: editors@cafeirreal.com. **Website:** www.cafeirreal.com. **Contact:** G.S. Evans, Alice Whittenburg, coeditors. Estab. 1998. "Our audience is composed of people who read or write literary fiction with fantastic themes, similar to the work of Franz Kafka, Kobo Abe, or Clarice Lispector. This is a type of fiction (irreal) that has difficulty finding its way into print in the English-speaking world and defies many of the conventions of American literature especially. As a result, ours is a fairly specialized literary publication, and we would strongly recommend that prospective writers look at our current issue and guidelines carefully."

○ Accepts 6-8 mss/issue; 24-32 mss/year. Recently published work by Marcel Béalu, Jeff Friedman, Daniel Chacón, Zdravka Evtimova, and Norman Lock.

NEEDS No horror or 'slice-of-life' stories; no genre or mainstream science fiction or fantasy. Length: 2,000 words (maximum).

HOW TO CONTACT Accepts submissions by e-mail. No attachments; include submission in body of e-mail. Include estimated word count.

PAYMENT/TERMS Pays 1¢/word, $2 minimum.

TIPS "Forget formulas. Write about what you don't know, take me places I couldn't possibly go, don't try to make me care about the characters. Read short fiction by writers such as Franz Kafka, Jorge Luis Borges, Donald Barthelme, Magnus Mills, Ana Maria Shua and Stanislaw Lem. Also read our website and guidelines."

CAKETRAIN

P.O. Box 82588, Pittsburgh, PA 15218. **E-mail:** editors@caketrain.org. **Website:** www.caketrain.org.

Contact: Amanda Raczkowski and Joseph Reed, editors. Estab. 2003. Price: $9.

○ *Caketrain* does not accept previously published pieces. Simultaneous submissions are permitted; please notify immediately if a piece is chosen for publication elsewhere. Response time can take up to 6 months but is often much shorter. Please do not submit additional work until a decision has been made regarding your current submission.

NEEDS "Please submit up to seven poems, works of fiction, or creative nonfiction (no book reviews), works of visual art, or any combination therein."

HOW TO CONTACT Send mss to editors@caketrain.org only; do not send work by mail. Submissions should include a cover letter with titles of pieces and a brief biographical statement.

PAYMENT/TERMS Contributors receive 1 complimentary copy. All rights revert to authors upon publication."

① CALYX

Calyx, Inc., P.O. Box B, Corvallis, OR 97339. (541)753-9384. **Fax:** (541)753-0515. **E-mail:** info@calyxpress.org; editor@calyxpress.org. **Website:** www.calyxpress.org. **Contact:** Rebecca Olson, senior editor. Estab. 1976. *"CALYX Journal* exists to publish fine literature and art by women and is committed to publishing the work of all women, including women of color, older women, working-class women, and other voices that need to be heard. We are committed to discovering and nurturing developing writers."

○ Annual open submission period is October 1-December 31.

NEEDS Length: no more than 5,000 words.

HOW TO CONTACT All submissions should include author's name on each page and be accompanied by a brief (50-word or less) biographical statement, phone number, and e-mail address. Submit using online submissions manager.

PAYMENT/TERMS "A contributor's payment for publication in *CALYX Journal* includes copies of the issue and a 1-volume subscription following that issue."

TIPS "A forum for women's creative work—including work by women of color, lesbian and queer women, young women, old women—*CALYX Journal* breaks new ground. Each issue is packed with new poetry, short stories, full-color artwork, photography, essays, and reviews."

② CANADIAN WRITER'S JOURNAL

Box 1178, New Liskeard ON P0J 1P0 Canada. (705)647-5424. **Fax:** (705)647-8366. **E-mail:** editor@cwj.ca. **Website:** www.cwj.ca. **Contact:** Deborah Ranchuk, editor. Estab. 1984. "Digest-size magazine for writers emphasizing short how-to articles, which convey easily understood information useful to both apprentice and professional writers. General policy and postal subsidies require that the magazine must carry a substantial Canadian content. We try for about 90% Canadian content, but prefer good material over country of origin, or how well you're known. Writers may query, but unsolicited mss are welcome."

NEEDS Fiction is published only through semi-annual short fiction contest with April 30 deadline. Send SASE for rules, or see guidelines on website. Does not want gratuitous violence or sex subject matters.

HOW TO CONTACT Accepts submissions by e-mail. Responds in 2 months to queries.

PAYMENT/TERMS Pays on publication for one-time rights.

TIPS "We prefer short, tightly written, informative how-to articles. US writers: note that US postage cannot be used to mail from Canada. Obtain Canadian stamps, use IRCs, or send small amounts in cash."

②①③ THE CAPILANO REVIEW

2055 Purcell Way, North Vancouver, BC V7J 3H5 Canada. (604)984-1712. **E-mail:** tcr@capilanou.ca. **Website:** www.thecapilanoreview.ca. **Contact:** Tamara Lee, managing editor. Estab. 1972. Tri-annual visual and literary arts magazine that "publishes only what the editors consider to be the very best fiction, poetry, drama, or visual art being produced. *TCR* editors are interested in fresh, original work that stimulates and challenges readers. Over the years, the magazine has developed a reputation for pushing beyond the boundaries of traditional art and writing. We are interested in work that is new in concept and in execution."

NEEDS No traditional, conventional fiction. Wants to see more innovative, genre-blurring work. Length: up to 6,000 words

HOW TO CONTACT Send complete ms with SASE and Canadian postage or IRCs. Does not accept submissions through e-mail or on disks.

PAYMENT/TERMS Pays $50-300.

⬤⬤⑤ ORSON SCOTT CARD'S INTERGALACTIC MEDICINE SHOW

Hatrack River Publications, P.O. Box 18184, Greensboro, NC 27419. **Website:** InterGalacticMedicine Show.com; oscIGMS.com. **Contact:** Edmund R. Schubert, editor. Estab. 2005. *"Orson Scott Card's InterGalactic Medicine Show* is an online fantasy and science fiction magazine. We are a bimonthly publication featuring content from both established, as well as talented new authors. In addition to our bimonthly issues, we offer weekly columns and reviews on books, movies, and video games, and writing advice."

NEEDS "We like to see well-developed milieus and believable, engaging characters. We also look for clear, unaffected writing." Length: up to 7,000 words.

HOW TO CONTACT Submit electronically using online submission form. Submit only 1 story at a time. Include estimated word count, e-mail address.

PAYMENT/TERMS Pays 6 cents a word up to 7,500 words and 5 cents a word thereafter.

TIPS "Please note: IGMS is a PG-13 magazine and website. That means that while stories can deal with intense and adult themes, we will not accept stories with explicit or detailed sex of the sort that would earn a movie rating more restrictive than PG-13; nor will there be language of the sort that earns an R rating."

⬤ CC&D: CHILDREN, CHURCHES & DADDIES: THE UNRELIGIOUS, NON-FAMILY-ORIENTED LITERARY AND ART MAGAZINE

Scars Publications and Design, 829 Brian Court, Gurnee, IL 60031. (847)281-9070. **E-mail:** ccandd96@ scars.tv. **Website:** http://scars.tv/ccd. **Contact:** Janet Kuypers. Estab. 1993. "Our biases are works that relate to issues such as politics, sexism, society, and the like, but are definitely not limited to such. We publish good work that makes you think, that makes you feel like you've lived through a scene instead of merely reading it. If it relates to how the world fits into a person's life (political story, a day in the life, coping with issues people face), it will probably win us over faster. We have received comments from readers and other editors saying that they thought some of our stories really happened. They didn't, but it was nice to know they were so concrete, so believable that people thought they were nonfiction. Do that to our readers." Publishes short shorts, essays, and stories. Also pub-

lishes poetry. Always comments on/critiques rejected mss, if asked.

🖵 Monthly literary magazine/journal: 5½" × 8½" perfect-bound, 84-page book. Contains illustrations and photographs as well as short stories, essays, and poetry. Has published Mel Waldman, Kenneth DiMaggio, Linda Webb Aceto, Brian Looney, Joseph Hart, Fritz Hamilton, G.A. Scheinoha, Ken Dean.

NEEDS Interested in many topics including adventure, ethnic/multicultural, experimental, feminist, gay, historical, lesbian, literary, mystery/suspense, new age, psychic/supernatural/occult, science fiction. Does not want religious or rhyming or family-oriented material. Average length: 1,000 words. "Contact us if you are interested in submitting very long stories or parts of a novel (if accepted, such a submission would appear in parts in multiple issues)."

HOW TO CONTACT Send complete ms with cover letter or query with clips of published work. Prefers submissions by e-mail. "If you have e-mail and send us a snail-mail submission, we will accept writing only if you e-mail it to us. 99.5% of all submissions are via e-mail only, so if you do not have electronic access, there is a strong chance you will not be considered. We recommend you e-mail submissions to us, either as an attachment (.txt, .rtf, or .doc—NOT .docx, and not .pdf) or by placing it directly in the e-mail letter). Send either SASE (or IRC) for return of ms or disposable copy of ms and #10 SASE for reply only, but if you have e-mail please send us an electronic submission instead. (If we accept your writing, we'll ask you to e-mail it to us anyway.)." Considers simultaneous submissions, previously published submissions, multiple submissions. Reviews fiction, essays, journals, editorials, short fiction.

⬤ CEMETERY MOON

Fortress Publishing, Inc., 3704 Hartzdale Dr., Camp Hill, PA 17011. **E-mail:** cemeterymoon@yahoo.com. **Website:** www.fortresspublishinginc.com. *Cemetery Moon* is a magazine filled with short stories and poetry devoted to horror, suspense, and gothic. This magazine brings to light what lurks in the darkness.

HOW TO CONTACT Send complete ms with cover letter by e-mail only.

TIPS "We want compelling stories—if we stop reading your story, so will the reader. We don't care about trick or twist endings; we're more concerned about how you take us there. Don't try to reinvent the wheel. Listen to advice with an open mind. Read your story, reread it, then read it again before you send it anywhere."

🌐🔵🎧 CHA

Hong Kong **E-mail:** editors@asiancha.com; j@asiancha.com. **E-mail:** submissions@asiancha.com. **Website:** www.asiancha.com. **Contact:** Tammy Ho Lai-Ming, founding co-editor; Jeff Zroback, founding co-editor; Eddie Tay, reviews editor. Estab. 2007. *Cha* is the first Hong Kong-based English online literary journal; it is dedicated to publishing quality poetry, fiction, creative nonfiction, reviews, photography, and art. *Cha* has a strong focus on Asian-themed creative work and work done by Asian writers and artists. It also publishes established and emerging writers/artists from around the world. *Cha* is an affiliated organization of the Asia-Pacific Writing Partnership and it is catalogued in the School of Oriental and African Studies (SOAS) Library, among other universities. *Cha* was named Best New Online Magazine of 2008. "At this time, we can only accept work in English or translated into English. If you want to review a book for *Cha*, please write for further information."

NEEDS Length: 100-5,000 words.

HOW TO CONTACT Submit via e-mail.

TIPS "Please read the guidelines on our website carefully before you submit work to us. Do not send attachments in your e-mail. Include all writing in the body of e-mail. Include a brief biography (100 words)."

🔵 CHAFFIN JOURNAL

English Department, Eastern Kentucky University, C, Richmond, KY 40475-3102. (859)622-3080. **E-mail:** robert.witt@eku.edu. **Website:** www.english.eku.edu/chaffin_journal. **Contact:** Robert Witt, editor. Estab. 1998. *The Chaffin Journal*, published annually in December, prints quality short fiction and poetry by new and established writers/poets. "We publish fiction on any subject; our only consideration is the quality."

○ Receives 20 unsolicited mss/month. Accepts 6-8 mss/year. Does not read mss October 1-May 31. Publishes 2-3 new writers/year. Has published work by Meridith Sue Willis, Marie Manilla, Raymond Abbott, Marjorie Bixler, Chris Helvey.

NEEDS No erotica, fantasy. Length: 10,000 words per submission period; average length: 5,000 words.

PAYMENT/TERMS Pays 1 contributor's copy.

TIPS "All mss submitted are considered."

🌐🔵 CHAPMAN

Chapman Publishing, 4 Broughton Place, Edinburgh EH1 3RX Scotland. (44)(131)557-2207. **E-mail:** chapman-pub@blueyounder.co.uk. **Website:** www.chapman-pub.co.uk. **Contact:** Joy Hendry, editor. Estab. 1970. Magazine published 3 times/year. "*Chapman*, Scotland's quality literary magazine, is a dynamic force in Scotland, publishing poetry, fiction, criticism, reviews, and articles on theater, politics, language, and the arts. Our philosophy is to publish new work, from known and unknown writers—mainly Scottish, but also worldwide."

○ Does not accept e-mail submissions.

NEEDS "Any length, any topic considered—the criterion is quality. Please do not send more than one item at a time. We are looking for fiction that is challenging, surprising, different ... in some way." No horror or science fiction. Length: 1,000-5,000 words.

PAYMENT/TERMS Negotiates payment individually.

TIPS "Submissions should be presented as double-spaced typescript, with indented paragraphs. Use double quotes for dialogue and quotations, indicate italics with underscore. Avoid using footnotes—we are not an academic journal."

"Keep your stories for six months and edit carefully. We seek challenging work which attempts to explore difficult/new territory in content and form, but lighter work, if original enough, is welcome. We have no plans at present to publish longer fiction or novels. We do not publish plays that have not been performed. If you would like to get a better impression of *Chapman*, individual copies of the magazine are available. Sample issue costs £3.45."

🔵 THE CHARITON REVIEW

Truman State University Press, 100 E Normal Ave., Kirksville, MO 63501. (800)916-6802. **E-mail:** chariton@truman.edu. **Website:** http://tsup.truman.edu/aboutChariton.asp. **Contact:** Barbara Smith-Mandell, managing editor. Estab. 1975. "Truman State University Press (TSUP) publishes peer-reviewed research in the humanities for the scholarly community and the broader public, and publishes creative literary works. TSUP is a resource to the Truman campus community, where students explore their publishing interests and scholars seek publishing advice." TSUP is now publishing *The Chariton Review*, an international literary journal.

James D'Agostino became editor in July 2010. He teaches at Truman State University and is the author of *Nude with Anything*. See also The Chariton Review Short Fiction Prize at http://tsup.truman.edu/prizes.asp.

HOW TO CONTACT Send a printout of the submission via snail mail; overseas authors may send submissions as e-mail attachments.

CHICAGO REVIEW

Taft House, 935 E. 60th St., Chicago, IL 60637. **E-mail:** chicago-review@uchcago.edu. **Website:** http://humanities.uchicago.edu/orgs/review. **Contact:** Chalcey Wilding, managing editor. Estab. 1946.

NEEDS "We will consider work in any literary style but are typically less interested in traditional narrative approaches." Length: no more than 5,000 words.

HOW TO CONTACT Submit one short story or up to 5 short short stories submitted in one file. Submit via online submissions manager or postal mail. Prefers electronic submissions.

PAYMENT/TERMS Pays in contributor's copies.

TIPS "We strongly recommend that authors familiarize themselves with recent issues of *Chicago Review* before submitting. Submissions that demonstrate familiarity with the journal tend to receive more attention than those that appear to be part of a carpet-bombing campaign."

CHIZINE: TREATMENT OF LIGHT AND SHADE IN WORDS

Canada. Estab. 1997. "Subtle, sophisticated dark fiction with a literary bent." Quarterly.

Received Bram Stoker Award for Other Media in 2000.

NEEDS Does not want "tropes of vampires, werewolves, mummies, monsters, or anything that's been done to death."

HOW TO CONTACT Send complete ms with cover letter.

CICADA MAGAZINE

Cricket Magazine Group, 70 E. Lake St., Suite 300, Chicago, IL 60601. (312)701-1720. **Fax:** (312)701-1728. **E-mail:** cicada@cicadamag.com. **Website:** www.cicadamag.com. **Contact:** Marianne Carus, editor-in-chief; Deborah Vetter, executive editor; John Sandford, art director. Estab. 1998. Bimonthly literary magazine for ages 14 and up. Publishes original short stories, poems, and first-person essays written for teens and young adults. *Cicada* publishes fiction and poetry with a genuine teen sensibility, aimed at the high school and college-age market. The editors are looking for stories and poems that are thought-provoking but entertaining.

Buys up to 42 mss/year.

NEEDS Young adults: adventure, contemporary, fantasy, historical, humor/satire, mainstream, multicultural, nature/environment, novel excerpts, novellas (1/issue), realistic, romance, science fiction, sports, suspense/mystery. The main protagonist should be at least 14 and preferably older. Stories should have a genuine teen sensibility and be aimed at readers in high school or college. Length: 5,000 words maximum (up to 9,000 words/novellas).

PAYMENT/TERMS Pays up to 25¢/word.

TIPS "Quality writing, good literary style, genuine teen sensibility, depth, humor, good character development, avoidance of stereotypes. Read several issues to familiarize yourself with our style."

CIMARRON REVIEW

205 Morrill Hall, English Department, Oklahoma State University, Stillwater, OK 74078. **E-mail:** cimarronreview@okstate.edu. **Website:** http://cimarronreview.com. **Contact:** Toni Graham, editor. Estab. 1967. "We want strong literary writing. We are partial to fiction in the modern realist tradition and distinctive poetry—lyrical, narrative, etc."

Magazine: 6" × 9"; 110 pages. Accepts 3-5 mss/issue; 12-15 mss/year. Publishes 2-4 new writers/year. Eager to receive mss from both established and less experienced writers "who intrigue us with their unusual perspective, language, imagery, and character." Has published work by Molly Giles, Gary Fincke, David Galef, Nona Caspers, Robin Beeman, Edward J. Delaney, William Stafford, John Ashbery, Grace Schulman, Barbara Hamby, Patricia Fargnoli, Phillip Dacey, Holly Prado, and Kim Addonizio.

NEEDS No juvenile or genre fiction. Length: 25 pages maximum.

HOW TO CONTACT Send complete ms with SASE; include cover letter. Accepts simultaneous submissions.

PAYMENT/TERMS Pays 2 contributor's copies.

TIPS "All work must come with SASE. A cover letter is encouraged. No e-mail submissions from authors living in North America. Query first and follow guidelines. In order to get a feel for the kind of work we publish, please read an issue or two before submitting."

●❸ THE CINCINNATI REVIEW

P.O. Box 210069, Cincinnati, OH 45221-0069. (513)556-3954. **E-mail:** editors@cincinnatireview.com. **Website:** www.cincinnatireview.com. **Contact:** Nicola Mason. Estab. 2003. A journal devoted to publishing the best new literary fiction, creative nonfiction, and poetry, as well as book reviews, essays, and interviews.

    Reads submissions August 15-April 5; mss arriving outside that period will not be read. *The Cincinnati Review* is 180-200 pages, digest size, perfect-bound, with matte paperback cover with full-color art; includes ads. Press run is 1,000. Single copy: $9 (current issue); subscription: $15.

NEEDS Does not want genre fiction. Length: 125-10,000 words.

HOW TO CONTACT Send complete mss with SASE. Does not consider e-mail submissions; does accept electronic submissions through submission manager at cincinnatireview.com/submissions. Accepts simultaneous submissions with notice.

PAYMENT/TERMS Pays $25/page and 2 contributor's copies.

TIPS "Each issue includes a translation feature. For more information on translations, please see our website."

○ THE CLAREMONT REVIEW

4980 Wesley Rd., Victoria V8Y 1Y9 B.C. (250)658-5221. **Fax:** (250)658-5387. **E-mail:** lmoran@telus.net. **Website:** www.theclaremontreview.ca. **Contact:** Linda Moran, managing editor. "We publish anything from traditional to post modern, but with a preference for works that reveal something of the human condition. By this we mean stories that explore real characters in modern settings. Who are we, what are we doing to the planet, what is our relationship to one another, the earth, or God. Also, reading samples on this website or from past issues will give you a clearer indication of what we are looking for."

NEEDS Does not want science fiction, fantasy, romance. Length: 5,000 maximum.

HOW TO CONTACT Send complete ms; should be double-spaced. Include SASE.

TIPS "Read guidelines before submitting."

● CLARK STREET REVIEW

P.O. Box 1377, Berthoud, CO 80513. **E-mail:** clarkreview@earthlink.net. **Contact:** Ray Foreman, editor. Estab. 1998. *Clark Street Review,* published 6 times/year, uses narrative poetry and short shorts. Tries "to give writers and poets cause to keep writing by publishing their best work."

    "Editor reads everything with a critical eye of 30 years of experience in writing and publishing small press work." *Clark Street Review* is 20 pages, digest size, photocopied, saddle stapled, with paper cover. Receives about 1,000 poems/year, accepts about 10%. Press run is 200. Single copy: $2; subscription: $10 for 10 issues postpaid for writers only. Make checks payable to R. Foreman. Has published poetry by Charles Ries, Anselm Brocki, Ed Galling, Ellaraine Lockie, and J. Glenn Evans.

NEEDS "Narrative poetry under 100 lines that reaches readers who are mostly published poets and writers. Subjects are open." Does not want "obscure or formalist work."

○ COAL CITY REVIEW

Coal City Press, University of Kansas, English Department, Lawrence, KS 66045. **E-mail:** coalcity@sunflower.com. **E-mail:** briandal@ku.edu. **Website:** www.coalcityreview.com. **Contact:** Brian Daldorph, founder and editor.

    Only accepts submissions by postal mail.

NEEDS "Flash/short shorts are happily considered. Usually, we don't publish novel excerpts, but if you've got a whiz-bang tight (and short) bit, you might give us a try." Length: no more than 4,000 words.

HOW TO CONTACT Submit one story at a time via postal mail. Does not accept e-mail submissions.

PAYMENT/TERMS Pays in contributor's copies.

TIPS "We are looking for artful stories—with great language and great heart. Please do not send work that has not been thoughtfully and carefully revised or edited."

COBBLESTONE

Carus Publishing, 30 Grove St., Suite C, Peterborough, NH 03458. (800)821-0115. **Fax:** (603)924-7380. **E-mail:** customerservice@caruspub.com. **Website:** www.cobblestonepub.com. "*Cobblestone* stands apart from other children's magazines by offering a solid look at one subject and stressing strong editorial content, color photographs throughout, and original illustrations. Each issue presents a particular theme, making it exciting as well as informative. All material must relate to monthly theme."

○ Prefers to work with published/established writers. *Cobblestone* themes and deadline are available on website or with SASE.

NEEDS "We are interested in articles of historical accuracy and lively, original approaches to the subject at hand. Writers are encouraged to study recent *Cobblestone* back issues for content and style. All material must relate to the theme of a specific upcoming issue in order to be considered." Length: 800 words maximum.

HOW TO CONTACT "To be considered, a query must accompany each individual idea (however, you can mail them all together) and must include the following: a brief cover letter stating the subject and word length of the proposed article, a detailed one-page outline explaining the information to be presented in the article, an extensive bibliography of materials the author intends to use in preparing the article, a SASE. Authors are urged to use primary resources and up-to-date scholarly resources in their bibliography. Writers new to *Cobblestone* should send a writing sample with the query. If you would like to know if your query has been received, please also include a stamped postcard that requests acknowledgment of receipt. In all correspondence, please include your complete address as well as a telephone number where you can be reached. A writer may send as many queries for one issue as he or she wishes, but each query must have a separate cover letter, outline, bibliography, and SASE. All queries must be typed. Please do not send unsolicited manuscripts—queries only!"

PAYMENT/TERMS Pays 20-25¢/word.

TIPS "Review theme lists and past issues to see what we're looking for."

◐ COLD MOUNTAIN REVIEW

Department of English, Appalachian State University, ASU Box 32052, Boone, NC 28608. **E-mail:** coldmountain@appstate.edu. **Website:** www.cold mountain.appstate.edu. **Contact:** Betty Miller Conway, managing editor. *Cold Mountain Review*, published twice/year (Spring and Fall), features poetry, interviews with poets, poetry book reviews, and black-and-white graphic art.

○ Has published poetry by Sarah Kennedy, Robert Morgan, Susan Ludvigson, Aleida Rodri

guez, R.T. Smith, and Virgil Suaárez. *Cold Mountain Review* is about 72 pages, digest size, neatly printed with one poem/page (or 2-page spread), perfect-bound, with light card-stock cover. Publishes only 10-12 poems/issue; "hence, we are extremely competitive: send only your best."

NEEDS Considers novel excerpts if the submission is "an exemplary stand-alone piece." Length: no more than 6,000 words.

COLORADO REVIEW

Center for Literary Publishing, Colorado State University, 9105 Campus Delivery, Fort Collins, CO 80523. (970)491-5449. **E-mail:** creview@colostate.edu. **Website:** http://coloradoreview.colostate.edu. **Contact:** Stephanie G'Schwind, editor-in-chief and nonfiction editor. Literary magazine published 3 times/year.

○ Work published in *Colorado Review* has been included in *Best American Poetry, Best New American Voices, Best Travel Writing, Best Food Writing,* and the *Pushcart Prize* anthology.

NEEDS No genre fiction. Length: under 30 ms pages.

HOW TO CONTACT Send complete ms. Fiction mss are read August 1-April 30. Mss received May 1-July 31 will be returned unread. Send no more than 1 story at a time.

PAYMENT/TERMS Pays $25 or $5/page, whichever is greater.

◑ COLUMBIA: A JOURNAL OF LITERATURE AND ART

Columbia University, New York, NY 10027. **Website:** http://columbiajournal.org. **Contact:** Binnie Kirshenbaum and William Wadsworth, faculty board. Estab. 1977. "*Columbia: A Journal of Literature and Art* is an annual publication that features the very best in poetry, fiction, nonfiction, and art. We were founded in 1977 and continue to be one of the few national literary journals entirely edited, designed, and produced by students. You'll find that our minds are open, our interests diverse. We solicit manuscripts from writers we love and select the most exciting finds from our virtual submission box. Above all, our commitment is to our readers—to producing a collection that informs, surprises, challenges, and inspires."

HOW TO CONTACT Submit using online submissions manager.

COMMON GROUND REVIEW

Western New England College, H-5132, Western New England College, 1215 Wilbraham Rd., Springfield, MA 01119. **E-mail:** editors@cgreview.org. **Website:** http://cgreview.org. **Contact:** Janet Bowdan, editor. Estab. 1999.

Common Ground Review, published semiannually (Spring/Summer, Fall/Winter), prints poetry and 1 short nonfiction piece in the Fall issue, 1 short fiction piece in Spring issue. Has published poetry by James Doyle, B.Z. Nidith, Ann Lauinger, Kathryn Howd Machan, and Sheryl L. Nelms.

NEEDS "We want poems with strong imagery, a love of language, a fresh message that evoke a sense of wonder. This is the official literary journal of Western New England College."

TIPS "For poems, use a few good images to convey ideas. Poems should be condensed and concise, free from words that do not contribute. The subject matter should be worthy of the reader's time and appeal to a wide range of readers. Sometimes the editors may suggest revisions."

THE COMSTOCK REVIEW

4956 St. John Dr., Syracuse, NY 13215. **E-mail:** poetry@comstockreview.org. **Website:** www.comstockreview.org. **Contact:** Georgia A. Popoff, managing editor. Estab. 1987.

CONFRONTATION

English Department, LIU Post, Brookville, NY 11548. (516)299-2720. **E-mail:** confrontationmag@gmail.com. **Website:** www.confrontationmagazine.org. **Contact:** Jonna Semeiks, editor-in-chief. Estab. 1968. "*Confrontation* has been in continuous publication since 1968. Our taste and our magazine is eclectic, but we always look for excellence in style, an important theme, a memorable voice. We enjoy discovering and fostering new talent. Each issue contains work by both well-established and new writers. In addition, *Confrontation* often features a thematic special section that 'confronts' a topic. The ensuing confrontation is an attempt to see the many sides of an issue or theme, rather than to present a formed conclusion."

Confrontation has garnered a long list of awards and honors, including the Editor's Award for Distinguished Achievement from CLMP (given to Martin Tucker, the founding editor of the magazine) and NEA grants. Work from the magazine has appeared in numerous anthologies, including the *Pushcart Prize, Best Short Stories*, and *The O. Henry Prize Stories*.

NEEDS "We publish theme issues. Upcoming themes are announced on our website and Facebook page and in our magazine." No "proselytizing" literature or conventional genre fiction. Length: Up to 7,200 words.

HOW TO CONTACT Send complete ms. "We prefer single submissions. Clear copy. No e-mail submissions unless writer resides outside the U.S. Mail submissions with a SASE. We read August 16-May 15. Do not send mss or e-mail submissions between May 16 and August 15.

PAYMENT/TERMS Pays $50-125; more for commissioned work.

TIPS "We look for literary merit. Keep honing your skills and keep trying."

CONNECTICUT REVIEW

Southern Connecticut State University, English Department, 501 Crescent St., New Haven, CT 06515. **E-mail:** ctreview@southernct.edu. **Website:** www.ctstateu.edu/ctreview/index.html. **Contact:** Vivian Shipley, editor (Southern); Jian-Zhong Lin, editor (Eastern); Lisa Siedlarz, managing editor. Estab. 1967. "*Connecticut Review* is a high-quality literary magazine. We take both traditional literary pieces and those on the cutting edge of their genres. We are looking for poetry, fiction, short shorts, creative essays, and scholarly articles accessible to a general audience. Each issue features an 8-page color fine art section with statements from the painters or photographers featured."

Poetry published in *Connecticut Review* has been included in *The Best American Poetry* and *the Pushcart Prize* anthologies; has received special recognition for Literary Excellence from Public Radio's series *The Poet and the Poem*; and has won the Phoenix Award for Significant Editorial Achievement from the Council of Editors of Learned Journals (CELJ). Has published work by John Searles, Michael Schiavone, Norman German, Tom Williams, Paul Ruffin, Dick Allen.

NEEDS "We're looking for the best in literary writing in a variety of genres. Some issues contain sections devoted to announced themes. The editors invite the submission of academic articles of general interest, creative essays, translations, short stories, short shorts, plays, poems and interviews. No 'entertainment' fiction, though we don't mind if you entertain us while you plumb for the truth." Length: 50-4,000 words.

HOW TO CONTACT Send complete ms, include SASE.

TIPS "We read manuscripts blind—stripping off the cover letter—but the biographical information should be there. Be patient. Our editors are spread over 4 campuses and it takes a while to move the manuscripts around."

●⑤ CONTRARY

3133 S. Emerald Ave., Chicago, IL 60616-3299. **E-mail:** chicago@contrarymagazine.com (no submissions). **Website:** www.contrarymagazine.com. **Contact:** Jeff McMahon, editor. Estab. 2003. "*Contrary* publishes fiction, poetry, literary commentary, and prefers work that combines the virtues of all those categories. Founded at the University of Chicago, it now operates independently and not-for-profit on the South Side of Chicago. We like work that is not only contrary in content, but contrary in its evasion of the expectations established by its genre. Our fiction defies traditional story form. For example, a story may bring us to closure without ever delivering an ending. We don't insist on the ending, but we do insist on the closure. And we value fiction as poetic as any poem."

○ Online literary magazine/journal. Contains illustrations. Receives 650 mss/month. Accepts 6 mss/issue; 24 mss/year. Publishes 1 new writer/year. Has published Sherman Alexie, Andrew Coburn, Amy Reed, Clare Kirwan, Stephanie Johnson, Laurence Davies, and Edward Mc-Whinney. Quarterly. Member CLMP.

NEEDS Length: 2,000 words (maximum); average length: 750 words. Publishes short shorts. Average length of short shorts: 750 words.

HOW TO CONTACT Accepts submissions through website only: www.contrarymagazine.com/Contrary/Submissions.html. Include estimated word count, brief bio, list of publications. Considers simultaneous submissions.

PAYMENT/TERMS Pays $20-60.

TIPS "Beautiful writing catches our eye first. If we realize we're in the presence of unanticipated meaning, that's what clinches the deal. Also, we're not fond of expository fiction. We prefer to be seduced by beauty, profundity, and mystery than to be presented with the obvious. We look for fiction that entrances, that stays

the reader's finger above the mouse button. That is, in part, why we favor microfiction, flash fiction, and short shorts. Also, we hope writers will remember that most editors are looking for very particular species of work. We try to describe our particular species in our mission statement and our submission guidelines, but those descriptions don't always convey nuance. That's why many editors urge writers to read the publication itself; in the hope that they will intuit an understanding of its particularities. If you happen to write the particular species of work we favor, your submission may find a happy home with us. If you don't, it does not necessarily reflect on your quality or your ability. It usually just means that your work has a happier home somewhere else."

① CONVERGENCE: AN ONLINE JOURNAL OF POETRY AND ART

An Online Journal of Poetry and Art, **E-mail:** clinville@csus.edu. **E-mail:** clinville@csus.edu. **Website:** www.convergence-journal.com. **Contact:** Cynthia Linville, managing editor. Estab. 2003. *Convergence* seeks to unify the literary and visual arts and draw new interpretations of the written word by pairing poems and flash fiction with complementary art. Quarterly. Estab. 2003. Circ. 200. "We look for well-crafted work with fresh images and a strong voice. Work from a series or with a common theme has a greater chance of being accepted."

○ Deadlines are January 5 and June 5. Recently published work by Oliver Rice, Simon Perchik, Mary Ocher.

NEEDS Accepts 5 mss/issue. Publishes ms 1-6 months after acceptance. Publishes short shorts. Also publishes poetry. Seasonally-themed work is appreciated (spring and summer for the January deadline, fall and winter for the June deadline).

HOW TO CONTACT Send complete ms. E-mail submissions only with "Convergence" in subject line. No simultaneous submissions. Responds in less than a week to queries; 6 months to mss. Writer's guidelines online. Submit no more than 5 fiction pieces, no longer than 1,000 words each. Please include a 75-word bio with your work (bios may be edited for length and clarity). A cover letter is not needed. Absolutely no simultaneous or previously published submissions."

PAYMENT/TERMS Acquires first rights.

TIPS "We look for freshness and originality and a mastery of the craft of flash fiction. Working with a common theme has a greater chance of being accepted."

● THE COPPERFIELD REVIEW

E-mail: copperfieldreview@aol.com. **Website:** www .copperfieldreview.com. **Contact:** Meredith Allard, executive editor. Estab. 2000. "We are a quarterly online literary journal that publishes historical fiction, reviews, and interviews related to historical fiction. We believe that by understanding the lessons of the past through historical fiction, we can gain better insight into the nature of our society today, as well as a better understanding of ourselves."

○ Receives 30 unsolicited mss/month. Accepts 7-10 mss/issue; 28-40 mss/year. Publishes 30-40% new writers/year.

NEEDS Essays, literary, literary criticism. "We will consider submissions in most fiction categories, but the setting must be historical in nature. We don't want to see anything not related to historical fiction." Publishes short shorts. Length: 500-3,000 words.

HOW TO CONTACT Send complete ms. Name and e-mail address should appear on the first page of the submission. Accepts submissions by e-mail or online submission. "Queries are not required. Send the complete ms according to our guidelines. Please submit online using our e-submissions manager or our Submission Guidelines page."

TIPS "We wish to showcase the very best in literary historical fiction. Stories that use historical periods and details to illuminate universal truths will immediately stand out. We are thrilled to receive thoughtful work that is polished, poised, and written from the heart. Be professional, and submit only your very best work. Be certain to adhere to a publication's submission guidelines, and always treat your e-mail submissions with the same care you would use with a traditional publisher. Above all, be strong and true to your calling as a writer. It is a difficult, frustrating but wonderful journey. It is important for writers to review our online submission guidelines prior to submitting."

●⊙ COSMOS MAGAZINE

Luna Media Pty Ltd., P.O. Box 302, Strawberry Hills NSW 2012, Sydney, Australia. (61)(2)9310-8500. **Fax:** (61)(2)9698-4899. **E-mail:** editorial@cosmosmaga zine.com. **E-mail:** fiction@cosmosmagazine.com. **Website:** www.cosmosmagazine.com. Estab. 2005. "An Australian brand with a global outlook, *COSMOS* is internationally respected for its literary writ-

ing, excellence in design and engaging breadth of content. *COSMOS* is the brainchild of Wilson da Silva, a former ABC TV science reporter and past president of the World Federation of Science Journalists. It is backed by an editorial advisory board that includes Apollo 11 astronaut Buzz Aldrin and ABC Radio's Robyn Williams. It is chaired by Dr. Alan Finkel, the neuroscientist and philanthropist who is the Chancellor of Monash University in Melbourne."

○ Won the 2009 Magazine of the Year and twice Editor of the Year at the annual Bell Awards for Publishing Excellence; the American Institute of Physics Science Writing Award; the Reuters/ IUCN Award for Excellence in Environmental Journalism; the City of Sydney Lord Mayor's Sustainability Award and an Earth Journalism Award.

NEEDS "*COSMOS* invites submissions of original fiction between 2,000 and 4,000 words in length. We seek well-written pieces, stylistically and imaginatively executed, and highly polished. A story should be based on scientific premises, principles, or possibilities. Characterization is valued, as is a story arc. We are, in short, looking for good science fiction. What we're not looking for: fantasy, literary allegory, magical realism, or lectures about science or politics lightly disguised as narrative. We do have some restrictions, since *COSMOS* has a wide readership, so please avoid profanity, explicit sex, or gratuitous violence." Length: 2,000-4,000 words.

PAYMENT/TERMS Pays flat $300 per story.

● COTTONWOOD

Room 400 Kansas Union, 1301 Jayhawk Blvd., University of Kansas, Lawrence, KS 66045. **E-mail:** tlorenz@ ku.edu. **Website:** www2.ku.edu/~englishmfa/cot tonwood. **Contact:** Tom Lorenz, fiction editor. Estab. 1965. "Established in the 1960s, *Cottonwood* is the nationally circulated literary review of the University of Kansas. We publish high-quality literary work in poetry, fiction, and creative nonfiction. Over the years authors such as William Stafford, Rita Dove, Connie May Fowler, Virgil Suarez, and Cris Mazza have appeared in the pages of *Cottonwood*, and recent issues have featured the work of Kim Chinquee, Quinn Dalton, Carol Lee Lorenzo, Jesse Kercheval, Joanne Lowery, and Oliver Rice. We welcome submissions from new and established writers. New issues appear once yearly, in the fall."

NEEDS Length: no more than 8,500 words.

HOW TO CONTACT Submit with SASE.

PAYMENT/TERMS Pays in contributor's copies.

TIPS "We're looking for depth and/or originality of subject matter, engaging voice and style, emotional honesty, command of the material and the structure. *Cottonwood* publishes high-quality literary fiction, and we are very open to the work of talented new writers. Write something honest that you care about and write it as well as you can. Don't hesitate to keep trying us. We sometimes take a piece from a writer we've rejected a number of times. We generally don't like clever, gimmicky writing. The style should be engaging but not claim all the the attention itself."

● THE COUNTRY DOG REVIEW

P.O. Box 1476, Oxford MS 38655. **E-mail:** country dogreview@gmail.com. **Website:** www.countrydog review.org. **Contact:** Danielle Sellers, editor. *The Country Dog Review*, published semiannually online, publishes "poetry, book reviews, and interviews with poets."

◗ Receives about 400 poems/year, accepts about 10%.

NEEDS "Poetry of the highest quality, not limited to style or region. Also accepts book reviews and interviews. Does not want translations, fiction, nonfiction.

HOW TO CONTACT "Query first."

CRAB ORCHARD REVIEW

Department of English, Southern Illinois University at Carbondale, Faner Hall 2380, Mail Code 4503, 1000 Faner Dr., Carbondale, IL 62901. (618)453-6833. **Fax:** (618)453-8224. **Website:** www.craborchardre view.siuc.edu. Estab. 1995. "We are a general interest literary journal published twice/year. We strive to be a journal that writers admire and readers enjoy. We publish fiction, poetry, creative nonfiction, fiction translations, interviews and reviews."

NEEDS No science fiction, romance, western, horror, gothic, or children's. Wants more novel excerpts that also stand alone. Length: 1,000-6,500 words.

HOW TO CONTACT Send SASE for reply, return of ms.

PAYMENT/TERMS Pays $100 minimum; $20/page maximum, 2 contributor's copies and a year subscription.

TIPS "We publish 2 issues per volume—1 has a theme (we read from May to November for the theme issue); the other doesn't (we read from January through April for the nonthematic issue). Consult our website for information about our upcoming themes."

CRAZYHORSE

College of Charleston, Department of English, 66 George St., Charleston, SC 29424. (843)953-4470. **E-mail:** crazyhorse@cofc.edu. **Website:** http://crazy horse.cofc.edu. Estab. 2,000. "We like to print a mix of writing regardless of its form, genre, school, or politics. We're especially on the lookout for original writing that doesn't fit the categories and that engages in the work of honest communication."

NEEDS Accepts all fiction of fine quality, including short shorts and literary essays.

PAYMENT/TERMS Pays 2 contributor's copies and $20 per page.

TIPS "Write to explore subjects you care about. The subject should be one in which something is at stake. Before sending, ask, 'What's reckoned with that's important for other people to read?'"

○ CREATIVE WITH WORDS PUBLICATIONS

P.O. Box 223226, Carmel, CA 93922. **Fax:** (831)655-8627. **E-mail:** geltrich@mbay.net. **Website:** creative withwords.tripod.com. **Contact:** Brigitta Gisella Geltrich-Ludgate, publisher and editor. Estab. 1975.

NEEDS No violence or erotica, overly religious fiction, or sensationalism.

HOW TO CONTACT Always include SASE with postal submissions.

TIPS "We offer a great variety of themes. We look for clean family-type fiction/poetry. Also, we ask the writer to look at the world from a different perspective, to research the topic thoroughly, be creative, apply brevity, tell the story from a character's viewpoint, tighten dialogue, be less descriptive, proofread before submitting, and be patient. We will not publish every manuscript we receive. It has to be in standard English, well written, proofread. We do not appreciate receiving manuscripts where we have to do the proofreading and the correcting of grammar."

CRICKET

Carus Publishing Co., 70 E. Lake St., Suite 300, Chicago, IL 60601. (312)701-1720, ext. 10. **Website:** www .cricketmag.com. **Contact:** Marianne Carus, editor-in-chief; Lonnie Plecha, editor; Alice Letvin, editorial director; Karen Kohn, senior art director. Estab. 1973.

Buys 70 mss/year. Recently published work by Aaron Shepard, Arnold Adoff, and Nancy Springer.

NEEDS "*Cricket* is looking for more fiction and nonfiction for the older end of its 9-14 age range, as well as contemporary stories set in other countries. It also seeks humorous stories and mysteries (not detective spoofs), fantasy and original fairy tales, stand-alone excerpts from unpublished novels, and well-written/researched science articles." Middle readers, young adults/teens: contemporary, fantasy, folk and fairy tales, history, humorous, legends/myths, realistic, science fiction, suspense/mystery. No didactic, sex, religious, or horror stories. Length: 200-2,000 words.

HOW TO CONTACT Submit complete ms.

PAYMENT/TERMS Pays 25¢/word maximum, and 6 contributor's copies; $2.50 charge for extras.

TIPS Writers: "Read copies of back issues and current issues. Adhere to specified word limits. *Please* do not query." Would currently like to see more fantasy and science fiction. Illustrators: "Send only your best work and be able to reproduce that quality in assignments. Put name and address on *all* samples. Know a publication before you submit."

⊕ CURA: A LITERARY MAGAZINE OF ART AND ACTION

441 E. Fordham Rd., English Department, Dealy 541W, Bronx, NY 10548. **E-mail:** curamag@fordham.edu. **Website:** www.curamag.com. **Contact:** Sarah Gambito, managing editor. Estab. 2011. "*CURA: A Literary Magazine of Art and Action* is a multimedia initiative based at Fordham University committed to integrating the arts and social justice. Featuring creative writing, visual art, new media, and video in response to current news, we seek to enable an artistic process that is rigorously engaged with the world at the present moment. *CURA* is taken from the Ignatian educational principle of 'cura personalis,' care for the whole person. On its own, the word *cura* is defined as guardianship, solicitude, and significantly, written work. Each year, *CURA* will feature a sustaining theme in dialogue with a nonprofit organization that reflects the vision of 'care for the whole person.' Our aim is to provide support for and to raise awareness of the critical work these organizations are undertaking. For information on this year's theme, please check out our website at curamag.com. All publication proceeds will directly benefit the featured nonprofit or-ganization. We seek to foster a movement of creative response guided by concrete and meaningful action— to celebrate informed and active citizenship where a republic of writers, filmmakers, visual and digital artists converge. What Martín Espada has written about the social responsibility of the 'Republic of Poetry' we believe applies to a Republic of all the Arts. It is "a place where creativity meets community, where the imagination serves humanity. It is a republic of justice because the practice of justice is the highest form of human expression."

○ Content is published in print and in online and Kindle editions.

NEEDS Length: no more than 6,000 words.

HOW TO CONTACT Submit complete ms.

PAYMENT/TERMS Pays 1 contributor's copy. *CURA* holds first serial rights on featured material.

◑◐ CURRENT ACCOUNTS

Current Accounts, Apt. 2D, Bradshaw Hall, Hardcastle Gardens, Bolton BL2 4NZ UK. **E-mail:** fjames hartnell@aol.com. **Website:** http://bankstreetwriters.webs.com/currentaccounts.htm. **Contact:** F. J. Hartnell. Estab. 1994. *Current Accounts*, published semiannually, prints poetry, fiction, and nonfiction by members of Bank Street Writers, and other contributors.

○ Considers poetry by children and teens. Has published poetry by Pat Winslow, M.R. Peacocke, and Gerald England. *Current Accounts* is 52 pages, A5, photocopied, saddle stapled, with card cover with black-and-white or color photo or artwork. Receives about 300 poems/year, accepts about 5%. Press run is 80; 8 distributed free to competition winners. Subscription: £6. Sample: £3. Make checks payable to Bank Street Writers (sterling checks only).

NEEDS Open to all types of poetry. "No requirements, although some space is reserved for members."

TIPS Bank Street Writers meets once/month and offers workshops, guest speakers, and other activities. Write for details."We like originality of ideas, images, and use of language. No inspirational or religious verse unless it's also good in poetic terms."

◐ CUTBANK

English Dept., University of Montana, LA 133, Missoula, MT 59812. **E-mail:** cutbank@umontana.edu. **Website:** www.cutbankonline.org. **Contact:** Andrew Martin, editor-in-chief. Estab. 1973.

Receives 200 unsolicited mss/month. Accepts 6-12 mss/year. Does not read mss March 1-September 30. **Publishes 4 new writers/year.** Recently published work by Kellie Wells and Danielle Dutton. Occasionally comments on rejected mss. Awards the Montana Prize for Fiction in the spring, as selected by the magazine's editors and an annual guest judge. Contest submissions accepted December-February. $17 entry fee includes subscription.

NEEDS No "science fiction, fantasy, or unproofed manuscripts. Innovative, challenging, well-written stories. We're always on the lookout for a boldness of form and a rejection of functional fixedness."

TIPS "Familiarity with the magazine is essential. *Cutbank* is very open to new voices—we have a legacy of publishing acclaimed writers early in their careers—but we will consider only your best work. *Cutbank* only accepts online submissions."

DALHOUSIE REVIEW

Dalhousie University, Halifax NS B3H 4R2 Canada. **E-mail:** dalhousie.review@dal.ca. **Website:** http://dalhousiereview.dal.ca. **Contact:** Poetry editor. Estab. 1921. *Dalhousie Review*, published 3 times/year, is a journal of criticism publishing poetry and fiction.

Considers poetry from both new and established writers. *Dalhousie Review* is 144 pages, digest size. Accepts about 5% of poems received. Press run is 500. Single copy: $15 CAD; subscription: $22.50 CAD, $28 USD. Make checks payable to *Dalhousie Review*.

DARGONZINE

E-mail: dargon@dargonzine.org. **Website:** dargonzine.org. **Contact:** Jon Evans, editor. "*DargonZine* is an e-zine that prints original fantasy fiction by aspiring fantasy writers. The Dargon Project is a shared world anthology whose goal is to provide a way for aspiring fantasy writers to meet and improve their writing skills through mutual contact and collaboration, as well as contact with a live readership via the Internet. Our goal is to write fantasy fiction that is mature, emotionally compelling, and professional. Membership in the Dargon Project is a requirement for publication."

Publishes 1-3 new writers/year.

PAYMENT/TERMS "As a strictly noncommercial magazine, our writers' only compensation is their growth and membership in a lively writing community.

TIPS "The Readers and Writers FAQs on our website provide much more detailed information about our mission, writing philosophy, and the value of writing for *DargonZine*."

THE DEAD MULE SCHOOL OF SOUTHERN LITERATURE

E-mail: deadmule@gmail.com. **E-mail:** submit.mule@gmail.com. **Website:** www.deadmule.com. **Contact:** Valerie MacEwan, publisher and editor; Helen Losse, poetry editor. "'No good southern fiction is complete without a dead mule.' Celebrating over 15 years online means *The Dead Mule* is one of the oldest, if not *the* oldest continuously published online literary journals alive today. Publisher and editor Valerie MacEwan welcomes submissions. *The Dead Mule School of Southern Literature* wants flash fiction, poetry, visual poetry, essays, and creative nonfiction. We usually publish new work on the 1st and 15th of the month, depending on whims, obligations, and mule-jumping contest dates. Helen Losse, poetry; Phoebe Kate Foster, fiction; Valerie MacEwan editor/publisher; Robert MacEwan, technical and design; and other volunteers who graciously donate their time and love to this fine journal."

"The Dead Mule School of Southern Literature Institutional Alumni Association recruits year-round. Want to join the freshman class of 2015? Submit today."

NEEDS "Always, always, stories about mules."

HOW TO CONTACT Send complete ms. "You can send it as a .doc attachment, but also include your submission in the body of your e-mail. Read and follow the guidelines online—you need a Southern Legitimacy Statement (SLS). It's mostly about you entertaining us and capturing our interest. Everyone is South of Somewhere, so go ahead, check us out."

TIPS "Read the site to get a feel for what we're looking to publish. Limit stories and essays to 1,000 words. All submissions must be accompanied by a 'southern legitimacy statement,' details of which can be seen within each page on *The Dead Mule* and within the submishmash entry page. We've been around for over 15 years, send us something original. Chapbooks published by invitation, also short fiction compilations. Sporadic payment to writers whenever cafepress/

deadmule sales reach an agreeable amount. Then we share!"

●☺ DENVER QUARTERLY

University of Denver, 2000 E. Asbury, Denver, CO 80208. (303)871-2892. **Website:** www.denverquarterly.com. **Contact:** Bill Ramke. Estab. 1996. "We publish fiction, articles, and poetry for a generally well-educated audience, primarily interested in literature and the literary experience. They read *DQ* to find something a little different from a stictly academic quarterly or a creative writing outlet."

○ *Denver Quarterly* received an Honorable Mention for Content from the American Literary Magazine Awards and selections have been anthologized in the *Pushcart Prize* anthologies. Quarterly. Reads between September 15 and May 15.

NEEDS "We are interested in experimental fiction (minimalism, magic realism, etc.) as well as in realistic fiction and in writing about fiction. No sentimental, science fiction, romance, or spy thrillers. No stories longer than 15 pages!"

HOW TO CONTACT Submit ms by mail, include SASE.

PAYMENT/TERMS Pays $5/page for fiction and poetry and 2 contributor's copies.

TIPS "We look for serious, realistic and experimental fiction; stories which appeal to intelligent, demanding readers who are not themselves fiction writers. Nothing so quickly disqualifies a manuscript as sloppy proofreading and mechanics. Read the magazine before submitting to it. We try to remain eclectic, but the odds for beginners are bound to be small considering the fact that we receive nearly 10,000 mss/year and publish only about ten short stories."

○ DESCANT

P.O. Box 314, Station P, Toronto, ON M5S 2S8 Canada. (416)593-2557. **Fax:** (416)593-9362. **E-mail:** info@descant.ca. **E-mail:** submit@descant.ca. **Website:** www.descant.ca. Estab. 1970.

NEEDS Short stories or book excerpts. Maximum length 6,000 words; 3,000 words or less preferred. No erotica, fantasy, gothic, horror, religious, romance, beat.

HOW TO CONTACT Send complete ms with cover letter. Include estimated word count and brief bio.

PAYMENT/TERMS Pays $100 (Canadian), plus 1-year subscription for accepted submissions of any kind.

TIPS "Familiarize yourself with our magazine before submitting."

◐☺ DESCANT: FORT WORTH'S JOURNAL OF POETRY AND FICTION

TCU Box 297270, Ft. Worth, TX 76129. (817)257-6537. **Fax:** (817)257-6239. **E-mail:** descant@tcu.edu. **Website:** www.descant.tcu.edu. **Contact:** David Kuhne, editor. Estab. 1956. "*Descant* seeks high-quality poems and stories in both traditional and innovative form." Member CLMP.

○ Magazine: 6" × 9"; 120-150 pages; acid-free paper; paper cover. Receives 20-30 unsolicited mss/month. Accepts 25-35 mss/year. Publishes ms 1 year after acceptance. Publishes 50% new writers/year. Recently published work by William Harrison, Annette Sanford, Miller Williams, Patricia Chao, Vonesca Stroud, and Walt McDonald. Several stories first published by *Descant* have appeared in *Best American Short Stories.*

NEEDS "No horror, romance, fantasy, erotica." Length: 1,000-5,000 words; average length: 2,500 words.

HOW TO CONTACT Send complete ms with cover letter. Include estimated word count and brief bio.

PAYMENT/TERMS Offers 4 cash awards: The $500 Frank O'Connor Award for the best story in an issue; the $250 Gary Wilson Award for an outstanding story in an issue; the $500 Betsy Colquitt Award for the best poem in an issue; the $250 Baskerville Publishers Award for outstanding poem in an issue.

TIPS "We look for character and quality of prose. Send your best short work."

DIAGRAM

Department of English, University of Arizona, P.O. Box 210067, Tucson, AZ 85721-0067. **E-mail:** editor@thediagram.com. **Website:** www.thediagram.com. "*DIAGRAM* is an electronic journal of text and art, found and created. We're interested in representations, naming, indicating, schematics, labeling and taxonomy of things; in poems that masquerade as stories; in stories that disguise themselves as indices or obituaries. We specialize in work that pushes the boundaries of traditional genre or work that is in some way schematic. We publish traditional fiction and poetry, too, but hybrid forms (short stories, prose poems, indexes, tables of contents, etc.) are particularly welcome! We also publish diagrams and schematics (original and found)."

◑   Receives 100 unsolicited mss/month. Accepts 2-3 mss/issue; 15 mss/year. Receives about 1,000 poems/year, accepts about 5%. Publishes 6 new writers/year. Bimonthly. Member CLMP. "We sponsor yearly contests for unpublished hybrid essays and innovative fiction. Guidelines on website."

NEEDS "We don't publish genre fiction, unless it's exceptional and transcends the genre boundaries." Average length: 250-2,000 words.

HOW TO CONTACT Send complete ms. Accepts submissions by Web submissions manager; no e-mail. If sending by snail mail, send SASE for return of the ms, or send disposable copy of the ms and #10 SASE for reply only.

PAYMENT/TERMS Acquires first, serial, electronic rights.

TIPS "Submit interesting text, images, sound, and new media. We value the insides of things, vivisection, urgency, risk, elegance, flamboyance, work that moves us, language that does something new, or does something old—well. We like iteration and reiteration. Ruins and ghosts. Mechanical, moving parts, balloons, and frenzy. We want art and writing that demonstrates/interaction; the processes of things; how functions are accomplished; how things become or expire, move or stand. We'll consider anything. We do not consider e-mail submissions, but we encourage electronic submissions via our submissions manager software. Look at the journal and submissions guidelines before submitting."

◐ THE DOS PASSOS REVIEW

Briery Creek Press, Longwood University, Department of English and Modern Languages, 201 High St., Farmville, VA 23909. **E-mail:** brierycreekpress@gmail.com. **Website:** http://brierycreekpress.word press.com/the-dos-passos-review.

NEEDS We do not accept novel excerpts. If submitting flash fiction (less than 1,000 words), you may submit up to 3 pieces.

HOW TO CONTACT Stories or essays should be typed, double-spaced, and paginated, with your name, address, phone number, and e-mail on the first page, title on subsequent pages. We are unable to read entire manuscripts, novellas, or submissions of more than one story (roughly 3,000 words) at a time. Reading periods vary: April 1-July 31 for Fall Issue, February 1-March 30 for Spring Issue. Submissions postmarked outside these reading periods will be returned unread.

PAYMENT/TERMS Pays 2 contributor's copies.

TIPS "We are looking for writing that demonstrates characteristics found in the work of John Dos Passos, such as an intense and original exploration of specifically American themes; an innovative quality; and a range of literary forms, especially in the genres of fiction and creative nonfiction. We are not interested in genre fiction or prose that is experiment for the sake of experiment. We are also not interested in nonfiction that is scholarly or critical in nature. Send us your best unpublished literary prose or poetry."

○ DOWN IN THE DIRT

829 Brian Court, Gurnee, IL 60031-3155. (847)281-9070. **E-mail:** dirt@scars.tv. **Website:** www.scars.tv. **Contact:** Janet Kuypers, editor. Estab. 2000. *Down in the Dirt*, published monthly online, prints "good work that makes you think, that makes you feel like you've lived through a scene instead of merely read it." Also considers poems. *Down in the Dirt* is published "electronically as well as in print, either as printed magazines sold through our printer over the Internet, on the Web (Internet web pages) or sold through our printer in e-book form (PDF file)."

◑   Literary magazine/journal: 5½" × 8½" perfect-bound, 84-page book. Contains illustrations and photographs as well as short stories, essays, and poetry." Has published work by Pat Dixon, Mel Waldman, Ken Dean, Aeon Logan, Helena Wolfe.

NEEDS No religious, rhyming, or family-oriented material. Average length: 1,000 words.

HOW TO CONTACT Query editor with e-mail submission. "99.5% of all submissions are via e-mail only, so if you do not have electronic access, there is a strong chance you will not be considered. We recommend you e-mail submissions to us, either as an attachment (.txt, .rtf, or .doc—NOT .docx, and not .pdf) or by placing it directly in the e-mail letter. For samples of what we've printed in the past, visit our website: http://scars.tv/dirt. Contact us if you are interested in submitting very long stories or parts of a novel (if accepted, it would appear in parts in multiple issues)." Accepts simultaneous, multiple submissions, and reprints.

PAYMENT/TERMS No payment.

TIPS Scars Publications sponsors a contest "where accepted writing appears in a collection book. Write or e-mail (dirt@scars.tv) for information." Also able to publish electronic chapbooks. Write for more information.

DOWNSTATE STORY

1825 Maple Ridge, Peoria, IL 61614. (309)688-1409. **E-mail:** ehopkins7@prodigy.net. **Website:** www.wiu .edu/users/mfgeh/dss; www.downstatestory.com. Estab. 1992.

NEEDS No porn. Length: 300-2,000 words.

HOW TO CONTACT Submit complete ms with cover letter and SASE. Submit via postal mail.

TIPS Wants more political fiction. Publishes short shorts and literary essays.

DRAMATICS MAGAZINE

Educational Theatre Association, 2343 Auburn Ave., Cincinnati, OH 45219. (513)421-3900. **E-mail:** dcorathers@edta.org. **Website:** www.edta.org. **Contact:** Don Corathers, editor. Estab. 1929. "*Dramatics* is for students (mainly high school age) and teachers of theater. Mix includes how-to (tech theater, acting, directing, etc.), informational, interview, photo feature, humorous, profile, technical. We want our student readers to grow as theater artists and become a more discerning and appreciative audience. Material is directed to both theater students and their teachers, with strong student slant."

NEEDS Young adults: drama (one-act and full-length plays). "We prefer unpublished scripts that have been produced at least once." Does not want to see plays that show no understanding of the conventions of the theater. No plays for children, no Christmas or didactic "message" plays. Length: 750-3,000 words.

HOW TO CONTACT Submit complete ms. Buys 5-9 plays/year. Emerging playwrights have better chances with résumé of credits.

PAYMENT/TERMS Pays $100-500 for plays.

TIPS "Obtain our writer's guidelines and look at recent back issues. The best way to break in is to know our audience—drama students, teachers, and others interested in theater—and write for them. Writers who have some practical experience in theater, especially in technical areas, have an advantage, but we'll

work with anybody who has a good idea. Some freelancers have become regular contributors."

◐ DUCTS

P.O. Box 3203, Grand Central Station, New York, NY 10163. **E-mail:** vents@ducts.org. **Website:** www.ducts .org. **Contact:** Jonathan Kravetz, editor-in-chief. Estab. 1999. *DUCTS* is a webzine of personal stories, fiction, essays, memoirs, poetry, humor, profiles, reviews, and art. "*DUCTS* was founded in 1999 with the intent of giving emerging writers a venue to regularly publish their compelling, personal stories. The site has been expanded to include art and creative works of all genres. We believe that these genres must and do overlap. *DUCTS* publishes the best, most compelling stories, and we hope to attract readers who are drawn to work that rises above."

◖ Semiannual.

NEEDS "Humor word count maximum is 1,200 words and, due to the large number of submissions we receive for this department, we are only able to respond to those submissions we accept for publication."

HOW TO CONTACT Submit to appropriate (by department) e-mail address. See website.

TIPS "We prefer writing that tells a compelling story with a strong narrative drive."

◉ ECHO INK REVIEW

E.I. Publishing Services, Published by Sildona Creative, 5920 Nall Ave., Suite 301, Mission, KS 66202. **E-mail:** editor@echoinkreview.com. **Website:** www .echoinkreview.com. **Contact:** Mary Stone Dockery, fiction editor; Don Balch, fiction editor; James Hagan, fiction editor; Magahn Lusk, poetry editor. Estab. 1997. "As of January 1, 2013, *Echo Ink Review* is changing its format from traditional print to digital mixed media. What does that mean? Simply put, it means video book. i.e., vBook. First, *Echo Ink Review* hires professional narrators who narrate manuscripts accepted for publication. Second, working in conjunction with Sildona Films, we combine that narration with a filmed narrative that seeks to expand upon the written (spoken) word for a full entertainment experience for the listener/viewer. It is our belief that the vBook is the modern expression of the ancient tradition of oral storytelling."

NEEDS Length: 250-1,500/words.

HOW TO CONTACT "Please use our online submission manager: the $2.00 submission fee helps support our journal— please support us instead of the post office. Other submission option: free postal submissions to office address."

PAYMENT/TERMS One contributor's copy.

TIPS "Read the online guidelines. Surprising, precise language + dynamic character arcs and character-driven plots that resonate = you have our attention. We publish quite a few stories by established writers, but we want to discover the best new talent out there. To that end, we reserve 50% of each issue to stories by new and moderately established writers. Additionally, we support our writers by paying them professional rates. Tips on judging your work: If you want to know where your writing stands in relation to that of your peers, compare your stories to those published by your favorite literary journal. If you don't have a favorite literary journal, get one. Entering our contests will also give you an idea of where your writing stands; in addition to posting winners (top 3), we post finalists (top 10), semifinalists (top 25), and quarter-finalists (top 25% of mss received). Stay positive; be persistent; keep writing."

ECLECTICA

E-mail: editors@eclectica.org. **Website:** www.eclectica.org. **Contact:** Tom Dooley, managing editor. Estab. 1996. "A sterling-quality literary magazine on the World Wide Web. Not bound by formula or genre, harnessing technology to further the reading experience and dynamic and interesting in content. *Eclectica* is a quarterly World Wide Web journal devoted to showcasing the best writing on the web, regardless of genre. 'Literary' and 'genre' work appear side-by-side in each issue, along with pieces that blur the distinctions between such categories. Pushcart Prize, National Poetry Series, and Pulitzer Prize winners, as well as Nebula Award nominees, have shared issues with previously unpublished authors."

NEEDS "High-quality work in any genre."

HOW TO CONTACT Submit via online submissions manager.

TIPS "We pride ourselves on giving everyone (high schoolers, convicts, movie executives, etc.) an equal shot at publication, based solely on the quality of their work. Because we like eclecticism, we tend to favor the varied perspectives that often characterize the work of international authors, people of color, women, alternative lifestylists—but others who don't fit into these categories often surprise us."

ECLIPSE

Glendale College, 1500 N. Verdugo Rd., Glendale, CA 91208. (818)240-1000. **Fax:** (818)549-9436. **E-mail:** eclipse@glendale.edu. **Website:** http://seco.glendale.edu/english/english.html. Magazine: 8½" × 5½"; 150-200 pages; 60 lb. paper. "*Eclipse* is committed to publishing outstanding fiction and poetry. We look for compelling characters and stories executed in ways that provoke our readers and allow them to understand the world in new ways."

Receives 50-100 unsolicited mss/month. Accepts 10 mss/year. Publishes ms 6-12 months after acceptance. **Publishes 8 new writers/year.** Sometimes comments on rejected mss. Recently published work by Amy Sage Webb, Ira Sukrungruang, Richard Schmitt, George Rabasa. Length: 6,000 words; average length: 4,000 words. Annual. Circ. 1,800. CLMP.

NEEDS Ethnic/multicultural, experimental, literary. "Does not want horror, religious, science fiction, or thriller mss." Publishes short shorts. Also publishes poetry. Length: 6,000 words.

HOW TO CONTACT Send complete ms. Responds in 2 weeks to queries; 4-6 weeks to mss. Accepts simultaneous submissions. Sample copy for $8. Writer's guidelines for #10 SASE or by e-mail. Send complete ms.

PAYMENT/TERMS Pays 2 contributor's copies; additional copies $7. Pays on publication for first North American serial rights.

TIPS "We look for well-crafted fiction, experimental or traditional, with a clear unity of elements. A good story is important, but the writing must transcend the simple act of conveying the story."

ECOTONE

Department of Creative Writing, University of North Carolina Wilmington, 601 S. College Rd., Wilmington, NC 28403. (910)962-2547. **Fax:** (910)962-7461. **E-mail:** info@ecotonejournal.com. **Website:** www.ecotonejournal.com. **Contact:** Sally J. Johnson, managing editor. "*Ecotone* is a literary journal of place that seeks to publish creative works about the environment and the natural world while avoiding the hushed tones and cliches of much of so-called nature writing. Reading period is August 15-April 15."

HOW TO CONTACT Send complete ms.

○ ⊘ ⑨ ELLERY QUEEN'S MYSTERY MAGAZINE

Dell Magazines, 267 Broadway, 4th Floor, New York, NY 10017. (212)686-7188. **Fax:** (212)686-7414. **E-mail:** elleryqueenmm@dellmagazines.com. **Website:** www.themysteryplace.com/eqmm. **Contact:** Jackie Sherbow, assistant editor. Estab. 1941. Magazine for lovers of mystery fiction. "*Ellery Queen's Mystery Magazine* welcomes submissions from both new and established writers. We publish every kind of mystery short story: the psychological suspense tale, the deductive puzzle, the private eye case, the gamut of crime and detection from the realistic (including the policeman's lot and stories of police procedure) to the more imaginative (including locked rooms and impossible crimes). *EQMM* has been in continuous publication since 1941. From the beginning, three general criteria have been employed in evaluating submissions: We look for strong writing, an original and exciting plot, and professional craftsmanship. We encourage writers whose work meets these general criteria to read an issue of *EQMM* before making a submission."

○ Magazine: 5⅞" × 8⅝", 112 pages with special 192-page combined March/April and September/October issues. Agented fiction 50%. **Publishes 10 new writers/year.** Recently published work by Jeffery Deaver, Joyce Carol Oates, and Margaret Maron. Sometimes comments on rejected mss.

NEEDS Mystery/suspense. No explicit sex or violence, no gore or horror. Seldom publishes parodies or pastiches. "We accept only mystery, crime, suspense and detective fiction." 2,500-8,000 words is the preferred range. Also publishes minute mysteries of 250 words; novellas up to 20,000 words from established authors. Publishes ms 6-12 months after acceptance. "We always need detective stories. Special consideration given to anything timely and original."

HOW TO CONTACT Send complete ms with SASE for reply. No e-mail submissions. No query necessary. Responds in 3 months to mss. Accepts simultaneous, multiple submissions. Sample copy for $5.50. Writer's guidelines for SASE or online. *EQMM* uses an online submission system (http://eqmm.magazinesubmissions.com) that has been designed to streamline our process and improve communication with authors. We ask that all submissions be made electronically, using this system, rather than on paper. All stories should be in standard manuscript format and submitted in .doc format. We cannot accept .docx, .rtf, or .txt files at this time. For detailed submission instructions, see http://eqmm.magazinesubmissions.com or our writers guidelines page (http://www.themysteryplace.com/eqmm/guidelines).

PAYMENT/TERMS Pays 5-8¢/ a word, occasionally higher for established authors. Pays on acceptance for first North American serial rights.

TIPS "We have a Department of First Stories to encourage writers whose fiction has never before been in print. We publish an average of 10 first stories every year. Mark subject line: Attn: Dept. of First Stories."

○ ⑨ ELLIPSIS MAGAZINE

Westminster College of Salt Lake City, 1840 S. 1300 East, Salt Lake City, UT 84105. (801)832-2321. **E-mail:** ellipsis@westminstercollege.edu. **Website:** www.westminstercollege.edu/ellipsis. **Contact:** Mikki Whitworth, managing editor; Lauren Johnson, editor-in-chief. Estab. 1967. **Contact:** Stephanie Peterson (revolving editor; changes every year).

○ Magazine: 6" × 9"; 110-120 pages; 60 lb. paper; 15 pt. cover stock; illustrations; photos. Annual. Circ. 2,000. Reads submissions August 1 to November 1. Receives 110 unsolicited mss/month. Accepts 4 mss/issue. Does not read mss November 1-July 31. Publishes ms 3 months after acceptance. **Publishes 2 new writers/year.** Rarely comments on rejected mss.

NEEDS "*Ellipsis Magazine* needs good literary poetry, fiction, essays, plays, and visual art." Length: 6,000 words; average length: 4,000 words.

HOW TO CONTACT Send complete ms. Send SASE (or IRC) for return of ms or send disposable copy of the ms and #10 SASE for reply only. Responds in 6 months to mss. Accepts simultaneous submissions. Sample copy for $7.50. Writer's guidelines online. Send complete ms.

PAYMENT/TERMS Pays $50 per story and one contributor's copy; additional copies $3.50. Pays on publication for first North American serial rights. Not copyrighted.

○ EPICENTER: A LITERARY MAGAZINE

P.O. Box 367, Riverside, CA 92502. **E-mail:** submissions@epicentermagazine.org. **Website:** www.epicentermagazine.org. **Contact:** Jeff Green, Cali Linfor, Rowena Silver, editors. Estab. 1994. *Epicenter: A Literary Magazine* published semiannually, is open to all styles of writing.

Epicenter is 100 pages, perfect-bound. Receives about 2,000 submissions/year, accepts about 5%. Press run is 800. Has published poetry by Virgil Suarez, Alba Cruz-Hacher, B.Z. Niditch, Egon Lass, and Zdravka Evtimova. Single copy: $9. Make checks payable to *Epicenter: A Literary Magazine.*

Needs "*Epicenter* is looking for poetry, essays, short stories, creative nonfiction, and artwork. We publish new and established writers." Considers translations. Does not want "angst-ridden, sentimental, or earthquake poetry. We are not adverse to graphic images as long as the work contains literary merit."

EPIPHANY: WHERE CREATIVITY AND INSPIRATION EVOLVE!

E-mail: contact@epiphmag.com. **E-mail:** submissions@epiphmag.com. **Website:** www.epiphmag.com. **Contact:** JW Smith, editor. Estab. 2010. *Epiphany* was started in 2010, solely to be an online venue in which writers and artists can display their works. "*Epiphany*'s dynamic formatting sets our publication apart from other online magazines. We strive to bring poetry, prose, fiction, nonfiction, artwork, and photography together to form a visually and creatively stimulating experience for our readers." Six issues/year in February, April, June, August, October, and December.

"*Epiphany* is a non-paying market at this time."
NEEDS Length: 500-4,000 words.
HOW TO CONTACT Accepts 40-70 mss/year. Send complete ms. "Please write 'Fiction' in the subject line of your e-mail."
TIPS "We are open to a variety of writing styles and content subject matter. Our audience includes writers, artists, students, teachers, and all who enjoy reading short fiction, poetry, and creative nonfiction. We will not publish any works which we feel have a derogatory nature. Please visit our submission guidelines page at www.epiphmag.com/guide.html for more details. "Please write the type of submission you are sending in the subject line of your e-mail."

EPOCH

251 Goldwin Smith Hall, Cornell University, Ithaca NY 14853. (607)255-3385. **Fax:** (607)255-6661. **Website:** http://english.arts.cornell.edu/publications/epoch. Estab. 1947. "Well-written literary fiction, poetry, personal essays. Newcomers always welcome. Open to mainstream and avant-garde writing."

Magazine: 6" × 9"; 128 pages; good quality paper; good cover stock. Receives 500 unsolicited mss/month. Accepts 15-20 mss/issue. **Reads submissions September 15-April 15.** Publishes 3-4 new writers/year. Has published work by Antonya Nelson, Doris Betts, Heidi Jon Schmidt.

NEEDS No genre fiction. "Would like to see more Southern fiction (Southern U.S.)."
HOW TO CONTACT Send complete ms.
PAYMENT/TERMS Pays $5 and up/printed page.
TIPS "Tell your story, speak your poem, straight from the heart. We are attracted to language and to good writing, but we are most interested in what the good writing leads us to, or where."

ESQUIRE

300 W. 57th St., 21st Floor, New York, NY 10019. (212)649-4020. **Website:** www.esquire.com. Estab. 1933. *Esquire* is geared toward smart, well-off men. General readership is college educated and sophisticated, between ages 30 and 45. Written mostly by contributing editors on contract. Rarely accepts unsolicited mss.

NEEDS "Literary excellence is our only criterion." No pornography, science fiction or 'true romance' stories.
HOW TO CONTACT Send complete ms. To submit a story, use online submission manager at http://esquiresubmissions.com.
TIPS "A writer has the best chance of breaking in at *Esquire* by querying with a specific idea that requires special contacts and expertise. Ideas must be timely and national in scope."

EUREKA LITERARY MAGAZINE

300 E. College Ave., Eureka College, Eureka, IL 61530. **E-mail:** elm@eureka.edu. **Website:** www.eureka.edu/arts/literary/literary.htm. Estab. 1992.

NEEDS Would like to see more "good literary fiction stories, good magical realism, historical fiction. We try to achieve a balance between the traditional and the experimental. We look for the well-crafted story, but essentially any type of story that has depth and substance to it is welcome." Length: 4,000-6,000 words.
HOW TO CONTACT Submit via e-mail.
TIPS "Do something that hasn't been done a thousand times already. Give us unusual but believable characters in unusual but believable conflicts—clear resolution isn't always necessary, but it's nice. We don't

hold to hard-and-fast rules about length, but most stories could do with some cutting. Make sure your title is relevant and eye-catching. Please do not send personal gifts or hate mail. We're a college-operated magazine, so we do not actually exist in summer. If we don't take a submission, that doesn't automatically mean we don't like it—we try to encourage authors who show promise to revise and resubmit. Order a copy if you can."

◑ $ EVANGEL

Light and Life Communications, 770 N. High School Rd., Indianapolis, IN 46214. (317)244-3660. **Contact:** Julie Innes, editor. Estab. 1897 by free Methodist denomination. *Evangel*, published quarterly, is an adult Sunday School paper. "Devotional in nature, it lifts up Christ as the source of salvation and hope. The mission of *Evangel* is to increase the reader's understanding of the nature and character of God and the nature of a life lived for Christ. Material that fits this mission and isn't longer than 1 page will be considered."

⚪   *Evangel* is 8 pages, 5½" × 8½", printed in 4-color, unbound, color and black-and-white photos. Does not want rhyming work. Accepts about 5% of poetry received. Fiction involves people coping with everyday crises, making decisions that show spiritual growth. Weekly distribution. Recently published work by Kelli Wise and Hope Byler. Press run is about 10,000. Subscription: $2.59/quarter (13 weeks).

NEEDS Receives 300 unsolicited mss/month. Accepts 3-4 mss/issue; 156-200 mss/year. Publishes 7 new writers/year. "No fiction without any semblance of Christian message or where the message clobbers the reader. Looking for devotional style short pieces 500 words or less."

HOW TO CONTACT Send complete ms. Accepts multiple submissions.

PAYMENT/TERMS Pays 4¢/word and 2 contributor's copies.

TIPS "We desire concise, tight writing that supports a solid thesis and fits the mission expressed in the guidelines."

◑ EVANSVILLE REVIEW

University of Evansville Creative Writing Deptartment, 1800 Lincoln Ave., Evansville, IN 47722. (812)488-1402. **E-mail:** evansvillereview@evansville.edu. **Website:** http://evansvillereview.evansville.edu. Estab. 1990.

NEEDS "We're open to all creativity. No discrimination. All fiction, screenplays, nonfiction, poetry, interviews, and anything in between." Does not want erotica, fantasy, experimental, or children's fiction. Length: no more than 10,000 words.

HOW TO CONTACT Submit through postal mail. Include a brief bio.

PAYMENT/TERMS Pays in contributor's copies.

TIPS "Because editorial staff rolls over every 1-2 years, the journal always has a new flavor."

◑ EVENING STREET REVIEW

Evening Street Press, Inc., 7652 Sawmill Rd. #352, Dublin, OH 43016. **E-mail:** editor@eveningstreet press.com. **Website:** www.eveningstreetpress.com. Estab. 2007. "Intended for a general audience, *Evening Street Press* is centered on Elizabeth Cady Stanton's 1848 revision of the Declaration of Independence: 'that all men—and women—are created equal,' with equal rights to 'life, liberty, and the pursuit of happiness.' It focuses on the realities of experience, personal and historical, from the most gritty to the most dreamlike, including awareness of the personal and social forces that block or develop the possibilities of this new culture."

HOW TO CONTACT Send complete ms. E-mail submissions preferred.

PAYMENT/TERMS Pays 1 contributor's copy.

TIPS "Does not want to see male chauvinism. Mss are read year-round. See website for chapbook and book competitions."

EXOTIC MAGAZINE

X Publishing Inc., 818 SW 3rd Ave., Suite 1324, Portland, OR 97204. (503)816-4174. **Fax:** (503)241-7239. **E-mail:** editorial@xmag.com. **Website:** www.xmag.com. Estab. 1993. "*Exotic* is pro-sex, informative, amusing, mature, and intelligent. Our readers rent and/or buy adult videos, visit strip clubs, and are interested in topics related to the adult entertainment industry and sexuality/culture. Don't talk down to them or fire too far over their heads. Many readers are computer literate and well traveled. We're also interested in insightful fetish material. We are not a 'hard-core' publication."

NEEDS "We are currently overwhelmed with fiction submissions. Please only send fiction if it's really amazing." Length: 1,000-1,800 words.

HOW TO CONTACT Send complete ms.

PAYMENT/TERMS Pays 10¢/word, up to $150.

TIPS "Read adult publications, spend time in the clubs doing more than just tipping and drinking. Look for new insights in adult topics. For the industry to continue to improve, those who cover it must also be educated consumers and affiliates. Please type, spell-check, and be realistic about how much time the editor can take 'fixing' your ms."

FACES MAGAZINE

Cobblestone Publishing, Editorial Dept., 30 Grove St., Suite C, Peterborough, NH 03458. (603)924-7209. **E-mail:** facesmag@yahoo.com. **Website:** www.cricket mag.com. *FACES Magazine*, published 9 times/year, features cultures from around the globe for children ages 9-14. "Readers learn how other kids live around the world and about the important inventions and ideas that a particular culture has given to the world. Subscription: $33.95/year (9 issues). Sample pages available on website.

NEEDS All material must relate to the theme of a specific upcoming issue in order to be considered." Wants "clear, objective imagery. Serious and light verse considered. Must relate to theme."

FAILBETTER.COM

2022 Grove Ave., Richmond, VA 23221. **E-mail:** tdi dato@failbetter.com; submissions@failbetter.com. **Website:** www.failbetter.com. **Contact:** Thom Didato, editor. Estab. 2000. "We are a quarterly online magazine published in the spirit of a traditional literary journal—dedicated to publishing quality fiction, poetry, and artwork. While the Web plays host to hundreds, if not thousands, of genre-related sites (many of which have merit), we are not one of them." Quarterly. Member CLMP.

NEEDS "If you're sending a short story or novel excerpt, send only one at a time. Wait to hear from us before sending another."

HOW TO CONTACT Submit work by pasting it into the body of an e-mail. Must put "Submission" in e-mail's subject line. Do not send attachments.

TIPS "Read an issue. Read our guidelines! We place a high degree of importance on originality, believing that even in this age of trends it is still possible. We are not looking for what is current or momentary. We are not concerned with length: One good sentence may find a home here, as the bulk of mediocrity will not. Most important, know that what you are saying could only come from you. When you are sure of this, please feel free to submit."

THE FAIRCLOTH REVIEW

E-mail: fairclothreview@gmail.com. **Website:** www .fairclothreview.com. **Contact:** Allen Coin, editor-in-chief; Lisa Pepin, managing editor. Estab. 2012. "*The Faircloth Review*, a weekly publication, is a paperless, online literary and arts journal with a wide range of focus. We accept fiction, nonfiction, poetry, photography, art, music, videos ... anything creative. We are open-minded, social media oriented, and specialize in previously unpublished artists."

NEEDS "No zombies, vampires, wizards, or werewolves, please, unless it's satirical." Length: 100-10,000 words.

HOW TO CONTACT Submit complete ms. "Please follow the submission guidelines on the site (include in your submission your name, location, a short blurb about yourself, your head shot, and a link to your personal website, if you have one). For photos: provide captions. For fiction/nonfiction: use .doc or .docx file and provide a very short summary."

FAULTLINE

University of California at Irvine, Department of English, 435 Humanities Instructional Building, Irvine, CA 92697. (949)824-1573. **E-mail:** faultline@ uci.edu. **Website:** http://faultline.sites.uci.edu. Estab. 1992. Reading period is September 15-February 15. Submissions sent at any other time will not be read. Editors change in September of each year.

NEEDS Length: up to 20 pages.

HOW TO CONTACT Send complete ms. "While simultaneous submissions are accepted, multiple submissions are not accepted. Please restrict your submissions to one story at a time, regardless of length."

PAYMENT/TERMS Pays in contributor copies.

TIPS "Our commitment is to publish the best work possible from well-known and emerging authors with vivid and varied voices."

FICKLE MUSES

315 Terrace Street SE, Albuquerque, NM 87106. **E-mail:** editor@ficklemuses.com. **Website:** www.fickle muses.com. "*Fickle Muses* is an online journal of poetry and fiction engaged with myth and legend. A poet or fiction writer is featured each week, with new selections posted on Sundays. Art is updated monthly."

HOW TO CONTACT Submit complete ms through online submissions manager. Query via e-mail. Submissions are accepted year-round.

TIPS "Originality. An innovative look at an old story. I'm looking to be swept away. Get a feel for our website."

THE FIDDLEHEAD

University of New Brunswick, Campus House, 11 Garland Court, Box 4400, Fredericton, NB E3B 5A3 Canada. (506)453-3501. **Fax:** (506) 453-5069. **E-mail:** fiddlehd@unb.ca. **Website:** www.thefiddlehead.ca. **Contact:** Kathryn Taglia, managing editor. Estab. 1945. "Canada's longest living literary journal, *The Fiddlehead* is published 4 times a year at the University of New Brunswick, with the generous assistance of the University of New Brunswick, the Canada Council for the Arts, and the Province of New Brunswick. It is experienced; wise enough to recognize excellence; always looking for freshness and surprise. *The Fiddlehead* publishes short stories, poems, book reviews, and a small number of personal essays. Our full-color covers have become collectors' items and feature work by New Brunswick artists and from New Brunswick museums and art galleries. *The Fiddlehead* also sponsors an annual writing contest. The journal is open to good writing in English from all over the world, looking always for freshness and surprise. Our editors are always happy to see new unsolicited works in fiction and poetry. Work is read on an ongoing basis; the acceptance rate is around 1-2%. Apart from our annual contest, we have no deadlines for submissions."

Magazine: 6" × 9"; 128-180 pages; ink illustrations; photos. "No criteria for publication except quality. For a general audience, including many poets and writers." Receives 100-150 unsolicited mss/month. Accepts 4-5 mss/issue; 20-40 mss/year. Agented fiction: small percentage. Publishes high percentage of new writers/year. Has published work by Marjorie Celona, Wasela Hiyate, Alexander MacLeod, and Erika Van Winden.

NEEDS Average length: 3,000-6,000 words. Also publishes short shorts.

HOW TO CONTACT Send SASE and *Canadian* stamps or IRCs for return of mss. No e-mail submissions. Simultaneous submissions only if stated on cover letter; must contact immediately if accepted elsewhere.

PAYMENT/TERMS Pays up to $40 (Canadian)/published page and 2 contributor's copies.

TIPS "If you are serious about submitting to *The Fiddlehead*, you should subscribe or read an issue or 2 to get a sense of the journal. Contact us if you would to order sample back issues ($10-15 plus postage)."

FILLING STATION

P.O. Box 22135, Bankers Hall, Calgary AB T2P 4J5 Canada. **E-mail:** mgmt@fillingstation.ca; poetry@fillingstation.ca; fiction@fillingstation.ca; nonfiction@fillingstation.ca. **Website:** www.fillingstation.ca. **Contact:** Caitlynn Cummings, managing editor. Estab. 1993. *filling Station*, published 3 times/year, prints contemporary poetry, fiction, visual art, interviews, reviews, and articles.

Has published poetry by Fred Wah, Larissa Lai, Margaret Christakos, Robert Kroetsch, Ron Silliman, Susan Holbrook, and many more. *filling Station* is 64 pages, 8½" × 11", perfect-bound, with card cover, includes photos and artwork. Receives about 100 submissions/issue, accepts approximately 10%. Press run is 700. Subscription: $20/3 issues; $36 for 6 issues. Sample: $8.

NEEDS "We are looking for all forms of contemporary writing. but especially that which is original and/or experimental. We receive any of the following fiction, or a combination thereof: flash fiction, postcard fiction, short fiction, experimental fiction, or a novel excerpt that can stand alone."

HOW TO CONTACT E-mail up to 10 pages to fiction@fillingstation.ca. "A submission lacking mailing address and/or bio will be considered incomplete."

TIPS "*filling Station* accepts singular or simultaneous submissions of previously unpublished poetry, fiction, creative nonfiction, nonfiction, or art. We are always on the hunt for great writing!"

FIRST CLASS

P.O. Box 86, Friendship IN 47021. **E-mail:** christopherm@four-sep.com. **Website:** www.four-sep.com. **Contact:** Christopher M, editor. Estab. 1995. *First Class* features short fiction and poetics from the cream of the small press and killer unknowns—mingling before your very hungry eyes. I publish plays, too."

NEEDS "No religious or traditional stories, or 'boomer angst'—therapy-driven self loathing." Length: 5,000-8,000 words.

HOW TO CONTACT Send SASE.

PAYMENT/TERMS Pays in contributor's copies.

TIPS "Don't bore me with puppy dogs and the morose/sappy feeling you have about death. Belt out a good, short, thought-provoking, graphic, uncommon piece."

THE FIRST LINE

Blue Cubicle Press, LLC, P.O. Box 250382, Plano, TX 75025. (972)824-0646. **E-mail:** submission@thefirstline.com. **Website:** www.thefirstline.com. **Contact:** Robin LaBounty, manuscript coordinator. Estab. 1999. "*The First Line* is an exercise in creativity for writers and a chance for readers to see how many different directions we can take when we start from the same place. The purpose of *The First Line* is to jump-start the imagination—to help writers break through the block that is the blank page. Each issue contains short stories that stem from a common first line; it also provides a forum for discussing favorite first lines in literature."

NEEDS "We only publish stories that start with the first line provided. We are a collection of tales—of different directions writers can take when they start from the same place." Length: 300-3,000 words.

HOW TO CONTACT Submit complete ms.

PAYMENT/TERMS Pays $30.

TIPS "Don't just write the first story that comes to mind after you read the sentence. If it is obvious, chances are other people are writing about the same thing. Don't try so hard. Be willing to accept criticism."

🌐❶ FIVE CHAPTERS

Five Chapters, Wales. **Website:** www.fivechapters.com. FiveChapters.com is the home of the most exciting original fiction on the web. A 5-part story will be published every week, serial-style, beginning on Monday and with a new installment every weekday.

HOW TO CONTACT Send complete ms.

FIVE POINTS

Georgia State University, P.O. Box 3999, Atlanta, GA 30302-3999. **E-mail:** info@langate.gsu.edu. **Website:** www.fivepoints.gsu.edu. Estab. 1996. "*Five Points* is committed to publishing work that compels the imagination through the use of fresh and convincing language."

◗ Magazine: 6" × 9"; 200 pages; cotton paper; glossy cover; photos. Receives 250 unsolicited mss/month. Accepts 4 mss/issue; 15-20 mss/year. Does not read mss April 30-September 1. Publishes 1 new writer/year. Sometimes comments on rejected mss. Recently published

work by Frederick Busch, Ursula Hegi, Melanie Rae Thon. Sponsors awards/contests. Sample copy for $7.

NEEDS List of upcoming themes available for SASE. Average length: 7,500 words.

HOW TO CONTACT Use online submission manager.

PAYMENT/TERMS Pays $15/page minimum ($250 maximum), free subscription to magazine and 2 contributor's copies; additional copies $4. Pays $15/page minimum; $250 maximum, free subscription to magazine and 2 contributor's copies; additional copies $4.

TIPS "We place no limitations on style or content. Our only criteria is excellence. If your writing has an original voice, substance, and significance, send it to us. We will publish distinctive, intelligent writing that has something to say and says it in a way that captures and maintains our attention."

❶ FLINT HILLS REVIEW

Dept. of English, Box 4019, Emporia State University, Emporia, KS 66801. **Website:** www.emporia.edu/fhr. **Contact:** Kevin Rabas. Estab. 1996. *Flint Hills Review*, published annually in late summer, is "a regionally focused journal presenting writers of national distinction alongside new authors. *FHR* seeks work informed by a strong sense of place or region, especially Kansas and the Great Plains region. We seek to provide a publishing venue for writers of the Great Plains and Kansas, while also publishing authors whose work evidences a strong sense of place, writing of literary quality, and accomplished use of language and depth of character development."

◗ Magazine: 9" × 6"; 115 pages; 60 lb. paper; glossy cover; illustrations; photos. Receives 5-15 unsolicited mss/month. Accepts 2-5 mss/issue; 2-5 mss/year. Does not read mss April-December. Recently published work by Kim Stafford, Elizabeth Dodd, Bart Edelman, and Jennifer Henderson.

NEEDS Ethnic/multicultural, gay, historical, regional (Plains), translations. "No religious, inspirational, children's." Want to see more "writing of literary quality with a strong sense of place." List of upcoming themes online. Short stories: Send 1 story, either short short (1-3 pages) or traditional length. Also publishes literary essays, literary criticism, short plays, poetry.

HOW TO CONTACT Send a disposable copy of ms and #10 SASE for reply only.

PAYMENT/TERMS Pays 2 contributor's copies; additional copies $5.50.

TIPS "Strong imagery and voice, writing that is informed by place or region, writing of literary quality with depth of character development. Hone the language down to the most literary depiction that is possible in the shortest space that still provides depth of development without excess length."

① THE FLORIDA REVIEW

Deptartment of English, University of Central Florida, P.O. Box 161346, Orlando, FL 32816. (407)823-5329. **E-mail:** flreview@mail.ucf.edu. **Website:** http://florida review.cah.ucf.edu/. **Contact:** Jocelyn Bartkevicius, editor. Estab. 1972. "We publish fiction of high 'literary' quality—stories that delight, instruct, and take risks. Our audience consists of avid readers of fiction, poetry, and creative nonfiction."

Ⓞ   Magazine: 6" × 9"; 185 pages; semigloss full color cover, perfect-bound. Recently published work by Gerald Vizenor, Billy Collins, Sherwin Bitsui, Kelly Clancy, Denise Duhamel, Tony Hoagland, Baron Wormser, Marcia Aldrich, and Patricia Foster.

NEEDS No genre fiction. Length: no limit. "We prefer prose that is between 3 and 25 manuscript pages." Short stories should be under 15 pages.

HOW TO CONTACT Send complete ms through postal mail or electronically on website.

TIPS "We're looking for writers with fresh voices and original stories. We like risk."

FLOYD COUNTY MOONSHINE

720 Christiansburg Pike, Floyd, VA 24091. (540)745-5150. **E-mail:** floydshine@gmail.com. **Contact:** Aaron Moore, editor-in-chief. Estab. 2008. *Floyd County Moonshine*, published biannually, is a "literary and arts magazine in Floyd, Virginia, and the New River Valley. We accept poetry, short stories, and essays addressing all manner of themes; however, preference is given to those works of a rural or Southern/Appalachian nature. We welcome cutting-edge and innovative fiction and poetry in particular."

Ⓞ   Has published poetry by Steve Kistulentz, Louis Gallo, Ernie Wormwood, R.T. Smith, Chelsea Adams, and Justin Askins. Single copy: $8; subscription: $16/1 year, $30/2 years.

NEEDS "Literature addressing rural or Appalachian themes."

① FLYWAY

Department of English, 206 Ross Hall, Iowa State University, Ames, IA 50011-1201. **E-mail:** flywayjournal@ gmail.com; flyway@iastate.edu. **Website:** www.flyway .org. Estab. 1995. "Based out of Iowa State University, *Flyway: Journal of Writing and Environment* publishes poetry, fiction, nonfiction, and visual art exploring the many complicated facets of the word *environment*— at once rural, urban, and suburban—and its social and political implications. We are also open to all different interpretations of *environment*."

Ⓞ   Has published work by Rick Bass, Jacob M. Appel, Madison Smartt Bell, Jane Smiley. Also sponsors the annual fall "Notes from the Field" nonfiction contest, and the spring "Sweet Corn Prize in Fiction" short story contest. Details on website.

NEEDS Length: 100-5,000 words. Average length: 3,000 words. Also publishes short shorts of up to 1,000 words. Average length: 500 words.

HOW TO CONTACT Submit mss only via online submission manager at https://flyway.submittable .com/submit. Submissions are closed May 1-August 31. Receives 50-100 mss/monthl Accepts 3-5 stories/issue; up to 10/year. Also reviews novels and short story collections. Send books for review to: *Flyway*, Department of English, 206 Ross Hall, Iowa State University, Ames, IA 50011-1201.

PAYMENT/TERMS Pays one-year subscription to *Flyway*.

TIPS "For *Flyway*, there should be tension between the environment or setting of the story and the characters in it. A well-known place should appear new, even alien and strange through the eyes and actions of the characters. We want to see an active environment, too—a setting that influences actions, triggers it's own events."

⊘⑤ FOGGED CLARITY

Fogged Clarity and Nicotine Heart Press, P.O. Box 1016, Muskegon, MI 49443-1016. (231)670-7033. **E-mail:** editor@foggedclarity.com. **E-mail:** submissions@foggedclarity.com. **Website:** www.foggedclarity .com. **Contact:** Ben Evans, executive editor/managing editor. Estab. 2008. "*Fogged Clarity* is an arts review that accepts submissions of poetry, fiction, nonfiction, music, visual art, and reviews of work in all mediums. We seek art that is stabbingly eloquent. Our print edition will be released once every year, while new issues of our online journal will come out the beginning of every month. Artists maintain the copyrights to their work until they are monetarily compensated for said work. If your work is selected for our print edition and you consent to its publication, you will be compensated."

"By incorporating music and the visual arts, and releasing a new issue monthly, *Fogged Clarity* aims to transcend the conventions of a typical literary journal. Our network is extensive and our scope is as broad as thought itself; we are, you are, unconstrained. With that spirit in mind *Fogged Clarity* examines the work of authors, artists, scholars, and musicians, providing a home for exceptional art and thought that warrants exposure."

NEEDS Does not want genre, experimental, religious, etc. "We tend to only publish literary fiction."

HOW TO CONTACT Send complete ms.

TIPS "The editors appreciate artists communicating the intention of their submitted work and the influences behind it, in a brief cover letter. Any artists with proposals for features or special projects should feel free to contact our editors directly at editor@fogged clarity.com."

FOLIATE OAK LITERARY MAGAZINE

University of Arkansas-Monticello, P.O. Box 3460, Monticello, AR 71656. (870)460-1247. **E-mail:** foli ateoak@uamont.edu. **Website:** www.foliateoak.ua mont.edu. Magazine: foliateoak.weebly.com. **Contact:** Online submission manager. Estab. 1973.

Magazine: 6" × 9"; 80 pages. Monthly. Receives 80 unsolicited mss/month. Accepts 20 mss/issue; 160 mss/year. Does not read mss May-August. Publishes ms 1 month after acceptance. Publishes 130 new writers/year. Rarely comments on rejected mss. Recently published work by David Barringer, Thom Didato, Joe Taylor, Molly Giles, Patricia Shevlin, Tony Hoagland.

NEEDS Adventure, comics/graphic novels, ethnic/multicultural, experimental, family saga, feminist, gay, historical, humor/satire, lesbian, literary, mainstream, science fiction (soft/sociological). No religious, sexist, or homophobic work. Length: 50-2,500 words; average length: 1,500 words. Publishes short shorts. Also publishes literary essays, literary criticism, poetry. Reviews fiction.

HOW TO CONTACT Use online submission manager to submit work. Postal submissions will not be read. Responds in 4 weeks. Only accepts submissions August through April. Accepts simultaneous submissions and multiple submissions. Please contact ASAP if work is accepted elsewhere. Sample copy with SASE and 6" × 8" envelope. Read writer's guidelines online.

PAYMENT/TERMS Pays contributor's copy if included in the annual print anthology. Acquires electronic rights. Sends galleys to author. Not copyrighted.

TIPS "We're open to honest, experimental, offbeat, realistic, and surprising writing, if it has been edited. Limit poems to five per submission, and one short story or creative nonfiction (less than 2,500 words). You may send up to three flash fictions. Please put your flash fiction in one attachment. Please don't send more writing until you hear from us regarding your first submission. We are also looking for artwork sent as .jpg or .gif files."

FOLIO

Department of Literature, American University, Washington DC 20016. **E-mail:** folio.editors@gmail .com; lit@american.edu. **Fax:** (202)885-2938. **Website:** www.american.edu/cas/literature/folio/. **Contact:** Abdul Ali, editor-in-chief. Estab. 1984. "*Folio* is a nationally recognized literary journal sponsored by the College of Arts and Sciences at American University in Washington, DC. Since 1984, we have published original creative work by both new and established authors. Past issues have included work by Michael Reid Busk, Billy Collins, William Stafford, and Bruce Weigl, and interviews with Michael Cunningham, Charles Baxter, Amy Bloom, Ann Beattie, and Walter Kirn. We look for well-crafted poetry and prose that is bold and memorable."

Poems and prose are reviewed by editorial staff and senior editors. *Folio* is 80 pages, digest size, with matte cover with graphic art. Receives about 1,000 poems/year, accepts about 25. Press run is 400; 50-60 distributed free to the American University community and contributors. Single copy: $6; subscription: $12/year. Make checks payable to *Folio* at American University. Reads submissions September 1-March 1.

NEEDS "Visit our website and read the journal for more information. We look for work that ignites and endures, is artful and natural, daring and elegant." Length: up to 5,000 words.

HOW TO CONTACT Submit via online submission form at https://foliolitjournal.submittable.com/submit. "Cover letters must contain all of the following: brief bio, e-mail address, snail mail address, phone number, and title(s) of work enclosed. SASE required for notification only; mss are not returned."

PAYMENT/TERMS Pays 2 contributor's copies.

FOURTEEN HILLS

Department of Creative Writing, San Francisco State University, 1600 Holloway Ave., San Francisco, CA 94132-1722. **E-mail:** hills@sfsu.edu. **Website:** www.14hills.net. Estab. 1994. "*Fourteen Hills* publishes the highest quality innovative fiction and poetry for a literary audience." Editors change each year.

Magazine: 6" × 9"; 200 pages; 60 lb. paper; 10-point C15 cover. Receives 300 unsolicited mss/month. Accepts 8-10 mss/issue; 16-20 mss/year. Does not usually read mss during the summer. Publishes ms 2-4 months after acceptance. Recently published work by Susan Straight, Yiyun Li, Alice LaPlante, Terese Svoboda, Peter Rock, Stephen Dixon, and Adam Johnson.

NEEDS "Innovative fiction and poetry for a literary audience." Publishes short shorts. Also publishes literary essays, flash fiction, creative nonfiction, poetry, and art.

HOW TO CONTACT Always sends prepublication galleys. Send 1 prose ms, max of 25 pages; visual art, experimental, and cross-genre literature also accepted; see website for guidelines. Writers may submit once per submission period. The submission periods are: September 1-January 1 for inclusion in the spring issue (released in May); March 1-July 1 for inclusion in the winter issue (released in Dec.). Response times vary from 4-9 months, "depending on where your submission falls in the reading period, but we will usually respond within 5 months. Mss and artwork may be mailed and addressed to the proper genre editor, and *must* be accompanied by an SASE for notification, in addition to an e-mail and telephone contact. Due to the volume of submissions, mss cannot be returned, so please do not send any originals. We accept simultaneous submissions; however, be sure to notify us immediately by e-mail should you need to withdraw submissions due to publication elsewhere.

Note that we accept electronic submissions at this time via our website: www.14hills.net. However, we do not accept submissions by e-mail. Check website for changes in submission policies."

PAYMENT/TERMS Pays 2 contributor's copies.

TIPS "Please read an issue of *Fourteen Hills* before submitting."

FREEFALL MAGAZINE

Freefall Literary Society of Calgary, 922 Ninth Ave. SE, Calgary AB T2G 0S4 Canada. **E-mail:** freefallmagazine@yahoo.com. **Website:** www.freefallmagazine.ca. **Contact:** Lynn S. Fraser, managing editor. Estab. 1990. "Magazine published biannually containing fiction, poetry, creative nonfiction, essays on writing, interviews, and reviews. We are looking for exquisite writing with a strong narrative."

NEEDS Prose of all types. Length: no more than 4,000 words.

HOW TO CONTACT Submit via e-mail. E-mail subject line should include your name and type of submission (poetry, fiction, nonfiction, creative nonfiction, flash fiction, short fiction, photo, art work, etc.) Include name, contact information, description, title, and 50 word bio in body of e-mail. Attach submission titled with your name and submission title.

PAYMENT/TERMS Pays $10 per printed page in the magazine, to a maximum of $100 and 1 contributor's copy.

TIPS "Our mission is to encourage the voices of new, emerging, and experienced Canadian writers and provide a platform for their quality work. Although we accept work from all over the world we maintain a commitment to 85% Canadian content."

FREE FLASH FICTION

E-mail: editor@freeflashfiction.com. **Website:** www.freeflashfiction.com. **Contact:** Jean Martin, managing editor. Estab. 2012. Literary online magazine. "*Free Flash Fiction* accepts flash fiction pieces that are between 200 and 1,000 words. We accept all genres. Our focus is on quality over previous publishing credits."

NEEDS "Even though flash fiction is short, it should still have a setting, character(s), plot, conflict, and resolution. We don't want to see anything that reads like a book report, blog post, or summary of a longer story." Length: minimum 200 words; maximum of 1,000.

TIPS "Read all guidelines and submit all fiction via our online form."

⊙◐ FREEXPRESSION

P.O. Box 4, West Hoxton NSW 2171 Australia. **E-mail:** editor@freexpression.com.au. **Website:** www.free xpression.com.au. **Contact:** Peter F. Pike, managing editor. Estab. 1993. *FreeXpresSion*, published monthly, contains "creative writing, how-to articles, short stories, and poetry including cinquain, haiku, etc., and bush verse."

Has published poetry by Ron Stevens, Ellis Campbell, John Ryan, and Ken Dean. *FreeXpresSion* is 28 pages, magazine size, offset printed, saddle stapled, with paper cover. Receives about 2,500 poems/year, accepts about 30%. Subscription: $15 AUS/3 months, $25 AUS/6 months, $42 AUS/1 year. *FreeXpresSion* also publishes books up to 200 pages **through subsidy arrangements with authors**. Some poems published throughout the year are used in *Yearbooks* (annual anthologies).

NEEDS Open to all forms. "Christian themes okay. Humorous material welcome. No gratuitous sex; bad language okay. We don't want to see anything degrading."

HOW TO CONTACT Submit prose via e-mail.

⊙◐ THE FROGMORE PAPERS

21 Mildmay Rd., Lewes, East Sussex BN7 1PJ England. **Website:** www.frogmorepress.co.uk. **Contact:** Jeremy Page, editor. Estab. 1983. *The Frogmore Papers*, published semiannually, is a literary magazine with emphasis on new poetry and short stories.

Has published poetry by Marita Over, Brian Aldiss, Carole Satyamurti, John Mole, Linda France, and Tobias Hill. *The Frogmore Papers* is 46 pages, photocopied in photo-reduced typescript, saddle stapled, with matte card cover. Accepts 2% of poetry received. Press run is 500. Subscription: £10/1 year (2 issues); £15/2 years (4 issues).

NEEDS Length: no more than 2,000 words. "Quality is generally the only criterion, although pressure of space means very long work (over 100 lines) is unlikely to be published."

◐◑ FRONT & CENTRE

573 Gainsborough Ave., Ottawa ON K2A 2Y6 Canada. (613)729-8973. **E-mail:** firth@istar.ca. **Website:** www .blackbilepress.com. **Contact:** Matthew Firth, editor. Estab. 1998.

Magazine: half letter-size; 40-50 pages; illustrations; photos. Receives 20 unsolicited mss/ month. Accepts 6-7 mss/issue; 10-20 mss/year. Publishes ms 6 months after acceptance. Always comments on rejected mss. Agented fiction 10%. **Publishes 8-9 new writers/year.** Recently published work by Len Gasparini, Katharine Coldiron, Salvatore Difalco, Gerald Locklin, Amanda Earl, Tom Johns. Three issues per year. Circ. 500.

NEEDS Literary (contemporary realism/gritty urban). "No science fiction, horror, mainstream, romance or religious. We look for new fiction from Canadian and international writers—bold, aggressive work that does not compromise quality." Publishes short shorts. Length: 50-4,000 words; average length: 2,500 words. Reviews fiction.

HOW TO CONTACT Send SASE (from Canada) (or IRCs from USA) for return of ms or send a disposable copy of ms with #10 SASE for reply only. Responds in 2 weeks to queries; 4 months to mss. Accepts multiple submissions. Sample copy for $5. Writer's guidelines for SASE or by e-mail.

PAYMENT/TERMS Acquires first rights. Not copyrighted.

TIPS "We look for attention to detail, unique voice, not overtly derivative, bold writing, not pretentious. We should like to see more realism. Read the magazine first—simple as that!"

①②③ FUGUE LITERARY MAGAZINE

200 Brink Hall, University of Idaho, P.O. Box 44110, Moscow, ID 83844. **E-mail:** fugue@uidaho.edu. **Website:** www.fuguejournal.org. **Contact:** Alexandra Teague, faculty advisor. Estab. 1990.

Work published in *Fugue* has won the Pushcart Prize and has been cited in *Best American Essays*. Biannual literary magazine. See website for submission instructions.

HOW TO CONTACT "Submissions are accepted online only. Poetry, nonfiction, and experiment submissions are accepted September 1 through May 1. Fiction Submissions are accepted September 1 to April 1. All material received outside of this period will not be read. Please send no more than 2 short shorts or one story at a time. Submissions in more than one genre should be submitted separately. We will consider simultaneous submissions (submissions that have been sent concurrently to another journal), but we will not consider multiple submissions. All multiple submissions will be returned unread. Once you have submitted a piece to us, wait for a response on this piece before submitting again." Submit using online submissions manager.

PAYMENT/TERMS All contributors receive payment and 2 complimentary copies of the journal.

TIPS "The best way, of course, to determine what we're looking for is to read the journal. As the name *Fugue* indicates, our goal is to present a wide range of literary perspectives. We like stories that satisfy us both intellectually and emotionally, with fresh language and characters so captivating that they stick with us and invite a second reading. We are also seeking creative literary criticism which illuminates a piece of literature or a specific writer by examining that writer's personal experience."

FUNNY TIMES

Funny Times, Inc., P.O. Box 18530, Cleveland Heights, OH 44118. (216)371-8600. **Fax:** (216)371-8696. **E-mail:** info@funnytimes.com. **Website:** www.funny times.com. **Contact:** Ray Lesser and Susan Wolpert, editors. Estab. 1985. "*Funny Times* is a monthly review of America's funniest cartoonists and writers. We are the *Reader's Digest* of modern American humor with a progressive/peace-oriented/environmental/politically activist slant."

NEEDS Wants anything funny. Length: 500-700 words.

HOW TO CONTACT Query with published clips.

PAYMENT/TERMS Pays $50-150.

TIPS "Send us a small packet (1-3 items) of only your very funniest stuff. If this makes us laugh, we'll be glad to ask for more. We particularly welcome previously published material that has been well received elsewhere."

✚ GARBANZO LITERARY JOURNAL

Seraphemera Books, 211 Greenwood Ave., Suite 224, Bethel, CT 06801. **E-mail:** storyteller@garbanzolit eraryjournal.org. **Website:** www.garbanzoliterary journal.org. **Contact:** Marc Moorash and Ava Dawn Heydt, co-editors. Estab. 2010. Limited edition hand-made book and iBookstore. "We are calling out to all who have placed word on page (and even those who still carry all their works in the mind). Stories of up to 1,172 words, poems of up to 43 lines, micro-fiction, macro-fiction, limericks, villanelles, cinquains, couplets, couplings, creative nonfiction, noncreative fictions ... and whatever form your moving, thoughtful, memorable tale wishes to take (which means disregard the rules, punk rock style). In our specific instance, there is always a light that shines through these works, always a redemption that happens in the end. We're whimsical and full of light, even though some of the subject matter and form is dark. If your work is full of sarcasm and cynicism, if your cover letter is full of the same, we're probably not a good fit to work with each other. We somewhat consider each issue of *Garbanzo* to be a moment in infinite space when a group of mostly disparate people wind up in the same room due to some strange space/time glitch. We're not all going to agree on everything, and we probably wouldn't all get along, but we're not going to waste that moment together in complaint ... we're going to celebrate each picking up a feather and causing this massive bird to fly ..."

NEEDS Length: 1-29,318 words.

HOW TO CONTACT Submit complete ms.

PAYMENT/TERMS Pays copies.

TIPS "Read our website and the various suggestions therein. We're not much for rules—so surprise us. In that same regard, if you send us certain things it will be immediately obvious that you are sending to us another long list and haven't bothered to learn about us. Those who pay attention to detail are far more interesting to work with—as we're very interactive with our published authors. We want people who want to work and play with our style of publishing, as much as we want good writing."

GARBLED TRANSMISSIONS MAGAZINE

5813 NW 20th St., Margate, FL 33063. **E-mail:** james robertpayne@yahoo.com. **E-mail:** editor@gar bledtransmission.com. **Website:** www.garbledtrans mission.com. **Contact:** James Payne, editor-in-chief. Estab. 2011. Daily online literary magazine featuring fiction and book, movie, and comic book reviews.

NEEDS "Stories should have a dark/strange/twisted slant to them and should be original ideas, or have such a twist to them that they redefine the genre. We like authors with an original voice. That being said, we like Stephen King, Richard Matheson, Neil Gaiman, A. Lee Martinez, Chuck Palahniuk, Clive Barker. Movies and TV shows that inspire us include *Lost*, *The Matrix*, *Fight Club*, *3:10 to Yuma*, *Dark City*, *The Sixth Sense*, *The X-Files*, and *Super 8*." No romance.

HOW TO CONTACT Send complete ms.

PAYMENT/TERMS Pays 1 contributor's copy. "We currently do not offer monetary payment, though we plan to in the future if all goes well. This is a labor of love, and although we currently do not pay, we expect nothing but your best."

TIPS "The best way to see what we like is to visit our website and read some of the stories we've published to get a taste of what style we seek."

GARGOYLE

Paycock Press, 3819 N. 13th St., Arlington, VA 22201. (703)525-9296. **E-mail:** hedgehog2@erols.com. **Website:** www.gargoylemagazine.com. **Contact:** Richard Peabody, editor, Lucinda Ebersole, co-editor. Estab. 1976. "*Gargoyle Magazine* has always been a scallywag magazine, a maverick magazine, a bit too academic for the underground and way too underground for the academics. We are a writer's magazine in that we are read by other writers and have never worried about reaching the masses."

Receives 50-200 unsolicited mss/month. Accepts 10-15 mss/issue. Accepts submissions during June, July, and August. Agented fiction 5%. **Publishes 2-3 new writers/year**. Sometimes comments on rejected mss Recently published work by Stephanie Allen, Tom Carson, Michael Casey, Kim Chinquee, Susan Cokal, Ramola D., Janice Eidus, Thaisa Frank, James Grady, Colette Inez, Susan Smith Nash, Zena Polin, Wena Poon, Pilar Quintana, Kris Saknussem, Tomaz Salamun, Lynda Sexson, Elisabeth Sheffield, Barry Silesky, Curtis Smith, Patricia Smith, Marilyn Stablein, Ronald Wallace. Annual.

NEEDS "Edgy realism or experimental works. We run both." Wants to see more Canadian, British, Australian, and Third World fiction. No romance, horror, science fiction. Length: 1,000-4,500 words, 30 pages maximum; average length: 5-10 pages. Publishes short shorts. Also publishes literary essays, literary criticism, poetry.

HOW TO CONTACT Query in an e-mail. "We prefer electronic submissions. Please use submission engine online." For snail mail, send SASE for reply, return of ms or send a disposable copy of ms.

TIPS "We have to fall in love with a particular fiction."

GATEWAY

Missouri History Museum, P.O. Box 11940, St. Louis, MO 63112. (314)746-4558. **Fax:** (314)746-4548. E-

mail: vwmonks@mohistory.org. **Website:** www.mohistory.org. **Contact:** Victoria Monks, editor. Estab. 1980. "*Gateway* is a popular cultural history magazine that is primarily a member benefit of the Missouri History Museum. Thus, we have a general audience with an interest in the history and culture of Missouri, and St. Louis in particular."

TIPS "You'll get our attention with queries reflecting new perspectives on historical and cultural topics."

GEORGETOWN REVIEW

Box 227, 400 East College St., Georgetown, KY 40324. (502)863-8308. **Fax:** (502)868-8888. **E-mail:** gtownreview@georgetowncollege.edu. **Website:** http://georgetownreview.georgetowncollege.edu. **Contact:** Steven Carter, editor. Estab. 1993. *Georgetown Review*, published annually in May, is a literary journal of poetry, fiction, and creative nonfiction.

Georgetown Review is 192 pages, digest size, offset printed, perfect-bound, with 60 lb. glossy 4-color cover with art/graphics, includes ads. Press run is 1,000. Single copy: $7. Make checks payable to *Georgetown Review*. Member CLMP. Receives 100-125 mss/month. Sometimes comments on/critiques rejected mss. Accepts 8-10 mss/issue; 15-20/year. Does not read January 1-August 31. Manuscript published 1 month-2 years after acceptance. No agented fiction. **Publishes 3-4 new writers/year.** Published Andrew Plattner, Sallie Bingham, Alison Stine.

NEEDS "We publish the best fiction we receive, regardless of theme or genre." Also publishes literary essays, poetry, short shorts. "Sponsors annual contest with $1,000 prize. Check website for guidelines." Does not want adventure, children's, fantasy, romance. Does not want "work that is merely sentimental, political, or inspirational." Average length: 4,000 words. Average length of short shorts: 500-1,500 words.

HOW TO CONTACT Send complete ms with cover letter. Include brief bio, list of publications.

PAYMENT/TERMS Writers receive 2 contributor's copies, free subscription to the magazine. Additional copies for $5.

TIPS "We look for fiction that is well written and that has a story line that keeps our interest. Don't send a first draft, and even if we don't take your first, second, or third submission, keep trying."

THE GEORGIA REVIEW

The University of Georgia, Athens, GA 30602. (706)542-3481. **Fax:** (706)542-0047. **E-mail:** garev@uga.edu. **Website:** www.uga.edu/garev. **Contact:** Stephen Corey, editor. Estab. 1947. "Our readers are educated, inquisitive people who read a lot of work in the areas we feature, so they expect only the best in our pages. All work submitted should show evidence that the writer is at least as well-educated and well-read as our readers. Essays should be authoritative but accessible to a range of readers."

NEEDS "We seek original, excellent writing not bound by type." "Ordinarily we do not publish novel excerpts or works translated into English, and we strongly discourage authors from submitting these."

HOW TO CONTACT Send complete ms. "We do not consider unsolicited manuscripts between May 15 and August 15. Submissions received during that period will be returned unread. Work previously published in any form or submitted simultaneously to other journals will not be considered." No simultaneous or electronic submissions.

PAYMENT/TERMS Pays $50/published page.

TIPS "Check website for submission guidelines."

THE GETTYSBURG REVIEW

Gettysburg College, Gettysburg, PA 17325. (717)337-6770. **Fax:** (717)337-6775. **Website:** www.gettysburgreview.com. **Contact:** Peter Stitt, editor. Estab. 1988. "Our concern is quality. Manuscripts submitted here should be extremely well written. Reading period September-May."

NEEDS High-quality, literary. "We require that fiction be intelligent and aesthetically written." Length: 2,000-7,000 words.

HOW TO CONTACT Send complete ms with SASE.

PAYMENT/TERMS Pays $30 per page.

GINOSKO

P.O. Box 246, Fairfax, CA 94978. **E-mail:** ginoskoeditor@aol.com.**Website:** www.ginoskoliteraryjournal.com. **Contact:** Robert Paul Cesaretti, editor. Estab. 2003. "*Ginosko* (ghin-océ-koe): To perceive, understand, realize, come to know; knowledge that has an inception, a progress, an attainment. The recognition of truth by experience."

○ Reads year-round. Length of articles flexible; accepts excerpts. Semiannual ezine. Check downloadable issues on website for tone and style. Downloads free; accepts donations. Also looking for books, art, and music to post on website, and links to exchange. Member CLMP.

NEEDS Accepting short fiction and poetry, creative nonfiction, interviews, social justice concerns, and spiritual insights for www.GinoskoLiteraryJournal.com.

PAYMENT/TERMS *Ginosko* Short Fiction Contest: Deadline is May 1; $12 entry fee; $500 prize.

GLIMMER TRAIN STORIES

Glimmer Train Press, Inc., P.O. Box 80430, Portland, OR 97280. **Fax:** (503)221-0837. **E-mail:** eds@glimmertrain.org. **Website:** www.glimmertrain.org. Estab. 1991.

○ Receives 4,000 unsolicited mss/month. Accepts 10 mss/issue; 40 mss/year. Agented fiction 5%. Publishes 20 new writers/year. Recently published work by Charles Baxter, Thisbe Nissen, Herman Carrillo, Andre Dubus III, William Trevor, Patricia Henley, Alberto Rios, Ann Beattie, Yiyun Li.

NEEDS "We are interested in literary short stories, particularly by new and lightly published writers." Length: 1,200-12,000 words.

HOW TO CONTACT Submit via the website. "In a pinch, send a hard copy and include SASE for response."

PAYMENT/TERMS Pays $700 for standard submissions, up to $2,500 for contest-winning stories.

TIPS "Make submissions using the online submission procedure on website. Saves paper, time, and allows you to track your submissions. See our contest listings in contest and awards section."

GOOD OLD DAYS

Annie's, 306 E. Parr Rd., Berne, IN 46711. **Fax:** (260)589-8093. **E-mail:** editor@goodolddaysmagazine.com. **Website:** www.goodolddaysmagazine.com. **Contact:** Mary Beth Weisenburger, editor.

NEEDS "We look for strong narratives showing life as it was in the middle decades of the 20th century. Our readership is composed of nostalgia buffs, history enthusiasts, and the people who actually lived and grew up in this era."

○ Queries accepted, but are not necessary.

TIPS "Most of our writers are not professionals. We prefer the author's individual voice, warmth, humor, and honesty over technical ability."

⊙⊙$ GRAIN

P.O. Box 67, Saskatoon SK S7K 3K1 Canada. (306)244-2828. **Fax:** (306)244-0255. **E-mail:** grainmag@sasktel.net. **Website:** www.grainmagazine.ca. **Contact:** Rilla Friesen, editor. Estab. 1973. "*Grain, The Journal Of Eclectic Writing*, is a literary quarterly that publishes engaging, diverse, and challenging writing and art by some of the best Canadian and international writers and artists. Every issue features superb new writing from both developing and established writers. Each issue also highlights the unique artwork of a different visual artist. *Grain* has garnered national and international recognition for its distinctive, cutting-edge content and design."

○ *Grain* is 112-128 pages, digest size, professionally printed. Press run is 1,100. Receives about 3,000 submissions/year. Subscription: $35 CAD/year, $55 CAD for 2 years. Sample: $13 CAD. (See website for U.S. and foreign postage fees.) Has published poetry by Lorna Crozier, Don Domanski, Cornelia Haeussler, Patrick Lane, Karen Solie, and Monty Reid.

NEEDS No romance, confession, science fiction, vignettes, mystery. Length: 5,000/words max; "stories at the longer end of the word count must be of exceptional quality."

HOW TO CONTACT "Submissions must be typed in readable font (ideally 12 point, Times Roman or Courier), free of typos, printed on 1 side only. No staples. Your name and address must be on every page. Pieces of more than 1 page must be numbered. Cover letter with all contact information, title(s), and genre of work is required."

TIPS "Submissions read September-May only. Mss postmarked between June 1 and August 31 will not be read. Only work of the highest literary quality is accepted. Read several back issues."

⊙ GRASSLIMB

P.O. Box 420816, San Diego, CA 92142. **E-mail:** editor@grasslimb.com. **Website:** www.grasslimb.com. **Contact:** Valerie Polichar, editor. Estab. 2002. "*Grasslimb* publishes literary prose, poetry, and art. Fiction is best when it is short and avant-garde or otherwise experimental."

○ Magazine: 14" × 20"; 8 pages; 60 lb. white paper; illustrations. Accepts 2-4 mss/issue; 4-8 mss/year. Publishes ms 3-6 months after acceptance. Publishes 4 new writers/year. Has pub-

lished work by Kuzhali Manickavel, Amanda Lyell. Semiannual.

NEEDS Publishes short shorts. Reviews fiction. Does not want romance or religious writings. Length: 500-2,000 words; average length: 1,500 words.

HOW TO CONTACT Send complete ms. Send SASE for return of ms or disposable copy of ms and #10 SASE for reply only. Accepts simultaneous and reprints, multiple submissions.

PAYMENT/TERMS Writers receive $10 minimum; $70 maximum, and 2 contributor's copies; additional copies $3.

TIPS "We publish brief fiction that can be read in a single sitting over a cup of coffee. Work is generally literary in nature, rather than mainstream. Experimental work welcome. Remember to have your work proofread and to send short work. We cannot read over 2,500 and prefer under 2,000 words. Include word count."

⊙ GREEN HILLS LITERARY LANTERN

McClain Hall, Truman State University, Kirksville, MO 63501. (660)785-4513. **E-mail:** jbeneven@truman.edu. **Website:** http://ll.truman.edu/ghllweb/. **Contact:** Joe Benevento, poetry editor. Estab. 1990. "The mission of *GHLL* is to provide a literary market for quality fiction writers, both established and beginners, and to provide quality literature for readers from diverse backgrounds. We also see ourselves as a cultural resource for North Missouri. Our publication works to publish the highest quality fiction—dense, layered, subtle—and, at the same time, fiction which grabs the ordinary reader. We tend to publish traditional short stories, but we are open to experimental forms."

○ Receives 40 unsolicited mss/month. Annual. The *GHLL* is now an online, open-access journal.

NEEDS "Our main requirement is literary merit. We wants more quality fiction about rural culture." No adventure, crime, erotica, horror, inspirational, mystery/suspense, romance. Length: 7,000 words; average length: 3,000 words. Also publishes short shorts.

GREEN MOUNTAINS REVIEW

Johnson State College, 337 College Hill, Johnson, VT 05656. (802)635.1350. **E-mail:** gmr@jsc.vsc.edu; Jacob.White@jsc.edu. **Website:** http://greenmountainsreview.com/. **Contact:** Elizabeth Powell, poetry editor; Jacob White, fiction editor. The editors are open to a wide rane of styles and subject matter.

○ "Manuscripts received between March 1 and September 1 will not be read and will be returned." Sometimes comments on rejected mss. Recently published work by Tracy Daugherty, Terese Svoboda, Walter Wetherell, T.M. McNally, J. Robert Lennon, Louis B. Jones, and Tom Whalen.

NEEDS Adventure, experimental, humor/satire, literary, mainstream, serialized novels, translations. Publishes short shorts. Also publishes literary criticism, poetry. Length: 1,000-7,500 words.

PAYMENT/TERMS Pays contributor's copies, 1-year subscription and small honorarium, depending on grants.

TIPS "We encourage you to order some of our back issues to acquaint yourself with what has been accepted in the past. Unsolicited mss are read from September 1 to March 1."

○ ○ THE GREENSBORO REVIEW

MFA Writing Program, 3302 HHRA Building, UNC-Greensboro, Greensboro, NC 27402. (336)334-5459. **E-mail:** jlclark@uncg.edu. **Website:** www.greensbororeview.org. **Contact:** Jim Clark, editor.

○ Stories for *the Greensboro Review* have been included in *Best American Short Stories, The O. Henry Awards Prize Stories, New Stories from The South* and *Pushcart Prize Anthology*. Does not accept e-mail submissions.

NEEDS Length: no more than 7,500 words.

HOW TO CONTACT Submit complete ms using online submission form or via postal mail. Include cover letter and estimated word count.

PAYMENT/TERMS Pays in contributor's copies.

TIPS "We want to see the best being written regardless of theme, subject or style."

THE GRIFFIN

Gwynedd-Mercy College, 1325 Sumneytown Pike, P.O. Box 901, Gwynedd Valley, PA 19437. (215)641-5518. **Fax:** (215)641-5552. **E-mail:** allego.d@gmc.edu. **Website:** www.gmc.edu/students/clubsorganizations/thegriffin.php. **Contact:** Dr. Donna M. Allegro, editor. Estab. 1999.

NEEDS All genres considered. Length: no more than 2,500 words.

HOW TO CONTACT Submit on disk with a hard copy or by e-mail. Include SASE and short bio.

TIPS "Looking for well-constructed works that explore universal qualities, respect for the individual and community, justice, and integrity. Check our description and criteria. Rewrite until you're sure every word counts. We publish the best work we find regardless of industry needs."

GUD MAGAZINE

Greatest Uncommon Denominator Publishing, P.O. Box 1537, Laconia, NH 03247. **E-mail:** editor@gudmagazine.com. **Website:** www.gudmagazine.com. Estab. 2006. L *"GUD Magazine* transcends and encompasses the audiences of both genre and literary fiction by featuring fiction, art, poetry, essays and reports, comics, and short drama."

NEEDS Length: up to 15,000 words.

HOW TO CONTACT Submit via online submissions manager.

PAYMENT/TERMS Pays $450.

TIPS "We publish work in any genre, plus artwork, factual articles, and interviews. We'll publish something as short as 20 words or as long as 15,000, as long as it grabs us. Be warned: We read a lot. We've seen it all before. We are not easy to impress. Is your work original? Does it have something to say? Read it again. If you genuinely believe it to be so, send it. We do accept simultaneous submissions, as well as multiple submissions, but read the guidelines first."

○ ○ GUERNICA MAGAZINE

112 W. 27th St., Suite 600, New York, NY 10001. **E-mail:** editors@guernicamag.com; art@guernicamag.com; publisher@guernicamag.com. **Website:** www.guernicamag.com. **Contact:** Erica Wright, poetry; Dan Eckstein, art/photography. Estab. 2005. *"Guernica* is called a 'great online literary magazine' by *Esquire. Guernica* contributors come from dozens of countries and write in nearly as many languages."

○ Received Caine Prize for African Writing, Best of the Net, cited by *Esquire* as a "great literary magazine." Accepts 26 mss/year. Has published Jesse Ball, Elizabeth Crane, Josh Weil, Justo Arroyo, Sergio Ramírez Mercado, Matthew Derby, E.C. Osondu (Winner of the 2009 Caine Prize for African Writing).

NEEDS Literary, preferably with an international approach. No genre fiction. Length: 700-2500 words.

HOW TO CONTACT Submit complete ms with cover letter, attn: Meakin Armstrong to fiction@guernicamag.com. In subject line (please follow this format exactly): "fiction submission." Include bio and list of previous publications.

TIPS "Please read the magazine first before submitting. Most stories that are rejected simply do not fit our approach. Submission guidelines available online."

GULF COAST: A JOURNAL OF LITERATURE AND FINE ARTS

University of Houston, Department of English, University of Houston, Houston, TX 77204-3013. (713)743-3223. **E-mail:** editors@gulfcoastmag.org. **Website:** www.gulfcoastmag.org. **Contact:** Zachary Martin, editor; Karyna McGlynn, managing editor; Michelle Oakes, Justine Post, Kimberly Bruss, poetry editors; Aja Gabel, D'Lynn Barham, Ashley Wurzbacher, fiction editors; Jameelah Lang, Beth Lyons, nonfiction editors. Estab. 1986.

Magazine: 7" × 9"; approximately 300 pages; stock paper, gloss cover; illustrations; photos. Receives 350 unsolicited mss/month. Accepts 6-8 mss/issue; 12-16 mss/year. Agented fiction: 5%. Publishes 2-8 new writers/year. Recently published work by Maggie Shipstead, Norman Dubie, Mary Biddinger, Bret Anthony Johnston, G.C. Waldrep, Clancy Martin, Steve Almond, Sam Lipsyte, Dean Young, Eula Biss, Sarah Manguso.

NEEDS "Please do not send multiple submissions; we will read only one submission per author at a given time, except in the case of our annual contests." No children's, genre, religious/inspirational. Publishes short shorts.

HOW TO CONTACT *Gulf Coast* reads general submissions, submitted by post or through the online submissions manager, September 1-March 1. Submissions e-mailed directly to the editors or postmarked March 1-September 1 will not be read or responded to. "Please visit our contest page for contest submission guidelines."

PAYMENT/TERMS Pays $150.

TIPS "Submit only previously unpublished works. Include a cover letter. Online submissions are strongly preferred. Stories or essays should be typed, double-spaced, and paginated with your name, address, and phone number on the first page, title on subsequent pages. Poems should have your name, address, and phone number on the first page of each." The Annual Gulf Coast Prizes awards publication and $1,500 each in poetry, fiction, and nonfiction; opens in January of each year. Honorable mentions in each category will

receive a $250 second prize. Postmark/online entry deadline: March 15 of each year. Winners and honorable mentions will be announced in May. **Entry fee:** $20 (includes 1-year subscription). Make checks payable to *Gulf Coast*. Guidelines available on website.

GULF STREAM MAGAZINE

English Department, FIU, Biscayne Bay Campus, 3000 NE 151 St., North Miami, FL 33181. **E-mail:** gulf streamfiu@yahoo.com. **Website:** www.gulfstream litmag.com. **Contact:** Jason Jones, editor. Estab. 1989. "*Gulf Stream Magazine* has been publishing emerging and established writers of exceptional fiction, nonfiction, and poetry since 1989. We also publish interviews and book reviews. Past contributors include Sherman Alexie, Steve Almond, Jan Beatty, Lee Martin, Robert Wrigley, Dennis Lehane, Liz Robbins, Stuart Dybek, David Kirby, Ann Hood, Ha Jin, B.H. Fairchild, Naomi Shihab Nye, F. Daniel Rzicznek, and Connie May Fowler. *Gulf Stream Magazine* is supported by the Creative Writing Program at Florida International University in Miami, Florida. Each year we publish 2 online issues."

NEEDS Does not want romance, historical, juvenile, or religious work.

PAYMENT/TERMS Pays contributor's copies.

TIPS "Looks for fresh, original writing—well plotted stories with unforgettable characters, fresh poetry, and experimental writing. Usually longer stories do not get accepted. There are exceptions, however."

THE G.W. REVIEW

The George Washington University, 800 21st St. NW, Marvin Center Box 20, Washington, DC 20052. (202)994-7779. **E-mail:** gwreview@gwu.edu. **Website:** http://thegwreview.weebly.com. **Contact:** Linda Cui, editor-in-chief. Estab. 1980. "*The G.W. Review* seeks to expose readers to new and emerging writers from both the United States and abroad. New, innovative writing—both in style and subject—is valued above the author's previous publishing history."

NEEDS "We do not publish genre fiction (i.e., romance, mystery, crime, etc.)." Length: 1,000-6,000 words.

HOW TO CONTACT Send complete ms. Publishes 6 mss/year.

TIPS "We enjoy work that is thought provoking and challenging in its subject matter and style."

HADASSAH MAGAZINE

50 W. 58th St., New York, NY 10019. (212)688-0227. **Fax:** (212)446-9521. **E-mail:** magazine@hadassah .org. **Website:** www.hadassah.org/magazine. **Contact:** Elizabeth Goldberg. Zelda Shluker, managing editor. Jewish general-interest magazine: 7" × 10½"; 64-80 pages; coated and uncoated paper; slick, medium weight coated cover; drawings and photos. "*Hadassah* is a general interest Jewish feature and literary magazine. We speak to our readers on a vast array of subjects ranging from politics to parenting, to midlife crisis to Mideast crisis. Our readers want coverage on social and economic issues, Jewish women's (feminist) issues, the arts, travel and health."

Receives 20-25 unsolicited mss/month. Publishes some new writers/year. Recently published work by Joanne Greenberg and Jennifer Traig. Short stories with strong plots and positive Jewish values. Bimonthly. Circ. 243,000.

NEEDS Ethnic/multicultural (Jewish). No personal memoirs, "schmaltzy" or shelter magazine fiction. Length: 1,500-2,000 words.

HOW TO CONTACT Must submit appropriate-sized SASE. Responds in 4 months to mss. Sample copy and writer's guidelines for 9" × 12" SASE. Stories can also be e-mailed to lbarnea@hadassah.org.

PAYMENT/TERMS Pays $700 minimum. Pays on acceptance for first North American serial, first rights. Pays $500 minimum

TIPS "Stories on a Jewish theme should be neither self-hating nor schmaltzy."

HAIGHT ASHBURY LITERARY JOURNAL

558 Joost Ave., San Francisco, CA 94127. (415)584-8264. **E-mail:** haljeditor@gmail.com. **Website:** http://haightashburyliteraryjournal.wordpress.com/; www .facebook.com/pages/Haight-Ashbury-Literary-Journal/365542018331. **Contact:** Alice Rogoff, Indigo Hotchkiss, Alice Rogoff, and Cesar Love, editors. Estab. 1979. *Haight Ashbury Literary Journal*, publishes "well-written poetry and fiction. HALJ's voices are often of people who have been marginalized, oppressed, or abused. HALJ strives to bring literary arts to the general public, to the San Francisco community of writers, to the Haight Ashbury neighborhood, and to people of varying ages, genders, ethnicities, and sexual preferences. *The Journal* is produced as a tabloid to maintain an accessible price for low-income people."

Haight Ashbury is 16 pages, includes ads. Includes fiction under 20 pages, 1 story/issue, and black-and-white drawings. Press run is 1,500. Subscription: $10/2 issues, $20/4 issues; $50 for a lifetime subscription. Sample: $4. Has published poetry by Dan O'Connell, Diane Frank, Dancing Bear, Lee Herrick, Al Young, and Laura Beausoleil.

HARDBOILED

Gryphon Publications, P.O. Box 209, Brooklyn, NY 11228. **Website:** www.gryphonbooks.com. Estab. 1988. "Hard-hitting crime fiction and private-eye stories—the newest and most cutting-edge work and classic reprints."

NEEDS "No pastiches, violence for the sake of violence." Length: 500-3,000 words.

HOW TO CONTACT Query or send complete ms.

PAYMENT/TERMS Pays $5-50.

TIPS "Your best bet for breaking in is short hard crime fiction filled with authenticity and brevity. Try a subscription to *Hardboiled* to get the perfect idea of what we are after."

HARPER'S MAGAZINE

666 Broadway, 11th Floor, New York, NY 10012. (212)420-5720. **Fax:** (212)228-5889. **E-mail:** readings@harpers.org. **Website:** www.harpers.org. Estab. 1850. "*Harper's Magazine* encourages national discussion on current and significant issues in a format that offers arresting facts and intelligent opinions. By means of its several shorter journalistic forms—Harper's Index, Readings, Forum, and Annotation—as well as with its acclaimed essays, fiction, and reporting, *Harper's* continues the tradition begun with its first issue in 1850: to inform readers across the whole spectrum of political, literary, cultural, and scientific affairs."

Magazine: 8" × 10¾"; 80 pages; illustrations. Monthly. Estab. 1850. Circ. 230,000. *Harper's Magazine* will neither consider nor return unsolicited nonfiction manuscripts that have not been preceded by a written query. Receives 50 unsolicited mss/month. Accepts 12 mss/year. Publishes ms 3 months after acceptance. **Publishes some new writers/year.** Recently published work by Rebecca Curtis, George Saunders, Haruki Murakami, Margaret Atwood, Allan Gurganus, Evan Connell, and Dave Bezmosgis. *Harper's* will consider unsolicited fiction. Unsolicited poetry will not be considered or returned. No queries or manuscripts will be considered unless they are accompanied by a SASE. All submissions and written queries (with the exception of Readings submissions) must be sent by mail to above address.

NEEDS Humor/satire. Stories on contemporary life and its problems. Length: 3,000-5,000 words.

HOW TO CONTACT Query by mail, except for submissions to the Readings section, which can be submitted via readings@harpers.org. Responds in 3 months to queries. Accepts reprints submissions. SASE required for all unsolicited material. Sample copy for $6.95.

PAYMENT/TERMS Generally pays 50¢-$1/word. Pays on acceptance. Vary with author and material. Sends galleys to author.

TIPS "Some readers expect their magazines to clothe them with opinions in the way that Bloomingdale's dresses them for the opera. The readers of *Harper's Magazine* belong to a different crowd. They strike me as the kind of people who would rather think in their own voices and come to their own conclusions."

HARPUR PALATE

English Department, P.O. Box 6000, Binghamton University, Binghamton, NY 13902-6000. **E-mail:** harpur.palate@gmail.com. **Website:** http://harpur palate.blogspot.com. **Contact:** Sara Erdmann and Jennie Case, editors. Estab. 2000. *Harpur Palate*, published biannually, is "dedicated to publishing the best poetry and prose, regardless of style, form, or genre. We have no restrictions on subject matter or form. Quite simply, send us your highest-quality fiction and poetry."

Ọ Magazine: 6" × 9"; 180-200 pages; coated or uncoated paper; 100 lb. coated cover; 4-color art portfolio insert. Receives 400 unsolicited mss/month. Accepts 5-10 mss/issue; 12-20 mss/year. Publishes ms 1-2 months after acceptance. Publishes 5 new writers/year. Has published work by Darryl Crawford and Tim Hedges, Jesse Goolsby, Ivan Faute, and Keith Meatto. Single copy: $10; subscription: $16/year (2 issues). Sample: $5. Make checks payable to *Harpur Palate*.

NEEDS Length: 250-8,000 words. Average length: 2,000-4,000 words.

HOW TO CONTACT Send complete ms with a cover letter. Include e-mail address on cover. Include estimated word count, brief bio, list of publications. Send a disposable copy of ms and #10 SASE for reply only. No more than 1 submission per envelope. Submission periods are July 15-November 15 for the winter issue, and December 15-April 15 for summer.

PAYMENT/TERMS Pays 2 contributor copies.

TIPS "*Harpur Palate* now accepts submissions all year; deadline for Winter issue is November 15, for Summer issue is April 15. We also sponsor a fiction contest for the Summer issue and a poetry and non-fiction contest for the Winter issue. We do not accept submissions via e-mail. We are interested in high quality writing of all genres, but especially literary poetry and fiction."

HARVARD REVIEW

Houghton Library of the Harvard College Library, Lamont Library, Harvard University, Cambridge, MA 02138. (617)495-9775. **Fax:** (617)496-3692. **E-mail:** info@harvard.edu. **Website:** www.hcl.harvard.edu/harvardreview/. Estab. 1992. "Previous contributors include John Updike, Alice Hoffman, Joyce Carol Oates, Miranda July, Jim Crace. We also publish the work of emerging and previously unpublished writers."

Ọ Does not accept e-mail submissions.

NEEDS Length: 7,000 words.

HOW TO CONTACT Submit using online submissions manager or by mail.

TIPS "There is no reading period. Include a cover letter citing recent publications or awards and SASE. Mss must be paginated and labeled with author's name on every page. Do not submit more than twice a year. We accept e-mail submissions through http://www.tellitslant.com."

HAWAII REVIEW

University of Hawaii Board of Publications, 2445 Campus Rd., Hemenway Hall 107, Honolulu, HI 96822. (808)956-3030. **Fax:** (808)956-3083. **E-mail:** hawaiireview@gmail.com. **Website:** www.kaleo.org/hawaii_review. Estab. 1973.

Ọ Offers yearly award with $500 prizes in poetry and fiction.

HOW TO CONTACT Send complete ms.

TIPS "Make it new."

🅞🎧💲 HAYDEN'S FERRY REVIEW

c/o Virginia G. Piper Center for Creative Writing, Arizona State University, P.O. Box 875002, Tempe, AZ 85287. (480)965-1337. **E-mail:** HFR@asu.edu. **Website:** www.haydensferryreview.org. **Contact:** Beth Staples, managing editor. Estab. 1986. *"Hayden's Ferry Review* publishes the best quality fiction, poetry, and creative nonfiction from new, emerging, and established writers."

🔾   Work from *Hayden's Ferry Review* has been selected for inclusion in *Pushcart Prize* anthologies and *Best Creative Nonfiction.*

NEEDS Word length open.

HOW TO CONTACT Send complete ms.

➕ HELLOHORROR

6609 Lindy Lane, Houston, TX 77023. **E-mail:** info@hellohorror.com. **Website:** www.hellohorror.com. **Contact:** Brent Armour, editor-in-chief. Estab. 2012. *"HelloHorror* is a recently created online literary magazine and blog. We are currently in search of literary pieces, photography, and visual art, including film from writers and artists that have a special knack for inducing goose bumps and raised hairs. This genre has become, especially in film, noticeably saturated in gore and high shock- value aspects as a crutch to avoid the true challenge of bringing about real, psychological fear to an audience that's persistently more and more numb to its tactics. While we are not opposed to the extreme, blood and guts need bones and cartilage. Otherwise it's just a sloppy mess."

NEEDS "We don't want fiction that can in no way be classified as horror. Some types of dark science fiction are acceptable, depending on the story."

HOW TO CONTACT Submit complete ms.

TIPS "We like authors that show consideration for their readers. A great horror story leaves an impression on the reader long after it is finished. The motivation behind creating the site was the current saturation of gore and shock value horror. A story that gives you goose bumps is a much greater achievement than a story that just grosses you out. We have television for that. Consider your reader and consider yourself. What really scares you as opposed to what's stereotypically supposed to scare you? Bring us and our readers into that place of fear with you."

HIGHLIGHTS FOR CHILDREN

803 Church St., Honesdale, PA 18431. (570)253-1080. **Fax:** (570)251-7847. **Website:** www.highlights.com.

Contact: Christine French Cully, editor-in-chief; Drew Hires, art director. Estab. 1946. "This book of wholesome fun is dedicated to helping children grow in basic skills and knowledge, in creativeness, in ability to think and reason, in sensitivity to others, in high ideals, and worthy ways of living—for children are the world's most important people. We publish stories for beginning and advanced readers. Up to 500 words for beginners (ages 3-7), up to 800 words for advanced (ages 8-12)."

NEEDS Meaningful stories appealing to both girls and boys, up to age 12. Vivid, full of action. Engaging plot, strong characterization, lively language. Prefers stories in which a child protagonist solves a dilemma through his or her own resources. Seeks stories that the child ages 8-12 will eagerly read, and the child ages 2-7 will like to hear when read aloud (500-800 words). Stories require interesting plots and a number of illustration possiblities. Also need rebuses (picture stories 120 words or under), stories with urban settings, stories for beginning readers (100-500 words), sports and humorous stories, adventures, holiday stories, and mysteries. We also would like to see more material of 1-page length (300 words), both fiction and factual. No war, crime, or violence.

HOW TO CONTACT Send complete ms.

PAYMENT/TERMS Pays $100 minimum plus 2 contributor's copies.

TIPS "Know the magazine's style before submitting. Send for guidelines and sample issue if necessary." Writers: "At *Highlights* we're paying closer attention to acquiring more nonfiction for young readers than we have in the past." Illustrators: "Fresh, imaginative work encouraged. Flexibility in working relationships a plus. Illustrators presenting their work need not confine themselves to just children's illustrations as long as work can translate to our needs. We also use animal illustrations, real and imaginary. We need crafts, puzzles, and any activity that will stimulate children mentally and creatively. We are always looking for imaginative cover subjects. Know our publication's standards and content by reading sample issues, not just the guidelines. Avoid tired themes, or put a fresh twist on an old theme so that its style is fun and lively. We'd like to see stories with subtle messages, but the fun of the story should come first. Write what inspires you, not what you think the market needs. We are pleased that many authors of children's literature report that their first published work was in the pages of *Highlights*. It is not our policy to consider fiction on the strength of the reputation of the author. We judge each submission on its own merits. With factual material, however, we do prefer that writers be authorities in their field or people with firsthand experience. In this manner we can avoid the encyclopedic article that merely restates information readily available elsewhere. We don't make assignments. Query with simple letter to establish whether the nonfiction subject is likely to be of interest. A beginning writer should first become familiar with the type of material that *Highlights* publishes. Include special qualifications, if any, of author. Write for the child, not the editor. Write in a voice that children understand and relate to. Speak to today's kids, avoiding didactic, overt messages. Even though our general principles haven't changed over the years, we are contemporary in our approach to issues. Avoid worn themes."

ALFRED HITCHCOCK'S MYSTERY MAGAZINE

Dell Magazines, 267 Broadway, 4th Floor, New York, NY 10007. (212)686-7188. **E-mail:** alfredhitchcockmm@dellmagazines.com. **Website:** www.themysteryplace.com/ahmm. Estab. 1956.

NEEDS "Original and well-written mystery and crime fiction. Because this is a mystery magazine, the stories we buy must fall into that genre in some sense or another. We are interested in nearly every kind of mystery: stories of detection of the classic kind, police procedurals, private eye tales, suspense, courtroom dramas, stories of espionage, and so on. We ask only that the story be about crime (or the threat or fear of one). We sometimes accept ghost stories or supernatural tales, but those also should involve a crime." No sensationalism. Length: up to 12,000 words.

HOW TO CONTACT Send complete ms.

PAYMENT/TERMS Payment varies.

TIPS "No simultaneous submissions, please. Submissions sent to *Alfred Hitchcock's Mystery Magazine* are not considered for or read by *Ellery Queen's Mystery Magazine*, and vice versa."

HOBART

P.O. Box 1658, Ann Arbor, MI 48103. **E-mail:** aaron@hobartpulp.com. **Website:** www.hobartpulp.com. "We tend to like quirky stories like truck driving, mathematics, and vagabonding. We like stories with humor (humorous but engaging, literary but not

stuffy). We want to get excited about your story and hope you'll send your best work."

◑ All submissions must go through our online submissions manager.

NEEDS "We publish nonstuffy, unpretentious, high-quality fiction that never takes itself too serious and always entertains." Length: 1,000-7,000 words.

HOW TO CONTACT Send complete ms with cover letter.

TIPS "We'd love to receive fewer run-of-the-mill relationship stories and more stories concerning truck drivers, lumberjacks, carnival workers, and gunslingers. In other words: Surprise us. Show us a side of life rarely depicted in literary fiction."

◐◑ HOME PLANET NEWS

P.O. Box 455, High Falls, NY 12440. (845)687-4084. **E-mail:** homeplanetnews@yahoo.com. **Website:** www.homeplanetnews.org. **Contact:** Donald Lev, editor. Estab. 1979. "*Home Planet News* publishes mainly poetry along with some fiction, as well as reviews (books, theater, and art) and articles of literary interest. We see *HPN* as a quality literary journal in an eminently readable format and with content that is urban, urbane, and politically aware."

◑ *HPN* has received a small grant from the Puffin Foundation for its focus on AIDS issues. Tabloid: 11½" × 16"; 24 pages; newsprint; illustrations; photos. Receives 12 unsolicited mss/month. Accepts 1 mss/issue; 3 mss/year. Has published work by Hugh Fox, Walter Jackman, Jim Story. Triannual.

NEEDS No children's or genre stories (except rarely some science fiction). Length: 500-2,500 words; average length: 2,000 words.

HOW TO CONTACT Send complete ms. Send SASE for reply, return of ms, or send a disposable copy of the ms. Publishes special fiction issue or anthology.

PAYMENT/TERMS Pays 3 contributor's copies; additional copies $1.

TIPS "We use very little fiction, and a story we accept just has to grab us. We need short pieces of some complexity, stories about complex people facing situations which resist simple resolutions."

◐ HOMESTEAD REVIEW

Box A-5, 156 Homestead Ave., Hartnell College, Salinas, CA 93901. (831)755-6943. **Website:** www.hartnell.edu/homestead_review. Estab. 1985. *Homestead Review*, published annually in April, seeks "avant-garde poetry as well as fixed-form styles of remarkable quality and originality."

○ Manuscripts are read by the staff and discussed. Poems/fiction accepted by majority consensus. Has published poetry by Sally Van Doren, Kathryn Kirkpatrick, Laura Le Hew, Allison Joseph, and Hal Sirowitz. Receives about 1,000 poems/year, accepts about 15%. Press run is 500 (300 subscribers/libraries); 200 are distributed free to poets, writers, bookstores. Single copy: $10; subscription: $10/year. Make checks payable to *Homestead Review*.

NEEDS Does not want "Hallmark-style writing or first drafts." Considers poetry written by children and teens.

HORIZONS

100 Witherspoon St., Louisville, KY 40202-1396. (502)569-5897. **Fax:** (502)569-8085. **E-mail:** yvonne .hileman@pcusa.org. **Website:** www.pcusa.org/ho rizons/. **Contact:** Yvonne Hileman, assistant editor. Estab. 1988. "Magazine owned and operated by Presbyterian women offering information and inspiration for Presbyterian women by addressing current issues facing the church and the world."

NEEDS Length: 600-1,800 words.

HOW TO CONTACT Send complete ms by mail, e-mail, or fax. Include contact information.

PAYMENT/TERMS Pays "an honorarium of no less than $50 per page printed in the magazine—amount will vary depending on time and research required for writing the article."

THE HUDSON REVIEW

The Hudson Review, Inc., 684 Park Ave., New York, NY 10065. **E-mail:** info@hudsonreview.com. **Website:** www.hudsonreview.com. **Contact:** Paula Deitz, editor. Estab. 1948.

NEEDS Reads between September 1 and November 30 only. Length: up to 10,000 words.

HOW TO CONTACT Send ms with SASE. Mss sent outside accepted reading period will be returned unread if SASE contains sufficient postage. "We do not consider simultaneous submissions. Unsolicited manuscripts submitted outside of specified reading times will be returned unread. Do not send submissions via e-mail."

TIPS "We do not specialize in publishing any particular 'type' of writing; our sole criterion for accepting unsolicited work is literary quality. The best way for

you to get an idea of the range of work we publish is to read a current issue.

❶⑤ HUNGER MOUNTAIN

Vermont College of Fine Arts, 36 College St., Montpelier, VT 05602. (802)828-8517. **E-mail:** hungermtn@ vcfa.edu. **Website:** www.hungermtn.org. Estab. 2002. Accepts high quality work from unknown, emerging, or successful writers.

○ *Hunger Mountain* is about 200 pages, 7" × 10", professionally printed, perfect-bound, with full-bleed color artwork on cover. Press run is 1,000; 10,000 visits online monthly. Single copy: $10; subscription: $12/year, $22/2 years. Make checks payable to Vermont College of Fine Arts. Member: CLMP.

NEEDS "We look for work that is beautifully crafted and tells a good story, with characters that are alive and kicking, story lines that stay with us long after we've finished reading, and sentences that slay us with their precision." No genre fiction, meaning science fiction, fantasy, horror, erotic, etc. Length: no more than 10,000 words.

HOW TO CONTACT Submit ms using online submissions manager. "Mss must be typed, prose double-spaced. Poets submit at least 3 poems. No multiple genre submissions."

PAYMENT/TERMS Pays $25-100.

TIPS "Fresh viewpoints and human interest are very important, as is originality. We are committed to publishing an outstanding journal of the arts. Do not send entire novels, mss, or short story collections. Do not send previously published work."

❶⑤ HUNGUR MAGAZINE

P.O. Box 782, Cedar Rapids, IA 52406-0782. **E-mail:** hungurmagazine@yahoo.com. **Website:** www.sams dotpublishing.com. **Contact:** Terrie Leigh Relf, editor. Estab. 2004. *Hungur Magazine*, published biannually, features "stories and poems about vampires, and especially about vampires on other worlds." Prefers a "decadent literary style."

○ *Hungur Magazine* is 32 pages, magazine size, offset printed, saddle stapled, with paper cover with color art, includes ads. Press run is 100/issue. Subscription: $13/year. $23/2 years. Make checks payable to Tyree Campbell/Sam's Dot Publishing. Member: The Speculative Literature Foundation (http://SpeculativeLiterature. org).

NEEDS Length: 2,500-6,000 words. Flash fiction: 1,000 words maximum.

HOW TO CONTACT No simultaneous submissions. Accepts e-mail submissions (pasted into body of message); no disk submissions. Reads submissions year-round.

PAYMENT/TERMS Pays $12 for stories; $4 for flash fiction.

●●⑤ THE IDAHO REVIEW

Department of English, Boise State University, 1910 University Dr., Boise, ID 83725. (208)426-1002. **Fax:** (208)426-4373. **E-mail:** idahoreview@boisestate.edu; mwieland@boisestate.edu. **Website:** http://idahoreview.org. **Contact:** Mitch Wieland, editor. Estab. 1998.

○ Recent stories reprinted in *The Best American Short Stories, The O. Henry Prize Stories, Pushcart Prize* anthology, and *New Stories from the South.*

NEEDS No genre fiction of any type.

HOW TO CONTACT Prefers submissions using online submissions manager but will accept submissions by postal mail.

PAYMENT/TERMS Pays in contributor's copies.

TIPS "We look for strongly crafted work that tells a story that needs to be told. We demand vision and intlligence and mystery in the fiction we publish."

IDEAGEMS

IdeaGems Publications, P.O. Box 4748, Portland, ME 04112. (202)746-5160. **E-mail:** ideagems@aol.com. **Website:** www.ideagems.com. **Contact:** Laurie Notch, managing editor. Estab. 2005. "Bimonthly magazine with 2 tracks: *IdeaGems Magazine*, with seasonal/holiday themes, and *Tough Lit*, devoted to crime/mystery, edge, fantasy, and sci-fi. Both issues seek short fiction, flash fiction, essay, anecdotal memoir, poetry, photography, artwork, and illustrations."

NEEDS "We accept pretty much anything in the way of fiction, nonfiction, poetry, photography, and artwork. We reserve the right to refuse to publish material that we deem unsuitable for our publication. We are open to any work of imagination and whimsy where women play central roles. We love stories that tackle issues; however, we do not invite stories with strong religions overtones, racial/gender prejudice, or political bents for the purposes of zealous expostulating. We are not able to review any full-length novels or graphic novels at this time, but you can always send a query and a sample chapter for us to consider running

as serialized material." Length: Flash fiction: 100-500 words. Article: 500-2,500 words. Novel excerpt: up to 3 chapters. Short story: 1,000-3,000 words.

HOW TO CONTACT "We ask all writers to format their submissions accordingly: Electronic formats, please! If you send us a print copy, we have to retype it in its entirety, which is quite labor intensive for us. Please use single-space lines with a paragraph indentation of no more than 4 spaces. Use font size Calibri 10, if possible (but not critical). All digital photography, authors' head shots, and scanned artwork should be sized at a minimum of 200 dpi. 300 dpi is preferred."

PAYMENT/TERMS "Due to economic downturn and radical reduction in sales, we are sad to say that we cannot pay for accepted work. However, we do our very best to give writers the platform they need in print, electronic, and online formats to showcase their work and get publishing credentials."

TIPS "As is true with any publication, check us out online and/or order a sample issue to understand the nature of our material. Check out our contests, and above all, be patient."

●●⑤ IDEOMANCER

Canada. **E-mail:** publisher@ideomancer.com. **Website:** www.ideomancer.com. **Contact:** Leah Bobet, publisher. Estab. 2001. "*Ideomancer* publishes speculative fiction and poetry that explores the edges of ideas; stories that subvert, refute, and push the limits. We want unique pieces from authors willing to explore nontraditional narratives and take chances with tone, structure, and execution, balance ideas and character, emotion, and ruthlessness. We also have an eye for more traditional tales told with excellence."

○ Quarterly online magazine. Contains illustrations. Receives 160 mss/month. Accepts 3 mss/issue; 9-12 mss/year. Does not read February, May, August, and November. Ms published within 12 months of acceptance. **Publishes 1-2 new writers/year.** Published Sarah Monette, Ruth Nestvold, Christopher Barzak, Nicole Kornher-Stace, Tobias Buckell, Yoon Ha Lee, and David Kopaska-Merkel.

NEEDS Also publishes book reviews, poetry. *Requests only* to have a novel or collection reviewed should be sent to the publisher. Does not want fiction without a speculative element. Length: 7,000 words (max). Average length: 4,000 words. Publishes short shorts. Average length of short shorts: 1,000 words.

HOW TO CONTACT Send complete ms with cover letter. Accepts submissions by e-mail only. Include estimated word count.

PAYMENT/TERMS Writers receive 3¢ per word, maximum of $40.

TIPS "Beyond the basics of formatting the fiction as per our guidelines, good writing and intriguing characters and plot, where the writer brings depth to the tale, make a ms stand out. We receive a number of submissions which showcase good writing, but lack the details that make them spring to life for us. Visit our website and read some of our fiction to see if we're a good fit. Read our submission guidelines carefully and use .rtf formatting as requested. We're far more interested in your story than your cover letter, so spend your time polishing that."

◒◯ IDIOM 23

Central Queensland University, Idiom 23 Literary Magazine, Rockhampton QLD 4702 Australia. **E-mail:** idiom@cqu.edu.au; l.hawryluk@cqu.edu .au. **Website:** www.cqu.edu.au/faculties/faculty-of-arts,-business,-informatics-and-education/schools/humanities-and-communication/idiom-23-literary-magazine. **Contact:** *Idiom 23* editorial board. Estab. 1988. *Idiom 23*, published annually, is "named for the Tropic of Capricorn and is dedicated to developing the literary arts throughout the Central Queensland region."

NEEDS "Submissions of original short stories, poems, articles, and black-and-white drawings and photographs are welcomed by the editorial collective."

TIPS "*Idiom 23* is not limited to a particular viewpoint but, on the contrary, hopes to encourage and publish a broad spectrum of writing. The collective seeks out creative work from community groups with as varied backgrounds as possible."

◑ ILLUMINATIONS

Dept. of English, College of Charleston, 26 Gleb St., Charleston, SC 29424. (843)953-4972. **E-mail:** scottcopsesm@cofc.edu. **Website:** www.cofc.edu/il luminations. **Contact:** Meg Scott-Copses, editor. Estab. 1982.

HOW TO CONTACT Send SASE for reply, return of ms or send a disposable copy of ms.

PAYMENT/TERMS Pays 2 contributor's copies of current issue; 1 of subsequent issue.

◑◉ IMAGE

3307 Third Ave. W., Seattle, WA 98119. (206)281-2988. **Fax:** (206)281-2979. **E-mail:** image@imagejournal .org. **Website:** www.imagejournal.org. **Contact:** Gregory Wolfe, publisher/editor. Estab. 1989. "*Image* is a unique forum for the best writing and artwork that is informed by—or grapples with—religious faith. We have never been interested in art that merely regurgitates dogma or falls back on easy answers or didacticism. Instead, our focus has been on writing and visual artwork that embody a spiritual struggle, that seek to strike a balance between tradition and a profound openness to the world. Each issue explores this relationship through outstanding fiction, poetry, painting, sculpture, architecture, film, music, interviews, and dance. *Image* also features 4-color reproductions of visual art."

◔ Magazine: 7" × 10"; 136 pages; glossy cover stock; illustrations; photos.

NEEDS "No sentimental, preachy, moralistic, obvious stories, or genre stories (unless they manage to transcend their genre)." Length: 4,000-6,000 words.

HOW TO CONTACT Send complete ms. Does not accept e-mail submissions.

PAYMENT/TERMS Pays $10/page ($150 maximum) and 4 contributor's copies.

TIPS "Fiction must grapple with religious faith, though subjects need not be overtly religious."

◑◔◉ INDIANA REVIEW

Ballantine Hall 465, 1020 E. Kirkwood, Indiana University, Bloomington, IN 47405. (812)855-3439. **E-mail:** inreview@indiana.edu. **Website:** www.indi ana.edu/~inreview. **Contact:** Jennifer Luebbers, editor. Estab. 1976. "*Indiana Review*, a nonprofit organization run by IU graduate students, is a journal of previously unpublished poetry and fiction. Literary interviews and essays are also considered. We publish innovative fiction, nonfiction, and poetry. We're interested in energy, originality, and careful attention to craft. While we publish many well-known writers, we also welcome new and emerging poets and fiction writers."

NEEDS "We look for daring stories that integrate theme, language, character, and form. We like polished writing, humor, and fiction that has consequence beyond the world of its narrator." No genre fiction. Length: 250-10,000 words.

HOW TO CONTACT Send complete ms. Cover letters should be *brief* and demonstrate specific familiarity with the content of a recent issue of *Indiana Review*. Include SASE.

PAYMENT/TERMS Pays $5/page ($10 minimum), plus 2 contributor's copies

TIPS "We're always looking for nonfiction essays that go beyond merely autobiographical revelation and utilize sophisticated organization and slightly radical narrative strategies. We want essays that are both lyrical and analytical where confession does not mean nostalgia. Read us before you submit. Often reading is slower in summer and holiday months. Submit work to journals you would proudly subscribe to, then subscribe to a few. Take care to read the latest 2 issues and specifically mention work you identify with and why. Submit work that 'stacks up' with the work we've published. Offers annual poetry, fiction, short-short/prose-poem prizes. See website for full guidelines."

INTERPRETER'S HOUSE

9 Glenhurst Rd., Mannamead, Plymouth PL3 5LT England. **Website:** www.interpretershouse.org.uk. **Contact:** Simon Curtis, editor. Estab. 1996. *Interpreter's House*, published 3 times/year in February, June, and October, prints short stories and poetry. Wants "good poetry, not too long." Does not want "Christmas-card verse or incomprehensible poetry." Has published poetry by Dannie Abse, Tony Curtis, Pauline Stainer, Alan Brownjohn, Peter Redgrove, and R.S. Thomas. *Interpreter's House* is 74 pages, A5, with attractive cover design. Receives about 1,000 poems/year, accepts up to 5%. Press run is 300 (200 subscribers). Single copy: £3 plus 55p. postage; subscription: £12 for 3 issues. Sample: £3.50.

NEEDS Length: no more than 2,000 words.

HOW TO CONTACT Submit up to 5 short stories.

THE IOWA REVIEW

308 EPB, The University of Iowa, Iowa City, IA 52242. (319)335-0462. **Website:** www.iowareview.org. **Contact:** Russell Scott Valentino, editor. Estab. 1970. *The Iowa Review*, published 3 times/year, prints fiction, poetry, essays, reviews, and, occasionally, interviews. *The Iowa Review* is 5½" × 8½", approximately 200 pages, professionally printed, flat spined, first-grade offset paper, Carolina CS1 10-point cover stock. Receives about 5,000 submissions/year, accepts up to 100. Press run is 2,900; 1,500 distributed to stores. Subscription: $25. Stories, essays, and poems for a general readership interested in contemporary literature.

"This magazine uses the help of colleagues and graduate assistants. Its reading period for unsolicited work is September 1-December 1. From January through April, we read entries to our annual Iowa Awards competition. Check our website for further information." Receives 600 unsolicited mss/month. Accepts 4-6 mss/issue; 12-18 mss/year. Does not read mss January-August. Publishes ms an average of 12-18 months after acceptance. Agented fiction less than 2%. **Publishes some new writers/year.** Recently published work by Bradley Bazzle, Chris Offutt, Alison Ruch.

NEEDS "We are open to a range of styles and voices and always hope to be surprised by work we then feel we need."

HOW TO CONTACT Send complete ms with cover letter. "Don't bother with queries." SASE for return of ms. SASE required. Responds in 4 months to mss. Accepts mss by snail mail and online submission form at https://iowareview.submittable.com/submit; no e-mail submissions. Simultaneous submissions accepted.

PAYMENT/TERMS Pays $.08 per word ($100 minimum), plus 2 contributor's copies.

TIPS "We publish essays, reviews, novel excerpts, stories, poems, and photography. We have no set guidelines as to content or length, but strongly recommend that writers read a sample issue before submitting. Buys 65-80 unsolicited ms/year. Submit complete ms with SASE."

IRREANTUM

The Association for Mormon Letters, P.O. Box 1315, Salt Lake City, UT 84110-1315. **E-mail:** editor@aml pubs.org. **Website:** www.irreantum.org. Estab. 1999. "While focused on Mormonism, *Irreantum* is a cultural, humanities-oriented magazine, not a religious magazine. Our guiding principle is that Mormonism is grounded in a sufficiently unusual, cohesive, and extended historical and cultural experience that it has become like a nation, an ethnic culture. We can speak of Mormon literature at least as surely as we can of a Jewish or Southern literature. *Irreantum* publishes stories, one-act dramas, stand-alone novel and drama excerpts, and poetry by, for, or about Mormons (as well as author interviews, essays, and reviews). The journal's audience includes readers of any or no religious faith who are interested in literary exploration of the Mormon culture, mind-set, and worldview through Mormon themes and characters either directly or by implication. *Irreantum* is currently the only magazine devoted to Mormon literature."

NEEDS Wants "high-quality work that explores the Mormon experience, directly or by implication, through literature. We acknowledge a broad range of experience with Mormonism, both as a faith and as a culture—on the part of devoted multigeneration Mormons, ethnic Mormons, new converts, and people outside the faith and culture who interact with Mormons and Mormon culture. We are committed to respectful exploration of Mormonism through literature." Length: 1,000-5,000 words. Also publishes short shorts, literary essays, literary criticism, and poetry.

PAYMENT/TERMS Pays $0-100.

TIPS "*Irreantum* is not interested in didactic or polemical fiction that primarily attempts to prove or disprove Mormon doctrine, history, or corporate policy. We encourage beginning writers to focus on human elements first, with Mormon elements introduced only as natural and organic to the story. Readers can tell if you are honestly trying to explore human experience or if you are writing with a propagandistic agenda either for or against Mormonism. For conservative, orthodox Mormon writers, beware of sentimentalism, simplistic resolutions, and foregone conclusions."

ISLAND

P.O. Box 210, Sandy Bay Tasmania 7006 Australia. (61)(3)6226-2325. **E-mail:** island.magazine@utas.edu.au. **Website:** www.islandmag.com. "*Island* seeks quality fiction, poetry, essays, and articles. A literary magazine with an environmental heart."

NEEDS Length: up to 2,500 words.

PAYMENT/TERMS Pays $150 (Australian).

JABBERWOCK REVIEW

Department of English, Mississippi State University, Drawer E, Mississippi State, MS 39762. **E-mail:** jabberwockreview@english.msstate.edu. **Website:** www.msstate.edu/org/jabberwock. **Contact:** Michael Kardos, editor. Estab. 1979.

Submissions will be accepted from August 15-October 20 and January 15-March 15.

NEEDS No science fiction, romance.

HOW TO CONTACT Submit complete ms with SASE and cover letter. Submit no more than 1 story at a time.

PAYMENT/TERMS Pays in contributor's copies.

TIPS "It might take a few months to get a response from us, but your manuscript will be read with care. Our editors enjoy reading submissions (really!) and will remember writers who are persistent and commited to getting a story 'right' through revision."

JACK AND JILL

U.S. Kids, 1100 Waterway Blvd., Indianapolis, IN 46206-0567. (317)634-1100. **E-mail:** editor@saturdayeveningpost.com. **Website:** www.jackandjillmag.org. Estab. 1938.

"Please do not send artwork. We prefer to work with professional illustrators of our own choosing."

NEEDS Length: 600-800 words.

HOW TO CONTACT Submit complete ms. Queries not accepted.

PAYMENT/TERMS Pays 30¢/word.

TIPS "We are constantly looking for new writers who can tell good stories with interesting slants—stories that are not full of outdated and timeworn expressions. We like to see stories about kids who are smart and capable, but not sarcastic or smug. Problem-solving skills, personal responsibility, and integrity are good topics for us. Obtain current issues of the magazine and study them to determine our present needs and editorial style."

JEWISH CURRENTS

P.O. Box 111, Accord NY 12404. (845)626-2427. **E-mail:** editor@jewishcurrents.org. **Website:** www.jewishcurrents.org. **Contact:** Lawrence Bush, editor. Estab. 1946. "*Jewish Currents*, published 4 times/year, is a progressive Jewish bimonthly magazine that carries on the insurgent tradition of the Jewish left through independent journalism, political commentary, and a 'countercultural' approach to Jewish arts and literature."

Jewish Currents is 48 pages, magazine size, offset printed, saddle stapled with a full-color arts section, "Jcultcha & Funny Pages." Press run is 700. Subscription: $25/year.

HOW TO CONTACT Send complete ms with cover letter. "Writers should include brief biographical information, especially their publishing histories."

PAYMENT/TERMS Pays contributor's copies.

⦿ J JOURNAL: NEW WRITING ON JUSTICE

524 West 59th St., 7th Floor, New York, NY 10019. (212) 327-8697. **E-mail:** jjournal@jjay.cuny.edu. **Website:** www.jjournal.org. **Contact:** Adam Berlin and Jeffrey Heiman, editors. Estab. 2008. "*J Journal* publishes literary fiction, creative nonfiction, and poetry on the subjects of crime, criminal justice, law and law enforcement. While the themes are specific, they need not dominate the work. We're interested in questions of justice from all perspectives."

○ Literary magazine/journal: 6" × 9"; 120 pages; 60 lb paper; 80 lb cover. Receives 100 mss/month. Accepts 20 mss/issue; 40 mss/year. Ms published 6 months after acceptance.

NEEDS Length: 750-6,000 words (max). Average length: 4,000 words.

HOW TO CONTACT Send complete ms with cover letter. Include estimated word count, brief bio, list of publications. Considers simultaneous submissions.

PAYMENT/TERMS Writers receive 2 contributor's copies. Additional copies $10.

TIPS "We're looking for literary fiction/memoir/personal narrative poetry with a connection, direct or tangential, to the theme of justice."

⦿❸ THE JOURNAL

The Ohio State University, 164 W. 17th Ave., Columbus, OH 43210. (614)292-4076. **Fax:** (614)292-7816. **E-mail:** managingeditor@thejournalmag.org. **Website:** http://thejournalmag.org. Estab. 1973. "We're open to all forms; we tend to favor work that gives evidence of a mature and sophisticated sense of the language."

○

NEEDS "We are interested in quality fiction, poetry, nonfiction, art, and reviews of new books of poetry, fiction, and nonfiction. We impose no restrictions on category, type, or length of submission for fiction, poetry, and nonfiction. We are happy to consider long stories and self-contained excerpts of novels. No romance, science fiction, or religious/devotional."

HOW TO CONTACT Does not accept queries. Send full ms via online submission system at http://the journal.submittable.com. "Please double-space all prose submissions. Please send 3-6 poems in 1 submission. We only accept online submissions and will not respond to mailed submissions."

PAYMENT/TERMS Pays 2 contributor's copies and 1-year subscription.

TIPS "Mss are rejected because of lack of understanding of the short story form, shallow plots, undeveloped characters. Cure: Read as much well-written fiction as possible. Our readers prefer 'psychological' fiction rather than stories with intricate plots. Take care to present a clean, well-typed submission."

⦿ KAIMANA: LITERARY ARTS HAWAI'I

Hawai'i Literary Arts Council, P.O. Box 11213, Honolulu, HI 96828. **E-mail:** reimersa001@hawaii.rr.com. **Website:** www.hawaii.edu/hlac. Estab. 1974. *Kaimana: Literary Arts Hawai'i*, published annually, is the magazine of the Hawai'i Literary Arts Council.

○ *Kaimana* is 64-76 pages, 7½ × 10", saddle stapled, with high-quality printing. Press run is 1,000. Subscription: $15, includes membership in HLAC. Sample: $10. Has published poetry by Kathryn Takara, Howard Nemerov, Anne Waldman, Reuel Denney, Haunani-Kay Trask, and Simon Perchik.

NEEDS Wants poems with "some Pacific reference—Asia, Polynesia, Hawai'i—but not exclusively."

TIPS "Poets published in Kaimana have received the Pushcart Prize, the Hawaii Award for Literature, the Stefan Baciu Award, the Cades Award, and the John Unterecker Award."

⦿◉❸ KALEIDOSCOPE

Kaleidoscope Press, 701 S. Main St., Akron, OH 44311-1019. (330)762-9755. **Fax:** (330)762-0912. **E-mail:** kaleidoscope@udsakron.org. **Website:** www.udsakron.org/services/kaleidoscope/index.asp. **Contact:** Gail Willmott, editor-in-chief. Estab. 1979. "*Kaleidoscope* magazine creatively focuses on the experiences of disability through literature and the fine arts. Unique to the field of disability studies, this award-winning publication expresses the experiences of disability from the perspective of individuals, families, health-care professionals, and society as a whole."

○ *Kaleidoscope* has received awards from the American Heart Association, the Great Lakes Awards Competition, and Ohio Public Images.

NEEDS Short stories with a well-crafted plot and engaging characters. No fiction that is stereotypical, patronizing, sentimental, erotic, or maudlin. No romance, religious, or dogmatic fiction; no children's literature. Length: no more than 5,000 words.

HOW TO CONTACT Submit complete ms by mail or e-mail. Include cover letter.

PAYMENT/TERMS Pays $10-125, plus 2 contributor's copies.

TIPS "The material chosen for *Kaleidoscope* challenges and overcomes stereotypical, patronizing, and sentimental attitudes about disability. We accept the work of writers with and without disabilities, however the work of a writer without a disability must focus on some aspect of disability. The criteria for good writing apply: effective technique, thought-provoking subject matter, and in general, a mature grasp of the art of story-telling. Writers should avoid using offensive language and always put the person before the disability."

●◉ KELSEY REVIEW

P.O. Box B, Liberal Arts Division, Trenton, NJ 08690. **E-mail:** kelsey.review@mccc.edu. **Website:** www.mccc.edu/community_kelsey-review.shtml. **Contact:** Ed Carmien. Estab. 1988. *Kelsey Review*, published annually in September by Mercer County Community College, serves as "an outlet for literary talent of people living and working in Mercer County, New Jersey only."

◐ *Kelsey Review* is about 90 glossy pages, 7" × 11", with paper cover. Receives 100+ submissions/year; accepts 10. Press run is 2,000; all distributed free to contributors, area libraries, bookstores, and schools. Black-and-white art. Has published poetry by Vida Chu, Carolyn Foote Edelmann, and Mary Mallery.

NEEDS Has no specifications as to form, subject matter, or style. Length: 5,000 word maximum.

HOW TO CONTACT Deadline is May 15. Submissions are limited to people who live, work, or give literary readings in Mercer County, New Jersey. Decisions on which material will be published are made by the 4-person editorial board in June and July. Contributors will be notified of submission acceptance determination(s) by the second week of August.

PAYMENT/TERMS Pays 3 contributor's copies.

TIPS "See the *Kelsey Review* website for current guidelines. Note: We only accept submissions from the Mercer County, New Jersey, area."

◉❸ KENTUCKY MONTHLY

P.O. Box 559, Frankfort, KY 40602-0559. (502)227-0053; (888)329-0053. **Fax:** (502)227-5009. **E-mail:** kymonthly@kentuckymonthly.com; steve@kentuckymonthly.com. **Website:** www.kentuckymonthly.com. **Contact:** Stephen Vest, editor. Estab. 1998. "We

publish stories about Kentucky and by Kentuckians, including stories written by those who live elsewhere."

NEEDS Adventure, historical, mainstream, novel excerpts. Publishes ms 3-5 months after acceptance. Length: 1,000-5,000 words.

HOW TO CONTACT Query with published clips. Accepts submissions by e-mail, fax. Responds in 3 weeks to queries; 1 month to mss. Accepts simultaneous submissions. Sample copy online. Writer's guidelines online. Query with published clips.

PAYMENT/TERMS Pays $50-100. Pays within 3 months of publication. Acquires first North American serial rights. Pays $50-100.

TIPS "Please read the magazine to get the flavor of what we're publishing each month. We accept articles via e-mail, fax, and mail."

❶❷❸ THE KENYON REVIEW

Finn House, 102 W. Wiggin, Gambier, OH 43022. (740)427-5208. **Fax:** (740)427-5417. **E-mail:** kenyonreview@kenyon.edu. **Website:** www.kenyonreview.org. **Contact:** Marlene Landefeld. Estab. 1939. "An international journal of literature, culture, and the arts, dedicated to an inclusive representation of the best in new writing (fiction, poetry, essays, interviews, criticism) from established and emerging writers."

◐ *The Kenyon Review* is 180 pages, digest size, and flat spined. Receives about 6,000 submissions/year. Also publishes *KR Online*, a separate and complementary literary magazine.

NEEDS Receives 900 unsolicited mss/month. Unsolicited mss read September 15-January 15 only. Recently published work by Alice Hoffman, Beth Ann Fennelly, Romulus Linney, John Koethe, Albert Goldbarth, Erin McGraw Length: 3-15 typeset pages preferred.

HOW TO CONTACT Only accepts mss via online submissions program; visit website for instructions. Do not submit via e-mail or snail mail.

PAYMENT/TERMS Pays $15-40/page.

TIPS "We no longer accept mailed or e-mailed submissions. Work will only be read if it is submitted through our online program on our website. Reading period is September 15-January 15. We look for strong voice, unusual perspective, and power in the writing."

◉ KEREM

Jewish Study Center Press, 3035 Porter St. NW, Washington, DC 20008. (202)364-3006. **E-mail:** langner@erols.com; kerem@simpatico.ca. **Website:** www.ker

em.org. **Contact:** Gilah Langner, co-editor; Sara R. Horowitz, co-editor. Estab. 1992.

NEEDS "*Kerem* publishes Jewish religious, creative, literary material—short stories, poetry, personal reflections, text study, prayers, rituals, etc."

HOW TO CONTACT Prefers submissions by e-mail.

PAYMENT/TERMS Pays one-year subscription and contributor's copies.

TIPS "Should have a strong Jewish content. We want to be moved by reading the manuscript!"

KRAX MAGAZINE

63 Dixon Lane, Leeds Yorkshire Br LS12 4RR United Kingdom. **Website:** http://editfast.com/english/writers_resources/magazines/Krax-93.htm. "*Krax* publishes lighthearted, humorous, and whimsical writing. It is for anyone seeking light relief at a gentle pace. Our audience has grown middle-aged along with us, especially now that we're annual and not able to provide the instant fix demanded by teens and twenties. Contemporary lighthearted poetry from Britain, America, and elsewhere. Currently over 68 pages of anything but stodgy poetry, short fiction, and glowingly brilliant graphics. Usually there is an interview with a writer of interest and a sizeable review section covering a vast range of related books, magazines, pamphlets, audio tape, and CDs."

NEEDS "No war stories, horror, space bandits, boy-girl soap opera."

HOW TO CONTACT Cover letter appreciated.

TIPS "Look at what you enjoy in all forms of fiction—from strip cartoons to novels, movies to music lyrics—then try to put some of this into your own writing. Go for the idea first, then find the scenery to set it in. There are plenty of unreal worlds out there."

LADYBUG

Carus Publishing Co., 700 E. Lake St., Suite 300, Chicago, IL 60601. (312)701-1720. **Website:** www.cricketmag.com. **Contact:** Marianne Carus, editor-in-chief; Suzanne Beck, managing art director. Estab. 1990. *LADYBUG Magazine*, published monthly, is a reading and listening magazine for young children (ages 2-6). "We look for quality literature and nonfiction."

Subscription: $35.97/year (12 issues). sample: $5; sample pages available on website.

NEEDS Picture-oriented material: adventure, animal, fantasy, folktales, humorous, multicultural, nature/environment, problem solving, science fiction, sports,

suspense/mystery. "Open to any easy fiction stories." Buys 50 mss/year. Length: 800 words maximum.

HOW TO CONTACT Submit complete ms, include SASE.

PAYMENT/TERMS Pays 25¢/word minimum.

TIPS "Reread manuscript before sending. Keep within specified word limits. Study back issues before submitting to learn about the types of material we're looking for. Writing style is paramount. We look for rich, evocative language and a sense of joy or wonder. Remember that you're writing for preschoolers—be age appropriate but not condescending or preachy. A story must hold enjoyment for both parent and child through repeated read-aloud sessions. Remember that people come in all colors, sizes, physical conditions, and have special needs. Be inclusive!"

LADY CHURCHILL'S ROSEBUD WRISTLET

150 Pleasant St., #306, Easthampton, MA 01027. **E-mail:** smallbeerpress@gmail.com. **Website:** www.smallbeerpress.com/lcrw. **Contact:** Gavin Grant, editor. Estab. 1996. "We accept fiction, nonfiction, poetry, and black-and-white art. The fiction we publish most of tends toward but is not limited to the speculative. This does not mean only quietly desperate stories. We will consider items that fall out with regular categories. We do not accept multiple submissions. We read everything, sometimes slow, sometimes fast. Our apologies for reading so slowly. At the moment we are only reading paper submissions. If 6 months has passed and you contact us, we will try to reply with our decision. We occasionally solicit work, but most of what we publish is work that comes in over the transom and we are very happy that we have generally published a couple of new writers in each issue. We recommend you read *Lady Churchill's Rosebud Wristlet* before submitting. You can procure a copy from us or from assorted book shops."

Zine: half legal size; 60 pages; 60 lb. paper; glossy cover; illustrations; photos. Receives 100 unsolicited mss/month. Accepts 4-6 mss/issue; 8-12 mss/year. Publishes 2-4 new writers/year. Also publishes literary essays, poetry. Has published work by Ted Chiang, Gwenda Bond, Alissa Nutting, Charlie Anders. Semiannual.

NEEDS "We do not publish gore, sword and sorcery, or pornography. We can discuss these terms if you like. There are places for them all, this is not one of them." Length: 200-7,000 words; average length: 3,500 words.

HOW TO CONTACT Send complete ms with a cover letter. Include estimated word count. Send SASE (or IRC) for return of ms, or send a disposable copy of ms and #10 SASE for reply only.

PAYMENT/TERMS Pays 1¢/word, $20 minimum, and 2 contributor's copies; additional copies contributor's discount 40%.

TIPS "I like fiction that tends toward the speculative. We recommend at least 1 rewrite for both our sanities. Please follow standard ms format: 12-point Courier, double-spaced, numbered pages, and a SASE (with a Forever Stamp) for our reply."

● LA KANCERKLINIKO

162 rue Paradis, P.O. Box 174, 13444 Marseille Cantini Cedex France. (33)2-48-61-81-98. **Fax:** (33)2-48-61-81-98. **E-mail:** lseptier@hotmail.com. **Contact:** Laurent Septier. An Esperanto magazine which appears 4 times annually. Each issue contains 32 pages. *La Kancerkliniko* is a political and cultural magazine. Accepts disk submissions. Accepts multiple submissions.

○ **Publishes 2-3 new writers/year.** Has published work by Mao Zifu, Manuel de Seabra, Peter Brown. and Aldo de'Giorgi.

PAYMENT/TERMS Pays in contributor's copies.

● LAKE EFFECT: A JOURNAL OF THE LITERARY ARTS

School of Humanities & Social Sciences, Penn State Erie, 4951 College Dr., Erie, PA 16563-1501. (814)898-6281. **Fax:** (814)898-6032. **E-mail:** gol1@psu.edu. **Website:** www.pserie.psu.edu/lakeeffect. **Contact:** George Looney, editor-in-chief. Estab. 1978.

NEEDS "*Lake Effect* is looking for stories that emerge from character and language as much as from plot. *Lake Effect* does not, in general, publish genre fiction, but literary fiction. For stories of longer than 15 pages or so, query first. *Lake Effect* seeks work from both established and new and emerging writers."

HOW TO CONTACT Submit complete ms with SASE.

● LAKE SUPERIOR MAGAZINE

Lake Superior Port Cities, Inc., P.O. Box 16417, Duluth, MN 55816-0417. (218)722-5002. **Fax:** (218)722-4096. **E-mail:** edit@lakesuperior.com. **Website:** www.lakesuperior.com. **Contact:** Konnie LeMay, editor. Estab. 1979.

NEEDS Ethnic, historic, humorous, mainstream, novel excerpts, slice-of-life vignettes, ghost stories. Must be targeted regionally. Wants stories that are Lake Superior related. Rarely uses fiction stories. Length: 300-2,500 words.

HOW TO CONTACT Query with published clips.

PAYMENT/TERMS Pays $50-125.

TIPS "Well-researched queries are attended to. We actively seek queries from writers in Lake Superior communities. We prefer manuscripts to queries. Provide enough information on why the subject is important to the region and our readers, or why and how something is unique. We want details. The writer must have a thorough knowledge of the subject and how it relates to our region. We prefer a fresh, unused approach to the subject which provides the reader with an emotional involvement. Almost all of our articles feature quality photography, color or black and white. It is a prerequisite of all nonfiction. All submissions should include a *short* biography of author/photographer; mug shot sometimes used. Blanket submissions need not apply."

● LANDFALL: NEW ZEALAND ARTS AND LETTERS

Otago University Press, P.O. Box 56, Dunedin, New Zealand. (64)(3)479-8807. **Fax:** (64)(3)479-8385. **E-mail:** landfall@otago.ac.nz. **Website:** www.otago.ac.nz/press/landfall. **Contact:** Richard Reeve, co-ordinator. Estab. 1947. *Landfall: New Zealand Arts and Letters* contains literary fiction and essays, poetry, extracts from work in progress, commentary on New Zealand arts and culture, work by visual artists including photographers and reviews of local books. (*Landfall* does not accept unsolicited reviews.)

○ "*Landfall* is published 6 issues/year. Submissions may be made at any time and will be considered for the next issue. We send acceptance/rejection letters once all submissions have been considered and the issue's contents list has been completely finalized (this is usually the month before or of publication). Submissions will not be held over for future issues unless you have been contacted and agree to this."

NEEDS Length: no more than 5,000 words.

HOW TO CONTACT Prefers e-mail submissions. Submit no more than 3 pieces per issue. Include word length and cover letter.

TIPS "*Landfall* is open to work by New Zealand and Pacific writers, or by writers whose work has a connection to the region in subject matter or location. Work from Australian writers is occasionally included as a special feature. The editor is interested in new work that has not been published before. While many established names appear in *Landfall*'s pages, the editor and *Landfall*'s readers are always on the lookout for exciting work from new writers and artists. If you are a new writer, find copies of Landfall in bookshops and libraries to get a sense of what is published."

◐ LANGUAGEANDCULTURE.NET

4000 Pimlico Dr., Suite 114-192, Pleasanton, CA 94588. **E-mail:** review@languageandculture.net. **Website:** www.languageandculture.net. **Contact:** Liz Fortini, editor. Estab. 2001.

◐ LA PETITE ZINE

E-mail: lapetitezine@gmail.com. **Website:** www.la petitezine.org. **Contact:** Melissa Broder, chief editor; D.W. Lichtenberg, managing editor. Member: CLMP. *La Petite Zine*, an online literary magazine founded in 1999, which currently publishes fierce poetry and petite prose pieces of 1,000 words or less. LPZ is not affiliated with a particular literary school or movement; we like what we like. Above all else, LPZ seeks to be unboring, a panacea for your emotional hangover."

◖ Has published work by Anne Boyer, Arielle Greenberg, Johannes Goransson, Joyelle McSweeney, Joshua Marie Wilkinson, and Jonah Winter. Receives about 3,000 poems/year, accepts about 150 (5%). Sample: free online; there is no subscription, but readers are invited to sign up for e-mail notification of new issues at the submission address. *La Petite Zine*'s home page "indexes all authors for each specific issue and offers links to past issues, as well as information about the journal, its interests and editors, and links to other sites. Art and graphics are supplied by Web del Sol. Additionally, we publish graphic poems, excerpts from graphic novels, and the like." Work published in *La Petite Zine* has appeared in *The Best American Poetry*. "Any deviation from our guidelines will result in the disposal of your submission."

NEEDS Length: no more than 1,000 words.

HOW TO CONTACT Considers simultaneous submissions, "but please notify us immediately if poems are accepted elsewhere"; no previously published poems. Only accepts submissions using submission manager on website. Cover letter is required. Include brief bio listing previous publications. Wait 4 months before submitting again. Reads year-round.

◉ ⑤ LEADING EDGE

4087 JKB, Provo, UT 84602. **E-mail:** editor@leading edgemagazine.com; fiction@leadingedgemagazine.com; art@leadingedgemagazine.com. **Website:** www.leadingedgemagazine.com. **Contact:** Nyssa Silvester, senior editor. Estab. 1980. "We strive to encourage developing and established talent and provide high-quality speculative fiction to our readers. *Leading Edge* is a magazine dedicated to new and upcoming talent in the field of science fiction and fantasy."

◖ Accepts unsolicited submissions.

NEEDS Does not accept mss with sex, excessive violence, or profanity. Length: 15,000 words maximum.

HOW TO CONTACT Send complete ms with cover letter and SASE. Include estimated word count.

PAYMENT/TERMS Pays 1¢/word; $10 minimum.

TIPS "Buy a sample issue to know what is currently selling in our magazine. Also, make sure to follow the writer's guidelines when submitting."

◐ THE LEDGE MAGAZINE

40 Maple Ave., Bellport, NY 11713. (631)286-5252. **E-mail:** info@theledgemagazine.com. **Website:** www.theledgemagazine.com. **Contact:** Tim Monaghan, editor-in-chief and publisher. Estab. 1988. "*The Ledge Magazine* publishes cutting-edge contemporary fiction by emerging and established writers."

◖ Annual. Receives 120 mss/month. Accepts 9 mss/issue. Manuscript published 6 months after acceptance. Published Pia Chatterjee, Xujun Eberlein, Clifford Garstang, Richard Jespers, William Luvaas, Michael Thompson. Rarely comments on/critiques rejected mss. Sample copy available for $10. Subscription: $20 (2 issues), $36 (4 issues). Guidelines available for SASE.

NEEDS "We are open to all styles and schools of writing. Excellence is our only criterion." Length: 2,500-7,500 words. Also publishes poetry.

HOW TO CONTACT Send complete ms with cover letter. Submit complete ms with SASE. Include estimated word count, brief bio. Send SASE (or IRC) for return of ms. Does not accept e-mail submissions.

PAYMENT/TERMS Writers receive 1 contributor's copy. Additional copies $6. Sends galleys to author. Publication is copyrighted.

TIPS "We seek compelling stories that employ innovative language and complex characterization. We especially enjoy poignant stories with a sense of purpose. We dislike careless or hackneyed writing."

◐ LE FORUM

University of Maine, Franco American Center, Orono, ME 04469-5719. (207)581-3764. **Fax:** (207)581-1455. **E-mail:** lisa_michaud@umit.maine.edu. **Website:** Francoamericanarchives.org. **Contact:** Lisa Michaud, managing editor. Estab. 1972. "We will consider any type of short fiction, poetry, and critical essays having to do with Franco-American experience. They must be of good quality in French or English. We are also looking for Canadian writers with French-North American experiences."

HOW TO CONTACT Include SASE.

PAYMENT/TERMS Pays 3 contributor's copies.

TIPS "Write honestly. Start with a strongly felt personal Franco-American experience. If you make us feel what you have felt, we will publish it. We stress that this publication deals specifically with the Franco-American experience."

◐ LEFT CURVE

P.O. Box 472, Oakland, CA 94604-0472. (510)763-7193. **E-mail:** editor@leftcurve.org. **Website:** www .leftcurve.org. **Contact:** Csaba Polony, editor. Estab. 1974. "*Left Curve* is an artist-produced journal addressing the problem(s) of cultural forms emerging from the crises of modernity that strive to be independent from the control of dominant institutions, based on the recognition of the destructiveness of commodity (capitalist) systems to all life."

◌ Magazine: 8½" × 11"; 144 pages; 60 lb. paper; 100 pt. C1S gloss lay flat lamination cover; illustrations; photos. Receives 50 unsolicited mss/month. Accepts 3-4 mss/issue. Has published work by Mike Standaert, Ilan Pappe, Terrence Cannon, John Gist. Published irregularly.

NEEDS "No topical satire, religion-based pieces, melodrama. We publish critical, open, social/political-conscious writing." Length: 500-5,000 words; average length: 1,200 words. Also publishes short shorts.

HOW TO CONTACT Send complete ms with cover letter. Include "statement of writer's intent, brief bio, and reason for submitting to *Left Curve*. We accept

electronic submissions and hard copy, though for accepted work we request e-mail copy, either in body of text or as attachments. For accepted longer work, we prefer submission of final draft in digital form via disk or e-mail."

PAYMENT/TERMS Pays in contributor's copies.

TIPS "We look for continuity, adequate descriptive passages, endings that are not simply abandoned (in both meanings). Dig deep; no superficial personalisms, no corny satire. Be honest and realistic, and gouge out the truth you wish to reaveal. Understand yourself and the world. Let writing be a means to achieve or realize what is real."

LIGHTHOUSE DIGEST

Lighthouse Digest, P.O. Box 250, East Machias, ME 04630. (207)259-2121. **E-mail:** Editor@LighthouseDigest.com. **Website:** www.lighthousedigest.com. **Contact:** Tim Harrison, editor. Estab. 1989.

NEEDS 2,500 words maximum.

HOW TO CONTACT Send complete ms.

TIPS "Read our publication and visit the website."

○ ◐ ⑤ LIGUORIAN

One Liguori Dr., Liguori, MO 63057. (636)464-2500. **Fax:** (636)464-8449; (636)464-2503. **E-mail:** liguo rianeditor@liguori.org. **Website:** www.liguorian.org. **Contact:** Cheryl Plass, managing editor. Estab. 1913. "Our purpose is to lead our readers to a fuller Christian life by helping them better understand the teachings of the gospel and the church, and by illustrating how these teachings apply to life and the problems confronting them as members of families, the church, and society."

NEEDS Length: 1,500-2,200 words.

HOW TO CONTACT Send complete ms.

PAYMENT/TERMS Pays 12-15¢/word and 5 contributor's copies.

TIPS "First read several issues containing short stories. We look for originality and creative input in each story we read. Since most editors must wade through mounds of manuscripts each month, consideration for the editor requires that the market be studied, the manuscript be carefully presented and polished before submitting. Our publication uses only one story a month. Compare this with the 25 or more we receive over the transom each month. Also, many fiction mss are written without a specific goal or thrust, i.e., an interesting incident that goes nowhere is *not a story*. We believe fiction is a highly effective mode for transmitting the Christian message and also provides a good balance in an unusually heavy issue."

LISSETTE'S TALES OF THE IMAGINATION

Lissette's Publishing LLC., P.O. Box 144, Danville, IN 46112. **E-mail:** lissette@lissettespublishing.com. **Website:** www.lissettespublishing.com. **Contact:** Kristin Roahrig, editor. "*Lissette* is dedicated to presenting the finest works of historical fiction with a twist, be it fantasy, horror, science fiction, or any other genre we haven't mentioned. We are not interested in world creation or invented cultures, but established mythologies and legendary realms (Olympus, Asgard, Camelot, etc.) are welcomed."

NEEDS "We like stories that feature historical, mythological and legendary characters, as well as ones from your own imagination. We won't be able to publish tales with established fictional characters like Sherlock Holmes, Conan the Barbarian, or the Frankenstein Monster. And even though we feel that vampires in general are overdone these days, we won't reject a work of quality so long as it reflects pre-Hollywood concepts of the living dead." Length: 3,000-8,000 words.

HOW TO CONTACT See website to answer questions and submit electronically, or print out form and submit via regular mail. Include SASE.

PAYMENT/TERMS Pays $12/story.

LITERAL LATTE

200 E. 10th St., Suite 240, New York, NY 10003. (212)260-5532. **E-mail:** litlatte@aol.com. **Website:** www.literal-latte.com. **Contact:** Jenine Gordon Bockman. Estab. 1994. Bimonthly online publication with an annual print anthology featuring the best of the website. "We want great writing in all styles and subjects. A feast is made of a variety of flavors."

NEEDS Length: no more than 6,000 words.

HOW TO CONTACT Send complete ms.

PAYMENT/TERMS Pays minimum of anthology copies and maximum of $1,000.

TIPS "Keeping free thought free and challenging entertainment are not mutually exclusive. Words make a manuscript stand out, words beautifully woven together in striking and memorable patterns."

LITERARY JUICE

Mishawaka, IN 46545. **E-mail:** info@literaryjuice.com. **E-mail:** srajan@literaryjuice.com. **Website:** www.literaryjuice.com. **Contact:** Sara Rajan, editor-in-chief; Andrea O'Connor and Dinesh Rajan, managing editors. Bimonthly online literary magazine. "*Literary Juice* publishes original works of short fiction, flash fiction, and poetry. We do not publish nonfiction material, essays, or interviews, nor do we accept previously published works."

NEEDS "We do not publish works with intense sexual content." Length: 100-2,500 words.

HOW TO CONTACT Submit complete ms.

TIPS "It is crucial that writers read our submission guidelines, which can be found on our website. Most important, send us your very best writing. We are looking for works that are not only thought-provoking, but venture into unconventional territory as well. For instance, avoid sending mainstream stories and poems (stories about wizards or vampires fall into this category). Instead, take the reader to a new realm that has yet to be explored."

LITERARY MAMA

E-mail: lminfo@literarymama.com. **Website:** www.literarymama.com. **Contact:** Caroline M. Grant, editor-in-chief. Estab. 2003. Departments include columns, creative nonfiction, fiction, Literary Reflections, poetry, Profiles & Reviews. We are interested in reading pieces that are long, complex, ambiguous, deep, raw, irreverent, ironic, body conscious.

NEEDS "We seek top-notch creative writing. We also look for quality literary criticism about mother-centric literature and profiles of mother writers. We publish writing with fresh voices, superior craft, vivid imagery. We tend to like stark revelation (pathos, humor, and joy), clarity, concrete details, strong narrative development; ambiguity, thoughtfulness, delicacy, irreverence, lyricism, sincerity; the elegant."

HOW TO CONTACT "Please send submission (copied into e-mail) to appropriate departmental editors. Include a brief cover letter. We need the submissions 3 months before the following months: October (Desiring Motherhood); May (Mother's Day Month); and June (Father's Day Month)."

THE LITERARY REVIEW

285 Madison Ave., Madison, NJ 07940. (973)443-8564. **Fax:** (973)443-8364. **E-mail:** editorial@theliteraryreview.org; info@theliteraryreview.org. **Website:** www.theliteraryreview.org. **Contact:** Minna Proctor, editor. Estab. 1957.

Work published in *the Literary Review* has been included in *Editor's Choice, Best Ameri-*

can *Short Stories,* and *Pushcart Prize* anthologies. Uses online submissions manager.

NEEDS Wants works of high literary quality only. Does not want to see "overused subject matter or pat resolutions to conflicts."

HOW TO CONTACT Submit electronically only. Does not accept paper submissions.

PAYMENT/TERMS Pays 2 contributor's copies and a 1-year subscription.

TIPS "We want original dramatic situations with complex moral and intellectual resonance and vivid prose. We don't want versions of familiar plots and relationships. Too much of what we are seeing today is openly derivative in subject, plot, and prose style. We pride ourselves on spotting new writers with fresh insight and approach."

⊙ ⑤ LIVE

Gospel Publishing House, 1445 N. Boonville Ave., Springfield, MO 65802-1894. (417)862-1447. **Fax:** (417)862-6059. **E-mail:** rl-live@gph.org. **Website:** www.gospelpublishing.com. Estab. 1928. "*LIVE* is a take-home paper distributed weekly in young adult and adult Sunday school classes. We seek to encourage Christians in living for God through fiction and true stories which apply Biblical principles to everyday problems."

NEEDS No preachy fiction, fiction about Bible characters, or stories that refer to religious myths (e.g., Santa Claus, Easter Bunny, etc.). No science or Bible fiction. No controversial stories about such subjects as feminism, war, or capital punishment. Length: 800-1,200 words.

HOW TO CONTACT Send complete ms.

PAYMENT/TERMS Pays 7-10¢/word.

TIPS "Don't moralize or be preachy. Provide human interest articles with Biblical life application. Stories should consist of action, not just thought life; interaction, not just insight. Heroes and heroines should rise above failures, take risks for God, prove that scriptural principles meet their needs. Conflict and suspense should increase to a climax! Avoid pious conclusions. Characters should be interesting, believable, and realistic. Avoid stereotypes. Characters should be active, not just pawns to move the plot along. They should confront conflict and change in believable ways. Describe the character's looks and reveal his personality through his actions to such an extent that the reader feels he has met that person. Readers should care

about the character enough to finish the story. Feature racial, ethnic, and regional characters in rural and urban settings."

⊙ ⑤ THE LONDON MAGAZINE

11 Queen's Gate, London En SW7 5ELU UK. +44 (0)20 7584 5977. **E-mail:** admin@thelondonmagazine.org. **Website:** www.thelondonmagazine.org. Estab. 1732.

NEEDS "Short fiction should address mature and sophisticated themes. Moreover, it should have an elegance of style, structure, and characterization. We do not normally publish science fiction or fantasy writing, or erotica." Length: no more than 4,000 words.

HOW TO CONTACT Send complete ms. Submit via e-mail, both as an attachment and in the body of the e-mail. Enclose SASE if submitting through postal mail.

TIPS "We look for poetry and short fiction that startles and entertains us. We are obviously interested in writing that has a London focus, but not exclusively so, since London is a world city with international concerns. Reviews, essays, memoir pieces and features should be erudite, lucid, and incisive. Please look at *The London Magazine* before you submit work, so that you can see the type of material we publish."

LONG LIFE

Longevity through technology, The Immortalist Society, 1437 Pineapple Ave., Melbourne, FL 32935. **E-mail:** 1cryoguy@gmail.com. **Website:** www.cryonics .org/immortalist/index.htm. **Contact:** John Bull, editor. Estab. 1968. "*Long Life* magazine is a publication for people who are particularly interested in cryonic suspension: the theory, practice, legal problems, etc., associated with being frozen when you die in the hope of eventual restoration to life and health. Many people who receive the publication have relatives who have undergone cryonic preparation or have made such arrangements for themselves or are seriously considering this option. Readers are also interested in other aspects of life extension such as anti-aging research and food supplements that may slow aging. Articles we publish include speculation on what the future will be like; problems of living in a future world and science in general, particularly as it may apply to cryonics and life extension."

NEEDS "Our magazine is primarily one of fact but we occasionally publish fiction (up to 2,500 words) that we feel our readers will find interesting. Generally, stories which one who believes strongly in the possibility of future life through science would find silly, morbid, or otherwise offensive are not welcome. We are not interested in horror, in stories where the future is portrayed as gloom and doom, end of the world stories, or those with an inspirational theme."

PAYMENT/TERMS Pays with contributor's copy.

TIPS "We are a small magazine but with a highly intelligent and educated readership which is socially and economically diverse. We currently don't pay for material but are seeking new authors and provide contributors with copies of the magazine with the contributor's published works. Look over a copy of *Long Life*, or talk with the editor to get the tone of the publication. There is an excellent chance that your ms will be accepted if it is well written and 'on theme.' Pictures to accompany the article are always welcome, and we like to publish photos of the authors with their first ms."

THE LONG STORY

18 Eaton St., Lawrence, MA 01843. (978)686-7638. **E-mail:** rpburnham@mac.com. **Website:** www.long storylitmag.com. **Contact:** R.P. Burnham. Estab. 1983. For serious, educated, literary people. We publish high literary quality of any kind but especially look for stories that have difficulty getting published elsewhere—committed fiction, working-class settings, left-wing themes, etc."

Annual magazine: 5½" × 8½"; 160 pages; 60 lb. cover stock; illustrations (black-and-white graphics). Receives 25-35 unsolicited mss/month. Accepts 6-7 mss/issue. Publishes 90% new writers/year.

NEEDS No science fiction, adventure, romance. Length: 8,000-20,000 words; average length: 8,000-12,000 words.

HOW TO CONTACT Include SASE.

PAYMENT/TERMS Pays 2 contributor's copies; $5 charge for extras.

TIPS "Read us first and make sure your material is the kind we're interested in. Send clear, legible mss. We're not interested in commercial success; rather we want to provide a place for long stories, the most difficult literary form to publish in our country."

THE LOS ANGELES REVIEW

P.O. Box 2458, Redmond, WA 98073. (626)356-4760. **Fax:** (626)356-9974. **E-mail:** larevieweditor@gmail .com. **Website:** http://losangelesreview.org. **Contact:** Kelly Davio, managing editor. Estab. 2003.

NEEDS "We're looking for hard-to-put-down shorties under 500 words and lengthier shorts up to 4,000 words—lively, vivid, excellent literary fiction." Does not accept multiple submissions. Does not want pornography.

HOW TO CONTACT Submishmash, our online submission form, is now our preferred method of submission, though you may still submit through postal mail. Please see our guidelines online.

TIPS "Read a recent issue or two to see what we're about. Pay close attention to the submission guidelines. We like cover letters, but please keep them brief."

LOUISIANA LITERATURE

SLU Box 10792, Southeastern Louisiana University, Hammond LA 70402. **E-mail:** lalit@selu.edu. **Website:** www.louisianaliterature.org. **Contact:** Jack B. Bedell, editor. Estab. 1984. Semiannual. "Essays should be about Louisiana; preference is given to fiction and poetry with Louisiana and Southern themes, but creative work can be set anywhere."

Magazine: 6" × 9"; 150 pages; 70 lb. paper; card cover; illustrations. Receives 100 unsolicited mss/month. May not read mss June-July. Publishes ms 6-12 after acceptance. Publishes 4 new writers/year. Publishes theme issues. Has published work by Anthony Bukowski, Aaron Gwyn, Robert Phillips, R.T. Smith.

NEEDS "No sloppy, ungrammatical mss." Length: 1,000-6,000 words; average length: 3,500 words. Reviews fiction.

HOW TO CONTACT Send ms by mail. Include SASE.

PAYMENT/TERMS Pays usually in contributor's copies.

TIPS "Cut out everything that is not a functioning part of the story. Make sure your ms is professionally presented. Use relevant, specific detail in every scene. We love detail, local color, voice, and craft. Any professional manuscript stands out."

THE LOUISIANA REVIEW

Division of Liberal Arts, Louisiana State University Eunice, P.O. Box 1129, Eunice, LA 70535. (337)550-1315. **E-mail:** bfonteno@lsue.edu. **Website:** web.lsue .edu/la-review. **Contact:** Dr. Billy Fontenot, fiction editor. Estab. 1999. *The Louisiana Review*, published annually during the fall or spring semester, offers "Louisiana poets, writers, and artists a place to showcase their most beautiful pieces. Others may submit Louisiana- or Southern-related poetry, stories, and black-and-white art, as well as interviews with Louisiana writers. We want to publish the highest-quality poetry, fiction, and art." Wants "strong imagery, metaphor, and evidence of craft."

○ *The Louisiana Review* is 100 pages, digest size, professionally printed, perfect-bound. Receives up to 2,000 poems/year, accepts 30-50. Press run is 300-600. Single copy: $5

NEEDS Receives 25 unsolicited mss/month. Accepts 5-7 mss/issue. Reads year-round. Has published work by Ronald Frame, Tom Bonner, Laura Cario, Sheryl St. Germaine. Also publishes short shorts. Length: up to 9,000 words; average length: 2,000 words.

HOW TO CONTACT Send SASE for return of ms. Accepts multiple submissions.

PAYMENT/TERMS Pays 1 contributor's copy.

TIPS "We do like to have fiction play out visually as a film would rather than static and undramatized. Louisiana or Gulf Coast settings and themes preferred."

LULLWATER REVIEW

Emory University, P.O. Box 122036, Atlanta, GA 30322. **E-mail:** lullwater@lullwaterreview.com. **Website:** www.lullwaterreview.com. **Contact:** Laura Kochman, editor-in-chief; Tonia Davis, managing editor. Estab. 1990. "We're a small, student-run literary magazine published out of Emory University in Atlanta, GA, with two issues yearly—once in the fall and once in the spring. You can find us in the *Index of American Periodical Verse*, the *American Humanities Index,* and as a member of the Council of Literary Magazines and Presses. We welcome work that brings a fresh perspective, whether through language or the visual arts."

○ Recently published work by Greg Jenkins, Thomas Juvik, Jimmy Gleacher, Carla Vissers, and Judith Sudnolt.

NEEDS No romance or science fiction, please. 5,000 words maximum.

HOW TO CONTACT Send complete ms via e-mail. *Does not accept postal mail submissions.*

PAYMENT/TERMS Pays 3 contributor's copies.

TIPS "We at the *Lullwater Review* look for clear cogent writing, strong character development and an engaging approach to the story in our fiction submissions. Stories with particularly strong voices and well-developed central themes are especially encouraged. Be sure that your manuscript is ready before mailing it off to us. Revise, revise, revise! Be original, honest, and of course, keep trying."

● THE MACGUFFIN

18600 Haggerty Rd., Livonia, MI 48152. (734)462-4400, ext 5327. **E-mail:** macguffin@schoolcraft.edu. **Website:** www.macguffin.org. **Contact:** Steven A. Dolgin, editor; Nicholle Cormier, managing editor; Elizabeth Kircos, fiction editor. Estab. 1984. "Our purpose is to encourage, support and enhance the literary arts in the Schoolcraft College community, the region, the state, and the nation. We also sponsor annual literary events and give voice to deserving new writers as well as established writers."

NEEDS Does not want "obvious pornographic material." Length: 5,000 words.

HOW TO CONTACT Submit 2 stories, maximum. Prose should be typed and double-spaced. Include word count. Send SASE or e-mail.

PAYMENT/TERMS Pays 2 contributor's copies.

TIPS "We strive to give promising new writers the opportunity to publish alongside recognized writers. Follow the submission guidelines, proofread your work, and be persistent. When we reject a story, we may accept the next one you send. When we make suggestions for a rewrite, we may accept the revision. Make your characters come to life. Even the most ordinary people become fascinating if they live for your readers."

● THE MADISON REVIEW

University of Wisconsin, 600 N, Park St., 6193 Helen C. White Hall, Madison, WI 53706. **E-mail:** madisonreview@gmail.com. **Website:** www.english.wisc.edu/madisonreview/madisonReviewHome.htm. **Contact:** Joe Malone and Anna Wehrwein, fiction editors; Joyce Edwards, poetry editor. Estab. 1972. *The Madison Review* is a student-run literary magazine that looks to publish the best available fiction and poetry.

NEEDS "Well-crafted, compelling fiction featuring a wide range of styles and subjects." Does not read May-September. No genre—horror, fantasy, erotica, etc., or unsolicited interviews. Length: 500-30,000 words.

HOW TO CONTACT Send complete ms.

PAYMENT/TERMS Pays 2 contributor's copies, $5 charge for extras.

TIPS "Our editors have very ecclectic tastes, so don't specifically try to cater to us. Above all, we look for original, high-quality work."

THE MAGAZINE OF FANTASY & SCIENCE FICTION

P.O. Box 3447, Hoboken, NJ 07030. (201) 876-2551. **E-mail:** fandsf@aol.com. **Website:** www.fandsf.com. **Contact:** Gordon Van Gelder, editor. Estab. 1949. *"The Magazine of Fantasy and Science Fiction* publishes various types of science fiction and fantasy short stories and novellas, making up about 80% of each issue. The balance of each issue is devoted to articles about science fiction, a science column, book and film reviews, cartoons, and competitions."

The *Magazine of Fantasy and Science Fiction* won a Nebula Award for Best Novelet for *What We Found*, by Geoff Ryman in 2012. Also won the 2012 World Fantasy Award for Best Short Story for *The Paper Menagerie*, by Ken Liu. Editor Van Gelder won the Hugo Award for Best Editor (short form), 2007 and 2008. Bimonthly.

NEEDS "Prefers character-oriented stories. We receive a lot of fantasy fiction, but never enough science fiction." Length: up to 25,000 words.

HOW TO CONTACT No electronic submissions. Send complete ms.

PAYMENT/TERMS Pays 7-10¢/word

TIPS "Good storytelling makes a submission stand out. Regarding manuscripts, a well-prepared manuscript (i.e., one that follows the traditional format, like that describted here: www.sfwa.org/writing/vonda/vonda.htm) stands out more than any gimmicks. Read an issue of the magazine before submitting. New writers should keep their submissions under 15,000 words—we rarely publish novellas by new writers."

THE MAIN STREET RAG

P.O. Box 690100, Charlotte, NC 28227-7001. (704)573-2516. **E-mail:** editor@mainstreetrag.com. **Website:** www.mainstreetrag.com. **Contact:** M. Scott Douglass, editor/publisher. Estab. 1996. *The Main Street Rag*, published quarterly, prints "poetry, short fiction, essays, interviews, reviews, photos, art. We like publishing good material from people who are interested in more than notching another publishing credit, people who support small independent publishers like ourselves."

The Main Street Rag is about 130 pages, digest size, perfect-bound, with 12-point laminated color cover. Receives about 5,000 submissions/year; publishes 50+ poems and 3-5 short stories/issue, a featured interview, photos, and an occasional nonfiction piece. Press run is about 500 (250 subscribers, 15 libraries). Single copy: $8; subscription: $24/year, $45/2 years.

NEEDS "Will consider almost anything, but prefers writing with an edge—either gritty or bitingly humorous. Contributors are advised to visit our website prior to submission to confirm current needs."

THE MALAHAT REVIEW

The University of Victoria, P.O. Box 1700, STN CSC, Victoria BC V8W 2Y2 Canada. (250)721-8524. **E-mail:** malahat@uvic.ca (for queries only). **Website:** www.malahatreview.ca. **Contact:** John Barton, editor. Estab. 1967. "We try to achieve a balance of views and styles in each issue. We strive for a mix of the best writing by both established and new writers."

NEEDS Length: 8,000 words maximum.

HOW TO CONTACT Send complete ms.

PAYMENT/TERMS Pays $35/magazine page

TIPS "Please do not send more than 1 submission at a time: 4-8 poems, 1 piece of creative nonfiction, or 1 short story (do not mix poetry and prose in the same submission). See *The Malahat Review*'s Open Season Awards for poetry and short fiction, creative nonfiction, long poem, and novella contests in the Awards section of our website."

MANOA

English Dept., University of Hawaii, Honolulu, HI 96822. (808)956-3070. **Fax:** (808)956-3083. **E-mail:** mjournal-l@listserv.hawaii.edu. **Website:** http://manoajournal.hawaii.edu. **Contact:** Frank Stewart, poetry editor. Estab. 1989. "High-quality literary fiction, poetry, essays, personal narrative. In general, each issue is devoted to new work from Pacific and Asian nations. Our audience is international. U.S. writing need not be confined to Pacific settings or subjects. Please note that we seldom publish unsolicited work."

Manoa has received numerous awards, and work published in the magazine has been selected for prize anthologies. See website for recently published issues.

NEEDS Query first and/or see website. No Pacific exotica. Length: 1,000-7,500 words.

HOW TO CONTACT Send complete ms.

PAYMENT/TERMS Pays $100-500 normally ($25/ printed page).

TIPS "Not accepting unsolicited manuscripts at this time because of commitments to special projects. See website for more information."

ⓞ ⓞ $ THE MASSACHUSETTS REVIEW

South College, University of Massachusetts, Amherst, MA 01003. (413)545-2689. **Fax:** (413)577-0740. **E-mail:** massrev@external.umass.edu. **Website:** www.massreview.org. **Contact:** Jim Hicks, editor. Estab. 1959.

🗨 Does not respond to mss without SASE. Has published work by Ahdaf Soueif, Elizabeth Denton, Nicholas Montemarano.

NEEDS Wants short stories. Length: "a maximum of 30 pages or 8,000 words."

HOW TO CONTACT Send complete ms. Accepts one short story per submission. "Please include your name and contact information on the first page, and we encourage page numbers. No manuscripts are considered May-September. Electronic submission process on website. No fax or e-mail submissions. No simultaneous submissions. Shorter rather than longer stories preferred (up to 28-30 pages)."

PAYMENT/TERMS Pays $50.

TIPS Looks for works that "stop us in our tracks." Manuscripts that stand out use "unexpected language, idiosyncrasy of outlook, and are the opposite of ordinary."

ⓞ $ MATURE LIVING

Lifeway Christian Resources, 1 Lifeway Plaza, Nashville, TN 37234. (615)251-2000. **E-mail:** matureliving@lifeway.com. **Website:** www.lifeway.com. **Contact:** Rene Holt. Estab. 1977. "Monthly leisure reading magazine for senior adults 55 and older. *Mature Living* is Christian in content, and the material required is what would appeal to 55 and over age group: inspirational, informational, nostalgic, humorous. Our magazine is distributed mainly through churches (especially Southern Baptist churches) that buy the magazine in bulk and distribute it to members in this age group."

NEEDS No reference to liquor, dancing, drugs, gambling; no pornography, profanity or occult. Length: 900-1,200 words preferred

HOW TO CONTACT Send complete ms.

PAYMENT/TERMS Pays $85-115; 3 contributor's copies.

TIPS "Mss are rejected because they are too long or subject matter is unsuitable. Our readers seem to enjoy an occasional short piece of fiction. It must be believable, however, and present senior adults in a favorable light."

ⓞ $ MATURE YEARS

The United Methodist Publishing House, 201 Eighth Ave. S., P.O. Box 801, Nashville, TN 37202-0801. (615)749-6292. **Fax:** (615)749-6512. **E-mail:** matureyears@umpublishing.org. Estab. 1954.

NEEDS "We don't want anything poking fun at old age, saccharine stories, or anything not for older adults. Must show older adults (age 55 plus) in a positive manner." Length: 1,000-2,000 words.

HOW TO CONTACT Send complete ms.

PAYMENT/TERMS Pays $60-125.

TIPS "Practice writing dialogue! Listen to people talk; take notes; master dialogue writing! Not easy, but well worth it! Most query letters are far too long. If you can't sell me an idea in a brief paragraph, you're not going to sell the reader on reading your finished article or story."

MCSWEENEY'S

849 Valencia St., San Francisco, CA 94110. **E-mail:** printsubmissions@mcsweeneys.net (print submissions); websubmissions@mcsweeneys.net (website submissions). **Website:** www.mcsweeneys.net. **Contact:** Christopher Monks, website edior; Jordan Bass, print editor. Online literary journal. "Timothy McSweeney's *Internet Tendency* is an offshoot of Timothy McSweeney's *Quarterly Concern*, a journal created by nervous people in relative obscurity, and published four times a year."

NEEDS Literate humor. Sometimes comments on rejected mss. Length: 1,500 words maximum; preference for pieces significantly shorter (700-1,000 words).

HOW TO CONTACT For submissions to the website, paste the entire piece into the body of an e-mail.

TIPS "Please read the writer's guidelines before submitting, and send your submissions to the appropriate address. Do not submit your work to both the print submissions address and the Web submissions address, as seemingly hundreds of writers have been doing lately. If you submit a piece of writing intended for the magazine to the Web submissions address, you will confuse us, and if you confuse us, we will accidentally delete your work without reading it."

MEMOIR

Memoir Journal, 1316 67th St. #8, Emeryville, CA 94608. (415)339-3142. **Website:** www.memoirjournal.com. Estab. 2006. *"Memoir publishes memoirs in many forms, from the traditional to the experimental."*

○ "We have 2 reading periods per year, with 3 prizes awarded in each: the Memoir Prizes for Prose and Poetry ($100, $250, $500, and publication in publication in print and online, plus 3-6 copies of the journal)."

NEEDS "The editors strive with each issue to include a selection of prose, poetry, graphic memoirs, narrative photography, lies, and more from both emerging and established authors."

HOW TO CONTACT Submit using online submissions manager.

TIPS "The editors particularly invite submissions that push the traditional boundaries of form and content in the exploration of the representation of self. They also just love a well-told memoir."

MENSBOOK JOURNAL

CQS Media, Inc., P.O. Box 418, Sturbridge, MA 01566. **Fax:** (508)347-8150. **E-mail:** features@mensbook.com. **Website:** www.mensbook.com. **Contact:** P.C. Carr, editor/publisher. Estab. 2008. "We target bright, inquisitive, discerning gay men who want more non-commercial substance from gay media. We seek primarily first-person autobiographical pieces—secondly: biographies, political and social analysis, cartoons, short fiction, commentary, travel, and humor."

NEEDS Length: 750-3,000 words.

HOW TO CONTACT Send complete ms.

TIPS "Be a tight writer with a cogent, potent message. Structure your work with well-organized progressive sequencing. Edit everything down before you send it over so we know it is the best you can do, and we'll work together from there."

○ METAL SCRATCHES

P.O. Box 685, Forest Lake, MN 55025. **E-mail:** metalscratches@metalscratches.com. **Website:** www.metalscratches.com. **Contact:** Kim Mark, editor. Estab. 2003. *"Metal Scratches* focuses on literary fiction that examines the dark side of humanity. We are not looking for anything that is cute or sweet."

○ Magazine: 5½" × 8½"; 35 pages; heavy cover-stock. Receives 20 unsolicited mss/month. Accepts 5-6 mss/issue; 20 mss/year. Publishes 3 new writers/year. Semiannual.

NEEDS Does not want horror (as in gore), science fiction, children's, religion, or poetry. Length: 3,500 words; average length: 3,000 words.

HOW TO CONTACT Send complete ms. Accepts submissions by e-mail (no attachments). Send disposable copy of ms and #10 SASE for reply only. Accepts simultaneous, multiple submissions.

PAYMENT/TERMS Pays 2 contributor's copies and 1-year subscription; additional copies for $3.

TIPS "Clean mss prepared according to guidelines are a must. Send us something new and inventive. Don't let rejections from any editor scare you. Keep writing and keep submitting."

●◐⑤ MICHIGAN QUARTERLY REVIEW

0576 Rackham Bldg., 915 E. Washington, University of Michigan, Ann Arbor, MI 48109-1070. (734)764-9265. **E-mail:** mqr@umich.edu. **Website:** www.michiganquarterlyreview.com. **Contact:** Jonathan Freedman, editor; Vicki Lawrence, managing editor. Estab. 1962. *"MQR* is an eclectic interdisciplinary journal of arts and culture that seeks to combine the best of poetry, fiction, and creative nonfiction with outstanding critical essays on literary, cultural, social, and political matters. The flagship journal of the University of Michigan, *MQR* draws on lively minds here and elsewhere, seeking to present accessible work of all varieties for sophisticated readers from within and without the academy."

○ The Laurence Goldstein Award is a $500 annual award to the best poem published in *MQR* during the previous year. The Lawrence Foundation Award is a $1,000 annual award to the best short story published in *MQR* during the previous year. The Page Davidson Clayton Award for Emerging Poets is a $500 annual award given to the best poet appearing in *MQR* during the previous year who has not yet published a book. Receives 300 unsolicited mss/month. Accepts 3-4 mss/issue; 12-16 mss/year. Publishes 1-2 new writers/year. Has published work by Rebecca Makkai, Peter Ho Davies, Laura Kasischke, Gerald Shapiro, Alan Cheuse.

NEEDS "No restrictions on subject matter or language. We are very selective. We like stories that are unusual in tone and structure, and innovative in language. No genre fiction written for a market. Would like to see more fiction about social, political, cultural matters, not just centered on a love relationship or dysfunctional family." Length: 1,500-7,000 words; average length: 5,000 words.

HOW TO CONTACT Send complete ms.

PAYMENT/TERMS Pays $10/published page.

TIPS "Read the journal and assess the range of contents and the level of writing. We have no guidelines to offer or set expectations; every manuscript is judged on its unique qualities. For essays—query with a very thorough description of the argument and a copy of the first page. Watch for announcements of special issues that are usually expanded issues and draw upon a lot of freelance writing. Be aware that this is a university quarterly that publishes a limited amount of fiction and poetry, and that it is directed at an educated audience, one that has done a great deal of reading in all types of literature."

◑ MICROHORROR: SHORT STORIES. ENDLESS NIGHTMARES

P.O. Box 32259, Pikesville, MD 21282-2259. (443) 670-6133. **E-mail:** microhorror@gmail.com. **Website:** www.microhorror.com. **Contact:** Nathan Rosen, editor. Estab. 2006. "*MicroHorror* is not a magazine in the traditional sense. Instead, it is a free online archive for short-short horror fiction."

◔ Golden Horror Award from Horrorfind.com in 2007.

NEEDS "With a strict limit of 666 words, *MicroHorror* showcases the power of the short-short horror to convey great emotional impact in only a few brief paragraphs." Length: no more than 666 words.

HOW TO CONTACT Send all submission through online submission form.

TIPS "This is horror. Scare me. Make shivers run down my spine. Make me afraid to look behind the shower curtain. Pack the biggest punch you can into a few well-chosen sentences. Read all the horror you can, and figure out what makes it scary. Trim away all the excess trappngs until you get right to the core, and use what you find."

◐◔ MID-AMERICAN REVIEW

Bowling Green State University, Department of English, Bowling Green, OH 43403. (419)372-2725. **E-mail:** mar@bgsu.edu. **Website:** www.bgsu.edu/midamericanreview. **Contact:** Abigail Cloud, editor-in-chief. Estab. 1981. "We aim to put the best possible work in front of the biggest possible audience. We publish contemporary fiction, poetry, creative nonfiction, translations, and book reviews."

◔ Magazine: 6" × 9"; 232 pages; 60 lb. bond paper; coated cover stock. Contests: The Fineline Competition for Prose Poems, Short Shorts, and Everything In Between (June 1 deadline, $10 per 3 pieces, limit 500 words each); The Sherwood Anderson Fiction Award (November 1 deadline, $10 per piece); and the James Wright Poetry Award (November 1 deadline, $10 per 3 pieces). "Visit our website!"

NEEDS Publishes traditional, character-oriented, literary, experimental, prose poem, and short-short stories. No genre fiction. Length: 6,000 words maximum.

HOW TO CONTACT Submit ms by post with SASE or with online submission manager. Selects 12 mss/year of 4,500 mss submitted. Agented fiction 5%. Recently published work by Matthew Eck and J. David Stevens.

PAYMENT/TERMS Pays $10/page up to $50, pending funding.

TIPS "We are seeking translations of contemporary authors from all languages into English; submissions must include the original and proof of permission to translate. We would also like to see more creative nonfiction."

◑ MIDWAY JOURNAL

P.O. Box 14499, St. Paul, MN 55114. (612) 825-4811. **E-mail:** editors@midwayjournal.com. **Website:** www.midwayjournal.com. **Contact:** Ralph Pennel, fiction editor. Estab. 2006.

HOW TO CONTACT Submit one piece of fiction or two pieces of flash/sudden fiction via online submissions manager.

TIPS "An interesting story with engaging writing, both in terms of style and voice, make a manuscript stand out. Round characters are a must. Writers who take chances either with content or with form grab an editor's immediate attention. Spend time with the words on the page. Spend time with the language. The language and voice are not vehicles, they, too, are tools."

◑◉ MINDFLIGHTS

Double-Edged Publishing Inc., 9618 Misty Brook Cove, Cordova, TN 38016. (901)213-3768. **E-mail:** editor@mindflights.com; MindFlightsEditors@gmail.com. **Website:** www.mindflights.com. **Contact:** Selena Thomason, managing editor. Estab. 2007.

"Paving new roads for Christ-reflected short fiction. Not preachy, but still a reflection of the truth and light. Examples of this are in the writings of C.S. Lewis and Tolkien. We strive to provide quality fiction and poetry, all in means that respect traditional values and Christian principles. Be uplifting, encouraging with something interesting to our audience—fans of sci-fi and fantasy who are comfortable with an environment committed to a Christian worldview."

◯ "No postal submissions accepted. See our portal entry and submission process online."

NEEDS Does not want to see any work that would be offensive to a Christian audience. Length: 50-5,000 words.

HOW TO CONTACT "We only accept submissions via our online form. Send complete ms. after August 1, when we plan to resume taking submissions."

PAYMENT/TERMS Pays $5-25

TIPS "Only a very small portion of the works accepted for *MindFlights* will appear in our annual print edition. Most will appear online only. Although our guidelines currently indicate that upon acceptance of a work we will ask for rights for either print, the web, or both, and our contracts clearly indicate which rights we are requesting, we are concerned that authors may assume that all works accepted will appear in the print edition."

● MISSISSIPPI REVIEW

University of Southern Mississippi, 118 College Dr., #5144, Hattiesburg, MS 39406-0001. (601)266-4321. **Fax:** (601)266-5757. **E-mail:** andrew.milward@usm .edu; msreview@usm.edu. **Website:** www.mississippi review.com. Estab. 1972.

◯ Publishes 25-30 new writers/year. Annual fiction and poetry competition: $1,000 awarded in each category, plus publication of all winners and finalists. Fiction entries 5,000 words or less. Poetry entry equals 1-3 poems; page limit is 10; $15 entry fee includes copy of prize issue. No limit on number of entries. Deadline October 1. No mss returned.

NEEDS No juvenile or genre fiction. 30 pages maximum.

HOW TO CONTACT "We do not accept unsolicited manuscripts except under the rules and guidelines of the *Mississippi Review* Prize Competition. See website for guidelines."

ⓘⓖⓢ THE MISSOURI REVIEW

357 McReynolds Hall, University of Missouri, Columbia, MO 65211. (573)882-4474. **Fax:** (573)884-4671. **E-mail:** question@moreview.com. **Website:** www .missourireview.com. **Contact:** Speer Morgan, editor. Estab. 1978. "We publish contemporary fiction, poetry, interviews, personal essays, cartoons, special features—such as History as Literature series and Found Text series—for the literary and the general reader interested in a wide range of subjects."

NEEDS No genre or flash fiction.

HOW TO CONTACT Send complete ms.

PAYMENT/TERMS Pays $30/printed page.

TIPS "Send your best work."

ⓘ MOBIUS: THE JOURNAL OF SOCIAL CHANGE

505 Christianson St., Madison, WI 53714. (608)242-1009. **E-mail:** fmschep@charter.net. **Website:** www .mobiusmagazine.com. **Contact:** Fred Schepartz, publisher and executive editor. Estab. 1989. *Mobius: The Journal of Social Change* became an online-only journal, published quarterly in March, June, September, and December, in 2009.

◯ *Mobius* is published quarterly online. Receives about 700 poems/year, accepts less than 30. Has published poetry by Rob Carney, Wade German, Michael Kriesel, Simon Perchik, Wendy Vardaman.

NEEDS Wants fiction dealing with themes of social change. "We like social commentary, but mainly we like good writing." "No porn, no racist, sexist, or any other kind of -ist. No Christian or spirituality proselytizing fiction." Length: no more than 5,000 words.

HOW TO CONTACT Submit no more than one story at a time via e-mail (preferred). Paste story in body of e-mail or send as an attachment.

TIPS "Note that fiction and poetry may be simultaneously published in e-version of *Mobius*. Due to space constraints of print version, some works may be accepted in e-version but not print version. We like high impact, we like plot and character-driven stories that function like theater of the mind. Looks for first and foremost, good writing. Prose must be crisp and polished; the story must pique my interest and make me care due to a certain intellectual, emotional aspect. Second, *Mobius* is about social change. We want stories that make some statement about the society we live in, either on a macro or micro level. Not that your story needs to preach from a soapbox (actually, we prefer that it doesn't), but your story needs to have *something* to say."

NEEDS Length: 5,000 maximum.

⦿ THE MOCHILA REVIEW

Missouri Western State University, 4525 Downs Dr., St. Joseph, MO 64507. **E-mail:** themochilareview@gmail.com. **Website:** www.missouriwestern.edu/orgs/mochila/homepage.htm. **Contact:** Bill Church, editor. Estab. 2000. "We are looking for writing that has respect for the sound of language. We value poems that have to be read aloud so your mouth can feel the shape of the words. Send us writing that conveys a sense of urgency, writing that the writer can't *not* write. We crave fresh and daring work."

NEEDS Length: no more than 5,000 words.

HOW TO CONTACT Submit complete ms by postal mail. Include cover letter, contact information, SASE.

PAYMENT/TERMS Pays in contributor's copies.

TIPS "Manuscripts with fresh language, energy, passion, and intelligence stand out. Study the craft and be entertaining and engaging."

☺ MOONSHOT MAGAZINE

E-mail: info@moonshotmagazine.org. **Website:** www.moonshotmagazine.org. **Contact:** JD Scott, editor. Estab. 2009. "*Moonshot*, a magazine of the literary and fine arts, was conceived in 2009 to provide an equal opportunity space for writers and artists based solely on the merits of their work. *Moonshot*'s mission is to eliminate the social challenges of publishing—encouraging all types of writers and artists to submit their work in the pursuit of exposing their creations to a wider range of audiences. It is our goal to utilize traditional printing techniques as well as new technologies and media arts to feature voices from all over the globe. *Moonshot* celebrates storytelling of all forms, embraces the dissemination of media, and champions diverse creators to construct an innovative and original literary magazine."

NEEDS Also publishes "fine arts as well as graphic narratives/comics." Does not want genre fiction.

PAYMENT/TERMS Pays 1 contributor's copy.

⦿◑ MORPHEUS TALES

116 Muriel St., London N1 9QU United Kingdom. **E-mail:** morpheustales@blueyonder.co.uk. **Website:** www.morpheustales.com. **Contact:** Adam Bradley, publisher. Estab. 2008. "We publish the best in hor-

ror, science fiction, and fantasy—both fiction and nonfiction."

NEEDS Length: 800-3,000 words.

HOW TO CONTACT Send complete ms.

◑◔⑨ MSLEXIA

Mslexia Publications Ltd., P.O. Box 656, Newcastle upon Tyne NE99 1PZ United Kingdom. (44)(191)204-8860. **E-mail:** submissions@mslexia.co.uk; postbag@mslexia.co.uk. **Website:** www.mslexia.co.uk. **Contact:** Debbie Taylor, editorial director. Estab. 1998. "*Mslexia* tells you all you need to know about exploring your creativity and getting into print. No other magazine provides *Mslexia*'s unique mix of advice and inspiration; news, reviews, interviews; competitions, events, grants; all served up with a challenging selection of new poetry and prose. *Mslexia* is read by authors and absolute beginners. A quarterly master class in the business and psychology of writing, it's the essential magazine for women who write."

◔ This publication accepts e-mail submissions, except from UK writers submitting to New Writing themed writing.

NEEDS Length: 50-2,200 words.

HOW TO CONTACT See guidelines on website. "Submissions not on one of our current themes will be returned (if submitted with a SASE) or destroyed." Send complete ms.

TIPS "Read the magazine; subscribe if you can afford it. *Mslexia* has a particular style and relationship with its readers which is hard to assess at a quick glance. The majority of our readers live in the UK, so feature pitches should be aware of this. We never commission work without seeing a written sample first. We rarely accept unsolicited manuscripts but prefer a short letter suggesting a feature, plus a brief bio and writing sample."

N+1

The Editors, 68 Jay St., Suite 405, Brooklyn, NY 11201. **E-mail:** editors@nplusonemag.com. **Website:** www.nplusonemag.com. **Contact:** Carla Blumenkranz, managing editor.

HOW TO CONTACT Submit queries or finished pieces by e-mail.

TIPS "Most of the slots available for a given issue will have been filled many months before publication. If you would like to brave the odds, the best submission guidelines are those implied by the magazine itself.

Read an issue or 2 through to get a sense of whether your piece might fit into *n+1*."

NA'AMAT WOMAN

505 8th Ave., Suite 2302, New York, NY 10018. (212)563-5222. **Fax:** (212)563-5710. **E-mail:** naamat@naamat.org; judith@naamat.org. **Website:** www.naamat.org. **Contact:** Judith Sokoloff, editor. Estab. 1926. "Magazine covering a wide variety of subjects of interest to the Jewish community—including political and social issues, arts, profiles; many articles about Israel and women's issues. Fiction must have a Jewish theme. Readers are the American Jewish community. "

Receives 10 unsolicited mss/month. Accepts 3-5 mss/year. Circ. 15,000.

NEEDS Ethnic/multicultural, historical, humor/satire, literary, novel excerpts, women oriented. "We want serious fiction with insight, reflection, and consciousness. We do not want fiction that is mostly dialogue. No corny Jewish humor. No Holocaust fiction." Length: 2,000-3,000 words.

HOW TO CONTACT Query with published clips or send complete mss. Responds in 6 months to queries; 6 months to mss. Sample copy for 9" × 11½" SAE and $2 postage. Sample copy for $2. Writer's guidelines for #10 SASE, or by e-mail. Query with published clips or send complete ms.

PAYMENT/TERMS Pays 10¢/word and 2 contributor's copies. Pays on publication for first North American serial, first, one-time, second serial (reprint) rights, makes work-for-hire assignments. Pays 10-20¢/word for assigned articles and for unsolicited articles.

TIPS "No maudlin nostalgia or romance; no hackneyed Jewish humor."

NARRATIVE MAGAZINE

2130 Fillmore St. #233, San Francisco, CA 94115. **Website:** www.narrativemagazine.com. Estab. 2003. "*Narrative* publishes high-quality contemporary literature in a full range of styles, forms, and lengths. We welcome submissions of previously unpublished mss of all lengths, ranging from short-short stories to complete book-length works for serialization."

Narrative has received recognitions in *New Stories from the South*, *Best American Mystery Stories*, *O. Henry Prize Stories*, *Best American Short Stories*, *Best American Essays*, and the *Pushcart Prize* anthology. In their first quarterly issue of 2010, the National Endowment

for the Arts featured an article on the business of books, with *Narrative*'s digital publishing model a key focus. Providing a behind-the-scenes look at the way in which *Narrative* functions and thrives, it is an essential read for anyone looking to learn more about the current state of publishing both in the print and digital arenas. Has published work by Amy Bloom, Tobias Wolff, Marvin Bell, Jane Smiley, Joyce Carol Oates, E.L. Doctorow, Min Jin Lee, and Alice Munro. Publishes new and emerging writers.

NEEDS "Submit poetry, fiction, and nonfiction, including stories, short shorts, novels, novel excerpts, novellas, personal essays, humor, sketches, memoirs, literary biographies, commentary, reportage, interviews, and short audio recordings of short-short stories and poems. In addition to submissions for issues of *Narrative* itself, we also encourage submissions for our Story of the Week, literary contests, and Readers' Narratives."

HOW TO CONTACT Send complete ms. "We accept submissions only through our electronic submission system. We do not accept submissions through postal services or e-mail. You may send us mss for the following submission categories: General Submissions, Narrative Prize, Story of the Week, Readers' Narrative, or a specific Contest. Your ms must be in one of the following file forms: .doc, .rtf, .pdf, .docx, .txt, .wpd, .odf, .mp3, .mp4, .mov, or .flv."

PAYMENT/TERMS Pays on publication between $150-1,000, $1,000-5,000 for book length, plus annual prizes of more than $32,000 awarded. Acquires first serial rights.

TIPS "Log on and study our magazine online. Narrative fiction, graphic art, and multimedia are selected, first and foremost, for quality."

NASSAU REVIEW

Nassau Community College, State University of New York, English Dept. Y9, 1 Education Dr., Garden City, NY 11530. **E-mail:** nassaureview@ncc.edu. **Website:** www.ncc.edu/nassaureview. **Contact:** Christina Rau, editor. Estab. 1964. "The Nassau Review welcomes submissions of many genres via our online system only. Please read all guidelines and details on the website: www.ncc.edu/nassaureview. All open submissions are under consideration for the Writer Awards."

NATURAL BRIDGE

Dept. of English, University of Missouri-St. Louis, One University Blvd., St. Louis, MO 63121. (314)516-7327. **E-mail:** natural@umsl.edu. **Website:** www.umsl.edu/~natural. Estab. 1999. *Natural Bridge*, published biannually, seeks "fresh, innovative poetry, both free and formal, on any subject. We want poems that work on first and subsequent readings—poems that entertain and resonate and challenge our readers. *Natural Bridge* also publishes fiction, essays, and translations."

No longer accepts submissions via e-mail. Accepts submissions through online submission form and postal mail only. Submit only July 1-August 31 and November 1-December 31. Sometimes comments on rejected mss. Recently published work by Tayari Jones, Steve Stern, Jamie Wriston Colbert, Lex Williford, and Mark Jay Mirsky.

NEEDS Literary. Also publishes literary essays, poetry.

HOW TO CONTACT Submit via postal mail or using online submission form. Send SASE for return of ms or send a disposable copy of ms and #10 SASE for reply only.

PAYMENT/TERMS Pays 2 contributor's copies and a one-year subscription; additional copies $5.

TIPS "The editors invite submissions of poetry, fiction, personal essays, and translations year-round. Because we are tied to the academic calendar, we will not read between May 1 and August 1."

NATURALLY

Internaturally, Inc., P.O. Box 317, Newfoundland, NJ 07435. (973)697-3552. **Fax:** (973)697-8313. **E-mail:** naturally@internaturally.com. **Website:** www.internaturally.com. Estab. 1980. "A full-color, glossy magazine with online editions, and the foremost naturist/nudist magazine in the U.S. with international distribution. *Naturally* focuses on the clothes-free lifestyle, publishing articles about worldwide destinations, first-time nudist experiences, with news information pertaining to the clothes-free lifestyle. Our mission is to demystify the human form and allow each human to feel comfortable in their own skin, in a nonsexual environment. We offer a range of books, DVDs, magazines, and other products useful to naturists/nudists in their daily lives, and for the education of nonnaturists. Travel DVDs featuring resorts to visit; books on Christianity and nudity, nudist plays, memoirs, cartoons, and novellas; and also towels, sandals, calendars, and more."

Write about nudists and naturists. More people stories than travel.

NEEDS No science fiction. Length: 800-2,000 words.

HOW TO CONTACT Send complete ms.

PAYMENT/TERMS Pays $0-80 per page.

TIPS "Become a nudist/naturist. Appreciate human beings in their natural state."

NEBO

Arkansas Tech University, Department of English, Russellville, AR 72801. (501)968-0256. **E-mail:** nebo@atu.edu. **Website:** www.atu.edu/worldlanguages/Nebo.php. **Contact:** Editor. Estab. 1983. "*Nebo* routinely publishes Arkansas Tech students and unpublished writers along side nationally known writers."

Literary jounral: 5" × 8"; 50-60 pages. For general, academic audience. Receives 20-30 unsolicited mss per month. *Nebo* is published in the spring and fall. Subscriptions: $10.

NEEDS Accepts all genres. Theme changes by semester. Contact editor for specifics. Does not read April 1-August 15. "Submissions deadlines for all work are November 1 and March 1 of each year."

PAYMENT/TERMS Pays 1 contributor's copy.

TIPS "Avoid pretentiousness. Write something you genuinely care about. Please edit your work for spelling, grammar, cohesiveness, and overall purpose. Many of the mss we receive should be publishable with a little polishing. Mss should never be submitted handwritten or on 'onion skin' or colored paper."

NECROLOGY SHORTS: TALES OF MACABRE AND HORROR

Isis International, P.O. Box 510232, St. Louis, MO 63151. **E-mail:** editor@necrologyshorts.com; submit@necrologyshorts.com. **Website:** www.necrologyshorts.com. **Contact:** John Ferguson, editor. Estab. 2009. Consumer publication published online daily and through Amazon Kindle. Also offers an annual collection. "*Necrology Shorts* is an online publication which publishes fiction, articles, cartoons, artwork, and poetry daily. Embracing the Internet, e-book readers, and new technology, we aim to go beyond the long time standard of a regular publication to bringing our readers a daily flow of entertainment. We will also be publishing an annual collection for each year in print, e-book reader, and Adobe PDF format. We also hold contests, judged by our readers, to select the top stories and artwork. Winners of contests receive various prizes, including cash."

NEEDS "Our main genre is suspense horror similar to H.P. Lovecraft and/or Robert E. Howard. We also publish science fiction and fantasy. We would love to see work continuing the Cthulhu Mythos, but we accept all horror." Length: 2,000 words minimum.

HOW TO CONTACT Send complete ms.

TIPS "*Necrology Shorts* is looking to break out of traditional publishing to use the Internet, e-book readers, and other technology. We not only publish works of authors and artists, we let them use their published works to brand themselves and further their profits of their hard work. We love to see traditional short fiction and artwork, but we also look forward to those that go beyond that to create multimedia works. The best way to get to us is to let your creative side run wild and not send us the typical fare. Don't forget that we publish horror, sci-fi, and fantasy. We expect deranged, warped, twisted, strange, sadistic, and things that question sanity and reality."

NERVE COWBOY

Liquid Paper Press, P.O. Box 4973, Austin, TX 78765. **Website:** www.jwhagins.com/nervecowboy.html. **Contact:** Joseph Shields or Jerry Hagins. Estab. 1996. "*Nerve Cowboy* publishes adventurous, comical, disturbing, thought-provoking, accessible poetry and fiction. We like to see work sensitive enough to make the hardest hard-ass cry, funny enough to make the most hopeless brooder laugh, and disturbing enough to make us all glad we're not the author of the piece."

NEEDS "No racist, sexist, or overly offensive work. Wants more unusual stories with rich description and enough twists and turns that leave the reader thinking." Length: 1,500 words.

HOW TO CONTACT Submit short-short stories (up to 5 pages) with SASE. Does not accept e-mail submissions.

PAYMENT/TERMS Pays 1 contributor's copy.

TIPS "We look for writing that is very direct and elicits a visceral reaction in the reader. Read magazines you submit to in order to get a feel for what the editors are looking for. Write simply and from the gut."

NEW DELTA REVIEW

Department of English, 15 Allen Hall, Louisiana State University, Baton Rouge, LA 70803. **E-mail:** newdelta@lsu.edu. **Website:** http://ndrmag.org. Estab. 1984. "We seek vivid and exciting work from new and established writers. We have published fiction from writers such as Stacy Richter, Mark Poirier, and George Singleton."

Semiannual. Editors change every year. Check website. Magazine: 6" × 9"; 75-125 pages; high-quality paper; glossy card cover; color artwork. *New Delta Review* also sponsors the Matt Clark Prizes for fiction and poetry. Work from the magazine has been included in the *Pushcart Prize* anthology.

NEEDS Publishes short shorts. Receives 150 unsolicited mss/month. Accepts 3-4 mss/issue; 6-8 mss/year. Reads from August 15-April 15. **Publishes 1-3 new writers/year.** Also publishes poetry. "No Elvis stories, overwrought Southern fiction, or cancer stories." Average length: 15 ms pages.

PAYMENT/TERMS Pays in contributor's copies. Charge for extras.

TIPS "Our staff is open-minded and youthful. We base decisions on merit, not reputation. The ms that's most enjoyable to read gets the nod. Be bold, take risks, surprise us."

NEW ENGLAND REVIEW

Middlebury College, Middlebury, VT 05753. (802)443-5075. **E-mail:** nereview@middlebury.edu. **E-mail:** Carolyn Kuebler, editor. **Website:** www.nereview.com. Estab. 1978. *New England Review* is a prestigious, nationally distributed literary journal. Reads September 1-May 31 (postmarked dates).

Literary only. *New England Review* is 200+ pages, 7" × 10", printed on heavy stock, flat spined, with glossy cover with art. Receives 3,000-4,000 poetry submissions/year, accepts about 70-80 poems/year. Receives 550 unsolicited mss/month. Accepts 6 mss/issue; 24 fiction mss/year. Does not accept mss June-August. Agented fiction less than 5%. Publishes approximately 10 new writers/year. Subscription: $30. Overseas shipping fees add $25 for subscription, $12 for Canada; international shipping $5 for single issues. Has published work by Steve Almond, Christine Sneed, Roy Kesey, Thomas Gough, Norman Lock, Brock Clarke, Carl Phillips, Lucia Perillo, Linda Gregerson, and Natasha Trethewey.

NEEDS Send 1 story at a time, unless it is very short. Serious literary only, novel excerpts. Prose length: not strict on word count.

HOW TO CONTACT Send complete ms via online submission manager or postal mail (with SASE). No e-mail submissions. "Will consider simultaneous submissions but must be stated as such, and you must notify us immediately if the ms accepted for publication elsewhere."

PAYMENT/TERMS Pays $10/page ($20 minimum), and 2 contributor's copies.

TIPS "We consider short fiction, including short-shorts, novellas, and self-contained extracts from novels in both traditional and experimental forms. In nonfiction, we consider a variety of general and literary but not narrowly scholarly essays; we also publish long and short poems; screenplays; graphics; translations; critical reassessments; statements by artists working in various media; testimonies; and letters from abroad. We are committed to the exploration of all forms of contemporary cultural expression in the U.S. and abroad. With few exceptions, we print only work not published previously elsewhere."

NEW LETTERS

University of Missouri-Kansas City, 5101 Rockhill Rd., Kansas City, MO 64110. (816)235-1168. **Fax:** (816)235-2611. **E-mail:** newletters@umkc.edu. **Website:** www.newletters.org. **Contact:** Robert Stewart, editor-in-chief. Estab. 1934.

Submissions are not read between May 1 and October 1.

NEEDS "We aren't interested in essays that are foot-noted or essays usually described as scholarly or critical. Our preference is for creative nonfiction or personal essays. We prefer shorter stories and essays to longer ones (an average length is 3,500-4,000 words)." No genre fiction. 5,000 words maximum.

HOW TO CONTACT Send complete ms.

PAYMENT/TERMS Pays $30-75.

TIPS We have no rigid preferences as to subject, style, or genre, although commercial efforts tend to put us off. Even so, our only fixed requirement is on good writing."

NEW MADRID

Murray State University, Department of English and Philosophy, 7C Faculty Hall, Murray, KY 42071-3341. (270)809-4730. **E-mail:** msu.newmadrid@murray state.edu. **Website:** http://newmadridjournal.org. **Contact:** Ann Neelon, editor. "*New Madrid* is the national journal of the low-residency MFA program at Murray State University. It takes its name from the

New Madrid seismic zone, which falls within the central Mississippi Valley and extends through western Kentucky."

"We have 2 reading periods, one from August 15-October 15, and one from January 15-March 15." Rarely comments on/critiques rejected mss.

NEEDS See website for guidelines and upcoming themes. Also publishes poetry and creative nonfiction.

HOW TO CONTACT Accepts submissions by online submissions manager only. Include brief bio, list of publications. Considers multiple submissions.

PAYMENT/TERMS Pays 2 contributor's copies on publication.

TIPS "Quality is the determining factor for breaking into *New Madrid*. We are looking for well-crafted, compelling writing in a range of genres, forms and styles."

NEW MILLENNIUM WRITINGS

New Messenger Writing and Publishing, P.O. Box 2463, Knoxville, TN 37901. (865)428-0389. **E-mail:** alexis.williams@hotmail.com. **Website:** http://new millenniumwritings.com. **Contact:** Alexis Williams, editor. Estab. 1996. "While we only accept general submissions January-March, we hold 4 contests twice each year for all types of fiction, nonfiction, short-short fiction, and poetry. Superior writing is the sole criterion. We have launched careers."

Annual anthology. 6" × 9", 204 pages, 50 lb. white paper, glossy 4-color cover. Contains illustrations. Includes photographs. Receives average of 200 mss/month. Accepts 60 mss/year. Agented fiction 0%. Publishes 10 new writers/year. Rarely comments on/critiques rejected mss. Has published work by Charles Wright, Ted Kooser, Pamela Uschuk, William Pitt Root, Allen Wier, Lucille Clifton, John Updike, and Don Williams.

NEEDS Length: 200-6,000 words. Average length: 4,000 words for fiction. Short-short fiction length: no more than 1,000 words.

HOW TO CONTACT Accepts mss through biannual *New Millennium Writing* Awards for Fiction, Poetry, and Nonfiction; also accepts general submissions January-March. Visit website for more information, or see listing for *New Millennium Writing* Awards in Contests & Awards section.

TIPS "Looks for originality, accessibility, musicality of language, psychological insight, mythic resonance. E-mail for list of writing tips or send SASE. "

NEW MOON GIRLS

New Moon Girl Media, P.O. Box 161287, Duluth, MN 55816. (218)728-5507. **Fax:** (218)728-0314. **E-mail:** newmoon@newmoon.com. **Website:** www.newmoon .org. Estab. 1992. "*New Moon Girls* is for every girl who wants her voice heard and her dreams taken seriously. *New Moon* celebrates girls, explores the passage from girl to woman, and builds healthy resistance to gender inequities. The *New Moon* girl is true to herself and *New Moon Girls* helps her as she pursues her unique path in life, moving confidently into the world."

⬤ In general, all material should be pro-girl and feature girls and women as the primary focus.

NEEDS Prefers girl-written material. All girl-centered. Length: 900-1,600 words.

HOW TO CONTACT Send complete ms.

PAYMENT/TERMS Pays 6-12¢/word.

TIPS "We'd like to see more girl-written feature articles that relate to a theme. These can be about anything the girl has done personally, or she can write about something she's studied. Please read *New Moon Girls* before submitting to get a sense of our style. Writers and artists who comprehend our goals have the best chance of publication. We love creative articles—both nonfiction and fiction—that are not condescending to our readers. Keep articles to suggested word lengths; avoid stereotypes. Refer to our guidelines and upcoming themes."

⬤ NEW OHIO REVIEW

English Department, 360 Ellis Hall, Ohio University, Athens OH 45701. (740)597-1360. **E-mail:** noreditors@ohio.edu. **Website:** www.ohiou.edu/nor. **Contact:** Jill Allyn Rosser, editor. Estab. 2007. *NOR*, published biannually in spring and fall, publishes fiction, nonfiction, and poetry.

⬤ Single: $9; Subscription: $16. Member: CLMP. Reading period is September 15-December 15 and January 15-April 1.

HOW TO CONTACT Send complete ms.

PAYMENT/TERMS Pays $30 minimum in addition to 2 contributor's copies and 1-year subscription.

⬤⬤⬤ NEW ORLEANS REVIEW

Box 195, Loyola University, New Orleans, LA 70118. (504)865-2295. **E-mail:** noreview@loyno.edu. **Website:** http://neworleansreview.org. **Contact:** Amberly Fox, managing editor. Estab. 1968. Biannual magazine publishing poetry, fiction, translations, photographs, and nonfiction on literature, art and film. Readership: those interested in contemporary literature and culture. *New Orleans Review* is a journal of contemporary literature and culture, publishing new poetry, fiction, nonfiction, art, photography, film and book reviews. The journal was founded in 1968 and has since published an eclectic variety of work by established and emerging writers including Walker Percy, Pablo Neruda, Ellen Gilchrist, Nelson Algren, Hunter S. Thompson, John Kennedy Toole, Richard Brautigan, Barry Spacks, James Sallis, Jack Gilbert, Paul Hoover, Rodney Jones, Annie Dillard, Everette Maddox, Julio Cortazar, Gordon Lish, Robert Walser, Mark Halliday, Jack Butler, Robert Olen Butler, Michael Harper, Angela Ball, Joyce Carol Oates, Diane Wakoski, Dermot Bolger, Roddy Doyle, William Kotzwinkle, Alain Robbe-Grillet, Arnost Lustig, Raymond Queneau, Yusef Komunyakaa, Michael Martone, Tess Gallagher, Matthea Harvey, D. A. Powell, Rikki Ducornet, and Ed Skoog.

NEEDS "Good writing, from conventional to experimental." Length: up to 6,500 words.

HOW TO CONTACT "We are now using an online submission system and require a $3 fee." See website for details.

PAYMENT/TERMS Pays $25-50 and 2 copies.

TIPS "We're looking for dynamic writing that demonstrates attention to the language, and a sense of the medium, writing that engages, surprises, moves us. We're not looking for genre fiction or academic articles. We subscribe to the belief that in order to truly write well, one must first master the rudiments: grammar and syntax, punctuation, the sentence, the paragraph, the line, the stanza. We receive about 3,000 manuscripts a year, and publish about 3% of them. Check out a recent issue, send us your best, proofread your work, be patient, be persistent."

⬤⬤ THE NEW QUARTERLY

St. Jerome's University, 290 Westmount Rd. N., Waterloo, ON N2L 3G3 Canada. (519)884-8111, ext. 28290. **E-mail:** editor@tnq.ca; pmulloy@tnq.ca. **Website:** www.tnq.ca. Estab. 1981. "Publishes Canadian writing only, fiction and poetry plus essays on writing. Emphasis on emerging writers and genres, but we publish more traditional work as well if the language and narrative structure are fresh."

Open to Canadian writers only.

NEEDS *"Canadian work only*. We are not interested in genre fiction. We are looking for innovative, beautifully crafted, deeply felt literary fiction." 20 pages maximum

HOW TO CONTACT Send complete ms. Does not accept submissions by e-mail. Accepts simultaneous submissions if indicated in cover letter.

PAYMENT/TERMS Pays $200/story.

TIPS "Reading us is the best way to get our measure. We don't have preconceived ideas about what we're looking for other than that it must be Canadian work (Canadian writers, not necessarily Canadian content). We want something that's fresh, something that will repay a second reading, something in which the language soars and the feeling is complexly rendered."

NEW SOUTH

Campus Box 1894, Georgia State University, MSC 8R0322 Unit 8, Atlanta, GA 30303-3083. (404)413-5874. **E-mail:** newsouth@gsu.edu. **Website:** www .review.gsu.edu. Estab. 1980. Semiannual magazine dedicated to finding and publishing the best work from artists around the world. Wants "original voices searching to rise above the ordinary." Seeks to publish high-quality work, regardless of genre, form, or regional ties.

New South is 160+ pages. Press run is 2,000; 500 distributed free to students. Single copy: $5; subscription: $8/year; $14/2 years. Single issue: $5. Sample:$3 (back issue). The *New South* Annual Writing Contest offers $1,000 for the best poem and $1,000 for the best story or essay; 1-year subscription to all who submit. Submissions must be unpublished. Submit up to 3 poems, 1 story, or 1 essay on any subject or in any form. Specify poetry or fiction on outside envelope." Guidelines available by e-mail or on website. **Deadline:** March 4. Competition receives 300 entries. Past judges include Sharon Olds, Jane Hirschfield, Anthony Hecht, Phillip Levine, and Jake Adam York. Winner will be announced in the fall issue.

NEEDS Receives 200 unsolicited mss/month. Publishes and welcomes short shorts. Length: 9,000 words.

HOW TO CONTACT Send complete ms. Include SASE for notification.

PAYMENT/TERMS Pays 2 contributor's copies.

TIPS *"New South* is now accepting submissions through Tell It Slant, an online submission manager. For a small fee that's roughly the cost of printing and posting paper submissions, Tell it Slant will save time, reduce paper waste, and increase our efficiency."

NEW WELSH REVIEW

P.O. Box 170, Aberystwyth, Ceredigion Wa SY23 1 WZ United Kingdom. 01970-626230. **E-mail:** editor@newwelshreview.com. **E-mail:** submissions@new welshreview.com. **Website:** www.newwelshreview .com. **Contact:** Gwen Davies, editor. *"NWR*, a literary quarterly ranked in the top five of British literary magazines, publishes stories, poems, and critical essays. The best of Welsh writing in English, past and present, is celebrated, discussed, and debated. We seek poems, short stories, reviews, special features/ articles and commentary." Quarterly.

HOW TO CONTACT Send hard copy only with SASE or international money order for return. Outside the UK, submission by e-mail only.

PAYMENT/TERMS Pays "check on publication and one free copy."

THE NEW WRITER

P.O. Box 60, Cranbrook Kent TN17 2ZR United Kingdom. (44)(158)021-2626. **E-mail:** editor@thenewwriter.com. **Website:** www.thenewwriter.com. **Contact:** Abegail Morley, poetry editor. Estab. 1996. "Contemporary writing magazine which publishes the best in fact, fiction, and poetry."

NEEDS *No unsolicited mss.* Accepts fiction from subscribers only. "We will consider most categories apart from stories written for children. No horror, erotic, or cozy fiction." Length: 2,000-5,000 words.

HOW TO CONTACT Query with published clips.

PAYMENT/TERMS Pays £10 per story by credit voucher; additional copies for £1.50.

TIPS "Hone it—always be prepared to improve the story. It's a competitive market."

THE NEW YORKER

4 Times Square, New York, NY 10036. (212) 286-5900. **E-mail:** beth_lusko@newyorker.com; toon@cartoon bank.com. **Website:** www.newyorker.com; www.cartoonbank.com. **Contact:** Bob Mankoff, cartoon; David Remnick, editor-in-chief. Estab. 1925. A quality weekly magazine of distinct news stories, articles, essays, and poems for a literate audience.

The New Yorker receives approximately 4,000 submissions per month. Subscription: $59.99/year (47 issues), $29.99 for 6 months (23 issues).

NEEDS Publishes 1 ms/issue.

HOW TO CONTACT Send complete ms. Fiction, poetry, Shouts & Murmurs, and newsbreaks should be sent as pdf attachments. Do not paste them into the message field. Submit at www.newyorker.com/contact/contactus.

PAYMENT/TERMS Payment varies.

TIPS "Be lively, original, not overly literary. Write what you want to write, not what you think the editor would like."

NITE-WRITER'S INTERNATIONAL LITERARY ARTS JOURNAL

158 Spencer Ave., Suite 100, Pittsburgh, PA 15227. (412)668-0691. **E-mail:** nitewritersliteraryarts@gmail.com. **Website:** http://nitewritersinternational.webs.com. **Contact:** John Thompson. Estab. 1994. *Nite-Writer's International Literary Arts Journal* is an online literary arts journal. "We are dedicated to the emotional intellectual with a creative perception of life."

Journal is open to beginners as well as professionals. Receives about 1,000 poems/year, accepts about 10-15%. Has published poetry by Lyn Lifshin, Rose Marie Hunold, Peter Vetrano, Carol Frances Brown, and Richard King Perkins II.

NEEDS Average length: 2,500 words.

HOW TO CONTACT Accepts simultaneous submissions and previously published work ("let us know when and where)."

PAYMENT/TERMS Does not pay but offers exposure to the individual artist.

TIPS "Read a lot of what you write—study the market. Don't fear rejection, but use it as learning tool to strengthen your work before resubmitting."

THE NORMAL SCHOOL

The Press at the California State University, Fresno, 5245 North Backer Ave., M/S PB 98, Fresno, CA 93740-8001. **E-mail:** editors@thenormalschool.com. **E-mail:** submissions@thenormalschool.com. **Website:** http://thenormalschool.com. **Contact:** Steven Church, editor. Estab. 2008. Semiannual magazine that accepts "outstanding work by beginning and established writers."

NEEDS "We also publish short shorts (fewer than 1,500 words). We sponsor The Normal Prizes in Fiction Contest and Creative Nonfiction Contest." Does not want any genre writing. Length: 12,000 words maximum.

HOW TO CONTACT Submit complete ms. "Manuscripts are read from September 1-December 1 and from January 15-April 15. Unsolicited manuscripts received outside of the designated reading periods will be printed out, sculpted into a political effigy, and burned ceremoniously in front of an unruly mob. Please address your submissions to the appropriate editor (i.e. Nonfiction Editor, Recipe Editor, Miscellaneous Editor, etc.). Please do not include pictures of yourself unless it is an extraordinarily funny picture of you wearing ridiculous glasses or unnecessarily tight pants with a large gravy stain. With any mailed submission, please tuck a SASE in along with your work. The trees would like you to submit online, but paper submissions are still welcome and there is no processing charge."

NORTH AMERICAN REVIEW

University of Northern Iowa, 1222 W. 27th St., Cedar Falls, IA 50614. (319)273-6455. **Fax:** (319)273-4326. **E-mail:** nar@uni.edu. **Website:** northamericanreview.org. **Contact:** Kim Groninga, nonfiction editor. Estab. 1815. "The *NAR* is the oldest literary magazine in America and one of the most respected; though we have no prejudices about the subject matter of material sent to us, our first concern is quality."

This is the oldest literary magazine in the country and one of the most prestigious. Also one of the most entertaining—and a tough market for the young writer. Reads fiction mss all year. Publishes ms an average of 1 year after acceptance. **Publishes 2 new writers/year.** Recently published work by Lee Ann Roripaugh, Dick Allen, Rita Welty Bourke.

NEEDS Open (literary). "No flat narrative stories where the inferiority of the character is the paramount concern." Wants to see more "well-crafted literary stories that emphasize family concerns. We'd also like to see more stories engaged with environmental concerns." No flat narrative stories where the inferiority of the character is the paramount concern.

HOW TO CONTACT Accepts submissions by USPS only. Send complete ms with SASE. Responds in 3 months to queries; 4 months to mss. No simultaneous submissions. Sample copy for $7.

PAYMENT/TERMS Pays $5/350 words; $20 minimum, $100 maximum.

TIPS "We like stories that start quickly and have a strong narrative arc. Poems that are passionate about subject, language, and image are welcome, whether they are traditional or experimental, whether in formal or free verse (closed or open form). Nonfiction should combine art and fact with the finest writing. We do not accept simultaneous submissions; these will be returned unread. We read poetry, fiction, and nonfiction year-round."

⑤ NORTH CAROLINA LITERARY REVIEW

East Carolina University, ECU Mailstop 555 English, Greenville, NC 27858-4353. (252)328-1537. **Fax:** (252)328-4889. **E-mail:** nclrsubmissions@ecu.edu. **Website:** www.nclr.ecu.edu. **Contact:** Gabrielle Freeman. Estab. 1992.

○ Uses online submission form.

NEEDS "Fiction submissions accepted during Doris Betts Prize Competition; see our submission guidelines for detail." Length: no more than 5,000 words.

HOW TO CONTACT Query electronically using online submission form.

PAYMENT/TERMS Pays $50-100 honorarium, extra copies, back issues or subscription (negotiable).

TIPS "By far the easiest way to break in is with special issue sections. We are especially interested in reports on conferences, readings, meetings that involve North Carolina writers, and personal essays or short narratives with a strong sense of place. See back issues for other departments. Interviews are probably the other easiest place to break in; no discussions of poetics/theory, etc., except in reader-friendly (accessible) language; interviews should be personal, more like conversations, that explore connections between a writer's life and his/her work."

ⓞⓠ NORTH DAKOTA QUARTERLY

276 Centennial Dr. Stop 7209, Merrifield Hall Room 15, Grand Forks, ND 58202. (701)777-3322. **E-mail:** und.ndq@email.und.edu. **Website:** www.und.nodak.edu/org/ndq. Estab. 1911.

○ Work published in *North Dakota Quarterly* was selected for inclusion in *The O. Henry Prize Stories,* the *Pushcart Prize* anthology and *Best American Essays.* Only reads fiction and poetry between September 1 and May 1.

NEEDS "*North Dakota Quarterly* does not have any submission guidelines, but we strive to publish the best fiction, poetry, and essays that in our estimation we can. Our tastes and interests are best reflected in what we have been recently publishing, and we suggest that you look at some current issues for guidance." No length restrictions.

HOW TO CONTACT Simultaneous submissions okay for fiction. Hard copies only.

NORTHWIND

Chain Bridge Press, LLC., 4201 Wilson Blvd., #110, Arlington, VA 22203. **E-mail:** info@northwindmagazine.com. **Website:** www.northwindmagazine.com. **Contact:** Tom Howard, managing editor. Estab. 2011. "Our focus is originality and provocative, compulsively readable prose and poetry, in any style or genre. We look for smart, lyrical writing that will appeal to an intelligent and culturally sophisticated audience."

NEEDS "We want the best that you've got. We want crazy beautiful characters, unforced and unsentimental prose, unexpected plots, great opening lines, and edgy dialogue. But mostly we want great, honest stories that move us and leave us shaken through the sheer force of narrative will. Surprise us." Does not want flash fiction or microfiction. Length: 3,000-8,000 words.

HOW TO CONTACT Submit complete ms using online submission form only.

PAYMENT/TERMS "*Northwind* pays $150 for the issue's featured story only. All contributors, however, will be provided with a dedicated page on the site for biographical information (including photo), any relevant website links, and an optional feedback form for readers."

ⓞⓠⓢ NOTRE DAME REVIEW

University of Notre Dame, 840 Flanner Hall, Notre Dame, IN 46556. (574)631-6952. **Fax:** (574)631-4795. **E-mail:** english.ndreview.1@nd.edu. **Website:** www.nd.edu/~ndr/review.htm. Estab. 1995. The *Notre Dame Review* is an indepenent, noncommercial magazine of contemporary American and international fiction, poetry, criticism, and art. We are especially interested in work that takes on big issues by making the invisible seen, that gives voice to the voiceless. In addition to showcasing celebrated authors like Seamus Heaney and Czelaw Milosz, the *Notre Dame Review* introduces readers to authors they may have never encountered before but who are doing innovative and important work. In conjunction with the *Notre Dame Review*, the online companion to the printed magazine, the *Notre Dame Review* engages readers as a community centered in literary rather than commercial concerns, a community we reach out to through critique and commentary as well as aesthetic experience.

NEEDS "We're eclectic. Upcoming theme issues planned. List of upcoming themes or editorial calendar available for SASE. Does not read mss May-August." No genre fiction. Length: 3,000 words.

HOW TO CONTACT Send complete ms with cover letter. Include 4-sentence bio. Send SASE for response, return of ms, or send a disposable copy of ms.

PAYMENT/TERMS Pays $5-25.

TIPS "We're looking for high-quality work that takes on big issues in a literary way Please read our back issues before submitting."

NOVA SCIENCE FICTION MAGAZINE

17983 Paseo Del Sol, Chino Hills, CA 91709. **Website:** http://novascifi.com/blog/. **Contact:** Wesley Kawato. Estab. 1999.

NOVA does not accept unsolicited manuscripts.

NEEDS "We publish religious science fiction short stories, no fantasy or horror. One story slot per issue will be reserved for a story written from an evangelical Christian viewpoint." Length: no more than 8,000 words.

HOW TO CONTACT Query first. "Send a query letter first, along with a list of previous story publications. If you are unpublished, list your training in creative writing."

PAYMENT/TERMS Pays 5¢/word.

TIPS "Make sure your plot is believable and describe your characters well enough so I can visualize them. If I like it, I buy it. I like happy endings and heroes with a strong sense of faith."

NOW & THEN; THE APPALACHIAN MAGAZINE

East Tennessee State University, Box 70556, Johnson City, TN 37614-1707. (423)439-5348. **Fax:** (423)439-6340. **E-mail:** nowandthen@etsu.edu. **E-mail:** wardenc@etsu.edu. **Website:** www.etsu.edu/cass/nowandthen. **Contact:** Jane Woodside, editor. Estab. 1984. Literary magazine published twice/year. "*Now & Then* accepts a variety of writing genres: fiction, poetry, nonfiction, essays, interviews, memoirs, and

book reviews. All submissions must relate to Appalachia and to the issue's specific theme. Our readership is educated and interested in the region."

Magazine: 8½" × 11"; 44-48 pages; coated paper and cover stock; illustrations; photos. *Now & Then* tells the stories of Appalachia and presents a fresh, revealing picture of life in Appalachia, past and present, with engaging articles, personal essays, fiction, poetry, and photography.

NEEDS Accepts 2-3 mss/issue. Publishes ms 4 months after acceptance. Publishes some new writers/year. Length: 1,000-1,500 words.

HOW TO CONTACT Send complete ms. Accepts submissions by mail, e-mail. Include "information we can use for contributor's note." SASE (or IRC). Responds in 5 months to queries; 5 months to mss. Accepts simultaneous submissions "but let us know when it has been accepted elsewhere right away." Sample copy for $5. Writer's guidelines online. Reviews fiction.

PAYMENT/TERMS Pays $30-100. Pays on publication.

TIPS "Keep in mind that *Now & Then* only publishes material related to the Appalachian region. Plus, we only publish fiction that has some plausible connection to a specific issue's themes. Get the guidelines. We like to offer first-time publication to promising writers."

NTH DEGREE

3502 Fernmoss Ct., Charlotte, NC 28269. **E-mail:** submissions@nthzine.com. **Website:** www.nthzine.com. **Contact:** Michael Pederson. Estab. 2002.

No longer accepts hard copy submissions.

NEEDS Length: no more than 7,500 words.

HOW TO CONTACT Submit complete ms via e-mail.

PAYMENT/TERMS Pays in contributor's copies.

TIPS "Don't submit anything that you may be ashamed of ten years later."

NUTHOUSE

P.O. Box 119, Ellenton, FL 34222. **Website:** www.nuthousemagazine.com. *Nuthouse*, published every 3 months, uses humor of all kinds, including homespun and political. Wants "humorous verse; virtually all genres considered." Has published poetry by Holly Day, Daveed Garstenstein-Ross, and Don Webb.

Nuthouse is 12 pages, digest size, photocopied from desktop-published originals. Receives about 500 poems/year, accepts about 100. Press run is 100. Subscription: $5 for 4 issues. Sample: $1.50. Make checks payable to Twin Rivers Press.

NEEDS "We publish all genres, from the homespun to the horrific. We don't automatically dismiss crudity or profanity. We're not prudes. Yet we consider such elements cheap and insulting unless essential to the gag. *Nuthouse* seeks submissions that are original, tightly written and laugh-out-loud funny." Length: no more than 1,000 words. "The shorter, the better."

HOW TO CONTACT Send complete ms with SASE and cover letter. Include estimated word count, bio (paragraph), and list of publications. No e-mail submissions.

🎧 NUVEIN ONLINE

(626)600-2780. **E-mail:** info@nuvein.org. **Website:** http://nuvein.org. Online magazine published by the Nuvein Foundation for Literature and the Arts. "We are open to short fiction, poetry, and essays that explore topics divergent from the mainstream. Our vision is to provide a forum for new and experienced voices rarely heard in our global community."

🗨 *Nuvein Online* has received the Visionary Media Award.

NEEDS Fiction, poetry, plays, movie/theater reviews/articles and art. Wants more "experimental fiction, ethnic works, and pieces dealing with the exploration of gender and sexuality, as well as works dealing with the clash of cultures."

HOW TO CONTACT Query. Accepts submissions by e-mail. Send work as attachment. Sample copy online.

TIPS "Read over each submission before sending it, and if you, as the writer, find the piece irresistable, e-mail it to us immediately!"

OBSIDIAN

North Carolina State University, Department of English, Box 8105, Raleigh, NC 27695. (919)515-4153. **E-mail:** obsidian@gw.ncsu.edu. **Website:** www.ncsu.edu/chass/obsidian/. **Contact:** Sheila Smith McKoy, editor. Estab. 1975.

🗨 Accepts submissions through online submission form ONLY. Accepts submissions from September 1-April 30.

NEEDS "Creative works in English by black writers, scholarly critical studies by all writers on black literature in English." Length: no more than 7,000 words.

HOW TO CONTACT Submit one story at a time using online submission form. Include word count.

PAYMENT/TERMS Pays in contributor's copies.

TIPS "Following proper format is essential. Your title must be intriguing and text clean. Never give up. Some of the writers we publish were rejected many times before we published them."

OCEAN MAGAZINE

P.O. Box 84, Rodanthe, NC 27968-0084. (252)256-2296. **E-mail:** diane@oceanmagazine.org. **Website:** www.oceanmagazine.org. Estab. 2004. "*OCEAN* magazine serves to celebrate and protect the greatest, most comprehensive resource for life on earth, our world's ocean. *OCEAN* publishes articles, stories, poems, essays, and photography about the ocean—observations, experiences, scientific and environmental discussions—written with fact and feeling, illustrated with images from nature."

NEEDS Length: 100-2,000 words.

HOW TO CONTACT Query.

PAYMENT/TERMS Pays $75-150.

TIPS "Submit with a genuine love and concern for the ocean and its creatures."

⬤ OHIO TEACHERS WRITE

1209 Heather Run, Wilmington, OH 45177. **E-mail:** karla.bisig@wilmington.k12.oh.us; ohioteacherswrite@octela.org. **Website:** http://otwonline.wordpress.com. Estab. 1995. "The purpose of the magazine is threefold: (1) to provide a collection of fine literature for the reading pleasure of teachers and other adult readers; (2) to encourage teachers to compose literary works along with their students; (3) to provide the literate citizens of Ohio a window into the world of educators not often seen by those outside the teaching profession."

🗨 Editors change every 3 years. Magazine: 8½" × 11"; 50 pages; 60 lb. white offset paper; 65 lb. blue cover stock; illustrations; photos. Has published work by Lois Spencer, Harry R. Noden, Linda J. Rice, June Langford Berkley. Annual.

NEEDS Submissions are limited to Ohio Educators. Receives 2 unsolicited mss/month. Accepts 7 mss/issue. "We read only in May when the editorial board meets." Often comments on rejected mss.

HOW TO CONTACT Send SASE with postage clipped for return of ms or send a disposable copy of ms. Accepts multiple submissions. Sample copy for $6.

PAYMENT/TERMS Pays 2 contributor's copies; additional copies $6.

⑤ ONE STORY

One Story, LLC, 232 3rd St., #A108, Brooklyn, NY 11215. **Website:** www.one-story.com. **Contact:** Maribeth Batcha, publisher. Estab. 2002. "*One Story* is a literary magazine that contains, simply, one story. It is a subscription-only magazine. Every 3 weeks subscribers are sent *One Story* in the mail. *One Story* is artfully designed, lightweight, easy to carry, and ready to entertain on buses, in bed, in subways, in cars, in the park, in the bath, in the waiting rooms of doctor's offices, on the couch, or in line at the supermarket. Subscribers also have access to a website, where they can learn more about *One Story* authors, and hear about *One Story* readings and events. There is always time to read *One Story.*"

NEEDS *One Story* only accepts short stories. Do not send excerpts. Do not send more than 1 story at a time. Length: 3,000-8,000 words.

HOW TO CONTACT Send complete ms using online submission form.

PAYMENT/TERMS Pays $250 and 25 contributor's copies.

TIPS "*One Story* is looking for stories that are strong enough to stand alone. Therefore they must be very good. We want the best you can give."

◐⑨ ON SPEC

P.O. Box 4727, Station South, Edmonton, AB T6E 5G6 Canada. (780)628-7121. **E-mail:** onspec@onspec.ca. **E-mail:** onspecmag@gmail.com. **Website:** www.on spec.ca. Estab. 1989. . "We publish speculative fiction and poetry by new and established writers, with a strong preference for Canadian authored works."

◯ See website guidelines for submission announcements.

NEEDS No media tie-in or shaggy-alien stories. No condensed or excerpted novels, religious/inspirational stories, fairy tales. Length: 1,000-6,000 words.

HOW TO CONTACT Send complete ms. Electronic submissions preferred.

TIPS "We want to see stories with plausible characters; a well-constructed, consistent, and vividly described setting; a strong plot and believable emotions; characters must show us (not tell us) their emotional responses to each other and to the situation and/or challenge they face. Also, don't send us stories written for television. We don't like media tie-ins, so don't watch TV for inspiration! Read, instead! Strong preference given to submissions by Canadians."

◐⑤ ON THE PREMISES: A GOOD PLACE TO START

On The Premises, LLC, 4323 Gingham Court, Alexandria, VA 22310. **E-mail:** questions@onthepremises .com. **Website:** www.OnThePremises.com. **Contact:** Tarl Roger Kudrick or Bethany Granger, co-publishers. Estab. 2006. "Stories published in *On the Premises* are winning entries in contests that are held every 4 months. Each contest challenges writers to produce a great story based on a broad premise that our editors supply as part of the contest. *On the Premises* aims to promote newer and/or relatively unknown writers who can write what we feel are creative, compelling stories told in effective, uncluttered, and evocative prose. Entrants pay no fees, and winners receive cash prizes in addition to publication."

◯ Does not read February, June, and October. Receives 50-125 mss/month. Accepts 3-6 mss/issue; 9-18 mss/year. Has published A'llyn Ettien, Cory Cramer, Mark Tullius, Michael Van Ornum, Ken Liu, and K. Stoddard Hayes. Member Small Press Promotions.

NEEDS Themes are announced the day each contest is launched. List of past and current premises available on website. "All genres considered. All stories must be based on the broad premise supplied as part of the contest. Sample premise, taken from the first issue: One or more characters are traveling in a vehicle, and never reach their intended destination. Why not? What happens instead?" No young adult, children's, or "preachy" fiction. "In general, we don't like stories that were written solely to make a social or political point, especially if the story seems to assume that no intelligent person could possibly disagree with the author. Save the ideology for editorial and opinion pieces, please. But above all, we *never ever* want to see stories that do not use the contest premise! Use the premise, and make it clear and obvious that you are using the premise." Length: 1,000-5,000 words. Average length: 3,500 words.

HOW TO CONTACT Send complete ms. "Submit stories only via submission form at http://onthepremis es.submittable.com/submit. We no longer accept e-mailed submissions."

PAYMENT/TERMS Pays $40-180.

TIPS "Make sure you use the premise, not just interpret it. If the premise is 'must contain a real live dog,' then think of a creative, compelling way to use a real dog. Revise your draft, then revise again and again.

Remember, we judge blindly, so craftmanship and creativity matter, not how well-known you are."

OUTER ART

The University of New Mexico, 200 College Rd., Gallup, NM 87301. **Website:** www.gallup.unm .edu/~smarandache/a/outer-art.htm. Estab. 2000. **NEEDS** Publishes short shorts.
HOW TO CONTACT Accepts submissions by e-mail. Send SASE (or IRC) for return of ms. Accepts simultaneous submissions and reprints.

OYEZ REVIEW

Roosevelt University, Dept. of Literature & Languages, 430 S. Michigan Ave., Chicago, IL 60605-1394. (312)341-3500. **E-mail:** oyezreview@roosevelt.edu. **Website:** legacy.roosevelt.edu/roosevelt.edu/oyezreview. Estab. 1965. Literary magazine/journal. "*Oyez Review* publishes fiction, creative nonfiction, poetry, and art. There are no restrictions on style, theme, or subject matter."

⌕ Reading period is August 1-October 1. Responds by mid-December. Recently published J. Weintraub, Lori Rader Day, Joyce Goldenstern, Norman Lock, Peter Obourn, Jotham Burrello.

NEEDS Publishes short stories and flash fiction from established authors and newcomers. Literary excellence is our goal and our primary criterion. Send us your best work, and you will receive a thoughtful, thorough reading. We publish short stories and flash fiction on their merit as contemporary literature rather than the category within the genre. 5,500 words maximum.
HOW TO CONTACT Accepts art and international submissions by e-mail. Sample copy available for $5. Guidelines available on website. Send complete ms.
PAYMENT/TERMS Writers receive 2 contributors copies. Acquires first North American serial rights.

OYSTER BOY REVIEW

P.O. Box 1483, Pacifica, CA 94044. **E-mail:** email_2014@oysterboyreview.com. **Website:** www .oysterboyreview.com. **Contact:** Damon Suave, editor/ publisher. Estab. 1993. Electronic and print magazine. *Oyster Boy Review*, published 4 times a year, is interested in "the underrated, the ignored, the misunderstood, and the varietal. We'll make some mistakes. 'All styles are good except the boring kind'—Voltaire."
NEEDS "Fiction that revolves around characters in conflict with themselves or each other; a plot that has a beginning, a middle, and an end; a narrative with a strong moral center (not necessarily 'moralistic'); a story with a satisfying resolution to the conflict; and an ethereal something that contributes to the mystery of a question but does not necessarily seek or contrive to answer it." No genre fiction.
TIPS "Keep writing, keep submitting, keep revising."

PACIFIC REVIEW

Dept. of English and Comparative Literature, San Diego State University, 5500 Campanile Dr., MC6020, San Diego, CA 92182-6020. **E-mail:** pacificreview_ sdsu@yahoo.com. **Website:** http://pacificREVIEW. sdsu.edu. "We welcome submissions of previously published poems, short stories, translations, and creative nonfiction, including essays and reviews."

⌕ For information on theme issues see website. **Publishes 15 new writers/year.** Recently published work by Ai, Alurista, Susan Daitch, Lawrence Ferlinghetti, William T. Vollmann.

PAYMENT/TERMS Pays 2 contributor's copies.
TIPS "We welcome all submissions, especially those created in or in the context of the West Coast/California and the space of our borders."

PACKINGTOWN REVIEW

111 S. Lincoln St., Batavia, IL 60510. **E-mail:** editors@ packingtownreview.com. **Website:** www.packing townreview.com. Estab. 2008. "*Packingtown Review* publishes imaginative and critical prose and poetry by emerging and established writers. We welcome submissions of poetry, scholarly articles, drama, creative nonfiction, fiction, and literary translation, as well as genre-bending pieces."

⌕ Annual. Magazine has revolving editor. Editorial term: 2 years. Next term: 2014. Literary magazine/journal. 8½" × 11", 250 pages. Press run: 500.

NEEDS Does not want to see uninspired or unrevised work. "We also would like to avoid fantasy, science fiction, overtly religious, or romantic pieces." Length: 3,000-8,000 words.
HOW TO CONTACT Send complete ms with cover letter. Include estimated word count, brief bio. Considers simultaneous submissions.
PAYMENT/TERMS Pays 2 contributor's copies.
TIPS "We are looking for well-crafted prose. We are open to most styles and forms. We are also looking for prose that takes risks and does so successfully. We will consider articles about prose."

🌓😊 PADDLEFISH

Mount Marty College, 1105 W. 8th St., Yankton, SD 57078. (605) 688-1362. **E-mail:** james.reese@mtmc .edu. **Website:** www.mtmc.edu/paddlefish. **Contact:** Dr. Jim Reese, Editor. Estab. 2007. Literary magazine/ journal. 6" × 9", 200 pages. Includes photographs. "We publish unique and creative pieces." Annual. Receives 300 mss/month. Accepts 30 mss/year. Submission period is November 1-February 28. Published David Lee, William Kloefkorn, David Allen Evans, Jack Anderson, and Maria Mazziotti Gillan. Length: 2,500 words (max).

Ⓞ   Does not accept e-mail submissions.

NEEDS Does not want excessive or gratuitous language, sex, or violence. Length: no more than 1,500 words.

HOW TO CONTACT Submit complete ms with SASE.

PAYMENT/TERMS Pays in contributor's copies.

🌓😊 PAINTED BRIDE QUARTERLY

Drexel University, Department of English and Philosophy, 3141 Chestnut St., Philadelphia, PA 19104. **E-mail:** pbq@drexel.edu. **Website:** www.webdelsol. com/pbq. Estab. 1973. *Painted Bride Quarterly* seeks literary fiction, experimental and traditional.

NEEDS Publishes theme-related work, check website; holds annual fiction contests. Length: up to 5,000 words.

HOW TO CONTACT Send complete ms.

PAYMENT/TERMS Pays contributor's copy.

TIPS "We look for freshness of idea incorporated with high-quality writing. We receive a lot of nicely written work with worn-out plots. We want quality—we hold experimental work to as strict a standard as anything else. Many of our readers write fiction; most of them enjoy a good reading. We hope to be an outlet for quality. A good story gives, first, enjoyment to the reader. We've seen a good many of them lately, and we've published the best of them."

🌓😊 PAKN TREGER

National Yiddish Book Center, 1021 West St., Amherst, MA 01002. (413)256-4900. **E-mail:** aatherley@ bikher.org; pt@bikher.org;. **Website:** www.yiddish bookcenter.org. **Contact:** Anne Atherley, editor's assistant. Estab. 1980.

NEEDS Length: 1,200-6,000 words.

HOW TO CONTACT Query first by e-mail.

PAYMENT/TERMS Pays $1,000-2,000

TIPS "Read the magazine and visit our website."

PALABRA

P.O. Box 86146, Los Angeles, CA 90086. **E-mail:** info@ palabralitmag.com. **Website:** www.palabralitmag .com. *"PALABRA* is about exploration, risk, and ganas—the myriad intersections of thought, language, story and art—*el mas alla of letters,* symbols, and spaces into meaning."

NEEDS No genre work, i.e., mystery, romance, suspense, science fiction, etc. Length: up to 4,000 words.

HOW TO CONTACT Send complete ms; unpublished work only via postal mail. If submitting in more than one genre, submit each one separately. Include brief cover letter and SASE. Submissions are accepted from September 1 through April 30.

PAYMENT/TERMS Pays $25-$40.

PANK

PANK, Department of Humanities, 1400 Townsend Dr., Houghton, MI 49931-1200. **Website:** www.pank magazine.com. **Contact:** M. Bartley Seigel, editor. Estab. 2007. *"PANK* Magazine fosters access to emerging and experimental poetry and prose, publishing the brightest and most promising writers for the most adventurous readers. To the end of the road, up country, a far shore, the edge of things, to a place of amalgamation and unplumbed depths, where the known is made and unmade, and where unimagined futures are born, a place inhabited by contradictions, a place of quirk and startling anomaly. [PANK], no soft pink hands allowed."

TIPS "To read *PANK* is to know *PANK.* Or, read a lot within the literary magazine and small press universe—there's plenty to choose from. Unfortunately, we see a lot of submissions from writers who have clearly read neither *PANK* nor much else. Serious writers are serious readers. Read. Seriously."

☾Ⓞ PAPERPLATES

19 Kenwood Ave., Toronto ON M6C 2R8 Canada. (416)651-2551. **E-mail:** magazine@paperplates.org. **Website:** www.paperplates.org. **Contact:** Bernard Kelly, publisher. Estab. 1990.

Ⓞ   No longer accepts IRCs.

NEEDS Length: no more than 7,500 words.

HOW TO CONTACT "Do not send fiction as an e-mail attachment. Copy the first 300 words or so into the body of your message. If you prefer not to send a fragment, you have the option of using snail mail." Include short bio with submission.

THE PARIS REVIEW

62 White St., New York, NY 10013. (212)343-1333. **E-mail:** queries@theparisreview.org. **Website:** www .theparisreview.org. **Contact:** Lorin Stein, editor. "Fiction and poetry of superlative quality, whatever the genre, style, or mode. Our contributors include prominent, as well as less well-known and previously unpublished writers. Writers at Work interview series includes important contemporary writers discussing their own work and the craft of writing."

NEEDS Study the publication. Annual Aga Khan Fiction Contest award of $1,000. Recently published work by Karl Taro Greenfeld, J. Robert Lennon, and Belle Boggs. Length: no limit.

HOW TO CONTACT Send complete ms. Address submissions to proper department. Do not make submissions via e-mail.

PAYMENT/TERMS Pays $500-1,000.

PASSAGES NORTH

English Department, Northern Michigan University, 1401 Presque Isle Ave., Marquette, MI 49855. (906)227-1203. **E-mail:** passages@nmu.edu. **Website:** www.passagesnorth.com. **Contact:** Jennifer A. Howard, editor-in-chief. Estab. 1979. *Passages North*, published annually in spring, prints poetry, short fiction, creative nonfiction, essays, and interviews.

Magazine: 7" × 10"; 200-300 pgs; 60 lb. paper. Publishes work by established and emerging writers. Has published poetry by Moira Egan, Frannie Lindsay, Ben Lerner, Bob Hicok, Gabe Gudding, John McNally, Steve Almond, Tracy Winn, and Midege Raymond. *Passages North* is 250 pages. Single copy: $13; subscription: $13/year, $23 for 2 years.

NEEDS "Don't be afraid to surprise us." No genre fiction, science fiction, "typical commercial press work." Length: up to 7,000 words.

HOW TO CONTACT Send one short story or as many as three short-short stories (paste them all into one document).

TIPS "We look for voice, energetic prose, writers who take risks. We look for an engaging story in which the author evokes an emotional response from the reader through carefully rendered scenes, complex characters, and a smart, narrative design. Revise, revise. Read what we publish."

PASSION

Crescent Moon Publishing, P.O. Box 393, Maidstone Kent ME14 5XU United Kingdom. (44)(162)272-9593. **E-mail:** cresmopub@yahoo.co.uk. **Website:** www .crmoon.com. Estab. 1988. *Passion*, published quarterly, features poetry, fiction, reviews, and essays on feminism, art, philosophy, and the media.

Has published poetry by Jeremy Reed, Penelope Shuttle, Alan Bold, D.J. Enright, and Peter Redgrove. Single copy: £2.50 ($4 USD); subscription: £10 ($17 USD). Make checks payable to Crescent Moon Publishing.

NEEDS "Wants "thought-provoking, incisive, polemical, ironic, lyric, sensual, and hilarious work." Does not want "rubbish, trivia, party politics, sport, etc."

THE PATERSON LITERARY REVIEW

Passaic County Community College, Cultural Affairs Dept., One College Blvd., Paterson, NJ 07505-1179. (973)684-6555. **Fax:** (973)523-6085. **E-mail:** mGillan@pccc.edu. **Website:** www.pccc.edu/poetry. **Contact:** Maria Mazziotti Gillan, editor/executive director. *Paterson Literary Review*, published annually, is produced by the The Poetry Center at Passaic County Community College. Wants poetry of "high quality; clear, direct, powerful work."

Paterson Literary Review is 300-400 pages, magazine size, professionally printed, perfect-bound, saddle stapled, with glossy 4-color card cover. Press run is 2,500. Has published poetry and work by Diane di Prima, Ruth Stone, Marge Piercy, Laura Boss, Robert Mooney, and Abigail Stone. Work for *PLR* has been included in the *Pushcart Prize* anthology and *Best American Poetry*.

NEEDS "We are interested in quality short stories, with no taboos on subject matter." Receives 60 unsolicited mss/month. Publishes 5% new writers/year.

HOW TO CONTACT Send SASE for reply or return of ms. "Indicate whether you want story returned."

PAYMENT/TERMS Pays in contributor's copies.

TIPS Looks for "clear, moving, and specific work."

THE PAUMANOK REVIEW

E-mail: editor@paumanokreview.com. **E-mail:** submissions@paumanokreview.com. **Website:** www .paumanokreview.com. Estab. 2000.

J.P. Maney's *Western Exposures* was selected for inclusion in the *E2INK Best of the Web Anthology*.

NEEDS Short story length: 1,000-6,000+ words. Short short story length: 200-1,000 words.

HOW TO CONTACT Submit complete ms by e-mail with cover letter.

TIPS "Though this is an English-language publication, it is not US-or UK-centric. Please submit accordingly. *TPR* is a publication of Wind River Press, which also publishes *Critique* magazine and select print and electronic books."

PAVEMENT SAW

Pavement Saw Press, 321 Empire St., Montpelier, OH 43543. **E-mail:** info@pavementsaw.org. **Website:** http://pavementsaw.org. **Contact:** David Baratier, editor. *Pavement Saw*, published annually in August. Dedicates 15-20 pages of each issue to a featured writer.

> *Pavement Saw* is 88 pages, digest size, perfectbound. Receives about 9,000 poems/year, accepts less than 1%. Press run is 550. Single copy: $8; subscription: $14. Sample: $7. Make checks payable to Pavement Saw Press.

NEEDS "Letters, short fiction, and poetry on any subject, especially work." Does not want "poems that tell; no work by a deceased writer, and no translations."

TIPS "Pavement Saw Press has been publishing steadily since the fall of 1993. Each year since 1999, we have published at least 4 full-length, paperback poetry collections, with some printed in library edition hard covers, 1 chapbook, and a yearly literary journal anthology. We specialize in finding authors who have been widely published in literary journals but have not published a chapbook or full-length book."

PEARL

3030 E. Second St., Long Beach, CA 90803. (562)434-4523. **E-mail:** pearlmag@aol.com. **Website:** www.pearlmag.com. **Contact:** Joan Jobe Smith and Marilyn Johnson, poetry editors. Estab. 1974. "*Pearl* is an eclectic publication, a place for lively, readable poetry and prose that speaks to real people about real life in direct, living language, profane or sublime."

> "Our annual fiction issue features the winner of our Pearl Short Story Prize contest as well as short shorts, and some of the longer stories in our contest. Length: 1,200 words. No obscure, experimental fiction. A $15 entry fee includes a copy of the magazine; all entries are considered for publication."

NEEDS Nothing sentimental, obscure, predictable, abstract, or cliché-ridden poetry or fiction. Length: 1,200 words.

HOW TO CONTACT Submissions are accepted from January-June only. Mss received between July and December will be returned unread. No e-mail submissions, except from countries outside the U.S. See guidelines.

PAYMENT/TERMS The winner of the Pearl Short Story Prize receives $250 and 10 copies of the issue the story appears in.

TIPS "We look for vivid, *dramatized* situations and characters, stories written in an original voice, that make sense and follow a clear narrative line. What makes a manuscript stand out is more elusive, though—more to do with feeling and imagination than anything else."

THE PEDESTAL MAGAZINE

6815 Honors Court, Charlotte, NC 28210. (704)643-0244. **E-mail:** pedmagazine@carolina.rr.com. **Website:** www.thepedestalmagazine.com. **Contact:** John Amen, editor-in-chief. Estab. 2000. "We are committed to promoting diversity and celebrating the voice of the individual."

NEEDS "We are receptive to all sorts of high-quality literary fiction. Genre fiction is encouraged as long as it crosses or comments upon its genre and is both character driven and psychologically acute.

HOW TO CONTACT "We encourage submissions of short fiction, no more than 3 flash fiction pieces at a time. There is no need to query prior to submitting; please submit via the submission form—no email to the editor." Length: 4,000 words.

PAYMENT/TERMS Pays $40/poem ; 8¢/word.

TIPS "If you send us your work, please wait for a response to your first submission before you submit again."

PENNSYLVANIA ENGLISH

Penn State DuBois, College Place, DuBois, PA 15801-3199. (814)375-4785. **Fax:** (814)375-4785. **E-mail:** avallone@psu.edu. **Website:** www.english.iup.edu/pcea/publications.htm. **Contact:** Dr. Jess Haggerty, editor; Tony Vallone, poetry editor. Estab. 1985. *Pennsylvania English*, published annually, is "sponsored by the Pennsylvania College English Association. Our philosophy is quality. We publish literary fiction (and poetry and nonfiction). Our intended audience is literate, college-educated people."

Magazine: 5¼" × 8¼"; up to 200 pages; perfect-bound; full-color cover featuring the artwork of a Pennsylvania artist. Reads mss during the summer. Publishes 4-6 new writers/year. Has published work by Dave Kress, Dan Leone, Paul West, Liz Rosenberg, Walt MacDonald, Amy Pence, Jennifer Richter, and Jeff Schiff.

NEEDS No genre fiction or romance.

HOW TO CONTACT Submit via the online submission manager at https://paenglish.submittable.com/submit. "For all submissions, please include a brief bio for the contributors' page. Be sure to include your name, address, phone number, e-mail address, institutional affiliation (if you have one), the title of your short story, and any other relevant information. We will edit if necessary for space."

PAYMENT/TERMS Pays 1 contributor's copy.

TIPS "Quality of the writing is our only measure. We're not impressed by long-winded cover letters detailing awards and publications we've never heard of. Beginners and professionals have the same chance with us. We receive stacks of competently written but boring fiction. For a story to rise out of the rejection pile, it takes more than the basic competence."

PENTHOUSE VARIATIONS

2 Penn Plaza, Suite 1125, New York, NY 10121. **Website:** http://variations.com/?penthousevariations.com. Estab. 1978. Online journal publishing erotic short stories.

HOW TO CONTACT Send complete ms; no queries.

TIPS "*Variations* publishes first-person, sex-positive narratives in which the author fully describes sex scenes squarely focused within one of the magazine's usual categories, in highly explicit erotic detail. To submit material to *Variations* you must be 18 years of age or older."

PEREGRINE

Amherst Writers & Artists Press, P.O. Box 1076, Amherst, MA 01004. (413)253-3307. **Fax:** (413)253-7764. **E-mail:** peregrine@amherstwriters.com. **Website:** www.amherstwriters.com. **Contact:** Jan Haag, editor. Estab. 1983. *Peregrine*, published annually, features poetry and fiction. "*Peregrine* has provided a forum for national and international writers since 1983 and is committed to finding excellent work by emerging as well as established writers. We welcome work reflecting diversity of voice. We like to be sur-

prised. We look for writing that is honest, unpretentious, and memorable. We like to be surprised. All decisions are made by the editors."

Magazine: 6" × 9"; 100 pages; 60 lb. white offset paper; glossy cover. Annual. Member CLMP. Only considers work submitted from March 15 to May 15.

NEEDS Length: up to 750 words.

HOW TO CONTACT Submit via e-mail. Include word count on first page of submissions. "Shorter stories have a better chance."

PAYMENT/TERMS Pays in contributor's copies.

TIPS "Check guidelines before submitting your work. Familiarize yourself with *Peregrine*. We look for heart and soul as well as technical expertise. Trust your own voice."

PERMAFROST: A LITERARY JOURNAL

c/o English Dept., Univ. of Alaska Fairbanks, P.O. Box 755720, Fairbanks, AK 99775. **Website:** www.uaf.edu/english/permafrost. Estab. 1977. *Permafrost: A Literary Journal*, published in May/June, contains poems, short stories, creative nonfiction, black-and-white drawings, photographs, and prints. "We survive on both new and established writers, hoping and expecting to see the best work out there. We publish any style of poetry provided it is conceived, written, and revised with care. While we encourage submissions about Alaska and by Alaskans, we also welcome poems about anywhere, from anywhere. We have published work by E. Ethelbert Miller, W. Loran Smith, Peter Orlovsky, Jim Wayne Miller, Allen Ginsberg, and Andy Warhol."

Permafrost is about 200 pages, digest-sized, professionally printed, flat-spined. Subscription: $9/year, $16/2 years, $22/3 years. Back-issues $5.

HOW TO CONTACT Submit up to 5 poems at a time. Considers simultaneous submissions. "Poems should be typed, with author's name, address, phone, and e-mail at the top of each page." Reads submissions September 1-March 15. Include SASE; "e-mail submissions will not be read." Sometimes comments on poems. Guidelines available on website. Responds in 2-3 months.

PAYMENT/TERMS Pays 1 contributor copy; reduced contributor rate on additional copies.

PERSIMMON TREE: MAGAZINE OF THE ARTS BY WOMEN OVER SIXTY

1534 Campus Dr., Berkeley, CA 94708. **E-mail:** editor@persimmontree.org; Submissions@persimmontree.org. **Website:** www.persimmontree.org. **Contact:** Nan Gefen, editor. *"Persimmon Tree*, an online magazine, is a showcase for the creativity and talent of women over sixty. Too often older women's artistic work is ignored or disregarded, and only those few who are already established receive the attention they deserve. Yet many women are at the height of their creative abilities in their later decades and have a great deal to contribute. *Persimmon Tree* is committed to bringing this wealth of fiction, nonfiction, poetry, and art to a broader audience, for the benefit of all."

NEEDS Length: 1,200-3,000 words.

HOW TO CONTACT Submit complete ms via e-mail.

TIPS "High quality of writing, an interesting or unique point of view, make a manuscript stand out. Make it clear that you're familiar with the magazine. Tell us why the piece would work for our audience."

PHILADELPHIA STORIES

Fiction/Art/Poetry of the Delaware Valley, 93 Old York Rd., Suite 1/#1-753, Jenkintown, PA 19046. (215) 551-5889. **E-mail:** christine@philadelphiastories.org; info@philadelphiastories.org. **Website:** www.philadelphiastories.org. **Contact:** Christine Weiser, executive director/co-publisher. Estab. 2004. *Philadelphia Stories*, published quarterly, publishes "fiction, poetry, essays, and art written by authors living in, or originally from, Pennsylvania, Delaware, or New Jersey. *"Philadelphia Stories* also hosts 2 national writing contests: The Marguerite McGlinn Short Story Contest ($2,000 prize) and the Sandy Crimmins National Poetry Contest ($1,000 1st place prize, $250 2nd place prize). Visi tour website for details. *"Philadelphia Stories* also launched a "junior" version in 2012 for Philadelphia-area writers ages 18 and younger. Visit www.philadelphiastories.org/junior for details.

Literary magazine/journal. 8½" × 11"; 24 pages; 70# matte text, all four-color paper; 70# matte text cover. Contains illustrations, photographs. Receives 45-80 mss/month. Accepts 3-4 mss/issue for print, additional 1-2 online; 12-16 mss/year for print, 4-8 online. Publishes 50% new writers/year. Also publishes book reviews. Send review queries to: info@philadelphiastories.org. Subscription: "We offer $20 memberships that include home delivery." Make checks payable to *Philadelphia Stories*. Member: CLMP.

NEEDS "We will consider anything that is well written but are most inclined to publish literary or mainstream fiction. We are *not*particularly interested in most genres (sci fi/fantasy, romance, etc.)." Length: 5,000 words (maximum). Average length: 4,000 words. Also publishes short shorts; average length: 800 words.

HOW TO CONTACT Send complete ms with cover letter via online submission form only. Include estimated word count, list of publications, and affiliation to the Philadelphia area. Considers simultaneous submissions.

PAYMENT/TERMS Writers receive 2+ contributor's copies.

TIPS "All work is screened by 3 editorial board members who rank the work. These scores are processed at the end of the quarterly submission period, and then the board meets to decide which pieces will be published in print and online. We look for exceptional, polished prose, a controlled voice, strong characters and place, and interesting subjects. Follow guidelines. We cannot stress this enough. Read every guideline carefully and thoroughly before sending anything out. Send out only polished material. We reject many quality pieces for various reasons; try not to take rejection personally. Just because your piece isn't right for one publication doesn't mean it's bad. Selection is an extremely subjective process."

PHOEBE: A JOURNAL OF LITERATURE AND ART

MSN 2C5, George Mason University, 400 University Dr., Fairfax, VA 22030. **E-mail:** phoebe@gmu.edu. **Website:** www.phoebejournal.com. Estab. 1972. "We publish mainly fiction and poetry with some visual art. *Phoebe* prides itself on supporting up-and-coming writers, whose style, form, voice, and subject matter demostrate a vigorous appeal to the senses, intellect, and emotions of our readers."

NEEDS "No romance or erotica." Length: no more than 4,000 words.

HOW TO CONTACT Submit one fiction submission via e-mail or mail. Include SASE.

PAYMENT/TERMS Pays in contributor's copies.

THE PINCH

Dept. of English, The University of Memphis, Memphis, TN 38152. (901)678-4591. **E-mail:** editor@

thepinchjournal.com. **Website:** www.thepinchjour
nal.com. **Contact:** Kristen Iverson, editor-in-chief;
Justin Luzader, managing editor. Estab. 1980. (Formerly *River City*). "We publish fiction, creative nonfiction, poetry, and art of literary quality by both established and emerging artists."

○ Magazine: 7" × 10"; 168 pages. Semiannual.
"Semiannual literary magazine."

NEEDS "Character-based stories, fresh use of language." No genre fiction. Length: up to 5,000 words.

HOW TO CONTACT "We do NOT accept submissions via e-mail. Submissions sent via e-mail will not
receive a response. To submit, see guidelines." Submit through mail or via online submissions manager.

PAYMENT/TERMS 2 copies of journal in which work
appears on publication.

TIPS "We have a new look and a new edge. We're soliciting work from writers with a national or international reputation as well as strong, interesting work
from emerging writers. The Pinch Literary Award
(previously River City Writing Award) in fiction offers a $1,500 prize and publication. Check our web-
site for details."

THE PINK CHAMELEON

E-mail: dpfreda@juno.com. **Website:** www.thepink
chameleon.com. **Contact:** Dorothy Paula Freda, edi-
tor/publisher. Estab. 2000. *The Pink Chameleon*, published annually online, contains "family-oriented, upbeat poetry and stories, any genre in good taste that
gives hope for the future."

○ Receives 20 unsolicited mss/month. Receives
about 50 poems/year, accepts about 50%. Publishes 50% new writers/year. Has published
work by Deanne F. Purcell, Martin Green, Albert J. Manachino, James W. Collins, Ron Arnold, Sally Kosmalski, Susan Marie Davniero,
and Glen D. Hayes.

NEEDS "No violence for the sake of violence." No
novels or novel excerpts. Length: 500-2,500 words;
average length: 2,000 words.

HOW TO CONTACT Send complete ms in the body
of the e-mail. No attachments. Accepts reprints. No
simultaneous submissions. Reading period is January
1-April 30 and September 1-October 31.

PAYMENT/TERMS No payment.

TIPS "Simple, honest, evocative emotion, upbeat fiction and nonfiction submissions that give hope for the
future; well-paced plots; stories, poetry, articles, es-

says that speak from the heart. Read guidelines carefully. Use a good, but not ostentatious, opening hook.
Stories should have a beginning, middle and end that
make the reader feel the story was worth his or her
time. This also applies to articles and essays. In the latter 2, wrap your comments and conclusions in a neatly
packaged final paragraph. Turnoffs include violence
and bad language. Simple, genuine and sensitive work
does not need to shock with vulgarity to be interesting and enjoyable."

⊙ PINYON

Mesa State College, Languages, Literature and Mass
Communications, Mesa State College, 1100 North
Ave., Grand Junction, CO 81501-3122. **E-mail:** rphil
lis@mesa5.mesa.colorado.edu. **Website:** http://my
home.coloradomesa.edu/~rphillis/. **Contact:** Randy
Phillis, editor. Estab. 1995. *Pinyon*, published annually in June, prints "the best available contemporary
American poetry and fiction. No restrictions other
than excellence. We appreciate a strong voice."

○ Literary magazine/journal: 8½" × 5½", 120
pages, heavy paper. Contains illustrations and
photographs. Press run is 300; 100 distributed
free to contributors, friends, etc. Annual. Subscription: $8/year. Sample: $5. Make checks
payable to Pinyon, MSC.

TIPS "Ask yourself if the work is something you would
like to read in a publication."

○ PISGAH REVIEW

Division of Humanities, Brevard College, 1 Brevard
College Dr., Brevard, NC 28712. (828)884-8349. **E-
mail:** tinerjj@brevard.edu. **Website:** www.pisgahre
view.com. **Contact:** Jubal Tiner, editor. Estab. 2005.
"*Pisgah Review* publishes primarily literary short fiction, creative nonfiction, and poetry. Our only criteria
is quality of work; we look for the best."

○ Literary magazine/journal: 5½ × 8½, 120 pages. Includes cover artwork. Published Ron
Rash, Thomas Rain Crowe, Joan Conner, Gary
Fincke, Steve Almond, Fred Bahnson. Publication is copyrighted. Receives 85 mss/month.
Accepts 6-8 mss/issue; 12-15 mss/year. Publishes 5 new writers/year.

NEEDS Does not want genre fiction or inspirational
stories. Length: 2,000-7,500 words. Average length:
4,000 words. Average length of short shorts: 1,000
words.

HOW TO CONTACT "Send complete ms to our submission manager on our website."

PAYMENT/TERMS Writers receive 2 contributor's copies. Additional copies $7.

TIPS "We select work of only the highest quality. Grab us from the beginning and follow through. Engage us with your language and characters. A clean ms goes a long way toward acceptance. Stay true to the vision of your work, revise tirelessly, and submit persistently."

PLAIN SPOKE

Blackdamp Press, 12211 State Route 43, Amsterdam, OH 43903. (740) 543-3345. **E-mail:** plainspoke@gmail.com. **Website:** www.plainspoke.net. **Contact:** Cindy Kelly, editor. Estab. 2007. "We publish work that has a sense of word economy, strong voice, Americana appeal, tightness, and shies away from the esoteric and expositional. We like to be surprised."

Plain Spoke is 36-60 digest size, laser printed, saddle stitched, with a color art on cardstock cover. Receives 80 mss/month; Accepts 2-3 mss/issue, 10-12 mss/year. Receives about 2,500 poems/year, accepts about 5%. Press run is 300. Single copy: $8; subscription: $30. Make checks payable to Cindy Kelly, editor. Has published poetry by Claudia Burbank, Deborah Bogen, Doug Ramspeck, Amy Sargent. Quarterly.

NEEDS Does not want science fiction, furry, cliché, plot driven, formulaic. Length: 1,500-3,000 words. Average length: 1,750 words. Also publishes short shorts; average length: fewer than 1,000 words.

HOW TO CONTACT Prefers electronic submissions. Send complete ms with cover letter. Accepts submissions by e-mail and on disk. Include estimated word count, brief bio in third person, list of publications. "Limit publication credits to 6." Send disposable copy of ms and #10 SASE for reply only. Considers simultaneous submissions, multiple submissions.

PAYMENT/TERMS Pays 1 contributor's copy; additional copies $4.

TIPS "Work that surprises us stands out. We don't like the predictable. We don't want to feel like we're reading a story, pull us in. Make every word count and don't rely on adverbs."

PLANET: THE WELSH INTERNATIONALIST

P.O. Box 44, Aberystwyth Ceredigion SY23 3ZZ United Kingdom. **E-mail:** planet.enquiries@planet magazine.org.uk. **Website:** www.planetmagazine.org.uk. **Contact:** Emily Trahair, associate editor. Estab. 1970. *Planet: The Welsh Internationalist*, published quarterly, is a cultural magazine "centered on Wales, but with broader interests in arts, sociology, politics, history, and science."

Planet is 128 pages, A5, professionally printed, perfect-bound, with glossy color card cover. Receives about 500 submissions/year, accepts about 5%. Has published poetry by Nigel Jenkins, Anne Stevenson, and Les Murray. Press run is 1,550 (1,500 subscribers, about 10% libraries, 200 shelf sales). Single copy: £6.75; subscription: £22 (£38 overseas). Sample available.

NEEDS Wants "good poetry in a wide variety of styles. No limitations as to subject matter; length can be a problem." Would like to see more inventive, imaginative fiction that pays attention to language and experiments with form. No magical realism, horror, science fiction. Length: 1,500-4,000 words.

HOW TO CONTACT No submissions returned unless accompanied by an SASE. Writers submitting from abroad should send at least 3 IRCs for return of typescript; 1 IRC for reply only. E-mail queries accepted.

PAYMENT/TERMS Pays £50/1,000 words.

TIPS "We do not look for fiction which necessarily has a 'Welsh' connection, which some writers assume from our title. We try to publish a broad range of fiction and our main criterion is quality. Try to read copies of any magazine you submit to. Don't write out of the blue to a magazine which might be completely inappropriate for your work. Recognize that you are likely to have a high rejection rate, as magazines tend to favor writers from their own countries."

PLEIADES

Pleiades Press, Department of English, University of Central Missouri, Martin 336, Warrensburg, MO 64093. (660)543-8106. **E-mail:** pleiades@ucmo.edu. **Website:** www.ucmo.edu/englphil/pleiades. **Contact:** Kevin Prufer, editor-at-large. Estab. 1991. "We publish contemporary fiction, poetry, interviews, literary essays, special-interest personal essays, reviews for a general and literary audience from authors from around the world."

"Also sponsors the Lena-Miles Wever Todd Poetry Series competition, a contest for the best book ms by an American poet. The winner receives $1,000, publication by Pleiades Press, and distribution by Louisiana State University Press. **Deadline:** September 30. Send SASE for guidelines."

NEEDS Reads fiction year-round. No science fiction, fantasy, confession, erotica. Length: 2,000-6,000 words. Accepts queries for book reviews.

HOW TO CONTACT Send complete ms. Include cover letter with brief bio and list of publications. Include SASE. Cover art is solicited directly from artists. For summer submissions, the poetry and nonfiction editors will no longer accept mss sent between June 1 and August 31. Any sent after May 31 will be held until the end of summer.

PAYMENT/TERMS Pays $10 and contributor's copies.

TIPS "Submit in only 1 genre at a time to appropriate editors. Show care for your material and your readers—submit quality work in a professional format. Please do not send your only copy of anything."

PLOUGHSHARES

Emerson College, Ploughshares, 120 Boylston St., Boston, MA 02116. **Website:** www.pshares.org. **Contact:** Ladette Randolph, editor-in-chief/executive director; Andrea Martucci, managing editor. Estab. 1971. *Ploughshares*, published 3 times/year, is "a journal of new writing guest edited by prominent poets and writers to reflect different and contrasting points of view. Translations are welcome if permission has been granted. "Our mission is to present dynamic, contrasting views on what is valid and important in contemporary literature and to discover and advance significant literary talent." Editors have included Carolyn Forché, Gerald Stern, Rita Dove, Chase Twichell, and Marilyn Hacker. Has published poetry by Donald Hall, Li-Young Lee, Robert Pinsky, Brenda Hillman, and Thylias Moss.

○ A competitive and highly prestigious market. Rotating and guest editors make cracking the lineup even tougher, since it's difficult to know what is appropriate to send. *Ploughshares* is 200 pages, digest size. Receives about 11,000 poetry, fiction, and essay submissions/year. Press run is 6,000. Subscription: $30 domestic, $30 plus shipping (see website) foreign. Sample: $14 current issue, $7 back issue, please inquire for shipping rates. Reads submissions June 1-January 15 (postmark); mss submitted January 16-May 31 will be returned unread.

Recently published work by ZZ Packer, Antonya Nelson, Stuart Dybek.

NEEDS "No genre (science fiction, detective, gothic, adventure, etc.), popular formula, or commerical fiction whose purpose is to entertain rather than to illuminate."

HOW TO CONTACT "We do accept electronic submissions—there is a $3 fee per submission, which is waived if you are a subscriber."

TIPS "We no longer structure issues around preconceived themes. If you believe your work is in keeping with our general standards of literary quality and value, submit at any time during our reading period."

POCKETS

The Upper Room, P.O. Box 340004, Nashville, TN 37203. (615)340-7333. **Fax:** (615)340-7267. **E-mail:** pockets@upperroom.org. **Website:** pockets.upperroom.org. **Contact:** Lynn W. Gilliam, editor. Estab. 1981. Magazine published 11 times/year. "*Pockets* is a Christian devotional magazine for children ages 8-12. All submissions should address the broad theme of the magazine. Each issue is built around one theme with material which can be used by children in a variety of ways. Scripture stories, fiction, poetry, prayers, art, graphics, puzzles, and activities are included. Submissions do not need to be overtly religious. They should help children experience a Christian lifestyle that is not always a neatly wrapped moral package but is open to the continuing revelation of God's will. Seasonal material, both secular and liturgical, is desired."

NEEDS Adventure, ethnic/multicultural, historical (general), religious/inspirational, slice-of-life vignettes. No violence, science fiction, romance, fantasy, or talking animal stories. Length: 600-1,000 words.

HOW TO CONTACT Send complete ms with SASE. Does not accept e-mail or fax submissions.

PAYMENT/TERMS Pays 14¢/word.

TIPS "Theme stories, role models, and retold scripture stories are most open to freelancers. Poetry is also open. It is very helpful if writers read our writers' guidelines and themes on our website."

POINTED CIRCLE

Portland Community College—Cascade, 705 N. Killing, Portland, OR 97217. **E-mail:** wendy.bourgeois@pcc.edu. **Contact:** Wendy Bourgeois, faculty advisor. Estab. 1980. Magazine: 80 pages; black-and-white illustrations; photos. "Anything of interest to educationally/culturally mixed audience. We will read whatever is sent, but encourage writers to remember we are a quality literary/arts magazine intended to promote the arts in the community. No pornography, nothing trite. Be mindful of deadlines and length limits."

NEEDS Length: Up to 3,000 words.

HOW TO CONTACT Accepts submissions by e-mail, mail; artwork in high-resolution digital form. Submitted materials will not be returned; SASE for notification only. Accepts multiple submissions. Accepts submissions only October 1-March 1, for July 1 issue.

PAYMENT/TERMS Pays 2 contributor's copies.

① THE PORTLAND REVIEW

Portland State University, P.O. Box 347, Portland, OR 97207-0347. (503)725-4533. **E-mail:** theportland review@gmail.com. **Website:** portlandreview.org. **Contact:** Tim Faiella, editor. Estab. 1956. Press run is 1,000 for subscribers, libraries, and bookstores nationwide. Single copy: $9; subscription: $27/year, $54/2 years. Sample: $8.

NEEDS No fantasy, detective, or western. Length: 5,000 words maximum.

HOW TO CONTACT Send complete ms.

PAYMENT/TERMS Pays contributor's copies.

TIPS "View website for current samples and guidelines."

① POST ROAD

P.O. Box 600725, Newtown, MA 02460. **E-mail:** postroad@bc.edu. **Website:** www.postroadmag.com. **Contact:** Chris Boucher, managing editor.

◐ Work from *Post Road* has received the following honors: honorable mention in the 2001 O. Henry Prize Issue guest edited by Michael Chabon, Mary Gordon, and Mona Simpson; the Pushcart Prize; honorable mention in *The Best American Nonfiction* series; and inclusion in the *Best American Short Stories* 2005.

HOW TO CONTACT Submit using online submission form. Accepts submissions February 1-April 1 and June 1-August 1.

PAYMENT/TERMS Pays 2 contributor's copies.

TIPS "Looking for interesting narrative, sharp dialogue, deft use of imagery and metaphor. Be persistent and be open to criticism."

◐①⑤ POSTSCRIPTS: THE A TO Z OF FANTASTIC FICTION

PS Publishing LTD., Grosvenor House, 1 New Road, Hornsea East Yorkshire HU18 1P9 England. 0-11-44-1964 537575. **Fax:** 0-11-44-1964 537535. **E-mail:** editor@pspublishing.co.uk. **Website:** www.pspublishing.co.uk. **Contact:** Peter Crowther, editor/publisher. Estab. 2004.

◐ *PS Publishing* has received 5 British Fantasy Awards, a World Fantasy Award, an International Horror Guild Award, and a Horror Writers Association Award.

NEEDS Wants "science fiction, fantasy, horror,, and crime/suspense. We focus on the cerebral rather than the visceral, with an emphasis on quality literary fiction within the specified areas." Length: 3,000-8,000 words.

HOW TO CONTACT Submit complete ms with cover letter. Submit by mail or e-mail.

PAYMENT/TERMS Pays 4-7¢/word, 2 contributor's copies.

TIPS "Read the magazine."

① POTOMAC REVIEW

Montgomery College, 51 Mannakee St., MT/212, Rockville, MD 20850. (301)251-7417. **Fax:** (301)738-1745. **E-mail:** PotomacReviewEditor@montgomerycollege.edu. **Website:** www.montgomerycollege.edu/potomacreview. **Contact:** Julie Wakeman-Linn, editor-in-chief. Estab. 1994. *Potomac Review* "reflects a view of our region looking out to the world, and in turn, seeks how the world views the region."

◐ Magazine: 5½" × 8½"; 175 pages; 50 lb. paper; 65 lb. color cover. Biannual.

NEEDS Prose. Length: up to 5,000 words.

HOW TO CONTACT Submit via online submissions manager. Reading period September 1-May 1; only one submission per genre per reading period.

PAYMENT/TERMS Pays in contributor's copies.

TIPS "Send us interesting, well-crafted stories. Have something to say in an original, provocative voice. Read recent issue to get a sense of the journal's new direction."

◐①⑤ THE PRAIRIE JOURNAL

P.O. Box 68073, 28 Crowfoot Terrace NW, Calgary AB Y3G 3N8 Canada. **E-mail:** editor@prairiejournal.org (queries only); prairiejournal@yahoo.com. **Website:** www.prairiejournal.org. **Contact:** A.E. Burke, literary editor. Estab. 1983. "The audience is literary, university, library, scholarly, and creative readers/writers."

◐ "Use our mailing address for submissions and queries with samples or for clippings."

NEEDS No genre (romance, horror, western—sagebrush or cowboys), erotic, science fiction, or mystery. Length: 100-3,000 words.

HOW TO CONTACT Send complete ms. No e-mail submissions.

PAYMENT/TERMS Pays $10-75.

TIPS "We publish many, many new writers and are always open to unsolicited submissions because we are 100% freelance. Do not send U.S. stamps, always use IRCs. We have poems, interviews, stories, and reviews online (query first)."

⓪ⓒ PRAIRIE SCHOONER

The University of Nebraska Press, Prairie Schooner, 123 Andrews Hall, University of Nebraska, Lincoln, NE 68588. (402)472-0911. **Fax:** (402)472-1817. **E-mail:** PrairieSchooner@unl.edu. **Website:** http://prairie schooner.unl.edu. **Contact:** Marianne Kunkel, managing editor. Estab. 1926. "We look for the best fiction, poetry, and nonfiction available to publish, and our readers expect to read stories, poems, and essays of extremely high quality. We try to publish a variety of styles, topics, themes, points of view, and writers with a variety of backgrounds in all stages of their careers. We like work that is compelling—intellectually or emotionally—either in form, language, or content."

NEEDS "We try to remain open to a variety of styles, themes, and subject matter. We look for high-quality writing, 3-D characters, well-wrought plots, setting, etc. We are open to realistic and/or experimental fiction."

HOW TO CONTACT Send complete ms with SASE and cover letter listing previous publications—where, when. Submissions must be received between September 1 and May 1.

PAYMENT/TERMS Pays 3 copies of the issue in which the writer's work is published.

TIPS "Send us your best, most carefully crafted work and be persistent. Submit again and again. Constantly work on improving your writing. Read widely in literary fiction, nonfiction, and poetry. Read *Prairie Schooner* to know what we publish."

⊕ PRAIRIE WINDS

Dakota Wesleyan University English Department, 1200 University Ave., Box 536, Mitchell, SD 57301. (605)995-2633. **E-mail:** prairiewinds@dwu.edu. **Website:** www.dwu.edu/prairiewinds. **Contact:** Joe Ditta, faculty advisor. Estab. 1946. *Prairie Winds* is a literary annual interested in poetry, fiction, creative nonfic-

tion, and essays of general interest. Selection of mss takes place in February, magazine goes to press in March, and is distributed in April of each year.

NEEDS No pornography. Length: 3,000 words maximum.

HOW TO CONTACT Submit complete ms. Include SASE, short bio, and e-mail address.

PAYMENT/TERMS Pays contributor's copies.

TIPS *Prairie Winds* accepts only a small proportion of works submitted. There are no restrictions on subject matter, except no pornography. There are no restrictions on style or form. Writers need to submit persuasively good work. Editors of *Prairie Winds* are eclectic and open-minded, and they like experimental as well as traditional work.

⊜⊘ PREMONITIONS

13 Hazely Combe, Arrenton Isle of Wight PO30 3AJ United Kingdom. **E-mail:** mail@pigasuspress.co.uk. **Website:** www.pigasuspress.co.uk. **Contact:** Tony Lee, editor.

NEEDS "No sword and sorcery, supernatural horror."

TIPS "Potential contributors are advised to study recent issues of the magazine."

✪⓪ⓒ⑤ PRISM INTERNATIONAL

Department of Creative Writing, Buch E462, 1866 Main Mall, University of British Columbia, Vancouver BC V6T 1Z1 Canada. (604)822-2514. **Fax:** (604)822-3616. **E-mail:** prismcirculation@gmail .com. **Website:** www.prismmagazine.ca. Estab. 1959. A quarterly international journal of contemporary writing—fiction, poetry, drama, creative nonfiction, and translation. Readership: public and university libraries, individual subscriptions, bookstores—a worldwide audience concerned with the contemporary in literature. "We have no thematic or stylistic allegiances: Excellence is our main criterion for acceptance of manuscripts."

🗨 *PRISM International* is 80 pages, digest size, elegantly printed, flat spined, with original color artwork on a glossy card cover. Receives 1,000 submissions/year, accepts about 80. Circulation is for 1,200 subscribers. Receives over 100 unsolicited mss/month. Accepts 70 mss/year. "*PRISM* publishes both new and established writers; our contributors have included Franz Kafka, Gabriel García Márquez, Michael Ondaatje, Margaret Laurence, Mark Anthony Jarman, Gail Anderson-Dargatz, and Eden

Robinson." Publishes ms 4 months after acceptance. **Publishes 7 new writers/year.** Recently published work by Ibi Kaslik, Melanie Little, Mark Anthony Jarman. Subscription: $35/year for Canadian subscriptions, $40/year for US subscriptions, $45/year for international. Sample: $12.

NEEDS Experimental, traditional. New writing that is contemporary and literary. Short stories and self-contained novel excerpts (up to 25 double-spaced pages). Works of translation are eagerly sought and should be accompanied by a copy of the original. Would like to see more translations. "No gothic, confession, religious, romance, pornography, or sci-fi." Also looking for creative nonfiction that is literary, not journalistic, in scope and tone. Publishes short shorts. Also publishes poetry. For Drama: one-acts/excerpts of no more than 1500 words preferred. Also interested in seeing dramatic monologues. "New writing that is contemporary and literary. Short stories and self-contained novel excerpts. Works of translation are eagerly sought and should be accompanied by a copy of the original.

HOW TO CONTACT Send complete ms by mail: Department of Creative Writing, Buch E462, 1866 Main Mall, University of British Columbia, Vancouver, BC V6T 1Z1 Canada; or submit online through prism magazine.ca. "Keep it simple. U.S. contributors take note: Do not send SASEs with U.S. stamps, they are not valid in Canada. Send IRCs instead." Responds in 4 months to queries; 3-6 months to mss. Sample copy for $12 or on website. Writer's guidelines online. Send complete ms.

PAYMENT/TERMS Pays $20/printed page of prose, $40/printed page of poetry, and 1-year subscription. Pays on publication for first North American serial rights. Selected authors are paid an additional $10/page for digital rights. Cover art pays $300 and 4 copies of issue. Sponsors awards/contests, including annual short fiction, poetry, and nonfiction contests. Pays $20/printed page, and 1-year subscription

TIPS "We are looking for new and exciting fiction. Excellence is still our No. 1 criterion. As well as poetry, imaginative nonfiction and fiction, we are especially open to translations of all kinds, very short fiction pieces and drama which work well on the page. Translations must come with a copy of the original language work. We pay an additional $10/printed

page to selected authors whose work we place on our online version of *PRISM*."

◐◑◉ PSEUDOPOD

Escape Artists, Inc., P.O. Box 965609, Marietta, GA 30066. **Fax:** (866)373-8739. **E-mail:** editor@pseudopod.org. **E-mail:** submit@pseudopod.org. **Website:** http://pseudopod.org. **Contact:** Shawn M. Garrett, editor. "*Pseudopod* is the premier horror podcast magazine. Every week we bring you chilling short stories from some of today's best horror authors, in convenient audio format for your computer or MP3 player."

NEEDS Length: 2,000-6,000 words (short fiction); 500-1,500 words (flash fiction).

HOW TO CONTACT Does not want multiple submissions. Paste submission in body of an e-mail you will use for correspondence. Include contact information, cover statement, and word count.

PAYMENT/TERMS Pays $100 for short fiction, $20 for flash fiction.

TIPS "Let the writing be guided by a strong sense of who the (hopefully somewhat interesting) protagonist is, even if zero time is spent developing any other characters. Preferably, tell the story using standard past tense, third person, active voice."

A PUBLIC SPACE

323 Dean St., Brooklyn, NY 11217. (718)858-8067. **E-mail:** general@apublicspace.org. **Website:** www.apublicspace.org. **Contact:** Brigid Hughes, editor. *A Public Space*, published quarterly, "is an independent magazine of literature and culture. In an era that has relegated literature to the margins, we plan to make fiction and poetry the stars of a new conversation. We believe that stories are how we make sense of our lives and how we learn about other lives. We believe that stories matter."

◖ Single copy: $15; subscription: $36/year or $60/2 years.

HOW TO CONTACT Submit one piece of fiction at a time via online submission form. Does not accept previously published ms. Accepts simultaneous submissions.

◖ THE PUCKERBRUSH REVIEW

University of Maine, English Department, 413 Neville Hall, Orono, ME 04469. **E-mail:** sanphip@aol.com. **Website:** http://puckerbrushreview.com. **Contact:** Sanford Phippen, Editor. Estab. 1979. *The Puckerbrush Review*, a print-only journal published twice/

year, looks for "freshness and simplicity." 9" × 12"; 80-100 pages; illustrations. Semiannual.

NEEDS "Wants to see more original, quirky, and well-written fiction. No genre fiction. Nothing cliché, nothing overly sensational except in its human interest."

HOW TO CONTACT Submit by clicking link on website.

TIPS "Please submit your poetry, short stories, literary essays, and reviews through our website link. Hard-copy submissions will no longer be accepted."

○ PUERTO DEL SOL

New Mexico State University, English Department, P.O.Box 30001, MSC 3E, Las Cruces, NM 88003. (505)646-3931. **E-mail:** contact@puertodelsol.org. **Website:** www.puertodelsol.org. **Contact:** Carmen Giménez Smith, editor-in-chief. Estab. 1964. "We publish innovative work from emerging and established writers and artists. "

○   Magazine: 7" × 9"; 200 pages; 60 lb. paper; 70 lb. cover stock. *Puerto del Sol* is 150 pages, digest size, professionally printed, flat spined, with matte card cover with art. Press run is 1,250 (300 subscribers, 25-30 libraries). Single copies: $10. Subscriptions: $20/1 year, $35/2 years, $45/3 years. Accepts 8-12 mss/issue; 16-24 mss/ year. Reading period is September 15-March 31. Publishes several new writers/year. Recently published work by David Trinidad, Molly Gaudry, Ray Gonzalez, Cynthia Cruz, Steve Tomasula, Denise Leto, Rae Bryant, Joshua Cohen, Blake Butler, Trinie Dalton, and Rick Moody.

NEEDS Poetry, fiction, nonfiction, drama, theory, artwork, interviews, reviews, and interesting combinations thereof.

HOW TO CONTACT Send complete ms. Submit 1 short story or 2-4 short short stories at a time through online submission manager.

PAYMENT/TERMS Pays 2 contributor's copies.

TIPS "We are especially pleased to publish emerging writers who work to push their art form or field of study in new directions."

○ ❸ PURPOSE

1251 Virginia Ave., Harrisonburg, VA 22802. **E-mail:** CarolD@MennoMedia.org; purposeeditor@mpn. net. **Website:** www.mennomedia.org. **Contact:** Carol Duerksen, editor. Estab. 1968. *Purpose*, published

monthly by Faith & Life Resources, an imprint of the Mennonite Publishing Network (the official publisher for the Mennonite Church in the US and Canada), is a "religious young adult/adult monthly." Focuses on "action-oriented, discipleship living."

Purpose is digest size, 5⅜" × 8⅜"; 8 pages, 4-color printing throughout. Press run is 8,000. Receives about 2,000 poems/year, accepts 150. Sample (with guidelines): $2 and 9" × 12" SAE. Receives 150 unsolicited mss/month. Accepts 12 mss/issue; 140 mss/ year. Publishes ms 1 year after acceptance. **Publishes 15-25 new writers/year.** Occasionally comments on rejected mss.

NEEDS Historical (related to discipleship theme), humor/satire, religious/inspirational. No militaristic, narrow patriotism, or racist themes. Length: 600 words; average length: 400 words. Produce the story with specificity so that it appears to take place somewhere and with real people. No militaristic/narrow patriotism or racism.

HOW TO CONTACT Send complete ms. Send all submissions by Word attachment via e-mail. Responds in 3 months to queries. Accepts simultaneous submissions, reprints, multiple submissions. Sample copy and writer's guidelines for $2, 6" × 9" SAE and 2 first-class stamps. Writer's guidelines online. Send complete ms.

PAYMENT/TERMS Pays up to 7¢/word for stories, and 2 contributor's copies. Pays on acceptance for one-time rights. Pays up to 7¢ for stories, and 2 contributor's copies.

TIPS "Many stories are situational, how to respond to dilemmas. Looking for first-person story lines. Write crisp, action moving, personal style, focused upon an individual, a group of people, or an organization. The story form is an excellent literary device to help readers explore discipleship issues. The first 2 paragraphs are crucial in establishing the mood/issue to be resolved in the story. Work hard on the development of these."

❶ QUARTER AFTER EIGHT

QAE, Ellis Hall, Ohio University, Athens, OH 45701. **Website:** www.quarteraftereight.org. **Contact:** Steve Coughlin.

NEEDS No traditional, convential fiction. Length: no more than 10,000 words.

HOW TO CONTACT Uses online submissions form.

PAYMENT/TERMS Pays 2 contributor's copies.

TIPS "We look for prose and poetry that is innovative, exploratory, and—most important—well written. Please subscribe to our journal and read what is published to get acquainted with the QAE aesthetic."

⬤◐⬤⑤ QUARTERLY WEST

University of Utah, 255 S. Central Campus Dr., Room 3500, Salt Lake City, UT 84112. **E-mail:** quarterly west@gmail.com. **Website:** www.quarterlywest.utah .edu. **Contact:** C.A. Schaefer & Sadie Hoagland, editors. Estab. 1976. "We publish fiction, poetry, and nonfiction in long and short formats, and will consider experimental as well as traditional works."

◯ *Quarterly West* was awarded first place for editorial content from the American Literary Magazine Awards. Work published in the magazine has been selected for inclusion in the *Pushcart Prize* anthology and *The Best American Short Stories* anthology.

NEEDS No preferred lengths; interested in longer, fuller short stories and short shorts. No detective, science fiction, or romance.

HOW TO CONTACT Send complete ms using online submissions manager.

PAYMENT/TERMS Pays $15-100 and 2 contributor's copies.

TIPS "We publish a special section of short shorts every issue, and we also sponsor a biennial novella contest. We are open to experimental work—potential contributors should read the magazine! Don't send more than 1 story per submission. Biennial novella competition guidelines available upon request with SASE. We prefer work with interesting language and detail—plot or narrative are less important. We don't do western themes or religious work."

◯◯⑤ QUEEN'S QUARTERLY

144 Barrie St., Queen's University, Kingston ON K7L 3N6 Canada. (613)533-2667. **Fax:** (613)533-6822. **E-mail:** queens.quarterly@queensu.ca. **Website:** www .queensu.ca/quarterly. **Contact:** Joan Harcourt, editor. Estab. 1893. *Queen's Quarterly* is "a general interest intellectual review featuring articles on science, politics, humanities, arts and letters, extensive book reviews, some poetry and fiction."

◯ Digest size, 224 pages. Press run is 3,500. Receives about 400 submissions of poetry/ year, accepts 40. Has published work by Gail Anderson-Dargatz, Tim Bowling, Emma Donohue, Viktor Carr, Mark Jarman, Rick

Bowers, and Dennis Bock. Subscription: $20 Canadian, $25 U.S. for U.S. and foreign subscribers. Sample: $6.50 U.S.

NEEDS Length: 2,500-3,000 words. "Submissions over 3,000 words shall not be accepted."

HOW TO CONTACT Send complete ms with SASE and/or IRC. No reply with insufficient postage. Accepts 2 mss/issue; 8 mss/year. Publishes 5 new writers/year.

PAYMENT/TERMS Pays on publication for first North American serial rights. Sends galleys to author.

THE RAG

11901 SW 34th Ave., Portland, OR 97219. **E-mail:** ra glitmag@gmail.com. **Website:** http://raglitmag.com. **Contact:** Seth Porter, editor; Dan Reilly, editor. Estab. 2011. "*The Rag* focuses on the grittier genres that tend to fall by the wayside at more traditional literary magazines. *The Rag*'s ultimate goal is to put the literary magazine magazine back into the entertainment market while rekindling the social and cultural value short fiction once held in North American literature."

NEEDS "We accept all styles and themes." Length: 2,000-10,000 words.

HOW TO CONTACT Send complete ms.

PAYMENT/TERMS Pays $50-300+.

TIPS "We like gritty material; material that is psychologically believable and that has some humor in it, dark or otherwise. We like subtle themes, original characters, and sharp wit."

⑤ RAINBOW RUMPUS

P.O. Box 6881, Minneapolis, MN 55406. (612)721-6442. **E-mail:** fictionandpoetry@rainbowrumpus .org; admin@rainbowrumpus.org. **Website:** www .rainbowrumpus.org. **Contact:** Beth Wallace, fiction editor. Estab. 2005. "*Rainbow Rumpus* is the world's only online literary magazine for children and youth with lesbian, gay, bisexual, and transgender (LGBT) parents. We are creating a new genre of children's and young adult fiction. Please carefully read and observe the guidelines on our website.

NEEDS "Stories should be written from the point of view of children or teens with lesbian, gay, bisexual, or transgender parents or other family members, or who are connected to the LGBT community. Stories for 4- to 12-year-old children should be approximately 800-2,500 words in length. Stories for 13- to 18-year-olds may be as long as 5,000 words. Stories featuring families of color, bisexual parents, transgender parents, family members with disabilities, and mixed-race families are particularly welcome."

HOW TO CONTACT "All fiction and poetry submissions should be sent via our contact page. Be sure to select the 'Submissions' category. A staff member will be in touch with you shortly to obtain a copy of your manuscript."

PAYMENT/TERMS Pays $75/story. "We purchase first North American online rights."

TIPS "Emerging writers encouraged to submit. You do not need to be a member of the LGBT community to participate."

⬤⬤ RATTAPALLAX

Rattapallax Press, 217 Thompson St., Suite 353, New York, NY 10012. (212)560-7459. **E-mail:** info@rattapallax.com. **Website:** www.rattapallax.com. **Contact:** Alan Cheuse, fiction editor. Estab. 1999. *Rattapallax*, published semiannually, is named for "Wallace Stevens's word for the sound of thunder." The magazine includes a DVD featuring poetry films and audio files. "*Rattapallax* is looking for the extraordinary in modern poetry and prose that reflect the diversity of world cultures. Our goals are to create international dialogue using literature and focus on what is relevant to our society."

○ *Rattapallax* is 112 pages, magazine size, offset printed, perfect-bound, with 12-pt. CS1 cover; some illustrations; photos. Press run is 2,000 (100 subscribers, 50 libraries, 1,200 shelf sales); 200 distributed free to contributors, reviews, and promos. Single copy: $7.95; no subscriptions. Make checks payable to *Rattapallax*. Receives 15 unsolicited mss/month. Accepts 3 mss/issue; 6 mss/year. Agented fiction 15%. Receives about 5,000 poems/year; accepts 2%. Publishes 3 new writers/year. Has published work by Stuart Dybek, Howard Norman, Molly Giles, Rick Moody, Anthony Hecht, Sharon Olds, Lou Reed, Marilyn Hacker, Billy Collins, and Glyn Maxwell.

NEEDS Length: up to 2,000 words.

HOW TO CONTACT Submit via Submittable at https://rattapallax.submittable.com/submit.

PAYMENT/TERMS Pays 2 contributor's copies.

TIPS "The editor-in-chief, senior editor, and associate editor review all the submissions and then decide on which to accept every week. Near publication time, all accepted work is narrowed, and unused work is kept for the next issue."

⬤⬤ THE RAVEN CHRONICLES

A Journal of Art, Literature, & the Spoken Word, 12346 Sand Point Way N.E., Seattle, WA 98125. (206)941-2955. **E-mail:** editors@ravenchronicles .org. **Website:** www.ravenchronicles.org. Estab. 1991.

NEEDS "Experimental work is always of interest." Length: 10-12 pages. "Check with us for maximum length. We do not print longer pieces."

HOW TO CONTACT Submit complete ms via postal mail with SASE.

TIPS "*The Raven Chronicles* publishes work which reflects the cultural diversity of the Pacific Northwest, Canada, and other areas of America. We promote art, literature, and the spoken word for an audience that is hip, literate, funny, informed, and lives in a society that has a multicultural sensibility. We publish fiction, talk art/spoken word, poetry, essays, reflective articles, reviews, interviews, and contemporary art. We look for work that reflects the author's experiences, perceptions, and insights."

⬤⬤ THE READER

The Reader Organisation, The Firary Centre, Bute St., Liverpool L5 3LA United Kingdom. **E-mail:** magazine@thereader.org.uk; info@thereader.org .uk. **Website:** www.thereader.org.uk. **Contact:** Philip Davis, editor. Estab. 1997. "*The Reader* is a quarterly literary magazine aimed at the intelligent 'common reader'—from those just beginning to explore serious literary reading to professional teachers, academics, and writers. As well as publishing short fiction and poetry by new writers and established names, the magazine features articles on all aspects of literature, language, and reading; regular features, including a literary quiz and 'Our Spy in NY', a bird's-eye view of literary goings-on in New York; reviews; and readers' recommendations of books that have made a difference to them. *The Reader* is unique among literary magazines in its focus on reading as a creative, important, and pleasurable activity, and in its combination of high-quality material and presentation with a genuine commitment to ordinary but dedicated readers."

○ Has published work by Karen King Arbisala, Ray Tallis, Sasha Dugdale, Vicki Seal, David Constantine, Jonathan Meades, Ramesh Avadhani.

NEEDS Length: 1,000-3,000 words. Average length: 2,300 words. Publishes short shorts. Average length of short shorts: 1,500 words. Also publishes literary essays, literary criticism, poetry.

HOW TO CONTACT No e-mail submissions. Send complete ms with cover letter. Include estimated word count, brief bio, list of publications.

TIPS "The style or polish of the writing is less important than the deep structure of the story (though of course, it matters that it's well written). The main persuasive element is whether the story moves us—and that's quite hard to quantify—it's something to do with the force of the idea and the genuine nature of enquiry within the story. When fiction is the writer's natural means of thinking things through, that'll get us. "

THE REALM BEYOND

Fortress Publishing, Inc., 3704 Hartzdale Dr., Camp Hill, PA 17011. **E-mail:** realm.beyond@yahoo.com. **Website:** www.fortresspublishinginc.com. **Contact:** Brian Koscienski, editor. Estab. 2010.

Magazine: 5½" × 8½"; 48-64 pages; white paper. Has published work by Jeff Young, Patrick Thomas, Kevin Wallis, and Richard Marsden. Publishes new writers. Accepts work by beginning and established writers. Sometimes comments on or critiques rejected mss.

NEEDS "No profanity. No graphic sex or violence." Length: 1,000-5,000 words. Average length: 3,000.

HOW TO CONTACT Send complete ms with cover letter via e-mail. Include estimated word count, brief bio, and list of publications. Does not accept multiple submissions.

PAYMENT/TERMS Pays 1 contributor's copy.

TIPS "We enjoy interesting and engaging stories. If it's a story about a 13-year-old girl named Mary coping with the change to womanhood while poignantly reflecting the recent passing of her favorite aunt Gertrude, we don't want it! Now, if Mary is the 13-year-old daughter of a vampire cowboy who stumbles upon a government conspiracy involving aliens and unicorns while investigating, hard-boiled style, the grizzly murder of her favorite aunt Gertrude, then we'll take a look at it."

REALPOETIK

E-mail: realpoetikblog@gmail.com. **Website:** www .realpoetik.org. Estab. 1993. "We do not want to see anything that fits neatly into categories. We subvert categories."

Publishes 20-30 new poets/year.

TIPS "Be different but interesting. Complexity and consciousness are always helpful. Write short. We're a postmodern e-zine. Query us before submitting at RealPoetikblog@gmail.com."

REDACTIONS: POETRY, POETICS, & PROSE

58 S. Main St., 3rd Floor, Brockport, NY 14420. **E-mail:** redactionspoetry@yahoo.com (poetry); reda tionsprose@yahoo.com (prose). **Website:** www.re dactions.com.

HOW TO CONTACT "We only accept submissions by e-mail. We read submissions throughout the year. E-mail us and attach submission into one Word, Wordpad, Notepad, .rtf, or .txt document, or place in the body of an e-mail. Include brief bio and your snail mail address. Query after 90 days if you haven't heard from us. See website for full guidelines for each genre, including artwork."

THE RED CLAY REVIEW

Dr. Jim Elledge, Director, M. A. in Professional Writing Program, Department of English, Kennesaw State University, 1000 Chastain Rd., #2701, Kennesaw, GA 30144. **E-mail:** redclay2013@gmail.com. **Website:** http://redclayreview.com. **Contact:** Dr. Jim Elledge, director, M.A. in Professional Writing Program. Estab. 2008.

NEEDS "We do not have any specific themes or topics, but keep in mind that we are a literary publication. We will read whatever is sent in. We will publish whatever we deem to be great literary writing. So in essence, every topic is open to submission, and we are all interested in a wide variety of subjects. We do not prohibit any topic or subject matter from being submitted. As long as submissions adhere to our guidelines, we are open to reading them. However, subject matter in any area that is too extreme may be less likely to be published because we want to include a broad collection of literary graduate work, but on the other hand, we cannot morally reject great writing." Length: no more than 10 pages.

HOW TO CONTACT Send complete ms with cover letter. Include brief bio, list of publications, and an e-mail address must be supplied for the student, as well as the student's advisor's contact information (to verify student status).

PAYMENT/TERMS Pays in contributor's copies.

TIPS "Because the editors of *RCR* are graduate student writers, we are mindful of grammatical proficiency, vocabulary, and the organizational flow of the submissions we receive. We appreciate a heightened level of writing from fellow graduate writing students; but we also hold it to a standard to which we have learned in our graduate writing experience. Have your submission(s) proofread by a fellow student or professor."

REDIVIDER

Department of Writing, Literature, and Publishing, Emerson College, 120 Boylston St., Boston, MA 02116. **E-mail:** editor@redividerjournal.org. **Website:** www.redividerjournal.org. Estab. 1986. *Redivider*, a journal of literature and art, is published twice a year by students in the graduate writing, literature, and publishing department of Emerson College. Editors change each year. Prints high-quality poetry, art, fiction, and creative nonfiction.

- *Redivider* is 100+ pages, digest size, offset printed, perfect-bound, with 4-color artwork on cover. Press run is 1,000. Single copy: $6; subscription: $10. Make checks payable to *Redivider* at Emerson College.

NEEDS Length: no more than 10,000 words.

HOW TO CONTACT Submit electronically. Include cover letter.

PAYMENT/TERMS Pays 2 contributor's copies.

TIPS "Our deadlines are July 1 for the Fall issue, and December 1 for the Spring issue."

RED ROCK REVIEW

College of Southern Nevada, CSN Department of English, J2A, 3200 E. Cheyenne Ave., North Las Vegas, NV 89030. (702)651-4094. **Fax:** (702)651-4639. **E-mail:** redrockreview@csn.edu. **Website:** sites.csn.edu/english/redrockreview/. **Contact:** Todd Moffett, senior editor. Estab. 1994. "We are dedicated to the publication of fine contemporary literature."

- *Red Rock Review* is about 130 pages, magazine sized, professionally printed, perfect-bound, with 10-pt. CS1 cover. Accepts about 15% of poems received/year. Press run is 2,350. Subscriptions: $9.50/year. Sample: $5.50.

NEEDS "We're looking for the very best literature. Stories need to be tightly crafted, strong in character development, built around conflict." Length: up to 7,500 words.

HOW TO CONTACT Submit with SASE.

PAYMENT/TERMS Pays 2 contributor's copies.

TIPS "Open to short fiction and poetry submissions from September 1-May 31. Include SASE and include brief bio. No general submissions between June 1 and August 31. See guidelines online."

REED MAGAZINE

San Jose State University, Dept. of English, One Washington Square, San Jose, CA 95192. (408) 927-4458. **E-mail:** mail@reedmag.org. **Website:** www.reedmag.org/drupal. **Contact:** Cathleen Miller, faculty advisor. Estab. 1944.

- Accepts electronic submissions only.

NEEDS Does not want children's, young adult, fantasy, or erotic. Length: no more than 6,000 words.

HOW TO CONTACT Include contact information on first page. Submit using online submissions manager.

PAYMENT/TERMS Writers receive free subscription to the magazine. Additional copies $5.

TIPS "Well-writen, original, clean grammatical prose is essential. Keep submitting! The readers are students and change every year."

REFORM JUDAISM

633 Third Ave., 7th Floor, New York, NY 10017-6778. (212)650-4240. **Fax:** (212)650-4249. **E-mail:** rjmagazine@urj.org. **Website:** www.reformjudaismmag.org. **Contact:** Joy Weinberg, managing editor. Estab. 1972. "*Reform Judaism* is the official voice of the Union for Reform Judaism, linking the institutions and affiliates of Reform Judaism with every Reform Jew. *RJ* covers developments within the Movement while interpreting events and Jewish tradition from a Reform perspective."

- Magazine: 8" × 10⅞"; 80-112 pages; illustrations; photos. Receives 75 unsolicited mss/month. Accepts 3 mss/year. Publishes ms 3 months after acceptance. Recently published work by Frederick Fastow and Bob Sloan. Quarterly.

NEEDS Humor/satire, religious/inspirational, sophisticated, cutting-edge, superb writing. Length: 600-2,500 words; average length: 1,500 words.

HOW TO CONTACT Send complete ms. SASE. "For quicker response time, send mss and stamped postcard with 'yes'; 'no'; 'maybe' options." Responds in 2 months to queries; 2 months to mss. Accepts simultaneous and reprints submissions. Sample copy for $3.50. Writer's guidelines online. Send complete ms.

PAYMENT/TERMS Pays 30¢/word. Pays on publication for first North American serial rights. Pays 30¢/published word.

TIPS "We prefer a stamped postcard including the following information/checklist: __Yes, we are interested in publishing; __No, unfortunately the submission doesn't meet our needs; __Maybe, we'd like to hold on to the article for now. Submissions sent this way will receive a faster response."

THE REJECTED QUARTERLY

P.O. Box 1351, Cobb, CA 95426. **E-mail:** bplankton@yahoo.com. **Website:** www.rejectedq.com. **Contact:** Daniel Weiss and Jeff Ludeke, fiction editors. Estab. 1998. "We want the best literature possible, regardless of genre. We do, however, have a bias toward the unusual and toward speculative fiction. We aim for a literate, educated audience. *The Rejected Quarterly* believes in publishing the highest quality rejected fiction and other writing that doesn't fit anywhere else. We strive to be different, but will go for quality every time, whether conventional or not."

NEEDS Length: 8,000 words.

HOW TO CONTACT Send SASE for reply, return of ms or send a disposable copy of ms. No longer accepting e-mail submissions. Responds in 2-4 weeks to queries; 1-9 months to mss. Accepts reprint submissions. Sample copy for $7.50 (IRCs for foreign requests). Reviews fiction.

PAYMENT/TERMS Pays $20 and 1 contributor's copy; additional copies $5.

TIPS "We read mss from June through August only. We are looking for high-quality writing that tells a story or expresses a coherent idea. We want unique stories, original viewpoints, and unusual slants. We are getting far too many inappropriate submissions. Please be familiar with the magazine. Be sure to include your rejection slips! Send out quality rather than quantity."

RESIDENTIAL ALIENS

ResAliens Press, P.O. Box 780203, Wichita, KS 67278. **E-mail:** resaliens@gmail.com. **Website:** www.resaliens.com; residentialaliens.blogspot.com. **Contact:** Lyn Perry, founding editor. Estab. 2007. "Because reading and writing speculative fiction is a strong interest of mine, I thought I'd contribute to the genre of faith-informed speculative fiction by offering other writers and readers of science fiction, fantasy, spiritual, and supernatural thrillers a quality venue in which to share their passion. You could say *ResAliens* is speculative fiction with a spiritual thread."

"Occasionally sponsors contests." Has published George L. Duncan (author of novel *A Cold and Distant Memory*), Patrick G. Cox (author of *Out of Time*), Merrie Destefano (editor of *Victorian Homes* magazine), Brandon Barr and Mike Lynch (authors of the science fiction novel *When the Sky Fell*).

NEEDS Receives 50 mss/month. Accepts 5-6 mss/issue; 65-75 mss/year. Publishes 25 new writers/year. Does not want straight horror, gore, erotica. Will publish another sci-fi/fantasy anthology. Length of short stories: 500-5,000 words. Average length: 3,500 words. Average length of short shorts: 900 words. Will take serial novellas of 2-5 installments (up to 20,000 words).

HOW TO CONTACT Send complete ms with cover letter via e-mail. Include estimated word count, brief bio.

PAYMENT/TERMS Writers receive PDF file as their contributor's copy. Sends galleys to author. Publication is copyrighted.

TIPS "We want stories that read well and move quickly. We enjoy all sorts of speculative fiction, and 'tried and true' forms and themes are fine as long as the author has a slightly different take or a fresh perspective on a topic. For example, time machine stories are great—how is yours unique or interesting?"

RHINO

The Poetry Forum, Inc., P.O. Box 591, Evanston, IL 60204. **E-mail:** editors@rhinopoetry.org. **E-mail:** Online submissions form: annsbrandon@gmail.com. **Website:** www.rhinopoetry.org. **Contact:** Ralph Hamilton, editor. "This eclectic annual journal of more than 30 years accepts poetry, flash fiction (750 words or less), and poetry-in-translation from around the world that experiments, provokes, compels. More than 80 poets are showcased."

Single copy: $12. Sample: $5 (back issue).

NEEDS Length: no more than 750 words.

HOW TO CONTACT Submit via online submissions manager (preferred) or postal mail. Include cover letter. Accepts general submissions April 1-August 31.

PAYMENT/TERMS Pays in contributor's copies.

TIPS "Our diverse group of editors looks for the very best in contemporary writing, and we have created a dynamic process of soliciting and reading new work by local, national, and international writers. We look for idiosyncratic, rigorous, lively, passionate, and funny work."

RIVER STYX MAGAZINE

Big River Association, 3547 Olive St., Suite 107, St. Louis, MO 63103. (314)533-4541. **E-mail:** bigriver@ riverstyx.org. **Website:** www.riverstyx.org. **Contact:** Richard Newman, editor. Estab. 1975. *"River Styx* publishes the highest quality fiction, poetry, interviews, essays, and visual art. We are an internationally distributed multicultural literary magazine. Mss read May-November."

Work published in *River Styx* has been selected for inclusion in past volumes of *New Stories From the South, The Best American Poetry, Beacon's Best, Best New Poets* and the *Pushcart Prize* anthology. Recently published work by George Singleton, Philip Graham, Katherine Min, Richard Burgin, Nancy Zafris, Jacob Appel, and Eric Shade.

NEEDS No genre fiction, less thinly veiled autobiography. Length: no more than 23-30 manuscript pages.

HOW TO CONTACT Send complete ms with SASE.

PAYMENT/TERMS Pays 2 contributor copies, plus 1-year subscription. Cash payment as funds permit.

R.KV.R.Y. QUARTERLY LITERARY JOURNAL

90 Meetings in 90 Days Press, 499 North Canon Dr., Suite 400, Beverly Hills, CA 90210. **E-mail:** r.kv.r.y.editor@gmail.com. **Website:** www.rkvry.com. **Contact:** Mary Akers, editor-in-chief. Estab. 2004. *"r.kv.r.y.* publishes 3 short stories of high literary quality every quarter. We publish fiction that varies widely in style. We prefer stories of character development, psychological penetration, and lyricism, without sentimentality or purple prose. We ask that all submissions address issues related to recovery from any type of physical, psychological, or cultural loss, dislocation or oppression. We include but do not limit ourselves to issues of substance abuse. We do not publish the standard 'what it was like, what happened, and what it is like now' recovery narrative. Works published by *r.kv.r.y.* embrace almost every area of adult interest related to recovery. Material should be presented in a fashion suited to a quarterly that is neither journalistic nor academic. We welcome academic articles from varying fields. We encourage our academic contributors to free themselves from the constraints imposed by academic journals, letting their knowledge, wisdom, and experience rock and roll on these pages. Our intended audience is people of discriminating taste, original ideas, heart, and love of narrative and language."

Receives 30 stories/month. Accepts 3 stories/issue; 12 stories/year. Agented fiction 10%. Publishes 5-6 new writers/year. Published Anthony Doerr, Margaret Atwood, Dylan Landis, T.J. Forrester, Kim Chinquee, Alicia Gifford, Andrew Tibbets, Jason Schneiderman.

NEEDS Length: 3,000 words (max). Average length: 2,000 words. Average length of short shorts: 1,000 words.

HOW TO CONTACT "Submit complete ms with cover letter through our online submission system."

TIPS "Wants strong focus on character development and lively writing style with strong voice. Read our present and former issues (archived online)."

ROANOKE REVIEW

Roanoke College, 221 College Lane, Salem, VA 24153-3794. **E-mail:** review@roanoke.edu. **Website:** http://roanokereview.wordpress.com. **Contact:** Paul Hanstedt, editor. Estab. 1967. "We're looking for fresh, thoughtful material that will appeal to a broader as well as literary audience. Humor encouraged."

Magazine: 6" × 9"; 200 pages; 60 lb. paper; 70 lb. cover. Receives 150 unsolicited mss/month. Accepts 10-115 mss/year. Does not read mss February 1-September 1. Publishes 1-5 new writers/year. Has published work by Siobhan Fallon, Jacob M. Appel, and JoeAnn Hart.

NEEDS Length: 1,000-5,000 words. Average length: 3,000 words.

HOW TO CONTACT Send SASE for return of ms or send a disposable copy of ms and #10 SASE for reply only.

PAYMENT/TERMS Pays $10-50/story (when budget allows) and 2 contributor's copies; additional copies $5.

TIPS "Pay attention to sentence-level writing—verbs, metaphors, concrete images. Don't forget, though, that plot and character keep us reading. We're looking for stuff that breaks the MFA story style. Be real. Know rhythm. Concentrate on strong images."

THE ROCKFORD REVIEW

The Rockford Writers Guild, P.O. Box 858, Rockford, IL 61105. **E-mail:** editors@rockfordwritersguild.com.

Website: www.rockfordwritersguild.com. **Contact:** Connie Kluntz. Estab. 1947. "Published twice/year. Members-only edition in summer-fall, winter-spring edition open to all writers. Open season to submit for the winter-spring edition of the Rock Review is August. If pubished in the winter-spring edition of the Rockford Review, payment is one copy of magazine and $5 per published piece. Credit line given. Check website for frequent updates. We are also on Facebook under Rockford Writers' Guild."

NEEDS Poetry 50 lines or less, prose 1,300 words or less. "Prose should express fresh insights into the human condition." No sexist, pornographic, or supremacist content. Length: no more than 1,300 words.

TIPS "We're wide open to new and established writers alike—particularly short satire."

ROMANCE FLASH

Romance Flash, N5610 County Road A, Lake Mills, WI 53551. **E-mail:** info@romanceflash.com. **E-mail:** submissions@romanceflash.com. **Website:** www.romanceflash.com. **Contact:** Kat de Falla and Rachel Green, editors. Estab. 2010.

NEEDS No heavy erotica. Length: 1,000/words or less.

PAYMENT/TERMS Pays $3 per story (paid via PayPay only).

☺️🌑💲 ROOM

P.O. Box 46160, Station D, Vancouver, BC V6J 5G5 Canada. **E-mail:** contactus@roommagazine.com. **Website:** www.roommagazine.com. Estab. 1975. "*Room* is Canada's oldest literary journal by, for, and about women. Published quarterly by a group of volunteers based in Vancouver, *Room* showcases fiction, poetry, reviews, art work, interviews, and profiles about the female experience. Many of our contributors are at the beginning of their writing careers, looking for an opportunity to get published for the first time. Some later go on to great acclaim. *Room* is a space where women can speak, connect, and showcase their creativity. Each quarter we publish original, thought-provoking works that reflect women's strength, sensuality, vulnerability, and wit."

○ *Room* is digest size; illustrations, photos. Press run is 1,000 (420 subscribers, 50-100 libraries, 350 shelf sales). Subscription: $22 ($32 US or foreign). Sample: $8 plus IRCs. Estab. 1975.

NEEDS Accepts literature that illustrates the female experience—short stories, creative nonfiction, poetry—by, for and about women.

HOW TO CONTACT "We accept e-mail submissions with some guidelines—see our full guidelines at our website. Or, send complete ms with a cover letter. Include estimated word count and brief bio. Do not send a SASE."

PAYMENT/TERMS Pays $50 (Canadian), 2 contributor's copies, and a 1-year subscription.

◑ ROSEBUD

N3310 Asje Rd., Cambridge WI 53523. (608)423-9780. **E-mail:** jrodclark@smallbytes.net. **Website:** www.rsbd.net. **Contact:** Roderick Clark, publisher/managing editor; John Lehman, founder/editor-at-large. Estab. 1993. *Rosebud*, published 3 times/year in April, August, and December, has presented "many of the most prominent voices in the nation and has been listed as among the very best markets for writers."

○ *Rosebud* is "elegantly" printed with full-color cover. Press run is 10,000. Single copy: $7.95 U.S. Subscription: $20/3 issues, $35/6 issues. Recently published work by Ray Bradbury, XJ Kennedy, and Nikki Giovanni.

NEEDS "We are seeking stories; articles; profiles; and poems of: love, alienation, travel, humor, nostalgia and unexpected revelation. Something has to 'happen' in the pieces we choose, but what happens inside characters is much more interesting to us than plot manipulation. We like good storytelling, real emotion and authentic voice." Publishes short shorts. Also publishes literary essays. Often comments on rejected mss. "No formula pieces."

HOW TO CONTACT Send complete ms. Include SASE for return of ms and $1 handling fee.

RUNNING TIMES

Rodale, Inc., 400 S. 10th St., Emmaus, PA 18098-0099. (610)967-5171. **Fax:** (610)967-8964. **E-mail:** editor@runningtimes.com. **Website:** www.runningtimes.com. **Contact:** Jonathan Beverly, editor-in-chief. Estab. 1977. "*Running Times* is the national magazine for the experienced running participant and fan. Our audience is knowledgeable about the sport and active in running and racing. All editorial relates specifically to running: improving performance, enhancing enjoyment, or exploring events, places, and people in the sport."

NEEDS Any genre, with running-related theme or characters. Buys 1 ms/year. Length: 1,500-3,000 words.

HOW TO CONTACT Send complete ms.

PAYMENT/TERMS Pays $100-500.

TIPS "Thoroughly get to know runners and the running culture, both at the participant level and the professional, elite level."

⊙⊙ SALMAGUNDI

Skidmore College, 815 North Broadway, Saratoga Springs, NY 12866. **Fax:** (518)580-5188. **E-mail:** salmagun@skidmore.edu. **E-mail:** salsubmit@skidmore.edu. **Website:** http://cms.skidmore.edu/salmagundi. Estab. 1965. "*Salmagundi* publishes an eclectic variety of materials, ranging from short-short fiction to novellas from the surreal to the realistic. Authors include Nadine Gordimer, Russell Banks, Steven Millhauser, Gordon Lish, Clark Blaise, Mary Gordon, Joyce Carol Oates, and Cynthia Ozick. Our audience is a generally literate population of people who read for pleasure."

○ Magazine: 8" × 5"; illustrations; photos. *Salmagundi* authors are regularly represented in *Pushcart* collections and *Best American Short Story* collections. Receives 300-500 unsolicited mss/month; "many sent, few accepted." Reads unsolicited mss February 1-April 15 "but from time to time close the doors even during this period because the backlog tends to grow out of control." Agented fiction 10%.

HOW TO CONTACT Send complete ms by e-mail to salsubmit@skidmore.edu.

PAYMENT/TERMS Pays 6-10 contributor's copies and 1 year free subscription to magazine.

TIPS "I look for excellence and a very unpredictable ability to appeal to the interests and tastes of the editors. Be brave. Don't be discouraged by rejection. Keep stories in circulation. Of course, it goes without saying: Work hard on the writing. Revise tirelessly. Study magazines and send only to those whose sensibility matches yours."

● SANDY RIVER REVIEW

University of Maine at Farmington, 238 Main St., Farmington, ME 04938. **E-mail:** srreview@gmail.com. **Website:** studentorgs.umf.maine.edu/~srreview. **Contact:** Kelsey Moore, editor. "*The Sandy River Review* seeks prose, poetry, and art submissions twice a year for our spring and fall issues. We publish a wide variety of work from students as well as professional, established writers. Your submission should be polished and imaginative with strongly drawn characters and an interesting, original narrative. The review is

the face of the University of Maine at Farmington's venerable BFA Creative Writing program, and we strive for the highest-quality prose and poetry standard."

NEEDS "The review is a literary journal—please, no horror, science fiction, romance." Length: 4,500-5,000 words.

HOW TO CONTACT Send complete ms. "Prose submissions may be either fiction or creative nonfiction and should be 15 pages or fewer in length; 12-point, Times Roman font; and double-spaced. Most of our art is published in black-and-white, and must be submitted as 300 dpi quaity, CMYK color mode, and saved as a .tif file."

PAYMENT/TERMS Pays 5 copies of the published issue.

TIPS "We recommend that you take time with your piece. As with all submissions to a literary journal, submissions should be fully completed, polished final drafts that require minimal to no revision once accepted. Double-check your prose pieces for basic grammatical errors before submitting."

SANTA CLARA REVIEW

Santa Clara Review, Santa Clara University, P.O. Box 3212, 500 El Camino Real, Santa Clara, CA 95053-3212. (408)554-4484. **Fax:** (408)554-4454. **E-mail:** info@santaclarareview.com. **Website:** www.santaclarareview.com. Estab. 1869. "SCR is one of the oldest literary publications in the West. Entirely student-run by undergraduates at Santa Clara University, the magazine draws upon submissions from SCU affiliates as well as contributors from around the globe. The magazine is published in February and May each year. In addition to publishing the magazine, the review staff organizes a writing practicum, open mic nights, retreats for writers and artists, and it hosts guest readers. Our printed magazine is also available to view free online. For contacts, queries, and general info, visit www.santaclarareview.com. SCR accepts submissions year-round.

NEEDS Length: 5,000 words or less. Excerpts from larger works accepted.

HOW TO CONTACT "Visual Art: Submit 2 works and provide us with a link to your online portfolio. Graphic Novels: 20 page max. Excerpts from larger works accepted. PDF format. Book or Album Reviews: 500-1,500 words."

ⓘ SANTA MONICA REVIEW

1900 Pico Blvd., Santa Monica, CA 90405. **Website:** www.smc.edu/sm_review/. Estab. 1989.

NEEDS "No crime and detective, mysogyny, footnotes, TV, dog stories. We want more self-conscious, smart, political, humorous, digressive, meta-fiction."

HOW TO CONTACT Submit complete ms with SASE. No e-mail submissions.

PAYMENT/TERMS Pays in contributor's copies.

ⓘ THE SARANAC REVIEW

CVH, Department of English, SUNY Plattsburgh, 101 Broad St., Plattsburgh, NY 12901. (518)564-2414. **Fax:** (518)564-2140. **E-mail:** saranacreview@plattsburgh .edu. **Website:** http://research.plattsburgh.edu/saranac review. **Contact:** J.L. Torres, editor. Estab. 2004. "*The Saranac Review* is committed to dissolving boundaries of all kinds, seeking to publish a diverse array of emerging and established writers from Canada and the U.S. *The Saranac Review* aims to be a textual clearing in which a space is opened for cross-pollination between American and Canadian writers. In this way the magazine reflects the expansive bright spirit of the etymology of its name, Saranac, meaning 'cluster of stars.'"

⊙ *The Saranac Review* is magazine size, with color photo or painting on cover, includes ads. Press run is 1,000. Make checks payable to Subscriptions/*The Saranac Review*. Published annually.

NEEDS Maximum length: 7,000 words.

HOW TO CONTACT "Please send one story at a time." Send complete ms. Send SASE (or IRC) for return of ms or send disposable copy of the ms and #10 SASE for reply only. Reads submissions September 1-February 15 (firm). Cover letter is appreciated. Include phone and e-mail contact information (if possible) in cover letter. No e-mail or disk submissions.

PAYMENT/TERMS Pays 2 contributor's copies; discount on extras.

TIPS "We publish serious, generous fiction."

ⓞ THE SAVAGE KICK LITERARY MAGAZINE

Murder Slim Press, 29 Alpha Rd., Gorleston Norfolk NR31 0EQ United Kingdom. **E-mail:** moonshine@ murderslim.com. **Website:** www.murderslim.com. Estab. 2005. "*Savage Kick* primarily deals with viewpoints outside the mainstream: honest emotions told in a raw, simplistic way. It is recommended that you are very familiar with the *SK* style before submitting.

We have only accepted 8 new writers in 4 years of the magazine. Ensure you have a distinctive voice and story to tell."

NEEDS "Real-life stories are preferred, unless the work is distinctively extreme within the crime genre. No poetry of any kind, no mainstream fiction, Oprah-style fiction, Internet/chat language, teen issues, excessive Shakespearean language, surrealism, overworked irony, or genre fiction (horror, fantasy, science fiction, western, erotica, etc.)." Length: 500-6,000 words.

HOW TO CONTACT Send complete ms.

PAYMENT/TERMS Pays $35.

THE SEATTLE REVIEW

Box 354330, University of Washington, Seattle, WA 98195. (206)543-2302. **E-mail:** seaview@uw.edu. **Website:** www.seattlereview.org. **Contact:** Andrew Feld, editor-in-chief. Estab. 1978. Includes general fiction, poetry, craft essays on writing, and one interview per issue with a Northwest writer.

⊙ *The Seattle Review* is 6" × 9"; 150 pages; illustrations; photos. Semiannual. Estab. 1978. Circ. 1,000. Receives 200 unsolicited mss/month. Accepts 2-4 mss/issue; 4-8 mss/year. Publishes ms 1-2½ years after acceptance. Subscriptions: $20/three issues, $32/five issues. Back issue: $4.

NEEDS *The Seattle Review* will publish, and will only publish, long poems and novellas. "Currently, we do not consider, use, or have a place for genre fiction (sci-fi, detective, etc.) or visual art." Length: 500-10,000 words.

HOW TO CONTACT Send complete ms.

TIPS "Know what we publish: no genre fiction; look at our magazine and decide if your work might be appreciated. Beginners do well in our magazine if they send clean, well-written manuscripts. We've published a lot of 'first stories' from all over the country and take pleasure in discovery."

ⓞⓢ SEEK

8805 Governor's Hill Dr., Suite 400, Cincinnati, OH 45239. (513)931-4050, ext. 351. **E-mail:** seek@stan dardpub.com. **Website:** www.standardpub.com. Estab. 1970.

⊙ Magazine: 5½" × 8½"; 8 pages; newsprint paper; art and photo in each issue.

HOW TO CONTACT Send complete ms. Prefers submissions by e-mail.

PAYMENT/TERMS Pays 7¢/word.

TIPS "Write a credible story with a Christian slant—no preachments; avoid overworked themes such as joy in suffering, generation gaps, etc. Most manuscripts are rejected by us because of irrelevant topic or message, unrealistic story, or poor character and/or plot development. We use fiction stories that are believable."

THE SEWANEE REVIEW

University of the South, 735 University Ave., Sewanee, TN 37383-1000. (931)598-1000. **Website:** www.sewanee.edu/sewanee_review. Estab. 1892. The *Sewanee Review* is America's oldest continuously published literary quarterly. Publishes "original fiction, poetry, essays on literary and related subjects, and book reviews for well-educated readers who appreciate good American and English literature." Only erudite work representing depth of knowledge and skill of expression is published.

Ⓞ Does not read mss June 1-August 31.

NEEDS No erotica, science fiction, fantasy or excessively violent or profane material. Length: 3,500-7,500 words.

HOW TO CONTACT Send query letter for reviews. Send complete ms for fiction.

PAYMENT/TERMS Pays $10-12/printed page, plus 2 contributor's copies.

⊕◯ SHADOWS EXPRESS

E-mail: managingeditor@shadowexpress.com. **E-mail:** fictioneditor@shadowexpress.com; nonfictioneditor@shadowexpress.com; poetryeditor@shadowexpress.com. **Website:** www.shadowexpress.com. **Contact:** K. Wall, managing editor. Estab. 2009. "*Shadows Express* is a magazine presenting new voices to discerning readers. In a demanding, fast-paced world, we need time to relax and feed our minds. Finding quality short stories, poetry, and articles that can be read in one sitting and shared with family members is becoming increasingly difficult. At *Shadows Express*, we strive to bring that quality to the reader: fiction both engaging and entertaining; poetry that speaks to the heart; and helpful, inspiring nonfiction. This is writing you will be eager to share with your spouse, parents, children, and friends."

NEEDS No gore, gratuitous sex, violence, or profanity. Length: 500-5,000 words.

HOW TO CONTACT Submit complete ms. Query if over 2,500 words.

TIPS "We are open to submissions by new authors. In fact, it is our mission to help new writers break into publishing. We urge all writers to read the guidelines carefully as we have specific editors for different departments. In addition, the author should always be professional and courteous. Proofread carefully and submit yout best work."

SHENANDOAH

Washington and Lee University, 17 Courthouse Square, Lexington, VA 24450. (540)458-8908. **Fax:** (540)458-8461. **E-mail:** shenandoah@wlu.edu. **Website:** http://shenandoahliterary.org. **Contact:** R.T. Smith, editor. Estab. 1950. "For over half a century, *Shenandoah* has been publishing splendid poems, stories, essays, and reviews which display passionate understanding, formal accomplishment and serious mischief."

Ⓞ Reads submissions September 1-May 15 only. Sponsors the annual James Boatwright III Prize for Poetry, a $1,000 prize awarded to the author of the best poem published in *Shenandoah* during a volume year.

NEEDS "No sloppy, hasty, slight fiction."

HOW TO CONTACT Send complete ms.

PAYMENT/TERMS Pays $25/page ($250 maximum).

SHINE BRIGHTLY

GEMS Girls' Clubs, P.O. Box 7259, Grand Rapids, MI 49510. (616)241-5616. **Fax:** (616)241-5558. **E-mail:** shinebrightly@gemsgc.org. **Website:** www.gemsgc.org. **Contact:** Jan Boone, executive director; Kelli Gilmore, managing editor. Estab. 1970. "Our purpose is to lead girls into a living relationship with Jesus Christ and to help them see how God is at work in their lives and the world around them. Puzzles, crafts, stories, and articles for girls ages 9-14."

NEEDS Does not want "unrealistic stories and those with trite, easy endings. We are interested in manuscripts that show how girls can change the world." Believable only. Nothing too preachy. Length: 700-900 words.

HOW TO CONTACT Submit complete ms in body of e-mail. No attachments.

PAYMENT/TERMS Pays up to $35, plus 2 copies.

TIPS Writers: "Please check our website before submitting. We have a specific style and theme that deals with how girls can impact the world. The stories should be current, deal with preadolescent problems and joys, and help girls see God at work in their lives through humor as well as problem solving." Prefers not to see anything on the adult level, secular material, or violence. Writers frequently oversimplify the articles and often write with a Pollyanna attitude. An author should be able to see his/her writing style as exciting and appealing to girls ages 9-14. The style can be fun but also teach a truth. Subjects should be current and important to *SHINE brightly* readers. Use our theme update as a guide. We would like to receive material with a multicultural slant."

SHORT STORY AMERICA

Short Story America, LLC, 66 Thomas Sumter St., Beaufort, SC 29907. (843)597-3220. **E-mail:** editors@ shortstoryamerica.com. **Website:** www.shortstory america.com. **Contact:** Tim Johnston, editor. Estab. 2010. "Our readers are fans of the short story. Our audience simply wants to enjoy reading great stories." **NEEDS** No erotica. Length: 500-12,000 words.
HOW TO CONTACT Send complete ms.
TIPS "We want stories that readers will remember and want to read again. If your story entertains from the first page forward, and the pacing and conflict engages the reader's interest from plot, character, and thematic standpoints, then please submit your story today! If the reader genuinely wants to know what eventually happens in your story and is still thinking about it 10 minutes after finishing, then your story works."

⊘ SHORT STUFF

Bowman Publications, 2001 I St., #5, Fairbury, NE 68352. (402)587-5003. **E-mail:** shortstf89@aol.com. Estab. 1989. "We are perhaps an enigma in that we publish only clean stories in any genre. We'll tackle any subject, but don't allow obscene language or pornographic description. Our magazine is for grownups, not X-rated 'adult' fare."
⌀ Receives 500 unsolicited mss/month. Accepts 9-12 mss/issue; 76 mss/year. Has published work by Bill Hallstead, Dede Hammond, Skye Gibbons.
NEEDS "We want to see more humor—not essay format—real stories with humor; 1,000-word mysteries, modern lifestyles. The 1,000-word pieces have the best chance of publication. No erotica; nothing morbid or pornographic." Length: 500-1,500 words.
HOW TO CONTACT Send complete ms.
PAYMENT/TERMS Payment varies.

TIPS "Don't send floppy disks or cartridges. We are holiday oriented; mark on outside of envelope if story is for Easter, Mother's Day, etc. We receive 500 mss each month. This is up about 200%. Because of this, I implore writers to send 1 ms at a time. I would not use stories from the same author more than once an issue and this means I might keep the others too long. Please don't e-mail your stories! If you have an e-mail address, please include that with cover letter so we can contact you. If no SASE, we destroy the ms."

◑ SIERRA NEVADA REVIEW

999 Tahoe Blvd., Incline Village, NV 89451. **E-mail:** sncreview@sierranevada.edu. **Website:** www.sier ranevada.edu/800. Estab. 1990. *Sierra Nevada Review*, published annually in May, features poetry and short fiction by new writers.
NEEDS Wants "image-oriented poems with a distinct, genuine voice. Although we don't tend to publish 'light verse,' we do appreciate, and often publish, poems that make us laugh. No limit on length, style, etc." Does not want "sentimental, clichéd, or obscure poetry."

◯ SLATE & STYLE

2861 S. 93 Plaza APT 8, Omaha, NE 68124. (402)350-1735. **E-mail:** bpollpeter@hotmail.com. **Website:** www.nfb-writers-division.net. **Contact:** Bridgit Pollpeter, editor; Robert Leslie Newman, president; Ross Pollpeter, layout and design editor. Estab. 1982. "*Slate & Style* is a quarterly publication of the Writers' division of the National Federation of the Blind (NFB Writers). It's dedicated to writing pursuits, including literary pieces along with resources and information about various writing styles. A majority of *Slate & Style*'s contributors are visually impaired, but we welcome submissions from any contributor, professional or amateur. We also accept submissions touching on any subject matter. *Slate & Style* accepts short fiction, short creative nonfiction, poetry, articles discussing and providing tips for various writing styles including literary, technical, editing, public relations and academic, literary criticism and resource information. Subject matter is not limited, though it will be up to the editor's discretion to publish."
⌀ Accepts material from adults and children. Prefers e-mail submission; no handwritten or Braille submissions. Annual subscription is $15; single copy for $5. Members of the Writer's Division receive issues free of charge. An

annual membership is $20. See website to pay via PayPal or e-mail newmanrl@cox.netf for other payment options.

NEEDS "*Slate & Style* will consider all submissions for publication. However, please be careful with graphic sexual and violent content, as well as language and antireligious, antigender, antiracial, and antihomosexual orientation content. Characterization and plot often require this type of material, but it must serve a purpose. Gratuitous material with no purpose or meant only for derogatory reasons will not be considered; however, material will be published according to the discretion of the editor though." Length: 3,000 maximum.

HOW TO CONTACT Accepts submissions January 1-September 1 only. "Include a title page, along with your submission with your name, title of piece, and contact info (phone, e-mail, address). Please include a brief bio of 150 words or less. Do not send an entire history; just include key items you feel are important for readers to know. Send submissions as attachments to bpollpeter@hotmail.com. Do not paste entries into the body of the e-mail; entries simply pasted into an e-mail will not be considered. In the subject line of your e-mail, write: *Slate & Style* Submission, your name, title, and genre. Example: *Slate & Style, Bridgit Kuenning-Pollpeter, Giving Directions, fiction.* Use Microsoft Word or create an .rtf document for all submissions. No other formats are accepted, and therefore will not be considered."

TIPS "Proofread and check your grammar and formatting before submitting. Submissions with too many errors will either be returned with corrections to be made if you wish to resubmit, or it will not be considered at all. All submissions are considered for publication, but not all pieces will be published. We may keep submissions to be used for later publication. The editor may respond with comments and suggestions, giving contributors an opportunity to resubmit. Please be patient and wait the full 6 weeks before contacting us about a submission. Please direct questions and comments to Bridgit Kuenning-Pollpeter at bpollpeter@hotmail.com."

◑ SLOW TRAINS LITERARY JOURNAL

P.O. 4741, Denver, CO 80155. **E-mail:** editor@slowtrains.com. **Website:** www.slowtrains.com. **Contact:** Susannah Grace Indigo, editor. Estab. 2000.

NEEDS "Genre writing is not encouraged. No sci-fi, erotica, horror, romance, though elements of those may naturally be included." Length: less than 5,000 words.

HOW TO CONTACT Submit via e-mail only.

TIPS "We are looking for fiction, essays, and poetry that reflect the spirit of adventure, the exploration of the soul, the energies of imagination, and the experience of Big Fun. Music, travel, sex, humor, love, loss, art, spirituality, childhood/coming of age, baseball, and dreams—these are a few of our favorite things—but most of all we want to read about the things you are passionate about."

◐⑤ SNOWY EGRET

The Fair Press, P.O. Box 9265, Terre Haute, IN 47808. **Website:** www.snowyegret.net. Estab. 1922. *Snowy Egret*, published in spring and autumn, specializes in work that is "nature oriented: poetry that celebrates the abundance and beauty of nature or explores the interconnections between nature and the human psyche." Has published poetry by Conrad Hilberry, Lyn Lifshin, Gayle Eleanor, James Armstrong, and Patricia Hooper.

◯ *Snowy Egret* is 60 pages, magazine size, offset printed, saddle stapled. Receives about 500 poems/year, accepts about 30. Press run is 400. Sample: $8; subscription: $15/year, $25 for 2 years. Semiannual.

NEEDS "We publish works which celebrate the abundance and beauty of nature and examine the variety of ways in which human beings interact with landscapes and living things. Nature writing from literary, artistic, psychological, philosophical and historical perspectives." "No genre fiction, e.g., horror, western, romance, etc."

HOW TO CONTACT Send complete ms with SASE. Cover letter optional: do not query. Responds in 2 months to mss. Accepts simultaneous submissions if noted.

PAYMENT/TERMS Pays $2/page plus 2 contributor's copies.

TIPS Looks for "honest, freshly detailed pieces with plenty of description and/or dialogue which will allow the reader to identify with the characters and step into the setting; fiction in which nature affects character development and the outcome of the story."

○ SNREVIEW

197 Fairchild Ave., Fairfield, CT 06825-4856. (203)366-5991. **E-mail:** editor@snreview.org. **Website:** www.snreview.org. **Contact:** Joseph Conlin, editor. Estab. 1999. "We search for material that not only has strong characters and plot but also a devotion to imagery." Quarterly.

○ Receives 300 unsolicited mss/month. Accepts 40+ mss/issue; 150 mss/year. Publishes 75 new writers/year. Has published work by Frank X. Walker, Adrian Louis, Barbara Burkhardt, E. Lindsey Balkan, Marie Griffin, and Jonathan Lerner. Print and Kindle editions are now available from an on-demand printer.

NEEDS Length: 1,000-7,000 words; average length: 4,000 words. Also publishes literary essays, literary criticism, poetry.

HOW TO CONTACT Accepts submissions by e-mail only. "Copy and paste work into the body of the e-mail. Don't send attachments." Include 100 word bio and list of publications. Accepts simultaneous submissions.

❶ SO TO SPEAK

George Mason University, 4400 University Dr., MSN 2C5, Fairfax, VA 22030-4444. **E-mail:** sts@gmu.edu (inquiries only). **Website:** http://sotospeakjournal.org. **Contact:** Kate Partridge, editor-in-chief. Estab. 1993. *So to Speak*, published semiannually, prints "high-quality work relating to feminism, including poetry, fiction, nonfiction (including book reviews and interviews), photography, artwork, collaborations, lyrical essays, and other genre-questioning texts."

○ *So to Speak* is 100-128 pages, digest size, photo offset printed, perfect-bound, with glossy cover; includes ads. Press run is 1,000 (75 subscribers, 100 shelf sales); 500 distributed free to students/contributors. Subscription: $12. Receives 100 unsolicited mss/month. Accepts 3-5 mss/issue; 6-10 mss/year. Publishes 7 new writers/year. Sponsors awards/contests.

NEEDS Wants "work that addresses issues of significance to women's lives and movements for women's equality and are especially interested in pieces that explore issues of race, class, and sexuality in relation to gender."No science fiction, mystery, genre romance. Length: 4,500 words maximum.

HOW TO CONTACT Accepts submissions only via submissions manager on website. Does not accept paper or e-mail submissions. "Fiction submitted during the August 1-October 15 reading period will be considered for our Spring Issue and requires no reading fee. Fiction submitted during the January 1-March 15 reading period will be considered for our fall annual fiction contest and must be accompanied by a $15 reading fee. See contest guidelines. Contest entries will not be returned."

PAYMENT/TERMS Pays contributor copies.

TIPS "We do not read between March 15 and August 15. Every writer has something they do exceptionally well; do that and it will shine through in the work. We look for quality prose with a definite appeal to a feminist audience. We are trying to move away from strict genre lines. We want high-quality fiction, nonfiction, poetry, art, innovative and risk-taking work."

❶ SOUTH CAROLINA REVIEW

Clemson University, Strode Tower Room 611, Box 340522, Clemson, SC 29634-0522. (864)656-5399. **Fax:** (864)656-1345. **E-mail:** cwayne@clemson.edu. **Website:** www.clemson.edu/cedp/cudp/scr/scrintro .htm. **Contact:** Wayne Chapman, editor.

○ Magazine: 6" × 9"; 200 pages; 60 lb. cream white vellum paper; 65 lb. color cover stock. Semiannual. Estab. 1967. Circ. 500. Literary, mainstream, poetry, essays, reviews. Does not read mss June-August or December. Receives 50-60 unsolicited mss/month.

NEEDS Recently published work by Thomas E. Kennedy, Ronald Frame, Dennis McFadden, Dulane Upshaw Ponder, and Stephen Jones. Rarely comments on rejected mss.

❶ SOUTH DAKOTA REVIEW

University of South Dakota, 414 E. Clark St., Vermillion, SD 57069. (605)677-5184. **E-mail:** sdreview@ usd.edu. **Website:** www.usd.edu/sdreview. **Contact:** Brian Bedard and Lee Ann Roripaugh, editors. Estab. 1963. *South Dakota Review*, published quarterly, prints "poetry, fiction, criticism, and scholarly and personal essays. When material warrants, emphasis is on the American West; writers from the West; Western places or subjects. There are frequent issues with no geographical emphasis; periodic special issues on one theme, one place, or one writer."

○ *Pushcart* and *Best American Essays* nominees. Press run is 500-600 (450 subscribers, half libraries). Single copy: $10; subscription: $30/ year, $45/2 years. Sample: $8.

NEEDS Wants "originality, sophistication, significance, craft—i.e., professional work." Ethnic/multicultural, literary, regional. "We like very well-written, thematically ambitious, character-centered short fiction. Contemporary Western American setting appeals but is not required if they story has a good sense of place.

HOW TO CONTACT Send complete ms and SASE. "We like cover letters that are not boastful and do not attempt to sell the stories but rather provide some personal information about the writer which can be used for a contributor's note."

PAYMENT/TERMS Pays 2 contributor's copies.

TIPS "No formula stories, horror, science fiction, or adolescent 'I' narrators. SDR rejects manuscripts because of careless writing, often careless typing, stories too personal ('I' confessional), aimlessness, unclear or unresolved conflicts, or subject matter that the editor finds clichéd, sensationalized, pretentious, or trivial."

SOUTHERN CALIFORNIA REVIEW

3501 Trousdale Pkwy., Mark Taper Hall, THH 355J, University of Southern California, Los Angeles, CA 90089. **E-mail:** scr@college.usc.edu. **Website:** http://dornsife.usc.edu/mpw/literary-journal. Estab. 1982.

NEEDS Length: no more than 7,000 words.

HOW TO CONTACT Submit complete ms with cover letter via postal mail or online submissions manager. Do not send more than one piece of any genre at one time.

PAYMENT/TERMS Pays in contributor's copies.

SOUTHERN HUMANITIES REVIEW

Auburn University, 9088 Haley Center, Auburn University, AL 36849. (334)844-9088. **Fax:** (334)844-9027. **E-mail:** shrengl@auburn.edu. **E-mail:** shrsubmissions@auburn.edu. **Website:** www.cla.auburn.edu/shr. **Contact:** Karen Beckwith, managing editor. Estab. 1967. *Southern Humanities Review* publishes fiction, poetry, and critical essays on the arts, literature, philosophy, religion, and history for a well-read, scholarly audience.

NEEDS Length: 3,500-15,000 words.

HOW TO CONTACT Send complete ms. Send only one story per submission. "It is wise to submit no more than 4 times per year unless editors ask to see more of your work. Translations are encouraged, but please include PDF scans of the original AND written permission from the copyright holder."

PAYMENT/TERMS Pays 2 contributor copies

TIPS "Send us the ms with SASE. If we like it, we'll take it or we'll recommend changes. If we don't like it, we'll send it back as promptly as possible. Read the journal. Send a typewritten, clean copy, carefully proofread. We also award the annual Hoepfner Prize of $100 for the best published essay or short story of the year. Let someone whose opinion you respect read your story and give you an honest appraisal. Rewrite, if necessary, to get the most from your story."

THE SOUTHERN REVIEW

Louisiana State University, Old President's House, Baton Rouge LA 70803-5001. (225)578-5108. **Fax:** (225)578-5098. **E-mail:** southernreview@lsu.edu. **Website:** http://thesouthernreview.com. Estab. 1935. Magazine: 6¼" × 10"; 240 pages; 50 lb. Glatfelter paper; 65 lb. #1 grade cover stock. Quarterly. Circ. 3,000. Reading period: September1-June 1. All mss. submitted during summer months will be recycled. Receives approximately 300 unsolicited mss/month. Accepts 4-6 mss/issue. Reading period: September-May. Publishes ms 6 months after acceptance. Agented fiction 1%. **Publishes 10-12 new writers/year.** Recently published work by Jack Driscoll, Don Lee, Peter Levine, and Debbie Urbanski.

NEEDS Literary. "We select fiction that conveys a unique and compelling voice and vision." Also publishes literary essays, literary criticism, poetry, and book reviews. Short stories of lasting literary merit, with emphasis on style and technique; novel excerpts. "We emphasize style and substantial content. No mystery, fantasy, or religious mss." Length: 4,000-8,000 words. "We rarely publish work that is longer than 8,000 words. We consider novel excerpts if they stand alone."

HOW TO CONTACT Mail hard copy of ms with cover letter and SASE. No queries. "Prefer brief letters giving author's prefessional information, including recent or notable publcations. Biographical info not necessary." Responds within 10 weeks to mss. Sample copy for $8. Writer's guidelines online. Reviews fiction, poetry. Submit one ms in any genre at a time.

PAYMENT/TERMS Pays $30/page. Pays on publication for first North American serial rights. Sends page proof to author via e-mail. Sponsors awards/contests. Pays $30/page

TIPS "Careful attention to craftsmanship and technique combined with a developed sense of the creation of story will always make us pay attention."

① SOUTHWEST REVIEW

P.O. Box 750374, Dallas, TX 75275-0374. (214)768-1037. **Fax:** (214)768-1408. **E-mail:** swr@smu.edu. **Website:** www.smu.edu/southwestreview. **Contact:** Willard Spiegelman, editor-in-chief. Estab. 1915. "The majority of our readers are well-read adults who wish to stay abreast of the latest and best in contemporary fiction, poetry, and essays in all but the most specialized disciplines." Quarterly.

Magazine: 6" × 9"; 150 pages. Receives 200 unsolicited mss/month. Has published work by Alice Hoffman, Sabina Murray, Alix Ohlin. Publishes fiction, literary essays, poetry.

NEEDS "High literary quality; no specific requirements as to subject matter but cannot use sentimental, religious, western, poor science fiction, pornographic, true confession, mystery, juvenile, or serialized or condensed novels." Length: 3,000-7,000 words preferred.

HOW TO CONTACT Submissions accepted online for a $2 fee. No fee for submissions sent by mail. No simultaneous or previously published work accepted. Submit one story at a time. Reading period: September 1-May 31.

PAYMENT/TERMS Accepted pieces receive nominal payment upon publication and copies of the issue.

TIPS "Despite the title, we are not a regional magazine. Before you submit your work, it's a good idea to take a look at recent issues to familiarize yourself with the magazine. We strongly advise all writers to include a cover letter. Keep your cover letter professional and concise and don't include extraneous personal information, a story synopsis, or a resume. When authors ask what we look for in a strong story submission the answer is simple regardless of graduate degrees in creative writing, workshops, or whom you know. We look for good writing, period."

① SOU'WESTER

Department of English, Box 1438, Southern Illinois University, Edwardsville, IL 62026. **Website:** http://souwester.org. Estab. 1960. *Sou'wester* appears biannually in spring and fall. "We lean toward poetry with strong imagery, successful association of images, and skillful use of figurative language."

Sou'wester has 30-40 pages of poetry in each digest size, 100-page issue. *Sou'wester* is professionally printed, flat spined, with textured matte card cover; press run is 300 for 500 subscribers of which 50 are libraries. Receives 3,000 poems (from 600 poets) each year, accepts 36-40, has a 6-month backlog. Subscription: $18/2 issues. Has published poetry by Robert Wrigley, Beckian Fritz Goldberg, Eric Pankey, Betsy Sholl, and Angie Estes.

HOW TO CONTACT Submit one piece of prose at a time. Uses online submission form.

PAYMENT/TERMS Pays 2 contributor's copies and a 1-year subscription.

① ⑤ SPACE AND TIME

458 Elizabeth Ave., Somerset, NJ 08873. **E-mail:** ww.spaceandtimemagazine.com. **Website:** www.spaceandtimemagazine.com. **Contact:** Hildy Silverman, editor-in-chief. Estab. 1966. "We love stories that blend elements—horror and science fiction, fantasy with science fiction elements, etc. We challenge writers to try something new and send us their unclassifiable works—what other publications reject because the work doesn't fit in their 'pigeonholes.'"

Magazine is 48 pages, matte paper, glossy cover. Contains illustrations.

NEEDS "We are looking for creative blends of science fiction, fantasy, and/or horror." "Do not send children's stories." Length: 1,000-10,000/words. Average length: 6,500 words. Average length of short shorts: 1,000.

HOW TO CONTACT Submit electronically as a Word doc or .rtf attachment.

PAYMENT/TERMS Pays a penny per word.

⊕ THE SPECULATIVE EDGE

E-mail: specedgeeditor@gmail.com. **Website:** https://sites.google.com/site/thespeculativeedge/home. **Contact:** Chloe Viner, editor; Shane R. Collins, managing editor. Estab. 2012. Monthly literary magazine. "Publishing stories and poems that are speculative is our primary goal, but ensuring they are also literary is a close second. Stories should balance characters with plot. They should be exciting but also written intelligently. Poetry should be insightful and imaginative but also accessible. Our mission at *The Speculative Edge* is to extinguish the false pretense that 'genre' and 'literary' are mutually exclusive."

NEEDS Length: 500-15,000 words.

HOW TO CONTACT Submit complete ms.

TIPS "Send us your best work. Grammar mistakes are a huge turnoff for us. If we find a glaring mistake in the first page of your ms—that might be it, depending on the editor's mood. Also, a professional, concise cover letter goes a long way. If you don't know how to write a cover letter, we have an explanation of what we want to see on the website. And finally, address your e-mail to the editor you're trying to contact. Our names are visible under the guidelines for submissions. Addressing us by name shows that you've done your homework and are a serious writer."

SPIDER

Cricket Magazine Group, 70 East Lake St., Suite 300, Chicago, IL 60601. (312)701-1720. **Fax:** (312)701-1728. **Website:** www.cricketmag.com. **Contact:** Marianne Carus, editor-in-chief; Suzanne Beck, managing art director. Estab. 1994. Monthly reading and activity magazine for children ages 6-9. "*Spider* introduces children to the highest quality stories, poems, illustrations, articles, and activities. It was created to foster in beginning readers a love of reading and discovery that will last a lifetime. We're looking for writers who respect children's intelligence."

NEEDS Stories should be easy to read. Recently published work by Polly Horvath, Andrea Cheng, and Beth Wagner Brust. No romance, horror, religious. Length: 300-1,000 words.

HOW TO CONTACT Submit complete ms and SASE.

PAYMENT/TERMS Pays 25¢/word maximum.

TIPS "We'd like to see more of the following: engaging nonfiction, fillers, and 'takeout page' activities; folktales, fairy tales, science fiction, and humorous stories. Most important, do not write down to children."

🌙 STAND MAGAZINE

School of English, University of Leeds, Leeds LS2 9JT United Kingdom. (44)(113)343-4794. **E-mail:** stand@leeds.ac.uk. **Website:** www.standmagazine.org. **Contact:** Jon Glover, managing editor. Estab. 1952. Quarterly literary magazine. "U.S. submissions can be made through the Virginia office."

🗨 Does not accept e-mail submissions.

NEEDS "*Stand Magazine* is concerned with what happens when cultures and literatures meet, with translation in its many guises, with the mechanics of language, with the processes by which the policy receives or disables its cultural makers. *Stand* promotes debate of issues that are of radical concern to the in-

tellectual community worldwide." No genre fiction. Length: up to 3,000 words.

HOW TO CONTACT Submit through postal mail only. Submit complete ms with SASE.

ST. ANTHONY MESSENGER

Franciscan Media, 28 W. Liberty St., Cincinnati, OH 45202-6498. (513)241-5615. **Fax:** (513)241-0399. **E-mail:** mageditors@franciscanmedia.org. **Website:** www.stanthonymessenger.org. **Contact:** John Feister, editor. Estab. 1893. "*St. Anthony Messenger* is a Catholic family magazine that aims to help its readers lead more fully human and Christian lives. We publish articles which report on a changing church and world, opinion pieces written from the perspective of Christian faith and values, personality profiles, and fiction which entertains and informs."

NEEDS "We do not want mawkishly sentimental or preachy fiction. Stories are most often rejected for poor plotting and characterization, bad dialogue (listen to how people talk), and inadequate motivation. Many stories say nothing, are 'happenings' rather than stories. No fetal journals, no rewritten Bible stories." Length: 2,000-2,500 words.

HOW TO CONTACT Send complete ms.

PAYMENT/TERMS Pays 20¢/word maximum and 2 contributor's copies; $1 charge for extras.

🌙🌕😮 STEAMPUNK MAGAZINE, PUTTING THE PUNK BACK INTO STEAMPUNK

Strangers in a Tangled Wilderness, Wales. **E-mail:** collective@steampunkmagazine.com. **Website:** www.steampunkmagazine.com.

NEEDS "We appreciate well-written, grammatically consistent fiction. That said, we are more interested in representing the underclasses and the exploited, rather than the exploiters." No misogynistic or racist work. Length: "We will work with fiction of nearly any length, although works longer than 6,000 words will be less likely to be accepted, as they may have to be split over multiple issues."

HOW TO CONTACT Submit ms as an e-mail attachment. Include word count.

TIPS "Please keep in mind before submitting that we publish under Creative Commons licensing, which means that people will be free to reproduce and alter your work for noncommercial purposes. We are not currently a paying market. Please introduce yourself in your introduction letter: We like to know that we're working with actual people. Surprise us! We're nicer people than we sound!"

STILL CRAZY

P.O. Box 777, Worthington, OH 43085. (614)746-0859. **E-mail:** editor@crazylitmag.com. **Website:** www.crazylitmag.com. **Contact:** Barbara Kussow, editor. "*Still Crazy* publishes writing by people over age 50 and writing by people of any age, if the topic is about people over 50 years old."

Accepts 3-4 mss/issue; 6-8/year. Occasionally considers previously published poems. "Do not submit material that has been published elsewhere online." Publication is not copyrighted. Reads submissions year-round. Paper copies $10; subscriptions $18 (2 issues/year); downloads $4.

NEEDS Publishes short shorts. Ms published 6-12 months after acceptance. Sometimes features a "First Story," a story by an author who has not been published before. Does not want material that is "too sentimental or inspirational, 'geezer' humor, or anything too grim." Length: 3,500 words (maximum), but stories fewer than 3,000 words are more likely to be published.

HOW TO CONTACT Upload submissions via submissions manager on website. Include estimated word count, brief bio, age of writer or "Over 50."

PAYMENT/TERMS Pays 1 contributor's copy.

TIPS Looking for "interesting characters and interesting situations that might interest readers of all ages. Humor and lightness welcomed."

STIRRING: A LITERARY COLLECTION

Stirring: A Literary Collection, c/o Erin Elizabeth Smith, Department of English, 301 McClung Tower, University of Tennessee, Knoxville, TN 37996. **E-mail:** eesmith81@gmail.com. **Website:** www.sundresspublications.com/stirring/. **Contact:** Erin Elizabeth Smith, managing and poetry editor. Estab. 1999.

"*Stirring* is one of the oldest continually published literary journals on the web. *Stirring* is a monthly literary magazine that publishes poetry, short fiction, creative nonfiction, and photography by established and emerging writers."

STONE SOUP

Children's Art Foundation, P.O. Box 83, Santa Cruz, CA 95063-0083. (831)426-5557. **E-mail:** editor@stonesoup.com. **Website:** http://stonesoup.com. **Con-**

tact: Ms. Gerry Mandel, editor. Estab. 1973. "We have a preference for writing and art based on real-life experiences; no formula stories or poems. We only publish writing by children ages 8-13. We do not publish writing by adults."

Stone Soup is 48 pages, 7" × 10", professionally printed in color on heavy stock, saddle stapled, with coated cover with full-color illustration. Receives 5,000 poetry submissions/year, accepts about 12. Press run is 15,000. Subscription: $37/year (U.S.). "Stories and poems from past issues are available online."

NEEDS "We do not like assignments or formula stories of any kind." Length: 150-2,500 words.

HOW TO CONTACT Send complete ms; no SASE.

PAYMENT/TERMS Pays $40 for stories, a certificate, and 2 contributor's copies, plus discounts.

TIPS "All writing we publish is by young people ages 13 and under. We do not publish any writing by adults. We can't emphasize enough how important it is to read a couple of issues of the magazine. You can read stories and poems from past issues online. We have a strong preference for writing on subjects that mean a lot to the author. If you feel strongly about something that happened to you or something you observed, use that feeling as the basis for your story or poem. Stories should have good descriptions, realistic dialogue, and a point to make. In a poem, each word must be chosen carefully. Your poem should present a view of your subject, and a way of using words that are special and all your own."

STORIE

Via Suor Celestina Donati 13/E, Rome 00167 Italy. (+39) 06 614 8777. **Fax:** (+39) 06 614 8777. **E-mail:** storie@tiscali.it. **Website:** www.storie.it. Estab. 1989. "*Storie* is one of Italy's leading literary magazines. Committed to a truly crossover vision of writing, the bilingual (Italian/English) review publishes high-quality fiction and poetry, interspersed with the work of alternative wordsmiths such as filmmakers and musicians. Through writings bordering on narratives and interviews with important contemporary writers, it explores the culture and craft of writing."

Italian magazine.

HOW TO CONTACT "Manuscripts may be submitted directly by regular post without querying first; however, we do not accept unsolicited manuscripts via e-mail. Please query via e-mail first. We only contact writers if their work has been accepted. We also arrange for and oversee a high-quality, professional translation of the piece."

PAYMENT/TERMS Pays $30-600 and 2 contributor's copies.

TIPS "More than erudite references or a virtuoso performance, we're interested in the recording of human experience in a genuine, original voice. *Storie* reserves the right to include a brief review of interesting submissions not selected for publication in a special column of the magazine."

STORY BYTES

E-mail: editor@storybytes.com. **Website:** www.storybytes.com. **Contact:** Mark Stanley Bubein. "A monthly e-zine and weekly electronic mailing list presenting the Internet's (and the world's) shortest stories—fiction ranging from 2 to 2,048 words.Just as eyes, art often provides a window to the soul. *Story Bytes'* very short stories offer a glimpse through this window into brief vignettes of life, often reflecting or revealing those things which make us human."

NEEDS "Story length must fall on a power of 2. That's 2, 4, 8, 16, 32, 64, 128, 256, 512, 1,024 and 2,048 words long. Stories must match one of these lengths exactly." See website for examples. No sexually explicit material. Length: 2-2048 words.

HOW TO CONTACT Submit story as plain text via e-mail. "The easiest way to do so is to simply copy it from your word processor and paste it into an e-mail message. Specify the word count below the title."

TIPS "In *Story Bytes* the very short stories themselves range in topic. Many explore a brief event—a vignette of something unusual, unique, and at times something even commonplace. Some stories can be bizarre, while others are quite lucid. Some are based on actual events, while others are entirely fictional. Try to develop conflict early on (in the first sentence, if possible!), and illustrate or resolve this conflict through action rather than description. I believe we'll find an audience for electronically published works primarily in the short story realm."

STORYSOUTH

5603B W. Friendly Ave., Suite 282, Greensboro, NC 27410. **E-mail:** terry@storysouth.com. **Website:** www.storysouth.com. **Contact:** Terry Kennedy, editor. Estab. 2001. "*storySouth* accepts unsolicited submissions of fiction, poetry, and creative nonfiction during two submission periods annually: March 15-June 15 and

September 15-December 15. Long pieces are encouraged. Please make only one submission in a single genre per reading period."

NEEDS No word limit.

HOW TO CONTACT Submit 1 story via online submissions manager.

TIPS "What really makes a story stand out is a strong voice and a sense of urgency—a need for the reader to keep reading the story and not put it down until it is finished."

THE STORYTELLER

2441 Washington Rd., Maynard, AR 72444. (870)647-2137. **E-mail:** storytellermag1@@yahoo.com. **Website:** www.thestorytellermagazine.com. Estab. 1996.

NEEDS Does not want anything graphic, religious, or bashing—even in fiction. Length: 1,500 words.

HOW TO CONTACT Send complete ms with SASE.

TIPS "*The Storyteller* is one of the best places you will find to submit your work, especially new writers. Our best advice, be professional. You have one chance to make a good impression. Don't blow it by being unprofessional."

THE STRAND MAGAZINE

P.O. Box 1418, Birmingham, MI 48012-1418. (248)788-5948. **Fax:** (248)874-1046. **E-mail:** strandmag@strandmag.com. **Website:** www.strandmag.com. Estab. 1998. "After an absence of nearly half a century, the magazine known to millions for bringing Sir Arthur Conan Doyle's ingenious detective, Sherlock Holmes, to the world has once again appeared on the literary scene. First launched in 1891, *The Strand*, included in its pages the works of some of the greatest writers of the 20th century: Agatha Christie, Dorothy Sayers, Margery Allingham, W. Somerset Maugham, Graham Greene, P.G. Wodehouse, H.G. Wells, Aldous Huxley, and many others. In 1950, economic difficulties in England caused a drop in circulation which forced the magazine to cease publication."

NEEDS We are not interested in submissions with any sexual content. Length: 2,000-6,000 words.

HOW TO CONTACT Query first. Include SASE.

PAYMENT/TERMS Pays $50-175.

TIPS No gratuitous violence, sexual content, or explicit language, please.

STRAYLIGHT

UW-Parkside, English Department, 900 Wood Rd., P.O. Box 2000, Kenosha, WI 53141. (262)595-2139. **Fax:** (262)595-2271. **E-mail:** submissions@stray lightmag.com. **Website:** www.straylightmag.com. **Contact:** Fiction editor. (Magazine has revolving editor. Editorial term: 1 year. Estab. 2005. *Straylight*, published biannually, seeks fiction and "poetry of almost any style as long as it's inventive." *Straylight* is digest size. Single copy: $10; subscription: $19. Make checks payable to *Straylight*.

○ Literary magazine/journal: 6" × 9", 115 pages, quality paper, uncoated index stock cover. Contains illustrations and photographs. Accepts 3-5 mss/issue; 6-10 mss/year. Does not read May-August. Agented fiction 10%.

NEEDS Publishes short shorts. Length: 2,500-6,000 words. Average length: 2,500 words.

HOW TO CONTACT Send complete ms with cover letter. Accepts submissions by e-mail. Include brief bio, list of publications. Send either SASE (or IRC) for return of ms or disposable copy of ms and #10 SASE for reply only.

PAYMENT/TERMS Writers receive 2 contributor's copies. Additional copies $3.

TIPS "We tend to publish character-based and inventive fiction with cutting-edge prose. We are unimpressed with works based on strict plot twists or novelties. Read a sample copy to get a feel for what we publish."

○ STRUGGLE: A MAGAZINE OF PROLETARIAN REVOLUTIONARY LITERATURE

P.O. Box 28536, Detroit, MI 48228. (313)273-9039. **E-mail:** timhall11@yahoo.com. **Website:** www.strugglemagazine.net. **Contact:** Tim Hall, editor. Estab. 1985. "A quarterly magazine featuring African American, Latino, and other writers of color, prisoners, disgruntled workers, activists in the antiwar, antiracist, and other mass movements, and many writers discontented with the Bush imperialist juggernaut and the Democratic and labor-leader capitulation to it. While we urge literature in the direction of revolutionary working-class politics and a vision of socialism as embodying a genuine workers' power, in distinction to the state-capitalist regimes of the former Soviet Union, present-day China, North Korea, Cuba, etc., we accept a broader range of rebellious viewpoints in order to encourage creativity and dialogue."

NEEDS "Readers would like fiction about anti-globalization, the fight against racism, prison conditions, neoconservatism and the Iraq and Afghanistan wars, the struggle of immigrants, and the disillusionment with the Obama Administration as it reveals it craven service to the billionaires. Would also like to see more fiction that depicts life, work, and struggle of the working class of every background; also the struggles of the 1930s and 1960s illustrated and brought to life." Length: 4,000 words; average length: 1,000-3,000 words.

HOW TO CONTACT Accepts submissions by e-mail, mail.

◐◑◔ SUBTERRAIN

Strong Words for a Polite Nation, P.O. Box 3008, MPO, Vancouver, BC V6B 3X5 Canada. (604)876-8710. **Fax:** (604)879-2667. **E-mail:** subter@portal.ca. **Website:** www.subterrain.ca. **Contact:** Brian Kaufman, editor-in-chief. Estab. 1988. "*subTerrain* magazine is published 3 times a year from modest offices just off of Main Street in Vancouver, BC. We strive to produce a stimulating fusion of fiction, poetry, photography, and graphic illustration from uprising Canadian, U.S., and international writers and artists."

○ Magazine: 8¼" × 10¾"; 72 pages; gloss stock paper; color gloss cover stock; illustrations; photos. Looking for unique work and perspectives from Canada and beyond. Receives 100 unsolicited mss/month. Accepts 4 mss/issue; 10-15 mss/year. Recently published work by John Moore. Needs Does not want genre fiction or children's fiction.

HOW TO CONTACT Send complete ms. Include disposable copy of the ms and #10 SASE for reply only. Accepts multiple submissions.

PAYMENT/TERMS Pays $25 per page for prose.

TIPS "Read the magazine first. Get to know what kind of work we publish."

SUBTROPICS

University of Florida, P.O. Box 112075, 4008 Turlington Hall, Gainesville, FL 32611-2075. **E-mail:** subtropics@english.ufl.edu. **Website:** www.english.ufl.edu/subtropics. **Contact:** David Leavitt. Estab. 2005. "Magazine published twice year through the University of Florida's English department. *Subtropics* seeks to publish the best literary fiction, essays, and poetry being written today, both by established and emerging authors. We will consider works of fiction of any length, from short shorts to novellas and self-contained novel excerpts. We give the same latitude to essays. We appreciate work in translation and, from time to time, republish important and compelling stories, essays, and poems that have lapsed out of print by writers no longer living." Member CLMP.

○ Literary magazine/journal: 9" × 6", 160 pages. Includes photographs. Receives 1,000 mss/ month. Accepts 5-6 mss/issue; 10-12 mss/year. Does not read May 1-August 31. Agented fiction 33%. Publishes 1-2 new writers/year. Has published John Barth, Ariel Dorfman, Tony D'Souza, Allan Gurganus, Frances Hwang, Kuzhali Manickavel, Eileen Pollack, Padgett Powell, Nancy Reisman, Jarret Rosenblatt, Joanna Scott, and Olga Slavnikova. Needs No genre fiction. Average length: 5,000 words. Average length of short shorts: 400 words.

HOW TO CONTACT Send complete ms with cover letter. Send disposable copy of ms. Replies via e-mail only. Do not include SASE. Considers simultaneous submissions.

PAYMENT/TERMS Writers receive $500-1,000, 2 contributor's copies. Additional copies $12.95. Pays on acceptance. Acquires first North American serial rights. Publication is copyrighted.

TIPS "We publish longer works of fiction, including novellas and excerpts from forthcoming novels. Each issue will include a short-short story of about 250 words on the back cover. We are also interested in publishing works in translation for the magazine's English-speaking audience."

○Ⓢ THE SUMMERSET REVIEW

25 Summerset Dr., Smithtown, NY 11787. **E-mail:** editor@summersetreview.org. **Website:** www.summersetreview.org. **Contact:** Joseph Levens, editor. Estab. 2002. "Our goal is simply to publish the highest quality literary fiction and essays intended for a general audience. This is a simple online literary journal of high-quality material, so simple you can call it unique."

○ Magazine: illustrations and photographs. Periodically releases print issues. Quarterly. Receives 150 unsolicited mss/month. Accepts 4 mss/issue; 18 mss/year. Publishes 5-10 new writers/year. Also publishes literary essays.

NEEDS No sci-fi, horror, or graphic erotica. Length: 8,000 words; average length: 3,000 words. Publishes short shorts.

HOW TO CONTACT Send complete ms. Accepts submissions by e-mail.

TIPS "Style counts. We prefer innovative or at least very smooth, convincing voices. Even the dullest of premises or the complete lack of conflict make for an interesting story if it is told in the right voice and style. We like to find little interesting facts and/or connections subtly sprinkled throughout the piece. Harsh language should be used only if/when necessary. If we are choosing between light and dark subjects, the light will usually win."

THE SUN

107 N. Roberson St., Chapel Hill, NC 27516. (919)942-5282. **Fax:** (919)932-3101. **Website:** www.thesunmagazine.org. **Contact:** Luc Sanders, assistant editor. Estab. 1974. "We are open to all kinds of writing, though we favor work of a personal nature."

○ Magazine: 8½" × 11"; 48 pages; offset paper; glossy cover stock; photos. Receives 800 unsolicited mss/month. Accepts 20 short stories/ year. Recently published work by Tony Hoagland, David James Duncan, Poe Ballantine, Linda McCullough Moore, Brenda Miller.

NEEDS No science fiction, horror, fantasy, or other genre fiction. "Read an issue before submitting." Length: 7,000 words maximum.

HOW TO CONTACT Send complete ms. Accepts reprint submissions.

PAYMENT/TERMS Pays $300-1,500.

TIPS "Do not send queries except for interviews. We're looking for artful and sensitive photographs that aren't overly sentimental. We're open to unusual work. Read the magazine to get a sense of what we're about. Send the best possible prints of your work. Our submission rate is extremely high. Please be patient after sending us your work. Send return postage and secure return packaging."

SUSPENSE MAGAZINE

JRSR Ventures, 26500 W. Agoura Rd., Suite 102-474, Calabasas, CA 91302. **Fax:** (310)626-9670. **E-mail:** editor@suspensemagazine.com; john@suspensemagazine.com. **Website:** www.suspensemagazine.com. **Contact:** John Raab, publisher/CEO/editor-in-chief. Estab. 2007.

NEEDS No explicit scenes. Length: 500-5,000 words.

HOW TO CONTACT Query.

TIPS "Unpublished writers are welcome and encouraged to query. Our emphasis is on horror, suspense, thriller, and mystery."

SYCAMORE REVIEW

Purdue University Dept. of English, 500 Oval Dr., West Lafayette, IN 47907. (765) 494-3783. **Fax:** (765)

494-3780. **E-mail:** sycamore@purdue.edu. **Website:** www.sycamorereview.com. **Contact:** Alisha Karabinus, managing editor; Jessica Jacobs, editor-in-chief. "Strives to publish the best writing by new and established writers. Looks for well-crafted and engaging work, works that illuminate our lives in the collective human search for meaning. We would like to publish more work that takes a reflective look at our national identity and how we are perceived by the world. We look for diversity of voice, pluralistic worldviews, and political and social context."

○ *Sycamore Review* is Purdue University's internationally acclaimed literary journal, affiliated with Purdue's College of Liberal Arts and the Department of English. Art should present politics in a language that can be felt.

PAYMENT/TERMS Pays in contributor's copies.

TIPS "We look for originality, brevity, significance, strong dialogue, and vivid detail. We sponsor the Wabash Prize for Poetry (deadline: mid-October) and Fiction (deadline: March 1). $1,000 award for each. All contest submissions will be considered for regular inclusion in the *Sycamore Review*. No e-mail submissions—no exception. Include SASE."

●⑤ TAKAHE

P.O. Box 13-335, Christchurch 8001 New Zealand. (03)359-8133. **E-mail:** admin@takahe.org.nz. **Website:** www.takahe.org.nz/index.php. The Takahe Collective Trust is a nonprofit organisation that aims to support emerging and published writers, poets, artists, and cultural commentators. *Takahē* appears three times a year and publishes short stories, poetry, and art by established and emerging writers and artists as well as essays and interviews (by invitation), and book reviews in these related areas.

NEEDS "We look for stories that have something special about them: an original idea, a new perspective, an interesting narrative style or use of language, an ability to evoke character and/or atmosphere. Above all, we like some depth, an extra layer of meaning, an insight—something more than just an anecdote or a straightforward narration of events. Humour of the understated, unforced variety is welcome." Length: 1,500-3,000 words. "Although we do occasionally accept shorter work."

HOW TO CONTACT E-mail submissions are preferred. Include cover letter with contact information and 40-word biography.

PAYMENT/TERMS Pays 1 contributor's copy.

TIPS "We pay a flat rate to each writer/poet appearing in a particular issue regardless of the number/length of items. Editorials and literary commentaries are by invitation only."

➕○ TALENT DRIPS EROTIC LITERARY EZINE

E-mail: talentdriseroticpublishing@yahoo.com. **Fax:** (216)799-9775. **Website:** http://eroticatalentdrips.wordpress.com. **Contact:** Kimberly Steele, founder. Estab. 2007. *Talent Drips*, published monthly online, focuses solely on showcasing new erotic fiction.

HOW TO CONTACT Submit short stories between 5,000 and 10,000 words by e-mail to talentdripserotic publishing@yahoo.com. Stories should be pasted into body of message. Reads submissions during publication months only.

PAYMENT/TERMS Pays $15 for each accepted short story.

TIPS "Please read our take on the difference between *erotica* and *pornography*; it's on the website. *Talent Drips* does not accept pornography. And please keep poetry 30 lines or less."

TALES OF THE TALISMAN

Hadrosaur Productions, P.O. Box 2194, Mesilla Park, NM 88047-2194. **E-mail:** hadrosaur@zianet.com. **Website:** www.talesofthetalisman.com. **Contact:** David Lee Summers, editor. Estab. 1995. *"Tales of the Talisman* is a literary science fiction and fantasy magazine. We publish short stories, poetry, and articles with themes related to science fiction and fantasy. Above all, we are looking for thought-provoking ideas and good writing. Speculative fiction set in the past, present, and future is welcome. Likewise, contemporary or historical fiction is welcome as long as it has a mythic or science fictional element. Our target audience includes adult fans of the science fiction and fantasy genres along with anyone else who enjoys thought-provoking and entertaining writing."

○ Fiction and poetry submissions are limited to reading periods of January 1-February 15 and July 1-August 15.

NEEDS "We do not want to see stories with graphic violence. Do not send 'mainstream' fiction with no science fictional or fantastic elements. Do not send stories with copyrighted characters, unless you're the copyright holder." Length: 1,000-6,000 words.

HOW TO CONTACT Send complete ms.

PAYMENT/TERMS Pays $6-10.

TIPS "Let your imagination soar to its greatest heights and write down the results. If we don't believe in the people living the story, we generally won't believe in the story itself."

⊙ TALKING RIVER

Division of Literature and Languages, 500 8th Ave., Lewiston, ID 83501. (208)792-2189. **Fax:** (208)792-2324. **E-mail:** talkingriver@lcmail.lcsc.edu. **Website:** www.lcsc.edu/talkingriverreview. **Contact:** Kevin Goodan, editorial advisor. Estab. 1994.

NEEDS "We look for new voices with something to say to a discerning general audience. Wants more well-written, character-driven stories that surprise and delight the reader with fresh, arresting yet unself-conscious language, imagery, metaphor, revelation."

◐   Reads mss September 1-May 1 only. Recently published work by X.J. Kennedy and Gary Fincke.

NEEDS Length: 4,000 words; average length: 3,000 words. Also publishes literary essays, poetry. Sometimes comments on rejected mss. No stories that are sexist, racist, homophobic, erotic for shock value; no genre fiction. Length: 4,000 words; average length: 3,000 words.

PAYMENT/TERMS Pays contributor's copies; additional copies $4.

HOW TO CONTACT Send complete manuscript with cover letter. Include estimated word count, 2-sentence bio and list of publications. Send SASE for reply, return of ms or send disposable copy of ms.

TIPS "We look for the strong, the unique; we reject clicheéd images and predictable climaxes."

TAMPA REVIEW

University of Tampa Press, 401 W. Kennedy Blvd., Tampa, FL 33606. (813)253-6266. **Fax:** (813)258-7593. **E-mail:** utpress@ut.edu. **Website:** www.ut.edu/tampareview. **Contact:** Richard Mathews, editor. Estab. 1988. An international literary journal publishing art and literature from Florida and Tampa Bay as well as new work and translations from throughout the world.

NEEDS "We are far more interested in quality than in genre. Nothing sentimental as opposed to genuinely moving, nor self-conscious style at the expense of human truth." Length: 200-5,000 words.

HOW TO CONTACT Send complete ms. Include brief bio.

PAYMENT/TERMS Pays $10/printed page.

TIPS "Send a clear cover letter stating previous experience or background. Our editorial staff considers submissions between September and December for publication in the following year."

⊙ TATTOO HIGHWAY

E-mail: submissions@tattoohighway.org. **Website:** www.tattoohighway.org. **Contact:** Sara McAulay, editor and graphics; Rochelle Nameroff, poetry editor. Estab. 1998.

NEEDS Welcomes "short 'screen reader-friendly' prose or cross-genre pieces." Length: no more than 1,000 words. "We do publish longer work if we can't live without it. (It happens!)"

HOW TO CONTACT "E-mail submissions to submissions@tattoohighway.org as a .rtf attachment or as plain text in the body of your message, and with TH and the issue number in the subject line."

PAYMENT/TERMS "We're sorry, but we don't pay contributors. We don't pay ourselves either."

TIPS "Interpret our themes literally or loosely, as you wish. Our tastes are eclectic. We like fresh, vivid language, and we like stories and poems that are actually about something—that acknowledge a world beyond the writer's own psyche. If they have an edge, if they provoke us to think or make us laugh, so much the better. We strongly suggest reading a previous issue or two before submitting."

⊙ TEXAS REVIEW

Texas Review Press, Department of English, Sam Houston State University, Box 2146, Huntsville, TX 77341-2146. (936)294-1992. **Fax:** (936)294-3070. **E-mail:** eng_pdr@shsu.edu; cww006@shsu.edu. **Website:** www.shsu.edu/~www_trp. **Contact:** Dr. Paul Ruffin, editor/director. Estab. 1976. "We publish top quality poetry, fiction, articles, interviews and reviews for a general audience."

◐   Magazine: 6" × 9"; 148-190 pages; best quality paper; 70 lb. cover stock; illustrations; photos. Receives 40-60 unsolicited mss/month. Accepts 4 mss/issue; 6 mss/year. **Publishes some new writers/year.** Does not read mss May-September. A member of the Texas A&M University Press consortium. Semiannual.

NEEDS "We are eager enough to consider fiction of quality, no matter what its theme or subject matter. No juvenile fiction."

HOW TO CONTACT Send complete ms. No mss accepted via fax. Send disposable copy of ms and #10 SASE for reply only. Accepts multiple submissions.
PAYMENT/TERMS Pays contributor's copies and 1-year subscription.

THEMA

Thema Literary Society, P.O. Box 8747, Metairie, LA 70011-8747. **E-mail:** thema@cox.net. **Website:** http://themaliterarysociety.com. **Contact:** Gail Howard, poetry editor. Estab. 1988. *"THEMA is designed to stimulate creative thinking by challenging writers with unusual themes, such as 'The Box Under the Bed' and 'Put It In Your Pocket, Lillian.' Appeals to writers, teachers of creative writing, and general reading audience."*

○ *THEMA* is 100 pages, digest size, professionally printed, with glossy card cover. Receives about 400 poems/year, accepts about 8%. Press run is 400 (230 subscribers, 30 libraries). Subscription: $20 U.S./$30 foreign. Has published poetry by Beverly Boyd, Elizabeth Creith, James Penha, and Matthew J. Spireng.

NEEDS No erotica.
HOW TO CONTACT Send complete ms with SASE, cover letter; include "name and address, brief introduction, specifying the intended target issue for the mss." SASE. Accepts simultaneous, multiple submissions, and reprints. Does not accept e-mailed submissions.
PAYMENT/TERMS Pays $10-25.

THE SOUTHEAST REVIEW

Florida State University, Tallahassee FL 32306-1036. **Website:** southeastreview.org. **Contact:** Katie Cortese, editor-in-chief. Estab. 1979. "The mission of *The Southeast Review* is to present emerging writers on the same stage as well-established ones. In each semi-annual issue, we publish literary fiction, creative non-fiction, poetry, interviews, book reviews and art. With nearly 60 members on our editorial staff, who come from throughout the country and the world, we strive to publish work that is representative of our diverse interests and aesthetics, and we celebrate the eclectic mix this produces. We receive approximately 400 submissions/month and we accept less than 1-2% of them. We will comment briefly on rejected mss when time permits."

○ Magazine: 6" × 9"; 160 pages; 70 lb. paper; 10 pt. Krome Kote cover; photos. Publishes 4-6 new writers/year. Has published work by Elizabeth Hegwood, Anthony Varallo, B.J. Hollars, Tina Karelson, and John Dufresne.

NEEDS Length: 7,500 words maximum.
HOW TO CONTACT "We try to respond to submissions within 2-4 months. If, after 4 months, you have not heard back regarding your submission, you may query the appropriate section editor. *SER* accepts simultaneous submissions, but we request that you withdraw the submission by way of our online submission manager if your piece is accepted elsewhere." Submit complete ms through online manager. "All submissions must be typed (prose doubled-spaced) and properly formatted, then uploaded to our online submission manager as a .doc or .rtf file only. Submission manager restricts you from sending us your work more than twice per year. Please wait until you receive a reply regarding a submission before you upload the next." Does not accept e-mail, paper, or previously published submissions. Accepts submissions year-round, "though please be advised that the response time is slower during the summer months."
PAYMENT/TERMS Pays 2 contributor's copies.
TIPS "Any breaks, hiatuses, or interruptions to the reading period will be announced online, and are more likely to occur during the summer months. *SER* does not, under any circumstances, accept work via e-mail. **Except during contest season, paper submissions sent through regular postal mail will not be read or returned**. Please note that, during contest season, entries to our World's Best Short Short Story, Poetry, and Creative Nonfiction competitions must still be sent through regular postal mail. Avoid trendy experimentation for its own sake (present-tense narration, observation that isn't also revelation). Fresh stories, moving, interesting characters and a sensitivity to language are still fiction mainstays. We also publish the winner and runners-up of the World's Best Short Story Contest, Poetry Contest, and Creative Nonfiction Contest."

THE STRAY BRANCH

6001 Munger Rd., Dayton, OH 45459. **E-mail:** thestraybranchlitmag@yahoo.com. **Website:** www.thestraybranch.org. **Contact:** Debbie Berk, editor/publisher. Estab. 2008. *The Stray Branch* is "open to form and style; however free verse is preferred. Shorter poems have a better chance of being published. Looking for edgy, darker material written from the gut, reflecting the heart and human condition known as 'existence.' Topics include depression, mental illness, loss, sorrow, addiction, recovery, abuse, survival, daily existence, self struggles, and discovery through words. Personal, confessional poems are welcomed and embraced here. Rhyming poems are okay. Does not want over-schooled, arrogant, self-rigteous, religious, political, sentimental, or happy and light pretty poetry. No erotic or sexually explicit poetry."

 ○ *The Stray Branch* does not accept work from children or teens, or work written for children or teens. E-mail submisssions only. Has published work by Andy Robertson, Keith Estes, Kate Sjostrand, Lena Vanelslander, Michael Grover, and Justin Blackburn. Issue price: $10; $7 for contributors with the use of a contributor discount code.

NEEDS "Please keep stories no longer than 2½ pages. Shorter pieces of fiction stand a better chance of being published."

HOW TO CONTACT Send submissions via e-mail; no more than 2 pieces of fiction per submission. "All fiction must be sent as attachments." No simultaneous submissions. Previously published fiction is okay. *The Stray Branch* also publishes flash fiction.

① THE WRITING DISORDER

P.O. Box 93613, Los Angeles, CA 90093. (323)336-5822. **E-mail:** submit@thewritingdisorder.com. **Website:** www.thewritingdisorder.com. **Contact:** C.E. Lukather, editor; Paul Garson, managing editor; Julianna Woodhead, poetry editor. Estab. 2009. Quarterly literary magazine featuring new and established writers. "*The Writing Disorder* is an online literary magazine devoted to literature, art, and culture. The mission of the magazine is to showcase new and emerging writers—particularly those in writing programs—as well as established ones. The magazine also features original artwork, photography, and comic art. Although it strives to publish original and experimental work, *The Writing Disorder* remains rooted in the classic art of storytelling."

NEEDS Does not want to see romance, religious, or fluff. Length: 7,500 words maximum.

HOW TO CONTACT Query.

PAYMENT/TERMS Pays contributor's copies.

TIPS "We are looking for work from new writers, writers in writing programs, and students and faculty of all ages."

① ⑤ THIRD WEDNESDAY: A LITERARY ARTS MAGAZINE

174 Greenside Up, Ypsilanti, MI 48197. (734) 434-2409. **E-mail:** submissions@thirdwednesday.org; LaurenceWT@aol.com. **Website:** http://thirdwednesday.org. **Contact:** Laurence Thomas, editor. Estab. 2007. "*Third Wednesday* publishes quality (a subjective term at best) poetry, short fiction, and artwork by experienced writers and artists. We welcome work by established writers/artists, as well as those who are not yet well known but headed for prominence."

 ○ Quarterly literary magazine/journal: 60-65 pages. Contains illustrations. Includes photographs. Receives 5-10 mss/month. Accepts 3-5 mss/issue. Receives 800 poems/year. Has published poetry by Wanda Coleman, Philip Dacey, Richard Luftig, Simon Perchik, Marge Piercy, Charles Harper Webb. Press run is 125. Single copy: $8; subscription: $30. Make checks payable to *Third Wednesday*.

NEEDS Does not want "purely anecdotal accounts of incidents, sentimentality, pointless conclusions, or stories without some characterization or plot development." Length: 1,500 words (maximum); average length: 1,000 words.

HOW TO CONTACT Send complete ms with cover letter. Include estimated word count and brief bio.

PAYMENT/TERMS Pays $3 and 1 contributor's copy.

TIPS "Of course, originality is important, along with skill in writing, deft handling of language, and meaning, which goes hand in hand with beauty—whatever that is. Short fiction is specialized and difficult, so the writer should read extensively in the field."

① 34TH PARALLEL

P.O. Box 4823, Irvine, CA 92623. **E-mail:** 34thParallel@gmail.com. **Website:** www.34thparallel.net. **Contact:** Tracey Boone Swan, Martin Chipperfield, editors. *34th Parallel*, published quarterly in print and online, seeks "to promote and publish the exceptional writing of new and emerging writers overlooked by large commercial publishing houses and mainstream presses. Wants work that experiments with and tests boundaries. Anything that communicates a sense of wonder, reality, tragedy, fantasy, and/or brilliance. Does not want historical romance, science fiction, erotica, Gothic horror, book reviews, or nonfiction."

NEEDS Length: 1,500-3,500 words.

HOW TO CONTACT "In the subject heading of your e-mail, type in 'story submissions' or 'poetry submission' or 'image submission.' Will discard as spam those submissions that do not contain one of these subject headings. Submit 1 story at a time."
PAYMENT/TERMS Pays 1 contributor's copy in PDF format.

TIMBER JOURNAL

E-mail: timberjournal@gmail.com. **Website:** www.timberjournal.com. **Contact:** Oren Silverman, managing editor; Caroline Davidson, poetry editor; Gabrielle Fuentes, fiction editor. *Timber* is a literary journal, run by students in the MFA program at the University of Colorado-Boulder, dedicated to the promotion of innovative literature. "We publish work that explores the boundaries of poetry, fiction, creative nonfiction, and digital literatures. We produce both an online journal, in which we explore the potentials of the digital medium, and a semiannual 'book object,' which is a venue for more traditional print-based work." Reading period September 1-February 15. Include 30-50 word bio with submission.
NEEDS Looking for innovative fiction. Length: up to 5,000 words.
PAYMENT/TERMS Pays one contributor copy.
TIPS "We are looking for innovative poetry, fiction, creative nonfiction, and digital lit (screenwriting, digital poetry, multimedia lit, etc.)."

TIN HOUSE

McCormack Communications, P.O. Box 10500, Portland, OR 97210. (503)219-0622. **Fax:** (503)222-1154. **E-mail:** info@tinhouse.com. **Website:** www.tinhouse.com. **Contact:** Cheston Knapp, managing editor; Holly Macarthur, founding editor. Estab. 1998. "We are a general-interest literary quarterly. Our watchword is quality. Our audience includes people interested in literature in all its aspects, from the mundane to the exalted."
NEEDS Length up to 5,000 words.
HOW TO CONTACT Send complete ms September 1-May 31 via regular mail or online submission form. No fax or e-mail submissions.
PAYMENT/TERMS Pays $200-800.
TIPS "Remember to send an SASE with your submission."

TOAD SUCK REVIEW

University of Central Arkansas, Department of Writing, Conway, AR 72035. **E-mail:** toadsuckre

view@gmail.com. **Website:** http://toadsuckreview.org. **Contact:** Mark Spitzer, editor. Estab. 2011. Prefers submissions from skilled, experienced poets; will consider work from beginning poets. "Born from the legendary *Exquisite Corpse Annual*, the innovative *Toad Suck Review* is a cutting-edge mixture of poetry, fiction, creative nonfiction, translations, reviews, and artwork with a provocative sense of humor and an interest in diverse cultures and politics. No previously published work. 'Previously published' work includes: poetry posted on a public website/blog/forum, and poetry posted on a private, password-protected forum. Reads mss in the summer. "

The journal received a Library Journal award for being one of the 10 best lit mags published in 2012. *Toad Suck Review* is a 6" × 11" magazine, 200 pages, perfect-bound flat spine. Lifetime subscription: $75. Has published work by Charles Bukowski, Lawrence Ferlinghetti, Edward Abbey, Gary Snyder, Anne Waldman, Ed Sanders, Tyrone Jaeger, Jean Genet, Louis-Ferdinand Céline, Antler, David Gessner, C.D. Wright, Amiri Baraka.

NEEDS No religious, straight-up realism, odes to dead dogs. Length: 200-10,000 words; average length: 5,000 words.
HOW TO CONTACT Send reviews of novels and short story collections to editor. Include cover letter with disposable copy of complete mss. Accepts 5 mss/year.
PAYMENT/TERMS Pays contributor's copies.
TIPS "Our guidelines are very open and ambiguous. Don't send us too much and don't make it too long. If you submit in an e-mail, use .rtf. We're easy. If it works, we'll be in touch. It's a brutal world—wear your helmet."

TOASTED CHEESE

E-mail: editors@toasted-cheese.com. **E-mail:** submit@toasted-cheese.com. **Website:** www.toasted-cheese.com. Estab. 2001. "*Toasted Cheese* accepts submissions of previously unpublished fiction, flash fiction, creative nonfiction, and poetry. Our focus is on quality of work, not quantity. Some issues will therefore contain fewer/more pieces than previous issues. We don't restrict publication based on subject matter. We encourage submissions from innovative writers in all genres."

Receives 150 unsolicited mss/month. Accepts 1-10 mss/issue; 5-30 mss/year. Publishes 15 new writers/year. Sponsors awards/contests.

NEEDS "No fan fiction. No chapters or excerpts unless they read as a stand-alone story. No first drafts."

HOW TO CONTACT Send complete ms in body of e-mail; no attachments. Accepts submissions by e-mail.

TIPS "We are looking for clean, professional writing from writers of any level. Accepted stories will be concise and compelling. We are looking for writers who are serious about the craft: tomorrow's literary stars before they're famous. Take your submission seriously, yet remember that levity is appreciated. You are submitting not to traditional editors but to fellow writers who appreciate the efforts of those in the trenches. Follow online submission guidelines."

TORCH: POETRY, PROSE AND SHORT STORIES BY AFRICAN AMERICAN WOMEN

3720 Gattis School Rd., Suite 800, Round Rock, TX 78664. **E-mail:** info@torchpoetry.org (inquiries), poetry@torchpoetry.org (submissions). **Website:** www.torchpoetry.org. **Contact:** Amanda Johnston, editor. Estab. 2006. *TORCH: Poetry, Prose, and Short Stories by African American Women*, published semiannually online, provides "a place to publish contemporary poetry, prose, and short stories by experienced and emerging writers alike. We prefer our contributors to take risks, and we offer a diverse body of work that examines and challenges preconceived notions regarding race, ethnicity, gender roles, and identity."

Has published poetry by Sharon Bridgforth, Patricia Smith, Crystal Wilkinson, Tayari Jones, and Natasha Trethewey. Reads submissions April 15-August 31 only. Sometimes comments on rejected poems.

PAYMENT/TERMS Always sends prepublication galleys. No payment.

TIPS "Within *TORCH*, we offer a special section called Flame that features an interview, biography, and work sample by an established writer as well as an introduction to their Spark—an emerging writer who inspires them and adds to the boundless voice of creative writing by Black women." A free online newsletter is available; see website.

TRAIL OF INDISCRETION

Fortress Publishing, Inc., Lemoyne, PA 17011. **E-mail:** fortresspublishinginc@yahoo.com. **E-mail:** realm.beyond@yahoo.com. **Website:** www.fortresspublishinginc.com.

NEEDS No profanity or graphic scenes. Length: no more than 5,000 words.

HOW TO CONTACT E-mail word document.

PAYMENT/TERMS Pays in contributor's copies.

TRANSITION: AN INTERNATIONAL REVIEW

104 Mount Auburn St., 3R, Cambridge, MA 02138. (617)496-2845. **Fax:** (617)496-2877. **E-mail:** transition@fas.harvard.edu. **Website:** http://dubois.fas.harvard.edu/transition-magazine. **Contact:** Sara Bruya, managing editor. Estab. 1961.

Essays first published in a recent issue of *Transition* were selected for inclusion in *Best American Essays 2008*, *Best American Nonrequired Reading 2008*, and *Best African American Writing 2009*. Four-time winner of the Alternative Press Award for international reporting (2001, 2000, 1999, 1995); finalist in the 2001 National Magazine Award in General Excellence category.

HOW TO CONTACT "For all submissions, please include the following information in your e-mail or cover letter and in the top left corner of the first page of all documents: name, address, e-mail address, word count, date of submission. Please also include a title with each work." E-mail submissions are preferred.

PAYMENT/TERMS Pays 1 contributor's copy.

TIPS "We look for a nonwhite, alternative perspective, dealing with issues of race, ethnicity, and identity in an unpredictable, provocative way."

U.S. CATHOLIC

Claretian Publications, 205 W. Monroe St., Chicago, IL 60606. (312)236-7782. **Fax:** (312)236-8207. **E-mail:** editors@uscatholic.org. **E-mail:** submissions@uscatholic.org. **Website:** www.uscatholic.org. Estab. 1935. "*U.S. Catholic* is dedicated to the belief that it makes a difference whether you're Catholic. We invite and help our readers explore the wisdom of their faith tradition and apply their faith to the challenges of the 21st century."

Please include SASE with written ms.

NEEDS Accepts short stories. "Topics vary, but unpublished fiction should be no longer than 2,500 words and should include strong characters and cause readers to stop for a moment and consider their relationships with others, the world, and/or God. Specifically religious themes are not required; subject matter is not restricted. E-mail literaryeditor@uscatholic.org. Usually responds in 8-10 weeks. Minimum payment is $300." Length: 2,500-3,000 words.

HOW TO CONTACT Send complete ms.

PAYMENT/TERMS Pays $300.

VAMPIRES 2 MAGAZINE

Man's Story 2 Publishing Co., 1321 Snapfinger Rd., Decatur, GA 30032. **E-mail:** mansstory2@aol.com. **Website:** www.vampires2.us. Estab. 1999. "Online e-zine that strives to re-create vampire romance in the pulp fiction style of the 1920s through the 1970s with strong emphasis on 3D graphic art." Also features illustrated stories, online magazine, online photo galleries, and more.

○ "We publish books, publish online, and operate websites. In 2000 we became one of *Writer's Digest*'s top 100 markets for fiction writers and have since become listed with 20 other outstanding writers organizations."

NEEDS Length: 3,500 words more or less.

HOW TO CONTACT Send complete ms.

PAYMENT/TERMS Pays $25.

TIPS "We suggest interested writers visit our website and read our writer's guidelines. Then read the pulp fiction stories posted in our online mini-magazine and/or read one of our magazines, or find an old pulp fiction magazine that was published in the 1960s. If all else fails, e-mail us. We accept submissions by e-mail year-round. Send submissions as a Word attachment."

○○ VERANDAH LITERARY & ART JOURNAL

Faculty of Arts, Deakin University, 221 Burwood Hwy., Burwood, Victoria 3125 Australia. (61)(3)9251-7134. **E-mail:** verandah@deakin.edu.au. **Website:** www.deakin.edu.au/verandah. Estab. 1985. *Verandah*, published annually in September, is "a high-quality literary journal edited by professional writing students. It aims to give voice to new and innovative writers and artists."

○ "The first edition of *Verandah* was launched in 1985, beneath the shade of the 'wide verandahs' of Victoria College. Established as a student-run publication, from its inception *Verandah* has attracted high-quality work by both established and emerging writers and artists for annual publication." Has published work by Christos Tsiolka, Dorothy Porter, Seamus

Heaney, Les Murray, Ed Burger, and John Muk Muk Burke. *Verandah* is 120 pages, professionally printed on glossy stock, flat-spined, with full-color glossy card cover.

NEEDS Length: 350-2,000 words.

HOW TO CONTACT "Submit by mail or e-mail. However, electronic version of work must be available if accepted by *Verandah*. Do not submit work without the required submission form (available for download on website)." Reads submissions by June 1 deadline (postmark).

VESTAL REVIEW

2609 Dartmouth Dr., Vestal NY 13850. **E-mail:** submissions@vestalreview.net. **Website:** www.vestalreview.net.

○ *Vestal Review*'s stories have been reprinted in the *Mammoth Book of Miniscule Fiction, Flash Writing, E2Ink Anthologies*, and in the *WW Norton Anthology Flash Fiction Forward*.

NEEDS Length: 50-500 words.

HOW TO CONTACT "We accept submissions only through our submission manager." Does not read new submissions in January, June, July, and December. All submissions received during these months will be returned unopened.

PAYMENT/TERMS Pays 3-10¢/word and 1 contributor's copy; additional copies for $10 (plus postage).

TIPS "We like literary fiction, with a plot, that doesn't waste words. Don't send jokes masked as stories."

○ THE VIEW FROM HERE MAGAZINE

Blam! Productions, **E-mail:** editor@viewfromheremagazine.com; rear.view.poetry@gmail.com. **Website:** www.viewfromheremagazine.com. **Contact:** Mike French, senior editor; Claire King, managing fiction editor. Estab. 2008. "We are a print and online literary magazine designed and edited by an international team. We bring an entertaining mix of wit and insight all packaged in beautifully designed pages."

NEEDS "We publish our fiction at The Front View, where we showcase the weird, unusual, thought provoking and occasionally bizarre. We classify ourselves as "Bohemian Eclectic." Our stories will make you wonder, laugh, cry, and generally feel something. We expect to elicit a valid emotional response from our readers." Nothing erotic. Length: up to 5,000 words, "but query if longer."

HOW TO CONTACT Send complete ms.

TIPS "Due to the amount of submissions, work sent without a brief cover letter or introduction will be dismissed."

VIRGINIA QUARTERLY REVIEW

University of Virginia, 5 Boar's Head Lane, P.O. Box 400223, Charlottesville, VA 22904. (434)243-4995. **Fax:** (434)924-1397. **E-mail:** editors@vqronline.org. **Website:** www.vqronline.org. **Contact:** Paul Reyes, deputy editor; Jane Friedman, web editor. Estab. 1925. A national journal of literature and thought. A lay, intellectual audience; people who are not out-and-out scholars but who are interested in ideas and literature. ◒ Check website for submissions schedule.
NEEDS Length: 2,000-8,000 words.
HOW TO CONTACT Send complete ms.
PAYMENT/TERMS Pays $100/page maximum.
TIPS "Submissions only accepted online."

WEST BRANCH

Stadler Center for Poetry, Bucknell University, Lewisburg, PA 17837-2029. (570)577-1853. **Fax:** (570)577-1885. **E-mail:** westbranch@bucknell.edu. **Website:** www.bucknell.edu/westbranch. *West Branch* publishes poetry, fiction, and nonfiction in both traditional and innovative styles.
NEEDS No genre fiction.
HOW TO CONTACT Send complete ms.
PAYMENT/TERMS Pays $20-100 ($10/page).
TIPS "All submissions must be sent via our online submission manager. Please see website for guidelines. We recommend that you acquaint yourself with the magazine before submitting."

WESTERN HUMANITIES REVIEW

University of Utah, English Department, 255 S. Central Campus Dr., Room 3500, Salt Lake City, UT 84112-0494. (801)581-6070. **Fax:** (801)585-5167. **E-mail:** whr@mail.hum.utah.edu. **Website:** www.hum.utah.edu/whr. **Contact:** Barry Weller, editor; Nate Liederbach, managing editor. Estab. 1947.
NEEDS Does not want genre (romance, sci-fi, etc.). Length: 5,000 words.
HOW TO CONTACT Send complete ms.
PAYMENT/TERMS Pays $5/published page (when funds available).
TIPS "Because of changes in our editorial staff, we urge familiarity with recent issues of the magazine. We do not publish writer's guidelines because we think that the magazine itself conveys an accurate

picture of our requirements. Please, no e-mail submissions."

WHISKEY ISLAND MAGAZINE

Rhodes Tower 1636, Cleveland, OH 44115. (216)687-2000. **E-mail:** whiskeyisland@csuohio.edu. **Website:** www.csuohio.edu/class/english/whiskeyisland. "This is a nonprofit literary magazine that has been published (in one form or another) by students of Cleveland State University for over 30 years. Also features the Annual Student Creative Writing Contest."
NEEDS No translations. "Please keep fiction submissions to 5,000 words or less."
HOW TO CONTACT "We accept original poetry, prose, and art submissions from August 15 through May 1 of each year. We accept simultaneous submissions and ask that you identify them as such in your cover letter. No multiple submissions, please, and no previously published work either. Reporting time is about 3 months."
TIPS "See submissions page. Wait at least a year before submitting again."

☻ ◐ ☻ WHITE FUNGUS: AN EXPERIMENTAL ARTS MAGAZINE

Room 5, Floor 9, No. 420, Sec. 2, Nantun Rd., Nantun District, Taichung City Taiwan **E-mail:** mail@whitefungus.com. **Website:** www.whitefungus.com. Estab. 2004. "*White Fungus* is an art magazine based in Taichung City, Taiwan. Founded by brothers Ron and Mark Hanson in Wellington, in 2004, as a quasi political manifesto, copies of the first issue were produced on a photocopier, wrapped in Christmas paper and hurled anonymously through the entrances of businesses throughout the city. Now a magazine featuring interviews, writing on art, new music, history and politics, *White Fungus* takes a dialogical approach to the work it covers. The name of the publication comes from a can of "white fungus" the Hansons found in their local supermarket in the industrial zone of Taichung City. Each cover of *White Fungus* is derived from a scan of the can."

◐ WILD VIOLET

P.O. Box 39706, Philadelphia, PA 19106. **E-mail:** wildvioletmagazine@yahoo.com. **Website:** www.wildviolet.net. **Contact:** Alyce Wilson, editor. Estab. 2001. Online magazine: illustrations, photos. "Our goal is to make a place for the arts: to make the arts more accessible and to serve as a creative forum for writers and artists. Our audience includes English-speaking readers from all over the world, who are interested in both 'high art' and pop culture."

○ Receives 30 unsolicited mss/month. Accepts 5 mss/issue; 20 mss/year. **Publishes 30 new writers/year.** Sometimes comments on rejected mss.

Recently published work by Rik Hunik, Wayne Scheer, Jane McDonald, Mark Joseph Kiewlak, T. Richard Williams, and Susan Snowden. Quarterly.

NEEDS Comics/graphic novels, ethnic/multicultural, experimental, fantasy (space fantasy, sword and sorcery), feminist, gay, horror (dark fantasy, futuristic, psychological, supernatural), humor/satire, lesbian, literary, New Age, psychic/supernatural/occult, science fiction. "No stories where sexual or violent content is just used to shock the reader. No racist writings." Length: 500-6,000 words; average length: 3,000 words. Also publishes literary essays, literary criticism, poetry. How to Contact Send complete ms. Accepts submissions by e-mail. Include estimated word count and brief bio. Send SASE for return of ms or send a disposable copy of ms and #10 SASE for reply only. Responds in 1 week to queries; 3-6 months to mss. Accepts simultaneous, multiple submissions. Sample copy online. Writer's guidelines by e-mail.

PAYMENT/TERMS Writers receive bio and links on contributor's page. Request limited electronic rights, for online publication and archival only. Sponsors awards/contests.

TIPS "We look for stories that are well-paced and show character and plot development. Even short shorts should do more than simply paint a picture. Manuscripts stand out when the author's voice is fresh and engaging. Avoid muddying your story with too many characters and don't attempt to shock the reader with an ending you have not earned. Experiment with styles and structures, but don't resort to experimentation for its own sake."

◑ WILLARD & MAPLE

163 S. Willard St., Freeman 302, Box 34, Burlington, VT 05401. (802)860-2700 ext.2462. **E-mail:** willardandmaple@champlain.edu. Estab. 1996. *Willard & Maple*, published annually in spring, is a student-run literary magazine from Champlain College's Professional Writing Program that considers short fiction, essays, reviews, fine art, and poetry by adults, children, and teens." Wants "creative work of the highest quality." Does not want any submissions over 10 typed pages in length; all submissions must be in English.

○ *Willard & Maple* is 200 pages, digest size, digitally printed, perfect-bound. Receives about 500 poems/year, accepts about 20%. Press run is 600 (80 subscribers, 4 libraries); 200 are distributed free to the Champlain College writing community. Single copy: $12. Contact Lulu Press for contributor's copy.

HOW TO CONTACT Send complete mss via e-mail or snail mail. Send SASE for return of ms or send disposable copy of mss and #10 SASE for reply only.

PAYMENT/TERMS Pays 2 contributor's copies.

TIPS "The power of imagination makes us infinite."

WILLOW REVIEW

College of Lake County Publications, College of Lake County, 19351 W. Washington St., Grayslake, IL 60030-1198. (847)543-2956. **E-mail:** com426@clcillinois.edu. **Website:** www.clcillinois.edu/community/willowreview.asp. **Contact:** Michael Latza, editor. Estab. 1969. *Willow Review*, published annually, is interested in poetry, creative nonfiction, and fiction of high quality. "We have no preferences as to form, style, or subject, as long as each poem stands on its own as art and communicates ideas."

○ The editors award prizes for best poetry and prose in the issue. Prize awards vary contingent on the current year's budget but normally ranges from $100-400. There is no reading fee or separate application for these prizes. All accepted mss are eligible. *Willow Review* is 88-96 pages, digest size, professionally printed, flat spined, with a 4-color cover featuring work by an Illinois artist. Press run is 1,000. Subscription: $18/3 issues, $30/6 issues. Sample: $5 (back issue). International: add $5 per issue. Has published poetry by Lisel Mueller, Lucien Stryk, David Ray, Louis Rodriguez, John Dickson, and Patricia Smith.

NEEDS Accepts short fiction. Considers simultaneous submissions, multiple submissions.

HOW TO CONTACT Send complete ms with cover letter. Include estimated word count, brief bio, list of publications. Send either SASE (or IRC) for return of ms or disposable copy of ms and #10 SASE for reply only.

PAYMENT/TERMS Pays 2 contributors copies.

TIPS "Include SASE. No e-mail submissions, please. *Willow Review* can be found on EBSCOhost databases, assuring a broader targeted audience for our authors' work. *Willow Review* is a nonprofit journal partially supported by a grant from the Illinois Arts Council (a state agency), College of Lake County Publications, private contributions, and sales."

WILLOW SPRINGS

501 N. Riverpoint Blvd., Suite 425, Spokane, WA 99202. (509)359-7435. **E-mail:** willowspringsewu@gmail.com. **Website:** http://willowsprings.ewu.edu. **Contact:** Samuel Ligon, editor. Estab. 1977. Willow Springs is published twice a year, in spring and fall. Submissions in all genres are closed between June 1 and August 31.

NEEDS We accept any good piece of literary fiction. Buy a sample copy. Does not want to see genre fiction that does not transcend its subject matter.

HOW TO CONTACT Send complete ms.

TIPS "Please submit all manuscripts with a cover letter and a brief bio. While we have no specific length restrictions, we generally publish fiction and nonfiction no longer than 10,000 words and poetry no longer than 120 lines, though those are not strict rules. *Willow Springs* values poems and essays that transcend the merely autobiographical and fiction that conveys a concern for language as well as story."

○ WINDHOVER

A Journal of Christian Literature, P.O. Box 8008, 900 College St., Belton, TX 76513. (254)295-4561. **E-mail:** windhover@umhb.edu. **Website:** http://undergrad.umhb.edu/english/windhover-journal. **Contact:** Dr. Nathaniel Hansen, editor. Estab. 1997. "*Windhover* is devoted to promoting writers and literature with a Christian perspective and with a broad definition of that perspective. We accept poetry, short fiction, nonfiction, creative nonfiction."

○ Magazine: 6" × 9"; white bond paper. Receives 30 unsolicited mss/month. Recently published work by Walt McDonald, Cleatus Rattan, Greg Garrett, Barbara Crooker.

NEEDS No erotica. Length: 1,500-4,000 words. Average length: 3,000 words.

HOW TO CONTACT Accepts electronic submissions only through online submission manager; no e-mailed submissions. Include estimated word count, brief bio, and list of publications. Reading period is February 1-September 1. Deadlines for submissions is June 1 for next issue.

PAYMENT/TERMS Pays 2 contributor's copies.

TIPS "We particularly look for convincing plot and character development."

○ WINDSOR REVIEW

Department of English, University of Windsor, Windsor, ON N9B 3P4 Canada. (519)253-3000; (519) 253-4232, ext. 2290. **Fax:** (519)971-3676. **E-mail:** uwrevu@uwindsor.ca. **Website:** www.uwindsor.ca. **Contact:** Marty Gervais, art editor. Estab. 1965. "We try to offer a balance of fiction and poetry distinguished by excellence."

NEEDS No genre fiction (science fiction, romance), but will consider if writing is good enough. Length: 1,000-5,000 words.

HOW TO CONTACT Send complete ms.

PAYMENT/TERMS Pays $25, 1 contributor's copy and a free subscription.

TIPS "Good writing, strong characters, and experimental fiction is appreciated."

○ WISCONSIN REVIEW

University of Wisconsin Oshkosh, 800 Algoma Blvd., Oshkosh, WI 54901. (920)424-2267. **E-mail:** wisconsinreview@uwosh.edu. **Website:** www.uwosh.edu/wisconsinreview. Estab. 1966. *Wisconsin Review*, published semiannually, is a "contemporary poetry, prose, and art magazine run by students at the University of Wisconsin Oshkosh." Wants all forms and styles of poetry. Does not want "poetry that is racist, sexist, or unnecessarily vulgar." Considers poetry by children and teens. "Minors may submit material by including a written letter of permission from a parent or guardian."

○ *Wisconsin Review* is around 100 pages, digest size, perfect-bound, with 4-color glossy cover stock. Receives about 400 poetry submissions/year, accepts about 50; Press run is 1,000. Single copy: $7.50; subscription: $10 plus $3 extra per issue for shipments outside the U.S.

NEEDS Send complete ms with cover letter and SASE.

PAYMENT/TERMS Pays with 2 contributor copies.

TIPS "We are open to any poetic form and style, and look for outstanding imagery, new themes, and fresh voices—poetry that induces emotions."

WITCHES AND PAGANS

BBI Media, Inc., P.O. Box 687, Forest Grove, OR 97116. (888)724-3966. **E-mail:** editor2@bbimedia

.com. **Website:** www.witchesandpagans.com. Estab. 2002. *Witches and Pagans* is dedicated to witches, wiccans, neo-pagans, and various other earth-based, pre-Christian, shamanic, and magical practitioners. "We hope to reach not only those already involved in what we cover, but the curious and completely new as well. Devoted exclusively to promoting and covering contemporary Pagan culture, *W&P* features exclusive interviews with the teachers, writers, and activists who create and lead our traditions; visits to the sacred places and people who inspire us; and in-depth discussions of our ever-evolving practices. You'll also find practical daily magic, ideas for solitary ritual and devotion, God/dess-friendly craft projects, Pagan poetry and short fiction, reviews, and much more in every 96-page issue. *W&P* is available in either traditional paper copy sent by postal mail or as a digital PDF e-zine download that is compatible with most computers and readers."

NEEDS Does not want "faction" (fictionalized retellings of real events). Avoid gratuitous sex, violence, sentimentality, and pagan moralizing. Don't beat our readers with the Rede or the Threefold Law. Length: 1,000-5,000 words.

HOW TO CONTACT Send complete ms.

PAYMENT/TERMS Pays 2¢/word minimum.

TIPS "Read the magazine, do your research, write the piece, send it in. That's really the only way to get started as a writer: Everything else is window dressing."

WOMAN'S WORLD

Bauer Publishing Co., 270 Sylvan Ave., Englewood Cliffs, NJ 07632. (201)569-6699. **Fax:** (201)569-3584. **E-mail:** dearww@bauerpublishing.com; dearww@aol.com. **Website:** http://winit.womansworldmag.com. **Contact:** Stephanie Saible, editor-in-chief. Estab. 1980. "We publish short romances and mini-mysteries for all women, ages 18-68."

Woman's World is not looking for freelancers to take assigments generated by the staff, but it will assign stories to writers who have made a successful pitch.

NEEDS "Short story, romance, and mainstream of 800 words and mini-mysteries of 1,000 words. Each of our stories has a light romantic theme and can be written from either a masculine or feminine point of view. Women characters may be single, married, or divorced. Plots must be fast moving with vivid dialogue and action. The problems and dilemmas inherent in them should be contemporary and realistic, handled with warmth and feeling. The stories must have a positive resolution. Specify Fiction on envelope. Always enclose SASE. Responds in 4 months. No phone or fax queries. Pays $1,000 for romances on acceptance for North American serial rights for 6 months. The 1,000 word mini-mysteries may feature either a 'whodunnit' or 'howdunnit' theme. The mystery may revolve around anything from a theft to murder. However, we are not interested in sordid or grotesque crimes. Emphasis should be on intricacies of plot rather than gratuitous violence. The story must include a resolution that clearly states the villain is getting his or her come uppance. Submit complete mss. Specify Mini-Mystery on envelope. Enclose SASE. No phone queries." Not interested in science fiction, fantasy, historical romance, or foreign locales. No explicit sex, graphic language, or seamy settings. Romances, 800 words; mysteries, 1,000 words.

HOW TO CONTACT Send complete ms.

PAYMENT/TERMS Pays $1,000/romances; $500/mysteries.

TIPS The whole story should be sent when submitting fiction. Stories slanted for a particular holiday should be sent at least 6 months in advance. "Familiarize yourself totally with our format and style. Read at least a year's worth of *Woman's World* fiction. Analyze and dissect it. Regarding romances, scrutinize them not only for content but tone, mood, and sensibility."

THE WORCESTER REVIEW

1 Ekman St., Worcester, MA 01607. (508)797-4770. **E-mail:** twr.diane@gmail.com. **Website:** www.theworcesterreview.org. **Contact:** Diane Mulligan, managing editor. Estab. 1972. *The Worcester Review*, published annually by the Worcester County Poetry Association, encourages "critical work with a New England connection; no geographic limitation on poetry and fiction." Wants "work that is crafted, intuitively honest and empathetic. We like high-quality, creative poetry, artwork, and fiction. Critical articles should be connected to New England."

The Worcester Review is 6" × 9"; 60 lb. white offset paper; 10 pt. CS1 cover stock; illustrations; photos. 160 pages, professionally printed in dark type on quality stock, perfect-bound, with matte card cover. Press run is 600. Subscription: $30 (includes membership in

WCPA). Recently published work by Robert Pinsky, Marge Piercy, Wes McNair, Ed Hirsch.

NEEDS Length: 1,000-4,000 words. Average length: 2,000 words.

HOW TO CONTACT Send complete ms. "Send only 1 short story—reading editors do not like to read 2 by the same author at the same time. We will use only 1."

PAYMENT/TERMS Pays 2 contributor's copies and honorarium if possible.

TIPS "We generally look for creative work with a blend of craftsmanship, insight, and empathy. This does not exclude humor. We won't print work that is shoddy in any of these areas."

THE WRITE PLACE AT THE WRITE TIME

E-mail: submissions@thewriteplaceatthewritetime .org. **Website:** www.thewriteplaceatthewritetime.org. **Contact:** Nicole M. Bouchard, editor-in-chief. Estab. 2008. "We encourage new and seasoned writers to send in submissions for the next issue, benefit from resources we provide, read the current issue and enjoy themselves. It is our personal touch, on everything from the feedback we give to our aesthetic to the lasting relationships we cultivate with our contributors, that distinguishes us as having a community-like atmosphere dedicated to a humanitarian approach to the arts. We publish 3 issues a year, and our writers range from previously unpublished to having written for *The New York Times*, *Time* magazine, *The Wall Street Journal*, *Glimmer Train*, *Newsweek*, and *Business Week*, and they come from all over the world."

NEEDS This online quarterly literary publication features fiction, poetry, Our Stories (memoir-style nonfiction), a Writers' Craft Box of writing essays and resources from professionals in the field, archives of past issues, Writers' Challenge, fine artwork from artists whose backgrounds include having done work for *The New York Times*, and best-selling author interviews such as Janet Fitch (*White Oleander*), Frances Mayes (*Under the Tuscan Sun*), Dennis Lehane (*Mystic River*), and Arthur Golden (*Memoirs of a Geisha*)—all of whom have had their works adapted into major motion pictures. Encourages beginning or unpublished writers to submit work for consideration. Accepts outstanding work by beginning and established writers. Email: editorialstaff@thewriteplaceatthewritetime. org. No erotica, explicit horror/gore/violence, political. Length: 3,500 words/max. Average length of

stories: 3,000 words. Average length of short shorts: 1,000 words.

HOW TO CONTACT Send complete ms with cover letter by e-mail. Include estimated word count and brief bio. Accepts multiple submissions, up to 3 stories at a time. Accepts 90-100 mss/year; receives 500-700 mss/year.

PAYMENT/TERMS "We are not currently offering monetary compensation."

TIPS "Visit the website for details before submitting. Our publication is copyrighted. We send pre-publication galleys to authors depending on whether the story underwent significant edits. We like to work closely with our writers. If the material is only slightly edited, then we don't."

🅞 WRITER'S BLOC

Texas A&M University-Kingsville, Dept. of Language and Literature, MSC 162, Fore Hall 201B, Kingsville, TX 78363. (361)593-2640. **E-mail:** octavio.quintanilla@tamuk.edu. **Website:** www.tamuk.edu/artsci/langlit/writers_bloc.html. **Contact:** Octavio Quintanilla. *Writer's Bloc*, published annually, prints poetry, fiction, creative nonfiction, and graphic art. "About half of our pages are devoted to the works of Texas A&M University-Kingsville students and half to the works of writers and artists from all over the world."

🅠 *Writer's Bloc* is 96 pages, digest size. Press run is 300. Subscription: $7. Sample: $7. Accepts about 6 mss/year. Does not read mss February-September.

NEEDS Wants quality poetry; no restrictions on content or form. Publishes short shorts. Also publishes literary essays, poetry. No pornography. No genre fiction. No work by children. Length: up to 3,500 words. Average length is 2,500 words.

THE WRITER'S CHRONICLE

Association of Writers & Writing Programs (AWP), Carty House MS 1E3, George Mason University, Fairfax, VA 22030-4444. (703)993-4301. **Fax:** (703)993-4302. **E-mail:** chronicle@awpwriter.org. **Website:** www.awpwriter.org. Estab. 1967. "*Writer's Chronicle* strives to: present the best essays on the craft and art of writing poetry, fiction, and nonfiction; help overcome the overspecialization of the literary arts by presenting a public forum for the appreciation, debate, and analysis of contemporary literature; present the diversity of accomplishments and points of view within contemporary literature; provide serious and committed writers and students of writing the best advice on how to manage their professional lives; provide writers who teach with new pedagogical approaches for their classrooms; provide the members and subscribers with a literary community as a compensation for a devotion to a difficult and lonely art; provide information on publishing opportunities, grants, and awards; and promote the good works of AWP, its programs, and its individual members."

TIPS "In general, the editors look for articles that demonstrate an excellent working knowledge of literary issues and a generosity of spirit that esteems the arguments of other writers on similar topics. When writing essays on craft, do not use your own work as an example. Keep in mind that 18,000 of our readers are students or just-emerging writers. They must become good readers before they can become good writers, so we expect essays on craft to show exemmplary close readings of a variety of contemporary and older works. Essays must embody erudition, generosity, curiosity, and discernment rather than self-involvement. Writers may refer to their own travails and successes if they do so modestly, in small proportion to the other examples. We look for a generosity of spirit—a general love and command of literature, as well as an expert, writerly viewpoint."

🅞 XAVIER REVIEW

Xavier University, 1 Drexel Dr., Box 89, New Orleans, LA 70125-1098. **Website:** www.xula.edu/review. **Contact:** Ralph Adamo, editor. Estab. 1980. "*Xavier Review* accepts poetry, fiction, translations, creative nonfiction, and critical essays. Content focuses on African American, Caribbean, and Southern literature, as well as works that touch on issues of religion and spirituality. We do, however, accept quality work on all themes. (Please note: This is not a religious publication.)"

NEEDS Has published work by Andrei Codrescu, Terrance Hayes, Naton Leslie, Patricia Smith. Also publishes literary essays and literary criticism.

HOW TO CONTACT Send complete ms. Include 2-3 sentence bio and SASE. E-mail submissions are generally not accepted; links to sites are ignored. "We rarely accepts mss over 20 pages.

PAYMENT/TERMS Pays 2 contributor's copies; offers 40% discount on additional copies.

THE YALE REVIEW

Yale University, P.O. Box 208243, New Haven, CT 06520. (203)432-0499. **Fax:** (203)432-0510. **Website:** www.yale.edu/yalereview. **Contact:** J.D. McClatchy, editor. Estab. 1911.

NEEDS Buys quality fiction. Length: 3,000-5,000 words.

HOW TO CONTACT Submit complete ms with SASE. All submissions should be sent to the editorial office.

PAYMENT/TERMS Pays $400-500.

THE YALOBUSHA REVIEW

University of Mississippi, P.O. Box 1848, Dept. of English, University, MS 38677. (662)915-3175. **E-mail:** yreditor@yahoo.com. **Website:** http://yr.olemiss .edu/. Estab. 1995.

NEEDS Length: 10,000 words.

HOW TO CONTACT Submit "one short story of traditional length (let's say 8-20 pages), of up to 3 pieces of shorter fiction (less than 5 pages a piece). If submitting 3 shorter works, please include all pieces in one file." Use online submissions manager.

PAYMENT/TERMS Pays honorarium when funding available.

🅞🅓 YEMASSEE

University of South Carolina, Department of English, Columbia, SC 29208. (803)777-2085. **Fax:** (803)777-9064. **E-mail:** editor@yemasseejournalonline.org. **Website:** http://yemasseejournalonline.org. **Contact:** Lauren Eyler, editor-in-chief. Estab. 1993. "*Yemassee* is the University of South Carolina's literary journal. Our readers are interested in high-quality fiction, poetry, drama, and creative nonfiction. We have no editorial slant; quality of work is our only concern. We publish in the fall and spring, printing 3-5 stories/issue and 12-15 poems/issue. We tend to solicit reviews, essays, and interviews but welcome unsolicited queries. We do not favor any particular aesthetic or school of writing."

🅠 Stories from *Yemassee* have been published in *New Stories From the South*. As of 2012, only accepts submissions through online submissions manager.

NEEDS "We are open to a variety of subjects and writing styles. We publish primarily fiction and poetry, but we are also interested in one-act plays, brief excerpts of novels, and interviews with literary figures. Our essential consideration for acceptance is the quality of the work. No romance, religious/inspirational,

young adult/teen, children's/juvenile, erotica. Wants more experimental work." Length: up to 5,000 words.
HOW TO CONTACT Send complete ms. "Submissions for all genres should include a cover letter that lists the titles of the pieces included, along with your contact information (including author's name, address, e-mail address, and phone number)."
PAYMENT/TERMS Pays in contributor copies.

ZOETROPE: ALL-STORY

Zoetrope: All-Story, The Sentinel Bldg., 916 Kearny St., San Francisco, CA 94133. (415)788-7500. **Website:** www.all-story.com. **Contact:** Michael Ray, editor. Estab. 1997. *Zoetrope: All Story* presents a new generation of classic stories.

- Does not accept submissions September 1-December 31 (with the exception of stories entered in the annual Short Fiction Contest, which are considered for publication in the magazine).

HOW TO CONTACT "Writers should submit only one story at a time and no more than two stories a year. Before submitting, nonsubscribers should read several issues of the magazine to determine if their works fit with *All-Story*. Electronic versions of the magazine are available to read, in part, at the website; and print versions are available for purchase by single-issue order and subscription. We consider unsolicited submissions of short stories and one-act plays no longer than 7,000 words. Excerpts from larger works, screenplays, treatments, and poetry will be returned unread. We do not accept artwork or design submissions. We do not accept unsolicited revisions nor do we respond to writers who don't include an SASE." Send complete ms.
PAYMENT/TERMS Pays up to $1,000.

ZYZZYVA

466 Geary Street, Suite 401, San Francisco, CA 94102. (415)440-1510. **E-mail:** editor@zyzzyva.org. **Website:** www.zyzzyva.org. **Contact:** Laura Cogan, editor; Oscar Villalon, managing editor. Estab. 1985. "We feature work by writers currently living on the West Coast or in Alaska and Hawaii only. We are essentially a literary magazine but of wide-ranging interests and a strong commitment to nonfiction."

- Accepts submissions year-round. Does not accept online submissions.

NEEDS Length: no maximum word count.
HOW TO CONTACT Send complete ms by mail. Include SASE and contact information.
PAYMENT/TERMS Pays $50.
TIPS "We are not currently seeking work about any particular theme or topic. That said, reading recent issues is perhaps the best way to develop a sense for the length and quality we are looking for in submissions."

BOOK PUBLISHERS

In this section, you will find many of the "big name" book publishers. Many of these publishers remain tough markets for new writers or for those whose work might be considered literary or experimental. Indeed, some only accept work from established authors, and then often only through an author's agent. Although having your novel published by one of the big commercial publishers listed in this section is difficult, it is not impossible. The trade magazine *Publishers Weekly* regularly features interviews with writers whose first novels are being released by top publishers. Many editors at large publishing houses find great satisfaction in publishing a writer's first novel.

On page 485, you'll find the publishing industry's "family tree," which maps out each of the large book publishing conglomerates' divisions, subsidiaries, and imprints. Remember, most manuscripts are acquired by imprints, not their parent company, so avoid submitting to the conglomerates themselves. (For example, submit to Dutton or Berkley Books, not their parent Penguin.)

Also listed here are "small presses," which publish four or more titles annually. Included among them are independent presses, university presses, and other nonprofit publishers. Introducing new writers to the reading public has become an increasingly important role of these smaller presses at a time when the large conglomerates are taking fewer chances on unknown writers. Many of the successful small presses listed in this section have built their reputations and their businesses in this way and have become known for publishing prize-winning fiction.

These smaller presses also tend to keep books in print longer than larger houses. And, since small presses publish a smaller number of books, each title is equally important to the publisher, and each is promoted in much the same way and with the same commitment.

Editors also stay at small presses longer because they have more of a stake in the business—often they own the business. Many smaller book publishers are writers themselves and know firsthand the importance of a close editor-author or publisher-author relationship.

TYPES OF BOOK PUBLISHERS

Large or small, the publishers in this section publish books "for the trade." That is, unlike textbook, technical, or scholarly publishers, trade publishers publish books to be sold to the general consumer through bookstores, chain stores, or other retail outlets. Within the trade book field, however, there are a number of different types of books.

The easiest way to categorize books is by their physical appearance and the way they are marketed. Hardcover books are the more expensive editions of a book, sold through bookstores and carrying a price tag of around $20 and up. Trade paperbacks are softbound books, also sold mostly in bookstores, but they carry a more modest price tag of usually around $10 to $20. Today a lot of fiction is published in this form because it means a lower financial risk than hardcover.

Mass-market paperbacks are another animal altogether. These are the smaller "pocket-size" books available at bookstores, grocery stores, drugstores, chain retail outlets, etc. Much genre or category fiction is published in this format. This area of the publishing industry is very open to the work of talented new writers who write in specific genres such as science fiction, romance, and mystery.

At one time, publishers could be easily identified and grouped by the type of books they produce. Today, however, the lines between hardcover and paperback books are blurred. Many publishers known for publishing hardcover books also publish trade paperbacks and have paperback imprints. This enables them to offer established authors (and a very few lucky newcomers) hard-soft deals in which their book comes out in both versions. Thanks to the mergers of the past decade, too, the same company may own several hardcover and paperback subsidiaries and imprints, even though their editorial focuses may remain separate.

CHOOSING A BOOK PUBLISHER

In addition to checking the bookstores and libraries for books by publishers that interest you, you may want to refer to the Category Index at the back of this book to find publishers divided by specific subject categories. The subjects listed in the index are general. Read individual listings to find which subcategories interest a publisher. For example, you will find several romance publishers listed, but you should read the listings to find which type of romance is considered: gothic, contemporary, regency, or futuristic.

The icons appearing before the names of the publishers will also help you in selecting a publisher. These codes are especially important in this section, because many of the publishing houses listed here require writers to submit through an agent. The Ⓐ symbol indicates that a publisher accepts agented submissions only. A ● icon identifies those that mostly publish established and agented authors, while a ○ points to publishers most open to new writers. See the inside front cover of this book for a complete list and explanations of symbols used in this book.

IN THE LISTINGS

As with other sections in this book, we identify new listings with a ⊕ symbol. In this section, most with this symbol are not new publishers, but they are established publishers who were unable to list last year (or decided not to) and are therefore new to this edition.

In addition to the ⊕ symbol indicating new listings, we include other symbols to help you narrow your search. English-speaking foreign markets are denoted by a ◉. The maple leaf symbol ✪ identifies Canadian presses. If you are not a Canadian writer but are interested in a Canadian press, check the listing carefully. Many small presses in Canada receive grants and other funds from their provincial or national government and are, therefore, restricted to publishing Canadian authors.

We also include editorial comments set off by a bullet (◑) within listings. This is where we include information about any special requirements or circumstances that will help you know even more about the publisher's needs and policies. The ◐ symbol identifies publishers who have recently received honors or awards for their books. The ☻ denotes publishers who produce comics and graphic novels.

Each listing includes a summary of the houses's editorial mission, an overarching principle that ties together what they publish. Under the heading Contact we list one or more editors, often with their specific area of expertise.

Book editors asked us again this year to emphasize the importance of paying close attention to the Needs and How to Contact subheads of listings for book publishers. Unlike magazine editors, who want to see complete manuscripts of short stories, most of the book publishers listed here ask that writers send a query letter with an outline and/or synopsis and several chapters of their novel. The Business of Fiction Writing, beginning on page 25 of this book, outlines how to prepare work to submit directly to a publisher.

There are no subsidy book publishers listed in *Novel & Short Story Writer's Market*. By subsidy, we mean any arrangement in which the writer is expected to pay all or part of the cost of producing, distributing, and marketing his book. We feel a writer should not be asked to share in any cost of turning his manuscript into a book. All the book publishers listed here told us that they do not charge writers for publishing their work. If any of the publishers listed here ask you to pay any part of publishing or marketing your manuscript, please let us know. See our Complaint Procedure on the copyright page of this book.

A NOTE ABOUT AGENTS

Some publishers are willing to look at unsolicited submissions, but most feel having an agent is in the writer's best interest. In this section more than any other, you'll find a number of publishers who prefer submissions from agents. That's why we've included a section of agents open to submissions from fiction writers (page 120). For even more agents, along with a great deal of helpful articles about approaching and working with them, refer to *Guide to Literary Agents* (Writer's Digest Books).

If you use the Internet or another resource to find an agent not listed in this book, be wary of any agents who charge large sums of money for reading a manuscript. Reading fees do not guarantee representation. Think of an agent as a potential business partner and feel free to ask tough questions about his or her credentials, experience, and business practices.

⊘ ABBEVILLE FAMILY

Abbeville Press, 137 Varick St., New York, NY 10013. (212)366-5585. **Fax:** (212)366-6966. **E-mail:** abbeville @abbeville.com. **Website:** www.abbeville.com. Estab. 1977. "Our list is full for the next several seasons."

O Not accepting unsolicited book proposals at this time.

NEEDS Picture books: animal, anthology, concept, contemporary, fantasy, folktales, health, hi-lo, history, humor, multicultural, nature/environment, poetry, science fiction, special needs, sports, suspense. Average word length 300-1,000 words.

HOW TO CONTACT Please refer to website for submission policy.

⊘ HARRY N. ABRAMS, INC.

115 W. 18th St., 6th Floor, New York, NY 10011. (212)206-7715. **Fax:** (212)519-1210. **E-mail:** abrams@ abramsbooks.com. **Website:** www.abramsbooks. com. **Contact:** Managing editor. Estab. 1951. Publishes hardcover and a few paperback originals.

O Does not accept unsolicited materials.

IMPRINTS Stewart, Tabori & Chang, Abrams Appleseed, Abrams Books for Young Readers, and Amulet Books.

NEEDS Publishes hardcover and "a few" paperback originals. Averages 150 total titles/year.

TIPS "We are one of the few publishers who publish almost exclusively illustrated books. We consider ourselves the leading publishers of art books and high-quality artwork in the U.S. Once the author has signed a contract to write a book for our firm, the author must finish the manuscript to agreed-upon high standards within the schedule agreed upon in the contract."

ACADEMY CHICAGO PUBLISHERS

363 W. Erie St., Suite 4W, Chicago, IL 60654. (312)751-7300. **Fax:** (312)751-7306. **E-mail:** zhanna@academy chicago.com. **Website:** www.academychicago.com. **Contact:** Zhanna Vaynberg, managing editor. Estab. 1975. Midsize independent publisher. Publishes hardcover originals and trade paperback reprints. Averages 15 total titles/year. "We publish quality fiction and nonfiction. Our audience is literate and discriminating. No novelized biography, history, or science fiction." No electronic submissions. Publishes hardcover and some paperback originals and trade

paperback reprints. Book catalog available online. Guidelines available online.

NEEDS Historical, mainstream/contemporary, military/war, mystery. "We look for quality work, but we do not publish experimental, avant-garde novels." Biography, history, academic, and anthologies. Only the most unusual mysteries, no private eyes or thrillers. No explicit sex or violence. Serious fiction, no romance/adventure. "We will consider historical fiction that is well researched. No science fiction/fantasy, no religious/inspirational, no how-to, no cookbooks. In general, we are very conscious of women's roles. We publish very few children's books." Published *Clean Start*, by Patricia Margaret Page (first fiction); *Cutter's Island: Caesar in Captivity*, by Vincent Panella (first fiction, historical); *Murder at the Paniomic Games*, by Michael B. Edward.PHI, PMS, PMW, PMYAccepts unsolicited mss. "We look for quality work, but we do not publish experimental, avant-garde, horror, science fiction, thrillers novels."

HOW TO CONTACT Do not submit by e-mail or fax. Accepts queries by mail. Include cover letter briefly describing the content of your work. Send SASE or IRC. "Manuscripts without envelopes will be discarded. *Mailers* are a *must* even from agents." Responds in 3 months to queries. No electronic submissions. Submit proposal package, synopsis, 3 sample chapters.

TERMS Pays 7-10% royalty on wholesale price. Average advance: modest. Publishes ms 18 months after acceptance. Ms guidelines online. Pays 7-10% royalty on wholesale price. Responds in 3 months.

TIPS "At the moment, we are looking for good nonfiction; we certainly want excellent original fiction, but we are swamped. No fax queries, no disks. No electronic submissions. We are always interested in reprinting good out-of-print books."

⊘⊘ ACE SCIENCE FICTION AND FANTASY

Imprint of the Berkley Publishing Group, Penguin Group (USA), Inc., 375 Hudson St., New York, NY 10014. (212)366-2000. **Website:** www.penguin.com. **Contact:** Ginjer Buchanan, editor-in-chief. Estab. 1953. Estab. 1953. Publishes hardcover, paperback, and trade paperback originals and reprints. Averages 75 total titles, 75 fiction titles/year. Ace publishes science fiction and fantasy exclusively. Publishes hardcover, paperback, and trade paperback originals and reprints

○ As imprint of Penguin, Ace is not open to unsolicited submissions.

NEEDS Does not accept unsolicited mss. No other genre accepted. No short stories.

HOW TO CONTACT Submit 1-2 sample chapter(s), synopsis. Send SASE or IRC. Responds in 2-3 months to queries. Due to the high volume of manuscripts received, most Penguin Group (USA) Inc. imprints do not normally accept unsolicited manuscripts. Query first with SASE. Editors will not respond unless interested.

TERMS Accepts simultaneous submissions. Pays royalty. Offers advance. Publishes ms 1-2 years after acceptance. Ms guidelines for #10 SASE. Pays royalty. Pays advance.

⊘ ALADDIN

Simon & Schuster, 1230 Avenue of the Americas, 4th Floor, New York, NY 10020. (212)698-7000. **Website:** www.simonsays.com. **Contact:** Acquisitions Editor. Aladdin publishes picture books, beginning readers, chapter books, middle-grade and tween fiction and nonfiction, and graphic novels and nonfiction in hardcover and paperback, with an emphasis on commercial, kid-friendly titles. Publishes hardcover/paperback imprints of Simon & Schuster Children's Publishing Children's Division.

HOW TO CONTACT Simon & Schuster does not review, retain, or return unsolicited materials or artwork. "We suggest prospective authors and illustrators submit their mss through a professional literary agent."

ALONDRA PRESS, LLC

4119 Wildacres Dr., Houston, TX 77072. **E-mail:** lark@alondrapress.com. **Website:** www.alondrapress.com. **Contact:** Pennelope Leight, fiction editor; Solomon Tager, nonfiction editor. Estab. 2007. Publishes trade paperback originals and reprints. Guidelines available online.

NEEDS "Just send us a few pages in an e-mail attachment, or the entire manuscript. We will look at it quickly and tell you if it interests us."

TERMS Responds in 1 month to queries/proposals; 3 months to mss.

TIPS "Be sure to read our guidelines before sending a submission. We will not respond to authors who do not observe our simple guidelines. Send your submissions in an e-mail attachment only."

AMERICAN CARRIAGE HOUSE PUBLISHING

P.O. Box 1130, Nevada City, CA 95959. (530)432-8860. **Fax:** (530)432-7379. **Website:** www.americancarriagehousepublishing.com. **Contact:** Lynn Taylor, editor (parenting, reference, child, women). Estab. 2004. Publishes trade paperback and electronic originals. Catalog free on request.

HOW TO CONTACT Query with SASE.

TERMS Pays outright purchase of $300-3,000. Responds in 3 months.

TIPS "We are looking for proposals, both fiction and nonfiction, preferably wholesome topics."

AMIRA PRESS

2721 N. Rosedale St., Baltimore, MD 21216 Wales. (704)858-7533. **E-mail:** submissions@amirapress.com. **Website:** www.amirapress.com. **Contact:** Yvette A. Lynn, CEO (any subgenre). Estab. 2007. "We are a small press which publishes sensual and erotic romance. Our slogan is 'Erotic and Sensual Romance. Immerse Yourself.' Our authors and stories are diverse." **Published 30 new writers last year.** Averages 50 fiction titles/year. Member EPIC. Distributes/promotes titles through Amazon, Mobipocket, Fictionwise, BarnesandNoble.com, Target.com, Amirapress.com, AllRomance Ebooks, and Ingrams. Format publishes in paperback originals, e-books, POD printing. Guidelines available online.

HOW TO CONTACT Submit complete ms with cover letter by e-mail. No snail mail. Include estimated word count, heat level, brief bio, list of publishing credits. Accepts unsolicited mss. Sometimes critiques/comments on rejected mss.

TERMS Pays royalties, 8½% of cover price (print)—30-40% of cover price (e-books). Responds in 3 months.

TIPS "Please read our submission guidelines thoroughly and follow them when submitting. We do not consider a work until we have all the requested information and the work is presented in the format we outline."

☻ ⊖ ANAPHORA LITERARY PRESS

104 Banff Dr., Apt. 101, Edinboro, PA 16412. (814)273-0004. **E-mail:** pennsylvaniajournal@gmail.com. **Website:** www.anaphoraliterary.com. **Contact:** Anna Faktorovich, editor-in-chief (general interest).

Estab. 2007. "We are actively seeking submissions at this time. Single and multiple-author books in fiction (poetry, novels, and short story collections). The genre is not as important as the quality of work. You should have a completed full-length ms ready to be e-mailed or mailed upon request." "In the winter of 2010, Anaphora began accepting book-length single-author submissions. We are actively seeking single and multiple-author books in fiction (poetry, novels, and short story collections) and nonfiction (academic, legal, business, journals, edited and un-edited dissertations, biographies, and memoirs). E-mail submissions. Profits are split 50/50 with single-author writers. There are no costs to have a book produced by Anaphora. We do not offer any free contributor copies." Format publishes in trade paperback originals and reprints; mass-market paperback originals and reprints. Catalog and guidelines available online at website.

NEEDS Short stories can be included in *Pennsylvania Literary Journal*. Two novellas might be published in a single book.

HOW TO CONTACT Looking for single and multiple-author books in fiction (poetry, novels, and short story collections). Query.

TERMS Pays 10-30% royalty on retail price. "We currently publish journals, which are authored by several people. If we publish a novel or a critical book by a single author, we will share our profits with the author." Pays 10-30% royalty on retail price. Responds in 1 month to queries, proposals, and mss.

TIPS "Our audience is academics, college students and graduates, as well as anybody who loves literature. Regardless of profits, we love publishing great books and we enjoy reading submissions. So, if you are reading this book because you love writing and hope to publish as soon as possible, send a query letter or a submission to us. But remember—proofread your work (most of our editors are English instructors)."

ANNICK PRESS, LTD.

15 Patricia Ave., Toronto, ON M2M 1H9 Canada. (416)221-4802. **Fax:** (416)221-8400. **E-mail:** annick press@annickpress.com. **Website:** www.annickpress.com. **Contact:** Rick Wilks, director; Colleen MacMillan, associate publisher; Sheryl Shapiro, creative director. "Annick Press maintains a commitment to high-quality books that entertain and challenge. Our publications share fantasy and stimulate imagination, while encouraging children to trust their judgment and abilities." Publishes 5 picture books/year; 6 young readers/year; 8 middle readers/year; 9 young adult titles/year. Publishes picture books, juvenile, and YA fiction and nonfiction; specializes in trade books. Book catalog and guidelines available online.

Does not accept unsolicited mss.

NEEDS Publisher of children's books. Publishes hardcover and trade paperback originals. Average print order: 9,000. First novel print order: 7,000. Plans 18 first novels this year. Averages 25 total titles/year. Distributes titles through Firefly Books Ltd. Juvenile, young adult. Recently published *The Apprentice's Masterpiece: A Story of Medieval Spain*, by Melanie Little, ages 12 and up; Chicken, Pig, Cow series, written and illustrated by Ruth Ohi, ages 2-5; Single Voices series, Melanie Little, editor, ages 14 and up; *Crusades*, by Laura Scandiffio, illustrated by John Mantha, ages 9-11. Not accepting picture books at this time.

TERMS Pays authors royalty of 5-12% based on retail price. Offers advances (average amount: $3,000). Pays illustrators royalty of 5% minimum.

ANTARCTIC PRESS

7272 Wurzbach, Suite 204, San Antonio, TX 78240. (210)614-0396. **E-mail:** submissions@antarctic-press .com. **Website:** www.antarctic-press.com. **Contact:** David Hutchison. Estab. 1985. "Antarctic Press is a Texas-based company that was started in 1984. Since then, we have grown to become one of the largest publishers of comics in the U.S. Over the years we have produced over 850 titles with a total circulation of over 5 million. Among our titles are some of the most respected and longest-running independent series in comics today. Since our inception, our main goal has been to establish a series of titles that are unique, entertaining, and high in both quality and profitability. The titles we currently publish exhibit all these traits and appeal to a wide audience." "Antarctic Press is among the top 10 publishers of comics in the United States. However, the difference in market shares between the top five publishers and the next five publishers is dramatic. Most of the publishers ranked above us have a far greater share of the market place. That being the case, we are an independent publisher with a small staff, and many of our employees have multiple responsibilities. Bigger companies would spread these responsibilities out among a larger staff. Additionally, we don't have the same financial power as a larger company. We cannot afford to pay high page rates; instead, we work on an advance and royalty system which is determined by sales or potential sales of a particular book. We pride ourselves on being a company that gives new talent a chance to get published and take a shot at comic stardom."

NEEDS Comic books, graphic novels.

TERMS Pays royalty on net receipts; ms guidelines online.

ANVIL PRESS

P.O. Box 3008 MPO, Vancouver, BC V6B 3X5 Canada. (604)876-8710. **Fax:** (604)879-2667. **E-mail:** info@anvilpress.com. **Website:** www.anvilpress.com. **Contact:** Brian Kaufman. Estab. 1988. "Three-person operation with volunteer editorial board." Publishes trade paperback originals. Books: offset or web printing; perfect-bound. **Published some debut authors within the last year.** Averages 8-10 total titles/year. Published *Stolen*, by Annette Lapointe (novel); *Suburban Pornography*, by Matthew Firth (stories); *Elysium and Other Stories*, by Pamela Stewart; *Dirtbags*, by Teresa McWhirter (novel); *Black Rabbit and Other Stories* by Salvatore DiFalco. Publishes ms 8 months after acceptance. Book catalog for 9" × 12" SAE with 2 first-class stamps. Ms guidelines online. "Anvil Press publishes contemporary adult fiction, poetry, and drama, giving voice to up-and-coming Canadian writers, exploring all literary genres, discovering, nurturing, and promoting new Canadian literary talent. Currently emphasizing urban/suburban-themed fiction and poetry; de-emphasizing historical novels." Publishes trade paperback originals. Book catalog for 9" × 12" SAE with 2 first-class stamps. Guidelines available online.

Canadian authors only. No e-mail submissions. **NEEDS** Experimental, literary, short story collections. Contemporary, progressive, modern literature—no formulaic or genre. Contemporary, modern literature; no formulaic or genre.

HOW TO CONTACT Accepts unsolicited mss, or query with SASE. Include estimated word count, brief bio. Send SASE for return of ms or send a disposable ms and SASE for reply only. No e-mail submissions. Responds in 2 months to queries; 6 months to mss. Accepts simultaneous submissions. Submit to: Anvil Press P.O. Box 3008, Main Post Office, Vancouver, BC V6B 3X5. Query with SASE.

TERMS Pays 15% royalty on net receipts. Average advance: $500. Pays advance. Responds in 6 months.

TIPS "Audience is young, informed, educated, aware, with an opinion, culturally active (films, books, the performing arts). No U.S. authors. Research the appropriate publisher for your work."

ARCADE PUBLISHING

Skyhorse Publishing, 307 W. 36th St., 11th Floor, New York, NY 10018. (212)643-6816. **Fax:** (212)643-6819. **E-mail:** arcadesubmissions@skyhorsepublishing.com. **Website:** www.arcadepub.com. **Contact:** Acquisitions Editor. Estab. 1988. "Arcade prides itself on publishing top-notch literary nonfiction and fiction, with a significant proportion of foreign writers." Publishes hardcover originals, trade paperback reprints. Book catalog and ms guidelines for #10 SASE.

NEEDS No romance, historical, science fiction.

HOW TO CONTACT Submit proposal with brief query, 1-2 page synopsis, chapter outline, market analysis, sample chapter, bio.

TERMS Pays royalty on retail price and 10 author's copies. Pays advance. Responds in 2 months if interested.

ARCHAIA

1680 Vine St., Suite 912, Los Angeles, CA 90028. **Website:** www.archaia.com. **Contact:** Mark Smylie, chief creative officer. Use online submission form.

NEEDS "Archaia publishes creator-owned comic books and graphic novels in the adventure, fantasy, horror, pulp noir, and science fiction genres that contain idiosyncratic and atypical writing and art. *Archaia does not generally hire freelancers or arrange for freelance work, so submissions should only be for completed book and series proposals.*" Looking for graphic novel submissions that include finished art. "Archaia Entertainment, LLC is a multi-award-winning graphic novel publisher with more than 50 renowned publishing brands, including such domestic and international hits as *Artesia, Mouse Guard, The Killer, Gunnerkrigg Court, Awakening, Titanium Rain, Days Missing, Tumor, Syndrome, Okko, The Secret History*, and a line of Jim Henson graphic novels including *Fraggle Rock* and *The Dark Crystal*. Archaia has built an unparalleled reputation for producing meaningful content that perpetually transforms minds, building one of the industry's most visually stunning and eclectic slates of graphic novels. Archaia is the reigning 2010 Graphic Novel Publisher of the Year according to *Ain't It Cool News, Graphic Policy*, and *Comic Related*. Archaia has also successfully emerged as a prolific storyteller in all facets of the entertainment industry, extending its popular brands into film, television, gaming, and branded digital media."

HOW TO CONTACT Query with outline/synopsis and photocopies of completed pages. Prefers e-mail submissions with PDF attachments. Accepts queries by snail mail. Include info on estimated page count, intended formats, and other technical details.

TERMS Submissions guidelines on website.

☼ ARSENAL PULP PRESS

#101-211 East Georgia St., Vancouver, BC V6A 1Z6 Canada. (604)687-4233. **Fax:** (604)687-4283. **E-mail:** info@arsenalpulp.com. **Website:** www.arsenalpulp .com. **Contact:** Editorial Board. Estab. 1980. Literary press. Publishes hardcover and trade paperback originals, and trade paperback reprints. **Published some debut authors within the last year.** Plans 2 first novels this year. Averages 20 total titles/year. Distributes titles through Whitecap Books (Canada) and Consortium (U.S.). Promotes titles through reviews, excerpts, and print advertising. Accepts unsolicited mss. Accepts 10% agented fiction. Responds in 2 months to queries; 4 months to mss. Accepts simultaneous submissions. Sometimes comments on rejected mss. Publishes ms 1 year after acceptance. Book catalog and submission guidelines on website. "We are interested in literature that traverses uncharted territories, and we publish books that challenge and stimulate and ask probing questions about the world around us. With a staff of five, located in a second-floor office in the historic Vancouver district of Gastown, we publish between 14-20 new titles/year, as well as an average of 12-15 reprints." Publishes trade paperback originals and trade paperback reprints. Book catalog for 9" × 12" SAE with IRCs or online. Guidelines available online.

IMPRINTS Tillacum Library, Advance Editions.

NEEDS Gay/lesbian, literary fiction and nonfiction, multicultural, regional (British Columbia), cultural studies, pop culture, political/sociological issues, cookbooks. No children's books or genre fiction, i.e., westerns, romance, horror, mystery, etc.

HOW TO CONTACT Submit proposoal package, outline, 2-3 sample chapter(s), synopsis. Include list of publishing credits. Send copy of ms and SASE (or with IRCs, if sent from outside Canada) or include e-mail address if manuscript does not need to be returned.

Address: Editorial Board, Arsenal Pulp Press, #101-211 East Georgia St., Vancouver, BC V6A 1Z6 Canada. No e-mail or fax submissions.

TERMS Responds in 2 months to queries. Responds in 4 months to proposals and mss.

◑ ARTE PUBLICO PRESS

University of Houston, 4902 Gulf Fwy, Bldg 19, Rm 100, Houston, TX 77204-2004. **Fax:** (713)743-3080. **E-mail:** submapp@mail.uh.edu. **Website:** www.lati noteca.com/arte-publico-press. **Contact:** Nicolas Kanellos, editor. Estab. 1979. "Small press devoted to the publication of contemporary U.S.-Hispanic literature." Publishes hardcover originals, trade paperback originals and reprints. Averages 36 total titles/year. Book catalog available free. Guidelines available online.

Arte Publico Press is the oldest and largest publisher of Hispanic literature for children and adults in the U.S. "We are a showcase for **Hispanic** literary creativity, arts and culture. Our endeavor is to provide a national forum for U.S.-Hispanic literature."

IMPRINTS Piñata Books.

NEEDS Ethnic, literary, mainstream/contemporary, written by U.S.-Hispanic authors. Recent publications include *Women Who Live in Coffee Shops and Other Stories*, by Stella Pope Duarte; *The Name Partner*, by Carlos Cisneros; and *The Party for Papá Luis/La fiesta para Papá Luis*, by Diane Gonzales Bertrand. "Written by U.S.-Hispanics."

HOW TO CONTACT Manuscripts must be submitted online at: www.artepublicopress.com. Agented fiction 1%. Responds in 2-4 months to queries; 3-6 months to mss. Accepts simultaneous submissions. Sometimes comments on rejected mss. Submissions made through online submission form.

TERMS Pays 10% royalty on wholesale price. Provides 20 author's copies; 40% discount on subsequent copies. Average advance: $1,000-3,000. Publishes ms 2 years after acceptance. Ms guidelines online. Pays 10% royalty on wholesale price. Responds in 1 month to queries and proposals. Responds in 4 months to mss.

TIPS "Include cover letter in which you 'sell' your book—why should we publish the book, who will want to read it, why does it matter, etc. Use our ms submission online form. Format files accepted are: Word, plain/text, rich/text files. Other formats will not be accepted. Manuscript files cannot be larger than 5MB. Once editors review your ms, you will receive an e-mail with the decision. Revision process could take up to four months."

ⒶⓏⒼ ATHENEUM BOOKS FOR YOUNG READERS

Simon & Schuster, 1230 Avenue of the Americas, New York, NY 10020. **Website:** imprints.simonand schuster.biz/atheneum; www.simonsayskids.com. **Contact:** Caitlyn Dlouhy, editorial director; Justin Chanda, vice president/publisher; Namrata Tripathi, executive editor; Anne Zafian, vice president. Estab. 1961. Atheneum Books for Young Readers is a hardcover imprint with a focus on literary fiction and fine picture books for preschoolers through young adults. Publishes special interest, first novels, and new talent. Publishes 20+ picture books/year; 20+ middle readers/year; 20+ young adult titles/year. "We do not need how-to pamphlets, ABC books, coloring books, or board books." Average print order is 10,000-15,000 for a first middle-grade or young adult book; 7,500-20,000 for a first picture book. Publishes hardcover originals. Guidelines for #10 SASE.

NEEDS Middle-grade and YA adventure, fantasy, humor, mainstream/contemporary, mystery, suspense, and picture books. All in juvenile versions. "We have few specific needs except for books that are fresh, interesting, and well written. Fad topics are dangerous, as are works you haven't polished to the best of your ability. We also don't need safety pamphlets, ABC books, coloring books and board books. In writing picture book texts, avoid the coy and cutesy, such as stories about characters with alliterative names." Agented submissions only. No paperback romance-type fiction.

HOW TO CONTACT "*We do not accept unsolicited queries, partial, or full manuscript submissions, unless from an agent.*"

TERMS Pays royalty on hardcover retail price: 10% fiction; 5% author, 5% illustrator (picture book). Offers $5,000-$8,000 advance for new authors. Publishes ms up to 3 years after acceptance.

TIPS "Study our titles."

ⒼⓈ AUTUMN HOUSE PRESS

87½ Westwood St., Pittsburgh, PA 15211. (412)381-4261. **E-mail:** info@autumnhouse.org. **Website:** www .autumnhouse.org. **Contact:** Michael Simms, editor-in-chief (fiction). Estab. 1998. "We are a nonprofit literary press specializing in high-quality poetry and fiction. Our editions are beautifully designed and printed, and they are distributed nationally. Approximately one-third of our sales are to college literature and creative writing classes." Member CLMP, AWP, Academy of American Poets. "We distribute our own titles. We do extensive national promotion through ads, web marketing, reading tours, bookfairs, and conferences. We are open to all genres. The quality of writing concerns us, not the genre." You can also learn about our annual Fiction Prize, Poetry Prize, and Chapbook Award competitions, as well as our online journal, *Coal Hill Review*. (Please note that Autumn House accepts unsolicited manuscripts *only* through these competitions.)" Hardcover, trade paperback, and electronic originals. Format: acid-free paper; offset printing; perfect and casebound (cloth) bound; sometimes contains illustrations. Average print order: 1,500. Debut novel print order: 1,500. Catalog free on request. Guidelines online at website; free on request; or for #10 SASE.

NEEDS Holds competition/award for short stories, novels, story collections, translations, memoirs, nonfiction "to identify and publish the best fiction, nonfiction, and poetry manuscripts we can find." *We ask that all submissions from authors new to Autumn House come through one of our annual contests.* Annual. Prize: $2,500 and book publication. Entries should be unpublished. Open to all writers over the age of 18. Length: approx 200-300 pages. Results announced September. Winners notified by mail, by phone, by e-mail. Results made available to entrants with SASE, by fax, by e-mail, on website. Published *New World Order*, by Derek Green (collection of stories) and *Drift and Swerve*, by Samuel Ligon (collection of stories). All submissions come through our annual contests; deadline June 30 each year. See website for official guidelines. Responds to queries in 2 days. Accepts mss only through contest. Never critiques/comments on rejected mss. Responds to mss by August. Questions answered through email at: info@ autumnhouse.org.

HOW TO CONTACT "Submit only through our annual contest. See guidelines online. Submit completed ms. Cover letter should include name, address, phone, e-mail, novel/story title. The mss are judged blind, so please include two cover pages, one with contact information and one without."

TERMS Pays 7% royalty on wholesale price. Pays $0-2,500 advance. Responds in 1-3 days on queries and proposals; 3 months on mss

TIPS "The competition to publish with Autumn House is very tough. Submit only your best work."

AVALON VBOOKS

Thomas Bouregy & Sons, Inc., 1202 Lexington Ave., Suite 283, New York, NY 10028. (212)598-0222. **Fax:** (212)979-1862. **E-mail:** editorial@avalonbooks.com. **Website:** www.avalonbooks.com. **Contact:** Lia Brown, editor. Estab. 1950. Publishes hardcover originals. Guidelines available online.

NEEDS "We publish contemporary romances, historical romances, mysteries, and westerns. Time period and setting are the author's preference. The historical romances will maintain the high level of reading expected by our readers. The books shall be wholesome fiction, without graphic sex, violence, or strong language."

HOW TO CONTACT "We do accept unagented material. We no longer accept e-mail queries. When submitting, include a query letter, a 2-3 page (and no longer) synopsis of the entire ms, and the first three chapters. All submissions must be typed and double spaced. If we think your novel might be suitable for our list, we will contact you and request that you submit the entire manuscript. **Please note that any unsolicited full manuscripts will not be returned.** There is no need to send your partial to any specific editor at Avalon. The editors read all the genres that are listed above. Address your letter to: The Editors."

TERMS Pays 10% royalty. Pays $1,000 advance. Responds in 2-3 months to queries.

TIPS "Avalon Books are geared and marketed for librarians to purchase and distribute."

AVON BOOKS

HarperCollins, 10 E. 53rd St., New York, NY 10022. **Website:** www.harpercollins.com. **Contact:** Editorial Submissions. Estab. 1941. Publishes trade and mass-market paperback originals and reprints.

NEEDS Only considers romance submissions. Print books 80,000-95,000 words; Avon Impulse (digital first) 50,000-60,000 words.

HOW TO CONTACT Submit via online form.

TERMS Royalty negotiable. Pays advance. Responds in 3 months.

AVON ROMANCE

Harper Collins Publishers, 10 E. 53 St., New York, NY 10022. **E-mail:** info@avonromance.com. **Website:** www.avonromance.com. Estab. 1941. "Avon has been publishing award-winning books since 1941. It is recognized for having pioneered the historical romance category and continues to bring the best of commercial literature to the broadest possible audience." Publishes paperback and digital originals and reprints.

HOW TO CONTACT Submit a query and ms via the online submission form at www.avonromance.com/impulse.

BAEN BOOKS

P.O. Box 1188, Wake Forest, NC 27588. (919)570-1640. **Website:** www.baen.com. Estab. 1983. "We publish only science fiction and fantasy. Writers familiar with what we have published in the past will know what sort of material we are most likely to publish in the future: powerful plots with solid scientific and philosophical underpinnings are the sine qua non for consideration for science fiction submissions. As for fantasy, any magical system must be both rigorously coherent and integral to the plot, and overall the work must strive for originality."

NEEDS "Style: Simple is generally better; in our opinion good style, like good breeding, never calls attention to itself. Length: 100,000-130,000 words. Generally we are uncomfortable with manuscripts under 100,000 words, but if your novel is really wonderful, send it along regardless of length."

HOW TO CONTACT "Query letters are not necessary. We prefer to see complete manuscripts accompanied by a synopsis. We prefer not to see simultaneous submissions. Electronic submissions are strongly preferred. *We no longer accept submissions by e-mail.* Send ms by using the submission form at: http://ftp.baen.com/Slush/submit.aspx. No disks unless requested. Attach ms as an .rtf file. Any other format will not be considered."

TERMS Responds to mss within 12-18 months.

BAKER BOOKS

6030 East Fulton Rd., Ada, MI 49301. (616)676-9185. **Website:** www.bakerbooks.com. Estab. 1939. "We will consider unsolicited work only through one of the following avenues: Materials sent through a literary agent will be considered. In addition, our staff attends various writers conferences at which prospective authors can develop relationships with those in the publishing industry." Publishes in hardcover and trade paperback originals, and trade paperback reprints. Book catalog for 9½" × 12½" envelope and 3 first-class stamps. Guidelines online.

⊖ "Baker Books publishes popular religious nonfiction reference books and professional books for church leaders. Most of our authors and readers are evangelical Christians, and our books are purchased from Christian bookstores, mail-order retailers, and school bookstores. Does not accept unsolicited queries."

TIPS "We are not interested in historical fiction, romances, science fiction, biblical narratives, or spiritual warfare novels. Do not call to 'pass by' your idea."

Ⓐ BALZER & BRAY

HarperCollins Children's Books, 10 E. 53rd St., New York, NY 10022. **Website:** www.harpercollinschildrens.com. Estab. 2008.

NEEDS Picture books, young readers: adventure, animal, anthology, concept, contemporary, fantasy, history, humor, multicultural, nature/environment, poetry, science fiction, special needs, sports, suspense. Middle readers, young adults/teens: adventure, animal, anthology, contemporary, fantasy, history, humor, multicultural, nature/environment, poetry, science fiction, special needs, sports, suspense.

HOW TO CONTACT Agented submissions only.

TERMS Offers advances. Pays illustrators by the project.

Ⓐ Ⓓ Ⓒ Ⓢ BANCROFT PRESS

P.O. Box 65360, Baltimore, MD 21209-9945. (410)358-0658. **Fax:** (410)764-1967. **E-mail:** bruceb@bancroftpress.com. **Website:** www.bancroftpress.com. **Contact:** Bruce Bortz, editor/publisher (health, investments, politics, history, humor, literary novels, mystery/thrillers, chick lit, young adult). "Small independent press publishing literary and commercial fiction." Publishes hardcover and trade paperback originals. Also packages books for other publishers (no fee to authors). **Published 5 debut authors within the last two years.** Averages 4-6 fiction titles/year. Published *The Re-Appearance of Sam Webber*, by Scott Fugua (literary); *Hume's Fork*, by Ron Cooper (literary); *The Case against My Brother*, by Libby Sternberg (historical/young adult); *Finn* by Matthew Olshan (young adult); and *The Sinful Life of Lucy Burns* by Elizabeth Leikness (fantasy/women's). Accepts unsolicited mss.

Agented fiction 100%. Responds in 6-12 months to mss. Accepts simultaneous submissions. Sometimes comments on rejected mss. Ms guidelines online. "Bancroft Press is a general trade publisher. We publish young adult fiction and adult fiction, as well as occasional nonfiction. Our only mandate is 'books that enlighten.'" Publishes hardcover and trade paperback originals. Guidelines available online

NEEDS PET, PFS, PFE, PGA, PGL, PHI, PHS, PLE, PLI, PMS, PMW, PMY, PNA, PRE, PSF, PYA.

HOW TO CONTACT Query with SASE or submit outline, 2 sample chapter(s), synopsis, by mail or e-mail or submit complete ms. Accepts queries by e-mail, fax. Include brief bio, list of publishing credits. Send SASE for return of ms or send a disposable ms and SASE for reply only.

TERMS Pays various royalties on retail price. Average advance: $1,500. Publishes ms up to 3 years after acceptance. Pays 6-8% royalty. Pays various royalties on retail price. Pays $750 advance. Responds in 6-12 months to queries, proposals, and manuscripts

TIPS "We advise writers to visit our website and to be familiar with our previous work. Patience is the number one attribute contributors must have. It takes us a very long time to get through submitted material, because we are such a small company. Also, we only publish 4-6 books per year, so it may take a long time for your optioned book to be published. We like to be able to market our books to be used in schools and in libraries. We prefer fiction that bucks trends and moves in a new direction. We are especially interested in mysteries and humor (especially humorous mysteries)."

Ⓐ Ⓞ BANTAM BOOKS

Imprint of Random House, Inc., 1745 Broadway, New York NY 10019. (212)782-9000. **Website:** www.randomhouse.com.

⊖ *Not seeking mss at this time.*

● BARBOUR PUBLISHING INC.

1810 Barbour Dr., P.O. Box 719, Urichsville, OH 44683. (740)922-6045. **E-mail:** editors@barbourbooks.com; aschrock@barbourbooks.com; fictionsubmit@barbourbooks.com. **Website:** www.barbourbooks.com. **Contact:** Ashley Schrock, creative director. Estab. 1981. Publishes hardcover, trade paperback, and mass-market paperback originals and reprints. Published 40% debut authors within the last year. Averages 250 total titles/year. All stories must have Christian faith as an underlying basis. Common writer's mistakes are a sketchy proposal, an unbelieveable story, and a story that doesn't fit our guidelines for inspirational romances." Published *The Journey*, by Wanda E. Brunstetter (fiction). From time to time, we do look for specific types of manuscripts. These are usually announced through various writers' organizations, including the American Christian Writers. You can follow a link for a submission form and e-mail address that you can send your questions to. Responds in 6 months to mss. Accepts simultaneous submissions. Book catalog online or for 9" × 12" SAE with 2 first-class stamps; ms guidelines for #10 SASE or online. "Barbour Books publishes inspirational/devotional material that is nondenominational and evangelical in nature. We're a Christian evangelical publisher." Specializes in short, easy-to-read Christian bargain books. "Faithfulness to the Bible and Jesus Christ are the bedrock values behind every book Barbour's staff produces."

○ "Please note that Barbour Publishing now only accepts book proposals via e-mail; paper proposals will not be reviewed by our editors and will ultimately be destroyed. Download the guidelines to ensure that your materials meet our specifications and will receive the proper attention from our editorial staff."

NEEDS Historical, contemporary, religious, romance, western, mystery. All submissions must be Christian mss. All stories must have Christian faith as an underlying basis. Common writer's mistakes are a sketchy proposal, an unbelievable story, and a story that doesn't fit our guidelines for inspirational romances."

HOW TO CONTACT Submit 3 sample chapter(s), synopsis by e-mail only. For submission of your manuscripts, please follow the link online to download the appropriate guidelines.

TERMS Pays 8-16% royalty on net price. Average advance: $1,000-8,000. Publishes ms 1-2 years after acceptance. Pays 0-16% royalty on net price or makes outright purchase of $500-6,000. Pays $500-10,000 advance. Purchases one-time rights, according to project. Responds in 1 month to queries, if interested.

TIPS "Audience is evangelical/Christian conservative, nondenominational, young and old. We're looking for great concepts, not necessarily a big-name author or agent. We want to publish books that will consistently sell large numbers, not just 'flash in the pan' releases. Send us your ideas!"

BAYLOR UNIVERSITY PRESS

One Bear Place 97363, Waco, TX 76798. (254)710-3164. **Fax:** (254)710-3440. **E-mail:** carey_newman@baylor.edu. **Website:** www.baylorpress.com. **Contact:** Dr. Carey C. Newman, director. Estab. 1897. "We publish contemporary and historical scholarly works about culture, religion, politics, science, and the arts." Publishes hardcover and trade paperback originals. Guidelines available online.

TERMS Pays 10% royalty on wholesale price. Responds in 2 months to proposals.

BEHRMAN HOUSE INC.

11 Edison Place, Springfield, NJ 07081. (973)379-7200. **Fax:** (973)379-7280. **Website:** www.behrmanhouse.com. Estab. 1921. Publishes books on all aspects of Judaism: history, cultural, textbooks, holidays. "Behrman House publishes quality books of Jewish content—history, Bible, philosophy, holidays, ethics—for children and adults." Book catalog free on request.

HOW TO CONTACT Submit outline/synopsis and sample chapters.

TERMS Pays authors royalty of 3-10% based on retail price or buys ms outright for $1,000-5,000. Offers advance. Pays illustrators by the project (range: $500-5,000). Responds in 1 month to queries; 2 months to mss.

TIPS Looking for "religious school texts" with Judaic themes or general trade Judaica.

FREDERIC C. BEIL, PUBLISHER, INC.

609 Whitaker St., Savannah, GA 31401. (912)233-2446. **Fax:** (912)233-6456. **E-mail:** books@beil.com. **Website:** www.beil.com. **Contact:** Mary Ann Bowman, editor. Estab. 1982. Frederic C. Beil publishes in the fields of history, literature, and biography. Publishes hardcover originals and reprints. Book catalog available free.

IMPRINTS The Sandstone Press; Hypermedia, Inc.

HOW TO CONTACT Query with SASE.

TERMS Pays 7.5% royalty on retail price. Responds in 1 week to queries.

TIPS "Our objectives are (1) to offer to the reading public carefully selected texts of lasting value; (2) to adhere to high standards in the choice of materials and in bookmaking craftsmanship; (3) to produce books that exemplify good taste in format and design; and (4) to maintain the lowest cost consistent with quality."

BELLEVUE LITERARY PRESS

New York University School of Medicine, Dept. of Medicine, NYU School of Medicine, 550 First Avenue, OBV A612, New York, NY 10016. (212) 263-7802. **E-mail:** BLPsubmissions@gmail.com. **Website:** blpress.org. Estab. 2005. Dept. of Medicine, NYU School of Medicine, 550 First Ave., OBV A-640, New York, NY 10016. (212) 263-7802. **Fax:** (212) 263-7803. **E-mail:** egoldman@blreview.org. **Contact:** Erika Goldman, editorial director (literary fiction); Leslie Hodgkins, editor (literary fiction). Estab. 2005. "We're a small literary press that publishes nonfiction and fiction that ranges the intersection of the sciences (or medicine) and the arts." Publishes hardcover originals, paperback originals. Debut novel print order: 3,000. Plans 2 debut novels this year. Averages 8 total titles/year; 2 fiction titles/year. Member CLMP. Distributes/promotes titles through Consortium. "Publishes literary and authoritative fiction and nonfiction at the nexus of the arts and the sciences, with a special focus on medicine. As our authors explore cultural and historical representations of the human body, illness, and health, they address the impact of scientific and medical practice on the individual and society."

NEEDS Literary. Published *The Cure*, by Varley O'Connor; *The Leper Compound*, by Paula Nangle (literary); *A Proper Knowledge*, by Michelle Latiolais; and *Tinkers*, by Paul Harding.

HOW TO CONTACT Send query letter or query with outline/synopsis and 3 sample chapters. Accepts queries by snail mail, e-mail. Include estimated word count, brief bio, list of publishing credits. Send disposable copy of ms and SASE for reply only. Agented fiction: 75%. Responds to queries in 2 weeks. Accepts unsolicited mss. Considers simultaneous submissions. Rarely critiques/comments on rejected mss. Responds to mss in 6 weeks.

TERMS Sends preproduction galleys to author. Manuscript published 8-12 months after acceptance. Writer's guidelines not available. Pays royalties 6-15%, advance $1,000. Book catalogs on website.

TIPS "We are a project of New York University's School of Medicine and while our standards reflect NYU's excellence in scholarship, humanistic medicine, and science, our authors need not be affiliated with NYU. We are not a university press and do not receive any funding from NYU. Our publishing operations are financed exclusively by foundation grants, private donors, and book sales revenue."

BERKLEY BOOKS

Penguin Group (USA) Inc., 375 Hudson St., New York, NY 10014. **Website:** us.penguingroup.com/. **Contact:** Leslie Gelbman, president and publisher. Estab. 1955. The Berkley Publishing Group publishes a variety of general nonfiction and fiction including the traditional categories of romance, mystery, and science fiction. Publishes paperback and mass-market originals and reprints.

"Due to the high volume of manuscripts received, most Penguin Group (USA) Inc., imprints do not normally accept unsolicited manuscripts. The preferred and standard method for having manuscripts considered for publication by a major publisher is to submit them through an established literary agent."

IMPRINTS Ace; Berkley; Jove.

NEEDS No occult fiction.

HOW TO CONTACT *Prefers agented submissions.*

BETHANY HOUSE PUBLISHERS

Baker Publishing Group, 6030 E. Fulton Rd., Ada, MI 49301. (616)676-9185. **Fax:** (616)676-9573. **Website:** www.bethanyhouse.com. Estab. 1956. Bethany House Publishers specializes in books that communicate Biblical truth and assist people in both spiritual and practical areas of life. While we do not accept unsolicited queries or proposals via telephone or e-mail, we will consider 1-page queries sent by fax and directed to adult nonfiction, adult fiction, or young adult/children. Publishes hardcover and trade paperback originals, mass-market paperback reprints. Book catalog for 9" × 12" envelope and 5 first-class stamps. Guidelines available online.

All unsolicited mss returned unopened.

TERMS Pays royalty on net price. Pays advance. Responds in 3 months to queries.

TIPS Bethany House Publishers' publishing program relates Biblical truth to all areas of life—whether in the framework of a well-told story, of a challenging book for spiritual growth, or of a Bible reference work. We are seeking high-quality fiction and nonfiction that will inspire and challenge our audience.

BIRCH BOOK PRESS

P.O. Box 81, Delhi, NY 13753. **Fax:** (607)746-7453. **E-mail:** birchbrook@copper.net. **Website:** www.birchbrookpress.info. **Contact:** Tom Tolnay, editor/publisher; Barbara dela Cuesta, associate editor. Estab. 1982. Birch Brook Press "is a letterpress book printer/

typesetter/designer that uses monies from these activities to publish several titles of its own each year with cultural and literary interest." Specializes in literary work, flyfishing, baseball, outdoors, theme anthologies, occasional translations of classics, and books about books. Specializes "mostly in anthologies with specific themes." Books are "hand-set letterpress editions printed in our own shop." Member, Small Press Center, Publishers Marketing Association, Academy of American Poets. Distributes titles through BarnesandNoble.com, Amazon.com, Gazelle Book Services in Europe, Multicultural Books in Canada. Abe Books, and Alibris Books online. Promotes titles through website, catalogs, direct mail, and group ads, book fairs. Occasionally publishes trade paperback originals. Book catalog available online.

IMPRINTS Birch Brook Press; Birch Brook Impressions. "Letterpress editions are printed in our own shop."

NEEDS "Mostly we do anthologies around a particular theme generated in-house. We make specific calls for fiction when we are doing an anthology."

HOW TO CONTACT Query with SASE or submit sample chapter(s), synopsis.

TERMS Pays modest royalty on acceptance. Responds in 3 to 6 months to mss.

TIPS "Write well on subjects of interest to BBP, such as outdoors, flyfishing, baseball, music, literary stories, fine poetry, and occasional novellas, books about books."

BKMK PRESS

University of Missouri - Kansas City, 5101 Rock hill Rd., Kansas City MO 64110-2499. (816)235-2558. **Fax:** (816)235-2611. **E-mail:** bkmk@umkc.edu. **Website:** www.umkc.edu/bkmk. **Contact:** Ben Furnish, managing editor. Estab. 1971. Ms guidelines online. "BkMk Press publishes fine literature. Reading period January-June." Publishes trade paperback originals Guidelines available online

NEEDS Literary, short story collections. Not currently acquiring novels.

HOW TO CONTACT Query with SASE or submit 2-3 sample stories between January 1 and June 30. Responds in 8 months to mss. Accepts simultaneous submissions. Query with SASE.

TERMS Pays 10% royalty on wholesale price. Publishes ms 1 year after acceptance. Responds in 4-6 months to queries

TIPS "We skew toward readers of literature, particularly contemporary writing. Because of our limited number of titles published per year, we discourage apprentice writers or `scattershot' submissions."

BLACK HERON PRESS

P.O. Box 13396, Mill Creek, WA 98082. **Website:** www.blackheronpress.com. **Contact:** Jerry Gold, publisher. Estab. 1984. "Black Heron Press publishes primarily literary fiction." Publishes hardcover and trade paperback originals, trade paperback reprints. Catalog available online and for 6" × 9" SAE with 3 first-class stamps. Guidelines available for #10 SASE.

NEEDS "All of our fiction is character driven. We don't want to see fiction written for the mass market. If it sells to the mass market, fine, but we don't see ourselves as a commercial press."

HOW TO CONTACT Submit proposal package, including cover letter and first 40-50 pages of your completed novel.

TERMS Pays 8% royalty on retail price. Responds in 6 months to queries and mss.

TIPS "Our readers love good fiction—they are scattered among all social classes, ethnic groups, and zip code areas. If you can't read our books, at least check out our titles on our website."

➕ 💲 BLACK MOUNTAIN PRESS

P.O. Box 9907, Asheville, NC 28815. (828)273-3332. **E-mail:** jackmoe@theBlackMountainPress.com. **Website:** www.theBlackMountainPress.com. **Contact:** Jack Moe, editor (how-to, poetry); James Robiningski (short story collections, novels). Estab. 1994. Publishes hardcover, trade paperback, and electronic originals. Book catalog and ms guidelines available online at website.

NEEDS "Creative literary fiction and poetry or collection of short stories are wanted for the next few years."

HOW TO CONTACT Submit complete ms.

TERMS Pays 5-10% royalty on retail price. Pays $100-500 advance. Responds in 4-6 months to mss.

TIPS "Don't be afraid of sending your antigovernment, antireligion, anti-art, antiliterature, experimental, avant-garde efforts here. But don't send your work before it's fully cooked. We do, however, enjoy fresh, natural, and sometimes even raw material, just don't send in anything that is 'glowing' unless it was savaged from a FoxNews book-burning event."

BLACK ROSE WRITING

P.O. Box 1540, Castroville, TX 78009. **E-mail:** creator@blackrosewriting.com. **Website:** www.blackrosewriting.com. **Contact:** Reagan Rothe. Estab. 2006. "We publish only one genre—our genre." Black Rose Writing is an independent publishing house that believes in developing a personal relationship with our authors. We don't see them as clients or just another number on a page, but rather as people. who we are willing to do whatever it takes to make them satisfied with their publishing choice.We are seeking growth in an array of different genres and searching for new publicity venues for our authors every day. Black Rose Writing doesn't promise our authors the world, leading them to become overwhelmed by the competitive and difficult venture. We are honest with our authors, and we give them the insight to generate solid leads without wasting their time. Black Rose Writing works with our authors along many lines of promotion, (examples: showcasing your titles at festivals, scheduling book events, and sending out press releases and review copies) and provides a broad distribution that covers many book buyers and allows interested parties access to our titles easily. We want to make our authors' journeys into the publishing world a success and eliminate the fear of a toilsome and lengthy experience." Publishes majority trade paperback, occasional hard cover or children's book. Please check submission guidelines before contacting by e-mail.

Online store: www.blackrosewritingbooks.com

HOW TO CONTACT Query via e-mail. Submit synopsis and author bio. Please allow 3-4 weeks for response.

TERMS Responds in 2-3 months to mss.

TIPS "Please query via e-mail first with synopsis and author bio. Allow 4-6 weeks for response. Always spell-check and try and send an edited manuscript. Do not forward your initial contact e-mails."

BLACK VELVET SEDUCTIONS PUBLISHING

1350-C W. Southport Rd., Box 249, Indianapolis, IN 46217. (319)241-6556. **E-mail:** lauriesanders@blackvelvetseductions.com. **Website:** www.blackvelvetseductions.com. **Contact:** Laurie Sanders, acquisitions editor. Estab. 2005. "We publish two types of material: 1) romance novels and short stories and 2) romantic stories involving spanking between consenting adults. We look for well-crafted stories with a high degree of emotional impact. **No first-person point of view.** All material must be in third-person point of view." Publishes trade paperback and electronic originals. "We have a high interest in republishing backlist titles in electronic and trade paperback formats once rights have reverted to the author." Accepts only complete manuscripts. Query with SASE. Submit complete ms. Publishes trade paperback and electronic originals and reprints. Catalog free or online. Guidelines online (guidelines@blackvelvetseductions.com).

IMPRINTS Forbidden Experiences (erotic romance of all types); Tender Destinations (sweet romance of all types); Sensuous Journeys (sensuous romance of all types); Amorous Adventures (romantic suspense); Erotic relationship stories (erotic short stories, usually including spanking, with a romantic relationship at their core).

NEEDS All stories must have a strong romance element. "There are very few sexual taboos in our erotic line. We tend to give our authors the widest latitude. If it is safe, sane, and consensual we will allow our authors latitude to show us the eroticism. However, we will not consider manuscripts with any of the following: bestiality (sex with animals), necrophilia (sex with dead people), pedophillia (sex with children)."

HOW TO CONTACT Only accepts electronic submissions.

TERMS Pays 10% royalty for paperbacks; 50% royalty for electronic books. Responds in 6 months to queries; 8 months to proposals; 8-12 months to mss.

TIPS "We publish romance and erotic romance. We look for books written in very deep point of view. Shallow point of view remains the number one reason we reject manuscripts in which the story line generally works."

JOHN F. BLAIR, PUBLISHER

1406 Plaza Dr., Winston-Salem, NC 27103. (336)768-1374. **Fax:** (336)768-9194. **Website:** www.blairpub.com. **Contact:** Carolyn Sakowski, president. Estab. 1954.

NEEDS "We specialize in regional books, with an emphasis on nonfiction categories such as history, travel, folklore, and biography. We publish only one or two works of fiction each year. Fiction submitted to us should have some connection with the Southeast. We do not publish children's books, poetry, or category fiction such as romances, science fiction, or spy thrillers. We do not publish collections of short stories, essays, or newspaper columns. Published *The Minotaur Takes a Cigarette Break*, by Steven Sherrill; *Rocks That Float*, by Kathy Steele."

HOW TO CONTACT "Accepts unsolicited mss. Any fiction submitted should have some connection with the Southeast, either through setting or author's background. Send a cover letter, giving a synopsis of the book. Include the first two chapters (at least 50 pages) of the manuscript. You may send the entire manuscript if you wish. If you choose to send only samples, please include the projected word length of your book and estimated completion date in your cover letter. Send a biography of the author, including publishing credits and credentials."

TERMS Pays royalties. Pays negotiable advance. Responds in 3-6 months.

TIPS "We are primarily interested in nonfiction titles. Most of our titles have a tie-in with North Carolina or the southeastern United States, we do not accept short story collections. Please enclose a cover letter and outline with the manuscript. We prefer to review queries before we are sent complete manuscripts. Queries should include an approximate word count."

✪ BLAZEVOX [BOOKS]

76 Inwood Place, Buffalo, NY 14209. **E-mail:** editor@blazevox.org. **Website:** www.blazevox.org. **Contact:** Geoffrey Gatza, editor/publisher. Estab. 2005. "We are a major publishing presence specializing in innovative fictions and wide-ranging fields of innovative forms of poetry and prose. Our goal is to publish works that are challenging, creative, attractive, and yet affordable to individual readers. Articles of submission depend on many criteria, but overall items submitted must conform to one ethereal trait—your work must not suck. This put plainly, bad art should be punished; we will not promote it. However, all submissions will be reviewed and the author will receive feedback. We are human, too." Guidelines online.

NEEDS Submit complete ms via e-mail.

TERMS Pays 10% royalties on fiction and poetry books, based on net receipts. This amount may be split across multiple contributors. "We do not pay advances."

TIPS "We actively contract and support authors who tour, read, and perform their work, play an active part of the contemporary literary scene, and seek a readership."

❹ BLOOMSBURY CHILDREN'S BOOKS

Imprint of Bloomsbury USA, 175 Fifth Ave., New York, NY 10010. **E-mail:** bloomsbury.kids@bloomsburyusa.com. **Website:** www.bloomsburykids.com. Book catalog available online. *Agented submissions only.* Guidelines available online.

🗩 No phone calls or e-mails.

NEEDS Picture books: adventure, animal, contemporary, fantasy, folktales, history, humor, multicultural, poetry, suspense/mystery. Young readers: adventure, animal, anthology, concept, contemporary, fantasy, folktales, history, humor, multicultural, suspense/mystery. Middle readers: adventure, animal, contemporary, fantasy, folktales, history, humor, multicultural, poetry, problem novels. Young adults: adventure, animal, anthology, contemporary, fantasy, folktales, history, humor, multicultural, problem novels, science fiction, sports, suspense/mystery.

HOW TO CONTACT Query with SASE. Submit clips, first 3 chapters with SASE.

TERMS Pays royalty. Pays advance. Responds in 6 months to queries; 6 months to ms.

TIPS "All Bloomsbury Children's Books submissions are considered on an individual basis. Bloomsbury Children's Books will no longer respond to unsolicited manuscripts or art submissions. Please include a telephone AND e-mail address where we may contact you if we are interested in your work. Do NOT send a self-addressed stamped envelope. We regret the inconvenience, but unfortunately, we are too understaffed to maintain a correspondence with authors. There is no need to send art with a picture book manuscript. Artists should submit art with a picture book manuscript. We do not return art samples. Please do not send us original art! Please note that we do accept simultaneous submissions but please be courteous and inform us if another house has made an offer on your work. Do not send originals or your only copy of anything. We are not liable for artwork or manuscript submissions. Please address all submissions to the attention of 'Manuscript Submissions.' Please make sure that everything is stapled, paper clipped, or rubber banded together. We do not accept e-mail or CD/DVD submissions. Be sure your work is appropriate for us. Familiarize yourself with our list by going to bookstores or libraries."

⬤🎧💲 BOA EDITIONS, LTD.

250 N. Goodman St., Suite 306, Rochester, NY 14607. (585)546-3410. **Fax:** (585)546-3913. **E-mail:** conners@boaeditions.org; hall@boaeditions.org. **Website:** www.boaeditions.org. **Contact:** Peter Conners, editor. Estab. 1976. "BOA Editions publishes distinguished collections of poetry, fiction and poetry in translation. Our goal is to publish the finest American contemporary poetry, fiction, and poetry in translation." Publishes hardcover and trade paperback originals. Book catalog available online. Guidelines available online.

NEEDS "We now publish literary fiction through our American Reader Series. While aesthetic quality is subjective, our fiction will be by authors more concerned with the artfulness of their writing than the twists and turns of plot. Our strongest current interest is in short story collections (and short-short story collections), although we will consider novels. We strongly advise you to read our first published fiction collections. *We are temporarily closed to novel/collection submissions.*"

TERMS Negotiates royalties. Pays variable advance. Responds in 1 week to queries; 5 months to mss.

➕💲 BOOKOUTURE

StoryFire Ltd., 23 Sussex Rd., Ickenham UB10 8P United Kingdom. **E-mail:** questions@bookouture.com. **E-mail:** pitch@bookouture.com. **Website:** www.bookouture.com. **Contact:** Oliver Rhodes, founder and publisher. Estab. 2012. Publishes mass-market paperback and electronic originals and reprints. Book catalog available online at website.

IMPRINTS Imprint of StoryFire Ltd.

NEEDS "We're looking for entertaining fiction targeted at modern women. That can be anything from Steampunk to erotica, historicals to thrillers. A distinctive author voice is more important than a particular genre or manuscript length."

HOW TO CONTACT Submit complete ms.

TERMS Pays 45% royalty on wholesale price. Responds in 1 month.

TIPS "The most important question that we ask of submissions is why would a reader buy the *next* book? What's distinctive or different about your storytelling that will mean readers will want to come back for more? We look to acquire global English language rights for eBook and Print on Demand."

⊘💭 BOREALIS PRESS, LTD.

8 Mohawk Crescent, Napean ON K2H 7G6 Canada. (613)829-0150. **Fax:** (613)829-7783. **E-mail:** drt@borealispress.com. **Website:** www.borealispress.com. Estab. 1972. Our mission is to publish work that will be of lasting interest in the Canadian book market. Currently emphasizing Canadian fiction, nonfiction, drama, poetry. De-emphasizing children's books. Publishes hardcover and paperback originals and reprints. Book catalog available online. Guidelines available online.

IMPRINTS Imprint: Tecumseh Press.

NEEDS Only material Canadian in content and dealing with significant aspects of the human situation.

HOW TO CONTACT Query with SASE. Submit clips, 1-2 sample chapters. *No unsolicited mss.*

TERMS Pays 10% royalty on net receipts; plus 3 free author's copies. Responds in 2 months to queries; 4 months to mss.

⊘ BRANDEN PUBLISHING CO., INC.

P.O. Box 812094, Wellesley, MA 02482. (781)235-3634. **Fax:** (781)235-3634. **E-mail:** branden@brandenbooks.com. **Website:** www.brandenbooks.com. **Contact:** Adolph Caso, editor. Estab. 1909. "Branden publishes books by or about women, children, military, Italian-American or African-American themes." Publishes hardcover and trade paperback originals, reprints, and software.

IMPRINTS International Pocket Library and Popular Technology; Four Seas and Brashear; Branden Books.

NEEDS Looking for contemporary, fast pace, modern society. No science, mystery, experimental, horor, or pornography. *No unsolicited mss.*

HOW TO CONTACT Query with SASE. Paragraph query only with author bio.

TERMS Responds in 1 month to queries.

Ⓐ BROADWAY BOOKS

The Crown Publishing Group/Random House, 1745 Broadway, New York, NY 10019. (212)782-9000. **Fax:** (212)782-9411. **Website:** www.broadwaybooks.com. **Contact:** William Thomas, editor-in-chief. Estab. 1995. Broadway publishes general-interest nonfiction and fiction for adults. Publishes hardcover and trade paperback originals and reprints. Publishes hardcover and trade paperback books.

💬 "Broadway publishes high-quality general-interest nonfiction and fiction for adults."

IMPRINTS Broadway Books; Broadway Business; Doubleday; Doubleday Image; Doubleday Religious Publishing; Main Street Books; Nan A. Talese.

NEEDS Broadway Books publishes a variety of non-fiction books across several categories, including memoir, health and fitness, inspiration and spirituality, history, current affairs and politics, marriage and relationships, animals, travel and adventure narrative, pop culture, humor, and personal finance. Publishes a limited list of commercial literary fiction. Published *Freedomland*, by Richard Price.

HOW TO CONTACT *Agented submissions only.*

TERMS Pays royalty on retail price. Pays advance.

☯ BROKEN JAW PRESS

Box 596, STN A, Fredericton, NB E3B 5A6 Canada. (506)454-5127. **E-mail:** editors@brokenjaw.com. **Website:** www.brokenjaw.com. "We publish poetry, fiction, drama, and literary nonfiction, including translations and multilingual books. Publishes almost exclusively Canadian-authored literary trade paperback originals and reprints." Book catalog for 6" × 9" SAE with 2 first-class Canadian stamps in Canada or download PDF from website. Guidelines available online.

○ *Currently not accepting unsolicited mss and queries.*

IMPRINTS Book Rat; Broken Jaw Press; SpareTime Editions; Dead Sea Physh Products; Maritimes Arts Projects Productions.

TERMS Pays 10% royalty on retail price. Pays $0-500 advance. Responds in 1 year to mss.

TIPS "Unsolicited queries and manuscripts are not welcome at this time."

☯ THE BRUCEDALE PRESS

P.O. Box 2259, Port Elgin, ON N0H 2C0 Canada. (519)832-6025. **E-mail:** brucedale@bmts.com. **Website:** brucedalepress.ca. The Brucedale Press publishes books and other materials of regional interest and merit, as well as literary, historical, and/or pictorial works. Publishes hardcover and trade paperback originals. Book catalog for #10 SASE (Canadian postage or IRC) or online. Guidelines available online.

○ *Accepts works by Canadian authors only. Submissions accepted in September and March ONLY.*

TERMS Pays royalty.

TIPS "Our focus is very regional. In reading submissions, I look for quality writing with a strong connec-

tion to the Queen's Bush area of Ontario. All authors should visit our website, get a catalog, and read our books before submitting."

○ ☺ BY LIGHT UNSEEN MEDIA

P.O. Box 1233, Pepperell, MA 01463. (978) 433-8866. **Fax:** (978) 433-8866. **E-mail:** vyrdolak@bylightun seenmedia.com. **E-mail:** vyrdolak@bylightunseen media.com. **Website:** www.bylightunseenmedia.com. **Contact:** Inanna Arthen, owner/editor-in-chief. Estab. 2006. Publishes hardcover, paperback, and electronic originals; trade paperback reprints. Catalog available online at website. Ms guidelines available online at website.

NEEDS "We are a niche small press that *only* publishes fiction relating in some way to vampires. Within that guideline, we're interested in almost any genre that includes a vampire trope, the more creative and innovative, the better. Restrictions are noted in the submission guidelines (no derivative fiction based on other works, such as Dracula, no gore for gore's sake "splatter" horror, etc.) We do not publish anthologies."

HOW TO CONTACT Submit proposal package including synopsis, 3 sample chapters, brief author bio. *We encourage electronic submissions. All unsolicited mss will be returned unopened.*

TERMS Pays royalty of 20-50% on net as explicitly defined in contract. Payment quarterly. Pays $200 advance. Responds in 3 months to queries/proposals/mss.

TIPS "We strongly urge authors to familiarize themselves with the vampire genre and not imagine that they're doing something new and amazingly different just because they're not imitating the current fad. Our submission guidelines list two online articles we recommend prospective authors read: '7 Wrong Things You Should Know About Vampire Folklore,'and 'Think Outside the Coffin: Writing the Vampire Novel.' We're looking for strong characters and good storytelling, not gimmicks. Our most successful promotional tag line is 'vampire stories for grown-ups.' That gives a good idea of what we're selling (and buying from authors)."

○ C&R PRESS

812 Westwood Ave., Chattanoog, TN 37405. (423)645-5375. **Website:** www.crpress.org. **Contact:** Chad Prevost, editorial director and publisher; Ryan G. Van Cleave, executive director and publisher. Estab. 2006. Publishes hardcover, trade paperback, mass-market

paperback, and electronic originals. Catalog and guidelines available online at website.

IMPRINTS Illumis Books

NEEDS "We want dynamic, exciting literary fiction and we want to work with authors (not merely books) who are engaged socially and driven to promote their work because of their belief in the product, and because it's energizing and exciting to do so and a vital part of the process."

HOW TO CONTACT Submit complete ms via e-mail.

TERMS Responds in up to 1 month on queries and proposals, 1-2 months on mss.

⊘ CALAMARI PRESS

Via Titta Scarpetta #28, Rome 00153 Italy. **E-mail:** derek@calamaripress.net. **Website:** www.calamari press.com. "Calamari Press publishes book objects of literary text and art and experimental fiction." Publishes paperback originals. Format: 60 lb. natural finch opaque paper; digital printing; perfect or saddle-stitched bound. Average print order: 500-1,000. Debut novel print order: 300. Averages 2-3 total titles/year; 2 fiction titles/year. Published *Land of the Snow Men*, by George Belden (Norman Lock) (fictional literary canard with illustrations); *The Singing Fish*, by Peter Markus (prose poem/short fiction collection); *The Night I Dropped Shakespeare on the Cat*, by John Olson; *The Revisionist*, by Miranda Mellis; *Part of the World*, by Robert Lopez; *Ever*, by Blake Butler; reissued *Motorman*, by David Ohle; and *Stories in the Worst Way*, by Gary Lutz. Responds to queries in 2 weeks. Accepts unsolicited mss. Considers e-mail submissions only. Sometimes critiques/comments on rejected mss. Responds to mss in 2 weeks. Sends preproduction galleys to author. Manuscript published 2-6 months after acceptance. Writer's guidelines on website. Calamari Press publishes books of literary text and art. Publishes 1-2 books/year. Manuscripts are selected by invitation. Occasionally has open submission period— check website. Helps to be published in *SleepingFish* first." See separate listing in magazines/journals. Order books through the website, Powell's, or SPD. Publishes paperback originals. Writer's guidelines on website.

NEEDS Adventure, comics/graphic novels, ethnic/multicultural, experimental, literary, short story collections.

HOW TO CONTACT Query with outline/synopsis and 3 sample chapters. Accepts queries by e-mail only.

Include brief bio. Send SASE or IRC for return of ms. Query with outline/synopsis and 3 sample chapters. Accepts queries by e-mail only. Include brief bio. Send SASE or IRC for return of ms.

TERMS Pays in author's copies. Responds to mss in 2 weeks.

CALKINS CREEK

Boyds Mills Press, 815 Church St., Honesdale, PA 18431. **Website:** www.calkinscreekbooks.com. Estab. 2004. We aim to publish books that are a well-written blend of creative writing and extensive research, which emphasize important events, people, and places in U.S. history." Guidelines available on website.

NEEDS All levels: history. Recently published *Healing Water*, by Joyce Moyer Hostetter (ages 10 and up, historical fiction); *The Shakeress*, by Kimberly Heuston (ages 12 and up, historical fiction).

HOW TO CONTACT Submit outline/synopsis and 3 sample chapters.

TERMS Pays authors royalty or work purchased outright.

TIPS "Read through our recently published titles and review our catalog. When selecting titles to publish, our emphasis will be on important events, people, and places in U.S. history. Writers are encouraged to submit a detailed bibliography, including secondary and primary sources, and expert reviews with their submissions."

⊘ CANDLEWICK PRESS

99 Dover St., Somerville, MA 02144. (617)661-3330. **Fax:** (617)661-0565. **E-mail:** bigbear@candlewick .com. **Website:** www.candlewick.com. **Contact:** Deb Wayshak, executive editor (fiction); Joan Powers, editor-at-large (picture books); Liz Bicknell, editorial director/associate publisher (poetry, picture books, fiction); Mary Lee Donovan, executive editor (picture books, nonfiction/fiction); Hilary Van Dusen, senior editor (nonfiction/fiction); Sarah Ketchersid, senior editor (board, toddler); Joan Powers, editor-at-large. Estab. 1991. "Candlewick Press publishes high-quality, illustrated children's books for ages infant through young adult. We are a truly child-centered publisher." Candlewick title *Good Masters! Sweet Ladies! Voices from a Medieval Village*, by Amy Schlitz, won the John Newbery Medal in 2008. Their title *Twelve Rounds to Glory: The Story of Muhammad Ali*, by Charles R. Smith Jr., illustrated by Bryan Collier, won a Coretta Scott King Author Honor Award

in 2008. Their title *The Astonishing Life of Octavian Nothing*, by M.T. Anderson, won the Boston Globe-Hornbook Award for Fiction and Poetry in 2007. Publishes hardcover and trade paperback originals and reprints.

○ *Candlewick Press is not accepting queries or unsolicited mss at this time.*

NEEDS Picture books: animal, concept, contemporary, fantasy, history, humor, multicultural, nature/environment, poetry. Middle readers, young adults: contemporary, fantasy, history, humor, multicultural, poetry, science fiction, sports, suspense/mystery.

HOW TO CONTACT "We do not accept editorial queries or submissions online. If you are an author or illustrator and would like us to consider your work, please read our submissions policy (online) to learn more."

TERMS Pays authors royalty of 2½-10% based on retail price. Offers advance.

TIPS *"We no longer accept unsolicited mss.* See our website for further information about us."

⊕ CANTERBURY HOUSE PUBLISHING, LTD.

225 Ira Harmon Rd., Vilas, NC 28692. (828)297-7127. **E-mail:** publisher@canterburyhousepublishing.com. **E-mail:** editor@canterburyhousepublishing.com. **Website:** www.canterburyhousepublishing.com. **Contact:** Wendy Dingwall, publisher; Sandra Horton, editor. Estab. 2009. "Our audience is made up of readers looking for wholesome fiction with good southern stories, with elements of mystery, romance, and inspiration and/or are looking for true stories of achievement and triumph over challenging circumstances." Publishes hardcover, trade paperback, and electronic originals. Book catalog available online at website. Guidelines availably online, free on request by e-mail.

○ *"We are very strict on our submission guidelines due to our small staff, and our target market of Southern regional settings. The setting needs to be a strong component in the stories. Authors need to be willing to actively promote their books in the beginning 9 months of publication via signing events and social media."*

HOW TO CONTACT Query with SASE and through website.

TERMS Pays 10-15% royalty on wholesale price. Responds in 1 month to queries; 3 months to mss.

TIPS "Because of our limited staff, we prefer authors who have good writing credentials and submit edited manuscripts. We also look at authors who are business and marketing savvy and willing to help promote their books."

CAROLINA WREN PRESS

120 Morris St., Durham, NC 27701. (919)560-2738. **E-mail:** carolinawrenpress@earthlink.net. **Website:** www.carolinawrenpress.org. **Contact:** Andrea Selch, president. Estab. 1976. "We publish poetry, fiction, and memoirs by, and/or about people of color, women, gay/lesbian issues, health and mental health topics in children's literature." Guidelines are available on our website in December, with information about electronic submissions.

○ Accepts simultaneous submissions, but "let us know if work has been accepted elsewhere."

NEEDS "We are no longer publishing children's literature of any topic." Books: 6" × 9" paper; typeset; various bindings; illustrations. **Published 2 debut authors within the last year.** Distributes titles through Amazon.com, Barnes & Noble, Baker & Taylor, and on their website. "We very rarely accept any unsolicited manuscripts, but we accept submissions for the Doris Bakwin Award for Writing by a Woman in January-March of even-numbered years." Published *Downriver*, by Jeanne Leiby in 2007, *All Eyes*, by Phoebe Hoss in 2009, *Relative Strangers*, by Margaret Hermes in 2012.

HOW TO CONTACT Query by mail. "We will accept e-mailed queries—a letter in the body of the e-mail describing your project—but please do not send large attachments."

TERMS Responds in 3 months to queries; 6 months to mss.

TIPS "Best way to get read is to submit to a contest."

⊘⊘ CARTWHEEL BOOKS

Imprint of Scholastic Trade Division, 557 Broadway, New York, NY 10012. (212)343-6100. **Website:** www.scholastic.com. Estab. 1991. Cartwheel Books publishes innovative books for children, up to age 8. We are looking for 'novelties' that are books first, play objects second. Even without its gimmick, a Cartwheel Book should stand alone as a valid piece of children's literature. Publishes novelty books, easy readers, board books, hardcover and trade paperback originals. Book catalog for 9" × 12" SASE. Guidelines available free.

NEEDS Again, the subject should have mass-market appeal for very young children. Humor can be helpful, but not necessary. Mistakes writers make: a reading level that is too difficult, a topic of no interest or too narrow, and manuscripts that are too long.

HOW TO CONTACT *Accepts mss from agents, previously publishes authors only.*

TIPS "Audience is young children, ages 0-8. Know what types of books the publisher does. Some manuscripts that don't work for one house may be perfect for another. Check out bookstores or catalogs to see where your writing would 'fit' best."

CAVE HOLLOW PRESS

P.O. Drawer J, Warrensburg, MO 64093. **E-mail:** gbcrump@cavehollowpress.com. **Website:** www.cavehollowpress.com. **Contact:** G.B. Crump, editor. Estab. 2001. "Our website is updated frequently to reflect the current type of fiction Cave Hollow Press is seeking." Publishes trade paperback originals. Book catalog for #10 SASE. Guidelines available free.

NEEDS "Our website is updated frequently to reflect the current type of fiction Cave Hollow Press is seeking."

HOW TO CONTACT Query with SASE.

TERMS Pays 7-12% royalty on wholesale price. Pays negotiable amount in advance. Responds in 1-2 months to queries and proposals. Responds in 3-6 months to manuscripts.

TIPS "Our audience varies based on the type of book we are publishing. We specialize in Missouri and Midwest regional fiction. We are interested in talented writers from Missouri and the surrounding Midwest. Check our submission guidelines on the website for what type of fiction we are interested in currently."

CEDAR FORT, INC.

2373 W. 700 S, Springville, UT 84663. (801)489-4084. **Fax:** (801)489-1097. **Website:** www.cedarfort.com. **Contact:** Shersta Gatica, acquisitions editor. Estab. 1986. "Each year we publish well over 100 books, and many of those are by first-time authors. At the same time, we love to see books from established authors. As one of the largest book publishers in Utah, we have the capability and enthusiasm to make your book a success, whether you are a new author or a returning one. We want to publish uplifting and edifying books that help people think about what is important in life, books people enjoy reading to relax and feel better about themselves, and books to help improve lives. We like to publish a wide variety of books. We are always on the lookout for new and exciting material that will capture the public's interest. However, there are a few genres with which we are very selective. We rarely take biographies, autobiographies, or memoirs, unless they have a very strong selling point (such as Mafia to Mormon). We do not publish poetry. Although we do put out several children's books each year, we are extremely selective. Our children's books must have strong religious or moral values, and must contain outstanding writing and an excellent story line." Publishes hardcover, trade paperback originals and reprints, mass-market paperback, and electronic reprints. Catalog and guidelines available online at website.

IMPRINTS Council Press, Sweetwater Books, Bonneville Books, Front Table Books, Hobble Creek Press, CFI.

HOW TO CONTACT Submit completed ms.

TERMS Pays 10-12% royalty on wholesale price. Pays $2,000-50,000 advance. Responds in 1 month on queries; 2 months on proposals; 4 months on mss.

TIPS "Our audience is rural, conservative, mainstream. The first page of your ms is very important because we start reading every submission, but good writing and plot keep us reading."

⊜ CHARLESBRIDGE PUBLISHING

85 Main St., Watertown, MA 02472. (617)926-0329. **Fax:** (617)926-5720. **E-mail:** tradeart@charlesbridge.com. **Website:** www.charlesbridge.com. Estab. 1980. "Charlesbridge publishes high-quality books for children, with a goal of creating lifelong readers and lifelong learners. Our books encourage reading and discovery in the classroom, library, and home. We believe that books for children should offer accurate information, promote a positive worldview, and embrace a child's innate sense of wonder and fun. To this end, we continually strive to seek new voices, new visions, and new directions in children's literature." Publishes hardcover and trade paperback nonfiction and fiction, children's books for the trade and library markets. Guidelines available online.

◯ "We're always interested in innovative approaches to a difficult genre, the nonfiction picture book."

IMPRINTS Charlesbridge, Imagine Publishing.

NEEDS Strong stories with enduring themes. Charlesbridge publishes both picture books and transitional bridge books (books ranging from early readers to middle-grade chapter books). Our fiction titles include lively, plot-driven stories with strong, engaging characters. No alphabet books, board books, coloring books, activity books, or books with audiotapes or CD-ROMs.

HOW TO CONTACT *Exclusive submissions only.* "Charlesbridge accepts unsolicited manuscripts submitted exclusively to us for a period of three months. 'Exclusive Submission' should be written on all envelopes and cover letters. Please submit only one or two manuscript(s) at a time. For picture books and shorter bridge books, please send a complete manuscript. For fiction books longer than 30 manuscript pages, please send a detailed plot synopsis, a chapter outline, and three chapters of text. Manuscripts should be typed and double-spaced. Please do not submit material by e-mail, by fax, or on a computer disk. Illustrations are not necessary. Please make a copy of your manuscript, as we cannot be responsible for submissions lost in the mail. Include your name and address on the first page of your manuscript and in your cover letter. Be sure to list any previously published work or relevant writing experience."

TERMS Pays royalty. Pays advance. Responds in 3 months. If you have not heard back from us after 3 months, you may assume we do not have a place for your project and submit it elsewhere.

TIPS "To become acquainted with our publishing program, we encourage you to review our books and visit our website (www.charlesbridge.com), where you will find our catalog. To request a printed catalog, please send a 9" × 12" SASE with $2.50 in postage."

CHILDREN'S BRAINS ARE YUMMY (CBAY) BOOKS

P.O. Box 92411, Austin, TX 78709. (512)789-1004. **Fax:** (512)473-7710. **E-mail:** submissions@cbaybooks.com. **Website:** www.cbaybooks.com. **Contact:** Madeline Smoot, publisher. Estab. 2008. "CBAY Books currently focuses on quality fantasy and science fiction books for the middle-grade and teen markets. Although we are exploring the possibility of publishing fantasy and science fiction books in the future, we are not seeking submissions for them at this time. We do welcome books that mix genres—a fantasy mystery for example—but since our press currently has a narrow focus, all submissions need to have fantasy or science fiction elements to fit in with our list." Brochure and guidelines available online at website.

HOW TO CONTACT Accepts international material. Submit outline/synopsis and 3 sample chapters.
TERMS Pays authors royalty 10-15% based on wholesale price. Offers advances against royalties. Average amount $500. Responds in 3 months to mss.
TIPS "CBAY Books only accepts unsolicited submissions from authors at specific times for specific genres. Please check the website to see if we are accepting books at this time. Manuscripts received when submissions are closed are not read."

CHRISTIAN BOOKS TODAY LTD

136 Main St., Buckshaw Village Chorley, Lancashire PR7 7BZ United Kingdom. **E-mail:** md@christian bookstoday.com. **E-mail:** submissions@christian bookstoday.com. **Website:** www.christianbooksto day.com. **Contact:** Jason Richardson, MD (nonfiction); Lynda McIntosh, editor (fiction). Estab. 2009. Publishes trade paperback originals/reprints and electronic originals/reprints. Catalog and guidelines available online.

NEEDS "We're looking for writers who write about life, failures and all! Tackle the big issues but in a tasteful way. Deal with divorce, blended families, ecumenism, atheists, creationism, crazy preachers, celebrity culture, sexuality. Life doesn't conform to expectations—neither did Christ. Tackle the difficult and brutal. How do we as Christians deal with the messiness? Moralizing doesn't appeal to a broader audience. In your cover letter, tell us how you intend to market the book, what sets it apart. No fantasy or sci-fi please."

HOW TO CONTACT Submit "cover Letter, chapter by chapter outline, first 3 chapters, and SASE. Or via the member section of our website."

TERMS Pays 10% royalty on retail price or 50% of title profit. Responds in 1 month to queries; 2 months to proposals and mss.

TIPS "We appeal to a general Christian readership. We are not interested in Hallmark stories, nor fantasy or mysticism. We want work by Christians rather than Christian writing. If you want to take a risk in subject, you are particularly encouraged to submit. We actively seek out writers who want to build a career with us and who understand we do what we do because we love it."

CHRISTIAN FOCUS PUBLICATIONS

Geanies House, Tain Ross-shire IV20 1TW United Kingdom. 44 (0) 1862 871 011. **Fax:** 44 (0) 1862 871 699.

E-mail: info@christianfocus.com. **Website:** www .christianfocus.com. **Contact:** Catherine Mackenzie, publisher. Estab. 1975. Specializes in Christian material, nonfiction, fiction, educational material.

NEEDS Picture books, young readers, adventure, history, religion. Middle readers: adventure, problem novels, religion. Young adult/teens: adventure, history, problem novels, religion. Average word length: young readers, 5,000; middle readers, max 10,000; young adult/teen, max 20,000. Recently published *Back Leg of a Goat*, by Penny Reeve, illustrated by Fred Apps (middle reader Christian/world issues); *Trees in the Pavement,* by Jennifer Grosser (teen fiction/Christian/Islamic, and multicultural issues); *The Duke's Daughter,* by Lachlan Mackenzie; illustrated by Jeff Anderson (young reader folk tale/Christian).

HOW TO CONTACT Query or submit outline/synopsis and 3 sample chapters. Will consider electronic submissions and previously published work.

TERMS Responds to queries in 2 weeks; mss in 3 months.

TIPS "Be aware of the international market as regards writing style/topics as well as illustration styles. Our company sells rights to European as well as Asian countries. Fiction sales are not as good as they were. Christian fiction for youngsters is not a product that is performing well in comparison to nonfiction, such as Christian biography/Bible stories/church history, etc."

CHRONICLE BOOKS

680 Second St., San Francisco, CA 94107. **E-mail:** submissions@chroniclebooks.com. **Website:** www .chroniclebooks.com. "We publish an exciting range of books, stationery, kits, calendars, and novelty formats. Our list includes children's books and interactive formats; young adult books; cookbooks; fine art, design, and photography; pop culture; craft, fashion, beauty, and home decor; relationships, mind-body-spirit; innovative formats such as interactive journals, kits, decks, and stationery; and much, much more." Book catalog for 9"× 12" SAE and 8 first-class stamps. Ms guidelines for #10 SASE.

NEEDS Only interested in fiction for children and young adults. No adult fiction.

HOW TO CONTACT Submit complete ms (picture books); submit outline/synopsis and 3 sample chapters (for older readers). Will not respond to submissions unless interested. Will not consider submissions by fax, e-mail or disk. Do not include SASE; do not send original materials. No submissions will be returned.

TERMS Generally pays authors in royalties based on retail price, "though we do occasionally work on a flat-fee basis." Advance varies. Illustrators paid royalty based on retail price or flat fee. Responds to queries in 1 month.

CHRONICLE BOOKS FOR CHILDREN

680 Second St., San Francisco, CA 94107. (415)537-4200. **Fax:** (415)537-4460. **E-mail:** frontdesk@ chroniclebooks.com. **Website:** www.chroniclekids .com. "Chronicle Books for Children publishes an eclectic mixture of traditional and innovative children's books. Our aim is to publish books that inspire young readers to learn and grow creatively while helping them discover the joy of reading. We're looking for quirky, bold artwork and subject matter. Currently emphasizing picture books. De-emphasizing young adult." Publishes hardcover and trade paperback originals. Book catalog for 9"× 12" envelope and 3 first-class stamps. Guidelines available online.

NEEDS Does not accept proposals by fax, via e-mail, or on disk. When submitting artwork, either as a part of a project or as samples for review, do not send original art.

TERMS Pays 8% royalty. Pays variable advance. Responds in 2-4 weeks to queries; 6 months to mss.

TIPS "We are interested in projects that have a unique bent to them—be it in subject matter, writing style, or illustrative technique. As a small list, we are looking for books that will lend our list a distinctive flavor. Primarily we are interested in fiction and nonfiction picture books for children ages up to eight years, and nonfiction books for children ages up to twelve years. We publish board, pop-up, and other novelty formats as well as picture books. We are also interested in early chapter books, middle-grade fiction, and young adult projects."

CLARION BOOKS

Houghton Mifflin Co., 215 Park Ave. S., New York, NY 10003. **Website:** www.houghtonmifflinbooks.com; www.hmco.com. **Contact:** Dinah Stevenson, vice president and publisher; Jennifer B. Greene, senior editor (contemporary fiction, picture books for all ages, nonfiction); Jennifer Wingertzahn, editor (fiction, picture books); Lynne Polvino, editor (fiction, nonfiction, picture books); Christine Kettner, art director. Estab. 1965. "Clarion is a strong presence in the fiction market for young readers. We are highly selective in the areas of historical and contemporary fiction. We publish chapter books for children ages 7-10 and middle-grade novels for ages 9-12, as well as picture books and nonfiction." Publishes hardcover originals for children. Averages 50 total titles/year. Mss are not responded to unless there is an interest in publishing. Published *A Taste for Red*, by Lewis Harris (contemporary, middle-grade); *The Wednesday Wars*, by Gary D. Schmidt (historical fiction); *Keeping Score*, by Linda Sue Park (middle-grade historical fiction). "Clarion Books publishes picture books, nonfiction, and fiction for infants through grade 12. Avoid telling your stories in verse unless you are a professional poet." Publishes hardcover originals for children. Guidelines for #10 SASE or online.

"We are no longer responding to your unsolicited submission unless we are interested in publishing it. Please do not include a SASE. Submissions will be recycled, and you will not hear from us regarding the status of your submission unless we are interested. We regret that we cannot respond personally to each submission, but we do consider each and every submission we receive."

NEEDS Adventure, historical, humor, mystery, suspense, strong character studies. Clarion is highly selective in the areas of historical fiction, fantasy, and science fiction. A novel must be superlatively written in order to find a place on the list. Accepts fiction translations.

HOW TO CONTACT Submit complete ms. Responds in 2 months to queries. Prefers no multiple submissions of mss. Submit complete ms. No queries, please. Send to only *one* Clarion editor.

TERMS Pays 5-10% royalty on retail price. Pays minimum of $4,000 advance. Average advance: start at $6,000. Publishes ms 2 years after acceptance. Ms guidelines available at website.

TIPS "Looks for freshness, enthusiasm—in short, life."

CLEIS PRESS

Cleis Press & Viva Editions, 2246 Sixth St., Berkeley, CA 94710. (510)845-8000 or (800)780-2279. **Fax:** (510)845-8001. **E-mail:** cleis@cleispress.com. **E-mail:** bknight@cleispress.com. **Website:** www.cleispress.com and www.vivaeditions.com. **Contact:** Brenda Knight, associate publisher. Estab. 1980. Cleis Press publishes provocative, intelligent books in the areas of sexuality, gay and lesbian studies, erotica, fiction, gender studies, and human rights. Publishes books that inform, enlighten, and entertain. Areas of interest include gift, inspiration, health, family and child care, self-help, women's issues, reference, cooking. "We do our best to bring readers quality books that celebrate life, inspire the mind, revive the spirit, and enhance lives all around. Our authors are practical visionaries; people who offer deep wisdom in a hopeful and helpful manner."

IMPRINTS Viva Edition

NEEDS "We are looking for high-quality fiction and nonfiction."

HOW TO CONTACT Submit complete ms. Include brief bio, list of publishing credits. Send SASE for return of ms or send a disposable ms and SASE for reply only.

TERMS Pays royalty on retail price. Responds in 2 month to queries.

TIPS "Be familiar with publishers' catalogs; be absolutely aware of your audience; research potential markets; present fresh new ways of looking at your topic; avoid 'PR' language and include publishing history in query letter."

COACH HOUSE BOOKS

80 bpNichol Lane, Toronto, ON M5S 3J4 Canada. (416)979-2217. **Fax:** (416)977-1158. **E-mail:** editor@chbooks.com. **Website:** www.chbooks.com. **Contact:** Alana Wilcox, editor. Publishes trade paperback originals by Canadian authors. Guidelines available online.

HOW TO CONTACT "Electronic submissions are welcome. Please send your complete manuscript, along with an introductory letter that describes your work and compares it to at least two current Coach House titles, explaining how your book would fit our list, and a literary CV listing your previous publications and relevant experience. If you would like your manuscript back, please enclose a large enough self-addressed envelope with adequate postage. If you don't want your ms back, a small stamped envelope or e-mail address is fine. We prefer electronic submissions. Please e-mail PDF files to editor@chbooks.com and include the cover letter and CV as a part of the ms. Please send your manuscript only once. Revised and updated versions will not be read, so make sure you're happy with your text before sending. You can also send your manuscript to 80 bpNichol Lane, Toronto, Ontario, M5S 3J4. Please do not send it by ExpressPost or Canada Post courier—regular Canada Post mail is much more likely to arrive here. Be patient. We try to respond promptly, but we do receive hundreds of submissions, so it may take us several months to get back to you. Please do not call or e-mail to check on the status of your submission. We will answer you as promptly as possible."

TERMS Pays 10% royalty on retail price. Responds in 6 months to queries.

TIPS "We are not a general publisher, and publish only Canadian poetry, fiction, artist books, and drama. We are interested primarily in innovative or experimental writing."

COFFEE HOUSE PRESS

79 13th NE, Suite 110, Minneapolis, MN 55413. (612)338-0125. **Fax:** (612)338-4004. **E-mail:** info@coffeehousepress.org. **Website:** www.coffeehouse press.org. **Contact:** Chris Fischbach, associate publisher. Estab. 1984. This successful nonprofit small press has received numerous grants from various organizations including the NEA, the McKnight Foundation, and Target. Books published by Coffee House Press have won numerous honors and awards. Example: *The Book of Medicines,* by Linda Hogan won the Colorado Book Award for Poetry and the Lannan Foundation Literary Fellowship. Publishes hardcover and trade paperback originals. Book catalog and ms guidelines online.

NEEDS Fiction. Seeks literary novels, short story collections and poetry.

HOW TO CONTACT Query first with outline and samples (20-30 pages).

TERMS Responds in 4-6 weeks to queries; up to 6 months to mss.

TIPS Look for our books at stores and libraries to get a feel for what we like to publish. No phone calls, e-mails, or faxes."

CONCORDIA PUBLISHING HOUSE

3558 S. Jefferson Ave., St. Louis, MO 63118. (314)268-1187. **Fax:** (314)268-1329. **E-mail:** publicity@cph.org; rosemary.parkinson@cph.org. **Website:** www.cph .org. **Contact:** Peggy Kuethe, senior editor (children's product, adult devotional, women's resources); Dawn Weinstock, managing production editor (adult nonfiction on Christian spirituality and culture, academic works of interest in Lutheran markets). Estab. 1869. "Concordia Publishing House produces quality resources that communicate and nurture the Christian faith and ministry of people of all ages, lay and professional. These resources include curriculum, worship aids, books, and religious supplies. We publish approximately 30 quality children's books each year. We boldly provide Gospel resources that are Christ centered, Bible based, and faithful to our Lutheran heritage." Publishes hardcover and trade paperback originals. Ms guidelines for 1 first-class stamp and a #10 envelope.

TERMS Pays authors royalties based on retail price or work purchased outright ($750-2,000). Responds in 1 month to queries; 3 months to mss.

TIPS "Do not send finished artwork with the manuscript. If sketches will help in the presentation of the manuscript, they may be sent. If stories are taken from the Bible, they should follow the Biblical account closely. Liberties should not be taken in fantasizing Biblical stories."

CONSTABLE & ROBINSON, LTD.

55-56 Russell Square, London WC1B 4HP United Kingdom. 0208-741-3663. **Fax:** 0208-748-7562. **E-mail:** reader@constablerobinson.com. **Website:** http://constablerobinson.co.uk/. **Contact:** Krystyna Green, editorial director (crime fiction). Constable & Robinson continues into the 21st century as a truly independent company. We publish a nonfiction list of current affairs, history and biography, military history, psychology and health, as well as literary novels and a constantly growing list of genre fiction in both hardback and paperback. Among our commercially successful series are the well-known Mammoth paperback anthologies, the best-selling and widely respected Overcoming list of CBT self-help titles, and the Brief History and Guide series. Our new fiction imprint, Corsair, launched in April 2010. Averages 160 total titles/year. Publishes hardcover and trade paperback originals Book catalog available free.

IMPRINTS Corsair, Constable Hardback; Robinson Paperback.

NEEDS Publishes "crime fiction (mysteries) and historical crime fiction." Length 80,000 words minimum; 130,000 words maximum. Recently published *Roma* and *The Judgement of Caesar,* by Steven Saylor; *The Yeane's Midnight,* by Ed O'Connor; *The More Deceived,* by David Roberts.

HOW TO CONTACT *Agented submissions only.* No e-mail submissions. Submit by post 3 sample chapter(s), synopsis, and cover letter. Responds in 1 month to queries; 3 months to mss. Accepts simultaneous submissions.

TERMS Pays royalty. Offers advance. Publishes ms 1 year after acceptance.

TIPS Constable & Robinson Ltd. is looking for "crime novels with good, strong identities. Think about what it is that makes your book(s) stand out from the others. We do not publish thrillers."

○ COTEAU BOOKS

Thunder Creek Publishing Co-operative Ltd., 2517 Victoria Ave., Regina, SK S4P 0T2 Canada. (306)777-0170. **Fax:** (306)522-5152. **E-mail:** coteau@coteau books.com. **Website:** www.coteaubooks.com. **Contact:** Geoffrey Ursell, publisher. Estab. 1975. "Coteau Books publishes the finest Canadian fiction, poetry, drama, and children's literature, with an emphasis on western writers." Publishes trade paperback originals and reprints. Books: offset printing; perfect-bound; 4-color illustrations. Averages 16 total titles, 4-6 fiction titles/year. Distributes titles through Fitzhenry & Whiteside. "Our mission is to publish the finest in Canadian fiction, nonfiction, poetry, drama, and children's literature, with an emphasis on Saskatchewan and prairie writers. De-emphasizing science fiction, picture books." Publishes trade paperback originals and reprints. Book catalog available free. Guidelines available online.

NEEDS Ethnic, fantasy, feminist, gay/lesbian, historical, humor, juvenile, literary, mainstream/contemporary, multicultural, multimedia, mystery, regional, short story collections, spiritual, sports, young adult. Canadian authors *only*. Published *The Knife Sharpener's Bell*, by Rhea Tregebov (novel); *Passchendaele: Canada's Triumph and Tragedy on the Fields of Flanders*, by Norman Leach (adult nonfiction); *We Want You to Know*, by Deborah Ellis (juvenile nonfiction); *Summer of Fire*, by Karen Bass (teen novel). *Canadian authors only*. No science fiction. No children's picture books.

HOW TO CONTACT Accepts unsolicited mss. Fiction accepted January 1-April 30; children's/teen novels May 1-August 31; poetry September 1-December 31; nonfiction accepted year-round. Submit complete manuscript, or 3-4 sample chapter(s), author bio. Responds in 2-3 months to queries; 6 months to mss. No simultaneous submissions. Sometimes comments on rejected mss. Submit bio, complete ms, SASE.

TERMS Pays 10% royalty on retail price. "We're a cooperative and receive subsidies from the Canadian, provincial and local governments. We do not accept payments from authors to publish their works." Publishes ms 1-2 years after acceptance. Ms guidelines online. Pays 10% royalty on retail price. Responds in 3 months to queries and manuscripts.

TIPS "Look at past publications to get an idea of our editorial program. We do not publish romance, horror, or picture books but are interested in juvenile and teen fiction from Canadian authors. Submissions, even queries, must be made in hard copy only. We do not accept simultaneous/multiple submissions. Check our website for new submission timing guidelines."

COVENANT COMMUNICATIONS, INC.

920 E. State Rd., American Fork, UT 84003. (801)756-9966. **Fax:** (801)756-1049. **E-mail:** submissionsdesk@ covenant-lds.com. **Website:** www.covenant-lds.com. **Contact:** Kathryn Jenkins, managing editor. Estab. 1958. Averages 80+ total titles/year. "Currently emphasizing inspirational, doctrinal, historical, biography. Our fiction is also expanding, and we are looking for new approaches to LDS literature and storytelling." Guidelines available online

NEEDS Historical fiction, suspense, mystery, romance, children's; all submissions must have strong LDS (Church of Jesus Christ of Latter-day Saints, or "Mormons") content. "We publish exclusively to the 'Mormon' (The Church of Jesus Christ of Latter-Day Saints) market. Fiction must feature characters who are members of that church, grappling with issues relevant to that religion."

HOW TO CONTACT E-mail your manuscript, along with a 1-page cover letter, a 1- to 2-page plot summary, and the Author Questionnaire. We request that all submissions be submitted via e-mail as Microsoft Word attachments. If you cannot e-mail your submission, please burn the Word document onto a CD and mail it. Follow submission guidelines on website. Requires electronic submission. Responds in 4 months to mss. Submit complete ms.

TERMS Pays 6½-15% royalty on retail price. Generally publishes ms 6-12 months after acceptance. Ms guidelines online. Responds in 1 month on queries and proposals; 4 months on manuscripts

TIPS "Our audience is exclusively LDS (Latter-Day Saints, 'Mormon')." We do not accept manuscripts that do not have a strong LDS theme or feature strong LDS characters.

CRESCENT MOON PUBLISHING

P.O. Box 393, Maidstone Kent ME14 5XU UK. (44) (162)272-9593. **E-mail:** cresmopub@yahoo.co.uk. **Website:** www.crescentmoon.org.uk. **Contact:** Jeremy Robinson, director (arts, media, cinema, literature); Cassidy Hushes (visual arts). Estab. 1988. "Our mission is to publish the best in contemporary work, in poetry, fiction, and critical studies, and selections from the great writers. Currently emphasizing nonfiction (media, film, music, painting). De-emphasizing children's books." Publishes hardcover and trade paperback originals. Book catalog and ms guidelines free.

IMPRINTS *Joe's Press, Pagan America Magazine, Passion Magazine.*

NEEDS "We do not publish much fiction at present but will consider high-quality new work."

HOW TO CONTACT Query with SASE. Submit outline, clips, 2 sample chapters, bio.

TERMS Pays royalty. Pays negotiable advance. Responds in 2 months to queries; 4 months to proposals and mss.

TIPS "Our audience is interested in new contemporary writing."

CRICKET BOOKS

Imprint of Carus Publishing, 70 E. Lake St., Suite 300, Chicago, IL 60601. (603)924-7209. **Fax:** (603)924-7380. **Website:** www.cricketmag.com. **Contact:** Submissions Editor. Estab. 1999. Cricket Books publishes picture books, chapter books, and middle-grade novels. Publishes hardcover originals.

◯ *Currently not accepting queries or mss. Check website for submissions details and updates.*

TERMS Pays up to 10% royalty on retail price. Average advance: $1,500 and up.

TIPS "Take a look at the recent titles to see what sort of materials we're interested in, especially for nonfiction. Please note that we aren't doing the sort of strictly educational nonfiction that other publishers specialize in."

CRIMSON ROMANCE

Adams Media, a division of F+W Media, Inc., 57 Littlefield St., Avon, MA 02322. (508)427-7100. **E-mail:** editorcrimson@gmail.com. **Contact:** Jennifer Lawler, editor. "Direct to e-book imprint of Adams Media." Publishes electronic originals.

NEEDS "We're open to romance submissions in five popular subgenres: romantic suspense, contemporary, paranormal, historical, and erotic romance. Within those subgenres, we are flexible about what happens. It's romance, so there must be a happily-ever-after, but we're open to how your characters get there. You won't come up against preconceived ideas about what can or can't happen in romance or what kind of characters you can or can't have. Our only rule is everyone has to be a consenting adult. Other than that, we're looking for smart, savvy heroines, fresh voices, and new takes on old favorite themes. We're looking for full-length novels, and while we prefer to work on the shorter end of the spectrum (50,000 words, give or take), we're not going to rule you out because you go shorter or longer."

HOW TO CONTACT "If you have a finished novel you'd like for us to consider, please just drop editor Jennifer Lawler a line at editorcrimson@gmail.com with a brief description of your work—please, no attachments until I know you're not a spambot. That's it! I'll get back to you as quickly as I can—within a few days for queries and within a few weeks if I request a full ms."

CROSSTIME

P.O. Box 23749, Santa Fe, NM 87502. (505)690-3923. **Fax:** (214)975-9715. **E-mail:** info@crossquarter.com. **Website:** www.crossquarter.com. **Contact:** Anthony Ravenscroft. Estab. 1985. Publishes paperback originals. Books: recycled paper; docutech or offset printing; perfect-bound.

NEEDS Mystery (occult), new age/mystic, pyschic/supernatural, romance (occult), science fiction, young adult (fantasy). Sponsors Short Science Fiction contest. Guidelines on website.

TERMS Pays 6-10% royalty.

CROWN BOOKS FOR YOUNG READERS

1745 Broadway, 10th Floor, New York, NY 10019. (212)572-2600 or (800)200-3552. **Website:** www.randomhouse.com/kids. See listing for Bantam, Doubleday, Dell/Delacorte, Knopf, and Crown Books for Young Readers.

◯ Random House Children's Publishing only accepts submissions through agents.

CROWN PUBLISHING GROUP

Random House, Inc., 1745 Broadway, New York, NY 10019. (212)782-9000. **E-mail:** CrownBiz@randomhouse.com. **Website:** www.randomhouse.com/crown.

Estab. 1933. "The group publishes a selection of popular fiction and nonfiction by both established and rising authors."

○ *Agented submissions only.* See website for more details.

IMPRINTS Bell Tower; Broadway Business; Clarkson Potter; Crown Business; Crown Forum; Harmony Books; Shaye Arehart Books; Three Rivers Press.

HOW TO CONTACT *Agented submissions only.*

⊕ CRYSTAL SPIRIT PUBLISHING, INC.

P.O. Box 12506, Durham, NC 27709. **E-mail:** crystal spiritinc@gmail.com. **Website:** www.crystalspiritinc .com. **Contact:** Vanessa S. O'Neal, senior editor; Elise L. Lattier, editor. Estab. 2004. "Our readers are lovers of high-quality books that are sold in book and gift stores and placed in libraries and schools. They support independent authors and they expect works that will provide them with entertainment, inspiration, romance, and education. Our audience loves to read and will embrace niche authors that love to write." Publishes hardcover, trade paperback, mass-market paperback, and electronic originals. Book catalog and ms guidelines available online at website.

HOW TO CONTACT Submit cover letter, synopsis, and 30 pages (or 30 chapters) **by USPS mail ONLY.**

TERMS Pays 20-45% royalty on retail price. Responds in 3-6 months to mss.

TIPS "Submissions are accepted for publication throughout the year, but the decisions for publishing considerations are made in March, June, September, and December. Works should be positive and non-threatening. Typed pages only. Nontyped entries will not be reviewed or returned. Ensure that all contact information is correct, abide by the submission guidelines, and do not send follow-up e-mails or calls."

⊕ CUP OF TEA BOOKS

PageSpring Publishing, P.O. Box 21133, Columbus, OH 43221. **E-mail:** weditor@pagespringpublishing .com. **Website:** www.cupofteabooks.com. Estab. 2012. "Cup of Tea Books publishes novel-length women's fiction. We are interested in finely drawn characters, a compelling story, and deft writing. We accept e-mail queries only; see our website for details." Publishes trade paperback and electronic originals. Guidelines online at website.

IMPRINTS Imprint of PageSpring Publishing.

HOW TO CONTACT Submit proposal package via e-mail. Include synopsis and the first 30 pages.

TERMS Pays royalty. Responds in 1 month to queries and mss.

⊛⊘ DAVID R. GODINE, PUBLISHER

15 Court Square, Suite 320, Boston, MA 02108. (617)451-9600. **Fax:** (617)350-0250. **E-mail:** info@ godine.com. **Website:** www.godine.com. Estab. 1970. "We publish books that matter for people who care."

○ This publisher is no longer considering unsolicited mss of any type. Only interested in agented material.

DAW BOOKS, INC.

Penguin Group (USA), 375 Hudson St., New York, NY 10014-3658. (212)366-2096. **Fax:** (212)366-2090. **Website:** www.dawbooks.com. **Contact:** Peter Stampfel, submissions editor. Estab. 1971. Publishes hardcover and paperback originals and reprints. Averages 60 total titles/year. DAW Books publishes science fiction and fantasy. Publishes hardcover and paperback originals and reprints. Guidelines available online

○ Simultaneous submissions not accepted, unless prior arrangements are made by agent.

NEEDS "We are interested in science fiction and fantasy novels. We are also interested in paranormal romantic fantasy. We like character-driven books. We accept both agented and unagented manuscripts. Long books are not a problem. We are not seeking short stories, poetry, or ideas for anthologies. We do not want any nonfiction manuscripts."

HOW TO CONTACT Submit entire ms, cover letter, SASE. Do not submit your only copy of anything. Responds within 3 months to mss. The average length of the novels we publish varies but is almost never less than 80,000 words. Send us the entire manuscript with a cover letter. We do not accept electronic submissions of any kind.

TERMS Pays in royalties with an advance negotiable on a book-by-book basis. Ms guidelines online.

DELACORTE PRESS

1745 Broadway, New York, NY 10019. (212)782-9000. **Website:** www.randomhouse.com/kids. Publishes middle-grade and young adult fiction in hard cover, trade paperback, mass-market, and digest formats.

○ All other query letters or ms submissions must be submitted through an agent or at the request of an editor. No e-mail queries.

ⒶⓄ DELACORTE PRESS BOOKS FOR YOUNG READERS

Imprint of Random House Children's Books/Random House, Inc., 1745 Broadway, New York, NY 10019. (212)782-9000. **Website:** www.randomhouse.com/kids; www.randomhouse.com/teens. Distinguished literary fiction and commercial fiction for the middle-grade and young adult categories.

◯ Not currently accepting unsolicited mss.

Ⓐ DEL REY BOOKS

Imprint of Random House Publishing Group, 1745 Broadway, 18th Floor, New York, NY 10019. (212)782-9000. **E-mail:** delrey@randomhouse.com. **Website:** www.randomhouse.com. Estab. 1977. "We are a long-established imprint with an eclectic frontlist. We're seeking interesting new voices to add to our best-selling backlist. Publishes hardcover, trade paperback, and mass-market originals and mass-market paperback reprints. Averages 120 total titles, 80 fiction titles/year. Del Rey publishes top-level fantasy, alternate history, and science fiction. Publishes hardcover, trade paperback, and mass-market originals and mass-market paperback reprints

IMPRINTS Del Rey/Manga, Del Rey/Lucas Books.

NEEDS Fantasy (should have the practice of magic as an essential element of the plot), science fiction (well-plotted novels with good characterizations and interesting extrapolations), alternate history. Published *Gentlemen of the Road*, by Michael Chabon; *Kraken*, by China Miéville; *His Majesty's Dragon*, by Naomi Novik; *The Man with the Iron Heart*, by Harry Turtledove; and *Star Wars: Order 66*, by Karen Traviss.

HOW TO CONTACT Does not accept unsolicited mss. *Agented submissions only.* Agented submissions only.

TERMS Pays royalty on retail price. Average advance: competitive. Publishes ms 1 year after acceptance. Ms guidelines online. Pays royalty on retail price. Pays competitive advance.

TIPS "Del Rey is a reader's house. Pay particular attention to plotting, strong characters, and dramatic, satisfactory conclusions. It must be and feel believable. That's what the readers like. In terms of mass-market, we basically created the field of fantasy best-sellers. Not that it didn't exist before, but we put the mass into mass-market."

DEMONTREVILLE PRESS, INC.

P.O. Box 835, Lake Elmo, MN 55042. **E-mail:** publisher@demontrevillepress.com. **Website:** www.demontrevillepress.com. **Contact:** Kevin Clemens, publisher (automotive fiction and nonfiction). Estab. 2006. Publishes trade paperback originals and reprints. Book catalog available online. Guidelines available online.

NEEDS "We want novel-length automotive or motorcycle historicals and/or adventures."

HOW TO CONTACT Submit proposal package, 3 sample chapters, clips, bio.

TERMS Pays 20% royalty on sale price. Responds in 3 months to queries; 4 months to proposals; 6 months to mss.

TIPS "Environmental, energy, and transportation nonfiction works are now being accepted. Automotive and motorcycle enthusiasts, adventurers, environmentalists, and history buffs make up our audience."

Ⓐ DIAL BOOKS FOR YOUNG READERS

Imprint of Penguin Group USA, 375 Hudson St., New York, NY 10014. (212)366-2000. **Website:** www.penguin.com/youngreaders. **Contact:** Lauri Hornik, president/publisher; Kathy Dawson, associate publisher; Kate Harrison, senior editor; Liz Waniewski, editor; Alisha Niehaus, editor; Jessica Garrison, editor; Lily Malcom, art director. Estab. 1961. "Dial Books for Young Readers publishes quality picture books for ages 18 months-6 years; lively, believable novels for middle readers and young adults; and occasional nonfiction for middle readers and young adults." Publishes hardcover originals. Book catalog for 9" × 12" envelope and 4 first-class stamps.

NEEDS Especially looking for lively and well-written novels for middle-grade and young adult children, involving a convincing plot and believable characters. The subject matter or theme should not be overworked in previously published books. The approach must not be demeaning to any minority group, nor should the roles of female characters (or others) be stereotyped, though we don't think books should be didactic, or in any way message-y. No topics inappropriate for the juvenile, young adult, and middle-grade audiences. No plays.

HOW TO CONTACT Accepts unsolicited queries and up to 10 pages for longer works and unsolicited mss for picture books.

TERMS Pays royalty. Pays varies advance. Responds in 4-6 months to queries.

TIPS "Our readers are anywhere from preschool age to teenage. Picture books must have strong plots, lots of action, unusual premises, or universal themes treated with freshness and originality. Humor works well in these books. A very well thought-out and intelligently presented book has the best chance of being taken on. Genre isn't as much of a factor as presentation."

⊘ DISKUS PUBLISHING

P.O. Box 475, Eaton, IN 47338. **E-mail:** editor@diskuspublishing.com. **Website:** www.diskuspublishing.com. **Contact:** Carol Davis, senior editor; Holly Janey, submissions editor. Estab. 1996. Publishes e-books and printed books. Book catalog is available online only. Guidelines for #10 SASE or online. "We prefer you get your guidelines online."

○ *"At this time DiskUs Publishing is closed for submissions. Keep checking our website for updates on the status of our submissions reopen date"*

NEEDS "We are actively seeking confessions for our Diskus Confessions line, as well as short stories for our Quick Pick line. We only accept e-mailed submissions for these lines."

HOW TO CONTACT Send your submission to diskuspublishing@aol.com with the word Diskus Submission in the subject line.

TERMS Pays 40% royalty.

DIVERSION PRESS

P.O. Box 3930, Clarksville, TN 37043. **E-mail:** diversionpress@yahoo.com. **Website:** www.diversionpress.com. Estab. 2008. Publishes hardcover, trade and mass-market paperback originals. Guidelines available online.

NEEDS "We will happily consider any children's or young adult books if they are illustrated. If your story has potential to become a series, please address that in your proposal. Fiction short stories and poetry will be considered for our anthology series. See website for details on how to submit your ms."

TERMS Pays 10% royalty on wholesale price. Responds in 2 weeks to queries. Responds in 1 month to proposals.

TIPS "Read our website and blog prior to submitting. We like short, concise queries. Tell us why your book is different, not like other books. Give us a realistic idea of what you will do to market your book—list the things you will actually do. We will ask for more information if we are interested."

DIVERTIR

P.O. Box 232, North Salem, NH 03073. **E-mail:** info@divertirpublishing.com; query@divertirpublishing.com. **Website:** www.divertirpublishing.com. **Contact:** Kenneth Tupper, publisher. Estab. 2009. Publishes trade paperback and electronic originals. Catalog available online at www.divertirpublishing.com/bookstore.html. Guidelines online at website: www.divertirpublishing.com/authorinfo.html.

NEEDS "We are particularly interested in the following: science fiction, fantasy, historical, alternate history, contemporary mythology, mystery and suspense, paranormal, and urban fantasy."

HOW TO CONTACT Electronically submit proposal package, including synopsis and query letter with author's bio.

TERMS Pays 10-15% royalty on wholesale price (for novels and nonfiction); outright purchase: $10-50 (for short stories) with additional bonus payments to authors when certain sales milestones are met. Responds in 1-2 months on queries; 3-4 months on proposals and mss.

TIPS "Please see our Author Info page (online) for more information."

DNA PRESS & NARTEA PUBLISHING

DNA Press, P.O. Box 9311, Glendale, CA 91226. **E-mail:** editors@dnapress.com. **Website:** www.dnapress.com. Estab. 1998. Book publisher for young adults, children, and adults. Publishes hardcover and trade paperback originals. Book catalog and ms guidelines free.

NEEDS All books should be oriented to explaining science, even if they do not fall 100% under the category of science fiction.

HOW TO CONTACT Submit complete ms.

TERMS Pays 10-15% royalty. Responds in 6 weeks to mss.

TIPS Quick response, great relationships, high commission/royalty.

DORAL PUBLISHING, INC.

3 Burroughs, Irvine, CA 92618. (800)633-5385. **E-mail:** doralpub@mindspring.com. **Website:** www.doralpub.com. **Contact:** Alvin Grossman, publisher; Joe Liddy, marketing manager (purebred dogs). Estab. 1986. Publishes hardcover and trade paperback originals. Book catalog available free. Guidelines for #10 SASE.

○ "Doral Publishing publishes only books about dogs and dog-related topics, mostly geared for purebred dog owners and showing. Currently emphasizing breed books."

NEEDS Subjects must center around dogs. Either the main character should be a dog or a dog should play an integral role.

HOW TO CONTACT Query with SASE.

TERMS Pays 10% royalty on wholesale price. Responds in 2 months to queries.

TIPS "We are currently expanding and are looking for new topics and fresh ideas while staying true to our niche. While we will steadfastly maintain that market—we are always looking for excellent breed books—we also want to explore more 'mainstream' topics."

DOUBLEDAY BOOKS FOR YOUNG READERS

1540 Broadway, New York, NY 10036. (212)782-9000. **Website:** www.randomhouse.com/kids.

○ Only accepts mss submitted by an agent. Trade picture book list, from preschool to age 8.

DOWN EAST BOOKS

Imprint of Down East Enterprise, Inc., P.O. Box 679, Camden, ME 04843. (207)594-9544, 800-766-1670. **Fax:** (207)594-7215. **E-mail:** editorial@downeast.com. **E-mail:** submissions@downeast.com. **Website:** www.downeast.com. **Contact:** Paul Doiron, editor-in-chief. Estab. 1967. Down East Books publishes books that capture and illuminate the unique beauty and character of New England's history, culture, and wild places. Publishes hardcover and trade paperback originals, trade paperback reprints. Send SASE for ms guidelines. Send 9" × 12" SASE for guidelines, plus recent catalog.

NEEDS We publish 2-4 juvenile titles/year (fiction and nonfiction), and 0-1 adult fiction titles/year.

HOW TO CONTACT Query with SASE.

TERMS Pays $500 average advance. Responds in 3 months to queries.

DOWN THE SHORE PUBLISHING

Box 100, West Creek NJ 08092. **Fax:** (609)597-0422. **E-mail:** dtsbooks@comcast.net. **Website:** www.down-the-shore.com. "Bear in mind that our market is regional New Jersey, the Jersey Shore, the mid-Atlantic, and seashore and coastal subjects." Publishes hardcover and trade paperback originals and reprints. Book catalog for 8" × 10" SAE with 2 first-class stamps or on website. Guidelines available online.

HOW TO CONTACT Query with SASE. Submit proposal package, clips, 1-2 sample chapters.

TERMS Pays royalty on wholesale or retail price, or makes outright purchase. Responds in 3 months to queries.

TIPS "Carefully consider whether your proposal is a good fit for our established market."

DREAMLAND BOOKS INC.

P.O. Box 1714, Minnetonka, MN 55345. (612)281-4704. **E-mail:** dreamlandbooks@inbox.com. **Website:** www.dreamlandbooksinc.com. Estab. 2008.

NEEDS "We are not accepting children's story submissions at this time. However, if you have a master or doctoral degree in creative writing, literature, or like field AND already have at least one nonvanity book published, we welcome query letters."

DUFOUR EDITIONS

P.O. Box 7, 124 Byers Road, Chester Springs, PA 19425. (610)458-5005 or (800)869-5677. **Fax:** (610)458-7103. **Website:** www.dufoureditions.com. Estab. 1948. **Contact:** Thomas Lavoie, associate publisher. Estab. 1948. Small, independent publisher, tending toward literary fiction. Publishes hardcover originals, trade paperback originals, and reprints. Averages 3-4 total titles, 1-2 fiction titles/year. Promotes titles through catalogs, reviews, direct mail, sales reps, Book Expo, and wholesalers. We publish literary fiction by good writers which is well received and achieves modest sales. De-emphsazing poetry and nonfiction. Publishes hardcover originals, trade paperback originals and reprints. Book catalog available free.

NEEDS Literary, short story collections. "We like books that are slightly offbeat, different, and well-written." Published *Tideland*, by Mitch Cullin; *The Case of the Pederast's Wife*, by Clare Elfman; *Last Love in Constantinople*, by Milorad Pavic; *Night Sounds and Other Stories*, by Karen Shoemaker; *From the Place in the Valley Deep in the Forest*, by Mitch Cullen (short stories); and *Beyond Faith and Other Stories*, by Tom Noyes.

HOW TO CONTACT Query with SASE. Accepts queries by e-mail, fax. Include estimated word count, brief bio, list of publishing credits. Responds in 3 months to queries; 6 months to mss. Accepts simultaneous submissions. Query with SASE.

TERMS Pays 6-10% royalty on net receipts. Average advance: $100-500. Publishes ms 18 months after acceptance. Responds in 3 months to queries. Responds in 6 months to manuscripts.

TIPS Audience is sophisticated, literate readers especially interested in foreign literature and translations, and a strong Irish-Celtic focus, as well as work from U.S. writers. Check to see if the publisher is really a good match for your subject matter.

♠ THOMAS DUNNE BOOKS

Imprint of St. Martin's Press, 175 Fifth Ave., New York, NY 10010. (212)674-5151. **Website:** www.thomasdun nebooks.com. Estab. 1986. "Thomas Dunne Books publishes popular trade fiction and nonfiction. With an output of approximately 175 titles each year, his group covers a range of genres including commercial and literary fiction, thrillers, biography, politics, sports, popular science, and more. The list is intentionally eclectic and includes a wide range of fiction and nonfiction, from first books to international bestsellers." Publishes hardcover and trade paperback originals, and reprints. Book catalog and ms guidelines free.

○ *Accepts agented submissions only.*

HOW TO CONTACT Agents submit query.

♠⊘ DUTTON ADULT TRADE

Imprint of Penguin Group (USA), Inc., 375 Hudson St., New York, NY 10014. (212)366-2000. **Website:** us.penguingroup.com. Estab. 1852. "*Dutton* publishes hardcover, original, mainstream, and contemporary fiction and nonfiction in the areas of memoir, self-help, politics, psychology, and science for a general readership. Dutton currently publishes 45 hardcovers/year, roughly half fiction and half nonfiction. It is currently home to many #1 *New York Times* best-selling authors, most notably **Harlan Coben**, author of *Hold Tight*, **Ken Follett**, author of *Pillars of the Earth* and *World Without End*, **Eckhart Tolle**, author of *A New Earth*, and **Al Franken**, author of *The Truth*. Dutton also publishes *The New York Times* best-selling authors **Eric Jerome Dickey**, author of *Pleasure* and *Waking with Enemies*, **Raymond Khoury**, author of *The Last Templar* and *The Sanctuary*, **John Lescroart**, author of *Betrayal* and *The Suspect*, **John Hodgman**, author of *The Areas of My Expertise* and *More Information Than You Require*, **John Jakes**, author of *Charleston* and *The Gods of Newport*, **Jenny McCarthy**, author of *Baby Laughs* and *Louder than Words*, and **Daniel Levitin**, author of *This is Your Brain on Music* and

The World in Six Songs." Publishes hardcover originals. Book catalog for #10 SASE.

○ *Does not accept unsolicited ms. Agented submissions only.* "Query letters **only** (must include SASE). A query letter should be typed and, ideally, fit on one page. Please include a brief synopsis of your ms and your publishing credits, if any."

HOW TO CONTACT Agented submissions only. *No unsolicited mss.*

TERMS Pays royalty. Pays negotiable advance.

TIPS "Write the complete ms and submit it to an agent or agents. They will know exactly which editor will be interested in a project."

DUTTON CHILDREN'S BOOKS

Penguin Group (USA), Inc., 375 Hudson St., New York, NY 10014. **E-mail:** duttonpublicity@ us.penguingroup.com. **Website:** www.penguin.com. **Contact:** Sara Reynolds, art director. Estab. 1852. Publishes hardcover originals as well as novelty formats. Averages 50 titles/year. 10% of books form first-time authors. Dutton Children's Books publishes high-quality fiction and nonfiction for readers ranging from preschoolers to young adults on a variety of subjects. Currently emphasizing middle-grade and young adult novels that offer a fresh perspective. De-emphasizing photographic nonfiction and picture books that teach a lesson. Approximately 80 new hardcover titles/year, fiction and nonfiction for babies through young adults. Publishes hardcover originals as well as novelty formats.

○ "Cultivating the creative talents of authors and illustrators and publishing books with purpose and heart continue to be the mission and joy at Dutton."

NEEDS Dutton Children's Books has a diverse general-interest list that includes picture books and fiction for all ages, from middle-grade to young adult novels. Published *Big Chickens Fly the Coop*, by Leslie Helakoski, illustrated by Henry Cole (picture book); *Antsy Does Time*, by Neal Shusterman (middle-grade novel); *Paper Towns*, by John Green (young adult novel).

HOW TO CONTACT Query letter only; include SASE.

TERMS Pays royalty on retail price. Offers advance.

EAKIN PRESS

P.O. Box 21235, Waco, TX 76702. (254)235-6161. **Fax:** (254)235-6230. **Website:** www.eakinpress.com. **Con-**

tact: Kris Gholson, associate publisher. Estab. 1978. "Our top priority is to cover the history and culture of the Southwest, especially Texas and Oklahoma. We also have successfully published titles related to ethnic studies. We publish very little fiction, other than for children." Publishes hardcover and paperback originals and reprints. Book catalog for $1.25. Guidelines available online.

○ No electronic submissions.

NEEDS Juvenile fiction for grades K-12, preferably relating to Texas and the Southwest or contemporary. No adult fiction.

HOW TO CONTACT Query or submit outline/synopsis

TERMS Responds in up to 1 year to queries.

◐◑ THE ECCO PRESS

10 E. 53rd St., New York, NY 10022. (212)207-7000. **Fax:** (212)702-2460. **Website:** www.harpercollins .com. **Contact:** Daniel Halpern, editor-in-chief. Estab. 1970. Publishes hardcover and trade paperback originals and reprints.

NEEDS Literary, short story collections. "We can publish possibly one or two original novels a year." Published *Blonde*, by Joyce Carrol Oates; *Pitching Around Fidel*, by S.L. Price.

HOW TO CONTACT *Does not accept unsolicited mss.*

TERMS Pays royalty. Pays negotiable advance.

TIPS "We are always interested in first novels and feel it's important that they be brought to the attention of the reading public."

EDCON PUBLISHING GROUP

30 Montauk Blvd., Oakdale, NY 11769. (631)567-7227. **Fax:** (631)567-8745. **E-mail:** dale@edconpublishing .com. **Website:** www.edconpublishing.com. Catalog available online.

○ Looking for educational games and nonfiction work in the areas of math, science, reading, and social studies.

HOW TO CONTACT Submit outline/synopsis and 1 sample chapter. Submission kept on file unless return is requested. Include SASE for return.

TERMS Work purchased outright from authors for up to $1,000.

◑ EDGE SCIENCE FICTION AND FANTASY PUBLISHING/TESSERACT BOOKS

Hades Publications, Box 1714, Calgary, AB T2P 2L7 Canada. (403)254-0160. **Fax:** (403)254-0456. **E-mail:**

publisher@hadespublications.com. **Website:** www .edgewebsite.com. **Contact:** Editorial Manager. Estab. 1996. "We are an independent publisher of science fiction and fantasy novels in hardcover or trade paperback format. We produce high-quality books with lots of attention to detail and lots of marketing effort. We want to encourage, produce, and promote thought-provoking and fun-to-read science fiction and fantasy literature by 'bringing the magic alive: one world at a time' (as our motto says) with each new book released." Books: natural offset paper; offset/web printing; HC/perfect-bound; black-and-white illustration only. Average print order: 2,000-3,000. Plans 20 first novels this year. Averages 16-20 total titles/year. Member of Book Publishers Association of Alberta (BPAA), Independent Publishers Association of Canada (IPAC), Publisher's Marketing Association (PMA), Small Press Center.

NEEDS Fantasy (space fantasy, sword and sorcery), science fiction (hard science/technological, soft/sociological). "We are looking for all types of fantasy and science fiction, horror except juvenile/young adult, erotica, religious fiction, short stories, dark/gruesome fantasy, or poetry." Length: 75,000-100,000/words. Published *Stealing Magic*, by Tanya Huff; *Forbidden Cargo*, by Rebecca K. Rowe, *The Hounds of Ash and Other Tales of Fool Wolf,* by Greg Keyes.

HOW TO CONTACT Accepts unsolicited mss. Submit first 3 chapters and synopsis, Check website for guidelines or send SAE and IRCs for same. Include estimated word count. Responds in 4-5 months to mss. No simultaneous submissions, electronic submissions. Rarely comments on rejected mss.

TERMS Pays 10% royalty on wholesale price. Average advance: negotiable. Publishes ms 18-20 months after acceptance. Ms guidelines online.

TIPS "Send us your best, polished, completed manuscript. Use proper manuscript format. Take the time before you submit to get a critique from people who can offer you useful advice. When in doubt, visit our website for helpful resources, FAQs, and other tips."

WILLIAM B. EERDMANS PUBLISHING CO.

2140 Oak Industrial Dr. NE, Grand Rapids, MI 49505. (616)459-4591. **Fax:** (616)459-6540. **E-mail:** info@ee rdmans.com. **Website:** www.eerdmans.com. **Contact:** Jon Pott, editor-in-chief. Estab. 1911. "The majority of our adult publications are religious and most of these are academic or semi-academic in character (as opposed to inspirational or celebrity books), though we also publish general trade books on the Christian life. Our nonreligious titles, most of them featuring regional history or social issues, aim, similarly, at an educated audience." Publishes hardcover and paperback originals and reprints. Book catalog and ms guidelines free.

○ Will not respond to or accept mss, proposals, or queries sent by e-mail or fax.

IMPRINTS Eerdmans Books for Young Readers.

HOW TO CONTACT Query with SASE.

TERMS Responds in 4 weeks to queries, possibly longer for mss. Please include e-mail and/or SASE.

⊕ ENETE ENTERPRISES

3600 Mission #10, San Diego, CA 92109. **E-mail:** EneteEnterprises@gmail.com. **Website:** www.EneteEnterprises.com. **Contact:** Shannon Enete, editor. Estab. 2011. Publishes trade paperback originals, mass-market paperback originals, electronic originals. Guidelines available on website.

HOW TO CONTACT Submit query, proposal, or ms by e-mail according to guidelines (do not forget a marketing plan).

TERMS Pays royalties of 1-15%. Responds to queries/proposals in 1 month; mss in 1-3 months.

TIPS "Send me your best work. Do not rush a draft."

ENGLISH TEA ROSE PRESS

The Wild Rose Press, P.O. Box 708, Adams Basin, NY 14410. (585)752-8770. **E-mail:** queryus@thewildrosepress.com. **Website:** www.thewildrosepress.com. **Contact:** Nicole D'Arienzo, editor. Estab. 2006. Member: EPIC, Romance Writers of America. Distributes/promotes titles through major distribution chains, including iTunes, Kobo, Sony, Amazon.com, Kindle, as well as smaller and online distributors. Publishes paperback originals, reprints, and e-books in a POD format. Guidelines available on website.

○ *Does not accept unsolicited mss.* Agented fiction less than 1%. Always comments on rejected mss. Sends prepublication galleys to author.

NEEDS "In the English Tea Rose line, we have conquering heroes, high seas adventure, and scandalous gossip: The love stories that will take you back in time. From the windswept moors of Scotland to the Emerald Isle to the elegant ballrooms of Regency England, the men and women of this time are larger than life and willing to risk it all for the love of a lifetime. English Tea Rose stories encompass historical romances

set before 1900 which are not set on American soil. Send us your medieval knights, Vikings, Scottish highlanders, marauding pirates, and ladies and gentlemen of the Ton. English Tea Rose romances should have strong conflict and be emotionally driven; and, whether the story is medieval, Regency, set during the Renaissance, or any other pre-1900 time, they must stay true to their period in historical accuracy and flavor. English Tea Roses can range from sweet to spicy, but should not contain overly explicit language."

HOW TO CONTACT Send query letter with outline and a list of publishing credits. Include estimated word count, brief bio, and list of publishing credits.

TERMS Pays royalty of 7% minimum; 35% maximum. Responds in 4 weeks to queries; 3 months to mss.

TIPS "Polish your manuscript, make it as error-free as possible, and follow our submission guidelines."

⊛⊘ EOS

Imprint of HarperCollins General Books Group, 10 E. 53rd St., New York, NY 10022. (212)207-7000. **Website:** www.eosbooks.com. Estab. 1998. **Contact:** Diana Gill, senior editor. Estab. 1998. Publishes hardcover originals, trade and mass-market paperback originals, and reprints. Averages 40-46 total titles, 40 fiction titles/year. Eos publishes quality science fiction/fantasy with broad appeal. Publishes hardcover originals, trade and mass-market paperback originals, and reprints. Guidelines for #10 SASE.

NEEDS Fantasy, science fiction. Published *The Isle of Battle*, by Sean Russell (fantasy); *Trapped*, by James Alan Gardner. No horror or juvenile.

HOW TO CONTACT *Agented submissions only.* Include list of publishing credits, brief synopsis. Agented fiction 99%. Responds in 6 months to queries. Never comments on rejected mss. *All unsolicited mss returned.*

TERMS Pays royalty on retail price. Average advance: variable. Publishes ms 18-24 months after acceptance. Ms guidelines for #10 SASE. Pays royalty on retail price. Pays variable advance.

TIPS "Query via e-mail. Your query should be brief—no more than a 2-page description of your book. Do not send chapters or full synopsis at this time. You will receive a response—either a decline or a request for more material—in approximately 1-2 months."

FABER & FABER LTD

Bloomsbury House, 74-77 Great Russell St., London WC1B 3DA United Kingdom. 020 7465 0045. **Fax:** 020 7465 0034. **Website:** www.faber.co.uk. **Contact:** Lee Brackstone, Hannah Griffiths, Angus Cargill, (fiction); Walter Donohue, (film); Dinah Wood, (plays); Julian Loose, Neil Belton, (nonfiction); Paul Keegan, (poetry); Belinda Matthews, (music); Suzy Jenvy, Julia Wells, (children's). Estab. 1925. Faber & Faber have rejuvenated their nonfiction, music and children's titles in recent years, and the film and drama lists remain market leaders. Publishes hardcover and paperback originals and reprints. Book catalog available online.

Faber & Faber will consider unsolicited proposals for poetry only.

HOW TO CONTACT *No unsolicited fiction submissions.*

TERMS Pays royalty. Pays varying advances with each project. Responds in 3 months to mss.

TIPS Explore the website and downloadable book catalogs thoroughly to get a feel for the lists in all categories and genres.

FANTAGRAPHICS BOOKS INC.

7563 Lake City Way NE, Seattle, WA 98115. (206)524-1967. **Fax:** (206)524-2104. **E-mail:** fbicomix@fanta graphics.com. **Website:** www.fantagraphics.com. **Contact:** Submissions editor. Estab. 1976. Publishes comics for thinking readers. Does not want mainstream genres of superhero, vigilante, horror, fantasy, or science fiction. Publishes original trade paperbacks. Book catalog available online. Guidelines available online.

NEEDS "Fantagraphics is an independent company with a modus operandi different from larger, factory-like corporate comics publishers. If your talents are limited to a specific area of expertise (i.e. inking, writing, etc.), then you will need to develop your own team before submitting a project to us. We want to see an idea that is fully fleshed out in your mind, at least, if not on paper. Submit a minimum of 5 fully inked pages of art, a synopsis, SASE, and a brief note stating approximately how many issues you have in mind."

TERMS Responds in 2-3 months to queries.

TIPS "Take note of the originality and diversity of the themes and approaches to drawing in such Fantagraphics titles as *Love & Rockets* (stories of life in Latin America and Chicano L.A.), *Palestine* (journalistic autobiography in the Middle East), *Eight-ball* (surrealism mixed with kitsch culture in stories alternately humorous and painfully personal), and *Naughty Bits* (feminist humor and short stories which both attack and commiserate). Try to develop your own, equally individual voice; originality, aesthetic maturity, and graphic story-telling skill are the signs by which Fantagraphics judges whether or not your submission is ripe for publication."

FARRAR, STRAUS & GIROUX

18 W. 18th St., New York, NY 10011. (646)307-5151. **E-mail:** fsg.editorial@fsgbooks.com. **Website:** us.macmillan.com. **Contact:** Children's Editorial Department. Estab. 1946. "We publish original and well-written materials for all ages." Publishes hardcover originals and trade paperback reprints. **Published some debut authors within the last year.** Averages 75 total titles/year. "We publish original and well-written material for all ages." Publishes hardcover originals and trade paperback reprints. For catalog fax request or email to: childrens.publicity@fsgbooks .com. Guidelines available online.

IMPRINTS Frances Foster Books.

NEEDS Children's/juvenile, picture books, middle grade, young adult, narrative nonfiction. "Do not query picture books; just send manuscript. Do not fax queries or manuscripts." Published *Adele and Simon*, by Barbara McClintock; *The Cabinet of Wonders*, by Marie Rutkoski.

HOW TO CONTACT For novels and other longer mss, query with SASE and three sample chapters. Do not query picture books, just send ms with cover letter. Include brief bio, list of publishing credits. Agented fiction 50%. Responds in 2 months to queries; 4 months to mss. Accepts simultaneous submissions. No electronic submissions or submissions on disk. Query with SASE. Hard copy submissions only.

TERMS Pays 2-6% royalty on retail price for paperbacks, 3-10% for hardcovers. Average advance: $3,000-25,000. Publishes ms 18 months after acceptance. Book catalog for 9" × 12" SAE with $2.00 postage. Ms guidelines for #10 SASE.

TIPS: "Study our list to avoid sending something inappropriate. Send query letters for long manuscripts; don't ask for editorial advice (just not possible, unfortunately); and send a SASE!" Audience is full age range, preschool to young adult. Specializes in literary fiction.

🎧 FARRAR, STRAUS & GIROUX FOR YOUNG READERS

18 W. 18th St., New York, NY 10011. (212)741-6900. **Fax:** (212)633-2427. **E-mail:** childrens-editorial@fsgbooks.com. **Website:** www.fsgkidsbooks.com. **Contact:** Margaret Ferguson, editorial director; Wesley Adams, executive editor; Janine O'Malley, senior editor; Frances Foster, Frances Foster Books; Robbin Gourley, art director. Estab. 1946. Farrar title *How I Learned Geography*, by Uri Shulevitz, won a Caldecott Honor in 2009. Farrar/Frances Foster title *The Wall: Growing Up Behind the Iron Curtain*, by Peter Siís, won a Caldecott Honor Medal in 2008. Farrar/Melanie Kroupa title *Rex Zero and the End of the World*, by Tim Wynne-Jones, won a Boston Globe-Horn Book Fiction and Poetry Honor Award in 2007. Farrar/Frances Foster title *Dreamquake: Book Two of the Dreamhunter Duet*, by Elizabeth Knox, won a Michael L. Printz Honor Award in 2008. Book catalog available for 9" × 12" SASE with $1.95 postage. Ms guidelines for SASE, with 1 first-class stamp, or go to www.fsgkidsbooks.com.

○ *As of January 2010, Farrar Straus & Giroux does not accept unsolicited manuscripts.* "We recommend finding a literary agent to represent you and your work."

NEEDS All levels: all categories. "Original and well-written material for all ages." Recently published *The Cabinet of Wonders*, by Marie Rutkoski; *Last Night*, by Hyewon Yum.

HOW TO CONTACT Submit cover letter, first 50 pages.

TIPS "Study our catalog before submitting. We will see illustrators' portfolios by appointment. Don't ask for criticism and/or advice—due to the volume of submissions we receive, it's just not possible. Never send originals. Always enclose SASE."

FENCE BOOKS

Science Library 320, Univ. of Albany, 1400 Washington Ave., Albany, NY 12222. (518)591-8162. **E-mail:** fence.fencebooks@gmail.com; robfence@gmail.com. **Website:** www.fenceportal.org. **Contact:** Rob Arnold, submissions manager. Hardcover originals. Guidelines available online.

○ *"Fence is closed to submissions right now.* We'll have another reading period in the spring. Fence Books offers 2 book contests (in addition to the National Poetry Series) with 2 sets of guidelines and entry forms on our website."

TIPS "At present Fence Books is a self-selecting publisher; mss come to our attention through our contests and through editors' investigations. We hope to become open to submissions of poetry and fiction mss in the near future."

💿 DAVID FICKLING BOOKS

31 Beamont St., Oxford En OX1 2NP United Kingdom. (018)65-339000. **Fax:** (018)65-339009. **E-mail:** DFickling@randomhouse.co.uk; tburgess@randomhouse.co.uk. **Website:** www.davidficklingbooks.co.uk.

NEEDS Considers all categories. Recently published *Once Upon a Time in the North*, by Phillip Pullman; *The Curious Incident of the Dog in the Night-time*, by Mark Haddon; *The Boy in the Striped Pyjamas*, by John Boyne.

HOW TO CONTACT Submit 3 sample chapters.

TERMS Responds to mss in 3 months.

➕ FIRST EDITION DESIGN PUBLISHING

5202 Old Ashwood Dr., Sarasota, FL 34233. (941)921-2607. **Fax:** (617)249-1694. **E-mail:** support@firsteditiondesign.com. **E-mail:** submission@firsteditiondesign.com. **Website:** www.firsteditiondesignpublishing.com. **Contact:** Deborah E. Gordon, executive editor; Tom Gahan, marketing director. Estab. 1985. Send SAE for catalog. Guidelines available free on request or online at website.

HOW TO CONTACT Submit complete ms electronically.

TERMS Pays royalty 30-70% on retail price.

TIPS "Follow our FAQs listed on our website."

FLORIDA ACADEMIC PRESS

P.O. Box 357425, Gainesville, FL 32635. (352)332-5104. **E-mail:** fapress@gmail.com. **Website:** www.floridaacademicpress.com. **Contact:** Max Vargas, CEO (nonfiction/scholarly); Linda Travis, assistant editor (fiction). Estab. 1997. Publishes trade paperback originals. Catalog available online.

NEEDS Serious fiction and scholarly social science manuscripts. Does not want "children's books, poetry, science fiction, religious tracts, anthologies, or booklets."

HOW TO CONTACT Submit completed ms by hard copy only.

TERMS Pays 6-10% royalty on retail price and higher on sales of 2,500+ copies a year. Responds in 3-4 months to mss.

TIPS Considers complete mss only. "Manuscripts we decide to publish must be resubmitted by the author in ready-to-print PDF files. Match our needs—do not send blindly. Books we accept for publication must be submitted in camera-ready format. The Press covers all publication/promotional expenditures."

FLUX

Llewellyn Worldwide, Ltd., Llewellyn Worldwide, Ltd., 2143 Wooddale Dr., Woodbury, MN 55125. (651)312-8613. **Fax:** (651)291-1908. **Website:** www.fluxnow.com; fluxnow.blogspot.com. **Contact:** Brian Farrey, acquisitions editor. Estab. 2005. "Flux seeks to publish authors who see YA as a point of view, not a reading level. We look for books that try to capture a slice of teenage experience, whether in real or imagined worlds." Book catalog and guidelines available on website.

○ *Does not accept unsolicited mss.*

NEEDS Young adult: adventure, contemporary, fantasy, history, humor, problem novels, religion, science fiction, sports, suspense. Average word length: 50,000.

TERMS Pays royalties of 10-15% based on wholesale price.

TIPS "Read contemporary teen books. Be aware of what else is out there. If you don't read teen books, you probably shouldn't write them. Know your audience. Write incredibly well. Do not condescend."

⊕ FOLDED WORD

5209 Del Vista Way, Rocklin, CA 95765. **Fax:** (916)624-5088. **E-mail:** editors@foldedword.com. **Website:** www.foldedword.com. Estab. 2008. "Folded Word is an independent literary press. Our focus? Connecting new voices to readers. Our goal? To make poetry and fiction accessible for the widest audience possible both on and off the page."

TIPS "E-mail is the best way to reach us."

FORWARD MOVEMENT

412 Sycamore St., Cincinnati, OH 45202. (513)721-6659; (800)543-1813. **Fax:** (513)721-0729. **E-mail:** rschmidt@forwarddaybyday.com. **Website:** www.forwardmovement.org. **Contact:** Rev. Dr. Richard H. Schmidt, editor and director. Estab. 1934. "Forward Movement was established to help reinvigorate the life of the church. Many titles focus on the life of prayer, where our relationship with God is centered, death, marriage, baptism, recovery, joy, the Episcopal Church, and more. Currently emphasizing prayer/spirituality." Book catalog and ms guidelines free. Guidelines available online.

○ "Forward Movement is an official agency of the Episcopal Church. In addition to Forward Day by Day, our daily devotional guide, we publish other books and tracts related to the life and concerns of the Christian church, especially within the Anglican Communion. These typically include material introducing the Episcopal Church, meditations and spiritual readings, prayers, liturgical resources, biblical reflections, and material on stewardship, church history, issues before the church, and Christian healing."

TERMS Responds in 1 month.

TIPS "Audience is primarily Episcopalians and other Christians."

◑ FOUR WAY BOOKS

Box 535, Village Station, New York, NY 10014. **E-mail:** editors@fourwaybooks.com. **Website:** www.fourwaybooks.com. **Contact:** Martha Rhodes, director. Estab. 1993. "Four Way Books is a not-for-profit literary press dedicated to publishing poetry and short fiction by emerging and established writers. Each year, Four Way Books publishes the winners of its national poetry competitions, as well as collections accepted through general submission, panel selection, and solicitation by the editors."

NEEDS Open reading period: June 1-30. Book-length story collections and novellas. Submission guidelines will be posted online at end of May. Does not want novels or translations.

◐ FRANCES LINCOLN CHILDREN'S BOOKS

Frances Lincoln, 74-77 White Lion St., Islington, London N1 9PF United Kingdom. 00-44-207-284-4009. **E-mail:** flcb@franceslincoln.com. **Website:** www.franceslincoln.com. Estab. 1977. "Our company was founded by Frances Lincoln in 1977. We published our first books two years later, and we have been creating illustrated books of the highest quality ever since, with special emphasis on gardening, walking and the outdoors, art, architecture, design, and landscape. In 1983, we started to publish illustrated books for children. Since then we have won many awards and prizes with both fiction and nonfiction children's books."

NEEDS Picture books, young readers, middle readers, young adults: adventure, animal, anthology, fantasy, folktales, health, history, humor, multicultural, nature/environment, special needs, sports. Average word length: picture books, 1,000; young readers, 9,788; middle readers, 20,653; young adults, 35,407. Recently published *The Sniper*, by James Riordan (young adult/teen novel); *Amazons! Women Warriors of the World*, by Sally Pomme Clayton, illustrated by Sophie Herxheimer (picture book); *Young Inferno*, by John Agard, illustrated by Satoshi Kitamura (graphic novel/picture book).

HOW TO CONTACT Query by e-mail.

TERMS Responds to mss in minimum of 6 weeks.

FREESTONE/PEACHTREE, JR.

1700 Chattahoochee Ave., Atlanta, GA 30318. (404)876-8761. **Fax:** (404)875-2578. **E-mail:** hello@peachtree-online.com. **Website:** www.peachtree-online.com. **Contact:** Helen Harriss, acquisitions; Loraine Joyner, art director; Melanie McMahon Ives, production manager. Estab. 1977.

Freestone and Peachtree, Jr., are imprints of Peachtree Publishers. See the listing for Peachtree for submission information. No e-mail or fax queries or submissions, please.

NEEDS Middle readers: adventure, animal, history, nature/environment, sports. Young adults: fiction, history, biography, mystery, adventure. Does not want to see science fiction, religion, or romance. Recent publications for comparison are: *This Girl is Different*, by J.J. Johnson (ages 12-16, young adult), *The Cheshire Cheese Cat,* by Carmen Agra Deedy and Randall Wright, illustrated by Barry Moser (ages 8 and up, middle reader), and *Grow,* by Juanita Havill, illustrated by Stanislawa Kodman (middle reader, ages 8-12).

HOW TO CONTACT Submit 3 sample chapters by postal mail only. No query necessary.

TERMS Responds in 6 months-1 year.

FRONT STREET

Boyds Mills Press, 815 Church St., Honesdale, PA 18431. **Website:** www.frontstreetbooks.com. **Contact:** Acquisitions Editor. Estab. 1994. "We are an independent publisher of books for children and young adults." Publishes hardcover originals and trade paperback reprints. Book catalog available online. Guidelines available online.

NEEDS "We look for fresh voices for children and young adults. Titles on our list entertain, challenge, or enlighten, always employing novel characters whose considered voices resonate."

HOW TO CONTACT Query with first 3 chapters and a plot summary and label the package "Manuscript Submission."

TERMS Pays royalty on retail price. Pays advance. Responds in 3 months.

TIPS "Read through our recently published titles and review our website. Check to see what's on the market and in our catalog before submitting your story. Feel free to query us if you're not sure."

FUTURECYCLE PRESS

Website: www.futurecycle.org. **Contact:** Diane Kistner, director/editor-in-chief. Estab. 2007. Guidelines available online at website.

NEEDS Flash fiction.

HOW TO CONTACT Submit complete ms.

TERMS Pays 10% royalty and 25 author's copies. Responds to mss in 3 months.

GASLIGHT PUBLICATIONS

P.O. Box 1344, Studio City, CA 91614. **Website:** playerspress.home.att.net/gaslight_catalogue.htm. **Contact:** Simon Waters, fiction editor (Sherlock Holmes only). Estab. 1950. Publishes hardcover and paperback originals and reprints.

NEEDS Sherlock Holmes only.

HOW TO CONTACT Query with SASE. Include estimated word count, brief bio, list of publishing credits.

TERMS Pays 8-10% royalty. Responds in 2 weeks to queries; 1 year to mss.

TIPS "Please send only Sherlock Holmes material. Other stuff just wastes time and money."

GENESIS PRESS, INC.

P.O. Box 101, Columbus, MS 39701. (888)463-4461. **Fax:** (662)329-9399. **E-mail:** customerservice@genesis-press.com. **Website:** www.genesis-press.com. Estab. 1993. Publishes hardcover and trade paperback originals and reprints. **Published 50% debut authors within the last year.** Genesis Press is the largest privately owned African-American book publisher in the country. Genesis has steadily increased its reach, and now brings its readers everything from suspense and science fiction to Christian-oriented romance and nonfiction. Publishes hardcover and trade paperback originals and reprints. Guidelines available online.

IMPRINTS Indigo (romance); Black Coral (fiction); Indigo Love Spectrum (interracial romance); Indigo after Dark (erotica); Obsidian (thriller/myster); Indigo Glitz (love stories for young adults); Indigo Vibe (for stylish audience under 35 years old); Mount Blue (Christian); Inca Books (teens); Sage (self-help/inspirational).

NEEDS Averages 30 total titles/year. Erotica, ethnic, literary, multicultural, romance, women's. Published *Cherish the Flame*, by Beverly Clark; *No Apologies*, by Seressia Glass.

HOW TO CONTACT Query with SASE or submit 3 sample chapter(s), synopsis. Responds in 2 months to queries; 4 months to mss. Submit clips, 3 sample chapters, SASE.

TERMS Pays 6-12% royalty on invoice price. Average advance: $750-5,000. Publishes ms 1 year after acceptance. Ms guidelines online. Responds in 2 months to queries. Responds in 4 months to manuscripts.

TIPS Be professional. Always include a cover letter and SASE. Follow the submission guidelines posted on our website or send SASE for a copy.

GIVAL PRESS

Gival Press, LLC, P.O. Box 3812, Arlington, VA 22203. (703)351-0079. **E-mail:** givalpress@yahoo.com. **Website:** www.givalpress.com. **Contact:** Robert L. Giron, editor-in-chief (area of interest: literary). Estab. 1998. A small, award-winning independent publisher that publishes quality works by a variety of authors from an array of walks of life. Works are in English, Spanish, and French and have a philosophical or social message. Publishes paperback originals and reprints and e-books. Books: perfect-bound. Average print order: 500. **Publishes established and debut authors.** Publishes 2 novels/year. Member AAP, PMA, Literary Council of Small Presses and Magazines. Distributes books through Ingram and BookMasters, Inc. Publishes trade paperback, electronic originals, and reprints. Book catalog available online, free on request/ for #10 SASE. Guidelines available online, by email, free on request/for #10 SASE.

IMPRINTS Gival Press.

NEEDS Literary, multicultural, GLBT. "Looking for French books with English translation." The Annual Gival Press Novel Award contest deadline is May 30. The Annual Gival Press Short Story Award contest deadline is August 8. Guidelines on website. Recently published *That Demon Life*, by Lowell Mick White;

Twelve Rivers of the Body, by Elizabeth Oness; and *A Tomb of the Periphery*, by John Domini.

HOW TO CONTACT Does not accept unsolicited mss. Query by e-mail first. Include description of project, estimated word count, brief bio, list of publishing credits. Agented fiction 5%. Responds by e-mail within 2-3 weeks. Rarely comments on rejected mss. Always query first via e-mail; provide description, author's bio, and supportive material.

TERMS Pays 20 contributor's copies. Offers advance. Publishes ms 1 year after acceptance. For book catalog send SASE and on website. Ms guidelines by SASE or on website. Royalties (% varies). Responds in 1 month to queries, 3 months to proposals and mss.

TIPS "Our audience is those who read literary works with depth to the work. Visit our website—there is much to be read/learned from the numerous pages."

THE GLENCANNON PRESS

P.O. Box 1428, El Cerrito, CA 94530. (510)528-4216. **Fax:** (510)528-3194. **E-mail:** merships@yahoo.com. **Website:** www.glencannon.com. **Contact:** Bill Harris (maritime, maritime children's). Estab. 1993. "We publish quality books about ships and the sea." Average print order: 1,000. Member PMA, BAIPA. Distributes titles through Baker & Taylor. Promotes titles through direct mail, magazine advertising, and word of mouth. Accepts unsolicited mss. Often comments on rejected mss. Publishes hardcover and paperback originals and hardcover reprints.

IMPRINTS Smyth: perfect binding; illustrations.

HOW TO CONTACT Submit complete ms. Include brief bio, list of publishing credits. Send SASE for return of ms or send a disposable ms and SASE for reply only.

TERMS Pays 10-20% royalty. Responds in 1 month to queries; 2 months to mss.

TIPS "Write a good story in a compelling style."

DAVID R. GODINE, PUBLISHER, INC.

15 Court Square, Suite 320, Boston, MA 02108. (617)451-9600. **Fax:** (617)350-0250. **E-mail:** info@ godine.com. **Website:** www.godine.com. Estab. 1970. Small, independent publisher (5-person staff). Publishes hardcover and trade paperback originals and reprints. Averages 35 total titles/year. "Our particular strengths are books about the history and design of the written word, literary essays, and the best of world fiction in translation. We also have an unusually strong list of children's books, all of them printed

in their entirety with no cuts, deletions, or sidestepping to keep the political watchdogs happy." Publishes hardcover and trade paperback originals and reprints. Book catalog for 5" × 8" envelope and 3 first-class stamps.

NEEDS children's/juvenile, historical, literary. *No unsolicited mss. No unsolicited mss.*

HOW TO CONTACT Does not accept unsolicited mss. Query with SASE.

TERMS Pays royalty on retail price. Publishes ms 3 years after acceptance.

TIPS "Please visit our website for more information about our books and detailed submission policy. No phone calls, please. Have your agent contact us."

GOOSE LANE EDITIONS

500 Beaverbrook Ct., Suite 330, Fredericton, NB E3B 5X4 Canada. (506)450-4251. **Fax:** (506)459-4991. **Website:** www.gooselane.com/submissions.php. **Contact:** Angela Williams, publishing assistant. Estab. 1954. Publishes hardcover and paperback originals and occasional reprints. Books: some illustrations. Average print order: 3,000. First novel print order: 1,500. Averages 16-18 total titles, 6-8 fiction titles/year. Distributes titles through University of Toronto Press (UTP). "Goose Lane publishes literary fiction and nonfiction from well-read and highly skilled Canadian authors." Publishes hardcover and paperback originals and occasional reprints.

NEEDS Literary (novels), mainstream/contemporary, short story collections. "Our needs in fiction never change: substantial, character-centered literary fiction." Published *Reading by Lightning,* by Joan Thomas. No children's, YA, mainstream, mass-market, genre, mystery, thriller, confessional, or science fiction.

HOW TO CONTACT Accepts unsolicited mss. Query with SASE. Responds in 6 months to queries. Responds in 6-8 months to mss. No simultaneous submissions. **Send submissions to:** Managing Editor, Goose Lane Editions, Suite 300, 500 Beaverbrook Court, Fredericton, NB E3B 5X4 CA. Query with SAE with Canadian stamps or IRCs. No U.S. stamps.

TERMS Pays 8-10% royalty on retail price. Average advance: $200-1,000, negotiable. Ms guidelines online.

TIPS "Writers should send us outlines and samples of books that show a very well-read author with highly developed literary skills. Our books are almost all

by Canadians living in Canada; we seldom consider submissions from outside Canada. If I were a writer trying to market a book today, I would contact the targeted publisher with a query letter and synopsis, and request manuscript guidelines. Purchase a recent book from the publisher in a relevant area, if possible. Always send an SASE with IRCs or suffient return postage in Canadian stamps for reply to your query and for any material you'd like returned should it not suit our needs. Specializes in high-quality Canadian literary fiction, poetry, and nonfiction. We consider submissions from outside Canada only when the author is Canadian and the book is of extraordinary interest to Canadian readers. We do not publish books for children or for the young adult market."

GRAYWOLF PRESS

250 Third Ave. N., Suite 600, Minneapolis, MN 55401. **E-mail:** wolves@graywolfpress.org. **Website:** www.graywolfpress.org. **Contact:** Katie Dublinski, editorial manager (nonfiction, fiction). Estab. 1974. Growing independent literary press, nonprofit corporation. Publishes trade cloth and paperback originals. Books: acid-free quality paper; offset printing; hardcover and soft binding. Average print order: 3,000-10,000. First novel print order: 3,000-7,500. Averages 27 total titles, 8-10 fiction titles/year. Distributes titles nationally through Farrar, Straus and Giroux. "Graywolf Press is an independent, nonprofit publisher dedicated to the creation and promotion of thoughtful and imaginative contemporary literature essential to a vital and diverse culture." Publishes trade cloth and paperback originals. Book catalog available free. Guidelines available online.

NEEDS Literary novels, short story collections. "Familiarize yourself with our list before submitting your work." Published *The Adderall Diaries,* by Stephen Elliot; *Castle,* by J. Robert Lennon; *The Heyday of the Insensitive Bastards,* by Robert Boswell; *I Am Not Sidney Poitier,* by Percival Everett. "Familiarize yourself with our list first." No genre books (romance, western, science fiction, suspense).

HOW TO CONTACT Send full ms during open submission period including SASE/IRC, estimated word count, brief bio, list of publishing credits. Agented fiction 90%. Does not accept unsolicited queries, book proposals, or sample chapters. Responds in 3-6 months to submissions. Accepts simultaneous submissions. Query with SASE. Please do not fax or e-mail.

TERMS Pays royalty on retail price, author's copies. Average advance: $2,500-15,000. Publishes ms 18-24 months after acceptance. Ms guidelines online. Pays royalty on retail price. Pays $1,000-25,000 advance. Responds in 3 months to queries.

⊘ GREENWILLOW BOOKS

HarperCollins Publishers, 10 E. 53rd St., New York, NY 10022. (212)207-7000. **Website:** www.greenwillowblog.com. **Contact:** Virginia Duncan, vice president/publisher; Paul Zakris, art director. Estab. 1974. Publishes hardcover originals, paperbacks, e-books, and reprints.

🖰 Does not accept unsolicited mss. "Unsolicited mail will not be opened and will not be returned."

TERMS Pays 10% royalty on wholesale price for first-time authors. Average advance: variable.

➕ 💲 GREY GECKO PRESS

565 S. Mason Rd., Suite 154, Katy, TX 77450. (866)535-6078. **Fax:** (866)535-6078. **E-mail:** info@greygeckopress.com. **E-mail:** submissions@greygeckopress.com. **Website:** www.greygeckopress.com. **Contact:** Hilary Comfort, editor-in-chief; Jason Aydelotte, executive director. Estab. 2011. Publishes hardcover, trade paperback, and electronic originals. Book catalog and ms guidelines for #10 SASE, by e-mail or online.

NEEDS "We do not publish extreme horror, erotica, or religious fiction. New and interesting stories by unpublished authors will always get our attention. Innovation is a core value of our company."

HOW TO CONTACT "We prefer electronic submissions but will accept query with SASE. Submit proposal package including outline, detailed, synopsis, and 3 sample chapters."

TERMS Pays 50-80% royalties on wholesale price. Responds in 1-3 months to queries, proposals, and mss.

TIPS "Be willing to be a part of the Grey Gecko family. Publishing with us is a partnership, not indentured servitude."

➕ GRIT CITY PUBLICATIONS

309 Hill St., Pittsburgh, PA 15140. (412)607-4592. **E-mail:** GritCityPublications@gmail.com. **Website:** www.GritCityPublications.com. **Contact:** Ron Gavalik, publisher. Estab. 2011. Publishes electronic originals. Book catalog and guidelines available online at website.

NEEDS "Please keep in mind we seek genre fiction for transformation into our unique fiction medium that's not published anywhere else. That's what makes EmotoBooks a hit with our fans. GCP publishes EmotoBooks. We seek shorter works of 6,000-10,000 words for EmotoSingles. We also seek works over 15,000 words for EmotoSerials. EmotoSerials are either short-term (novella length) or long-term (novel length). Writers are also required to read our 'How To Create EmotoBooks Handbook.' This is a free download from the Write Emotobooks page on the website."

HOW TO CONTACT Query EmotoSerials through e-mail; submit completed EmotoSingles only by e-mail.

TERMS Pays 11.7-18.4% royalty on retail price. Does not offer advance. Responds to queries in 1 month; mss in 3 months.

TIPS "We ask writers to experience already published EmotoBooks to discover the new medium and learn our style."

🅐 ⊘ GROSSET & DUNLAP PUBLISHERS

Penguin Putnam Inc., 375 Hudson St., New York, NY 10014. **Website:** www.penguingroup.com. **Contact:** Francesco Sedita, vice president/publisher. Estab. 1898. Grosset & Dunlap publishes children's books that show children that reading is fun, with books that speak to their interests and that are affordable so that children can build a home library of their own. Focus on licensed properties, series, and readers. "Grosset & Dunlap publishes high-interest, affordable books for children ages 0-10 years. We focus on original series, licensed properties, readers, and novelty books." Publishes hardcover (few) and mass-market paperback originals.

🖰 *Not currently accepting submissions.*

NEEDS All book formats except for picture books. Submit a summary and the first chapter or two for longer works. **Recently published series:** Frankly Frannie; George Brown, Class Clown; Bedeviled; Hank Zipzer; Camp Confidential; Katie Kazoo; Magic Kitten; Magic Puppy; The Hardy Boys; Nancy Drew; The Little Engine That Could. **Upcoming series:** Splurch Academy for Disruptive Boys; Gladiator Boy; Dinkin Dings; Hello, Gorgeous! **Licensed series:** Angelina Ballerina; Disney Club Penguin; Charlie & Lola; Star Wars: The Clone Wars; WWE; Disney's Classic Pooh;

Max & Ruby; The Penguins of Madagascar; Batman: The Brave and the Bold; Strawberry Shortcake.

HOW TO CONTACT Agented submissions only.

TERMS Pays royalty. Pays advance.

TIPS "Nonfiction that is particularly topical or of wide interest in the mass market; new concepts for novelty format for preschoolers; and very well-written easy readers on topics that appeal to primary graders have the best chance of selling to our firm."

ⓞ GROUNDWOOD BOOKS

110 Spadina Ave. Suite 801, Toronto, ON M5V 2K4 Canada. (416)363-4343. **Fax:** (416)363-1017. **E-mail:** ssutherland@groundwoodbooks.com. **Website:** www .houseofanansi.com. Publishes 13 picture books/year; 3 young readers/year; 5 middle readers/year; 5 young adult titles/year, approximately 2 nonfiction titles/year. Visit website for guidelines: www.houseofan ansi.com/Groundwoodsubmissions.aspx.

NEEDS Recently published: *One Year in Coal Harbour*, by Polly Horvath; *That Night's Train*, by Ahmad Akbarpour; *Nobody Knows*, by Shelley Tanaka; *My Name is Parvana*, by Deborah Ellis; *My Book of Life by Angel*, by Martine Leavitt.

HOW TO CONTACT Submit synopsis and sample chapters.

TERMS Offers advances. Responds to mss in 6-8 months.

ⓞⓞ ⓞ GROVE/ATLANTIC, INC.

841 Broadway, 4th Floor, New York, NY 10003. (212)614-7850. **Fax:** (212)614-7886. **E-mail:** info@ groveatlantic.com. **Website:** www.groveatlantic.com. Estab. 1917. "Due to limited resources of time and staffing, Grove/Atlantic cannot accept manuscripts that do not come through a literary agent. In today's publishing world, agents are more important than ever, helping writers shape their work and navigate the main publishing houses to find the most appropriate outlet for a project." Publishes hardcover and trade paperback originals, and reprints. Book catalog available online.

IMPRINTS Black Cat, Atlantic Monthly Press, Grove Press.

HOW TO CONTACT Agented submissions only.

TERMS Pays 7½-12½% royalty. Makes outright purchase of $5-500,000. Responds in 1 month to queries; 2 months to proposals; 4 months to mss.

GRYPHON PUBLICATIONS

P.O. Box 209, Brooklyn, NY 11228. **Website:** www .gryphonbooks.com. **Contact:** Gary Lovisi, owner/publisher. "I publish very genre-oriented work (science fiction, crime, pulps) and nonfiction on these topics, authors, and artists. It's best to query with an idea first." Publishes trade paperback originals and reprints. Book catalog and ms guidelines for #10 SASE.

IMPRINTS Paperback Parade Magazine; Hardboiled Magazine; Gryphon Books; Gryphon Doubles.

NEEDS "We want cutting-edge fiction, under 3,000 words with impact."

TERMS Makes outright purchase by contract, price varies. Pays no advance. Responds in 1 month to queries.

TIPS "We are very particular about novels and book-length work. A first timer has a better chance with a short story or article. For anything over 4,000 words do not send manuscript, send only query letter with SASE. Always query **first** with an SASE."

ⓞⓞ GUERNICA EDITIONS

Box 117, Station P, Toronto, ON M5S 2S6 Canada. (416)576-9403. **Fax:** (416)981-7606. **E-mail:** mich aelmirolla@guernicaeditions.com. **Website:** www .guernicaeditions.com. **Contact:** Antonio D'Alfonso, editor/publisher (poetry, nonfiction, novels). Estab. 1978. Guernica Editions is a literary press that produces works of poetry, fiction, and nonfiction often by writers who are ignored by the mainstream. Publishes trade paperback originals and reprints. Book catalog available online.

NEEDS "We wish to open up into the fiction world and focus less on poetry. We specialize in European, especially Italian, translations."

HOW TO CONTACT Query with SASE. *All unsolicited mss returned unopened.*

TERMS Pays 8-10% royalty on retail price, or makes outright purchase of $200-5,000. Pays $200-2,000 advance. Responds in 1 month to queries. Responds in 6 months to proposals. Responds in 1 year to manuscripts

ⓞⓞⓞ HADLEY RILLE BOOKS

PO Box 25466, Overland Park, KS 66225. **E-mail:** subs@hadleyrillebooks.com. **Website:** www.hadley rillebooks.com. **Contact:** Eric T. Reynolds, editor/publisher. Estab. 2005.

ⓞ   Currently closed to submissions. Check website for future reading periods.

TIPS "We aim to produce books that are aligned with current interest in the genres. Anthology markets are somewhat rare in science fiction these days, we feel there aren't enough good anthologies being published each year and part of our goal is to present the best that we can. We like stories that fit well within the guidelines of the particular anthology for which we are soliciting manuscripts. Aside from that, we want stories with strong characters (not necessarily characters with strong personalities, flawed characters are welcome). We want a sense of wonder and awe. We want to feel the world around the character, so scene description is important (however, this doesn't always require a lot of text, just set the scene well so we don't wonder where the character is). We strongly recommend workshopping the story or having it critiqued in some way by readers familiar with the genre. We prefer clichés be kept to a bare minimum in the prose and avoid reworking old story lines."

HAMPTON ROADS PUBLISHING CO., INC.

665 Third Street, Suite 400, San Francisco, CA 94107. **E-mail:** submissions@hrpub.com; submissions@ redwheelweiser.com. **Website:** www.hrpub.com. **Contact:** Ms. Pat Bryce, Acquisitions Editor. Estab. 1989. 1125 Stoney Ridge Rd., Charlottesville, VA 22902. (434)296-2772. **Fax:** (434)296-5096. **E-mail:** editorial@hrpub.com. **Website:** www.hampton roadspub.com **Contact:** Frank Demarco, chief editor. Estab. 1989. "We work as a team to produce the best books we are capable of producing; those which will impact, uplift and contribute to positive change in the world. We publish what defies or doesn't quite fit the usual genres. We are noted for visionary fiction." Publishes and distributes hardcover and paperback originals on subjects including metaphysics, health, complementary medicine, visionary fiction, and other related topics. Average print order: 3,000-5,000. **Published 6 debut authors within the last year.** Averages 24-30 total titles, 4 fiction titles/year. Distributes titles through distributors. Promotes titles through advertising, representatives, author signings, and radio-TV interviews with authors. "Our reason for being is to impact, uplift, and contribute to positive change in the world. We publish books that will enrich and empower the evolving consciousness of mankind. Though we are not necessarily limited in scope, we are most interested in manuscripts on the following subjects: body/mind/spirit, health and heal-ing, self-help. Please be advised that at the moment we are not accepting: fiction or novelized material that does not pertain to body/mind/spirit, channeled writing." Guidelines available online.

"Please know that we only publish a handful of books every year, and that we pass on many well-written, important works, simply because we cannot publish them all. We review each and every proposal very carefully. However, due to the volume of inquiries, we cannot respond to them all individually. Please give us 30 days to review your proposal. If you do not hear back from us within that time, this means we have decided to pursue other book ideas that we feel fit better within our plan."

NEEDS Literary, new age/mystic, psychic/supernatural, spiritual, visionary fiction, past-life fiction, based on actual memories. "Fiction should have one or more of the following themes: spiritual, inspirational, metaphysical, i.e., past-life recall, out-of-body experiences, near death experience, paranormal." Published *Rogue Messiahs*, by Colin Wilson; *Spirit Matters*, by Michael Lerner; and *The Authenticator*, by William M. Valtos.

HOW TO CONTACT Accepts unsolicited mss. Submit outline, 2 sample chapter(s), synopsis. Accepts queries by e-mail, fax. Send SASE for return of ms or send a disposable ms and SASE for reply only. Agented fiction 5%. Responds in 2-4 months to queries; 6-12 months to mss. Accepts simultaneous submissions.

TERMS Pays royalty. Average advance: less than $10,000. Publishes ms 1 year after acceptance. Ms guidelines online. Pays royalty. Pays $1,000-50,000 advance.

HARCOURT, INC., TRADE DIVISION

Imprint of Houghton Mifflin Harcourt Book Group, 215 Park Ave. S., New York, NY 10003. **Website:** www .harcourtbooks.com. Publishes hardcover and trade paperback originals and trade paperback reprints. Book catalog for 9" × 12" envelope and first-class stamps. Guidelines available online.

HOW TO CONTACT Agented submissions only.

TERMS Pays 6-15% royalty on retail price. Pays $2,000 minimum advance.

HARK! NEW ERA PUBLISHING, LLC

Williamsburg, VA **E-mail:** staff@harknewerapub lishing.com. **Website:** www.harknewerapublishing .com. **Contact:** Jonathan Katora, editor/co-managing member; Amana Katora, editor/co-managing member. Estab. 2012. "We are targeting the growing eBook market. Our audience will be people who appreciate quality fiction." Publishes electronic originals. Catalog and guidelines available online at website.

○ *Accepts electronic submissions only.*

NEEDS "We are neither for, nor adverse to genre submissions of fiction. We look for quality fiction. Writers must be willing to work closely with our editors and staff. They must also be comfortable working with our virtual company and will be expected to navigate this medium."

HOW TO CONTACT Submit query, 20 sample pages, 1 page author biography. Do not send SASE.

TERMS Pays competitive royalties on retail sales. Responds to queries and mss in 1 month.

TIPS "Follow our submission guidelines on our website. Unsolicited submissions that do not follow our guidelines will not be considered. We are interested in writers who enjoy working with others."

⊘○ HARPERCOLLINS CANADA, LTD.

2 Bloor St. E., 20th Floor, Toronto, ON M4W 1A8 Canada. (416)975-9334. **Fax:** (416)975-5223. **Website:** www.harpercollins.ca. Estab. 1989. 2 Bloor St. East, 20th Floor, Toronto ON M4W 1A8 Canada. (416)975-9334. **Fax:** (416)975-5223. **Website:** www.harpercan ada.com. Harpercollins is not accepting unsolicited material at this time.

○ HarperCollins Canada is not accepting unsolicited material at this time.

IMPRINTS HarperCollinsPublishers; HarperPerennialCanada (trade paperbacks); HarperTrophyCanada (children's); Phyllis Bruce Books.

HARPERCOLLINS CHILDREN'S BOOKS/ HARPERCOLLINS PUBLISHERS

10 E. 53rd, New York, NY 10022. (212)207-6901. **E-mail:** Dana.fritts@Harpercollins.com; Kate.eng bring@Harpercollins.com. **Website:** www.harpercol lins.com. **Contact:** Kate Engbring, assistant designer; Dana Fritts, designer. HarperCollins, one of the largest English language publishers in the world, is a broad-based publisher with strengths in academic, business and professional, children's, educational, general interest, and religious and spiritual books, as well as multimedia titles. Publishes hardcover and paperback originals and paperback reprints. Catalog available online.

IMPRINTS HarperCollins Australia/New Zealand: Angus & Robertson, Fourth Estate, HarperBusiness, HarperCollins, HarperPerenniel, HarperReligious, HarperSports, Voyager; **HarperCollins Canada:** HarperFlamingoCanada, PerennialCanada; **HarperCollins Children's Books Group:** Amistad, Julie Andrews Collection, Avon, Joanna Cotler Books, Eos, Laura Geringer Books, Greenwillow Books, HarperAudio, HarperCollins Children's Books, HarperFestival, HarperTempest, HarperTrophy, Rayo, Katherine Tegen Books; **HarperCollins General Books Group:** Access, Amistad, Avon, Caedmon, Ecco, Eos, Fourth Estate, HarperAudio, HarperBusiness, HarperCollins, HarperEntertainment, HarperLargePrint, HarperResource, HarperSanFrancisco, HarperTorch, Harper Design International, Perennial, PerfectBound, Quill, Rayo, ReganBooks, William Morrow, William Morrow Cookbooks; **HarperCollins UK:** Collins Bartholomew, Collins, HarperCollins Crime & Thrillers, Collins Freedom to Teach, HarperCollins Children's Books, Thorsons/Element, Voyager Books; **Zondervan:** Inspirio, Vida, Zonderkidz, Zondervan.

NEEDS "We look for a strong story line and exceptional literary talent."

HOW TO CONTACT Agented submissions only. *All unsolicited mss returned.*

TERMS Negotiates a flat fee upon acceptance. Responds in 1 month, will contact if interested.

TIPS "We do not accept any unsolicited material."

⊘⊘ HARVEST HOUSE PUBLISHERS

990 Owen Loop N, Eugene, OR 97402. (541)343-0123. **Fax:** (541)302-0731. **Website:** www.harvesthousepub lishers.com. Estab. 1974. Publishes hardcover, trade paperback, and mass-market paperback originals and reprints.

NEEDS *No unsolicited mss, proposals, or artwork.*

HOW TO CONTACT Agented submissions only.

TERMS Pays royalty.

TIPS "For first-time/nonpublished authors we suggest building your literary résumé by submitting to magazines, or perhaps accruing book contributions."

HENDRICK-LONG PUBLISHING CO., INC.

10635 Tower Oaks, Suite D, Houston, TX 77070. (832)912-READ. **Fax:** (832)912-7353. **E-mail:** hen drick-long@att.net. **Website:** hendricklongpublish ing.com. **Contact:** Vilma Long. Estab. 1969. Only considers manuscripts with Texas theme. Publishes hardcover and trade paperback originals and hardcover reprints. Averages 4 total titles/year. "Hendrick-Long publishes historical fiction and nonfiction about Texas and the Southwest for children and young adults." Publishes hardcover and trade paperback originals and hardcover reprints Book catalog for 8½" × 11" or 9" × 12" SASE with 4 first-class stamps. Guidelines available online.

NEEDS Juvenile, young adult.

HOW TO CONTACT Submit outline, 2 sample chapter(s), synopsis. Responds in 3 months to queries. No simultaneous submissions. Please, no e-mail submissions. Query with SASE. Submit outline, clips, 2 sample chapters.

TERMS Pays royalty on selling price. Offers advance. Publishes ms 18 months after acceptance. Pays royalty on selling price. Pays advance.

○ ⊕ HIGHLAND PRESS PUBLISHING

P.O. Box 2292, High Springs, FL 32655. (386) 454-3927. **Fax:** (386) 454-3927. **E-mail:** The.Highland.Press@gmail.com; Submissions.hp@gmail.com. **Website:** www.highlandpress.org. **Contact:** Leanne Burroughs, CEO (fiction); she will forward all mss to appropriate editor. Estab. 2005. "With our focus on historical romances, Highland Press Publishing is known as your 'Passport to Romance.' We focus on historical romances and our award-winning anthologies. Many people have told us they can once again delight in reading with the anthologies, since they do not have to feel guilty about reading and then putting a book down before it is finished. With the short stories/novellas, they can read a heartwarming story, yet still get back to the demands of today's busy lives. As for our historicals, we publish historical novels like the ones many of us grew up with and loved. History is a big part of the story and is tactfully woven throughout the romance." Publishes paperback originals, paperback reprints. Format: offset printing; perfect-bound. Average print order: 1,000. Debut novel print order: 1,000. **Published 15 new writers last year.** Plans 25 debut authors this year. Averages 30 total titles/year; 30 fiction titles/year. Distributes/promotes titles through Ingrams, Baker & Taylor, Nielsen, Powells. We have recently opened our submissions up to all genres, with the exception of erotica. Our newest lines are inspirational, regency, and young adult. Paperback originals catalog and guidelines available online at website.

○ *Blue Moon Enchantment* won the 2007 P.E.A.R.L. Award (two separate stories). *Christmas Wishes* received the 2007 Linda Howard Award of Excellence. *Her Highland Rogue* received the 2006 Reviewer's International Award, the 2006 National Readers Choice Award. *Cat O'Nine Tales* had several stories as finalists or won the 2007 P.E.A.R.L. Award, 2007 Linda Howard Award of Excellence, and the 2007 Reviewers International Organization Award of Excellence. *Highland Wishes* was a Finalist, 2005 Readers and Booksellers Best and 2006 Winner, Reviewers International Award of Excellence. *Faery Special Romances* was a nominee for 2007 Night Owl Romances. *Blue Moon Enchantment* won the 2007 P.E.A.R.L. Award (two separate stories). *Christmas Wishes* had several stories nominated for the 2007 P.E.A.R.L. Award and received the 2007 Linda Howard Award of Excellence. *Her Highland Rogue* recieved the 2006 Reviewer's International Award, the 2006 National Readers Choice Award, and was a 2007 finalist for Readers and Booksellers Best. *Cat O'Nine Tales* had several stories as finalists or win the 2007 P.E.A.R.L. Award, 2007 Linda Howard Award of Excellence, and the 2007 Reviewers International Organization Award of Excellence.

NEEDS Children's/juvenile (adventure, animal, easy-to-read, fantasy, historical, mystery, preschool/picture book, series), comedy (romance/suspense), contemporary (romance/mystery/suspense); family saga, fantasy (space fantasy), historical, horror (dark fantasy, futuristic, supernatural), mainstream, military/war, mystery/suspense (amateur/sleuth, cozy, police, private eye/hard-boiled), religious (children's, general, family, inspirational, fantasy, mystery/suspense, thriller, romance), romance (contemporary, futuristic/time travel, gothic, historical, regency period, suspense), short story collections, thriller/espionage, western (frontier saga, traditional), young adult/teen (adventure, paranormal, fantasy/science fiction, historical, horror, mystery/suspense, romance, series, western, chapter books).

HOW TO CONTACT Send query letter. Query with outline/synopsis and sample chapters. Accepts queries by snail mail, e-mail. Include estimated word count, target market. Send disposable copy of ms and SASE for reply only. Agented fiction: 10%. Responds to queries in 8 weeks. Accepts unsolicited mss. Considers simultaneous submissions, e-mail submissions. Sometimes critiques/comments on rejected mss.

Responds to mss in 3-12 months. Send query letter. Query with outline/synopsis and sample chapters. Accepts queries by snail mail, e-mail. Include estimated word count, target market.

TERMS Sends preproduction galleys to author. Ms published within 12 months after acceptance. Writer's guidelines on website. Pays royalties 7½-8%. Book catalogs on website. Pays royalties 7½-8% Responds in 8 weeks to queries; responds in 3-12 months to mss

TIPS Special interests: Children's ms must come with illustrator. "We will always be looking for good historical manuscripts. In addition, we are actively seeking inspirational romances and Regency period romances." Numerous romance anthologies are planned. Topics and word count are posted on the website. Writers should query with their proposal. After the submission deadline has passed, editors select the stories. "I don't publish based on industry trends. We buy what we like and what we believe readers are looking for. However, often this proves to be the genres and time periods larger publishers are not currently interested in. Be professional at all times. Present your manuscript in the best possible light. Be sure you have run spell-checker and that the manuscript has been vetted by at least one critique partner, preferably more. Many times we receive manuscripts that have wonderful stories involved but would take far too much time to edit to make it marketable."

HIS WORK CHRISTIAN PUBLISHING

P.O. Box 563, Ward Cove, AK 99928. (206)274-8474. **Fax:** (614)388-0664. **E-mail:** hiswork@hisworkpub .com. **Website:** www.hisworkpub.com. **Contact:** Angela J. Perez, acquisitions editor. Estab. 2005. Publishes trade paperback and electronic originals and reprints; also, hardcover originals. Book catalog available online. "Guidelines available online and updated regularly. Please check these before submitting to see what we are looking for."

HOW TO CONTACT Submit query/proposal package, 3 sample chapters, clips.

TERMS Pays 10-20% royalty on wholesale price. Responds in 1-3 months to queries; 1-2 months to *requested* manuscripts.

TIPS "Audience is children and adults who are looking for the entertainment and relaxation you can only get from jumping into a good book. Submit only your best work to us. Submit only in the genres we are interested in publishing. Do not submit work that is not suitable for a Christian audience."

HOLIDAY HOUSE, INC.

425 Madison Ave., New York, NY 10017. (212)688-0085. **Fax:** (212)421-6134. **E-mail:** info@holiday house.com. **Website:** holidayhouse.com. **Contact:** Mary Cash, editor-in-chief. Estab. 1935. Publishes 35 picture books/year; 3 young readers/year; 15 middle readers/year; 8 young adult titles/year. 20% of books by first-time authors; 10% from agented writers. Mission Statement: "To publish high-quality books for children." "Holiday House publishes children's and young adult books for the school and library markets. We have a commitment to publishing first-time authors and illustrators. We specialize in quality hardcovers from picture books to young adult, both fiction and nonfiction, primarily for the school and library market." Publishes hardcover originals and paperback reprints. Guidelines for #10 SASE.

NEEDS All levels of young readers: adventure, contemporary, fantasy, folktales, ghost, historical, humor, literary, multicultural, school, suspense/mystery, sports. Recently published *Anansi's Party Time*, by Eric Kimmel, illustrated by Janet Stevens; *The Blossom Family* series, by Betsy Byars; *Washington at Valley Forge*, by Russell Freedman. Children's books only.

HOW TO CONTACT Send queries only to editor. Responds to queries in 3 months; mss in 4 months. "If we find your book idea suits our present needs, we will notify you by mail. Once a ms has been requested, the writers should send in the exclusive submission. Please send the entire manuscript, whether submitting a picture book or novel. All submissions should be directed to the Editorial Department, Holiday House, 425 Madison Ave., New York, NY 10017. Send your manuscript via U.S. Mail. We do not accept certified or registered mail. There is no need to include a SASE. We do not consider submissions by e-mail or fax. Please note that you do not have to supply illustrations. However, if you have illustrations you would like to include with your submission, you may send detailed sketches or photocopies of the original art. Do not send original art. Query with SASE. No phone calls, please."

TERMS Pays authors and illustrators an advance against royalties. Originals returned at job's completion. Book catalog, ms guidelines available for a SASE.

Pays royalty on list price, range varies. Agent's royalty. Responds in 4 months.

TIPS "We need manuscripts with strong stories and writing."

◐◑◓⑤ HOPEWELL PUBLICATIONS

P.O. Box 11, Titusville, NJ 08560. **Website:** www.hopepubs.com. **Contact:** E. Martin, publisher. Estab. 2002. "Hopewell Publications specializes in classic reprints—books with proven sales records that have gone out of print—and the occasional new title of interest. Our catalog spans from 1-60 years of publication history. We print fiction and nonfiction, and we accept agented and unagented materials. Books are only accepted after a formal e-mail query." Format publishes in hardcover, trade paperback, and electronic originals; trade paperback and electronic reprints. Catalog online at website. Guidelines online at website (e-mail query guidelines).

IMPRINTS Egress Books, Legacy Classics.

HOW TO CONTACT Query online using our online guidelines.

TERMS Pays royalty on retail price. Responds in 3 months to queries; 6 months to proposals; 9 months to mss.

HOUGHTON MIFFLIN HARCOURT BOOKS FOR CHILDREN

Imprint of Houghton Mifflin Trade & Reference Division, 222 Berkeley St., Boston, MA 02116. (617)351-5000. **Fax:** (617)351-1111. **E-mail:** children's_books@hmco.com. **Website:** www.houghtonmifflinbooks.com. **Contact:** Erica Zappy, associate editor; Kate O'Sullivan, senior editor; Anne Rider, executive editor; Margaret Raymo, editorial director. Houghton Mifflin Harcourt gives shape to ideas that educate, inform, and above all, delight. Query with SASE. Submit sample chapters, synopsis. Faxed or e-mailed manuscripts and proposals are not considered. Complete submission guidelines available on website. Publishes hardcover originals and trade paperback originals and reprints. Guidelines available online.

○ Does not respond to or return mss unless interested.

IMPRINTS Sandpiper Paperback Books; Graphia.

HOW TO CONTACT Submit complete ms.

TERMS Pays 5-10% royalty on retail price. Pays variable advance. Responds in 4-6 months to queries.

TIPS Faxed or e-mailed manuscripts and proposals are not considered. Complete submission guidelines available on website.

Ⓐ HOUGHTON MIFFLIN HARCOURT CO.

222 Berkeley St., Boston, MA 02116. (617)351-5000. **Website:** www.hmhco.com; www.hmhbooks.com. Estab. 1832. Publishes hardcover originals and trade paperback originals and reprints. **Published 5 debut authors within the last year.** Averages 250 total titles/year. Publishes hardcover originals and trade paperback originals and reprints.

○ "Houghton Mifflin Harcourt gives shape to ideas that educate, inform, and delight. In a new era of publishing, our legacy of quality thrives as we combine imagination with technology, bringing you new ways to know."

IMPRINTS American Heritage Dictionaries; Clarion Books; Great Source Education Group; Houghton Mifflin; Houghton Mifflin Books for Children; Houghton Mifflin Paperbacks; Mariner Books; McDougal Littell; Peterson Field Guides; Riverside Publishing; Sunburst Technology; Taylor's Gardening Guides; Edusoft; Promissor; Walter Lorraine Books; Kingfisher.

NEEDS Literary. "We are not a mass-market publisher. Study the current list." Published *Extremely Loud and Incredibly Close*, by Jonathan Safran Foer; *The Plot against America*, by Philip Roth; *Heir to the Glimmering World*, by Cynthia Ozick.

HOW TO CONTACT Does not accept unsolicited mss. *Agented submissions only.* Accepts simultaneous submissions.

TERMS Hardcover: pays 10-15% royalty on retail price, sliding scale, or flat rate based on sales; paperback: 7½% flat rate, but negotiable. Average advance: variable. Publishes ms 3 years after acceptance.

HQN BOOKS

Imprint of Harlequin, 233 Broadway, Suite 1001, New York, NY 10279. **Website:** e.harlequin.com; www.hqn.com. **Contact:** Tara Parsons, senior editor. Publishes hardcover, trade paperback, and mass-market paperback originals.

○ "HQN publishes romance in all subgenres—historical, contemporary, romantic suspense, paranormal—as long as the story's central focus is romance. Prospective authors can familiarize themselves with the wide range of books we publish by reading work by some of our current authors. These include Susan Andersen, Beth Ciotta, Nicola Cornick, Victoria Dahl, Susan Grant, Kristan Higgins, Susan Mallery, Kasey Michaels, Linda Lael Miller, Diana Palmer, Carly Phillips, Rosemary Rogers, Meryl Sawyer, Gena Showalter, Christina Skye, and Bertrice Small. The imprint is looking for a wide range of authors from known romance stars to first-time authors. At the moment, we are accepting only agented submissions. Unagented authors may send a query letter to determine if their project suits our needs. Please send your projects to our New York editorial office."

HOW TO CONTACT Accepts unagented material. Length: 90,000 words.

TERMS Pays royalty. Pays advance.

IDEALS CHILDREN'S BOOKS AND CANDYCANE PRESS

2630 Elm Hill Pike, Suite 100, Nashville, TN 37214. **Website:** www.idealsbooks.com. Estab. 1944.

NEEDS Picture books: animal, concept, history, religion. Board books: animal, history, nature/environment, religion. Average word length: picture books, 1,500; board books, 200.

☺ IDW PUBLISHING

5080 Santa Fe, San Diego, CA 92109. **E-mail:** letters@idwpublishing.com. **Website:** www.idwpublishing.com. Estab. 1999. IDW Publishing currently publishes a wide range of comic books and graphic novels including titles based on Angel, Doctor Who, GI Joe, Star Trek, Terminator: Salvation, and Transformers. Creator-driven titles include *Fallen Angel*, by Peter David and JK Woodward, *Locke & Key*, by Joe Hill and Gabriel Rodriguez, and a variety of titles by writer Steve Niles including *Wake the Dead, Epilogue*, and *Dead, She Said*. Publishes hardcover, mass-market, and trade paperback originals.

ILIUM PRESS

2407 S. Sonora Dr., Spokane, WA 99037. (509)928-7950. **E-mail:** contact@iliumpress.com; submissions@iliumpress.com. **Website:** www.iliumpress.com. **Contact:** John Lemon, owner/editor (literature, epic poetry, how-to). Estab. 2010. Publishes trade paperback originals and reprints, electronic originals and reprints. Guidelines available on website www.iliumpress.com.

NEEDS "See website for guidelines and preferred styles."

HOW TO CONTACT Query with SASE or submit proposal package with outline, first 20 pages, and SASE.

TERMS Pays 20-50% royalties on receipts. Responds in 6 months to queries/proposals/mss.

TIPS "Read submission guidelines and literary preferences on the website: www.iliumpress.com."

☺ IMAGE COMICS

2134 Allston Way, 2nd Floor, Berkeley, CA 94704. **E-mail:** submissions@imagecomics.com. **Website:** www.imagecomics.com. **Contact:** Eric Stephenson, publisher. Estab. 1992. "We are looking for good, well-told stories and exceptional artwork that run the gamut in terms of both style and genre. Image is a comics and graphic novels publisher formed by seven of Marvel Comics' best-selling artists: Erik Larsen, Jim Lee, Rob Liefeld, Todd McFarlane, Whilce Portacio, Marc Silvestri, and Jim Valentino. Since that time, Image has gone on to become the third-largest comics publisher in the U.S." Publishes comic books, graphic novels. See this company's website for detailed guidelines.

◑ Does not accept writing samples without art.

NEEDS "We are not looking for any specific genre or type of comic book. We are looking for comics that are well written and well drawn, by people who are dedicated and can meet deadlines."

HOW TO CONTACT Query with 1 page synopsis and 5 pages or more of samples. "We do not accept writing (that is plots, scripts, whatever) samples! If you're an established pro, we might be able to find somebody willing to work with you but it would be nearly impossible for us to read through every script that might find its way our direction. Do not send your script or your plot unaccompanied by art—it will be discarded, unread." Accepts queries by snail mail, e-mail. Sometimes critiques/comments on rejected mss.

TERMS Writer's guidelines on website.

IMAGES SI, INC

109 Woods of Arden Rd., Staten Island, NY 10312. (718)966-3964. **Fax:** (718)966-3695. **Website:** www.imagesco.com. Estab. 1990.

TERMS Pays 10-20% royalty on wholesale price.

◐ IMMEDIUM

P.O. Box 31846, San Francisco, CA 94131. (415)452-8546. **Fax:** (360)937-6272. **E-mail:** submissions@

immedium.com. **Website:** www.immedium.com. **Contact:** Amy Ma, acquisitions editor. Estab. 2005. "*Immedium* focuses on publishing eye-catching children's picture books, Asian-American topics, and contemporary arts, popular culture, and multicultural issues." Publishes hardcover and trade paperback originals. Catalog available online. Guidelines available online.

HOW TO CONTACT Submit complete ms.

TERMS Pays 5% royalty on wholesale price. Pays on publication. Responds in 1 month to queries; 2 months to proposals; 3 months to mss.

TIPS "Our audience is children and parents. Please visit our site."

◑ INGALLS PUBLISHING GROUP, INC

P.O. Box 2500, Banner Elk, NC 28604. (828)297-6884. **Fax:** (828)297-6880. **E-mail:** editor@ingallspublishinggroup.com; sales@ingallspublishinggroup.com. **Website:** www.ingallspublishinggroup.com. **Contact:** Rebecca Owen. Estab. 2001. Estab. 2001. "We are a small regional house focusing on popular fiction and memoir. At present, we are most interested in regional fiction, historical fiction, and mystery fiction." Publishes hardcover originals, paperback originals and paperback reprints. Exploring digital technologies for printing and e-books. Member IBPA, MWA, SIBA. "We are a small regional house focusing on popular fiction and memoir. At present, we are most interested in regional fiction, historical fiction, and mystery fiction." Exploring digital technologies for printing and e-books. Member IBPA, MWA, SIBA. Accepts unsolicited mss. Query first. Will specifically request if interested in reading synopsis and 3 sample chapters. Accepts queries by e-mail. Include estimated word count, brief bio, list of publishing credits. Agented fiction 10%. Accepts electronic submissions. No submissions on disk. Often comments on rejected mss. Publishes hardcover originals, paperback originals and paperback reprints. Guidelines available online.

NEEDS Regional (southeast U.S.), mystery (amateur sleuth, cozy, police procedural, private eye/hardboiled), regional (southern Appalachian), romance (contemporary, historical, romantic suspense adventure). Upcoming list for 2011 includes: *Corpus Conundrum: A Third Case from the Notebooks of Pliny the Younger*, by Albert A. Bell, Jr.; *The Chamomile*, by Susan F. Craft; *The Ninth Man*, by Brad Crowther;

One Shot Too Many, by Maggie Bishop; *The Ocean Forest*, by Troy Nooe; *Naked and Hungry*, by Ashley Memory and *Getorix: Games of the Underworld*, by Judith Geary.

HOW TO CONTACT Accepts unsolicited mss. Query first. Will specifically request if interested in reading synopsis and 3 sample chapters. Accepts queries by e-mail. Include estimated word count, brief bio, list of publishing credits. Agented fiction 10%. Responds in 6 weeks to queries or mss. Accepts simultaneous submissions, electronic submissions. No submissions on disk. Often comments on rejected mss. Query first.

TERMS Pays 10% royalty. Publishes ms 6 months-2 years after acceptance. Ms guidelines online. Pays 10% royalty. Responds in 6 weeks to queries or mss

⊕ INNOVATIVE PUBLISHERS INC.

44 Highland St., Boston, MA 02119. (617)963-0886. **Fax:** (617)861-8533. **E-mail:** pub@innovative-publishers.com. **Website:** www.innovative-publishers.com. Estab. 2000. Publishes hardcover, trade paperback, mass-market, and electronic originals; trade paperback and mass-market reprints. Book catalog for 9" × 12" SASE with 7 first-class stamps. Guidelines for #10 SASE.

NEEDS "Primarily seeking artists that are immersed in their topic. If you live, eat, and sleep your topic, it will show. Our focus is a wide demographic."

HOW TO CONTACT Query with SASE.

TERMS Pays 5-17% royalty on retail price. Offers $1,500-$125,000 advance. Responds in 3 months to queries; 4-6 months to mss and proposals.

◐ INSOMNIAC PRESS

520 Princess Ave., London, ON N6B 2B8 Canada. (416)504-6270. **E-mail:** mike@insomniacpress.com. **Website:** www.insomniacpress.com. **Contact:** Mike O'Connor, publisher. Estab. 1992. "Midsize independent publisher with a mandate to produce edgy experimental fiction." Publishes trade paperback originals and reprints, mass-market paperback originals, and electronic originals and reprints. First novel print order: 3,000. **Published 15 debut authors within the last year.** Plans 4 first novels this year. Averages 20 total titles, 5 fiction titles/year. We publish a mix of commercial (mysteries) and literary fiction. Published *Pray for Us Sinners*, by Patrick Taylor (novel). Agented fiction 5%. Responds in 1 week to queries; 2 months to mss. Accepts simultaneous submissions. Sometimes comments on rejected mss. Ms guidelines on-

line. Publishes trade paperback originals and reprints, mass-market paperback originals, and electronic originals and reprints. Guidelines available online

NEEDS Comic books, ethnic, experimental, gay/lesbian, humor, literary, mainstream/contemporary, multicultural, mystery, suspense. "We publish a mix of commercial (mysteries) and literary fiction."

HOW TO CONTACT Accepts unsolicited mss. Accepts queries by e-mail. Include estimated word count, brief bio, list of publishing credits. Send SASE for return of ms or send a disposable ms and SASE for reply only. Query via e-mail, submit proposal.

TERMS Pays 10-15% royalty on retail price. Average advance: $500-1,000. Publishes ms 6 months after acceptance. Pays 10-15% royalty on retail price. Pays $500-1,000 advance.

TIPS "We envision a mixed readership that appreciates up-and-coming literary fiction and poetry as well as solidly researched and provocative nonfiction. Peruse our website and familiarize yourself with what we've published in the past."

⊙ INTERLINK PUBLISHING GROUP, INC.

46 Crosby St., Northampton, MA 01060. (413)582-7054. **Fax:** (413)582-7057. **E-mail:** info@interlinkbooks.com; editor@interlinkbooks.com. **Website:** www.interlinkbooks.com. **Contact:** Michel Moushabeck, publisher; Pam Thompson, editor. Estab. 1987. "Midsize independent publisher specializing in world travel, world literature, world history, and politics." Publishes hardcover and trade paperback originals. Books: 55 lb. Warren Sebago Cream white paper; web offset printing; perfect-bound. Average print order: 5,000. Published new writers within the last year. Averages 50 total titles, 2-4 fiction titles/year. Distributes titles through Baker & Taylor. Promotes titles through book mailings to extensive, specialized lists of editors and reviews; authors read at bookstores and special events across the country. Interlink is a independent publisher of a general trade list of adult fiction and nonfiction with an emphasis on books that have a wide appeal while also meeting high intellectual and literary standards. Publishes hardcover and trade paperback originals Book catalog and guidelines available free online

IMPRINTS Crocodile Books, USA; Codagan Guides, USA; Interlink Books; Olive Branch Press; Clockroot Books.

NEEDS Ethnic, international. "We are looking for translated works relating to the Middle East, Africa, or Latin America." Recently published *Everything Good Will Come*, by Sefi Atta (first novel); *The Gardens of Light*, by Amin Maalouf (novel translated from French); *War in the Land of Egypt*, by Yusef Al-Qaid (novel translated from Arabic). No science fiction, romance, plays, erotica, fantasy, horror."

HOW TO CONTACT "Become familiar with the kinds of books we publish. Request a catalog or read them at your local library, If you believe your ms might fit our list, please send a query letter to the attention of Pam Thompson. The query letter may (but doesn't have to) include any of the following: a writing sample (preferably the opening of the book) of no more than 10 pages, a brief synopsis and bio. Send an SASE as well. The only fiction we publish falls into our 'Interlink WorldFiction' series. Most of these books, as you can see in our catalog, are translated fiction from around the world. The idea behind the series is to bring fiction from other countries to a North American audience. So unless you were born outside the United States, your novel will not fit into the series. All of our children's books are picture books designed for ages 3-8. We publish very few of them, and most are co-published with overseas publishing houses. We do not consider unsolicited manuscripts of children's books." Query with SASE and a brief sample. Responds in 3 months to queries. Accepts simultaneous submissions. No electronic submissions. Interlink Publishing Group, Inc., 46 Crosby St., Northampton MA 01060. Query with SASE. Submit outline, sample chapters.

TERMS Pays 6-8% royalty on retail price. Average advance: small. Publishes ms 18 months after acceptance. Ms guidelines online. Pays 6-8% royalty on retail price. Pays small advance. Responds in 3-6 months to queries

TIPS "Any submissions that fit well in our publishing program will receive careful attention. A visit to our website, your local bookstore, or library to look at some of our books before you send in your submission is recommended."

⊙ INVERTED-A

P.O. Box 267, Licking, MO 65542. **E-mail:** amnfn@well.com. **Contact:** Aya Katz, chief editor (poetry, novels, political); Nets Katz, science editor (scientific, academic). Estab. 1985. Books: offset printing. Average print order: POD. Distributes through Baker & Taylor, Amazon, Bowker. Publishes paperback originals. Guidelines for SASE.

HOW TO CONTACT Does not accept unsolicited mss. Query with SASE. Reading period open from January 2 to March 15. Accepts queries by e-mail. Include estimated word count.

TERMS Pays 10 author's copies. Responds in 1 month to queries; 3 months to mss.

TIPS "Read our books. Read the *Inverted-A Horn*. We are different. We do not follow industry trends."

◐ ITALICA PRESS

595 Main St., Suite 605, New York, NY 10044-0047. (917)371-0563. **E-mail:** inquiries@italicapress.com. **Website:** www.italicapress.com. **Contact:** Ronald G. Musto and Eileen Gardiner, publishers. Estab. 1985. Small, independent publisher of Italian fiction in translation. "First-time translators published. We would like to see translations of Italian writers who are well-known in Italy who are not yet translated for an American audience." Publishes trade paperback originals. Books: 50-60 lb. natural paper; offset printing; illustrations. Average print order: 1,500. Averages 6 total titles, 2 fiction titles/year. Distributes/promotes titles through website. "Italica Press publishes English translations of modern Italian fiction and medieval and Renaissance nonfiction." Publishes trade paperback originals. Book catalog and guidelines available online.

NEEDS Translations of 20th-century Italian fiction. Published *Game Plan for a Novel*, by Gianna Manzini; *The Great Bear*, by Ginevra Bompianai; *Sparrow*, by Giovanni Verga.

HOW TO CONTACT Accepts unsolicited mss. Query with SASE. Accepts queries by e-mail, fax. Responds in 1 month to queries; responds in 4 months to msss. Accepts simultaneous submissions, electronic submissions, submissions on disk. **Mail:** Italica Press, 595 Main Street, Suite 605, New York, NY 10044, **Fax:** 212-838-7812. **E-mail:** inquiries@italicapress.com. Query with SASE.

TERMS Pays 7-15% royalty on wholesale price. Pays author's copies. Publishes ms 1 year after acceptance. Ms guidelines online.

TIPS "We are interested in considering a wide variety of medieval and Renaissance topics (not historical fiction). For modern works we are only interested in translations from Italian fiction by well-known Ital-

ian authors." *Only* fiction that has been previously published in Italian. A *brief* call saves a lot of postage. 90% of proposals we receive are completely off base—but we are very interested in things that are right on target. Please send return postage if you want your ms returned.

JEWISH LIGHTS PUBLISHING

LongHill Partners, Inc., Sunset Farm Offices, Rt. 4, P.O. Box 237, Woodstock, VT 05091. (802)457-4000. **Fax:** (802)457-4004. **E-mail:** editorial@jewishlights.com; sales@jewishlights.com. **Website:** www.jewishlights.com. **Contact:** Tim Holtz, art acquisitions. Estab. 1990. "Jewish Lights publishes books for people of all faiths and all backgrounds who yearn for books that attract, engage, educate, and spiritually inspire. Our authors are at the forefront of spiritual thought and deal with the quest for the self and for meaning in life by drawing on the Jewish wisdom tradition. Our books cover topics including history, spirituality, life cycle, children, self-help, recovery, theology and philosophy. We do not publish autobiography, biography, fiction, Haggadah, poetry, or cookbooks. At this point we plan to do only two books for children annually, and one will be for younger children (ages 4-10)." Fiction/nonfiction: Query with outline/synopsis and 2 sample chapters; submit complete ms for picture books. Include SASE. Responds to queries/mss in 4 months. Publishes hardcover and trade paperback originals, trade paperback reprints. Book catalog and ms guidelines online.

NEEDS Picture books, young readers, middle readers: spirituality. "We are not interested in anything other than spirituality." Recently published *God's Paintbrush*, by Sandy Eisenberg Sasso, illustrated by Annette Compton (ages 4-9).

TERMS Pays authors royalty of 10% of revenue received; 15% royalty for subsequent printings. Responds in 3 months to queries.

TIPS "We publish books for all faiths and backgrounds that also reflect the Jewish wisdom tradition. Explain in your cover letter why you're submitting your project to us in particular. Make sure you know what we publish."

JOURNEYFORTH

Imprint of BJU Press, 1700 Wade Hampton Blvd., Greenville, SC 29614. (864)242-5100, ext. 4350. **Fax:** (864)298-0268. **E-mail:** jb@bju.edu. **Website:** www.journeyforth.com. **Contact:** Nancy Lohr. Estab. 1974.

"Small independent publisher of excellent, trustworthy novels for readers preschool through high school. We desire to develop in our children a love for and understanding of the written word, ultimately helping them love and understand God's word." Publishes paperback originals. Average print order varies. Published some debut authors within the last year. Averages 20-24 total titles/year. Distributes titles through Genesis/Spring Arbor and Appalachian. "Small independent publisher of trustworthy novels and biographies for readers preschool through high school from a conservative Christian perspective, Christian living books, and Bible studies for adults." Publishes paperback originals. Book catalog available free guidelines available online at www.bjupress.com/books/freelance.php.

NEEDS Adventure (children's/juvenile, young adult), historical (children's/juvenile, young adult), juvenile (animal, easy-to-read, series), mystery (children's/juvenile, young adult), sports (children's/juvenile, young adult), suspense (young adult), western (young adult), young adult (series). "Our fiction is all based on a moral and Christian worldview." Published *Susannah and the Secret Coins*, by Elaine Schulte (historical children's fiction); *Arby Jenkins Meets His Match*, by Sharon Hambrick (contemporary children's fiction); *Over the Divide*, by Catherine Farnes (young adult fiction); *Beyond the Smoke*, by Terry Burns (young adult western); *What about Cimmaron?* by Laurain Snelling (youth fiction). "Our fiction is all based on a moral and Christian worldview." Does not want short stories.

HOW TO CONTACT Accepts unsolicited mss. Query with SASE or submit outline or synopsis and 5 sample chapters, or complete ms. Include estimated word count, brief bio, list of publishing credits. Send SASE for return of ms or send a disposable ms and SASE for reply only. Responds 3 months to mss.

TERMS Pays royalty. Publishes ms 12-18 months after acceptance. Ms guidelines online. Guidelines at www.bjupress.com/books/freelance.php. Pays royalty. Responds in 1 month to queries. Responds in 3 months to manuscripts

TIPS "Study the publisher's guidelines. No picture books and no submissions by e-mail."

JUPITER GARDENS PRESS

Jupiter Gardens, LLC, PO Box 191, Grimes, IA 50111. **E-mail:** submissions@jupitergardens.com. **Website:** www.jupitergardens.com. **Contact:** Mary Wilson, publisher (romance, sci-fi, fantasy, new age). Estab. 2007. Format publishes in trade paperback originals and reprints; electronic originals and reprints. Catalog available online at website. Guidelines available online at website.

IMPRINTS Pink Petal Books, Mary Wilson, publisher; Jupiter Storm, Sasha Vivelo, senior editor.

NEEDS "We only publish romance (all sub-genres), science fiction, fantasy, and metaphysical fiction. Our science fiction and fantasy covers a wide variety of topics, such as feminist fantasy, or more hard science fiction and fantasy, which looks at the human condition. Our young adult imprint, Jupiter Storm, with thought-provoking reads that explore the full range of speculative fiction, includes science fiction or fantasy and metaphysical fiction. These readers enjoy edgy contemporary works. Our romance readers love seeing a couple, no matter the gender, overcome obstacles and grow in order to find true love. Like our readers, we believe that love can come in many forms."

HOW TO CONTACT "To submit your work for consideration, please e-mail submissions@jupitergardens.com with a cover letter detailing your writing experience (if any, we do welcome new authors), and attach in .doc or .rtf format, a 2-4 page synopsis, and the first 3 chapters."

TERMS Pays 40% royalty on retail price. Responds in 1 months on proposals, 2 months on mss.

TIPS "No matter which line you're submitting to, know your genre and your readership. We publish a diverse catalog, and we're passionate about our main focus. We want romance that takes your breath away and leaves you with that warm feeling that love does conquer all. Our science fiction takes place in wild and alien worlds, and our fantasy transports readers to mythical realms and finds strange worlds within our own. And our metaphysical nonfiction will help readers gain new skills and awareness for the coming age. We want authors who engage with their readers and who aren't afraid to use social media to connect. Read and follow our submission guidelines."

KAEDEN BOOKS

P.O. Box 16190, Rocky River, OH 44116. **Website:** www.kaeden.com. **Contact:** Lisa Stenger, editor. Estab. 1986. "Children's book publisher for education K-3 market: reading stories, fiction/nonfiction, chapter books, science, and social studies materials." Publishes paperback originals. Book catalog and guide-lines available online.

NEEDS "We are looking for stories with humor, surprise endings, and interesting characters that will appeal to children in kindergarten through third grade. No sentence fragments. Please do not submit: queries, manuscript summaries, or résumés, manuscripts that stereotype or demean individuals or groups, manuscripts that present violence as acceptable behavior."

HOW TO CONTACT Submit complete ms. "Can be as minimal as 25 words for the earliest reader or as much as 2,000 words for the fluent reader. Beginning chapter books are welcome. Our readers are in kindergarten to third grade, so vocabulary and sentence structure must be appropriate for young readers. Make sure that all language used in the story is of an appropriate level for the students to read independently. Sentences should be complete and grammatically correct."

TERMS Work purchased outright from authors. Pays royalties to previous authors. Responds only if interested.

TIPS "We are an educational publisher. We are particularly interested in humorous stories with surprise endings and beginning chapter books."

KAMEHAMEHA PUBLISHING

567 S. King St., Honolulu, HI 96813. **Website:** www .KamehamehaPublishing.org. Estab. 1933. "Kamehameha Schools Press publishes in the areas of Hawaiian history, Hawaiian culture, Hawaiian language, and Hawaiian studies." Call or write for book catalog.

NEEDS Young reader, middle readers, young adults: biography, history, multicultural, Hawaiian folklore.

TERMS Work purchased outright from authors or by royalty agreement. Responds in 3 months to queries and mss.

TIPS "Writers and illustrators must be knowledgeable in Hawaiian history/culture and be able to show credentials to validate their proficiency. Greatly prefer to work with writers/illustrators available in the Honolulu area."

🅐🅒🅞🅢 KANE/MILLER BOOK PUBLISHERS

Kane/Miller: A Division of EDC Publishing, 4901 Morena Blvd., Suite 213, San Diego, CA 92117. (858)456-0540. **Fax:** (858)456-9641. **E-mail:** info@ kanemiller.com. **E-mail:** submissions@kanemiller .com. **Website:** www.kanemiller.com. **Contact:** Kira Lynn, editorial department. Estab. 1985. "Kane/Miller Book Publishers is a division of EDC Publishing, specializing in award-winning children's books from around the world. Our books bring the children of the world closer to each other, sharing stories and ideas, while exploring cultural differences and similarities. Although we continue to look for books from other countries, we are now actively seeking works that convey cultures and communities within the U.S. We are looking for picture book fiction and nonfiction on those subjects that may be defined as particularly American: sports such as baseball, historical events, American biographies, American folktales, etc. We are committed to expanding our early and middle-grade fiction list. We're interested in great stories with engaging characters in all genres (mystery, fantasy, adventure, historical, etc.) and, as with picture books, especially those with particularly American subjects. All submissions sent via USPS should be sent to: Editorial Department. Please do not send anything requiring a signature. Work submitted for consideration may also be sent via e-mail. Please send either the complete picture book ms, the published book (with a summary and outline in English, if that is not the language of origin), or a synopsis of the work and two sample chapters. Do not send originals. Illustrators may send color copies, tear sheets, or other non-returnable illustration samples. If you have a website with additional samples of your work, please include the web address. Please do not send original artwork or samples on CD. A SASE must be included if you send your submission via USPS; otherwise you will not receive a reply. If we wish to follow up, we will notify you."

🗩 "We like to think that a child reading a Kane/Miller book will see parallels between his own life and what might be the unfamiliar setting and characters of the story. And that by seeing how a character who is somehow or in some way dissimilar—an outsider—finds a way to fit comfortably into a culture or community or situation while maintaining a healthy sense of self and self-dignity, she might be empowered to do the same."

NEEDS Picture Books: concept, contemporary, health, humor, multicultural. Young Readers: contemporary, multicultural, suspense. Middle Readers: contemporary, humor, multicultural, suspense.

TERMS Responds in 90 days

🜂 KAR-BEN PUBLISHING

Lerner Publishing Group, 1251 Washington Ave. N., Minneapolis, MN 55401. (612)332-3344, ext. 229. **Fax:** 612-332-7615. **E-mail:** Editorial@Karben.com. **Website:** www.karben.com. Estab. 1974. Publishes hardcover, trade paperback, and electronic originals. Book catalog available online; free upon request. Guidelines available online.

NEEDS "We seek picture book mss of about 1,000 words on Jewish-themed topics for children." Picture books: Adventure, concept, folktales, history, humor, multicultural, religion, special needs; must be on a Jewish theme. Average word length: picture books—1,000. Recently published *Engineer Ari and the Rosh Hashanah Ride*, by Deborah Bodin Cohen, illustrated by Shahar Kober; and *The Wedding That Saved a Town*, by Yale Strom, illustrated by Jenya Prosmitsky.

HOW TO CONTACT Submit full ms. Picture books only.

TERMS Pays 3-5% royalty on NET price. Pays $500-2,500 advance. Responds in 6 weeks.

TIPS "Authors: Do a literature search to make sure a similar title doesn't already exist. Illustrators: Look at our online catalog for a sense of what we like—bright colors and lively composition."

🜂 🜃 KELLY POINT PUBLISHING LLC

Martin Sisters Publishing LLC, P.O. Box 1154, Barbourville, KY 40906. **E-mail:** publisher@kellypoint publishing.com. **E-mail:** submissions@kellypoint publishing.com. **Website:** www.kellypointpublish ing.com. **Contact:** Melissa Newman, publisher. Estab. 2012. Subsidiary of Martin Sisters Publishing, LLC. Publishes trade paperback, mass-market, and electronic originals. Book catalog available online at website. Guidelines available online at website or by e-mail at submissions e-mail address.

🜄 *All unsolicited mss returned unopened.*

IMPRINTS Kelly Point Books, KP Mystery, KP Romance.

NEEDS "Please visit our website and read the submissions guidelines for aspiring authors before submitting your query."

HOW TO CONTACT Query with SASE.

TERMS Pays 7.5% royalty on retail price. Responds in 1 month to queries; 2 months to proposals; 4 months to mss.

TIPS "Write a good query letter with a hook and follow the submissions guidelines on our website."

🜂 KIDS CAN PRESS

25 Dockside Dr., Toronto, ON M5A 0B5 Canada. (416)479-7000. **Fax:** (416)960-5437. **E-mail:** info@ kidscan.com; kkalmar@kidscan.com. **Website:** www .kidscanpress.com. **Contact:** Corus Quay, acquisitions. Estab. 1973.

🜄 *Kids Can Press is currently accepting unsolicited mss from Canadian adult authors only.*

NEEDS Picture books, young readers: concepts. We do not accept young adult fiction or fantasy novels for any age. Adventure, animal, contemporary, folktales, history, humor, multicultural, nature/environment, special needs, sports, suspense/mystery. Average word length: picture books 1,000-2,000; young readers 750-1,500; middle readers 10,000-15,000; young adults over 15,000. Recently published *Rosie & Buttercup* by Chieri Ugaki, illustrated by Shephane Jorisch (picture book); *The Landing* by John Ibbitson (novel); *Scaredy Squirrel* by Melanie Watt, illustrated by Melanie Watt (picture book).

HOW TO CONTACT Submit outline/synopsis and 2-3 sample chapters. For picture books submit complete ms.

TERMS Responds in 6 months only if interested.

🜂 🜃 ALFRED A. KNOPF

1745 Broadway, 21st Floor, New York, NY 10019. **Website:** knopf.knopfdoubleday.com. Estab. 1915. Publishes hardcover and paperback originals.

NEEDS Publishes book-length fiction of literary merit by known or unknown writers. Length: 40,000-150,000 words. Published *Gertrude and Claudius*, by John Updike; *The Emperor of Ocean Park*, by Stephen Carter; *Balzac and the Little Chinese Seamstress*, by Dai Sijie.

HOW TO CONTACT *Agented submissions only.* Query with SASE or submit sample chapter(s).

TERMS Royalties vary. Offers advance. Responds in 2-6 months to queries.

KNOPF PUBLISHING GROUP

Imprint of Random House, 1745 Broadway, New York, NY 10019. (212)751-2600. **Website:** www.ran domhouse.com/knopf. **Contact:** Senior Editor. Estab. 1915. Division of Random House, Inc. "Throughout history, Knopf has been dedicated to publishing distinguished fiction and nonfiction." Publishes hardcover and paperback originals. "We usually only accept work through an agent, but you may still send a query to our slush pile." Publishes hardcover and paperback originals.

⊙ Knopf is a general publisher of quality nonfiction and fiction. "We usually only accept work through an agent, but you may still send a query to our slush pile.

IMPRINTS Alfred A. Knopf; Everyman's Library; Pantheon Books; Schocken Books; Vintage Anchor Publishing (Vintage Books, Anchor Books).

NEEDS Publishes book-length fiction of literary merit by known or unknown writers. Length: 40,000-150,000 words.

HOW TO CONTACT Submit query, 25-page sample, SASE.

KNOX ROBINSON PUBLISHING

244 Fifth Ave., Suite 1861, New York, NY 10001. **E-mail:** sales@knoxrobinsonpublishing.com. **Website:** www.knoxrobinsonpublishing.com. **Contact:** Dana Celeste Robinson, managing director (historical fiction, historical romance, fantasy). Estab. 2010. Knox Robinson Publishing is an international, independent, specialist publisher of historical fiction, historical romance, and fantasy. Guidelines free on request.

⊙ "KRP publishes historical fiction and historical romance; any story set in an era prior to 1960 is acceptable. We also publish medieval fantasy. We do not publish science fiction. We do not publish fantasy with children and/or animal protagonists. We do not publish novels that involve any aspects of time travel. We welcome the submission of a well-written, detailed synopsis and the first 3 chapters of completed mss directly from authors."

NEEDS "We are seeking historical fiction featuring obscure historical figures."

HOW TO CONTACT Submit first 3 chapters and author questionnaire found on website.

TERMS Pays royalty. Responds in 2 months to submissions of first 3 chapters. "We do not accept proposals."

KREGEL PUBLICATIONS

Kregel, Inc., P.O. Box 2607, Grand Rapids, MI 49501. (616)451-4775. **Fax:** (616)451-9330. **E-mail:** kregel books@kregel.com. **Website:** www.kregelpublica tions.com. **Contact:** Dennis R. Hillman, publisher. Estab. 1949. "Our mission as an evangelical Christian publisher is to provide—with integrity and excellence—trusted, Biblically based resources that challenge and encourage individuals in their Christian lives. Works in theology and Biblical studies should reflect the historic, orthodox Protestant tradition." Publishes hardcover and trade paperback originals and reprints. Guidelines available online.

IMPRINTS Editorial Portavoz (Spanish-language works); Kregel Academic & Professional; Kregel Kidzone.

NEEDS Fiction should be geared toward the evangelical Christian market. Wants books with fast-paced, contemporary story lines presenting a strong Christian message in an engaging, entertaining style.

TERMS Pays royalty on wholesale price. Pays negotiable advance.

TIPS "Our audience consists of conservative, evangelical Christians, including pastors and ministry students."

WENDY LAMB BOOKS

Imprint of Random House Children's Books/Random House, Inc., 1745 Broadway, New York, NY 10019. (212)782-9000. **Fax:** (212)782-9452. **E-mail:** wlamb@randomhouse.com; cmeckler@random house.com. **Website:** www.randomhouse.com. Estab. 2001. "Query letter with SASE for reply. A query letter should briefly describe the book you have written, the intended age group, and your brief biography and publishing credits, if any. Please send the first 10 pages (or to the end of the chapter) of your manuscript. Our turn around time is approximately 4-8 weeks." Publishes hardcover originals. Guidelines for #10 SASE.

⊙ Literary fiction and nonfiction for readers 8-15.

NEEDS Recently published *When You Reach Me*, by Rebecca Stead; *Love, Aubrey*, by Suzanne LaFleur; *Eyes of the Emperor*, by Graham Salisbury; *A Brief Chapter in My Impossible Life*, by Dana Reinhardt; *What They Found: Love on 145th Street*, by Walter Dean Myers; *Eleven*, by Patricia Reilly Giff. Other WLB authors include Christopher Paul Curtis, Gary Paulsen, Donna Jo Napoli, Peter Dickinson, Marthe Jocelyn, Graham McNamee.

TERMS Pays royalty.

TIPS "Please note that we do not publish picture books. Please send the first 10 pages of your ms (or until the end of the first chapter) along with a cover letter, synopsis, and SASE. Before you submit, please take a look at some of our recent titles to get an idea of what we publish."

Ⓐ⊘ LAUREL-LEAF

Imprint of Random House Children's Books/Random House, Inc., 1745 Broadway, New York, NY 10019. (212)782-9000. **Website:** www.randomhouse.com/teens.

💬   Quality reprint paperback imprint for young adult paperback books. *Does not accept unsolicited mss.*

⊕ LEDGE HILL PUBLISHING

P.O. Box 337, Alton, NH 03809. **E-mail:** info@ledgehillpublishing.com. **Website:** www.ledgehillpublishing.com. **Contact:** Amanda Eason. Estab. 2011. Publishes hardcover, trade paperback, and mass-market paperback originals. Book catalog available online at website. Guidelines free on request by e-mail or online at website.

HOW TO CONTACT Submit proposal package, including syopsis and 4 sample chapters or submit complete ms.

TERMS Pays 2-15% royalty. Responds in 1 month to queries and proposals; 2 months to mss.

Ⓓ LEE & LOW BOOKS

95 Madison Ave., #1205, New York, NY 10016. (212)779-4400. **E-mail:** general@leeandlow.com. **Website:** www.leeandlow.com. **Contact:** Louise May, editor-in-chief (multicultural children's fiction/nonfiction). Estab. 1991. "Our goals are to meet a growing need for books that address children of color and to present literature that all children can identify with. We only consider multicultural children's books. Currently emphasizing material for 5-12 year olds. Sponsors a yearly New Voices Award for first-time picture book authors of color. Contest rules online at website or for SASE." Publishes hardcover originals and trade paperback reprints. Book catalog available online. Guidelines available online or by written request with SASE.

NEEDS Picture books, young readers: anthology, contemporary, history, multicultural, poetry. Picture book, middle reader: contemporary, history, multicultural, nature/environment, poetry, sports. Average word length: picture books—1,000-1,500 words. Recently published *Gracias~Thanks*, by Pat Mora; *Balarama*, by Ted and Betsy Lewin; *Yasmin's Hammer*, by Ann Malaspina; *Only One Year*, by Andrea Cheng (chapter book). "We do not publish folklore or animal stories."

HOW TO CONTACT Submit complete ms.

TERMS Pays net royalty. Pays authors advances against royalty. Pays illustrators advance against royalty. Photographers paid advance against royalty. Responds in 6 months to mss if interested.

TIPS "Check our website to see the kinds of books we publish. Do not send mss that don't fit our mission."

⊕ LES FIGUES PRESS

P.O. Box 7736, Los Angeles, CA 90007. **E-mail:** info@lesfigues.com. **Website:** www.lesfigues.com. **Contact:** Teresa Carmody and Vanessa Place, co-directors. Les Figues Press is an independent, nonprofit publisher of poetry, prose, visual art,conceptual writing, and translation. With a mission to create aesthetic conversations between readers, writers, and artists, Les-Figues Press favors projects which push the boundaries of genre, form, and general acceptability. Submissions are only reviewed through its annual NOS Book Contest.

⊘ LETHE PRESS

118 Heritage Ave., Maple Shade, NJ 08052. (609)410-7391. **E-mail:** editor@lethepressbooks.com. **Website:** www.lethepressbooks.com. **Contact:** Steve Berman, publisher. Estab. 2001. "Named after the Greek river of memory and forgetfulness (and pronounced Lee-Thee), Lethe Press is a small press devoted to ideas that are often neglected or forgotten by mainstream, profit-oriented publishers." Distributes/promotes titles. Lethe Books are distributed by Ingram Publications and Bookazine, and are available at all major bookstores, as well as the major online retailers.

NEEDS *Rarely accepts unsolicited mss.* Primarily interested in gay fiction, poetry, and nonfiction titles. Has imprint for gay spirituality titles. Also releases work of occult and supernatural, sci-fi, and east asian interests.

HOW TO CONTACT Send query letter. Accepts queries by e-mail.

Ⓓ⊙ ARTHUR A. LEVINE BOOKS

Scholastic, Inc., 557 Broadway, New York, NY 10012. (212)343-4436. **Fax:** (212)343-6143. **E-mail:** arthuralevinebooks@scholastic.com. **Website:** www.arthuralevinebooks.com. **Contact:** Arthur A. Levine, VP/publisher; Cheryl Klein, executive editor; Emily Clement, assistant editor. Estab. 1996. Imprint of Scholastic, Inc. Publishes hardcover, paperback, and e-book editions.

NEEDS "Arthur A. Levine is looking for distinctive literature, for children and young adults, for whatever's extraordinary." Averages 18-20 total titles/year.

TERMS Responds in 1 month to queries; 5 months to mss.

⬤ LILLENAS PUBLISHING CO.

Imprint of Lillenas Drama Resources, P.O. Box 419527, Kansas City, MO 64109. (816)931-1900. **Fax:** (816)412-8390. **E-mail:** drama@lillenas.com. **Website:** www.lillenasdrama.com. "We purchase only original, previously unpublished materials. Also, we require that all scripts be performed at least once before they are submitted for consideration. We do not accept scripts that are sent via fax or e-mail. Direct all manuscripts to the Drama Resources Editor." Publishes mass-market paperback and electronic originals. See guidelines online at website.

NEEDS "Looking for sketch and monologue collections for all ages: adults, children and youth. For these collections, we request 12-15 scripts to be submitted at one time. Unique treatments of spiritual themes, relevant issues, and biblical messages are of interest. Contemporary full-length and one-act plays that have conflict, characterization, and a spiritual context that is neither a sermon nor an apologetic for youth and adults. We also need wholesome so-called secular full-length scripts for dinner theaters and schools." No musicals.

TERMS Pays royalty on net price. Makes outright purchase. Responds in 4-6 months to material.

TIPS "We never receive too many manuscripts."

➕ R.C. LINNELL PUBLISHING

2100 Tyler Ln., Louisville, KY 40205. **E-mail:** info@LinnellPublishing.com. **Website:** www.linnellpublishing.com. **Contact:** Cheri Powell, owner. Estab. 2010. "We are currently very small and have published a limited number of books. If a book is well-written and has an audience, we will consider it." Publishes print on demand paperbacks. Book catalog and guidelines available online at website.

HOW TO CONTACT Submit complete ms.

TERMS Pays 10-40% royalty on retail price. Responds in 1 month to mss.

TIPS "Visit our website to understand the business model and the relationship with authors. All sales are through the Internet. Author should have a marketing plan in mind. We can help expand the plan but we do not market books. Author should be comfortable with using the Internet and should know their intended readers. We offer translation services for English to Spanish and Spanish to English. We are especially interested in books that inspire, motivate, amuse, and challenge readers."

LIQUID SILVER BOOKS

10509 Sedgegrass Dr., Indianapolis, IN 46235. **E-mail:** tracey@liquidsilverbooks.com. **Website:** www.liquidsilverbooks.com. **Contact:** Tracey West, acquisitions editor; Terri Schaefer, editorial director. Estab. 1999. Liquid Silver Books is an imprint of Atlantic Bridge Publishing, a royalty paying, full-service ePublisher. Atlantic Bridge has been in business since June 1999. Liquid Silver Books is dedicated to bringing high-quality erotic romance to our readers.

IMPRINTS Liquid Silver Books, Romance's Silver Lining.

⬤ "We are foremost an e-publisher. We believe the market will continue to grow for e-books. It is our prime focus. At this time our print publishing is on hiatus. We will update the submission guidelines if we reinstate this aspect of our publishing."

NEEDS Needs contemporary, gay and lesbian, paranormal, supernatural, sci-fi, fantasy, historical, suspense, and western romances. We do not accept literary erotica submissions.

HOW TO CONTACT E-mail entire ms as an attachment in .rtf format in Arial 12pt. "Include in the body of the email: author bio, your thoughts on e-publishing, a blurb of your book, including title and series title if applicable. Ms must include pen name, real name, snail mail, and e-mail contact information on the first page, top left corner." More writer's guidelines available online at website.

TERMS Responds to mss in 4-6 weeks.

Ⓐ LITTLE, BROWN AND CO. ADULT TRADE BOOKS

237 Park Ave., New York, NY 10017. **E-mail:** publicity@littlebrown.com. **Website:** www.hachettebookgroup.com. **Contact:** Michael Pietsch, publisher. Estab. 1837. "The general editorial philosophy for all divisions continues to be broad and flexible, with high quality and the promise of commercial success always the first considerations." Publishes hardcover originals and paperback originals and reprints. Guidelines available online.

NEEDS Literary, mainstream/contemporary. Published *Cross Country*, by James Patterson; *Outliers*, by Malcolm Gladwell; *The Historian*, by Elizabeth Kostova; *When You Are Engulfed in Flames*, by David Sedaris.

HOW TO CONTACT *Agented submissions only.*

TERMS Pays royalty. Offer advance.

⊕ LITTLE, BROWN AND CO. BOOKS FOR YOUNG READERS

Hachette Book Group USA, 237 Park Ave., New York, NY 10017. (212)364-1100. **Fax:** (212)364-0925. **E-mail:** pamela.gruber@hbgusa.com. **Website:** www.lb-kids.com; www.lb-teens.com. Estab. 1837. "Little, Brown and Co. Children's Publishing publishes all formats including board books, picture books, middle-grade fiction, and nonfiction YA titles. We are looking for strong writing and presentation, but no predetermined topics." *Only interested in solicited agented material.* Fiction: Submit complete ms. Nonfiction: Submit cover letter, previous publications, a proposal, outline, and 3 sample chapters. Do not send originals.

NEEDS Picture books: humor, adventure, animal, contemporary, history, multicultural, folktales. Young adults: contemporary, humor, multicultural, suspense/mystery, chick lit. Multicultural needs include "any material by, for, and about minorities." Average word length: picture books, 1,000; young readers, 6,000; middle readers, 15,000-50,000; young adults, 50,000 and up.

HOW TO CONTACT *Agented submissions only.*

TERMS Pays authors royalties based on retail price. Pays illustrators and photographers by the project or royalty based on retail price. Sends galleys to authors; dummies to illustrators. Pays negotiable advance. Responds in 1 month to queries; 2 months to proposals and mss.

TIPS "In order to break into the field, authors and illustrators should research their competition and try to come up with something outstandingly different."

⊘ LIVINGSTON PRESS

University of West Alabama, Station 22, Livingston, AL 35470. **E-mail:** jwt@uwa.edu. **Website:** www.livingstonpress.uwa.edu. **Contact:** Joe Taylor, director. Estab. 1974. "Small university press specializing in offbeat and/or Southern literature." Publishes hardcover and trade paperback originals. Books: acid-free; offset; some illustrations. Average print order: 2,500.

First novel print order: 2,500. Plans 5 first novels this year. Averages 10 fiction titles/year. "Like all literary presses, Livingston Press looks for authorial excellence in style. Currently emphasizing novels. Except for Tartts Contest, we read in June only." Our standing policy is to read over-the-transom, open submission, ONLY in June of every year. When we are reading over-the-transom, we accept only fiction—either story collections or novels. Publishes hardcover and trade paperback originals Book catalog for SASE. Guidelines available online.

IMPRINTS Swallow's Tale Press.

NEEDS Experimental, literary, short story collections, offbeat or Southern. "We are interested in form and, of course style." Published *The Gin Girl*, by River Jordan (novel); *Pulpwood*, by Scott Ely (stories); *Live Cargo*, by Paul Toutonghi (stories). We are especially interested in novels and story collections that intertwine in one way or another.

HOW TO CONTACT Query with SASE. Include estimated word count, brief bio, list of publishing credits. Send SASE for return of ms or send a disposable ms and SASE for reply only. Responds in 1 month to queries; 1 year to mss. Accepts simultaneous submissions.

TERMS Pays 10% of 1,500 print run, 150 copies; thereafter pays a mix of royalties and books. Publishes ms 18 months after acceptance. Book catalog for SASE. Ms guidelines online. Pays 150 contributor's copies, after sales of 1,500, standard royalty. Responds in 1 month to queries. Responds in 6 months-1 year to manuscripts.

TIPS "Our readers are interested in literature, often quirky literature that emphasizes form and style. Please visit our website for current needs."

⑤ LOOSE ID

P.O. Box 425690, San Francisco, CA 94142-5960. **E-mail:** submissions@loose-id.com. **Website:** www.loose-id.com. **Contact:** Treva Harte, editor-in-chief. Estab. 2004. "*Loose Id* is love unleashed. We're taking romance to the edge." Publishes e-books and some print books. Distributes/promotes titles. "The company promotes itself through web and print advertising wherever readers of erotic romance may be found, creating a recognizable brand identity as the place to let your id run free and the people who unleash your fantasies. It is currently pursuing licensing agreements for foreign translations and has a print program of 2-5 titles/month." Guidelines available online at website.

"Loose Id is actively acquiring stories from both aspiring and established authors."

NEEDS Wants nontraditional erotic romance stories, including gay, lesbian, heroes and heroines, multi-culturalism, cross-genre, fantasy, and science fiction, straight contemporary or historical romances.

HOW TO CONTACT Query with outline/synopsis and three sample chapters. Accepts queries by e-mail. Include estimated word count, list of publishing credits, and why your submission is "Love Unleashed." "Before submitting a query or proposal, please read the guidelines on our website. Please don't hesitate to contact us at submissions@loose-id.com for any information you don't see there."

TERMS Pays e-book royalties of 35%. Responds to queries in 1 month.

LOST HORSE PRESS

105 Lost Horse Lane, Sandpoint, ID 83864. (208)255-4410. **E-mail:** losthorsepress@mindspring.com. **Website:** www.losthorsepress.org. **Contact:** Christine Holbert, publisher; Carolyne Wright, editor; Christi Kramer, editor. Estab. 1998. Distributed by University of Washington Press. Publishes hardcover and paperback originals.

"Does not accept unsolicited mss. However, we welcome submissions for the *Idaho Prize for Poetry*, a national competition offering $1,000 prize money plus publication for a book-length manuscript. Please check the submission guidelines for the *Idaho Prize for Poetry* online."

LUCKY MARBLE BOOKS

PageSpring Publishing, P.O. Box 21133, Columbus, OH 43221 **E-mail:** yaeditor@pagespringpublishing.com. **Website:** www.luckymarblebooks.com. Estab. 2012. "Lucky Marble Books publishes novel-length young adult and middle-grade fiction. We are looking for engaging characters and well-crafted plots that keep our readers turning the page. We accept e-mail queries only; see our website for details." Publishes trade paperback and electronic originals. Guidelines available on website.

IMPRINTS Imprint of PageSpring Publishing

HOW TO CONTACT Submit proposal package via e-mail. Include synopsis and 3 sample chapters.

TERMS Pays royalty. Responds in 1 month to queries and mss.

TIPS "We love books that jump right into the story and sweep us along!"

MAGINATION PRESS

750 First St. NE, Washington, DC 20002. (202)336-5618. **Fax:** (202)336-5624. **E-mail:** rteeter@apa.org. **Website:** www.apa.org. **Contact:** Kristine Enderle, managing editor. Estab. 1988. Magination Press is an imprint of the American Psychological Association. "We publish books dealing with the psycho/therapeutic resolution of children's problems and psychological issues with a strong self-help component." Submit complete ms. Materials returned only with SASE.

NEEDS All levels: psychological and social issues, self-help, health, parenting concerns and, special needs. Picture books, middle school readers. Recently published *Nobody's Perfect: A Story for Children about Perfection*, by Ellen Flanagan Burns, illustrated by Erica Peltron Villnave (ages 8-12); *Murphey's Three Homes: A Story for Children in Foster Care*, by Jan Levinson Gilman, illustrated by Kathy O'Malley (ages 4-8).

TERMS Responds to queries in 1-2 months; mss in 2-6 months.

MANDALA PUBLISHING

Mandala Publishing and Earth Aware Editions, 10 Paul Dr., San Rafael, CA 94903. **E-mail:** info@mandalapublishing.com. **Website:** www.mandalapublishing.com. Estab. 1989. "In the traditions of the East, wisdom, truth, and beauty go hand in hand. This is reflected in the great arts, music, yoga, and philosophy of India. Mandala Publishing strives to bring to its readers authentic and accessible renderings of thousands of years of wisdom and philosophy from this unique culture-timeless treasures that are our inspirations and guides. At Mandala, we believe that the arts, health, ecology, and spirituality of the great Vedic traditions are as relevant today as they were in sacred India thousands of years ago. As a distinguished publisher in the world of Vedic literature, lifestyle, and interests today, Mandala strives to provide accessible and meaningful works for the modern reader." Publishes hardcover, trade paperback, and electronic originals. Book catalog available online.

HOW TO CONTACT Query with SASE.

TERMS Pays 3-15% royalty on retail price. Responds in 6 months to queries, proposals, and mss.

MARTIN SISTERS PUBLISHING, LLC

P.O. Box 1749, Barbourville, KY 40906-1499. **E-mail:** submissions@martinsisterspublishing.com. **Website:** www.martinsisterspublishing.com. **Contact:** Denise Melton, publisher/editor (fiction/nonfiction); Melissa Newman, publisher/editor (fiction/nonfiction). Estab. 2011. Firm/imprint publishes trade and mass-market paperback originals; electronic originals. Catalog and guidelines available online.

IMPRINTS Ivy House Books (literary/mainstream fiction); rainshower books (Christian fiction and nonfiction); Skyvine Books (science fiction/fantasy/paranormal romance); Martin Sisters Books (nonfiction/short story collections/coffee table books/cookbooks); Barefoot Books (young adult). Query Ms. Newman or Ms. Melton for all imprints listed at submissions@martinsisterspublishing.com.

NEEDS Adventure, confession, fantasy, historical, humor, juvenile, literary, mainstream, military, mystery, poetry in translation, regional, religious, romance, science fiction, short story collections, spiritual, sports, suspense, war, western, young adult.

HOW TO CONTACT Send query letter only to submissions@martinsisterspublishing.com; publisher@martinsisterspublishing.com.

TERMS Pays 7.5% royalty/max on retail price. No advance offered. Time between acceptance of ms and publication is 6 months. Accepts simultaneous submissions. No SASE returns. Responds in 1 month on queries, 2 months on proposals, 3-6 months on mss. Catalog and guidelines available online. Pays 7.5% royalty/max on retail price. No advance offered.

MAVERICK MUSICALS AND PLAYS

89 Bergann Rd., Maleny QLD 4552 Australia. **Fax:** (61)(7)5494-4007. **E-mail:** helen@mavmuse.com. **Website:** www.mavmuse.com. Estab. 1978. Guidelines available online.

NEEDS "Looking for two-act musicals and one- and two-act plays. See website for more details."

MCBOOKS PRESS

ID Booth Building, 520 N. Meadow St., Ithaca, NY 14850. (607)272-2114. **Fax:** (607)273-6068. **E-mail:** mcbooks@mcbooks.com. **Website:** www.mcbooks.com. **Contact:** Alexander G. Skutt, publisher. Estab. 1979. Publishes trade paperback and hardcover originals and reprints guidelines available online.

"Currently not accepting submissions or queries for fiction or nonfiction."

NEEDS Publishes Julian Stockwin, John Biggins, Colin Sargent, and Douglas W. Jacobson. Distributes titles through Independent Publishers Group.

TIPS "We are currently only publishing authors with whom we have a preexisting relationship. If this policy changes, we will announce the change on our website."

THE MCDONALD & WOODWARD PUBLISHING CO.

431 E. College St., Granville, OH 43023. (740)321-1140. **Fax:** (740)321-1141. **E-mail:** mwpubco@mwpubco.com. **Website:** www.mwpubco.com. **Contact:** Jerry N. McDonald, publisher. Estab. 1986. McDonald & Woodward publishes books in natural history, cultural history, and natural resources. Currently emphasizing travel, natural and cultural history, and natural resource conservation. Publishes hardcover and trade paperback originals. Book catalog available online. Guidelines free on request; by e-mail.

HOW TO CONTACT Query with SASE.

TERMS Pays 10% royalty. Responds in less than 1 month to queries, proposals, and mss.

TIPS Our books are meant for the curious and educated elements of the general population.

MARGARET K. MCELDERRY BOOKS

Imprint of Simon & Schuster Children's Publishing Division, Simon & Schuster, 1230 Sixth Ave., New York, NY 10020. (212)698-7200. **Website:** www.simonsayskids.com. **Contact:** Justin Chanda, vice president; Karen Wojtyla, editorial director; Gretchen Hirsch, associate editor; Emily Fabre, assistant editor. Ann Bobco, executive art director. Estab. 1971. "Margaret K. McElderry Books publishes hardcover and paperback trade books for children from preschool age through young adult. This list includes picture books, middle-grade and teen fiction, poetry, and fantasy. The style and subject matter of the books we publish is almost unlimited. We do not publish textbooks, coloring and activity books, greeting cards, magazines, pamphlets, or religious publications." Guidelines for #10 SASE.

NEEDS We will consider any category. Results depend on the quality of the imagination, the artwork, and the writing. Average word length: picture books, 500; young readers, 2,000; middle readers, 10,000-20,000; young adults, 45,000-50,000. Recently Published: *Monster Mess*, by Margery Cuyler, illustrated by S. D. Schindler (picture book); *The Joy of Spooking: Fiendish Deeds*, by P. J. Bracegirdle (MGF); *Identical*, by Ellen Hopkins (teen); *Where Is Home, Little Pip?*, by Karma Wilson; illustrated by Jane Chapman (picture book); *Dr. Ted*, by Andrea Beaty, illustrated by Pascal LeMaitre (picture book); *To Be Mona*, by Kelly Easton (teen). *No unsolicited mss.*

HOW TO CONTACT Send query letter with SASE.

TERMS Pays authors royalty based on retail price. Pays illustrator royalty by the project. Pays photographers by the project. Original artwork returned at job's completion. Offers $5,000-8,000 advance for new authors.

TIPS "Read! The children's book field is competitive. See what's been done and what's out there before submitting. We look for high quality: an originality of ideas, clarity, and felicity of expression, a well-organized plot, and strong character-driven stories. We're looking for strong, original fiction, especially mysteries and middle-grade humor. We are always interested in picture books for the youngest age reader. Study our titles."

MC PRESS

3695 W. Quail Heights Ct., Boise, ID 83703. **Fax:** (208)639-1231. **E-mail:** duptmor@mcpressonline .com. **Website:** www.mcpressonline.com. **Contact:** David Uptmor, publisher. Estab. 2001. Publishes trade paperback originals. Book catalog and ms guidelines free.

IMPRINTS MC Press, IBM Press.

TERMS Pays 10-16% royalty on wholesale price. Responds in 1 month to queries/proposals/mss.

MEDALLION MEDIA GROUP

100 S. River St., Aurora, IL 60506. (630)513-8316. **E-mail:** emily@medallionpress.com; submissions@ medallionpress.com. **Website:** http://medallionme diagroup.com. **Contact:** Emily Steele, editorial director. Estab. 2003. "We are an independent, innovative publisher looking for compelling, memorable stories told in distinctive voices." Online submission form: http://medallionmediagroup.com/submissions. Publishes trade paperback, hardcover, e-book originals, book apps, and TREEbook™. Guidelines available online at website.

NEEDS Minimum word count: 60,000. (40,000 for YA). No short stories, anthologies, erotica.

HOW TO CONTACT Submit first 3 consecutive chapters and a synopsis through our online submission form, http://medallionmediagroup.com/submissions.

TERMS Offers advance. Responds in 2-3 months to mss.

TIPS "We are not affected by trends. We are simply looking for well-crafted, original, compelling works of fiction and nonfiction. Please visit our website at http://medallionmediagroup.com/submissions/ for the most current guidelines prior to submitting anything to us."

MERIWETHER PUBLISHING LTD.

885 Elkton Dr., Colorado Springs, CO 80907. (719)594-9916. **Fax:** (719)594-4422. **E-mail:** editor@ meriwether.com. **Website:** www.meriwether.com. **Contact:** Ted Zapel; Rhonda Wray. Estab. 1969. "Our niche is drama. Our books cover a wide variety of theater subjects from play anthologies to theater craft. We publish books of monologues, duologues, one-act plays, scenes for students, acting textbooks, how-to speech and theater textbooks, improvization and theater games. We also publish anthologies of Christian sketches. We do not publish works of fiction or devotionals."

NEEDS Middle readers, young adults: anthology, contemporary, humor, religion. "We publish plays, not prose fiction. Our emphasis is comedy plays instead of educational themes."

TERMS Pays authors royalty of 10% based on retail or wholesale price. Responds to queries in 3 weeks, mss in 2 months or less.

TIPS "We are currently interested in finding unique treatments for theater arts subjects: scene books, how-to books, musical comedy scripts, monologues and short comedy plays for teens."

MERRIAM PRESS

133 Elm St., Suite 3R, Bennington, VT 05201. (802)447-0313. **E-mail:** ray@merriam-press.com. **Website:** www.merriam-press.com. Estab. 1988. "Merriam Press specializes in military history—particularly World War II history. We are also branching out into other genres." Publishes hardcover and softcover trade paperback originals and reprints Book catalog available for $5 or visit website to view all available titles and access writer's guidelines and info.

NEEDS Especially but not limited to military, war, World War II.

HOW TO CONTACT Query with SASE or by e-mail first.

TERMS Pays 10% royalty on actual selling price. Responds quickly (e-mail preferred) to queries.

TIPS "Our military history books are geared for military historians, collectors, model kit builders, war gamers, veterans, general enthusiasts. We now publish some historical fiction and poetry, and will consider well-written books on a variety of non-military topics."

MESSIANIC JEWISH PUBLISHERS

6120 Day Long Lane, Clarksville, MD 21029. (410)531-6644. **E-mail:** website@messianicjewish.net. **Website:** www.messianicjewish.net. **Contact:** Janet Chaier, managing editor. Publishes hardcover and trade paperback originals and reprints. Guidelines available via e-mail.

IMPRINTS Lederer Books.

NEEDS "We publish very little fiction. Jewish or Biblical themes are a must. Text must demonstrate keen awareness of Jewish culture and thought."

HOW TO CONTACT Query with SASE. Unsolicited mss are not return.

TERMS Pays 7-15% royalty on wholesale price.

MILKWEED EDITIONS

1011 Washington Ave. S., Suite 300, Minneapolis, MN 55415. (612)332-3192. **Fax:** (612)215-2550. **E-mail:** submissions@milkweed.org. **Website:** www.milkweed.org. Estab. 1979. "Milkweed Editions publishes with the intention of making a humane impact on society, in the belief that literature is a transformative art uniquely able to convey the essential experiences of the human heart and spirit. To that end, Milkweed Editions publishes distinctive voices of literary merit in handsomely designed, visually dynamic books, exploring the ethical, cultural, and esthetic issues that free societies need continually to address." Publishes hardcover, trade paperback, and electronic originals; trade paperback and electronic reprints. Book catalog available online. Guidelines available online.

NEEDS Novels for adults and for readers 8-13. High literary quality. For adult readers: literary fiction, nonfiction, poetry, essays. Middle readers: adventure, contemporary, fantasy, multicultural, nature/environment, suspense/mystery. Does not want to see folktales, health, hi-lo, picture books, poetry, religion, romance, sports. Average length: middle readers—90-200 pages. Recently published *Perfect*, by Natasha Friend (contemporary); *The Linden Tree*, by Ellie Mathews (contemporary); *The Cat*, by Jutta Richter (contemporary/translation). No romance, mysteries, science fiction.

HOW TO CONTACT Query with SASE, submit completed ms.

TERMS Pays authors variable royalty based on retail price. Offers advance against royalties. Pays varied advance from $500-10,000. Responds in 6 months to queries, proposals, and mss.

TIPS "We are looking for excellent writing with the intent of making a humane impact on society. Please read submission guidelines before submitting and acquaint yourself with our books in terms of style and quality before submitting. Many factors influence our selection process, so don't get discouraged. Nonfiction is focused on literary writing about the natural world, including living well in urban environments."

MILKWEED FOR YOUNG READERS

Milkweed Editions, Open Book Building, 1011 Washington Ave. S., Suite 300, Minneapolis, MN 55415. (612)332-3192. **Fax:** (612)215-2550. **E-mail:** submissions@milkweed.org. **Website:** www.milkweed.org. Estab. 1984. "We are looking first of all for high-quality literary writing. We publish books with the intention of making a humane impact on society." Publishes hardcover and trade paperback originals. Book catalog for $1.50. Guidelines for #10 SASE or on the website.

HOW TO CONTACT Query with SASE. "Milkweed Editions now accepts manuscripts online through our submission manager. If you're a first-time submitter, you'll need to fill in a simple form and then follow the instructions for selecting and uploading your manuscript. Please make sure that your manuscript follows the submission guidelines."

TERMS Pays 7% royalty on retail price. Pays variable advance. Responds in 6 months to queries.

MONDIAL

203 W. 107th St., Suite 6C, New York, NY 10025. (212)851-3252. **Fax:** (208)361-2863. **E-mail:** contact@mondialbooks.com. **Website:** www.mondialbooks.com; www.librejo.com. **Contact:** Andrew Moore, editor. Estab. 1996. Publishes trade paperback originals and reprints. Guidelines available online.

HOW TO CONTACT Query through online submission form.

TERMS Pays 10% royalty on wholesale price. Responds to queries in 3 months.

MOODY PUBLISHERS

Moody Bible Institute, 820 N. LaSalle Blvd., Chicago, IL 60610. (800)678-8812. **Fax:** (312)329-4157. **E-mail:**

authors@moody.edu. **Website:** www.moodypublish ers.org. Estab. 1894. "The mission of Moody Publishers is to educate and edify the Christian and to evangelize the non-Christian by ethically publishing conservative, evangelical Christian literature, and other media for all ages around the world, and to help provide resources for Moody Bible Institute in its training of future Christian leaders." Publishes hardcover, trade, and mass-market paperback originals. Book catalog for 9" × 12" envelope and 4 first-class stamps. Guidelines for SASE and on website.

IMPRINTS Northfield Publishing; Lift Every Voice (African-American interest).

HOW TO CONTACT Submit query letter, bio, one-page description of book, word count, table of contents, two chapters fully written, marketing information and SASE. "Mss should be neatly typed, double-spaced, on white letter-size typing paper. Grammar, style, and punctuation should follow normal English usage. We use The Chicago Manual of Style (University of Chicago Press) for fine points."

TERMS Royalty varies. Responds in 2-3 months to queries.

TIPS "In our fiction list, we're looking for Christian storytellers rather than teachers trying to present a message. Your motivation should be to delight the reader. Using your skills to create beautiful works is glorifying to God."

MY GREEN PUBLISHER LLC

P.O. Box 702, Richland, MT 49083. **E-mail:** mygreen publisher@gmail.com. **Website:** www.mygreenpub lisher.com. **Contact:** Fiona Thomas, editor-in-chief. Estab. 2011. Publishes trade paperback and electronic originals. Book catalog available online. Guidelines availble online or by e-mail.

HOW TO CONTACT Submit complete ms.

TERMS Pays 15% royalty on wholesale price (paperback); 20% royalty on wholesale price (e-book). Responds in 3 days to queries; 1 month to proposals and mss.

NBM PUBLISHING

160 Broadway, Suite 700, East Bldg., New York, NY 10038. **E-mail:** nbmgn@nbmpub.com. **Website:** nbm pub.com. **Contact:** Terry Nantier, editor/art director. Estab. 1976. "One of the best-regarded quality graphic novel publishers. Our catalog is determined by what will appeal to a wide audience of readers." Publishes hardcover originals, paperback originals. Format: offset printing; perfect-bound. Average print order: 3,000-4,000; average debut writer's print order: 2,000. Publishes 1-2 debut writers/year. Publishes 30 titles/year. Member: PMA, CBC. Distributed/promoted by IPG. Imprints: ComicsLit (literary comics), Eurotica (erotic comics). Publishes graphic novels for an audience of adults. Types of books include fiction, mystery, and social parodies.

NEEDS Literary fiction mostly, children's/juvenile (especially fairy tales, classics), creative nonfiction (especially true crime), erotica, ethnic/multicultural, humor (satire), manga, mystery/suspense, translations, young adult/teen. Does not want superhero or overly violent comics.

HOW TO CONTACT Prefers submissions from writer-artists, creative teams. Send a 1-page synopsis of story along with a few pages of comics (copies, NOT originals) and a SASE. Attends San Diego Comicon. Agented submissions: 2%. Responds to queries in 1 week; to ms/art packages in 3-4 weeks. Sometimes comments on rejected manuscripts.

TERMS Royalties and advance negotiable. Publishes ms 6 months to 1 year after acceptance. Writer's guidelines on website. Artist's guidelines on website. Book catalog free upon request.

NEW AFRICA BOOKS

New Africa Books (Pty) Ltd, P.O. Box 46962, Glosderry 7702 South Africa. (27)(21)467-5860. **Fax:** (27)(21)467-5895. **E-mail:** info@newafricabooks.co.za. **Website:** www.newafricabooks.co.za. **Contact:** David Philip, publisher. "New Africa Books strives to be the leading African publisher—the world's definitive gateway to African content and information."

TERMS Pays royalty.

NEW ISSUES POETRY & PROSE

Western Michigan University, 1903 W. Michigan Ave., Kalamazoo, MI 49008-5463. (269)387-8185. **Fax:** (269)387-2562. **E-mail:** new-issues@wmich.edu. **Website:** wmich.edu/newissues. **Contact:** Managing Editor. Estab. 1996. Publishes hardcover originals and trade paperback originals. Averages 8 titles/year. Has recently published *Vivisect*, by Lisa Lewis; *Pima Road Notebook*, by Keith Ekiss; and *Tocqueville*, by Khaled Mattawa. Guidelines available online, by e-mail, or by SASE.

NEEDS Literary, poetry, translations.

HOW TO CONTACT Query first. All unsolicited mss returned unopened. 50% of books published are by first time authors. Agented submissions: less than 5%. Responds to mss in 6 months.

TERMS Manuscript published 18 months after acceptance. Accepts simultaneous submissions. Writer's guidelines by SASE, e-mail, or online.

NEW LIBRI PRESS

4230 95th Ave. SE, Mercer Island, WA 98040. **E-mail:** query@newlibri.com. **Website:** http://www.newlibri.com. **Contact:** Michael Muller, editor (nonfiction and foreign writers); Stanislav Fritz (literary). Estab. 2011. Publishes hardcover, trade paperback, mass-market paperback, electronic original, electronic reprints. Catalog not available yet.

NEEDS "Open to most ideas right now; this will change as we mature as a press." As a new press, we are more open than most and time will probably shape the direction. That said, trite as it is, we want good writing that is fun to read. While we currently are not looking for some subgenres, if it is well written and a bit off the beaten path, submit to us. We are e-book friendly, which means some fiction may be less likely to currently sell (e.g. picture books would work only on an iPad or Color Nook as of this writing)."

HOW TO CONTACT Submit proposal package, including synopsis. Prefers complete ms.

TERMS Pays 20-35% royalty on wholesale price. No advance. Responds in 1 month to ms. No proposals; only complete mss.

TIPS "Our audience is someone who is comfortable reading an e-book, or someone who is tired of the recycled authors of mainstream publishing but still wants a good, relatively fast, reading experience. The industry is changing, while we accept the traditional model, we are searching for writers who are interested in sharing the risk and controlling their own destiny. We embrace writers with no agent."

NEW VICTORIA PUBLISHERS

2455 W. Warner Ave., Chicago, IL 60613. (773)793-2244. **E-mail:** newvictoriapub@att.net. **Website:** www.newvictoria.com. **Contact:** Patricia Feuerhaken, president. Estab. 1976. "Publishes mostly lesbian fiction—strong female protagonists. Most well known for Stoner McTavish mystery series." Distributes titles through Amazon Books, Bella books, Bulldog Books (Sydney, Australia), and Women and Children First Books (Chicago). Promotes titles "mostly through lesbian feminist media." Publishes trade paperback originals. Catalog free on request; for #10 SASE; or online at website. Guidelines free on request; for #10 SASE; or online.

Mommy Deadest, by Jean Marcy, won the Lambda Literary Award for Mystery.

NEEDS Lesbian, feminist fiction including adventure, erotica, fantasy, historical, humor, mystery (amateur sleuth), or science fiction.

HOW TO CONTACT Accepts unsolicited mss, but prefers query first. Submit outline, synopsis, and sample chapters (50 pages). No queries by e-mail or fax; please send SASE or IRC. No simultaneous submissions.

TERMS Pays 10% royalty.

TIPS "We are especially interested in lesbian or feminist novels, ideally with a character or characters who can evolve through a series of books. Stories should involve a complex plot, accurate details, and protagonists with full emotional lives. Pay attention to plot and character development. Read guidelines carefully. We advise you to look through our catalog or visit our website to see our past editorial decisions as well as what we are currently marketing. Our books average 80-100,000 words, or 200-220 single-spaced pages."

NORTH ATLANTIC BOOKS

2526 MLK Jr. Way, Berkeley, CA 94704. **Website:** www.northatlanticbooks.com. **Contact:** Douglas Reil, associate publisher; Erin Wiegand, senior acquisitions editor. Estab. 1974. Publishes hardcover, trade paperback, and electronic originals; trade paperback and electronic reprints. Book catalog free on request (if available). Guidelines online.

IMPRINTS Evolver Editions, Blue Snake Books.

NEEDS "We only publish fiction on rare occasions."

HOW TO CONTACT Submit proposal package including an outline, 3-4 sample chapters, and "a 75-word statement about the book, your qualifications as an author, marketing plan/audience, for the book, and comparable titles."

TERMS Pays royalty percentage on wholesale price. Responds in 3-6 months to queries, proposals, mss.

NORTIA PRESS

Mission Viejo, CA **E-mail:** acquisitions@nortiapress.com. **Website:** www.NortiaPress.com. Estab. 2009. Publishes trade paperback and electronic originals.

NEEDS "We focus mainly on nonfiction as well as literary and historical fiction, but are open to other genres. No vampire stories, science fiction, or erotica, please."

HOW TO CONTACT "Submit a brief e-mail query. Please include a short bio, approximate word count of book, and expected date of completion (fiction titles should be completed before sending a query and should contain a sample chapter in the body of the e-mail). All unsolicited snail mail or attachments will be discarded without review.

TERMS Pays negotiable royalties on wholesale price. Responds in 1 month to queries and proposals.

TIPS "We specialize in working with experienced authors who seek a more collaborative and fulfilling relationship with their publisher. As such, we are less likely to accept pitches form first-time authors, no matter how good the idea. As with any pitch, please make your e-mail very brief and to the point, so the reader is not forced to skim it. Always include some biographic information. Your life is interesting."

W.W. NORTON & COMPANY, INC.

500 Fifth Ave., New York, NY 10110. (212)354-5500. **Fax:** (212)869-0856. **Website:** www.wwnorton.com. **Contact:** Trish Marks. Estab. 1923. "W. W. Norton & Company, the oldest and largest publishing house owned wholly by its employees, strives to carry out the imperative of its founder to "publish books not for a single season, but for the years" in fiction, nonfiction, poetry, college textbooks, cookbooks, art books, and professional books."

○ "Due to the workload of our editorial staff and the large volume of materials we receive, *Norton is no longer able to accept unsolicited submissions.* If you are seeking publication, we suggest working with a literary agent who will represent you to the house."

○ ○ OAK TREE PRESS

140 E. Palmer, Taylorville, IL 62568. (217)824-6500. **E-mail:** oaktreepub@aol.com. **E-mail:** queryotp@aol.com. **Website:** www.oaktreebooks.com. **Contact:** Billie Johnson, publisher (mysteries, romance, nonfiction); Sarah Wasson, acquisitions editor (all); Barbara Hoffman, senior editor (children's, young adult, educational). Estab. 1998. "Oak Tree Press is an independent publisher that celebrates writers, and is dedicated to the many great unknowns who are just waiting for the opportunity to break into print. We're looking for mainstream, genre fiction, narrative nonfiction, how-to. Sponsors 3 contests annually: Dark Oak Mystery, Timeless Love Romance and CopTales for true crime and other stories of law enforcement professionals."

Publishes trade paperback and hardcover books. Catalog and guidelines available online.

○ "I am always on the lookout for good mysteries, ones that engage quickly. I definitely want to add to our Timeless Love list. I am also looking at a lot of nonfiction, especially in the how-to category. We are one of a few publishers who will consider memoirs, especially memoirs of folks who are not famous, and this is because I enjoy reading them myself. In addition, plans are in progress to launch a political/current affairs imprint, and I am actively looking for titles to build this list. Then, of course, there is always that special something book that you can't quite describe, but you know it when you see it. "

NEEDS Adventure, confession, ethnic, fantasy (romance), feminist, humor, mainstream/contemporary, mystery (amateur sleuth, cozy, police procedural, private eye/hard-boiled), new age/mystic, picture books, romance (contemporary, futuristic/time travel, romantic suspense), suspense, thriller/espionage, young adult (adventure, mystery/suspense, romance). Emphasis on mystery and romance novels. Recently published *The Poetry of Murder*, by Bernadette Steele (mystery); *Media Blitz* by Joe Nowlan(mystery); *Lake Meade*, by Heather Mosko (romance); *Secrets by the Sea*, by Mary Montague Sikes (paranormal romance); *Easy Money*, by Norm Maher (memoir-police officer), and *The Last Stop: Lincoln and the Mud Circuit*, by Alan Bower (history). "No science fiction or fantasy novels, or stories set far into the future. Novels substantially longer than our stated word count are not considered, regardless of genre. We look for manuscripts of 70,000-90,000 words. If the story really charms us, we will bend some on either end of the range. No right-wing political or racist agenda, gratuitous sex or violence, especially against women, or depicting the harm of animals."

HOW TO CONTACT Does not accept or return unsolicited mss. Query with SASE. Accepts queries by e-mail. Include estimated word count, brief bio, list of publishing credits, brief description of ms. Send SASE for return of ms or send a disposable ms and SASE for reply only.

TERMS Royalties based on sales. No advance. Responds in 4-6 weeks.

TIPS "Perhaps my most extreme pet peeve is receiving queries on the kinds of projects we've clearly stated we don't want: science fiction, fantasy, epic tomes, big-oted diatribes and so on. Second to that is a practice I call 'over-taping,' or the use of yards and yards of tape, or worse yet, the filament tape so that it takes forever to open the package. Finding story pitches on my voice mail is also annoying."

OCEANVIEW PUBLISHING

595 Bay Isles Rd., Suite 120-G, Longboat Key, FL 34228. **E-mail:** submissions@oceanviewpub.com. **Website:** www.oceanviewpub.com. **Contact:** Robert Gussin, CEO. Estab. 2006. "Independent publisher of nonfiction and fiction, with primary interest in original mystery, thriller, and suspense titles. Accepts new and established writers." Publishes hardcover and electronic originals. Catalog and guidelines available online.

NEEDS Accepting adult mss with a primary interest in the mystery, thriller, and suspense genres—from new and established writers. No children's or YA literature, poetry, cookbooks, technical manuals, or short stories.

HOW TO CONTACT Within body of e-mail only, include author's name and brief bio (indicate if this is an agent submission), ms title and word count, author's mailing address, phone number, and e-mail address. Attached to the e-mail should be the following: A synopsis of 750 words or fewer and the first 30 pages of the ms. Please note that we accept only Word documents as attachments to the submission e-mail. Do not send query letters or proposals.

TERMS Responds in 3 months on mss.

ONSTAGE PUBLISHING

190 Lime Quarry Rd., Suite 106-J, Madison, AL 35758-8962. (256)461-0661. **E-mail:** onstage123@ knology.net. **Website:** www.onstagepublishing.com. **Contact:** Dianne Hamilton, senior editor. Estab. 1999. At this time, we only produce fiction books for ages 8-18. We are adding an e-book only side of the house for mysteries for grades 6-12. See our website for more information. We will not do anthologies of any kind. Query first for nonfiction projects as nonfiction projects must spark our interest. Now accepting e-mail queries and submissions. For submissions: Put the first 3 chapters in the body of the e-mail. Do not use attachments! We will no longer return any mss. Only an SASE envelope is needed. Send complete ms if under 20,000 words, otherwise send synopsis and first 3 chapters.

To everyone who has submitted a ms, we are currently about 6 months behind. We should get back on track eventually. Please feel free to submit your ms to other houses. OnStage Publishing understands that authors work very hard to produce the finished ms, and we do not have to have exclusive submission rights. Please let us know if you sell your ms. Meanwhile, keep writing and we'll keep reading for our next acquisitions.

NEEDS Middle readers: adventure, contemporary, fantasy, history, nature/environment, science fiction, suspense/mystery. Young adults: adventure, contemporary, fantasy, history, humor, science fiction, suspense/mystery. Average word length: chapter books—4,000-6,000 words; middle readers—5,000 words and up; young adults—25,000 and up. Recently published *China Clipper* by Jamie Dodson (an adventure for boys ages 12+); *Huntsville, 1892: Clara* (a chapter book for grades 3-5). "We do not produce picture books."

TERMS Pays authors/illustrators/photographers advance plus royalties.

TIPS "Study our titles and get a sense of the kind of books we publish, so that you know whether your project is likely to be right for us."

OOLIGAN PRESS

369 Neuberger Hall, 724 SW Harrison St., Portland, OR 97201. (503)725-9410. **E-mail:** ooligan@ooligan press.pdx.edu. **Website:** www.ooliganpress.pdx.edu. Estab. 2001. Publishes trade paperback, and electronic originals and reprints. Book catalog available online. Guidelines available online.

NEEDS "Ooligan Press is a general trade press at Portland State University. As a teaching press, Ooligan makes as little distinction as possible between the press and the classroom. Under the direction of professional faculty and staff, the work of the press is done by students enrolled in the Book Publishing graduate program at PSU. We are especially interested in works with social, literary, or educational value. Though we place special value on local authors, we are open to all submissions, including translated works and writings by children and young adults. We do not currently publish picture books, board books, easy readers, pop-up books, or middle-grade readers."

HOW TO CONTACT Query with SASE. *"At this time we cannot accept science fiction or fantasy submissions."*

TERMS Pays negotiable royalty on retail price.

TIPS "For children's books, our audience will be middle grades and young adult, with marketing to general trade, libraries, and schools. Good marketing ideas increase the chances of a manuscript succeeding."

ORCA BOOK PUBLISHERS

P.O. Box 5626, Stn. B, Victoria, BC V8R 6S4 Canada. **Fax:** (877)408-1551. **E-mail:** orca@orcabook.com. **Website:** www.orcabook.com. **Contact:** Christi Howes, editor (picture books); Sarah Harvey, editor (young readers); Andrew Wooldridge, editor (juvenile and teen fiction); Bob Tyrrell, publisher (YA, teen). Estab. 1984. Publishes hardcover and trade paperback originals, and mass-market paperback originals and reprints. Book catalog for 8½" × 11" SASE. Guidelines available online.

Only publishes Canadian authors.

NEEDS Picture books: animals, contemporary, history, nature/environment. Middle readers: contemporary, history, fantasy, nature/environment, problem novels, graphic novels. Young adults: adventure, contemporary, hi-lo (Orca Soundings), history, multicultural, nature/environment, problem novels, suspense/mystery, graphic novels. Average word length: picture books, 500-1,500; middle readers, 20,000-35,000; young adult, 25,000-45,000; Orca Soundings, 13,000-15,000; Orca Currents, 13,000-15,000. Published *Tall in the Saddle*, by Anne Carter, illustrated by David McPhail (ages 4-8, picture book); *Me and Mr. Mah*, by Andrea Spalding, illustrated by Janet Wilson (ages 5 and up, picture book); *Alone at Ninety Foot*, by Katherine Holubitsky (young adult). No romance, science fiction.

HOW TO CONTACT Query with SASE. Submit proposal package, outline, clips, 2-5 sample chapters, SASE.

TERMS Pays 10% royalty. Responds in 1 month to queries; 2 months to proposals and mss.

TIPS "Our audience is students in grades K-12. Know our books, and know the market."

ORCHARD BOOKS

557 Broadway, New York, NY 10012. **E-mail:** mcroland@scholastic.com. **Website:** www.scholastic.com. **Contact:** Ken Geist, vice president/editorial director; David Saylor, vice president/creative director.

Orchard is not accepting unsolicited manuscripts.

NEEDS Picture books, early readers, and novelty: animal, contemporary, history, humor, multicultural, poetry.

TERMS Most commonly offers an advance against list royalties.

TIPS "Read some of our books to determine first whether your manuscript is suited to our list."

OUR CHILD PRESS

P.O. Box 4379, Philadelphia, PA 19118. **Fax:** (610)308-8088. **E-mail:** info@ourchildpress.com. **Website:** www.ourchildpress.com. **Contact:** Carol Perrott, president. Book catalog for business-size SAE and 67 cents.

NEEDS All levels: adoption, multicultural, special needs. Published *Like Me*, written by Dawn Martelli, illustrated by Jennifer Hedy Wharton; *Is That Your Sister?*, by Catherine and Sherry Burin; *Oliver: A Story About Adoption*, by Lois Wichstrom.

TERMS Pays authors royalty of 5-10% based on wholesale price. Pays illustrators royalty of 5-10% based on wholesale price. Responds to queries/mss in 6 months.

OUTRIDER PRESS, INC.

2036 North Winds Dr., Dyer, IN 46311. (219)322-7270. **Fax:** (219)322-7085. **E-mail:** outriderpress@sbcglobal.net. **Website:** www.outriderpress.com. **Contact:** Whitney Scott, editor. Estab. 1988. Publishes trade paperback originals. Guidelines available online.

Accepts unsolicited mss. Query with SASE. Accepts queries by mail. Include estimated word count, brief bio, list of publishing credits. Accepts simultaneous submissions, electronic submissions, submissions on disk. Sometimes comments on rejected mss. In affiliation with Tallgrass Writers Guild, publishes an annual anthology with $1,000 in cash prizes for short fiction, nonfiction, and poetry. Anthology theme for 2013 was Music to my ear. "As always, broadly interpreted; we welcome nature's music as subjects as well as human-made compositions and whatever constitutes music to your ears." Guidelines via e-mail at outriderpress@sbcglobal.net. Was a *Small Press Review* pick for 2000. Sponsors an anthology competition for short stories, poetry, and creative nonfiction.

NEEDS Ethnic, experimental, family saga, fantasy (space fantasy, sword and sorcery), feminist, gay/lesbian, historical, horror (psychological, supernatural), humor, lesbian, literary, mainstream/contemporary, mystery (amateur sleuth, cozy, police procedural, private eye/hard-boiled), new age/mystic, psychic/supernatural, romance (contemporary, futuristic/time travel, gothic, historical, regency period, romantic suspense), science fiction (soft/sociological), short story collections, thriller/espionage, western (frontier saga, traditional). Published *Telling Time*, by Cherie Caswell Dost; *If Ever I Cease to Love*, by Robert Klein Engler; *62,000 Reasons*, by Paul Miller; *Aquarium Octopus*, by Claudia Van Gerven; and *Heat*, by Deborah Thompson.

HOW TO CONTACT Query with SASE.

TERMS Pays honorarium. Responds in 6 weeks to queries; 4 months to proposals and mss.

TIPS "It's always best to familiarize yourself with our publications. We're especially fond of humor/irony."

🅐 THE OVERLOOK PRESS

141 Wooster St., New York, NY 10012. (212)673-2210. **Fax:** (212)673-2296. **E-mail:** sales@overlookny .com. **Website:** www.overlookpress.com. Estab. 1971. "Overlook Press publishes fiction, children's books, and nonfiction." Publishes hardcover and trade paperback originals and hardcover reprints. Book catalog available free.

HOW TO CONTACT Agented submissions only.

🅓 RICHARD C. OWEN PUBLISHERS, INC.

P.O. Box 585, Katonah, NY 10536. (914)232-3903; (800)262-0787. **E-mail:** richardowen@rcowen.com. **Website:** www.rcowen.com. **Contact:** Richard Owen, publisher. Estab. 1982. "We publish child-focused books, with inherent instructional value, about characters and situations with which five-, six-, and seven-year-old children can identify—books that can be read for meaning, entertainment, enjoyment, and information. We include multicultural stories that present minorities in a positive and natural way. Our stories show the diversity in America." Not interested in lesson plans or books of activities for literature studies or other content areas. Submit complete ms and cover letter. Book catalog available with SASE. Ms guidelines with SASE or online.

🔾 "Due to high volume and long production time, we are currently limited to reading nonfiction submissions only."

TERMS Pays authors royalty of 5% based on net price or outright purchase (range: $25-500). Offers no advances. Pays illustrators by the project (range: $100-2,000) or per photo (range: $100-150). Responds to mss in 1 year.

TIPS "We don't respond to queries or e-mails. Please do not fax or e-mail us. Because our books are so brief, it is better to send an entire manuscript. We publish story books with inherent educational value for young readers—books they can read with enjoyment and success. We believe students become enthusiastic, independent, lifelong learners when supported and guided by skillful teachers using good books. The professional development work we do and the books we publish support these beliefs."

🖂 PETER OWEN PUBLISHERS

81 Ridge Rd., London N8 9NP United Kingdom. (44)(208)350-1775. **Fax:** (44)(208)340-9488. **E-mail:** aowen@peterowen.com. **Website:** www.peterowen.com. **Contact:** Antonia Owen, editorial director. "We are far more interested in proposals for nonfiction than fiction at the moment. No poetry or short stories." Publishes hardcover originals and trade paperback originals and reprints. Book catalog for SASE, SAE with IRC or on website.

NEEDS "No first novels. Authors should be aware that we publish very little new fiction these days. Will consider excerpts from novels of normal length from established authors if they submit sample chapters and synopses."

HOW TO CONTACT Query with SASE or by e-mail.

TERMS Pays 7½-10% royalty. Pays negotiable advance. Responds in 2 months to queries; 3 months to proposals and mss.

PACIFIC PRESS PUBLISHING ASSOCIATION

Trade Book Division, 1350 N. Kings Rd., Nampa, ID 83687. (208)465-2500. **Fax:** (208)465-2531. **E-mail:** booksubmissions@pacificpress.com. **Website:** www .pacificpress.com. **Contact:** Scott Cady, acquisitions editor (children's stories, biography, Christian living, spiritual growth); David Jarnes, book editor (theology, doctrine, inspiration). Estab. 1874. "We publish books that fit Seventh-day Adventist beliefs only. All titles are Christian and religious. For guidance, see www.adventist.org/beliefs/index.html. Our books fit into the categories of this retail site: www.adventistbookcenter.com." Publishes hardcover and trade paperback originals and reprints. Guidelines available online.

NEEDS "Pacific Press rarely publishes fiction, but we're interested in developing a line of Seventh-Day Adventist fiction in the future. Only proposals accepted; no full manuscripts."

TERMS Pays 8-16% royalty on wholesale price. Responds in 3 months to queries.

TIPS "Our primary audience is members of the Seventh-Day Adventist denomination. Almost all are written by Seventh-Day Adventists. Books that do well for us relate the biblical message to practical human concerns and focus more on the experiential rather than theoretical aspects of Christianity. We are assigning more titles, using less unsolicited material—although we still publish manuscripts from freelance submissions and proposals."

PALARI PUBLISHING

P.O. Box 4, Montpelier, VA 23192. (866)570-6724. **Fax:** (866)570-6724. **E-mail:** dave@palaribooks.com. **Website:** www.palaribooks.com. **Contact:** David Smitherman, publisher/editor. Estab. 1998. "Palari provides authoritative, well-written nonfiction that addresses topical consumer needs and fiction with an emphasis on intelligence and quality. We accept solicited and unsolicited manuscripts, however we prefer a query letter and SASE, describing the project briefly and concisely. This letter should include a complete address and telephone number. Palari Publishing accepts queries or any other submissions by e-mail, but prefers queries submitted by U.S. mail. All queries must be submitted by mail according to our guidelines. Promotes titles through book signings, direct mail and the Internet." Publishes hardcover and trade paperback originals. Guidelines available online.

O Member of Publishers Marketing Association.

NEEDS Tell why your idea is unique or interesting. Make sure we are interested in your genre before submitting.

HOW TO CONTACT Query with SASE. Submit bio, estimated word count, list of publishing credits. Accepts queries via e-mail (prefer U.S. Mail), fax.

TERMS Pays royalty. Responds in 1 month to queries; 2-3 months to mss.

TIPS "Send a good bio. I'm interested in a writer's experience and unique outlook on life."

A PANTHEON BOOKS

Random House, Inc., 1745 Broadway, 3rd Floor, New York, NY 10019. **E-mail:** pantheonpublicity@randomhouse.com. **Website:** www.pantheonbooks.com. Estab. 1942. Publishes hardcover and trade paperback originals and trade paperback reprints.

O Pantheon Books publishes both Western and non-Western authors of literary fiction and important nonfiction. "We only accept mss submitted by an agent. You may still send a 20-50 page sample and a SASE to our slushpile. Allow 2-6 months for a response."

HOW TO CONTACT *Does not accept unsolicited mss.* Agented submissions only.

PARADISE CAY PUBLICATIONS

P.O. Box 29, Arcata, CA 95518-0029. (800)736-4509. **Fax:** (707)822-9163. **E-mail:** info@paracay.com; jim@paracay.com. **Website:** www.paracay.com. **Contact:** Matt Morehouse, publisher. "Paradise Cay Publications, Inc., is a small independent publisher specializing in nautical books, videos, and art prints. Our primary interest is in manuscripts that deal with the instructional and technical aspects of ocean sailing. We also publish and will consider fiction if it has a strong nautical theme." Publishes hardcover and trade paperback originals and reprints. Book catalog and ms guidelines free on request or online.

IMPRINTS Pardey Books.

NEEDS All fiction must have a nautical theme.

HOW TO CONTACT Query with SASE. Submit proposal package, clips, 2-3 sample chapters.

TERMS Pays 10-15% royalty on wholesale price. Makes outright purchase of $1,000-10,000. Does not normally pay advances to first-time or little-known authors. Responds in 1 month to queries/proposals; 2 months to mss.

TIPS Audience is recreational sailors. Call Matt Morehouse (publisher).

PAUL DRY BOOKS

1700 Sansom St., Suite 700, Philadelphia, PA 19103. (215)231-9939. **Fax:** (215)231-9942. **E-mail:** pdry@pauldrybooks.com; editor@pauldrybooks.com. **Website:** http://pauldrybooks.com. "We publish fiction, both novels and short stories, and nonfiction, biography, memoirs, history, and essays, covering subjects from Homer to Chekhov, bird watching to jazz music, New York City to shogunate Japan." Hardcover and trade paperback originals, trade paperback reprints.

Book catalog available online. Guidelines available online.

◯ "Take a few minutes to familiarize yourself with the books we publish. Then if you think your book would be a good fit in our line, we invite you to submit the following: A one- or two-page summary of the work. Be sure to tell us how many pages or words the full book will be; a sample of 20 to 30 pages; your bio. A brief description of how you think the book (and you, the author) could be marketed."

HOW TO CONTACT Submit sample chapters, clips, bio.

TIPS "Our aim is to publish lively books 'to awaken, delight, and educate'—to spark conversation."

◐ PAYCOCK PRESS

3819 N. 13th St., Arlington, VA 22201. (703)525-9296. **E-mail:** gargoyle@gargoylemagazine.com. **Website:** www.gargoylemagazine.com. **Contact:** Lucinda Ebersole and Richard Peabody. Estab. 1976. "Too academic for underground, too outlaw for the academic world. We tend to be edgy and look for ultraliterary work." Publishes paperback originals. Books: POD printing. Average print order: 500. Averages 1 total title/year. Member CLMP. Distributes through Amazon and website.

NEEDS Wants: experimental, literary, short story collections.

HOW TO CONTACT Accepts unsolicited mss. Accepts queries by e-mail. Include brief bio. Send SASE for return of ms or send a disposable ms and SASE for reply only.

TERMS Responds to queries in 1 month; mss in 4 months.

TIPS "Check out our website. Two of our favorite writers are Paul Bowles and Jeanette Winterson."

PEACE HILL PRESS

Affiliate of W.W. Norton, 18021 The Glebe Ln., Charles City, VA 23030. (804)829-5043. **Fax:** (804)829-5704. **E-mail:** info@peacehillpress.com. **Website:** www.peacehillpress.com. **Contact:** Peter Buffington, acquisitions editor. Estab. 2001. Publishes hardcover and trade paperback originals.

HOW TO CONTACT Submit proposal package, outline, 1 sample chapter.

TERMS Pays 6-10% royalty on retail price. Pays $500-1,000 advance.

◐ PEACHTREE CHILDREN'S BOOKS

Peachtree Publishers, Ltd., 1700 Chattahoochee Ave., Atlanta, GA 30318-2112. (404)876-8761. **Fax:** (404)875-2578. **E-mail:** hello@peachtree-online.com. **Website:** www.peachtree-online.com. **Contact:** Helen Harriss, submissions editor. "We publish a broad range of subjects and perspectives, with emphasis on innovative plots and strong writing." Publishes hardcover and trade paperback originals. Book catalog for 6 first-class stamps. Guidelines available online.

IMPRINTS Freestone; Peachtree Jr.

NEEDS Looking for very well-written middle-grade and young adult novels. Juvenile, picture books, young adult. No adult fiction. No short stories or poetry; no romance or science fiction. Published *Martina the Beautiful Cockroach, Night of the Spadefoot Toads, The Boy Who Was Raised by Librarians*.

HOW TO CONTACT Submit complete ms with SASE.

TERMS Pays royalty on retail price. Responds in 6 months and mss.

PEACHTREE PUBLISHERS, LTD.

1700 Chattahoochee Ave., Atlanta, GA 30318. (404)876-8761. **Fax:** (404)875-2578. **E-mail:** hello@peachtree-online.com; jackson@peachtree-online.com. **Website:** www.peachtree-online.com. **Contact:** Helen Harriss, acquisitions editor; Loraine Joyner, art director; Melanie McMahon Ives, production manager. Estab. 1977.

NEEDS Picture books, young readers: adventure, animal, concept, history, nature/environment. Middle readers: adventure, animal, history, nature/environment, sports. Young adults: fiction, mystery, adventure. Does not want to see science fiction, romance.

HOW TO CONTACT Submit complete ms or 3 sample chapters by postal mail only.

TERMS Responds to queries and mss in 6-7 months.

◐◑ PEDLAR PRESS

113 Bond St., St. John's NL A16 1T6 Canada. (709)738-6702. **E-mail:** feralgrl@interlog.com. **Website:** www.pedlarpress.com. **Contact:** Beth Follett, owner/editor. Distributes in Canada through LitDistCo.; in the U.S. distributes directly through publisher.

NEEDS Experimental, feminist, gay/lesbian, literary, short story collections. Canadian writers only. Published *Black Stars in a White Night Sky*, by Jonarno Lawson, illustrated by Sherwin Tjia.

HOW TO CONTACT Query with SASE, sample chapter(s), synopsis.

TERMS Pays 10% royalty on retail price. Average advance: $200-400.

TIPS "I select manuscripts according to my taste, which fluctuates. Be familiar with some if not most of Pedlar's recent titles."

● ○ PELICAN PUBLISHING COMPANY

1000 Burmaster St., Gretna, LA 70053. (504)368-1175. **Fax:** (504)368-1195. **E-mail:** editorial@pelicanpub.com. **Website:** www.pelicanpub.com. **Contact:** Nina Kooij, editor-in-chief. Estab. 1926. "We believe ideas have consequences. One of the consequences is that they lead to a best-selling book. We publish books to improve and uplift the reader. Currently emphasizing business and history titles." Publishes 20 young readers/year; 1 middle reader/year. "Our children's books (illustrated and otherwise) include history, biography, holiday, and regional. Pelican's mission is to publish books of quality and permanence that enrich the lives of those who read them." Publishes hardcover, trade paperback and mass-market paperback originals and reprints. Book catalog and ms guidelines online.

NEEDS We publish no adult fiction. Young readers: history, holiday, science, multicultural, and regional. Middle readers: Louisiana History. Multicultural needs include stories about African-Americans, Irish-Americans, Jews, Asian-Americans, and Hispanics. Does not want animal stories, general Christmas stories, "day at school" or "accept yourself" stories. Maximum word length: young readers—1,100; middle readers—40,000. No young adult, romance, science fiction, fantasy, gothic, mystery, erotica, confession, horror, sex, or violence. Also no psychological novels.

HOW TO CONTACT Query with SASE. Submit outline, clips, 2 sample chapters, SASE.

TERMS Pays authors in royalties; buys ms outright rarely. Illustrators paid by "various arrangements." Advance considered. Responds in 1 month to queries; 3 months to mss.

TIPS "We do extremely well with cookbooks, popular histories, and business. We will continue to build in these areas. The writer must have a clear sense of the market and knowledge of the competition. A query letter should describe the project briefly, give the author's writing and professional credentials, and promotional ideas."

○ PEMMICAN PUBLICATIONS, INC.

90 Sutherland Ave., Winnipeg, MB R2W 3C7 Canada. (204)589-6346. **Fax:** (204)589-2063. **E-mail:** pemmi-can@pemmican.mb.ca. **Website:** www.pemmicanpublications.ca. **Contact:** Randal McIlroy, managing editor (Metis culture and heritage). Estab. 1980. "Pemmican Publications is a Metis publishing house, with a mandate to publish books by Metis authors and illustrators and with an emphasis on culturally relevant stories. We encourage writers to learn a little about Pemmican before sending samples. Pemmican publishes titles in the following genres: adult fiction, which includes novels, story collections and anthologies; nonfiction, with an emphasis on social history and biography reflecting Metis experience; children's and young adult titles; Aboriginal languages, including Michif and Cree." Publishes trade paperback originals and reprints. Book catalog available free with SASE. Guidelines available online.

NEEDS All manuscripts must be Metis culture and heritage related.

HOW TO CONTACT Submit proposal package including outline and 3 sample chapters.

TERMS Pays 10% royalty on retail price. Responds to queries, proposals, and mss in 3 months.

TIPS "Our mandate is to promote Metis authors, illustrators, and stories. No agent is necessary."

● ● ● ○ PENGUIN GROUP USA

375 Hudson St., New York NY 10014. (212)366-2000. **Website:** www.penguin.com. **Contact:** Peter Stampfel, submission editor (DAW Books). General interest publisher of both fiction and nonfiction. Guidelines available online at website.

○ "We publish first novels, if they are of professional quality. A literary agent is not required for submission. We will not consider mss that are currently on submission to another publisher unless prior arrangements have been made with a literary agent."

IMPRINTS Exceptions are DAW Books and G.P. Putnam's Sons Books for Young Readers, which are accepting submissions. See individual listings for more information. **Penguin Adult Division:** Ace Books, Alpha Books, Avery, Berkley Books, Dutton, Gotham Books, HPBooks, Hudson Street Press, Jove, New American Library, Penguin, The Penguin Press, Perigee, Plume, Portfolio, G.P. Putnam's Sons, Riverhead, Sentinel, Jeremy P. Tarcher, Viking; **Penguin Children's Division:** Dial Books for Young Readers, Dutton Children's Books, Firebird, Grosset & Dunlap, Philomel, Price Stern Sloan, Puffin Books, G.P. Putnam's Sons, Speak, Viking Children's Books, Frederick Warne.

NEEDS "DAW Books is currently accepting manuscripts in the science fiction/fantasy genre. The average length of the novels we publish varies but is almost never less than 80,000 words. Do not submit handwritten material." We do not want short stories, short story collections, novellas, or poetry.

HOW TO CONTACT "Due to the high volume of mss we receive, Penguin Group (USA) Inc., imprints do not normally accept unsolicited mss. On rare occasion, however, a particular imprint may be open to reading such. The Penguin Group (USA) website features a listing of which imprints (if any) are currently accepting unsolicited manuscripts. Please enclose a SASE with your submission for our correspondence. We ask that you only send us disposable copies of your ms, which will be recycled in the event they are not found suitable for publication. We regret that we are no longer able to return submitted ms copies, as the process resulted in too many difficulties with the postal service and unnecessary expense for the prospective authors. It may require up to three months or more for our editors to review a submission and come to a decision. If you want to be sure we have received your manuscript, please enclose a stamped, self-addressed postcard that we will return when your ms. It is not necessary for you to register or copyright your work before publication. It is protected by law as long as it has not been published. When published, we will copyright the book in the author's name and register that copyright with the Library of Congress. Continue to check website for updates to the list. **TERMS** Responds in 3 months generally."

☺ PENNY-FARTHING PRESS INC.

2000 W. Sam Houston Pkwy. S, Houston, TX 77042. (713)780-0300 or (800)926-2669. **Fax:** (713)780-4004. **E-mail:** submissions@pfpress.com; corp@pf press.com. **Website:** www.pfpress.com. **Contact:** Ken White, publisher; Marlaine Maddox, editor-in-chief. Estab. 1998. "Penny-Farthing Press officially opened its doors in 1998 with a small staff and a plan to create comic books and children's books that exemplified quality storytelling, artwork, and printing. Starting with only one book, *The Victorian*, Penny-Farthing Press has expanded its line to six titles, but keeps its yearly output small enough to maintain the highest quality. This "boutique approach" to publishing has

won the recognition of the comics and fine arts industries, and PFP has won numerous awards including the Gutenberg D'Argent Medal and several Spectrum Awards." Guidelines available online at website.

HOW TO CONTACT "Please make sure all submissions include a synopsis that is brief and to the point. Remember, the synopsis is the "first impression" of your submission and you know what they say about first impressions. If you are submitting just one single-issue story (standard 32 pages), you may send the full script with your submission. If you are submitting a story for any kind of series or graphic novel, please send only the first chapter of the series. If we like what we see, we will contact you to see more. If you are submitting a completed work (script, artwork, and lettering) copies of this may be sent instead."

ⒶⓄ PERENNIAL

HarperCollins Publishers, 10 E. 53rd St., New York, NY 10022. (212)207-7000. **Website:** www.harpercol lins.com. **Contact:** Acquisitions Editor. Estab. 1963. Perennial publishes a broad range of adult literary fiction and nonfiction paperbacks that create a record of our culture. Publishes trade paperback originals and reprints. Book catalog available free.

○ "With the exception of Avon romance, HarperCollins does not accept unsolicited submissions or query letters. Please refer to your local bookstore, the library, or a book entitled *Literary Marketplace* on how to find the appropriate agent for you."

HOW TO CONTACT Agented submissions only.

TIPS See our website for a list of titles or write to us for a free catalog.

Ⓓ THE PERMANENT PRESS

Attn: Judith Shepard, 4170 Noyac Rd., Sag Harbor, NY 11963. (631)725-1101. **Fax:** (631)725-8215. **E-mail:** ju dith@thepermanentpress.com; shepard@theperma nentpress.com. **Website:** www.thepermanentpress .com. **Contact:** Judith and Martin Shepard, acquisitions/co-publishers. Estab. 1978. Midsize, independent publisher of literary fiction. "We keep titles in print and are active in selling subsidiary rights." Average print order: 1,500. Averages 14 total titles. Accepts unsolicited mss. Pays 10-15% royalty on wholesale price. Offers $1,000 advance. Publishes hardcover originals.

○ *Will NOT accept simultaneous submissions.*

NEEDS Promotes titles through reviews. Literary, mainstream/contemporary, mystery. Especially looking for high-line literary fiction, "artful, original, and arresting." Accepts any fiction category as long as it is a "well-written, original full-length novel."

TERMS Pays 10-15% royalty on wholesale price. Offers $1,000 advance. Responds in weeks or months to queries and submissions.

TIPS "We are looking for good books—be they 10th novels or first ones, it makes little difference. The fiction is more important than the track record. Send us the first 25 pages; it's impossible to judge something that begins on page 302. Also, no outlines—let the writing present itself."

⊕ PERSEA BOOKS

277 Broadway, Suite 708, New York, NY 10007. (212)260-9256. **Fax:** (212)267-3165. **E-mail:** info@ perseabooks.com. **Website:** www.perseabooks.com. Estab. 1975. "We are pleased to receive query letters from authors and literary agents for fiction and nonfiction manuscripts." Guidelines online.

HOW TO CONTACT Queries should include a cover letter, author background, and publication history, a detailed synopsis of the proposed work, and a sample chapter. Please indicate if the work is simultaneously submitted.

TERMS Responds in 8 weeks to proposals; 10 weeks to mss.

⊘ PHILOMEL BOOKS

Imprint of Penguin Group (USA), Inc., 375 Hudson St., New York, NY 10014. (212)414-3610. **Website:** www.us.penguingroup.com. **Contact:** Michael Green, president/publisher; Annie Ericsson, junior designer. Estab. 1980. "We look for beautifully written, engaging manuscripts for children and young adults." Publishes hardcover originals. Book catalog for 9" × 12" envelope and 4 first-class stamps. Guidelines for #10 SASE.

NEEDS All levels: adventure, animal, boys, contemporary, fantasy, folktales, historical fiction, humor, sports, multicultural. Middle readers, young adults: problem novels, science fiction, suspense/mystery. No concept picture books, mass-market "character" books, or series. Average word length: picture books, 1,000; young readers, 1,500; middle readers, 14,000; young adult, 20,000. No series or activity books. No generic, mass-market oriented fiction.

HOW TO CONTACT *No unsolicited mss.*

TERMS Pays authors in royalties. Average advance payment "varies." Illustrators paid by advance and in royalties. Pays negotiable advance.

TIPS Wants "unique fiction or nonfiction with a strong voice and lasting quality. Discover your own voice and own story and persevere." Looks for "something unusual, original, well written. Fine art or illustrative art that feels unique. The genre (fantasy, contemporary, or historical fiction) is not so important as the story itself and the spirited life the story allows its main character."

PIANO PRESS

P.O. Box 85, Del Mar, CA 92014. (619)884-1401. **Fax:** (858)755-1104. **E-mail:** pianopress@pianopress.com. **Website:** www.pianopress.com. **Contact:** Elizabeth C. Axford, editor. Estab. 1998. "We publish music-related books, either fiction or nonfiction, coloring books, songbooks, and poetry." Book catalog available for #10 SASE and 2 first-class stamps.

NEEDS Picture books, young readers, middle readers, young adults: folktales, multicultural, poetry, music. Average word length: picture books, 1,500-2,000. Recently published *Strum a Song of Angels*, by Linda Oatman High and Elizabeth C. Axford; *Music and Me*, by Kimberly White and Elizabeth C. Axford.

TERMS Pays authors, illustrators, and photographers royalty of 5-10% based on retail price. Responds to queries in 3 months; mss in 6 months.

TIPS "We are looking for music-related material only for any juvenile market. Please do not send material that is not related. Query first before submitting anything."

TIPS "Study our list before submitting your work."

⊕⊙⊕ PICADOR USA

MacMillan, 175 Fifth Ave., New York, NY 10010. (212)674-5151. **E-mail:** david.saint@picadorusa.com; pressinquiries@macmillanusa.com. **Website:** www .picadorusa.com. **Contact:** Frances Coady, publisher (literary fiction). Estab. 1994. Picador publishes high-quality literary fiction and nonfiction. "We are open to a broad range of subjects, well written by authoritative authors." Publishes hardcover and trade paperback originals and reprints. Averages 70-80 total titles/year. Titles distributed through Von Holtzbrinck Publishers. Titles promoted through national print advertising and bookstore co-op. Book catalog for 9" × 12" SASE and $2.60 postage. Ms guidelines for #10 SASE or online.

○ Does not accept unsolicited mss. *Agented submissions only.*

TERMS Pays 7-15% on royalty. Advance varies. Responds to queries in 2 months.

PICCADILLY PRESS

5 Castle Rd., London NW1 8PR United Kingdom. (44)(207)267-4492. **Fax:** (44)(207)267-4493. **E-mail:** books@piccadillypress.co.uk. **Website:** www.picca dillypress.co.uk. "Piccadilly Press is the perfect choice for variety of reading for everyone aged 2-16! We're an independent publisher, celebrating 26 years of specialising in teen fiction and nonfiction, children's fiction, picture books and parenting books by highly acclaimed authors and illustrators, and fresh new talents, too. We hope you enjoy reading the books as much as we enjoy publishing them."

NEEDS Picture books: animal, contemporary, fantasy, nature/environment. Young adults: contemporary, humor, problem novels. Average word length: picture books—500-1,000; young adults—25,000-35,000.

HOW TO CONTACT Submit complete ms for picture books or submit outline/synopsis and 2 sample chapters for YA. Enclose a brief cover letter and SASE for reply.

TERMS Responds to mss in 6 weeks.

TIPS "Take a look in bookshops to see if there are many other books of a similar nature to yours—this is what your book will be competing against, so make sure there is something truly unique about your story. Looking at what else is available will give you ideas as to what topics are popular, but reading them will also give you a sense of the right styles, language, and length appropriate for the age group."

PINEAPPLE PRESS, INC.

P.O. Box 3889, Sarasota, FL 34230. (941)739-2219. **Fax:** (941)739-2296. **E-mail:** info@pineapplepress.com. **Website:** www.pineapplepress.com. **Contact:** June Cussen, executive editor. Estab. 1982. "We are seeking quality nonfiction on diverse topics for the library and book trade markets. Our mission is to publish good books about Florida." Publishes hardcover and trade paperback originals. Book catalog for 9" × 12" SAE with $1.25 postage. Guidelines available online.

NEEDS Picture books, young readers, middle readers, young adults: animal, folktales, history, nature/environment. Recently published *The Treasure of Amelia Island*, by M.C. Finotti (ages 8-12).

HOW TO CONTACT Query or submit outline/synopsis and 3 sample chapters.

TERMS Pays authors royalty of 10-15%. Responds to queries/samples/mss in 2 months.

TIPS "Quality first novels will be published, though we usually only do one or two novels per year and they must be set in Florida. We regard the author/editor relationship as a trusting relationship with communication open both ways. Learn all you can about the publishing process and about how to promote your book once it is published. A query on a novel without a brief sample seems useless."

PITSPOPANY PRESS

Simcha Media, P.O. Box 5329, Englewood, NJ 07631. (212)444-1657. **Fax:** (866)205-3966. **E-mail:** pitspop@ netvision.net.il. **Website:** www.pitspopany.com. Estab. 1992. "Pitspopany Press is dedicated to bringing quality children's books of Jewish interest into the marketplace. Our goal is to create titles that will appeal to the esthetic senses of our readers and, at the same time, offer quality Jewish content to the discerning parent, teacher, and librarian. While the people working for Pitspopany Press embody a wide spectrum of Jewish belief and opinion, we insist that our titles be respectful of the mainstream Jewish viewpoints and beliefs. We are especially interested in chapter books for kids. Most of all, we are committed to creating books that all Jewish children can read, learn from, and enjoy." Catalog on website. Writer's guidelines available for SASE.

NEEDS Picture books: animal, anthology, fantasy, folktales, history, humor, multicultural, nature/environment, poetry. Young readers: adventure, animal, anthology, concept, contemporary, fantasy, folktales, health, history, humor, multicultural, nature/environment, poetry, religion, science fiction, special needs, sports, suspense. Middle readers: animal, anthology, fantasy, folktales, health, hi-lo, history, humor, multicultural, nature/environment, poetry, religion, science fiction, special needs, sports, suspense. Young adults/teens: animal, anthology, contemporary, fantasy, folktales, health, hi-lo, history, humor, multicultural, nature/environment, poetry, religion, science fiction, special needs, sports, suspense. Recently published *Hayyim's Ghost*, by Eric Kimmel, illustrated by Ari Binus (ages 6-9); *The Littlest Pair*, by Syliva Rouss, illustrated by Hally Hannan (ages 3-6); *The*

Converso Legacy, by Sheldon Gardner (ages 10-14, historical fiction).

HOW TO CONTACT Submit outline/synopsis.

TERMS Pays authors royalty or work purchased outright. Responds to queries/mss in 6 weeks.

⊘ PLAN B PRESS

P.O. Box 4067, Alexandria, VA 22303. (215)732-2663. **E-mail:** planbpress@gmail.com. **Website:** www.plan bpress.com. **Contact:** Steven Allen May, president. Estab. 1999. Plan B Press is a "small publishing company with an international feel. Our intention is to have Plan B Press be part of the conversation about the direction and depth of literary movements and genres. Plan B Press's new direction is to seek out authors rarely-to-never published, sharing new voices that might not otherwise be heard. Plan B Press is determined to merge text with image, writing with art." Publishes poetry and short fiction. Wants "experimental poetry, concrete/visual work." Has published poetry by Lamont B. Steptoe, Michele Belluomini, Jim Mancinelli, Lyn Lifshin, Robert Miltner, and Steven Allen May. Publishes 1 poetry book/year and 5-10 chapbooks/year. Manuscripts are selected through open submission and through competition (see below). Books/chapbooks are 24-48 pages, with covers with art/graphics.

TERMS Pays author's copies. Responds to queries in 1 month; mss in 3 months.

PLEXUS PUBLISHING, INC.

143 Old Marlton Pike, Medford, NJ 08055. (609)654-6500. **Fax:** (609)654-4309. **E-mail:** jbryans@plexus publishing.com. **Website:** www.plexuspublishing .com. **Contact:** John B. Bryans, editor-in-chief/publisher. Estab. 1977. Plexus publishes regional-interest (southern New Jersey and the greater Philadelphia area) fiction and nonfiction including mysteries, field guides, nature, travel, and history. Also a limited number of titles in health/medicine, biology, ecology, botany, astronomy. Publishes hardcover and paperback originals. Book catalog and book proposal guidelines for 10" × 13" SASE.

NEEDS Mysteries and literary novels with a strong regional (southern New Jersey) angle.

HOW TO CONTACT Query with SASE.

TERMS Pays $500-1,000 advance. Responds in 3 months to proposals.

❶❷ POCKET BOOKS

Simon & Schuster, 1230 Avenue of the Americas, New York, NY 10020. (212)698-7000. **Website:** www .simonsays.com. **Contact:** Jennifer Bergstrom, editor-in-chief. Estab. 1939. Pocket Books publishes commercial fiction and genre fiction (WWE, Downtown Press, Star Trek). Publishes paperback originals and reprints, mass-market and trade paperbacks. Book catalog available free. Guidelines available online.

○ Pocket Books remains the mass-market imprint of Simon & Schuster in the Gallery family, publishing titles from authors like Stephen King, Mary Higgins Clark, Vince Flynn, Sandra Brown, Greg Iles, Kresley Cole, and Julia London.

HOW TO CONTACT *Agented submissions only.*

○ POCOL PRESS

P.O. Box 411, Clifton, VA 20124. (703)830-5862. **Website:** www.pocolpress.com. **Contact:** J. Thomas Hetrick, editor. Estab. 1999. "Pocol Press is dedicated to producing high-quality print books and e-books from first-time, non-agented authors. However, all submissions are welcome. We're dedicated to good storytellers and to the written word, specializing in short fiction and baseball. Several of our books have been used as literary texts at universities and in book group discussions around the nation. Pocol Press does not publish children's books, romance novels, or graphic novels." Publishes trade paperback originals. Book catalog and guidelines available online.

○ "Our authors are comprised of veteran writers and emerging talents."

NEEDS "We specialize in thematic short fiction collections by a single author and baseball fiction. Expert storytellers welcome." Horror (psychological, supernatural), literary, mainstream/contemporary, short story collections, baseball. Published *Gulf*, by Brock Adams (short fiction); *The Last of One* by Stephan Solberg (novel); *A Good Death* by David E. Lawrence.

HOW TO CONTACT Does not accept or return unsolicited mss. Query with SASE or submit 1 sample chapter.

TERMS Pays 10-12% royalty on wholesale price. Responds in 1 month to queries; 2 months too mss.

TIPS "Our audience is aged 18 and over. Write the best stories you can. Read them to your friends/peers. Note their reactions. Publishes some of the finest fiction by a small press."

✛ ◗ THE POISONED PENCIL

Poisoned Pen Press, 6962 E. 1st Ave., Suite 103, Scottsdale, AZ 85251. (480)945-3375. **Fax:** (480)949-1707. **E-mail:** info@thepoisonedpencil.com. **E-mail:** www .thepoisonedpencil.submittable.com/submit. **Website:** www.thepoisonedpencil.com. **Contact:** Ellen Larson, editor. Estab. 2012. Publishes trade paperback and electronic originals. Guidelines available online at website.

◗   *Accepts young adult mysteries only.*

IMPRINTS Imprint of Poisoned Pen Press.

NEEDS "We publish only young adult mystery novels, 45,000 to 90,000 words in length. For our purposes, a young adult book is a book with a protagonist between the ages of 12 and 18. We are looking for both traditional and cross-genre young adult mysteries. We encourage offbeat approaches and narrative choices that reflect the complexity and ambiguity of today's world. Submissions from teens are very welcome. Avoid serial killers, excessive gore, and vampires (and other heavy supernatural themes). We only consider authors who live in the U.S. or Canada, due to practicalities of marketing promotion. Avoid coincidence in plotting. Avoid having your sleuth leap to conclusions rather than discover and deduce. Pay attention to the resonance between character and plot; between plot and theme; between theme and character. We are looking for clean style, fluid storytelling, and solid structure. Unrealistic dialog is a real turnoff."

HOW TO CONTACT Submit proposal package including synopsis, complete ms, and cover letter.

TERMS Pays 9-15% for trade paperback; 25-35% for e-books. Pays advance of $1,000. Responds in 6 weeks to mss.

TIPS "Our audience is young adults and adults who love YA mysteries."

◗ ◗ ⦿ POISONED PEN PRESS

6962 E. 1st Ave., Suite 103, Scottsdale, AZ 85251. (480)945-3375. **Fax:** (480)949-1707. **E-mail:** submissions@poisonedpenpress.com. **Website:** www.poisonedpenpress.com. **Contact:** Jessica Tribble, publisher; Barbara Peters, editor-in-chief. Estab. 1996. "Our publishing goal is to offer well-written mystery novels of crime and/or detection where the puzzle and its resolution are the main forces that move the story forward." Publishes hardcover originals, and hardcover and trade paperback reprints. Book catalog and guidelines available online at website.

◗   *Not currently accepting submissions. Check website.*

IMPRINTS The Poisoned Pencil.

NEEDS Mss should generally be longer than 65,000 words and shorter than 100,000 words. Member Publishers Marketing Associations, Arizona Book Publishers Associations, Publishers Association of West. Distributes through Ingram, Baker & Taylor, Brodart. Does not want novels centered on serial killers, spousal or child abuse, drugs, or extremist groups, although we do not entirely rule such works out.

HOW TO CONTACT Accepts unsolicited mss. Electronic queries only. "Query with SASE. Submit clips, first 3 pages. We must receive both the synopsis and ms pages electronically as separate attachments to an e-mail message or as a disk or CD, which we will not return."

TERMS Pays 9-15% royalty on retail price. Responds in 2-3 months to queries and proposals; 6 months to mss.

TIPS "Audience is adult readers of mystery fiction."

◗ ◗ PRAIRIE JOURNAL PRESS

P.O. Box 68073, Calgary AB T3G 3N8 Canada. **E-mail:** prairiejournal@yahoo.com. **Website:** www .geocities.com/prairiejournal/. **Contact:** Anne Burke, literary editor. Estab. 1983.

◗   Prairie Journal Press authors have been nominees for The Journey Prize in fiction and finalists and honorable mention for the National Magazine awards.

NEEDS Literary, short story collections. Published *Prairie Journal Fiction, Prairie Journal Fiction II* (anthologies of short stories); *Solstice* (short fiction on the theme of aging); and *Prairie Journal Prose.*

HOW TO CONTACT Submit with SAE with IRC for individuals. No U.S. stamps please. Accepts unsolicited mss. Sometimes comments on rejected mss.

TERMS Pays 1 author's copy; honorarium depends on grant/award provided by the government or private/corporate donations.

TIPS "We wish we had the means to promote more new writers. We look for something different each time and try not to repeat types of stories if possible. We receive fiction of very high quality. Short fiction is preferable although excerpts from novels are considered if they stand alone on their own merit."

PRESS 53

P.O. Box 30314, Winston-Salem, NC 27101. **E-mail:** kevin@press53.com. **Website:** www.press53.com. **Contact:** Kevin Morgan Watson, publisher. "Press 53 was founded in October 2005 and quickly began earning a reputation as a quality publishing house of short story and poetry collections." Open submission period in November each year. Guidelines online.

NEEDS "We publish roughly 8 short story collections each year by writers who are active and earning recognition through publication and awards." Collections should include 10-15 short stories with 70% or more of those stories previously published. Does not want novels.

HOW TO CONTACT November submission period. Submit via Submittable on site with a letter of introduction (information about yourself and your collection), where the stories have been published, a few ideas for marketing your book, and the complete ms.

TERMS Responds in 6 months to mss.

TIPS "We are looking for writers who are actively involved in the writing community, writers who are submitting their work to journals, magazines, and contests, and who are getting published and earning a reputation for their work."

PUFFIN BOOKS

Imprint of Penguin Group (USA), Inc., 375 Hudson St., New York, NY 10014. (212)366-2000. **Website:** www.penguinputnam.com. **Contact:** Kristin Gilson, editorial director. "Puffin Books publishes high-end trade paperbacks and paperback reprints for preschool children, beginning and middle readers, and young adults." Publishes trade paperback originals and reprints. Book catalog for 9" × 12" SAE with 7 first-class stamps.

IMPRINTS Speak, Firebird, Sleuth.

NEEDS Picture books, young adult novels, middle grade and easy-to-read grades 1-3: fantasy and science fiction, graphic novels, classics. Recently published *Three Cups of Tea* (young readers edition), by Greg Mortenson and David Oliver Relin, adapted for young readers by Sarah Thomson; *The Big Field*, by Mike Lupica; *Geek Charming*, by Robin Palmer.

HOW TO CONTACT *No unsolicited mss.* Submit 3 sample chapters with SASE.

TERMS Royalty varies. Pays varies advance. Responds in 5 months.

TIPS "Our audience ranges from little children 'first books' to young adult (ages 14-16). An original idea has the best luck."

PUSH

Scholastic, 557 Broadway, New York, NY 10012. **E-mail:** DLevithan@Scholastic.com. **Website:** www thisispush.com. Estab. 2002. PUSH publishes new voices in teen literature.

PUSH does not accept unsolicited mss or queries, only agented or referred fiction/memoir.

NEEDS Young adults: contemporary, multicultural, poetry. Recently published *Splintering*, by Eireann Corrigan; *Never Mind the Goldbergs*, by Matthue Roth; *Perfect World*, by Brian James.

HOW TO CONTACT *Does not accept unsolicited mss.*

TIPS "We only publish first-time writers (and then their subsequent books), so authors who have published previously should not consider PUSH. Also, for young writers in grades 7-12, we run the PUSH Novel Contest with the Scholastic Art & Writing Awards. Every year it begins in October and ends in March. Rules can be found on our website."

G.P. PUTNAM'S SONS HARDCOVER

Imprint of Penguin Group (USA), Inc., 375 Hudson, New York, NY 10014. (212)366-2000. **Fax:** (212)366-2664. **Website:** www.penguinputnam.com. Publishes hardcover originals. Request book catalog through mail order department.

HOW TO CONTACT Agented submissions only. *No unsolicited mss.*

TERMS Pays variable royalties on retail price. Pays varies advance.

QUIXOTE PRESS

3544 Blakslee St., Wever IA 52658. (800)571-2665. **Fax:** (319)372-7485. **Website:** www.heartsntummies .com. **Contact:** Bruce Carlson. Quixote Press specializes in humorous and/or regional folklore and special-interest cookbooks. Publishes trade paperback originals and reprints. **Published many debut authors within the last year.**

NEEDS Humor, short story collections. Published *Eating Ohio*, by Rus Pishnery (short stories about Ohio); *Lil' Red Book of Fishing Tips*, by Tom Whitecloud (fishing tales); *How to Talk Hoosier*, by Netha Bell (humor); *Cow Whisperer*, by Skip Holmes (humor); *Flour Sack Bloomers*, by Lucy Fetterhoff (history).

HOW TO CONTACT Query with SASE. Accepts simultaneous submissions. www.heartsntummies.com. Contact: Bruce Carlson.

TERMS Pays 10% royalty on wholesale price. Publishes ms 1 year after acceptance.

TIPS "Carefully consider marketing considerations. Audience is women in gift shops, on farm sites, direct retail outlets, wineries, outdoor sport shops, etc. Contact us at *your idea* stage, not complete ms stage. Be receptive to design input by us."

⊘◌ RAINCOAST BOOK DISTRIBUTION, LTD.

2440 Viking Way, Richmond, BC V6V 1N2 Canada. (604)448-7100. **Fax:** (604)270-7161. **E-mail:** info@raincoast.com. **Website:** www.raincoast.com. Publishes hardcover and trade paperback originals and reprints. Book catalog for #10 SASE.

IMPRINTS Raincoast Books; Polestar Books (fiction, poetry, literary nonfiction).

NEEDS *No unsolicited mss.*

TERMS Pays 8-12% royalty on retail price. Pays $1,000-6,000 advance.

RAIN TOWN PRESS

1111 E. Burnside St. #309, Portland, OR 97214. (503)962-9612. **E-mail:** submissions@raintownpress .com. **Website:** www.raintownpress.com. **Contact:** Misty V'Marie, acquisitions editor; Ellery Harvey, art director. Estab. 2009. Catalog available on website. Imprints included in a single catalog. Guidelines available on website for writers, artists, and photographers.

◌   "We are Portland, Oregon's first independent press dedicated to publishing literature for middle grade and young adult readers. We hope to give rise to their voice, speaking directly to the spirit they embody through our books and other endeavors. The gray days we endure in the Pacific Northwest are custommade for reading a good book—or in our case, making one. The rain inspires, challenges, and motivates us. To that end, we say: Let it drizzle. We will soon publish picture books."

IMPRINTS In The Future: Raintown Kids, Mary Darcy, Misty V'Marie, William Softich, Leah Brown.

NEEDS Middle Readers/YA/Teens: Wants adventure, animal, contemporary, fantasy, folktales, graphic novels, health, hi-lo, history, humor, multicultural, nature/environment, problem novels, sci-fi, special needs, sports. Catalog available on website.

HOW TO CONTACT Query. Submit complete ms. See online submission guide for detailed instructions.

TERMS Pays 8-15% royalty on net sales. Does not pay advance. Responds to queries and mss in 1-6 months.

TIPS "The middle-grade and YA markets have sometimes very stringent conventions for subject matter, theme, etc. It's most helpful if an author knows his/her genre inside and out. Read, read, read books that have successfully been published for your genre. This will ultimately make your writing more marketable. Also, follow a publisher's submission guidelines to a tee. We try to set writers up for success. Send us what we're looking for."

⊘⊘ RANDOM HOUSE CHILDREN'S BOOKS

1745 Broadway, New York, NY 10019. (212)782-9000. **Website:** www.randomhouse.com. Estab. 1925. "Producing books for preschool children through young adult readers, in all formats from board to activity books to picture books and novels, Random House Children's Books brings together world-famous franchise characters, multimillion-copy series and topflight, award-winning authors, and illustrators."

◌   Submit mss through a literary agent.

IMPRINTS BooksReportsNow.com, GoldenBooks. com, Junie B. Jones, Seussville, Kids@Random, Teachers@Random, Teens@Random; **Knopf/Delacorte/ Dell Young Readers Group:** Bantam, Crown, David Fickling Books, Delacorte Press, Dell Dragonfly, Dell Laurel-Leaf, Dell Yearling, Doubleday, Alfred A. Knopf, Wendy Lamb Books; **Random House Young Readers Group:** Akiko, Arthur, Barbie, Beginner Books, The Berenstain Bears, Bob the Builder, Disney, Dragon Tales, First Time Books, Golden Books, Landmark Books, Little Golden Books, Lucas Books, Mercer Mayer, Nickelodeon, Nick, Jr., pat the bunny, Picturebacks, Precious Moments, Richard Scarry, Sesame Street Books, Step Into Reading, Stepping Stones, Star Wars, Thomas the Tank Engine and Friends.

NEEDS "Random House publishes a select list of first chapter books and novels, with an emphasis on fantasy and historical fiction." Chapter books, middle-grade readers, young adult.

HOW TO CONTACT *Does not accept unsolicited mss.*

TIPS "We look for original, unique stories. Do something that hasn't been done before."

◐○ RANSOM PUBLISHING

Radley House, 8 St. Cross Road, Winchester Hampshire SO23 9HX United Kingdom. +44 (0) 01962 862307. **Fax:** +44 (0) 05601 148881. **E-mail:** ransom@ransom.co.uk. **Website:** www.ransom.co.uk. **Contact:** Jenny Ertle, editor. Estab. 1995. Independent UK publisher with distribution in English speaking markets throughout the world. Specializes in books for reluctant and struggling readers. Our high-quality, visually stimulating, age-appropriate material has achieved wide acclaim for its ability to engage and motivate those who either can't or won't read. One of the few English language publishers to publish books with very high interest age and very low reading age. Has a developing list of children's books for home and school use. Specializes in phonics and general reading programs. Publishes paperback originals. Ms guidelines by e-mail.

NEEDS Easy reading for young adults. Books for reluctant and struggling readers.

HOW TO CONTACT Accepts unsolicited mss. Query with SASE or submit outline/proposal. Prefers queries by e-mail. Include estimated word count, brief bio, list of publishing credits.

TERMS Pays 10% royalty on net receipts. Responds to mss in 3-4 weeks.

RAZORBILL

Penguin Group, 375 Hudson St., New York, NY 10014. (212)414-3448. **Fax:** (212)414-3343. **E-mail:** laura.schechter@us.penguingroup.com; Ben.Schrank@us.penguingroup.com. **Website:** www.razorbillbooks.com. **Contact:** Gillian Levinson, assistant edtor; Jessica Rothenberg, editor; Brianne Mulligan, editor. Estab. 2003. "This division of Penguin Young Readers is looking for the best and the most original of commercial contemporary fiction titles for middle-grade and YA readers. A select quantity of nonfiction titles will also be considered."

NEEDS Middle Readers: adventure, contemporary, graphic novels, fantasy, humor, problem novels. Young adults/teens: adventure, contemporary, fantasy, graphic novels, humor, multicultural, suspense, paranormal, science fiction, dystopian, literary, romance. Average word length: middle readers—40,000; young adult—60,000. Recently published *Thirteen Reasons Why*, by Jay Asher (ages 14 and up, a *New York Times*

bestseller); Vampire Academy series by Richelle Mead (ages 12 and up; *New York Times* best-selling series); *The Teen Vogue Handbook* (ages 12 and up; a *New York Times* bestseller); and *I Am a Genius of Unspeakable Evil and I Want to Be Your Class President*, by Josh Lieb (ages 12 and up; a *New York Times* bestseller).

HOW TO CONTACT Submit outline/synopsis and 3 sample chapters along with query and SASE.

TERMS Offers advance against royalties. Responds to queries/mss in 1-3 months.

TIPS "New writers will have the best chance of acceptance and publication with original, contemporary material that boasts a distinctive voice and well-articulated world. Check out www.razorbillbooks.com to get a better idea of what we're looking for."

◑ RECLINER BOOKS

P.O. Box 64128, Calgary, AB T2K 1A9 Canada. (403)668-9746. **E-mail:** info@reclinerbooks.com. **E-mail:** submission@reclinerbooks.com. **Website:** www.reclinerbooks.com. **Contact:** Dustin Smith, editor (fiction, literary nonfiction). Estab. 2009. Publishes trade paperback originals. Soon available online at www.writtenindust.com/catalogue.html. Guidelines available online at www.writtenindust.com/submission.

NEEDS "We are not currently accepting anything targeted at children, young adults, or science fiction readers."

HOW TO CONTACT Submit proposal package, including: synopsis, 3 sample chapters, completed mss.

TERMS Pays 10-15% royalty on retail price. Pays $250-500 advance. Responds in 3 months to queries and proposals; 6 months to mss.

TIPS "Our audience is 24 years and older, 70% female, 30% male, 90% Canadian."

◑◐◑ RED DEER PRESS

195 Allstate Pkwy., Markham, ON L3R 4TB Canada. (905)477-9700. **Fax:** (905)477-9179. **E-mail:** rdp@reddeerpress.com; dionne@reddeerpress.com; val@reddeerpress.com. **Website:** www.reddeerpress.com. **Contact:** Richard Dionne, publisher. Estab. 1975. Book catalog for 9" × 12" SASE.

◑   Red Deer Press has received numerous honors and awards from the Book Publishers Association of Alberta, Canadian Children's Book Centre, the Governor General of Canada, and the Writers Guild of Alberta.

BOOK PUBLISHERS

NEEDS Publishes young adult, adult nonfiction, science fiction, fantasy, and paperback originals "focusing on books by, about, or of interest to Canadians." Books: offset paper; offset printing; hardcover/perfect-bound. Average print order: 5,000. First novel print order: 2,500. Distributes titles in Canada and the U.S., the UK, Australia, and New Zealand. Young adult (juvenile and early reader), contemporary. No romance or horror. Published *A Fine Daughter*, by Catherine Simmons Niven (novel); *The Kappa Child*, by Hiromi Goto (novel); *The Dollinage*, by Martine Leavitt; and *The Game*, by Teresa Toten (nominated for the Governor General's Award); *The Drum Calls Softly*, by David Bouchard (Aboriginal Picture Book); *Greener Grass*, by Caroline Pignat (Winner of the Governor General's Award); *Big Big Sky*, by Kristyn Dunnion (novel).

HOW TO CONTACT Accepts unsolicited mss. Query with SASE. No submissions on disk.

TERMS Pays 8-10% royalty. Responds to queries in 6 months.

TIPS "We're very interested in young adult and children's fiction from Canadian writers with a proven track record (either published books or widely published in established magazines or journals) and for manuscripts with regional themes and/or a distinctive voice. We publish Canadian authors exclusively."

⊘ RED HEN PRESS

P.O. Box 3537, Granada Hills, CA 91394. (818)831-0649. **Fax:** (818)831-6659. **E-mail:** redhenpressbooks.com. **Website:** www.redhen.org. **Contact:** Mark E. Cull, publisher/editor (fiction). Estab. 1993. "*Red Hen Press is not currently accepting unsolicited material.* At this time, the best opportunity to be published by Red Hen is by entering one of our contests. Please find more information in our award submission guidelines." Publishes trade paperback originals. Book catalog available free. Guidelines available online.

NEEDS Ethnic, experimental, feminist, gay/lesbian, historical, literary, mainstream/contemporary, short story collections. "We prefer high-quality literary fiction." Published *The Misread City: New Literary Los Angeles*, edited by Dana Gioia and Scott Timberg; *Rebel*, by Tom Hayden

HOW TO CONTACT Currently not accepting submissions.

TERMS Responds in 1 month to queries; 2 months to proposals; months to mss.

TIPS "Audience reads poetry, literary fiction, intelligent nonfiction. If you have an agent, we may be too small since we don't pay advances. Write well. Send queries first. Be willing to help promote your own book."

RED SAGE PUBLISHING, INC.

P.O. Box 4844, Seminole, FL 33775. (727)391-3847. **E-mail:** submissions@eredsage.com. **Website:** www.eredsage.com. **Contact:** Alexandria Kendall, publisher; Theresa Stevens, managing editor. Estab. 1995. Publishes books of romance fiction, written for the adventurous woman. Guidelines available online.

HOW TO CONTACT Submission guidelines online at http://www.eredsage.com/store/RedSageSubmissionGuidelines_HowToSendSubmission.html

TERMS Pays advance.

◐◑ RED TUQUE BOOKS, INC.

477 Martin St., Unit #6, Penticton, BC V2A 5L2 Canada. (778)476-5750. **Fax:** (778)476-5651. **Website:** www.redtuquebooks.ca. **Contact:** David Korinetz, executive editor.

HOW TO CONTACT Submit a query letter and first five pages. Include total word count. A one-page synopsis is optional. Accepts queries by e-mail and mail. SASE for reply only.

TERMS Pays 5-7% royalties on net sales. Pays $250 advance. Responds in 3 weeks.

TIPS "Well-plotted, character-driven stories, preferably with happy endings, will have the best chance of being accepted. Keep in mind that authors who like to begin sentences with 'and, or, and but' are less likely to be considered. Don't send anything gruesome or overly explicit; tell us a good story, but think PG."

RENAISSANCE HOUSE

465 Westview Ave., Englewood, NJ 07631. (201)408-4048. **E-mail:** info@renaissancehouse.net. **Website:** www.renaissancehouse.net. Publishes biographies, folktales, coffee table books, instructional, textbooks, adventure, picture books, juvenile, and young adult. Specializes in multicultural and bilingual titles, Spanish-English. Submit outline/synopsis. Will consider e-mail submissions. Children's, educational, multicultural, and textbooks. Represents 80 illustrators. 95% of artwork handled is children's book illustration. Currently open to illustrators seeking representation. Open to both new and established illustrators.

NEEDS Picture books: animal, folktales, multicultural. Young readers: animal, anthology, folktales, multicultural. Middle readers, young adult/teens: anthology, folktales, multicultural, nature/environment. **TERMS** Responds to queries/mss in 2 months.

REPUBLIC OF TEXAS PRESS

Imprint of Taylor Trade Publishing, and part of Rowman and Littlefield Publishing Group, 5360 Manhattan Circle, #101, Boulder, CO 80303. (303)543-7835, ext. 318. **E-mail:** tradeeditorial@rowman.com. **Website:** www.rlpgtrade.com. **Contact:** Rick Rinehart, editorial director. Publishes trade and paperback originals.

TERMS Pays industry-standard royalty on net receipts. Pays small advance. Responds in 2 months to queries.

TIPS "Do not submit any original materials, as they will not be returned. Our market is adult."

✚ RING OF FIRE PUBLISHING LLC

6523 California Ave. SW #409, Seattle, WA 98136. **E-mail:** contact@ringoffirebooks.com. **E-mail:** submissions@ringoffirebooks.com. **Website:** www.ringoffirebooks.com. Estab. 2011. "Our audience is comprised of well-read fiction enthusiasts. Let us tell your story." Book catalog and ms guidelines available online at website.

IMPRINTS Publishes trade paperback and electronic originals.

HOW TO CONTACT Query online. Submit synopsis and 3 sample chapters.

TERMS Pays royalties. Responds in 1 month to queries; 2 months to mss.

❶ ⚙ RIVER CITY PUBLISHING

1719 Mulberry St., Montgomery, AL 36106. **E-mail:** fnorris@rivercitypublishing.com. **Website:** www.rivercitypublishing.com. **Contact:** Fran Norris, editor. Estab. 1989. Midsize independent publisher (8-10 books/year). River City primarily publishes narrative nonfiction that reflects the South. "We are looking for mainly narrative histories, sociological accounts, and travel. Only biographies and memoirs from noted persons will be considered; we are closed to all personal memoir submissions." Publishes hardcover and trade paperback originals.

NEEDS Literary fiction, narrative nonfiction, regional (southern), short story collections. No poetry, memoir, or children's books. Published *Murder Creek*, by Joe Formichella (true crime); *Breathing Out the Ghost*, by Kirk Curnutt (novel); *The Bear Bryant Funeral Train*, by Brad Vice (short story collection).

HOW TO CONTACT See nonfiction submission guidelines.

TERMS Pays 10-15% royalty on retail price. Pays $500-5,000 advance. Responds to mss in 9 months.

TIPS "Only send your best work after you have received outside opinions. From approximately 1,000 submissions each year, we publish no more than 8 books and few of those come from unsolicited material. Competition is fierce, so follow the guidelines exactly. All first-time novelists should submit their work to the Fred Bonnie Award contest."

❶ ❷ ⚙ RIVERHEAD BOOKS

Penguin Putnam, 375 Hudson St., Office #4079, New York, NY 10014. **E-mail:** ecommerce@us.penguingroup.com. **E-mail:** riverhead.web@us.penguingroup.com. **Website:** www.riverheadbooks.com. **Contact:** Megan Lynch, senior editor.

NEEDS Literary, mainstream, contemporary. Among the award-winning writers whose careers Riverhead has launched so far are Pearl Abraham (*The Romance Reader*; *Giving Up America*), Jennifer Belle (*Going Down*; *High Maintenance*), Adam Davies (*The Frog King*), Junot Díaz (*Drown*), Alex Garland (*The Beach*; *The Tesseract*), Nick Hornby (*High Fidelity*; *About a Boy*; *How to Be Good*), Khaled Hosseini (*The Kite Runner*), ZZ Packer (*Drinking Coffee Elsewhere*), Iain Pears (*The Dream of Scipio*; *Instance of the Fingerpost*), Danzy Senna (*Caucasia*), Gary Shteyngart (*The Russian Debutante's Handbook*), Aryeh Lev Stollman (*The Far Euphrates*; *The Illuminated Soul*; *The Dialogues of Time and Entropy*), Sarah Waters (*Tipping the Velvet*; *Affinity*; *Fingersmith*).

HOW TO CONTACT *Submit through agent only. No unsolicited mss.*

❶ ROARING BROOK PRESS

175 Fifth Ave., New York, NY 10010. (646)307-5151. **E-mail:** david.langva@roaringbrookpress.com. **E-mail:** press.inquiries@macmillanusa.com. **Website:** http://us.macmillan.com/RoaringBrook.aspx. **Contact:** David Langva. Estab. 2000. Roaring Brook Press is an imprint of MacMillan, a group of companies that includes Henry Holt and Farrar, Straus & Giroux. Roaring Brook is not accepting unsolicited manuscripts. Roaring Brook title *First the Egg*, by Laura Vaacaro Seeger, won a Caldecott Honor Medal and a Theodor Seuss Geisel Honor in 2008. Their title *Dog and Bear:*

Two Friends, Three Stories, also by Laura Vaccaro Seeger, won the Boston Globe-Horn Book Picture Book Award in 2007.

NEEDS Picture books, young readers, middle readers, young adults: adventure, animal, contemporary, fantasy, history, humor, multicultural, nature/environment, poetry, religion, science fiction, sports, suspense/mystery. Recently published *Happy Birthday Bad Kitty*, by Nick Bruel; *Cookie*, by Jacqueline Wilson.

HOW TO CONTACT *Not accepting unsolicited mss or queries.*

TERMS Pays authors royalty based on retail price.

TIPS "You should find a reputable agent and have him/her submit your work."

◐ RONSDALE PRESS

3350 W. 21st Ave., Vancouver, BC V6S 1G7 Canada. (604)738-4688. **Fax:** (604)731-4548. **E-mail:** rons dale@shaw.ca. **Website:** http://ronsdalepress.com. **Contact:** Ronald B. Hatch (fiction, poetry, nonfiction, social commentary); Veronica Hatch (young adult novels and short stories). Estab. 1988. "Ronsdale Press is a Canadian literary publishing house that publishes 12 books/year, four of which are young adult titles. Of particular interest are books involving children exploring and discovering new aspects of Canadian history." Publishes trade paperback originals. Book catalog for #10 SASE. Guidelines available online.

NEEDS Young adults: Canadian novels. Average word length: middle readers and young adults—50,000. Recently published *Torn from Troy*, by Patrick Bowman (ages 10-14); *Hannah & The Salish Sea*, by Carol Anne Shaw (ages 10-14); *Dark Times*, edited by Ann Walsh (anthology of short stories, ages 10 and up); *Outlaw in India*, by Philip Roy; *Freedom Bound*, by Jean Rae Baxter (ages 10-14).

HOW TO CONTACT Submit complete ms.

TERMS Pays 10% royalty on retail price. Responds to queries in 2 weeks; mss in 2 months.

TIPS "Ronsdale Press is a literary publishing house, based in Vancouver and dedicated to publishing books from across Canada, books that give Canadians new insights into themselves and their country. We aim to publish the best Canadian writers."

ROSE ALLEY PRESS

4203 Brooklyn Ave. NE, #103A, Seattle, WA 98105. (206)633-2725. **E-mail:** rosealleypress@juno.com. **Website:** www.rosealleypress.com. **Contact:** David D. Horowitz. Estab. 1995. "Rose Alley Press primarily publishes books featuring rhymed metrical poetry and an annually updated booklet about writing and publication. We do not read or consider unsolicited manuscripts."

SAINT MARY'S PRESS

702 Terrace Heights, Winona, MN 55987. (800)533-8095. **Fax:** (800)344-9225. **E-mail:** submissions@smp .org. **Website:** www.smp.org. Ms guidelines online or by e-mail.

TIPS "Request product catalog and/or see Saint Mary Press book lists online before submitting proposal."

➕ ✪ SAKURA PUBLISHING & TECHNOLOGIES

P.O. Box 1681, Hermitage, PA 16148. (330)360-5131. **E-mail:** skpublishing124@gmail.com. **Website:** www .sakura-publishing.com. **Contact:** Derek Vasconi, talent finder and CEO. Estab. 2010. Publishes hardcover, trade paperback, mass-market paperback and electronic originals and reprints. Book catalog available for #10 SASE. Guidelines available online at website or by e-mail.

TERMS Pays royalty of 20-60% on wholesale price or retail price. Responds in 1 month to queries, mss, proposals.

⊘ SALVO PRESS

E-mail: schmidt@salvopress.com. **E-mail:** query@ salvopress.com. **Website:** www.salvopress.com. **Contact:** Scott Schmidt, publisher. Estab. 1998. Book catalog and ms guidelines online.

NEEDS "We are a small press specializing in mystery, suspense, espionage, and thriller fiction. Our press publishes in trade paperback and most e-book formats." Publishes hardcover, trade paperback originals and e-books in most formats. Books: 5½" × 8½" or 6" × 9" printing; perfect-bound. **Published 6 debut authors within the last year.** Averages 6-12 fiction total titles/year, mostly fiction. "Our needs change, check our website."

HOW TO CONTACT Currently closed to submissions.

TERMS Pays 10% royalty. Responds in 5 minutes to 1 month to queries; 2 months to mss.

◐ ◑ ⚲ SAMHAIN PUBLISHING, LTD

11821 Mason Montgomery Rd., Cincinnati, OH 45249. (478)314-5144. **Fax:** (478)314-5148. **E-mail:** editor@ samhainpublishing.com. **Website:** www.samhain

publishing.com. **Contact:** Heather Osborn, editorial director. Estab. 2005. "A small, independent publisher, Samhain's motto is 'It's all about the story.' We look for fresh, unique voices who have a story to share with the world. We encourage our authors to let their muse have its way and to create tales that don't always adhere to current trends. One never knows what the next hot genre will be or when it will start, so write what's in your soul. These are the books that, whether the story is based on formula or is an original, when written from the heart will earn you a lifetime readership." Publishes e-books and paperback originals. POD/offset printing; line illustrations. Guidelines available online.

○ Preditor and Editors Best Publisher 2006.

NEEDS Needs erotica and all genres and all heat levels of romance (contemporary, futuristic/time travel, gothic, historical, paranormal, regency period, romantic suspense, fantasy, action/adventure, etc.), as well as fantasy, urban fantasy or science fiction with strong romantic elements, with word counts between 12,000 and 120,000 words. "Samhain is now accepting submissions for our line of horror novels. We are actively seeking talented writers who can tell an exciting, dramatic, and frightening story, and who are eager to promote their work and build their community of readers. We are looking for novels either supernatural or not, contemporary or historical that are original and compelling. Authors can be previously unpublished or established, agented or un-agented. Content can range from subtle and unsettling to gory and shocking. The writing is what counts."

HOW TO CONTACT Accepts unsolicited mss. Query with outline/synopsis and either 3 sample chapters or the full ms. Accepts queries by e-mail only. Include estimated word count, brief bio, list of publishing credits, and "how the author is working to improve craft: association, critique groups, etc."

TERMS Pays royalties 30-40% for e-books, average of 8% for trade paper, and author's copies (quantity varies). Responds in 4 months to queries and mss.

TIPS "Because we are an e-publisher first, we do not have to be as concerned with industry trends and can publish less popular genres of fiction if we believe the story and voice are good and will appeal to our customers. Please follow submission guidelines located on our website, include all requested information, and proof your query/manuscript for errors prior to submission."

SARABANDE BOOKS, INC.

2234 Dundee Rd., Suite 200, Louisville, KY 40205. (502)458-4028. **Fax:** (502)458-4065. **E-mail:** info@sarabandebooks.org. **Website:** www.sarabandebooks.org. **Contact:** Sarah Gorham, editor-in-chief. Estab. 1994. "Sarabande Books was founded to publish poetry, short fiction, and creative nonfiction. We look for works of lasting literary value. Please see our titles to get an idea of our taste. Accepts submissions through contests and open submissions." Publishes trade paperback originals. Book catalog available free. Contest guidelines for #10 SASE or on website.

○ Charges $10 handling fee with alternative option of purchase of book from website (email confirmation of sale must be included with submission).

NEEDS Literary, novellas, short novels, 250 pages maximum, 150 pages minimum. We consider novels and non-fiction in a wide variety of genres and subject matters with a special emphasis on mysteries and crime fiction. We do not consider science fiction, fantasy, or horror. Our target length is 70,000-90,000 words. Submissions to Mary McCarthy Prize in Short Fiction accepted January through February. Published *Other Electricities*, by Ander Monson; *More Like Not Running Away*, by Paul Shepherd, and *Water: Nine Stories*, by Alyce Miller.

HOW TO CONTACT Queries can be sent via e-mail, fax, or regular post. Ms guidelines for #10 SASE.

TERMS Pays royalty of 10% on actual income received. Pays $500-1000 advance. Also pays in author copies. Publishes ms 18 months after acceptance.

TIPS "Make sure you're not writing in a vacuum, that you've read and are conscious of contemporary literature. Have someone read your manuscript, checking it for ordering, coherence. Better a lean, consistently strong manuscript than one that is long and uneven. We like a story to have good narrative, and we like to be engaged by language."

SASQUATCH BOOKS

1904 Third Ave., Suite 710, Seattle, WA 98101. (206)467-4300. **Fax:** (206)467-4301. **E-mail:** ttabor@sasquatchbooks.com. **Website:** www.sasquatchbooks.com. **Contact:** Gary Luke, editorial director; Terence Maikels, acquisitions editor; Heidi Lenze, acquisitions editor. Estab. 1986. "Sasquatch Books publishes books for and from the Pacific Northwest, Alaska, and California is the nation's premier regional press.

Sasquatch Books' publishing program is a veritable celebration of regionally written words. Undeterred by political or geographical borders, Sasquatch defines its region as the magnificent area that stretches from the Brooks Range to the Gulf of California and from the Rocky Mountains to the Pacific Ocean. Our top-selling *Best Places®* travel guides serve the most popular destinations and locations of the West. We also publish widely in the areas of food and wine, gardening, nature, photography, children's books, and regional history, all facets of the literature of place. With more than 200 books brimming with insider information on the West, we offer an energetic eye on the lifestyle, landscape, and worldview of our region. Considers queries and proposals from authors and agents for new projects that fit into our West Coast regional publishing program. We can evaluate query letters, proposals, and complete mss." Publishes regional hardcover and trade paperback originals. Book catalog for 9" × 12" envelope and 2 first-class stamps. Guidelines available online.

○ "When you submit to Sasquatch Books, please remember that the editors want to know about you *and* your project, along with a sense of who will want to read your book."

NEEDS Young readers: adventure, animal, concept, contemporary, humor, nature/environment. Recently published *Amazing Alaska*, by Deb Vanasse, illustrated by Karen Lewis; *Sourdough Man*, by Cherie Stihler, illustrated by Barbara Lavallee.

TERMS Pays royalty on cover price. Pays wide range advance. Responds to queries in 3 months.

TIPS "We sell books through a range of channels in addition to the book trade. Our primary audience consists of active, literate residents of the West Coast."

Ⓐ SCHOLASTIC PRESS

Imprint of Scholastic, Inc., 557 Broadway, New York, NY 10012. (212)343-6100. **Fax:** (212)343-4713. **Website:** www.scholastic.com. **Contact:** David Saylor, editorial director, Scholastic Press, creative director and associate publisher for all Scholastic hardcover imprints. Scholastic Press publishes fresh, literary picture book fiction and nonfiction; fresh, literary non-series or nongenre-oriented middle-grade and young adult fiction. Currently emphasizing subtly handled treatments of key relationships in children's lives; unusual approaches to commonly dry subjects, such as biography, math, history, or science. De-emphasizing

fairy tales (or retellings), board books, genre, or series fiction (mystery, fantasy, etc.). Publishes hardcover originals.

NEEDS Looking for strong picture books, young chapter books, appealing middle-grade novels (ages 8-11) and interesting and well-written young adult novels. Wants fresh, exciting picture books and novels—inspiring, new talent. Published *Chasing Vermeer*, by Blue Balliet; *Here Today*, by Ann M. Martin; *Detective LaRue*, by Mark Teague.

HOW TO CONTACT *Agented submissions and previously published authors only.*

TERMS Pays royalty on retail price. Pays variable advance. Responds in 3 months to queries; 6-8 months to mss.

TIPS Read *currently* published children's books. Revise, rewrite, rework, and find your own voice, style, and subject. We are looking for authors with a strong and unique voice who can tell a great story and have the ability to evoke genuine emotion. Children's publishers are becoming more selective, looking for irresistible talent and fairly broad appeal, yet still very willing to take risks, just to keep the game interesting."

SEAL PRESS

1700 4th St., Berkeley, CA 94710. (510)595-3664. **E-mail:** Seal.Press@perseusbooks.com. **E-mail:** sealacquisitions@avalonpub.com. **Website:** www.sealpress.com. Estab. 1976. "Seal Press is an imprint of Avalon Publishing Group, feminist book publisher interested in original, lively, radical, empowering, and culturally diverse nonfiction by women addressing contemporary issues from a feminist perspective or speaking positively to the experience of being female. Currently emphasizing women outdoor adventurists, young feminists, political issues for women, health issues, and surviving abuse. *Not accepting fiction at this time.*" Publishes trade paperback originals. Book catalog and ms guidelines for SASE or online.

NEEDS Ethnic, feminist, gay/lesbian, literary, multicultural. "We are interested in alternative voices." Published *Valencia*, by Michelle Tea (fiction); *Navigating the Darwin Straits*, by Edith Forbes (fiction); and *Bruised Hibiscus*, by Elizabeth Nunez (fiction).

HOW TO CONTACT *Does not accept fiction at present.* Query with SASE or submit outline, 2 sample chapters, synopsis.

TERMS Pays 7-10% royalty on retail price. Pays variable royalty on retail price. Pays $3,000-10,000 advance. Pays variable advance. Responds in 2 months to queries.

TIPS "Our audience is generally composed of women interested in reading about women's issues addressed from a feminist perspective."

SECOND STORY PRESS

20 Maud St., Suite 401, Toronto, ON M5V 2M5 Canada. (416)537-7850. **Fax:** (416)537-0588. **E-mail:** info@secondstorypress.ca; marketing@secondstorypress.com. **Website:** www.secondstorypress.ca.

NEEDS Considers nonsexist, nonracist, and nonviolent stories, as well as historical fiction, chapter books, picture books. **Recently published:** *Writing the Revolution*, by Michele Landsberg; *Shannen and the Dream for a School*, by Janet Wilson.

HOW TO CONTACT *Accepts appropriate material from residents of Canada only.* Submit outline and sample chapters by postal mail only. No electronic submissions or queries.

SEEDLING PUBLICATIONS, INC.

Continental Press, Inc., 520 E. Bainbridge St., Elizabethtown, PA 17022. (800)233-0759. **E-mail:** MBergonzi@continentalpress.com. **Website:** www.continentalpress.com. **Contact:** Megan Bergonzi, managing editor. Estab. 1937. "We are an education niche publisher, producing books for beginning readers. Stories must include language that is natural to young children and story lines that are interesting to 5-7-year-olds and written at their beginning reading level. Continental Press's Seedling product line focuses on fiction and nonfiction leveled readers and other materials that support early literacy in prekindergarten through second grade. Familiarity with reading recovery, guided reading, and other reading intervention programs will give you a sense of the kinds of materials needed for Seedling products." Publishes Seedling books in an 8-, 12-, or 16-page format for beginning readers. Guidelines for #10 SASE.

Does not accept mss via fax. Does not accept queries at all.

HOW TO CONTACT Submit complete ms.

TERMS Makes outright purchase.

TIPS "Follow our guidelines. Do not submit full-length picture books or chapter books."

SERIOUSLY GOOD BOOKS

999 Vanderbilt Beach Rd., Naples, FL 34119. **E-mail:** seriouslygoodbks@aol.com. **Website:** www.seriouslygoodbks.net. Estab. 2010. Publishes historial fiction only. Publishes trade paperback and electronic originals. Book catalog and writers guidelines online at website.

HOW TO CONTACT Query by e-mail.

TERMS Pays 15% minimum royalties. Respons in 1 month to queries.

TIPS "Looking for historial fiction with substance. We seek well-researched historical fiction in the vein of Rutherfurd, Mary Renault, Maggie Anton, Robert Harris, etc. Please don't query with historical fiction mixed with other genres (romance, time travel, vampires, etc.)."

SEVEN STORIES PRESS

140 Watts St., New York, NY 10013. (212)226-8760. **Fax:** (212)226-1411. **E-mail:** anna@sevenstories.com. **Website:** www.sevenstories.com. **Contact:** Daniel Simon; Anna Lui. Estab. 1995. Founded in 1995 in New York City, and named for the seven authors who committed to a home with a fiercely independent spirit, Seven Stories Press publishes works of the imagination and political titles by voices of conscience. While most widely known for its books on politics, human rights, and social and economic justice, Seven Stories continues to champion literature, with a list encompassing both innovative debut novels and National Book Award-winning poetry collections, as well as prose and poetry translations from the French, Spanish, German, Swedish, Italian, Greek, Polish, Korean, Vietnamese, Russian, and Arabic. Publishes hardcover and trade paperback originals. Book catalog and ms guidelines free.

HOW TO CONTACT "We are currently unable to accept any unsolicited full manuscripts. We do accept query letters and sample chapters. Please send no more than a cover letter and two sample chapters, along with a first-class-stamped SASE or postcard for reply. (If you would like your submission materials returned to you, please include sufficient postage.)"

TERMS Pays 7-15% royalty on retail price. Pays advance. Responds in 1 month to queries and mss.

TIPS "Each year we also publish an annual compilation of censored news stories by Project Censored. Features of this series include the Top 25 Censored News Stories of the year—which has a history of identifying important neglected news stories and which is widely disseminated in the alternative press—as well as the "Junk Food News" chapter and chapters on hot-button topics for the year. Seven Stories also maintains a publishing partnership with Human Rights Watch through the yearly publication of the World Report, a preeminent account of human rights abuse around the world—a report card on the progress of the world's nations towards the protection of human rights for people everywhere."

ⓐ⬤ SEVERN HOUSE PUBLISHERS

Salatin House, 19 Cedar St., Sutton, Surrey SM2 5DA United Kingdom. (44)(208)770-3930. **Fax:** (44)(208)770-3850. **Website:** www.severnhouse.com. **Contact:** Amanda Stewart, editorial director. Severn House is currently emphasizing suspense, romance, mystery. Large print imprint from existing authors. Publishes hardcover and trade paperback originals and reprints. Book catalog available free.

IMPRINTS Creme de la Crime.

NEEDS Adventure, fantasy, historical, horror, mainstream/contemporary, mystery, romance, short story collections, suspense. Recently published *Future Scrolls*, by Fern Michaels (historical romance); *Weekend Warrios*, by Fern Michaels; *The Hampton Passion*, by Julie Ellis (romance); *Looking Glass Justice*, by Jeffrey Ashford (crime and mystery); and *Cold Tactics*, by Ted Allbeury (thriller).

HOW TO CONTACT *Agented submissions only.*

TERMS Pays 7½-15% royalty on retail price. Pays $750-5,000 advance. Responds in 3 months to proposals.

ⓘ SILVER LEAF BOOKS, LLC

P.O. Box 6460, Holliston, MA 01746. **E-mail:** editor@silverleafbooks.com. **Website:** www.silverleafbooks.com. **Contact:** Brett Fried, editor. "Silver Leaf Books is a small press featuring primarily new and upcoming talent in the fantasy, science fiction, mystery, thrillers, suspense, and horror genres. Our editors work closely with our authors to establish a lasting and mutually beneficial relationship, helping both the authors and company continue to grow and thrive." Publishes hardcover originals, trade paperback originals, paperback originals, electronic/digital books. Average print order: 3,000. Debut novel print order: 3,000. **Published 1 new writer last year.** Plans 4 debut novels this year. Averages 6 total titles/year; 6 fiction titles/year. Distributes/promotes titles through Baker & Taylor Books and Ingram. Guidelines available online at website.

NEEDS Fantasy (space fantasy, sword and sorcery), horror (dark fantasy, futuristic, psychological, supernatural), mystery/suspense (amateur sleuth, cozy, police procedural, private eye/hard-boiled), science fiction (hard science/technological, soft/sociological), young adult (adventure, fantasy/science fiction, horror, mystery/suspense). Published *The Apprentice of Zoldex* and *The Darkness Within*, by Clifford B. Bowyer; *When the Sky Fell,* by Mike Lynch and Brandon Barr.

HOW TO CONTACT Query with outline/synopsis and 3 sample chapters. Accepts queries by snail mail. Include estimated word count, brief bio and marketing plan. Send SASE or IRC for return of ms or disposable copy of ms and SASE/IRC for reply only.

TERMS Pays royalties and provides author's copies. Responds to queries in 6 months; mss in 4 months.

TIPS "Follow the online guidelines, be thorough and professional."

ⓐ SIMON & SCHUSTER

1230 Avenue of the Americas, New York, NY 10020. (212)698-7000. **Website:** www.simonsays.com. ⬤ *Accepts agented submissions only.*

ⓐ SIMON & SCHUSTER ADULT PUBLISHING GROUP

1230 Avenue of the Americas, New York, NY 10020. **E-mail:** ssonline@simonsays.com; Lydia.Frost@simonandschuster.com. **Website:** www.simonsays.com. Estab. 1924. (formerly Simon & Schuster Trade Division, Division of Simon & Schuster), The Simon & Schuster Adult Publishing Group includes a number of publishing units that offer books in several formats. Each unit has its own publisher, editorial group, and publicity department. Common sales and business departments support all the units. The managing editorial, art, production, marketing, and subsidiary rights departments have staff members dedicated to the individual imprints.

HOW TO CONTACT *Agented submissions only.*

ⓞ SIMON & SCHUSTER BOOKS FOR YOUNG READERS

Imprint of Simon & Schuster Children's Publishing, 1230 Avenue of the Americas, New York, NY 10020. (212)698-7000. **Fax:** (212)698-2796. **Website:** www.simonsayskids.com. "Simon and Schuster Books For Young Readers is the Flagship imprint of the S&S Children's Division. We are committed to publishing a wide range of contemporary, commercial, award-winning fiction and nonfiction that spans every age of children's publishing. Books for Young Readers is constantly looking to the future, supporting our foundation authors and franchises, but always with an eye for breaking new ground with every publication. We publish high-quality fiction and nonfiction for a variety of age groups and a variety of markets. Above all, we strive to publish books that we are passionate about." Publishes hardcover originals. Guidelines for #10 SASE.

⚪ *No unsolicited mss. All unsolicited mss returned unopened. Queries are accepted via mail.*

IMPRINTS Paula Wiseman Books.

HOW TO CONTACT Query with SASE only.

TERMS Pays variable royalty on retail price. Responds in 2 months to queries and mss.

TIPS "We're looking for picture books centered on a strong, fully-developed protagonist who grows or changes during the course of the story; YA novels that are challenging and psychologically complex; also imaginative and humorous middle-grade fiction. And we want nonfiction that is as engaging as fiction. Our imprint's slogan is 'Reading You'll Remember.' We aim to publish books that are fresh, accessible, and family-oriented; we want them to have an impact on the reader."

SKINNER HOUSE BOOKS

The Unitarian Universalist Association, 25 Beacon St., Boston, MA 02108. (617)742-2100 ext. 603. **Fax:** (617)742-7025. **E-mail:** info@uua.org. **Website:** www.uua.org/skinner. **Contact:** Mary Benard, senior editor. Estab. 1975. "We publish titles in Unitarian Universalist faith, liberal religion, history, biography, worship, and issues of social justice. Most of our children's titles are intended for religious education or worship use. They reflect Unitarian Universalist values. We also publish inspirational titles of poetic prose and meditations. Writers should know that Unitarian Universalism is a liberal religious denomination committed to progressive ideals. Currently emphasizing social justice concerns." Publishes trade paperback originals and reprints. Book catalog for 6" × 9" SAE with 3 first-class stamps. Guidelines available online.

NEEDS All levels: anthology, multicultural, nature/environment, religion. Recently published *A Child's Book of Blessings and Prayers*, by Eliza Blanchard (ages 4-8, picture book); *Meet Jesus: The Life and Lessons of a Beloved Teacher*, by Lynn Gunney (age's 5-8,

picture book); *Magic Wanda's Travel Emporium*, by Joshua Searle-White (ages 9 and up, stories).

HOW TO CONTACT Query or submit outline/synopsis and 2 sample chapters.

TERMS Responds to queries in 3 weeks.

TIPS "From outside our denomination, we are interested in manuscripts that will be of help or interest to liberal churches, Sunday School classes, parents, ministers, and volunteers. Inspirational/spiritual and children's titles must reflect liberal Unitarian Universalist values."

⚪⚪ SMALL BEER PRESS

150 Pleasant St., #306, Easthampton, MA 01027. (413)203-1636. **Fax:** (413) 203-1636. **E-mail:** info@smallbeerpress.com. **Website:** www.smallbeerpress.com. **Contact:** Gavin J. Grant, acquisitions. Estab. 2000.

⚪ Small Beer Press also publishes the zine *Lady Churchill's Rosebud Wristlet*. "SBP's books have recently received the Tiptree and Crawford Awards."

NEEDS Literary, experimental, speculative, story collections. Recently published *The Monkey's Wedding and Other Stories*, by Joan Aiken; *Meeks*, by Julia Holmes; *What I Didn't See and Other Stories*, by Karen Joy Fowler.

HOW TO CONTACT "We do not accept unsolicited novel or short story collection manuscripts. Queries are welcome. Please send queries with an SASE by mail."

TIPS "Please be familiar with our books first to avoid wasting your time and ours, thank you."

SOFT SKULL PRESS INC.

Counterpoint, 1919 Fifth St., Berkeley, CA 94710. (510)704-0230. **Fax:** (510)704-0268. **E-mail:** info@softskull.com. **Website:** www.softskull.com. "Here at Soft Skull we love books that are new, fun, smart, revelatory, quirky, groundbreaking, cage-rattling, and/or otherwise unusual." Publishes hardcover and trade paperback originals. Book catalog and guidelines on website.

NEEDS Does not consider poetry.

HOW TO CONTACT Soft Skull Press no longer accepts digital submissions. Send a cover letter describing your project in detail and a completed ms. For graphic novels, send a minimum of five fully inked pages of art, along with a synopsis of your story line. "Please do not send original material, as it will not be returned."

TERMS Pays 7-10% royalty. Average advance: $100-15,000. Responds in 2 months to proposals; 3 months to mss.

TIPS "See our website for updated submission guidelines."

SOHO PRESS, INC.

853 Broadway, New York, NY 10003. **E-mail:** soho@sohopress.com. **Website:** www.sohopress.com. **Contact:** Bronwen Hruska, publisher; Katie Herman, editor. Estab. 1986. Soho Press publishes primarily fiction, as well as some narrative literary nonfiction and mysteries set abroad. No electronic submissions, only queries by e-mail. Publishes hardcover and trade paperback originals; trade paperback reprints. Guidelines available online.

NEEDS Adventure, ethnic, feminist, historical, literary, mainstream/contemporary, mystery (police procedural), suspense, multicultural. Published *Thirty-Three Teeth*, by Colin Cotterill; *When Red Is Black*, by Qiu Xiaolong; *Murder on the Ile Saint-Louis*, by Cara Black; *The Farming of Bones*, by Edwidge Danticat; *The Darkest Child*, by Delores Phillips; *The First Wave*, by James R. Benn.

HOW TO CONTACT Submit 3 sample chapters and cover letter with synopsis, author bio, SASE. *No e-mailed submissions.*

TERMS Pays 10-15% royalty on retail price (varies under certain circumstances). Responds in 3 months to queries and mss.

TIPS "Soho Press publishes discerning authors for discriminating readers, finding the strongest possible writers and publishing them. Before submitting, look at our website for an idea of the types of books we publish, and read our submission guidelines."

SOUNDPRINTS/STUDIO MOUSE

Palm Publishing. LLC, 50 Washington St., 12th Floor, Norwalk, CT 06854. (800)228-7839. **Fax:** (203)864-1776. **E-mail:** info@soundprints.com. **Website:** www.soundprints.com. Estab. 1947. Catalog available on website. Guidelines for SASE.

NEEDS Picture books, young readers: adventure, animal, fantasy, history, multicultural, nature/environment, sports. Recently published *Smithsonian Alphabet of Earth*, by Barbie Heit Schwaeber, and illustrated by Sally Vitsky (ages preschool to 2, hardcover and paperback available with audio CD plus bonus audiobook and e-book downloads); *First Look at Insects*, by Laura Gates Galvin, illustrated by Charlotte Oh.

Ages 18 months-5 years board book plus e-book and activities download.

HOW TO CONTACT Query or submit complete ms.

TERMS Responds to queries and mss in 6 months.

Ⓐ SOURCEBOOKS LANDMARK

Sourcebooks, Inc., 232 Madison Ave., Suite 1100, New York, NY 10016. **E-mail:** romance@sourcebooks.com. **Website:** www.sourcebooks.com. **Contact:** Leah Hultenschmidt. "Our fiction imprint, Sourcebooks Landmark, publishes a variety of commercial fiction, including specialties in historical fiction and Austenalia. We are interested first and foremost in books that have a story to tell."

> "We publish a variety of titles. We are currently only reviewing agented fiction manuscripts with the exception of romance fiction. Find out more information about our romance fiction submission guidelines online at our website."

NEEDS "We are actively acquiring single-title and single-title series romance fiction (90,000 to 120,000 actual digital words) for our Casablanca imprint. We are looking for strong writers who are excited about marketing their books and building their community of readers, and whose books have something fresh to offer in the genre of romance." Receipt of e-mail submissions will be acknowledged within 21 days via e-mail.

HOW TO CONTACT Responds to queries in 6-8 weeks. Email: romance@sourcebooks.com. Or mail hard copy to: Leah Hulltenschmidt, Sourcebooks, Inc., 390 Fifth Ave., Suite 907, New York, NY 10018. If you have any questions about our guidelines, please don't hesitate to email deb.werksman@sourcebooks.com. Please allow 21 days for response.

Ⓞ SPEAK UP PRESS

P.O. Box 100506, Denver, CO 80250. (303)715-0837. **Fax:** (303)715-0793. **E-mail:** info@speakuppress.org. **E-mail:** submit@speakuppress.org. **Website:** www.speakuppress.org. Estab. 1999. As a 501(c)3 nonprofit organization, Speak Up Press is supported by individuals, corporations, and foundations from across the country. Speak Up Press publishes *Speak Up Online* quarterly, featuring the original fiction, nonfiction, and poetry of teens (13-19 years old).

> *Only accepts submissions via e-mail.*

TIPS "Follow submission guidelines."

STARCHERONE BOOKS

Dzanc Books, P.O. Box 303, Buffalo, NY 14201. (716)885-2726. **E-mail:** starcherone@gmail.com; publisher@starcherone.com. **Website:** www.starcherone.com. **Contact:** Ted Pelton, publisher; Carra Stratton, acquisitions editor. Estab. 2000. Nonprofit publisher of literary and experimental fiction. Publishes paperback originals and reprints. Books: acid-free paper; perfect-bound; occasional illustrations. Average print order: 1,000. Average first novel print order: 1,000. **Published 2 debut authors within the last year.** Member CLMP. Titles distributed through website, Small Press Distribution, Amazon, independent bookstores. Catalog and guidelines available online at website.

HOW TO CONTACT Accepts queries by mail or e-mail during August and September of each year. *We will not be accepting any mss or queries outside of our contest until annual contest is concluded.* Submissions of unsolicited mss will risk being returned or discarded, unread. Include brief bio, list of publishing credits. Always query before sending ms.

TERMS Pays 10-12.5% royalty. Responds in 2 months to queries; 6-10 months to mss.

TIPS During the late summer/early fall each year, after our contest has concluded, we have an **open consideration period** of approximately six weeks. During this time, we read queries from authors who already have established their credentials in some way, generally through prior publication, awards, and the like. We ask for queries from writers describing their projects and their writing credentials. From these, we invite submissions. Our next period for receiving queries will be in the late summer/early fall. In October of each year, we begin our **annual contest**. "Become familiar with our interests in fiction. We are interested in new strategies for creating stories and fictive texts. Do not send genre fiction unless it is unconventional in approach."

STEEPLE HILL BOOKS

Imprint of Harlequin Enterprises, 233 Broadway, Suite 1001, New York, NY 10279. (212)553-4200. **Fax:** (212)227-8969. **Website:** www.eharlequin.com. **Contact:** Joan Marlow Golan, executive editor; Melissa Endlich, senior editor (inspirational contemporary romance, historical romance, romantic suspense); Tina James, senior editor (inspirational romantic suspense and historical romance); Emily Rodmell, asso-ciate editor. Estab. 1997. "This series of contemporary, inspirational love stories portrays Christian characters facing the many challenges of life, faith, and love in today's world." Publishes mass-market paperback originals and reprints. Guidelines available online, free on request, for #10 SASE.

IMPRINTS Love Inspired; Love Inspired Suspense; Love Inspired Historical.

NEEDS "We are looking for authors writing from a Christian worldview and conveying their personal faith and ministry values in entertaining fiction that will touch the hearts of believers and seekers everywhere."

HOW TO CONTACT Query with SASE and synopsis, submit completed ms.

TERMS Pays royalty on retail price. Pays advance. Respinds in 3 months to proposals and mss.

TIPS "Drama, humor, and even a touch of mystery all have a place in Steeple Hill. Subplots are welcome and should further the story's main focus or intertwine in a meaningful way. Secondary characters (children, family, friends, neighbors, fellow church members, etc.) may all contribute to a substantial and satisfying story. These wholesome tales include strong family values and high moral standards. While there is no premarital sex between characters, in the case of romance, a vivid, exciting tone presented with a mature perspective is essential. Although the element of faith must clearly be present, it should be well integrated into the characterizations and plot. The conflict between the main characters should be an emotional one, arising naturally from the well-developed personalities you've created. Suitable stories should also impart an important lesson about the powers of trust and faith."

ⒶⓄ ST. MARTIN'S PRESS, LLC

Holtzbrinck Publishers, 175 Fifth Ave., New York, NY 10010. (212)674-5151. **Fax:** (212)420-9314. **Website:** www.stmartins.com. Estab. 1952. General interest publisher of both fiction and nonfiction. Publishes hardcover, trade paperback, and mass-market originals.

IMPRINTS Minotaur; Thomas Dunne Books; Griffin; Palgrave MacMillan (division); Priddy Books; St. Martin's Press Paperback & Reference Group; St. Martin's Press Trade Division; Truman Talley Books.

HOW TO CONTACT Agented submissions only. *No unsolicited mss.*

TERMS Pays royalty. Pays advance.

⊕ STONE BRIDGE PRESS

P.O. Box 8208, Berkeley, CA 94707. **Website:** www .stonebridge.com. **Contact:** Peter Goodman, publisher. Estab. 1989. "Independent press focusing on books about Japan and Asia in English (business, language, culture, literature, animation)." Publishes hardcover and trade paperback originals. Books: 60-70 lb. offset paper; web and sheet paper; perfect-bound; some illustrations. Averages 12 total titles/year. Distributes titles through Consortium. Promotes titles through Internet announcements, special-interest magazines and niche tie-ins to associations. Book catalog for 2 first-class stamps and SASE. Ms guidelines online.

◑   Stone Bridge Press received a Japan-U.S. Friendship Prize for *Life in the Cul-de-Sac*, by Senji Kuroi.

NEEDS Experimental, gay/lesbian, literary, Japan-themed. "Primarily looking at material relating to Japan. Translations only."

HOW TO CONTACT Does not accept unsolicited mss. Query with SASE. Accepts queries by e -mail, fax. "If you need to send hard copy or other materials, send it to P.O. Box 8208, Berkeley, CA 94707. Use media mail or priority mail ONLY. IMPORTANT: If you require a certificate of delivery or are using Express Mail or a delivery service like UPS, (**do not use the post office box address and make the editor stand in line**); instead use our street address: 1393 Solano Avenue, Suite C, Albany, CA 94706. We will be **very** unhappy if you don't do this. Please note that we are primarily interested in books with a Japan/Asia connection (however tenuous). No materials can be returned to you unless you provide us with sufficient return postage. **We prefer to reply by e-mail.**"

TERMS Pays royalty on wholesale price. Responds to queries in 4 months, mss in 8 months.

TIPS "Fiction translations only for the time being. No poetry."

⊕ STONESLIDE BOOKS

Stoneslide Media LLC, P.O. Box 8331, New Haven, CT 06530. **E-mail:** editors@stoneslidecorrective.com. **E-mail:** submissions@stoneslidecorrective.com. **Website:** www.stoneslidecorrective.com. **Contact:** Jonathan Weisberg, editor; Christopher Wachlin, editor. Estab. 2012. Publishes trade paperback and electronic originals. Book catalog and guidelines available online.

NEEDS "We will look at any genre. The important factor for us is that the story use plot, characters, emotions, and other elements of storytelling to move the mind forward."

HOW TO CONTACT Submit proposal package via e-mail including: synopsis and 3 sample chapters.

TERMS Pays royalty of 20% minimum to 80% maximum. Responds in 1 month to queries/proposals; 2 months to mss.

TIPS "Read the Stoneslide Corrective (stoneslidecorrective.com) to see if your work fits with our approach."

⊕ SUBITO PRESS

University of Colorado at Boulder, Dept. of English, 226 UCB, Boulder, CO 80309-0226. **E-mail:** subito pressucb@gmail.com. **Website:** www.subitopress.org. Subito Press is a nonprofit publisher of literary works. Each year Subito publishes one work of fiction and one work of poetry through its contest. Submissions are open annually during the month of July. Trade paperback originals. Guidelines online.

HOW TO CONTACT Submit complete ms to contest.

TIPS "We publish two books of innovative writing a year through our poetry and fiction contests. All entries are also considered for publication with the press."

⊜ SUNBURY PRESS, INC.

50 W. Main St., Mechanicsburg, PA 17055. **E-mail:** info@sunburypress.com. **E-mail:** proposals@sun burypress.com. **Website:** www.sunburypress.com. Estab. 2004. Publishes trade paperback originals and reprints; electronic originals and reprints. Catalog and guidelines available online at website.

◑   "Please use our online submission form."

NEEDS "We are especially seeking historical fiction regarding the Civil War and books of regional interest."

TERMS Pays 10% royalty on wholesale price. Responds in 2 months.

TIPS "Our books appeal to very diverse audiences. We are building our list in many categories, focusing on many demographics. We are not like traditional publishers—we are digitally adept and very creative. Don't be surprised if we move quicker than you are accustomed to!"

SWAN ISLE PRESS

P.O. Box 408790, Chicago, IL 60640. (773)728-3780. **E-mail:** info@swanislepress.com. **Website:** www

.swanislepress.com. Estab. 1999. Publishes hardcover and trade paperback originals. Book catalog available online. Guidelines available online.

🖸 *"We do not accept unsolicited mss."*

HOW TO CONTACT Query with SASE. Submit complete mss.

TERMS Pays 7½-10% royalty on wholesale price. Responds in 6 months to queries. Responds in 12 months to manuscripts.

SYLVAN DELL PUBLISHING

612 Johnnie Dodds, Suite A2, Mt. Pleasant, SC 29464. (843)971-6722. **Fax:** (843)216-3804. **E-mail:** don nagerman@sylvandellpublishing.com. **Website:** www.sylvandellpublishing.com. **Contact:** Donna German, editor. Estab. 2004. "The picture books we publish are usually, but not always, fictional stories that relate to animals, nature, the environment, and science. All books should subtly convey an educational theme through a warm story that is fun to read and that will grab a child's attention. Each book has a 3-5 page *'For Creative Minds'* section to reinforce the educational component. This section will have a craft and/or game, as well as 'fun facts' to be shared by the parent, teacher, or other adult. Authors do not need to supply this information. Mss should be less than 1,500 words and meet all of the following 4 criteria: Fun to read—mostly fiction with nonfiction facts woven into the story; national or regional in scope; must tie into early elementary school curriculum; must be marketable through a niche market such as a zoo, aquarium, or museum gift shop." Publishes hardcover, trade paperback, and electronic originals. Book catalog and guidelines available online.

NEEDS Picture books: animal, folktales, nature/environment, math related. Word length—picture books: no more than 1,500. Recently published *Whistling Wings,* by first-time author Laura Goering, illustrated by Laura Jacques; *Sort it Out!,* by Barbara Mariconda, illustrated by Sherry Rogers; *River Beds: Sleeping in the World's Rivers,* by Gail Langer Karwoski, illustrated by Connie McLennan; *Saturn for My Birthday,* by first-time author John McGranaghan, illustrated by Wendy Edelson.

HOW TO CONTACT Accepts electronic submissions only. Snail mail submissions are discarded without being opened.

TERMS Pays 6-8% royalty on wholesale price. Pays small advance. Acknowledges receipt of ms submission within one week.

TIPS "Please make sure you have looked at our website to read our complete submission guidelines and to see if we are looking for a particular subject. Manuscripts must meet all four of our stated criteria. We look for fairly realistic, bright, and colorful art—no cartoons. We want the children excited about the books. We envision the books being used at home and in the classroom."

SYNERGEBOOKS

948 New Highway 7, Columbia, TN 38401. (863)956-3015. **Fax:** (863)588-2198. **E-mail:** synergebooks@ aol.com. **Website:** www.synergebooks.com. **Contact:** Debra Staples, publisher/acquisitions editor. Estab. 1999. "SynergEbooks is first and foremost a digital publisher, so most of our marketing budget goes to those formats. Authors are required to direct sell a minimum of 100 digital copies of a title before it's accepted for print." Publishes trade paperback and electronic originals. Book catalog and guidelines available online.

NEEDS SynergEbooks publishes at least 40 new titles a year, and only 1-5 of those are put into print in any given year. "SynergEbooks is first and foremost a digital publisher, so most of our marketing budget goes to those formats."

HOW TO CONTACT Submit proposal package, including synopsis, 1-3 sample chapters, and marketing plans.

TERMS Pays 15-40% royalty; makes outright purchase.

TIPS "At SynergEbooks, we work with the author to promote their work."

🝳 TAFELBERG PUBLISHERS

Imprint of NB Publishers, P.O. Box 879, Cape Town 8000 South Africa. (27)(21)406-3033. **Fax:** (27)(21)406-3812. **E-mail:** nb@nb.co.za. **Website:** www .tafelberg.com. **Contact:** Danita van Romburgh, editorial secretary; Louise Steyn, publisher. General publisher best known for Afrikaans fiction, authoritative political works, children's/youth literature, and a variety of illustrated and nonillustrated nonfiction.

NEEDS Picture books, young readers: animal, anthology, contemporary, fantasy, folktales, hi-lo, humor, multicultural, nature/environment, scient fiction, special needs. Middle readers, young adults:

animal (middle reader only), contemporary, fantasy, hi-lo, humor, multicultural, nature/environment, problem novels, science fiction, special needs, sports, suspense/mystery. Average word length: picture books—1,500-7,500; young readers—25,000; middle readers—15,000; young adults—40,000. Recently published *Because Pula Means Rain*, by Jenny Robson (ages 12-15, realism); *BreinBliksem*, by Fanie Viljoen (ages 13-18, realism); *SuperZero*, by Darrel Bristow-Bovey (ages 9-12, realism/humor).

HOW TO CONTACT Query or submit complete ms.

TERMS Pays authors royalty of 15-18% based on wholesale price. Responds to queries in 2 weeks; mss in 6 months.

TIPS "Writers: Story needs to have a South African or African style. Illustrators: I'd like to look, but the chances of getting commissioned are slim. The market is small and difficult. Do not expect huge advances. Editorial staff attended or plans to attend the following conferences: IBBY, Frankfurt, SCBWI Bologna."

Ⓐ NAN A. TALESE

Imprint of Doubleday, Random House, Inco, 1745 Broadway, New York NY 10019. (212)782-8918. **Fax:** (212)782-8448. **Website:** www.nanatalese.com. **Contact:** Nan A. Talese, publisher and editorial director; Ronit Feldman, assistant editor. Publishes hardcover originals. Averages 15 total titles/year. Nan A. Talese publishes nonfiction with a powerful guiding narrative and relevance to larger cultural interests, and literary fiction of the highest quality. Publishes hardcover originals.

○ "Nan A. Talese publishes nonfiction with a powerful guiding narrative and relevance to larger cultural trends and interests, and literary fiction of the highest quality."

NEEDS Literary. "We want well-written narratives with a compelling story line, good characterization and use of language. We like stories with an edge." *Agented submissions only.* Published *The Blind Assassin*, by Margaret Atwood; *Atonement*, by Ian McEwan; *Great Shame*, Thomas Keneally.

HOW TO CONTACT Responds in 1 week to queries; 2 weeks to mss. Accepts simultaneous submissions.

TERMS Pays variable royalty on retail price. Average advance: varying. Publishes ms 1 year after acceptance. Agented submissions only. Pays variable royalty on retail price. Pays varying advance.

TIPS "Audience is highly literate people interested in story, information, and insight. We want well-written material submitted by agents only. See our website."

TANGLEWOOD BOOKS

P.O. Box 3009, Terre Haute, IN 47803. **E-mail:** ptierney@tanglewoodbooks.com. **Website:** www.tanglewoodbooks.com. **Contact:** Kairi Hamlin, acquisitions editor; Peggy Tierney, publisher. Estab. 2003. "Tanglewood Press strives to publish entertaining, kid-centric books."

NEEDS Picture books: adventure, animal, concept, contemporary, fantasy, humor. Average word length: picture books—800. Recently published *68 Knots*, by Micheal Robert Evans (young adult); *The Mice of Bistrot des Sept Freres*, written and illustrated by Marie Letourneau; *Chester Raccoon and the Acorn Full of Memories*, by Audrey Penn and Barbara Gibson.

HOW TO CONTACT Query with 3-5 sample chapters.

TERMS Responds to mss in up to 18 months.

TIPS "Please see lengthy 'Submissions' page on our website."

TEXAS TECH UNIVERSITY PRESS

P.O. Box 41037, 3003 15th St., Suite 201, Lubbock, TX 79409. (806)742-2982. **Fax:** (806)742-2979. **E-mail:** judith.keeling@ttu.edu. **Website:** www.ttupress.org. **Contact:** Judith Keeling, editor-in-chief; Robert Mandel, director. Estab. 1971. Texas Tech University Press, the book publishing office of the university since 1971 and an AAUP member since 1986, publishes nonfiction titles in the areas of natural history and the natural sciences; eighteenth-century and Joseph Conrad studies; studies of modern Southeast Asia, particularly the Vietnam War; costume and textile history; Latin American literature and culture; and all aspects of the Great Plains and the American West, especially history, biography, memoir, sports history, and travel. In addition, the Press publishes several scholarly journals, acclaimed series for young readers, an annual invited poetry collection, and literary fiction of Texas and the West. Guidelines online.

NEEDS Fiction rooted in the American West and Southwest, Jewish literature, Latin American and Latino fiction (in translation or English).

◎ THISTLEDOWN PRESS LTD.

118 20th Street West, Saskatoon, SK S7M 0W6 Canada. (306)244-1722. **Fax:** (306)244-1762. **E-mail:** editorial@thistledownpress.com. **Website:** www.this

tledownpress.com. **Contact:** Allan Forrie, publisher. Book catalog free on request. Guidelines available for #10 envelope and IRC.

🖸 "Thistledown originates books by Canadian authors only, although we have co-published titles by authors outside Canada. We do not publish children's picture books."

NEEDS Middle readers, young adults: adventure, anthology, contemporary, fantasy, humor, poetry, romance, science fiction, suspense/mystery, short stories. Average word length: young adults—40,000. Recently published *Up All Night*, edited by R.P. MacIntyre (young adult, anthology); *Offside*, by Cathy Beveridge (young adult, novel); *Cheeseburger Subversive*, by Richard Scarsbrook; *The Alchemist's Daughter*, by Eileen Kernaghan.

HOW TO CONTACT Submit outline/synopsis and sample chapters. *Does not accept mss.* Do not query by e-mail.

TERMS Pays authors royalty of 10-12% based on net dollar sales. Pays illustrators and photographers by the project (range: $250-750). Responds to queries in 4 months.

TIPS "Send cover letter including publishing history and SASE."

TIA CHUCHA PRESS

c/o Tia Chucha's Centro Cultural, 13197-A Gladstone Blvd., Sylmar, CA 91342. **E-mail:** info@tiachucha .com. **Website:** www.tiachucha.com. **Contact:** Luis Rodriguez, director. Estab. 1989. Tia Chucha's Centro Cultural is a nonprofit learning and cultural arts center. We support andpromote the continued growth, development, and holistic learning of our community through the many powerful means of the arts. Tia Centro provides a positive space for people to activate what we all share as humans: the capacity to create, to imagine, and to express ourselves in an effort to improve the quality of life for our community. Publishes hardcover and trade paperback originals. Guidelines available free.

TERMS Pays 10% royalty on wholesale price. Responds in 9 months to mss.

TIPS "We will cultivate the practice. Audience is those interested."

🖸⊘ TIGHTROPE BOOKS

602 Markham St., Toronto, ON M6G 2L8 Canada. (647)348-4460. **E-mail:** info@tightropebooks.com. **Website:** www.tightropebooks.com. **Contact:** Shirarose Wilensky, editor. Estab. 2005. Publishes hardcover and trade paperback originals. Catalog and guidelines free on request and online.

🖸 Temporarily suspending all submissions.

IMPRINTS Zurita, Latino-Canadian imprint, Halli Villegas, Publisher.

TERMS Pays 5-15% royalty on retail price. Pays advance of $200-300. Responds if interested.

TIPS "Audience is young, urban, literary, educated, unconventional."

🅐🅞 TIN HOUSE BOOKS

2617 NW Thurman St., Portland, OR 97210. (503)473-8663. **Fax:** (503)473-8957. **E-mail:** meg@tinhouse .com. **Website:** www.tinhouse.com. **Contact:** Meg Storey, editor; Tony Perez, editor; Masie Cochran, associate editor. "We are a small independent publisher dedicated to nurturing new, promising talent as well as showcasing the work of established writers. Our Tin House New Voice series features work by authors who have not previously published a book." Distributes/promotes titles through Publishers Group West. Publishes hardcover originals, paperback originals, paperback reprints. Guidelines available on website.

HOW TO CONTACT *Agented mss only.* We no longer read unsolicited submissions by authors with no representation. We will continue to accept submissions from agents.

TERMS Responds to queries in 2-3 weeks; mss in 2-3 months.

🅞 TITAN PRESS

PMB 17897, Encino, CA 91416. **E-mail:** titan91416@ yahoo.com. **Website:** www.calwriterssfv.com. **Contact:** Stefanya Wilson, editor. Estab. 1981. Publishes hardcover and paperback originals. Ms guidelines for #10 SASE.

NEEDS Literary, mainstream/contemporary, short story collections. Published *Orange Messiahs*, by Scott Sonders (fiction).

HOW TO CONTACT Does not accept unsolicited mss. Query with SASE. Include brief bio, social security number, list of publishing credits.

TERMS Pays 20-40% royalty. Responds to queries in 3 months.

TIPS "Look, act, sound, and *be* professional."

⊘ TOP COW PRODUCTIONS, INC.

3812 Dunn Dr., Culver City, CA 90232. **Website:** www .topcow.com.

HOW TO CONTACT *No unsolicited submissions.* Prefers submissions from artists. See website for details and advice on how to break into the market.

TOP PUBLICATIONS, LTD.

12221 Merit Dr., Suite 950, Dallas, TX 75251. (972)628-6414. Fax: (972)233-0713. **E-mail:** info@toppub.com. **E-mail:** submissions@toppub.com. **Website:** www.toppub.com. Estab. 1999. Primarily a mainstream fiction publisher. Publishes hardcover and paperback originals. Tear sheets available on new titles. Guidelines available online.

○ "It is imperative that our authors realize they will be required to promote their book extensively for their books to be a success. Unless they are willing to make this commitment, they shouldn't submit to TOP."

TERMS Pays 15% royalty on wholesale price. Pays $250-$1,000 advance. Acknowledges receipt of queries but only responds if interested in seeing ms. Responds in 6 months to mss.

TIPS "We recommend that our authors write books that appeal to a large mainstream audience to make marketing easier and increase the chances of success. We only publish a few titles a year so the odds at getting published at TOP are slim. If we don't offer you a contract, it doesn't mean we didn't like your submission. We have to pass on a lot of good material each year simply by the limitations of our time and budget."

TOR BOOKS

175 Fifth Ave., New York, NY 10010. **Website:** www.tor-forge.com. **Contact:** Juliet Pederson, publishing coordinator. Book catalog available for 9" × 12" SAE and 3 first-class stamps. See website for latest submission guidelines.

○ Tor Books is the "world's largest publisher of science fiction and fantasy, with strong category publishing in historical fiction, mystery, western/Americana, thriller, YA."

IMPRINTS Forge, Orb, Starscape, Tor Teen.

NEEDS Average word length: middle readers, 30,000; young adults, 60,000-100,000.

HOW TO CONTACT We do not accept queries.

TERMS Pays author royalty. Pays illustrators by the project.

TIPS "Know the house you are submitting to, familiarize yourself with the types of books they are publishing. Get an agent. Allow him/her to direct you to

publishers who are most appropriate. It saves time and effort."

TORQUERE PRESS

P.O. Box 2545, Round Rock, TX 78680. (512)586-3553. **Fax:** (866)287-2968. **E-mail:** editor@torquerepress.com. **E-mail:** submissions@torquerepress.com. **Website:** www.torquerepress.com. **Contact:** Shawn Clements, submissions editor (homoerotica, suspense, gay/lesbian); Lorna Hinson, senior editor (gay/lesbian romance, historicals). Estab. 2003. "We are a gay and lesbian press focusing on romance and genres of romance. We particularly like paranormal and western romance." Publishes trade paperback originals and electronic originals and reprints. Book catalog available online. Guidelines available online.

IMPRINTS Top Shelf (Shawn Clements, editor); Single Shots (Kil Kenny, editor); Screwdrivers (M. Rode, editor); High Balls (Vincent Diamond, editor).

NEEDS All categories gay and lesbian themed. Adventure, erotica, historical, horror, mainstream, multicultural, mystery, occult, romance, science fiction, short story collections, suspense, western. Published *Broken Road*, by Sean Michael (romance); *Soul Mates: Bound by Blood*, by Jourdan Lane (paranormal romance). Imprints accepting submissions.

HOW TO CONTACT Submit proposal package, 3 sample chapters, clips.

TERMS Pays 8-40% royalty. Pays $35-75 for anthology stories. Responds in 1 month to queries and proposals; 2-4 months to mss.

TIPS "Our audience is primarily people looking for a familiar romance setting featuring gay or lesbian protagonists. Please read guidelines carefully and familiarize yourself with our lines."

🌑 TORREY HOUSE PRESS, LLC

2806 Melony Dr., SLC, UT 84124. (801)810-9THP. **E-mail:** mark@torreyhouse.com. **Website:** http://torreyhouse.com. **Contact:** Mark Bailey, publisher. Estab. 2010. See the website at www.torreyhouse.com for guidelines about submitting your work; peruse the columns and book reviews and read some of THP's favorite fiction and nonfiction excerpts to get a sense of the writing that the company seeks. Follow us at Torrey House Press on Facebook and on our website for contest updates, and please contact us any time with questions." Publishes hardcover, trade paperback, and electronic originals. Catalog online at website. Guidelines online at website.

NEEDS "Torrey House Press publishes literary fiction and creative nonfiction about the world environment and the American West."

HOW TO CONTACT Submit proposal package including: synopsis, complete ms, bio.

TERMS Pays 5-15% royalty on retail price. Responds in 3 months to queries, proposals, and mss.

TIPS "Include writing experience (none okay)."

⊕🌑🌓 TOTAL-E-BOUND PUBLISHING

Total-e-Ntwined Limited, 1 Faldingworth Road, Spridlington, Market Rasen, Lincolnshire LN8 2DE United Kingdom. **Website:** http://www.total-e-bound .com; http://www.forum.totalebound.com. **Contact:** Claire Siemaszkiewicz, editor; Michele Paulin, editor; Janice Bennett, editor. "The team at Total-e-bound came together to provide a unique service to our authors and readers. We are a royalty paying, full-service e-publisher. This means that there are no fees to the author. Brought together by a mutual love of outstanding erotic fiction, we offer a mass of business experience in the form of editors, artists, marketeers, IT technicians, and support staff to meet all of your needs. We love what we do and are totally dedicated, committed, and loyal to providing the best service that we can to our authors and our readers. TEB publishes, markets, and promotes top-quality erotic romance e-books and paperback books." Publishes paperback and e-book originals. Book catalog online at website.

NEEDS "We are currently accepting manuscripts between 10,000 and 100,000+ words in the following genres: action/adventure, bondage/BDSM, comedy/humor, contemporary, cowboy/western, fantasy/fairytale, futuristic/sci-fi, gay/lesbian, historical/rubenesque, mènage-á-trois/multiple Partners, multicultural, older woman/younger man, paranormal/time travel, thriller/crime, shape-shifters/morphers, vampire/werewolf." Throughout the year we do special themed short stories. General guidelines: 10,000-15,000 word count. Any genre (see below for specific themes). Anthologies are released every quarter—each with a distinctive theme. "We produce a series of four anthologies per year, six short stories in each. Published Campus Cravings Series, by Carol Lynne (gay/contemporary); *Sink or Swim*, by Alexis Fleming (paranormal); and *Wild in the Country*, by Portia Da Costa (contemporary/erotica). Current and planned series include Campus Cravings (M/M), Good-time Boys (M/M), Cattle Valley (M/M), Horsemen of Apocalypse Island (fantasy), Wives R Us (contemporary), The Goddess Grind (contemporary/paranormal), Sons of Olympus (paranormal), Psychic Detective (paranormal), and The Watchers (paranormal/fantasy).

HOW TO CONTACT Query with outline/synopsis and first 3 and last chapters. Accepts queries by online submission e-mail. Include estimated word count, brief bio, list of publishing credits.

TERMS Pays royalties 40% e-book, 10% print. Responds to queries in 2 weeks, mss in 2 months.

TIPS "First impressions are important. Send in a good intro letter with your synopsis and manuscript, giving details of what you will do yourself to promote your work. Always read and follow the submission guidelines."

☯ TOUCHWOOD EDITIONS

The Heritage Group, 340-1105 Pandora Ave., Victoria, BC V8V 3P9 Canada. (250)360-0829. **Fax:** (250)386-0829. **E-mail:** info@touchwoodeditions.com. **Website:** www.touchwoodeditions.com. Publishes trade paperback originals and reprints. Book catalog and submission guidelines available online for free.

HOW TO CONTACT Submit TOC, outline, word count.

TERMS Pays 15% royalty on net price. Responds in 3 months to queries

TIPS "Our area of interest is Western Canada. We would like more creative nonfiction and books about people of note in Canada's history."

☯ TRADEWIND BOOKS

202-1807 Maritime Mews, Granville Island, Vancouver, BC V6H 3W7 Canada. (604)662-4405. **E-mail:** tradewindbooks@mail.lycos.com. **Website:** www .tradewindbooks.com. **Contact:** Michael Katz, publisher; Carol Frank, art director; R. David Stephens, senior editor. "Tradewind Books publishes juvenile picture books and young adult novels. Requires that submissions include evidence that author has read at least 3 titles published by Tradewind Books." Publishes hardcover and trade paperback originals. Book catalog and ms guidelines online.

NEEDS Picture books: adventure, multicultural, folktales. Average word length: 900 words. Recently published *City Kids*, by X.J. Kennedy and illustrated by Phillpe Beha; *Roxy* by PJ Reece; *Viva Zapata!* by Emilie Smith and illustrated by Stefan Czernecki.

HOW TO CONTACT Send complete ms for picture books. *YA novels by Canadian authors only. Chapter books by U.S. authors considered.*

TERMS Pays 7% royalty on retail price. Pays variable advance. Responds to mss in 2 months.

TRISTAN PUBLISHING

2355 Louisiana Ave. N, Golden Valley, MO 55427. (763)545-1383. **Fax:** (763)545-1387. **E-mail:** info@ tristanpublishing.com or manuscripts@tristanpub lishing.com. **Website:** www.tristanpublishing.com. **Contact:** Brett Waldman, publisher. Estab. 2002. Publishes hardcover originals. Catalog and guidelines free on request. Guidelines available online at website.

IMPRINTS Tristan Publishing; Waldman House Press; Tristan Outdoors.

HOW TO CONTACT Query with SASE; submit completed mss.

TERMS Pays royalty on wholesale or retail price; outright purchase. Responds in 3 months on queries/proposals/mss.

TIPS "Our audience is adults and children."

TUPELO PRESS

P.O. Box 1767, North Adams, MA 01247. (413)664-9611. **E-mail:** publisher@tupelopress.org. **E-mail:** www.tupelopress.org/submissions. **Website:** www .tupelopress.org. **Contact:** Jeffrey Levine, publish/editor-in-chief; Elyse Newhouse, associate publisher; Jim Schley, managing editor. Estab. 2001. "We're an independent nonprofit literary press. Also sponsor these upcoming competitions: Dorset Prize: $10,000. Entries must be postmarked between September 1 and December 31. Guidelines are online; Snowbound Series chapbook Award: $1,000 and 50 copies of chapbook. See website for submission period and guidelines. Every July we have Open Submissions. We accept book-length poetry, poetry collections (48+ pages), short story collections, novellas, literary nonfiction/memoirs and up to 80 pages of a novel." Guidelines available online.

NEEDS "For Novels—submit no more than 100 pages along with a summary of the entire book. If we're interested we'll ask you to send the rest. We accept very few works of prose (1 or 2/year)."

HOW TO CONTACT Submit complete ms. **Charges a $45 reading fee.**

TURNSTONE PRESS

206-100 Arthur St., Winnipeg MB R3B 1H3 Canada. (204)947-1555. **Fax:** (204)942-1555. **E-mail:** info@ turnstonepress.com. **E-mail:** editor@turnstonepress .com. **Website:** www.turnstonepress.com. Estab. 1976. "Turnstone Press is a literary publisher, not a general publisher, and therefore we are only interested in literary fiction, literary nonfiction—including literary criticism—and poetry. We do publish literary mysteries, thrillers, and noir under our Ravenstone imprint. We publish only Canadian authors or landed immigrants we strive to publish a significant number of new writers, to publish in a variety of genres, and to have 50% of each year's list be Manitoba writers and/ or books with Manitoba content." Guidelines available online at website.

HOW TO CONTACT "Samples must be 40-60 pages, typed/printed in a minimum 12 point serif typeface such as Times, Book Antiqua, or Garamond."

TERMS Responds in 4-7 months.

TIPS "As a Canadian literary press, we have a mandate to publish Canadian writers only. Do some homework before submitting works to make sure your subject matter/genre/writing style falls within the publishers area of interest."

TURN THE PAGE PUBLISHING LLC

P.O. Box 3179, Upper Montclair, NJ 07043. **E-mail:** rlentin@turnthepagepublishing.com. **E-mail:** in quiry@turnthepagepublishing.com. **Website:** www .turnthepagepublishing.com. **Contact:** Roseann Lentin, editor-in-chief; Ann Kolakowski, editor. Estab. 2009. Publishes hardcover, trade paperback, electronic originals and trade paperback, electronic reprints. Book catalog available online at website. Guidelines by e-mail.

NEEDS "We like new, fresh voices who are not afraid to 'step outside the box,' with unique ideas and story lines. We prefer 'edgy' rather than 'typical.'"

HOW TO CONTACT Submit proposal package including synopsis and 3 sample chapters.

TERMS Pays 8-15% royalty on retail price. Responds in 3 months to queries; 2 months to proposals/mss.

TIPS "Our audience is made up of intelligent, sophisticated, forward-thinking, progressive readers, who are not afraid to consider reading something different to Turn the Page of their lives. We're an independent publisher, we're avant-garde, so if you're looking for run of the mill, don't submit here."

TWILIGHT TIMES BOOKS

P.O. Box 3340, Kingsport, TN 37664. **Website:** www .twilighttimesbooks.com. **Contact:** Andy M. Scott, managing editor. Estab. 1999. "We publish compelling literary fiction by authors with a distinctive voice." Published 5 debut authors within the last year. Averages 120 total titles; 15 fiction titles/year. Member: AAP, PAS, SPAN, SLF. Guidelines available online.

HOW TO CONTACT Accepts unsolicited mss. Do not send complete mss. Queries via e-mail only. Include estimated word count, brief bio, list of publishing credits, marketing plan.

TERMS Pays 8-15% royalty. Responds in 4 weeks to queries; 2 months to mss.

TIPS "The only requirement for consideration at Twilight Times Books is that your novel must be entertaining and professionally written."

Ⓐⴲ TYNDALE HOUSE PUBLISHERS, INC.

351 Executive Dr., Carol Stream, IL 60188. (800)323-9400. **Fax:** (800)684-0247. **Website:** www.tyndale.com. **Contact:** Katara Washington Patton, acquisitions; Talinda Iverson, art acquisitions. Estab. 1962. "Tyndale House publishes practical, user-friendly Christian books for the home and family." Publishes hardcover and trade paperback originals and mass-paperback reprints. Guidelines for 9" × 12" SAE and $2.40 for postage, or visit website.

NEEDS "Christian truths must be woven into the story organically. No short story collections. Youth books: character building stories with Christian perspective. Especially interested in ages 10-14. We primarily publish Christian historical romances, with occasional contemporary, suspense, or stand alones."

HOW TO CONTACT Agented submissions only. *No unsolicited mss.*

TERMS Pays negotiable royalty. Pays negotiable advance.

TIPS "All accepted manuscripts will appeal to Evangelical Christian children and parents."

�O UNBRIDLED BOOKS

200 N. Ninth Street, Suite A, Columbia, MO 65201. **Website:** http://unbridledbooks.com. Estab. 2004. "Unbridled Books is a premier publisher of works of rich literary quality that appeal to a broad audience."

HOW TO CONTACT Please query first by e-mail. Due to the heavy volume of submissions, we regret that at this time we are not able to consider uninvited mss. Please query either Fred Ramey or Greg Michalson, but NOT BOTH.

TIPS "We try to read each ms that arrives, so please be patient."

UNITY HOUSE

Unity, 1901 N.W. Blue Pkwy., Unity Village, MO 64065-0001. (816)524-3550. **Fax:** (816)347-5518. **E-mail:** unity@unityonline.org. **E-mail:** sartinson@unityonline.org. **Website:** www.unityonline.org. **Contact:** Sharon Sartin, executive assistant. Estab. 1889. Unity House publishes metaphysical Christian books based on Unity principles, as well as inspirational books on metaphysics and practical spirituality. All manuscripts must reflect a spiritual foundation and express the Unity philosophy, practical Christianity, universal principles, and/or metaphysics. Publishes hardcover, trade paperback, and electronic originals. Catalog free on request and online at website: http://unityonline.org/publications/pdf/productcatalog.pdf. Guidelines free and available online and by e-mail.

NEEDS "We are a bridge between traditional Christianity and New Age spirituality. Unity is based on metaphysical Christian principles, spiritual values, and the healing power of prayer as a resource for daily living."

HOW TO CONTACT Submit complete mss (3 copies).

TERMS Pays 10-15% royalty on retail price. Pays advance. Responds in 6-8 months.

TIPS "We target an audience of spiritual seekers."

UNIVERSITY OF GEORGIA PRESS

Main Library, Third Floor, 320 S. Jackson St., Athens, GA 30602. (706)369-6130. **Fax:** (706)369-6131. **E-mail:** books@ugapress.uga.edu. **Website:** www.ugapress.org. Estab. 1938. University of Georgia Press is a midsize press that publishes fiction only through the Flannery O'Connor Award for Short Fiction competition. Publishes hardcover originals, trade paperback originals, and reprints. Book catalog and ms guidelines for #10 SASE or online.

NEEDS Short story collections published in Flannery O'Connor Award Competition.

HOW TO CONTACT Mss for Flannery O'Connor Award for Short Fiction accepted in April and May.

TERMS Pays 7-10% royalty on net receipts. Pays rare, varying advance. Responds in 2 months to queries.

TIPS "Please visit our website to view our book catalogs and for all manuscript submission guidelines."

UNIVERSITY OF IOWA PRESS

100 Kuhl House, 119 W. Park Rd., Iowa City, IA 52242. (319)335-2000. **Fax:** (319)335-2055. **E-mail:** uipress@uiowa.edu. **Website:** www.uiowapress.org. **Contact:** Holly Carver, director; Joseph Parsons, acquisitions editor. Estab. 1969. "We publish authoritative, original nonfiction that we market mostly by direct mail to groups with special interests in our titles, and by advertising in trade and scholarly publications." Publishes hardcover and paperback originals. Book catalog available free. Guidelines available online.

NEEDS Currently publishes the Iowa Short Fiction Award selections.

TERMS Pays 7-10% royalty on net receipts.

UNIVERSITY OF NEBRASKA PRESS

1111 Lincoln Mall, Lincoln, NE 68588. (800)755-1105. **Fax:** (402)472-6214. **E-mail:** pressmail@unl.edu. **E-mail:** arold1@unl.edu. **Website:** nebraskapress.unl.edu. **Contact:** Heather Lundine, editor-in-chief; Alison Rold, production manager. "We primarily publish nonfiction books and scholarly journals, along with a few titles per season in contemporary and regional prose and poetry. On occasion, we reprint previously published fiction of established reputation, and we have several programs to publish literary works in translation." Publishes hardcover and trade paperback originals and trade paperback reprints. Book catalog available free. Guidelines available online.

IMPRINTS Bison Books (paperback reprints of classic books).

NEEDS Series and translation only. Occasionally reprints fiction of established reputation.

UNIVERSITY OF NEVADA PRESS

Morrill Hall, Mail Stop 0166, Reno, NV 89557. (775)784-6573. **Fax:** (775)784-6200. **Website:** www.unpress.nevada.edu. **Contact:** Joanne O'Hare, director. Estab. 1961. "Small university press. Publishes fiction that primarily focuses on the American West." Member: AAUP Publishes hardcover and paperback originals and reprints. Guidelines available online.

NEEDS "We publish in Basque studies, gambling studies, Western literature, Western history, natural science, environmental studies, travel and outdoor books, archeology, anthropology, and political studies, all focusing on the West." The Press also publishes creative nonfiction and books on regional topics for a general audience. Has published *The Mechanics of Falling and Other Stories*, by Catherine Brady; *Little*

Lost River, by Pamela Johnston; *Moon Lily*, by Susan Lang.

HOW TO CONTACT Submit proposal package, outline, clips, 2-4 sample chapters. Include estimated word count, brief bio, list of publishing credits. Send SASE or IRC. No e-mail submissions.

TERMS Responds in 2 months.

⊛ UNIVERSITY OF NEW MEXICO PRESS

1717 Roma Ave., Albuquerque, NM 87106. (505)277-3324 or (800)249-7737. **Fax:** (505)277-3343. **E-mail:** clark@unm.edu. **E-mail:** wcwhiteh@unm.edu. **Website:** www.unmpress.com. **Contact:** W. Clark Whitehorn, editor-in-chief. Estab. 1929. "The Press is well-known as a publisher in the fields of anthropology, archeology, Latin American studies, art and photography, architecture and the history and culture of the American West, fiction, some poetry, Chicano/a studies and works by and about American Indians. We focus on American West, Southwest, and Latin American regions." Publishes hardcover originals and trade paperback originals and reprints. Book catalog available for free. Please read and follow the submission query guidelines on the Author Information page online. Do not send your entire ms or additional materials until requested. If your book is accepted for publication, you will be notified.

TERMS Pays variable royalty. Pays advance.

⊕ UNIVERSITY OF WISCONSIN PRESS

1930 Monroe St., 3rd Floor, Madison, WI 53711. (608)263-1110. **Fax:** (608)263-1132. **E-mail:** uwiscpress@uwpress.wisc.edu. **E-mail:** kadushin@wisc.edu. **Website:** www.wisc.edu/wisconsinpress. **Contact:** Raphael Kadushin, senior acquisitions editor; Gwen Walker, acquisitions editor. Estab. 1937. Publishes hardcover originals, paperback originals, and paperback reprints. **Published 5-8 debut authors within the last year.** Averages 98 total titles, 15 fiction titles/year. Member, AAUP. Distributes titles through ads, reviews, catalog, sales reps, etc. Publishes hardcover originals, paperback originals, and paperback reprints. Guidelines online.

◐ Check online guidelines for latest submission guidelines.

NEEDS Gay/lesbian, historical, lesbian, mystery, regional (Wisconsin), short story collections. Recently published *A Friend of Kissinger*, by David Milofsky; *Beijing*, by Philip Gambone; *Latin Moon in Manhattan*, by Jaime Manrique. Gay/lesbian, historical,lesbian, mystery, regional (Wisconsin), short story collections.

HOW TO CONTACT Does not accept unsolicited mss. Query with SASE or submit outline, 1-2 sample chapter(s), synopsis. Accepts queries by e-mail, mail, fax. See website for more contact info. Responds in 2 weeks to queries; 8 weeks to mss. Rarely comments on rejected mss.

TERMS Pays royalty. Publishes ms 9-18 months after acceptance. Ms guidelines online.

TIPS "Make sure the query letter and sample text are well-written, and read guidelines carefully to make sure we accept the genre you are submitting to."

UNLIMITED PUBLISHING LLC

P.O. Box 99, Nashville, IN 47448. **E-mail:** acquisitions@unlimitedpublishing.com. **Website:** www.unlimitedpublishing.com. Estab. 2000. "We prefer short nonfiction and fiction with a clear audience, and expect authors to be actively involved in publicity. A detailed marketing plan is required with all submissions. Moderate to good computer skills are necessary." Catalog online at website.

◯ "We publish mostly short nonfiction books, often in collaboration with other book publishers, or with nonprofit, charitable, and educational institutions worldwide. Our focus on quality and support of worthy causes gives UP books more credibility and public exposure than typical POD book publishing fare."

IMPRINTS Harvardwood Books.

HOW TO CONTACT Submit proposal package by e-mail, including: outline and 10-page excerpt in rich text format, author bio, and detailed marketing plan.

TERMS Pays 10-20% Royalty on retail price. 1 month on queries, proposal, and mss.

TIPS "The growth of online bookselling allows authors and publishers to jointly cultivate a tightly targeted grassroots audience in specialty or niche markets before expanding to mainstream book industry channels based on proven public demand."

UNTREED READS PUBLISHING

506 Kansas St., San Francisco, CA 94107. (415)621-0465. **Fax:** (415)621-0465. **E-mail:** general@untreedreads.com. **E-mail:** submissions@untreedreads.com. **Website:** www.untreedreads.com. **Contact:** Jay A. Hartman, editor-in-chief (fiction: all genres). Estab. 2009. Publishes electronic originals and reprints. Catalog and guidelines available online at website.

NEEDS "We look forward to long-terms relationships with our authors. We encourage works that are either already a series or could develop into a series. We are one of the few publishers publishing short stories and are happy to be a resource for these good works. We welcome short story collections. Also, we look forward to publishing children's books, cookbooks, and other works that have been known for illustrations in print as the technology in the multiple ereaders improves. We hope to be a large platform for diverse content and authors. We seek mainstream content, but if you're an author or have content that doesn't seem to always 'fit' into traditional market we'd like to hear from you." No erotica, picture books, poetry, poetry in translation, or romance.

HOW TO CONTACT Submit porposal package with 3 sample chapters. Submit completed ms.

TERMS Pays 50-60% royalty on retail price. Responds in 2 weeks on queries, 1 month on proposals, and 6 weeks on mss.

TIPS "For our fiction titles, we lean toward a literary audience. For nonfiction titles, we want to be a platform for business people, entrepreneurs, and speakers to become well known in their fields of expertise. However, for both fiction and nonfiction we want to appeal to many audiences."

◐ USBORNE PUBLISHING

83-85 Saffron Hill, London En EC1N 8RT United Kingdom. (44)(020)7430-2800. **Fax:** (44)(020)7430-1562. **E-mail:** mail@usborne.co.uk; pippas@usborne.co.uk; alicep@usborne.co.uk; Graeme@usborne.co.uk. **Website:** www.usborne.com. "Usborne Publishing is a multiple-award-winning, worldwide children's publishing company specializing in superbly researched and produced information books with a unique appeal to young readers."

NEEDS Young readers, middle readers: adventure, contemporary, fantasy, history, humor, multicultural, nature/environment, science fiction, suspense/mystery, strong concept-based or character-led series. Average word length: young readers—5,000-10,000; middle readers—25,000-50,000. Recently published *Secret Mermaid* series by Sue Mongredien (ages 7 and up); *School Friends*, by Ann Bryant (ages 9 and up).

TERMS Pays authors royalty.

TIPS "Do not send any original work and, sorry, but we cannot guarantee a reply."

☉ VÉHICULE PRESS

3861 Boulevard St-Laurent, P.O.B. 42094 BP Roy, Montreal, QC H2W 2T3 Canada. (514)844-6073. **Fax:** (514)844-7543. **E-mail:** vp@vehiculepress.com. **Website:** www.vehiculepress.com. **Contact:** Simon Dardick, president/publisher. Estab. 1973. "Montreal's Véhicule Press has published the best of Canadian and Quebec literature-fiction, poetry, essays, translations, and social history." Publishes trade paperback originals by Canadian authors mostly. Book catalog for 9" × 12" SAE with IRCs.

IMPRINTS Signal Editions (poetry); Dossier Quebec (history, memoirs); Esplanade Editions (fiction).

NEEDS Contact Andrew Steinmetz. Literary, regional, short story collections. Published *Optique*, by Clayton Bailey; *Seventeen Tomatoes: Tales from Kashmir*, by Jaspreet Singh; *A Short Journey by Car*, by Liam Durcan. No romance or formula writing.

HOW TO CONTACT Query with SASE.

TERMS Pays 10-15% royalty on retail price. Pays $200-500 advance. Responds in 4 months to queries.

TIPS "Quality in almost any style is acceptable. We believe in the editing process."

⊘☺ VERTIGO

DC Universe, Vertigo-DC Comics, 1700 Broadway, New York, NY 10019. **Website:** www.dccomics.com.

NEEDS "The DC TALENT SEARCH program is designed to offer aspiring artists the chance to present artwork samples directly to the DC editors and art directors. The process is simple: During your convention visit, drop off photocopied samples of your work and enjoy the show! No lines, no waiting. If the DC folks like what they see, a time is scheduled for you the following day to meet a DC representative personally and discuss your artistic interests and portfolio. At this time, DC Comics does not accept unsolicited writing submissions by mail. See submission guidelines online. "We're seeking artists for all our imprints, including the DC Universe, Vertigo, WildStorm, Mad magazine, Minx, kids comics, and more!"

❶ VIKING

Imprint of Penguin Group (USA), Inc., 375 Hudson St., New York, NY 10014. (212)366-2000. **Website:** us.penguingroup.com/static/pages/publishers/adult/viking.html. Estab. 1925. Viking publishes a mix of academic and popular fiction and nonfiction. Publishes hardcover and originals.

NEEDS Literary, mainstream/contemporary, mystery, suspense. Published *Lake Wobegon Summer 1956*, by Garrison Keillor; *A Day Late and A Dollar Short*, by Terry McMillian; *A Common Life*, by Jan Karon; *In the Heart of the Sea*, by Nathaniel Philbrick.

HOW TO CONTACT Agented submissions only.

TERMS Pays 10-15% royalty on retail price.

❶❶ VIKING CHILDREN'S BOOKS

375 Hudson St., New York NY 10014. **E-mail:** averystudiopublicity@us.penguingroup.com. **Website:** www.penguingroup.com. **Contact:** Catherine Frank, executive editor. "Viking Children's Books is known for humorous, quirky picture books, in addition to more traditional fiction. We publish the highest-quality fiction, nonfiction, and picture books for preschoolers through young adults." Publishes hardcover originals.

○ *Does not accept unsolicited submissions.*

NEEDS All levels: adventure, animal, contemporary, fantasy, history, humor, multicultural, nature/environment, poetry, problem novels, romance, science fiction, sports, suspense/mystery. Recently published *Llama Llama Misses Mama*, by Anna Dewdney (ages 2 up, picture book); *Wintergirls*, by Laurie Halse Anderson (ages 12 and up); *Good Luck Bear*, by Greg Foley (ages 2 up); *Along for the Ride*, by Sarah Dessen (ages 12 up).

HOW TO CONTACT *Accepts agented mss only.*

TERMS Pays 2-10% royalty on retail price or flat fee. Pays negotiable advance. Responds to queries/mss in 6 months.

TIPS No "cartoony" or mass-market submissions for picture books.

❶ VILLARD BOOKS

Imprint of Random House Publishing Group, 1745 Broadway, New York, NY 10019. (212)572-2600. **Website:** www.atrandom.com. Estab. 1983. Publishes hardcover and trade paperback originals. Averages 40-50 total titles/year. "Villard Books is the publisher of savvy and sometimes quirky, best-selling hardcovers and trade paperbacks." Publishes hardcover and trade paperback originals.

NEEDS Commercial fiction.

HOW TO CONTACT *Agented submissions only.* Agented fiction 95%. Accepts simultaneous submissions.

TERMS Pays negotiable royalty. Average advance: negotiable.

ⓐ VINTAGE ANCHOR PUBLISHING

1745 Broadway, New York, NY 10019. **E-mail:** vintageanchorpublicity@randomhouse.com. **Website:** www.randomhouse.com. **Contact:** Furaha Norton, editor.

NEEDS Literary, mainstream/contemporary, short story collections. Published *Snow Falling on Cedars*, by David Guterson (contemporary); *Martin Dressler*, by Steven Millhauser (literary).

HOW TO CONTACT *Agented submissions only.* Accepts simultaneous submissions. No electronic submissions.

TERMS Pays 4-8% royalty on retail price. Average advance: $2,500 and up.

VIZ MEDIA LLC

P.O. Box 77010, 295 Bay St., San Francisco, CA 94133. (415)546-7073. **E-mail:** evelyn.dubocq@viz.com. **Website:** www.viz.com. "VIZ Media, LLC, is one of the most comprehensive and innovative companies in the field of manga (graphic novel) publishing, animation and entertainment licensing of Japanese content. Owned by three of Japan's largest creators and licensors of manga and animation, Shueisha Inc., Shogakukan Inc., and Shogakukan-Shueisha Productions, Co., Ltd., VIZ Media is a leader in the publishing and distribution of Japanese manga for English-speaking audiences in North America, the United Kingdom, Ireland, and South Africa, and is a global ex-Asia licensor of Japanese manga and animation. The company offers an integrated product line, including magazines such as *SHONEN JUMP* and *SHOJO BEAT*, graphic novels, and DVDs, and develops, markets, licenses, and distributes animated entertainment for audiences and consumers of all ages."

HOW TO CONTACT VIZ Media is currently accepting submissions and pitches for original comics. Keep in mind that all submissions must be accompanied by a signed release form.

WAKESTONE PRESS

200 Brook Hollow Rd., Nashville, TN 37205. (615)739-6428. **E-mail:** submissions@wakestonepress.com. **Website:** www.wakestonepress.com. **Contact:** Frank Daniels III, editor. Estab. 2010. Publishes hardcover, trade paperback and electronic originals. Catalog free by request. Guidelines free by request.

IMPRINTS Wakestone Press LLC; Moonshadow Press (subsidiary): Fiction imprint targeting young adults (10 and up).

HOW TO CONTACT Submit in Microsoft Word file(s) a proposal package, including: book outline several (2-3) sample chapter(s) and author bio(s).

TERMS Pays 7½-20% on wholesale price. Outright purchases $10,000-$20,000 maximum. Pays $2,000-$5,000 advance. Responds 1 month to queries and proposals; 2 months to mss.

WALKER AND CO.

Walker Publishing Co., 175 Fifth Ave., 7th Floor, New York, NY 10010. (212)727-8300. **Fax:** (212)727-0984. **E-mail:** rebecca.mancini@bloomsburyusa.com. **Website:** bloomsbury.com/us/children. **Contact:** Emily Easton, publisher (picture books, middle-grade and young adult novels); Stacy Cantor, associate editor (picture books, middle-grade, and young adult novels); Mary Kate Castellani, assistant editor (picture books, middle-grade, and young adult novels). Estab. 1959. "Walker publishes general nonfiction on a variety of subjects, as well as children's books." Publishes hardcover trade originals. Book catalog for 9" × 12" envelope and 3 first-class stamps.

NEEDS Accepts unsolicited mss. Query with SASE. Include "a concise description of the story line, including its outcome, word length of story, writing experience, publishing credits, particular expertise on this subject and in this genre. Common mistake: not researching our publishing program and forgetting SASE."

HOW TO CONTACT Query with SASE. Send complete ms for picture books.

TERMS Pays 5-10% royalty.

⊕ WALTSAN PUBLISHING

P.O. Box 821803, Vancouver, WA 98682. **E-mail:** williamkercher@gmail.com. **E-mail:** acqs@WaltsanPublishing.com. **Website:** www.WaltsanPublishing.com. **Contact:** William Kercher, acquisitions editor. Estab. 2010. Waltsan publishing publishes biographies, general nonfiction, how-tos, and illustrated, reference, scholary, self-help, technical books, and textbooks. Trade paperback originals, mass-market paperback originals, electronic originals. Cataog available for SAE with 1 first class stamp. Guidelines available online at website.

"Waltsan looks at author credentials, manuscript length, suitability of topic, believability, marketability, and writing skills. Looking for appropriate number and quality of graphics when appropriate."

NEEDS Interested in all topics. "Make sure your writing is polished, believable, and the manuscript is not too short. Pay attention to details and don't try to fool the readers. Check for continuity of details by making sure what is written in one chapter coincides with what is written in other chapters. Don't guess. Check your facts."

HOW TO CONTACT Accepts electronic submissions ONLY. "See website for details."

TERMS Pays royalty minimum of 20%, maximum of 50% Does not pay advance. Responds in 1 month on queries, proposals, and mss.

TIPS "Waltsan Publishing's audience is the on-the-go person, electronic reader or android in hand, that wants to read whenever and wherever they get a chance. Generally younger, technologically savvy, and intelligent. Truly a 21st century individual."

Ⓐ WATERBROOK MULTNOMAH PUBLISHING GROUP

Random House, 12265 Oracle Blvd., Suite 200, Colorado Springs, CO 80921. (719)590-4999. **Fax:** (719)590-8977. **Website:** www.waterbrookmult nomah.com. Estab. 1996. Publishes hardcover and trade paperback originals. Book catalog available online.

NEEDS Adventure, historical, literary, mainstream/contemporary, mystery, religious (inspirational, religious mystery/suspense, religious thriller, religious romance), romance (contemporary, historical), science fiction, spiritual, suspense. Published *A Name of Her Own*, by Jane Kirkpatrick (historical); *Women's Intuition*, by Lisa Samson (contemporary); *Thorn in My Heart*, by Liz Curtis Higgs (historical).

HOW TO CONTACT Agented submissions only.

TERMS Pays royalty. Responds in 2-3 months to queries/proposals/mss.

WESTERN PSYCHOLOGICAL SERVICES

625 Alaska Ave., Torrance, CA 90503. (424)201-8800 or (800)648-8857. **Fax:** (424)201-6950. **E-mail:** re view@wpspublish.com. **Website:** www.wpspublish .com; www.creativetherapystore.com. Estab. 1948. "Western Psychological Services publishes psychological and educational assessments that practitioners trust. Our products allow helping professionals to accurately screen, diagnose, and treat people in need. WPS publishes practical books and games used by therapists, counselors, social workers, and others in the helping professionals who work with children and adults." Publishes psychological and educational assessments and some trade paperback originals. Book catalog available free. Guidelines available online.

NEEDS Children's books dealing with feelings, anger, social skills, autism, family problems, etc.

HOW TO CONTACT Submit complete ms.

TERMS Pays 5-10% royalty on wholesale price. Responds in 2 months to queries.

WHITE MANE KIDS

73 W. Burd St., P.O. Box 708, Shippensburg, PA 17257. (717)532-2237. **Fax:** (717)532-6110. **E-mail:** market ing@whitemane.com. **Website:** www.whitemane.com. **Contact:** Harold Collier, acquisitions editor. Estab. 1987. Book catalog and writer's guidelines available for SASE.

IMPRINTS White Mane Books, Burd Street Press, White Mane Kids, Ragged Edge Press.

NEEDS Middle readers, young adults: history (primarily American Civil War). Average word length: middle readers—30,000. Does not publish picture books. Recently published *The Witness Tree and the Shadow of the Noose: Mystery, Lies, and Spies in Manassas*, by K.E.M. Johnston, and *Drumbeat: The Story of a Civil War Drummer Boy*, by Robert J. Trout (grades 5 and up).

HOW TO CONTACT Query.

TERMS Pays authors royalty of 7-10%. Pays illustrators and photographers by the project. Responds to queries in 1 month, mss in 3 months.

TIPS "Make your work historically accurate. We are interested in historically accurate fiction for middle and young adult readers. We do *not* publish picture books. Our primary focus is the American Civil War and some America Revolution topics."

Ⓘ WILD CHILD PUBLISHING

PO Box 4897, Culver City, CA 90231. (310) 721-4461. **E-mail:** admin@wildchildpublishing.com. **Website:** www.wildchildpublishing.com. **Contact:** Marci Baun, editor-in-chief (genres not covered by other editors); Faith Bicknell-Brown, managing editor (horror and romance); S.R. Howen, editor (science fiction and nonfiction). Estab. 1999. Wild Child Publishing is a small, independent press that started out as a magazine in September 1999. We are known for working with newer/unpublished authors and editing to the standards of NYC publishers. Publishes paperback originals, e-books. Format: POD printing; perfect-bound. Average print order: 50-200. Member EPIC.

Distributes/promotes titles through Ingrams and own website, Mobipocket Kindle, Amazon, and soon with Fictionwise. Freya's Bower already distributes through Fictionwise. Book catalogs on website.

○ Was named a Top 101 Writers' Websites in 2005.

NEEDS Adventure, children's/juvenile, erotica for Freya's Bower only, ethnic/multicultural, experimental, fantasy, feminist, gay, historical, horror, humor/satire, lesbian, literary, mainstream, military/war, mystery/suspense, New Age/mystic, psychic/supernatural, romance, science fiction, short story collections, thriller/espionage, western, young adult/teen (fantasy/science fiction). Multiple anthologies planned.

HOW TO CONTACT Query with outline/synopsis and 1 sample chapter. Accepts queries by e-mail only. Include estimated word count, brief bio. Often critiques/comments on rejected mss. Published *Weirdly: A Collection of Strange Tales*, by Variety (horror/psychological thriller); *Quits: Book 2: Devils*, by M.E. Ellis (horror, psychological thriller, paranormal).

TERMS Pays royalties 10-40%. Responds in 1 month to queries and mss.

TIPS "Read our submission guidelines thoroughly. Send in entertaining, well-written stories. Be easy to work with and upbeat."

○○ THE WILD ROSE PRESS

P.O. Box 708, Adams Basin, NY 14410. (585) 752-8770. **E-mail:** queryus@thewildrosepress.com; rpenders@thewildrosepress.com. **Website:** www.thewildrosepress.com. **Contact:** Nicole D'Arienzo, editor. Estab. 2006. Publishes paperback originals, reprints, and e-books in a POD format. Guidelines available on website.

○ "The American Rose line publishes stories about the French and Indian wars; Colonial America; the Revolutionary War; the war of 1812; the War Between the States; the Reconstruction era; the dawn of the new century. These are the struggles at the heart of the American Rose story. The central romantic relationship is the key driving force, set against historically accurate backdrop. These stories are for those who long for the courageous heroes and heroines who fought for their freedom and settled the new world; for gentle southern belles with spines of steel and the gallant gentlemen who sweep them away. This line is wide open for writers with a love of American history." Published 5 debut authors last year. Member: EPIC, Romance Writers of America. Has received two Eppie Awards (2007) for First Place, and the New Jersey Golden Leaf Award for 2006 and 2007.

NEEDS Distributes/promotes titles through major distribution chains, including Ingrams, Baker & Taylor, Sony, Kindle, Amazon.com, as well as smaller and online distributors. Please do not submit women's fiction, poetry, science fiction, fanfiction, or any type of nonfiction.

HOW TO CONTACT *Does not accept unsolicited mss.* Send query letter with outline and synopsis of up to 5 pages. Accepts all queries by e-mail. Include estimated word count, brief bio, and list of publishing credits. Agented fiction less than 1%. Always comments on rejected mss. Sends prepublication galleys to author. Only our full-length (over 65,000 words) will go to print. For information on distribution visit our FAQ section. We only publish **romance**. For more information on how we define romance, please read the articles listed in the FAQ section . We may or may not respond to a query for something that is NOT a romance.

TERMS Pays royalty of 7% minimum; 35% maximum. Responds in 1 month to queries; 3 months to mss.

TIPS "Polish your manuscript, make it as error-free as possible, and follow our submission guidelines."

⊘ WILDSTORM

DC Universe, 1700 Broadway, New York, NY 10019. **Website:** http://www.dccomics.com/wildstorm. (212)636-5400. Wildstorm is part of the DC Universe.

○ *Does not accept unsolicited mss.*

HOW TO CONTACT "At this time, DC Comics does not accept unsolicited artwork or writing submissions."

▲⊘ WILLIAM MORROW

HarperCollins, 10 E. 53rd St., New York, NY 10022. (212)207-7000. **Fax:** (212)207-7145. **Website:** www.harpercollins.com. Estab. 1926. "William Morrow publishes a wide range of titles that receive much recognition and prestige—a most selective house." Book catalog available free.

NEEDS Publishes adult fiction. Morrow accepts only the highest quality submissions in adult fiction. *No unsolicited mss or proposals.*

HOW TO CONTACT Agented submissions only.
TERMS Pays standard royalty on retail price. Pays varying advance.

⊙ WILSHIRE BOOK COMPANY

9731 Variel Ave., Chatsworth, CA 91311. (818)700-1522. **Fax:** (818)700-1527. **E-mail:** mpowers@mpowers.com. **Website:** www.mpowers.com. **Contact:** Rights Department. Estab. 1947. Publishes trade paperback originals and reprints. Ms guidelines online.
NEEDS "You are not only what you are today, but also what you choose to become tomorrow." Looking for adult fables that teach principles of psychological growth. Distributes titles through wholesalers, bookstores, and mail order. Promotes titles through author interviews on radio and television. Wants adult allegories that teach principles of psychological growth or offer guidance in living. Minimum 30,000 words. No standard fiction.
HOW TO CONTACT Submit 3 sample chapters. Submit complete ms. Include outline, author bio, analysis of book's, competition and SASE.
TERMS Pays standard royalty. Pays advance. Responds in 2 months.
TIPS "We are vitally interested in all new material we receive. Just as you are hopeful when submitting your manuscript for publication, we are hopeful as we read each one submitted, searching for those we believe could be successful in the marketplace. Writing and publishing must be a team effort. We need you to write what we can sell. We suggest you read the successful books similar to the one you want to write. Analyze them to discover what elements make them winners. Duplicate those elements in your own style, using a creative new approach and fresh material, and you will have written a book we can catapult onto the bestseller list. You are welcome to telephone or e-mail us for immediate feedback on any book concept you may have. To learn more about us and what we publish, and for complete manuscript guidelines, visit our website."

WINDRIVER PUBLISHING, INC.

3280 Madison Ave., Ogden, UT 84403. (801)689-7440. **E-mail:** info@windriverpublishing.com. **Website:** www.windriverpublishing.com. **Contact:** E. Keith Howick, Jr., president; Gail Howick, vice president/editor-in-chief. Estab. 2003. "Authors who wish to submit book proposals for review must do so according to our submissions guidelines, which can be found on our website, along with an online submission form, which is our preferred submission method. *We do not accept submissions of any kind by e-mail.*" Publishes hardcover originals and reprints, trade paperback originals, and mass-market originals. Book catalog available online. Guidelines available online.
HOW TO CONTACT *Does not accept unsolicited mss.*
TERMS Responds in 1-2 months to queries; 4-6 months to proposals/mss.
TIPS "We do not accept manuscripts containing graphic or gratuitous profanity, sex, or violence. See online instructions for details."

WISDOM PUBLICATIONS

199 Elm St., Somerville, MA 02144. (617)776-7416, ext. 28. **Fax:** (617)776-7841. **E-mail:** editors@wisdompubs.org. **Website:** www.wisdompubs.org. **Contact:** David Kittlestrom, senior editor. Estab. 1976. "Wisdom Publications is dedicated to making available authentic Buddhist works for the benefit of all. We publish translations, commentaries, and teachings of past and contemporary Buddhist masters and original works by leading Buddhist scholars. Currently emphasizing popular applied Buddhism, scholarly titles." Publishes hardcover originals and trade paperback originals and reprints. Book catalog and ms guidelines online.
TERMS Pays 4-8% royalty on wholesale price. Pays advance.
TIPS "We are basically a publisher of Buddhist books—all schools and traditions of Buddhism. Please see our catalog or our website before you send anything to us to get a sense of what we publish."

WIZARDS OF THE COAST BOOKS FOR YOUNG READERS

P.O. Box 707, Renton, WA 98057. (425)254-2287. **E-mail:** nina.hess@wizards.com. **Website:** www.wizards.com. **Contact:** Nina Hess. Estab. 2003. Wizards of the Coast publishes only science fiction and fantasy shared-world titles. Currently emphasizing solid fantasy writers. De-emphasizing gothic fiction. Dragonlance; Forgotten Realms; Magic: The Gathering; Eberron. Wizard of the Coast publishes games as well, including Dungeons & Dragons® role-playing game. Publishes hardcover and trade paperback originals and trade paperback reprints. Catalog available on website. Ms guidelines available on website.
NEEDS Young readers, middle readers, young adults: fantasy only. Average word length: middle readers—30,000-40,000; young adults—60,000-75,000.

Recently published *A Practical Guide to Dragon-Riding*, by Lisa Trumbauer (ages 6 and up); *The Stow-away*, by R.A. Salvatore and Geno Salvatore (10 and up), *Red Dragon Codex*, by R. Henham (ages 8-12).

HOW TO CONTACT Query with samples.

TERMS Pays authors 4-6% based on retail price. Pays illustrators by project. Offers advances (average amount: $4,000).

TIPS Editorial staff attended or plans to attend ALA conference.

WORDSONG

815 Church St., Honesdale PA 18431. **Fax:** (570)253-0179. **E-mail:** submissions@boydsmillspress.com; eagarrow@boydsmillspress.com. **Website:** www.wordsongpoetry.com. Estab. 1990. "We publish fresh voices in contemporary poetry."

NEEDS Submit complete ms or submit through agent. Label package "Manuscript Submission" and include SASE. "Please send a book-length collection of your own poems. Do not send an initial query."

TERMS Pays authors royalty or work purchased outright. Responds to mss in 3 months.

TIPS "Collections of original poetry, not anthologies, are our biggest need at this time. Keep in mind that the strongest collections demonstrate a facility with multiple poetic forms and offer fresh images and insights. Check to see what's already on the market and on our website before submitting."

○ YELLOW SHOE FICTION SERIES

P.O. Box 25053, Baton Rouge, LA 70894. **Website:** www.lsu.edu/lsupress. **Contact:** Michael Griffith, editor. Estab. 2004.

○ "Looking first and foremost for literary excellence, especially good manuscripts that have fallen through the cracks at the big commercial presses. I'll cast a wide net."

HOW TO CONTACT Does not accept unsolicited mss. Accepts queries by mail, Attn: Rand Dotson. No electronic submissions.

TERMS Pays royalty. Offers advance.

Ⓐ ZEBRA BOOKS

Kensington, 119 W. 40th St., New York, NY 10018. (212)407-1500. **E-mail:** mrecords@kensingtonbooks.com. **Website:** www.kensingtonbooks.com. **Contact:** Megan Records, associate editor. Zebra Books is dedicated to women's fiction, which includes, but is not limited to, romance. Publishes hardcover originals, trade paperback and mass-market paperback originals and reprints. Book catalog available online.

NEEDS Mostly historical romance. Some contemporary romance, westerns, horror, and humor.

HOW TO CONTACT Agented submissions only. You may QUERY ONLY by e-mail. Do not attach manuscripts or proposals to e-mail queries. An editor will respond if he or she is interested in seeing your material based on your query. SUBMIT TO ONE EDITOR ONLY. For fiction, send cover letter, first three chapters, and synopsis (no more than five pages). Note that we do not publish science fiction or fantasy. We do not publish poetry.

ZONDERVAN, A HARPERCOLLINS COMPANY

Division of HarperCollins Publishers, 5300 Patterson Ave. SE, Grand Rapids MI 49530. (616)698-6900. **Fax:** (616)698-3454. **E-mail:** submissions@zondervan.com. **E-mail:** christianmanuscriptsubmissions.com. **Website:** www.zondervan.com. Estab. 1931. "Our mission is to be the leading Christian communications company meeting the needs of people with resources that glorify Jesus Christ and promote biblical principles." Publishes hardcover and trade paperback originals and reprints. Guidelines available online.

IMPRINTS Zondervan, Zonderkidz, Youth Specialties, Editorial Vida.

NEEDS Refer to nonfiction. Inklings-style fiction of high literary quality. Christian relevance in all cases. Will not consider collections of short stories or poetry.

HOW TO CONTACT Submit TOC, curriculum vitae, chapter outline, intended audience.

TERMS Pays 14% royalty on net amount received on sales of cloth and softcover trade editions; 12% royalty on net amount received on sales of mass-market paperbacks. Pays variable advance. Responds in 2 months to queries; 3 months to proposals; 4 months to mss.

CONTESTS & AWARDS

In addition to honors and, quite often, cash prizes, contests and awards programs offer writers the opportunity to be judged on the basis of quality alone, without the outside factors that sometimes influence publishing decisions. New writers who win contests may be published for the first time, while more experienced writers may gain public recognition for an entire body of work.

Listed here are contests for almost every type of fiction writing. Some focus on form, such as short stories, novels, or novellas, while others feature writing on particular themes or topics. Still others are prestigious prizes or awards for work that must be nominated, such as the Pulitzer Prize in Fiction. Chances are, no matter what type of fiction you write, there is a contest or award program that may interest you.

SELECTING & SUBMITTING TO A CONTEST

Use the same care in submitting to contests as you would sending your manuscript to a publication or book publisher. Deadlines are very important, and where possible, we've included this information. For some contests, deadlines were only approximate at our press deadline, so be sure to write, call, or look online for complete information.

Follow the rules to the letter. If, for instance, contest rules require your name on a cover sheet only, you will be disqualified if you ignore this and put your name on every page. Find out how many copies to send. If you don't send the correct amount, by the time you are contacted to send more, it may be past the submission deadline. An increasing number of contests invite writers to query by e-mail, and many post contest information on their websites. Check listings for e-mail and website addresses.

One note of caution: Beware of contests that charge entry fees that are disproportionate to the amount of the prize. Contests offering a $10 prize and charging $7 in entry fees are a waste of your time and money.

If you are interested in a contest or award that requires your publisher to nominate your work, it's acceptable to make your interest known. Be sure to leave the publisher plenty of time, however, to make the nomination deadline.

24-HOUR SHORT STORY CONTEST

WritersWeekly.com, 5726 Cortez Rd. W., #349, Bradenton, FL 34210. **E-mail:** writersweekly@writersweekly.com. **Website:** www.writersweekly.com/misc/contest.php. **Contact:** Angela Hoy. "Quarterly contest in which registered entrants receive a topic at start time (usually noon Central Time) and have 24 hours to write a story on that topic. All submissions must be returned via e-mail. Each contest is limited to 500 people. Guidelines via e-mail or online." **Deadline:** Quarterly—see website for dates. **Prize:** 1st Place: $300; 2nd Place: $250; 3rd Place: $200. There are also 20 honorable mentions and 60 door prizes. The top 3 winners' entries are posted on WritersWeekly.com (nonexclusive electronic rights only). Writers retain all rights to their work. Angela Hoy (publisher of WritersWeekly.com and Booklocker.com).

AEON AWARD

Albedo One/Aeon Press, Aeon Award, Albedo One, 2 Post Road, Lusk, Dublin, Ireland. +353 1 8730177. **E-mail:** fraslaw@yahoo.co.uk. **Website:** www.albedo1.com. **Contact:** Frank Ludlow, event coordinator. "We aim to encourage new writers into the genre and to encourage existing writers to push at their boundaries" Annual. Competition/award for short stories. "Categories: any speculative genre, "i.e. fantasy, SF horror or anything in between or unclassifiable (like slipstream)." **Deadline:** November 30. **Prize:** Grand prize €1,000; second €200;, and third €100. The top three stories are guaranteed publication in *Albedo One*.

AESTHETICA CREATIVE WORKS COMPETITION

P.O. Box 371, York YO23 1WL United Kingdom. **E-mail:** pauline@aestheticamagazine.com. **E-mail:** submissions@aestheticamagazine.com. **Website:** www.aestheticamagazine.com. The Aesthetica Creative Works Competition represents the scope of creative activity today and provides an opportunity for both new and established artists to nurture their reputations on an international scale. There are three categories: Short Film Festival, Art Prize, and Creative Writing. Art Prize has four subcategories, Creative writing has two. See website for guidelines and more details. The Aesthetica Creative Works Competition is looking to discover talented artists and writers. The editor of Aesthetica is a Fellow of the Royal Society of Arts. See guidelines online. **Deadline:** August 31. **Prize:** £500-1,000, Each winner will receive an additional prize from our competition partners. Winners will be published in the Aesthetica Creative Works Annual. Winners will receive a complimentary copy of the Aesthetica Creative Works Annual and publication of the work in their creative section (3 winners).

AHWA FLASH & SHORT STORY COMPETITION

AHWA (Australian Horror Writers Association), **E-mail:** ahwacomps@australianhorror.com. **E-mail:** ahwa@australianhorror.com. **Website:** http://australianhorror.com. **Contact:** David Carroll, competitions officer. Competition/award for short stories and flash fiction. "We're after horror stories, tales that frighten, yarns that unsettle us in our comfortable homes. All themes in this genre will be accepted, from the well-used (zombies, vampires, ghosts, etc.) to the highly original, so long as the story is professional and well written. No previously published entries will be accepted—all tales must be an original work by the author. Stories can be as violent or as bloody as the story line dictates, but those containing gratuitous sex or violence will not be considered. Please check your entries for spelling and grammar mistakes and follow standard submission guidelines (eg, 12 pt font, Ariel, Times New Roman, or Courier New, one and a half spacing between lines, with title and page number on each page)." **Deadline:** May 31. **Prize:** The authors of the winning Flash Fiction and Short Story entries will each receive paid publication in *Midnight Echo*; The Magazine of the AHWA and an engraved plaque.

ALABAMA STATE COUNCIL ON THE ARTS INDIVIDUAL ARTIST FELLOWSHIP

201 Monroe St., Montgomery, AL 36130. (334)242-4076, ext. 236. **Fax:** (334)240-3269. **E-mail:** anne.kimzey@arts.alabama.gov. **Website:** www.arts.state.al.us. **Contact:** Anne Kimzey, literature program manager. Purpose: To recognize the achievements and potential of Alabama writers. **Deadline:** March 1. Applications must be submitted online by eGRANT. Judged by independent peer panel. Winners notified by mail and announced on website in June.

THE AMERICAN GEM LITERARY FESTIVAL

Film*Makers* Magazine/Write Brothers, **Website:** www.filmmakers.com/contests/short/. Estab. 2004. **Deadlines:** March 1 (early bird deadline); June 1 (regular deadline); August 1 (late deadline); September (final deadline).

AMERICAN MARKETS NEWSLETTER SHORT STORY COMPETITION

1974 46th Ave., San Francisco, CA 94116. **E-mail:** sheila.oconnor@juno.com. Award is "to give short story writers more exposure." Accepts fiction and nonfiction up to 2,000 words. Entries are eligible for cash prizes, and all entries are eligible for worldwide syndication whether they win or not. "Send double-spaced mss with your story/article title, byline, word count, and address on the first page above your article/story's first paragraph (no need for separate cover page). There is no limit to the number of entries you may send." **Prize:** 1st Place: $300; 2nd Place: $100; 3rd Place: $50. Judged by a panel of independent judges. **Entry fee:** $12 per entry; $20 for 2; $25 for 3; $30 for 4; $5 each entry thereafter. For guidelines, send SASE, fax or e-mail. **Deadline:** June 30 and December 31. Contest offered biannually. Published and unpublished stories are actively encouraged. Add a note of where and when previously published. Open to any writer. "All kinds of fiction are considered. We especially want women's pieces—romance, with a twist in the tale—but all will be considered." Results announced within 3 months of deadlines. Winners notified by mail if they include SASE. Award is "to give short story writers more exposure."

A MIDSUMMER TALE

E-mail: editors@toasted-cheese.com. **Website:** www.toasted-cheese.com. **Contact:** Theryn Fleming, editor. Entries must be unpublished. Accepts inquiries by e-mail. Cover letter should include name, address, e-mail, word count, and title. Word limit varies each year. Open to any writer. Guidelines available in April on website. June 21 Amazon gift certificates and publication in Toasted Cheese. Entries are blind judged.

THE SHERWOOD ANDERSON FOUNDATION FICTION AWARD

12330 Ashton Mill Terrace, Glen Allen, VA 23059. **E-mail:** sherwoodandersonfoundation@gmail.com. **Website:** sherwoodandersonfoundation.org. **Contact:** Anna McKean, foundation president. Contest is to honor, preserve, and celebrate the memory and literary work of Sherwood Anderson, American realist for the first half of the 20th century. Annual award supports developing writers of short stories and novels. Entrants must have published at least one book of fiction or have had several short stories published in major literary and/or commercial publication. Self-

published stories do not qualify. Send a detailed resumé that includes a bibliography of your publications. Include a cover letter that provides a history of your writing experience and your plans for writing projects. Also, submit 2 or 3 examples of what you consider to be your best work. Do not send manuscripts by e-mail. Only mss in English will be accepted. Open to any writer who meets the qualifications listed above. Accepts inquiries by e-mail. Mail your application to the above address. No mss or publications will be returned. **Deadline:** April 1. **Prize:** $20,000 grant award.

ART AFFAIR SHORT STORY AND WESTERN SHORT STORY CONTESTS

Art Affair - Contest, P.O. Box 54302, Oklahoma City, OK 73154. **E-mail:** artaffair@aol.com. **Website:** www.shadetreecreations.com. The annual Art Affair Writing Contests include (General) Short Story and Western Short Story categories. Open to any writer. All short stories must be unpublished. Multiple entries accepted in both categories with separate entry fees for each. Submit original stories on any subject and time frame for general Short Story category, and submit original western stories for Western Short Story—word limit for all entries is 5,000 words. Guidelines available on website. **Deadline:** postmarked by October 1. **Prize:** $50, $25, $15.

ARTIST TRUST FELLOWSHIP AWARD

1835 12th Ave., Seattle, WA 98122. (209)467-8734 ext. 9. **Fax:** (866)218-7878. **E-mail:** miguel@artisttrust.org. **Website:** artisttrust.org. **Contact:** Miguel Guillen, Program Manager. "Artist Trust Fellowship awards practicing professional Washington State artists of exceptional talent and demonstrated ability." Annual. **Deadline:** February 18. **Prize:** $7,500. Receives about 175 entries per category. Entries are judged by work samples as specified in the guidelines. Winners are selected by a multidisciplinary panel of artists and arts professionals. No entry fee. Guidelines available around December, please check website. Accepts inquiries by e-mail, phone. Submission period is December-February. Website should be consulted for the exact date. Entries can be unpublished or previously published. Washington State residents only. Length: up to 15 pages for poetry, fiction, graphic novels, experimental, works and creative nonfiction, and up to 20 pages for screen plays, film scripts, and teleplays. All mss must be typed with a 12-pt font size or larger and cannot be single-spaced (except for poetry). Include artist statement and resume with name, address, phone, e-mail, and novel/story title. "The Fellowship awards are highly competitive. Please follow guidelines with care." Results announced in the spring. Winners notified by mail. Results made available to entrants on website. Literature fellowships are offered every other year, in even years. The award is made on the basis of work of the past 5 years. Applicants must be individual artists; Washington State residents; not matriculated students; and generative artists. Guidelines and application online."

THE ART OF MUSIC BIENNIAL WRITING CONTEST

P.O. Box 85, Del Mar, CA 92014. (619)884-1401. **Fax:** (858)755-1104. **E-mail:** info@theartofmusicinc.org. **E-mail:** eaxford@aol.com. **Website:** www.theartof musicinc.org; www.pianopress.com. **Contact:** Elizabeth C. Axford. Offered biannually. Categories are: essay, short story, poetry, song lyrics, and illustrations for cover art. Acquires one-time rights. All entries must be accompanied by an entry form indicating category and age; parent signature is required of all writers under age 18. Poems may be of any length and in any style; essays and short stories should not exceed 5 double-spaced, typewritten pages. All entries shall be previously unpublished (except poems and song lyrics) and the original work of the author. Inquiries accepted by e-mail, phone. Open to any writer. "Make sure all work is fresh and original. Music-related topics only." Results announced October 31. Winners notified by mail. For contest results, send SASE or visit website. "The purpose of the contest is to promote the art of music through writing." **Deadline:** June 30. **Prize:** Trophy, certificate, publication online and in the e-book, *The Art of Music: A Collection of Writings*. Judged by a panel of published poets, authors, and songwriters.

THE ATHENAEUM LITERARY AWARD

The Athenaeum of Philadelphia, 219 S. Sixth St., Philadelphia, PA 19106-3794. (215)925-2688. **Fax:** (215)925-3755. **E-mail:** jilly@PhilAthenaeum.org. **Website:** www.PhilaAthenaeum.org. **Contact:** Jill Lee, Circulation Librarian. The Athenaeum Literary Award was established in 1950 to recognize and encourage literary achievement among authors who are "bona fide residents of Philadelphia or Pennsylvania living within a radius of 30 miles of City Hall" at the time their book was written or published. Any volume of general literature is eligible; technical, scientific, and juvenile books are not included. Nominated works are reviewed on the basis of their significance and importance to the general public as well as for literary excellence. **Deadline:** December 31.

ATLANTIC WRITING COMPETITION FOR UNPUBLISHED MANUSCRIPTS

Writers' Federation of Nova Scotia, 1113 Marginal Rd., Halifax, NS B3H 4P7. (902)423-8116. **Fax:** (902)422-0881. **E-mail:** programs@writers.ns.ca. **Website:** www.writers.ns.ca. **Contact:** Hillary Titley. Estab. 1975. "Annual contest for beginners to try their hand in a number of categories: novel, short story, poetry, writing for younger children, writing for juvenile/young adult. Only 1 entry/category is allowed. Established writers are also eligible but must work in an area that's new to them. Because our aim is to help Atlantic Canadian writers grow, judges return written comments when the competition is concluded. Anyone residing in the Atlantic Provinces for at least 6 months prior to the contest deadline is eligible to enter." $35 fee for novel ($30 for WFNS members); $25 fee for all other categories ($20 for WFNS members). Needs poetry, essays, juvenile, novels, articles, short stories. "We encourage writers in Atlantic Canada to explore and expand their talents by sending in their new, untried work." **Deadline:** November 9. Prizes vary based on categories. See website for details.

AUTUMN HOUSE POETRY, FICTION, AND NONFICTION PRIZES

P.O. Box 60100, Pittsburgh, PA 15211. (412)381-4261. **E-mail:** msimms@autumnhouse.org. **Website:** http://autumnhouse.org. **Contact:** Michael Simms, editor. Estab. 1999. Offers annual prize of $2,500 and publication of book-length ms with national promotion. Submission must be unpublished as a collection, but individual poems, stories, and essays may have been previously published elsewhere. Considers simultaneous submissions. Submit 50-80 pages of poetry or 200-300 pages of prose ("blind judging—2 cover sheets requested"). Guidelines available for SASE, by e-mail, or on website. Competition receives 1,500 entries/year. Winners announced through mailings, website, and ads in *Poets & Writers*, *American Poetry Review*, and *Writer's Chronicle* (extensive publicity for winner). Copies of winning books available from Amazon. com, Barnes & Noble, and other retailers. "Autumn

House is a nonprofit corporation with the mission of publishing and promoting poetry and other fine literature. We have published books by Gerald Stern, Ruth L. Schwartz, Ed Ochester, Andrea Hollander Budy, George Bilgere, Jo McDougall, and others." **Deadline:** June 30, annually. 2012 judges were Stephen Dunn, Stewart O'Nan, and Phillip Lopate.

○ AWP AWARD SERIES

Association of Writers & Writing Programs, George Mason University, 4400 University Drive, MSN 1E3, Fairfax, VA 22030. **E-mail:** supriya@awpwriter.org. **Website:** www.awpwriter.org. **Contact:** Supriya Bhatnagar, director of publications. AWP sponsors the Award Series, an annual competition for the publication of excellent new book-length works. The competition is open to all authors writing in English regardless of nationality or residence, and is available to published and unpublished authors alike. Offered annually to foster new literary talent. **Deadline:** Postmarked between January 1 and February 28. **Prize:** AWP Prize for the Novel: $2,000; Donald Hall Prize for Poetry: $5,000; Grace Paley Prize in Short Fiction: $5,000; and AWP Prize for Creative Nonfiction: $2,000.

○ MILDRED L. BATCHELDER AWARD

50 E. Huron St., Chicago IL 60611-2795. **Website:** www.ala.org/alsc. **Contact:** Jean Hatfield, Chair. Estab. 1966. This award honors Mildred L. Batchelder, a former executive director of the Association for Library Service to Children, a believer in the importance of good books for children in translation from all parts of the world. This award is a citation awarded to an American publisher for a children's book considered to be the most outstanding of those books originally published in a foreign language in a foreign country, and subsequently translated into English and published in the U.S. ALSC gives the award to encourage American publishers to seek out superior children's books abroad and to promote communication among the peoples of the world. **Deadline:** December 31.

BELLEVUE LITERARY REVIEW GOLDENBERG PRIZE FOR FICTION

Bellevue Literary Review, NYU Dept of Medicine, 550 First Ave., OBV-A612, New York, NY 10016. (212)263-3973. **E-mail:** info@blreview.org; stacy@blreview.org. **Website:** www.blreview.org. **Contact:** Stacy Bodziak, managing editor. The BLR prizes award outstand-

ing writing related to themes of health, healing, illness, the mind, and the body. Annual. Competition/award for short stories. Receives about 200-300 entries per category. Send credit card information or make checks payable to Bellevue Literary Review. Guidelines available in February. Accepts inquiries by e-mail, phone, mail. Submissions open in February. Results announced in December and made available to entrants with SASE, by e-mail, on website. Winners notified by mail, by e-mail. **Deadline:** July 1 $1,000 and publication in *The Bellevue Literary Review*. BLR editors select semifinalists to be read by an independent judge who chooses the winner. Previous judges include Amy Hempel, Rick Moody, Rosellen Brown, and Andre Dubus III.

○ GEORGE BENNETT FELLOWSHIP

Phillips Exeter Academy, Phillips Exeter Academy, 20 Main St., Exeter, NH 03833. **E-mail:** teaching_opportunities@exeter.edu. **Website:** www.exeter.edu. Annual award for fellow and family "to provide time and freedom from material considerations to a person seriously contemplating or pursuing a career as a writer. Applicants should have a manuscript in progress which they intend to complete during the fellowship period." Duties: To be in residency at the Academy for the academic year; to make oneself available informally to students interested in writing. The committee favors writers who have not yet published a book with a major publisher. **Deadline for application:** December 1. A choice will be made, and all entrants notified in mid-April. **Prize:** Cash stipend, room, and board. Judged by committee of the English department.

● BINGHAMTON UNIVERSITY JOHN GARDNER FICTION BOOK AWARD

Creative Writing Program, Binghamton University, Binghamton University, Department of English, General Literature, and Rhetoric, Library North Room 1149, P.O. Box 6000, Binghamton, NY 13902-6000. (607)777-2713. **E-mail:** cwpro@binghamton.edu. **Website:** http://binghamton.edu/english/creative-writing/. **Contact:** Maria Mazziotti Gillan, director. Estab. 2001. Contest offered annually for a novel or collection of short stories published that year in a press run of 500 copies or more. Each book submitted must be accompanied by an application form. Publisher may submit more than 1 book for prize consideration. Send 3 copies of each book. Guidelines available on website. Award's purpose is "to serve the literary community by calling attention to outstanding books of fiction." **Deadline:** March 1. **Prize:** $1,000. Judged by a professional writer not on Binghamton University faculty.

JAMES TAIT BLACK MEMORIAL PRIZES

University of Edinburgh, David Hume Tower, George, Edinburgh EH8 9JX Scotland. **Website:** www.englit.ed.ac.uk/jtbinf.htm. **Prize:** "Two prizes each of £10,000 are awarded: one for the best work of fiction, one for the best biography or work of that nature, published during the calendar year January 1 to December 31." Judged by professors of English literature with the assistance of teams of postgraduate readers. Accepts inquiries by fax, e-mail, phone. Entries must be previously published. "Eligible works are those written in English and first published or co-published in Britain in the year of the award. Works should be submitted by publishers." Open to any writer. Winners notified by phone, via publisher. Contact department of English literature for list of winners or check website. **Deadline:** December 1

BURNABY WRITERS' SOCIETY CONTEST

E-mail: info@bws.bc.ca. **Website:** www.bws.bc.ca; http:burnabywritersnews.blogspot.com. **Contact:** Eileen Kernaghan. "Offered annually for unpublished work. Open to all residents of British Columbia. Categories vary from year to year. Send SASE for current rules. For complete guidelines see website or burnabywritersnews.blogspot.com." Purpose is to encourage talented writers in all genres. **Deadline:** May 31. **Prize:** 1st Place: $200; 2nd Place: $100; 3rd Place: $50; and public reading.

THE CAINE PRIZE FOR AFRICAN WRITING

51 Southwark St., London SE1 1RU United Kingdom. **E-mail:** info@caineprize.com. **Website:** www.caineprize.com. **Contact:** Jenny Casswell. Estab. 2000. Entries must have appeared for the first time in the 5 years prior to the closing date for submissions, which is January 31 each year. Publishers should submit 6 copies of the published original with a brief cover note (no pro forma application). "Please indicate nationality or passport held." The Caine Prize is open to writers from anywhere in Africa for work published in English. Its focus is on the short story, reflecting the

contemporary development of the African story-telling tradition. **Deadline:** January 31. **Prize:** £10,000.

JOHN W. CAMPBELL MEMORIAL AWARD FOR BEST SCIENCE FICTION NOVEL OF THE YEAR

English Department, University of Kansas, Lawrence, KS 66045. (785)864-3380. **Fax:** (785)864-1159. **E-mail:** cmckit@ku.edu. **Website:** www.ku.edu/~sfcenter. **Contact:** Chris McKitterick. Estab. 1973. Award to "honor the best science fiction novel of the year." **Prize:** Trophy. Winners receive an expense-paid trip to the university to receive their award. Their names are also engraved on a permanent trophy. Categories: novels. Judged by a jury. No entry fee. **Deadline:** see website. Entries must be previously published. Open to any writer. Accepts inquiries by e-mail and fax. "Ordinarily publishers should submit work, but authors have done so when publishers would not. Send for list of jurors." Results announced in July. For contest results, send SASE.

JAMIE CAT CALLAN HUMOR PRIZE

Category in the Soul Making Keats Literary Competition, The Webhallow House, 1544 Sweetwood Dr., Broadmoor Village, CA 94015-2029. **E-mail:** Eileen Malone@comcast.net. **Website:** www.soulmakingcontest.us. **Contact:** Eileen Malone. **Deadline:** November 30. **Prize:** First Place: $100; Second Place: $50; Third Place: $25. Judged by Jamie Cat Callan.

KAY CATTARULLA AWARD FOR BEST SHORT STORY

Texas Institute of Letters, P.O. Box 609, Round Rock TX 78680. **E-mail:** tilsecretary@yahoo.com. **Website:** http://texasinstituteofletters.org. Offered annually for work published January 1-December 31 of previous year to recognize the best short story. The story submitted must have appeared in print for the first time to be eligible. Writers must have been born in Texas, must have lived in Texas for at least 2 consecutive years, or the subject matter of the work must be associated with Texas. See website for guidelines. **Deadline:** See website for exact date. **Prize:** $1,000.

COLORADO BOOK AWARDS

Colorado Center for the Book, 1490 Lafayette St., Suite 101, Denver, CO 80218. (303)894-7951, ext. 21. **Fax:** (303)864-9361. **E-mail:** goff@coloradohumanities.org. **Website:** www.coloradohumanities.org. **Contact:** Christine Goff. An annual program that celebrates the accomplishments of Colorado's outstanding authors, editors, illustrators, and photographers. Awards are presented in at least ten categories including anthology/collection, biography, children's, creative nonfiction, fiction, history, nonfiction, pictorial, poetry, and young adult. To celebrate books and their creators, and promote them to readers.

COWBOY UP SHORT STORY CONTEST

Moonlight Mesa Associates, Inc., 18620 Moonlight Mesa Rd., Wickenburg, AZ 85390. **E-mail:** orders@ moonlightmesaassociates.com. **Website:** www .moonlightmesaassociates.com. Estab. 2006. Fiction only: 3,500 words maximum. Open March 1-September 1. **Prize:** $75-250

> "Contest will be held every two years on even years beginning in 2014. Check website for details."

◯ CRAZYHORSE FICTION PRIZE

College of Charleston, Department of English, 66 George St., Charleston, SC 29424. (843)953-4470. **Fax:** (843)953-7740. **E-mail:** crazyhorse@cofc.edu. **Website:** http://crazyhorse.cofc.edu. The journal's mission is to publish the entire spectrum of today's fiction, essays, and poetry—from the mainstream to the avant-garde, from the established to the undiscovered writer. The editors are especially interested in original writing that engages in the work of honest communication. *Crazyhorse* publishes writing of fine quality regardless of style, predilection, subject. Contest open to any writer. **Deadline:** January 31 of each year; see website. **Prize:** $2,000 and publication in *Crazyhorse*. Judged by anonymous writer whose identity is disclosed when the winners are announced in April. Past judges: Diana Abu-Jaber (2004), T.M. McNally (2005), Dan Chaon (2006), Antonya Nelson (2007), Ha Jin (2008); Ann Pratchett (2009).

THE CRUCIBLE POETRY AND FICTION COMPETITION

Crucible, Barton College, College Station, Wilson, NC 27893. (800)345-4973 x6450. **E-mail:** cru cible@barton.edu. **Website:** www.barton.edu/ SchoolofArts&Sciences/English/Crucible.htm. **Contact:** Terrence L. Grimes, editor. "Offered annually for unpublished mss. Fiction is limited to 8,000 words; poetry is limited to 5 poems. Guidelines online or by e-mail or for SASE. All submissions should be electronic." **Deadline:** May 1. **Prize:** 1st Place: $150; 2nd Place: $100 (for both poetry and fiction). Winners are

also published in *Crucible*. Judged by in-house editorial board.

DANA AWARDS IN THE NOVEL, SHORT FICTION, ESSAY AND POETRY

www.danaawards.com, 200 Fosseway Dr., Greensboro, NC 27445. (336)644-8028. **E-mail:** dan aawards@pipeline.com. **E-mail:** danaawards@gmail .com. **Website:** www.danaawards.com. **Contact:** Mary Elizabeth Parker, chair. Four awards offered annually for unpublished work written in English. Purpose is monetary award for work that has not been previously published or received monetary award, but will accept work published simply for friends and family. Works previously published online are not eligible. No work accepted by or for persons under 16 for any of the 4 awards: **Novel**—For the first 40 pages of a novel completed or in progress; **Fiction**—short fiction (no memoirs) up to 10,000 words; **Essay**—personal essay, memoir, or creative nonfiction up to 10,000 words; **Poetry**—for best group of 5 poems based on excellence of all 5 (no light verse, no single poem over 100 lines). **Deadline:** October 31 (postmarked). **Prizes:** $1,000 for each of the 4 awards.

◯ DEAD OF WINTER

E-mail: editors@toasted-cheese.com. **Website:** www .toasted-cheese.com. **Contact:** Stephanie Lenz, editor. The contest is a winter-themed horror fiction contest with a new topic each year. Topic and word limit announced October 1. The topic is usually geared toward a supernatural theme. Categories: Short stories. No entry fee. Results announced January 31. Winners notified by e-mail. List of winners on website. **Deadline:** December 21. **Prize:** Amazon gift certificates and publication in *Toasted Cheese*. Also offers honorable mention. Judged by 2 *Toasted Cheese* editors who blind judge each contest. Each judge uses her own criteria to rate entries.

◐ DIAGRAM/NEW MICHIGAN PRESS CHAPBOOK CONTEST

Department of English, P.O. Box 210067, University of Arizona, Tucson, AZ 85721-0067. **E-mail:** nmp@ thediagram.com. **Website:** thediagram.com/contest .html. **Contact:** Ander Monson, editor. Estab. 1999. The annual *DIAGRAM*/New Michigan Press Chapbook Contest offers $1,000, plus publication and author's copies, with discount on additional copies. Also publishes 2-4 finalist chapbooks each year. **Deadline:** April 1. **Prize:** $1,000 plus publication.

DOBIE PAISANO PROJECT

The Graduate School, The University of Texas at Austin, Attn: Dobie Paisano Program, 110 Inner Campus Drive Stop G0400, Austin, TX 78712-0531. (512)232-3609. **Fax:** (512)471-7620. **E-mail:** gbarton@austin .utexas.edu. **Website:** www.utexas.edu/ogs/Paisano. **Contact:** Gwen Barton. "Sponsored by the Graduate School at The University of Texas at Austin and the Texas Institute of Letters, the Dobie Paisano Fellowship Program provides solitude, time, and a comfortable place for Texas writers or writers who have written significantly about Texas." **Deadline:** January 15. **Prizes:** "The Ralph A. Johnston memorial Fellowship is for a period of 4 months with a stipend of $5,000 per month. It is aimed at writers who have already demonstrated some publishing and critical success. The Jesse H. Jones Writing Fellowship is for a period of approximately 6 months with a stipend of $3,000 per month. It is aimed at, but not limited to, writers who are early in their careers."

JACK DYER FICTION PRIZE

Crab Orchard Review, Department of English, Mail Code 4503, Faner Hall 2380, Southern Illinois University at Carbondale, 1000 Faner Drive, Carbondale, IL 62901. **E-mail:** jtribble@siu.edu. **Website:** www .craborchardreview.siu.edu. **Contact:** Jon C. Tribble, man. editor. Offered annually for unpublished short fiction. *Crab Orchard Review* acquires first North American serial rights to all submitted work. **Deadline:** May 4. **Prize:** $2,000, publication and 1-year subscription to *Crab Orchard Review*. Judged by editorial staff (pre-screening); winner chosen by genre editor.

MARY KENNEDY EASTHAM FLASH FICTION PRIZE

Category in the Soul Making Keats Literary Competition, The Webhallow House, 1544 Sweetwood Dr., Broadmoor Village, CA 94015-2029. **E-mail:** Eileen Malone@comcast.net. **Website:** www.soulmaking contest.us. **Contact:** Eileen Malone. "Keep each story under 500 words. Three stories per entry. One story per page, typed, double-spaced, and unidentified. Send me your best stuff but, more than that, make my heart beat faster. Surprise me. Read great writing daily and WRITE. WRITE. WRITE. To be successful you need to do your best every day for a very long time." **Deadline:** November 30. **Prizes:** 1st Place: $100; 2nd Place: $50; 3rd Place: $25.

EATON LITERARY AGENCY'S ANNUAL AWARDS PROGRAM

Eaton Literary Agency, P.O. Box 49795, Sarasota, FL 34230-6795. (941)366-6589. **Fax:** (941)365-4679. **E-mail:** eatonlit@aol.com. **Website:** www.eatonliter ary.com. **Contact:** Richard Lawrence, V.P. Offered biannually for unpublished mss. **Prize:** $2,500 (over 10,000 words); $500 (under 10,000 words). Judged by an independent agency in conjunction with some members of Eaton's staff. No entry fee. Guidelines available for SASE, by fax, e-mail, or on website. Accepts inquiries by fax, phone and e-mail. **Deadline: March 31** (mss under 10,000 words); **August 31** (mss over 10,000 words). Entries must be unpublished. Open to any writer. Results announced in April and September. Winners notified by mail. For contest results, send SASE, fax, e-mail, or visit website. Offered biannually for unpublished mss. Entries must be unpublished.

THE EMILY CONTEST

18207 Heaton Dr., Houston, TX 77084. **E-mail:** em ily.contest@whrwa.com. **Website:** www.whrwa.com. "The Emily Contest was first established by the West Houston Chapter of RWA® in 1990 in order to promote publication of previously unpublished writers of romance. The contest is unusual in that it does not limit its entrants to members of RWA. Rather, it is open to any writer who has not published in a given category within the past three years." The mission of The Emily is to professionally support writers and guide them toward a path to publication. **Deadline:** September 30. Final judging done by an editor and an agent.

☉ THE FAR HORIZONS AWARD FOR SHORT FICTION

The Malahat Review, University of Victoria, P.O. Box 1700, Stn CSC, Victoria, BC V8W 2Y2 Canada. (250)721-8524. **Fax:** (250)472-5051. **E-mail:** malahat@ uvic.ca. **Website:** www.malahatreview.ca. **Contact:** John Barton, editor. Open to "emerging short fiction writers from Canada, the U.S., and elsewhere" who have not yet published their fiction in a full-length book (48 pages or more). 2011 winner: Zoey Peterson. Winner and finalists contacted by e-mail. **Deadline:** May 1 of odd-numbered years. **Prize:** Offers $1,000 CAD, publication in fall issue of *The Malahat Review* (see separate listing in Magazines/Journals).

Announced in fall on website, Facebook page, and in quarterly e-newsletter, *Malahat Lite*.

THE VIRGINIA FAULKNER AWARD FOR EXCELLENCE IN WRITING

Prairie Schooner, 123 Andrews Hall, University of Nebraska-Lincoln, Lincoln, NE 68588-0334. (402)472-0911. **Fax:** (402)472-1817. **E-mail:** PrairieSchooner@unl.edu. **Website:** www.prairieschooner.unl.edu. **Contact:** Kwame Dawes. Offered annually for work published in *Prairie Schooner* in the previous year. Categories: short stories, essays, novel excerpts, and translations. Guidelines for SASE or on website. **Prize:** $1,000. Judged by Editorial Board.

FIRSTWRITER.COM INTERNATIONAL SHORT STORY CONTEST

firstwriter.com, United Kingdom. **Website:** www.firstwriter.com. **Contact:** J. Paul Dyson, managing editor. "Accepts short stories up to 3,000 words on any subject and in any style." **Deadline:** April 1. **Prize:** about $300. Ten special commendations will also be awarded and all the winners will be published in *firstwriter* magazine and receive a $36 subscription voucher, allowing an annual subscription to be taken out for free. All submissions are automatically considered for publication in *firstwriter* magazine and may be published there online. Judged by *firstwriter* magazine editors.

◐◯ FISH PUBLISHING FLASH FICTION COMPETITION

Durrus, Bantry, County Cork Ireland. **E-mail:** info@fishpublishing.com. **Website:** www.fishpublishing.com. The Fish Flash Fiction Prize has been an annual event since 2004. "This is an opportunity to attempt what is one of the most difficult and rewarding tasks—to create, in a tiny fragment, a completely resolved and compelling story in 300 words or less." **Deadline:** February 28. **First Prize:** €1,000. The ten published authors will receive five copies of the anthology and will be invited to read at the launch during the West Cork Literary Festival in July. 2013 competition judged by Peter Benson.

◯ FLORIDA FIRST COAST WRITERS' FESTIVAL NOVEL, SHORT FICTION, PLAYWRITING & POETRY AWARDS

Florida Community College at Jacksonville, 4501 Capper Road, Jacksonville, FL 32218-4499. (904)766-6601. **Fax:** (904)766-6654. **Website:** opencampus.fccj.org/WF/. Conference and contest "to create a healthy writing environment, honor writers of merit, and find a novel manuscript to recommend to New York publishers for 'serious consideration." **Deadline:** December 1.

H.E. FRANCIS SHORT STORY COMPETITION

Ruth Hindman Foundation, University of Alabama in Huntsville, Department of English, Morton Hall Room 222, Huntsville, AL 35899. **Website:** www.hefranciscompetition.com. "Offered annually for unpublished work, not to exceed 5,000 words. Acquires first-time publication rights." **Deadline:** December 31. $2,000. Judged by a panel of nationally recognized, award-winning authors, directors of creative writing programs, and editors of literary journals.

SOEURETTE DIEHL FRASER AWARD FOR BEST TRANSLATION OF A BOOK

P.O. Box 609, Round Rock, TX 78680. **E-mail:** tilsecretary@yahoo.com. **Website:** http://texasinstituteofletters.org. Offered every 2 years to recognize the best translation of a literary book into English. Translator must have been born in Texas or have lived in the state for at least 2 consecutive years at some time. **Deadline:** early January; see website for exact date. **Prize:** $1,000.

◯ FREEFALL SHORT PROSE AND POETRY CONTEST

Freefall Literary Society of Calgary, 922 9th Ave. SE, Calgary, AB T2G 0S4 Canada. **E-mail:** freefallmagazine@yahoo.ca. **Website:** www.freefallmagazine.ca. **Contact:** Lynn C. Fraser, managing editor. Offered annually for unpublished work in the categories of poetry (5 poems/entry) and prose (3,000 words or less). The purpose of the award in both categories is to recognize writers and offer publication credits in a literary magazine format. Contest rules and entry form online. Acquires first Canadian serial rights; ownership reverts to author after one-time publication. **Deadline:** December 31. **Prize:** 1st Place: $300 (CAD); 2nd Place: $150 (CAD); 3rd Place: $75; Honourable Mention: $25. All prizes include publication in the spring edition of *FreeFall Magazine*. Winners will also be invited to read at the launch of that issue, if such a launch takes place. Honorable mentions in each category will be published and may be asked to read. Travel expenses not included. Judged by current guest editor for issue (a published author in Canada).

THE FRENCH-AMERICAN AND THE FLORENCE GOULD FOUNDATIONS TRANSLATION PRIZES

French-American Foundation, 28 W. 44th St., Suite 1420, New York, NY 10036. (646)588-6786. **E-mail:** ebriet@frenchamerican.org. **Website:** www.frencha merican.org. **Contact:** Eugenie Briet. (212)829-8800. **Fax:** (212)829-8810. **E-mail:** ebriet@frenchamerican .org. **Website:** www.frenchamerican.org. **Contact:** Emma Archer. Annual contest to "promote French literature in the U.S., to give translators and their craft more visibility, and encouraging the American publishers who bring significant French texts to the English reading audience." Entries must have been published the year before the prizes are awarded. Judged by a jury committee made up of translators, writers, and scholars in French literature and culture. Annual contest to promote French literature in the United States. To "give translators and their craft more visibility, and to encourage the American publishers who bring significant French texts to the English reading audience." **Deadline:** December 31. **Prize:** "The foundation presents a $10,000 cash award for the best English translation of French in both fiction and nonfiction."

⚪ GEORGETOWN REVIEW

Georgetown Review, 400 East College St., Box 227, Georgetown, KY 40324. (502) 863-8308. **Fax:** (502) 863-8888. **E-mail:** gtownreview@georgetowncollege .edu. **Website:** georgetowncolleged.edu/georgetown review. **Contact:** Steve Carter, editor. Our magazine is a collaboration between English faculty at Georgetown College and undergrads who learn the editing business as they go and who always amaze their elders with their dedication and first-rate work. **Deadline:** October 15. **Prize:** $1,000 and publication; runners-up receive publication.

GIVAL PRESS NOVEL AWARD

Gival Press, LLC, P.O. Box 3812, Arlington, VA 22203. (703)351-0079. **E-mail:** givalpress@yahoo.com. **Website:** www.givalpress.com. **Contact:** Robert L. Giron. Offered annually for a previously unpublished original novel (not a translation). Guidelines by phone, on website, via e-mail, or by mail with SASE. Results announced late fall of same year. Winners notified by phone. Results made available to entrants with SASE, by e-mail, on website. "To award the best literary novel." **Deadline:** May 30. **Prize:** $3,000, plus publication

of book with a standard contract and author's copies. Final judge is announced after winner is chosen. Entries read anonymously.

GLIMMER TRAIN'S FAMILY MATTERS

Glimmer Train, 4763 SW Maplewood Rd., P.O. Box 80430, Portland, OR 97280. (503)221-0836. **Fax:** (503)221-0837. **E-mail:** eds@glimmertrain.org. **Website:** www.glimmertrain.org. **Contact:** Susan Burmeister-Brown. "This contest is now held twice a year, during the months of April and October. Winners are contacted two months after the close of each contest, and results officially announced one week later. Submit online at www.glimmertrain.org. **Prize:** 1st Place: $1,500, publication in *Glimmer Train Stories*, and 20 copies of that issue; 2nd Place: $500; 3rd Place: $300.

⚪ Represented in recent editions of *The Pushcart Prize*, *New Stories from the Midwest*, *The PEN/O. Henry Prize Stories*, *New Stories from the South*, *Best of the West*, and *Best American Short Stories Anthologies*.

GLIMMER TRAIN'S VERY SHORT FICTION AWARD (JANUARY)

Glimmer Train Press, Inc., 4763 SW Maplewood Rd., P.O. Box 80430, Portland, OR 97280. (503)221-0836. **Fax:** (503)221-0837. **E-mail:** eds@glimmertrain.org. **Website:** www.glimmertrain.org. **Contact:** Susan Burmeister-Brown. "Offered to encourage the art of the very short story. Word count: 3,000 maximum. Submit by January 31. Submit online at www.glimmertrain.org. Winners will be called on March 31." **Prize:** 1st Place: $1,500, publication in *Glimmer Train Stories*, and 20 copies of that issue; 2nd Place: $500; 3rd Place: $300.

⚪ Represented in recent editions of *The Pushcart Prize*, *New Stories from the Midwest*, *The PEN/O. Henry Prize Stories*, *New Stories from the South*, *Best of the West*, and *Best American Short Stories Anthologies*.

GLIMMER TRAIN'S VERY SHORT FICTION CONTEST (JULY)

Glimmer Train Press, Inc., 4763 SW Maplewood Rd., P.O. Box 80430, Portland, OR 97280. (503)221-0836. **Fax:** (503)221-0837. **E-mail:** eds@glimmertrain.org. **Website:** www.glimmertrain.org. **Contact:** Susan Burmeister-Brown. "Offered to encourage the art of the very short story. Word count: 3,000 maximum. Open July 1-31. Submit online at www.glimmertrain

.org." Winners are contacted by September 30 and results are officially announced one week later. **Prize:** 1st Place: $1,500, publication in *Glimmer Train Stories*, and 20 copies of that issue; 2nd Place: $500; 3rd Place: $300.

Ⓞ Represented in recent editions of *The Pushcart Prize*, *New Stories from the Midwest*, *The PEN/O. Henry Prize Stories*, *New Stories from the South*, *Best of the West*, and *Best American Short Stories* Anthologies.

Ⓞ GOVERNOR GENERAL'S LITERARY AWARD FOR FICTION

Canada Council for the Arts, 350 Albert St., P.O. Box 1047, Ottawa, ON K1P 5V8 Canada. (613)566-4414, ext. 5573. **Fax:** (613)566-4410. **Website:** www.canadacouncil.ca/prizes/ggla. Offered annually for the best English-language and the best French-language work of fiction by a Canadian. Publishers submit titles for consideration. **Deadline:** depends on the book's publication date. Books in English: March 15, June 1, or August 7. Books in French: March 15 or July 15. **Prize:** Each laureate receives $25,000; nonwinning finalists receive $1,000.

THE GRUB STREET NATIONAL BOOK PRIZE

Grub Street, 162 Boylston Street, 5th Floor, Boston ,MA 02116. (617) 695-0075. **Fax:** (617) 695-0075. **E-mail:** info@grubstreet.org. **Website:** http://grubstreet .org. **Contact:** Christopher Castellani, artistic director. The Grub Street National Book Prize for nonfiction is awarded once annually to an American writer outside New England publishing his or her second, third, fourth (or beyond) book. First books are not eligible. Writers whose primary residence is Massachusetts, Vermont, Maine, New Hampshire, Connecticut, or Rhode Island are also not eligible. **Deadline:** October 15. **Prize:** $5,000.

HAMMETT PRIZE

International Association of Crime Writers, North American Branch, 328 Eighth Ave., #114, New York, NY 10001. **E-mail:** mfrisque@igc.org. **Website:** www .crimewritersna.org. **Contact:** Mary A. Frisque, executive director, North American Branch. Award established "to honor a work of literary excellence in the field of crime writing by a U.S. or Canadian author." Award for novels, story collections, nonfiction by one author. Judged by committee. "Our reading committee seeks suggestions from publishers, and they also ask the membership for recommendations. Eligible books are read by a committee of members of the organization. The committee chooses 5 nominated books, which are then sent to 3 outside judges for a final selection. Judges are outside the crime writing field." **Deadline:** December 1. **Prize:** Trophy.

WILDA HEARNE FLASH FICTION CONTEST

Big Muddy: A Journal of the Mississippi River Valley, WHFF Contest, Southeast Missouri State University Press, One University Plaza, MS 2650, Cape Girardeau, MO 63701. **Website:** www6.semo.edu/ universitypress/hearne.htm. "We're searching for the best short-short story of any theme." **Deadline:** October 1. **Prize:** $300 and publication in *Big Muddy: A Journal of the Mississippi River Valley*. Semifinalists will be chosen by a regional team of published writers. The final manuscript will be chosen by Susan Swartwout, publisher of the Southeast Missouri State University Press.

DRUE HEINZ LITERATURE PRIZE

University of Pittsburgh Press, Eureka Building, 5th Floor, 3400 Forbes Ave., Eureka Bldg., 5th Floor, Pittsburgh, PA 15260. (412)383-2492. **Fax:** (412)383-2466. **Website:** www.upress.pitt.edu. Estab. 1981. Offered annually to writers who have published a book-length collection of fiction or a minimum of 3 short stories or novellas in commercial magazines or literary journals of national distribution. Does not return mss. **Deadline:** Submit May 1-June 30 only. **Prize:** $15,000. Judged by anonymous nationally known writers such as Robert Penn Warren, Joyce Carol Oates, and Margaret Atwood.

LORIAN HEMINGWAY SHORT STORY COMPETITION

Hemingway Days Festival, P.O. Box 993, Key West, FL 33041. **E-mail:** shortstorykw@gmail.com. **Website:** www.shortstorycompetition.com. **Contact:** Eva Eliot, editorial assistant. Estab. 1981. Award to "encourage literary excellence and the efforts of writers whose voices have yet to be heard." Offered annually for unpublished short stories up to 3,500 words. Guidelines available via mail, e-mail, or online. **Deadline:** May 15. **Prize:** 1st Place: $1,500, plus publication of his or her winning story in *Cutthroat: A Journal of the Arts*; 2nd-3rd Place: $500; honorable mentions will also be awarded. Judged by a panel of writers, editors, and literary scholars selected by author Lorian Hemingway. (Lorian Hemingway is the competition's final judge.)

Results announced at the end of July during Hemingway Days festival. Winners notified by phone prior to announcement. For contest results, send e-mail or visit website.

TONY HILLERMAN PRIZE

Wordharvest, 1063 Willow Way, Santa Fe, NM 87507. (505)471-1565. **E-mail:** wordharvest@wordharvest .com. **Website:** www.wordharvest.com. **Contact:** Anne Hillerman and Jean Schaumberg, coorganizers. Annual competition/award for novels. Categories: Unpublished mystery novels set in the American southwest, written by a first-time author in the mystery genre. Results announced at the Tony Hillerman Writers Conference. St. Martin's Press notifies the winner by phone or by e-mail 2-3 weeks prior to the conference. Results made available to entrants on website. All entries must be mailed to St. Martin's Press at the address below. Entry form is online at the website. For additional copies of the rules and to request an entry form, please send a SASE to: **St. Martin's Press/Hillerman Mystery Competition Thomas Dunne Books, 175 Fifth Ave., New York, NY 10010**. "To honor the contributions made by Tony Hillerman to the art and craft of the mystery." **Deadline:** June 1. **Prize:** $10,000 advance and publication by St. Martin's Minotaur imprint. Nominees will be selected by judges chosen by the editorial staff of St. Martin's Press, with the assistance of independent judges selected by organizers of the Tony Hillerman Writers Conference (Wordharvest), and the winner will be chosen by St. Martin's editors.

THE HODDER FELLOWSHIP

Lewis Center for the Arts, 185 Nassau Street, Princeton, NJ 08544. (609)258-1500. **E-mail:** anikolop@ princeton.edu. **Website:** www.princeton.edu/arts/ lewis_center/society_of_fellows. **Contact:** Angelo Nikolopoulos, program assistant, creative writing. The Hodder Fellowship will be given to writers of exceptional promise to pursue independent projects at Princeton University during the current academic year. Typically the fellows are poets, playwrights, novelists, creative nonfiction writers, and translators who have published one highly acclaimed work and are undertaking a significant new project that might not be possible without the "studious leisure" afforded by the fellowship. **Deadline:** November 1 (postmarked). **Prize:** $68,000 stipend.

TOM HOWARD/JOHN H. REID SHORT STORY CONTEST

c/o Winning Writers, 351 Pleasant St., PMB 222, Northampton, MA 01060-3961. (866)946-9748. **Fax:** (413)280-0539. **E-mail:** adam@winningwriters.com. **Website:** www.winningwriters.com. **Contact:** Adam Cohen, President. Estab. 1993. Now in its 20th year. Open to all writers. Submit any type of short story, essay, or other work of prose. "You may submit work that has been published or won prizes elsewhere, as long as you own the online publication rights." **Entry fee:** $15. Make checks payable to Winning Writers ("U.S. funds only, please"). Submit online or by mail. Early submission encouraged. Contest is sponsored by Tom Howard Books and assisted by Winning Writers. Judges: John H. Reid and Dee C. Konrad. See the complete guidelines and past winners. Guidelines available in July on website. Prefers inquiries by e-mail. Length: 5,000 words max per entry. Cover letter should include name, address, phone, e-mail, story title, and place(s) where story was previously published (if any). Only the title should be on the actual ms. Writers may submit own work. Read past winning entries at www.winningwriters.com/contests/tom story/ts_pastwinners.php. Winners notified by e-mail. Results made available to entrants on website. Contest is sponsored by Tom Howard Books and assisted by Winning Writers. **Deadline:** April 30, 2014. **Prizes:** 1st Place: $3,000; 2nd Place: $1,000; 3rd Place: $400; 4th Place: $250; and 6 Most Highly Commended Awards of $150 each. The winners will be published on the Winning Writers website.

THE JULIA WARD HOWE/BOSTON AUTHORS AWARD

The Boston Authors Club, 45 Pine Crest Rd., Newton, MA 02459. (617)244-0646. **E-mail:** bostonauthors@ aol.com; SarahM45@aol.com. **Website:** www.bostonauthorsclub.org. **Contact:** Sarah Lamstein. Estab. 1900. This annual award honors Julia Ward Howe and her literary friends who founded the Boston Authors Club in 1900. It also honors the membership over 110 years, consisting of novelists, biographers, historians, governors, senators, philosophers, poets, playwrights, and other luminaries. Authors must live within 100 miles of Boston the year their book is published. Works of fiction, nonfiction, memoir, poetry, and biography published in the year prior to the award (2013 for 2014 award) are eligible. Authors must live within

100 miles of Boston the year their book is published. Picture books, textbooks, and self-published works are not eligible. **Entry fee:** $25 per title. **Deadline:** January 15, 2014. **Prizes:** $1,000 each for 2 books.

○ L. RON HUBBARD'S WRITERS OF THE FUTURE CONTEST

P.O. Box 1630, Los Angeles, CA 90078. (323)466-3310. **Fax:** (323)466-6474. **E-mail:** contests@authorservicesinc.com. **Website:** www.writersofthefuture.com. **Contact:** Joni Labaqui, contest director. Estab. 1983. Foremost competition for new and amateur writers of unpublished science fiction or fantasy short stories or novelettes. Offered "to find, reward, and publicize new speculative fiction writers so they may more easily attain professional writing careers." Open to writers who have not professionally published a novel or short novel, more than 1 novelette, or more than 3 short stories. Entries must be unpublished. Limit 1 entry per quarter. Open to any writer. Results announced quarterly in e-newsletter. Winners notified by phone. **Deadline:** December 31, March 31, June 30, September 30. **Prize:** (awards quarterly) 1st Place: $1,000; 2nd Place: $750; and 3rd Place: $500. Annual grand prize: $5,000. "Contest has 4 quarters. There shall be 3 cash prizes in each quarter. In addition, at the end of the year, the 4 first-place, quarterly winners will have their entries rejudged, and a grand prize winner shall be determined." Judged by K.D. Wentworth (initial judge), then by a panel of 4 professional authors.

INDEPENDENT PUBLISHER BOOK AWARDS

Jenkins Group/Independent Publisher Online, 1129 Woodmere Ave., Ste. B, Traverse City, MI 49686. (231)933-4954, ext. 1011. **Fax:** (231)933-0448. **E-mail:** jimb@bookpublishing.com. **Website:** www.independentpublisher.com. **Contact:** Jim Barnes. "The Independent Publisher Book Awards were conceived as a broad-based, unaffiliated awards program open to all members of the independent publishing industry. The staff at *Independent Publisher* magazine saw the need to bring increased recognition to the thousands of exemplary independent, university, and self-published titles produced each year." The IPPY Awards reward those who exhibit the courage, innovation, and creativity to bring about change in the world of publishing. Independent spirit and expertise comes from publishers of all areas and budgets,

and we judge books with that in mind. Entries will be accepted in 67 categories, visit website to see details. Open to any published writer. **Deadline:** March 16. **Prize:** Gold, silver and bronze medals for each category; foil seals available to all. Judged by a panel of experts representing the fields of design, writing, bookselling, library, and reviewing.

INDIANA REVIEW 1/2 K (SHORT-SHORT/PROSE-POEM) CONTEST

Indiana Review, Ballantine Hall 465, 1020 E. Kirkwood Ave., Indiana University, Bloomington, IN 47405-7103. (812)855-3439. **Fax:** (812)855-9535. **E-mail:** inreview@indiana.edu. **Website:** http://indianareview.org. **Contact:** Jennifer Luebers, editor. Offered annually for unpublished work. Maximum story/poem length is 500 words. Guidelines available in March for SASE, by phone, e-mail, on website, or in publication. **Deadline:** May 31. **Prize:** $1,000, plus publication, contributor's copies, and a year's subscription to *Indiana Review*.

○ INDIANA REVIEW FICTION CONTEST

Ballantine Hall 465, Indiana University, 1020 E. Kirkwood Ave., Bloomington, IN 47405-7103. (812)855-3439. **Fax:** (812)855-4253. **E-mail:** inreview@indiana.edu. **Website:** http://indianareview.org. **Contact:** Deborah Kim, editor. Contest for fiction in any style and on any subject. Open to any writer. "We look for a command of language and structure, as well as a facility with compelling and unusual subject matter. It's a good idea to obtain copies of issues featuring past winners to get a more concrete idea of what we are looking for." **Deadline:** Mid-October. **Prize:** $1,000, publication in the *Indiana Review* and contributor's copies. Judged by guest judges.

○◐ INTERNATIONAL 3-DAY NOVEL CONTEST

Box 2106 Station Terminal, Vancouver, BC V6B 3T5 Canada. **E-mail:** info@3daynovel.com. **Website:** www.3daynovel.com. **Contact:** Melissa Edwards, managing editor. Estab. 1977. "Can you produce a masterwork of fiction in three short days? The 3-Day Novel Contest is your chance to find out. For more than 30 years, hundreds of writers step up to the challenge each Labour Day weekend, fueled by nothing but adrenaline and the desire for spontaneous literary nirvana. It's a thrill, a grind, a 72-hour kick in the pants and an awesome creative experience. How many crazed plotlines, coffee-stained pages, pangs of doubt, and moments of genius will next year's contest bring forth? And what will you think up under pressure?" Entrants write in whatever setting they wish, in whatever genre they wish, anywhere in the world. You may start writing as of midnight on Friday night, and must stop by midnight on Monday night. Then you print up your entry and mail it in to the contest for judging. **Deadline:** Friday before Labor Day weekend. **Prize:** 1st place receives publication; 2nd place receives $500; 3rd place receives $100.

INTERNATIONAL READING ASSOCIATION CHILDREN'S BOOK AWARDS

P.O. Box 8139, 800 Barksdale Rd., Newark, DE 19714-8139. (302)731-1600, ext. 221. **E-mail:** exec@reading .org. **E-mail:** committees@reading.org. **Website:** reading.org. **Contact:** Kathy Baughman. Children's and Young Adults' Book Awards is intended for newly published authors who show unusual promise in the children's and young adults' book field. Awards are given for fiction and nonfiction in each of three categories: primary, intermediate, and young adult. Books from all countries and published in English for the first time during the previous calendar year will be considered. **Deadline:** November 1. **Prize:** $1,000.

◐ THE IOWA REVIEW AWARD IN POETRY, FICTION, AND NONFICTION

308 EPB, University of Iowa, Iowa City, IA 52242. **E-mail:** iowa-review@uiowa.edu. **Website:** www .iowareview.org. **Prize:** *The Iowa Review* Award in Poetry, Fiction, and Nonfiction presents $1,500 to each winner in each genre, $750 to runners-up. Winners and runners-up published in *The Iowa Review*. **Deadline:** Submit January 1-31 (postmark). 2013 Judges: Mary Jo Bang, Z.Z. Packer, Susan Orlean.

THE IOWA SHORT FICTION AWARD

Iowa Writers' Workshop, 507 N. Clinton St., 102 Dey House, Iowa City, IA 52242-1000. **Website:** www .uiowapress.org. **Contact:** Jim McCoy, director. Annual award "to give exposure to promising writers who have not yet published a book of prose." Open to any writer. Current University of Iowa students are not eligible. No application forms are necessary. Announcement of winners made early in year following competition. Winners notified by phone. No application forms are necessary. Do not send original ms. Include SASE for return of ms. **Deadline:** September 30. Submission period: August 1-September 30. Packages must be postmarked by September 30. **Prize:** publi-

cation by University of Iowa Press. Judged by senior Iowa Writers' Workshop members who screen mss; published fiction author of note makes final selections.

⊗ TILIA KLEBENOV JACOBS RELIGIOUS ESSAY PRIZE

Category in the Soul Making Keats Literary Competition, The Webhallow House, 1544 Sweetwood Dr., Broadmoor Village, CA 94015-2029. **E-mail:** SoulKeats@mail.com. **Website:** www.soulmak ingcontest.us. **Contact:** Eileen Malone. Estab. 2012. "Call for thoughtful writings of up to 3,000 words. No preaching, no proselytizing." Open annually to any writer. **Deadline:** November 30. **Prize:** 1st Place: $100; 2nd Place $50; 3rd Place $25.

JERRY JAZZ MUSICIAN NEW SHORT FICTION AWARD

Jerry Jazz Musician, 2207 NE Broadway, Portland, OR 97232. **E-mail:** jm@jerryjazzmusician.com. **Website:** www.jerryjazz.com. Three times a year, *Jerry Jazz Musician* awards a writer who submits, in our opinion, the best original, previously unpublished work of approximately 3,000-5,000 words. The winner will be announced via a mailing of our *Jerry Jazz* newsletter. Publishers, artists, musicians, and interested readers are among those who subscribe to the newsletter. Additionally, the work will be published on the home page of *Jerry Jazz Musician* and featured there for at least 4 weeks. The *Jerry Jazz Musician* reader tends to have interests in music, history, literature, art, film, and theater—particularly that of the counterculture of mid-20th century America. Guidelines available online. **Deadline:** September, January, and May. **Prize:** $100. Judged by the editors of *Jerry Jazz Musician*.

JESSE JONES AWARD FOR FICTION

P.O. Box 609, Round Rock, TX 78680. **E-mail:** tilsec retary@yahoo.com. **Website:** http://texasinstituteo fletters.org. Offered annually by Texas Institute of Letters for work published January 1-December 31 of year before award is given to recognize the writer of the best book of fiction entered in the competition. Writers must have been born in Texas, have lived in the state for at least 2 consecutive years at some time, or the subject matter of the work should be associated with the state. President changes every 2 years. See website for guidelines. **Deadline:** See website for exact date. **Prize:** $6,000.

JAMES JONES FIRST NOVEL FELLOWSHIP

Wilkes University, Creative Writing Department, Wilkes University, 84 West South Street, Wilkes-Barre, PA 18766. (570)408-4547. **Fax:** (570)408-3333. **E-mail:** Jamesjonesfirstnovel@wilkes.edu. **Website:** www.wilkes.edu/pages/1159.asp. Offered annually for unpublished novels, novellas, and closely linked short stories (all works in progress). The competition is open to all American writers who have not previously published novels. The award is intended to honor the spirit of unblinking honesty, determination, and insight into modern culture exemplified by the late James Jones. **Deadline:** March 1. **Prize:** $10,000; 2 runners-up get $750 honorarium.

JUST DESERTS SHORT-SHORT FICTION PRIZE

Passages North, NMU, 1401 Presque Isle Ave., Marquette, MI 49855. **E-mail:** passages@nmu.edu. **Website:** www.passagesnorth.com. Offered every other year—check website for details. **Prize:** $1,000 1st Prize and 2 honorable mentions. **Entry fee:** $15 for up to 2 stories; includes contest issue. Make checks payable to Northern Michigan University. **Deadline:** Submission period is October 15-February 15. Entries should be unpublished. Anyone may enter contest. Length: Maximum of 1,000 words. Cover letter should include name, address, phone, e-mail; may also be submitted online at www.passagesnorth.com. Writers may submit own work. Winners notified by e-mail. Results made available to entrants with SASE. Offered every other year—check website for details.

LAWRENCE FOUNDATION PRIZE

Michigan Quarterly Review, 0576 Rackham Bldg., 915 E. Washington Street, Ann Arbor, MI 48109-1070. (734)764-9265. **E-mail:** mqr@umich.edu. **Website:** www.umich.edu/~mqr. **Contact:** Vicki Lawrence, Managing Editor. This annual $1000 cash prize is awarded by the Michigan Quarterly Review editorial board to the author of the best short story published in MQR that year. Established in 1978, the prize is sponsored by University of Michigan alumnus and fiction writer Leonard S. Bernstein, a trustee of the Lawrence Foundation of New York. Approximately eight short stories are published in MQR each year. **Prize:** $1,000. Judged by editorial board.

LEAGUE OF UTAH WRITERS CONTEST

The League of Utah Writers, P.O. Box 88, Logan, UT 84323. (435)755-7609. **E-mail:** luwcontest@gmail .com. **Website:** www.luwriters.org. **Contact:** Tim Keller, Contest Chair. Open to any writer, the LUW Contest provides authors an opportunity to get their work read and critiqued. Multiple categories are offered; see webpage for details. Entries are judged by professional authors and editors from outside the League. Entries must be the original and unpublished work of the author. Winners are announced at the Annual Writers Round-Up in September. Those not present will be notified by e-mail. **Deadline:** Contest submission period opens March 1 and closes June 1. **Prize:** Cash prizes are awarded.

LET'S WRITE LITERARY CONTEST

The Gulf Coast Writers Association, P.O. Box 10294, Gulfport, MS 39505. **E-mail:** writerpllevin@gmail .com. **Website:** www.gcwriters.org. **Contact:** Philip Levin. "The Gulf Coast Writers Association sponsors this nationally recognized contest, which accepts unpublished poems and short stories from authors all around the U.S. This is an annual event which has been held for over 20 years." **Deadline:** April 15. **Prize:** 1st Place: $100; 2nd Place: $60; 3rd Place: $25.

LITERAL LATTÉ FICTION AWARD

Literal Latté, 200 E. 10th St., Suite 240, New York, NY 10003. (212)260-5532. **E-mail:** litlatte@aol.com. **Website:** www.literal-latte.com. **Contact:** Edward Estlin, contributing editor. "Award to provide talented writers with 3 essential tools for continued success: money, publication, and recognition. Offered annually for unpublished fiction (maximum 10,000 words). Guidelines online. Open to any writer." **Deadline:** January 15. **Prize:** 1st Place: $1,000 and publication in *Literal Latté*; 2nd Place: $300; 3rd Place: $200; also up to seven honorable mentions.

LITERAL LATTE SHORT SHORTS CONTEST

Literal Latte, 200 E. 10th St., Suite 240, New York, NY 10003. (212)260-5532. **E-mail:** litlatte@aol.com. **Website:** www.literal-latte.com. **Contact:** Jenine Gordon Bockman, editor. Annual contest. Send unpublished shorts. 2,000 words max. All styles welcome. Postmark by June 30. Name, address, phone number, e-mail address (optional) on cover page only. Include SASE or e-mail address for reply. All entries considered for publication **Deadline:** June 30. **Prize:** $500. Judged by the editors.

THE MARY MACKEY SHORT STORY PRIZE

Category in the Soul-Making Keats Literary Competition under the auspice of the National League of American Pen Women, The Webhallow House, 1544 Sweetwood Dr., Broadmoor Village CA 94015. **E-mail:** SoulKeats@aol.com. **Website:** www.soulmakingcontest.us. **Contact:** Eileen Malone. Open annually to any writer. **Deadline:** November 30 (annually) Cash prizes.

☯☯ THE MALAHAT REVIEW NOVELLA PRIZE

The Malahat Review, University of Victoria, P.O. Box 1700 STN CSC, Victoria, BC V8W 2Y2 Canada. (250)721-8524. **E-mail:** malahat@uvic.ca. **Website:** malahatreview.ca. **Contact:** John Barton, editor. "Held in alternate years with the Long Poem Prize. Offered to promote unpublished novellas. Obtains first world rights. After publication rights revert to the author. Open to any writer." Submit novellas between 10,000 and 20,000 words in length. Include separate page with author's name, address, e-mail, and novella title; no identifying information on mss. pages. No e-mail submissions. Do not include SASE for results; mss will not be returned. Guidelines available on website. **Deadline:** February 1 (even years). **Prize:** $1,500 CAD and one year's subscription. Winner and finalists contacted by e-mail. Winner published in summer issue of *The Malahat Review* and announced on website, Facebook page, and in quarterly e-newsletter, *Malahat Lite*.

☯ MARSH AWARD FOR CHILDREN'S LITERATURE IN TRANSLATION

Dartmouth House, 37 Charles St., London W1J 5ED United Kingdom. 020 7233 3112. **Fax:** 020 7222 0294. **Website:** www.marshchristiantrust.org. The Award is presented biennially and recognizes the best translation into English of a children's book published within the previous two years. The purpose of the Award is to celebrate the best translation of a children's book from a foreign language into English, thereby promoting children's literature across different cultures, making great stories more accessible to young readers. It also highlights the important role of the translator, who can often be overlooked.

MARY MCCARTHY PRIZE IN SHORT FICTION

Sarabande Books, P.O. Box 4456, Louisville, KY 40204. (502)458-4028. **Fax:** (502)458-4065. **E-mail:** info@sarabandebooks.org. **Website:** www.sarabandebooks.org. **Contact:** Kirby Gann, managing editor. Offered annually to publish an outstanding collection of stories, novellas, or a short novel (less than 250 pages). All finalists considered for publication. **Deadline:** January 1-February 15. **Prize:** $2,000 and publication (standard royalty contract).

⊘ THE MCGINNIS-RITCHIE MEMORIAL AWARD

Southwest Review, P.O. Box 750374, Dallas, TX 75275-0374. (214)768-1037. **Fax:** (214)768-1408. **E-mail:** swr@mail.smu.edu. **Website:** www.smu.edu/southwestreview. **Contact:** Jennifer Cranfill, senior editor, and Willard Spiegelman, editor-in-chief. "The McGinnis-Ritchie Memorial Award is given annually to the best works of fiction and nonfiction that appeared in the magazine in the previous year. Mss are submitted for publication, not for the prizes themselves. Guidelines for SASE or online." **Prize:** $500. Judged by Jennifer Cranfill and Willard Spiegelman.

MEMPHIS MAGAZINE FICTION CONTEST

Memphis Magazine, Davis-Kidd Booksellers, Burke's Books, Midtown Books, 460 Tennessee St., Memphis, TN 38103. (901)521-9000. **Fax:** (901)521-0129. **E-mail:** sadler@memphismagazine.com. **Website:** www.memphismagazine.com. **Contact:** Marilyn Sadler. **Deadline:** February 15. **Prize:** $1,000 grand prize, along with being published in the annual Cultural Issue; two honorable-mention awards of $500 each will be given if the quality of entries warrants.

DAVID NATHAN MEYERSON PRIZE FOR FICTION

Southwest Review, P.O. Box 750374, Dallas, TX 75275-0374. (214) 768-1037. **Fax:** (214) 768-1408. **E-mail:** swr@smu.edu. **Website:** www.smu.edu/southwestreview. **Contact:** Jennifer Cranfill, senior editor. Annual award given to a writer who has not published a first book of fiction, either a novel or collection of stories. All contest entrants will receive a copy of the issue in which the winning piece appears. **Deadline:** Postmarked deadline for entry is May 1. **Prize:** $1,000 and publication in the *Southwest Review*.

MIDLAND AUTHORS AWARD

Society of Midland Authors, Society of Midland Authors, P.O. Box 10419, Chicago, IL 60610-0419. **E-mail:** loerzel@comcast.net. **Website:** www.midlandauthors.com. **Contact:** Robert Loerzel, President.

Since 1957, the Society has presented annual awards for the best books written by Midwestern authors. "Established in 1915, the Society of Midland Authors Award (SMA) is presented to one title in each of six categories 'to stimulate creative effort,' one of SMA's goals, to be honored at the group's annual awards banquet in May." **Deadline:** February 1. **Prize:** Cash prize of at least $300 and a plaque that is awarded at the SMA banquet.

MILLION WRITERS AWARD

E-mail: lapthai@yahoo.com. **Website:** www.storysouth.com. **Contact:** Jason Sanford, editor emeritus. "The reason for Million Writers Award is that most of the literary prizes for short fiction have traditionally ignored web-published fiction. This award aims to show that world-class fiction is being published online and to promote to the larger reading and literary community." **Deadline for nominations of stories:** March 26-April 9. **Prize:** $600 for the overall winner, $200 for the runner-up, and $100 for the honorable mention/third place in 2011. Prize is subject to donations.

◑ MISSISSIPPI REVIEW PRIZE

Mississippi Review, 118 College Dr., #5144, Hattiesburg, MS 39406-0001. (601)266-4321. **Fax:** (601)266-5757. **E-mail:** msreview@usm.edu; rief@mississippireview.com. **Website:** www.mississippireview.com. "Our annual contest awards prizes of $1,000 in fiction and in poetry. Winners and finalists will make up next winter's print issue of the national literary magazine *Mississippi Review*. Contest is open to all writers in English except current or former students or employees of The University of Southern Mississippi. Fiction entries should be 1,000-5,000 words; poetry entries should be three poems totaling 10 pages or less. There is no limit on the number of entries you may submit. Entry fee is $15 per entry, payable to the *Mississippi Review*. Each entrant will receive a copy of the prize issue. No manuscripts will be returned. Previously published work is ineligible. Contest opens April 2. **Deadline:** October 1. Winners will be announced in late January and publication is scheduled for May next year. Entries should have 'MR Prize,' author name, address, phone, e-mail, and title of work on page 1."

MONTANA PRIZE IN FICTION

Cutbank Literary Magazine, English Dept., LA 133, UMT, Missoula, MT 59812. **Website:** www.cutbankonline.org. **Contact:** Andrew Martin, editor-in-chief; fiction editors: Beth Ambury, Sean Cleary, Jordan Rossen, Peter Schumacher. "Since *CutBank* was founded in 1973, we have watched as the landscape for literary and small magazines has broadened considerably, resulting in more quality short stories, essays, and poems finding their way to an audience each year. Occasionally, we come across a submission that seems to stand above the already impressive work being published in its genre, the sort of piece that serves to credit the wide field of literary publications generally. The goal of *CutBank*'s annual contests it to provoke, identify, and reward work of that caliber." Annual. Competition/award for short stories. **Prize:** $500 and publication in the summer issue of *CutBank*. Entries are narrowed down to a pool of five to ten submissions which are then submitted to a guest judge for selection of the winner. Limit of one work of fiction per submitter (though writers may also submit work to our contests in other genres). Make checks payable to *Cutbank Literary Magazine*. Entries are accepted online only. Guidelines available in November. Accepts inquiries by e-mail. Entries should be unpublished. Anyone may enter contest. Please submit no more than 40 double-spaced pages. Cover letter should include name, address, phone, e-mail, novel/story title. Only name and title on ms. Writers may submit own work. "Read the magazine and get a sense of our style. We are seeking work that showcases an authentic voice, a boldness of form, and a rejection of functional fixedness." Results announced June. Winners notified by e-mail. Results made available to entrants on website.

● NATIONAL BOOK AWARDS

The National Book Foundation, 90 Broad St., Suite 604, New York, NY 10004. (212)685-0261. **E-mail:** nationalbook@nationalbook.org. **Website:** www.nationalbook.org. **Deadline:** See website for current year's deadline. **Prize:** Presents $10,000 in each of 4 categories (fiction, nonfiction, poetry, and young people's literature), plus 16 short-list prizes of $1,000 each to finalists. Submissions must be previously published and **must be entered by the publisher**. General guidelines available on website; interested publishers should phone or e-mail the Foundation.

NATIONAL READERS' CHOICE AWARDS

Oklahoma Romance Writers of America (OKRWA), **E-mail:** nrca@okrwa.com. **Website:** www.okrwa.com. Contest "to provide writers of romance fiction with a competition where their published novels are judged by readers." See the website for categories and descriptions. Additional award for best first book. All entries must have an original copyright date during the current contest year. Entries will be accepted from authors, editors, publishers, agents, readers, whoever wants to fill out the entry form, pay the fee, and supply the books. No limit to the number of entries, but each title may be entered only in one category. Open to any writer published by an RWA approved non-vanity/non-subsidy press. For guidelines, send e-mail or visit website. **Deadline:** January 15. **Prize:** Plaques and finalist certificates awarded at the awards banquet hosted at the Annual National Romance Writers Convention.

○ NATIONAL WRITERS ASSOCIATION NOVEL WRITING CONTEST

The National Writers Association, 10940 S. Parker Rd. #508, Parker, CO 80134. (303)841-0246. **E-mail:** natlwritersassn@hotmail.com. **Website:** www.nationalwriters.com. **Contact:** Sandy Whelchel, director. Categories: Open to any genre or category. Entry fee: $35. Opens December 1. Open to any writer. Annual contest to help develop creative skills, to recognize and reward outstanding ability, and to increase the opportunity for the marketing and subsequent publication of novel mss. **Deadline:** April 1. **Prize:** 1st Place: $500; 2nd Place: $250; 3rd Place: $150. Judged by editors and agents.

NATIONAL WRITERS ASSOCIATION SHORT STORY CONTEST

The National Writers Association, 10940 S. Parker Rd. #508, Parker, CO 80134. (303)841-0246. **E-mail:** natlwritersassn@hotmail.com. **Website:** www.nationalwriters.com. **Contact:** Sandy Whelchel, director. Annual contest to encourage writers in this creative form, and to recognize those who excel in fiction writing. **Deadline:** July 1. **Prize:** 1st Place: $200; 2nd Place: $100; 3rd Place: $50.

THE NELLIGAN PRIZE FOR SHORT FICTION

Colorado Review/Center for Literary Publishing, 9105 Campus Delivery, Dept. of English, Colorado State University, Ft. Collins, CO 80523-9105. (970)491-5449. **E-mail:** creview@colostate.edu. **Website:** http://nelliganprize.colostate.edu. **Contact:** Stephanie G'Schwind, editor. "The Nelligan Prize for Short Fiction was established in memory of Liza Nelligan,

a writer, editor, and friend of many in Colorado State University's English department, where she received her master's degree in literature in 1992. By giving an award to the author of an outstanding short story each year, we hope to honor Liza Nelligan's life, her passion for writing, and her love of fiction." Annual. Competition/award for short stories. Receives approximately 900 stories. All entries are read blind by *Colorado Review*'s editorial staff. 15 entries are selected to be sent on to a final judge. Send credit card information or make checks payable to Colorado Review. Payment also accepted via our online submission manager link from website. **Deadline:** March 12. **Prize:** $1,500 and publication of story in *Colorado Review*.

NEW MILLENNIUM AWARDS FOR FICTION, POETRY, AND NONFICTION

New Millennium Writings, NMW, Room M2, P.O. Box 2463, Knoxville, TN 37901. (423)428-0389. **Website:** www.newmillenniumwritings.com/awards. "No restrictions as to style, content, or number of submissions. Previously published pieces accepted if online or under 5,000 print circulation. **Deadline:** June 17 for the Summer Awards program; January 31 for the Winter Awards. **Prize:** $1,000 for Best Poem; $1,000 for Best Fiction; $1,000 for Best Nonfiction; $1,000 for Best Short-Short Fiction. Simultaneous and multiple submissions welcome. Each fiction or nonfiction piece is a separate entry and should total no more than 6,000 words, except for the Short-Short Fiction Award, which should total no more than 1,000 words. (Nonfiction includes essays, profiles, memoirs, interviews, creative nonfiction, travel, humor, etc.) Each poetry entry may include up to 3 poems, not to exceed 5 pages total. All 20 poetry finalists will be published. Include name, phone, address, e-mail, and category on cover page only."

NEW SOUTH WRITING CONTEST

English Department, Georgia State University, P.O. Box 3970, Atlanta, GA 30302-3970. **E-mail:** newsouth@gsu.edu. **Website:** newsouthjournal.com/contest. **Contact:** Matt Sailor, editor-in-chief. Offered annually to publish the most promising work of up-and-coming writers of poetry (up to 3 poems) and fiction (9,000 word limit). Rights revert to writer upon publication. Guidelines online. **Deadline:** March 15. **Prize:** 1st Place: $1,000 in each category; 2nd Place: $250; and publication to winners. Judged by Marily Kallet in poetry and Amber Sparks in prose.

NORTH CAROLINA WRITERS' FELLOWSHIPS

North Carolina Arts Council, North Carolina Arts Council, Writers' Fellowships, Department of Cultural Resources, Raleigh, NC 27699-4632. (919)807-6512. **Fax:** (919)807-6532. **E-mail:** debbie.mcgill@nc mail.net. **Website:** www.ncarts.org. **Contact:** Debbie McGill, literature director. The North Carolina Arts Council offers grants in two categories to writers, spoken-word artists, playwrights, and screenwriters: fellowships (every other year) and residency grants (every year). Offered every even year to support writers of fiction, poetry, literary nonfiction, literary translation, and spoken word. See website for guidelines and other eligibility requirements. **Deadline:** November 1. **Prize:** $10,000 grant. Reviewed by a panel of literature professionals (writers and editors).

SEAN O'FAOLAIN SHORT STORY COMPETITION

The Munster Literature Centre, Frank O'Connor House, 84 Douglas Street, Cork, Ireland. +353-0214319255. **E-mail:** munsterlit@eircom.net. **Website:** www.munsterlit.ie. **Contact:** Patrick Cotter, artistic director. "To reward writers of outstanding short stories." **Deadline:** July 31. **Prize:** 1st prize €1500 (approx U.S. $2,200); 2nd prize €500 (approx $730). Four runners-up prizes of €100 (approx $146). All six stories to be published in *Southword Literary Journal*.

OHIOANA WALTER RUMSEY MARVIN GRANT

Ohioana Library Association, 274 E. First Ave., Suite 300, Columbus, OH 43201. (614)466-3831. **Fax:** (614)728-6974. **E-mail:** ohioana@ohioana.org. **Website:** www.ohioana.org. **Contact:** Linda Hengst. Award "to encourage young, unpublished writers 30 years of age or younger." Competition for short stories or novels in progress. Open to unpublished authors born in Ohio or who have lived in Ohio for a minimum of 5 years. Guidelines for SASE or on website. Winner notified in May or June. Award given in October. **Deadline:** January 31. **Prize:** $1,000.

ON THE PREMISES CONTEST

On The Premises, LLC, 4323 Gingham Court, Alexandria VA, 22310. (202) 262-2168. **E-mail:** questions@onthepremises.com. **Website:** www.onthepremises .com. **Contact:** Tarl Roger Kudrick or Bethany Granger, co-publishers. "*On the Premises* aims to promote newer and/or relatively unknown writers who can write what we feel are creative, compelling stories told in effective, uncluttered and evocative prose. Each contest challenges writers to produce a great story based on a broad premise that our editors supply as part of the contest." Competition/award for short stories. **Deadline:** Contests held every four months, check website for exact dates. **Prize:** 1st Place: $180; 2nd Place: $140; 3rd Place: $100; Honorable Mentions recieve $40. All prize winners are published in *On the Premises* magazine in HTML and PDF format. Entries are judged blindly by a panel of judges with professional editing and writing experience. Open to everyone. No entry fee. Contests held every 4 months. Check website for exact dates. Submissions are accepted by e-mail only. Entries should be unpublished. Length: minimum 1,000 words; maximum 5,000. E-mail should include name, address, e-mail, and novel/story title, with ms attached. No name or contact info should be in ms. Writers may submit own work. "Write something compelling, creative, and well-crafted. Above all, clearly use the contest premise." Results announced within 2 weeks of contest deadline. Winners notified via newsletter and with publication of *On the Premises*. Results made available to entrants on website and in publication.

OPEN SEASON AWARDS

The Malahat Review, University of Victoria, P.O. Box 1700, Stn CSC, Victoria, BC V8V 2Y2 Canada. **Fax:** (250)472-5051. **E-mail:** malahat@uvic.ca. **Website:** www.malahatreview.ca. **Contact:** John Barton, editor. The annual Open Season Awards offers $1,000 CAD and publication in *The Malahat Review*. The Open Season Awards accepts entries of poetry, fiction, and creative nonfiction. Submissions must be unpublished. No simultaneous submissions. Submit up to 3 poems per entry, each poem not to exceed 100 lines; one piece of fiction (2,500 words max.), or one piece of creative nonfiction (2,500 words max.); no restrictions on subject matter or aesthetic approach. Include separate page with writer's name, address, e-mail, and title(s); no identifying information on mss pages. No e-mail submissions. Do not include SASE for results; mss will not be returned. Guidelines available on website. Winner and finalists contacted by e-mail. Winners published in spring issue of *Malahat Review* announced in winter on website, facebook page, and in quarterly e-newsletter, *Malahat lite*. **Deadline:** November 1 of each year. **Prize:** $1,000 CAD and publication in *The Malahat Review* in each category.

✚ ⑤ KENNETH PATCHEN AWARD FOR THE INNOVATIVE NOVEL

Eckhard Gerdes Publishing, Civil Coping Mechanisms, 12 Simpson Street, Apt. D, Geneva, IL 60134. **E-mail:** egerdes@experimentalfiction.com. **Website:** www.experimentalfiction.com. **Contact:** Eckhard Gerdes. "This award will honor the most innovative novel submitted during the previous calendar year. Kenneth Patchen is celebrated for being among the greatest innovators of American fiction, incorporating strategies of concretism, asemic writing, digression, and verbal juxtaposition into his writing long before such strategies were popularized during the height of American postmodernist experimentation in the 1970s." **Deadline:** All submissions must be postmarked between January 1 and July 31. **Prize:** $1,000, 20 complimentary copies.

THE PATERSON FICTION PRIZE

The Poetry Center at Passaic Community College, One College Blvd., Paterson, NJ 07505. (973)684-6555. **Fax:** (973)523-6085. **E-mail:** mgillan@pccc.edu. **Website:** www.pccc.edu/poetry. **Contact:** Maria Mazziotti Gillan, executive director. Offered annually for a novel or collection of short fiction published the previous calendar year. For more information, visit the website or send SASE. **Deadline:** April 1. **Prize:** $1,000.

⭘ PEARL SHORT STORY PRIZE

3030 E. Second St., Long Beach, CA 90803. (562)434-4523. **E-mail:** Pearlmag@aol.com. **Website:** www.pearlmag.com. **Contact:** Marilyn Johnson, fiction editor. Award to "provide a larger forum and help widen publishing opportunities for fiction writers in the small press and to help support the continuing publication of *Pearl*." Include a brief bio and SASE for reply or return of mss. Accepts simultaneous submissions but asks to be notified if story is accepted elsewhere. Entries must be unpublished. "Although we are open to all types of fiction, we look most favorably on coherent, well-crafted narratives containing interesting, believable characters in meaningful situations." Length: 4,000 words maximum. Open to any writer. Guidelines for SASE or on website. Accepts queries by e-mail or fax. Results announced in September. Winners notified by mail. For contest results, send SASE, e-mail, or visit website. April 1-May 31 submission period. **Prize:** $250, publication in *Pearl* and 10 copies

of the journal. Judged by the editors of *Pearl*: Marilyn Johnson, Joan Jobe Smith, Barbara Hauk.

⭘ JUDITH SIEGEL PEARSON AWARD

Judith Siegel Pearson Award, c/o Department of English, Wayne State University, Attn: Rhonda Agnew, 5057 Woodward Ave, Ste. 9408, Detroit, MI 48202. (313)577-2450. **Fax:** (313)577-8618. **E-mail:** ad2073@wayne.edu. **Contact:** Rhonda Agnew. Offers an annual award of up to $500 for the best creative or scholarly work on a subject concerning women. The type of work accepted rotates each year: Poetry in 2013 (poetry, 20 pages maximum); essays in 2014; fiction in 2015. Open to all interested writers and scholars. Submissions must be unpublished. Guidelines available by e-mail. No late or electronic submissions accepted. The award is an annual prize for the best creative or scholarly work on a subject concerning women. **Deadline:** February 25.

THE PINCH LITERARY AWARD IN FICTION AND POETRY

Fiction/Poetry Contest, The Pinch, Department of English, The University of Memphis, Memphis, TN 38152-6176. (901)678-4591. **E-mail:** editor@thepinchjournal.com. **Website:** www.thepinchjournal.com. Offered annually for unpublished short stories of 5,000 words maximum or up to three poems. Guidelines on website. Cost: $20, which is put toward one issue of *The Pinch*. Offered annually for unpublished short stories of 5,000 words maximum or up to three poems. Guidelines on website. **Deadline:** April 5. **Prizes:** $1,000 for 1st place in both competitions.

PNWA LITERARY CONTEST

Pacific Northwest Writers Association, PMB 2717-1420 NW Gilman Blvd., Suite 2, Issaquah, WA 98027. (425)673-2665. **Fax:** (425)961-0768. **E-mail:** pnwa@pnwa.org. **Website:** www.pnwa.org. **Contact:** Kelli Liddane. **Open to students.** Annual contest. Purpose of contest: "Valuable tool for writers as contest submissions are critiqued (2 critiques)." Unpublished submissions only. Submissions made by author. **Deadline:** February 18. **Prize:** 1st: $700; 2nd: $300.

⭘ POCKETS FICTION-WRITING CONTEST

P.O. Box 340004, Nashville, TN 37203-0004. (615)340-7333. **Fax:** (615)340-7267. **E-mail:** pockets@upperroom.org. **Website:** www.pockets.upperroom.org. **Contact:** Lynn W. Gilliam, senior editor.

Designed for 6- to 12-year-olds, *Pockets* magazine offers wholesome devotional readings that teach about God's love and presence in life. The content includes fiction, scripture stories, puzzles and games, poems, recipes, colorful pictures, activities, and scripture readings. Freelance submissions of stories, poems, recipes, puzzles and games, and activities are welcome. The primary purpose of Pockets is to help children grow in their relationship with God and to claim the good news of the gospel of Jesus Christ by applying it to their daily lives. Pockets espouses respect for all human beings and for God's creation. It regards a child's faith journey as an integral part of all of life and sees prayer as undergirding that journey. **Deadline:** November 1. **Prize:** $500 and publication in magazine.

ⓘ EDGAR ALLAN POE AWARD

1140 Broadway, Suite 1507, New York, NY 10001. (212)888-8171. **Fax:** (212)888-8107. **E-mail:** mwa@ mysterywriters.org. **Website:** www.mysterywriters .org. Estab. 1945. Mystery Writers of America is the leading association for professional crime writers in the U.S. Members of MWA include most major writers of crime fiction and nonfiction, as well as screenwriters, dramatists, editors, publishers, and other professionals in the field. Purpose of the award: to honor authors of distinguished works in the mystery field. Previously published submissions only. Submissions made by the author, author's agent; "normally by the publisher." Work must be published/produced the year of the contest. **Deadline:** November 30. **Prize:** Awards ceramic bust of "Edgar" for winner; scrolls for all nominees. Judged by professional members of Mystery Writers of America (writers).

THE KATHERINE ANNE PORTER PRIZE FOR FICTION

Nimrod International Journal, The University of Tulsa, 800 S. Tucker Dr., Tulsa, OK 74104. (918)631-3080. **Fax:** (918)631-3033. **E-mail:** nimrod@utulsa.edu. **Website:** www.utulsa.edu/nimrod. **Contact:** Eilis O'Neal. **Deadline:** April 30. **Prizes:** 1st Place: $2,000 and publication; 2nd Place: $1,000 and publication. The *Nimrod* editors select the finalists and a recognized author selects the winners.

○ Submissions must be unpublished. Work must be in English or translated by original author. Author's name must not appear on ms. Include cover sheet with title, author's name, address,

phone number, and e-mail address (author must have a U.S. address by October of contest year to enter). Mark "Contest Entry" on submission envelop and cover sheet. Include SASE for results only; mss will not be returned. Guidelines available for #10 SASE or on website.

PRAIRIE SCHOONER BOOK PRIZE

Prairie Schooner and the University of Nebraska Press, Prairie Schooner Prize Series, Attn: Fiction, 123 Andrews Hall, Lincoln, NE 68588-0334. (402)472-0911. **E-mail:** PSBookPrize@unl.edu. **Website:** prairie schooner.unl.edu. **Contact:** Kwame Dawes, editor. Annual competition/award for story collections. **Deadline:** March 15. **Prize:** $3,000 and publication through the University of Nebraska Press.

⊕ PRESS 53 OPEN AWARDS

Press 53, 411 W. Fourth St., Suite 101A, Winston-Salem, NC 27101. **E-mail:** kevin@press53.com. **Website:** www.press53.com. **Contact:** Kevin Morgan Watson, publisher. The Press 53 Open Awards Writing Contest is open to writers anywhere in the world who write in English (excluding Press 53 employees and family members). Previously published pieces are accepted so long as any previous publishing agreements do not prohibit Press 53 from publishing the work in the winning anthology. **Deadline:** March 31. **Prize:** 1st Place: Press 53 Open Award, publication, 2 complimentary copies of anthology; 2nd Place: Personalized certificate, complimentary copy of anthology; Honorable Mention: Personalized certificate, complimentary copy of anthology.

☯ PRISM INTERNATIONAL ANNUAL SHORT FICTION, POETRY, AND LITERARY NONFICTION CONTESTS

Prism International, Creative Writing Program, UBC, Buch. E462, 1866 Main Mall, Vancouver, BC V6T 1Z1 Canada. **E-mail:** prismwritingcontest@gmail.com. **Website:** www.prismmagazine.ca/contests. **Contact:** Andrea Hoff, Contest Manager. "Offered annually for unpublished work to award the best in contemporary fiction, poetry, drama, translation, and nonfiction. Works of translation are eligible. Guidelines are available on website. Acquires first North American serial rights upon publication, and limited Web rights for pieces selected for website. Open to any writer except students and faculty in the Creative Writing Department at UBC, or people who have taken a creative writing course at UBC within 2 years of the contest deadline." **Costs:** $28 per entry; $7 each additional entry (outside Canada pay US currency); includes subscription. **Deadline:** January 27 (poetry, short fiction; November 30 (nonfiction). **Prize:** 1st Place: $1,000-2,000; runners-up (3): $200-300 each (depends on contest); winners published. You may pay entry fees via check or online through our store. Download a PDF entry form and guidelines."

PUSHCART PRIZE

Pushcart Press, P.O. Box 380, Wainscott, NY 11975. (631)324-9300. **Website:** www.pushcartprize.com. **Contact:** Bill Henderson. Estab. 1976. Published every year since 1976, The Pushcart Prize—Best of the Small Presses series "is the most honored literary project in America. Hundreds of presses and thousands of writers of short stories, poetry, and essays have been represented in the pages of our annual collections." Little magazine and small book press editors (print or online) may make up to six nominations from their year's publications by the deadline. The nominations may be any combination of poetry, short fiction, essays, or literary whatnot. Editors may nominate self-contained portions of books — for instance, a chapter from a novel. **Deadline:** December 1.

DAVID RAFFELOCK AWARD FOR PUBLISHING EXCELLENCE

National Writers Association, 10940 S. Parker Rd., #508, Parker, CO 80134. (303)841-0246. **E-mail:** natl writersassn@hotmail.com. **Website:** www.national writers.com. **Contact:** Sandy Whelchel. "Contest is offered annually for books published the previous year." Published works only. Open to any writer. Guidelines for SASE, by e-mail, or on website. Winners announced in June at the NWAF conference and notified by mail or phone. List of winners available for SASE or visit website. Its purpose is to assist published authors in marketing their works and to reward outstanding published works. **Deadline:** May 15. **Prize:** Publicity tour, including airfare, valued at $5,000.

RANDOM HOUSE, INC. CREATIVE WRITING COMPETITION

c/o Scholarship America, One Scholarship Way, P.O. Box 297, St. Peter, MN 56082. (212)782-0316. **Fax:** (212)940-7590. **E-mail:** creativewriting@random house.com. **Website:** www.randomhouse.com/creativewriting. **Contact:** Melanie Fallon Hauska, director. Offered annually for unpublished work to NYC

public high school seniors. Applicants must be seniors (under age 21) at a New York high school. Four categories: poetry/spoken word, fiction/drama, personal essay/memoir, graphic novel. Judged by various city officials, executives, authors, editors. No entry fee. Guidelines available in October on website and in publication. Entries must be unpublished. Word length: 2,500 words or less. No college essays or class assignments will be accepted. Results announced mid-May. Winners notified by mail and phone. For contest results, send SASE, fax, e-mail or visit website. **Deadline:** February 10. **Prize:** 1st Place: $10,000 awarded to 1 entry in each category; 2nd Place: $5,000 awarded to 1 entry in each category; 3rd Place: $1,000 awarded to to 1 entry in each category; Best of Borough: $1,000 awarded to 1 entry per category for each borough; Artist Recognition Awards: $500 awarded to 3 entries chosen from each borough in any of the categories.

THE RBC BRONWEN WALLACE AWARD FOR EMERGING WRITERS

The Writers' Trust of Canada, 90 Richmond St. East, Suite 200, Toronto, ON M5C 1P1 Canada. (416)504-8222. **Fax:** (416)504-9090. **E-mail:** info@writerstrust.com. **Website:** www.writerstrust.com. **Contact:** Amanda Hopkins. Presented annually to "a Canadian writer under the age of 35 who is not yet published in book form. The award, which alternates each year between poetry and short fiction, was established in memory of poet Bronwen Wallace." **Deadline:** January 31. **Prize:** $5,000 and $1,000 to 2 finalists.

THE RED HOUSE CHILDREN'S BOOK AWARD

Red House Children's Book Award, 123 Frederick Road, Cheam, Sutton, Surrey SM1 2HT United Kingdom. **E-mail:** info@rhcba.co.uk. **Website:** www.red housechildrensbookaward.co.uk. **Contact:** Sinead Kromer, national co-ordinator. (formerly The Children's Book Award), Owned and co-ordinated by the Federation of Children's Book Groups (Reg. Charity No. 268289). Purpose of the award is to enable children choose the best works of fiction published in the UK. **Prize:** trophy and silver bookmarks, portfolio of children's letters and pictures. Categories: Books for Younger Children, Books for Younger Readers, Books for Older Readers. No entry fee. **Deadline:** Closing date is December 31. Either author or publisher may nominate title. Guidelines available on website. Accepts inquiries by e-mail and phone. Shortlist announced in February and winners announced in May. Winners notified at award ceremony and dinner at the Birmingham Botanical Gardens and via the publisher. For contest results, visit the website.

☼ REGINA BOOK AWARD

Saskatchewan Book Awards, Inc., P.O. Box 20025, Regina SK S4P 4J7 Canada. (306)569-1585. **E-mail:** director@bookawards.sk.ca. **Website:** www.boo kawards.sk.ca. Estab. 1993. Offered annually. "In recognition of the vitality of the literary community in Regina, this award is presented to a Regina author for the best book, judged on the quality of writing." Books from the following categories will be considered: children's; drama; fiction (short fiction by a single author, novellas, novels); nonfiction (all categories of nonfiction writing except cookbooks, directories, how-to books, or bibliographies of minimal critical content); poetry. **Deadline:** November 1. **Prize:** $2,000 (CAD).

☼ THE ROGERS WRITERS' TRUST FICTION PRIZE

The Writers' Trust of Canada, 90 Richmond St. E., Suite 200, Toronto ON M5C 1P1 Canada. (416)504-8222. **Fax:** (416)504-9090. **E-mail:** info@writerstrust .com. **Website:** www.writerstrust.com. **Contact:** Amanda Hopkins. "Awarded annually for a distinguished work of fiction—either a novel or short story collection—published within the previous year. Presented at the Writers' Trust Awards event held in Toronto each fall. Open to Canadian citizens and permanent residents only." **Deadline:** August. **Prize:** $25,000 and $2,500 to 4 finalists.

☺ LOIS ROTH AWARD FOR A TRANSLATION OF A LITERARY WORK

Modern Language Association, 26 Broadway, 3rd Floor, New York, NY 10004. (646)576-5141. **Fax:** (646)458-0030. **E-mail:** awards@mla.org. **Website:** www.mla.org. Offered every 2 years (odd years) for an outstanding translation into English of a book-length literary work published the previous year. Translators need not be members of the MLA. **Deadline:** April 1 **Prize:** A cash award and a certificate to be presented at the Modern Language Association's annual convention in January.

☼ SASKATCHEWAN FICTION AWARD

Saskatchewan Book Awards, Inc., P.O. Box 20025, Regina SK S4P 4J7 Canada. (306)569-1585. **E-mail:** director@bookawards.sk.ca. **Website:** www.boo kawards.sk.ca. Estab. 1995. Offered annually. "This award is presented to a Saskatchewan author for the best book of fiction (novel or short fiction), judged on the quality of writing." **Deadline:** November 1. **Prize:** $2,000 (CAD).

☼ SASKATCHEWAN FIRST BOOK AWARD

Saskatchewan Book Awards, Inc., P.O. Box 20025, Regina SK S4P 4J7 Canada. (306)569-1585. **E-mail:** director@bookawards.sk.ca. **Website:** www.boo kawards.sk.ca. Estab. 1993. Offered annually. "This award is presented to a Saskatchewan author for the best first book, judged on the quality of writing." Books from the following categories will be considered: children's; drama; fiction (short fiction by a single author, novellas, novels); nonfiction (all categories of nonfiction writing except cookbooks, directories, how-to books, or bibliographies of minimal critical content); and poetry. **Deadline:** November 1. **Prize:** $2,000 (CAD).

⊕ THE SATURDAY EVENING POST GREAT AMERICAN FICTION CONTEST

The Saturday Evening Post Society, 1100 Waterway Blvd., Indianapolis, IN 46202. **E-mail:** fictioncon test@saturdayeveningpost.com. **Website:** www.sat urdayeveningpost.com/fiction-contest. "In its nearly 3 centuries of publication, *The Saturday Evening Post* has included fiction by a who's who of American authors, including F. Scott Fitzgerald, William Faulkner, Kurt Vonnegut, Ray Bradbury, Louis L'Amour, Sinclair Lewis, Jack London, and Edgar Allan Poe. The *Post*'s fiction has not just entertained us; it has played a vital role in defining who we are as Americans. In launching this contest, we are seeking America's next great, unpublished voices." **Deadline:** July 1. **Prize:** The winning story will receive $500 and publication in the magazine and online. Five runners-up will be published online and receive $100 each.

ALDO AND JEANNE SCAGLIONE PRIZE FOR A TRANSLATION OF A LITERARY WORK

Modern Language Association, 26 Broadway, 3rd Floor, New York, NY 10004-1789. (646)576-5141. **Fax:** (646)458-0030. **E-mail:** awards@mla.org. **Website:**

www.mla.org. **Contact:** Coordinator of Book Prizes. The Committee on Honors and Awards of the Modern Language Association invites translators and publishers to compete for the Aldo and Jeanne Scaglione Prize for a Translation of a Literary Work. The prize, established by the Aldo and Jeanne Scaglione Endowment Fund, is awarded each even-numbered year for an outstanding translation into English of a book-length literary work. **Deadline:** April 1. **Prize:** A cash award and a certificate to be presented at the Modern Language Association's annual convention in January.

○ THE SCARS EDITOR'S CHOICE AWARDS

829 Brian Court, Gurnee, IL 60031-3155. **E-mail:** editor@scars.tv. **Website:** http://scars.tv. **Contact:** Janet Kuypers, editor/publisher (whom all reading fee checks need to be made out to). Award "to showcase good writing in an annual book." Categories: short stories, poetry. **Entry fee:** $19/short story and $15/poem. **Deadline:** Revolves for appearing in different upcoming books as winners. **Prize:** Publication of story/essay and 1 copy of the book. Entries may be unpublished or previously published, "as long as you retain the rights to your work." Open to any writer. For guidelines, visit website. Accepts inquiries by e-mail. "E-mail is always preferred for inquiries and submissions. (If you have access to e-mail, we will request that you e-mail your contest submission, and we will hold it until we receive the reading fee payment for the submission.)" Length: "We appreciate shorter works. Shorter stories, more vivid and more real story lines in writing have a good chance." Results announced at book publication, online. Winners notified by mail when book is printed. For contest results, send SASE or e-mail, or look at the contest page at website. " Award to showcase good writing in an annual book.

THE MONA SCHREIBER PRIZE FOR HUMOROUS FICTION & NONFICTION

3940 Laurel Canyon Blvd., #566, Studio City, CA 91604. **E-mail:** brad.schreiber@att.net. **Website:** www.bradschreiber.com. **Contact:** Brad Schreiber. Estab. 2000. "The purpose of the contest is to award the most creative humor writing, in any form less than 750 words, in either fiction or nonfiction, including but not limited to stories, articles, essays, speeches, shopping lists, diary entries, and anything else writers dream up." **Deadline:** December 1. **Prize:** 1st Place: $500; 2nd Place: $250; 3rd Place: $100.

A. DAVID SCHWARTZ FICTION PRIZE

cream city review, Dept. of English; University of Wisconsin-Milwaukee, PO Box 413, Milwaukee, WI 53201. (414) 229-4708. **E-mail:** info@creamcityreview.org. **Website:** www.creamcityreview.org. **Contact:** Ching-In Chen, editor-in-chief. *cream city review* is a volunteer based, nonprofit literary magazine devoted to publishing memorable and energetic pieces that push the boundaries of "literature." Continually seeking to explore the relationship between form and content, the magazine features fiction, poetry, creative non-fiction, comics, reviews of contemporary literature and criticism, as well as author interviews and artwork. "To recognize what the judge determines to be the most original, well-crafted work of previously unpublished short fiction. We are devoted to publishing memorable and energetic fiction, poetry, and creative nonfiction by new and established writers. *cream city review* is particularly interested in publishing new voices; our reputation and long publishing history attracts well-known writers, often leading to unpublished writers appearing next to poet laureates. Our contest is open to all writers in all places, so long as the work is in English, original, and previously unpublished." **Deadline:** December 31. **Prize:** $1,000.

SCRIPTAPALOOZA TELEVISION WRITING COMPETITION

7775 Sunset Blvd., Suite #200, Hollywood, CA 90046. (323)654-5809. **E-mail:** info@scriptapalooza.com. **Website:** www.scriptapaloozatv.com. "Biannual competition accepting entries in 4 categories: Reality shows, sitcoms, original pilots, and 1-hour dramas. There are more than 25 producers, agents, and managers reading the winning scripts. Two past winners won Emmys because of Scriptapalooza and 1 past entrant now writes for Comedy Central." Winners announced February 15 and August 30. For contest results, visit website. **Deadline:** October 1 and April 15. **Prize:** 1st Place: $500; 2nd Place: $200; 3rd Place: $100 (in each category); production company consideration.

MICHAEL SHAARA AWARD FOR EXCELLENCE IN CIVIL WAR FICTION

Civil War Institute at Gettysburg College, 300 N. Washington St., Campus Box 435, Gettysburg, PA 17325. (717)337-6574. **Fax:** (717)337-6596. **E-mail:**

civilwar@gettysburg.edu. **Website:** www.gettysburg .edu/cwi. **Contact:** Diane Brennan. Estab. 1997. Offered annually for fiction published January 1-December 31. Contest "to encourage examination of the Civil War from unique perspectives or by taking an unusual approach." All Civil War novels are eligible. Publishers should make nominations, but authors and critics can nominate as well. Entries must be previously published. Judged for presentation of unique perspective, use of unusual approach, effective writing, contribution to existing body of Civil War literature. Competition open to authors of Civil War novels published for the first time in the year designated by the award (i.e., for 2013 award, only novels published in 2013 are eligible). Guidelines available on website. Accepts inquiries by fax, e-mail, and phone. Cover letter should include name, address, phone, e-mail, and title. Need 4 copies of novel. "Enter well before deadline. Results announced in July. Winners notified by phone. For contest results, visit website." Self published books are not eligible. This includes books printed and bound by a company hired and paid by the author to publish his/her work in book form. **Deadline:** December 31. **Prize:** $5,000.

SKIPPING STONES HONOR (BOOK) AWARDS

P.O. Box 3939, Eugene, OR 97403. Phone/fax: (541)342-4956. **E-mail:** editor@skippingstones.org. **Website:** www.skippingstones.org. **Contact:** Arun N. Toké. Estab. 1994. Annual awards since 1994 to "promote multicultural and/or nature awareness through creative writings for children and teens and their educators. We seek authentic, exceptional, child/youth-friendly books that promote intercultural, international, intergenerational harmony, and understanding through creative ways. Writings that come out of your own experiences and cultural understanding seem to have an edge." February 1. **Prize:** Honor certificates; gold seals; reviews; press release/publicity. Judged by "a multicultural committee of teachers, librarians, parents, students and editors."

THE BERNICE SLOTE AWARD

Prairie Schooner, 123 Andrews Hall, P.O. Box 880334, Lincoln, NE 68588-0334. (402)472-0911. **Fax:** (402)472-1817. **E-mail:** PrairieSchooner@unl.edu. **Website:** www.prairieschooner.unl.edu. **Contact:** Kwame Dawes. Offered annually for the best work by a beginning writer published in *Prairie Schooner* in

the previous year. Celebrates the best and finest writing that they have published for the year. **Prize:** $500.

KAY SNOW WRITING CONTEST

Willamette Writers, Willamette Writers, 2108 Buck St., West Linn, OR 97068. (503)305-6729. **Fax:** (503)344-6174. **E-mail:** wilwrite@willamettewriters .com. **Website:** www.willamettewriters.com. **Contact:** Lizzy Shannon, contest director. "Willamette Writers is the largest writers' organization in Oregon and one of the largest writers' organizations in the United States. It is a nonprofit, tax-exempt Oregon corporation led by volunteers. Elected officials and directors administer an active program of monthly meetings, special seminars, workshops, and annual writing conference. Continuing with established programs and starting new ones is only made possible by strong volunteer support. The purpose of this annual writing contest, named in honor of Willamette Writer's founder, Kay Snow, is to help writers reach professional goals in writing in a broad array of categories and to encourage student writers." **Deadline:** April 23. **Prize:** One 1st prize of $300, one 2nd place prize of $150, and a 3rd place prize of $50 per winning entry in each of the six categories.

STONY BROOK SHORT FICTION PRIZE

Stony Brook Southampton, 239 Montauk Highway, Southampton, NY 11968. **Website:** www.stonybrook .edu/fictionprize. **Deadline:** March 1. **Prize:** $1,000.

THEODORE STURGEON MEMORIAL AWARD FOR BEST SHORT SF OF THE YEAR

English Department, University of Kansas, Lawrence, KS 66045. (785)864-3380. **Fax:** (785)864-1159. **E-mail:** jgunn@ku.edu. **Website:** sfcenter.ku.edu/sturgeon .htm. **Contact:** James Gunn, professor and director. Award to "honor the best science fiction short story of the year." **Prize:** Trophy. Winners receive expense-paid trip to the University and have their names engraved on the pernmanent trophy.

THREE CHEERS AND A TIGER

E-mail: editors@toasted-cheese.com. **Website:** www .toasted-cheese.com. **Contact:** Stephanie Lenz, editor. Purpose of contest is to write a short story (following a specific theme) within 48 hours. Contests are held first weekend in spring (mystery) and first weekend in fall (sci-fi/fantasy). Category: short stories. No entry fee. Word limit announced at the start of the contest. Contest-specific information is announced 48 hours before the contest submission deadline. Results announced in April and October. Winners notified by e-mail. List of winners on website. **Prize:** Amazon gift certificates and publication. Blind judged by 2 *Toasted Cheese* editors. Each judge uses his or her own criteria to choose entries.

WABASH PRIZE FOR FICTION

Sycamore Review, Department of English, 500 Oval Dr., Purdue University, West Lafayette, IN 47907. **E-mail:** sycamore@purdue.edu. **Website:** www.sycamorereview.com/contest/. **Contact:** Jessica Jacobs, editor-in-chief. **Deadline:** March 22. **Prize:** $1,000 and publication.

⭕ THE ROBERT WATSON LITERARY PRIZE IN FICTION AND POETRY

MFA Writing Program, 3302 MHRA Building, Greensboro, NC 27402-6170. (336)334-5459. **E-mail:** jlclark@uncg.edu. **Website:** www.greensbororeview.org. **Contact:** Jim Clark, editor. Offered annually for fiction (7,500 word limit) and poetry (3-5 poems). Entries must be unpublished. No submissions by e-mail. Open to any writer. Winners notified by mail, phone, or e-mail. List of winners published in spring issue. "All manuscripts meeting literary award guidelines will be considered for cash award as well as for publication in the spring issue of *The Greensboro Review*." **Deadline:** September 15. **Prize:** $1,000 each for best short story and poem. Judged by editors of *The Greensboro Review*.

WESTERN WRITERS OF AMERICA

271CR 219, Encampment, WY 82325. (307)329-8942. **Fax:** (307)327-5465 (call first). **E-mail:** wwa.moulton@gmail.com. **Website:** www.westernwriters.org. **Contact:** Candy Moulton, executive director. Estab. 1953. "17 Spur Award categories in various aspects of the American West. The nonprofit Western Writers of America has promoted and honored the best in Western literature with the annual Spur Awards, selected by panels of judges. Awards, for material published last year, are given for works whose inspirations, image, and literary excellence best represent the reality and spirit of the American West."

WILLA LITERARY AWARD

Women Writing the West, 8547 East Arapaho Rd., #J-541, Greenwood Village, CO 80112-1436. **E-mail:** pamtartaglio@yahoo.com. **Website:** www.womenwritingthewest.org. **Contact:** Pam Tartaglio. The WILLA Literary Award honors the best in literature featuring women's or girls' stories set in the West published each year. Women Writing the West (WWW), a nonprofit association of writers and other professionals writing and promoting the Women's West, underwrites and presents the nationally recognized award annually (for work published between January 1 and December 31). The award is named in honor of Pulitzer Prize winner Willa Cather, one of the country's foremost novelists. The award is given in 7 categories: Historical fiction, contemporary fiction, original softcover fiction, creative nonfiction, scholarly nonfiction, poetry, and children's/young adult fiction/nonfiction. **Deadline:** February 1. **Prize:** Winner receives $100 and a trophy. Finalist receives a plaque. Award announcement is in early August, and awards are presented to the winners and finalists at the annual WWW Fall Conference. Judged by professional librarians not affiliated with WWW.

WORLD FANTASY AWARDS

P.O. Box 43, Mukilteo, WA 98275. **E-mail:** sfexecsec@gmail.com. **Website:** www.worldfantasy.org. **Contact:** Peter Dennis Pautz, president. Awards "to recognize excellence in fantasy literature worldwide." Offered annually for previously published work in several categories, including life achievement, novel, novella, short story, anthology, collection, artist, special award—pro, and special award—nonpro. Works are recommended by attendees of current and previous 2 years' conventions and a panel of judges. Judged by panel. No entry fee. Guidelines available in December for SASE or on website. Entries must be previously published. Published submissions from previous calendar year. Word length: 10,000-40,000 for novella, 10,000 for short story. "All fantasy is eligible, from supernatural horror to Tolkien-esque to sword and sorcery to the occult, and beyond." Cover letter should include name, address, phone, e-mail, word count, title, and publications where submission was previously published, submitted to the address above and the panel of judges when they appear on the website. Results announced November 1 at annual convention. For contest results, visit website. Awards "to recognize excellence in fantasy literature worldwide." **Prize:** Bust of HP Lovecraft. **Deadline:** June 1.

WOW! WOMEN ON WRITING QUARTERLY FLASH FICTION CONTEST

WOW! Women on Writing, P.O. Box 41104, Long Beach, CA 90853. **E-mail:** contestinfo@wow-womenonwriting.com. **Website:** www.wow-womenonwriting.com/contest.php. **Contact:** Angela Mackintosh, editor. Contest offered quarterly. "We are open to all themes and genres, although we do encourage writers to take a close look at our literary agent guest judge for the season, if you are serious about winning." Entries must be 250-750 words. **Deadline:** August 31, November 30, February 28, May 31. **Prize:** 1st place: $350 cash prize, $25 Amazon gift certificate, book from our sponsor, story published on WOW! Women On Writing, interview on blog; 2nd place: $250 cash prize, $25 Amazon gift certificate, book from our sponsor, story published on WOW! Women On Writing, interview on blog; 3rd place: $150 cash prize, $25 Amazon gift certificate, book from our sponsor, story published on WOW! Women On Writing, interview on blog; 7 runners up: $25 Amazon gift certificate, book from our sponsor, story published on WOW! Women on Writing, interview on blog;10 honorable mentions: $20 gift certificate from Amazon, book from our sponsor, story title and name published on WOW!Women On Writing.

WRITER'S DIGEST INTERNATIONAL SELF-PUBLISHED BOOK AWARDS

Writer's Digest, 700 E. State St., Iola, WI 54990. (715)445-4612, ext. 13430. **E-mail:** WritersDigest WritingCompetition@fwmedia.com. **Website:** www.writersdigest.com. **Contact:** Nicole Florence. Contest open to all English-language self-published books for which the authors have paid the full cost of publication, or the cost of printing has been paid for by a grant or as part of a prize. Categories include: Mainstream/Literary Fiction, Genre Fiction, Nonfiction, Inspirational (spiritual/new age), Life Stories (biographies/autobiographies/family histories/memoirs), Children's Books, Reference Books (directories/encyclopedias/guide books), Poetry, Middle-Grade/Young Adult Books. **Deadline:** May 1; Early bird deadline: April 1. **Prizes:** Grand Prize: $3,000, promotion in *Writer's Digest* and *Publisher's Weekly*, and 10 copies of the book will be sent to major review houses with a guaranteed review in *Midwest Book Review*; 1st Place (9 winners): $1,000, promotion in *Writer's Digest*; Honorable Mentions: promotion in *Writer's Digest*, $50 of Writer's Digest Books, and a certificate.

ZOETROPE SHORT STORY CONTEST

Zoetrope: All-Story, Attn: Fiction Editor, 916 Kearny St., San Francisco, CA 94133. (415)788-7500. **E-mail:** contests@all-story.com. **Website:** www.all-story.com. Annual contest for unpublished short stories. Opens on July 1. **Prizes:** 1st place: $1,000; 2nd place: $500; 3rd place: $250.

CONFERENCES & WORKSHOPS

//

Why are conferences so popular? Writers and conference directors alike tell us it's because writing can be such a lonely business—at conferences writers have the opportunity to meet (and commiserate) with fellow writers, as well as meet and network with publishers, editors, and agents. Conferences and workshops provide some of the best opportunities for writers to make publishing contacts and pick up valuable information on the business, as well as the craft, of writing.

The bulk of the listings in this section are for conferences. Most conferences last from one day to one week and offer a combination of workshop-type writing sessions, panel discussions, and a variety of guest speakers. Topics may include all aspects of writing from fiction to poetry to scriptwriting, or they may focus on a specific type of writing, such as those conferences sponsored by the Romance Writers of America (RWA) for writers of romance or by the Society of Children's Book Writers and Illustrators (SCBWI) for writers of children's books.

Workshops, however, tend to run longer—usually one to two weeks. Designed to operate like writing classes, most require writers to be prepared to work on and discuss their fiction while attending. An important benefit of workshops is the opportunity they provide writers for an intensive critique of their work, often by professional writing teachers and established writers.

Each of the listings here includes information on the specific focus of an event as well as planned panels, guest speakers, and workshop topics. It is important to note, however, some conference directors were still in the planning stages for 2014 when we contacted them. If it was not possible to include 2014 dates, fees, or topics, we have provided information from 2013 so you can get an idea of what to expect. For the most current information, it's best to check the conference website or send a self-addressed, stamped envelope to the director in question about three months before the date(s) listed.

FINDING A CONFERENCE

Many writers try to make it to at least one conference a year, but cost and location count as much as subject matter or other considerations when determining which conference to attend. There are conferences in almost every state and province, and even some in Europe open to North Americans.

To make it easier for you to find a conference close to home—or to find one in an exotic locale to fit into your vacation plans—we've divided this section into geographic regions. The conferences appear in alphabetical order under the appropriate regional heading.

Note that conferences appear under the regional heading according to where they will be held, which is sometimes different from the address given as the place to register or send for information. The regions are as follows:

Northeast (page 467): Connecticut, Maine, Massachusetts, New Hampshire, New York, Rhode Island, Vermont

Midatlantic (page 469): Washington DC, Delaware, Maryland, New Jersey, Pennsylvania

Midsouth (page 471): North Carolina, South Carolina, Tennessee, Virginia, West Virginia

Southeast (page 472): Alabama, Arkansas, Florida, Georgia, Louisiana, Mississippi, Puerto Rico

Midwest (page 474): Illinois, Indiana, Kentucky, Michigan, Ohio

North Central (page 475): Iowa, Minnesota, Nebraska, North Dakota, South Dakota, Wisconsin

South Central (page 476): Colorado, Kansas, Missouri, New Mexico, Oklahoma, Texas

West (page 479): Arizona, California, Hawaii, Nevada, Utah

Northwest (page 481): Alaska, Idaho, Montana, Oregon, Washington, Wyoming

Canada (page 482)

International (page 483)

To find a conference based on the month in which it occurs, check out our Conference Index by Date at the back of this book.

LEARNING & NETWORKING

Besides learning from workshop leaders and panelists in formal sessions, writers at conferences also benefit from conversations with other attendees. Writers on all levels enjoy sharing insights. A conversation over lunch can reveal a new market for your work or let you know which editors are most receptive to the work of new writers. You can find out about recent editor changes and about specific agents. A casual chat could lead to a new contact or resource in your area.

Many editors and agents make visiting conferences a part of their regular search for new writers. A cover letter or query that starts with "I met you at the Green Mountain Writers Conference," or "I found your talk on your company's new romance line at the Moonlight and Magnolias Writer's Conference most interesting ..." may give you a small leg up on the competition.

While a few writers have been successful in selling their manuscripts at a conference, the availability of editors and agents does not usually mean these folks will have the time to read your novel or six best short stories (unless, of course, you've scheduled an individual meeting with them in advance). While editors and agents are glad to meet writers and discuss work in general terms, usually they don't have the time (or energy) to give an extensive critique during a conference. In other words, use the conference as a way to make a first, brief contact.

SELECTING A CONFERENCE

Besides the obvious considerations of time, place, and cost, choose your conference based on your writing goals. If, for example, your goal is to improve the quality of your writing, it will be more helpful to you to choose a hands-on craft workshop rather than a conference offering a series of panels on marketing and promotion. If, on the other hand, you are a science fiction novelist who would like to meet your fans, try one of the many science fiction conferences or "cons" held throughout the country and the world.

Look for panelists and workshop instructors whose work you admire and who seem to be writing in your general area. Check for specific panels or discussions of topics relevant to what you are writing now. Think about the size—would you feel more comfortable with a small workshop of eight people or a large group of one hundred or more attendees?

If your funds are limited, start by looking for conferences close to home, but you may want to explore those that offer contests with cash prizes—and a chance to recoup your expenses. A few conferences and workshops also offer scholarships, but the competition is stiff and writers interested in these should seek out the requirements early. Finally, students may want to look for conferences and workshops that offer college credit. You will find these options included in the listings here. Again, send a self-addressed, stamped envelope for the most current details.

BACKSPACE AGENT-AUTHOR SEMINAR

P.O. Box 454, Washington, MI 48094-0454. (732)267-6449. **Fax:** (586)532-9652. **E-mail:** chrisg@bksp.org. **E-mail:** karendionne@bksp.org. **Website:** www.bksp.org. **Contact:** Karen Dionne. Estab. 2006. Last event held May 23-25, 2013

COSTS All 3 days: May 23-25, 2013; includes Agent-Author Seminar, Conference Program, Book Signing & Cocktail Reception, Donald Maass workshop—$720. **Backspace Members Receive a $100 discount on a 3-day registration! First 2 days:** May 23-24; includes Agent-Author Seminar, Conference Program, Book Signing & Cocktail Reception—$580. **Friday only:** May 24; Two-track conference program with literary agents, editors, and authors. Includes keynote address, booksigning, and cocktail reception—$275. **Saturday only:** May 25; Back-to-back craft workshops with best-selling author Jonathan Maberry in the morning and literary agent Donald Maass in the afternoon—$200.

ACCOMMODATIONS Held in the Radisson Martinique, at 49 West 32nd Street, New York, NY 10001. Telephone: (212) 736-3800. Fax: (212) 277-2702. You can call to book a reservation, based on a two-person occupancy.

ADDITIONAL INFORMATION The Backspace Agent-Author Seminar offers plenty of face time with attending agents. This casual, no-pressure seminar is a terrific opportunity to network, ask questions, talk about your work informally, and listen from the people who make their lives selling books.

BREAD LOAF WRITERS' CONFERENCE

Middlebury College, Middlebury College, Middlebury, VT 05753. (802)443-5286. **Fax:** (802)443-2087. **E-mail:** ncargill@middlebury.edu. **E-mail:** blwc@middlebury.edu. **Website:** www.middlebury.edu/blwc. **Contact:** Michael Collier, Director. Estab. 1926. Last event held August 14-24, 2013.

COSTS $2,714 (includes tuition, housing).

ACCOMMODATIONS Bread Loaf Campus in Ripton, Vermont.

ADDITIONAL INFORMATION Location: mountain campus of Middlebury College. Average attendance: 230.

CAPE COD WRITERS CENTER ANNUAL CONFERENCE

P.O. Box 408, Osterville, MA 02655. **E-mail:** writers@capecodwriterscenter.org. **Website:** www.capecodwriterscenter.org. **Contact:** Nancy Rubin Stuart, executive director. Last event held August 4-9, 2013.

COSTS Vary, depending on the number of courses selected.

THE GLEN WORKSHOP

Image, 3307 Third Ave. W., Seattle, WA 98119. (206)281-2988. **Fax:** (206)281-2335. **E-mail:** glenworkshop@imagejournal.org. **Website:** glenworkshop.com. Estab. 1995. **E-mail:** glenworkshop@imagejournal.org; jmullins@imagejournal.org. **Website:** www.imagejournal.org/glen. "The Glen Workshop, sponsored by *Image* journal, is an innovative and enriching program combining the best elements of a workshop, an arts festival, and a conference. Daily classes, taught by nationally known authors and artists, offer close attention to artists of all levels. Afternoons and evenings feature readings, lectures, concerts, and worship services incorporating the arts. Like its sponsor, *Image*, the Glen is grounded in a Christian perspective, but its tone is informal and hospitable to all spiritual wayfarers." Last events held: Glen East 2013 (June 9, 2013-June 16, 2013) in South Hadley, MA; Glen West 2013 (Jul 28, 2013-August 4, 2013) in Santa Fe, New Mexico. Faculty has included Robert Clark (fiction), Barry Moser (life drawing), Patricia Hampl (memoir), Sedrick Huckaby (painting), and Over the Rhine (songwriting).

COSTS See costs online. A limited number of partial scholarships are available.

ACCOMMODATIONS Offers dorm rooms, dorm suites, and apartments.

ADDITIONAL INFORMATION Depending on the teacher, participants may need to submit workshop material prior to arrival (usually 10-25 pages).

GOTHAM WRITERS' WORKSHOP

WritingClasses.com, 555 Eighth Ave., Suite 1402, New York NY 10018. (212)974-8377. **Fax:** (212)307-6325. **E-mail:** dana@write.org. **Website:** www.writingclasses.com. **Contact:** Dana Miller, director of student relations. Estab. 1993.

COSTS $420/10-week workshops; $159 for the 4-week online selling seminars and $125 for 1-day intensive courses; $299 for 6-week creative writing and business writing classes.

ADDITIONAL INFORMATION "Participants do not need to submit workshop material prior to their first class." Sponsors a contest for a free 10-week online creative writing course (valued at $420) offered each term. Students should fill out a form online at www.writingclasses.com to participate in the contest. The winner is randomly selected. For brochure send e-mail, visit website, or call. Accepts inquiries by e-mail and phone.

GREEN MOUNTAIN WRITERS CONFERENCE

47 Hazel St., Rutland, VT 05701. (802)236-6133. E-mail: ydaley@sbcglobal.net. E-mail: yvonnedaley@me.com. Website: vermontwriters.com. Contact: Yvonne Daley, director. Estab. 1999.

COSTS $600 before June 30; $650 after June 30. Partial scholarships are available.

ACCOMMODATIONS "We have made arrangements with a major hotel in nearby Rutland and two area bed-and-breakfast inns for special accommodations and rates for conference participants. You must make your own reservations."

ADDITIONAL INFORMATION Participants' mss can be read and commented on at a cost. Sponsors contests. Conference publishes a literary magazine featuring work of participants. Brochures available in January on website or for SASE, e-mail. Accepts inquiries by SASE, e-mail, phone. "We offer the opportunity to learn from some of the nation's best writers at a small, supportive conference in a lakeside setting that allows one-to-one feedback. Participants often continue to correspond and share work after conferences." Further information available on website, by e-mail, or by phone.

THE MACDOWELL COLONY

100 High St., Peterborough, NH 03458. (603)924-3886. Fax: (603)924-9142. E-mail: admissions@macdowellcolony.org. Website: www.macdowellcolony.org. Estab. 1907.

COSTS Travel reimbursement and stipends are available for participants of the residency, based on need. There are no residency fees.

⊙ ODYSSEY FANTASY WRITING WORKSHOP

P.O. Box 75, Mont Vernon, NH 03057. E-mail: jcavelos@sff.net. Website: www.odysseyworkshop.org. Estab. 1996. Last event held June 10-July 19, 2013.

COSTS In 2012: $1,900 tuition, $790 housing (double room), $1,580 (single room); $35 application fee, $400-600 food (approximate), $550 processing fee to receive college credit.

ADDITIONAL INFORMATION Students must apply and include a writing sample. Students' works are critiqued throughout the 6 weeks. Workshop information available in October. For brochure/guidelines, send SASE, e-mail, visit website, or call. Accepts inquiries by SASE, e-mail, phone.

RT BOOKLOVERS CONVENTION

55 Bergen St., Brooklyn, NY 11201. (718)237-1097 or (800)989-8816, ext. 12. Fax: (718)624-2526. E-mail: jocarol@rtconvention.com. E-mail: nancy@rtbookreviews.com. Website: rtconvention.com.

COSTS See website for pricing and other information.

ACCOMMODATIONS Rooms available at a nearby Sheraton and Westin. Check online to reserve a room.

THRILLERFEST

P.O. Box 311, Eureka, CA 95502. E-mail: infocentral@thrillerwriters.org. Website: www.thrillerfest.com. Contact: Kimberley Howe, executive director. Estab. 2006.

COSTS Price will vary from $300-1,100, depending on which events are selected. Various package deals are available offering savings, and Early Bird pricing is offered beginning August of each year.

ACCOMMODATIONS Grand Hyatt in New York City.

VERMONT STUDIO CENTER

P.O. Box 613, 80 Pearl Street, Johnson, VT 05656. (802)635-2727. Fax: (802)635-2730. E-mail: info@vermontstudiocenter.org. Website: www.vermontstudiocenter.org. Contact: Gary Clark, writing program director. Estab. 1984. Ongoing residencies. Conference duration: From 2-12 weeks. Average attendance: 55 writers and visual artists/month. "The Vermont Studio Center is an international creative community located in Johnson, VT, and serving more than 600 American and international artists and writers each year (50 per month). A Studio Center Residency features secluded, uninterrupted writing time, the companionship of dedicated and talented peers, and access to a roster of two distinguished Visiting Writers each month. All VSC Residents receive three meals a day, private, comfortable housing, and the company of an international community of painters, sculptors, poets, printmakers, and writers. Writers attending residencies at the Studio Center may work on whatever they choose—no matter what month of the year they attend." Visiting writers have included Ron Carlson, Donald Revell, Jane Hirshfield, Rosanna Warren, Chris Abani, Bob Shacochis, Tony Hoagland, and Alice Notley.

ACCOMMODATIONS "The cost of a 4-week residency is $3,750. Generous fellowship and grant assistance available. Accommodations available on site. "Residents live in single rooms in ten modest, comfortable houses adjacent to the Red Mill Building. Rooms are simply furnished and have shared baths. Complete linen service is provided. The Studio Center is unable to accommodate guests at meals, overnight guests, spouses, children, or pets."

ADDITIONAL INFORMATION Fellowships application deadlines are February 15, June 15, and October 1. Writers encouraged to visit website for more information. May also e-mail, call, fax.

WESLEYAN WRITERS CONFERENCE

Wesleyan University, 294 High St., Room 207, Middletown, CT 06459. (860)685-3604. **Fax:** (860)685-2441. **E-mail:** agreene@wesleyan.edu. **Website:** www.wesleyan.edu/writing/conference. Estab. 1956.

ACCOMMODATIONS Meals are provided on campus. Lodging is available on campus or in town.

ADDITIONAL INFORMATION Ms critiques are available but not required. Scholarships and teaching fellowships are available, including the Joan Jakobson Awards for fiction writers and poets; and the Jon Davidoff Scholarships for nonfiction writers and journalists. Inquire via e-mail, fax, or phone.

WRITER'S DIGEST CONFERENCE

F+W Media, Inc., 10151 Carver Road, Suite 200, Blue Ash, OH 45242. **E-mail:** jill.ruesch@fwmedia.com. **Website:** www.writersdigestconference.com. "Energize your writing—and your writing career. You'll make real connections with fellow writers, experience the thrill of pitching your work to literary agents and editors, and get practical publishing-industry advice and writing inspiration from successful authors at the Writer's Digest Conference." Writer's Digest Conference East held in New York City. Writer's Digest Conference West held in Los Angeles. Last event (WDC East) held April 5-7, 2013.

COSTS See website for more information on costs.

WRITERS OMI AT LEDIG HOUSE

55 Fifth Ave., 15th Floor, New York, NY 10003. (212)206-6114. **E-mail:** writers@artomi.org. **Website:** www.artomi.org.

ACCOMMODATIONS Residents provide their own transportation. Offers overnight accommodations.

ADDITIONAL INFORMATION "Agents and editors from the New York publishing community are invited for dinner and discussion. Bicycles, a swimming pool, and nearby tennis court are available for use."

MIDATLANTIC

BALTIMORE COMIC-CON

Baltimore Convention Center, One West Pratt St., Baltimore, MD 21201. (410)526-7410. **E-mail:** press@baltimorecomiccon.com. **Website:** www.baltimorecomiccon.com. **Contact:** Marc Nathan. Estab. 1999.

ACCOMMODATIONS Does not offer overnight accommodations. Provides list of area hotels or lodging options.

ADDITIONAL INFORMATION For brochure, visit website.

GREATER LEHIGH VALLEY WRITERS GROUP 'THE WRITE STUFF' WRITERS CONFERENCE

3650 Nazareth Pike, PMB #136, Bethlehem, PA 18020-1115. **E-mail:** writestuffchair@glvwg.org. **Website:** www.glvwg.org. **Contact:** Donna Brennan, chair. Estab. 1993.

COSTS Members: $110 (includes Friday evening session and all Saturday workshops, 2 meals, and a chance to pitch to an editor or agent); nonmembers: $130. Late registration: $145. Pre-conference workshops require an additional fee.

ADDITIONAL INFORMATION "The Writer's Flash contest is judged by conference participants. Write 100 words or less in fiction, creative nonfiction, or poetry. Brochures available in January by SASE, or by phone, e-mail, or on website. Accepts inquiries by SASE, e-mail, or phone. Agents and editors attend conference. For updated info refer to the website. Greater Lehigh Valley Writers Group hosts a friendly conference and gives you the most for your money. Break-out rooms offer craft topics, business of publishing, editor and agent panels. Book fair with book signing by published authors and presenters."

HIGHLIGHTS FOUNDATION FOUNDERS WORKSHOPS

814 Court St., Honesdale, PA 18431. (570)253-1122. **Fax:** (570)253-0179. **E-mail:** klbrown@high lightsfoundation.org; jo.lloy@highlightsfoundation.org. **Website:** highlightsfoundation.org. **Contact:** Kent L. Brown, Jr. Estab. 2000.

COSTS Prices vary based on workshop. Check website for details.

ACCOMMODATIONS Coordinates pickup at local airport. Offers overnight accommodations. Participants stay in guest cabins on the wooded grounds surrounding Highlights Founders' home adjacent to the house/conference center.

ADDITIONAL INFORMATION Some workshops require pre-workshop assignment. Brochure available for SASE, by e-mail, on website, by phone, by fax. Accepts inquiries by phone, fax, e-mail, SASE. Editors attend conference. "Applications will be reviewed and accepted on a first-come, first-served basis, applicants must demonstrate specific experience in writing area of workshop they are applying for—writing samples are required for many of the workshops."

HIGHLIGHTS FOUNDATION WRITERS WORKSHOP AT CHAUTAUQUA

814 Court St., Honesdale, PA 18431. (570)253-1192. **Fax:** (570)253-0179. **E-mail:** klbrown@highlights foundation.org; jo.lloyd@highlightsfoundation.org. **Website:** highlightsfoundation.org. Estab. 1985.

ACCOMMODATIONS We coordinate ground transportation to and from airports, trains, and bus stations in the Erie, PA and Jamestown/Buffalo, NY area. We also coordinate accommodations for conference attendees.

ADDITIONAL INFORMATION "We offer the opportunity for attendees to submit a ms for review at the conference. Workshop brochures/guidelines are available upon request."

JENNY MCKEAN MOORE COMMUNITY WORKSHOPS

English Department, George Washingtion University, 801 22nd St. NW, Rome Hall, Suite 760, Washington, DC 20052. (202) 994-6180. **Fax:** (202) 994-7915. **E-mail:** tvmallon@gwu.edu. **Website:** www.gwu.edu/~english/creative_jennymckeanmoore.html. **Contact:** Thomas Mallon, director of creative writing. Estab. 1976.

ADDITIONAL INFORMATION Admission is competitive and by ms.

MONTROSE CHRISTIAN WRITERS' CONFERENCE

218 Locust St., Montrose, PA 18801. (570)278-1001 or (800)598-5030. **Fax:** (570)278-3061. **E-mail:** info@montrosebible.org. **Website:** montrosebible.org. Estab. 1990.

COSTS Tuition is $175.

ACCOMMODATIONS Will meet planes in Binghamton, NY and Scranton, PA. On-site accommodations: room and board $305-350/conference; $60-70/day including food (2009 rates). RV court available.

ADDITIONAL INFORMATION "Writers can send work ahead of time and have it critiqued for a small fee." The attendees are usually church related. The writing has a Christian emphasis. Conference information available in April. For brochure send SASE, visit website, e-mail, call, or fax. Accepts inquiries by SASE, e-mail, fax, phone.

WILLIAM PATERSON UNIVERSITY SPRING WRITER'S CONFERENCE

English Department, Atrium 232, 300 Pompton Rd., Wayne, NJ 07470. (973)720-3067. **Fax:** (973)720-2189. **E-mail:** liut@wpunj.edu. **Website:** wpunj.edu/cohss/departments/english/writers-conference/.

COSTS $55 (includes lunch).

PHILADELPHIA WRITERS' CONFERENCE

P.O. Box 7171, Elkins Park, PA 19027-0171. (215) 619-7422. **E-mail:** dresente@mc3.edu. **E-mail:** info@pwcwriters.org. **Website:** www.pwcwriters.org. **Contact:** Dana Resente. Estab. 1949.

COSTS Advance registration is $205; walk-in registration is $225. The banquet and buffet are $40 each. Master classes are $50.

ACCOMMODATIONS Holiday Inn, Independence Mall, Fourth and Arch Streets, Philadelphia, PA 19106-2170. "Hotel offers discount for early registration."

ADDITIONAL INFORMATION Sponsors contest. "Length is generally 2,500 words for fiction or nonfiction. 1st Prize, in addition to cash and certificate, gets free tuition for following year." Also offers ms critique. Accepts inquiries by e-mail and SASE. Agents and editors attend conference. Visit us on the web for further agent and speaker details."

○ SCBWI–NEW JERSEY; ANNUAL SUMMER CONFERENCE

SCBWI-New Jersey: Society of Children's Book Writers & Illustrators, New Jersey **Website:** www.newjerseyscbwi.com. **Contact:** Kathy Temean, regional advisor.

WINTER POETRY & PROSE GETAWAY

18 N. Richards Ave., Ventnor, NJ 08406. (888)887-2105. **E-mail:** info@wintergetaway.com. **Website:** www.wintergetaway.com. **Contact:** Peter Murphy. Estab. 1994.

ACCOMMODATIONS See website or call for current fee information.

ADDITIONAL INFORMATION Previous faculty has included Julianna Baggott, Christian Bauman, Laure-Anne Bosselaar, Kurt Brown, Mark Doty (National Book Award winner), Stephen Dunn (Pulitzer Prize winner), Dorianne Laux, Carol Plum-Ucci, James Richardson, Mimi Schwartz, Terese Svoboda, and more.

MIDSOUTH

AMERICAN CHRISTIAN WRITERS CONFERENCES

P.O. Box 110390, Nashville, TN 37222-0390. (800)219-7483. **Fax:** (615)834-7736. **E-mail:** acwriters@aol.com. **Website:** www.acwriters.com. **Contact:** Reg Forder, director. Estab. 1981.

COSTS Costs vary based on conference. Prices also depend on whether it is a conference or a mentoring retreat.

ACCOMMODATIONS Special rates are available at the host hotel (usually a major chain like Holiday Inn).

ADDITIONAL INFORMATION All events in 2014 will be mentoring retreats where editors and professional writers will work with you in putting your manuscript into publishable form: April 4-5, 2014, Nashville, TN; April 11-12, 2014, Oklahoma City, OK; June 6-7, 2014, Grand Rapids, MI; July 11-12, 2014, Atlanta, GA; August 1-2, 2014, Minneapolis, MN; September 26-27, 2014, Spokane, WA; Oct 31-November 1, 2014, Phoenix, AZ; November 21-22, 2014, Orlando, FL. Send a SASE for conference brochures/guidelines.

CELEBRATION OF SOUTHERN LITERATURE

Southern Lit Alliance, 3069 S. Broad St., Suite 2, Chattanooga, TN 37408-3056. (423)267-1218 or (800)267-4232. **Fax:** (423)267-1018. **E-mail:** srobinson@southernlitalliance.org. **Website:** www.southernlitalliance.org. **Contact:** Susan Robinson. Last event held April 18-20, 2013.

COST See website for information on pricing.

ACCOMODATIONS The 2013 Celebration of Southern Literature (CSL) official hotel was the Sheraton Read House.

ADDITIONAL Information "On average, 1,000 people from across the country attend the Celebration of Southern Literature. There are scheduled book signings and breaks between events, at which time many writers mingle with attendees."

HIGHLAND SUMMER CONFERENCE

Box 7014, Radford University, Radford, VA 24142-7014. (540)831-5366. **Fax:** (540)831-5951. **E-mail:** tburriss@radford.edu; rbderrick@radford.edu. **Website:** www.radford.edu/content/cehd/home/departments/appalachian-studies.html. **Contact:** Dr. Theresa Burriss, Ruth Derrick. Estab. 1978.

ACCOMMODATIONS "We do not have special rate arrangements with local hotels. We do offer accommodations on the Radford University campus in a recently refurbished residence hall."

ADDITIONAL INFORMATION Conference leaders typically critique work done during the 1-week conference, and because of the 1-week format, students will be asked to bring preliminary work when they arrive at the conference, as well as submit a portfolio following the conference. Brochures/guidelines are available in March by request.

⊙ KILLER NASHVILLE

P.O. Box 680759, Franklin, TN 37068-0686. (615)599-4032. **E-mail:** contact@killernashville.com. **Website:** www.killernashville.com. **Contact:** Clay Stafford. Estab. 2006.

COSTS Early Bird Registration: $160 (February 16); Advanced Registration: $170 (May 1); $180 for 3-day full registration.

ACCOMMODATIONS The Hutton Hotel has all rooms available for the Killer Nashville Conference.

ADDITIONAL INFORMATION Additional information about registration is provided online.

NORTH CAROLINA WRITERS' NETWORK FALL CONFERENCE

P.O. Box 21591, Winston-Salem, NC 27120. (336)293-8844. **E-mail:** mail@ncwriters.org. **Website:** www.nc

writers.org. Estab. 1985. Next event held November 15-17, 2013 in Wrightsville Beach, NC.

COSTS Approximately $250 (includes 4 meals).

ACCOMMODATIONS Special rates are usually available at the conference hotel, but conferees must make their own reservations.

ADDITIONAL INFORMATION "The Fall Conference attracts hundreds of writers from around the country and provides a weekend full of activities that include lunch and dinner banquets with readings, keynotes, tracks in several genres, open mic sessions, and the opportunity for 1-on-1 manuscript critiques with editors or agents. Conference faculty include professional writers from North Carolina and beyond. Held every year in a major hotel, the conference rotates annually."

SEWANEE WRITERS' CONFERENCE

735 University Ave., 119 Gailor Hall, Stamler Center, Sewanee, TN 37383-1000. (931) 598-1654. **E-mail:** allatham@sewanee.edu. **Website:** www.sewaneewriters.org. **Contact:** Adam Latham. Estab. 1990.

COSTS $1,000 for tuition and $700 for room, board, and activity costs.

ACCOMMODATIONS Participants are housed in single rooms in university dormitories. Bathrooms are shared by small groups. Motel or bed-and-breakfast housing is available, but not abundantly so.

SHEVACON

P.O. Box 7622, Roanoke, VA 24019. (540)248-4152. **E-mail:** shevacon@shevacon.org. **Website:** www.shevacon.org. **Contact:** Lynn Bither, chairperson. Estab. 1993. Average attendance: 400. "We are one of the smaller conventions in the sci-fi/fantasy genre, but we have a lot of big convention qualities." Conference focuses on writing (science fiction and fantasy, some horror), art (science fiction and fantasy), gaming (science fiction and fantasy). Past fiction-related panels have included Stolen Stories: The Use of Historical Models; Blood on the Bulkhead: Is New Fiction Too Graphic?; Bad Guys We Want to Win: Writing Good Villians; Scare Me, Thrill Me: Is Horror More Difficult to Write than Fiction?"

COSTS Contact Shevacon for rates.

ACCOMMODATIONS There is special rate at the Sheraton Roanoke Hotel & Conference Center, Virginia. "Shuttles from the airport are available; we do not have airline discounts." Offers overnight accomodations; "individuals must make their own reservations."

For brochure, send SASE or visit website. Accepts inquiries by mail, e-mail, or phone.

ADDITIONAL INFORMATION "Shevacon is the largest multimedia science fiction and fantasy convention in Southwestern Virginia. We offer many fun events and great programming focusing on sci-fi, fantasy, and horror. Workshops, panel discussions, art show and artist alley, dealer's room, costumed fandom groups, auctions, computer and console gaming, RPG/LARP gaming, Video and Anime screenings ... and so much more! Confirmed guests are listed on the website and we are updating regularly."

STELLARCON

Box F4, Brown Annex, Elliott University Center, UNCG, Greensboro, NC 27412. (336)294-8041. **E-mail:** info@stellarcon.org. **Website:** www.stellarcon.com. **Contact:** Mike Monaghan, convention manager. Estab. 1976. Annual. Last conference held March 1-3, 2013. Average attendance: 500. Conference focuses on "general science fiction and fantasy (horror also) with an emphasis on literature." See website for 2013 speakers.

COSTS At-the-door rate for weekend pass: $35.

ACCOMMODATIONS Make a reservation at the Greensboro-High Point Airport Mariott. Call 336-852-6450 for StellarCon room block reservations.

VIRGINIA FESTIVAL OF THE BOOK

Virginia Festival of the Book Foundation for the Humanities, 145 Ednam Dr., Charlottesville, VA 22903-4629. (434)924-3296. **Fax:** (434)296-4714. **E-mail:** vabook@virginia.edu; spcoleman@virginia.edu. **Website:** www.vabook.org. **Contact:** Nancy Damon, program director. Estab. 1995.

COSTS Most events are free and open to the public. Two luncheons, a breakfast, and a reception require tickets.

ACCOMMODATIONS Overnight accommodations available.

ADDITIONAL INFORMATION "The festival is a 5-day event featuring authors, illustrators, and publishing professionals. Authors must apply to the festival to be included on a panel. Applications accepted only online.

SOUTHEAST

ALABAMA WRITERS' CONCLAVE

137 Sterling Dr, Hueytown, AL 35023. **Website:** www.alabamawritersconclave.org. **Contact:** Richard Mod-

lin, president. Estab. 1923. **E-mail:** rfm1937@earth
link.net. **Website:** www.alabamawritersconclave.org.
Last event held April 25-27, 2013. Conference to promote all phases of writing. Also offers ms critiques
and eight writing contests.

COSTS Fees for conference are $150 (member)/$175
(nonmember), includes 2 meals. Critique fee $25
(member)/$30 (nonmember). Membership $25.

ACCOMMODATIONS 2013 conference held at
Hampton Inn-Mobile Bay, Fairhope, AL. Special
conference rates.

ADDITIONAL INFORMATION "We have major
speakers and faculty members who conduct intensive, energetic workshops. Our annual writing contest guidelines and all other information is available
at www.alabamawritersconclave.org."

HOW TO BE PUBLISHED WORKSHOPS

P.O. Box 100031, Irondale, AL 35210-3006. **E-mail:**
mike@writing2sell.com. **Website:** www.writing2sell
.com. **Contact:** Michael Garrett. Estab. 1986.
COSTS $79-99.

MONTEVALLO LITERARY FESTIVAL

Sta. 6420, University of Montevallo, Montevallo, AL
35115. (205)665-6420. **Fax:** (205)665-6422. **E-mail:**
murphyj@montevallo.edu. **Website:** www.monte
vallo.edu/english. **Contact:** Dr. Jim Murphy, director. Estab. 2003.

COSTS Readings are free. Readings, plus lunch, reception, and dinner is $20. Master Class only is $30.
Master Class with everything else is $50.

ACCOMMODATIONS Offers overnight accommodations at Ramsay Conference Center on campus.
Call (205)665-6280 for reservations. Free on-campus
parking. Additional information available at www
.montevallo.edu/cont_ed/ramsay.shtm.

ADDITIONAL INFORMATION To enroll in a fiction
workshop, contact Bryn Chancellor (bchancellor@
montevallo.edu). Information for upcoming festival
available in February. For brochure, visit website. Accepts inquiries by mail (with SASE), e-mail, phone,
and fax. Editors participate in conference. "This is a
friendly, relaxed festival dedicated to bringing literary
writers and readers together on a personal scale." Poetry workshop participants submit up to 5 pages of poetry; e-mail as Word doc to Jim Murphy (murphyj@
montevallo.edu) at least 2 weeks prior to festival.

OZARK CREATIVE WRITERS, INC. CONFERENCE

P.O. Box 424, Eureka Springs, AR 72632. **E-mail:**
ozarkcreativewriters@gmail.com. **Website:** www
.ozarkcreativewriters.org.

UNIVERSITY OF NORTH FLORIDA WRITERS CONFERENCE

12000 Alumni Dr., Jacksonville, FL 32224-2678.
(904)620-4200. **E-mail:** sharon.y.cobb@unf.edu.
Website: www.unfwritersconference.com. **Contact:**
Sharon Y. Cobb, conference director. Estab. 2009. Annual conference held in August.

COSTS See website for current registration fees.

ACCOMMODATIONS Nearby accommodations are
listed on website. There is free parking provided at the
University Center.

ADDITIONAL INFORMATION Conference duration: 3 days. Average attendance: 200. Full conference
attendees receive: workshops, critiques by faculty and
fellow students, lunches, Friday wine/cheese reception, and book signings. Short workshops in craft,
genre, marketing, and getting published. See website
for current registration fees. Nearby accommodations
with special conference discounts are listed on website. There is free parking provided at the University
Center. Workshops include fiction, young adult, children's, nonfiction, romance, and screenwriting held at
the University Center on campus at the University of
North Florida. Writers may submit pitches to agents,
editors, and film producers through the Writers Pitch
Book. Brochures and guidelines available for SASE
and on website (www.unfwritersconference.com), or
by e-mail.

WRITERS IN PARADISE

Eckerd College, 4200 54th Ave. South, St. Petersburg,
FL 33711. (727) 864-7994. **Fax:** (727) 864-7575. **E-mail:** cayacr@eckerd.edu. **Website:** www.writersin
paradise.com. **Contact:** Christine Koryta, conference
coordinator. Estab. 2005. Next event held January 18-
25, 2014.

COSTS 2014 tuition fee: $700.

ACCOMMODATIONS Block of rooms at area hotel with free shuttle to and from conference; $582.24.

ADDITIONAL INFORMATION Application materials are required of all attendees. Acceptance is based
on a writing sample and a letter detailing your writing background. Submit 1 short story (25 page max)
or the opening 25 pages of a novel-in-progress, plus

a 2-page synopsis of the book. Deadline for application materials is December 1. "Writers in Paradise is a conference for writers of various styles and approaches. While admission is selective, the admissions committee accepts writers with early potential as well as those with strong backgrounds in writing." Information available in August. For brochure, send SASE, call, e-mail. Agents participate in conference. Editors participate in conference. "The tranquil seaside landscape sets the tone for this informal gathering of writers, teachers, editors, and literary agents. After 8 days of workshopping and engagement with peers and professionals in your field, you will leave this unique opportunity with solid ideas about how to find an agent and get published, along with a new and better understanding of your craft."

MIDWEST

FESTIVAL OF FAITH AND WRITING

Department of English, Calvin College, 1795 Knollcrest Circle, SE, Grand Rapids, MI 49546. (616)526-6770. **E-mail:** ffw@calvin.edu. **Website:** festival.calvin.edu. Estab. 1990. Next event held April 10-12, 2014.
COSTS Consult festival website.
ACCOMMODATIONS Shuttles are available to and from local hotels. Shuttles are also available for overflow parking lots. A list of hotels with special rates for conference attendees is available on the festival website. High school and college students can arrange on-campus lodging by e-mail.
ADDITIONAL INFORMATION Online registration opens in October. Accepts inquiries by e-mail and phone.

FLATHEAD RIVER WRITERS CONFERENCE

P.O. Box 7711, Kalispeil, MT 59904-7711. (406)881-4066. **E-mail:** answers@authorsoftheflathead.org. **Website:** www.authorsoftheflathead.org/conference.asp. Estab. 1990. Next event held September 28-29, 2013.
COSTS Contact for cost information, not currently listed on website.
ACCOMMODATIONS Rooms are available at a discounted rate.
ADDITIONAL INFORMATION Watch website for additional speakers and other details. Register early as seating is limited.

INDIANA UNIVERSITY WRITERS' CONFERENCE

464 Ballantine Hall, 1020 E. Kirkwood Ave., Bloomington, IN 47405-7103. (812)855-1877. **Fax:** (812)855-9535. **E-mail:** writecon@indiana.edu. **Website:** www.indiana.edu/~writecon. **Contact:** Bob Bledsoe, director. Estab. 1940. Last event held May 26-31, 2013.
COSTS 2013: Workshop, $550/week; classes only, $300/week.
ACCOMMODATIONS Information on accommodations available on website.
ADDITIONAL INFORMATION Fiction workshop applicants must submit up to 25 pages of prose. Registration information available for SASE, by e-mail, or on website.

KENYON REVIEW WRITERS WORKSHOP

Kenyon College, Gambier, OH 43022. (740)427-5207. **Fax:** (740)427-5417. **E-mail:** kenyonreview@kenyon.edu; writers@kenyonreview.org. **Website:** www.kenyonreview.org. **Contact:** Anna Duke Reach, director. Estab. 1990.
COSTS $1,995; includes tuition, room, and board.
ACCOMMODATIONS The workshop operates a shuttle to and from Gambier and the airport in Columbus, OH. Offers overnight accommodations. Participants are housed in Kenyon College student housing. The cost is covered in the tuition.
ADDITIONAL INFORMATION Application includes a writing sample. Admission decisions are made on a rolling basis. Workshop information is available online at www.kenyonreview.org/workshops in November. For brochure send e-mail, visit website, call, fax. Accepts inquiries by SASE, e-mail, phone, fax.

LOVE IS MURDER

Chicago, IL. **E-mail:** hanleyliz@wideopenwest.com. **Website:** loveismurder.net.
COSTS Full conference including panels, discussions, entertainment, and all meals: $369.
ACCOMMODATIONS Held at InterContinental Chicago O'Hare. You can register for a room through the website.
ADDITIONAL INFORMATION Banquet and Lovey Awards for best first novel, historical novel, series, crime-related nonfiction, private investigator/police procedural, paranormal/science fiction/horror, traditional/amateur sleuth, suspense thriller, romance/fantasy, and short story.

◉ MAGNA CUM MURDER

Magna Cum Murder Crime Writing Festival, The E.B. and Bertha C. Ball Center, Ball State University, Muncie, IN 47306. (765)285-8975. **Fax:** (765)747-9566. **E-mail:** magnacummurder@yahoo.com; kennisonk@aol.com. **Website:** www.magnacummurder.com. Estab. 1994.
COSTS Check website for updates.

MIDWEST WRITERS WORKSHOP

Ball State University, Department of Journalism, Muncie, IN 47306. (765)282-1055. **E-mail:** midwestwriters@yahoo.com. **Website:** www.midwestwriters.org. **Contact:** Jama Kehoe Bigger, director.
COSTS $135-360. Most meals included.
ADDITIONAL INFORMATION Offers scholarships. See website for more information.

☺ SPACE (SMALL PRESS AND ALTERNATIVE COMICS EXPO)

Back Porch Comics, P.O. Box 20550, Columbus, OH 43220. **E-mail:** bpc13@earthlink.net. **Website:** www.backporchcomics.com/space.htm.
COSTS Admission: $5 per day or $8 for weekend.
ADDITIONAL INFORMATION For brochure, visit website. Editors participate in conference.

WESTERN RESERVE WRITERS & FREELANCE CONFERENCE

7700 Clocktower Dr., Kirtland, OH 44094. (440)525-7812. **E-mail:** deencr@aol.com. **Website:** www.deannaadams.com. **Contact:** Deanna Adams, director/conference coordinator. Estab. 1983.
COSTS Fall all-day conference includes lunch: $95. Spring half-day conference, no lunch: $69.
ADDITIONAL INFORMATION Brochures for the conferences are available by January (for spring conference) and July (for fall). Accepts inquiries by e-mail and phone. Check Deanna Adams' website for all updates. Editors and agents often attend the conferences.

WILLAMETTE WRITERS CONFERENCE

2108 Buck St., Portland, OR 97068. (503)305-6729. **Fax:** (503)344-6174. **E-mail:** wilwrite@willamettewriters.com. **Website:** www.willamettewriters.com. Estab. 1981.
COSTS Pricing schedule available online.
ACCOMMODATIONS If necessary, arrangements can be made on an individual basis through the conference hotel. Special rates may be available.

ADDITIONAL INFORMATION Brochure/guidelines are available for a catalog-sized SASE.

WOMEN WRITERS WINTER RETREAT

Homestead House Bed and Breakfast, 38111 West Spaulding, Willoughby, OH 44094. (440)946-1902. **E-mail:** deencr@aol.com. **Website:** www.deannaadams.com. Estab. 2007.
COSTS Single room: $315; shared room: $235 (includes complete weekend package, with B&B stay and all meals and workshops); weekend commute: $165; Saturday only: $125 (prices include lunch and dinner).
ADDITIONAL INFORMATION Brochures for the writers retreat are available by December. Accepts inquiries and reservations by e-mail or phone. See Deanna's website for additional information and updates.

WRITE-TO-PUBLISH CONFERENCE

WordPro Communication Services, 9118 W. Elmwood Dr., Suite 1G, Niles, IL 60714-5820. (847)296-3964. **Fax:** (847)296-0754. **E-mail:** lin@writetopublish.com. **Website:** www.writetopublish.com. **Contact:** Lin Johnson, director. Estab. 1971.
COSTS Approximately $485; includes conference and banquet.
ACCOMMODATIONS On-campus residence halls. Cost is approximately $280-360.
ADDITIONAL INFORMATION Optional ms evaluation available. College credit available. Conference information available in January. For details, visit website, or e-mail brochure@writetopublish.com. Accepts inquiries by e-mail, fax, phone.

NORTH CENTRAL

GREEN LAKE CHRISTIAN WRITERS CONFERENCE

W2511 State Road 23, Green Lake Conference Center, Green Lake, WI 54941-9599. (920)294-3323. **E-mail:** program@glcc.org. **E-mail:** janet.p.white@gmail.com. **Website:** glcc.org. **Contact:** Janet White, Conference Director. Estab. 1948.
COSTS Short Track (2 days): $65 per person. Full Track: Writers' $225 per person; Artists' $40 per person.
ACCOMMODATIONS Hotels, lodges, and all meeting rooms are a/c. Affordable rates, excellent meals.

ADDITIONAL INFORMATION Brochure and scholarship info from website or contact Jan White (920-294-7327). To register, call 920-294-3323.

IOWA SUMMER WRITING FESTIVAL

The University of Iowa, C215 Seashore Hall, University of Iowa, Iowa City, IA 52242. (319)335-4160. **Fax:** (319)335-4743. **E-mail:** iswfestival@uiowa.edu. **Website:** uiowa.edu/~iswfest. Estab. 1987.

COSTS $590 for full week; $305 for weekend workshop. Housing and meals are separate.

ACCOMMODATIONS Accommodations available at area hotels. Information on overnight accommodations available by phone or on website.

ADDITIONAL INFORMATION Brochures are available in February. Inquire via e-mail or on website.

UW-MADISON WRITERS' INSTITUTE

21 North Park St., Room 7331, Madison, WI 53715. (608)265-3972. **Fax:** (608)265-2475. **E-mail:** lscheer@dcs.wisc.edu. **Website:** www.uwwritersinstitute.org. **Contact:** Laurie Scheer. Estab. 1989.

COSTS $155-255; includes materials, breaks.

ACCOMMODATIONS Provides a list of area hotels or lodging options.

ADDITIONAL INFORMATION Sponsors contest.

WISCONSIN REGIONAL WRITERS' ASSOCIATION CONFERENCES

P.O Box 085270, Racine, WI 53408-5270. **E-mail:** cfreg@wiwrite.org. **Website:** www.wiwrite.org. **Contact:** Nate Scholze, Fall Conference Coordinator; Roxanne Aehl, Spring Conference Coordinator. Estab. 1948. Annual. Conferences held in May and September "are dedicated to self-improvement through speakers, workshops, and presentations. Topics and speakers vary with each event." Average attendance: 100-150. "We honor all genres of writing. Fall conference is a 2-day event featuring the Jade Ring Banquet and awards for six genre categories. Spring conference is a 1-day event."

COSTS $40-75.

ACCOMMODATIONS Provides a list of area hotels or lodging options. "We negotiate special rates at each facility. A block of rooms is set aside for a specific time period."

ADDITIONAL INFORMATION Award winners receive a certificate and a cash prize. First place winners of the Jade Ring contest receive a jade ring. Must be a member to enter contests. For brochure, call, e-mail or visit website in March/July.

SOUTH CENTRAL

ASPEN SUMMER WORDS LITERARY FESTIVAL & WRITING RETREAT

Aspen Writers' Foundation, 110 E. Hallam St., #116, Aspen, CO 81611. (970)925-3122. **Fax:** (970)925-5700. **E-mail:** info@aspenwriters.org. **Website:** www.aspenwriters.org. **Contact:** Natalie Lacy, programs coordinator. Estab. 1976. Last event held June 16-21, 2013. "Aspen Summer Words (ASW) is the place to be for anyone with a passion for the written word. Hailed as one of the nation's "Top Ten Literary Gatherings" by *USA Today*, this six-day celebration of words, stories, and ideas consists of a morning writing retreat, afternoon literary festival events, and 1-on-1 professional consultations with agents and editors. Simply, Aspen Summer Words offers an invigorating opportunity for booklovers from around the world to engage in an array of experiences and events in a stunning mountain setting. From author readings and behind-the-book panel discussions to live music and social gatherings, this literary sojourn examines the craft of writing and celebrates the literary arts."

COSTS Check website each year for updates.

ACCOMMODATIONS Discount lodging at the conference site will be available. 2014 rates to be announced. Free shuttle around town.

ADDITIONAL INFORMATION Check website for details on when to buy tickets and passes.

CRESTED BUTTE WRITERS CONFERENCE

P.O. Box 1361, Crested Butte, CO 81224. **E-mail:** coordinator@conf.crestedbuttewriters.org. **Website:** www.crestedbuttewriters.org/conf.php. **Contact:** Barbara Crawford or Theresa Rizzo, co-coordinators. Estab. 2006. Last event held June 21-23, 2013.

COSTS $330 nonmembers; $300 members; $297 Early Bird; The Sandy Writing Contest Finalist $280; and groups of 5 or more $280.

ACCOMMODATIONS The conference is held at The Elevation Hotel, located at the Crested Butte Mountain Resort at the base of the ski mountain (Mt. Crested Butte, CO). The quaint historic town lies nestled in a stunning mountain valley 3 short miles from the resort area of Mt. Crested Butte. A free bus runs frequently between the 2 towns. The closest airport is 30 miles away, in Gunnison, CO. Our website lists 3 lodging options besides rooms at the event facility. All condos, motels, and hotel options offer special conference rates. No special travel arrangements are made through the conference; however, information for car rental from Gunnison airport or the Alpine Express shuttle is listed on the conference FAQ page.

ADDITIONAL INFORMATION "Our conference workshops address a wide variety of writing craft and business. Our most popular workshop is Our First Pages Readings—with a twist. Agents and editors read opening pages volunteered by attendees—with a few best-selling authors' openings mixed in. Think the A/E can identify the bestsellers? Not so much. Each year one of our attendees has been mistaken for a bestseller and obviously garnered requests from some on the panel. Agents attending in 2013: Carlie Webber—CK Webber Associates and TBDs. The agents will be speaking and available for meetings with attendees through our Pitch and Pages system. Editors attending in 2013: Christian Trimmer, senior editor at Disney Hyperion Books, and Jessica Williams of Harper Collins. Award-winning authors: Mark Coker, CEO of Smashwords; Kristen Lamb, social media guru, Kim Killion, book cover designer; Jennifer Jakes; Sandra Kerns; and Annette Elton. Writers may request additional information by e-mail."

EAST TEXAS CHRISTIAN WRITERS CONFERENCE

The School of Humanities, Dr. Jerry L. Summers, Dean, Scarborough Hall, East Texas Baptist University, 1 Tiger Dr., Marshall, TX 75670. (903)923-2083. **E-mail:** jhopkins@etbu.edu; contest@etbu.edu. **Website:** www.etbu.edu/News/CWC. **Contact:** Sally Roden, humanities secretary. Estab. 2002.

ACCOMMODATIONS Visit website for a list of local hotels offering a discounted rate.

NATIONAL WRITERS ASSOCIATION FOUNDATION CONFERENCE

10940 S. Parker Rd., #508, Parker, CO 80138. (303)841-0246. **E-mail:** natlwritersassn@hotmail.com. **Website:** www.nationalwriters.com. **Contact:** Sandy Whelchel, executive director. Estab. 1926.

COSTS Approximately $100.

ADDITIONAL INFORMATION Awards for previous contests will be presented at the conference. Brochures/guidelines are online, or send an SASE.

THE NEW LETTERS WEEKEND WRITERS CONFERENCE

University of Missouri-Kansas City, 5101 Rock hill Rd., Kansas City, MO 64110-2499. (816)235-1168.

Fax: (816)235-2611. **E-mail:** newletters@umkc.edu. **Website:** http://cas.umkc.edu/ce/. **Contact:** Robert Stewart, director. Estab. 1970s (as The Longboat Key Writers Conference).

COSTS Participants may choose to attend as a noncredit student or they may attend for 1 hour of college credit from the University of Missouri-Kansas City. Conference registration includes Friday evening reception and keynote speaker, Saturday and Sunday continental breakfast and lunch.

ACCOMMODATIONS Registrants are responsible for their own transportation, but information on area accommodations is available.

ADDITIONAL INFORMATION Those registering for college credit are required to submit a ms in advance. Ms reading and critique are included in the credit fee. Those attending the conference for noncredit also have the option of having their ms critiqued for an additional fee. Brochures are available for a SASE after March. Accepts inquiries by e-mail and fax.

NIMROD ANNUAL WRITERS' WORKSHOP

800 S. Tucker Dr., Tulsa, OK 74104. (918)631-3080. **E-mail:** nimrod@utulsa.edu. **Website:** www.utulsa.edu/nimrod. **Contact:** Eilis O'Neal, managing editor. Estab. 1978.

COSTS Approximately $50. Lunch provided. Scholarships available for students.

ADDITIONAL INFORMATION *Nimrod International Journal* sponsors *Nimrod* Literary Awards: The Katherine Anne Porter Prize for fiction and The Pablo Neruda Prize for poetry. Poetry and fiction prizes: $2,000 each and publication (1st prize); $1,000 each and publication (2nd prize). Deadline: must be postmarked no later than April 30.

ROCKY MOUNTAIN FICTION WRITERS COLORADO GOLD

Rocky Mountain Fiction Writers, P.O. Box 735, Confier, CO 80433. **E-mail:** conference@rmfw.org. **Website:** www.rmfw.org. Estab. 1982. Next event: September 20-22, 2013.

COSTS Available online.

ACCOMMODATIONS Special rates will be available at conference hotel.

ADDITIONAL INFORMATION Editor-conducted workshops are limited to 8 participants for critique, with auditing available. Pitch appointments available at no charge. Friday morning master classes available.

New for 2013: Writers' retreat available immediately following conference; space is limited.

SCIENCE FICTION WRITERS WORKSHOP

English Department/University of Kansas, Wesoce Hall, 1445 Jayhawk Blvd., Room 3001, Lawrence, KS 66045-7590. (785)864-2508. **E-mail:** cmckit@ku.edu. **Website:** www.sfcenter.ku.edu/SFworkshop.htm. Estab. 1985.

COSTS $500, exclusive of meals and housing.

ACCOMMODATIONS Housing information is available. Several airport shuttle services offer reasonable transportation from the Kansas City International Airport to Lawrence.

ADDITIONAL INFORMATION Admission to the workshop is by submission of an acceptable story, usually by May. Two additional stories are submitted by the middle of June. These 3 stories are distributed to other participants for critiquing and are the basis for the first week of the workshop. One story is rewritten for the second week, when students also work with guest authors. See website for guidelines. This workshop is intended for writers who have just started to sell their work or need that extra bit of understanding or skill to become a published writer.

STEAMBOAT SPRINGS WRITERS GROUP

P.O. Box 774284, Steamboat Springs, CO 80477. (970)879-8079. **E-mail:** susan@steamboatwriters.com. **Website:** www.steamboatwriters.com. **Contact:** Susan de Wardt, director. Estab. 1982.

COSTS $50 before May 25, $60 after. Fee covers all seminars and luncheon.

ACCOMMODATIONS Lodging available at Steamboat Resorts.

ADDITIONAL INFORMATION Optional dinner and activities during evening preceding conference. Accepts inquiries by e-mail, phone, mail.

⊕ STORY WEAVERS CONFERENCE

Oklahoma Writer's Federation, (405)682-6000. **E-mail:** president@owfi.org. **Website:** www.OWFI.org. **Contact:** Linda Apple, president. Last event held May 2-4, 2013.

⊙ "The theme of our conference is to create good stories with strong bones. We will be exploring cultural writing and cultural sensitivity in writing. This year we will also be looking at the cutting edge of publishing and the options it is producing."

COSTS Cost is $150 before March 15. $175 after March 15 (2013 cost). Cost includes awards banquet and famous author banquet.

ACCOMMODATIONS The site is at the Embassy Suite using their meeting halls. There are very few stairs and the rooms are close together for easy access.

ADDITIONAL INFORMATION "We have 20 speakers, five agents, and nine publisher/editors. For a full list and bios, please see website."

SUMMER WRITING PROGRAM

Naropa University, 2130 Arapahoe Ave., Boulder, CO 80302. (303)245-4600. **Fax:** (303)546-5287. **E-mail:** swpr@naropa.edu. **Website:** www.naropa.edu/swp. **Contact:** Kyle Pivarnik, administrative coordinator. Estab. 1974.

COSTS In 2013: $500/week, $2,000 for all 4 weeks (noncredit students).

ACCOMMODATIONS Housing is available at Snow Lion Apartments. Additional info is available on the housing website: www.naropa.edu/student-life/housing/index.php.

ADDITIONAL INFORMATION Writers can elect to take the Summer Writing Program for noncredit, graduate, or undergraduate credit. The registration procedure varies, so consider whether or not you'll be taking the SWP for academic credit. All participants can elect to take any combination of the first, second, third, and/or fourth weeks. To request a catalog of upcoming program or to find additional information, visit www.naropa.edu/swp. Naropa University also welcomes participants with disabilities. Contact Andrea Rexilius at (303)546-5296 or arexilius@naropa.edu before May 15 to inquire about accessibility and disability accommodations needed to participate fully in this event.

TAOS SUMMER WRITERS' CONFERENCE

Department of English Language and Literature, MSC 03 2170, 1 University of New Mexico, Albuquerque, NM 87131-0001. (505)277-5572. **Fax:** (505)277-2950. **E-mail:** taosconf@unm.edu. **Website:** www.unm.edu/~taosconf. **Contact:** Sharon Oard Warner. Estab. 1999.

COSTS Weeklong workshop registrations are $650.

ACCOMMODATIONS Held at the Sagebrush Inn and Conference Center.

TONY HILLERMAN WRITER'S CONFERENCE

1063 Willow Way, Santa FE, NM 87505. (505)471-1565. **E-mail:** wordharvest@wordharvest.com. **Website:** www.wordharvest.com. **Contact:** Jean Schaumberg, co-director. Estab. 2004.

COSTS Previous year's costs: $395 per registration.

ACCOMMODATIONS Hilton Santa Fe Historic Plaza offers $119 single or double occupancy. November 6-10. Book online with the hotel.

ADDITIONAL INFORMATION Sponsors a $10,000 first mystery novel contest with St. Martin's Press. Brochures available in July for SASE, by phone, e-mail, and on website. Accepts inquiries by SASE, phone, e-mail. Deadline for the Hillerman Mystery Competition is June 1.

WRITING FOR THE SOUL

Jerry B. Jenkins Christian Writers Guild, 5525 N. Union Blvd., Suite 101, Colorado Springs, CO 80918. (866)495-5177. **Fax:** (719)495-5181. **E-mail:** contactus@christianwritersguild.com. **Website:** www.christianwritersguild.com/conference.

COSTS See website for pricing.

ACCOMMODATIONS The Broadmoor in Colorado Springs.

THE HELENE WURLITZER FOUNDATION

P.O. Box 1891, Taos, NM 87571. (575)758-2413. **Fax:** (575)758-2559. **E-mail:** hwf@taosnet.com. **Website:** www.wurlitzerfoundation.org. **Contact:** Michael A. Knight, executive director. Estab. 1953. Residence duration: 3 months.

ACCOMMODATIONS "Provides individual housing in fully furnished studio/houses (casitas), rent-and utility-free. Artists are responsible for transportation to and from Taos, their meals, and the materials for their work. Bicycles are provided upon request."

WEST

BLOCKBUSTER PLOT INTENSIVE WRITING WORKSHOPS (SANTA CRUZ)

Santa Cruz, CA **E-mail:** contact@blockbusterplots.com. **Website:** www.blockbusterplots.com. **Contact:** Martha Alderson M.A. (also known as the Plot Whisperer), instructor. Estab. 2000.

COSTS $95 per day.

ACCOMMODATIONS Provides list of area hotels and lodging options.

ADDITIONAL INFORMATION Brochures available by e-mail or on website. Accepts inquiries by e-mail.

CALIFORNIA CRIME WRITERS CONFERENCE

Pasadena, CA. **E-mail:** sistersincrimela@gmail.com. **Website:** www.ccwconference.org. Estab. 1995. Co-sponsored by Sisters in Crime/Los Angeles and the Southern California Chapter of Mystery Writers of America. Last event held June 22-23, 2013. "A weekend of outstanding workshops geared to the needs of both emerging and established mystery writers."

ADDITIONAL INFORMATION Conference information is available at www.ccwconference.org.

LAS VEGAS WRITERS CONFERENCE

Henderson Writers' Group, 614 Mosswood Dr., Henderson, NV 89015. (702)564-2488; or, toll-free, (866)869-7842. **E-mail:** marga614@mysticpublishers.com. **Website:** www.lasvegaswritersconference.com.

COSTS $400 before December 31, $450 until conference, and $500 at the door. 1day registration is $275.

ADDITIONAL INFORMATION Sponsors contest. Agents and editors participate in conference.

LEAGUE OF UTAH WRITERS' ANNUAL WRITER'S CONFERENCE

Dianne Hardy, League of Utah Writers, 420 W. 750 N., Logan, UT 84321. **E-mail:** writerscache435@gmail.com. **Website:** www.luwriters.org/index.html. **Contact:** Tim Keller, president; Irene Hastings, president-elect; Caroll Shreeve, secretary.

MENDOCINO COAST WRITERS CONFERENCE

1211 Del Mar Dr., Fort Bragg, CA 95437. (707)937-9983. **E-mail:** info@mcwc.org. **Website:** www.mcwc.org. Estab. 1988.

COSTS $525+ (includes panels, meals, 2 socials with guest readers, 4 public events, 3 morning intensive workshops in 1 of 6 subjects, and a variety of afternoon panels and lectures).

ACCOMMODATIONS Information on overnight accommodations is made available.

ADDITIONAL INFORMATION Emphasis is on writers who are also good teachers. Registration opens March 15. Send inquiries via e-mail.

⊙ MOUNT HERMON CHRISTIAN WRITERS CONFERENCE

P.O. Box 413, Mount Hermon, CA 95041. **E-mail:** info@mounthermon.org. **Website:** mounthermon .org. Estab. 1970.

COSTS Registration fees include tuition, all major morning sessions, keynote sessions, and refreshment breaks. Room and board varies depending on choice of housing options. Costs vary from $617 to $1,565 based on housing rates.

ACCOMMODATIONS Registrants stay in hotel-style accommodations. Meals are buffet style, with faculty joining registrants. See website for cost updates.

ADDITIONAL INFORMATION "The residential nature of our conference makes this a unique setting for one-on-one interaction with faculty/staff. There is also a decided inspirational flavor to the conference, and general sessions with well-known speakers are a highlight. Registrants may submit 2 works for critique in advance of the conference, then have personal interviews with critiquers during the conference. All conference information is online by December 1 of each year. Send inquiries via e-mail. Tapes of past conferences are also available online."

NAPA VALLEY WRITERS' CONFERENCE

Napa Valley College, 1088 College Ave., St. Helena, CA 94574. (707)967-2900. **Website:** www.napawrit ersconference.org. **Contact:** John Leggett and Anne Evans, program directors. Estab. 1981.

COSTS Total participation fee is $900.

ADDITIONAL INFORMATION The conference is held at the Upper Valley Campus of Napa Valley College, located in the heart of California's Wine Country. During the conference week, attendees' meals are provided by the Napa Valley Cooking School, which offers high-quality, intensive training for aspiring chefs.

PACIFIC COAST CHILDREN'S WRITERS WHOLE-NOVEL WORKSHOP

P.O. Box 244, Aptos, CA 95001. **Website:** www.child renswritersworkshop.com. Estab. 2003.

PIMA WRITERS' WORKSHOP

Pima College, 2202 W. Anklam Rd., Tucson, AZ 85709. (520)206-6084. **Fax:** (520)206-6020. **E-mail:** mfiles@pima.edu. **Contact:** Meg Files, director.

SAN DIEGO STATE UNIVERSITY WRITERS' CONFERENCE

SDSU College of Extended Studies, 5250 Campanile Dr., San Diego State University, San Diego, CA 92182-1920. (619)594-2517. **Fax:** (619)594-8566. **E-mail:** sd suwritersconference@mail.sdsu.edu. **Website:** ces .sdsu.edu/writers. Estab. 1984.

COSTS Approximately $365-485

ACCOMMODATIONS Attendees must make their own travel arrangements.

SAN FRANCISCO WRITERS CONFERENCE

1029 Jones St., San Francisco, CA 94109. (415)673-0939. **Fax:** (415)673-0367. **E-mail:** Barabara@sfwrit ers.org. **Website:** sfwriters.org. **Contact:** Barbara Santos, marketing director. Estab. 2003.

COSTS Early price (until September) is $575. Check the website for pricing on later dates.

ACCOMMODATIONS The Intercontinental Mark Hopkins Hotel is a historic landmark at the top of Nob Hill in San Francisco. The hotel is located so that everyone arriving at the Oakland or San Francisco airport can take BART to either the Embarcadero or Powell Street exits, then walk or take a cable car or taxi directly to the hotel.

ADDITIONAL INFORMATION "Present yourself in a professional manner and the contact you will make will be invaluable to your writing career. Brochures and registration are online."

ACCOMMODATIONS "The conference will be in meeting rooms at the Denver Marriott City Place."

SANTA BARBARA WRITERS CONFERENCE

27 W. Anapamu St., Suite 305, Santa Barbara, CA 93101. (805)568-1516. **E-mail:** info@sbwriters.com. **Website:** www.sbwriters.com. Estab. 1972.

COSTS Conference registration is $550 on or before March 16 and $625 after March 16.

ACCOMMODATIONS Hyatt Santa Barbara.

ADDITIONAL INFORMATION Register online or contact for brochure and registration forms.

SCBWI—VENTURA/SANTA BARBARA; FALL CONFERENCE

Simi Valley, CA 93094-1389. **E-mail:** alexisinca@aol .com. **Website:** www.scbwicencal.org. **Contact:** Alexis O'Neill, regional advisor. Estab. 1971.

SCBWI WINTER CONFERENCE ON WRITING AND ILLUSTRATING FOR CHILDREN

8271 Beverly Blvd., Los Angeles, CA 90048. (323)782-1010. **Fax:** (323)782-1892. **E-mail:** scbwi@scbwi.org. **Website:** www.scbwi.org. **Contact:** Stephen Mooser. Estab. 2000.

COSTS See website for current cost and conference information.

ADDITIONAL INFORMATION SCBWI also holds an annual summer conference in August in Los Angeles. See the listing in the West section or visit website for details.

⊙ SOCIETY OF CHILDREN'S BOOK WRITERS & ILLUSTRATORS ANNUAL SUMMER CONFERENCE ON WRITING AND ILLUSTRATING FOR CHILDREN

8271 Beverly Blvd., Los Angeles, CA 90048-4515. (323)782-1010. **Fax:** (323)782-1892. **E-mail:** scbwi@scbwi.org. **Website:** www.scbwi.org. Estab. 1972.

COSTS Approximately $450 (does not include hotel room).

ACCOMMODATIONS Information on overnight accommodations is made available.

ADDITIONAL INFORMATION Ms and illustration critiques are available. Brochure/guidelines are available in June online or for SASE.

TMCC WRITERS' CONFERENCE

Truckee Meadows Community College, 5270 Neil Rd., Reno, NV 89502. (775)829-9010. **Fax:** (775)829-9032. **E-mail:** wdce@tmcc.edu. **Website:** wdce.tmcc.edu. Estab. 1991.

COSTS $119 for a full-day seminar; $32 for a 10-minute one-on-one appointment with an agent or editor.

ACCOMMODATIONS The Silver Legacy, in downtown Reno, offers a special rate and shuttle service to the Reno/Tahoe International Airport, which is less than 20 minutes away.

ADDITIONAL INFORMATION "The conference is open to all writers, regardless of their level of experience. Brochures are available online and mailed in January. Send inquiries via e-mail."

UCLA EXTENSION WRITERS' PROGRAM

10995 Le Conte Ave., #440, Los Angeles, CA 90024. (310)825-9415 or (800)388-UCLA. **Fax:** (310)206-7382. **E-mail:** writers@uclaextension.edu. **Website:** www.uclaextension.org/writers. Estab. 1891. **Contact:** Cindy Lieberman, program manager. Courses held year-round with 1-day or intensive weekend workshops to 12-week courses. Writers Studio held in February. 9-month master classes are also offered every fall. "The diverse offerings span introductory seminars to professional novel and script completion workshops. The annual Writers Studio and a number of 1-, 2- and 4-day intensive workshops are popular with out-of-town students due to their specific focus and the chance to work with industry professionals. The most comprehensive and diverse continuing education writing program in the country, offering over 550 courses a year, including screenwriting, fiction, writing for the youth market, poetry, nonfiction, playwriting and publishing. Adult learners in the UCLA Extension Writers' Program study with professional screenwriters, fiction writers, playwrights, poets, and nonfiction writers, who bring practical experience, theoretical knowledge and a wide variety of teaching styles and philosophies to their classes." **Site:** Courses are offered in Los Angeles on the UCLA campus, in the 1010 Westwood Center in Westwood Village, at the Figueroa Courtyard in downtown Los Angeles, as well as online.

COSTS Depends on length of the course.

ACCOMMODATIONS Students make their own arrangements. Out-of-town students are encouraged to take online courses.

ADDITIONAL INFORMATION Some advanced-level classes have ms submittal requirements; see the UCLA Extension catalog or see website.

NORTHWEST

ASSOCIATION OF WRITERS & WRITING PROGRAMS ANNUAL CONFERENCE

Association of Writers & Writing Programs, George Mason University, 4400 University Drive, MSN 1E3, Fairfax, VA 22030-4444. (703)993-4317. **Fax:** (703)993-4302. **E-mail:** conference@awpwriter.org. **Website:** www.awpwriter.org. **Contact:** Anne Le, conference coordinator. Estab. 1992.

ADDITIONAL INFORMATION Upcoming conference locations include Seattle (February 26-March 1, 2014), Minneapolis (April 8-11, 2015), Los Angeles (March 30-April 2, 2016), and Washington, D.C. (February 8-11, 2017).

JACKSON HOLE WRITERS CONFERENCE

PO Box 1974, Jackson, WY 83001. (307)413-3332. E-mail: nicole@jacksonholewritersconference.com. Website: jacksonholewritersconference.com. Estab. 1991.

COSTS $365 if registered by May 12. Accompanying teen writer: $175. Pre-conference writing workshop: $150.

ADDITIONAL INFORMATION Held at the Center for the Arts in Jackson, Wyoming and online.

NORWESCON

100 Andover Park W. PMB 150-165, Tukwila, WA 98188-2828. (425)243-4692. Fax: (520)244-0142. E-mail: info@norwescon.org. Website: www.norwescon.org. Estab. 1978.

ACCOMMODATIONS Conference is held at the Doubletree Hotel Seattle Airport.

ADDITIONAL INFORMATION Brochures are available online or for a SASE. Send inquiries via e-mail.

SITKA CENTER FOR ART AND ECOLOGY

56605 Sitka Dr., Otis, OR 97368. (541)994-5485. Fax: (541)994-8024. E-mail: info@sitkacenter.org. Website: www.sitkacenter.org. Contact: Caroline Brooks, program manager. Estab. 1970.

COSTS Workshops are generally $65-500; they do not include meals or lodging.

ACCOMMODATIONS Does not offer overnight accommodations. Provides a list of area hotels or lodging options.

ADDITIONAL INFORMATION Brochure available in February of each year; request a copy by e-mail or phone, or visit website for listing. Accepts inquiries in-person or by e-mail, phone, fax.

SOUTH COAST WRITERS CONFERENCE

Southwestern Oregon Community College, P.O. Box 590, 29392 Ellensburg Ave., Gold Beach, OR 97444. (541)247-2741. Fax: (541)247-6247. E-mail: scwc@socc.edu. Website: www.socc.edu/scwriters. Estab. 1996.

ADDITIONAL INFORMATION See website for cost and additional details.

WRITE ON THE SOUND WRITERS' CONFERENCE

Edmonds Arts Commission, 700 Main St., Edmonds, WA 98020. (425)771-0228. Fax: (425)771-0253. E-mail: sarah.cocker@edmondswa.gov. Website: www.writeonthesound.com. Estab. 1985.

COSTS See website for more information to view costs.

ADDITIONAL INFORMATION Brochures are available in July. Accepts inquiries via phone, e-mail, and fax.

CANADA

BLOODY WORDS MYSTERY CONFERENCE

E-mail: chair@bloodywords.com. Website: www.bloodywords.com. Contact: Cheryl Freedman, chair. Estab. 1999.

COSTS $195 (includes the banquet and all panels, readings, dealers' room, and workshop).

ACCOMMODATIONS Offers block of rooms in hotel; list of optional lodging available. Check website for details.

ADDITIONAL INFORMATION Sponsors short mystery story contest—5,000 word limit; judges are experienced editors of anthologies; fee is $5 (entrants must be registered). Also sponsors The Bony Blithe Award for light mysteries; see website for details. Conference information is available now. For brochure, visit website. Accepts inquiries by e-mail and phone. Agents and editors participate in conference.

BOOMING GROUND ONLINE WRITERS STUDIO

Buch E-462, 1866 Main Mall, UBC, Vancouver, BC V6T 1Z1 Canada. Fax: (604)648-8848. E-mail: contact@boomingground.com. Website: www.boomingground.com. Contact: Robin Evans, director.

CLARION WEST WRITERS WORKSHOP

P.O. Box 31264, Seattle, WA 98103-1264. (206)322-9083. E-mail: info@clarionwest.org. Website: www.clarionwest.org. Contact: Leslie Howle, workshop director. "The 2013 Clarion West Six-Week Writers Workshop was held June 23-August 2, 2013, in Seattle, Washington."

COSTS $3,600 (for tuition, housing, most meals). Limited scholarships are available based on financial need.

ACCOMMODATIONS Students stay on-site in workshop housing at one of the University of Washington's sorority houses. "Students write their own stories every week while preparing critiques of all the other students' work for classroom sessions. This gives participants a more focused, professional approach to their writing. The core of the workshop remains speculative fiction, and short stories (not novels) are the focus." Conference information available in fall. For brochure/guidelines send SASE, visit website, e-mail or call. Accepts inquiries by e-mail, phone, SASE. Limited scholarships are available, based on financial need. Students must submit 20-30 pages of ms with 4-page biography and $40 fee ($30, if received prior to February 10) for applications sent by mail or e-mail to qualify for admission.

ADDITIONAL INFORMATION This is a critique-based workshop. Students are encouraged to write a story every week; the critique of student material produced at the workshop forms the principal activity of the workshop. Students and instructors critique mss as a group. Conference guidelines are available for a SASE. Visit the website for updates and complete details.

SAGE HILL WRITING EXPERIENCE

Box 1731, Saskatoonm, SK S7K 3S1 Canada. (306)652-7395. **E-mail:** sage.hill@sasktel.net. **Website:** sage hillwriting.ca. **Contact:** Philip Adams, executive director.

COSTS Summer program: $1,295 (includes instruction, accommodation, meals). Fall Poetry Colloquium: $1,495. Scholarships and bursaries are available.

ACCOMMODATIONS Located at Lumsden, 45 kilometers outside Regina.

ADDITIONAL INFORMATION For Introduction to Creative Writing, send a 5-page sample of your writing or a statement of your interest in creative writing and a list of courses taken. For workshop and colloquium programs, send a résumé of your writing career and a 12-page sample of your work, plus 5 pages of published work. Guidelines are available for SASE. Inquire via e-mail or fax.

SASKATCHEWAN FESTIVAL OF WORDS

217 Main St. N., Moose Jaw SK S6J 0W1 Canada. **Website:** www.festivalofwords.com. Estab. 1997.

ACCOMMODATIONS Information available at www.templegardens.sk.ca, campgrounds, and bed-and-breakfast establishments. Complete information about festival presenters, events, costs, and schedule also available on website.

THE SCHOOL FOR WRITERS SUMMER WORKSHOP

The Humber School for Writers, Humber Institute of Technology & Advanced Learning, 3199 Lake Shore Blvd. W., Toronto, ON M8V 1K8 Canada. (416)675-6622. **E-mail:** antanas.sileika@humber.ca; hilary.higgins@humber.ca. **Website:** www.creativeandper formingarts.humber.ca/content/writers.html.

COSTS Around $800 (in 2013). Some limited scholarships are available.

ACCOMMODATIONS Nearby hotels are available.

ADDITIONAL INFORMATION Accepts inquiries by e-mail, phone, and fax.

THE WRITERS RETREATS' NETWORK

15 Canusa St., Stanstead, QC J0B 3E5 Canada. **Website:** www.writersretreat.com.

INTERNATIONAL

ABROAD WRITERS CONFERENCES

17363 Sutter Creek Rd., Sutter Creek, CA 95685. (209)296-4050. **E-mail:** abroadwriters@yahoo.com. **Website:** www.abroad-crwf.com/index.html. Next event held December 9-16, 2013 at Lismore Castle, Ireland.

COSTS Prices start at $2,750. Discounts and upgrades may apply. Participants must apply to program no later than 3 months before departure. To secure a place you must send in a deposit of $1,000. Balance must be paid in full 12 weeks before departure. See website for pricing details.

ADDITIONAL INFORMATION Agents participate in conference. Application is online at website.

ART WORKSHOPS IN GUATEMALA

4758 Lyndale Ave. S., Minneapolis, MN 55419-5304. (612)825-0747. **E-mail:** info@artguat.org. **Website:** www.artguat.org. **Contact:** Liza Fourre, director. Estab. 1995. "Art Workshops in Guatemala strives to provide a new and renewing experience for creative souls. Through contact with a world so different from our own, we expand our horizons—not only artistically—but also in many other ways. Our hope is that our participants will leave Guatemala with a greater understanding for other ways of life and a renewed enthusiasm and appreciation for their own."

COSTS See website. Includes tuition, lodging, breakfast, ground transportation.

ACCOMMODATIONS All transportation and accommodations included in price of conference.
ADDITIONAL INFORMATION Conference information available. For brochure/guidelines visit website, e-mail, or call. Accepts inquiries by e-mail, phone.

● INTERNATIONAL CREATIVE WRITING CAMP

111-11th Ave.SW, Minot, ND 58701-6081. (701)838-8472. **Fax:** (701)838-1351. **E-mail:** info@internation almusiccamp.com. **Website:** www.internationalmu siccamp.com. **Contact:** Joseph Alme, interim director.

COSTS Before May 1, $375; after May 1—$390. Write for more information.

● WINCHESTER WRITERS' CONFERENCE, FESTIVAL AND BOOKFAIR, AND IN-DEPTH WRITING WORKSHOPS

University of Winchester, Winchester Hampshire WA S022 4NR United Kingdom. 44 (0) 1962 827238. **E-mail:** Barbara.Large@winchester.ac.uk. **Website:** www.writersconference.co.uk. **Contact:** Barbara Large.

PUBLISHERS & THEIR IMPRINTS

The publishing world is in constant transition. With all the buying, selling, reorganizing, consolidating, and dissolving, it's hard to keep publishers and their imprints straight. To help make sense of these changes, here's a breakdown of major publishers (and their divisions)—who owns whom and which imprints are under each company umbrella. Keep in mind that this information changes frequently. The website of each publisher is provided to help you keep an eye on this ever-evolving business.

HACHETTE BOOK GROUP USA

www.hachettebookgroup.com

CENTER STREET

FAITHWORDS

   Jericho Books

GRAND CENTRAL PUBLISHING

   5 Spot

   Business Plus

   Forever

   Forever Yours

   Grand Central Life & Style

   Twelve

   Vision

HACHETTE DIGITAL MEDIA

HACHETTE AUDIO

LITTLE, BROWN AND COMPANY

   Back Bay Books

   Mulholland Books

   Reagan Arthur Books

LITTLE, BROWN BOOKS FOR YOUNG READERS

   LB Kids

   Poppy

ORBIT

YEN PRESS

HARLEQUIN ENTERPRISES

www.harlequin.com

CARINA PRESS

HARLEQUIN

Harlequin American Romance

Harlequin Blaze

Harlequin Desire

Harlequin Heartwarming

Harlequin Historical

Harlequin Intrigue

Harlequin Kimani Romance

Harlequin KISS

Harlequin Medical Romance

Harlequin Nocturne

Harlequin Presents

Harlequin Romance

Harlequin Romance Suspense

Harlequin Special Edition

Harlequin Superromance

Love Inspired

Love Inspired Historical

Love Inspired Suspense

HARLEQUIN HQN

HARLEQUIN KIMANI ARABESQUE

HARLEQUIN KIMANI TRU

HARLEQUIN KIMANI PRESS

HARLEQUIN TEEN

HARLEQUIN LUNA

HARLEQUIN MIRA

SILHOUETTE SPECIAL RELEASES

Silhouette Desire

Silhouette Romantic Suspense

Silhouette Special Edition

SPICE

Spice Briefs (e-book only)

WORLDWIDE LIBRARY WORLDWIDE MYSTERY

HARLEQUIN CANADA

HARLEQUIN U.K.

Mills & Boon

HARPERCOLLINS

www.harpercollins.com

HARPERCOLLINS GENERAL BOOKS GROUP

Amistad

Avon

    Avon Impulse

    Avon Inspire

    Avon Red

Ecco

Fourth Estate

Harper

Harper Business

Harper Design

Harper Luxe

Harper Paperbacks

Harper Perennial

Harper Perennial Modern Classics

Harper Voyager

HarperAudio

HarperOne

ItBooks

William Morrow

William Morrow Trade Paperbacks

HARPERCOLLINS CHILDREN'S BOOKS

Amistad

Balzer + Bray

Collins

Greenwillow Books

HarperChildren's Audio

HarperCollins Children's Books

HarperFestival

HarperTeen

Katherine Tegen Books

Rayo

Walden Pond Press

HARPERCOLLINS U.K.

4th Estate

Avon

Blue Door

Collins Education

Collins Geo

Collins Language

Harper

Harper Audio

Harper NonFiction

HarperCollins Children's Books

The Friday Project

Voyager

William Collins

HARPERCOLLINS CANADA

Amistad

Avon Impulse

Avon Romance

Broadside Books

Ecco

Greenwillow

Harper Business

Harper Design

Harper Perennial

Harper Voyager

HarperAudio

HarperCollins Children's

HarperOne

It Books

Katherine Tegen Books

Morrow Cookbooks

Walden Pond Press

William Morrow Paperbacks

HARPERCOLLINS AUSTRALIA

HARPERCOLLINS INDIA

HARPERCOLLINS NEW ZEALAND

ZONDERVAN

Zonderkidz

MACMILLAN US (HOLTZBRINCK)

http://us.macmillan.com

FARRAR, STRAUS AND GIROUX

North Point Press

Hill and Wang

Faber and Faber, Inc.

Sarah Crichton Books

FSG Originals

Scientific American

FIRST SECOND

HENRY HOLT & CO.

Henry Holt Books for Young Readers

Holt Paperbacks

Metropolitan Books

Times

MACMILLAN AUDIO

MACMILLAN CHILDREN'S

FSG Books for Young Readers

Feiwel & Friends

Holt Books for Young Readers

Kingfisher

Roaring Brook

Priddy Books

Starscape/Tor Teen

Square Fish

Young Listeners

Macmillan Children's Publishing Group

PICADOR

QUICK AND DIRTY TIPS

ST. MARTIN'S PRESS
Griffin
Minotaur
St. Martin's Paperbacks
Let's Go
Thomas Dunne Books
Truman Talley Books

TOR/FORGE BOOKS
Forge
Paranormal Romance
Orb
Tor/Seven Seas

PENGUIN GROUP (USA), INC.

www.penguingroup.com

PENGUIN ADULT DIVISION
Ace Books
Alpha Books
Amy Einhorn Books/Putnam
Avery
Berkley Books
Blue Rider Press
C.A. Press
Current
Dutton Books
Gotham Books
G.P. Putnam's Sons
HP Books
Hudson Street Press
Jeremy P. Tarcher
Jove
NAL
Pamela Dorman Books
Penguin

Penguin Press
Perigree
Plume
Portfolio
Prentice Hall Press
Riverhead
Sentinel
Tarcher
The Viking Press

YOUNG READERS DIVISION
Dial Books for Young Readers
Dutton Children's Books
Firebird
Frederick Warne
G.P. Putnam's Sons Books for Young Readers
Grosset & Dunlap
Nancy Paulsen Books
Philomel
Prentice Hall Press
Price Stern Sloan
Puffin Books
Razorbill
Speak
Viking Books for Young Readers

RANDOM HOUSE, INC. (BERTELSMANN)

www.randomhouse.com

CROWN PUBLISHING GROUP
Amphoto Books
Back Stage Books
Billboard Books
Broadway Business
Clarkson Potter
Crown
Crown Archetype

Crown Business

Crown Forum

Doubleday Religion

Harmony Books

Image Books

Potter Craft

Potter Style

Ten Speed Press

Three Rivers Press

Waterbrook Multnomah

Watson-Guptill

KNOPF DOUBLEDAY PUBLISHING GROUP

Alfred A. Knopf

Anchor Books

Doubleday

Everyman's Library

Nan A. Talese

Pantheon Books

Schocken Books

Vintage

RANDOM HOUSE PUBLISHING GROUP

Ballantine Books

Bantam

Del Rey/Lucas Books

Del Rey/Manga

Delacorte

Dell

The Dial Press

The Modern Library

One World

Presidio Press

Random House Trade Group

Random House Trade Paperbacks

Spectra

Spiegel and Grau

Triumph Books

Villard Books

RANDOM HOUSE CHILDREN'S BOOKS

Kids@Random (RH Children's Books)

Golden Books

Princeton Review

Sylvan Learning

RANDOM HOUSE DIGITAL PUBLISHING GROUP

Books on Tape

Fodor's Travel

Living Language

Listening Library

Random House Audio

RH Large Print

RANDOM HOUSE INTERNATIONAL

Random House Australia

Random House of Canada

The Random House Group (UK)

Random House India

Random House Mondadori (Argentina)

Random House Mondadori (Chile)

Random House Mondadori (Columbia)

Random House Mondadori (Mexico)

Random House Mondadori (Spain)

Random House Mondadori (Uruguay)

Random House Mondadori (Venezuela)

Random House New Zealand

Random House Struik (South Africa)

Transworld Ireland

SIMON & SCHUSTER

www.simonandschuster.com

SIMON & SCHUSTER ADULT PUBLISHING

Atria Books/Beyond Words

Folger Shakespeare Library

Free Press

Gallery Books

Howard Books

Pocket Books

Scribner

Simon & Schuster

Threshold Editions

Touchstone

SIMON & SCHUSTER CHILDREN'S PUBLISHING

Aladdin

Atheneum Books for Young Readers

Bench Lane Books

Little Simon

Margaret K. McElderry Books

Paula Wiseman Books

Simon & Schuster Books for Young Readers

Simon Pulse

Simon Spotlight

SIMON & SCHUSTER AUDIO

Simon & Schuster Audio

Pimsleur

SIMON & SCHUSTER INTERNATIONAL

Simon & Schuster Australia

Simon & Schuster Canada

Simon & Schuster UK

GLOSSARY

ADVANCE. Payment by a publisher to an author prior to the publication of a book, to be deducted from the author's future royalties.

ADVENTURE STORY. A genre of fiction in which action is the key element, overshadowing characters, theme, and setting. The conflict in an adventure story is often man against nature. A secondary plot that reinforces this kind of conflict is sometimes included.

ALL RIGHTS. The rights contracted to a publisher permitting a manuscript's use anywhere and in any form, including movie and book club sales, without additional payment to the writer.

AMATEUR SLEUTH. The character in a mystery, usually the protagonist, who does the detection but is not a professional private investigator or police detective.

ANTHOLOGY. A collection of selected writings by various authors.

ASSOCIATION OF AUTHORS' REPRESENTATIVES (AAR). An organization for literary agents committed to maintaining excellence in literary representation.

AUCTION. Publishers sometimes bid against each other for the acquisition of a manuscript that has excellent sales prospects.

BACKLIST. A publisher's books not published during the current season but still in print.

BIOGRAPHICAL NOVEL. A life story documented in history and transformed into fiction through the insight and imagination of the writer. This type of novel melds the elements of biographical research and historical truth into the framework of a novel, complete with dialogue, drama, and mood. A biographical novel resembles historical fiction, save for one aspect: Characters in a historical novel may be fabricated and then placed into an authentic setting; characters in a biographical novel have actually lived.

BOOK PRODUCER/PACKAGER. An organization that may develop a book for a publisher based upon the publisher's idea or may plan all elements of a book, from its initial concept to writing and marketing strategies, and then sell the package to a book publisher and/or movie producer.

CLIFFHANGER. Fictional event in which the reader is left in suspense at the end of a chapter or episode, so that interest in the story's outcome will be sustained.

CLIP. Sample, usually from a newspaper or magazine, of a writer's published work.

CLOAK-AND-DAGGER. A melodramatic, romantic type of fiction dealing with espionage and intrigue.

COMMERCIAL. Publishers whose concern is salability, profit, and success with a large readership.

CONTEMPORARY. Material dealing with popular current trends, themes, or topics.

CONTRIBUTOR'S COPY. Copy of an issue of a magazine or published book sent to an author whose work is included.

COPUBLISHING. An arrangement in which the author and publisher share costs and profits.

COPYEDITING. Editing a manuscript for writing style, grammar, punctuation and factual accuracy.

COPYRIGHT. The legal right to exclusive publication, sale, or distribution of a literary work.

COVER LETTER. A brief letter sent with a complete manuscript submitted to an editor.

"COZY" (OR "TEACUP") MYSTERY. Mystery usually set in a small British town, in a bygone era, featuring a somewhat genteel, intellectual protagonist.

ELECTRONIC RIGHTS. The right to publish material electronically, either in book or short story form.

ELECTRONIC SUBMISSION. A submission of material by e-mail or on computer disk.

ETHNIC FICTION. Stories whose central characters are black, Native American, Italian-American, Jewish, Appalachian, or members of some other specific cultural group.

EXPERIMENTAL FICTION. Fiction that is innovative in subject matter and style; avant-garde, non-formulaic, usually literary material.

EXPOSITION. The portion of the story line, usually the beginning, where background information about character and setting is related.

E-ZINE. A magazine that is published electronically.

FAIR USE. A provision in the copyright law that says short passages from copyrighted material may be used without infringing on the owner's rights.

FANZINE. A noncommercial, small-circulation magazine usually dealing with fantasy, horror or science-fiction literature and art.

FICTIONAL BIOGRAPHY. The biography of a real person that goes beyond the events of a person's life by being fleshed out with imagined scenes and dialogue. The writer of fictional biographies strives to make it clear that the story is, indeed, fiction and not history.

FIRST NORTH AMERICAN SERIAL RIGHTS. The right to publish material in a periodical before it appears in book form, for the first time, in the United States or Canada.

FLASH FICTION. *See* short short stories.

GALLEYS. The first typeset version of a manuscript that has not yet been divided into pages.

GENRE. A formulaic type of fiction such as romance, western, or horror.

GOTHIC. This type of category fiction dates back to the late eighteenth and early nineteenth centuries. Contemporary gothic novels are characterized by atmospheric, historical settings and feature young, beautiful women who win the favor of handsome, brooding heroes—simultaneously dealing successfully with some life-threatening menace, either natural or supernatural. Gothics rely on mystery, peril, romantic relationships, and a sense of foreboding for their strong, emotional effect on the reader. A classic early gothic novel is Emily Bronte's *Wuthering Heights.*

GRAPHIC NOVEL. A book (original or adapted) that takes the form of a long comic strip or heavily illustrated story of forty pages or more, produced in paperback. Though called a novel, these can also be works of nonfiction.

HARD-BOILED DETECTIVE NOVEL. Mystery novel featuring a private eye or police detective as the protagonist; usually involves a murder. The emphasis is on the details of the crime, and the tough, unsentimental protagonist usually takes a matter-of-fact attitude toward violence.

HARD SCIENCE FICTION. Science fiction with an emphasis on science and technology.

HIGH FANTASY. Fantasy with a medieval setting and a heavy emphasis on chivalry and the quest.

HISTORICAL FICTION. A fictional story set in a recognizable period of history. As well as telling the stories of ordinary people's lives, historical fiction may involve political or social events of the time.

HORROR. Howard Phillips (H.P.) Lovecraft, generally acknowledged to be the master of the horror tale in the twentieth century and the most important American writer of this genre since Edgar Allan Poe, maintained that "the oldest and strongest emotion of mankind is fear, and the oldest and strongest kind of fear is fear of the unknown. These facts few psychologists will dispute, and their admitted truth must establish for all time the genuineness and dignity of the weirdly horrible tale as a literary form." Lovecraft distinguishes horror literature from fiction based entirely on physical fear and the merely gruesome. It is that atmosphere—the creation of a particular sensation or emotional level—that, according to Lovecraft, is the most important element in the creation of horror literature. Contemporary writers enjoying considerable success in horror fiction include Stephen King, Robert Bloch, Peter Straub, and Dean Koontz.

HYPERTEXT FICTION. A fictional form, read electronically, which incorporates traditional elements of storytelling with a nonlinear plot line, in which the reader determines the direction of the story by opting for one of many author-supplied links.

IMPRINT. Name applied to a publisher's specific line (e.g. Owl, an imprint of Henry Holt).

INTERACTIVE FICTION. Fiction in book or computer-software format where the reader determines the path the story will take by choosing from several alternatives at the end of each chapter or episode.

INTERNATIONAL REPLY COUPON (IRC). A form purchased at a post office and enclosed with a letter or manuscript to an international publisher, to cover return postage costs.

JUVENILES, WRITING FOR. This includes works intended for an audience usually between the ages of two and eighteen. Categories of children's books are usually divided in this way: (1) picture books and storybooks (ages two to eight); (2) young readers or easy-to-read books (ages five to eight); (3) middle readers or middle grade (ages nine to eleven); (4) young adult books (ages twelve and up).

LIBEL. Written or printed words that defame, malign, or damagingly misrepresent a living person.

LITERARY AGENT. A person who acts for an author in finding a publisher or arranging contract terms on a literary project.

LITERARY FICTION. The general category of fiction that employs more sophisticated technique, driven as much or more by character evolution than action in the plot.

MAINSTREAM FICTION. Fiction that appeals to a more general reading audience, versus literary or genre fiction. Mainstream is more plot-driven than literary fiction and less formulaic than genre fiction.

MALICE DOMESTIC NOVEL. A mystery featuring a murder among family members, such as the murder of a spouse or a parent.

MANUSCRIPT. The author's unpublished copy of a work, usually typewritten, used as the basis for typesetting.

MASS MARKET PAPERBACK. Softcover book on a popular subject, usually around 4" × 7", directed to a general audience and sold in drugstores and groceries as well as in bookstores.

MIDDLE READER. Also called *middle grade*. Juvenile fiction for readers aged nine to eleven.

MS(S). Abbreviation for *manuscript(s)*.

MULTIPLE SUBMISSION. Submission of more than one short story at a time to the same editor. Do not make a multiple submission unless requested.

MYSTERY. A form of narration in which one or more elements remain unknown or unexplained until the end of the story. The modern mystery story contains elements of the serious novel: a convincing account of a character's struggle with various physical and psychological obstacles in an effort to achieve his goal, good characterization, and sound motivation.

NARRATION. The account of events in a story's plot as related by the speaker or the voice of the author.

NARRATOR. The person who tells the story, either someone involved in the action or the voice of the writer.

NEW AGE. A term including categories such as astrology, psychic phenomena, spiritual healing, UFOs, mysticism, and other aspects of the occult.

NOIR. A style of mystery involving hardboiled detectives and bleak settings.

NOM DE PLUME. French for "pen name"; a pseudonym.

NONFICTION NOVEL. A work in which real events and people are written [about] in novel form, but are not camouflaged, as they are in the roman à clef. In the nonfiction novel, reality is presented imaginatively; the writer imposes a novelistic structure on the actual events, keying sections of narrative around moments that are seen (in retrospect) as symbolic. In this way, he creates a coherence that the actual story might not have had. *The Executioner's Song*, by Norman Mailer, and *In Cold Blood*, by Truman Capote, are notable examples of the nonfiction novel.

NOVELLA (ALSO NOVELETTE). A short novel or long story, approximately 20,000–50,000 words.

#10 ENVELOPE. 4" × 9½" envelope, used for queries and other business letters.

OFFPRINT. Copy of a story taken from a magazine before it is bound.

ONETIME RIGHTS. Permission to publish a story in periodical or book form one time only.

OUTLINE. A summary of a book's contents, often in the form of chapter headings with a few sentences outlining the action of the story under each one; sometimes part of a book proposal.

OVER THE TRANSOM. A phrase referring to unsolicited manuscripts, or those that come in "over the transom."

PAYMENT ON ACCEPTANCE. Payment from the magazine or publishing house as soon as the decision to print a manuscript is made.

PAYMENT ON PUBLICATION. Payment from the publisher after a manuscript is printed.

PEN NAME. A pseudonym used to conceal a writer's real name.

PERIODICAL. A magazine or journal published at regular intervals.

PLOT. The carefully devised series of events through which the characters progress in a work of fiction.

POPULAR FICTION. Generally, a synonym for category or genre fiction; i.e., fiction intended to appeal to audiences for certain kinds of novels. Popular, or category, fiction is defined as such primarily for the convenience of publishers, editors, reviewers, and booksellers who must identify novels of different areas of interest for potential readers.

PRINT ON DEMAND (POD). Novels produced digitally one at a time, as ordered. Self-publishing through print on demand technology typically involves some fees for the author.

Some authors use POD to create a manuscript in book form to send to prospective traditional publishers.

PROOFREADING. Close reading and correction of a manuscript's typographical errors.

PROOFS. A typeset version of a manuscript used for correcting errors and making changes, often a photocopy of the galleys.

PROPOSAL. An offer to write a specific work, usually consisting of an outline of the work and one or two completed chapters.

PROTAGONIST. The principal or leading character in a literary work.

PSYCHOLOGICAL NOVEL. A narrative that emphasizes the mental and emotional aspects of its characters, focusing on motivations and mental activities rather than on exterior events. The psychological novelist is less concerned about relating what happened than about exploring why it happened. The term is most often used to describe twentieth-century works that employ techniques such as interior monologue and stream of consciousness. Two examples of contemporary psychological novels are Judith Guest's *Ordinary People* and Mary Gordon's *The Company of Women*.

PUBLIC DOMAIN. Material that either was never copyrighted or whose copyright term has expired.

PULP MAGAZINE. A periodical printed on inexpensive paper, usually containing lurid, sensational stories or articles.

QUERY. A letter written to an editor to elicit interest in a story the writer wants to submit.

READER. A person hired by a publisher to read unsolicited manuscripts.

READING FEE. An arbitrary amount of money charged by some agents and publishers to read a submitted manuscript.

REGENCY ROMANCE. A subgenre of romance, usually set in England between 1811 and 1820.

REMAINDERS. Leftover copies of an out-of-print book, sold by the publisher at a reduced price.

REPORTING TIME. The number of weeks or months it takes an editor to report back on an author's query or manuscript.

REPRINT RIGHTS. Permission to print an already published work whose rights have been sold to another magazine or book publisher.

ROMAN À CLEF. French "novel with a key." A novel that represents actual living or historical characters and events in fictionalized form.

ROMANCE NOVEL. A type of category fiction in which the love relationship between a man and a woman pervades the plot. The story is often told from the viewpoint of the heroine, who meets a man (the hero), falls in love with him, encounters a conflict that hinders their relationship, then resolves the conflict. Romance is the overriding element in this kind of story: The couple's relationship determines the plot and tone of the book.

ROYALTIES. A percentage of the retail price paid to an author for each copy of the book that is sold.

SAE. Self-addressed envelope.

SASE. Self-addressed stamped envelope.

SCIENCE FICTION (VS. FANTASY). It is generally accepted that, to be science fiction, a story must have elements of science in either the conflict or setting (usually both). Fantasy, on the other hand, rarely utilizes science, relying instead on magic, mythological and neomythological beings, and devices and outright invention for conflict and setting.

SECOND SERIAL (REPRINT) RIGHTS. Permission for the reprinting of a work in another periodical after its first publication in book or magazine form.

SELF-PUBLISHING. In this arrangement, the author keeps all income derived from the book, but he pays for its manufacturing, production, and marketing.

SERIAL RIGHTS. The rights given by an author to a publisher to print a piece in one or more periodicals.

SERIALIZED NOVEL. A book-length work of fiction published in sequential issues of a periodical.

SETTING. The environment and time period during which the action of a story takes place.

SHORT SHORT STORY. A condensed piece of fiction, usually under 1,000 words.

SIMULTANEOUS SUBMISSION. The practice of sending copies of the same manuscript to several editors or publishers at the same time. Some editors refuse to consider such submissions.

SLANT. A story's particular approach or style, designed to appeal to the readers of a specific magazine.

SLICE OF LIFE. A presentation of characters in a seemingly mundane situation that offers the reader a flash of illumination about the characters or their situation.

SLUSH PILE. A stack of unsolicited manuscripts in the editorial offices of a publisher.

SOCIAL FICTION. Fiction written with the purpose of bringing positive changes in society.

SOFT/SOCIOLOGICAL SCIENCE FICTION. Science fiction with an emphasis on society and culture versus scientific accuracy.

SPACE OPERA. Epic science fiction with an emphasis on good guys versus bad guys.

SPECULATION (OR SPEC). An editor's agreement to look at an author's manuscript with no promise to purchase.

SPECULATIVE FICTION (SPECFIC). The all-inclusive term for science fiction, fantasy, and horror.

SUBSIDIARY. An incorporated branch of a company or conglomerate (e.g. Alfred Knopf, Inc., a subsidiary of Random House, Inc.).

SUBSIDIARY RIGHTS. All rights other than book publishing rights included in a book contract, such as paperback, book club, and movie rights.

SUBSIDY PUBLISHER. A book publisher who charges the author for the cost of typesetting, printing, and promoting a book. Also called a *vanity publisher*.

SUBTERFICIAL FICTION. Innovative, challenging, nonconventional fiction in which what seems to be happening is the result of things not so easily perceived.

SUSPENSE. A genre of fiction where the plot's primary function is to build a feeling of anticipation and fear in the reader over its possible outcome.

SYNOPSIS. A brief summary of a story, novel or play. As part of a book proposal, it is a comprehensive summary condensed in a page or page and a half.

TABLOID. Publication printed on paper about half the size of a regular newspaper page (e.g. the *National Enquirer*).

TEARSHEET. Page from a magazine containing a published story.

THEME. The dominant or central idea in a literary work; its message, moral, or main thread.

THRILLER. A novel intended to arouse feelings of excitement or suspense. Works in this genre are highly sensational, usually focusing on illegal activities, international espionage, sex, and violence. A thriller is often a detective story in which the forces of good are pitted against the forces of evil in a kill-or-be-killed situation.

TRADE PAPERBACK. A softbound volume, usually around 5" × 8", published and designed for the general public, available mainly in bookstores.

TRADITIONAL FANTASY. Fantasy with an emphasis on magic, using characters with the ability to practice magic, such as wizards, witches, dragons, elves, and unicorns.

UNSOLICITED MANUSCRIPT. A story or novel manuscript that an editor did not specifically ask to see.

URBAN FANTASY. Fantasy that takes magical characters, such as elves, fairies, vampires, or wizards, and places them in modern-day settings, often in the inner city.

VANITY PUBLISHER. See subsidy publisher.

VIEWPOINT. The position or attitude of the first- or third-person narrator or multiple narrators, which determines how a story's action is seen and evaluated.

WESTERN. Genre with a setting in the West, usually between 1860 and 1890, with a formula plot about cowboys or other aspects of frontier life.

WHODUNIT. Genre dealing with murder, suspense, and the detection of criminals.

WORK-FOR-HIRE. Work that another party commissions you to do, generally for a flat fee. The creator does not own the copyright and therefore cannot sell any rights.

YOUNG ADULT. The general classification of books written for readers twelve and up.

ZINE. Often one- or two-person operations run from the home of the publisher/editor. Themes tend to be specialized, personal, experimental, and often controversial.

PROFESSIONAL ORGANIZATIONS

AGENTS' ORGANIZATIONS

ASSOCIATION OF AUTHORS' AGENTS (AAA) Rogers, Coleridge & White Ltd. 20 Powis Mews, London W11 1JN. (020)7221-3717. **E-mail:** Peters@rcwlitagency.com. **Website:** www.agentsassoc.co.uk.

ASSOCIATION OF AUTHORS' REPRESENTATIVES (AAR) 676-A 9th Ave., Suite 312, New York, NY 10036. **E-mail:** administrator@aaron line.org. **Website:** www.aar-online.org.

ASSOCIATION OF TALENT AGENTS (ATA) 9255 Sunset Blvd., Suite 930, Los Angeles, CA 90069. (310)274-0628. **Fax:** (310)274-5063. **E-mail:** rnoval@agentassociation.com. **Website:** www.agentassociation.com.

WRITERS' ORGANIZATIONS

ACADEMY OF AMERICAN POETS 75 Maiden Lane, Suite 901, New York, NY 10038. (212)274-0343. **Fax:** (212)274-9427. **E-mail:** academy@poets.org. **Website:** www.poets.org.

AMERICAN CRIME WRITERS LEAGUE (ACWL) 17367 Hilltop Ridge Dr., Eureka, MO 63205. **Website:** www.acwl.org.

AMERICAN MEDICAL WRITERS ASSOCIATION (AMWA) 30 West Gude Drive, Suite 525, Rockville, MD 20850-4347. (240)238-0940. **Fax:** (301)294-9006. **E-mail:** amwa@amwa .org. **Website:** www.amwa.org.

AMERICAN SCREENWRITERS ASSOCIATION (ASA), 269 S. Beverly Dr., Suite 2600, Beverly Hills, CA 90212-3807. (866)265-9091. **E-mail:** asa@goasa.com. **Website:** www .asascreenwriters.com.

AMERICAN TRANSLATORS ASSOCIATION (ATA) 225 Reinekers Lane, Suite 590, Alexandria, VA 22314. (703)683-6100. **Fax:** (703)683-6122. **E-mail:** ata@atanet.org. **Website:** www .atanet.org.

EDUCATION WRITERS ASSOCIATION (EWA) 3516 Connecticut Avenue NW, Washington, DC

20008. (202)452-9830. **E-mail:** ewa@ewa.org. **Website:** www.ewa.org.

GARDEN WRITERS ASSOCIATION (GWA) 7809 FM 179, Shallowater, TX 79363. (806)832.1870. **Fax:** (806)832.5244. **E-mail:** info@gardenwriters.org. **Website:** www.gardenwriters.org.

HORROR WRITERS ASSOCIATION (HWA) 244 Fifth Ave., Suite 2767, New York, NY 10001. **E-mail:** hwa@horror.org. **Website:** www.horror.org.

THE INTERNATIONAL WOMEN'S WRITING GUILD (IWWG) 317 Madison Avenue, Suite 1704, New York, NY 10017. **E-mail:** iwwgquestions@gmail.com. **Website:** www.iwwg.com.

MYSTERY WRITERS OF AMERICA (MWA) 1140 Broadway, Suite 1507, New York, NY 10001. (212)888-8171. **Fax:** (212)888-8107. **E-mail:** mwa@mysterywriters.org. **Website:** www.mysterywriters.org.

NATIONAL ASSOCIATION OF SCIENCE WRITERS (NASW) P.O. Box 7905, Berkeley, CA 94707. (510)647-9500. **E-mail:** editor@nasw.org. **Website:** www.nasw.org.

ORGANIZATION OF BLACK SCREENWRITERS (OBS) 3010 Wilshire Blvd., #269, Los Angeles, CA 90010. (323)735-2050. **Website:** www.obswriter.com.

OUTDOOR WRITERS ASSOCIATION OF AMERICA (OWAA) 615 Oak St., Ste. 201, Missoula, MT 59801. (406)728-7434. **E-mail:** info@owaa.org. **Website:** www.owaa.org.

POETRY SOCIETY OF AMERICA (PSA) 15 Gramercy Park, New York, NY 10003. (212)254-9628. **Fax:** (212)673-2352. **Website:** www.poetrysociety.org.

POETS & WRITERS 90 Broad St., Suite 2100, New York, NY 10004. (212)226-3586. **Fax:** (212)226-3963. **Website:** www.pw.org.

ROMANCE WRITERS OF AMERICA (RWA) 114615 Benfer Road, Houston, TX 77069. (832)717-5200. **Fax:** (832)717-5201. **E-mail:** info@rwa.org. **Website:** www.rwa.org.

SCIENCE FICTION AND FANTASY WRITERS OF AMERICA (SFWA) P.O. Box 3238, Enfield, MD 06083-3238. **Website:** www.sfwa.org.

SOCIETY OF AMERICAN BUSINESS EDITORS & WRITERS (SABEW) Walter Cronkite School of Journalism and Mass Communication, Arizona State University, 555 N. Central Ave., Suite 302, Phoenix, AZ 85004-1248 (602) 496-7862. **Fax:** (602)796-7041. **E-mail:** sabew@sabew.org. **Website:** www.sabew.org.

SOCIETY OF AMERICAN TRAVEL WRITERS (SATW) 11950 W. Lake Park Drive, Suite 320, Milwaukee, WI 53224-3049. (414)359-1625. **Fax:** (414)768-8001. **E-mail:** info@satw.org. **Website:** www.satw.org.

SOCIETY OF CHILDREN'S BOOK WRITERS & ILLUSTRATORS (SCBWI) 8271 Beverly Blvd., Los Angeles, CA 90048. (323)782-1010. **Fax:** (323)782-1892. **E-mail:** scbwi@scbwi.org. **Website:** www.scbwi.org.

WESTERN WRITERS OF AMERICA (WWA) **E-mail:** wwa.moulton@gmail.com. **Website:** www.westernwriters.org.

INDUSTRY ORGANIZATIONS

AMERICAN BOOKSELLERS ASSOCIATION (ABA)
333 Westchester Avenue, Suite S202, White Plains, NY 10604. (914)406-7500. **Fax:** (914)417-4013. **E-mail:** info@bookweb.org. **Website:** www.bookweb.org.

AMERICAN SOCIETY OF JOURNALISTS & AUTHORS (ASJA) Times Square, 1501 Broadway, Suite 403, New York, NY 10036. **Website:** www.asja.org.

ASSOCIATION FOR WOMEN IN COMMUNICATIONS (AWC), 3337 Duke St., Alexandria VA 22314. (703)370-7436. **Fax:** (703)342-4311. **E-mail:** info@womcom.org. **Website:** www.womcom.org.

ASSOCIATION OF AMERICAN PUBLISHERS (AAP), 71 Fifth Ave., 2nd Floor, New York NY 10003. (212)255-0200. **Fax:** (212)255-7007. Or: 50 F St. NW, Suite 400, Washington, DC 20001. (202)347-3375. **Fax:** (202)347-3690. **Website:** www.publishers.org.

THE ASSOCIATION OF WRITERS & WRITING PROGRAMS (AWP) George Mason University, 4400 University Drive, MSN 1E3, Fairfax, VA 22030. (703)993-4301. **Fax:** (703)993-4302. **E-mail:** awp@awpwriter.org. **Website:** www.awpwriter.org.

THE AUTHORS GUILD, INC., 31 E. 32nd St., 7th Floor, New York, NY 10016. (212)563-5904. **Fax:** (212)564-5363. **E-mail:** staff@authorsguild.org. **Website:** www.authorsguild.org.

CANADIAN AUTHORS ASSOCIATION (CAA) 74 Mississaga St East, Orillia, ON L3V 1V5 Canada. (705)653-0323. **E-mail:** admin@canauthors.org. **Website:** www.canauthors.org.

CHRISTIAN BOOKSELLERS ASSOCIATION (CBA)
9240 Explorer Drive, Suite 200, Colorado Springs, CO 80920. (800)252-1950. **Fax:** (719)272-3510. **E-mail:** info@cbaonline.org. **Website:** www.cbaonline.org.

THE DRAMATISTS GUILD OF AMERICA 1501 Broadway, Suite 701, New York, NY 10036. (212)398-9366. **Fax:** (212)944-0420. **Website:** www.dramatistsguild.com.

NATIONAL LEAGUE OF AMERICAN PEN WOMEN (NLAPW) Pen Arts Building, 1300 17th St. NW, Washington DC 20036-1973. (202)785-1997. **Fax:** (202)452-8868. **E-mail:** contact@nlapw.org. **Website:** www.americanpenwomen.org.

NATIONAL WRITERS ASSOCIATION (NWA)
10940 S. Parker Rd., #508, Parker, CO 80134. (303)841-0246. **E-mail:** natlwritersassn@hotmail.com. **Website:** www.nationalwriters.com

NATIONAL WRITERS UNION (NWU) 256 West 38th Street, Suite 703, New York, NY 10018. (212)254-0279. **Fax:** (212)254-0673. **E-mail:** nwu@nwu.org. **Website:** www.nwu.org.

PEN AMERICAN CENTER 588 Broadway, Suite 303, New York, NY 10012-3225. (212)334-1660. **Fax:** (212)334-2181. **E-mail:** pen@pen.org. **Website:** www.pen.org.

THE PLAYWRIGHTS GUILD OF CANADA (PGC) 401 Richmond Street West, Suite 350, Toronto, Ontario M5V 3A8 Canada. (416)703-0201. **Fax:** (416)703-0059. **E-mail:** info@playwrightsguild.ca. **Website:** http://www.playwrightsguild.ca.

VOLUNTEER LAWYERS FOR THE ARTS (VLA) 1 E. 53rd St., Sixth Floor, New York, NY 10022. (212)319-2787, ext.1. **Fax:** (212)752-6575. **E-mail:** vlany@vlany.org. **Website:** www.vlany.org.

WOMEN IN FILM (WIF) 6100 Wilshire Blvd., Suite 710, Los Angeles, CA 90048. (323)935-2211. **Fax:** (323)935-2212. **E-mail:** info@wif.org. **Website:** www.wif.org.

WOMEN'S NATIONAL BOOK ASSOCIATION (WNBA) P.O. Box 237, FDR Station, New York NY 10150. (212)208-4629. **Fax:** (212)208-4629. **E-mail:** publicity@bookbuzz.com. **Website:** www.wnba-books.org.

WRITERS GUILD OF ALBERTA (WGA) Percy Page Centre, 11759 Groat Rd., Edmonton AB T5M 3K6 Canada. (780)422-8174. **Fax:** (780)422-2663 (attn: WGA). **E-mail:** mail@writersguild.ab.ca. **Website:** writersguild.ab.ca.

WRITERS GUILD OF AMERICA-EAST (WGA) 250 Hudson Street, Suite 700, New York, NY 10013. (212)767-7800. **Fax:** (212)582-1909. **E-mail:** info@wgaeast.org. **Website:** www.wgaeast.org.

WRITERS GUILD OF AMERICA-WEST (WGA) 7000 W. Third St., Los Angeles CA 90048. (323)951-4000. **Fax:** (323)782-4800. **Website:** www.wga.org.

WRITERS UNION OF CANADA (TWUC) 90 Richmond St. E., Suite 200, Toronto, ON M5C 1P1 Canada. (416)703-8982. **Fax:** (416)504-9090. **E-mail:** info@writersunion.ca. **Website:** www.writersunion.ca.

GENRE GLOSSARY

Definitions of Fiction Subcategories

The following were provided courtesy of The Extended Novel Writing Workshop, created by the staff of Writers Online Workshops (www.writersonlineworkshops.com).

MYSTERY SUBCATEGORIES

The major mystery subcategories are listed below, each followed by a brief description and the names of representative authors, so you can sample each type of work. Note that we have loosely classified "suspense/thriller" as a mystery category. While these stories do not necessarily follow a traditional "whodunit" plot pattern, they share many elements with other mystery categories.

AMATEUR DETECTIVE. As the name implies, the detective is not a professional detective (private or otherwise), but is almost always a professional something. This professional association routinely involves the protagonist in criminal cases (in a support capacity), gives him or her a special advantage in a specific case, or provides the contacts and skills necessary to solve a particular crime. (Jonathan Kellerman, Patricia Cornwell, Jan Burke)

CLASSIC MYSTERY (WHODUNIT). A crime (almost always a murder) is solved. The detective is the viewpoint character; the reader never knows any more or less about the crime than the detective, and all the clues to solving the crime are available to the reader.

COURTROOM DRAMA. The action takes place primarily in the courtroom; protagonist is generally a defense attorney out to prove the innocence of his or her client by finding the real culprit.

COZY. A special class of the amateur detective category that frequently features a female protagonist. (Agatha Christie's Miss Marple stories are the classic example.) There is less onstage violence than in other categories, and the plot is often wrapped up in a final scene where the detective identifies the murderer and explains how the crime was solved. In contemporary stories, the protagonist can be anyone from a chronically curious housewife to a mystery-buff clergyman to a college professor, but he or she is usually quirky, even eccentric. (Susan Isaacs, Andrew Greeley, Lillian Jackson Braun)

ESPIONAGE. The international spy novel is less popular since the end of the Cold War, but stories can still revolve around political intrigue in unstable regions. (John le Carré, Ken Follett)

HEISTS AND CAPERS. The crime itself is the focus. Its planning and execution are seen in detail, and the participants are fully drawn characters that may even be portrayed sympathetically. One character is the obvious leader of the group (the "brains"); the other members are often brought together by the leader specifically for this job and may or may not have a previous association. In a heist, no matter how clever or daring the characters are, they are still portrayed as criminals, and the expectation is that they will be caught and punished (but not always). A caper is more lighthearted, even comedic. The participants may have a noble goal (something other than personal gain) and often get away with the crime. (Eric Ambler, Tony Kenrick, Leslie Hollander)

HISTORICAL. May be any category or subcategory of mystery, but with an emphasis on setting, the details of which must be diligently researched. But beyond the historical details (which must never overshadow the story), the plot develops along the lines of its contemporary counterpart. (Candace Robb, Caleb Carr, Anne Perry)

JUVENILE/YOUNG ADULT. Written for the 8–12 age group (middle grade) or the 12 and up age group (young adult), the crime in these stories may or may not be murder, but it is serious. The protagonist is a kid (or group of kids) in the same age range as the targeted reader. There is no graphic violence depicted, but the stories are scary and the villains are realistic. (Mary Downing Hahn, Wendy Corsi Staub, Cameron Dokey, Norma Fox Mazer)

MEDICAL THRILLER. The plot can involve a legitimate medical threat (such as the outbreak of a virulent plague) or the illegal or immoral use of medical technology. In the former scenario, the protagonist is likely to be the doctor (or team) who identifies the virus and procures the antidote; in the latter he or she could be a patient (or the relative of a victim) who uncovers the plot and brings down the villain. (Robin Cook, Michael Palmer, Michael Crichton, Stanley Pottinger)

POLICE PROCEDURALS. The most realistic category, these stories require the most meticulous research. A police procedural may have more than one protagonist since cops rarely work alone. Conflict between partners, or between the detective and his or her superiors, is a common theme. But cops are portrayed positively as a group, even though there may be a couple of bad or ineffective law enforcement characters for contrast and conflict. Jurisdictional disputes are still popular sources of conflict as well. (Lawrence Treat, Joseph Wambaugh, Ridley Pearson, Julie Smith)

PRIVATE DETECTIVE. When described as "hard-boiled," this category takes a tough stance. Violence is more prominent, characters are darker, the detective—while almost always licensed by the state—operates on the fringes of the law, and there is often open resentment between the detective and law enforcement. More "enlightened" male detectives and a crop of contemporary females have brought about new trends in this category. (For female P.I.s: Sue Grafton, Sara Paretsky; for male P.I.s: John D. MacDonald, Lawrence Sanders)

SUSPENSE/THRILLER. Where a classic mystery is always a whodunit, a suspense/thriller novel may deal more with the intricacies of the crime, what motivated it, and how the villain (whose identity may be revealed to the reader early on) is caught and brought to justice. Novels in this category frequently employ multiple points of view and have broader scopes than more traditional murder mysteries. The crime may not even involve murder—it may be a threat to global economy or regional ecology; it may be technology run amok or abused at the hands of an unscrupulous scientist; it may involve innocent citizens victimized for personal or corporate gain. Its perpetrators are kidnappers, stalkers, serial killers, rapists, pedophiles, computer hackers, or just about anyone with an evil intention and the means to carry it out. The protagonist may be a private detective or law enforcement official, but is just as likely to be a doctor, lawyer, military officer, or other individual in a unique position to identify the villain and bring him or her to justice. (James Patterson, John J. Nance)

TECHNO-THRILLER. These are replacing the traditional espionage novel and feature technology as an integral part of not just the setting but the plot as well.

WOMAN IN JEOPARDY. A murder or other crime may be committed, but the focus is on the woman (and/or her children) currently at risk, her struggle to understand the nature of the danger, and her eventual victory over her tormentor. The protagonist makes up for her lack of physical prowess with intellect or special skills and solves the problem on her own or with the help of her family (but she runs the show). Closely related to this category is romantic suspense. But, while the heroine in a romantic suspense is certainly a "woman in jeopardy," the mystery or suspense element is subordinate to the romance. (Mary Higgins Clark, Mary Stewart, Jessica Mann)

ROMANCE SUBCATEGORIES

These categories and subcategories of romance fiction have been culled from the *Romance Writer's Sourcebook* (Writer's Digest Books) and Phyllis Taylor Pianka's *How to Write Romances* (Writer's Digest Books). We've arranged the "major" categories below, with the subcategories beneath them, each followed by a brief description and the names of authors who write in each category, so you can sample representative works.

CATEGORY OR SERIES. These are published in "lines" by individual publishing houses (such as Harlequin); each line has its own requirements as to word length, story content, and amount of sex. (Debbie Macomber, Nora Roberts, Glenda Sanders)

CHRISTIAN. With an inspirational Christian message centering on the spiritual dynamic of the romantic relationship and faith in God as the foundation for that relationship; sensuality is played down. (Janelle Burnham, Ann Bell, Linda Chaikin, Catherine Palmer, Dee Henderson, Lisa Tawn Bergen)

GLITZ. So called because they feature generally wealthy characters with high-powered positions in careers that are considered glamorous—high finance, modeling/acting, publishing, fashion—and are set in exciting or exotic (often metropolitan) locales, such as Monte Carlo, Hollywood, London, or New York. (Jackie Collins, Judith Krantz)

HISTORICAL. Can cover just about any historical (or even prehistorical) period. Setting in the historical is especially significant, and details must be thoroughly researched and accurately presented. For a sampling of a variety of historical styles, try Laura Kinsell (*Flowers from the Storm*), Mary Jo Putney (*The Rake and the Reformer*), and Judy Cuevas (*Bliss*). Some currently popular periods/themes in historicals are:

- **GOTHIC:** Historical with a strong element of suspense and a feeling of supernatural events, although these events frequently have a natural explanation. Setting plays an important role in establishing a dark, moody, suspenseful atmosphere. (Phyllis Whitney, Victoria Holt)
- **HISTORICAL FANTASY:** With traditional fantasy elements of magic and magical beings, frequently set in a medieval society. (Amanda Glass, Jayne Ann Krentz, Kathleen Morgan, Jessica Bryan, Taylor Quinn Evans, Carla Simpson, Karyn Monk)
- **EARLY AMERICAN:** Usually Revolution to Civil War, set in New England or the South, but "frontier" stories set in the American West are quite popular as well. (Robin Lee Hatcher, Elizabeth Lowell, Heather Graham)
- **NATIVE AMERICAN:** Where one or both of the characters are Native Americans; the conflict between cultures is a popular theme. (Carol Finch, Elizabeth Grayson, Karen Kay, Kathleen Harrington, Genell Dellim, Candace McCarthy)
- **REGENCY:** Set in England during the Regency period from 1811 to 1820. (Carol Finch, Elizabeth Elliott, Georgette Heyer, Joan Johnston, Lynn Collum)

MULTICULTURAL. Most currently feature African-American or Hispanic couples, but editors are looking for other ethnic stories as well. Multiculturals can be contemporary or historical and fall into any subcategory. (Rochelle Alers, Monica Jackson, Bette Ford, Sandra Kitt, Brenda Jackson)

PARANORMAL. Containing elements of the supernatural or science fiction/fantasy. There are numerous subcategories (many stories combine elements of more than one) including:

- **TIME TRAVEL:** One or more of the characters travels to another time—usually the past—to find love. (Jude Devereaux, Linda Lael Miller, Diana Gabaldon, Constance O'Day Flannery)
- **SCIENCE FICTION/FUTURISTIC:** S/F elements are used for the story's setting: imaginary worlds, parallel universes, Earth in the near or distant future. (Marilyn Campbell, Jayne Ann Krentz, J.D. Robb [Nora Roberts], Anne Avery)
- **CONTEMPORARY FANTASY:** From modern ghost and vampire stories to "New Age" themes such as extraterrestrials and reincarnation. (Linda Lael Miller, Anne Stuart, Antoinette Stockenberg, Christine Feehan)

ROMANTIC COMEDY. Has a fairly strong comic premise and/or a comic perspective in the author's voice or the voices of the characters (especially the heroine). (Jennifer Crusie, Susan Elizabeth Phillips)

ROMANTIC SUSPENSE. With a mystery or psychological thriller subplot in addition to the romance plot. (Mary Stewart, Barbara Michaels, Tami Hoag, Nora Roberts, Linda Howard, Catherine Coulter)

SINGLE TITLE. Longer contemporaries that do not necessarily conform to the requirements of a specific romance line and therefore feature more complex plots and nontraditional characters. (Mary Ruth Myers, Nora Roberts, Kathleen Gilles Seidel, Kathleen Korbel)

YOUNG ADULT. Focus is on first love with very little, if any, sex. These can have bittersweet endings, as opposed to the traditional romance happy ending, since first loves are often lost loves. (YA historical: Nancy Covert Smith, Louise Vernon; YA contemporary: Kathryn Makris)

SCIENCE FICTION SUBCATEGORIES

Peter Heck, in his article "Doors to Other Worlds: Trends in Science Fiction and Fantasy," which appears in the 1996 edition of *Science Fiction and Fantasy Writer's Sourcebook* (Writer's Digest Books), identifies some science fiction trends that have distinct enough characteristics to be defined as categories. These distinctions are frequently the result of marketing decisions as much as literary ones, so understanding them is important in deciding where your novel idea belongs. We've supplied a brief description and the names of authors who write in each category. In those instances where the author writes in more than one category, we've included titles of appropriate representative works.

ALTERNATE HISTORY. Fantasy, sometimes with science fiction elements, that changes the accepted account of actual historical events or people to suggest an alternate view of history.

(Ted Mooney, *Traffic and Laughter*; Ward Moore, *Bring the Jubilee*; Philip K. Dick, *The Man in the High Castle*)

CYBERPUNK. Characters in these stories are tough outsiders in a high-tech, generally near-future society where computers have produced major changes in the way society functions. (William Gibson, Bruce Sterling, Pat Cadigan, Wilhelmina Baird)

HARD SCIENCE FICTION. Based on the logical extrapolation of real science to the future. In these stories the scientific background (setting) may be as, or more, important than the characters. (Larry Niven)

MILITARY SCIENCE FICTION. Stories about war that feature traditional military organization and tactics extrapolated into the future. (Jerry Pournelle, David Drake, Elizabeth Moon)

NEW AGE. A category of speculative fiction that deals with subjects such as astrology, psychic phenomena, spiritual healing, UFOs, mysticism, and other aspects of the occult. (Walter Mosley, *Blue Light*; Neil Gaiman)

SCIENCE FANTASY. Blend of traditional fantasy elements with scientific or pseudoscientific support (genetic engineering, for example, to "explain" a traditional fantasy creature like the dragon). These stories are traditionally more character driven than hard science fiction. (Anne McCaffrey, Mercedes Lackey, Marion Zimmer Bradley)

SCIENCE FICTION MYSTERY. A cross-genre blending that can either be a more-or-less traditional science fiction story with a mystery as a key plot element, or a more-or-less traditional whodunit with science fiction elements. (Philip K. Dick, Lynn S. Hightower)

SCIENCE FICTION ROMANCE. Another genre blend that may be a romance with science fiction elements (in which case it is more accurately placed as a subcategory within the romance genre) or a science fiction story with a strong romantic subplot. (Anne McCaffrey, Melanie Rawn, Kate Elliot)

SOCIAL SCIENCE FICTION. The focus is on how the characters react to their environments. This category includes social satire. (George Orwell's *1984* is a classic example.) (Margaret Atwood, *The Handmaid's Tale*; Ursula K. Le Guin, *The Left Hand of Darkness*; Marge Piercy, *Woman on the Edge of Time*)

SPACE OPERA. From the term "horse opera," describing a traditional good-guys-versus-bad-guys western, these stories put the emphasis on sweeping action and larger-than-life characters. The focus on action makes these stories especially appealing for film treatment. (The Star Wars series is one of the best examples; also Samuel R. Delany.)

STEAMPUNK. A specific type of alternate-history science fiction set in Victorian England in which characters have access to 20th-century technology. (William Gibson; Bruce Sterling, *The Difference Engine*)

YOUNG ADULT. Any subcategory of science fiction geared to a YA audience (12–18), but these are usually shorter novels with characters in the central roles who are the same age as (or slightly older than) the targeted reader. (Jane Yolen, Andre Norton)

FANTASY SUBCATEGORIES

Before we take a look at the individual fantasy categories, it should be noted that, for purposes of these supplements, we've treated fantasy as a genre distinct from science fiction. While these two are closely related, there are significant enough differences to warrant their separation for study purposes. We have included here those science fiction categories that have strong fantasy elements, or that have a significant amount of crossover (these categories appear in both the science fiction and the fantasy supplements), but "pure" science fiction categories are not included below. If you're not sure whether your novel is fantasy or science fiction, consider this definition by Orson Scott Card in *How to Write Science Fiction and Fantasy* (Writer's Digest Books): "Here's a good, simple, semi-accurate rule of thumb: If the story is set in a universe that follows the same rules as ours, it's science fiction. If it's set in a universe that doesn't follow our rules, it's fantasy. Or in other words, science fiction is about what could be but isn't; fantasy is about what couldn't be."

But even Card admits this rule is only "semi-accurate." He goes on to say that the real boundary between science fiction and fantasy is defined by how the impossible is achieved: "If you have people do some magic, impossible thing [like time travel] by stroking a talisman or praying to a tree, it's fantasy; if they do the same thing by pressing a button or climbing inside a machine, it's science fiction."

Peter Heck, in his article "Doors to Other Worlds: Trends in Science Fiction and Fantasy," which appears in the 1996 edition of the *Science Fiction and Fantasy Writer's Sourcebook* (Writer's Digest Books), does note some trends that have distinct enough characteristics to be defined as separate categories. These categories are frequently the result of marketing decisions as much as literary ones, so understanding them is important in deciding where your novel idea belongs. We've supplied a brief description and the names of authors who write in each category, so you can sample representative works.

ARTHURIAN. Reworking of the legend of King Arthur and the Knights of the Round Table. (T.H. White, *The Once and Future King*; Marion Zimmer Bradley, *The Mists of Avalon*)

CONTEMPORARY (ALSO CALLED "URBAN") FANTASY. Traditional fantasy elements (such as elves and magic) are incorporated into an otherwise recognizable modern setting. (Emma

Bull, *War for the Oaks*; Mercedes Lackey, *The SERRAted Edge*; Terry Brooks, the Knight of the Word series)

DARK FANTASY. Closely related to horror but generally not as graphic. Characters in these stories are the "darker" fantasy types: vampires, witches, werewolves, demons, etc. (Anne Rice; Clive Barker, *Weaveworld*, *Imajica*; Fred Chappell)

FANTASTIC ALTERNATE HISTORY. Set in an alternate historical period (in which magic would not have been a common belief) where magic works, these stories frequently feature actual historical figures. (Orson Scott Card, *Alvin Maker*)

GAME-RELATED FANTASY. Plots and characters are similar to high fantasy, but are based on a particular role-playing game. (Dungeons and Dragons; Magic: The Gathering; World of Warcraft)

HEROIC FANTASY. The fantasy equivalent to military science fiction, these are stories of war and its heroes and heroines. (Robert E. Howard, the Conan the Barbarian series; Elizabeth Moon, *Deed of Paksenarion*; Michael Moorcock, the Elric series)

HIGH FANTASY. Emphasis is on the fate of an entire race or nation, threatened by an ultimate evil. J.R.R. Tolkien's Lord of the Rings trilogy is a classic example. (Terry Brooks, David Eddings, Margaret Weis, Tracy Hickman)

HISTORICAL FANTASY. The setting can be almost any era in which the belief in magic was strong; these are essentially historical novels where magic is a key element of the plot and/or setting. (Susan Schwartz, *Silk Road and Shadow*; Margaret Ball, *No Earthly Sunne*; Tim Powers, *The Anubis Gates*)

JUVENILE/YOUNG ADULT. Can be any type of fantasy, but geared to a juvenile (8–12) or YA audience (12–18); these are shorter novels with younger characters in central roles. (J.K. Rowling, Christopher Paolini, C.S. Lewis)

SCIENCE FANTASY. A blend of traditional fantasy elements with scientific or pseudoscientific support (genetic engineering, for example, to "explain" a traditional fantasy creature like the dragon). These stories are traditionally more character driven than hard science fiction. (Anne McCaffrey, Mercedes Lackey, Marion Zimmer Bradley)

HORROR SUBCATEGORIES

Subcategories in horror are less well defined than in other genres and are frequently the result of marketing decisions as much as literary ones. But being familiar with the terms used to describe different horror styles can be important in understanding how your own novel might be best presented to an agent or editor. What follows is a brief description of the most commonly used terms, along with names of authors and, where necessary, representative works.

DARK FANTASY. Sometimes used as a euphemistic term for horror in general, but also refers to a specific type of fantasy, usually less graphic than other horror subcategories, that features more "traditional" supernatural or mythical beings (vampires, werewolves, zombies, etc.) in either contemporary or historical settings. (Contemporary: Stephen King, *Salem's Lot*; Thomas Tessier, *The Nightwalker*. Historical: Brian Stableford, *The Empire of Fear*; Chelsea Quinn Yarbro, *Werewolves of London*.)

HAUNTINGS. "Classic" stories of ghosts, poltergeists, and spiritual possessions. The level of violence portrayed varies, but many writers in this category exploit the reader's natural fear of the unknown by hinting at the horror and letting the reader's imagination supply the details. (Peter Straub, *Ghost Story*; Richard Matheson, *Hell House*)

JUVENILE/YOUNG ADULT. Can be any horror style, but with a protagonist who is the same age as, or slightly older than, the targeted reader. Stories for middle grades (8–12 years old) are scary, with monsters and violent acts that might best be described as "gross," but stories for young adults (12–18) may be more graphic. (R.L. Stine, Christopher Pike, Carol Gorman)

PSYCHOLOGICAL HORROR. Features a human monster with horrific, but not necessarily supernatural, aspects. (Thomas Harris, *The Silence of the Lambs*, *Hannibal*; Dean Koontz, *Whispers*)

SPLATTERPUNK. Very graphic depiction of violence—often gratuitous—popularized in the 1980s, especially in film. (*Friday the 13th*, *Halloween*, *Nightmare on Elm Street*, etc.)

SUPERNATURAL/OCCULT. Similar to the dark fantasy, but may be more graphic in its depiction of violence. Stories feature satanic worship, demonic possession, or ultimate evil incarnate in an entity or supernatural being that may or may not have its roots in traditional mythology or folklore. (Ramsey Campbell; Robert McCammon; Ira Levin, *Rosemary's Baby*; William Peter Blatty, *The Exorcist*; Stephen King, *Pet Sematary*)

TECHNOLOGICAL HORROR. "Monsters" in these stories are the result of science run amok or technology turned to purposes of evil. (Dean Koontz, *Watchers*; Michael Crichton, *Jurassic Park*)

LITERARY AGENTS SPECIALITIES INDEX

CATEGORY INDEX

MAGAZINES

FAMILY SAGA

FANTASY

MILITARY/WAR

MYSTERY/SUSPENSE

GENERAL INDEX